Judicial Review: Law & Practice

Second Edition

Judicial Review: Law & Practice

Second Edition

General Editors

The Hon Mrs Justice Patterson DBE

Sam Karim
Barrister, Kings Chambers

Assistant Editor

Justin Leslie
Barrister and Assistant Parliamentary Counsel

Published by
Jordan Publishing Limited
21 St Thomas Street
Bristol BS1 6JS

Whilst the publishers and the author have taken every care in preparing the material included in this work, any statements made as to the legal or other implications of any transaction, any particular method of litigation or any kind of compensation claim are made in good faith purely for general guidance and cannot be regarded as a substitute for professional advice. Consequently, no liability can be accepted for loss or expense incurred as a result of relying in particular circumstances on statements made in this work.

© Jordan Publishing Limited 2015

All rights reserved. No part of this publication may be reproduced, stored in a retrieval system, or transmitted in any way or by any means, including photocopying or recording, without the written permission of the copyright holder, application for which should be addressed to the publisher.

Crown Copyright material is reproduced with kind permission of the Controller of Her Majesty's Stationery Office.

British Library Cataloguing-in-Publication Data

A catalogue record for this book is available from the British Library.

ISBN 978 1 84661 914 4

Typeset by Letterpart Limited, Caterham on the Hill, Surrey CR3 5XL

Printed in Great Britain by Hobbs the Printers Limited, Totton, Hampshire SO40 3WK

CONTRIBUTORS

Simon Burrows
Barrister, Kings Chambers
Chapter 4 The Tribunal System;
Chapter 8 Mental Health

Colin Crawford
Barrister, Kings Chambers
Chapter 13 Central/Local Government

Jonathan Easton
Barrister, Kings Chambers
Chapter 7 Housing

Adam Fullwood
Barrister, Kings Chambers
Chapter 16 Healthcare

Anthony Gill
Barrister, Kings Chambers
Chapter 2 Remedies; Chapter 3 Practice and Procedure (first edition only); Chapter 5 Planning Law

David Hercock
Barrister, 6 Pump Court
Chapter 12 Licensing (first edition only)

Freddie Humphreys
Barrister, Kings Chambers
Chapter 5 Planning Law

Sam Karim
Barrister, Kings Chambers
Chapter 1 Grounds of Judicial Review; Chapter 2 Remedies; Chapter 3 Practice and Procedure; Chapter 6 Community Care

Justin Leslie
Barrister and Assistant Parliamentary Counsel
Chapter 1 Grounds of Judicial Review; Chapter 2 Remedies; Chapter 3 Practice and Procedure; Chapter 15 Professional Regulation

Jesse Nicholls
Barrister, Garden Court Chambers
Chapter 10 Prison Law

The Hon Mrs Justice Patterson DBE
Chapter 1 Grounds of Judicial Review; Chapter 2 Remedies; Chapter 3 Practice and Procedure; Chapter 4 The Tribunal System; Chapter 5 Planning Law

Melanie Plimmer
Tribunal Judge, First-tier Tribunal
Chapter 14 Immigration Law

Hugh Southey QC
Matrix Chambers
Chapter 9 Criminal Law

Matthew Stanbury
Barrister, Garden Court North
Chapter 10 Prison Law

Matthew Stockwell
Barrister, St Johns Buildings
Chapter 11 Education

Abigail Telford
Pupil Barrister, Zenith Chambers, Leeds
Chapter 1 Grounds of Judicial Review; Chapter 3 Practice and Procedure

Ben Williams
Barrister, Kings Chambers
Chapter 12 Licensing

PREFACE

The advent of the regionalisation project of the Administrative Court was the catalyst that led to the first edition of this book. Indeed, it was now some six years ago, while we were both discussing the embryonic stages of establishing the Northern Administrative Law Association (NALA) at Kings Chambers, Manchester that it was plain that there was a gap in the market: a book that provides a comprehensive introduction to the law and practice of judicial review proceedings together with in-depth analysis of areas where judicial review is readily used as a mean of redress, including town and country planning, community care and social welfare, immigration, housing, mental health, education and licensing.

The first edition sought to provide a wide-ranging coverage of administrative law and its niche practice areas including essential procedural rules, forms and guidance issued by the Administrative Court. The second edition seeks to update practitioners on the specific practice areas while building upon the foundations and principles of judicial review in Part One.

There is no doubt that the regionalisation of the Administrative Court has been a success. With the six-year anniversary fast approaching it is important to remember its rationale. The report of the Judicial Working Group convened by then Vice-President of the Queen's Bench Division (now President), May LJ in January 2007 stated:

> 'The present system discriminates against those who are not in the South of England. Nearly all judicial review and other claims in the Administrative Court have to be brought in London, with the obvious inconvenience and additional expense that this causes for claimants, defendants, interested parties and their lawyers. Proper access to justice is not achieved if those in the regions can only bring judicial review and other claims in the Administrative Court in London.'

The position was aptly summarised by Sarah Nason and Maurice Sunkin (2013) 76(2) MLR 223–53 at 250:

> 'The establishment of regional centres for handling Administrative Court matters and enabling regional access to judicial review, while achieved as an administrative change, is a potentially significant step in the development of judicial review in England and Wales. It creates a new procedural architecture for dealing with judicial reviews and marks an additional welcome step away from the highly centralist conception of the judicial review system epitomised by

Lord Dipock's judgment in *O'Reilly v Mackman*. As such regionalisation recognises the need to improve the ability of citizens from across England and Wales to gain access to public law redress.'

At an event hosted by NALA at Kings Chambers marking the anniversary of the regionalisation project, Langstaff J, former Presiding Judge of the Leeds and Manchester Centres, noted that: 'The future is the Admin Court; it gives a tremendous social advantage to those who want access to justice.'[1] We wholeheartedly agree.

We wish to thank the co-authors for their dedicated and excellent contributions, each being highly experienced in the topics that they have covered. We have endeavoured to state the law as at 1 December 2014. We hope that this book provides an indispensable source of reference and a guide.

For our part, this experience has been a pleasure, albeit as with all projects of substance, somewhat time consuming.

The Hon Mrs Justice Frances Patterson

Sam Karim
(Sheikh MS Karim)

Justin Leslie

December 2014

---

[1] http://www.kingschambers.com/news/latest/admin_court_flourishing_in_the_regions/.

INTRODUCTION

This book is designed to provide a source for public law practitioners who practise across the broad spectrum of laws in which judicial review is used as an avenue of redress. It is also of value to others who appear less frequently in the Administrative Court but need a convenient reference point. Part 1 seeks to concentrate primarily on the central subject matter, namely, judicial review. Part 2 considers how judicial review is currently utilised to review the lawfulness of the powers and duties of those exercising public function in various areas.

Because of the ever-evolving nature of judicial review and administrative law this work does not seek to be a comprehensive encyclopaedia on judicial review. Indeed, it is hard to think that any work could be so. What this work does is to cover the main subject areas where judicial review claims are brought.

WHAT IS JUDICIAL REVIEW?

The Bowman Report[1] summarised judicial review as, 'the means by which those with a "sufficient interest" can challenge the exercise or non-exercise of powers by public bodies on the grounds of illegality, irrationality or procedural impropriety'.

Although originally a cause of action against central or local government, judicial review now extends to cover many non-governmental organisations and into the commercial world. Put another way, administrative law determines the powers and duties of administrative authorities. As set out by Sir Ivor Jennings, administrative law should be defined according to its subject matter: the law of public administrative or administrative law.[2] Carnwath LJ has said recently 'Judicial review is the court's response to allegations of abuse of power adversely affecting the rights or interests of those bringing the claim. The starting point must therefore be to identify the legal source of the power in question and the practical consequences of its exercise'.[3]

---

[1] Review of Crown Office work carried out by Sir Jeffrey Bowman who reported to the Lord Chancellor in 2000. The Crown Office was the predecessor of the Administrative Court.
[2] Jennings, *The Law and the Constitution* (5th edn), p 217.
[3] *R (Hillingdon BC) v SS for Transport* [2010] EWHC 626.

The importance of the Administrative Court and its function cannot be understated. Sir Thomas Bingham MR (as he then was) in *R v Ministry of Justice ex p Smith* described the Court as having, '... the constitutional role and duty of ensuring that the rights of citizens are not abused by the unlawful exercise of executive power ...'.[4]

At the Administrative Court an individual seeks to challenge a decision of an administrative body by way of achieving one or more of the various remedies that are potentially available, namely (a) a quashing order (formerly known as certiorari); (b) a prohibiting order (formerly known as prohibition); (c) a mandatory order (formerly know as mandamus); (d) a declaration; (e) an interim declaration; (f) an injunction; and (g) a substitutionary remedy.

Judicial review, therefore, is a process by which the above remedies may be applied for in a specialist part of the High Court (Queens Bench Division), which considers public law and administrative law cases, namely, the Administrative Court.

The supervisory jurisdiction of the Administrative Court is not to be underestimated. The unique nature has been described by commentators as '... the question is not whether the judge disagrees with what the public body has done, but whether there is some recognisable public law wrong ...'. As aptly put by Professor Paul Craig who explained the conceptual justification for judicial intervention within the context of the supervisory role as:

> 'It is readily apparent that the execution of legislation may require the grant of discretionary power to a minister or an agency. Parliament may not be able to foresee all the eventualities and flexibility may be required to implement the legislation. The legislature will of necessity grant power subject to conditions [...] Herein lies the modern conceptual justification for judicial intervention. It was designed to ensure that those to whom such grants of power were made did not transgress the sovereign will of Parliament.'[5]

Lord Clyde in *Reid v Secretary of State for Scotland* [1999] 2 AC 512 said that:

> '... [judicial review] does not allow the court ... to examine the evidence with a view to forming its own view about the substantial merits of the case. It may be that the tribunal whose decision is being challenged has done something which it had no lawful authority to do. It may have abused or misused the authority which it had. It may have departed from the procedures which either by statute or at common law as matter of fairness it ought to have observed. As regards the decision itself it may be found to be perverse, or

---

[4] [1996] 2 WLR 305 at 338.
[5] Professor P P Craig, *Administrative Law* (5th edn, 2003), p 5.

irrational, or grossly disproportionate to what was required. Or the decision may be found to be erroneous in respect of a legal deficiency, as for example, through the absence of evidence, or of sufficient evidence, to support it, or through account being taken of irrelevant matter, or through a failure for any reason to take account of a relevant matter, or through some misconstruction of the terms of the statutory provision which the decision-maker is required to apply. But while the evidence may have to be explored in order to see if the decision is vitiated by such legal deficiencies it is perfectly clear that in a case of review, as distinct from an ordinary appeal, the court may not set about forming its own preferred view of the evidence.'

The 2000 edition of the Treasury Solicitors' publication, *The Judge Over Your Shoulder* provides a useful description of who is affected by administrative law stating that:

'1.2 "Administrative" or "public" law governs the acts of public bodies and the exercise of public functions. Public bodies include "non-departmental public bodies", such as the Committee on Standards in Public Life, and Next Steps Agencies like HM Prison Service.

1.3 Private sector bodies may also be subject to administrative law when they exercise a public function. Generally, bodies exercise public functions when they act and have authority to act for the collective benefit of the general public. The activities of City institutions with market regulatory functions, like the London Stock Exchange, are a good example.'[6]

The fourth edition of the publication also provides that:

'The Human Rights Act 1998 is part of administrative law because it governs the exercise of statutory powers by public authorities. For example, the Act has an important bearing on the way in which those powers are to be interpreted. The devolution legislation is part of administrative law for the same reason. Likewise European Community (EC) law may be relevant to the exercise of statutory Powers.'[7]

---

[6] Treasury Solicitor, *The Judge Over Your Shoulder, A Guide to Judicial Review for UK Government Administrators* (3rd edn, 2000).
[7] Treasury Solicitor, *The Judge Over Your Shoulder, A Guide to Judicial Review for UK Government Administrators* (4th edn, 2006).

HISTORY

The present jurisdiction of the High Court extends the continuous lineage from the earliest periods of the English common law initiated by the separation of the King's Council around 1200 into the King's Bench (which grew out of the King's Court or *Curia Regis*) that was also granted jurisdiction to supervise and correct the actions of inferior courts and officials.[8] At some unknown stage, a Court independent of the King's personal presence grew out of the *Curia Regis*, consisting of a number of Royal judges who would hear cases themselves around the country. However, in 1215 the King's Court was formally recognised by way of the Magna Carta, as was the Common Bench (later Court of Common Pleas). At this stage, the King's Bench was theoretically a *movable* Court.[9] Increasingly, however, the King's Bench became a fixed Court, even though it could in theory meet anywhere in England, and from 1421 it appears not to have moved from Westminster Hall. The Court of Queen's Bench became the Queen's Bench Division of the High Court of Justice in 1873.

The growth of judicial review is a relatively recent phenomenon:

> '... the extension of judicial control of the administrative process has provided over the 30 years the most striking feature of the development of common law in those countries of whose legal systems it provides the source; and although it is a development that has already gone a long way towards providing a system of administrative law as comprehensive in its content as the droit administrative of countries of the civil law, albeit differing in procedural approach, it is a development that is still continuing.'[10]

This assertion by Lord Diplock in 1984 regarding the organic development of administrative law remains accurate in the contemporary usage of the Administrative Court. Prior to this 'striking development' since the Second World War, administrative law was an unknown specialism. Lord Reid stated in *Ridge v Baldwin*[11] that, '... we do not have a developed system of administrative law – perhaps because until fairly recently we did not need it'. This view was clearly reflected by Mr Maudling (Secretary of State for the Home Department) when in 1971 he said in debating the Immigration Bill 1971 that, '... I have never seen the sense of administrative law in our country, because it merely means someone else taking the Government's decision for them ...'.[12] It is clear that matters have since moved on!

---

[8] Pollard, Parpworth & Hughes, *Constititional and Administrative Law* (4th edn), p 461.
[9] One may argue, therefore, that there is historical underpinning to the recent regionalisation of the Administrative Court that occurred in April 2009.
[10] Lord Diplock in *Mahon v Air New Zealand* [1984] AC 808.
[11] [1964] AC 40, HL.
[12] Official Report, Standing Committee B, 25 May 1971, col 1508.

There have been three milestones in the development of this area of law, namely (i) the introduction of Rules of the Supreme Court 1977 of a codified process by which to challenge the decision of a administrative body (subsequently giving legislative effect to the new procedure contained in the RSC Ord 53 by the Supreme Court Act 1981, section 31); (ii) the House of Lords (as it then was) decision of *Mahon*[13] which defined that actions or powers exercised by an administrative body must be categorised as raising questions of 'public law' and its distinction with 'private law'; and (iii) the explosion of government post the Second World War.[14] Lord Diplock described the development in *R v Inland Revenue*[15] as, '... that progress towards a comprehensive system of administrative law that I regard as having been the greatest achievement of the English courts in my judicial lifetime ...'. In equal terms, Lord Goff stated in *Kleinwort Benson Ltd v Lincoln City Council*[16] that:

> 'Occasionally, a judicial development of the law will be of a more radical nature, constituting a departure, even a major departure, from what has previously been considered to be established principle, and leading to a realignment of subsidiary principles within that branch of the law. Perhaps the most remarkable example of such a development is to be found in the decisions of this House in the middle of this century which led to the creation of our modern system of administrative law. It is into this category that the present case falls; but it must nevertheless be seen as a development of the law, and treated as such.'

Finally, it is worth noting the impact of government policies during 1997 to 2010 and the accompanying increase of litigation in the Administrative Court with the introduction of a major package of constitutional reform such as devolution, human rights, reform of the House of Lords and freedom of information. As a result, there has been an expansion of judicial influence, as stated by Professor Robert Stevens:

> '[T]he most obvious and public change concerned the expansion of judicial review to provide an extensive power for the courts to intervene in procedural due process over a wide range of public and quasi public matter[s].'[17]

The 2000 edition of *The Judge Over Your Shoulder* indicated that judicial review was, '... [A] growth industry. In 1974 there were 160 applications for leave to seek judicial review in England and Wales. By 1998 the figure was

---

[13] *Mahon v Air New Zealand* [1984] AC 808.
[14] See Bradley & Ewing, *Constitutional & Administrative Law* (14th edn), pp 662–4 'reform of the administrative law' for more information.
[15] [1982] AC 617 at 641C–D.
[16] [1999] AC 349 at 378E.
[17] Robert Stevens, *The English Judges – Their role in the changing constitution* (2002).

4,539 ...'.[18] As set out in para 3.0 in 2010 there were over 13,000 applications for permission lodged: a figure which could not have been anticipated just over 10 years ago.

De Smith, Woolf and Jowell described the changes from the 1970s, stating that:

'... From the 1970s onwards a number of pressure groups consciously adopted "test case strategies" in which judicial review, in conjunction with other forms of legal proceedings and together with conventional forms of political action, was used to seek changes in government policy [...] Success, however, was often temporary, limited and indirect: judicial review generated publicity and was capable of inflicting political embarrassment on ministers. The response of government however, was often to nullify or sidestep the effects of an unpalatable judicial decision by enacting primary legislation [...].'[19]

THE PRESENT DAY

The Administrative Court and Administrative Court Office were established on the 2 October 2000. The changes were introduced after a review of the Crown Office by Sir Jeffrey Bowman and which was submitted to the Lord Chancellor in March 2000. It recommended that the Crown Office and the Crown Office List be renamed as the Administrative Court to emphasise the principal work of the Court.

The Bowman review had been instigated after the rapid expansion of administrative law and consequential growth of judicial review during the 1980s and 1990s. As a result there was increasing concern about how cases were dealt with and delays in dealing with cases. The Law Commission had recommended in 1994[20] that the procedure and remedies for judicial review be reformed and observed that there was a public interest in the prompt adjudication of disputes through the courts.

The Bowman Report hoped that its recommendations would achieve such a solution. It said, 'We believe that its work would be dealt with more efficiently and effectively by a smaller number of nominated judges working in the Crown Office List for a majority of the year in a similar fashion to the Commercial Court.'

The Report could not have foreseen the explosion of work in the Administrative Court during the 2000s which at one time threatened the

---

[18] Treasury Solicitor, *The Judge Over Your Shoulder, A Guide to Judicial Review for UK Government Administrators* (3rd edn, 2000).
[19] De Smith, Woolf and Jowell, *Judicial Review of Administrative Action* (5th edn, 1995).
[20] *Administrative Law: Judicial Review and Statutory Appeals* (Law Commission No 226).

efficient and effective running of the court with which Bowman was concerned. The delays before cases reached any substantive hearing were the subject of widespread concern and complaint.

By 2013 the number of judicial review cases lodged had grown to more than 16,000 from a figure of 4,300 in 2000. The Government was becoming increasingly concerned. The Secretary of State for Justice said:

> 'I believe in protecting judicial review as a check on unlawful executive action, but I am equally clear that it should not be abused, to act as a brake on growth. In my view judicial review has extended far beyond its original concept, and too often cases are pursued as a campaigning tool, or simply to delay legitimate proposals. That is bad for the economy and the taxpayer, and also bad for public confidence in the justice system.'

As a result reforms to the system have been introduced and a series of significant steps have been taken to relieve the pressure on the Administrative Court. First, most of the immigration and asylum cases have been transferred to the Upper Tribunal. Second, more specialist judges have been appointed (there are in excess of 50 nominated High Court judges for Administrative Court work and significant numbers of suitably qualified Deputy High Court judges). Third, as a result of the Report by May LJ (President of the Queen's Bench Division) and the Senior Judicial Working Group[21] looking at Justice Outside London Regionalisation of the Administrative Court has occurred so that from the 21 April 2009 public law cases arising in the Regions can be tried at the venue most local to them (Birmingham, Leeds, Liverpool and Manchester[22]) thus spreading the work from London, relieving pressure on the Administrative Court List in London and making the Administrative Court more accessible to all. More recently the government has introduced further reforms, such as the introduction of the Planning Court, increased use of the totally without merit criteria when considering whether to grant permission to

---

[21] Report of the Judicial Working Group in January 2007 ('report'). In a News Release dated 17 November 2007, The Working Group in their report, *Justice Outside of London*, said: 'Nearly all judicial review and other claims in the Administrative Court have to be brought in London, with the obvious inconvenience and additional expense that this causes for claimants, defendants, interested parties and their lawyers. The essential point is proper access to justice is not achieved if those in the regions can only bring judicial review and other claims in the Administrative Court in London. The present system discriminates against those who are not in the South of England.' May LJ, President of the Queen's Bench Division also has said in a interview, 'The move is not just a pragmatic one ... It is also that it is right, in itself, for these cases to be heard locally ... the important thing is that claimants based in the regions will be able to have their cases dealt with at the centre that they regard as most convenient, instructing – if they wish – lawyers also based in the region' (*The Times*, 9 April 2009, 'Administrative Court takes asylum cases out to the regions').

[22] Manchester (Civil Justice Centre, 12th Floor, 1 Bridge Street, Manchester, M3 3FX), Leeds (Leeds Combined Court, 1 Oxford Row, Leeds, LS1 3BG), Birmingham (Civil Justice Centre, Priory Courts, 5th Floor, 33 Bull Street, Birmingham, B4 6DS) and Cardiff (Civil Justice Centre, 2 Park Street, Cardiff, CF10 1ET).

bring judicial review proceedings, a strict framework for Protective Costs Order cases (in non-environmental matters) and has limited the availability of legal aid.

All of these initiatives mean that there is now a framework in place for the Administrative Court to resume its role as a specialist court to be able to work expeditiously and effectively[23] whilst the government believes retaining access to justice.

The Court operates under a lead nominated judge with overall responsibility for the speed, efficiency and economy with which the work of the Administrative Court is undertaken.[24] There are lead judges for the Administrative Court in the regions. The Administrative Court Office is responsible for the running of the Administrative Court. In London there is a team of lawyers, each of which is responsible for different areas of work. Each of the regional centres has its own dedicated office and all Administrative Court centres are linked to a central computer system so that each Administrative Court centre is aware of proceedings in other centres to secure efficiency and to avoid 'forum shopping'.[25]

Parallel with changes to the way the Administrative Court is administered amendments have been made to what was RSC Ord 53. Those changes are now encompassed in RSC Ord 54 which in turn modifies Part 8 of the Civil Procedure Rules. Together, and read with the Practice Directions that

---

[23] Paragraph 5.2 of the 53D Practice Direction (Venue) provides the following guidance:
'The general expectation is that proceedings will be administered and determined in the region with which the Claimant has the closest connection, subject to the following considerations as applicable:
(a) any reason expressed by any party for preferring a particular venue;
(b) the region in which the Defendants or any relevant office or department where the Defendant is based;
(c) the region in which the Claimant's legal representatives are based;
(d) the ease and cost of travel to a hearing;
(e) the availability and suitability of alternative means of attending a hearing (for example by video link);
(f) the extent and nature of media interest in the proceedings in any particular locality;
(g) the time within which it is appropriate for the proceedings to be determined;
(h) whether it is desirable to administer or determine the claim in another region in the light of the volume of claims issued at, and the capacity, resources and workload of, the Court at which it is issued;
(i) whether the claim issued is sufficiently similar to those in another outstanding claim to make it desirable that they should be determined together with, or immediately following the other claim; and
(j) whether the claim raises devolution issues and for that reason whether it should more appropriately be determined in London or Cardiff.'
[24] Currently Ouseley J.
[25] All four regional centres have their own dedicated administrative staff including an Administrative Court Office lawyer. In addition, all regional centres (including London) use the same computer network system, COINS. This is a confidential and secure system, which enables all five centres to act cohesively. As such, the system prevents the possibility of two or more of the same claims being issued more than once in the respective regional centre.

accompany RSC Ord 54, and s 31 of the Senior Courts Act 1981 they provide the procedural rules for judicial review. These are dealt with in greater detail later in this work.

WORK OF THE ADMINISTRATIVE COURT

The work of the Administrative Court is described by the Court itself as:

> 'varied, consisting of the administrative law jurisdiction of England and Wales as well as a supervisory jurisdiction over inferior courts and tribunals. The supervisory jurisdiction, exercised in the main through the procedure of Judicial Review, covers persons or bodies exercising a public law function – a wide and still growing field.'[26]

Annex A to the HMCS website lists the work of the Administrative Court as follows:

> 'Judicial review – of decisions of inferior courts and tribunals, public bodies and persons exercising a public function. Criminal cases may arise from decisions of magistrates' courts or the Crown Court when it is acting in its appellate capacity.
>
> Statutory appeals and applications – the right given by certain statutes to challenge decisions of e.g. Ministers, Local Government, Tribunals.
>
> Statutory review challenge to decisions of the IAT to refuse leave to appeal.
>
> Appeals by way of case stated – appeals against decisions of magistrates' courts and the Crown Court (predominantly criminal cases).
>
> Applications for habeas corpus.
>
> Applications for committal for contempt.
>
> Applications for an order preventing a vexatious litigant from instituting or continuing proceedings without the leave of a judge.
>
> Applications under the Coroners Act 1988.
>
> Some matters are required by statute or rules of Court to be heard by a Divisional Court (i.e. a court of two or more judges):

---

[26] HMCS website.

1. Applications for committal for contempt where the contempt (a) is committed in connection with (i) proceedings before a Q.B. Divisional Court, (ii) criminal proceedings (except where it is in the face of the court or disobedience to an order), (iii) proceedings in an inferior court or (b) is committed otherwise than in any proceedings;
2. Appeals from the Law Society Disciplinary Tribunal. Such appeals are heard by a three judge court unless the Lord Chief Justice otherwise directs. By convention these appeals are heard by a Court presided over by the Lord Chief Justice;
3. Applications under s 13 of the Coroners Act 1988 (with fiat of the Attorney General);
4. Applications for vexatious litigant orders under s 42 of the Supreme Court Act 1981;
5. Applications relating to parliamentary and local government elections under the Representation of the People Acts (unless exercisable by a single judge by express statutory provision).

Others can be, and usually are, heard by a Divisional Court:

1. Applications for judicial review in a criminal cause or matter;
2. Applications for leave to apply for judicial review in a criminal cause or matter, after refusal by a single judge (whether on paper or after oral argument);
3. Appeals by way of case stated in a criminal cause or matter, whether from the Crown Court or from a magistrates' court;

The remaining matters in the Administrative Court List will generally be heard by a single judge.'

CONTENTS

Contributors v
Preface vii
Introduction ix
Table of Cases xxxiii
Table of Statutes cxiii
Table of Statutory Instruments cxxiii

Part 1
General Principles

Chapter 1
Grounds of Judicial Review 3
Introduction 3
  Classifying the principles of judicial review 3
  Structure of this chapter 5
Category 1: Irrationality 5
  Unreasonableness 5
    Principle 5
    Key case 5
    Commentary 5
    Recent examples 9
  Proportionality 10
    Principle 10
    Key cases 10
    Commentary 10
    Recent examples 17
  Bad faith/improper motive 18
    Principle 18
    Key case 18
    Explanation 18
    Recent examples 19
Category 2: Illegality 20
  Ultra vires 21
    Principle 21
    Key cases 21
    Explanation 21
    Recent examples 25
  Unlawful delegation of powers 25
    Principle 25

Key case	25
Explanation	26
Recent examples	27
Fettering discretion	28
Principle	28
Key case	28
Explanation	28
Error of fact	29
Principle	29
Key cases	29
Explanation	29
Recent examples	31
Relevant/irrelevant considerations	32
Principle	32
Key case	32
Explanation	32
Recent example	33
Frustrating legislative purpose	34
Principle	34
Key case	34
Explanation	34
Recent examples	35
Sufficient inquiry	35
Principle	35
Key case	35
Explanation	36
Policy challenges	36
Principle	36
Key case	37
Explanation	37
Category 3: Procedural impropriety	38
Procedural fairness	39
Principle	39
Key case	39
Explanation	39
Bias	43
Principle	43
Key cases	43
Explanation	43
Recent examples	44
Legitimate expectations	45
Principle	45
Key cases	45
Explanation	45
Recent examples	47
Consultation	47
Principle	47
Key cases	47

Explanation	48
Recent examples	49
Reasons	50
Principle	50
Key case	50
Explanation	50
Recent examples	53
Category 4: Rights and freedoms	53
ECHR rights	54
Principle	54
Key provision	54
Explanation	54
Common law rights	64
Principle	64
Key cases	65
Explanation	65
EU law rights	68
Principle	68
Key case	68
Explanation	68

Chapter 2
Remedies

Introduction	73
Interim relief	73
Procedure	73
Actions against the Crown	74
Principles on interim relief	74
Cross undertaking in damages	75
Injunctions	75
The European dimension	77
Interim declarations	77
Stays	77
Bail	77
The prerogative remedies: mandatory, prohibiting and quashing orders	78
Mandatory order	78
Prohibiting order	81
Examples of when a prohibiting order has been granted	81
Earliest time for application	82
Quashing orders	82
Severance	85
Restrictions on quashing orders	86
Examples of where quashing orders have been granted	87
Injunctions to restrain a person from acting in office	88
Declarations and injunctions	88
Injunction	88
Declarations	89
Orders against the Crown	91

Damages and restitution	92
Damages	92
Restitution	94
HRA damages	96
Discretion	97
Conduct of the claimant	97
Delay	98
The role of mediation and other alternative remedies in judicial review	102
Mediation	103
Introduction	103
Support for mediation	104
General	104
The pre-action protocol for judicial review	107
The view in *The Judge Over Your Shoulder*	107
Suggestions that courts and ombudsman should have power to require mediation	108
Particular advantages in public law	108
Objections to the use of mediation in public law	109
It is wrong to consider public law as a single category	109
Duties and discretions	110
Not just two parties but the public as well	110
Authority to settle	111
Other tailor-made processes/remedies	112
Summary	112
Other alternative remedies	113
Tribunals	113
Inquiries	113
Internal complaints systems	114
Standards	115
Audit	115
Ombudsmen	117

Chapter 3
Practice and Procedure

Practice and Procedure	**121**
Judicial review in the administrative court	121
Pre-Action Protocol	121
Pre-issue considerations	122
Standing	123
Duty of candour/disclosure	123
Time limits for bringing a claim	125
Alternative remedy	126
Academic challenges	127
The claim form and service	128
Issuing the claim	128
Service	129
Acknowledgement of service	130
Urgent cases	131

Interim orders	132
Directions	132
Interim relief	133
Permission	133
Renewal of the application for permission	135
The oral hearing	135
Appeal on permission	135
Substantive hearing	136
Additional grounds	137
Skeleton arguments	137
The hearing	138
Conversion to a common law claim	138
Consent orders	139
Appeals	139
Costs	141
The permission stage	141
Substantive hearing	141
Protective costs order	144

Chapter 4
The Tribunal System

Introduction	147
The role of the tribunal system	147
Background	147
Legislation	148
Review of decisions	150
Appeals to the Upper Tribunal	152
Judicial Review in the UT	153
Judicial review of UT as a 'superior court of record'	154
The Tribunal system: an overview of appeals	155
Onward Appeals – pre and post transfer	155
First-tier Tribunal	155
Upper Tribunal	159

Part 2
Specific Areas

Chapter 5
Planning and Environment

Introduction	163
The Planning Court	163
Other amendments	165
Statutory framework	166
Planning decisions	166
Compulsory purchase decisions	170
Judicial review proceedings	171
The influence of EC law	171
Sufficient interest/person aggrieved	174
The need to be prompt and avoid undue delay	175

Grounds of review	175
Ministerial statements and policy	177
Error of law	180
Duty to give reasons for the grant of planning permission	180
The interpretation of planning policy	180
EC-based challenges	182
Irrationality	183
Procedural unfairness	185
Protective costs orders	188

Chapter 6
Community Care

Preface	191
Introduction	192
Part 1 – an overview of community care law	193
The community care decision-making process	193
The statutory framework	195
The assessment	195
Eligibility	198
The decision and care planning	200
Services	201
Direct payments	205
Personalisation and independent living	206
Part 2 – specific and significant areas of community care law	209
Children	209
Statutory framework	209
The assessment process	214
Leaving care	215
Eligible and relevant child	216
Former relevant child	216
Young people over 16 and qualifying children	217
Guidance	217
Leaving care decisions and judicial review	218
Carers	221
The social care and healthcare overlap	222
Cooperation	222
Division between social care and medical care services	223
Can a local authority provide healthcare provision?	224
Section 117 after care service	224
Analysis	228
Community care support for asylum seekers and migrants	228
Statutory framework	229
Section 21 support	230
Unaccompanied asylum-seeking children	231
Further representations by failed asylum seekers	235
Private care homes	237
Scope of judicial review	237
Rates disputes	238

Part 3 – common examples of judicial review challenges of community care decisions 239

Chapter 7
Housing 247
Introduction 247
The role of public law in social housing 247
Jurisdiction 249
Judicial attitude 252
Homelessness 253
   Exceptional circumstances 253
   Decisions outside the statutory code 255
      Interim accommodation 255
      Challenge to policy 256
      Statutory appeal ineffective 257
      Refusal to extend time to review 258
      Local connection 258
      Refusal to entertain a homelessness application 258
      Advice and assistance 259
      Pre-emptive strikes 259
Allocation 260
Introductory tenancies 263
Procedure 265
   Interim relief 265
   Costs 267

Chapter 8
Mental Health 271
Introduction 271
Public law and the Mental Health Act 1983 272
Legal review of the lawfulness of detention 277
   The hospital managers and nearest relatives 278
Treatment and the continuing duty to review 281
Treatment in the community 283
The Tribunal 285
   The Upper Tribunal 287
   The First-tier Tribunal 288
The Mental Capacity Act and the Court of Protection 293
Conclusion 296

Chapter 9
Criminal Law 299
Introduction 299
Whether the matter is a criminal cause or matter 299
   The importance of knowing whether a matter is a criminal cause or matter 299
   The decision that determines whether a matter is a criminal cause or matter 299

Determining whether a matter is a criminal cause or matter	300
Decisions that cannot be challenged	302
Interim decisions	302
Decisions of the Crown Court	304
Grounds for applying for judicial review	308
Decisions of prosecutors	308
Legitimate expectation	310
Alternative remedies	311
Appeal to the Crown Court	311
Appeal by way of case stated	311
Procedure	313
Bail as a form of interim relief	313
Role of the defendant	315
Relief at the conclusion of proceedings	315
Costs against magistrates' courts	316
Costs from central funds	317
Appeal to the Supreme Court	317
Concluding remarks	318

Chapter 10
Prison Law

Prison Law	319
Introduction	319
Regime	320
Categorisation and recategorisation	320
Allocation	321
Mother and baby units	322
Vulnerable prisoner units and segregation	322
Close supervision centres	323
Sentence planning	323
Offending behaviour programmes	323
Dangerous and severe personality disorder units	325
Reasonable adjustments	325
Living conditions	326
Property	326
Association	326
Incentives and earned privileges	326
Correspondence and visits	327
Reasonable adjustments	329
Health and social care	329
Overview	329
Mental health transfers	329
Release and recall	330
Licence and recall	330
The Parole Board	331
Home detention curfew	333
Early removal scheme	334
Tariff expired removal scheme	335

Prison discipline	335
The prison disciplinary system	335
Governor adjudications	336
Independent adjudications	337
Challenging findings of guilt	337
Complaints processes	339
The internal complaints system	339
The Prison and Probation Ombudsman	340
Investigations/Failures to investigate	341
Use of force	341
Assaults	343
Deaths	344
Near deaths	346
Litigation practicalities	348
Exhausting alternative remedies	348
Identifying the correct defendant	349
Public funding	349

Chapter 11
Education   351

Introduction	351
Overview	351
The legislative framework	351
Categorisation of schools and colleges	352
State schools	352
Academies and free schools	354
Independent schools	355
Further education	355
Higher education	356
Substantive areas of challenge	357
School organisation	357
School admissions	359
Introduction	359
The legal framework	359
Co-ordination of school admissions	359
The schools adjudicator	361
Parental preference, admission numbers and oversubscription	363
School admission appeals	370
Special educational needs and learning disability	374
Introduction	374
The Tribunal	375
Residual jurisdiction of the High Court	378
Pupil discipline and exclusion	379
Introduction	379
Exclusion	380
Challenging RP decisions	380
School uniform	385

Particular considerations 387
    Standing and funding 387
    Delay 387
Human rights 388
Conclusions 389

Chapter 12
Licensing 391
Introduction 391
    Local decision-making 391
    Specialist tribunals 391
    Chapter outline 391
Status of a licence 391
    Permission/authorisation 391
    Possession or property? 392
    Summary of the principles 395
Role of local licensing bodies 395
    Quasi-judicial function? 395
    Local decision-making 396
    Local knowledge 396
Role of local councillors 397
    Strong and robust opinions 397
    A closed mind approach? 398
    A less strict approach? 399
    Summary of the general principles 399
Role of the appeal courts 400
    Time periods for appealing 400
    The nature of the appeal 401
    Admissibility of fresh evidence 401
    The appeal – a true rehearing? 402
    The appeal – an alternative remedy 404
    Case stated or judicial review? 405
Policies and guidance 405
    Licensing policies – an overview 405
    Policies – summary of general principles 406
    Statutory guidance – an overview 408
    Guidance – summary of general principles 408
Objectors and representors 410
    Objections and representations – an overview 410
    The *Miss Behavin'* litigation 411
    Importance of the statutory context 412
    The strength of opposition 413
    Fair notice of objection or representation 414
Hearings and evidence 415
    Being properly heard by the decision-maker 415
    The procedure at the meeting or hearing 416
    Matters are generally heard in public 416
    The approach of the decision-maker 417

Judgment and the decision-maker's discretion	418
The future	419

Chapter 13
Local/Central Government — 421

Introduction	421
The legal basis of central and local government	421
Residual and prerogative powers for central government	421
Residual prerogative powers for local government?	430
General power of competence	430
Multifunctional government and judicial review	436
Democratic issues	437
Political considerations	437
Fiduciary duty	437
Interests and probity	442
Relationship with officers	443
Role of standing orders	446
Concluding remarks	449

Chapter 14
Immigration Law — 451

Introduction	451
Overview of the immigration, asylum and nationality law framework	451
Appellate structure	453
Judicial review jurisdiction of the UT	454
Pre-action matters to consider	455
Pre-action protocol letters	455
Time limits	456
Alternative remedies	456
Procedure in the UT	456
Urgent applications and interim relief	456
Lodging the application	457
Removal directions	458
Responding to the application – the acknowledgment of service ('AoS')	458
Permission	459
Substantive hearing	459
Consent orders	459
Costs	460
Common judicial review applications before the UT	460
Fresh claims	460
Certification	461
Delay	462
Article 8 ECHR/refusal to issue an appealable decision	463
Other challenges	464
Detention	464
Secondary legislation or the immigration rules	465
Decisions of the UT	465

National security/SIAC 465

Chapter 15
Professional Regulation 467
Introduction 467
Regulation and the regulators 467
  What is regulation? 467
    Self regulation v statutory regulation 467
    Who are the regulators? 469
  Key regulatory functions 472
Judicial review and the regulators 473
  The limits of judicial review 473
    Targets 473
    Timing 475
    Amenability 476
    Alternative remedies 478
    Restraint 480
    Standing 481
  The grounds of judicial review 481
    Entry onto the register 482
    Issues regarding registration 482
    Exams 483
    Recognition of certain qualifications 484
    Maintaining the register 485
  Removal from the register 485
    Allegations 485
    Investigations 488
    The role of judicial review at the investigation stage 489
    Data issues 490
    Delay 491
    Reopening cases 492
    Adjudication 493
  Preliminary issues 494
    Adjournments 494
    Charges 495
  The substantive hearing 497
    Standard of proof 497
    Legal assessors 497
    Natural justice 498
    Article 6 of the European Convention on Human Rights 501
    Unreasonableness 505
    Illegality 506
  Sanctions 508
  Appeals 509
  Costs 510
  Postscript: Judicial review of the regulators by the regulators 511

Chapter 16
Healthcare — 515
Introduction — 515
NHS reconfiguration and consultation — 515
NHS continuing healthcare funding — 518
Medical treatment policies — 520
Individual funding requests — 521
After-care services — 522
Immigration and healthcare — 525
Prisoners and healthcare — 526
Conclusion — 526

Part 3
Appendices
Appendix 1
Procedural Guide — 529
Claims for Judicial Review — 529

Appendix 2
Statutory Materials — 537
Senior Courts Act 1981, s 31 — 537
Tribunal Courts and Enforcement Act 2007, ss 15–18 — 539
First-tier Tribunal and Upper Tribunal (Chambers) (Amendment No 2) Order 2013, SI 2013/2068 — 542
Upper Tribunal (Immigration and Asylum Chamber) (Judicial Review) (England and Wales) Fees (Amendment) Order 2013, SI 2013/2069 — 543

Appendix 3
Civil Procedure Rules — 545
Practice Directions — 553
Practice Direction 54A – Judicial Review — 553
Practice Direction 54B – Applications for Statutory Review under section 103A of the Nationality, Immigration and Asylum Act 2002 — 558
Practice Direction 54C – References by the Legal Services Commission — 558
Practice Direction 54D – Administrative Court (Venue) — 558
Practice Direction 54E – Planning Court Claims — 561
Pre Action Protocol for Judicial Review — 562

Appendix 4
Administrative Court Guidance — 571
Notes for guidance on applying for judicial review — 571
Administrative Court – guidance as to how the court will approach applications for costs following settlement of claims for judicial review — 589

R (on the application of Hamid) v Secretary of State for the Home
    Department [2012] EWHC 3070 — 591
R (Butt and Others) v SSHD [2014] EWHC 264 (Admin) — 594

Appendix 5
Forms — 599
N461 – Judicial Review Claim Form — 600
N462 – Judicial Review Acknowledgment of Service — 606
N463 – Judicial Review Application for Urgent Consideration — 610
T480 – Judicial Review Claim Form in the Upper Tribunal
    Immigration and Asylum Chamber — 612
T481 – Accompanying Notes to T480 — 618
T482 – Acknowledgment of Service in the Upper Tribunal Immigration
    and Asylum Service — 622
T483 – Judicial Review Application for Urgent Consideration in the
    Upper Tribunal Immigration and Asylum Chamber — 625

Index — 629

TABLE OF CASES

References are to paragraph numbers.

A Company, Re [1981] AC 374, [1980] 3 WLR 181, [1980] 2 All ER 634	1.76
A Solicitor No 4 of 2009, Re, Afsar [2009] EWCA Civ 842	15.75
A Solicitor Nos 21 and 22 of 2007, Re, Ali and Naeem [2008] EWCA Civ 769	15.75
A v Chief Constable of West Yorkshire [2004] UKHL 21, [2005] 1 AC 51, [2004] 2 WLR 1209, [2004] 3 All ER 145, [2004] 2 CMLR 37, [2004] Eu LR 841, [2004] ICR 806, [2004] IRLR 573, [2004] 2 FCR 160, [2004] HRLR 25, [2004] UKHRR 694, 17 BHRC 585, (2004) 101(20) LSG 34, (2004) 154 NLJ 734, (2004) 148 SJLB 572, (2004) Times, 7 May	1.204
A v Essex County Council [2010] UKSC 33, [2010] 4 All ER 199, [2010] 3 WLR 509, [2010] PTSR 1332, (2010) Times, 15 July, 154 Sol Jo 30, [2010] All ER (D) 140 (Jul)	2.100, 11.157
A v Secretary of State for the Home Department [2004] UKHL 56, [2005] 2 AC 68, [2005] 2 WLR 87, [2005] 3 All ER 169, [2005] HRLR 1, [2005] UKHRR 175, 17 BHRC 496, [2005] Imm AR 103, (2005) 155 NLJ 23, (2005) 149 SJLB 28, (2004) Times, 17 December, (2004) Independent, 21 December	1.55, 1.201
A v Secretary of State for the Home Department [2005] UKHL 71, [2006] 2 AC 221, [2005] 3 WLR 1249, [2006] 1 All ER 575, [2006] HRLR 6, [2006] UKHRR 225, 19 BHRC 441, (2005) 155 NLJ 1924, (2005) Times, 9 December, (2005) Independent, 14 December	1.55, 1.201
A v Secretary of State for the Home Department [2010] UKSC 2, [2010] 2 AC 534, [2010] 2 WLR 378, [2010] 4 All ER 745, [2010] HRLR 15, [2010] UKHRR 204, [2010] Lloyd's Rep FC 217, (2010) 154(4) SJLB 28, (2010) Times, 29 January	1.01
Aegis Group plc v IRC, sub nom Aegis, Re [2005] EWHC 1468 (Ch), [2005] All ER (D) 209 (May), [2006] STC 23, [2005] SWTI 989	3.78
AH v Sudan [2007] UKHL 49, [2008] 1 AC 678, [2007] 3 WLR 832, [2008] 4 All ER 190, [2008] Imm AR 289, [2008] INLR 100, (2007) 151 SJLB 1500, (2007) Times, 15 November	8.55
AHK v Secretary of State for the Home Department, FM v Secretary of State for the Home Department [2009] EWCA Civ 287, [2009] 1 WLR 2049, [2009] All ER (D) 35 (Apr)	14.58
Ahmed v HM Treasury [2010] UKSC 2, [2010] 2 AC 534, [2010] 2 WLR 378, [2010] 4 All ER 745, [2010] HRLR 15, [2010] UKHRR 204, [2010] Lloyd's Rep FC 217, (2010) 154(4) SJLB 28, (2010) Times, 29 January	1.01, 1.55, 1.201
Aintree University NHS Foundation Trust v James [2013] UKSC 67, [2013] 3 WLR 1299, [2014] 1 All ER 573, [2014] 1 FCR 153, (2013) 16 CCL Rep 554, [2014] Med LR 1, (2014) 135 BMLR 1, (2013) 163(7583) NLJ 16, (2013) 157(43) SJLB 53, (2013) Times, 19 November	16.32

Akenzua (Administrators of the Estate of Laws (decd)) v Secretary of State
   for the Home Department [2002] EWCA Civ 1470, [2003] 1 All ER
   35, [2003] 1 WLR 741, [2002] 47 LS Gaz R 29, (2002) *Times*, 30
   October, 146 Sol Jo LB 243, [2002] All ER (D) 327 (Oct) 2.89
Akewushola v Secretary of State for the Home Department [2000] 1 WLR
   2295, [2000] 2 All ER 148, [1999] Imm AR 594, [1999] INLR 433,
   (1999) *Times*, 3 November 15.132, 15.223
Akhtar v Birmingham City Council [2011] EWCA Civ 383, [2011] HLR 28,
   (2011) *Times*, 22 April 1.154
Aksoy v Turkey (App 21987/93) (1997) 23 EHRR 553 . . . . 1.169
AL (Serbia) v Secretary of State for the Home Department [2008] UKHL 42,
   [2008] 1 WLR 1434, [2008] 4 All ER 1127, [2008] HRLR 41, [2008]
   UKHRR 917, 24 BHRC 738, [2008] Imm AR 729, [2008] INLR 471,
   (2008) 152(26) SJLB 29, (2008) *Times*, 2 July 1.193
Al Rawi v Security Service [2011] UKSC 34, [2012] 1 AC 531, [2011] 3
   WLR 388, [2012] 1 All ER 1, [2011] UKHRR 931, (2011) 108(30)
   LSG 23, (2011) 155(28) SJLB 31, (2011) *Times*, 15 July 1.55, 1.123, 1.201
Ali v Birmingham City Council [2010] UKSC 8, [2010] 2 AC 39, [2010] 2
   WLR 471, [2010] 2 All ER 175, [2010] PTSR 524, [2010] HRLR 18,
   [2010] UKHRR 417, [2010] HLR 22, [2010] BLGR 401, (2010)
   154(7) SJLB 37, (2010) *Times*, 19 February 1.178, 1.179
Alice Woodhall, ex p (1888) 20 QBD 832 . . . . 9.05
Allman v Coroner for West Sussex [2012] EWHC 534 (Admin), (2012) 176
   JP 285 . . . . 2.116
Allsop v North Tyneside Metropolitan Borough Council (1992) 90 LGR 462,
   [1992] ICR 639, [1992] RVR 104 . . . . 13.48
Alnwick DC v Secretary of State for the Environment, Transport and the
   Regions (2000) 79 P & CR 130, [1999] 4 PLR 43, [2000] JPL 474,
   (1999) 96(34) LSG 35, (1999) 96(32) LSG 35 . . . . 5.51, 5.52
Alstom Transport v Eurostar International Ltd [2012] EWHC 28 (Ch),
   [2012] 3 All ER 263, [2012] 2 All ER (Comm) 869, [2013] PTSR
   454, 140 Con LR 1, [2012] Eu LR 425, (2012) 162 NLJ 215 . . . . 1.205
Alvi v SSHD [2012] UKSC 33, [2012] 1 WLR 2208, [2012] 4 All ER 1041,
   [2012] Imm AR 998, [2012] INLR 504 . . . . 14.06
AM v South London & Maudsley NHS Foundation Trust, Secretary of State
   for Health [2013] UKUT 365 (AAC) 8.80
Amand v Home Secretary and Minister of Defence of Royal Netherlands
   Government [1943] AC 147, [1942] 2 All ER 381, HL 3.51, 9.06, 9.64
American Cyanamid Co v Ethicon Ltd [1975] AC 396, [1975] 2 WLR 316,
   [1975] 1 All ER 504, [1975] RPC 513, HL 2.10, 3.42, 7.98
Andreou v Institute of Chartered Accountants in England and Wales [1998]
   1 All ER 14 . . . . 15.37, 15.43
Anisminic Ltd v Foreign Compensation Commission and Another [1969] 2
   AC 147, [1969] 2 WLR 163, [1969] 1 All ER 208, (1968) 113 SJ 55,
   (1968) *Times*, 18 December 1.04, 1.67, 1.75, 4.22, 8.58
Ansari v General Pharmaceutical Council [2012] All ER (D) 126 (Apr) 2.72
Anufrijeva v Southwark London Borough Council, R (N) v Secretary of State
   for the Home Department, R (M) v Same [2003] EWCA Civ 1406,
   [2004] QB 1124, [2004] 1 All ER 833, [2004] 2 WLR 603, [2004]
   LGR 184, [2003] 3 FCR 673, [2004] 1 FLR 8, [2004] Fam Law 12,
   [2003] 44 LS Gaz R 30, (2003) *Times*, 17 October, 15 BHRC 526,
   [2003] All ER (D) 288 (Oct) 1.163, 1.183, 2.99, 2.101, 2.103, 2.104
Anya v University of Oxford [2001] EWCA Civ 405, [2001] ICR 847,
   [2001] IRLR 377, [2001] Emp LR 509, [2001] ELR 711, (2001)
   Times, 4 May 1.153
Aparau v Iceland Frozen Foods Plc [2000] 1 All ER 228, [2000] ICR 341,
   [2000] IRLR 196, (1999) 96(45) LSG 31, *Times*, November 11, 1999 . . . . 1.77
Application for Judicial Review by JR17, Re [2010] UKSC 27, [2010] NI
   105, [2010] HRLR 27, [2010] UKHRR 984, [2010] ELR 764, (2010)
   13 CCL Rep 357, (2010) 154(25) SJLB 41 . . . . 1.123

Arben Simoni v Secretary of State for Communities and Local Government
    [2012] EWHC 323, Admin ... 5.31
Ardagh Glass v Chester City Council [2009] EWHC 745 (Admin), [2009]
    Env LR 34, [2009] NPC 59 ... 5.106
Asher v Secretary of State for the Environment [1974] Ch 208, [1974] 2 All
    ER 156, [1974] 2 WLR 466, 72 LGR 333, 118 Sol Jo 258 ... 2.193
Ashley v SSCLG & LB Greenwich & Taylor Wimpey (CA) [2012] EWCA
    Civ 547 ... 5.124, 5.125, 5.126
Ashraf v SSHD [2013] EWHC 4028 (Admin) ... 14.17
Ashton, Re [1994] AC 9, [1993] 2 WLR 846, 97 Cr App Rep 203, [1993]
    Crim LR 959 ... 9.28, 9.34
ASM Shipping Ltd v Harris [2007] EWHC 1513 (Comm), [2008] 1 Lloyd's
    Rep 61, [2007] 1 CLC 1017, (2007) 23 Const LJ 533, [2007] Bus LR
    D105, (2007) *Times*, 6 August ... 1.132
Assessor for Renfrewshire v Mitchell and Others 1965 SC 271, Lands Val
    AC ... 1.04, 1.09, 1.102
Associated Provincial Picture Houses Ltd v Wednesbury Corporation [1948]
    1 KB 223, [1947] 2 All ER 680, (1947) 63 TLR 623, (1948) 112 JP
    55, 45 LGR 635, [1948] LJR 190, (1947) 177 LT 641, (1948) 92 SJ
    26 ... 1.04, 1.09, 1.11, 1.12, 1.102, 6.131, 8.16, 8.23, 8.40, 12.101, 12.103, 13.88, 13.97, 13.99, 13.123, 15.190
Association of British Civilian Internees v Secretary of State for Defence
    [2003] EWCA Civ 473, [2003] QB 1397, [2003] 3 WLR 80, [2003]
    ACD 51, (2003) 100(23) LSG 38, (2003) *Times*, 19 April, (2003)
    Independent, 10 April ... 1.41, 1.55, 1.201
Aston Cantlow and Wilmcote with Billesley Parochial Church Council v
    Wallbank [2003] UKHL 37, [2004] 1 AC 546, [2003] 3 WLR 283,
    [2003] 3 All ER 1213, [2003] HRLR 28, [2003] UKHRR 919, [2003]
    27 EG 137 (CS), (2003) 100(33) LSG 28, (2003) 153 NLJ 1030,
    (2003) 147 SJLB 812, [2003] NPC 80, (2003) *Times*, 27 June ... 7.22, 15.41
Attorney-General (at the relation of Allen) v Colchester Corpn [1955] 2 QB
    207, [1955] 2 All ER 124, [1955] 2 WLR 913, 53 LGR 415, 99 Sol
    Jo 291 ... 2.67
Attorney-General v Blake [2001] 1 AC 268, [2000] 3 WLR 625, [2000] 4
    All ER 385, [2000] 2 All ER (Comm) 487, [2001] IRLR 36, [2001]
    Emp LR 329, [2000] EMLR 949, (2000) 23(12) IPD 23098, (2000)
    97(32) LSG 37, (2000) 150 NLJ 1230, (2000) 144 SJLB 242, (2000)
    Times, 3 August, (2000) *Independent*, 6 November ... 1.55, 1.201
Attorney-General v Great Eastern Railway (1880) 5 App Cas 473 ... 13.45
Attorney-General v Leicester Corporation [1943] 1 Ch 86, [1943] 1 All ER
    146, 41 LGR 82, 107 JP 65, 112 LJ Ch 97, 87 Sol Jo 57, 168 LT
    229, 59 TLR 118 ... 13.42
Attorney-General v London and Home Counties Joint Electricity Authority
    [1929] 1 Ch 513, 27 LGR 337, 93 JP 115, 98 LJ Ch 162, 140 LT
    578, 45 TLR 235 ... 2.69
Attorney-General v Manchester Corporation [1906] 1 Ch 643, 4 LGR 365,
    70 JP 201, 75 LJ Ch 330, 54 WR 307, 22 TLR 261 ... 13.41
Attorney-General v Wilts United Dairies Ltd (1922) 91 LJKB 897, 66 Sol Jo
    630, 127 LT 822, 38 TLR 781, [1922] All ER Rep Ext 845 ... 13.49
Austin v Commissioner of Police of the Metropolis [2009] UKHL 5, [2009]
    1 AC 564, [2009] 2 WLR 372, [2009] 3 All ER 455, [2009] HRLR
    16, [2009] UKHRR 581, 26 BHRC 642, [2009] Po LR 66, (2009)
    153(4) SJLB 29, (2009) *Times*, 29 January ... 1.163, 1.173, 1.174
Awuku v SSHD [2012] EWHC 3690 (Admin), [2013] ACD 26 ... 14.24
AXA General Insurance Ltd v HM Advocate [2011] UKSC 46, [2012] 1 AC
    868, [2011] 3 WLR 871, 2012 SC (UKSC) 122, 2011 SLT 1061,
    [2012] HRLR 3, [2011] UKHRR 1221, (2011) 122 BMLR 149,
    (2011) 108(41) LSG 22, (2011) *Times*, 19 October ... 1.01, 1.197, 1.201
Azzam v General Medical Council [2008] EWHC 2711 (Admin), [2009] LS
    Law Medical 28, (2009) 105 BMLR 142 ... 15.153

B & J v SSHD [2012] EWHC 3770 (Admin), [2013] ACD 28   14.24
B (A Child), Re [2013] UKSC 33, [2013] 1 WLR 1911, [2013] 3 All ER
    929, [2013] 2 FLR 1075, [2013] 2 FCR 525, [2013] HRLR 29,
    [2013] Fam Law 946, (2013) 157(24) SJLB 37   1.18, 1.184, 1.187
B v Barking, Havering and Brentwood Community Healthcare NHS Trust
    [1999] 1 FLR 106, CA   8.44
B v Croydon Health Authority [1995] Fam 133, [1995] 1 All ER 683,
    [1995] 2 WLR 294, [1995] 1 FCR 662, [1995] 1 FLR 470, [1995]
    Fam Law 244, 22 BMLR 13, [1994] NLJR 1696, [1995] PIQR P 145   8.20, 8.40
B v Secretary of State for Justice [2000] 2 CMLR 1086, [2000] Eu LR 687,
    [2000] HRLR 439, [2000] UKHRR 498, [2000] Imm AR 478, [2000]
    INLR 361, (2000) *Independent*, 26 June   1.201
B v Secretary of State for Justice [2011] EWCA Civ 1608, [2012] 1 WLR
    2043, (2012) 124 BMLR 13, [2012] MHLR 131, (2012) *Times*, 19
    January   1.55
B v Secretary of State for the Home Department [2000] 2 CMLR 1086,
    [2000] Eu LR 687, [2000] HRLR 439, [2000] UKHRR 498, [2000]
    Imm AR 478, [2000] INLR 361, (2000) *Independent*, 26 June   1.207
B, Re [2008] UKHL 35, [2009] 1 AC 11, [2008] 3 WLR 1, [2008] 4 All ER
    1, [2008] 2 FLR 141, [2008] 2 FCR 339, [2008] Fam Law 619,
    [2008] Fam Law 837, (2008) *Times*, 12 June   15.155
BAA Ltd v Competition Commission [2010] EWCA Civ 1097, [2011]
    UKCLR 1   1.132
Balogh v Secretary of State for the Environment [1996]1 PLR 32   5.19
Bank Mellat v HM Treasury, No 2 [2011] EWCA Civ 1, [2012] QB 101,
    [2011] 3 WLR 714, [2011] 2 All ER 802, [2011] HRLR 13, [2011]
    UKHRR 208, [2011] Lloyd's Rep FC 168   1.157
Banks v Royal Borough of Kingston upon Thames [2008] EWCA Civ 1443,
    [2009] LGR 536, [2009] PTSR 1354, [2009] HLR 482, (2009) *Times*,
    10 March, [2008] All ER (D) 185 (Dec)   7.10
Baraona v Portugal (1991) 13 EHRR 329   1.179
Barker v Hambleton DC [2012] EWCA Civ 610, [2013] PTSR 41, [2012]
    CP Rep 36, [2013] 1 P & CR 1, [2012] 2 EGLR 101, [2012] 28 EG
    85, [2012] 20 EG 92 (CS), (2012) *Times*, August 21   5.22
Barnard v Gorman [1941] AC 378, [1941] 3 All ER 45   1.98
Barnard v National Dock Labour Board [1953] 2 QB 18, [1953] 2 WLR
    995, [1953] 1 All ER 1113, [1953] 1 Lloyd's Rep 371, (1953) 97 SJ
    331   1.84
Barrett v Enfield London Borough Council [2001] 2 AC 550, [1999] 3 WLR
    79, [1999] 2 FLR 426, [1999] 3 All ER 193, HL   2.83
Barty-King v Ministry of Defence [1979] 2 All ER 80, [1979] STC 218   2.72
Baxendale-Walker v Law Society [2006] EWHC 643 (Admin), [2006] 3 All
    ER 675, [2006] 5 Costs LR 696, (2006) 156 NLJ 601, (2006) *Times*,
    17 May, (2006) *Independent*, 5 April   15.217, 15.221
BB v Cygnet Health Care & Lewisham LBC [2008] EWHC 1259 (Admin),
    [2008] All ER (D) 35 (Mar)   8.13
BBC v Johns (Inspector of Taxes) [1965] Ch 32, [1964] 1 All ER 923,
    [1964] 2 WLR 1071, 41 TC 471, 43 ATC 38, 10 RRC 239, [1964]
    TR 45, 108 Sol Jo 217, [1964] RVR 579   13.07
Begum (Nipa) v Tower Hamlets London Borough Council [2000] 1 WLR
    306, [1999] 44 LS Gaz R 41, 143 Sol Jo LB 277, [1999] All ER (D)
    1189   7.37
Belfast City Council v Miss Behavin' Ltd [2007] UKHL 19, [2007] 1 WLR
    1420, [2007] 3 All ER 1007, [2007] NI 89, [2007] HRLR 26, [2008]
    BLGR 127, (2007) 104(19) LSG 27, (2007) 151 SJLB 575, (2007)
    Times, 1 May   1.123
Belgian Linguistics Case (No 2) (Applications 1474/62, 1691/62, 1769/63,
    1994/63, 2126/64 and 1677/62) (1968) 1 EHRR 252   11.155
Belize Bank Ltd v Attorney General of Belize [2011] UKPC 36   1.130, 1.131
Benthem v Netherlands (8848/80) (1986) 8 EHRR 1   1.179

Beresford v Solicitors Regulation Authority [2009] EWHC 3155 (Admin)   15.217
Berkeley v Secretary of State for the Environment, Transport and the Regions [2000] UKHL 36, [2001] 2 AC 603, [2000] 3 WLR 420, [2000] 3 All ER 897, HL   2.123, 5.58, 5.60
Bhatt v General Medical Council [2011] EWHC 783 (Admin)   15.102
Bilbie v Lumley (1802) 2 East 469, 102 ER 448, [1775–1802] All ER Rep 425   2.93
Bilston Corporations v Wolverhampton Corps [1942] Ch 391, [1942] 2 All ER 447, 40 LGR 167, 106 JP 181, 111 LJ Ch 268, 167 LT 61   2.69
Birkdale District Electricity Supply Co Ltd v Southport Corporation [1926] AC 355   1.82
Birmingham City Council v (1) Clue, (2) Secretary of State for the Home Department, & (3) Shelter [2010] EWCA Civ 460   6.136
Birmingham City Council v Qasim [2009] EWCA Civ 1080, [2010] LGR 253, [2010] PTSR 471, [2010] HLR 327, [2009] 43 EG 104 (CS), [2010] 1 P & CR D41, [2009] All ER (D) 206 (Oct)   7.69
Black v UK (App No 60682/00)   10.86
Blackburn-Smith v Lambeth London Borough Council [2007] EWHC 767 (Admin), [2007] All ER (D) 64 (Apr)   6.52
Blackpool Council v Howitt [2008] EWHC 3300 (Admin), [2009] 4 All ER 154, [2009] PTSR 1458, 173 JP 101, [2008] All ER (D) 28 (Dec)   12.63
Bloomsbury International Ltd v Department for Environment, Food and Rural Affairs [2011] UKSC 25, [2011] 1 WLR 1546, [2011] 4 All ER 721, [2011] 3 CMLR 32, (2011) 161 NLJ 883   1.203
Blyth, ex p [1944] 1 KB 532   9.63
Board of Education v Rice [1911] AC 179, 9 LGR 652, 75 JP 393, 80 LJKB 796, [1911–13] All ER Rep 36, 55 Sol Jo 440, 104 LT 689, 27 TLR 378   1.56, 1.122, 2.61
Boddington v British Transport Police [1999] 2 AC 143, [1998] 2 WLR 639, [1998] 2 All ER 203, (1998) 162 JP 455, (1998) 10 Admin LR 321, (1998) 148 NLJ 515, (1998) Times, 3 April   1.05, 1.67, 1.78, 1.127, 8.32, 9.42
Bolton Metropolitan Borough Council v Secretary of State for the Environment (1991) 61 P & CR 343, [1991] JPL 241, [1990] EG 106 (CS)   5.30, 5.32, 5.70
Bolton Metropolitan Borough Council v Secretary of State for the Environment [1995] 1 WLR 1176, [1996] 1 All ER 184, [1995] 3 PLR 37, [1996] JPL 300, [1995] EG 126 (CS), (1995) Times, 17 July   1.155, 5.32
Bolton v Law Society [1994] 1 WLR 512, [1994] 2 All ER 486, [1994] COD 295, (1993) Times, 8 December   15.05, 15.61, 15.209, 15.210
Brabazon-Drenning v United Kingdom Central Council for Nursing, Midwifery and Health Visiting [2001] HRLR 6, (2000) Telegraph, 28 November   1.155
Bradbury v London Borough of Enfield [1967] 3 All ER 434, [1967] 1 WLR 1311, 66 LGR 115, 132 JP 15, 111 Sol Jo 701   2.68
Bradley v Jockey Club [2005] EWCA Civ 1056, (2005) Times, 14 July   15.19
Brennan v Health Professions Council [2011] EWHC 41 (Admin), (2011) 119 BMLR 1   15.204
British Medical Association v Secretary of State for Health [2008] EWHC 599 (Admin)   1.149
British Oxygen Co Ltd v Minister of Technology [1971] AC 610, [1970] 3 All ER 165, [1970] 3 WLR 488, 49 ATC 154, [1970] TR 143, 114 Sol Jo 682   1.89, 1.90, 12.61
Bromley London Borough Council v Greater London Council, sub nom R v Greater London Council, ex p Bromley London Borough Council [1983] 1 AC 768, [1982] 1 All ER 129, [1982] 2 WLR 62, 80 LGR 1, [1982] RA 47, 125 Sol Jo 809   1.20, 13.91, 13.94, 13.97, 13.99, 13.100
Brown v Stott (Procurator Fiscal, Dunfermline) and Another [2003] 1 AC 681, [2001] 2 WLR 817, [2001] UKHRR 333, [2001] 2 All ER 97, [2001] SC (PC) 43, 2000 JC 328, PC   1.47

Bryant v Law Society [2007] EWHC 3043 (Admin), [2009] 1 WLR 163, (2008) 105(3) LSG 28, (2008) 158 NLJ 66 .... 15.151
Budd v Office of the Independent Adjudicator for Higher Education [2010] EWHC 1056 (Admin), [2010] ELR 579 .... 11.26
Bultitude v Law Society [2004] EWCA Civ 1853, (2005) 102(9) LSG 29, (2005) *Times*, 14 January 15.151
Burnip v Birmingham City Council [2012] EWCA Civ 629, [2013] PTSR 117, [2012] HRLR 20, [2012] Eq LR 701, [2013] HLR 1, [2012] BLGR 954, (2012) *Times*, 21 August 1.193
Bushell v Secretary of State for the Environment [1981] AC 75, [1980] 3 WLR 22, [1980] 2 All ER 608, 78 LGR 269, (1980) 40 P & CR 51, [1980] JPL 458, (1981) 125 SJ 168 .... 1.123
Butt v Solicitors Regulation Authority [2010] EWHC 1381 (Admin) 15.74
Byrne v Kinematograph Renters Society Ltd [1958] 1 WLR 762, [1958] 2 All ER 579, (1958) 102 SJ 509 .... 1.58

C (A Minor: Medical Treatment: Court's Jurisdiction) [1997] 2 FLR 180 .... 8.20
Cala Homes (South) Ltd v Secretary of State for Communities and Local Government [2010] EWHC 2866, (Admin), [2010] All ER (D) 102 (Nov) 2.20
Calhaem v General Medical Council [2007] EWHC 2606 (Admin), [2008] LS Law Medical 96 .... 15.151, 15.152
Campbell v MGN Ltd [2004] UKHL 22, [2004] 2 AC 457, [2004] 2 WLR 1232, [2004] 2 All ER 995, [2004] EMLR 15, [2004] HRLR 24, [2004] UKHRR 648, 16 BHRC 500, (2004) 101(21) LSG 36, (2004) 154 NLJ 733, (2004) 148 SJLB 572, *Times*, May 7, 2004, (2004) *Independent*, 11 May 1.189
Cannan v Governor of Sutton Prison [2009] EWHC 1517 (Admin), [2010] 2 Prison LR 166 .... 10.22
Cannock Chase District Council v Kelly [1978] 1 WLR 1, [1978] 1 All ER 152, 76 LGR 67, (1978) 36 P & CR 219, (1977) 244 EG 211, [1977] JPL 655, (1977) 121 SJ 593 .... 1.59
Canterbury City Council v Ali [2013] EWHC 2360 (Admin) 12.49
Carltona Ltd v Commissioner of Works [1943] 2 All ER 560 .... 1.81, 1.85, 13.122, 13.125, 13.127
Carr v Atkins [1987] QB 963, [1987] 3 WLR 529, [1987] 3 All ER 684, CA 9.04, 9.09, 9.14
Cart v The Upper Tribunal (Rev 1) [2011] UKSC 28, [2012] 1 AC 663, [2011] 3 WLR 107, [2011] 4 All ER 127, [2011] PTSR 1053, [2011] STC 1659, [2012] 1 FLR 997, [2011] Imm AR 704, [2011] MHLR 196, [2012] Fam Law 398, [2011] STI 1943, (2011) 161 NLJ 916, (2011) 155(25) SJLB 35, (2011) *Times*, 23 June 1.80
Carter-Pascoe (Mark) v Birmingham Justices [2002] EWHC 1202 (Admin), [2002] All ER (D) 104 (Jun) 12.100
Case of Sutton's Hospital (1612) 10 Co Rep 1 .... 13.41
Centros Ltd v Erhvervs-og Selskabsstyrelsen (Case C-212/97) [1999] ECR I-1459, [2000] Ch 446, [2000] 2 WLR 1048, [1999] 2 CMLR 551, ECJ 1.206, 1.207
Ceylon University v Fernando [1960] 1 WLR 223, [1960] 1 All ER 631, (1960) 104 SJ 230 .... 1.123
CF v Secretary of State for the Home Department [2004] EWHC 111 (Fam), [2004] 2 FLR 517, [2004] 1 FCR 577, [2005] 1 Prison LR 104, [2004] Fam Law 639 .... 10.15
Charles Terence Estates v Cornwall County Council [2012] EWCA Civ 1439, [2013] 1 WLR 466, [2013] PTSR 175, [2013] HLR 12, [2013] BLGR 97 .... 13.103
Chaudery v Solicitors Regulation Authority [2012] EWHC 372 (Admin) 15.75
Chauffeur Bikes Limited v Leeds City Council [2005] EWHC 2369 (Admin), [2006] RTR 74, 170 JPN 373, (2005) *Times*, 20 October, [2005] All ER (D) 106 (Oct) 12.21

Cheatle v General Medical Council [2009] EWHC 645 (Admin), [2009] LS
  Law Medical 299 .... 15.168
Cheshire West and Chester Council v P [2011] EWCA Civ 1257, [2012]
  PTSR 1447, [2012] 1 FLR 693, (2012) 15 CCL Rep 48, [2013] Med
  LR 421, [2011] MHLR 430, [2012] Fam Law 137 .... 1.173, 1.174
Chester v Secretary of State for Justice [2013] UKSC 63, [2013] 3 WLR
  1076, [2014] 1 All ER 683, 2014 SLT 143, [2014] 1 CMLR 45,
  [2014] HRLR 3, 2013 GWD 34-676 .... 1.163
Chevrol v France (49636/99) 1.179
Chief Constable of Hertfordshire Police v Van Colle, Smith v Chief
  Constable of Sussex Police [2008] 3 WLR 593, [2008] UKHL 50,
  [2009] AC 225, [2008] 3 All ER 977, [2009] 1 Cr App Rep 146,
  [2009] PIQR P9, (2008) *Times*, 1 August, (2008) *Times*, 4 August,
  152 Sol Jo (no 32) 31, [2009] 3 LRC 272, [2008] All ER (D) 408
  (Jul) 2.87
Chief Constable of North Wales Police v Evans [1982] 1 WLR 1155, [1982]
  3 All ER 141, HL 2.121
Chyc v General Medical Council [2008] EWHC 1025 (Admin) 15.211
City of Edinburgh Council v Secretary of State for Scotland [1997] 1 WLR
  1447, [1998] 1 All ER 174, 1998 SC (HL) 33, 1998 SLT 120, 1997
  SCLR 1112, [1997] 3 PLR 71, [1998] JPL 224, [1997] EG 140 (CS),
  (1997) 94(42) LSG 31, (1997) 141 SJLB 228, [1997] NPC 146, 1997
  GWD 33-1693, (1997) *Times*, 31 October 1.155
Clifford and O'Sullivan, Re [1921] 2 AC 570, 90 LJPC 244, 27 Cox CC
  120, 65 Sol Jo 792, 126 LT 97, 37 TLR 988 .... 2.60
Clue v Birmingham City Council [2010] EWCA Civ 460, [2011] 1 WLR 99,
  [2010] 4 All ER 423, [2010] PTSR 2051, [2010] 2 FLR 1011, [2010]
  3 FCR 475, [2010] BLGR 485, (2010) 13 CCL Rep 276, [2010] Fam
  Law 802, (2010) 154(18) SJLB 29, (2010) *Times*, 7 May 1.163
Clunis v Camden and Islington Health Authority [1998] QB 978, [1998] 2
  WLR 902, [1998] 3 All ER 180, CA 6.118
Cohen v General Medical Council [2008] EWHC 581 (Admin), [2008] LS
  Law Medical 246, (2008) 105(15) LSG 27 .... 15.153
Colman v General Medical Council [2010] EWHC 1608 (QB), [2011] ACD
  38 .... 15.171
Commissioner for HM Revenue and Customs v IDT Card Services Ireland
  [2006] EWCA Civ 29, [2006] STC 1252, [2006] BTC 5175, [2006]
  BVC 244, [2006] STI 239 .... 5.56
Compton v General Medical Council [2008] EWHC 2868 (Admin) 15.158
Condron v National Assembly for Wales [2006] EWCA Civ 1573, [2007]
  BLGR 87, [2007] 2 P & CR 4, [2007] JPL 938, [2006] 49 EG 94
  (CS), [2006] NPC 127, [2007] Env LR D7, (2006) *Times*, 13
  December, (2006) *Independent*, 29 November 5.116
Connolly v Law Society [2007] EWHC 1175 .... 15.148
Cooke v Secretary of State for Social Security [2001] EWCA Civ 734, [2002]
  3 All ER 279, (2001) Telegraph, 1 May 8.55
Cooper v Wandsworth Board of Works 143 ER 414, (1863) 14 CB NS 180 .... 1.122
Corby Borough Council v Scott [2012] EWCA Civ 276, [2013] PTSR 141,
  [2012] HLR 23, [2012] BLGR 493, [2012] 2 EGLR 38, [2012] 21 EG
  100, [2012] 12 EG 92 (CS), [2012] 1 P & CR DG23 .... 1.184, 1.186
Corporation of the Hall of Arts and Science v Albert Court Residents'
  Association [2011] EWCA Civ 430 .... 12.68
Council for the Regulation of Health Care Professionals v Ruscillo [2004]
  EWCA Civ 1356, [2005] 1 WLR 717, [2005] Lloyd's Rep Med 65,
  [2005] ACD 69, [2005] ACD 99, (2004) 148 SJLB 1248, (2004)
  Times, 27 October, (2004) *Independent*, 28 October 15.102
Council for the Regulation of Healthcare Professionals v General Dental
  Council [2006] EWHC 1870 (Admin), (2006) 92 BMLR 36, [2007]
  ACD 18 .... 15.169

Council for the Regulation of Healthcare Professionals v General Dental
    Council and Fleischmann [2005] EWHC 87 (QB), (2005) *Times*, 8
    February   15.75
Council of Civil Service Unions v Minister for the Civil Service [1985] AC
    374, [1984] 3 WLR 1174, [1984] 3 All ER 935, [1985] ICR 14,
    [1985] IRLR 28, (1985) 82 LSG 437, (1984) 128 SJ 837   1.04, 1.14, 1.31, 1.78, 1.122,
                                1.123, 1.137, 2.78, 7.09, 13.09, 13.10, 13.11, 13.15, 13.17
Council of the Law Society of Scotland v Scottish Legal Complaints
    Commission [2010] CSIH 79, 2011 SC 94, 2011 SLT 31, 2010 SCLR
    781, 2010 GWD 33-687   15.98
County Durham & Darlington NHS Foundation Trust v PP & Others
    [2014] EWCOP 9   16.32
Cranage Parish Council v First Secretary of State [2004] EWHC 2949   5.97
Crawley Borough Council v Attenborough [2006] EWHC 1278 (Admin),
    170 JP 593, 171 JPN 69, [2006] All ER (D) 104 (May)   12.04
Credit Suisse v Allerdale Borough Council [1997] QB 306, [1996] 4 All ER
    129, [1996] 3 WLR 894, [1996] 2 Lloyd's Rep 241   13.50
Creednz Inc v Governor General [1981] 1 NZLR 172   1.102
Crofton v NHS Litigation Authority [2007] EWCA Civ 71   6.01
Crompton (t/a David Crompton Haulage) v Department of Transport North
    Western Area [2003] EWCA Civ 64, [2003] RTR 517, (2003) *Times*,
    7 February, [2003] All ER (D) 311 (Jan)   12.12, 12.15
Crompton v General Medical Council [1981] 1 WLR 1435, [1982] 1 All ER
    35   1.123, 15.161, 15.162
Cullen v Chief Constable of the Royal Ulster Constabulary (Northern
    Ireland) [2003] UKHL 39, [2004] 2 All ER 237, [2003] 1 WLR 1763,
    [2003] 35 LS Gaz R 38, (2003) *Times*, 11 July, 147 Sol Jo LB 873,
    [2004] 3 LRC 231, [2003] All ER (D) 174, Jul   2.88
Cullen v General Medical Council [2005] EWHC 353 (Admin)   15.168
Cumings v Birkenhead Corporation [1972] 1 Ch 12   11.71

D v East Berkshire Community Health NHS Trust, K v Dewsbury
    Healthcare NHS Trust, K v Oldham NHS Trust [2003] EWCA Civ
    1151, [2004] QB 558, [2003] 4 All ER 796, [2004] 2 WLR 58,
    [2003] 3 FCR 1, [2003] 2 FLR 1166, [2003] Fam Law 816, 76
    BMLR 61, [2003] 36 LS Gaz R 37, (2003) *Times*, 22 August, [2003]
    All ER (D) 547 (Jul)   2.86
D'Souza v Law Society [2006] EWHC 987 (Admin), [2006] ACD 72   15.169
Dad v General Dental Council [2000] 1 WLR 1538, [2000] Lloyd's Rep
    Med 299, (2000) 56 BMLR 130, (2000) *Times*, 19 April   15.204
Daraghmeh v General Medical Council [2011] EWHC 2080 (Admin)   15.203
Darlington Borough Council v Paul Wakefield [1989] 153 JP 481   12.40
Davidson v Scottish Ministers [2004] UKHL 34, 2005 1 SC (HL) 7, 2004
    SLT 895, 2004 SCLR 991, [2004] HRLR 34, [2004] UKHRR 1079,
    [2005] ACD 19, 2004 GWD 27-572, (2004) *Times*, 16 July   1.130
Davidson v Scottish Ministers [2005] UKHL 74, (2005) *Times*, 19 December,
    2006 SLT 110, 2006 SCLR 249   2.09
Davies v Solicitors Regulation Authority [2010] EWHC 3645 (Admin)   15.75
Davis v West Sussex County Council [2012] EWHC 2152 (Admin), [2013]
    PTSR 494, (2012) 156(34) SJLB 27   6.139
Day v Grant, Note [1987] QB 972, [1987] 3 WLR 537, [1987] 3 All ER
    678, CA   9.14
De Falco v Crawley BC [1980] QB 460, [1980] 1 All ER 913, [1980] 2
    WLR 664, [1980] 1 CMLR 437, 78 LGR 180, 124 Sol Jo 82   7.98
de Freitas v Permanent Secretary of Ministry of Agriculture, Fisheries, Lands
    and Housing and Others [1999] 1 AC 69, [1999] 1 AC 69, [1998] 3
    WLR 675, 4 BHRC 563, (1998) 142 SJLB 219   1.29, 1.36, 1.38
De Keyser's Royal Hotel Ltd (1920) AC 508   13.31

Dennis v United Kingdom Central Council for Nursing Midwifery & Health
  Visiting [1993] 4 Med LR 252, (1993) 137 SJLB 131, (1993) *Times*, 2
  April, (1993) *Independent*, 23 March 15.165
Deumeland v Germany (Application No 9384/81) (1986) 8 EHRR 448,
  ECHR 1.179
Devon County Council v Secretary of State for Communities and Local
  Government [2010] EWHC 1456 (Admin), [2011] BLGR 64, [2010]
  ACD 83 . . . . 1.143
Dimes v Proprietors of Grand Junction Canal 10 ER 301, (1852) 3 HL Cas
  759 . . . . 1.133
DN v Northumberland, Tyne & Wear NHS Foundation Trust [2011] UKUT
  327 (AAC), [2011] MHLR 249 . . . . 8.80
Doherty v Birmingham City Council (Secretary of State for Communities and
  Local Government intervening) [2008] UKHL 57, [2009] AC 367,
  [2009] 1 All ER 653, [2008] 3 WLR 636, [2008] LGR 695, [2009] 1
  P & CR 213, [2008] HLR 785, (2008) *Times*, 14 August, 152 Sol Jo
  (no 31) 30, [2008] All ER (D) 425 (Jul) 7.28
Doherty, Re [2008] UKHL 3, [2008] 1 AC 805, [2008] 2 WLR 299, [2008]
  2 All ER 207, [2008] 2 CMLR 8, [2008] Extradition LR 61, (2008)
  152(6) SJLB 30, (2008) *Times*, 1 February 15.155
Doll-Steinberg v Society of Lloyd's [2002] EWHC 419 (Admin) 15.46
Donkin v Law Society [2007] EWHC 414 (Admin), (2007) 157 NLJ 402 . . . . . . 15.151
Dorot Properties Ltd v London Borough of Brent [1990] COD 378, [1990]
  RA 137 . . . . 2.107
Dorset Healthcare NHS Foundation Trust v MH [2009] UKUT 4 (AAC),
  [2009] PTSR 1112, 111 BMLR 1 . . . . 4.21, 8.63
Douglas v Hello! Ltd, No 3 [2005] EWCA Civ 595, [2006] QB 125, [2005]
  3 WLR 881, [2005] 4 All ER 128, [2005] EMLR 28, [2005] 2 FCR
  487, [2005] HRLR 27, (2005) 28(8) IPD 28057, (2005) 155 NLJ
  828, (2005) *Times*, 24 May, (2005) *Independent*, 26 May 1.55, 1.189, 1.201
Dowty Boulton Paul Ltd v Wolverhampton Corps [1971] 2 All ER 277,
  [1971] 1 WLR 204, 69 LGR 192, 135 JP 333, 115 Sol Jo 76 . . . . 2.67
DPP v Hutchinson, DPP v Smith [1990] 2 AC 783 . . . . 2.56, 2.57, 2.59
Duff v Minister of Agriculture [1996] ECR I-4559 . . . . 1.206
Durham County Council v D [2012] EWCA Civ 1654, [2013] 1 WLR 2305,
  [2013] 2 All ER 213, [2013] CP Rep 15, [2013] BLGR 315, [2013]
  Fam Law 795 . . . . 3.12
Durity v Attorney General of Trinidad and Tobago [2008] UKPC 59 . . . . . . 1.123
Duthie v The Nursing and Midwifery Council [2012] EWHC 3021 (Admin) 2.72
Dyason v Secretary of State for the Environment (1998) 75 P & CR 506,
  [1998] 2 PLR 54, [1998] JPL 778, [1998] EG 11 (CS), (1998) 142
  SJLB 62, [1998] NPC 9, (1998) *Independent*, 30 January 1.116
Dymocks Franchise Systems (NSW) Pty Ltd v Todd [2004] UKPC 39, [2004]
  1 WLR 2807, [2005] 4 All ER 195, PC 3.78

E v Chief Constable of the Royal Ulster Constabulary [2008] UKHL 66,
  [2009] 1 AC 536, [2008] 3 WLR 1208, [2009] 1 All ER 467, [2009]
  NI 141, [2009] HRLR 8, [2009] UKHRR 277, 25 BHRC 720, [2008]
  Po LR 350, (2008) 152(45) SJLB 27, (2008) *Times*, 19 November 1.170
E v Secretary of State for the Home Department, R v Secretary of State for
  the Home Department [2004] EWCA Civ 49, [2004] QB 1044,
  [2004] 2 WLR 1351, [2004] All ER (D) 16 (Feb), CA 1.92, 1.94, 1.95, 1.123, 3.72
Eagil Trust Co Ltd v Pigott-Brown and Another [1985] 3 All ER 119, CA . . . 1.154
Eba v Advocate General for Scotland [2011] UKSC 29, [2012] 1 AC 710,
  [2011] 3 WLR 149, [2011] PTSR 1095, [2011] STC 1705, 2012 SC
  (UKSC) 1, 2011 SLT 768, [2011] Imm AR 745, [2011] STI 1941,
  (2011) 108(27) LSG 24, (2011) 161 NLJ 917 . . . . 8.58
Edwards v Bairstow [1956] AC 14, [1955] 3 WLR 410, [1955] 3 All ER 48,
  48 R & IT 534, 36 TC 207, (1955) 34 ATC 198, [1955] TR 209,
  (1955) 99 SJ 558 . . . . 1.13

Edwards v UK (2002) 35 EHRR 19, 12 BHRC 190, [2002] MHLR 220,
    [2002] Po LR 161, (2002) *Times*, 1 April   10.124, 10.134
Edwards v United States [2012] EWHC 3771 (Admin)   1.89
El-Masri v Macedonia (App No 39630/09)   10.120
Ellis v Dubowski [1921] 3 KB 621   1.87
Emmot v Minister for Social Welfare and the Att-Gen (Case 33/76) [1991]
    ECR I-4269   3.14
Engel v The Netherlands (1976) 1 EHRR 647   1.172
English v Emery Reimbold and Strick Ltd [2002] EWCA Civ 605, [2002] 1
    WLR 2409, [2002] 3 All ER 385, [2002] CPLR 520, [2003] IRLR
    710, [2002] UKHRR 957, (2002) 99(22) LSG 34, (2002) 152 NLJ
    758, (2002) 146 SJLB 123, (2002) *Times*, 10 May, (2002)
    Independent, 7 May   1.154
Enterprise Inns plc v Secretary of State for the Environment, Transport and
    the Regions and Liverpool CC [2002] EWHC 921 (Admin), [2002] 21
    EG 143 (CS), (2002) 99(21) LSG 33, [2002] NPC 67   5.40
Eren v Turkey (Application No 60856/00) (2006) 44 EHRR 619, [2006]
    ELR 155, [2006] ECHR 60856/00   11.156
Eshugbayi Eleko v Government of Nigeria [1931] AC 662   1.96, 1.201
EU Plants Ltd v Wokingham Borough Council [2012] EWHC 3305, Admin   5.118
European Commission v United Kingdom of Great Britain and Northern
    Ireland Case C-530/11   5.132
Everett v Griffiths [1924] 1 KB 941, 22 LGR 330, 88 JP 93, 93 LJKB 583,
    68 Sol Jo 562, 131 LT 405, 40 TLR 477   2.63
Ewing v Office of the Deputy Prime Minister [2005] EWCA Civ 1583,
    [2006] 1 WLR 1260, [2005] All ER (D) 315 (Dec)   3.03, 3.30
EY v General Medical Council [2013] EWHC 860 (Admin), [2013] Med LR
    227, (2013) 163(7560) NLJ 16   15.68
Ezeh and Connors v UK (2004) 39 EHRR 3, [2003] Info TLR 372, [2003]
    Po LR 355, (2003) *Times*, 26 August   10.86

FA (Iraq) v Secretary of State for the Home Department [2011] UKSC 2,
    [2011] 1 WLR 268, [2011] 1 All ER 744, [2011] PTSR 337, [2011]
    Env LR 19, [2011] BLGR 271, [2011] JPL 865, [2011] 4 EG 101
    (CS), (2011) 108(5) LSG 20, (2011) *Times*, January 26   1.205
Fairmount Investments Ltd v Secretary of State for the Environment [1976] 1
    WLR 1255, [1976] 2 All ER 865, 75 LGR 33, (1976) 120 SJ 801   1.123
Fawdry v Murfitt [2002] EWCA Civ 643, [2003] QB 104, [2002] 3 WLR
    1354, [2003] 4 All ER 60, [2002] CP Rep 62, [2002] CPLR 593,
    (2002) *Independent*, 23 May   15.197
Financial Services Authority v Sinaloa Gold [2013] UKSC 11, [2013] 2 AC
    28, [2013] 2 WLR 678, [2013] 2 All ER 339, [2013] 1 All ER
    (Comm) 1089, [2013] Bus LR 302, [2013] 1 BCLC 353, [2013]
    Lloyd's Rep FC 305, (2013) 163 NLJ 267, (2013) 157(9) SJLB 31,
    (2013) *Times*, 29 March   2.11
Findlay, Re, Re Hogben, Re Honeyman, Re Matthews [1985] AC 318,
    [1984] 3 WLR 1159, [1984] 3 All ER 801, HL   1.90, 1.102
Finegan v General Medical Council [1987] 1 WLR 121, (1987) 84 LSG 577,
    (1987) 131 SJ 196   15.206
Fitzgerald v Northcote (1865) 4 F & F 656   11.123
Flaherty v National Greyhound Racing Club Ltd [2005] EWCA Civ 1117,
    (2005) 102(37) LSG 31, *Times*, October 5, 2005   15.19
Flannery v Halifax Estate Agencies Ltd (t/a Colleys Professional Services)
    [2000] 1 WLR 377, [2000] 1 All ER 373, (1999) 11 Admin LR 465,
    CA   1.154
Fleming v Revenue and Customs Commissioners [2008] UKHL 2, [2008] 1
    WLR 195, [2008] 1 All ER 1061, [2008] STC 324, [2008] 1 CMLR
    48, [2008] Eu LR 455, [2008] BTC 5096, [2008] BVC 221, [2008]
    STI 181, (2008) 158 NLJ 182, (2008) 152(5) SJLB 30, [2008] NPC 5,
    (2008) *Times*, 25 January   1.72

Fox Strategic Land and Property Ltd v Secretary of State for Communities
and Local Government & Cheshire East Council [2012] EWHC 444
(Admin), [2012] JPL 920, on appeal [2012] EWCA Civ 1198, [2013]
1 P & CR 6, CA   5.111
Fredin v Sweden (Application 12033/86) (1991) 13 EHRR 784   12.07
Fry, ex p [1954] 2 All ER 118, [1954] 1 WLR 730   2.117
Fullbrook v Berkshire Magistrates' Court Committee (1970) 69 LGR 75   2.117

G v E [2010] EWCA Civ 822   8.07, 8.77
GD v Manager of the Dennis Scott Unit (QBD Admin, 27 June 2008)   8.13
General Dental Council v Jamous [2013] EWHC 1428 (Admin), (2013) 134
BMLR 79, [2013] ACD 115   15.16
General Dental Council v Savery [2011] EWHC 3011 (Admin), [2012] Med
LR 204, [2012] ACD 11   15.119, 15.120, 15.121, 15.122, 15.123
General Medical Council v Meadow [2006] EWCA Civ 1390, [2007] QB
462, [2007] 2 WLR 286, [2007] 1 All ER 1, [2007] ICR 701, [2007]
1 FLR 1398, [2006] 3 FCR 447, [2007] LS Law Medical 1, (2006) 92
BMLR 51, [2007] Fam Law 214, [2006] 44 EG 196 (CS), (2006)
103(43) LSG 28, (2006) 156 NLJ 1686, (2006) Times, 31 October,
(2006) Independent, 31 October   15.153
General Medical Council v Spackman [1943] AC 627, [1943] 2 All ER 337,
(1943) 59 TLR 412, (1943) 169 LT 226, (1943) 87 SJ 298   1.127, 15.163
Georgiadis v Greece (21522/93) (1997) 24 EHRR 606   1.179
Georgiou v Enfield London Borough Council [2004] LGR 779   5.116
Ghaidan v Godin-Mendoza [2004] UKHL 30, [2004] 2 AC 557, [2004] 3
WLR 113, [2004] 3 All ER 411, [2004] 2 FLR 600, [2004] 2 FCR
481, [2004] HRLR 31, [2004] UKHRR 827, 16 BHRC 671, [2004]
HLR 46, [2005] 1 P & CR 18, [2005] L & TR 3, [2004] 2 EGLR
132, [2004] Fam Law 641, [2004] 27 EG 128 (CS), (2004) 101(27)
LSG 30, (2004) 154 NLJ 1013, (2004) 148 SJLB 792, [2004] NPC
100, [2004] 2 P & CR DG17, (2004) Times, 24 June   1.72, 1.163, 1.205, 5.56
Ghosh v General Medical Council [2001] UKPC 29, [2001] 1 WLR 1915,
[2001] UKHRR 987, [2001] Lloyd's Rep Med 433, (2001) Times, 25
June   1.55, 15.55, 15.211, 15.212
Gibb v Maidstone & Tunbridge Wells NHS Trust [2010] EWCA Civ 678,
[2010] IRLR 786, [2010] Med LR 458, (2010) 107(27) LSG 15,
(2010) 160 NLJ 942   1.66, 1.67
Gillan v United Kingdom (4158/05) (2010) 50 EHRR 45   1.173
Gillick v West Norfolk and Wisbech Area Health Authority and Another
[1986] AC 112, [1986] 1 FLR 224, [1985] 3 All ER 402, [1985] 3
WLR 830, HL, [1985] FLR 736, [1985] 1 All ER 533, [1985] 2 WLR
413, CA   1.121, 2.47, 2.65, 2.72
Gillies v Secretary of State for Work and Pensions [2006] UKHL 2, [2006] 1
WLR 781, [2006] 1 All ER 731, 2006 SC (HL) 71, 2006 SLT 77,
2006 SCLR 276, [2006] ICR 267, (2006) 9 CCL Rep 404, (2006)
103(9) LSG 33, (2006) 150 SJLB 127, 2006 GWD 3-66, (2006)
Times, 30 January   1.125
GJ v Foundation Trust [2009] EWHC 2972 (Fam), [2010] Fam 70, [2010] 3
WLR 840, [2010] Fam Law 139, [2010] 1 FLR 1251   8.20, 8.21, 8.40, 8.64, 8.79
Glowacki v Long and Chief Constable of Lancashire [1998] EWCA Civ
1034   10.111
Glynn v Keele University [1971] 1 WLR 487, [1971] 2 All ER 89, sub nom
Glynn v University of Keele (1970) 115 SJ 173   2.122
Gokool v Permanent Secretary for the Ministry of Health and Quality of Life
[2008] UKPC 54   1.138
Golder v UK [1975] 1 EHRR 524   10.40
Goordin v Secretary of State for the Home Department (1981) 125 Sol Jo
624   2.117
Goose v Wilson Sandford and Co (1998) Times, 19 February   1.123

Gopakumar v General Medical Council [2008] EWCA Civ 309, (2008) 101
    BMLR 121 .... 15.157
Governing Body of the London Oratory School v Schools Adjudicator [2005]
    EWHC 1842 (Admin), [2005] ELR 484, [2005] 35 LS Gaz R 43,
    [2005] All ER (D) 61 (Aug), Admin Ct 11.46, 11.50
Gransden v Secretary of State for the Environment (1987) 54 P & CR 86,
    [1986] JPL 519 .... 1.153
Grunwick Processing Laboratories Ltd v Advisory Conciliation and
    Arbitration Service, sub nom Advisory Conciliation and Arbitration
    Service v Grunwick Processing Laboratories Ltd [1978] AC 655,
    [1978] 1 All ER 338, [1978] 2 WLR 277, [1978] ICR 231, [1977]
    IRLR 38, 122 Sol Jo 46 .... 2.47
Guardian of the Poor of Gateshead Union v Durham County Council [1918]
    1 Ch 146, 16 LGR 33, 82 JP 53, 87 LJ Ch 113, 62 Sol Jo 86, 117 LT
    796, 34 TLR 65 .... 11.123
Gulshan (Article 8 – new Rules – correct approach) [2013] UKUT 640 (IAC) ... 14.50
Gupta v General Medical Council [2001] UKPC 61, [2002] 1 WLR 1691,
    [2002] ICR 785, [2002] Lloyd's Rep Med 82, (2002) 64 BMLR 56,
    (2002) Times, 9 January 1.153, 1.154, 15.55, 15.168, 15.211, 15.212, 15.213
Guzzardi v Italy (Application No 7367/76) (1981) 3 EHRR 333, ECHRGW
    v United Kingdom, Le Petit v United Kingdom (Application Nos
    34155/96 and 35574/97), 15 June 2004, ECHR 1.172

H v Belgium (1986) 8 EHRR CD510 .... 1.179
H v Lord Advocate [2012] UKSC 24, [2013] 1 AC 413, [2012] 3 WLR 151,
    [2012] 4 All ER 600, 2012 SC (UKSC) 308, 2012 SLT 799, 2012 SCL
    635, 2012 SCCR 562, [2012] HRLR 24, (2012) 109(27) LSG 19,
    2012 GWD 21-432, (2012) Times, 3 July 1.201
Hackney London Borough Council v Sareen [2003] EWCA Civ 351, [2003]
    HLR 800, (2003) Times, 9 April, 147 Sol Jo LB 353, [2003] All ER
    (D) 274 (Mar) 7.57
Hadmor Productions Ltd v Hamilton [1983] 1 AC 191, [1982] 2 WLR 322,
    [1982] 1 All ER 1042, [1982] ICR 114, [1982] IRLR 102, (1982) 126
    SJ 134 .... 1.123
Hall & Co Ltd v Shoreham-by-Sea UDC [1964] 1 All ER 1, [1964] 1 WLR
    240, 62 LGR 206, 15 P & CR 119, 128 JP 120, 107 Sol Jo 1001 .... 2.58
Hall v City of Westminster [2010] EWCA Civ 817, [2011] 1 WLR 504,
    [2011] Costs LR Online 13, (2010) 107(30) LSG 12, [2010] NPC 83,
    (2010) Times, 28 July 1.189
Hall v Wandsworth London Borough Council, Carter v Wandsworth London
    Borough Council [2004] EWCA Civ 1740, [2005] 2 All ER 192,
    [2005] LGR 350, (2005) Times, 7 January, [2004] All ER (D) 293
    (Dec) 7.10
Halsey v Milton Keynes General NHS Trust, Steel v Joy [2004] EWCA Civ
    576, [2004] 4 All ER 920, [2004] 1 WLR 3002, 81 BMLR 108,
    [2004] 22 LS Gaz R 31, [2004] NLJR 769, (2004) Times, 27 May,
    148 Sol Jo LB 629, [2004] 3 Costs LR 393, [2004] All ER (D) 125
    (May) 3.78
Hamid v SSHD [2012] EWHC 3070 (Admin), [2013] CP Rep 6, [2013]
    ACD 27 .... 14.24
Hanson v Church Comrs for England [1978] QB 823, [1977] 3 All ER 404,
    [1977] 2 WLR 848, 34 P & CR 158, 120 Sol Jo 837 .... 2.117
Hardwick (EF), Re (1883) 12 QBD 148, 53 LJQB 64, 32 WR 191, 49 LT
    584 .... 9.13
Harmon CFEM Facades (UK) Ltd v Corporate Officer of the House of
    Commons 1.207
Harris v Solicitors Regulation Authority [2011] EWHC 2173 (Admin) 15.210

Hashwani v Jivraj [2011] UKSC 40, [2011] 1 WLR 1872, [2012] 1 All ER
  629, [2012] 1 All ER (Comm) 1177, [2011] Bus LR 1182, [2011] 2
  Lloyd's Rep 513, [2011] 2 CLC 427, [2012] 1 CMLR 12, [2011] ICR
  1004, [2011] IRLR 827, [2011] Eq LR 1088, [2011] Arb LR 28,
  [2011] CILL 3076, [2011] 32 EG 54 (CS), (2011) Times, 4 August ... 1.205
Hassan v Secretary of State for Justice [2011] EWHC 1359 (Admin) ... 10.18
Hazelhurst v Solicitors Regulation Authority [2011] EWHC 462 (Admin),
  [2011] NPC 29 ... 15.205
Hazell v Hammersmith and Fulham LBC [1992] 2 AC 1, [1991] 2 WLR
  372, [1991] 1 All ER 545, HL ... 13.42, 13.48, 13.50
Health and Safety Executive v Wolverhampton City Council [2012] UKSC
  34, [2012] 1 WLR 2264, [2012] 4 All ER 429, [2012] PTSR 1362,
  [2012] BLGR 843, [2013] JPL 43, [2012] 30 EG 74 (CS), (2012) 162
  NLJ 1000, (2012) 156(29) SJLB 27, (2012) Times, 24 July ... 1.102, 5.48
Heath v Home Office Policy and Advisory Board for Forensic Pathology
  [2005] EWHC 1793 (Admin), (2005) Times, 18 October ... 15.116
Helow v Secretary of State for the Home Department [2008] UKHL 62,
  [2008] 1 WLR 2416, [2009] 2 All ER 1031, 2009 SC (HL) 1, 2008
  SLT 967, 2008 SCLR 830, (2008) 152(41) SJLB 29, 2008 GWD
  35-520, (2008) Times, 5 November ... 1.130, 1.131, 15.170
Hemming (t/a Simply Pleasure Ltd) v Westminster City Council [2012]
  EWHC 1260 (Admin), [2012] PTSR 1676, (2012) 109(23) LSG 16 ... 2.98
Hemns v Wheeler [1948] 2 KB 61, 64 TLR 236, [1948] LJR 1024, (1948)
  92 SJ 194 ... 1.95
Henry Boot v Bassetlaw [2002] EWCA Civ 983, [2003] 1 P & CR 23,
  [2002] 4 PLR 108, [2003] JPL 1030, [2002] 50 EG 112 (CS), (2002)
  99(49) LSG 20, (2002) 146 SJLB 277, [2002] NPC 156, (2002)
  Times, 16 December ... 5.114
Henshall v General Medical Council [2005] EWCA Civ 1520, [2006] Lloyd's
  Rep Med 103, (2006) 88 BMLR 146, (2006) Times, 9 January ... 15.107, 15.113
Herbage, Re (1985) Times, 25 October ... 9.38
Herczegfalvy v Austria (Applications 10533/83) (1992) 15 EHRR 437, 18
  BMLR 48 ... 8.40
Hertfordshire CC, City and District of St Albans v SSCLG [2009] EWHC
  1280 (Admin), [2010] JPL 70 ... 5.107
Hewlett v Secretary of State for Justice [2009] EWHC 2979 (Admin) ... 10.22
Hinde v Rugby BC and SSCLS [2011] EWHC 3684 (Admin), [2012] JPL
  816 ... 5.22
HL v United Kingdom (Application 45508/99) (2004) 40 EHRR 761, 81
  BMLR 131, (2004) Times, 19 October, 17 BHRC 418, [2004] ECHR
  45508/99, [2004] All ER (D) 39 (Oct) ... 8.08
HMB Holdings Ltd v Antigua and Barbuda [2007] UKPC 37 ... 1.17
Hoekstra v HM Advocate 2000 JC 391, 2000 SLT 605, 2000 SCCR 367,
  [2000] HRLR 410, [2000] UKHRR 578, 2000 GWD 12-417, (2000)
  Times, 14 April ... 1.180
Hoffmann-La Roche (F) & Co AG v Secretary of State for Trade and
  Industry [1975] AC 295, [1974] 3 WLR 104, [1974] 2 All ER 1128,
  [1975] 3 All ER 945, (1973) 117 SJ 713, (1974) 118 SJ 500 ... 1.123, 2.69
Holgate-Mohammed v Duke [1984] AC 437, [1984] 1 All ER 1054, [1984]
  2 WLR 660, 79 Cr App Rep 120, [1984] Crim LR 418, 128 Sol Jo
  244, [1984] LS Gaz R 1286, [1984] NLJ Rep 523, HL ... 1.58
Holmes v Royal College of Veterinary Surgeons [2011] UKPC 48 ... 15.171
Holton v General Medical Council [2006] EWHC 2960 (Admin), (2007) 93
  BMLR 74, [2007] ACD 66 ... 15.152
Horner v Lancashire County Council [2007] EWCA Civ 784, [2008] Env LR
  10, [2008] 1 P & CR 5, [2008] JPL 209, [2007] NPC 99 ... 5.56

Hounslow London Borough Council v Powell [2011] UKSC 8, [2011] 2 AC
    186, [2011] 2 WLR 287, [2011] 2 All ER 129, [2011] PTSR 512,
    [2011] HRLR 18, [2011] UKHRR 548, [2011] HLR 23, [2011]
    BLGR 363, [2011] 1 P & CR 20, [2011] 9 EG 164 (CS), (2011)
    155(8) SJLB 31, [2011] NPC 24, (2011) *Times*, 1 March 1.184
HS2 Action Alliance Ltd v Secretary of State for Transport [2013] EWHC
    481 (Admin), [2013] PTSR D25 .... 1.151
Huang v Secretary of State for the Home Department [2007] UKHL 11,
    [2007] 2 AC 167, [2007] 2 WLR 581, [2007] 4 All ER 15, [2007] 1
    FLR 2021, [2007] HRLR 22, [2007] UKHRR 759, 24 BHRC 74,
    [2007] Imm AR 571, [2007] INLR 314, [2007] Fam Law 587, (2007)
    151 SJLB 435, (2007) *Times*, 22 March 1.29, 1.44, 1.50, 7.29
Huddersfield Police Authority v Watson [1947] KB 842, [1947] 2 All ER
    193, 63 TLR 415, (1947) 111 JP 463, [1948] LJR 182, 177 LT 114,
    (1947) 91 SJ 421 .... 8.55
Hunston Properties Ltd and another v St Albans City and District Council
    [2013] EWCA Civ 1610, [2014] JPL 599 .... 5.101
Hunt v North Somerset Council [2013] EWCA Civ 1320, [2014] BLGR 1,
    (2013) 16 CCL Rep 502 .... 6.25
Hurst v Leeming [2002] EWHC 1051(Ch), [2003] 1 Lloyd's Rep 379, [2003]
    2 Costs LR 153, [2002] All ER (D) 135 (May) 2.145
Hutchinson v General Dental Council [2008] EWHC 2896 (Admin) 15.155

Ighalo v Solicitors Regulation Authority [2013] EWHC 661 (Admin), (2013)
    157(14) SJLB 31 .... 1.134, 15.171
Inco Europe Ltd v First Choice Distribution (a firm) [2000] 1 WLR 586,
    [2000] 2 All ER 109, [2000] 1 All ER (Comm) 674, [2000] 1 Lloyd's
    Rep 467, [2000] CLC 1015, [2000] BLR 259, (2000) 2 TCLR 487,
    74 Con LR 55, (2000) 97(12) LSG 39, (2000) 144 SJLB 134, [2000]
    NPC 22, (2000) *Times*, March 10, (2000) *Independent*, March 15 .... 1.71
IRC v Nat Fed of Self-Employed and Small Businesses Ltd [1982] AC 617,
    [1981] 2 All ER 93, [1981] 2 WLR 722, [1981] STC 260, 55 TC
    133, 125 Sol Jo 325 .... 3.44
Ireland v United Kingdom [1978] 2 EHRR 25 .... 1.168
Islam v Bar Standards Board [2012] All ER (D) 05 (Aug) 15.74
Islington LBC v Secretary of State for Communities and Local Government
    [2013] EWHC 2320 (Admin), [2014] JPL 206 .... 5.100

James v UK (2013) 56 EHRR 12, 33 BHRC 617, (2012) 109(37) LSG 20 ..... 10.01, 10.23, 10.25
Janik v Standards Board for England [2007] EWHC 835 (Admin), (2007)
    104(14) LSG 22 .... 15.143
Jideofo v Law Society [2007] WL 511 6865 .... 15.75
Johansen v Norway (No 17383/90) (1996) 23 EHRR 33, (1996) III RJD
    1008, ECtHR 1.184
Johnson v Leicestershire Constabulary (1998) *Times*, 7 October 9.59
Jones v Commission for Social Care Inspection [2004] EWCA Civ 1713,
    [2005] 1 WLR 2461, (2005) 149 SJLB 59, (2005) *Times*, 4 January 15.74
Jones v Department of Employment [1989] QB 1, [1988] 1 All ER 725,
    [1988] 2 WLR 493, 132 Sol Jo 128, [1988] 4 LS Gaz R 35, [1987]
    NLJ Rep 1182 .... 2.84
Jones v Ministry of Interior of Saudi Arabia [2006] UKHL 26, [2007] 1 AC
    270, [2006] 2 WLR 1424, [2007] 1 All ER 113, [2006] HRLR 32,
    [2007] UKHRR 24, 20 BHRC 621, (2006) 156 NLJ 1025, (2006)
    150 SJLB 811, (2006) *Times*, 15 June, (2006) *Independent*, 22 June 1.163, 1.201
Jordan v UK [2001] 37 EHRR 52 .... 10.123

K and T v Finland (2001) 36 EHRR 18 .... 1.184
K v Newham London Borough Council, *sub nom* R (K) v Newham London
    Borough Council [2002] EWHC 405 (Admin), [2002] ELR 390,
    (2002) *Times*, 28 February, [2002] All ER (D) 252 (Feb) 11.65, 11.161

Kakoulli v Turkey (2007) 45 EHRR 12   10.124
Kanda v Government of Malaya [1962] AC 322, [1962] 2 WLR 1153,
    (1962) 106 SJ 305   1.123, 1.127, 15.161, 15.162
Karagozlu v Commissioner of Police for the Metropolis [2006] EWCA Civ
    1691, [2007] 2 All ER 1055, [2007] 1 WLR 1881, (2006) Times, 26
    December, [2006] All ER (D) 166 (Dec)   2.89
Kavanagh v Chief Constable of Devon and Cornwall [1974] QB 624, [1974]
    2 All ER 697, [1974] 2 WLR 762, 138 JP 618, 118 Sol Jo 347   12.97, 12.98
Kay v Lambeth Borough Council [2006] UKHL 10, [2006] 2 AC 465,
    [2006] 2 WLR 570, [2006] 4 All ER 128, [2006] 2 FCR 20, [2006]
    HRLR 17, [2006] UKHRR 640, 20 BHRC 33, [2006] HLR 22,
    [2006] BLGR 323, [2006] 2 P & CR 25, [2006] L & TR 8, [2006]
    11 EG 194 (CS), (2006) 150 SJLB 365, [2006] NPC 29, (2006)
    Times, 10 March, (2006) Independent, 14 March   15.53
Kemper Reinsurance Company v Minister of Finance [2000] 1 AC 1, [1998]
    3 WLR 630, (1998) 142 SJLB 175, (1998) Times, May 18   1.93
Kensington and Chelsea RLBC, ex p Byfield (1997) 31 HLR 913, QBD   7.49
Khan v General Teaching Council for England [2010] EWHC 3404 (Admin)   15.141
Khan v Newport Borough Council [1991] COD 157   5.20
Khan v Solicitors Regulation Authority [2010] EWHC 1555 (Admin)   15.75
Kjeldsen, Busk Madsen and Pedersen v Denmark (1976) 1 EHRR 711,
    ECHR   1.193
Klamecki v Poland [2003] 2 FCR 97, (2004) 39 EHRR 7   10.42
Kleinwort Benson Ltd v Lincoln City Council, Kleinwort Benson Ltd v
    Birmingham City Council, Kleinwort Benson Ltd v Southwark LBC,
    Kleinwort Benson Ltd v Kensington and Chelsea RLBC [1999] 2 AC
    349, [1998] 4 All ER 513, [1998] 3 WLR 1095, [1998] Lloyds Rep
    Bank 387, [1999] CLC 332, (1999) 1 LGR 148, (1999) 11 Admin LR
    130, [1998] RVR 315, (1998) 148 NLJ 1674, (1998) 142 SJLB 279,
    [1998] NPC 145, (1998) Times, October 30, HL   2.93, 2.94, 2.96, 2.97
Klensch v Secretary of State [1986] ECR 3477   1.206

L (Hughes) v Hereford and Worcester CC [2000] ELR 375   11.161
L v Birmingham City Council [2007] UKHL 27, [2008] 1 AC 95, [2007] 3
    WLR 112, [2007] 3 All ER 957, [2007] HRLR 32, [2008] UKHRR
    346, [2007] HLR 44, [2008] BLGR 273, (2007) 10 CCL Rep 505,
    [2007] LS Law Medical 472, (2007) 96 BMLR 1, (2007) 104(27)
    LSG 29, (2007) 157 NLJ 938, (2007) 151 SJLB 860, [2007] NPC 75,
    (2007) Times, 21 June   6.138, 6.141, 7.23
Laker Airways Inc v FLS Aerospace Ltd [2000] 1 WLR 113, [1999] 2
    Lloyd's Rep 45, [1999] CLC 1124, (1999) Times, 21 May, (1999)
    Independent, 24 May   1.129
Laker Airways Ltd v Department of Trade [1977] QB 643, [1977] 2 WLR
    234, [1977] 2 All ER 182, (1976) 121 SJ 52, (1976) Times, 16
    December   1.06, 1.88, 6.34, 13.31
Lam v UK, Application No 4167/98   3.14
Lambeth London Borough Council v Johnston [2008] EWCA Civ 690,
    (2008) Times, 30 June, [2008] All ER (D) 242 (Jun)   7.10
Lambeth London Borough Council v Kay, Price v Leeds City Council [2006]
    UKHL 10, [2006] 2 AC 465, [2006] 4 All ER 128, [2006] 2 WLR
    570, [2006] LGR 323, [2006] 2 P & CR 511, [2006] 2 FCR 20,
    (2006) Times, 10 March, 150 Sol Jo LB 365, 20 BHRC 33, [2006] 5
    LRC 158, [2006] All ER (D) 120 (Mar)   7.28
Larkfleet Ltd v SSCLG & South Kesteven DC [2012] EWHC 3592   5.91
Law Society of Scotland v The Scottish Legal Complaints Commission
    [2010] ScotCS CSIH 79   15.28
Law Society v Salsbury [2008] EWCA Civ 1285, [2009] 1 WLR 1286,
    [2009] 2 All ER 487, (2008) 105(47) LSG 18, (2008) 158 NLJ 1720,
    (2008) 152(46) SJLB 30, (2009) Times, 15 January   15.210

Law v National Greyhound Racing Club Ltd [1983] 1 WLR 1302, [1983] 3
    All ER 300, (1983) 80 LSG 2367, (1983) 127 SJ 619   2.71, 15.19, 15.49
Lawal v Northern Spirit Ltd [2003] UKHL 35, [2004] 1 All ER 187, [2003]
    ICR 856, [2003] IRLR 538, HL   1.131
Lawrence v Financial Services Commission [2009] UKPC 49   1.123
Leathley v Bar Standards Board [2012] All ER (D) 110 (Jan) 15.171
Leech v Deputy Governor of Parkhurst Prison [1988] AC 533, [1988] 2
    WLR 290, [1988] 1 All ER 485, (1988) 85(11) LSG 42, (1988) 138
    NLJ Rep 38, (1988) 132 SJ 191   2.61, 15.52
Libman v GMC [1972] AC 217, [1972] 2 WLR 272, [1972] 1 All ER 798,
    (1971) 116 SJ 123   15.157
Lipkin Gorman (a Firm) v Karpnale Ltd [1991] 2 AC 548, [1991] 3 WLR
    10, [1992] 4 All ER 512, HL, [1989] 1 WLR 1340, [1992] 4 All ER
    409, [1989] BCLC 756, CA, [1987] 1 WLR 987, [1992] 4 All ER 331 2.96
Little France Limited v Ealing London Borough Council [2013] EWHC 2144
    (Admin)   12.47
Liversidge v Anderson and Another [1942] AC 206, [1941] 3 All ER 338,
    HL   1.96
Livingstone v Adjudication Panel for England [2006] EWHC 2533 (Admin),
    [2006] LGR 799, [2006] NLJR 1650, (2006) Times, 9 November,
    [2006] All ER (D) 230 (Oct)   13.113
Locabail (UK) Ltd v Bayfield Properties Ltd and Another, Locabail (UK) Ltd
    and Another v Waldorf Investment Corporation and Others, Timmins
    v Gormley, Williams v HM Inspector of Taxes and Others, R v Bristol
    Betting and Gaming Licensing Committee ex p O'Callaghan [2000]
    QB 451, [2000] 2 WLR 870, [2000] UKHRR 300, [2000] 1 All ER
    65, [2000] IRLR 96, CA   1.129, 1.133
Local Government Board v Arlidge [1915] AC 120, HL   1.04
Lomax and Others v Secretary of State for Transport, Local Government and
    the Regions and Rochdale Metropolitan Borough Council [2002] 21
    EG 143   5.39
London and Henley (Middle Brook Street) Ltd v Secretary of State for
    Communities and Local Government [2013] EWHC 4207   5.09
London Corps v Cox (1867) LR 2 HL 239, 36 LJ Ex 225, 16 WR 44 2.39
Loutfi v General Medical Council [2010] EWHC 1762 (Admin)   15.190
Lumba (WL) (Congo) v SSHD [2011] UKSC 12, [2012] 1 AC 245, [2011] 2
    WLR 671, [2011] 4 All ER 1, [2011] UKHRR 437, (2011) 108(14)
    LSG 20, (2011) 155(12) SJLB 30, (2011) Times, 24 March   10.03
Luthra v General Medical Council [2013] EWHC 240 (Admin)   15.204

M v Croydon LBC [2012] EWCA Civ 595, [2012] 1 WLR 2607, [2012] 3
    All ER 1237, [2012] 4 Costs LR 689, [2012] 3 FCR 179, [2012]
    BLGR 822,   7.102
M v Home Office [1994] 1 AC 377, [1993] 3 WLR 433, [1993] 3 All ER
    537, HL   2.08, 2.09, 2.33, 2.68, 2.72, 2.79, 3.41, 13.10
M v Scottish Ministers [2012] UKSC 58, [2012] 1 WLR 3386, 2013 SC
    (UKSC) 139, 2013 SLT 57, 2013 SCLR 98, 2012 GWD 40-774   1.114
M v South West Hospital & St Georges Mental Health Trust [2008] EWCA
    Civ 1112   8.40
M, Re [1994] 1 AC 377, [1993] 3 WLR 433, [1993] 3 All ER 537, HL 2.03
Macarthur v Secretary of State for Communities and Local Government
    [2013] EWHC 3 (Admin)   1.94, 1.99
Macarthys Ltd v Smith [1979] 1 WLR 1189, [1979] 3 All ER 325, [1979] 3
    CMLR 44, [1979] 3 CMLR 381, [1979] ICR 785, [1979] IRLR 316,
    (1979) 123 SJ 603   1.70
MacLeod v Royal College of Veterinary Surgeons [2006] UKPC 39, (2006)
    150 SJLB 1023   15.204

Magill v Porter [2001] UKHL 67, [2002] 2 AC 357, [2002] 2 WLR 37,
  [2002] 1 All ER 465, [2002] HRLR 16, [2002] HLR 16, [2002]
  BLGR 51, (2001) 151 NLJ 1886, [2001] NPC 184, (2001) *Times*, 14
  December, (2002) *Independent*, 4 February, (2001) Telegraph, 20
  December   1.62, 1.127, 1.130
Mahmood v General Medical Council [2007] EWHC 474 (Admin), (2007)
  95 BMLR 229   15.143
Malcolm v Benedict Mackenzie and Another [2004] EWHC 339 (Ch),
  [2004] 1 WLR 1803, [2004] BPIR 747, [2004] All ER (D) 433 (Feb),
  ChD   1.193
Malloch v Aberdeen Corporation [1971] 1 WLR 1578, [1971] 2 All ER
  1278, 1971 SC (HL) 85, 1971 SLT 245, (1971) 115 SJ 756   1.123
Malone v Metropolitan Police Commissioner [1979] Ch 344, [1979] 2 WLR
  700, 143 JP 473, [1979] 2 All ER 620, ChD   13.21
Manchester City Council v Cochrane [1999] 1 WLR 809, [1999] LGR 626,
  31 HLR 810, 143 Sol Jo LB 37, [1998] All ER (D) 793   7.87
Manchester City Council v Pinnock (No 1) [2010] UKSC 45, [2011] 2 AC
  104, [2010] 3 WLR 1441, [2011] 1 All ER 285, [2011] PTSR 61,
  [2011] HRLR 3, [2010] UKHRR 1213, 31 BHRC 670, [2011] HLR
  7, [2010] BLGR 909, [2011] L & TR 2, [2010] 3 EGLR 113, [2010]
  45 EG 93 (CS), (2010) 107(44) LSG 16, (2011) 108(8) LSG 20,
  (2010) 154(42) SJLB 30, [2010] NPC 109, (2010) *Times*, 4 November   1.163, 1.184, 7.85
Manning v Ramjohn [2011] UKPC 20   1.123
Marcic v Thames Water Utilities Ltd [2003] UKHL 66, [2004] 2 AC 42,
  [2003] 3 WLR 1603, [2004] 1 All ER 135, [2004] BLR 1, 91 Con LR
  1, [2004] Env LR 25, [2004] HRLR 10, [2004] UKHRR 253, [2003]
  50 EG 95 (CS), (2004) 101(4) LSG 32, (2003) 153 NLJ 1869, (2003)
  147 SJLB 1429, [2003] NPC 150, (2003) *Times*, 5 December, (2003)
  Independent, 9 December   1.197
Marcus v Nursing and Midwifery Council [2011] All ER (D) 104 (Nov)   15.30, 15.109
Marleasing SA v La Comercial Internacional de Alimentación SA (C-106/89)
  [1990] ECR I-4135, [1992] 1 CMLR 305, [1993] BCC 421, 135 Sol
  Jo 15   1.205, 3.81, 5.55
Marlowe, ex p [1973] Crim LR 294   9.34
Matadeen v Pointu [1999] 1 AC 98, [1998] 3 WLR 18, (1998) 142 SJLB
  100   1.201
Matthew Taylor v Manchester City Council & TCG Bars Limited [2012]
  EWHC 3467 (Admin), [2013] 2 All ER 490, (2013) 177 JP 1, [2013]
  ACD 36   12.20
McCartan Turkington Breen v Times Newspapers Ltd [2001] 2 AC 277,
  [2000] 3 WLR 1670, [2000] 4 All ER 913, [2000] NI 410, [2001]
  EMLR 1, [2001] UKHRR 184, 9 BHRC 497, (2000) 97(47) LSG 40,
  (2000) 150 NLJ 1657, (2000) 144 SJLB 287, (2000) *Times*, 3
  November, (2000) *Independent*, 7 November   1.55, 1.161, 1.201
McCarthy v Visitors to the Inns of Court [2013] EWHC 3253 (Admin)   15.162
McCaughey, Re [2011] UKSC 20, [2012] 1 AC 725, [2011] 2 WLR 1279,
  [2011] 3 All ER 607, [2011] NI 122, [2011] HRLR 25, [2011]
  UKHRR 720, [2011] Inquest LR 22, (2011) 155(20) SJLB 35, (2011)
  Times, 20 May   1.163
McCool v Rushcliffe Borough Council [1998] 3 All ER 889, (1998) 162 JPN
  883, QBD   12.96, 12.97
McCormick v Horsepower Ltd [1981] 1 WLR 993, [1981] 2 All ER 746,
  [1981] ICR 535, [1981] IRLR 217, (1981) 125 SJ 375   1.70
McCotter v UK (1993) 15 EHRR CD 98   10.11
McDaid v Nursing and Midwifery Council [2013] EWHC 586 (Admin),
  (2013) 132 BMLR 190   15.166
McEldowney v Forde [1971] AC 632, [1969] 3 WLR 179, [1969] 2 All ER
  1039, [1970] NI 11, (1969) 113 SJ 566   1.110, 1.201
McFarland, Re [2004] UKHL 17, [2004] 1 WLR 1289, [2004] NI 380,
  (2004) 148 SJLB 541, (2004) *Times*, 30 April   1.71

McFarlane v Relate Avon Limited [2010] EWCA Civ 880, [2010] IRLR 872,
    29 BHRC 249   1.55, 1.201
McInnes v Onslow Fane [1978] 1 WLR 1520, [1978] 3 All ER 211, (1978)
    122 SJ 844   15.19
McKeown v British Horseracing Authority [2010] EWHC 508 (QB)   15.19
MD v Nottinghamshire Health Care NHS Trust [2010] UKUT 59   8.19
Meade v Haringey LBC [1979] 1 WLR 637, [1979] 2 All ER 1016, [1979]
    ICR 494, CA   2.30
Meadow v General Medical Council [2006] EWCA Civ 1390, [2007] QB
    462, [2007] 2 WLR 286, [2007] 1 All ER 1, [2007] ICR 701, [2007]
    1 FLR 1398, [2006] 3 FCR 447, [2007] LS Law Medical 1, (2006) 92
    BMLR 51, [2007] Fam Law 214, [2006] 44 EG 196 (CS), (2006)
    103(43) LSG 28, (2006) 156 NLJ 1686, (2006) *Times*, 31 October,
    (2006) *Independent*, 31 October   15.204
Medicaments and Related Classes of Goods (No 2), Re, *sub nom* Director
    General of Fair Trading v Proprietary Association for Great Britain
    [2001] 1 WLR 700, [2001] ICR 564, [2000] All ER (D) 2425   1.129, 11.138
Meerabus v Attorney General of Belize [2005] UKPC 12, [2005] 2 AC 513,
    [2005] 2 WLR 1307, (2005) *Times*, 20 April   1.133
Mendizabel v France (2010) 50 EHRR 50   14.47
Mengiste v Endowment Fund [2013] EWCA Civ 1003, [2014] CP Rep 5,
    [2013] 5 Costs LR 841, [2014] PNLR 4, (2013) 157(34) SJLB 40   1.134
Meredith, Re (1973) 57 Cr App R 451, DC   9.29
MF (Nigeria) v SSHD [2013] EWCA Civ 1192, [2014] 1 WLR 544, [2014]
    Imm AR 211, [2014] INLR 18, (2013) *Times*, December 17   14.50
MH v Nottinghamshire CC [2009] UKUT 178   11.118
Michalak v London Borough of Wandsworth [2002] EWCA Civ 271, [2003]
    1 WLR 617, [2002] 4 All ER 1136, [2003] 1 FCR 713, [2002] HLR
    39, [2002] NPC 34   1.193
Michelle Williamson's Application for Judicial Review, Re (NI Unreported
    Judgments, Court of Appeal, 16 March 2010)   13.07
Milk Marketing Board of England and Wales v Tom Parker Farms Ltd
    [1999] EuLR 154   1.206
Miller v General Medical Council [2013] EWHC 1934 (Admin)   15.167
Mills v London City Council [1925] 1 KB 213   1.87
Minister of Health v R, ex p Yaffé, *sub nom* R v Minister of Health, ex p
    Yaffé [1931] AC 494, 29 LGR 305, 95 JP 125, 100 LJKB 306, [1931]
    All ER Rep 343, 75 Sol Jo 232, 145 LT 98, 47 TLR 337   2.77
Miss Behavin' Ltd v Belfast City Council [2007] UKHL 19, [2007] NI 89,
    [2007] 3 All ER 1007, [2007] 1 WLR 1420, [2008] LGR 127, (2007)
    Times, 1 May, 151 Sol Jo LB 575, [2007] All ER (D) 219 (Apr), HL,
    reversing Miss Behavin' Ltd's Application for Judicial Review, Re
    [2005] NICA 35, [2006] NI 181, NI CA   12.16, 12.70, 12.82, 12.83
MK v Secretary of State for the Home Department [2012] EWHC 1896
    (Admin)   1.121
ML (Nigeria) v Secretary of State for the Home Department [2013] EWCA
    Civ 844   1.99
MN v London Borough of Hackney [2013] EWHC 1205 (Admin)   6.52
Modahl v British Athletic Federation [2001] EWCA Civ 1447, [2002] 1
    WLR 1192, (2001) 98(43) LSG 34, (2001) 145 SJLB 238   15.19
Mohamed v Alaga [1998] 2 All ER 720, (1998) 95(17) LSG 29, (1998) 142
    SJLB 142, (1998) *Times*, 2 April, (1998) *Independent*, 27 March   15.196
Mohammed v Department of Work and Pensions [2012] EWHC 4220
    (Admin)   1.89
Mohit v Director of Public Prosecutions of Mauritius [2006] UKPC 20,
    [2006] 1 WLR 3343   15.41
Molkerei-Zentrale Westfalen v Hauptzollamt Paderborn [1968] ECR 143,
    [1968] CMLR 187   1.204
Montes v Secretary of State for the Home Department [2004] EWCA Civ
    404, [2004] Imm AR 250   1.94

Moyna v Secretary of State for Work and Pensions [2003] UKHL 44, [2003]
1 WLR 1929, [2003] 4 All ER 162, [2003] 73 BMLR 201, HL ... 1.73
Mulla v Solicitors Regulation Authority [2010] EWHC 3077 (Admin) ... 15.75
Murrell v British Leyland Trustees [1989] COD 389 ... 2.60
Muscat v Health Professions Council [2008] EWHC 2798 (QB) ... 15.155, 15.172
Mustafa v France (63056/00) ... 1.179

Nadarajah v Secretary of State for the Home Department [2005] EWCA Civ
1363, (2005) *Times*, 14 December ... 1.140
Nagiub v General Medical Council [2011] EWHC 366 (Admin) ... 15.211
Nagre v SSHD [2013] EWHC 720 (Admin) ... 14.50
Napier, ex p (1852) 18 QB 692 ... 2.35
Naraynsingh v Commissioner of Police [2004] UKPC 20, (2004) 148 SJLB
510 ... 1.116
Nelms v Roe [1969] 3 All ER 1379, [1970] 1 WLR 4, [1970] RTR 45, 54
Cr App Rep 43, 113 Sol Jo 942 ... 13.125, 13.127
NHS Foundation Trust v (1) M (2) K [2013] EWHC 2402 (COP) ... 16.32
Nichol v Gateshead Metropolitan Council (1988) 87 LGR 435 ... 1.145
Noble Organisation Limited, The v City of Glasgow District Council (No 3)
1991 SCLR 380, 1991 SC 131, 1991 SLT 213 ... 12.78, 12.81
Noble Organisation Limited, The v Kilmarnock and Loudoun District
Council [1992] SCLR 1006, 1993 SLT 759 ... 12.78
Noor Mohammed Khan v Coventry Magistrates' Court and Coventry City
Council [2011] EWCA Civ 751, (2011) 175 JP 429 ... 12.42
Norris v Government of the United States for America (No 2) [2010] UKSC
9, [2010] 2 AC 487, [2010] 2 WLR 572, [2010] 2 All ER 267, [2010]
HRLR 20, [2010] UKHRR 523, [2010] Lloyd's Rep FC 325, (2010)
Times, 25 February ... 1.184
North Range Shipping Ltd v Seatrans Shipping Corp [2002] EWCA Civ 405,
[2002] 1 WLR 2397, [2002] 4 All ER 390, [2002] 2 All ER (Comm)
193, [2002] 2 Lloyd's Rep 1, [2002] CLC 992, (2002) 99(20) LSG
31, (2002) *Times*, 18 April, (2002) Telegraph, 13 May ... 1.153
North West Leicestershire DC v East Midlands Housing Association [1981]
3 All ER 364, [1981] 1 WLR 1396, 80 LGR 84, 125 Sol Jo 513 ... 13.132
North Wiltshire District Council v Secretary of State for the Environment
and Others (1993) 65 P & CR 137, [1992] 3 PLR 113, [1992] JPL
955, [1992] EG 65 (CS), [1992] NPC 57, (1992) *Times*, 21 April ... 5.110
Northavon District Council v Secretary of State for the Environment [1993]
JPL 761 ... 5.96
Nottinghamshire County Council v Secretary of State for the Environment
[1986] AC 240, [1986] 1 All ER 199, [1986] 2 WLR 1, 84 LGR 305,
130 Sol Jo 36, [1985] NLJ Rep 1257, HL ... 2.73
NS v Secretary of State for the Home Department [2010] EWCA Civ 990,
[2010] Eq LR 183 ... 1.208
NS v Secretary of State for the Home Department [2011] EUECJ C-493/10 ... 1.208
Nuran Aksu & Mrat Yazgan v London Borough of Enfield [2013] EWHC
249 (Admin) ... 12.63

O'Neill (Charles Bernard) v HM Advocate [2013] UKSC 36, [2013] 1 WLR
1992, 2013 SC (UKSC) 266, 2013 SLT 888, 2013 SCL 678, 2013
SCCR 401, [2013] 2 Cr App R 34, [2013] HRLR 25, 2013 GWD
21-410 ... 1.134
O'Reilly v Coventry Coroner (1996) 160 JP 749, (1997) 35 BMLR 48,
[1996] COD 268, (1996) *Times*, 3 April ... 1.116
O'Reilly v Mackman [1983] 2 AC 237, [1982] 3 WLR 1096, [1982] 3 All
ER 1124, (1982) 126 SJ 820 ... 1.76, 1.80, 1.123, 2.65
O'Rourke v London Borough of Camden [1998] AC 188, [1997] 3 All ER
23, [1997] 3 WLR 86, 29 HLR 793, [1997] 26 LS Gaz R 30, 141 Sol
Jo LB 139 ... 2.25
Odeola v SSHD [2009] UKHL 25, [2009] 1 WLR 1230 ... 14.06

Office of Fair Trading v IBA Health Ltd [2004] EWCA Civ 142, [2004] 4
All ER 1103, [2005] 1 All ER (Comm) 147, [2004] UKCLR 683,
[2005] ECC 1, [2004] ICR 1364, (2004) 101(11) LSG 33, (2004) 154
NLJ 352, (2004) *Times*, February 25, (2004) *Independent*, March 29 ... 1.157
Ogango v Nursing and Midwifery Council [2008] EWHC 3115 (Admin) ... 15.169
Ogunnowo v Solicitors Regulation Authority [2013] EWHC 1882 (Admin) ... 1.56
Okolo v Secretary of State for the Environment [1997] 4 All ER 242, [1997]
JPL 1009, [1998] COD 8 ... 5.40
Olotu v Home Office [1997] 1 All ER 385, [1997] 1 WLR 328, [1997] 1 LS
Gaz R 24, 141 Sol Jo LB 14 ... 2.88
Oneryildiz v Turkey (48939/99) (No 2) (2005) 41 EHRR 20 ... 1.170
Osborn v The Parole Board [2013] UKSC 61, [2013] 3 WLR 1020, [2014] 1
All ER 369, [2014] HRLR 1, (2013) 157(39) SJLB 37 ... 1.123, 1.125, 1.199
Osman v United Kingdom (23452/94) [1999] 1 FLR 193, (2000) 29 EHRR
245, 5 BHRC 293, (1999) 1 LGLR 431, (1999) 11 Admin LR 200,
[2000] Inquest LR 101, [1999] Crim LR 82, [1998] HRCD 966,
[1999] Fam Law 86, (1999) 163 JPN 297, (1998) *Times*, 5 November ... 1.166, 1.179
Oxton Farms v Selby District Council [1997] EGCS 60 ... 12.88
Ozyurekliler v Secretary of State for Communities and Local Government
[2013] EWHC 2648 (Admin) ... 1.158

P (A Barrister) v General Council of the Bar [2005] 1 WLR 3019, [2005]
PNLR 32 ... 15.171
Padfield v Minister of Agriculture Fisheries and Food [1968] AC 997, [1968]
1 All ER 694, [1968] 2 WLR 924, 112 Sol Jo 171 ... 1.04, 1.62, 1.107, 1.108, 2.22, 2.26, 12.61
Palacegate Properties Ltd v Camden London Borough Council (2001) 3
LGLR 18, (2001) 82 P & CR 17, [2000] 4 PLR 59, [2001] JPL 373
(Note), [2001] ACD 23, ... 1.76
Paponette v Attorney General of Trinidad and Tobago [2010] UKPC 32,
[2012] 1 AC 1, [2011] 3 WLR 219, (2010) *Times*, 15 December ... 1.102, 1.137
Parsipoor v Secretary of State for the Home Department [2011] EWCA Civ
276, [2011] 1 WLR 3187, [2011] CP Rep 30, [2011] ACD 85 ... 3.20, 3.47
Patmalniece v Secretary of State for Work and Pensions [2011] UKSC 11,
[2011] 1 WLR 783, [2011] 3 All ER 1, [2011] PTSR 680, [2011] 2
CMLR 45, [2011] Eq LR 508, (2011) 108(13) LSG 23, (2011)
155(11) SJLB 31, (2011) *Times*, 23 March ... 1.206
Pepper v Hart [1993] AC 593, [1992] 3 WLR 1032, [1993] 1 All ER 42,
[1992] STC 898, [1993] ICR 291, [1993] IRLR 33, [1993] RVR 127,
(1993) 143 NLJ 17, [1992] NPC 154, (1992) *Times*, 30 November,
(1992) *Independent*, 26 November ... 1.71, 1.111, 1.139
Percy v Board of National Mission of the Church of Scotland [2005] UKHL
73, [2006] 2 AC 28, [2006] 2 WLR 353, [2006] 4 All ER 1354, 2006
SC (HL) 1, 2006 SLT 11, [2006] ICR 134, [2006] IRLR 195, (2006)
150 SJLB 30, (2005) *Times*, 16 December, (2005) *Independent*, 20
December ... 1.55, 1.201
Perry v Nursing and Midwifery Council [2012] EWHC 2275 (Admin),
[2012] Med LR 723 ... 15.199
Persimmon Homes Teesside Ltd v R (Lewis) [2008] EWCA Civ 746, [2009]
1 WLR 83, [2008] BLGR 781, [2008] 2 P & CR 21, [2009] JPL 402,
[2008] NPC 78 ... 5.120, 13.83
Phelps v London Borough of Hillingdon, Anderton v Clwyd County Council,
Jarvis v Hampshire County Council, Re G (A Minor) [2001] 2 AC
619, [2000] 4 All ER 504, [2000] 3 WLR 776, [2000] LGR 651,
[2000] 3 FCR 102, [2000] ELR 499, 56 BMLR 1, [2000] NLJR
1198, 144 Sol Jo LB 241, [2000] All ER (D) 1076 ... 2.83
Phipps v General Medical Council (Application for Permission to Appeal)
[2006] EWCA Civ 397, [2006] Lloyd's Rep Med 345 ... 15.169

Pickwell v Camden London Borough Council [1983] QB 962, [1983] 1 All
    ER 602, [1983] 2 WLR 583, 80 LGR 798, 126 Sol Jo 397, [1982]
    RVR 140   13.95, 13.97
Pioneer Aggregates (UK) Ltd v SSE [1985] 1 AC 132   5.114
Plymouth City Council v Quietlynn Ltd and other appeals [1988] QB 114,
    [1987] 2 All ER 1040, [1987] 3 WLR 189, 85 LGR 856, 151 JP 810,
    131 Sol Jo 940, [1987] LS Gaz R 2119   12.72, 12.83
Pomiechowski v District Court of Legnica [2012] UKSC 20, [2012] 1 WLR
    1604, [2012] 4 All ER 667, [2012] HRLR 22, [2013] Crim LR 147,
    (2012) 162 NLJ 749, (2012) *Times*, 7 June   1.55, 1.180, 1.201
Porter v Magill (1998) 96 LGR 157   1.64, 1.113
Porter v Magill [2001] UKHL 67, [2002] 2 AC 357, [2002] 2 WLR 37,
    [2002] 1 All ER 465, [2002] HRLR 16, [2002] HLR 16, [2002]
    BLGR 51, (2001) 151 NLJ 1886, [2001] NPC 184, (2001) *Times*, 14
    December, (2002) *Independent*, 4 February, (2001) Telegraph, 20
    December   5.116, 12.30, 12.33, 15.170
PR (Bateman) v Legal Services Commission [2001] EWHC Admin 797,
    [2001] All ER (D) 293 (Oct)   3.78
PR (Sri Lanka) v SSHD [2011] EWCA Civ 988, [2012] 1 WLR 73, [2011]
    CP Rep 47, [2011] Imm AR 904, [2012] INLR 92   14.57
Practice Direction (Administrative Court) [2000] 1 WLR 1654   3.21
Practice Statement (Administrative Court: Annual Statement) [2002] 1 All
    ER 633   3.49
Practice Statement (Administrative Court: annual statement) [2002] 1 All ER
    633   7.92
Practice Statement (Administrative Court: Listings and Urgent Cases) [2002]
    1 WLR 810   2.04, 3.32
Preiss v General Dental Council [2001] UKPC 36, [2001] 1 WLR 1926,
    [2001] IRLR 696, [2001] HRLR 56, [2001] Lloyd's Rep Med 491,
    (2001) 98(33) LSG 31, (2001) *Times*, 14 August   15.204
Prescott v Birmingham Corporation [1955] Ch 210, [1954] 3 All ER 698, 53
    LGR 68, 119 JP 48, 98 Sol Jo 886   13.89
Preston, Re [1985] AC 835, [1985] 2 WLR 836, [1985] 2 All ER 327,
    [1985] STC 282, 59 TC 1   15.54
Pretty v United Kingdom (Application No 2346/02) [2002] ECHR 427,
    (2002) 35 EHRR 1, [2002] 2 FLR 45, (2002) 12 BHRC 149, ECHR   1.169
Price v United Kingdom [1988] 55 DR 224   1.168
Primecrown Ltd v Medicines Control Agency [1997] EuLR 657   15.53
Principal Reporter v K [2010] UKSC 56, [2011] 1 WLR 18, 2011 SC
    (UKSC) 91, 2011 SLT 271, [2011] HRLR 8, 33 BHRC 352, 2011
    Fam LR 2, (2011) 108(1) LSG 15, (2011) 161 NLJ 63, 2011 GWD
    3-112, (2010) *Times*, 20 December   1.163, 1.183
Procola v Luxembourg (1996) 22 EHRR 193   1.179
Pulhofer v Hillingdon London Borough Council [1986] AC 484, [1986] 1
    All ER 467, [1986] 2 WLR 259, 84 LGR 385, [1986] 2 FLR 5,
    [1986] Fam Law 218, 18 HLR 158, 130 Sol Jo 143, [1986] LS Gaz R
    785, [1986] NLJ Rep 140   6.20, 7.50

Quinn Direct Insurance Ltd v Law Society [2010] EWCA Civ 805, [2011] 1
    WLR 308, [2010] Lloyd's Rep IR 655, (2010) 160 NLJ 1044, (2010)
    154(29) SJLB 33, [2010] NPC 80   1.55, 1.201

R (4 Wins Leisure Limited) v Licensing Committee for Blackpool Council
    [2007] EWHC 2213 (Admin), [2007] All ER (D) 185 (Aug)   12.24, 12.63, 12.76, 12.101
R (A & B) v East Sussex County Council No 2 (2003) 6 CCLR 194   6.42
R (A (by his litigation friend Valbona Mejzninin)) v Croydon London
    Borough Council [2008] EWHC 2921 (Admin), [2009] LGR 113,
    [2009] 3 FCR 499, [2009] 2 FLR 173, [2009] Fam Law 579, [2008]
    All ER (D) 19 (Dec)   6.131

R (A) v Bromley LBC [2008] EWHC 2449 (Admin), [2008] All ER (D) 86
  (Sep) 11.120
R (A) v Coventry CC [2009] EWHC 34 (Admin), [2009] LGR 486, [2009] 1
  FCR 501, [2009] 1 FLR 1202, [2009] Fam Law 289, [2009] All ER
  (D) 04 (Feb) 6.58
R (A) v Croydon LBC & R (WK) v Secretary of State for the Home
  Department and Kent CC [2009] EWHC 939 (Admin) 6.131
R (A) v Croydon LBC [2008] EWHC 2921 (Admin), [2009] LGR 113,
  [2009] 3 FCR 499, [2009] 2 FLR 173, [2009] Fam Law 579, [2008]
  All ER (D) 19 (Dec) 6.55
R (A) v Croydon LBC [2009] UKSC 8, [2009] 1 WLR 2557, [2010] 1 All
  ER 469, [2010] PTSR 106, [2010] 1 FLR 959, [2009] 3 FCR 607,
  [2010] HRLR 9, [2010] UKHRR 63, [2010] BLGR 183, (2009) 12
  CCL Rep 552, [2010] Fam Law 137, (2009) 159 NLJ 1701, (2009)
  153(46) SJLB 34, (2009) *Times*, 30 November 1.92, 1.96, 1.97, 1.98
R (A) v Croydon LBC, R (M) v London Borough of Lambeth [2008] EWCA
  Civ 1445, [2009] LGR 24, [2009] PTSR 1011, [2009] 1 FCR 317,
  [2009] 1 FLR 1324, [2009] Fam Law 290, [2008] All ER (D) 236
  (Dec) 6.56, 6.131
R (A) v Head Teacher of North Westminster Community School and others
  [2002] EWHC 2351 (Admin), [2003] ELR 378, [2002] All ER (D)
  260 (Oct) 11.136
R (A) v Independent Appeal Panel for Sutton London Borough Council
  [2009] EWHC 1223 (Admin), [2009] ELR 321, [2009] All ER (D) 26
  (Jun) 11.135
R (A) v Lord Saville of Newidgate [2001] EWCA Civ 2048, [2002] 1 WLR
  1249, [2002] ACD 22, (2001) *Times*, 21 December, (2002)
  Independent, 11 January, (2002) Telegraph, 11 January 1.125
R (A) v North Somerset Council [2009] EWHC 3060 (Admin), [2010] ELR
  139, [2009] All ER (D) 323 (Nov) 11.120
R (A) v Partnerships in Care Ltd [2002] EWHC 529 (Admin), [2002] 1
  WLR 2610, (2002) 5 CCL Rep 330, [2002] MHLR 298, (2002)
  99(20) LSG 32, (2002) 146 SJLB 117, (2002) *Times*, 23 April 15.41
R (A) v Secretary of State for the Home Department [2002] EWHC 1618
  (Admin), [2003] 1 WLR 330, [2003] MHLR 54, [2003] ACD 7,
  (2002) *Times*, 5 September, (2002) *Independent*, 18 November 1.175
R (AA) v Lambeth LBC [2001] EWCA Admin 741 .... 6.17
R (AB and SB) v Nottingham City Council (2001) 4 CCLR 294, [2001]
  EWHC Admin 235, [2001] 3 FCR 350, [2001] All ER (D) 359 (Mar) ... 6.65, 6.68, 6.86
R (AB) v Secretary of State for Justice [2009] EWHC 2220 (Admin), [2010]
  2 All ER 151, [2009] HRLR 35, (2010) 11 BMLR 70, [2010] ACD
  27, (2009) 106(37) LSG 16, (2009) 159 NLJ 1251 .... 1.184
R (Abassi) v Secretary of State for Foreign and Commonwealth Affairs
  [2002] EWCA Civ 1598, [2003] UKHRR 76, (2002) 99(47) LSG 29,
  (2002) *Times*, 8 November, (2002) *Independent*, 8 November 1.69, 1.201
R (Adams) v Commissioner for Local Administration [2011] EWHC 2971 ... 1.155
R (Adetoro) v Secretary of State for Justice, Parole Board [2012] EWHC
  2576 (Admin), [2013] ACD 16 .... 10.08, 10.64
R (Adow) v LB Newham [2010] EWHC 951, Admin [2010] All ER (D) 73
  (Apr) 7.32
R (AF) v Brent and Vassie LBC [2000] ELR 550 .... 11.141
R (Afework) v London Borough of Camden [2013] EWHC 1637 (Admin),
  (2013) MHLO 51 .... 16.44, 16.45
R (Aga) v General Medical Council [2012] EWHC 782 (Admin) 15.59
R (Agogo) v North Somerset Magistrates' Court [2011] EWHC 518
  (Admin), [2011] ACD 47 .... 1.123
R (Aguiar) v Newham LBC [2003] EWHC 1325 .... 7.53
R (Ahmad) v Newham LBC [2009] UKHL 14, [2009] 3 All ER 755, [2009]
  LGR 627, [2009] PTSR 632, [2009] HLR 516, (2009) *Times*, 6
  March, 153 Sol Jo (no 9) 29, [2009] All ER (D) 43 (Mar) 7.31, 7.75

R (Ahmed (Ashfaq)) v Waltham Forest London Borough Council [2001]
    EWHC Admin 540, [2001] All ER (D) 331 (Jun) 7.37, 7.46
R (Akhtar) v Governor of Newhall Prison [2001] ACD 69 .... 9.62
R (Al Hasan) v Secretary of State for the Home Department [2005] UKHL
    13, [2005] 1 WLR 688, [2005] 1 All ER 927, [2005] HRLR 12, 19
    BHRC 282, [2005] 2 Prison LR 120, (2005) 102(15) LSG 35, *Times*,
    February 18, 2005 .... 1.132, 2.39
R (Al Rawi) v Secretary of State for Foreign and Commonwealth Affairs
    [2006] EWCA Civ 1279, [2008] QB 289, [2007] 2 WLR 1219,
    [2006] HRLR 42, [2007] UKHRR 58, (2006) 103(41) LSG 33,
    (2006) *Times*, 18 October 1.103
R (Al Sweady) v Secretary of State for Defence, *sub nom* Regina (Al-Sweady)
    v Secretary of State for Defence (No 2) [2009] EWHC 2387 (Admin),
    (2009) *Times*, 14 October 3.12
R (Al-Zayyat) v General Medical Council [2010] EWHC 3213 (Admin) 15.191
R (Albert Court Residents' Association) v Westminster City Council [2011]
    EWCA Civ 430, [2012] PTSR 604, [2011] BLGR 616, [2011] 2
    EGLR 49, [2011] 24 EG 110, [2011] 16 EG 79 (CS), (2011) 108(17)
    LSG 14, (2011) 155(15) SJLB 38, (2011) *Times*, 21 April 1.139
R (Alconbury Developments) v Secretary of State for the Environment
    Transport and the Regions [2001] UKHL 23, [2003] 2 AC 295,
    [2001] 2 WLR 1389, [2001] 2 All ER 929, [2002] Env LR 12, [2001]
    HRLR 45, [2001] UKHRR 728, (2001) 3 LGLR 38, (2001) 82
    P & CR 40, [2001] 2 PLR 76, [2001] JPL 920, [2001] 20 EG 228
    (CS), (2001) 98(24) LSG 45, (2001) 151 NLJ 727, (2001) 145 SJLB
    140, [2001] NPC 90, (2001) *Times*, 10 May, (2001) *Independent*, 25
    June, (2001) Telegraph, 15 May 1.40, 1.99, 1.100, 1.180, 5.103
R (Alhy) v General Medical Council [2011] EWHC 2277 (Admin), [2011]
    ACD 114 .... 15.207
R (Ali) v Director of High Security Prisons [2009] EWHC 1732 (Admin),
    [2010] 2 All ER 82, [2010] 2 Prison LR 263 .... 1.154
R (Alistair Lockwood Thompson) v Oxford City Council [2013] EWHC
    1819 (Admin), [2013] 3 EGLR 75 .... 12.33
R (Allen) v Parole Board [2009] EWHC 3492 (Admin) 10.60
R (Alvi) v Secretary of State for the Home Department [2012] UKSC 33,
    [2012] 1 WLR 2208, [2012] 4 All ER 1041, [2012] Imm AR 998,
    [2012] INLR 504 .... 1.92
R (AM) v Director of Public Prosecutions [2012] EWHC 470 (Admin) ... 1.55, 1.201
R (AM) v Secretary of State for the Home Department [2009] EWCA Civ
    219, [2009] UKHRR 973, [2009] Prison LR 133, [2009] ACD 38,
    Times, March 20, 2009 .... 10.120
R (Amin) v Secretary of State for the Home Department [2003] UKHL 51,
    [2004] 1 AC 653, [2003] 3 WLR 1169, [2004] UKHRR 75, [2003] 4
    All ER 1264, 15 BHRC 362, HL 1.55, 1.201, 10.123, 10.124, 10.133
R (Amraf Training Plc) v Secretary of State for Education and Employment
    (2001) *Times*, 28 June 1.59
R (Anderson) v Independent Adjudicator [2010] EWHC 2260 (Admin) 10.88
R (Anderson) v Secretary of State for the Home Department [2002] UKHL
    46, [2002] 3 WLR 1800, [2003] UKHRR 112, [2002] 4 All ER 1089,
    HL 1.180
R (Anglian Water Services Ltd) v Environment Agency [2003] EWHC 1506
    (Admin), [2004] Env LR 15 .... 1.117
R (Animal Defenders International) v Secretary of State for Culture, Media
    and Sport [2008] UKHL 15, [2008] 1 AC 1312, [2008] 2 WLR 781,
    [2008] 3 All ER 193, [2008] EMLR 8, [2008] HRLR 25, [2008]
    UKHRR 477, 24 BHRC 217, (2008) 152(12) SJLB 30, (2008) *Times*,
    17 March 1.189, 1.190
R (Anufrijeva) v Secretary of State for the Home Department [2003] UKHL
    36, [2004] 1 AC 604, [2003] 3 WLR 252, [2003] 3 All ER 827, HL 1.55, 1.123, 1.201

R (Ariemuguvbe) v Islington London Borough Council [2009] EWCA Civ
    1308, [2009] All ER (D) 281 (Feb) 7.78
R (Arratoon) v Office of the Independent Adjudicator [2008] EWHC 3125
    (Admin), [2009] ELR 186, [2008] All ER (D) 160 (Nov) 11.26
R (Aru) v Chief Constable of Merseyside [2004] EWCA Civ 199, [2004] 1
    WLR 1697, [2004] 06 LS Gaz R 33, [2004] 7 LS Gaz R 36, (2004)
    Times, 5 February, [2004] All ER (D) 313 (Jan) 9.08
R (AS) v Great Yarmouth Youth Court [2011] EWHC 2059 (Admin), [2012]
    Crim LR 478 .... 1.123
R (Asha Foundation) v Millennium Commission [2003] EWCA Civ 88,
    [2003] ACD 50, (2003) 100(11) LSG 31, *Times*, January 24, 2003 .... 1.155
R (Ashby) v Royal Pharmaceutical Society of Great Britain [2008] EWHC
    1739 (Admin) 15.172
R (Ashworth Hospital Authority) v Mental Health Review Tribunal for the
    West Midland and North West Region [2001] EWHC Admin 901,
    (2002) 5 CCL Rep 78, [2002] MHLR 13 .... 1.155, 2.18
R (Ashworth Hospital Authority) v Mental Health Review Tribunal for West
    Midlands and the North West Region [2002] EWCA Civ 923, [2003]
    1 WLR 127, 70 BMLR 40, [2002] 34 LS Gaz R 29, (2002) *Times*, 10
    July, [2002] All ER (D) 252 (Jun), CA 8.70
R (Associated Newspapers Ltd) v Lord Justice Leveson [2012] EWHC 57
    (Admin), [2012] ACD 23 .... 15.37
R (AT) v Parole Board [2004] EWHC 515 (Admin), [2004] Prison LR 369 .... 10.59
R (Atamewan) v Secretary of State for the Home Department [2013] EWHC
    2727 (Admin) 2.28
R (Attfield) v Barnet London Borough Council [2013] EWHC 2089
    (Admin), [2014] 1 All ER 304, [2013] PTSR 1559, [2013] RTR 33,
    [2013] BLGR 633, [2014] ACD 22 .... 1.114
R (Aujla & Others) v Slough Borough Council [2005] EWHC 1866
    (Admin), [2005] All ER (D) 162 (Jul) 12.32, 12.33, 12.35
R (Aurangzeh) v Law Society of England and Wales [2003] EWHC 1286
    (Admin) 15.114, 15.116
R (Austin) v Parole Board [2011] EWHC 2384 (Admin) 10.58
R (Aweys) v Birmingham City Council [2009] EWCA Civ 1308, [2010] HLR
    14 .... 7.78
R (B and C) v Lambeth LBC [2001] HWHC 515 .... 11.30
R (B) v Birmingham City Council Education Appeals Committee, ex p B
    [1999] ELR 305, (1998) *Times*, 13 October 11.94
R (B) v Camden London Borough Council [2005] EWHC 1366 (Admin),
    [2006] LGR 19, 85 BMLR 28, [2005] All ER (D) 43 (Jul) 8.67
R (B) v Cornwall CC & The Brandon Trust [2009] EWHC 491 (Admin),
    (2009) 12 CCL Rep 381 .... 6.17
R (B) v DPP [2009] EWHC 106 (Admin), [2009] 1 WLR 2072, [2009] 1 Cr
    App R 38, [2009] UKHRR 669, (2009) 106 BMLR 152, [2009]
    MHLR 61, [2009] Crim LR 652, [2009] ACD 19, (2009) 153(5)
    SJLB 29, (2009) *Times*, March 24 .... 9.44
R (B) v Dr SS (RMO) SOAD & Secretary of State for Health [2006] EWCA
    Civ 28 .... 8.41
R (B) v Head Teacher of Alperton Community School, R (T) v Head Teacher
    of Wembley High School and Others, R (C) v The Governing Body of
    Cardinal Newman High School and Others [2001] EWHC 229
    (Admin), [2001] ELR 359, [2002] BLGR 132, [2002] ACD 15, QBD 11.132, 11.137,
                                                                              11.151, 11.161
R (B) v London Borough of Lambeth [2006] EWHC 262 (QB) 16.43
R (B) v London Borough of Southwark, *sub nom* Binomugisha v London
    Borough of Southwark [2006] EWHC 2254 (Admin), [2007] 3 FCR
    457, [2007] 1 FLR 916, [2006] All ER (D) 83 (Sep) 6.134
R (B) v Merton London Borough Council [2003] EWHC 1689 (Admin),
    [2003] 4 All ER 280, [2003] 2 FLR 888, [2005] 3 FCR 69, (2003) 6
    CCL Rep 457, [2003] Fam Law 813, (2003) *Times*, 18 July 1.156, 11.142

R (B) v Nursing and Midwifery Council [2012] EWHC 1264 (Admin)	1.140, 2.72, 15.131, 15.222
R (B) v Rochdale MBC [2000] Ed CR 117	11.152
R (BA) v Secretary of State for the Home Department [2011] EWHC 2748 (Admin)	1.169
R (Badger Trust) v Secretary of State for the Environment, Food and Rural Affairs [2012] EWHC 1904 (Admin)	1.116
R (Badger Trust) v Welsh Ministers [2010] EWCA Civ 807, [2010] 6 Costs LR 896, (2010) 107(30) LSG 12, [2010] NPC 79	1.102
R (Bahta) v Secretary of State for the Home Department [2011] EWCA Civ 895, [2011] CP Rep 43, [2011] 5 Costs LR 857, [2011] ACD 116	3.65, 15.228
R (Bailey) v London Borough of Brent [2011] EWHC 2572 (Admin)	1.145
R (Baker) v North East Somerset District Council [2009] EWHC 595 (Admin), [2009] Env LR 27, [2010] 1 P & CR 4, [2009] JPL 1498, [2009] ACD 37	5.104
R (Bancoult) v Secretary of State for Foreign & Commonwealth Affairs (No 2) [2008] UKHL 61, [2009] 1 AC 453, [2008] 3 WLR 955, [2008] 4 All ER 1055, (2008) 105(42) LSG 20, (2008) 158 NLJ 1530, (2008) 152(41) SJLB 29, (2008) *Times*, 23 October	1.55, 1.67, 1.137, 1.138, 1.201, 13.05, 13.13, 13.82
R (Bancoult) v Secretary of State for Foreign and Commonwealth Affairs [2013] EWHC 1502 (Admin), [2014] Env LR 2, [2013] ACD 83	1.151
R (Bancoult) v Secretary of State for the Foreign and Commonwealth Office [2001] QB 1067, [2001] 2 WLR 1219, [2001] ACD 18, (2000) 97(47) LSG 39, (2000) *Times*, 10 November	1.55, 1.65, 1.66, 1.67, 1.201
R (Bandtock) v Secretary of State for Education [2001] ELR 333	11.151
R (Banks) v Secretary of State for Environment, Food and Rural Affairs [2004] EWHC 416 (Admin), (2004) *Times*, 19 April, [2004] All ER (D) 265 (Mar)	3.78
R (Bantamagbari) v Westminster City Council [2003] EWHC 1350 (Admin), [2003] All ER (D) 163 (May)	7.58
R (Barker) v Bromley London Borough Council [2006] UKHL 52	5.46
R (Barnsley MBC) v Secretary of State for Communities and Local Government [2012] EWHC 1366 (Admin), [2013] PTSR 23, [2012] BLGR 933, [2012] 2 EGLR 1, [2012] 34 EG 48, [2012] ACD 101, (2012) 156(22) SJLB 31	13.60
R (Bary) v Secretary of State for Justice [2010] EWHC 587 (Admin), [2010] ACD 59	10.19
R (Bashir) v Cranfield University [1999] ELR 317	11.26
R (Bassetlaw District Council) v Worksop Magistrates' Court [2008] EWHC 3530 (Admin), 173 JP 599, [2008] All ER (D) 65 (Nov)	12.63
R (Batantu) v Islington London Borough [2000] All ER (D) 1744	6.17
R (Bates) v Independent Adjudicator, Secretary of State for Justice [2011] EWHC 3236 (Admin)	10.88, 10.93
R (BBC) v Secretary of State for Justice [2012] EWHC 13 (Admin), [2013] 1 WLR 964, [2012] 2 All ER 1089, [2012] EMLR 18, [2012] ACD 33, (2012) 162 NLJ 94, (2012) *Times*, 13 April	1.189
R (Bealey) v Secretary of State for the Home Department [2005] EWHC 1618 (Admin), [2006] 1 Prison LR 175	10.26
R (Beaumont) v Kirklees MBC [2001] LGR 187, [2001] ELR 204, (2000) *Times*, 22 November	11.30
R (Beer) v Hampshire Farmers Market Ltd [2003] EWCA Civ 1056, [2004] 1 WLR 233, [2004] UKHRR 727, [2003] 31 EG 67 (CS), (2003) 100(36) LSG 40, (2003) 147 SJLB 1085, [2003] NPC 93, (2003) *Times*, 25 August, (2003) *Independent*, 30 July	15.40
R (Beeson) v Dorset County Council [2001] EWHC 986 (Admin)	1.153
R (Beever) v Independent Adjudicator of HMP Frankland [2010] EWHC 1559 (Admin)	10.92
R (Begbie) v Secretary of State for Education and Employment [2000] 1 WLR 1115, [2000] ELR 445, [1999] 35 LS Gaz R 39, 143 Sol Jo LB 240, [1999] All ER (D) 983	11.161

R (Begum (Amirun)) v Tower Hamlets London Borough Council [2002]
EWHC 633 (Admin), [2003] HLR 70, [2002] All ER (D) 308 (Apr)   7.68
R (Begum) v Headteacher and Governors of Denbigh High School, *sub nom*
R (SB) v Governors of Denbigh High School [2006] UKHL 15, [2007]
1 AC 100, [2006] 2 All ER 487, [2006] 2 WLR 719, [2006] 2 FCR
613, [2006] NLJR 552, (2006) *The Times*, 23 March, 150 Sol Jo LB
399, 23 BHRC 276, [2006] 4 LRC 543, [2006] All ER (D) 320 (Mar)   11.145, 11.156
R (Begum) v Tower Hamlets London Borough Council [2003] UKHL 5,
[2003] 2 AC 430, [2003] 2 WLR 388, [2003] 1 All ER 731, [2003]
HRLR 16, [2003] UKHRR 419, 14 BHRC 400, [2003] HLR 32,
[2003] BLGR 205, 2003 Hous LR 20, [2003] ACD 41, (2003)
100(13) LSG 28, (2003) 147 SJLB 232, [2003] NPC 21, (2003)
Times, February 17, (2003) *Independent*, 18 February   1.180
R (Bentley) v HM Coroner District of Avon [2001] EWHC Admin 170   1.123
R (Bernard) v Enfield Borough Council [2002] EWHC 2282 (Admin), [2003]
LGR 423, [2003] HLR 354, [2002] 48 LS Gaz R 27, (2002) *Times*, 8
November, 5 CCL Rep 577, [2002] All ER (D) 383 (Oct)   2.101, 2.102
R (Betting Shop Services Ltd) v Southend on Sea Borough Council [2007]
EWHC 105 (Admin), [2008] All ER (D) 15 (Jan)   12.63
R (Bhatt Murphy) v Independent Assessor [2008] EWCA Civ 755, (2008)
152(29) SJLB 29, (2008) *Times*, 21 July   1.137, 1.138, 1.143
R (Bhatti) v Bury MBC [2013] EWHC 3093 (Admin), (2014) 17 CCL Rep
64   3.17
R (Bibi) v Newham London Borough Council [2001] EWCA Civ 607,
[2002] 1 WLR 237, (2001) 33 HLR 84, (2001) 98(23) LSG 38,
[2001] NPC 83, (2001) *Times*, 10 May   1.102, 1.135, 1.137, 1.138
R (Birmingham and Solihull Taxi Association) v Birmingham International
Airport [2009] EWHC 1913 (Admin)   1.59
R (Birmingham City Council) v Birmingham Crown Court [2009] EWHC
3329 (Admin), [2010] 1 WLR 1287, [2010] PTSR 1229, (2010) 174
JP 185, [2010] ACD 34, (2010) *Times*, 5 January   1.153, 1.154
R (Black) v Secretary of State for Justice [2009] 1 AC 949, [2009] UKHL 1,
[2009] AC 949, [2009] 4 All ER 1, [2009] 2 WLR 282, (2009) *Times*,
30 January, 153 Sol Jo (no 4) 27, 26 BHRC 664, [2009] All ER (D)
138 (Jan)   1.173, 9.12
R (Blackwood) v Birmingham Magistrates' Court & Others [2006] EWHC
1800 (Admin), 170 JP 613, 171 JPN 19, [2006] All ER (D) 324 (Jun)   12.40
R (Bonhoeffer) v General Medical Council [2011] EWHC 1585 (Admin),
[2012] IRLR 37, [2011] Med LR 519, [2011] ACD 104   1.123, 15.166
R (Booker) v NHS Oldham [2010] EWHC 2593 (Admin), (2011) 14 CCL
Rep 315, [2011] Med LR 10   16.17
R (Botmeh and Alami) v Parole Board [2008] EWHC 1115 (Admin), [2009]
Prison LR 83   10.59
R (Bourgass) v Secretary of State for Justice [2011] EWHC 286 (Admin)   10.18
R (Bourke) v Secretary of State for Justice [2012] EWHC 4041 (Admin)   10.61
R (Bramall) v Law Society [2005] EWHC 1570 (Admin), [2006] PNLR 4   15.100
R (Breckland District Council) v The Boundary Committee [2009] EWCA
Civ 239, [2009] PTSR 1611, [2009] BLGR 589, (2009) 153(12) SJLB
28   1.146
R (Britannic Asset Management Ltd) v Pensions Ombudsman [2002] EWHC
441 (Admin), [2002] OPLR 175, (2002) 99(20) LSG 32, (2002)
Times, 16 April   1.98
R (British Beer & Pub Association & Others) v Canterbury City Council
[2005] EWHC 1318 (Admin), [2006] LGR 596, 169 JP 521, (2005)
Times, 11 July, [2005] All ER (D) 285 (Jun)   12.61
R (British Sky Broadcasting Ltd) v Central Criminal Court [2011] EWHC
3451 (Admin), [2012] QB 785, [2012] 3 WLR 78   1.123
R (Broadbent) v Parole Board [2005] EWHC 1207 (Admin), [2006] 1 Prison
LR 137, (2005) *Times*, 22 June   10.54

R (Brooks) v Parole Board [2003] EWHC 1458 (Admin), [2003] Prison LR 376	1.125
R (Brooks) v Secretary of State for Justice, Isle of Wight Primary Care Trust [2008] EWHC 3041 (Admin), [2010] 1 Prison LR 266	10.46
R (Brown) v Secretary of State for Work and Pensions [2008] EWHC 3158 (Admin), [2009] PTSR 1506	1.83
R (BSB Ltd) v Chelmsford Crown Court [2012] EWHC 1295 (Admin), [2012] 2 Cr App R 33, [2012] EMLR 30, [2012] Crim LR 888, [2012] ACD 68	1.189
R (Buckinghamshire County Council) v Kingston upon Thames London Borough Council [2011] EWCA Civ 457, [2012] PTSR 854, (2011) 14 CCL Rep 426, [2011] ACD 83, [2011] Fam Law 814	1.123
R (Buckinghamshire County Council) v Royal Borough of Kingston upon Thames [2010] EWHC 1703 (Admin), [2010] All ER (D) 115 (Jul)	6.33
R (Buckinghamshire County Council) v School Admissions Independent Appeal Panel for Buckinghamshire [2009] EWHC 1679 (Admin), [2010] ELR 172, [2009] All ER (D) 136 (Jul)	11.34
R (Buglife) v Medway Council [2011] EWHC 746 (Admin), [2011] 3 CMLR 39, [2011] Env LR 27, [2011] 24 EG 108 (CS)	3.14
R (Buglife, The Invertebrate Conservation Trust) v Thurrock Thames Gateway Development Corpn [2008] EWCA Civ 1209, [2008] 45 EG 101 (CS), (2008) *Times*, 18 November, 152 Sol Jo (no 43) 29, [2009] 1 Costs LR 80, [2008] All ER (D) 30 (Nov)	3.80
R (Bunce) v Pensions Appeal Tribunal [2009] EWCA Civ 451, (2009) *Times*, April 15	1.77
R (Burkett) v London Borough of Hammersmith and Fulham [2002] UKHL 23, [2002] 1 WLR 1593, [2002] 3 All ER 97, [2002] CP Rep 66, [2003] Env LR 6, [2003] 1 P & CR 3, [2002] 2 PLR 90, [2002] JPL 1346, [2002] ACD 81, [2002] 22 EG 136 (CS), (2002) 99(27) LSG 34, (2002) 152 NLJ 847, (2002) 146 SJLB 137, [2002] NPC 75, (2002) *Times*, 24 May, (2002) *Independent*, 28 May	3.54, 5.67
R (Butt and others) v SSHD [2014] EWHC 264 (Admin)	14.24
R (C and another) v Nottingham City Council [2010] EWCA Civ 790, [2011] 1 FCR 127, [2010] All ER (D) 82 (Dec)	2.143
R (C and others) v Bromley LBC [1992] 1 FLR 174	11.73
R (C) v Admission Panel of Nottinghamshire CC and another [2004] EWHC 2988 (Admin), [2005] ELR 182, [2004] All ER (D) 15 (Dec)	11.95
R (C) v Brent London Borough Council [2006] EWCA Civ 728, [2006] ELR 435, [2006] All ER (D) 189 (Apr)	11.55, 11.119
R (C) v Financial Services Authority [2012] EWHC 1417 (Admin), [2012] ACD 97	1.155
R (C) v Financial Services Authority [2013] EWCA Civ 677	15.51, 15.53, 15.57
R (C) v IAP of Sefton MBC and Governors of Hillside High School [2001] ELR 393	11.136
R (C) v Lambeth London Borough Council [2008] EWHC 1230 (Admin), [2008] All ER (D) 277 (May)	6.88
R (C) v Lewisham London Borough Council [2003] EWCA Civ 927, [2003] 3 All ER 1277, [2004] HLR 27, [2003] 34 LS Gaz R 30, [2003] NLJR 1064, (2003) *Times*, 12 August, 147 Sol Jo LB 818, [2003] All ER (D) 87 (Jul)	7.54
R (C) v Mental Health Review Tribunal [2001] EWCA Civ 1110, [2002] 1 WLR 176, [2002] 2 FCR 181, [2001] 29 LS Gaz R 39, (2001) *Times*, 11 July, 145 Sol Jo LB 167, [2001] All ER (D) 24 (Jul)	8.62
R (C) v Merton London Borough Council [2005] EWHC 1753 (Admin), [2005] 3 FCR 42	1.153
R (C) v Secretary of State for Justice [2009] EWHC 2671 (Admin), [2010] HRLR 3	10.53
R (C) v South Gloucestershire Appeals Committee [2000] ELR 220	11.95
R (C) v The Upper Tribunal [2010] EWCA Civ 859	4.23

R (Cala Homes (South) Ltd) v Secretary of State for Communities and Local
  Government [2010] EWHC 2866 (Admin), [2011] BLGR 204, [2010]
  46 EG 116 (CS), [2010] NPC 110, [2011] PTSR D15   1.112, 5.80, 5.87
R (Cala Homes (South) Ltd) v Secretary of State for Communities and Local
  Government [2011] EWCA Civ 639, [2011] 2 EGLR 75, [2011] 34
  EG 68, [2011] JPL 1458, [2011] 22 EG 103 (CS), [2011] NPC 57   5.80, 5.88
R (Cali, Abdi and Hassan) v Waltham Forest London Borough Council
  [2006] EWHC 302 (Admin), [2006] All ER (D) 124 (Apr)   7.74
R (Campbell) v General Medical Council [2005] EWCA Civ 250, [2005] 1
  WLR 3488, [2005] 2 All ER 970, [2005] Lloyd's Rep Med 353,
  (2005) 83 BMLR 30, (2005) Times, 18 April, (2005) Independent, 12
  April   15.157
R (Cannan) v Governor of HMP Full Sutton [2009] EWHC 1517 (Admin),
  [2010] 2 Prison LR 166   10.36
R (Capenhurst) v Leicester City Council [2004] EWHC 2124 (Admin),
  (2004) 7 CCL Rep 557, [2004] ACD 93   1.146
R (Capital Care Services (UK) Ltd v Secretary of State for the Home
  Department [2012] EWCA Civ 1151   1.140
R (Care North East Northumberland) v Northumberland County Council
  [2013] EWCA Civ 1740, [2014] PTSR 758, (2014) 17 CCL Rep 117,
  (2013) 157(46) SJLB 37   6.146
R (Carman) v Secretary of State for the Home Department [2004] EWHC
  2400 (Admin), [2005] 2 Prison LR 172, (2004) Times, 11 October   10.02, 10.53
R (Carnell) v Regents Park College and Conference of Colleges Appeal
  Tribunal [2008] EWHC 739 (Admin), [2008] ELR 268   3.17, 11.21, 11.24
R (Carroll and Al-Hasan) v Secretary of State for the Home Department
  [2005] UKHL 13, [2005] 1 WLR 688, [2005] 1 All ER 927, [2005]
  HRLR 12, 19 BHRC 282, [2005] 2 Prison LR 120, (2005) 102(15)
  LSG 35, (2005) Times, 18 February   10.83
R (Carson) v Secretary of State for Work and Pensions [2005] UKHL 37,
  [2006] 1 AC 173, [2005] 2 WLR 1369, [2005] 4 All ER 545, [2005]
  HRLR 23, [2005] UKHRR 1185, 18 BHRC 677, (2005) Times, 27
  May   1.194
R (Cart) v Upper Tribunal [2009] EWHC 3052 (Admin), [2010] 2 WLR
  1012, [2010] 1 All ER 908, [2010] PTSR 824, [2010] STC 493,
  [2010] 2 FCR 309, [2010] MHLR 35, [2010] ACD 36, [2009] STI
  3167   1.01, 1.04, 1.76
R (Cart) v Upper Tribunal [2011] UKSC 28, [2012] 1 AC 663, [2011] 3
  WLR 107, [2011] 4 All ER 127, [2011] PTSR 1053, [2011] STC
  1659, [2012] 1 FLR 997, [2011] Imm AR 704, [2011] MHLR 196,
  [2012] Fam Law 398, [2011] STI 1943, (2011) 161 NLJ 916, (2011)
  155(25) SJLB 35, (2011) Times, 23 June   3.44, 8.58, 12.52, 14.57, 15.52
R (Cart) v Upper Tribunal (Secretary of State for Justice, interested party)
  (Public Law Project intervening) [2010] EWCA Civ 859, [2010] 4 All
  ER 714, [2011] 2 WLR 36, [2010] STC 2556, [2010] NLJR 1115,
  (2010) Times, 4 October, [2010] SWTI 2272, [2010] All ER (D) 246
  (Jul)   8.57, 8.63
R (Casey) v Restormel Borough Council [2007] EWHC 2554 (Admin),
  [2007] All ER (D) 96 (Nov)   7.96, 7.97
R (Cash) v Northamptonshire Coroner [2007] EWHC 1354 (Admin), [2007]
  4 All ER 903, [2007] UKHRR 1037, [2007] Inquest LR 147, (2007)
  157 NLJ 895   1.154
R (Cathco Property Holdings Ltd) v Cygnor Gwynedd Council [2008]
  EWHC 1462 (Admin), [2009] JPL 230   1.79
R (Cawser) v Secretary of State for the Home Department [2003] EWCA Civ
  1522, [2004] UKHRR 101, [2004] Prison LR 166, (2003) 100(48)
  LSG 18, (2003) Times, 25 November   10.24
R (CC West Midlands) v Birmingham Justices [2002] EWHC 1087 (Admin),
  [2002] Po LR 157, [2003] Crim LR 37, [2003] ACD 18, (2002)
  99(28) LSG 32, (2002) 146 SJLB 159, (2002) Times, June 5   1.83

R (CF) v Secretary of State for the Home Department [2004] EWHC 111
(Fam), [2004] 2 FLR 517, [2004] 1 FCR 577, [2005] 1 Prison LR
104, [2004] Fam Law 639 .... 1.183
R (Chandler) v London Borough of Camden & Others [2009] EWHC 219
(Admin) 11.27, 12.35
R (Charlton) v Secretary of State for Education and Skills [2005] EWHC
1378 (Admin), [2006] 1 FLR 175, [2005] 2 FCR 603, [2005] Fam
Law 861, (2005) Times, 12 August 1.140
R (Che) v Secretary of State for the Home Department [2013] EWHC 2220
(Admin) 1.142
R (Chelfat) v Tower Hamlets LBC [2006] EWHC 313 (Admin), [2006] All
ER (D) 139 (Feb) 7.12, 7.86
R (Cheltenham Builders Ltd) v South Gloucestershire District Council [2003]
EWHC 2803 (Admin), [2003] 4 PLR 95, [2004] 1 EGLR 85, [2004]
JPL 975 .... 15.52
R (Cherkley Campaign Ltd) v Mole Valley District Council [2013] EWHC
2582 (Admin), [2014] 1 P & CR 12, [2014] ACD 42, (2013) 157(34)
SJLB 40, [2014] PTSR D1 .... 5.100
R (Chester) v Secretary of State for Justice [2013] UKSC 63, [2013] 3 WLR
1076, [2014] 1 All ER 683, 2014 SLT 143, [2014] 1 CMLR 45,
[2014] HRLR 3, 2013 GWD 34-676 .... 1.163
R (Chief Constable of Avon and Somerset Police) v Police Appeals Tribunal
[2004] EWHC 220 (Admin), [2004] Po LR 116, (2004) Times, 11
February 15.214
R (Chief Constable of the West Midlands Police) v Birmingham Justices
[2002] EWHC 1087 (Admin), [2003] Crim LR 37, [2002] 28 LS Gaz
R 32, (2002) Times, 5 June, 146 Sol Jo LB 159, [2002] All ER (D)
502 (May) 13.123, 13.126
R (Children's Rights Alliance for England) v Secretary of State for Justice
[2012] EWHC 8 (QB), [2012] CTLC 158 .... 1.183
R (Chisnell) v Richmond Upon Thames London Borough Council [2005]
EWHC 134 (Admin), [2005] 5 EG 203 (CS) 1.152, 5.110
R (Chong) v Law Society [2007] EWHC 641 (Admin) 15.193
R (Chowdhury) v Newham LBC [2003] EWHC 2837 (Admin), [2003] All
ER (D) 397 (Nov) 7.84
R (Clark & others) v Rotherham Metropolitan Borough Council (1997) 96
LGR 214, [1998] 1 FCR 509, [1998] ELR 152 .... 11.64
R (Clarke) v Cardiff University [2009] NPC 105, [2009] EWHC 2148
(Admin), 153 Sol Jo (no 33) 32, [2009] All ER (D) 147 (Aug) 11.24
R (Clegg) v Secretary of State for Trade and Industry [2002] EWCA Civ
519, [2003] BCC 128 .... 1.127
R (Clift) v Secretary of State for the Home Department [2006] UKHL 54,
[2007] 1 AC 484, [2007] 2 WLR 24, [2007] 2 All ER 1, [2007]
HRLR 12, [2007] UKHRR 348, 21 BHRC 704, [2007] Prison LR
125, [2007] ACD 27, (2006) Times, 21 December 1.193
R (Coghlan) v Chief Constable of Greater Manchester Police [2004] EWHC
2801 (Admin), [2005] 2 All ER 890, [2005] ACD 34 .... 1.103, 15.205
R (Coke-Wallis) v Institute of Chartered Accountants in England and Wales
[2011] UKSC 1, [2011] 2 AC 146, [2011] 2 WLR 103, [2011] 2 All
ER 1, [2011] ICR 224, (2011) 108(5) LSG 18, (2011) Times, 31
January 15.43, 15.102
R (Collins) v Lincolnshire Health Authority [2001] EWHC Admin 685,
[2001] All ER (D) 08 (Sep) 6.152
R (Commissioner of Police of the Metropolis) v Police Appeals Tribunal and
Peart [2011] EWHC 3421 (Admin), [2012] ACD 43 .... 15.34
R (Conde) v Lambeth London Borough Council [2005] EWHC 62 (Admin),
[2005] 2 FLR 198, [2005] 1 FCR 189, [2005] HLR 29, (2005) 8 CCL
Rep 486, [2005] Fam Law 455, ... 1.207

R (Condliff) v North Staffordshire Primary Care Trust [2011] EWCA Civ
910, [2012] 1 All ER 689, [2012] PTSR 460, [2011] HRLR 38,
(2011) 14 CCL Rep 656, [2011] Med LR 572, (2011) 121 BMLR
192, [2011] ACD 113, (2011) 155(30) SJLB 31 .... 1.184, 16.36
R (Connolly) v Secretary of State for Communities and Local Government
[2009] EWCA Civ 1059, [2010] 2 P & CR 1, [2009] NPC 114 .... 1.94
R (Core Issues Trust) v Transport for London [2013] EWHC 651 (Admin),
[2013] PTSR 1161, [2013] HRLR 22, [2013] Eq LR 508, [2013]
ACD 71 .... 1.189
R (Corner House Research) v Director of Serious Fraud [2008] EWHC 714
(Admin), [2009] AC 756, [2008] 4 All ER 927, [2008] NLJR 556,
(2008) *Times*, 16 April, [2009] 1 LRC 343, [2008] All ER (D) 151
(Apr) 6.131, 9.44, 9.91
R (Corner House Research) v Secretary of State for Trade and Industry
[2005] EWCA Civ 192, [2005] 4 All ER 1, [2005] 1 WLR 2600,
(2005) *Times*, 7 March, 149 Sol Jo LB 297, [2005] 3 Costs LR 455,
[2005] All ER (D) 07 (Mar) 3.79, 3.81, 5.132
R (Cornwall Council) v Wiltshire Council [2012] EWHC 3739 (Admin),
[2013] 2 FCR 369, [2013] BLGR 197, (2013) 16 CCL Rep 82,
(2013) 131 BMLR 1, [2013] ACD 39 .... 6.119
R (Council for the Regulation of Health Care Professionals) v Nursing &
Midwifery Council [2007] EWHC 1806 (Admin), (2007) 98 BMLR
60, [2007] ACD 79 .... 15.148
R (Countryside Alliance) v Attorney General [2007] UKHL 52, [2008] 1 AC
719, [2007] 3 WLR 922, [2008] 2 All ER 95, [2008] Eu LR 359,
[2008] HRLR 10, [2008] UKHRR 1, (2007) 104(48) LSG 23, (2007)
157 NLJ 1730, (2007) 151 SJLB 1564, [2007] NPC 127, (2007)
Times, 29 November 1.182, 1.206, 1.207
R (Cowl) v Plymouth City Council, *sub nom* Cowl v Plymouth City Council,
Cowl (Practice Note), Re [2001] EWCA Civ 1935, [2002] 1 WLR
803, [2002] CP Rep 18, [2002] ACD 11, CA 2.137, 2.143, 2.144, 2.148, 3.17, 3.18
R (Cox) v Independent Adjudicator [2013] EWHC 2753 (Admin) 10.88
R (CPS) v Sedgmoor Magistrates' Court [2007] EWHC Admin 1803 .... 9.20
R (Craven) v Secretary of State for the Home Department [2001] EWHC
Admin 850, [2002] Po LR 18 .... 10.53
R (CS) v Mental Health Review Tribunal [2004] EWHC 2958 (Admin),
[2004] All ER (D) 87 (Dec) 8.44
R (Culkin) v Wirral Independent Appeal Panel [2009] EWHC 868 (Admin),
[2009] ELR 287, [2009] All ER (D) 216 (Apr) 11.135, 11.138, 11.140, 11.141
R (D & K) v SSHD [2006] EWHC 980 (Admin) 14.54
R (D'Cunha) v Parole Board [2011] EWHC 128 (Admin) 10.58, 10.62
R (D) v General Medical Council [2013] EWHC 2839 (Admin), (2013) 134
BMLR 118 .... 15.92, 15.93
R (D) v Haringey London Borough Council, R (D) v Haringey Primary Care
Trust [2005] EWHC 2235 (Admin), [2005] All ER (D) 256 (Oct) 6.107
R (D) v Northamptonshire CC [1998] ELR 291 .... 11.95
R (D) v Secretary of State for the Home Department [2003] EWHC 155
(Admin), [2003] 1 FLR 979, [2003] Prison LR 220, [2003] ACD 69,
[2003] Fam Law 315, (2003) *Times*, 27 January 1.184
R (D) v Secretary of State for the Home Department [2006] EWCA Civ 143,
[2006] 3 All ER 946, [2006] HRLR 24, [2006] Inquest LR 35, [2006]
ACD 66, (2006) *Times*, 21 March, (2006) *Independent*, 2 March 10.133, 10.134,
10.135, 10.137
R (D) v Secretary of State for the Home Department [2012] EWHC 2501
(Admin), [2012] ACD 120 .... 1.169
R (Daly) v Secretary of State for the Home Department [2001] UKHL 26,
[2001] 2 AC 532, [2001] 2 WLR 1622, [2001] 3 All ER 433, [2001]
HRLR 49, [2001] UKHRR 887, [2001] Prison LR 322, [2001] ACD
79, (2001) 98(26) LSG 43, (2001) 145 SJLB 156, (2001) *Times*, 25
May, (2001) Telegraph, 29 May 1.46, 10.41

R (Daniel Thwaites plc) v Wirral Borough Magistrates' Court [2008] EWHC
838 (Admin), [2009] 1 All ER 239, 172 JP 301, [2008] NLJR 707,
[2008] All ER (D) 61 (May) ... 12.25, 12.63, 12.102
R (Das) v Secretary of State for the Home Department [2013] EWHC 682
(Admin) ... 1.116
R (Davey) v Aylesbury Vale District Council [2007] EWCA Civ 1166, [2008]
2 All ER 178, [2008] 1 WLR 878, [2008] 1 Costs LR 60, [2007] All
ER (D) 259 (Nov) ... 3.44
R (David) v General Medical Council [2004] EWHC 2977 (Admin), (2005)
84 BMLR 30, (2005) Times, 12 January ... 15.111, 15.115
R (Davies) v Financial Services Authority [2003] EWCA Civ 1128, [2004] 1
WLR 185, [2003] 4 All ER 1196, [2004] 1 All ER (Comm) 88,
[2005] 1 BCLC 286, [2003] ACD 83, (2003) 100(38) LSG 34, (2003)
Times, 6 October ... 15.51, 15.57
R (Davies) v Revenue and Customs Commissioners [2011] UKSC 47, [2011]
1 WLR 2625, [2012] 1 All ER 1048, [2011] STC 2249, 81 TC 134,
[2011] BTC 610, [2012] WTLR 215, [2011] STI 2847, (2011)
155(40) SJLB 31, [2011] NPC 107, (2011) Times, 24 October ... 1.137
R (Davies) v Secretary of State for the Home Department [2005] 1 Prison
LR 228 ... 10.53
R (Derbyshire Constabulary) v The Police Appeals Tribunal [2012] EWHC
2280 (Admin), [2012] ACD 126 ... 15.150
R (Derwent Holdings Ltd) v Trafford BC [2011] EWHC 491 (Admin),
[2011] 11 EG 103 (CS) ... 5.122
R (Developing Retail Limited) v East Hampshire Magistrates' Court [2011]
EWHC 618 (Admin) ... 12.48
R (Devon County Council) v Secretary of State for Communities and Local
Government [2010] EWHC 1456 (Admin), [2011] BLGR 64, [2010]
ACD 83 ... 1.150
R (Director of Public Prosecutions) v Birmingham City Justices [2003]
EWHC 2352 ... 1.67
R (Dixon) v Somerset CC [1998] Env LR 111 ... 3.06
R (DK) v Secretary of State for Justice [2010] EWHC 82 (Admin), (2010)
112 BMLR 116, [2010] MHLR 64 ... 10.48
R (DL) v Newham Borough Council [2011] EWHC 1127 (Admin), [2011] 2
FLR 1033, [2011] ACD 95, [2011] Fam Law 922, (2011) 108(24)
LSG 19 ... 1.183
R (Domb) v London Borough of Hammersmith & Fulham [2009] EWCA
Civ 941, [2009] BLGR 843, [2010] ACD 20, (2009) 153(34) SJLB 30 ... 1.83
R (Doshi) v Southend on Sea Primary Care Trust [2007] EWHC 1361
(Admin), [2007] LS Law Medical 418, [2007] ACD 70 ... 15.155
R (Downs) v Secretary of State for Justice [2011] EWCA Civ 1422, [2012]
ACD 38 ... 1.123
R (DR) v Head Teacher of St George's Catholic School, R (AM) v Governing
Body of Kingsmead School [2002] EWCA Civ 1822, [2003] LGR
371, (2002) Times, 19 December, [2002] All ER (D) 209 (Dec) ... 11.126
R (E) v DPP [2011] EWHC 1465 (Admin), [2012] 1 Cr App R 6, [2012]
Crim LR 39, (2011) 155(24) SJLB 43 ... 9.41
R (E) v Education Appeal Committee of Lancashire County Council [1994]
3 FCR 1, [1994] ELR 530 ... 11.95
R (E) v Governing Body of the Jews Free School (The United Synagogue
intervening), R (E) v Office of The Schools Adjudicator (British
Humanist Association intervening) [2009] EWCA Civ 626, [2009] 4
All ER 375, [2009] PTSR 1442, [2009] ELR 407, [2009] NLJR 963,
(2009) Times, 8 July, [2009] All ER (D) 260 (Jun), CA ... 11.75
R (E) v Nottinghamshire Healthcare NHS Trust [2009] EWCA Civ 795,
[2010] PTSR 674, [2009] HRLR 31, [2009] UKHRR 1442, (2009)
110 BMLR 87, [2009] MHLR 266, (2009) Times, 10 August ... 1.201
R (East Midlands Care Ltd) v Leicestershire County Council [2011] EWHC
3096 (Admin) ... 6.146

R (Eastenders Cash & Carry Plc) v Revenue & Customs Commissioners [2012] EWCA Civ 15, [2012] 1 WLR 2067, [2012] STC 817, [2014] BVC 7 .... 1.55, 1.201

R (Edwards and Anor) v Environment Agency and others [2008] UKHL 22, [2009] 1 All ER 57, [2008] 1 WLR 1587, [2008] 16 EG 153 (CS), (2008) *Times*, 6 May, [2008] All ER (D) 219 (Apr) 2.106

R (Edwards) v Environment Agency [2004] EWHC 736 (Admin), [2004] 3 All ER 21, [2004] Env LR 43, [2004] 2 P & CR 20, [2004] JPL 1691, [2004] ACD 82, [2004] NPC 56 .... 5.64

R (Eisai Ltd) v National Institute for Health and Clinical Excellence [2008] EWCA Civ 438, (2008) 11 CCL Rep 385, [2008] LS Law Medical 333, (2008) 101 BMLR 26, [2008] ACD 77, (2008) 105(19) LSG 27, (2008) 152(19) SJLB 31, (2008) *Times*, 7 May 1.123

R (Electoral Commission) v City of Westminster Magistrates' Court [2009] EWHC 78 (Admin), [2009] ACD 23 .... 1.55

R (Elphinstone) v Westminster CC and others [2008] EWCA Civ 1069, [2009] LGR 158, [2009] ELR 24, [2008] All ER (D) 101 (Oct) 1.150, 11.30

R (EO & Ors) v Secretary of State for the Home Department [2013] EWHC 1236 (Admin), [2013] ACD 116 .... 1.201, 14.54

R (ES) v London Borough of Barking and Dagenham [2013] EWHC 691 (Admin) 3.36, 6.52

R (Essex County Council) v Secretary of State for Education [2012] EWHC 1460 (Admin), [2012] ELR 383, [2012] ACD 93 .... 1.83

R (Evans) v Chief Constable of Sussex [2011] EWHC 2329 (Admin) 1.123

R (F (A Child)) v Secretary of State for the Home Department [2010] UKSC 17, [2010] 2 All ER 707, [2011] 1 AC 331, 113 BMLR 209, 174 CL&J 301, (2010) *Times*, 22 April, 154 Sol Jo (no 16) 27, [2010] All ER (D) 123 (Apr) 1.163, 1.184, 9.10

R (Faithfull) v Ipswich Crown Court [2007] EWHC 2763 (Admin), [2008] 3 All ER 749, [2008] 1 WLR 1636, [2007] All ER (D) 403 (Oct) 9.34, 9.37

R (Farrakhan) v Secretary of State for the Home Department [2002] EWCA Civ 606, [2002] QB 1391, [2002] 3 WLR 481, [2002] 4 All ER 289, [2002] UKHRR 734, 12 BHRC 497, [2002] Imm AR 447, [2002] INLR 257, [2002] ACD 76, (2002) 99(22) LSG 33, (2002) 152 NLJ 708, (2002) 146 SJLB 124, (2002) *Times*, 6 May, (2002) *Independent*, 8 May 1.189

R (Faulkner) v Secretary of State for Justice [2005] EWHC 2567 (Admin), [2006] INLR 502 .... 1.153, 1.173

R (Faulkner) v Secretary of State for Justice [2013] UKSC 23, [2013] 2 AC 254, [2013] 2 WLR 1157, [2013] 2 All ER 1013, [2013] HRLR 24, 35 BHRC 378, (2013) 157(18) SJLB 31, (2013) *Times*, June 4 .... 2.102

R (FDA) v Secretary of State for Work and Pensions [2012] EWCA Civ 332, [2013] 1 WLR 444, [2012] 3 All ER 301, [2012] Pens LR 215, (2012) *Times*, 20 June 1.106

R (FH) v SSHD [2007] EWHC 1571 (Admin) 14.48

R (FL, a child, by her litigation friend the Official Solicitor) v Lambeth London Borough Council [2010] EWHC 49 (Admin), [2010] 1 FCR 269, [2010] All ER (D) 117 (Jan) 6.55

R (Fleurose) v Securities and Futures Authority [2001] EWCA Civ 2015, [2002] IRLR 297, (2002) *Times*, 15 January, (2002) Telegraph, 17 January 1.181

R (Forest Care Home Ltd) v Pembrokeshire County Council [2010] EWHC 3514 (Admin), (2011) 14 CCL Rep 103, [2011] ACD 58 .... 6.144, 6.145

R (Foster) v Secretary of State for Justice [2013] EWHC 1951 (Admin) .. 10.68

R (Fox) v Secretary of State for Justice [2012] EWHC 2411 (Admin) 10.07

R (Friends of Basildon Golf Course) v Basildon District Council [2009] EWHC 66 (Admin), [2009] All ER (D) 92 (Mar) 3.38

Table of Cases   lxv

R (FZ) v Croydon London Borough Council [2011] EWCA Civ 59, [2011]
PTSR 748, [2011] 1 FLR 2081, [2011] HLR 22, [2011] BLGR 445,
(2011) 14 CCL Rep 289, [2011] Fam Law 355, (2011) 108(7) LSG
16   1.96, 1.97, 6.131
R (G and B) v Brighouse School Appeal Committee [1997] ELR 39   11.87
R (G) v Barnet London Borough Council [2003] UKHL 57, [2004] 2 AC
208, [2004] 1 All ER 97, [2003] 3 WLR 1194, [2003] LGR 569,
[2003] 3 FCR 419, [2004] 1 FLR 454, [2004] Fam Law 21, [2004]
HLR 117, [2003] 45 LS Gaz R 29, (2003) Times, 24 October, 147 Sol
Jo LB 1242, [2003] All ER (D) 385 (Oct)   6.52, 6.54
R (G) v Immigration Appeal Tribunal, R (M) v Immigration Appeal Tribunal
[2004] EWHC 588 (Admin), [2004] 3 All ER 286, [2004] 1 WLR
2953, (2004) Times, 13 May, [2004] All ER (D) 493 (Mar)   11.116, 15.52
R (G) v Independent Appeal Panel of Bexley London Borough Council
[2008] EWHC 3051 (Admin), [2009] ELR 100, [2008] All ER (D) 98
(Dec)   11.135
R (G) v Lambeth LBC [1994] ELR 207   11.72
R (G) v Southwark London Borough Council [2008] EWCA Civ 877   6.58
R (G) v Southwark London Borough Council [2009] UKHL 26, [2009] 3 All
ER 189, [2009] 1 WLR 1299, [2009] LGR 673, [2009] PTSR 1080,
[2009] 2 FCR 459, [2009] 2 FLR 380, [2009] Fam Law 668, [2009]
NLJR 791, (2009) Times, 4 June, 153 Sol Jo (no 20) 42, [2009] All
ER (D) 178 (May)   6.55
R (G) v Westminster City Council [2004] EWCA Civ 45, [2004] 1 WLR
1113, [2004] ELR 135, [2004] All ER (D) 312 (Jan), CA   11.55
R (Gallagher) v Basildon District Council [2010] EWHC 2824 (Admin),
[2011] PTSR 731, [2011] BLGR 227   1.105
R (Gallastegui) v Westminster City Council [2013] EWCA Civ 28, [2013] 1
WLR 2377, [2013] 2 All ER 579, [2013] HRLR 15, [2013] BLGR
337   1.56
R (Gardiner) v Haringey London BC [2009] EWHC 2699 (Admin), [2009]
All ER (D) 301 (Oct)   7.60
R (Gardner) v Harrogate BC (Mr and Mrs Atkinson) [2008] EWHC 2942
(Admin), [2009] JPL 872   5.121
R (Garland) v Secretary of State for Justice [2011] EWCA Civ 1335, [2012]
1 WLR 1879   10.78
R (Garner) v Elmbridge Borough Council [2011] EWCA Civ 891, [2012]
JPL 119, [2012] PTSR D7   1.104, 3.81, 5.132
R (Gates Hydraulics Ltd) v Secretary of State for Communities and Local
Government [2009] EWHC 2187 (Admin)   1.123
R (Gavin) v Haringey London Borough Council [2003] EWHC 2591
(Admin), [2004] 2 P & CR 209, [2003] All ER (D) 57 (Nov)   2.115
R (GC) v Metropolitan Police Commissioner [2011] UKSC 21, [2011] 1
WLR 1230, [2011] 3 All ER 859, [2011] 2 Cr App R 18, [2011]
HRLR 26, [2011] UKHRR 807, [2011] Crim LR 964, (2011) 108(22)
LSG 18, (2011) 155(20) SJLB 35, (2011) Times, 19 May   1.184
R (Georgiou) v Enfield London Borough Council, sub nom Georgiou v
Enfield London Borough Council (Cygnet Healthcare Ltd, interested
parties) [2004] EWHC 779 (Admin), [2004] LGR 497, [2004] 2
P & CR 380, [2004] 17 LS Gaz R 33, [2004] All ER (D) 135 (Apr)   1.118, 12.31, 12.33
R (Geraldo) v SSHD [2013] EWHC 2763 (Admin)   14.49
R (Gifford) v Governor HMP Bure & Secretary of State for Justice [2014]
EWHC 911 (Admin)   10.140
R (Giles) v Fareham Borough Council [2002] EWHC 2951 (Admin), [2003]
HLR 36, (2003) Times, 11 February   1.154
R (Gill) v Secretary of State for Justice [2010] EWHC 364 (Admin), [2010]
Eq LR 296, (2010) 13 CCL Rep 193, [2010] MHLR 135   10.21, 10.29

R (Gillan) v Commissioner of Police of the Metropolis [2006] UKHL 12,
[2006] 2 AC 307, [2006] 2 WLR 537, [2006] 4 All ER 1041, [2006]
2 Cr App R 36, [2006] HRLR 18, [2006] UKHRR 740, 21 BHRC
202, [2006] Po LR 26, [2006] Crim LR 752, (2006) 150 SJLB 366,
(2006) *Times*, 9 March 1.173
R (Godfrey) v Southwark London Borough Council [2012] EWCA Civ 500,
[2012] BLGR 683 1.137, 5.75
R (Goldsmith) v Wandsworth London Borough Council [2000] 3 CCLR 354,
[2004] EWCA Civ 1170, 148 Sol Jo LB 1065, [2004] All ER (D) 154
(Aug) 1.157, 2.14, 6.152
R (Gordon) v Parole Board [2000] Prison LR 275, [2001] ACD 47 10.58, 10.62
R (Gordon-Jones) v The Secretary of State for Justice [2014] EWHC 3997
(Admin) 12.61
R (Gorlov) v Institute of Chartered Accountants in England and Wales
[2001] EWHC Admin 220, [2001] ACD 73 15.43, 15.149, 15.217, 15.218
R (Governing Body of Drayton Manor High School) v Office of the Schools
Adjudicator [2008] EWHC 3119 (Admin), [2009] ELR 127, (2008)
Times, 24 December, [2008] All ER (D) 270 (Oct) 11.51
R (Governing Body of Queensmead School) v Hillingdon LBC [1997] ELR
331 11.120
R (Governors of John Ball Primary School) v Greenwich LBC (1990) 88
LGR 589 11.71, 11.72
R (GP) v Derby City Council & Derbyshire Mental Health NHS Foundation
Trust [2012] EWHC 1451 (Admin), [2012] MHLR 252 8.12
R (Great Yarmouth Port Co Limited) v Marine Management Organisation
[2013] EWHC 3052 (Admin), [2014] ACD 23 12.55
R (Green) v Gloucestershire County Council [2011] EWHC 2687 (Admin),
[2012] Eq LR 225, [2012] BLGR 330, (2011) 108(46) LSG 19,
[2012] PTSR D19 1.147
R (Green) v Secretary of State for the Home Department [2004] EWHC 596
(Admin), [2004] Prison LR 376 10.36
R (Greenfield) v Secretary of State for the Home Department [2005] UKHL
14, [2005] 1 WLR 673, [2005] UKHRR 323, [2005] 2 All ER 240,
HL 1.163, 1.178, 2.102
R (Greenpeace Ltd) v Secretary of State for the Environment, Food and
Rural Affairs [2005] EWCA Civ 1656, [2006] Env LR 27 1.103
R (Greenwich London Borough Council) v Secretary of State for Health
[2006] EWHC 2576 (Admin), [2006] All ER (D) 178 (Jul) 6.33
R (Gregson) v Parole Board [2009] EWHC 3639 (Admin) 10.59
R (Griffiths) v Lewisham College [2007] EWHC 809 (Admin), [2007] All ER
(D) 297 (Mar) 11.21
R (Griggs) v Financial Services Authority [2008] EWHC 2587 (Admin),
[2009] ACD 28 15.51, 15.57
R (Ground Rents (Regisport) Ltd) v Upper Tribunal (Administrative Appeals
Chamber) [2013] EWHC 2638, Admin 1.99
R (Guardian News and Media Ltd) v City of Westminster Magistrates' Court
[2011] EWCA Civ 1188, [2011] 1 WLR 3253, [2012] CP Rep 5,
[2012] EMLR 11, (2011) 108(43) LSG 21 9.14
R (Guardian News and Media Ltd) v City of Westminster Magistrates' Court
[2012] EWCA Civ 420, [2013] QB 618, [2012] 3 WLR 1343, [2012]
3 All ER 551, [2012] CP Rep 30, [2012] EMLR 22, (2012) 109(16)
LSG 22, (2012) 162 NLJ 619, (2012) *Times*, 12 July 1.55, 1.80, 1.199, 1.201
R (Guittard) v Secretary of State for Justice [2009] EWHC 2951 (Admin) 10.08
R (Gulliver) v Parole Board [2007] EWCA Civ 1386, [2008] 1 WLR 1116,
[2007] Prison LR 376, (2007) 151 SJLB 928, (2007) *Times*, 20
August 10.54
R (Gunn) v Secretary State for Justice and the Nottinghamshire Multi
Agency Public Protection Arrangements Board [2009] EWHC 1812
(Admin), [2009] Po LR 300, [2010] 2 Prison LR 281 10.53

R (Gwynn) v General Medical Council [2007] EWHC 3145 (Admin), [2008]
  LS Law Medical 112 . . . . 15.93, 15.133
R (H) v A [2013] EWHC 2506 (Admin) 11.88
R (H) v Ashworth Hospital Authority [2001] EWHC Admin 872, [2002] 1
  FCR 206, (2002) 64 BMLR 124, [2001] MHLR 241, [2002] ACD 19 . . 1.91, 2.20
R (H) v Brent London Borough Council [2002] EWHC 1105 (Admin),
  [2002] ELR 509, [2002] All ER (D) 348 (May) 11.120, 11.121
R (H) v Camden LBC and the Governors of Hampstead School [1996] ELR
  360 . . . . 11.139
R (H) v Deputy Prosecutor of the Italian Republic, Genoa [2012] UKSC 25,
  [2013] 1 AC 338, [2012] 3 WLR 90, [2012] 4 All ER 539, [2012]
  HRLR 25, (2012) 156(25) SJLB 31, (2012) Times, 2 July 1.211
R (H) v Hull City Council [2011] EWCA Civ 403, [2011] UKHRR 599,
  [2011] BLGR 590, (2011) 14 CCL Rep 381, [2011] ACD 76, (2011)
  108(17) LSG 13, (2011) 155(16) SJLB 31 . . . . 1.45
R (H) v Independent Appeal Panel for Y College [2004] EWHC 1193
  (Admin), [2005] ELR 25, [2004] All ER (D) 364 (May) 11.135, 11.141
R (H) v Kingston upon Thames Royal London Borough Council [2002] All
  ER (D) 477 (May), [2002] EWHC 3158 . . . . 7.105
R (H) v MHRT [2001] EWCA Civ 415 . . . . 8.15
R (H) v Parole Board [2011] EWHC 2081 (Admin) 10.60
R (H) v Secretary of State for the Home Department [2002] EWCA Civ 646,
  [2003] QB 320, [2002] 3 WLR 967, [2002] 25 LS Gaz R 35, (2002)
  Times, 24 May, 146 Sol Jo LB 146, [2002] All ER (D) 219 (May) 3.72
R (H) v Secretary of State for the Home Department [2003] UKHL 59,
  [2004] 2 AC 253, [2003] 3 WLR 1278, [2004] 1 All ER 412, [2004]
  HRLR 5, [2004] UKHRR 115, 15 BHRC 571, (2004) 7 CCL Rep
  147, (2004) 76 BMLR 179, [2004] MHLR 51, (2004) 101(2) LSG
  30, (2003) 147 SJLB 1365, (2003) Times, 14 November, (2003)
  Independent, 18 November 1.163, 6.116
R (H) v Wandsworth London Borough Council [2007] EWHC 1082
  (Admin), [2007] 2 FCR 378, [2007] 2 FLR 822, [2007] Fam Law
  802, [2007] All ER (D) 08 (Jun) 6.54, 6.82
R (HA (Nigeria)) v Secretary of State for the Home Department [2012]
  EWHC 979 (Admin), [2012] Med LR 353 . . . . 1.17, 1.169
R (Halite Energy Group Ltd) v Secretary of State for Climate Change and
  Energy [2014] EWHC 17 . . . . 5.127
R (Hall) v University College London Hospitals NHS Foundation Trust,
  Secretary of State for Justice [2013] EWHC 198 (Admin), [2013]
  ACD 55 . . . . 10.44, 10.47
R (Hamid) v Secretary of State for the Home Department [2012] EWHC
  3070 (Admin), [2013] CP Rep 6, [2013] ACD 27 . . . . 7.92, 7.95
R (Hammia) v Wandsworth London Borough Council [2005] EWHC 1127
  (Admin), [2005] HLR 735, [2005] All ER (D) 244 (May) 7.51
R (Hampshire County Council) v Independent Appeal Panel for Hampshire
  [2006] EWHC 2460 (Admin), [2007] ELR 266 . . . . 11.91
R (Haney) v Secretary of State for Justice [2013] EWHC 803 (Admin),
  [2013] ACD 78 . . . . 10.25
R (Hasan) v Secretary of State for Trade and Industry [2008] EWCA Civ
  1312, [2009] 3 All ER 539, (2008) 152(46) SJLB 29 . . . . 1.153
R (Haworth) v Northumbria Police Authority [2012] EWHC 1225 (Admin) 1.108, 1.112
R (Heather) v Leonard Cheshire Foundation and Another [2002] EWCA Civ
  366, [2002] 2 All ER 936, [2002] UKHRR 883, [2002] HRLR 30,
  CA 3.64
R (Hereford Waste Watchers Ltd) v Hereford Council [2005] EWHC 191
  (Admin), [2005] Env LR 29, [2005] JPL 1469, [2005] 9 EG 188 (CS) . . . 1.156
R (Hewitson) v Guildford Borough Council [2011] EWHC 3440 (Admin),
  [2012] BLGR 637, [2012] JPL 951 . . . . 1.157, 5.122
R (Hewlett) v Secretary of State for Justice [2009] EWHC 2979 (Admin) . . . 10.36

R (HH) v Westminster City Magistrates' Court [2012] UKSC 25, [2013] 1
  AC 338, [2012] 3 WLR 90, [2012] 4 All ER 539, [2012] HRLR 25,
  (2012) 156(25) SJLB 31, (2012) Times, 2 July   1.184, 1.186
R (Hicks) v Court At Snaresbrook & Anor [2012] EWCA Crim 2515   3.53
R (Hicks) v Metropolitan Police Commissioner [2012] EWHC 1947
  (Admin), [2012] ACD 102   1.64, 1.65, 1.113
R (Hilali) v Governor of Whitemoor Prison [2008] UKHL 3, [2008] 1 AC
  805, [2008] 2 WLR 299, [2008] 2 All ER 207, [2008] 2 CMLR 8,
  [2008] Extradition LR 61, (2008) 152(6) SJLB 30, (2008) Times,
  February 1   1.201
R (Hill) v Institute of Chartered Accountants in England and Wales [2012]
  EWHC 1731 (QB)   15.43
R (Hill) v Institute of Chartered Accountants in England and Wales [2013]
  EWCA Civ 555, [2014] 1 WLR 86, (2013) Times, 10 July   1.124, 15.173
R (Hill) v Parole Board [2012] EWHC 809 (Admin)   10.58
R (Hillingdon London Borough Council) v Lord Chancellor [2008] EWHC
  2683 (Admin), [2009] CP Rep 13, [2009] 1 FLR 39, [2009] 1 FCR 1,
  [2009] BLGR 554, [2009] Fam Law 13, (2008) 158 NLJ 1602,
  [2009] PTSR (CS) 20   1.123
R (Hillingdon London Borough Council) v Secretary of State for Transport
  (Transport for London, interested party) [2010] EWHC 626 (Admin),
  [2010] 15 LS Gaz R 17, [2010] All ER (D) 253 (Mar)   13.27
R (Hindawi) v Secretary of State for Justice [2011] EWHC 830 (QB), [2011]
  ACD 80   1.118
R (Hirst) v Secretary of State for the Home Department [2001] EWCA Civ
  378, [2001] Prison LR 147, (2001) 98(18) LSG 45, (2001) 145 SJLB
  107, (2001) Times, 22 March, (2001) Independent, 30 April   1.123
R (Hirst) v Secretary of State for the Home Department and Another [2002]
  EWHC 602 (Admin), [2002] 1 WLR 2929, [2002] UKHRR 758,
  [2002] Prison LR 260, [2002] ACD 93, (2002) 99(19) LSG 32,
  (2002) 146 SJLB 100, (2002) Times, 10 April   1.189
R (Hoffmann) v Commissioner of Inquiry [2012] UKPC 17   15.38
R (Holmes) v General Medical Council [2001] EWHC Admin 321, [2001]
  Lloyd's Rep Med 366, (2002) 63 BMLR 131   15.97
R (Holmes) v General Medical Council [2002] EWCA Civ 1838   15.112
R (Holub) v Secretary of State for the Home Department [2001] 1 WLR
  1359, [2001] ELR 401, [2001] Imm AR 282, [2000] All ER (D) 239   11.160
R (Hooper) v Secretary of State for Work and Pensions [2002] EWHC 191
  (Admin), [2002] UKHRR 785, QBD, [2003] EWCA Civ 813, [2003]
  1 WLR 2623, [2003] UKHRR 1268, [2003] 3 All ER 673, CA,
  [2005] UKHL 29, [2005] 1 WLR 1681, [2005] 2 FCR 183, [2006] 1
  All ER 487, HL   2.103
R (Hope and Glory Public House Ltd) v City of Westminster Magistrates'
  Court & Others [2009] EWHC 1996 (Admin)   12.47
R (Hope and Glory Public House Ltd) v City of Westminster Magistrates'
  Court & Others [2011] EWCA Civ 31 (CA), [2011] All ER (D) 206
  (Jan)   12.20, 12.47
R (Hounslow London Borough Council) v Schools Admissions Appeal Panel
  for Hounslow [2002] 1 WLR 3147, [2002] EWCA Civ 900, [2002]
  LGR 501, [2002] 3 FCR 142, [2002] ELR 602, (2002) Times, 3
  October, [2002] All ER (D) 189 (Jun)   11.85, 11.91
R (Howard League for Penal Reform) v Secretary of State for the Home
  Department [2002] EWHC 2497 (Admin), [2003] 1 FLR 484, (2003)
  6 CCL Rep 47, [2003] Prison LR 128, [2003] Fam Law 149, (2003)
  100(3) LSG 30, (2003) 147 SJLB 61, (2002) Times, 5 December   1.183
R (HR) v Medway Council [2010] ELR 513   11.119
R (HS) v Upper Tribunal [2012] EWHC 3126 (Admin), [2013] Imm AR 579   14.57
R (HSMP Forum Ltd) v Secretary of State for the Home Department [2008]
  EWHC 664 (Admin), [2008] INLR 262, (2008) Times, 29 May   1.137

R (HSMP Forum Ltd) v Secretary of State for the Home Department (No 2)
 [2008] EWHC 711 ... 1.140
R (Huitson) v Revenue and Customs Commissioners [2011] EWCA Civ 893,
 [2012] QB 489, [2012] 2 WLR 490, [2011] STC 1860, [2011] BTC
 456, 14 ITL Rep 90, [2011] STI 2307, [2011] NPC 91 ... 1.197
R (Hurst) v London Northern District Coroner [2007] UKHL 13, [2007] 2
 AC 189, [2007] 2 WLR 726, [2007] 2 All ER 1025, [2007] HRLR
 23, [2007] UKHRR 797, [2007] Inquest LR 29, (2007) 157 NLJ 519,
 (2007) 151 SJLB 466, (2007) *Times*, 29 March ... 1.102, 10.125
R (Husain) v Asylum Support Adjudicator [2001] EWHC Admin 852,
 [2002] ACD 10, (2001) *Times*, 15 November ... 1.181
R (I) v IAP for G Technology College [2005] EWHC 558 (Admin), [2005]
 ELR 490, [2005] All ER (D) 240 (Mar) ... 11.95, 11.137
R (I) v IAP for G Technology College [2005] EWHC 558 (Admin), [2005]
 ELR 490 ... 1.157
R (I) v Secretary of State for the Home Department [2005] EWHC 1025
 (Admin), (2005) *Times*, 10 June ... 1.153
R (Iceland Foods Ltd) v Newport City Council [2010] EWHC 2502 (Admin) ... 5.43
R (Iftikhar Ahmed) v SSHD [2014] EWHC 300 ... 14.50
R (Independent Police Complaints Commission) v Assistant Commissioner
 Hayman [2008] EWHC 2191 (Admin), [2008] Po LR 263 ... 15.156
R (Independent Police Complaints Commission) v Commissioner of Police of
 the Metropolis [2009] EWHC 1566 (Admin), [2009] Po LR 281 ... 15.134, 15.135, 15.136
R (Infinis Plc) v Gas and Electricity Markets Authority [2011] EWHC 1873 ... 1.196
R (Interbrew SA) v Competition Commission [2001] EWHC Admin 367,
 [2001] UKCLR 954, [2001] ECC 40, (2001) Telegraph, 29 May ... 1.17
R (International Transport Roth GmbH) v Secretary of State for the Home
 Department [2002] EWCA Civ 158, [2003] QB 728, [2002] 3 WLR
 344, [2002] 1 CMLR 52, [2002] Eu LR 74, [2002] HRLR 31, [2002]
 UKHRR 479, [2002] ACD 57, (2002) *Times*, 26 February, (2002)
 Telegraph, 7 March ... 1.207, 9.16
R (Ireneschild) v Lambeth London Borough Council [2007] EWCA Civ 234,
 [2007] HLR 34, [2007] BLGR 619, (2007) 10 CCL Rep 243, [2007]
 NPC 31 ... 1.103, 6.19, 6.20, 6.152
R (Island Farm Development Ltd) v Bridgend County Borough Council
 [2006] EWHC 2189 (Admin), [2007] LGR 60, [2006] All ER (D) 118
 (Aug) ... 5.116, 12.34, 12.35
R (Ivlev) v Entry Clearance Officer, New York [2013] EWHC 1162 (Admin) ... 2.49
R (J) v Caerphilly County Borough Council [2005] EWHC 586 (Admin),
 [2005] 2 FCR 153, [2005] 2 FLR 860, [2005] Fam Law 528, [2005]
 Fam Law 611, (2005) *Times*, 21 April, [2005] All ER (D) 94 (Apr) ... 6.84
R (J) v Newham LBC [2001] EWHC Admin 992, [2001] All ER (D) 291
 (Oct) ... 6.69
R (Jackowski) v Poland [2012] EWHC 3935 (Admin) ... 1.65
R (Jackson) v Attorney General [2005] UKHL 56, [2006] 1 AC 262, [2005]
 3 WLR 733, [2005] 4 All ER 1253, (2005) 155 NLJ 1600, [2005]
 NPC 116, (2005) *Times*, 14 October, (2005) *Independent*, 20 October ... 1.01
R (Jackson) v General Medical Council [2013] EWHC 2595 (Admin) ... 1.158
R (Jackson) v Stratford-on-Avon DC and others [1985] 3 All ER 769, [1985]
 1 WLR 1319, 84 LGR 287, 51 P & CR 76, 129 Sol Jo 854, [1985]
 LS Gaz R 3533 ... 11.153
R (Jacobs) v Essex CC [1997] ELR 190 ... 11.88
R (James) v Secretary of State for Justice [2009] UKHL 22, [2010] 1 AC
 553, [2009] 2 WLR 1149, [2009] 4 All ER 255, [2009] HRLR 23,
 [2009] UKHRR 809, 26 BHRC 696, [2009] Prison LR 371, (2009)
 Times, 8 May ... 10.25
R (Javed) v Secretary of State for the Home Dept [2001] EWCA Civ 789,
 [2002] QB 129, [2001] 3 WLR 323, [2001] Imm AR 529, [2001] 26
 LS Gaz R 44, 145 Sol Jo LB 149, [2001] All ER (D) 215 (May) ... 2.76

R (JC) v Richmond LBC [2001] LGR 146, [2001] ELR 21, [2000] All ER
 (D) 1127 11.92, 11.151, 11.161
R (JD Wetherspoon PLC) v Guildford Borough Council [2006] EWHC 815
 (Admin), [2007] 1 All ER 400, [2006] LGR 767, [2006] 16 EG 147
 (CS), (2006) Times, 14 April, [2006] All ER (D) 147 (Apr) 12.54, 12.61, 12.64
R (Jenkinson) v Nursing and Midwifery Council [2009] EWHC 1111
 (Admin) 15.131
R (JK) v Haringey LBC [2009] ELR 421 11.120
R (JL a child, by his mother and litigation friend LL(1), LL(2)) v Islington
 London Borough Council and Others [2009] EWHC 458 (Admin),
 [2009] 2 FLR 515, [2009] Fam Law 485, [2009] All ER (D) 140
 (Mar) 6.26, 6.152
R (JL) v Secretary of State for the Home Department [2007] EWCA Civ
 767, [2008] 1 WLR 158, (2007) Times, 2 October, [2007] All ER (D)
 362 (Jul) 6.54, 6.56
R (JL) v Secretary of State for the Home Department [2008] UKHL 68,
 [2009] 1 AC 588, [2008] 3 WLR 1325, [2009] 2 All ER 521, [2009]
 HRLR 9, [2009] UKHRR 415, 27 BHRC 24, [2008] Inquest LR 88,
 (2008) 158 NLJ 1719, (2008) 152(46) SJLB 31, (2008) Times, 2
 December 10.123, 10.135, 10.137
R (JM) v London Borough of Hammersmith & Fulham, and R
 (Hertfordshire CC) v London Borough of Hammersmith & Fulham
 [2010] EWHC 562 (Admin), [2010] LGR 678, 116 BMLR 46, [2010]
 All ER (D) 218 (Mar) 6.119
R (Johns) v Derby City Council [2011] EWHC 375 (Admin), [2011] 1 FLR
 2094, [2011] 1 FCR 493, [2011] HRLR 20, [2011] Eq LR 361,
 [2011] Fam Law 471, (2011) 161 NLJ 364, (2011) 155(9) SJLB 31 1.55, 1.201
R (Jones and others) v Ceredigion County Council [2004] EWHC 1376
 (Admin), [2004] LGR 881, [2004] ELR 506, (2004) Times, 8 July,
 [2004] All ER (D) 175 (Jun) 11.55
R (Jones) v Mansfield District Council [2003] EWCA Civ 1408, [2004] Env
 LR 21, [2004] 2 P & CR 14, (2003) 147 SJLB 1209, [2003] NPC
 119, (2003) Times, 31 October 5.61
R (Jorgenson) v Secretary of State for Justice [2011] EWHC 977 (Admin),
 [2011] ACD 81 10.02
R (JW through his litigation friend, DW) v Learning Trust [2009] UKUT
 1997 (AAC), [2010] ELR 115 11.117
R (K & AC Jackson and Son) v Department for the Environment Food and
 Rural Affairs [2011] EWHC 956 (Admin) 1.94
R (K and S) v Admissions Appeal Panel of Cardiff County Council [2003]
 EWHC 436 (Admin), [2003] ELR 495, [2003] All ER (D) 182 (Mar) 11.95
R (K) v Beatrix Potter School [1997] ELR 468 11.88
R (K) v Bow Street Magistrates' Court (2005) Times, 27 July 9.18
R (K) v Camden and Islington Health Authority [2001] EWCA Civ 240,
 [2002] QB 198, [2001] 3 WLR 553, [2001] UKHRR 1378, (2001) 4
 CCL Rep 170, [2001] Lloyd's Rep Med 152, (2001) 61 BMLR 173,
 [2001] MHLR 24, (2001) 98(16) LSG 34, (2001) 145 SJLB 69,
 (2001) Times, 15 March, (2001) Independent, 28 February 6.118, 8.67, 8.70, 16.43
R (K) v Governors of the W School and West Sussex CC [2001] ELR 311 11.126, 11.132
R (K) v Mental Health Review Tribunal [2002] EWHC 639 (Admin), [2002]
 All ER (D) 182 (Apr) 8.62
R (K) v University of Nottingham [1998] ELR 184 11.152
R (Kaiyam) v Secretary of State for Justice [2014] UKSC 66 10.25
R (Kanssen) v Secretary of State for the Environment, Food and Rural
 Affairs [2005] EWHC 1024 (Admin), [2005] NPC 76 1.116
R (Kashyap) v General Medical Council [2009] EWHC 2873 (Admin) 15.38
R (Kaur) v Institute of Legal Executives Appeal Tribunal [2011] EWCA Civ
 1168, [2012] 1 All ER 1435, [2012] 1 Costs LO 23, [2011] ELR 614,
 (2011) 108(45) LSG 20, (2011) 155(40) SJLB 31, [2011] NPC 106,
 [2012] PTSR D1 1.133, 15.171

R (KB) v Secretary of State for Justice [2010] EWHC 15 (Admin)	10.76
R (Kelly and Mehari) v Birmingham City Council [2009] EWHC 3240 (Admin)	7.47
R (Kelly) v Liverpool City Council [2009] EWCA Civ 191	12.04
R (Kelly) v Liverpool City Council (unreported), 5 September 2008	12.04
R (Kelly) v Warley Magistrates' Court [2007] EWHC 1836 (Admin), [2008] 1 WLR 2001, [2008] 1 Cr App R 14, (2007) 171 JP 585, [2008] Lloyd's Rep FC 37, [2008] Crim LR 643, [2007] ACD 89, (2008) 172 JPN 83, (2007) 157 NLJ 1155	1.55, 1.201
R (Kelway) v Newcastle upon Tyne Combined Court [2013] EWHC 2574 (Admin)	1.65
R (Kemp) v Denbighshire Local Health Board [2006] EWHC 181 (Admin), [2006] 3 All ER 141, [2007] 1 WLR 639, [2006] All ER (D) 230 (Feb)	3.03
R (Kensington & Chelsea Royal London Borough Council) v Secretary of State for Communities and Local Government [2012] EWHC 1785 (Admin), [2012] 28 EG 81 (CS), (2012) 162 NLJ 963	1.94
R (Khan) v Secretary of State for the Home Department [2011] EWHC 2763 (Admin)	3.23
R (Khana) v Southwark LBC [2001] EWCA Civ 999	6.152
R (Khatun) v London Borough of Newham [2004] EWCA Civ 55, [2005] QB 37, [2004] 3 WLR 417, [2004] Eu LR 628, [2004] HLR 29, [2004] BLGR 696, [2004] L & TR 18, (2004) 148 SJLB 268, [2004] NPC 28, (2004) *Times*, 27 February, (2004) *Independent*, 4 March	1.17, 1.18, 1.103, 1.116, 1.123
R (Kides) v South Cambridgeshire DC [2002] EWCA Civ 1370, [2003] 1 P & CR 19, [2002] 4 PLR 66, [2003] JPL 431, [2002] 42 EG 160 (CS), (2002) 99(43) LSG 35, (2002) 146 SJLB 230, [2002] NPC 121, (2002) *Times*, 15 October, (2002) *Independent*, 16 October	5.65
R (King) v Secretary of State for Justice [2012] EWCA Civ 376, [2012] 1 WLR 3602, [2012] 4 All ER 44, [2012] HRLR 17, (2012) *Times*, 27 June	10.18, 10.32
R (Kingwell) v Royal Borough of Kingston-upon-Thames [1992] 1 FLR 182, [1992] Fam Law 193	11.73
R (KM) v Cambridgeshire County Council [2012] UKSC 23, [2012] 3 All ER 1218, [2012] PTSR 1189, [2012] BLGR 913, (2012) 15 CCL Rep 374, (2012) 126 BMLR 186, (2012) 162 NLJ 780	1.157, 6.37
R (KSS) v Northampton Crown Court [2010] EWHC 723 (Admin), [2010] 2 Cr App Rep 175, [2010] All ER (D) 65 (May)	9.38
R (Kumar) v SSHD (Acknowledgment of Service, Tribunal Arrangements) IJR [2014] UKUT 00104 (IAC)	14.33
R (L) v Barking and Dagenham LBC [2001] EWCA Civ 533	6.19, 6.20
R (L) v Commissioner of Police of the Metropolis [2009] UKSC 9, [2010] 1 AC 464, [2009] 3 WLR 1270, [2010] HRLR 10, [2010] UKHRR 86, (2009) 159 NLJ 1737, (2009) *Times*, 2 December	1.184
R (L) v Governors of the Buss Foundation Camden School for Girls [1991] COD 98	11.96
R (L) v Independent Appeal Panel of St Edward's College [2001] EWHC 108 (Admin), [2001] ELR 542	11.94, 11.95, 11.96
R (L) v Leeds City Council [2010] EWHC 3324 (Admin)	6.58
R (L) v Nottinghamshire CC [2007] EWHC 2364 (Admin), [2007] All ER (D) 158 (Sep)	6.54
R (L) v Prosthetists and Orthotists Board [2001] EWCA Civ 837, (2001) 61 BMLR 128, [2001] ACD 72, (2001) Telegraph, 19 June	15.99
R (L) v Secretary of State for the Home Department [2003] EWCA Civ 25, [2003] 1 WLR 1230, [2003] 1 All ER 1062, [2003] Imm AR 330, [2003] INLR 224, (2003) 100(11) LSG 33, (2003) *Times*, 30 January, (2003) *Independent*, 28 January	1.87, 1.123
R (L) v Waltham Forest London Borough Council [2007] EWHC 2060 (Admin), [2008] LGR 495, [2007] All ER (D) 393 (Jun)	11.120
R (Lakareber) v University of Portsmouth [1999] ELR 135	11.152, 11.153

R (Lambeth LBC) v IAP for Lambeth [2012] EWHC 943 (Admin), [2013]
    ELR 145 .... 11.86
R (Laporte) v Newham London Borough Council [2004] EWHC 227
    (Admin), [2004] All ER (D) 309 (Jan) 7.84
R (Latham) v Northampton Magistrates' Court [2008] EWHC 245 (Admin),
    [2008] All ER (D) 66 (Feb) 9.22
R (Law Society) v Legal Services Commission [2010] EWHC 2550 (Admin),
    [2011] Costs LR Online 57, [2011] ACD 16, (2010) 107(40) LSG 22,
    (2011) Times, 1 February 1.115, 3.15
R (Law Society) v Master of the Rolls [2005] EWHC 146 (Admin), [2005] 1
    WLR 2033, [2005] 2 All ER 640, (2005) 155 NLJ 246, (2005) Times,
    21 February 15.76
R (Lawer) v Restormel Borough Council [2007] EWHC 2299 (Admin),
    [2008] HLR 327 .... 3.41, 7.95, 7.96, 7.97
R (LE (Jamaica)) v Secretary of State for the Home Department [2012]
    EWCA Civ 597 .... 1.69, 1.120, 1.157
R (Leach) v Parole Board [2011] EWHC 2470 (Admin) 10.58, 10.62
R (Lepage) v HM Assistant Deputy Coroner for Inner South London [2012]
    EWHC 1485 (Admin) 10.125
R (Leung) v Imperial College of Science, Technology and Medicine [2002]
    EWHC 1358 (Admin), [2002] ELR 653, [2002] ACD 100 .... 1.156
R (Lewis) v Persimmon Homes Teesside Ltd, sub nom R (Lewis) v Redcar &
    Cleveland Borough Council [2008] EWCA Civ 746, [2009] 1 WLR
    83, [2008] LGR 781, [2008] 2 P & CR 436, [2008] All ER (D) 11
    (Jul) 12.34, 12.35
R (Lewis) v Redcar and Cleveland Borough Council (No 2) [2010] UKSC
    11, [2010] 2 AC 70, [2010] 2 WLR 653, [2010] 2 All ER 613, [2010]
    BLGR 295, [2010] 2 P & CR 16, [2010] 1 EGLR 153, [2010] JPL
    1135, [2010] 10 EG 116 (CS), (2010) 160 NLJ 390, (2010) 154(9)
    SJLB 30, [2010] NPC 27, (2010) Times, 4 March 1.79
R (Lewisham LBC) v Secretary of State for Health [2013] EWCA Civ 1409,
    [2014] 1 WLR 514, [2014] PTSR 273, (2014) 135 BMLR 78 .... 16.12
R (Lewisham LBC) v Secretary of State for Health [2013] EWHC 2381
    (Admin), [2013] PTSR 1298, [2013] BLGR 665, [2014] ACD 11 ... 1.81, 16.10, 16.11
R (LG) v Independent Appeal Panel for Tom Hood School (Secretary of State
    for Children, Schools and Families, interested party) [2010] EWCA
    Civ 142, [2010] PTSR 1462, [2010] ELR 291, [2010] All ER (D) 292
    (Feb) 11.134
R (LH and MH) v Lambeth [2006] EWHC 1190 (Admin), [2006] 2 FCR
    348, [2006] 2 FLR 1275, [2006] Fam Law 931, [2006] All ER (D) 83
    (Jun) 6.69
R (Li) v General Medical Council [2013] EWHC 522 (Admin) 15.192
R (Lichfield Securities Ltd) v Lichfield District Council [2001] EWCA Civ
    304, (2001) 3 LGLR 35, [2001] 3 PLR 33, [2001] PLCR 32, [2001]
    JPL 1434 (Note), [2001] 11 EG 171 (CS), (2001) 98(17) LSG 37,
    (2001) 145 SJLB 78, (2001) Times, 30 March 1.137
R (Lichniak) v Secretary of State for the Home Department, R v Lichniak, R
    (Pyrah) v Secretary of State for the Home Department, R v Pyrah
    [2001] EWHC Admin 294, [2002] QB 296, [2001] 4 All ER 934,
    [2001] 3 WLR 933, 145 Sol Jo LB 127, [2001] All ER (D) 22 (May) 9.31
R (Limbuela) v Secretary of State for the Home Department [2005] UKHL
    66, [2006] 1 AC 396, [2005] 3 WLR 1014, [2007] 1 All ER 951,
    [2006] HRLR 4, [2006] HLR 10, (2006) 9 CCL Rep 30, (2005)
    102(46) LSG 25, (2005) 149 SJLB 1354, (2005) Times, 4 November 1.169, 1.201
R (Liverpool City Council) v Hillingdon London Borough Council [2009]
    EWCA Civ 43, [2009] LGR 289, [2009] PTSR 1067, [2009] 3 FCR
    46, [2009] 1 FLR 1536, [2009] Fam Law 394, (2009) Times, 13
    February, [2009] All ER (D) 81 (Feb) 6.131
R (London Borough of Lewisham) v Secretary of State for Health [2013]
    EWHC 2329 (Admin) 2.54

R (London Christian Radio Ltd) v Radio Advertising Clearance Centre
[2012] EWHC 1043 (Admin), [2012] HRLR 19, [2013] CTLC 41,
[2012] ACD 82 .... 1.189
R (London Fire and Emergency Planning Authority) v Secretary of State for
Communities and Local Government [2007] EWHC 1176 (Admin),
[2007] BLGR 591 .... 1.155
R (London Reading College Ltd) v Secretary of State for the Home
Department [2010] EWHC 2561 (Admin), [2010] ELR 809, [2011]
ACD 31 .... 1.123, 1.196
R (Lord Carlile of Berriew) v Secretary of State for the Home Department
[2013] EWCA Civ 199 .... 1.56, 1.189
R (Lord) v Secretary of State for the Home Department [2003] EWHC 2073
(Admin), [2004] Prison LR 65 .... 10.09
R (Louden) v Bury School Organisation Committee [2002] EWHC 2749
(Admin), [2002] All ER (D) 313 (Dec) 11.30
R (Low) v Independent Adjudicator [2009] EWHC 2253 (Admin), [2010] 2
Prison LR 329 .... 10.88
R (Low) v Secretary of State for the Home Department [2010] EWCA Civ 4,
[2010] 2 CMLR 34, [2010] Eu LR 415, [2010] ICR 755 .... 1.207
R (Lowe) v Governor HMP Liverpool [2008] EWHC 2167 (Admin), [2009]
Prison LR 197, (2008) 105(37) LSG 20 .... 10.09
R (Lowther) v Durham County Council & Others [2001] EWCA Civ 781,
[2002] 1 P & CR 283, [2001] 3 PLR 83, [2001] 22 EGCS 154,
[2001] All ER (D) 318 (May) 12.89
R (LT) v Rotherham MBC [2000] LGR 338, [2000] ELR 76 .... 11.73
R (Lumba) v Secretary of State for the Home Department [2011] UKSC 2,
[2011] 1 WLR 268, [2011] 1 All ER 744, [2011] PTSR 337, [2011]
Env LR 19, [2011] BLGR 271, [2011] JPL 865, [2011] 4 EG 101
(CS), (2011) 108(5) LSG 20, (2011) Times, 26 January 1.108
R (Lumba) v Secretary of State for the Home Department [2011] UKSC 12,
[2012] 1 AC 245, [2011] 2 WLR 671, [2011] 4 All ER 1, [2011]
UKHRR 437, (2011) 108(14) LSG 20, (2011) 155(12) SJLB 30,
(2011) Times, 24 March 1.55, 1.90, 1.102, 1.120, 1.123, 1.173, 1.201, 14.53, 14.54
R (Lunn) v Revenue & Customs Commissioners [2011] EWHC 240
(Admin), [2011] STC 1028, [2011] BTC 104, [2011] STI 526 .... 1.123, 1.153, 1.154
R (Lunt & Others) v Liverpool City Council [2009] EWHC 2356 (Admin),
[2010] 1 CMLR 431, [2010] RTR 38, [2009] All ER (D) 07 (Aug) 12.21, 12.26, 12.103
R (Luton Borough Council) v Secretary of State for Education [2011] EWHC
217 (Admin), [2011] Eq LR 481, [2011] BLGR 553, [2011] ELR 222,
[2011] ACD 43 .... 1.143, 1.147
R (Lynch) v Lambeth London Borough Council [2006] EWHC 2737
(Admin), [2007] HLR 225, [2006] All ER (D) 177 (Oct) 7.37, 7.38
R (M) v Barking and Dagenham Borough Council [2002] EWHC 2483
(Admin), [2003] ELR 144, [2002] All ER (D) 64 (Aug) 11.152
R (M) v Board of Governors of Stoke Newington School [1994] ELR 131 ..... 11.138
R (M) v Criminal Injuries Compensation Authority [2002] EWHC 2646
(Admin), (2003) 100(2) LSG 31, (2002) Times, 25 November 1.17
R (M) v Gateshead MBC [2006] EWCA Civ 221, [2006] QB 650, [2007] 1
All ER 1262, [2006] 3 WLR 108, [2006] 2 FLR 379, [2006] Fam
Law 444, (2006) Times, 27 April, 150 Sol Jo LB 397, [2006] All ER
(D) 198 (Mar) 6.56
R (M) v Governors of St Gregory's RC Aided High School [1995] ELR 290 ..... 11.126
R (M) v Hammersmith and Fulham London Borough Council [2008] UKHL
14, [2008] 4 All ER 271, [2008] 1 WLR 535, [2008] LGR 159,
[2008] 3 FCR 688, [2008] 1 FLR 1384, [2008] Fam Law 383, [2008]
Fam Law 515, [2008] NLJR 370, (2008) Times, 3 March, 152 Sol Jo
(no 9) 28, [2008] All ER (D) 390 (Feb) 6.54, 6.61
R (M) v Haringey Independent Appeal Panel [2010] EWCA Civ 1103,
[2010] ELR 823, [2011] PTSR D10, (2010) Times, 5 November 1.156, 11.82

R (M) v Isleworth Crown Court [2005] EWHC 363 (Admin), [2005] All ER
   (D) 42 (Mar)   9.38
R (M) v Lambeth London Borough Council, R (A) v Croydon London
   Borough Council [2009] UKSC 8, [2010] 1 All ER 469, [2009] 1
   WLR 2557, [2010] LGR 183, [2010] PTSR 106, [2009] 3 FCR 607,
   [2010] 1 FLR 959, [2010] Fam Law 137, [2009] NLJR 1701, (2009)
   Times, 30 November, 153 Sol Jo (no 46) 34, [2009] All ER (D) 288
   (Nov)   6.131
R (M) v Lancashire County Council [1995] ELR 136   11.94, 11.95
R (M) v London Borough of Barnet [2008] EWHC 2354 (Admin), [2009] 2
   FLR 725, [2008] Fam Law 1197   6.58, 6.65
R (M) v Secretary of State for Home Department [2001] EWHC Admin 245   11.152
R (M) v Slough Borough Council [2008] UKHL 52, [2008] 4 All ER 831,
   [2008] 1 WLR 1808, [2008] LGR 871, [2008] HLR 763, (2008)
   Times, 5 September, 152 Sol Jo (no 32) 30, [2008] All ER (D) 412
   (Jul)   6.125, 6.127
R (MA) v Independent Adjudicator [2013] EWHC 438 (Admin)   10.79, 10.91
R (MA) v National Probation Service [2011] EWHC 1332 (Admin), [2011]
   ACD 86   10.53
R (Mackay) v Secretary of State for Justice [2011] EWCA Civ 522   10.07
R (Mackenzie) v Secretary of State for Justice [2009] EWCA Civ 669, [2010]
   1 Prison LR 109   1.116
R (Macrae) v Herefordshire District Council [2012] EWCA Civ 457, [2012]
   JPL 1356   1.152, 1.156
R (Madan) v General Medical Council (No 1) [2001] EWHC Admin 322   15.105
R (Madan) v Secretary of State for the Home Department [2007] EWCA Civ
   770, [2008] 1 All ER 973, [2007] 1 WLR 2891, (2007) Times, 27
   August, [2007] All ER (D) 387 (Jul)   3.35
R (Madden) v Bury Metropolitan Borough Council [2002] EWHC 1882
   (Admin), (2002) 5 CCL Rep 622   1.146
R (Maftah) v Secretary of State for Foreign and Commonwealth Affairs
   [2011] EWCA Civ 350, [2012] QB 477, [2012] 2 WLR 251, (2011)
   108(17) LSG 14, (2011) Times, 21 April   1.179
R (Mahfouz) v General Medical Council [2004] EWCA Civ 233, [2004]
   Lloyd's Rep Med 377, (2004) 80 BMLR 113, (2004) 101(13) LSG 35,
   (2004) Times, 19 March   1.125, 15.34, 15.36
R (Malik) v Manchester Crown Court [2008] EWHC 1362 (Admin), [2008]
   4 All ER 403, [2008] EMLR 19, [2008] UKHRR 1151   1.93, 1.189
R (Malik) v Waltham Forest NHS [2007] EWCA Civ 265, [2007] 1 WLR
   2092, [2007] 4 All ER 832, [2007] ICR 1101, [2007] IRLR 529,
   [2007] HRLR 24, [2007] UKHRR 1105, [2007] LS Law Medical 335,
   (2007) Times, 10 April   1.195
R (Maloney) v Governor of HMP Rochester [2000] Prison LR 23   10.93
R (Manchester City Council) v Secretary of State for Environment, Food &
   Rural Affairs [2007] EWHC 3167 (Admin)   1.104, 3.81, 5.132
R (Manhire) v Secretary of State for Justice [2009] EWHC 1788 (Admin),
   [2010] 2 Prison LR 275   10.09
R (Manydown Co Ltd) v Basingstoke and Deane Borough Council [2012]
   EWHC 977 (Admin), [2012] JPL 1188, [2012] 17 EG 111 (CS)   1.112, 5.23
R (Mavalon Care Ltd) v Pembrokeshire County Council [2011] EWHC 3371
   (Admin), (2012) 15 CCL Rep 229, [2012] ACD 45   1.156, 6.144
R (Maxwell) v Office of the Independent Adjudicator & University of
   Salford [2010] EWHC 1889 (Admin), [2010] ELR 637, [2010] All ER
   (D) 248 (Jul)   11.25
R (May) v Birmingham City Council [2012] EWHC 1399, Admin   1.29
R (Mayor and Citizens of Westminster City Council) v Metropolitan
   Stipendary Magistrate [2008] EWHC 1202 (Admin), 172 JP 462, 172
   JPN 660, [2008] All ER (D) 62 (May)   12.04
R (McCarthy) v Secretary of State for Education and Employment (1996)
   Times, 24 July   11.120

R (McDonagh) v Salisbury District Council [2001] EWHC Admin 567,
  (2001) *Times*, 15 August, [2001] All ER (D) 58 (Jul) 7.88
R (McDonald) v Kensington & Chelsea LBC [2009] EWHC 1582 (Admin),
  [2010] All ER (D) 127 (Oct) 6.36
R (McDonald) v Kensington and Chelsea Royal London Borough Council
  [2011] UKSC 33, [2011] 4 All ER 881, [2011] PTSR 1266, [2011]
  HRLR 36, [2011] Eq LR 974, [2012] BLGR 107, (2011) 14 CCL Rep
  341, (2011) 121 BMLR 164, (2011) 108(29) LSG 17, (2011) 161
  NLJ 1026, (2011) 155(27) SJLB 39, (2011) *Times*, 7 July 1.183, 1.184
R (McDougal) v Liverpool City Council [2009] EWHC 1821 (Admin),
  [2009] ELR 510, [2009] All ER (D) 225 (Jul) 11.30
R (McFetrich) v Secretary of State for the Home Department [2003] EWHC
  1542 (Admin), [2003] 4 All ER 1093, [2003] 34 LS Gaz R 29, (2003)
  Times, 28 July, [2003] All ER (D) 386 (Jun) 9.02
R (McGetrick) v Parole Board, Secretary of State for Justice [2013] EWCA
  Civ 182, [2013] 1 WLR 2064, [2013] 3 All ER 636, [2013] ACD 79 ..... 10.59
R (McIntyre) v Gentoo Group Ltd [2010] EWHC 5 (Admin), (2010) 154(2)
  SJLB 29, [2010] 2 P & CR DG6 ..... 7.28
R (McLeod) v HM Prison Service [2002] EWHC 390 (Admin), [2002] Po
  LR 211 ..... 10.07, 10.09
R (McNicholas) v Nursing and Midwifery Council [2009] EWHC 627 ..... 15.108
R (MD (Gambia)) v SSHD [2011] EWCA Civ 121 ..... 14.44
R (Medhanye) v Secretary of State for the Home Department [2012] EWHC
  1799 (Admin) 1.211
R (Medical Justice) v Secretary of State for the Home Department [2010]
  EWHC 1925 (Admin) 1.121, 1.123
R (Medical Justice) v Secretary of State for the Home Department [2011]
  EWCA Civ 1710 ..... 1.55, 1.201
R (Mehmet) v London Probation Board [2007] EWHC 2223 (Admin),
  [2008] Prison LR 196 ..... 10.53
R (Mei Ling Lin) v Barnet LBC [2007] EWCA Civ 132, [2007] HLR 30 ..... 7.72
R (Mellor) v Secretary of State for Communities & Local Government
  [2009] EWCA Civ 1201 ..... 5.105
R (Melton and others) v Oxford CC [2001] EWHC Admin 245 ..... 11.152
R (Metropolitian Borough of Wirral) v Chief Schools Adjudicator [2001]
  ELR 574 ..... 1.157
R (Middleton) v Cambridge Magistrates' Court [2012] EWHC 2122
  (Admin), (2012) 176 JP 569, [2012] CTLC 100 ..... 1.55
R (Middleton) v West Somerset Coroner [2004] UKHL 10, [2004] 2 AC
  182, [2004] 2 WLR 800, [2004] UKHRR 501, [2004] 2 All ER 465,
  HL 1.166, 1.167, 10.123, 10.125
R (Miller) v North Yorkshire County Council & Others [2009] EWHC 2172
  (Admin), [2009] All ER (D) 189 (Aug) 12.89
R (Milner) v South Central Strategic Health Authority [2011] EWHC 218
  (Admin), [2011] PTSR D27 ..... 1.91
R (Mirza) v Secretary of State for the Home Department [2013] EWHC
  2207 (Admin) 1.158
R (Misick) v Secretary of State for Foreign and Commonwealth Affairs
  [2009] EWCA Civ 1549 ..... 1.55, 1.201
R (MM) v Greenwich LBC & Bromley LBC [2010] EWHC 1462 (Admin),
  [2010] LGR 868, [2010] NLJR 905, [2010] All ER (D) 124 (Jun) 6.118
R (MM) v LB Lewisham [2009] EWHC 416 (Admin) 6.62
R (MM) v Secretary of State for the Home Department [2012] EWCA Civ
  668 ..... 10.120
R (MM) v Secretary of State for Work and Pensions [2012] EWHC 2106
  (Admin) 3.55
R (MM) v Secretary of State for Work and Pensions [2013] EWCA Civ
  1565, [2014] 1 WLR 1716, [2014] 2 All ER 289, [2014] Eq LR 34 ..... 6.17
R (MM) v SSHD [2013] EWHC 1900 (Admin), [2013] WLR(D) 280 ..... 2.79, 14.07, 14.56
R (MN (Tanzania)) v SSHD [2011] EWCA Civ 193, [2011] 1 WLR 3200,
  [2011] 2 All ER 772, (2011) 108(11) LSG 20, (2011) *Times*, 21 April 1.98, 14.45, 14.46

R (Modaresi) v Secretary of State for Health [2013] UKSC 53, [2013] 4 All
    ER 318, [2013] PTSR 1031, [2013] HRLR 35, (2013) 133 BMLR 1 — 8.64
R (Mohamed) v Secretary of State for Foreign and Commonwealth Affairs
    (No 1) [2008] EWHC 2048 (Admin), [2009] 1 WLR 2579, (2008)
    105(34) LSG 22 — 1.201
R (Mohamed) v Secretary of State for Foreign and Commonwealth Affairs
    (No 2) [2010] EWCA Civ 158, [2011] QB 218, [2010] 3 WLR 554,
    [2010] 4 All ER 177, [2010] CP Rep 28 — 1.55, 1.201
R (Molinaro) v Kensington and Chelsea Royal London Borough Council
    [2001] EWHC Admin 896, [2002] LGR 336, [2001] All ER (D) 420
    (Oct) — 13.100
R (Mongan) v Isleworth Crown Court [2007] EWHC Admin 1087 — 9.38
R (Moos) v Commissioner of Police of the Metropolis [2012] EWCA Civ 12 — 1.173
R (Morgan Grenfell & Co Ltd) v Inland Revenue Commissioners [2002]
    UKHL 21, [2003] 1 AC 563, [2002] 2 WLR 1299, [2002] 3 All ER 1,
    [2002] STC 786, [2002] HRLR 42, 74 TC 511, [2002] BTC 223, 4
    ITL Rep 809, [2002] STI 806, (2002) 99(25) LSG 35, (2002) 146
    SJLB 126, [2002] NPC 70, (2002) *Times*, 20 May, (2002)
    Independent, 21 May — 1.55, 1.201
R (Morris) v Newport City Council [2009] EWHC 3051 (Admin), [2010]
    BLGR 234, [2010] ACD 33, [2010] PTSR (CS) 11, (2010) *Times*, 5
    January — 1.148, 1.155
R (Mount Cook Land Ltd et al) v Westminster City Council [2003] EWCA
    Civ 1346, [2004] 2 P & CR 405, [2003] 43 EGCS 137, (2003) *Times*,
    16 October, 147 Sol Jo LB 1272, [2004] 2 Costs LR 211, [2003] All
    ER (D) 222 (Oct) — 3.43, 3.50, 3.75, 3.76
R (Mousa) v Secretary of State for Defence [2010] EWHC 3304 (Admin),
    [2011] UKHRR 268, [2011] ACD 32 — 10.120
R (Mousa) v Secretary of State for Defence [2011] EWCA Civ 1334, [2012]
    HRLR 6, (2011) 161 NLJ 1669, (2011) *Times*, 28 December — 1.170
R (MP) v Secretary of State for Justice [2012] EWHC 214 (Admin), [2012]
    ACD 58, (2012) 109(9) LSG 17 — 1.91, 1.120
R (Mullaney) v Adjudication Panel for England [2009] EWHC 72 (Admin),
    [2010] LGR 354, [2009] PTSR (CS) 28, [2009] All ER (D) 102 (Feb) — 13.113
R (Mullins) v Jockey Club Appeal Board [2005] EWHC 2197 (Admin),
    [2006] ACD 2, (2005) *Times*, 24 October — 15.19, 15.45
R (Munjaz) v Ashworth Hospital Authority [2005] UKHL 58, [2006] 2 AC
    148, [2005] 3 WLR 793, [2006] 4 All ER 736, [2005] HRLR 42,
    [2006] Lloyd's Rep Med 1, (2005) 86 BMLR 84, [2005] MHLR 276,
    (2005) *Times*, 18 October, (2005) *Independent*, 18 October — 1.69, 1.92, 1.120, 1.121, 8.16
R (Muwonge) v SSHD (Consent Orders: Costs: Guidance) [2014] UKUT
    00514 (IAC) — 14.38
R (Muwonge) v SSHD (consent orders: costs: guidance) [2014] UKUT 00514
    (IAC) — 14.40
R (Mwanza) v (1) Greenwich LBC (2) Bromley LBC [2010] EWHC 1462
    (Admin), [2011] PTSR 965, [2010] BLGR 868, (2010) 13 CCL Rep
    454, [2010] MHLR 226, [2010] ACD 86 — 16.40, 16.41, 16.42
R (N and E) v Governors of the Hasmonean High School [1994] ELR 343 — 11.59, 11.78
R (N) v Coventry City Council [2008] EWHC 2786 (Admin) — 6.127
R (N) v Governing Body of A School [2014] EWHC 1238 (Admin) — 11.120
R (N) v Lambeth LBC [2006] EWHC 3427 — 6.134
R (N) v Leeds CC [1999] ELR 324 — 11.30, 11.152
R (N) v M and others [2002] EWCA Civ 1789, [2003] 1 WLR 562, [2003]
    1 FCR 124, [2003] 1 FLR 667, [2003] Fam Law 160, 72 BMLR 81,
    [2003] 08 LS Gaz R 29, (2002) *Times*, 12 December, [2002] All ER
    (D) 75 (Dec) — 3.10, 8.40
R (N) v North Tyneside Borough Council (IPSEA Intervening) [2010] EWCA
    Civ 135, [2010] ELR 312, [2010] All ER (D) 115 (Jun) — 11.120

R (Nadarajah) v Secretary of State for the Home Department [2005] EWCA
    Civ 1363, (2005) *Times*, 14 December   1.134, 1.135
R (Naik) v Secretary of State for the Home Department [2011] EWCA Civ
    1546, [2012] Imm AR 381   1.189
R (Nash) v Chelsea College of Art and Design [2000] Ed CR 571, [2000]
    ELR 686   1.156
R (Nash) v Chelsea College of Art and Design [2001] EWHC Admin 538,
    (2001) *Times*, 25 July, [2001] All ER (D) 133 (Jul)   11.142
R (Nealon & Sims) v Governor HMP Wakefield, unreported, 19 April 2010   10.35
R (New London College Ltd) v Secretary of State for the Home Department
    [2013] UKSC 51, [2013] 1 WLR 2358, [2013] 4 All ER 195, [2013]
    PTSR 995, [2014] Imm AR 151, [2014] INLR 66   1.69, 13.07, 13.23, 13.36, 13.37
R (Newsmith Stainless Ltd) v Secretary of State for the Environment,
    Transport and the Regions [2001] EWHC Admin 74   5.32, 5.108
R (Nicholls) v Security Industry Authority [2006] EWHC 1792 (Admin),
    [2007] 1 WLR 2067, [2007] ICR 1076, [2006] All ER (D) 259 (Jul)   12.15, 12.61
R (NM) v London Borough of Islington [2012] EWHC 414 (Admin), [2012]
    2 All ER 1245, [2012] PTSR 1582, [2012] BLGR 435, (2012) 15
    CCL Rep 563, (2012) *Times*, 25 April   6.17
R (NM) v Secretary of State for Justice [2012] EWCA Civ 1182, [2012]
    MHLR 390   10.118, 10.119, 10.120
R (Noble Organisation) v Thanet District Council [2005] EWCA Civ 782,
    [2006] 1 P & CR 197, [2005] All ER (D) 322 (Jun)   3.06
R (Noone) v Secretary of State for Justice [2010] UKSC 30, [2010] 1 WLR
    1743, [2010] 4 All ER 463, (2010) 107(28) LSG 16, (2010) 154(26)
    SJLB 28, (2010) *Times*, 2 July   10.51
R (Northern Cyprus Tourism Centre Ltd) v Transport for London [2005]
    EWHC 1698 (Admin), [2005] UKHRR 1231, [2005] ACD 101,
    (2005) *Times*, 24 August   1.189
R (Nottingham Healthcare NHS Trust) v Mental Health Review Tribunal
    [2008] EWHC 2445 (Admin), [2008] MHLR 326   1.153
R (O'Sullivan) v Parole Board [2009] EWHC 2370 (Admin), [2010] 2 Prison
    LR 235   10.60, 10.62
R (O) v Barking and Dagenham London Borough Council [2010] EWHC
    634 (Admin); on appeal [2010] EWCA Civ 1101, CA   6.90, 6.92
R (O) v East Riding of Yorkshire County Council [2010] EWHC 489
    (Admin), [2010] 2 FCR 204, [2010] ELR 318, [2010] All ER (D) 109
    (Mar)   11.120
R (O) v Hackney London Borough Council [2006] EWHC 3405 (Admin),
    [2007] ELR 405, [2006] All ER (D) 36 (Dec)   11.55
R (O) v London Borough of Hammersmith and Fulham [2011] EWHC 679
    (Admin)   6.58
R (Oakes) v Secretary of State for Justice [2009] EWHC 3470 (Admin)   10.54
R (Oge Dengbe) v Secretary of State for Justice [2011] EWHC 266 (Admin) 10.09
R (Okondu and Abdussalam) v SSHD [2014] UKUT 377 (IAC)   14.24
R (Osborn) v Parole Board [2013] UKSC 61, [2013] 3 WLR 1020, [2014] 1
    All ER 369, [2014] HRLR 1, (2013) 157(39) SJLB 37   10.07, 10.57
R (Othman) v Secretary of State for Work and Pensions [2001] EWHC
    Admin 1022, (2002) 5 CCL Rep 148   1.201
R (Oyston) v Parole Board [2000] EWCA Crim 3552   10.58, 10.61
R (P) v Newham LBC [2004] EWHC 2210 (Admin), [2005] 2 FCR 171,
    [2004] All ER (D) 89 (Sep)   6.83
R (P) v Schools Adjudicator [2007] BLGR 346   11.30
R (P) v Secretary of State for Justice [2009] EWCA Civ 701, [2010] QB 317,
    [2010] 2 WLR 967, [2009] UKHRR 1496, [2009] MHLR 201,
    [2009] Prison LR 151, [2010] 2 Prison LR 221, (2009) *Times*, 23 July   10.120, 10.136
R (P) v Windsor & Maidenhead RBC and the Learning & Skills Council
    [2010] EWHC 1408 (Admin)   11.120
R (Pal) v General Medical Council [2009] EWHC 1061 (Admin)   15.96
R (Palmer) v Secretary of State for the Home Department [2004] EWHC
    1817 (Admin), [2005] 2 Prison LR 165, (2004) *Times*, 13 September 1.123, 10.07, 10.09

R (Parish) v Pensions Ombudsman [2009] EWHC 969 (Admin)   1.77
R (Parr) v Hertfordshire County Council [2008] EWHC 3379 (Admin),
   [2009] All ER (D) 268 (Jan)   11.30
R (Partridge Farms Ltd) v Secretary of State for Environment, Food & Rural
   Affairs [2008] EWHC 1645 (Admin), [2008] Eu LR 840, [2008] NPC
   84   1.206
R (Pascoe) v First Secretary of State [2006] EWHC 2356   5.62
R (Patel) v General Medical Council [2013] EWCA Civ 327, [2013] 1 WLR
   2801, (2013) 133 BMLR 14, (2013) *Times*, 21 June   1.142, 15.84, 15.85
R (Patel) v Secretary of State for the Home Department [2012] EWHC 2100
   (Admin)   1.102
R (Patmore) v Brentwood Borough Council [2012] EWHC 1244 (Admin)   1.79
R (Paul-Coker) v Southwark London Borough Council [2006] EWHC 497
   (Admin), [2006] HLR 573, [2006] All ER (D) 39 (Mar)   7.47
R (Peacock) v General Medical Council [2007] EWHC 585 (Admin), [2007]
   LS Law Medical 284   15.93
R (Peries) v Secretary of State for the Home Department [1997] EWHC 712   10.07, 10.09
R (Persaud) v Cambridge University [2001] ELR 480, [2001] EWCA Civ
   534, [2001] All ER (D) 103 (Apr)   11.26
R (Pharis) v Secretary of State for the Home Department [2004] EWCA Civ
   654, [2004] 3 All ER 310, [2004] 1 WLR 2590, [2004] 26 LS Gaz R
   28, (2004) *Times*, 27 May, [2004] All ER (D) 353 (May)   2.15
R (Pharmacy Care Plus Ltd) v Family Health Services Appeals Unit [2013]
   EWHC 824 (Admin)   1.99
R (Playfoot) v Governing Body of Millais School [2007] ELR 484, [2007]
   EWHC 1698 (Admin), [2007] LGR 851, [2007] 3 FCR 754, (2007)
   Times, 23 July, [2007] All ER (D) 234 (Jul)   11.148
R (PM) v Hertfordshire County Council [2010] EWHC 2056 (Admin),
   [2010] NLJR 1191, (2010) *Times*, 18 November, [2010] All ER (D)
   28 (Aug)   6.131
R (Preston) v Wandsworth London Borough Council [2011] EWHC 3174
   (Admin), [2012] 2 WLR 1134, [2012] PTSR 765   1.55, 1.201, 1.207
R (Primary Health Investment Properties Ltd) v Secretary of State for Health
   [2009] EWHC 519 (Admin), [2009] PTSR 1563, [2009] LS Law
   Medical 315, [2010] RVR 63, [2009] ACD 57, [2009] NPC 52   1.123
R (ProLife Alliance) v BBC [2003] UKHL 23, [2004] 1 AC 185, [2003] 2
   WLR 1403, [2003] 2 All ER 977, [2003] EMLR 23, [2003] HRLR
   26, [2003] UKHRR 758, [2003] ACD 65, (2003) 100(26) LSG 35,
   (2003) 153 NLJ 823, (2003) 147 SJLB 595, (2003) *Times*, 16 May   1.49
R (Prothero) v Secretary of State for the Home Department [2013] EWHC
   2830 (Admin), (2013) 157(37) SJLB 37   1.56
R (Public and Commercial Services Union) v Minister for the Civil Service
   (No 3) [2011] EWHC 2041 (Admin), [2012] 1 All ER 985, [2011]
   IRLR 903, [2011] ACD 115, (2011) 108(33) LSG 27   1.195
R (Purja) v Ministry of Defence [2003] EWCA Civ 1345, [2004] 1 WLR
   289, [2004] UKHRR 309, (2003) 100(41) LSG 33, (2003) *Times*, 16
   October   1.193
R (Q) v Secretary of State for the Home Department [2003] EWCA Civ 364,
   [2004] QB 36, [2003] 3 WLR 365, [2003] 2 All ER 905, [2003]
   HRLR 21, [2003] UKHRR 607, 14 BHRC 262, [2003] HLR 57,
   (2003) 6 CCL Rep 136, [2003] ACD 46, (2003) 100(21) LSG 29,
   (2003) *Times*, 19 March, (2003) *Independent*, 21 March   1.78, 1.116
R (Q, D, KH, OK, JK H, T and S) v Secretary of State for the Home
   Department [2003] EWHC 2507   3.35
R (Quark Fishing) v Secretary of State for Foreign and Commonwealth
   Affairs [2002] EWCA Civ 1409   1.118
R (Quila) v Secretary of State for the Home Department [2010] EWCA Civ
   1482, [2011] 3 All ER 81, [2011] 1 FLR 1187, [2011] 2 FCR 462,
   [2011] HRLR 11, [2011] UKHRR 183, [2011] Imm AR 423, [2011]
   Fam Law 232, (2011) *Times*, 10 January   1.55, 1.197, 1.201

R (Quila) v Secretary of State for the Home Department [2011] UKSC 45,
[2012] 1 AC 621, [2011] 3 WLR 836, [2012] 1 All ER 1011, [2012]
1 FLR 788, [2011] 3 FCR 575, [2012] HRLR 2, [2011] UKHRR
1347, 33 BHRC 381, [2012] Imm AR 135, [2011] INLR 698, [2012]
Fam Law 21, (2011) 108(41) LSG 15, (2011) 155(39) SJLB 31,
(2011) *Times*, 20 October ... 1.53
R (R and other) v Leeds City Council [2005] EWHC 2495 (Admin), [2006]
LGR 579, [2006] ELR 25, [2005] All ER (D) 369 (Nov) ... 11.55
R (R) v A Chief Constable [2013] EWHC 2864 (Admin), [2014] 1 Cr App R
16, (2013) 134 BMLR 98, ... 1.56
R (R) v Kent County Council [2007] ELR 648, [2007] EWHC 2135 (Admin) ... 11.55
R (R) v Muntham House School [2000] LGR 255, [2000] LGR 269, [2000]
ELR 287, (2000) *Times*, 26 January ... 11.18
R (Ramda) v Secretary of State for the Home Department [2002] EWHC
1278 (Admin) ... 1.123
R (Rank) v East Cambridgeshire District Council [2003] JPL 454 ... 5.70
R (Raphael) v Highbury Corner Magistrates' Court [2011] EWCA Civ 462,
[2012] PTSR 427 ... 1.89
R (Raw) v London Borough of Lambeth [2010] EWHC 507 (Admin) ... 3.20
R (Rawnsley) v Parole Board [2010] EWHC 2689 (Admin) ... 10.59
R (Razazan) v Wiltshire CC [1997] ELR 370 ... 11.73
R (Razgar) v Secretary of State for the Home Department [2003] EWCA Civ
840, [2003] INLR 543, [2003] Imm AR 529, [2003] All ER (D) 249
(Jun), CA, [2004] UKHL 27, [2004] 2 AC 368, [2004] 3 WLR 58,
[2004] INLR 349, [2004] 3 All ER 821, [2004] UKHL 27, [2004]
INLR 349, HL ... 1.184
R (RB) v The First-tier Tribunal [2010] UKUT 160, AAC ... 4.14, 8.51, 8.53, 8.63
R (RC) v Manchester City Council (unreported), 21 June 2014 ... 11.120
R (Reading Borough Council) v Admissions Appeal Panel for Reading
Borough Council [2005] EWHC 2378 (Admin), [2006] ELR 186 ... 1.155, 11.95
R (Redcar and Cleveland Independent Providers Association and Others) v
Redcar and Cleveland Borough Council [2013] EWHC 4 (Admin),
[2013] PTSR 1096 ... 6.146
R (Redgrave) v Commissioner of Police for the Metropolis [2003] EWCA
Civ 4, [2003] 1 WLR 1136, [2003] Po LR 25, (2003) 100(11) LSG
34, (2003) 147 SJLB 116, (2003) *Times*, 30 January ... 15.102
R (Refugee Legal Centre) v Secretary of State for the Home Department
[2004] EWCA Civ 1481, [2005] 1 WLR 2219, [2005] INLR 236,
[2005] ACD 52, (2005) 102(1) LSG 16, *Times*, November 24, 2004 ... 1.120, 1.121
R (Regentford) Ltd v Canterbury Crown Court [2001] HRLR 18 ... 9.30
R (Reilly) v Secretary of State for Work and Pensions [2013] EWCA Civ 66,
[2013] 1 WLR 2239, [2013] 3 All ER 67, (2013) 163 NLJ 236 ... 1.81
R (Remedy UK Ltd) v General Medical Council [2010] EWHC 1245
(Admin), [2010] Med LR 330, [2010] ACD 72 ... 15.96, 15.103, 15.151, 15.152
R (Rex Cart) v The Upper Tribunal and others [2010] EWCA Civ 859,
[2010] 2 WLR 1012, CA, [2009] EWHC 3052 (Admin), QB ... 4.22
R (Rhodes) v Police and Crime Commissioner for Lincolnshire [2013]
EWHC 1009 (Admin), [2013] ACD 98 ... 1.29
R (Richards) v General Medical Council [2001] Lloyd's Rep Med 47, (2001)
Times, 24 January ... 15.112
R (Richards) v Pembrokeshire County Council [2004] EWCA Civ 1000,
[2005] BLGR 105 ... 1.64, 1.113, 1.156
R (RJM) v Secretary of State for Work and Pensions [2007] EWCA Civ 614,
[2007] 1 WLR 3067, [2007] HRLR 35, [2007] UKHRR 1061, [2007]
ACD 104, (2007) 151 SJLB 894 ... 1.193
R (RJM) v Secretary of State for Work and Pensions [2008] UKHL 63,
[2009] 1 AC 311, [2008] 3 WLR 1023, [2009] 2 All ER 556, [2009]
PTSR 336, [2009] HRLR 5, [2009] UKHRR 117, 26 BHRC 587,
(2008) *Times*, 27 October ... 1.195

R (Roberts) v Parole Board [2005] UKHL 45, [2005] 2 AC 738, [2005] 3
 WLR 152, [2006] 1 All ER 39, [2005] HRLR 38, [2005] UKHRR
 939, (2005) 155 NLJ 1096, (2005) Times, 8 July, (2005) Independent,
 12 July 1.123
R (Roberts) v Secretary of State for the Home Department [2003] EWHC
 3120 (Admin), [2004] 2 All ER 776, [2004] Prison LR 257, [2004]
 ACD 60 .... 10.21, 10.22
R (Roose) v Parole Board [2010] EWHC 1780 (Admin), (2010) Times, 1
 September 10.27
R (Rowe) v Parole Board [2012] EWHC 1272 (Admin) 10.59
R (Rowen) v Governor of Kirkham Prison [2009] EWHC 3756 (Admin),
 [2010] 2 Prison LR 210 .... 1.154, 10.09, 10.66
R (Royal Brompton and Harefield NHS Foundation Trust) v Joint
 Committee of Primary Care Trusts [2012] EWCA Civ 472, (2012)
 126 BMLR 134, (2012) 109(18) LSG 20 .... 1.132, 1.137, 15.35
R (Royden) v Wirral Metropolitan Borough Council [2002] EWHC Admin
 2484, [2003] LGR 290, [2002] All ER (D) 256 (Oct) 12.08, 12.61
R (RP) v Brent London Borough Council [2011] EWHC 3251 (Admin) 1.116
R (Rudi) v Secretary of State for the Home Department [2007] EWCA Civ
 132, [2007] HLR 30, [2007] BLGR 454, (2007) 104(10) LSG 28,
 (2007) 151 SJLB 297 .... 1.55, 1.201
R (Russell) v General Medical Council [2008] EWHC 2546 (Admin) 15.206
R (Russell) v Secretary of State for the Home Department [2000] Prison LR
 145, (2000) Times, 31 August 10.88
R (Rutter) v The General Teaching Council for England [2008] EWHC 133
 (Admin) 15.195
R (Rycroft) v Royal Pharmaceutical Society of Great Britain [2010] EWHC
 2832 (Admin), [2011] Med LR 23 .... 15.111, 15.127
R (S (by his litigation friend the Official Solicitor)) v Secretary of State for
 the Home Department [2014] EWHC 50 (Admin) 16.51, 16.52
R (S and B) v Independent Appeal Panel of Birmingham City Council [2006]
 EWHC 2369 (Admin), [2007] ELR 57, [2006] All ER (D) 139 (Aug) 11.95, 11.140
R (S) v Brent London Borough Council, R (T) v Head Teacher of Wembley
 High School, R (P) v Oxfordshire County Council Exclusion Appeals
 Panel [2002] EWCA Civ 693, [2002] ELR 556, (2002) Times, 4 June,
 [2002] All ER (D) 277 (May) 11.132
R (S) v Chief Constable of the South Yorkshire Police [2004] UKHL 39,
 [2004] 1 WLR 2196, [2004] 4 All ER 193, [2004] HRLR 35, [2004]
 UKHRR 967, 21 BHRC 408, [2004] Po LR 283, [2005] Crim LR
 136, (2004) 101(34) LSG 29, (2004) 154 NLJ 1183, (2004) 148 SJLB
 914, (2004) Times, 23 July, (2004) Independent, 29 July 1.193
R (S) v Cobham Hall School [1998] ELR 389 1014 .... 11.18
R (S) v General Teaching Council for England [2013] EWHC 2779 (Admin) 3.65
R (S) v Governing Body of YP School [2003] EWCA Civ 1306, [2004] ELR
 37, [2003] All ER (D) 202 (Jul) 11.135
R (S) v Governors of Dame Alice Owens School [1998] Ed CR 101, [1998]
 COD 108 .... 11.86
R (S) v Hampshire County Council [2009] EWHC 2537 (Admin) 2.143, 2.148
R (S) v Headteacher of C High School [2001] EWHC Admin 513, [2002]
 ELR 73 .... 11.137
R (S) v Independent Appeal Panel of St Thomas Catholic Primary School
 [2010] EWHC 3785 (Admin), 153 Sol Jo (no 36) 29, [2009] All ER
 (D) 116 (Sep) 11.86
R (S) v Knowsley NHS Primary Care Trust [2006] EWHC 26 (Admin),
 [2006] Lloyd's Rep Med 123, [2006] ACD 60, (2006) Times, 2
 February 1.123
R (S) v London Borough of Brent [2002] EWCA Civ 693, [2002] ELR 556,
 [2002] ACD 90, (2002) 99(26) LSG 38, (2002) 146 SJLB 137, (2002)
 Times, 4 June, (2002) Independent, 30 May, ... 1.123

Table of Cases   lxxxi

R (S) v Norfolk County Council [2004] EWHC 404 (Admin), [2004] ELR 259   2.15
R (S) v Roman Catholic Schools [1998] ELR 304   11.136
R (S) v Royal Borough of Kensington & Chelsea [2010] EWCA Civ 1209, CA   6.45
R (S) v Royal Borough of Kensington & Chelsea [2010] EWHC 414 (Admin), [2010] All ER (D) 118 (Mar)   6.44
R (S) v Secretary of State for Justice [2013] EWHC 2889 (Admin)   10.42
R (S) v Secretary of State for the Home Department [2007] EWCA Civ 546, [2007] Imm AR 781, [2007] INLR 450, [2007] ACD 94, (2007) 104(27) LSG 30, (2007) 151 SJLB 858   1.90
R (S) v Secretary of State for the Home Department [2011] EWHC 2120 (Admin), (2011) 108(35) LSG 20   1.169
R (S) v Special Educational Needs Tribunal and City of Westminster [1996] 1 All ER 171, [1995] 1 WLR 1627, [1996] 2 FCR 310, [1996] ELR 102   11.112, 11.151
R (S) v Sutton London Borough Council [2007] EWCA Civ 790, [2007] All ER (D) 422 (Jul)   6.60
R (S, H & Q) v SSHD [2009] EWCA Civ 142   14.49
R (S, T and P) v Brent LBC, Oxfordshire CC, Head Teacher of Elliott School and the Secretary of State for Education and Skills [2002] EWCA Civ 693, [2002] ELR 556, (2002) *Times*, 4 June, [2002] All ER (D) 277 (May)   11.137
R (Saadat) v Rent Service [2001] EWCA Civ 1559, [2002] HLR 32, (2001) 98(44) LSG 36, *Times*, November 6, 2001   1.108
R (Saadi) v Secretary of State for the Home Department [2002] UKHL 41, [2002] 1 WLR 3131, [2002] 4 All ER 785, [2003] UKHRR 173, [2002] INLR 523, [2003] ACD 11, (2002) 146 SJLB 250, (2002) *Times*, 1 November, (2002) *Independent*, 5 November   1.55, 1.173, 1.201
R (Sacker) v West Yorkshire Coroner [2004] UKHL 11, [2004] 1 WLR 796, [2004] 2 All ER 487, [2004] HRLR 30, [2004] UKHRR 521, [2004] Lloyd's Rep Med 281, [2004] 79 BMLR 40, [2004] Inquest LR 28, [2003] Inquest LR 15, (2004) 101(16) LSG 28, (2004) 148 SJLB 354, (2004) *Times*, 12 March   10.123, 10.124, 10.134
R (Sacupima) v Newham LBC [2001] 1 WLR 563, (2000) *Times*, 1 December, [2000] All ER (D) 1947   2.120
R (Sainsbury's Supermarkets Ltd) v Wolverhampton City Council [2010] UKSC 20, [2011] 1 AC 437, [2010] 2 WLR 1173, [2010] 4 All ER 931, [2010] PTSR 1103, [2010] BLGR 727, [2011] 1 P & CR 1, [2010] 2 EGLR 103, [2010] RVR 237, [2010] JPL 1259, [2010] 20 EG 144 (CS), (2010) 154(20) SJLB 36, [2010] NPC 66, (2010) *Times*, 13 May   1.55, 1.104, 1.201
R (Samaroo) v Secretary of State for the Home Department [2001] EWCA Civ 1139, [2001] UKHRR 1150, [2002] INLR 55, (2001) 98(34) LSG 40, (2001) 145 SJLB 208, (2001) *Times*, 18 September   1.105
R (Sandhar) v Office of the Independent Adjudicator for Higher Education [2011] EWCA Civ 1614, [2012] ELR 160   1.123
R (Sardar) v Watford Borough Council [2006] EWHC 1590 (Admin), [2007] ACD 19   1.145
R (Savage) v Hillingdon LBC [2010] EWHC 88 (Admin), [2010] PTSR 1859   7.61
R (SAVE Britain's Heritage and the Victorian Society) v Sheffield City Council and the University of Sheffield [2013] EWCA Civ 1108   5.100
R (Save Our Parkland Appeal) v East Devon DC & Axminster Carpets [2013] EWHC 22   5.91
R (Save our Surgery Ltd) v Joint Committee of Primary Care Trusts [2013] EWHC 439 (Admin), [2013] Med LR 150, (2013) 131 BMLR 166, [2013] ACD 70, [2013] PTSR D16   1.151
R (Savva) v Kensington and Chelsea Royal London Borough Council [2010] EWCA Civ 1209, [2011] PTSR 761, [2011] BLGR 150, (2011) 14 CCL Rep 75, (2010) *Times*, 15 November   1.154, 1.156

R (Saxon) v Criminal Cases Review Commission [2001] EWCA Civ 1384 — 9.07
R (Scholten) v General Medical Council [2013] EWHC 173 (Admin) — 15.169
R (Scott) v London Borough of Hackney [2009] EWCA Civ 217, [2009] All ER (D) 124 (Jan) — 7.103
R (SD) v Governors of Denbigh High School [2006] UKHL 15 — 5.62
R (Secretary of State for Defence) v Pensions Appeal Tribunal [2008] EWHC 3248 (Admin) — 1.77
R (Secretary of State for the Home Department) v Assistant Deputy Coroner for Inner West London [2010] EWHC 3098 (Admin), [2011] 1 WLR 2564, [2011] 3 All ER 1001, (2010) 174 JP 593, [2010] Inquest LR 211, [2011] ACD 23, (2010) 107(48) LSG 14, (2010) 160 NLJ 1717, (2011) Times, 12 January — 1.55, 1.201
R (Sefton Care Association) v Sefton Council [2011] EWHC 2676 (Admin), [2012] PTSR D13 — 6.146
R (Sezuk) v SSHD [2001] INLR 675 — 14.55
R (Shaffi) v Secretary of State for the Home Department [2011] EWHC 3113 (Admin) — 1.123
R (Shaheen) v Secretary of State for Justice [2008] EWHC 1195 (Admin), [2009] Prison LR 91, [2008] ACD 75 — 10.11
R (Shanks (t/a Blue Line Taxis)) v Northumberland County Council [2012] EWHC 1539 (Admin), [2013] PTSR 154, [2012] RTR 36, [2012] ACD 107 — 1.81
R (Shaw) v HM Coroner for Leicester City and South Leicestershire [2013] EWHC 386 (Admin) — 1.134
R (Shepherd) v Governor of HMP Whatton [2010] EWHC 2474 (Admin) — 10.90
R (Shi) v King's College London [2008] EWHC 857 (Admin), [2008] ELR 414, [2008] All ER (D) 136 (Apr) — 11.24
R (Shields) v Crown Court at Liverpool and the Lord Chancellor [2001] UKHRR 610, [2001] EWHC Admin 90, [2001] All ER (D) 190 (Jan) — 9.30
R (Shoesmith) v Ofsted [2011] EWCA Civ 642, [2011] PTSR 1459, [2011] ICR 1195, [2011] IRLR 679, [2011] BLGR 649, (2011) 108(23) LSG 16, (2011) 155(22) SJLB 35 — 1.123, 1.125, 15.53
R (Shreeve) v Secretary of State for Justice [2007] EWHC 2431 (Admin), [2008] Prison LR 229, [2008] ACD 9 — 10.78
R (Shrewsbury and Atcham BC) v Secretary of State for Communities and Local Government, [2008] EWCA Civ 148, [2008] 3 All ER 548, (2008) Times, 12 March, [2008] All ER (D) 25 (Mar) — 13.05, 13.23
R (Shutt) v Governor HMP Albany [2012] EWHC 851 (Admin) — 10.37
R (Siborurema) v Office of the Independent Adjudicator [2007] EWCA Civ 1365, [2008] ELR 209, (2008) 152(2) SJLB 31, (2008) Times, 10 January — 1.127, 11.26
R (Simpson) v Chief Constable of Greater Manchester [2013] EWHC 1858 (Admin), [2014] ACD 20 — 1.142
R (Sinclair Collis Ltd) v Secretary of State for Health [2011] EWCA Civ 437, [2012] QB 394, [2012] 2 WLR 304, [2011] 3 CMLR 37, [2012] Eu LR 50, (2012) 123 BMLR 36, [2011] ACD 98, (2011) Times, 28 June — 1.52, 1.53, 1.54, 1.55, 1.206, 1.207
R (Singh) v Cardiff City Council [2012] EWHC 1852 (Admin) — 12.61
R (Singh) v Stratford Magistrates' Court [2007] EWHC 1582 (Admin), [2007] 1 WLR 3119, [2007] 4 All ER 407, [2008] 1 Cr App R 2, (2007) 171 JP 557, [2007] ACD 72, (2008) 172 JPN 69, (2007) Times, 13 August — 15.34
R (Sivasubramaniam) v Wandsworth County Court [2002] EWCA Civ 1738, [2003] 1 WLR 475, [2003] 2 All ER 160, [2003] CP Rep 27, (2003) 100(3) LSG 34, (2002) Times, 30 November — 1.80
R (Slaiman) v Richmond-Upon-Thames LBC [2006] EWHC 329 (Admin), [2006] All ER (D) 132 (Feb) — 7.54
R (Smith) v East Kent Hospital NHS Trust [2002] EWHC 2640 (Admin), (2003) 6 CCL Rep 251 — 1.148, 1.150
R (Smith) v Governor HMP Lindholme [2010] EWHC 1356 (Admin) — 10.09

R (Smith) v Governor of HMP Belmarsh and Secretary of State for the
  Home Department [2009] EWHC 109 (Admin), [2010] 1 Prison LR
  126 .... 10.77, 10.91
R (Smith) v Independent Adjudicator [2011] EWHC 3981 (Admin) ... 10.88, 10.90
R (Smith) v Oxfordshire Assistant Deputy Coroner [2010] UKSC 29, [2011]
  1 AC 1, [2010] 3 WLR 223, [2010] 3 All ER 1067, [2010] HRLR 28,
  [2010] UKHRR 1020, 29 BHRC 497, [2010] Inquest LR 119, (2010)
  107(28) LSG 17, (2010) 160 NLJ 973, (2010) 154(26) SJLB 28,
  (2010) *Times*, 8 July 1.167
R (Smith) v Parole Board [2003] EWCA Civ 1014, [2003] 1 WLR 2548,
  [2003] 34 LS Gaz R 31, [2003] 38 LS Gaz R 34, [2003] NLJR 1427,
  (2003) *Times*, 9 July, [2003] All ER (D) 401 (Jun) 3.45
R (Snelgrove) v Woolwich Crown Court [2004] EWHC 2172 (Admin),
  [2005] 1 WLR 3223, [2005] 1 Cr App Rep 253, [2004] All ER (D)
  177 (Sep) 9.34
R (South Glamorgan CC) v Special Educational Needs Tribunal [1996] ELR
  326 .... 11.117
R (South Northamptonshire Council) v Towcester Magistrates' Court [2008]
  EWHC 381 (Admin), [2008] All ER (D) 76 (Feb) 12.63
R (South West Care Homes Ltd) v Devon County Council [2012] EWHC
  1867 (Admin), [2012] ACD 108 .... 6.146
R (Southern) v Oxfordshire County Council [2004] EWHC 133 (Admin),
  [2004] ELR 489, (2004) *Times*, 3 March, [2004] All ER (D) 219 (Jan) 11.55
R (SP) v Secretary of State for the Home Department [2004] EWCA Civ
  1750, [2005] 1 Prison LR 84, (2005) 102(7) LSG 27, (2005) *Times*,
  21 January 1.123
R (Spath Holme Ltd) v Secretary of State for the Environment, Transport
  and the Regions [2001] 2 AC 349, [2001] 2 WLR 15, [2001] 1 All
  ER 195, (2001) 33 HLR 31, [2001] 1 EGLR 129, [2000] EG 152
  (CS), (2001) 98(8) LSG 44, (2000) 150 NLJ 1855, (2001) 145 SJLB
  39, [2000] NPC 139, (2000) *Times*, 13 December 1.71, 1.111
R (Spencer) v Lambeth LBC [2006] EWHC 3611 .... 7.47
R (Sporting Options Plc) v Horserace Betting Levy Board [2003] EWHC
  1943 (Admin) 1.123
R (Srinivasans Solicitors) v Croydon County Court [2011] All ER (D) 108
  (Oct) 1.77
R (Staff Side of the Police Negotiating Board) v Secretary of State for Work
  and Pensions [2011] EWHC 3175 (Admin), [2012] Eq LR 124,
  [2012] Pens LR 31, [2012] ACD 39 .... 1.149
R (Stanley) v HM Coroner for Inner North London [2003] EWHC 1180
  (Admin), [2003] Inquest LR 38, (2003) *Times*, 12 June 10.124
R (Stellato) v Secretary of State for Justice [2007] UKHL 5, [2007] 2 AC 70,
  [2007] 2 All ER 737, [2007] 2 WLR 531, (2007) *Times*, 16 March,
  151 Sol Jo LB 395, [2007] All ER (D) 251 (Mar) 9.10
R (Stennett) v Manchester City Council [2002] UKHL 34, [2002] 2 AC
  1127, [2002] 4 All ER 124, [2002] 3 WLR 584, [2002] LGR 557, 68
  BMLR 247, (2002) *Times*, 29 August, [2002] All ER (D) 366 (Jul) 6.118
R (Stern) v Horsham District Council [2013] EWHC 1460 (Admin), [2013]
  3 All ER 798, [2013] PTSR 1502, [2013] ACD 118 .... 2.122
R (Strickson) v Preston County Court [2007] EWCA Civ 1132 .... 1.75
R (Sturnham) v Parole Board [2013] UKSC 23, [2013] 2 AC 254, [2013] 2
  WLR 1157, [2013] 2 All ER 1013, [2013] HRLR 24, 35 BHRC 378,
  (2013) 157(18) SJLB 31, (2013) *Times*, 4 June 1.173
R (Sullivan) v Warwick District Council [2003] EWHC 606 (Admin), [2003]
  2 PLR 56, [2003] JPL 1545, (2003) *Times*, June 12 .... 1.79
R (Sunderland City Council) v South Tyneside Council [2011] EWHC 2355
  (Admin), [2011] MHLR 374 .... 16.39
R (Sunderland City Council) v South Tyneside Council [2012] EWCA Civ
  1232, [2013] 1 All ER 394, [2013] PTSR 549, [2013] BLGR 51,
  (2012) 15 CCL Rep 701, [2012] MHLR 404 .... 6.119

R (Sunspell Ltd (t/a Superlative Travel)) v Association of British Travel
    Agents [2001] ACD 16, (2000) *Independent*, 27 November   15.49
R (Suppiah) v Secretary of State for the Home Department [2011] EWHC 2
    (Admin), (2011) 108(4) LSG 18   1.121
R (Supportways Community Services Ltd) v Hampshire County Council
    [2006] EWCA Civ 1035, [2006] BLGR 836, (2006) 9 CCL Rep 484   6.140
R (Suzuluk) v Governor HM Prison Full Sutton [2004] EWHC 514 (Admin),
    [2004] Prison LR 386, [2004] ACD 45   1.184
R (T) v Chief Constable of Greater Manchester [2013] EWCA Civ 25,
    [2013] 1 WLR 2515, [2013] 2 All ER 813, [2013] 1 Cr App R 27,
    [2013] HRLR 14   1.163
R (T) v Governors of Haberdashers' Aske's Hatcham College Trust [1995]
    ELR 350   11.18
R (T) v Governors of La Sainte Union Convent School [1996] ELR 98   11.74, 11.153
R (T) v Hackney LBC [1991] COD 454   11.94, 11.151
R (T) v Head Teacher of Elliott School [2002] ELR 556, [2002] All ER (D)
    537 (Jul), [2002] EWCA Civ 1349   11.132, 11.133, 11.138
R (T) v IAP for Devon CC and Governing Body of X College [2007] ELR
    499   11.95, 11.141
R (T) v Secretary of State for Education [2000] Ed CR 652   11.30
R (T) v Secretary of State for the Home Department [2010] EWHC 435
    (Admin)   1.55, 1.201
R (T) v Sheffield City Council [2013] EWHC 2953 (QB), (2013) 16 CCL
    Rep 580   1.151
R (T, D and B) v Haringey LBC [2005] EWHC 2235 (Admin)   6.52
R (Tabbakh) v The Staffordshire and West Midlands Probation Trust [2013]
    EWHC 2492 (Admin)   1.118, 1.121
R (Tarmohamed) v Education Committee of Leicester CC [1997] ELR 48,
    [1996] COD 286   11.93
R (Taylor) v Education Committee of Blackpool BC [1999] ELR 237   11.76, 11.95, 11.152
R (Taylor) v Haydn-Smith etc [2005] EWHC 1668 (Admin), [2005] All ER
    (D) 460 (May)   8.40
R (Thakrar) v Secretary of State for Justice [2012] EWHC 3538 (Admin),
    [2013] ACD 38   10.40
R (Theophilus) v London Borough of Lewisham [2002] EWHC 1371
    (Admin), [2002] 3 All ER 851, [2002] Eu LR 563, [2003] BLGR 98,
    [2002] ELR 719, (2002) *Independent*, 14 October   1.207
R (Thompson) v General Chiropractic Council [2008] EWHC 2499 (Admin) 15.145
R (Thompson) v Law Society [2004] EWCA Civ 167, [2004] 1 WLR 2522,
    [2004] 2 All ER 113, (2004) 101(13) LSG 35, (2004) 154 NLJ 307,
    (2004) 148 SJLB 265, (2004) *Times*, 1 April, (2004) *Independent*, 29
    March   15.38
R (ToTel Ltd) v First-tier Tribunal (Tax Chamber) [2012] EWCA Civ 1401,
    [2013] QB 860, [2013] 2 WLR 1136, [2013] STC 1557, [2012] BVC
    333, [2012] STI 3230, (2012) *Times*, 27 December   1.81
R (Townlink Limited) v Thames Magistrates' Court [2011] EWHC 898
    (Admin)   12.48
R (Tracey) v Cambridge University Hospital NHS Foundation Trust [2014]
    EWCA Civ 33   16.30, 16.31
R (Tucker) v Director General of the National Crime Squad [2003] EWCA
    Civ 2, (2003) 147 SJLB 114, [2003] NPC 14   1.154
R (TW Logistics) v Tendring District Council and Anglia Maltings
    (Holdings) Ltd [2013] EWCA Civ 9, [2013] 2 P & CR 9, [2013] 1
    EGLR 83, [2013] 14 EG 88, [2013] JPL 832   5.100
R (Uddin) v Crown Court at Isleworth [2013] EWHC Admin 2752   9.38
R (UK Real Estate Ltd) v London Borough of Camden [2013] EWHC 3505
    (Admin)   9.24
R (UK Uncut Legal Action Ltd) v Revenue and Customs Commissioners
    [2013] EWHC 1283 (Admin), [2013] STC 2357, 81 TC 890, [2013]
    BTC 467, [2013] STI 1849   1.107

R (Ullah) v Special Adjudicator, Do v Immigration Appeal Tribunal [2002]
EWCA Civ 1856, [2003] 1 WLR 770, [2003] INLR 74, [2003]
UKHRR 302, [2003] 3 All ER 1174, CA, [2004] UKHL 26, [2004] 2
AC 323, [2004] 3 WLR 23, [2004] UKHRR 995, [2004] INLR 381,
[2004] 3 All ER 785, HL 1.163, 1.170
R (Unison) v NHS Shared Business Services Ltd [2012] EWHC 624 (Admin),
[2012] ACD 84 .... 3.06
R (V) v Secretary of State for the Home Department [2013] EWHC 765
(Admin) 1.29
R (Van der Stolk) v Camden London Borough Council [2002] All ER (D)
309 (May), [2002] EWHC 1261 (Admin) 7.41
R (Van Hoogstraten) v Governor of HMP Belmarsh [2002] EWHC 1965
(Admin), [2003] 1 WLR 263, [2003] 4 All ER 309, [2003] Prison LR
6, [2003] ACD 19, (2002) 99(42) LSG 38, (2002) 152 NLJ 1531,
(2002) 146 SJLB 213, (2002) Times, 5 November, (2002)
Independent, 25 November 2.31, 10.91
R (Varma) v Duke of Kent [2004] EWHC 1705 (Admin), [2004] ELR 616,
[2004] ACD 81, (2004) Times, 23 July 1.127
R (VC) v Newcastle City Council [2011] EWHC 2673 (Admin), [2012] 2 All
ER 227, [2012] PTSR 546, [2012] 1 FLR 944, [2012] 1 FCR 206,
(2012) 15 CCL Rep 194, [2012] Fam Law 280 .... 1.108
R (Vieira and Saph) v London Borough of Camden & Bozi [2012] EWHC
287 .... 5.71
R (Vijayatunga) v Her Majesty the Queen in Council, sub nom R v
University of London Visitor, ex p Vijayatunga [1990] 2 QB 444,
[1989] 2 All ER 843, [1989] 3 WLR 13, 133 Sol Jo 818, [1989] 28
LS Gaz R 40 .... 11.26
R (W (A Minor)) v Education Appeal Committee of Lancashire CC [1994]
ELR 530, [1994] 3 FCR 1 .... 11.82
R (W) v Croydon London Borough Council [2011] EWHC 696 (Admin),
(2011) 14 CCL Rep 247, [2011] ACD 64 .... 1.123
R (W) v Doncaster Metropolitan Borough Council [2003] EWHC 192
(Admin), (2003) Times, 12 March, [2003] All ER (D) 177 (Feb) 8.25
R (W) v Governors of Bacon's City Technology College [1998] ELR 488 ..... 11.132
R (W) v Gwynedd County Council (1993) Times, 25 June 11.55
R (W) v Independent Appeal Panel of Bexley LBC [2008] EWHC 758
(Admin), [2008] ELR 301, [2008] All ER (D) 244 (Apr) 11.132, 11.141
R (W) v Kent County Council [2009] EWHC 1790 (Admin), [2009] ELR
536, [2009] All ER (D) 176 (Jul) 11.116
R (W) v Metropolitan Police Commissioner [2005] EWHC 1586 (Admin),
[2005] 1 WLR 3706, [2005] 3 All ER 749, (2005) 169 JP 473, [2005]
Po LR 202, (2005) 169 JPN 718, (2005) 155 NLJ 1184, (2005)
Times, 21 July, (2005) Independent, 22 July 1.201
R (W) v Northamptonshire County Council [1998] ELR 291 .... 11.139, 11.141
R (W) v Sheffield City Council [2005] EWHC 720 (Admin) 7.42
R (W) v Solihull BC [1997] ELR 489 .... 11.139
R (W) v Stockton on Tees BC [2000] ELR 93 .... 11.62
R (Wagstaff) v Secretary of State for Health [2001] 1 WLR 292, [2000]
HRLR 646, [2000] UKHRR 875, (2000) 56 BMLR 199, [2001] ACD
24, (2000) 97(37) LSG 39, (2000) 144 SJLB 249, (2000) Times, 31
August, (2000) Independent, 30 October 1.123
R (Waite) v Hammersmith and Fulham London Borough Council [2002]
EWCA Civ 482, [2003] HLR 3 .... 1.193
R (Wandsworth BC) v SSTLGR [2003] EWHC 622 (Admin), [2004] 1
P & CR 32, [2004] JPL 291, [2003] NPC 11 .... 5.115
R (Wandsworth LBC) v Schools Adjudicator [2003] EWHC 2969 (Admin),
[2004] ELR 274, [2003] All ER (D) 125 (Dec) 11.49
R (Warren) v HM Assistant Coroner for Northamptonshire [2008] EWHC
966 (Admin), [2008] Inquest LR 65 .... 10.124

R (Watford Grammar School for Girls) v Adjudicator for Schools [2003]
EWHC 2480 (Admin), [2004] ELR 40, (2003) *Times*, 27 October,
[2003] All ER (D) 135 (Oct)   11.50
R (Watkins-Singh) v Governing Body of Aberdare Girls' High School [2008]
EWHC 1865 (Admin), [2008] 3 FCR 203, [2008] ELR 561, [2008]
All ER (D) 376 (Jul)   11.149, 11.161
R (Watt) v Kesteven County Council [1955] 1 QB 408, [1955] 1 All ER 473,
[1955] 2 WLR 499, 53 LGR 254, 119 JP 220, 99 Sol Jo 149   11.55, 11.56
R (WB) v School Organisation Committee for Leeds [2002] EWHC 1927
(Admin), [2003] ELR 67, (2002) *Times*, 22 October, [2002] All ER
(D) 72 (Sep)   11.30
R (Weaver) v London & Quadrant Housing Trust [2008] EWHC 1377
(Admin), [2009] 1 All ER 17, (2008) 158 NLJ 969, [2008] NPC 74,
(2008) *Times*, 8 July   1.138
R (Weaver) v London & Quadrant Housing Trust [2009] EWCA Civ 587,
[2010] 1 WLR 363, [2009] 4 All ER 865, [2010] PTSR 1, [2009]
HRLR 29, [2009] UKHRR 1371, [2009] HLR 40, [2009] BLGR 962,
[2009] L & TR 26, [2009] 25 EG 137 (CS), (2009) 153(25) SJLB 30,
[2009] NPC 81, (2009) *Times*, 26 August   1.163, 7.20, 7.26, 7.28, 15.41
R (Webb) v Bristol CC [2001] EWHC 696 (Admin)   3.47
R (Weddle) v Secretary of State for Justice [2013] EWHC 2323 (Admin),
[2014] ACD 18   1.29, 10.24, 10.25
R (West) v Lloyd's of London [2004] EWCA Civ 506, [2004] 3 All ER 251,
[2004] 2 All ER (Comm) 1, [2004] 2 CLC 649, [2004] HRLR 27,
[2004] Lloyd's Rep IR 755, (2004) 148 SJLB 537   15.46
R (West) v Parole Board [2005] UKHL 1, [2005] 1 WLR 350, [2005] 1 All
ER 755, [2005] HRLR 8, 18 BHRC 267, [2005] 2 Prison LR 14,
(2005) 102(12) LSG 26, (2005) 149 SJLB 145, (2005) *Times*, 28
January, (2005) *Independent*, 2 February   10.57
R (Westminster City Council) v Middlesex Crown Court & Chorion PLC &
Fred Proud [2002] EWHC 1104 (Admin), [2002] All ER (D) 457
(May)   12.50, 12.61
R (Westminster City Council) v National Asylum Support Service [2001]
EWCA Civ 512, (2001) 33 HLR 938, CA, [2002] UKHL 38, [2002] 1
WLR 2956, [2002] 4 All ER 654, [2002] HLR 58, HL   1.139
R (Westwater) v Secretary of State for Justice [2010] EWHC 2403 (Admin),
[2011] 1 FLR 1989, [2011] Fam Law 13   10.43
R (Weszka) v Parole Board [2012] EWHC 827 (Admin)   10.59
R (Wheeler) v Assistant Commissioner of the Metropolitan Police [2008]
EWHC 439 (Admin), [2008] Po LR 48   15.147, 15.169
R (Wheeler) v Office of the Prime Minister [2008] EWHC 1409 (Admin),
[2008] ACD 70, (2008) 105(26) LSG 22   1.139
R (Whiston) v Secretary of State for Justice [2012] EWCA Civ 1374, [2014]
QB 306, [2013] 2 WLR 1080   10.68
R (Wildie) v Wakefield Metropolitan District Council [2013] EWHC 2769
(Admin)   1.158
R (Wilkinson) v Broadmoor Special Hospital Authority and Others [2001]
EWCA Civ 1545, [2002] 1 WLR 419, [2002] UKHRR 390, CA   3.10, 3.61, 6.131, 8.25, 8.40
R (Wilkinson) v Home Office [2013] EWHC 2889 (Admin)   10.42
R (Wilmot) v Secretary of State for Justice [2012] EWHC 3139 (Admin)   10.64
R (WK) v Secretary of State for the Home Department [2009] EWHC 939
(Admin), [2010] 1 FLR 193, [2009] Fam Law 659, 153 Sol Jo (no 20)
40, [2009] All ER (D) 70 (May)   6.131
R (Wood) v Commissioner of Police of the Metropolis [2009] EWCA Civ
414, [2010] 1 WLR 123, [2009] 4 All ER 951, [2010] EMLR 1,
[2009] HRLR 25, [2009] UKHRR 1254, [2009] Po LR 203, [2009]
ACD 75, (2009) 106(22) LSG 24, (2009) 153(21) SJLB 30, (2009)
Times, 1 June   1.184

R (Wood) v Secretary of State for Education [2011] EWHC 3256 (Admin),
[2012] ELR 172, [2012] ACD 24 .... 1.55, 1.140, 15.132
R (Wooder) v Feggetter [2002] EWCA Civ 554, [2003] QB 219, [2002] 3
WLR 591, [2002] MHLR 178, [2002] ACD 94, (2002) 99(22) LSG
33, (2002) 146 SJLB 125, (2002) Times, 28 May, (2002) Independent,
3 May 1.153, 1.154
R (Woods) v General Medical Council [2002] EWHC 1484 (Admin) 15.97
R (Woolas) v Parliamentary Election Court [2010] EWHC 3169 (Admin),
[2012] QB 1, [2011] 2 WLR 1362, [2011] ACD 20 .... 1.80
R (Wright) v Secretary of State for Health [2009] UKHL 3, [2009] 1 AC
739, [2009] 2 WLR 267, [2009] 2 All ER 129, [2009] PTSR 401,
[2009] HRLR 13, [2009] UKHRR 763, 26 BHRC 269, (2009) 12
CCL Rep 181, (2009) 106 BMLR 71, (2009) 106(5) LSG 15, (2009)
153(4) SJLB 30, (2009) Times, 23 January 1.163, 1.180
R (Wye Valley Action Association Ltd) v Herefordshire Council [2011]
EWCA Civ 20, [2011] PTSR 1011, [2011] Env LR 20, [2011] 2
P & CR 3, [2011] JPL 941, (2011) 155(4) SJLB 39, [2011] NPC 12 .... 1.152
R (X) v Governing Body of Gateway Primary School [2001] ELR 321 .... 11.152
R (X) v The Headteacher of Y School [2007] EWHC 298 (Admin), [2008] 1
All ER 249, [2007] LGR 698, [2007] ELR 278, [2007] All ER (D)
267 (Feb) 11.145
R (Yogathas) v SSHD [2003] 1 AC 920 .... 14.44
R (Young) v Oxford City Council [2002] EWCA Civ 990, [2002] 3 PLR 86,
[2003] JPL 232 .... 1.156
R (Zeqiri) v Secretary of State for the Home Department [2002] UKHL 3,
[2002] Imm AR 296, [2002] INLR 291, [2002] ACD 60, (2002)
Times, 15 February 1.201
R (Zia) v General Medical Council [2011] EWCA Civ 743, [2012] 1 WLR
504, [2012] ICR 146 .... 15.15, 15.137
R (ZO (Somalia)) v Secretary of State for the Home Department [2010]
UKSC 36, [2010] 1 WLR 1948, [2010] 4 All ER 649, [2010] INLR
503, (2010) Times, 25 October 1.203
R (Zurich Assurance Ltd t/a Threadneedle Property Investments) v North
Lincolnshire Council [2012] EWHC 3708 (Admin) 5.100
R and H v United Kingdom [2011] 2 FLR 1236, (2012) 54 EHRR 2, [2011]
Fam Law 924 .... 1.184
R v A (No 2) [2001] UKHL 25, [2002] 1 AC 45, [2001] 2 WLR 1546,
[2001] UKHRR 825, [2001] 3 All ER, HL 1.163
R v Abdroikov [2007] UKHL 37, [2007] 1 WLR 2679, [2008] 1 All ER
315, [2008] 1 Cr App R 21, [2008] Inquest LR 1, [2008] Crim LR
134, (2007) 151 SJLB 1365, (2007) Times, 8 November 1.130
R v Advertising Standards Authority, ex p City Trading [1997] COD 202 .... 3.45
R v Agricultural Dwelling-House Advisory Committee for Bedfordshire
Cambridgeshire and Northamptonshire, ex p Brough (1986) 19 HLR
367, [1987] 1 EGLR 106, 282 Estates Gazette 1542 .... 2.47
R v Amber Valley District Council, ex p Jackson [1984] 3 All ER 501,
[1985] 1 WLR 298, 50 P & CR 136, 128 Sol Jo 853, [1983] JPL 742 .... 12.35
R v Aylesbury Vale District Council ex p Chaplin (1998) 76 P & CR 207,
[1997] 3 PLR 55, [1998] JPL 49, (1997) Times, 19 August, (1997)
Independent, 6 October 5.110
R v Bacon's School Governors, ex p Inner London Education Authority
[1990] COD 414, (1990) Independent, 29 March 2.124
R v Barnes (1910) 102 LT 860 .... 9.53
R v Barnet London Borough Council ex p Shah [1983] 2 AC 309, [1983] 2
WLR 16, [1983] 1 All ER 226, 81 LGR 305, (1983) 133 NLJ 61,
(1983) 127 SJ 36 .... 16.39
R v Barnet London Borough Council, ex p Babalola (1996) 28 HLR 196 .... 1.117
R v Barnet Magistrates' Court, ex p Cantor [1998] 2 All ER 333, [1999] 1
WLR 334 .... 2.22

R v Barnsley MBC, ex p Hook [1976] 3 All ER 452, [1976] 1 WLR 1052,
   74 LGR 493, 140 JP 638, 120 Sol Jo 182 — 2.61
R v Berkshire County Council, ex p Parker (1996) 95 LGR 449 — 6.14, 6.17, 6.152
R v Birmingham City Council and Birmingham University [2009] EWHC
   688 (Admin), [2009] All ER (D) 68 (Jul) — 6.36
R v Birmingham City Council, ex p Ferrero Ltd [1993] 1 All ER 530, 89
   LGR 977, 155 JP 721, [1991] 26 LS Gaz R 32 — 3.18
R v Birmingham City Council, ex p Taj Mohammed (1998) 1 CCLR 441 — 6.17
R v Birmingham City Justice, ex p Chris Foreign Foods (Wholesalers) Ltd
   [1970] 1 WLR 1428, [1970] 3 All ER 945, 68 LGR 737, (1970) 114
   SJ 682 — 1.86
R v Birmingham Mental Health Trust, ex p Phillips (C/O/1501/95) — 8.12
R v Blundeston Board of Visitors, ex p Fox-Taylor [1982] 1 All ER 646,
   [1982] Crim LR 119, (1981) *Times*, 29 October — 2.61, 10.89
R v Board of Visitors of Dartmoor Prison, ex p Smith [1987] QB 106,
   [1986] 2 All ER 651, [1986] 3 WLR 61, 130 Sol Jo 505 — 2.38, 10.78
R v Board of Visitors of Hull Prison, ex p St Germain [1979] QB 425,
   [1979] 1 All ER 701, [1979] 2 WLR 42, 68 Cr App Rep 212, 122 Sol
   Jo 697 — 9.13
R v Boundary Commission for England, ex p Foot [1983] QB 600, [1983] 1
   All ER 1099, [1983] 2 WLR 458, 127 Sol Jo 155 — 2.119
R v Bournemouth Crown Court, ex p Weight [1984] 1 WLR 980, 148 JP
   335, [1984] Crim LR 293 — 9.26
R v Bournewood Community and Mental Health NHS Trust, ex p L [1999]
   1 AC 458, [1998] 3 All ER 289, [1998] 3 WLR 107, [1998] 2 FCR
   501, [1998] 2 FLR 550, [1998] Fam Law 592, 44 BMLR 1, [1998]
   29 LS Gaz R 27, [1998] NLJR 1014, 142 Sol Jo LB 195 — 8.09, 8.77
R v Bow Street Metropolitan Stipendiary Magistrate, ex p Pinochet Ugarte
   (No 2) [2000] 1 AC 119, [1999] 2 WLR 272, [1999] 1 All ER 577, 6
   BHRC 1, (1999) 11 Admin LR 57, (1999) 96(6) LSG 33, (1999) 149
   NLJ 88, (1999) *Times*, 18 January, (1999) *Independent*, 19 January — 1.133
R v Boxall v Mayor and Burgess of Waltham Forest London Borough
   Council (2001) 4 CCLR 258 — 3.78
R v Bradford MBC, ex p Skiandar Ali [1994] ELR 299, [1993] 40 LS Gaz R
   42, 137 Sol Jo LB 232 — 11.152
R v Brent Health Authority, ex p Francis [1985] QB 869, [1985] 1 All ER
   74, [1984] 3 WLR 1317, 128 Sol Jo 815 — 2.118
R v Brent LBC, ex p Baruwa [1997] 3 FCR 97, (1997) 29 HLR 915, [1997]
   COD 450, (1997) *Independent*, 27 February — 1.155, 1.157
R v Brent LBC, ex p Gunning (1985) 84 LGR 168 — 1.142, 1.144
R v Brent LBC, ex p O'Connor (1999) 31 HLR 923 — 7.37, 7.39
R v Brent LBC, ex p O'Malley (1997) 30 HLR 328, (1997) 10 Admin LR
   265 — 2.116
R v Brent LBC, ex p Sadiq (2001) 33 HLR 47 — 7.37, 7.40
R v Brentford General Cssrs, ex p Chan [1986] STC 46 — 3.18
R v Bristol CC, ex p Penfold [1998] 1 CCLR 315 — 6.17, 6.32
R v Bristol Corpn, ex p Hendy [1974] 1 All ER 1047, [1974] 1 WLR 498,
   72 LGR 405, 27 P & CR 180, 117 Sol Jo 912 — 2.30
R v Bristol Magistrates' Court, ex p Hodge [1997] QB 974, [1996] 4 All ER
   924, [1997] 2 WLR 756, [1997] 1 FCR 412, [1997] 1 FLR 88,
   [1997] Fam Law 89 — 9.80
R v Broadcasting Complaints Commission, ex p Owen [1985] QB 1153,
   [1985] 2 All ER 522, [1985] 2 WLR 1025, 129 Sol Jo 349 — 3.63
R v Bromley Licensing Justices, ex p Bromley Licensed Victuallers [1984] 1
   All ER 794, [1984] 1 WLR 585, 148 JP 496, 128 Sol Jo 264, [1984]
   LS Gaz R 663 — 2.120
R v Bromley London Borough Council, ex p Lambeth London Borough
   Council (1984) *Times*, 16 June — 2.71, 2.74
R v Bromley Magistrates' Court, ex p Smith [1995] 4 All ER 146, [1995] 1
   WLR 944, [1995] 2 Cr App Rep 285, 159 JP 251, [1995] Crim LR
   248, [1995] 02 LS Gaz R 36 — 2.120

Table of Cases   lxxxix

R v Cambourne Justices, ex p Pearce [1954] 2 All ER 850 . . . . 9.75
R v Camden LBC, ex p Mohammed (1998) 30 HLR 315 . . . . 7.37, 7.45, 7.47
R v Canterbury City Council ex p Springimage Ltd [1993] 3 PLR 58 . . . . 5.66
R v Cardiff City Council, ex p Barry (1990) 22 HLR 261, [1990] COD 94 . . . . 7.98
R v Cardiff Crown Court, ex p Jones [1974] QB 113, [1973] 3 All ER 1027,
    [1973] 3 WLR 497, 58 Cr App Rep 85, 138 JP 75, 117 Sol Jo 634 . . . . 9.33
R v Central Arbitration Committee, ex p BTP Tioxide Ltd [1981] ICR 843,
    [1982] IRLR 60 . . . . 15.62
R v Central Criminal Court and Nadir, ex p Director of the Serious Fraud
    Office [1993] 2 All ER 399, [1993] 1 WLR 949, 96 Cr App Rep 248,
    [1993] Crim LR 134 . . . . 9.32
R v Central Criminal Court, ex p Crook [1995] 1 All ER 537, [1995] 1
    WLR 139, [1995] 2 Cr App Rep 212, [1995] 2 FCR 153, [1995] 1
    FLR 132, [1995] Fam Law 73, 159 JP 295, [1995] Crim LR 509,
    [1994] 39 LS Gaz R 38, 138 Sol Jo LB 199 . . . . 9.34
R v Central Criminal Court, ex p Raymond [1986] 2 All ER 379, [1986] 1
    WLR 710, 83 Cr App Rep 94, 130 Sol Jo 430, [1986] LS Gaz R
    1553, [1986] NLJ Rep 395 . . . . 9.34
R v Central London County Court, ex p London [1999] QB 1260, [1999] 3
    All ER 991, [1999] 3 WLR 1, [1999] 2 FLR 161, [1999] Fam Law
    452, [1999] 15 LS Gaz R 30 . . . . 8.32
R v Chance, ex p Coopers & Lybrand [1995] BCC 1095, (1995) 7 Admin
    LR 821, (1995) Times, 28 January 1.123, 15.34
R v Charity Commissioners for England and Wales, ex p Baldwin (2001) 33
    HLR 538 . . . . 1.80
R v Chelmsford Crown Court, ex p Chief Constable of the Essex Police
    [1994] 1 All ER 325, [1994] 1 WLR 359, 99 Cr App Rep 59, [1994]
    Crim LR 56 . . . . 9.25
R v Chelsea College of Art and Design, ex p Nash [2000] Ed CR 571,
    [2000] ELR 686 . . . . 1.127
R v Chester City Council, ex p Quietlynn (1983) Times, 19 October   12.72, 12.74, 12.86, 12.87
R v Chester Crown Court, ex p Pascoe & Jones (1987) 151 JP 752, [1987]
    BSMD 237 . . . . 12.61
R v Chesterfield Borough Council, ex p Darker Enterprises Ltd [1992] COD
    466 . . . . 12.28, 12.33
R v Chichester Crown Court, ex p Abodunrin and Sogbanmu (1984) 79 Cr
    App Rep 293, 149 JP 54, [1984] Crim LR 240 . . . . 9.28
R v Chief Constable of Kent, ex p L [1993] 1 All ER 756, 93 Cr App Rep
    416, 155 JP 760, [1991] Crim LR 841 . . . . 9.22, 9.41
R v Chief Constable of Lancashire, ex p Parker [1993] QB 577, [1993] 2 All
    ER 56, [1993] 2 WLR 428, 97 Cr App Rep 90, [1993] Crim LR 204,
    [1992] 20 LS Gaz R 37, [1992] NLJR 635, 136 Sol Jo LB 136 . . . . 2.105
R v Chief Constable of Merseyside Police, ex p Bennion [2001] ACD 114 . . . . . . 3.18
R v Chief Constable of Ministry of Defence Police, ex p Sweeney [1999]
    COD 122 CA 15.37, 15.56
R v Chief Constable of North Wales and Others, ex p Thorpe [1999] QB
    396, [1998] 3 All ER 310, [1998] 3 WLR 57, [1998] 3 FCR 371,
    [1998] 2 FLR 571, [1998] Fam Law 529, [1998] 17 LS Gaz R 29 . . . . 9.13
R v Chief Constable of Sussex, ex p International Trader's Ferry Ltd [1999]
    2 AC 418, [1998] 3 WLR 1260, [1999] 1 All ER 129, [1999] 1
    CMLR 1320, (1999) 11 Admin LR 97, (1998) 95(47) LSG 29, (1998)
    148 NLJ 1750, (1998) 142 SJLB 286, (1998) Times, 16 November 1.207
R v Chief Constable of the Merseyside Police, ex p Calveley [1986] QB 424,
    [1986] 2 WLR 144, [1986] 1 All ER 257, [1986] IRLR 177, (1985)
    Times, 28 November 15.128
R v Chief Constable of the Merseyside Police, ex p Merrill [1989] 1 WLR
    1077, [1990] COD 61, (1989) 153 LG Rev 1010, (1989) Times, 19
    May 15.127
R v Chief Constable of the Thames Valley Police, ex p Cotton [1990] IRLR
    344, (1989) Times, 28 December, (1989) Independent, 22 December 1.126

R v Chief Constable of the Thames Valley Police, ex p Police Complaints
Authority [1996] COD 324 .... 1.86, 15.199
R v Chief Constable of the West Midlands Police, ex p Carroll (1995) 7
Admin LR 45, (1994) *Times*, 20 May, (1994) *Independent*, 6 June 15.163
R v Chief Immigration Officer, Gatwick Airport, ex p Kharrazi [1980] 1
WLR 1396 .... 2.61
R v Chief Immigration Officer, Lympne Airport, ex p Amrik Singh [1969] 1
QB 333, [1968] 3 All ER 163, [1968] 3 WLR 945, 112 Sol Jo 657 .... 2.61
R v Chief National Insurance Commissioner, ex p Connor [1981] QB 758,
[1981] 1 All ER 769, [1981] 2 WLR 412, [1980] Crim LR 579, 124
Sol Jo 478 .... 2.24, 2.117
R v Chief Rabbi, ex p Wachmann [1992] 1 WLR 1036, [1993] 2 All ER
249, (1991) 3 Admin LR 721, [1991] COD 309, (1991) *Times*, 7
February 1.80, 15.41, 15.49
R v City & County of Swansea, ex p Julie Amanda Jones (1996)
CO1996/3187/95 unreported 12.61
R v City of Westminster Housing Benefit Review Board, ex p Mehanne
[2001] UKHL 11, [2001] 1 WLR 539, [2001] 2 All ER 690, (2001)
33 HLR 46, [2001] NPC 51, (2001) *Independent*, 30 April 1.104
R v Clerkenwell Stipendiary Magistrate, ex p DPP [1984] QB 821, [1984] 2
All ER 193, [1984] 2 WLR 244, 79 Cr App Rep 141, 148 JP 39, 128
Sol Jo 33, [1984] LS Gaz R 359 .... 9.61
R v Commission for Racial Equality, ex p Hillingdon London Borough
Council [1982] AC 779, [1982] 3 WLR 159, 80 LGR 737, [1982]
IRLR 424, 126 Sol Jo 449, HL, Affirming [1982] QB 276, [1981] 3
WLR 520, 80 LGR 157, 125 Sol Jo 623, CA 2.54, 2.61
R v Commissioners of Customs and Excise, ex p Lunn Poly Ltd [1999]
EuLR 653 .... 1.98
R v Committee of Lloyd's, ex p Moran (1983) *Times*, 24 June 15.47, 15.48
R v Committee of Lloyd's, ex p Posgate (1983) *Times*, 12 January 15.47, 15.48
R v Commonwealth Public Services Commission, ex p Killeen (1914) 18
CLR 586 (Aust) 2.119
R v Commr for Local Administration, ex p Croydon London Borough
Council, *sub nom* R v Local Ombudsman, ex p London Borough of
Croydon [1989] 1 All ER 1033, [1989] Fam Law 187, [1989] COD
226 .... 11.82, 11.87
R v Commr for Local Administration, ex p Field [2000] COD 58 .... 3.55
R v Commr of the Police for the Metropolis, ex p Blackburn [1968] 2 QB
118, [1968] 1 All ER 763, [1968] 2 WLR 893, 112 Sol Jo 112 .... 9.44
R v Comptroller-General of Patents [1899] 1 QB 909, 68 LJQB 568, 16
RPC 233, 47 WR 567, 80 LT 777, 15 TLR 310 .... 9.46
R v Cornwall County Council, ex p Huntingdon [1992] 3 All ER 566,
[1992] NLJR 348 .... 3.08
R v Cornwall County Council, ex p Nicholls [1989] COD 507 .... 2.121
R v Costwold DC, ex p Kissel (1997) Unreported, 28 February 3.78
R v Council of Legal Education Board of Examiners, ex p Joseph [1994]
COD 318 .... 15.77
R v Council of Lloyd's, ex p Johnson, unreported, 16 August 1996 .... 15.46
R v Coventry CC, ex p Phoenix Aviation [1995] 3 All ER 37, [1995] NLJR
559 .... 2.105
R v CPS, ex p Waterworth (1995) Unreported 9.44
R v Criminal Injuries Compensation Board, ex p A [1999] 2 AC 330, [1999]
2 WLR 974, [1999] COD 244, 143 Sol Jo LB 120 .... 2.109, 3.16, 3.29
R v Criminal Injuries Compensation Board, ex p Lain [1967] 2 QB 864,
[1967] 2 All ER 770, [1967] 3 WLR 348, 111 Sol Jo 331 .... 2.42, 2.46
R v Cripps, ex p Muldoon [1984] QB 68, [1983] 3 All ER 72, [1983] 3
WLR 465, 82 LGR 439, 127 Sol Jo 427, 133 NLJ 848 .... 2.61
R v Crown Court at Knightsbridge, ex p Marcrest Ltd [1983] 1 All ER
1148, [1983] 1 WLR 300 .... 2.117

R v Crown Court at Southwark, ex p Bowles [1998] AC 641, [1998] 2 WLR 715, [1998] 2 All ER 193, [1998] 2 Cr App R 187, [1999] Crim LR 220, (1998) 95(18) LSG 32, (1998) 148 NLJ 588, (1998) 142 SJLB 126, (1998) *Times*, 7 April	1.64, 1.113
R v Crown Court at Stafford, ex p Wil Gilbert (Staffs) Ltd [1999] 2 All ER 955, [1999] COD 26	1.156
R v Crown Court of Southwark, ex p Samuel [1995] COD 249	1.156
R v Croydon, ex p AW [2005] EWHC 2950 (Admin), [2006] LGR 159, [2005] All ER (D) 251 (Dec)	6.133
R v Customs and Excise Commissioners (1836) 5 Ad & El 380	2.79
R v Customs and Excise Commissioners, ex p Cooke and Stevenson [1970] 1 All ER 1068, [1970] 1 WLR 450, 114 Sol Jo 34	2.79
R v Dacorum District Council ex p Cannon [1996] 2 PLR 45	5.20
R v Dairy Produce Quota Tribunal for England and Wales, ex p Caswell [1990] AC 738	2.111, 2.112
R v Dairy Produce Quota Tribunal, ex p S Dimelow Farms (1988) *Times*, 7 November	2.61
R v Dairy Produce Quota Tribunal, ex p Wynn Jones [1987] 2 EGLR 9, 283 Estates Gazette 643	3.15
R v Department for Education and Employment, ex p Begbie [2000] 1 WLR 1115, [2000] Ed CR 140, [2000] ELR 445, (1999) 96(35) LSG 39, (1999) *Times*, 14 September	1.21, 1.67, 1.138, 1.139
R v Deputy Governor of Parkhurst Prison, ex p Hague [1992] 1 AC 58, [1991] 3 All ER 733, [1991] 3 WLR 340, 135 Sol Jo LB 102	2.88, 2.122
R v Derbyshire County Council ex p Woods [1998] Env LR 277, [1997] JPL 958	5.95, 5.100
R v Derbyshire County Council, ex p Times Supplements Ltd (1991) 3 Admin LR 241, [1991] COD 129, (1991) 155 LG Rev 123, (1990) 140 NLJ 1421, (1990) *Times*, 19 July	1.58, 1.59
R v Devon County Council, ex p Baker [1995] 1 All ER 73, 91 LGR 479, (1994) 6 Admin LR 113, [1993] COD 253, (1993) *Times*, 21 January, (1993) *Independent*, 22 February	1.147, 6.152
R v Devon County Council, ex p O, Adoption [1997] 2 FLR 388, [1997] 3 FCR 411, [1997] COD 369, [1997] Fam Law 390	1.123
R v Director of Public Prosecutions, ex p Association of First Division Civil Servants (1988) 138 NLJ Rep 158, (1988) *Times*, 24 May, (1988) *Independent*, 24 May, (1988) Guardian, 24 May	1.83
R v Director of Public Prosecutions, ex p Kebilene [2000] 2 AC 326, [1999] 3 WLR 972, [1999] 4 All ER 801, [2000] 1 Cr App R 275, [2000] HRLR 93, [2000] UKHRR 176, (2000) 2 LGLR 697, (1999) 11 Admin LR 1026, [2000] Crim LR 486, (1999) 96(43) LSG 32, (1999) *Times*, 2 November	1.48
R v Director of Public Prosecutions, ex p Manning [2001] QB 330, [2000] 3 WLR 463, [2001] HRLR 3, [2000] Inquest LR 133, [2000] Po LR 172, (2000) *Times*, 19 May, (2000) *Independent*, 6 June	1.153
R v Director of the Serious Fraud Office, ex p Smith [1993] AC 1, [1992] 3 WLR 66, [1992] 3 All ER 456, [1992] BCLC 879, (1992) 95 Cr App R 191, [1992] Crim LR 504, [1992] COD 270, (1992) 89(27) LSG 34, (1992) 142 NLJ 895, (1992) 136 SJLB 182, (1992) *Times*, 16 June, (1992) *Independent*, 12 June, (1992) *Financial Times*, 17 June, (1992) *The Guardian*, 1 July	1.55, 1.201
R v Disciplinary Committee of the Jockey Club, ex p Aga Khan [1993] 1 WLR 909, [1993] 2 All ER 853, [1993] COD 234, (1993) 143 NLJ 163, (1992) *Times*, 9 December, (1992) *Independent*, 22 December	15.19, 15.41, 15.45
R v Disciplinary Committee of the Jockey Club, ex p Massingberd-Mundy [1993] 2 All ER 207, (1990) 2 Admin LR 609, [1990] COD 260	15.41, 15.45
R v District Auditor, ex p Leicester City Council [1985] RVR 191	2.197
R v District Auditor, ex p West Yorkshire Metropolitan CC [1986] RVR 24	2.197
R v Doncaster Justices, ex p Langfield (1984) 149 JP 26, [1985] BSMD 46	12.99, 12.100

R v Doncaster Metropolitan Borough Council, ex p Nortrop (1996) 28 HLR
    862 .... 1.157
R v Dorking Justices, ex p Harrington [1984] AC 743, [1984] 3 WLR 142,
    [1984] 2 All ER 474, (1984) 79 Cr App R 305, (1985) 149 JP 211,
    [1984] Crim LR 622, (1984) 81 LSG 2142, (1984) 134 NLJ 567,
    (1984) SJ 434 .... 1.77
R v Dorset Police Authority, ex p Vaughan [1995] COD 153, (1994)
    Independent, 10 October 1.77
R v DPP, ex p Burke [1997] 2 CL 184 .... 9.41
R v DPP, ex p Camelot plc (1998) 10 Admin L Rep 93 .... 3.51, 9.44, 9.45
R v DPP, ex p Kebilene [2000] 2 AC 326, [1999] 3 WLR 972, [1999] 4 All
    ER 801, [2000] 1 Cr App R 275, [2000] HRLR 93, [2000] UKHRR
    176, (2000) 2 LGLR 697, (1999) 11 Admin LR 1026, [2000] Crim
    LR 486, (1999) 96(43) LSG 32, (1999) *Times*, 2 November 1.48, 1.139
R v DPP, ex p M and R v CPS ex p Hitchins (1997) Unreported 9.44
R v DPP, ex p Panayiotu [1997] COD 83 .... 9.44
R v DPP, ex p Treadway (1997) *Times*, 31 October 9.44
R v Drew [2003] UKHL 25, [2003] All ER (D) 100 (May), HL 8.21, 8.34
R v Dudley Justices, ex p Curlett [1974] 2 All ER 38, [1974] 1 WLR 457,
    138 JP 335, 118 Sol Jo 220 .... 2.61
R v Durham County Council, ex p Huddleston [2000] 1 WLR 1484, [2000]
    2 CMLR 229, [2000] 1 PLR 122, [2000] 13 LS Gaz R 43, [2000]
    EGCS 39, [2000] JPL 1125, [2000] All ER (D) 297 .... 2.11, 5.57
R v Ealing Local Health Authority, ex p Fox [1993] 3 All ER 170, [1993] 1
    WLR 373, 11 BMLR 59, 136 Sol Jo LB 220 .... 2.53
R v East Dereham Justices, ex p Clark [1996] COD 196, (1996)
    Independent, 29 January 1.127
R v East Sussex CC ex p Reprotech (Pebsham) [2002] UKHL 8, [2003] 1
    WLR 348, [2002] 4 All ER 58, [2003] 1 P & CR 5, [2002] 2 PLR
    60, [2002] JPL 821, [2002] 10 EG 158 (CS), [2002] NPC 32, (2002)
    Times, 5 March 5.115
R v Edmunsbury and Ipswich Diocese (Chancellor), ex p White [1948] 1 KB
    195, [1947] 2 All ER 170, 63 TLR 523, 177 LT 488, (1947) 91 SJ
    369 .... 1.80
R v Electricity Cssrs, ex p London Electricity Joint Committee Co (1920) Ltd
    [1924] 1 KB 171 .... 2.38
R v Elmbridge Borough Council, ex p Activeoffice Ltd [1998] 01 LS Gaz R
    24, (1997) *Times*, 29 December 9.41
R v Elmbridge Borough Council, ex p Health Care Corporation (1992) 4
    Admin LR 242, (1992) 63 P & CR 260, [1991] 3 PLR 63, [1992] JPL
    39, [1992] COD 85, (1992) 156 LG Rev 462, (1991) *Times*, 2 July 15.62, 15.115
R v Environment Agency, ex p Mayer Parry Recycling Ltd [2000] EWHC
    Admin 388, [2003] ECR I-6163, [2005] All ER (EC) 647, [2004] 1
    WLR 538, [2003] 3 CMLR 195, (2003) *Times*, 14 July, [2003] All
    ER (D) 276 (Jun) 2.13, 2.18
R v Essex Quarter Sessions, ex p Thomas [1966] 1 All ER 353, [1966] 1
    WLR 359, 130 JP 121, 110 Sol Jo 188 .... 12.44
R v Falmouth and Truro Port Health Authority ex p South West Water
    [2001] QB 445, [2000] 3 WLR 1464, [2000] 3 All ER 306, [2000]
    Env LR 658, [2000] EHLR 306, [2000] 2 LGLR 1061, [2000] JPL
    1174 (Note), [2000] EG 50 (CS), (2000) 97(23) LSG 41, [2000] NPC
    36, (2000) *Times*, 24 April 5.38, 15.53
R v Feltham Justices, ex p Rees [2001] 2 Cr App R 1, [2001] Crim LR 47,
    [2000] All ER (D) 1623 .... 9.50
R v Fernhill Manor School, ex p A [1994] 1 FCR 146, [1993] 1 FLR 620,
    [1993] Fam Law 202, [1994] ELR 67, [1992] COD 446, (1992)
    Times, 5 June, (1992) *Independent*, 25 June 11.18, 11.126
R v Flintshire CC, ex p Armstrong-Braun [2001] EWCA Civ 345   13.133, 13.134, 13.135,
                                                                    13.136, 13.137, 13.138, 13.139

R v Football Association Ltd, ex p Football League Ltd [1993] 2 All ER 833, (1992) 4 Admin LR 623, [1992] COD 52, (1991) *Times*, 22 August 15.41
R v Fulham, Hammersmith and Kensington Rent Tribunal, ex p Zerek [1951] 2 KB 1, [1951] 1 All ER 482, 49 LGR 275, 115 JP 132, 95 Sol Jo 237, [1951] 1 TLR 423 2.61
R v Gaming Board for Great Britain, ex p Benaim and Khaida [1970] 2 QB 417, [1970] 2 All ER 528, [1970] 2 WLR 1009, 134 JP 513, 114 Sol Jo 266 2.61
R v General Council of the Bar, ex p Percival [1991] 1 QB 212, [1990] 3 WLR 323, [1990] 3 All ER 137, (1990) 2 Admin LR 711, (1990) 87(24) LSG 44 15.50, 15.65, 15.197
R v General Medical Council, ex p Colman [1990] 1 All ER 489, (1990) 2 Admin LR 469, (1990) 9 Tr LR 108, [1990] COD 202, (1989) 139 NLJ 1753, (1989) *Times*, 8 December, (1989) *Independent*, 12 December, (1989) *The Guardian*, 12 December 15.201
R v General Medical Council, ex p Richards [2001] Lloyd's Rep Med 47, (2001) *Times*, 24 January 15.27, 15.65, 15.97
R v General Medical Council, ex p St Georges University, unreported, 30 November 1994, DC 15.83
R v General Medical Council, ex p Toth [2000] 1 WLR 2209, [2000] Lloyd's Rep Med 368, (2001) 61 BMLR 149, R (Woods) v General Medical Council [2002] EWHC 1484 (Admin) 15.97, 15.113
R v GLC, ex p Royal Borough of Kensington and Chelsea (1982) *Times*, 7 April 2.117
R v Gloucester Crown Court, ex p Chester (1998) *Independent*, 6 July 9.55, 9.75
R v Gloucestershire CC, ex p Barry [1997] AC 584, [1997] 2 All ER 1, [1997] 2 WLR 459, 95 LGR 638, 36 BMLR 69, [1997] NLJR 453, 141 Sol Jo LB 91, 1 CCL Rep 40 6.17, 6.24, 6.27, 6.29, 6.152
R v Gough [1993] AC 646, [1993] 2 WLR 883, [1993] 2 All ER 724, (1993) 97 Cr App R 188, (1993) 157 JP 612, [1993] Crim LR 886, (1993) 157 JPN 394, (1993) 143 NLJ 775, (1993) 137 SJLB 168, (1993) *Times*, 24 May, (1993) *Independent*, 26 May, (1993) *The Guardian*, 22 May 1.127, 1.129, 1.133, 11.138
R v Governor HMP Frankland, ex p Russell & Wharrie, unreported, 10 July 2000 10.35
R v Governor of Brixton Prison, ex p Armah [1968] AC 192, [1966] 3 WLR 828, [1966] 3 All ER 177, (1967) 131 JP 43, (1966) 110 SJ 890 1.75
R v Governor of Brixton Prison, ex p Levin [1997] AC 741, [1997] 3 WLR 117, [1997] 3 All ER 289, [1998] 1 Cr App R 22, [1997] Crim LR 891, (1997) 94(30) LSG 28, (1997) 147 NLJ 990, (1997) 141 SJLB 148, (1997) *Times*, 21 June, (1997) *Independent*, 2 July 1.79
R v Governor of Brockhill Prison, ex p Evans (No 2) [1999] QB 1043, [1998] 4 All ER 993, [1999] 2 WLR 103, [1998] 33 LS Gaz R 35, 142 Sol Jo LB 196, [1998] All ER (D) 286 2.105
R v Governor of Durham Prison, ex p Hardial Singh [1984] 1 WLR 704 14.53, 14.54
R v Governors of Dunraven School, ex p B [2000] ELR 156, [2000] LGR 494, [2000] 04 LS Gaz R 32, 144 Sol Jo LB 51, [2000] All ER (D) 02 11.132, 11.133
R v Governors of the Bishop Challoner Roman Catholic Comprehensive Girls' School, ex p Purkayastha, *sub nom* Choudhury v Governors of Bishop Challoner Roman Catholic Comprehensive School [1992] 2 AC 182, [1992] 3 All ER 277, [1992] 3 WLR 99, 90 LGR 445, [1992] 2 FCR 507, [1992] 2 FLR 444, [1993] Fam Law 23, [1992] 27 LS Gaz R 36 11.70, 11.74
R v Great Yarmouth BC, ex p Botton Bros Arcades Ltd (1987) 56 P & CR 99, [1988] JPL 18 2.45
R v H [2003] UKHL 1, [2003] 1 WLR 411, [2003] 1 All ER 497, [2003] 2 Cr App R 2, (2003) 167 JP 125, [2003] HRLR 19, (2003) 71 BMLR 146, [2003] MHLR 209, [2003] Crim LR 817, (2003) 167 JPN 155, (2003) 100(12) LSG 30, (2003) 147 SJLB 146, (2003) *Times*, 31 January, (2003) *Independent*, 4 February 1.178

R v Hackney LBC, ex p Structadene Ltd [2001] 2 All ER 225, [2001] LGR
204, 82 P & CR 328, [2001] 12 EG 168, [2001] 01 LS Gaz R 23,
[2000] All ER (D) 1800 .... 13.99, 13.102
R v Hammersmith and Fulham LBC, ex p Fleck (1997) 30 HLR 679 .... 7.47
R v Hammersmith and Fulham London Borough Council, ex p Burkett
[2002] UKHL 23, [2002] 1 WLR 1593, [2002] 3 All ER 97, [2002]
CP Rep 66, [2003] Env LR 6, [2003] 1 P & CR 3, [2002] 2 PLR 90,
[2002] JPL 1346, [2002] ACD 81, [2002] 22 EG 136 (CS), (2002)
99(27) LSG 34, (2002) 152 NLJ 847, (2002) 146 SJLB 137, [2002]
NPC 75, (2002) Times, 24 May, (2002) Independent, 28 May 3.07, 7.13, 7.39, 15.52
R v Hampshire County Council, ex p W [1994] ELR 460 .... 1.91
R v Harrow Crown Court ex p Perkins (1998) Times, 28 April 9.26, 9.29, 9.34
R v Harrow London Borough Council, ex p Chavad [2007] EWHC 3064
(Admin), [2008] LGR 657, 100 BMLR 27, [2007] All ER (D) 337
(Dec) 6.25
R v Hatfield Justices, ex p Castle [1980] 3 All ER 509, [1981] 1 WLR 217,
71 Cr App Rep 287, 145 JP 265, [1980] Crim LR 579, 125 Sol Jo
165 .... 9.23
R v Health and Safety Commission, ex p Spelthorne Borough Council (1983)
Times, 18 July 2.61
R v Hendon Justices, ex p DPP [1994] QB 167, [1993] 1 All ER 411, [1993]
2 WLR 862, 96 Cr App Rep 227, 157 JP 181, [1993] Crim LR 215,
[1992] NLJR 1303 .... 2.49
R v Hereford and Worcester County Council, ex p Smith (Tommy) [1994]
COD 129 .... 2.118
R v Hereford Magistrates' Court, ex p Rowlands and Ingram, R v Harrow
Youth Court, ex p Prussia [1998] QB 110, [1997] 2 WLR 854, 161
JP 258 .... 9.52, 9.53
R v Higher Education Funding Council, ex p Institute of Dental Surgery
[1994] 1 WLR 242, [1994] 1 All ER 651, [1994] COD 147, (1993)
Independent, 28 September 1.153, 15.83
R v Hillingdon Health Authority, ex p Goodwin [1984] ICR 800 .... 2.118
R v Hillingdon LBC, ex p Royco Homes Ltd [1974] 2 QB 720, [1974] 2 All
ER 643 .... 2.52, 2.61
R v Hillingdon LBC, ex p Streeting [1980] 3 All ER 413, [1980] 1 WLR
1425, 79 LGR 167, 10 Fam Law 249, 124 Sol Jo 514 .... 2.42
R v Hillingdon LBC, ex p Tinn (1988) 152 LGR 750, [1988] Fam Law 388,
20 HLR 305 .... 7.63
R v Hillingdon London Borough Council, ex p Puhlhofer [1986] AC 484,
[1986] 2 WLR 259, [1986] 1 All ER 467, [1986] 1 FLR 22, (1986)
18 HLR 158, [1986] Fam Law 218, (1986) 83 LSG 785, (1986) 136
NLJ 140, (1986) 130 SJ 143 .... 1.20, 7.30
R v HM Treasury, ex p Daily Mail & General Trust Plc [1989] QB 446,
[1989] 2 WLR 908, [1989] 1 All ER 328, [1988] STC 787, [1988]
ECR 5483, [1989] BCLC 206, [1988] 3 CMLR 713, (1989) 133 SJ
693, (1988) Times, 29 September 1.207
R v HM Treasury, ex p Petch [1990] COD 19 .... 2.84
R v HM Treasury, ex p Smedley [1985] QB 657, [1985] 1 All ER 589,
[1985] 2 WLR 576, [1985] 1 CMLR 665, 129 Sol Jo 48 .... 2.50
R v Honourable Society of the Middle Temple, ex p Bullock [1996] ELR
349, [1996] COD 376 .... 15.195
R v Horncastle [2009] UKSC 14, [2010] 2 AC 373, [2010] 2 WLR 47,
[2010] 2 All ER 359, [2010] 1 Cr App R 17, [2010] HRLR 12,
[2010] UKHRR 1, [2010] Crim LR 496, (2009) 153(48) SJLB 32,
(2009) Times, 10 December 1.163
R v Horseferry Road Justices, ex p Independent Broadcasting Authority
[1987] QB 54, [1986] 2 All ER 666, [1986] 3 WLR 132, 130 Sol Jo
446, [1986] LS Gaz R 1553, [1986] NLJ Rep 139 .... 2.37, 2.38, 2.54, 9.22

R v Horseferry Road Magistrates' Court, ex p Bennet [1994] 1 AC 42, [1993] 3 All ER 138, [1993] 3 WLR 90, 98 Cr App Rep 114, 137 Sol Jo LB 159, [1993] 3 LRC 94 . . . 9.22
R v Horsham District Council and West Sussex County Council, ex p Wenman [1994] 4 All ER 681, [1995] 1 WLR 680, [1993] NLJR 1477, 159 LG Rev 365 . . . 2.35, 6.131
R v Hospital Managers of the Park Royal Hospital, ex p Robinson (QBD Admin 26 November 2007) . . . 8.13
R v Hull University Visitor, ex p Page [1993] AC 682, [1992] 3 WLR 1112, [1993] 1 All ER 97, [1993] ICR 114, (1993) 143 NLJ 15, (1993) 137 SJLB 45, (1992) *Times*, 15 December, (1992) *Independent*, 9 December . . . 1.67, 1.78, 1.79, 1.80, 15.50
R v Humberside CC, ex p Bogdal [1992] COD 467 . . . 3.08, 3.19
R v Humphries [1977] AC 1, [1976] 2 All ER 497, [1976] 2 WLR 857, [1976] RTR 339, 63 Cr App Rep 95, 140 JP 386, [1977] Crim LR 421, 120 Sol Jo 420 . . . 9.42
R v Huntingdon District Council, ex p Cowan and another [1984] 1 All ER 58, [1984] 1 WLR 501, 82 LGR 342, 148 JP 367, 128 Sol Jo 246 . . . 12.53, 12.83
R v Huntingdon Magistrates' Court, ex p Percy [1994] COD 323 . . . 9.83
R v Immigration Appeal Tribunal, ex p Sui Rong Suen [1997] Imm AR 355 . . . 1.123
R v Immigration Officer, ex p Shah [1982] 2 All ER 264, [1982] 1 WLR 544, 126 Sol Jo 173 . . . 2.45
R v Independent Television Commission, ex p TVNI Limited (1991) *Times*, 20 December . . . 3.14
R v Independent Television Commission, ex p TVNI Limited [1996] JR 60 . . . 3.15
R v Independent Television Commission, ex p Virgin Television Limited [1996] EMLR 318 . . . 1.94
R v Inland Revenue Commissioners, ex p Mead [1993] 1 All ER 772, [1992] STC 482, [1992] COD 361, (1992) *Independent*, 7 April, (1992) *The Guardian*, 27 March . . . 15.53
R v Inland Revenue Commissioners, ex p National Federation of Self Employed and Small Businesses [1982] AC 617, [1981] 2 All ER 93, [1981] 2 WLR 722, [1981] STC 260, 55 TC 133, 125 Sol Jo 325 . . . 3.38
R v Inland Revenue Commissioners, ex p Unilever Plc [1996] STC 681, 68 TC 205, [1996] COD 421 . . . 1.123, 15.23
R v Inner Crown Court, ex p Provis (2000) *Times*, 11 July . . . 12.82, 12.83
R v Inner London Crown Court, ex p Benjamin (1987) 85 Cr App R 267 . . . 9.35
R v Inner London Education Authority, ex p Ali and Murshid [1990] COD 317, [1990] 2 Admin LR 822 . . . 2.30, 2.119, 11.55
R v Inspectorate of Pollution, ex p Greenpeace [1993] EWCA Civ 9, [1994] 4 All ER 321, [1994] 1 WLR 570 . . . 2.11
R v Institute of Chartered Accountants in England and Wales, ex p Andreou (1996) 8 Admin LR 557, [1996] COD 489 . . . 15.37
R v Institute of Chartered Accountants in England and Wales, ex p Brindle [1994] BCC 297, (1994) *Times*, 12 January . . . 15.43
R v Institute of Chartered Accountants in England and Wales, ex p Friend & Co, unreported, 30 June 2000 . . . 15.43
R v Institute of Chartered Accountants in England and Wales, ex p Nawaz [1997] CLY 1 . . . 1.84, 15.26, 15.43
R v Institute of Chartered Accountants, ex p Bruce, unreported, 22 October 1986, CA . . . 15.78
R v International Stock Exchange, ex p Else [1993] QB 534, [1993] 2 WLR 70, [1993] 1 All ER 420, [1993] BCC 11, [1993] BCLC 834, [1993] 2 CMLR 677, (1994) 6 Admin LR 67, [1993] COD 236, (1992) *Times*, 2 November, (1992) *Independent*, 24 November . . . 1.203
R v IRC, ex p Woolwich Equitable Building Society [1991] 4 All ER 92, [1990] 1 WLR 1400, [1990] STC 682 . . . 2.57
R v Isleworth Crown Court, ex p Irwin (1991) *Times*, 5 December . . . 9.51
R v Islington London Borough Council, ex p Rixon [1997] ELR 66, 32 BMLR 136, [1998] 1 CCL Rep 119 . . . 1.153, 6.34, 6.66, 6.152

R v Islington North Juvenile Court, ex p Daley [1983] 1 AC 347, [1982] 3 WLR 344, [1982] 2 All ER 974, (1982) 75 Cr App R 280, [1982] Crim LR 760, (1982) 79 LSG 1412, (1982) 126 SJ 524	1.55, 1.201
R v Jockey Club Licensing Committee, ex p Wright (Barrie John) [1991] COD 306	3.07
R v Jockey Club, ex p RAM Racecourse Ltd [1993] 2 All ER 225, (1991) 5 Admin LR 265, [1990] COD 346	15.40, 15.45
R v Kensington and Chelsea Royal London Borough Council, ex p Grillo (1996) 28 HLR 94, [1995] NPC 85, (1995) Times, 13 May, (1995) Independent, 13 June	1.153, 1.154
R v Kensington and Chelsea Royal London Borough Council, ex p Hammell [1989] QB 518, [1989] 1 All ER 1202, [1989] 2 WLR 90, 87 LGR 145, [1989] FCR 323, [1989] 2 FLR 223, [1989] Fam Law 430, 20 HLR 666, 133 Sol Jo 45, [1989] 3 LS Gaz R 43	2.34
R v Kensington and Chelsea Royal London Borough Council, ex p Kujtim [1999] 4 All ER 161, [1999] LGR 761, 32 HLR 579, (1999) Times, 5 August, 2 CCLR 340	6.152
R v Kensington Income Tax Commissioners, ex p Princess Edmond de Polignac [1917] 1 KB 486, 86 LJKB 257, 61 Sol Jo 182, 116 LT 136, 33 TLR 113	2.108, 3.07
R v Kent Police Authority, ex p Godden [1971] 2 QB 662, [1971] 3 All ER 20, [1971] 3 WLR 416, 135 JP 543, 115 Sol Jo 640, 69 LGR 553, CA	2.38, 2.39
R v Kirk (1983) 76 Cr App R 194	9.28
R v Kirkham MBC, ex p Daykin and Daykin (1997–8) 1 CCLR 512	6.14, 6.17
R v Knightsbridge Crown Court, ex p Marcrest Properties [1983] 1 All ER 1148, [1983] 1 WLR 300	2.122
R v Knowsley Metropolitan Borough Council, ex p Maguire (1992) 90 LGR 653, [1992] NLJR 1375	2.82
R v Lambeth London Borough Council, ex p Crookes (1995) 29 HLR 28	2.210
R v Lambeth London Borough Council, ex p Crookes (1997) 29 HLR 29	1.123
R v Lambeth London Borough Council, ex p K (2000) 3 CCLR 141	1.116
R v Lancashire CC, ex p F [1995] ELR 33	11.77
R v Lancashire CC, ex p Guyer [1980] 2 All ER 520, [1980] 1 WLR 1024, 78 LGR 454, 40 P & CR 376, 124 Sol Jo 375	2.30
R v Lancashire CC, ex p Huddlestone [1986] 2 All ER 941, [1986] NLJ Rep 562	3.09
R v Lancashire County Council, ex p M [1995] ELR 136	1.156
R v Law Society, ex p Bratsky Lesopromyshlenny Complex [1995] COD 216	15.56
R v Law Society, ex p Kingsley [1996] COD 59	15.56
R v Leeds City Council, ex p Cobleigh [1997] COD 69	1.62
R v Leeds City Council, ex p Gnezele, R (Dayina) v Leeds CC [2007] EWHC 3275 (Admin), [2007] All ER (D) 163 (Dec)	6.129, 6.135
R v Leeds City Council, ex p Hendry (1994) Times, 20 January	12.53
R v Legal Aid Board, ex p Kaim Todner [1999] QB 966, [1998] 3 WLR 925, [1998] 3 All ER 541, (1998) 95(26) LSG 31, (1998) 148 NLJ 941, (1998) 142 SJLB 189, (1998) Times, 15 June, (1998) Independent, 12 June	15.167
R v Leicester City Justices, ex p Barrow [1991] 2 QB 260, [1991] 3 WLR 368, [1991] 3 All ER 935, (1991) 155 JP 901, [1991] RA 205, [1991] Crim LR 556, (1991) 155 JPN 736, (1991) 141 NLJ 1145, (1991) Times, 5 August, (1991) Independent, 7 August, (1991) The Guardian, 14 August	1.127
R v Leominster District Council ex p Pothecary [1998] P & CR 346	5.109
R v Lewes Crown Court, ex p Sinclair (1993) 5 Admin LR 1	9.36
R v Lewisham LBC, ex p Pajaziti [2007] EWCA Civ 1351, [2007] All ER (D) 261 (Dec)	6.128
R v Licensing Justices at North Tyneside, ex p Todd and Lewis (1988) 153 JP 100	12.61
R v Licensing Justices of East Gwent, ex p Chief Constable of Gwent (2000) 164 JP 339	12.98

R v Lincoln Justices, ex p Count (1996) 8 Admin LR 233	9.81
R v Liverpool CC, ex p Muldoon [1996] 3 All ER 498, [1996] 1 WLR 1103, 29 HLR 163, [1996] 33 LS Gaz R 25, [1996] NLJR 1057, 140 Sol Jo LB 184	3.28, 3.57
R v Liverpool City Corps, ex p Ferguson and Ferguson [1985] IRLR 501	2.31
R v Liverpool City Council, ex p Baby Products Association & Others [2000] LGR 171, (1999) *Times*, 1 December	13.50
R v Liverpool City Council, ex p Coade (1986) *Times*, 10 October	2.24, 2.105
R v Liverpool City Council, ex p Luxury Leisure Limited [1999] LGR 345, [1998] All ER (D) 446	12.79
R v Liverpool City Council, ex p Newman [1993] COD 65, (1993) 5 Admin LR 669	3.78
R v Liverpool City Council, ex p Ramm (unreported) 28 January 1998	12.87
R v Liverpool City Council, ex p Secretary of State for Employment [1989] COD 404, 154 JPN 118	2.45
R v Liverpool Corps, ex p Liverpool Taxi Fleet Operators' Assoc [1972] 2 QB 299, [1972] 2 All ER 589, [1972] 2 WLR 1262, 71 LGR 387, 116 Sol Jo 201	2.38
R v Lloyd's of London, ex p Briggs [1993] 1 Lloyd's Rep 176, [1993] COD 66	3.07, 15.46
R v Local Commissioner for Administration for North and North-East England, ex p Liverpool City Council [2000] All ER (D) 235, [2001] 1 All ER 462, [2000] LGR 571	2.210, 13.114
R v London Borough of Ealing, ex p Times Newspapers [1987] IRLR 129, 85 LGR 316, (1987) 151 LG Rev 530, (1986) *Times*, 6 November	1.62
R v London Borough of Hackney, ex p Decordova (1995) 27 HLR 108	1.123
R v London Borough of Islington, ex p Hinds (1995) 27 HLR 65, [1994] COD 494	1.152
R v London Borough of Wandsworth, ex p Darker Enterprises Limited (unreported) 15 January 1999	12.19, 12.93
R v London County Council, ex p Entertainments Protection Association [1931] 2 KB 215, 29 LGR 252, 95 JP 89, 100 LJKB 760, 75 Sol Jo 138, 144 LT 464, 47 TLR 227	2.61
R v London Transport Executive, ex p Greater London Council [1983] QB 484, [1983] 2 All ER 262, [1983] 2 WLR 702, 81 LGR 474, 127 Sol Jo 106	2.72, 13.92, 13.94
R v Lord Chancellor, ex p Maxwell [1997] 1 WLR 104, [1996] 4 All ER 751, [1996] 2 BCLC 324 Ch, (1996) 8 Admin LR 603, [1997] COD 22, (1996) 146 NLJ 986, (1996) 140 SJLB 157, (1996) *Times*, 27 June, (1996) *Independent*, 25 June	1.20
R v Lord Chancellor, ex p Witham [1998] QB 575, [1998] 2 WLR 849, [1997] 2 All ER 779, [1997] COD 291, (1997) 147 NLJ 378, (1997) 141 SJLB 82, (1997) *Times*, 13 March, (1997) *Independent*, 21 March	1.55, 1.201
R v Lord Saville of Newdigate, ex p A [2000] 1 WLR 1855, [1999] 4 All ER 860, [1999] COD 436, (1999) 149 NLJ 1201, (1999) *Times*, 29 July	1.24, 1.125, 15.37
R v Maidstone Crown Court, ex p Clark [1995] 3 All ER 513, [1995] 1 WLR 831, [1995] 06 LS Gaz R 37	9.22
R v Maidstone Crown Court, ex p Gill [1987] 1 All ER 129, [1986] 1 WLR 1405, [1987] RTR 35, 84 Cr App Rep 96, [1986] Crim LR 737, 130 Sol Jo 712, [1986] LS Gaz R 2750, [1986] NLJ Rep 823	9.35
R v Maidstone Crown Court, ex p Harrow London Borough Council [2000] QB 719, [1999] 3 All ER 542, [2000] 2 WLR 237, [2000] 1 Cr App Rep 117, [1999] Crim LR 838, [1999] 21 LS Gaz R 38	9.25, 9.37
R v Maidstone Crown Court, ex p Shanks & McEwan (Southern) Ltd [1993] Env LR 340	9.34
R v Managers of South Western Hospital, ex p M [1993] QB 683, [1993] 3 WLR 376, QBD	8.29
R v Manchester City Justices, ex p McHugh [1989] RTR 285	12.61
R v Manchester Crown Court, ex p DPP [1994] 1 AC 9, [1993] 1 WLR 1524	9.28, 9.32, 9.34

R v Manchester Crown Court, ex p H [2000] 2 All ER 166, [2000] 1 WLR
  760, [2000] 1 Cr App Rep 262, (1999) *Times*, August 13 — 9.33, 9.35
R v Manchester Stipendiary Magistrate, ex p Hill [1983] 1 AC 328, [1982] 3
  WLR 331, [1982] 2 All ER 963, (1982) 75 Cr App R 346, [1982]
  RTR 449, [1982] Crim LR 755, (1982) 126 SJ 526 — 1.77, 1.84
R v Mansfield Justices, ex p Sharkey [1985] QB 613, [1985] 1 All ER 193,
  [1984] 3 WLR 1328, [1984] IRLR 496, 149 JP 129, [1985] Crim LR
  148, 128 Sol Jo 872 — 2.122
R v Medical Appeal Tribunal, ex p Gilmore [1957] 1 QB 574, [1957] 1 All
  ER 796, [1957] 2 WLR 498, 101 Sol Jo 248 — 2.61
R v Mendip District Council ex p Fabre (2000) 80 P & CR 500, [2000] JPL
  810, [2000] COD 372 — 5.110
R v Mental Health Act Commission, ex p W (1988) 9 BMLR 77 — 2.61, 8.38
R v Mental Health Review Tribunal for South Thames Region, ex p Smith
  [1998] EWHC 832 — 8.15
R v Mental Health Review Tribunal, ex p Hall (1999) 2 CCLR 383, [1999]
  MHLR 63, CA — 6.117, 8.68
R v Merseyside County Council, ex p Great Universal Stores (1982) 80 LGR
  639, [1982] RVR 83 — 13.92
R v Merton LBC, ex p Sembi (2000) 32 HLR 439 — 7.37
R v Metropolitan Stipendiary Magistrate, ex p Ali (1997) *Independent*, 12
  May — 9.83
R v Mid-Hertfordshire Justices, ex p Cox (1996) 160 JP 507, (1996) 8
  Admin LR 409 — 1.105
R v Mid-Worcestershire Justices, ex p Hart [1989] COD 397 — 3.08, 9.53
R v Milling (Medical Referee), ex p West Yorkshire Police Authority [1997]
  8 Med LR 392, (1996) *Times*, 24 December — 15.62
R v Minister of Health, ex p Davis [1929] 1 KB 619, 27 LGR 677, 93 JP
  49, 98 LJKB 636, 141 LT 6, 45 TLR 345 — 2.38
R v Ministry for Agriculture Fisheries & Food, ex p Hamble Fisheries
  (Offshore) Ltd [1995] 2 All ER 714, [1995] 1 CMLR 533, (1995) 7
  Admin LR 637, [1995] COD 114 — 1.92, 1.206
R v Ministry of Agriculture Fisheries and Food, ex p Live Sheep Traders Ltd
  [1995] COD 297 — 2.119
R v Ministry of Agriculture, Fisheries and Food, ex p FEDESA [1990] I-4023 — 1.206
R v Ministry of Agriculture, Fisheries and Food, ex p First City Trading Ltd
  [1997] 1 CMLR 250 — 2.08
R v Ministry of Agriculture, Fisheries and Food, ex p Hedley Lomas
  (Ireland) Ltd [1997] QB 139, [1996] 3 WLR 787, [1996] All ER (EC)
  493, [1996] ECR I-2553, [1996] 2 CMLR 391, [1996] CEC 979,
  (1996) 15 Tr LR 364, (1996) *Times*, 6 June, (1996) *Independent*, 24
  June — 1.207
R v Ministry of Defence Police, ex p Byrne [1994] COD 429 DC — 15.58, 15.162
R v Ministry of Defence, ex p Smith [1996] QB 517, [1996] 2 WLR 305,
  [1996] 1 All ER 257, [1996] ICR 740, [1996] IRLR 100, (1996) 8
  Admin LR 29, [1996] COD 237, (1995) 145 NLJ 1689, (1995)
  Times, 6 November, (1995) *Independent*, 7 November — 1.22, 1.23, 1.27
R v Ministry of Defence, ex p Walker [2000] 1 WLR 806, [2000] 2 All ER
  917, [2000] COD 153, (2000) 97(19) LSG 43, (2000) 144 SJLB 198,
  (2000) *Times*, 7 April, (2000) *Independent*, 11 April — 1.138
R v MMC, ex p Milk Marque Ltd and NFU [2000] COD 329 — 3.28
R v Monopolies & Mergers Commission, ex p South Yorkshire Transport
  Ltd [1993] 1 WLR 23, [1993] 1 All ER 289, [1993] BCC 111, [1994]
  ECC 231, (1993) 143 NLJ 128, (1992) *Times*, 17 December — 1.95, 5.108
R v Monopolies and Mergers Commission, ex p Argyll Group plc [1986] 2
  All ER 257, [1986] 1 WLR 763, 130 Sol Jo 467, [1986] LS Gaz R
  1225 — 2.125, 3.15
R v Monopolies and Mergers Commission, ex p Brown (Matthew) [1987] 1
  All ER 463, [1987] 1 WLR 1235, 4 BCC 171, 131 Sol Jo 1120,
  [1987] LS Gaz R 2606 — 2.121

R v Morpeth Ward Justices, ex p Ward (1992) 95 Cr App Rep 215, 156 JP 529	9.54
R v N [2012] EWCA Crim 189, [2013] QB 379, [2012] 3 WLR 1159, [2012] 1 Cr App R 35, [2012] Crim LR 958, (2012) *Times*, 10 April	9.42
R v Nailsworth Licensing Justices, ex p Bird [1953] 2 All ER 652, [1953] 1 WLR 1046, 51 LGR 532, 117 JP 426, 97 Sol Jo 541	2.117
R v Newcastle under Lyme Justices, ex p Massey [1995] 1 All ER 120, [1994] 1 WLR 1684, 158 JP 1037, [1994] NLJR 1444	9.83
R v Newham LBC, ex p Lumley (2001) 33 HLR 11	7.47
R v Norfolk County Council Social Services Department, ex p M [1989] QB 619, [1989] 2 All ER 359, [1989] 3 WLR 502, 87 LGR 598, [1989] FCR 667, [1989] 2 FLR 120, [1989] Fam Law 310, [1989] NLJR 293	2.46
R v North and East Devon Health Authority, ex p Coughlan [2001] QB 213, [2000] 2 WLR 622, [2000] 3 All ER 850, (2000) 2 LGLR 1, [1999] BLGR 703, (1999) 2 CCL Rep 285, [1999] Lloyd's Rep Med 306, (2000) 51 BMLR 1, [1999] COD 340, (1999) 96(31) LSG 39, (1999) 143 SJLB 213, (1999) *Times*, 20 July, (1999) *Independent*, 20 July	1.134, 1.140, 1.142, 1.144, 1.146, 6.106, 6.109, 6.111, 12.61
R v North East Thames Regional Health Authority, ex p De Groot [1988] COD 25	2.108
R v North Hertfordshire DC, ex p Cobbold [1985] 3 All ER 486	2.45, 2.58
R v North West Lancashire Health Authority, ex p A [2000] 1 WLR 977, [2000] 2 FCR 525, (1999) 2 CCL Rep 419, [1999] Lloyd's Rep Med 399, (2000) 53 BMLR 148, (1999) *Times*, 24 August, (1999) *Independent*, 5 October	1.91, 1.120
R v North Yorkshire CC, ex p William Hargreaves (1997–98) 1 CCL Rep 104	6.152
R v Northampton Magistrates, ex p Commissioners for Customs and Excise [1994] COD 382	9.23
R v Northavon DC, ex p Palmer (1993) 25 HLR 674, [1993] 42 LS Gaz R 43	2.119
R v Northumberland Compensation Appeal Tribunal, ex p Shaw [1952] 1 KB 338, [1952] 1 All ER 122, [1952] 1 TLR 161, (1952) 116 JP 54, 50 LGR 193, (1951-52) 2 P & CR 361, (1952) 96 SJ 29	1.75, 1.93, 2.44
R v Norwich Crown Court, ex p Cox (1993) 5 Admin LR 689	9.35
R v Nottingham City Council, ex p Howitt [1999] COD 530	12.53, 12.61
R v Nottingham County Court, ex p Byers [1985] 1 All ER 735, [1985] 1 WLR 403, [1985] FLR 695, 128 Sol Jo 873	2.23
R v Nottingham Magistrates' Court, ex p Davidson [2000] 1 Cr App R 167	9.48
R v Oldham Justices, ex p Cawley [1997] QB 1, [1996] 1 All ER 464, [1996] 2 WLR 681, 160 JP 133	9.75
R v Oxenden (1691) 89 ER 545	2.60
R v Paddington Valuation Officer, ex p Peachey Property Corps Ltd [1966] 1 QB 380, [1965] 2 All ER 836, [1965] 3 WLR 426, 63 LGR 353, [1965] RA 177, 11 RRC 141, 129 JP 447, 109 Sol Jo 475, [1965] RVR 384, CA, Affirming [1964] 3 All ER 200, [1964] 1 WLR 1186, 62 LGR 549, [1964] RA 165, 10 RRC 330, 128 JP 550, 108 Sol Jo 692, [1964] CLY 3112, [1964] RVR 500, QBD	2.61, 2.121
R v Panel on Take-overs and Mergers, ex p Datafin Plc [1987] QB 815, [1987] 2 WLR 699, [1987] 1 All ER 564, (1987) 3 BCC 10, [1987] BCLC 104, [1987] 1 FTLR 181, (1987) 131 SJ 23	2.46, 2.121, 15.41, 15.48
R v Panel on Take-overs and Mergers, ex p Guinness plc [1990] 1 QB 146, [1989] 2 WLR 863, [1989] 1 All ER 509, (1988) 4 BCC 714, [1989] BCLC 255, (1988) 138 NLJ Rep 244, (1989) 133 SJ 660	1.125
R v Panel on Takeovers and Mergers, ex p Fayed (1992) *Times*, 15 April	9.41
R v Parliamentary Commissioner for Administration, ex p Balchin [1998] 1 PLR 1, [1997] JPL 917, [1997] COD 146, [1996] EG 166 (CS), [1996] NPC 147	1.17, 1.106

R v Parliamentary Commissioner for Administration, ex p Dyer [1994] 1
    WLR 621, [1994] 1 All ER 375, [1994] COD 331, (1993) 137 SJLB
    259, (1993) *Times*, 27 October, (1993) *Independent*, 26 October,
    (1993) *The Guardian*, 25 October   1.77
R v Parole Board, ex p Hart, unreported, 24 May 2000   10.62
R v Parole Board, ex p Higgins, unreported, 1998   10.59
R v Parole Board, ex p Watson [1996] 1 WLR 906, [1996] 2 All ER 641,
    (1996) 8 Admin LR 460, [1997] COD 72, (1996) *Times*, 11 March   1.86
R v Pateley Bridge Justices, ex p Percy [1994] COD 453   9.78
R v Peak Park Joint Planning Board (1976) 74 LGR 376   2.121
R v Pembrokeshire Justices, ex p Bennell [1969] 1 QB 386, [1968] 1 All ER
    940, [1968] 2 WLR 858, 66 LGR 394, 132 JP 216, 112 Sol Jo 114   12.38
R v Peterborough Magistrates' Court, ex p Dowler [1997] QB 911, [1997] 2
    WLR 843, [1996] 2 Cr App Rep 561, 160 JP 561   9.53
R v Police Complaints Board, ex p Madden [1983] 1 WLR 447, [1983] 2 All
    ER 353, [1983] Crim LR 263, (1983) 127 SJ 85   1.91, 2.52, 2.61, 15.205
R v Poplar MBC, ex p Metropolitan Asylums Board (No 2) [1922] 1 KB 95,
    19 LGR 731, 85 JP 259, 91 LJKB 174, [1921] All ER Rep 437, 126
    LT 138, 38 TLR 5, 66 Sol Jo (WR) 10   2.32, 2.33
R v Port Talbot BC, ex p Jones [1988] 2 All ER 207, 20 HLR 265   2.45, 2.117
R v Postmaster General, ex p Carmichael [1928] 1 KB 291, 91 JP 43, 96
    LJKB 347, 137 LT 26, 43 TLR 228, 21 BWCC 226   2.42
R v Powell (1841) 1 QB 352, 5 JP 465, 10 LJQB 148, Arn & H 290, 5 Jur
    605, 4 Per & Dav 719   2.79
R v Preston Borough Council, ex p Quietlynn Ltd (1984) 83 LGR 308   12.20, 12.86
R v Preston Crown Court, ex p Chief Constable of Lancashire & Others
    [2001] EWHC Admin 928, [2002] 1 WLR 1332, [2001] All ER (D)
    166 (Nov)   12.46
R v Race Relations Board, ex p Selvarajan [1975] 1 WLR 1686, [1976] 1 All
    ER 12, [1975] IRLR 281, (1975) 119 SJ 644   1.84, 15.25
R v Reading Borough Council, ex p Johnson [2004] EWHC 765 (Admin),
    [2004] All ER (D) 90 (Apr)   12.22, 12.23
R v Reading Borough Council, ex p Quietlynn (1986) 85 LGR 387   12.28, 12.29, 12.33, 12.35
R v Recorder of Liverpool, ex p McCann (1994) *Times*, 4 May   9.26
R v Registrar-General, ex p Smith [1990] 2 WLR 782   2.24
R v Restormel Borough Council, ex p Parkyn, R v Restormel Borough
    Council, ex p Corbett [2001] EWCA Civ 330, [2001] 1 PLR 108   2.125
R v Richmond Upon Thames London Borough Council, ex p McCarthy &
    Stone (Developments) Ltd [1992] 2 AC 48, [1990] 2 All ER 852,
    [1990] 2 WLR 1294, 60 P & CR 174, [1990] 27 LS Gaz R 41,
    [1990] NLJR 362   13.49
R v Rochdale MBC, ex p Schemet (1992) 91 LGR 425, [1994] ELR 89,
    (1992) 91 LGR 425, [1993] 1 FCR 306, [1993] COD 113   2.72, 2.117, 2.121
R v Rochford [2010] EWCA Crim 1928, [2011] 1 WLR 534, [2011] 1 Cr
    App R 11   1.55, 1.201
R v Royal Borough of Kensington and Chelsea, ex p Ghrebregiosis (1994)
    27 HLR 602, [1994] COD 502   3.78
R v Royal Borough of Kensington and Chelsea, ex p Kassam (1994) 26 HLR
    455   1.106, 1.155
R v Royal Pharmaceutical Society of Great Britain, ex p Mahmood [2001]
    EWCA Civ 1245, [2002] 1 WLR 879, (2001) 98(37) LSG 39, (2001)
    145 SJLB 217, (2001) *Times*, 9 August   15.79
R v Save Guana Cay Reef Association [2009] UKPC 44   1.143
R v Secretary for State for the Environment & Anr, ex p Kirkstall Valley
    Campaign Ltd [1996] 3 All ER 304, [1997] 1 PLR 8, [1996] JPL
    1042, [1996] COD 337, (1996) 160 JP Rep 699, [1996] EG 46 (CS),
    (1996) 146 NLJ 478, [1996] NPC 41, (1996) *Times*, 20 March   5.116
R v Secretary of State for Education and Employment, ex p National Union
    of Teachers, unreported, 14 July 2000   1.147

R v Secretary of State for Education and Science, ex p Avon [1991] 1 QB 558, [1991] 1 All ER 282, [1991] 2 WLR 702, 89 LGR 121, [1990] NLJR 781	2.20, 3.40
R v Secretary of State for Education and Science, ex p Birmingham CC (1984) 83 LGR 79	2.107, 2.117
R v Secretary of State for Education and Science, ex p Islam (1993) 5 Admin LR 177, [1992] COD 448, (1993) 157 LG Rev 104, *Times*, May 22, 1992	1.93
R v Secretary of State for Education, ex p London Borough of Southwark [1995] ELR 308	1.116
R v Secretary of State for Education, ex p Prior [1994] ELR 231	1.84
R v Secretary of State for Employment, ex p Equal Opportunities Commission [1995] 1 AC 1, [1994] 2 WLR 409, [1994] 1 All ER 910, [1995] 1 CMLR 391, [1994] ICR 317, [1994] IRLR 176, 92 LGR 360, [1994] COD 301, (1994) 91(18) LSG 43, (1994) 144 NLJ 358, (1994) 138 SJLB 84, (1994) *Times*, 4 March, (1994) *Independent*, 9 March, (1994) *The Guardian*, 7 March	1.207, 2.42, 2.71
R v Secretary of State for Employment, ex p Seymour-Smith [1999] 2 AC 554, [1999] 3 WLR 460, [1999] All ER (EC) 97, [1999] ECR I-623, [1999] 2 CMLR 273, [1999] CEC 79, [1999] ICR 447, [1999] IRLR 253, (1999) *Times*, 25 February	1.207
R v Secretary of State for Foreign Affairs, ex p World Development Movement Ltd [1995] 1 WLR 386, [1995] 1 All ER 611, [1995] COD 211, (1995) 145 NLJ 51, (1994) *Times*, 27 December, (1995) *Independent*, 11 January	1.110
R v Secretary of State for Foreign and Commonwealth Affairs, ex p Everett [1989] QB 811, [1989] 2 WLR 224, [1989] 1 All ER 655, [1989] Imm AR 155, [1989] COD 291, (1989) 86(8) LSG 43, (1989) 133 SJ 151, (1988) *Times*, 1 November, (1988) *Independent*, 26 October	1.127, 2.46, 2.78, 2.121, 2.126
R v Secretary of State for Foreign and Commonwealth Affairs, ex p World Development Movement Ltd [1995] 1 WLR 386, [1995] 1 All ER 611, [1995] COD 211, (1995) 145 NLJ 51, (1994) *Times*, 27 December, (1995) *Independent*, 11 January	1.62
R v Secretary of State for Health and Others, ex p Harrison [2009] EWHC 574 (Admin), [2009] All ER (D) 216 (Mar)	6.38
R v Secretary of State for Health, ex p C [2000] 1 FCR 471, [2000] 10 LS Gaz R 35, [2000] All ER (D) 215	13.27, 13.34
R v Secretary of State for Health, ex p Imperial Tobacco Ltd [2002] QB 161, [2000] 2 WLR 834, [2000] 1 CMLR 307, [2000] 02 LS Gaz R 29, 144 Sol Jo LB 31	2.17
R v Secretary of State for Health, ex p Pfizer Ltd (1999) 2 CCLR 270	1.206
R v Secretary of State for Health, ex p United States Tobacco Inc [1992] QB 353, [1992] 1 All ER 212, [1991] 3 WLR 529	2.76
R v Secretary of State for Home Deptartment, ex p Dannenberg [1984] QB 766, [1984] 2 All ER 481, [1984] 2 WLR 855, [1984] 2 CMLR 456, 148 JP 321, [1984] Crim LR 362, [1984] Imm AR 33, 128 Sol Jo 349	9.12
R v Secretary of State for Social Security, ex p Joint Council for the Welfare of Immigrants [1997] 1 WLR 275, [1996] 4 All ER 385, (1997) 29 HLR 129, (1997) 9 Admin LR 1, (1996) 146 NLJ 985, (1996) *Times*, 27 June, (1996) *Independent*, 26 June	1.201
R v Secretary of State for Social Services, ex p Association of Metropolitan Authorities (1992) 25 HLR 131, 5 Admin LR 6	2.125
R v Secretary of State for Social Services, ex p Association of Metropolitan Authorities [1986] 1 All ER 164, [1986] 1 WLR 1, 83 LGR 796, 130 Sol Jo 35	2.72, 2.119
R v Secretary of State for the Environment ex p Royal Society for the Protection of Birds [1997] QB 206	5.47

R v Secretary of State for the Environment v Rose Theatre Trust Co [1990]
1 QB 504, [1990] 2 WLR 186, [1990] 1 All ER 754, (1990) 59
P & CR 257, [1990] 1 PLR 39, [1990] JPL 360, [1990] COD 186,
[1989] EG 107 (CS), (1990) 87(6) LSG 41, (1990) 134 SJ 425, (1989)
Times, 18 July, (1989) *Independent*, 18 July, (1989) *The Guardian*, 18
July 5.66
R v Secretary of State for the Environment, ex p Binney [1984] JPL 871 .... 2.61
R v Secretary of State for the Environment, ex p Brent LBC [1982] QB 593,
[1983] 3 All ER 321, [1982] 2 WLR 693, 80 LGR 357, 126 Sol Jo
118, [1981] RVR 279 .... 2.61
R v Secretary of State for the Environment, ex p Greater London Council
[1985] JPL 868 .... 2.75
R v Secretary of State for the Environment, ex p Lancashire County Council
[1994] 4 All ER 165, 93 LGR 29, [1994] COD 347, (1994) 158 LG
Rev 541, (1994) 91(9) LSG 40, (1994) 138 SJLB 53, (1994) *Times*, 3
February 1.88
R v Secretary of State for the Environment, ex p LBI [1997] JR 21 .... 6.131
R v Secretary of State for the Environment, ex p Nottinghamshire County
Council [1986] AC 240, [1986] 2 WLR 1, [1986] 1 All ER 199, 84
LGR 305, (1986) 83 LSG 359, (1985) 135 NLJ 1257, (1986) 130 SJ
36, (1985) *Financial Times*, 13 December 1.20, 1.26, 1.67
R v Secretary of State for the Environment, ex p Oldham Metropolitan
Borough Council [1998] ICR 367, (1996) *Times*, 16 December 1.206
R v Secretary of State for the Environment, ex p Powis [1981] 1 All ER 788,
[1981] 1 WLR 584, 79 LGR 318, 42 P & CR 73, 125 Sol Jo 324,
258 Estates Gazette 57, [1981] JPL 270 .... 3.61
R v Secretary of State for the Environment, ex p Shelter and the Refugee
Council [1997] COD 49 .... 7.52
R v Secretary of State for the Home Department and the Govenor of HMP
Swaledale, ex p Francois [1999] 1 AC 43, [1998] 1 All ER 929,
[1998] 2 WLR 530, [1998] 2 Cr App Rep (S) 370, [1998] 16 LS Gaz
R 24, [1998] NLJR 402, 142 Sol Jo LB 123 .... 9.10
R v Secretary of State for the Home Department, ex p Adams [1995] All ER
(EC) 177, (1994) *Times*, 10 August, (1994) *Independent*, 27 July 1.207
R v Secretary of State for the Home Department, ex p Anderson [1984] QB
778, [1984] 2 WLR 725, [1984] 1 All ER 920, [1984] Crim LR 295,
(1984) 81 LSG 658, (1984) 128 SJ 62, (1983) *Times*, 22 December   1.55, 1.201, 2.31
R v Secretary of State for the Home Department, ex p Bentley [1994] QB
349, [1993] 4 All ER 442, [1994] 2 WLR 101, [1993] 37 LS Gaz R
49, [1993] NLJR 1025, 137 Sol Jo LB 194, [1993] 4 LRC 15 .... 13.13
R v Secretary of State for the Home Department, ex p Brind [1991] 1 AC
696, [1991] 2 WLR 588, [1991] 1 All ER 720, (1991) 3 Admin LR
486, (1991) 141 NLJ 199, (1991) 135 SJ 250, (1991) *Times*, 8
February, (1991) *Independent*, 8 February, (1991) *The Guardian*, 8
February 1.06, 1.18, 1.30, 1.35, 1.39, 1.67
R v Secretary of State for the Home Department, ex p Bugdaycay [1987] AC
514, [1987] 1 All ER 940, [1987] 2 WLR 606, [1987] Imm AR 250,
131 Sol Jo 297, [1987] LS Gaz R 902, [1987] NLJ Rep 199 ...... 1.98, 2.119
R v Secretary of State for the Home Department, ex p Chinoy (1991) 4
Admin LR 457, [1991] COD 381, DC 3.07, 3.47
R v Secretary of State for the Home Department, ex p Daly [2001] UKHL
26, [2001] 2 AC 532, [2001] 2 WLR 1622, [2001] 3 All ER 433,
[2001] HRLR 49, [2001] UKHRR 887, [2001] Prison LR 322, [2001]
ACD 79, (2001) 98(26) LSG 43, (2001) 145 SJLB 156, (2001) *Times*,
25 May, (2001) Telegraph, 29 May 1.32, 1.184
R v Secretary of State for the Home Department, ex p Dannenberg [1984]
QB 766, [1984] 2 WLR 855, [1984] 2 All ER 481, (1984) 148 JP
321, [1984] 2 CMLR 456, [1984] Imm AR 33, [1984] Crim LR 362,
(1984) 128 SJ 349 .... 1.206, 2.61

R v Secretary of State for the Home Department, ex p Doody [1994] 1 AC
531, [1993] 3 WLR 154, [1993] 3 All ER 92, (1995) 7 Admin LR 1,
(1993) 143 NLJ 991, (1993) *Times*, 29 June, (1993) *Independent*, 25
June 1.84, 1.122, 1.123, 1.153

R v Secretary of State for the Home Department, ex p Doorga [1990] COD
109, [1990] Imm AR 98, CA 3.42

R v Secretary of State for the Home Department, ex p Duggan [1994] 3 All
ER 277, [1994] COD 258, (1993) *Times*, 9 December, (1994)
Independent, 28 January, (1993) *The Guardian*, 13 December 1.153, 10.07

R v Secretary of State for the Home Department, ex p Fire Brigades Union
[1995] 2 AC 513, [1995] 2 WLR 464, [1995] 2 All ER 244, (1995) 7
Admin LR 473, [1995] PIQR P228, (1995) 145 NLJ 521, (1995) 139
SJLB 109, (1995) *Times*, 6 April, (1995) *Independent*, 6 April 1.108, 13.08

R v Secretary of State for the Home Department, ex p Garner [1990] COD
457, 3 Admin LR 33 ..... 9.07

R v Secretary of State for the Home Department, ex p Georghiades (1993) 5
Admin LR 457, [1992] COD 412, (1992) *Times*, 3 June, (1992)
Independent, 27 May 1.127

R v Secretary of State for the Home Department, ex p H [2003] UKHL 59,
[2004] 2 AC 253, [2004] 1 All ER 412, [2003] 3 WLR 1278, 76
BMLR 179, [2004] 02 LS Gaz R 30, (2003) *Times*, 14 November,
147 Sol Jo LB 1365, 15 BHRC 571, [2003] All ER (D) 192 (Nov) 8.71

R v Secretary of State for the Home Department, ex p Hepworth [1997]
EWHC (Admin) 32 ..... 10.61

R v Secretary of State for the Home Department, ex p Hindley [2001] 1 AC
410, [2000] 2 WLR 730, [2000] 2 All ER 385, [2000] Prison LR 71,
[2000] COD 173, (2000) 97(15) LSG 39, (2000) 144 SJLB 180,
(2000) *Times*, 31 March 1.138

R v Secretary of State for the Home Department, ex p Iyadurai [1998] Imm
AR 470, [1998] INLR 472, [1998] COD 410, (1998) *Times*, 16 June 1.116

R v Secretary of State for the Home Department, ex p Kelso [1998] INLR
603 ..... 9.65

R v Secretary of State for the Home Department, ex p Khawaja [1984] AC
74, [1983] 2 WLR 321, [1983] 1 All ER 765, [1982] Imm AR 139,
(1983) 127 SJ 137 ..... 1.55, 1.98, 1.201

R v Secretary of State for the Home Department, ex p Launder [1997] 1
WLR 839, [1997] 3 All ER 961, (1997) 94(24) LSG 33, (1997) 147
NLJ 793, (1997) 141 SJLB 123, (1997) *Times*, 26 May, (1997)
Independent, 3 June 1.93

R v Secretary of State for the Home Department, ex p Leech [1994] QB 198,
[1993] 3 WLR 1125, [1993] 4 All ER 539, (1993) 137 SJLB 173,
(1993) *Times*, 20 May, (1993) *Independent*, 20 May 1.55, 1.201

R v Secretary of State for the Home Department, ex p Northumbria Police
Authority [1989] QB 26, [1987] 2 All ER 282, [1987] 2 WLR 998,
131 Sol Jo 505, [1987] LS Gaz R 1571 ..... 13.07, 13.31

R v Secretary of State for the Home Department, ex p Oladehinde, R v
Secretary of State for the Home Department, ex p Alexander, *sub nom*
Oladehinde v Secretary of State for the Home Department, Alexander
v Secretary of State for the Home Department [1991] 1 AC 254,
[1990] 3 All ER 393, [1990] 3 WLR 797, 134 Sol Jo 1264, [1990] 41
LS Gaz R 36, [1990] NLJR 1498 ..... 1.85, 13.122

R v Secretary of State for the Home Department, ex p Pierson [1998] AC
539, [1997] 3 WLR 492, [1997] 3 All ER 577, (1997) 94(37) LSG
41, (1997) 147 NLJ 1238, (1997) 141 SJLB 212, (1997) *Times*, 28
July, (1997) *Independent*, 31 July 1.55, 1.123, 1.201

R v Secretary of State for the Home Department, ex p Popatia [2001] Imm
AR 46, [2000] INLR 587, (2000) *Times*, 18 July 1.138

R v Secretary of State for the Home Department, ex p Potter [2001] EWHC
Admin 1041, [2002] Po LR 120, [2002] ACD 27 ..... 10.36

R v Secretary of State for the Home Department, ex p Rukshanda Begum
[1990] Imm AR 1, [1990] COD 107   3.44
R v Secretary of State for the Home Department, ex p Sezek [2001] EWCA
Civ 795, [2002] 1 WLR 348, [2001] Imm AR 657, [2001] All ER (D)
336 (May)   2.21
R v Secretary of State for the Home Department, ex p Sholola [1992] Imm
AR 135   3.07
R v Secretary of State for the Home Department, ex p Simms [2000] 2 AC
115, [1999] 3 WLR 328, [1999] 3 All ER 400, [1999] EMLR 689, 7
BHRC 411, (1999) 11 Admin LR 961, [1999] Prison LR 82, [1999]
COD 520, (1999) 96(30) LSG 28, (1999) 149 NLJ 1073, (1999) 143
SJLB 212, (1999) *Times*, 9 July   1.72, 1.197, 1.201
R v Secretary of State for the Home Department, ex p Swati [1986] 1 All ER
717, [1986] 1 WLR 477, [1986] Imm AR 88, 130 Sol Jo 186, [1986]
LS Gaz R 780, [1986] NLJ Rep 189   3.17, 3.19, 3.44
R v Secretary of State for the Home Department, ex p Tarrant [1985] QB
251, [1984] 2 WLR 613, [1984] 1 All ER 799, (1984) 81 LSG 1045,
(1984) SJ 223, (1983) *Times*, 9 November   1.123, 10.80
R v Secretary of State for the Home Department, ex p Turkoglu [1988] QB
398, [1987] 2 All ER 823, [1987] 3 WLR 992, [1987] Imm AR 484,
131 Sol Jo 1186, [1987] LS Gaz R 2692   9.64, 9.69
R v Secretary of State for the Home Department, ex p Zakrocki (1997–98) 1
CCL Rep 374   6.152
R v Secretary of State for Trade and Industry, ex p Eastaway [2001] 1 All
ER 27, [2000] 1 WLR 2222, 144 Sol Jo LB 282   3.54
R v Secretary of State for Trade and Industry, ex p Lonrho (1989) *Times*, 18
January, (1989) 5 BCC 284, [1989] NLJR 150   2.27
R v Secretary of State for Trade and Industry, ex p Lonrho plc [1989] 1
WLR 525, [1989] 2 All ER 609, (1989) 5 BCC 633, (1989) 139 NLJ
717, (1989) 133 SJ 724, (1989) *Times*, 19 May, (1989) *Independent*,
19 May, (1989) *The Guardian*, 19 May, (1989) Telegraph, 22 May   1.86
R v Secretary of State for Transport, ex p Factortame Ltd (No 2) [1991] 1
AC 603, [1990] 3 WLR 818, [1991] 1 All ER 70, [1991] 1 Lloyd's
Rep 10, [1990] 3 CMLR 375, (1991) 3 Admin LR 333, (1990) 140
NLJ 1457, (1990) 134 SJ 1189   1.201, 1.204, 2.12, 2.13
R v Secretary of State for Transport, ex p Greater London Council [1986]
QB 556, [1985] 3 All ER 300, [1985] 3 WLR 574, 129 Sol Jo 590,
[1986] JPL 513   2.55
R v Secretary of State for Transport, ex p Sherriff & Sons (1986) *Times*, 18
December, (1988) *Independent*, 12 January   2.105
R v Secretary of State for War [1891] 2 QB 326, 56 JP 105, 60 LJQB 457,
40 WR 5, 64 LT 764, 7 TLR 579   2.79
R v Sedgemoor District Council, ex p McCarthy (1996) 28 HLR 607   1.117
R v Sefton Metropolitan Borough Council, ex p Help the Aged (1997) 36
BMLR 110, [1997] NLJR 490   6.152
R v Shayler [2002] UKHL 11, [2003] 1 AC 247, [2002] 2 WLR 754, [2002]
UKHRR 603, [2002] 2 All ER 477, HL   1.55, 1.163, 1.201
R v Sheffield City Council ex p Mansfield 77 LGR 126, (1979) 37 P & CR
1, (1978) 247 EG 52, [1978] JPL 465   5.01
R v Sheffield City Council, ex p H, *sub nom* R v Sheffield City Council, ex p
Hague [1999] ELR 511, [1999] 32 LS Gaz R 32, [1999] All ER (D)
859   11.85
R v Sheffield Magistrates' Court, ex p Ojo (2000) 164 JP 659   9.85
R v Smith, M [1975] QB 531   9.34
R v Snaresbrook Crown Court, ex p Director of the Serious Fraud Office
(1998) *Times*, 26 October   9.32
R v Somerset County Council, ex p Dixon [1998] Env LR 111, (1998) 75
P & CR 175, [1997] JPL 1030, [1997] COD 323, [1997] NPC 61   1.01, 5.64
R v South Northamptonshire District Council, ex p Crest Homes Plc (1995)
93 LGR 205   1.127

R v South Yorkshire Police Authority, ex p Booth [2000] Po LR 335, (2000)
  Times, 10 October 15.216
R v Southampton Justices, ex p Green [1976] QB 11, [1975] 2 All ER 1073,
  [1975] 3 WLR 277, 139 JP 667, 119 Sol Jo 541 .... 9.14
R v Southwark Crown Court, ex p Brooke [1997] COD 81 .... 9.60
R v Southwark Crown Court, ex p Ward [1996] Crim LR 123 .... 9.34
R v Spear [2001] EWCA Crim 2, [2001] QB 804, [2001] 2 WLR 1692,
  [2001] Crim LR 485, (2001) 98(12) LSG 43, (2001) 145 SJLB 38,
  (2001) Times, 30 January 1.181
R v St Lawrence's Hospital Statutory Visitors, ex p Pritchard [1953] 2 All
  ER 766, [1953] 1 WLR 1158, 117 JP 458, 97 Sol Jo 590 .... 2.42, 2.47
R v Staffordshire County Council, ex p Ashworth [1997] COD 132, [1997]
  9 Admin LR 373 .... 3.45
R v Staffordshire County Council, ex p Farley (1987) 6.152
R v Statutory Committee of the Pharmaceutical Society of Great Britain, ex
  p Pharmaceutical Society of Great Britain [1981] 1 WLR 886, [1981]
  2 All ER 805, (1981) 125 SJ 428 .... 15.102, 15.225, 15.234
R v Sutton LBC, ex p Tucker (1998) 1 CCLR 251 .... 6.152
R v Swale Borough Council Medway Ports Authority, ex p RSPB (1991) 2
  Admin LR 790, [1991] 1 PLR 6, [1990] COD 263, [1991] JPL 39 .... 2.114
R v Swansea City Council, ex p Main (1981) Times, 23 December 3.15
R v Tanbridge District Council, ex p Al Fayed [2000] EHLR 257, (2000) 80
  P & CR 90, [2000] 1 PLR 58, [2000] JPL 604, [2000] EG 1 (CS),
  [1999] NPC 161, [2000] Env LR D23, (2000) Times, 1 February 1.127
R v Teignmouth District Council, ex p Teignmouth Quay Co Ltd [1995] 2
  PLR 1 .... 1.86
R v Thanet Justices, ex p Dass [1996] COD 77 .... 9.15
R v Thomas [1892] 1 QB 426, 56 JP 151, 61 LJMC 141, 40 WR 478, 66
  LT 289, 8 TLR 299 .... 2.32
R v Tottenham and District Rent Tribunal, ex p Northfield (Highgate) Ltd
  [1957] 1 QB 103, [1956] 2 All ER 863, [1956] 3 WLR 462, 54 LGR
  421, 120 JP 472, 100 Sol Jo 552 .... 2.38, 2.39
R v Tower Hamlets London Borough Council, ex p Chetnik Developments
  Ltd, sub nom Tower Hamlets London Borough Council v Chetnik
  Developments Ltd [1988] AC 858, [1988] 1 All ER 961, [1988] 2
  WLR 654, 86 LGR 321, [1988] RA 45, 132 Sol Jo 462, [1988] 2
  EGLR 195, [1988] 16 LS Gaz R 44, [1988] NLJR 89, [1988] 28 EG
  69, HL, Affirming [1987] 1 WLR 593, 85 LGR 713, [1987] RA 57,
  131 Sol Jo 692, [1987] 1 EGLR 180, [1987] LS Gaz R 1058, 282
  Estates Gazette 455, CA, Reversing [1985] RVR 87, QBD 2.23, 2.51, 2.97
R v Transport Secretary, ex p Factortame (No) 2 [1991] 1 AC 603, [1991] 1
  All ER 70, [1990] 3 WLR 818, [1990] 3 CMLR 375, [1990] 2
  Lloyd's Rep 365n, [1991] 1 Lloyd's Rep 10, 134 Sol Jo 1189, [1990]
  41 LS Gaz R 36, [1990] NLJR 1457 .... 2.29
R v Treasury Lords Cssrs (1872) LR 7 QB 387 .... 2.79
R v University of Cambridge (1723) 1 Stra 557 .... 1.122
R v University of Cambridge, ex p Evans [1998] Ed CR 151, [1998] ELR
  515 .... 1.152
R v Vaccine Damage Tribunal, ex p Loveday [1985] 2 Lancet 1137, (1985)
  Times, 20 April, CA 2.44
R v Visitors to the Inns of Court, ex p Calder & Persaud [1994] QB 1,
  [1993] 3 WLR 287, [1993] 2 All ER 876, [1993] COD 242, (1993)
  143 NLJ 164, (1993) Times, 26 January, (1993) Independent, 29
  January 1.80, 15.50
R v Waltham Forest LBC ex p Vale (1985) Times, 25 February 6.119
R v Wandsworth BC v Secretary of State for Transport, Local Government
  and the Regions [2003] EWCA Civ 142, [2003] 9 EG 196 (CS),
  (2003) 100(8) LSG 31, [2003] NPC 24 .... 5.35

R v Wandsworth London Borough Council, ex p O [2000] 1 WLR 2539,
  [2000] 4 All ER 590, (2001) 33 HLR 39, [2000] BLGR 591, (2000) 3
  CCL Rep 237, (2000) *Times*, 18 July, (2000) *Independent*, 28 June   1.201
R v Warrington Crown Court, ex p RBNB (a company) [2002] UKHL 24,
  [2002] 4 All ER 131, [2002] 1 WLR 1954, [2002] BCC 697, (2002)
  Times, 21 June, [2002] All ER (D) 136 (Jun)   12.96
R v Warwickshire County Council, ex p Collymore [1995] ELR 217   1.91, 1.120
R v Weir [2001] 2 All ER 216, [2001] 1 WLR 421, [2001] 2 Cr App Rep
  141, (2001) *Times*, February 9, 145 Sol Jo LB 61, [2001] All ER (D)
  121 (Feb)   9.87
R v Westminster City Council, ex p Augustin [1993] 1 WLR 730, 91 LGR
  89   2.14
R v Westminster City Council, ex p Ermakov [1996] 2 All ER 302, [1996] 2
  FCR 208, (1996) 28 HLR 819, (1996) 8 Admin LR 389, [1996] COD
  391, (1996) 160 JP Rep 814, (1996) 140 SJLB 23, (1995) *Times*, 20
  November   1.152, 1.157
R v Wigan MBC, ex p Tammadge (1998) 1 CCLR 581   6.24, 6.29, 6.32
R v Williams, ex p Phillips [1914] 1 KB 608, 78 JP 148, 83 LJKB 528, 110
  LT 372   2.117
R v Wirral Borough Council, ex p F, J, S, R & Others [2009] EWHC 1626
  (Admin), [2009] LGR 905, [2009] All ER (D) 160 (Jul)   6.02, 6.20, 6.151
R v Wirral MBC, ex p The Wirral Licensed Taxi Owners Association [1983]
  3 CMLR 150   12.61
R v Wolverhampton MBC, ex p Watters [1997] 3 FCR 747, 29 HLR 931   7.73
R v Worthing Borough Council, ex p Burch (1985) 50 P & R 53   1.88
R v York City Justices, ex p Farmery (1988) 153 JP 257   9.80
Rabone v Pennine Care NHS Trust [2012] UKSC 2, [2012] 2 AC 72, [2012]
  2 WLR 381, [2012] 2 All ER 381, [2012] PTSR 497, [2012] HRLR
  10, 33 BHRC 208, (2012) 15 CCL Rep 13, [2012] Med LR 221,
  (2012) 124 BMLR 148, [2012] MHLR 66, (2012) 162 NLJ 261,
  (2012) 156(6) SJLB 31, (2012) *Times*, 20 February   1.55, 1.163, 1.166, 1.199
Rahman v Bar Standards Board [2013] EWHC 4202 (QB)   15.87
Rahmattullah v Secretary of State of Foreign and Commonwealth Affairs
  [2011] EWCA Civ 1540, [2012] 1 WLR 1462, [2012] 1 All ER 1290,
  [2012] HRLR 9, (2012) 109(2) LSG 15   1.55, 1.201
Raji v General Medical Council [2003] UKPC 24, [2003] 1 WLR 1052,
  [2003] Lloyd's Rep Med 280, [2003] ACD 63, (2003) 100(21) LSG
  30, (2003) *Times*, 31 March   15.89
Raschid v General Medical Council [2007] EWCA Civ 46, [2007] 1 WLR
  1460, [2007] ICR 811, (2007) 104(5) LSG 29, (2007) 151 SJLB 127   15.137, 15.204, 15.213
Raymond v Honey [1981] QB 874, [1981] 3 WLR 218, [1981] 2 All ER
  1084, (1981) 73 Cr App R 242, (1981) *Times*, 8 April   10.03
Redland Bricks Ltd v Morris and Another [1970] AC 652, [1969] 2 WLR
  1487, [1969] 2 All ER 576, HL   2.66
Reid v Secretary of State for Scotland [1999] 2 AC 512, [1999] 2 WLR 28,
  [1999] 1 All ER 481, 1999 SC (HL) 17, 1999 SLT 279, 1999 SCLR
  74, (1999) 96(4) LSG 37, 1998 GWD 40-2075, (1998) *Times*, 7
  December, (1998) *Independent*, 8 December   1.20
Reid v UK (2003) 37 EHRR 9   8.62
Rewe-Zentralfinanz GmbH v Landwirtschaftskammer für Saarland: 33/76
  [1976] ECR 1989, [1977] 1 CMLR 533, CMR 8382   3.14
Rey v Government of Switzerland [1999] 1 AC 54, [1998] 3 WLR 1, (1998)
  142 SJLB 167   1.154
Reyners v Belgium [1974] ECR 631, [1974] 2 CMLR 305   1.204
Richardson v Solihull Metropolitan Borough Council, White v Ealing
  London Borough Council [1998] 1 FCR 344, [1998] ELR 203   11.118
Riche v Ashbury Railway Carriage and Iron Co (1874) LR 9 Exch 224, 43
  LJ Ex 177, 23 WR 7, 31 LT 339   13.41
Richmond Borough Council v Watson [2000] EWCA Civ 239   6.118

Ridge v Baldwin [1964] AC 40, [1963] 2 WLR 935, [1963] 2 All ER 66,
(1963) 127 JP 295, (1963) 127 JP 251, 61 LGR 369, 37 ALJ 140,
234 LT 423, 113 LJ 716, (1963) 107 SJ 313 .... 1.04, 1.122, 15.160
Rikha Begum v London Borough of Tower Hamlets [2005] 1 WLR 2103 .... 7.60
Ringeisen v Austria, No 1 (1979-80) 1 EHRR 455 .... 1.179
Risk Management Partners Ltd v Brent London Borough Council [2009]
EWCA Civ 490, [2009] LGR 99, [2010] PTSR 349, [2009] All ER
(D) 109 (Jun) 13.58, 13.59, 13.64
RK v Chief Constable of South Yorkshire [2013] EWHC 1555 (Admin),
[2013] ACD 121 .... 1.55
Roberts v Hopwood [1925] AC 578, 23 LGR 337, 89 JP 105, 94 LJKB 542,
[1925] All ER Rep 24, 69 Sol Jo 475, 133 LT 289, 41 TLR 436 .... 13.87, 13.88, 13.89,
13.91, 13.95
Robin Murray & Co v The Lord Chancellor [2011] EWHC 1528 (Admin),
[2011] ACD 103, [2011] NPC 64 .... 1.146
Roche v United Kingdom (32555/96) (2006) 42 EHRR 30 .... 1.179
Rodrigues Da Silva & Hoogkamer v Netherlands (2007) 44 EHRR 34 .... 14.50
Roose v Parole Board and Secretary of State for Justice [2010] EWHC 1780
(Admin), (2010) Times, 1 September 10.57
Rowland v Environment Agency [2002] EWHC 2785 (Ch), [2003] Ch 581,
[2003] 2 WLR 1233, [2003] 1 All ER 625, [2003] 1 Lloyd's Rep 427,
(2003) 100(9) LSG 28, (2002) Times, 28 December 1.139
Rowland v Environment Agency [2003] EWCA Civ 1885, [2005] Ch 1,
[2004] 3 WLR 249, [2004] 2 Lloyd's Rep 55, (2004) 101(8) LSG 30,
[2003] NPC 165, (2004) Times, 20 January 1.137, 1.195
Rowley v Secretary of State for Work and Pensions [2007] EWCA Civ 598,
[2007] 1 WLR 2861, [2007] 3 FCR 431, [2007] 2 FLR 945, [2007]
Fam Law 896, (2007) Times, 6 July, 151 Sol Jo LB 856, [2007] All
ER (D) 186 (Jun) 2.84
Royal College of Nursing of the United Kingdom v Dept of Health and
Social Security [1981] AC 800, [1981] 1 All ER 545, [1981] 2 WLR
279, 125 Sol Jo 149, 1 BMLR 40 .... 2.72
Roylance v General Medical Council (No 2) [2000] 1 AC 311, [1999] 3
WLR 541, [1999] Lloyd's Rep Med 139, (1999) 47 BMLR 63, (1999)
143 SJLB 183, (1999) Times, 26 March 15.172
Rrapaj v Director of Legal Aid Casework [2013] EWHC 1837 (Admin) 3.36
Runa Begum v Tower Hamlets London Borough Council (First Secretary of
State Intervening) [2003] UKHL 5, [2003] 2 AC 430, [2003] 2 WLR
388, [2003] UKHRR 419, [2003] 1 All ER 731, HL 1.95
Rushbridger v HM Attorney General [2003] UKHL 38, [2004] 1 AC 357,
[2003] 3 WLR 232, [2003] 3 All ER 784, [2003] HRLR 32, (2003)
153 NLJ 1029, (2003) 147 SJLB 812, (2003) Times, 27 June 1.55, 1.201
Rushmoor Borough Council v Richards (1996) Times, 5 February 12.40, 12.42
Russell v Bar Standards Board [2012] All ER (D) 122 .... 15.197
Russell v Transocean International Resources Ltd [2011] UKSC 57, [2012] 2
All ER 166, 2012 SC (UKSC) 250, 2012 SLT 239, 2012 SCLR 238,
[2012] 1 CMLR 53, [2012] ICR 185, [2012] IRLR 149, (2011) 161
NLJ 1743, (2011) 155(47) SJLB 31, (2011) Times, 8 December 1.205

S-C (Mental Patient: Habeas Corpus), Re [1996] QB 599, CA 8.30, 8.32
Sagnata Investments Ltd v Norwich Corporation [1971] 2 QB 614, [1971] 3
WLR 133, [1971] 2 All ER 1441, CA 12.39, 12.44, 12.47
Sahardid v Camden LBC [2005] HLR 11 .... 7.70
Sainsbury's Supermarket Limited sub nom Sainsbury's Supermarket Limited v
Winemark the Wine Merchants and others [2012] NIQB 45 .... 12.41
Salha v General Medical Council [2003] UKPC 80, [2004] ECDR 12, (2004)
80 BMLR 169 .... 15.148
Salontaji-Drobnjak v Serbia (ECtHR) 36500/05 .... 8.26
Sampson, Re [1987] 1 WLR 194 .... 9.28, 9.29, 9.33
Samuda v Secretary of State for Work & Pensions & Harris [2014] EWCA
Civ 1, [2014] CP Rep 18 .... 8.51

Sanders v Ethical Standards Officer [2005] EWHC 2132 (Admin), [2006]
  BLGR 111, (2005) 102(44) LSG 33, (2005) Times, 14 November 15.205
Sanders v Kingston [2005] EWHC 1145 .... 13.113
Sardar & Others v Watford Borough Council [2006] EWHC 1590, Admin 12.61
Savage v Hillingdon LBC [2010] EWHC 88 (Admin) 7.51
Savva v Royal London Borough of Kensington and Chelsea [2010] EWHC
  414 (Admin), (2010) 13 CCL Rep 227 .... 1.179
Sayce v TNT (UK) Ltd [2011] EWCA Civ 1583, [2012] 1 WLR 1261,
  [2012] RTR 22, [2012] Lloyd's Rep IR 183, [2012] PIQR P8 .... 1.123
Scholarastica UMO v Commissioner for Local Administration [2003] EWHC
  3202 (Admin) 2.210
Scrivens v Ethical Standards Officer [2005] EWHC 124, Admin 13.114
Seal v Chief Constable of South Wales [2007] UKHL 31 .... 8.25, 8.26
Secretary of State for Education and Science v Tameside Metropolitan
  Borough Council [1977] AC 1014, [1976] 3 WLR 641, [1976] 3 All
  ER 665, (1976) 120 SJ 735 .... 1.17, 1.19, 1.102, 1.114, 1.115
Secretary of State for Justice v B [2011] EWCA Civ 1608, [2012] 1 WLR
  2043, (2012) 124 BMLR 13, [2012] MHLR 131, (2012) Times, 19
  January 8.53
Secretary of State for Justice v RB & Lancashire Care NHS Foundation
  Trust [2010] UKUT 454 (AAC), [2011] MHLR 37 .... 8.53, 8.55
Secretary of State for the Home Department v AF (No 3) [2009] UKHL 28,
  [2010] 2 AC 269, [2009] 3 WLR 74, [2009] 3 All ER 643, [2009]
  HRLR 26, [2009] UKHRR 1177, 26 BHRC 738, (2009) 106(25) LSG
  14, (2009) Times, 11 June 1.123, 1.180
Secretary of State for the Home Department v AP (No 1) [2010] UKSC 24,
  [2011] 2 AC 1, [2010] 3 WLR 51, [2010] 4 All ER 245, [2010]
  HRLR 25, [2010] UKHRR 748, 29 BHRC 296, (2010) 107(26) LSG
  17, (2010) 160 NLJ 903, (2010) Times, 17 June 1.105, 1.173
Secretary of State for the Home Department v E [2007] UKHL 46, [2008] 1
  AC 440, [2007] 3 WLR 681, [2008] 1 All ER 657, [2008] HRLR 6,
  [2008] UKHRR 119, [2008] Crim LR 491, (2007) 157 NLJ 1577,
  (2007) 151 SJLB 1437, (2007) Times, 6 November 1.173
Secretary of State for the Home Department v GG [2009] EWCA Civ 786,
  [2010] QB 585, [2010] 2 WLR 731, [2010] 1 All ER 721, (2009)
  Times, 21 October 1.201
Secretary of State for the Home Department v JJ [2007] UKHL 45, [2008] 1
  AC 385, [2007] 3 WLR 642, [2008] 1 All ER 613, [2008] HRLR 5,
  [2008] UKHRR 80, 24 BHRC 531, [2008] Crim LR 489, (2007) 157
  NLJ 1576, (2007) 151 SJLB 1432, (2007) Times, 5 November 1.172, 1.173
Secretary of State for the Home Department v Lim [2007] EWCA Civ 733 .... 14.23
Secretary of State for the Home Department v MB [2007] UKHL 47, [2008]
  1 AC 499, [2007] 3 WLR 720, [2008] 1 All ER 699, [2008] HRLR 7,
  [2008] UKHRR 69, [2008] Crim LR 486, (2007) 157 NLJ 1578,
  (2007) 151 SJLB 1433, Times, November 13, 2007 .... 1.173
Security Industry Authority v Stewart & Others [2007] EWHC 2338
  (Admin) 12.13, 12.15
Selmouni v France [1988] EHRLR 510 .... 1.168
Sempra Metals Ltd (formerly Metallgesellschaft Ltd) v Inland Revenue Cssrs
  [2008] 1 AC 561 .... 2.94
SH (Iran) v SSHD [2014] EWCA Civ 1469 .... 14.49
Shah v General Pharmaceutical Council [2011] EWHC 73 (Admin) 15.67
Shahzad (Art 8: legitimate aim) [2014] UKUT 00085 (IAC) 14.50
Sheill v General Medical Council [2008] EWHC 2967 (Admin) 15.211
Singleton v Law Society [2005] EWHC 2915 .... 15.148
Sinha v General Medical Council [2009] EWCA Civ 80 .... 15.101, 15.158
SL v Westminster City Council [2013] UKSC 27, [2013] 1 WLR 1445,
  [2013] 3 All ER 191, [2013] PTSR 691, [2013] HLR 30, [2013]
  BLGR 423, (2013) 16 CCL Rep 161 .... 6.129
Smalley, Re [1985] AC 622, [1985] 2 WLR 538, [1985] 1 All ER 769, HL 9.26, 9.28, 9.34, 9.35

Smirek v Williams [2000] EWCA Civ 3025   8.15
Smith & others v SSTI and London Development Agency [2007] EWHC
   1013   5.62
Smith v East Ello Rural District Council [1956] AC 736, [1956] 2 WLR 888,
   [1956] 1 All ER 855, (1956) 120 JP 263, 54 LGR 233, (1956) 6
   P & CR 102, (1956) 100 SJ 282   1.56
Smith v Inner London Education Authority [1978] 1 All ER 411   2.10
Smith v United Kingdom (No 1) (2000) 29 EHRR 493, ECHR   1.33
Somerville v Scottish Ministers [2007] UKHL 44, [2007] 1 WLR 2734, 2008
   SC (HL) 45, 2007 SLT 1113, 2007 SCLR 830, [2008] HRLR 3,
   [2008] UKHRR 570, (2007) 151 SJLB 1398, 2007 GWD 37-656   1.42
South Buckinghamshire District Council v Porter (No 2) [2004] UKHL 33,
   [2004] 1 WLR 1953, [2004] 4 All ER 775, [2005] 1 P & CR 6,
   [2004] 4 PLR 50, [2004] 28 EG 177 (CS), (2004) 101(31) LSG 25,
   (2004) 148 SJLB 825, [2004] NPC 108, (2004) *Times*, 2 July, (2004)
   Independent, 6 July   1.151, 1.155, 5.32
South Bucks District Council v Flanagan [2002] EWCA Civ 690, [2002] 1
   WLR 2601, [2002] 3 PLR 47, [2002] JPL 1465, (2002) 99(25) LSG
   35, (2002) 146 SJLB 136, [2002] NPC 71   1.139
Southall v General Medical Council [2010] EWCA Civ 40, [2010] 1 WLR
   1508, [2010] 4 All ER 680, [2010] 4 Costs LR 481, (2010) 160 NLJ
   217, (2010) *Times*, 2 March   15.168, 15.169
Sporrong v Sweden [1982] 5 EHRR 35   12.07
Stec v United Kingdom (65731/01) (2006) 43 EHRR 47, 20 BHRC 348,
   (2006) *Times*, 26 May   1.193
Steele v Home Office [2010] EWCA Civ 724, (2010) 115 BMLR 218   10.46
Stefan v General Medical Council [1999] 1 WLR 1293, [2000] HRLR 1, 6
   BHRC 487, [1999] Lloyd's Rep Med 90, (1999) 49 BMLR 161,
   (1999) 143 SJLB 112, (1999) *Times*, 11 March   1.153, 1.154, 15.168
Stepney Borough Council v Joffe, Stepney Borough Council v Diamond,
   Stepney Borough Council v White [1949] 1 KB 599, [1949] 1 All ER
   256, [1949] LJR 561, 113 JP 124, QBD   12.43, 12.47
Stockton on Tees Borough Council v Latif [2009] EWHC 228, Admin   12.38
Streames v Copping [1985] QB 920, [1985] 2 WLR 993, [1985] 2 All ER
   122, QBD   9.17
Stringer v Minister of Housing and Local Government and Another [1970] 1
   WLR 1281, [1971] 1 All ER 65, QBD   5.70
Stuart Bracking v Secretary of State for Work and Pensions [2013] EWCA
   Civ 1345, [2014] Eq LR 60, (2013) 16 CCL Rep 479   6.45
Sullivan v United States [2012] EWHC 1680 (Admin), (2012) 156(25) SJLB
   31   1.173
Sunworld Ltd v Hammersmith and Fulham London Borough Council, R v
   Blackfriars Crown Court ex p Sunworld Ltd [2000] 1 WLR 2102,
   [2000] 2 All ER 837, [2000] Crim LR 593, QBD   5.70
Suratt and others v Att-Gen of Trinidad and Tobago [2008] 2 WLR 262   2.60
Surrey County Council v CA [2011] EWCA Civ 190, [2012] Fam 170,
   [2012] 2 WLR 1056, [2012] PTSR 727, [2011] 2 FLR 583, [2011] 1
   FCR 559, [2011] HRLR 19, [2011] UKHRR 584, (2011) 14 CCL
   Rep 209, [2011] MHLR 125, [2011] Fam Law 475   1.174
Swain v Law Society [1983] 1 AC 598, [1982] 3 WLR 261, [1982] 2 All ER
   827, (1982) 79 LSG 887, (1982) 126 SJ 464   15.196

Tan Te Lam v Superintendant of Tai A Chau Detention Centre [1997] AC
   97, [1996] 2 WLR 863, [1996] 4 All ER 256, (1996) 140 SJLB 106   1.98
Tariq v Home Office [2011] UKSC 35, [2012] 1 AC 452, [2011] 3 WLR
   322, [2012] 1 All ER 58, [2012] 1 CMLR 2, [2011] ICR 938, [2011]
   IRLR 843, [2011] HRLR 37, [2011] UKHRR 1060, (2011) *Times*, 18
   July   1.123, 1.205
Taylor v General Chiropractic Council [2009] EWHC 301 (Admin)   15.86
Taylor v Munrow [1960] 1 WLR 151   13.98

Tehrani v United Kingdom Central Council for Nursing Midwifery and
    Health Visiting 2001 SC 581, 2001 SLT 879, [2001] IRLR 208, 2001
    GWD 4-165   15.33
Terry v LB Tower Hamlets (2009) Unreported, 15 December, QBD   3.78
Tesco Stores Ltd v Dundee City Council [2012] UKSC 13, [2012] PTSR 983,
    2012 SC (UKSC) 278, 2012 SLT 739, [2012] 2 P & CR 9, [2012] JPL
    1078, [2012] 13 EG 91 (CS), 2012 GWD 12-235   1.79, 5.97, 5.98, 5.99
Tesco Stores Ltd v Secretary of State for the Environment and Others [1995]
    1 WLR 759, [1995] 2 All ER 636, 93 LGR 403, (1995) 70 P & CR
    184, [1995] 2 PLR 72, [1995] 2 EGLR 147, [1995] 27 EG 154,
    [1995] EG 82 (CS), (1995) 92(24) LSG 39, (1995) 145 NLJ 724,
    (1995) 139 SJLB 145, (1995) *Times*, 13 May   1.105, 5.32, 5.92
Tewkesbury Borough Council v Secretary of State for Communities and
    Local Government [2013] EWHC 286, Admin   5.91
Thaker v Solicitors Regulation Authority [2011] EWHC 660 (Admin)   15.146
Thames Water Utilities Ltd v Transport for London [2013] EWHC 187
    (Admin), [2013] PTSR 627, [2013] RTR 16   1.89
Thobani v Solicitors Regulation Authority [2011] All ER (D) 12 (Dec)   15.88
Thoburn v Sunderland City Council [2002] EWHC 195 (Admin), [2003] QB
    151, [2002] 3 WLR 247, [2002] 4 All ER 156, (2002) 166 JP 257,
    [2002] 1 CMLR 50, [2002] Eu LR 253, (2002) 99(15) LSG 35,
    (2002) 152 NLJ 312, (2002) 146 SJLB 69, (2002) *Times*, 22 February   1.161, 1.202, 1.204
Thomas v Bridgend County Borough Council [2011] EWCA Civ 862   1.196
Three Rivers DC v Governors of the Bank of England [2003] 1 AC 1   2.89
Threlfall v General Optical Council [2004] EWHC 2683 (Admin), [2005]
    Lloyd's Rep Med 250, [2005] ACD 70, (2004) 101(48) LSG 25,
    (2004) *Times*, 2 December   15.55, 15.168, 15.213
Thurrock Borough Council v West [2012] EWCA Civ 1435, [2013] HLR 5,
    [2013] 1 P & CR 12, [2013] L & TR 11, [2013] 1 P & CR DG9   1.184
Times Investment Ltd v SOSE (1991) 61 P & CR 98, [1990] 3 PLR 111,
    [1991] JPL 67, [1991] COD 158, (1991) 155 LG Rev 870, (1990)
    Times, 21 June   5.26
Tinnelly v United Kingdom (20390/92) (1999) 27 EHRR 249   1.179
Tinsa v General Medical Council [2008] EWHC 1284 (Admin), (2008) 103
    BMLR 41   15.144
Tower Hamlets LBC v Begum (Runa) [2003] UKHL 5, [2003] 2 AC 430,
    [2003] 2 WLR 388, [2003] UKHRR 419, [2003] 1 All ER 731, HL   7.39
TP and KM v United Kingdom Application No 28945/95 (2002) 34 EHRR
    2, [2001] 2 FLR 549, [2001] Fam Law 590, (2001) 3 LGLR 52,
    ECHR   2.86
Tre Trakoter Aktiebolag v Sweden [1991] EHRR 309   12.09, 12.11, 12.12, 12.17
Trent Strategic Health Authority v Jain [2009] UKHL 4, [2009] AC 853,
    [2009] 1 All ER 957, [2009] 2 WLR 248, [2009] PTSR 382, 106
    BMLR 88, (2009) *Times*, 22 January, 153 Sol Jo (no 4) 27, [2009] All
    ER (D) 148 (Jan)   2.84
TTM v Hackney LBC, East London NHS Foundation Trust and Secretary of
    State for Health [2010] EWHC 1349 (Admin)   8.31
TTM v Hackney LBC, East London NHS Foundation Trust and Secretary of
    State for Health [2011] EWCA Civ 4   8.33
Twinsectra Ltd v Yardley and Others [2002] UKHL 12, [2002] 2 AC 164,
    [2002] 2 WLR 802, [2002] 2 All ER 377, [2002] PNLR 30, [2002]
    WTLR 423, [2002] 38 EG 204 (CS), (2002) 99(19) LSG 32, (2002)
    152 NLJ 469, (2002) 146 SJLB 84, [2002] NPC 47, (2002) *Times*, 25
    March   15.151

Uddin v General Medical Council [2012] EWHC 2669 (Admin)   2.21
Udom v General Medical Council [2009] EWHC 3242 (Admin), [2010] Med
    LR 37, (2010) 112 BMLR 47   15.203

UK Coal Mining Ltd v Secretary of State for Communities and Local
    Government [2013] EWHC 2142 (Admin), [2014] JPL 14 .... 5.100
Uniplex (UK) Ltd v NHS Business Services Authority (C-406/09) 3.14
United Kingdom Association of Fish Producer Organisations v Secretary of
    State for Environment, Food and Rural Affairs [2013] EWHC 1959
    (Admin) 1.142
University of Bristol v North Somerset Council [2013] EWHC 231 (Admin),
    [2013] JPL 940 .... 5.24

Van Colle v Chief Constable of Hertfordshire [2008] UKHL 50, [2009] 1 AC
    225, [2008] 3 WLR 593, [2008] 3 All ER 977, [2009] 1 Cr App R
    12, [2008] HRLR 44, [2008] UKHRR 967, [2009] PIQR P2, [2009]
    LS Law Medical 1, [2008] Inquest LR 176, [2008] Po LR 151, (2008)
    152(32) SJLB 31, (2008) *Times*, 1 August, (2008) *Times*, 4 August ... 1.166
Varma v General Medical Council [2008] EWHC 753 (Admin), [2008] LS
    Law Medical 313, (2008) 102 BMLR 84, (2008) 152(18) SJLB 30 ..... 15.144
Venton v Solicitors Regulation Authority [2010] EWHC 1377 (Admin) 15.75
Veolia ES Nottinghamshire Ltd v Nottinghamshire County Council [2009]
    EWHC 2382 (Admin) 2.200
Vigon v DPP [1998] Crim LR 289, DC 9.56
Virdi v Law Society [2010] EWCA Civ 100, [2010] 1 WLR 2840, [2010] 3
    All ER 653, [2010] ACD 38, (2010) 107(9) LSG 14   1.131, 15.158, 15.170, 15.195
Virgin Cinema Properties Ltd v Secretary of State for the Environment
    [1998] 2 PLR 24, [1998] PLCR 1, [1997] EG 135 (CS), [1997] NPC
    139, (1997) *Independent*, 20 October 5.96
Vodafone 2 v Revenue and Customs Commissioners [2009] EWCA Civ 446,
    [2010] Ch 77, [2010] 2 WLR 288, [2010] Bus LR 96, [2009] STC
    1480, [2010] Eu LR 110, [2009] BTC 273, [2009] STI 1795, (2009)
    Times, 26 June 1.205
Vranicki v Architects Registration Board [2007] EWHC 506 (Admin), [2007]
    13 EG 254 (CS) 15.152

W v Doncaster MBC [2004] EWCA Civ 378 .... 8.68
Wainhomes (South West) Holdings Ltd v SSCLG [2012] EWHC 914
    (Admin) 5.112
Wainwright v Home Office [2003] UKHL 53, [2004] 2 AC 406, [2003] 3
    WLR 1137, [2004] UKHRR 154, [2003] 4 All ER 969, HL 1.55, 1.201
Walker v General Medical Council [2010] EWHC 3849 (Admin) 15.190
Waltham Forest NHS Primary Care Trust & Others v Malik [2007] EWCA
    Civ 265 .... 12.12, 12.13, 12.14, 12.15
Walton v Scottish Ministers [2012] UKSC 44, [2013] PTSR 51, 2013 SC
    (UKSC) 67, 2012 SLT 1211, [2013] 1 CMLR 28, [2013] Env LR 16,
    [2013] JPL 323, 2012 GWD 34-689 .... 5.59
Wandsworth LBC v Winder [1985] AC 461, 17 HLR 196, HL 7.87
Warner v Suckerman 81 ER 101, (1615) 3 Bulst 119 .... 1.04
Warwickshire CC v British Railways Board [1969] 3 All ER 631, [1969] 1
    WLR 1117, CA 2.67
Watkins v Home Office [2006] 2 AC 395 .... 2.89
Weeks v UK (1988) 10 EHRR 293, (1987) *Times*, 5 March 10.56
Wells v Secretary of State for Transport, Local Government and the Regions
    (Case C-201/02) [2004] ECR 1-273 .... 5.46
Westley v Hertfordshire County Council (1998) Unreported 9.89
Westminster City Council v O'Reilly [2003] EWCA Civ 1007 .... 12.57
Wheeler v Leicester City Council [1985] AC 1054, [1985] 3 WLR 335,
    [1985] 2 All ER 1106, 83 LGR 725, (1985) 129 SJ 558 .... 1.56, 1.60
Whelan v R [1921] 2 IR 310 .... 2.117
Whitfield v UK (App Nos 46387/99, 48906/99, 57410/00 and 57419/00) 10.86
William Sinclair v English Nature [2001] EWHC 408 (Admin) 2.15

Wilson v First County Trust Ltd (No 2) [2003] UKHL 40, [2004] 1 AC 816,
    [2003] 3 WLR 568, [2003] 4 All ER 97, [2003] 2 All ER (Comm)
    491, [2003] HRLR 33, [2003] UKHRR 1085, (2003) 100(35) LSG
    39, (2003) 147 SJLB 872, (2003) *Times*, 11 July, (2003) *Independent*,
    3 November 1.71, 1.111, 1.139, 1.163, 1.197
Windsor and Maidenhead Royal Borough Council v Brandrose Investments
    Ltd [1983] 1 WLR 509 .... 2.107
Winterwerp v The Netherlands (1979) 2 EHRR 387 .... 8.07, 8.10, 8.21
Wiseman v Borneman [1971] AC 297, [1969] 3 All ER 275, [1969] 3 WLR
    706, 113 SJ 838, 45 TC 540, [1969] TR 279, HL, affirming [1968]
    Ch 429, [1967] 3 All ER 1045, [1968] 2 WLR 320, 46 ATC 237, 111
    SJ 892, [1967] TR 415, CA, affirming [1968] Ch 334, [1967] 3 All
    ER 546, [1967] 3 WLR 1372, 46 ATC 439, 111 SJ 606, [1967] TR 1.123
WM (DRC) v SSHD [2006] EWCA Civ 1495, [2007] Imm AR 337, [2007]
    INLR 126, (2006) 103(45) LSG 27, (2006) *Times*, 1 December 14.41
Woolwich Building Society v Inland Revenue Cssrs (No 2) [1993] AC 70 ..... 2.91, 2.92, 2.97

X v Bedfordshire County Council [1995] 2 AC 633 .... 2.82, 2.83, 2.85, 2.88

Yanah v General Medical Council [2006] EWHC 3843 (Admin), [2007] LS
    Law Medical 143 .... 15.168
YC v United Kingdom [2012] 2 FLR 332, [2013] 2 FCR 36, (2012) 55
    EHRR 33, [2012] Fam Law 932 .... 1.184
Yeong v General Medical Council [2009] EWHC 1923 (Admin), [2010] 1
    WLR 548, [2009] LS Law Medical 582, (2009) 110 BMLR 125,
    Times, August 25, 2009 .... 15.153
YH (Iraq) v SSHD [2010] 4 All ER 448 .... 14.44
Yildiz v Secretary of State for Social Security [2001] EWCA Civ 309, (2001)
    Independent, 9 March 1.201
YL v Birmingham City Council [2007] UKHL 27, [2008] 1 AC 95, [2007] 3
    WLR 112, [2007] 3 All ER 957, [2007] HRLR 32, [2008] UKHRR
    346, [2007] HLR 44, [2008] BLGR 273, (2007) 10 CCL Rep 505,
    [2007] LS Law Medical 472, (2007) 96 BMLR 1, (2007) 104(27)
    LSG 29, (2007) 157 NLJ 938, (2007) 151 SJLB 860, [2007] NPC 75,
    (2007) *Times*, 21 June 1.163, 15.41
Young v UK (App No 56745/00) 10.86
Younger Homes (Northern) Ltd v FSS and Calderdale MBC [2004] EWCA
    Civ 1060, [2005] Env LR 12, [2005] 1 P & CR 14, [2005] 3 PLR 21,
    [2005] JPL 354 .... 5.61
Youssef v Secretary of State for Foreign and Commonwealth Affairs [2011]
    EWHC 3014 (Admin), [2012] ACD 3 .... 3.37

Z v United Kingdom (2002) 34 EHRR 97 .... 2.86
Z v United Kingdom (29392/95) [2001] 2 FLR 612 .... 1.170
Zalewska v Department of Social Security [2008] UKHL 67, [2008] 1 WLR
    2602, [2009] 2 All ER 319, [2009] NI 116, [2009] 1 CMLR 24,
    [2009] Eu LR 344, (2008) 158 NLJ 1643, (2008) 152(45) SJLB 27,
    (2008) *Times*, 14 November 1.206
ZH (Tanzania) v SSHD [2011] UKSC 4, [2011] 2 AC 166, [2011] 2 WLR
    148, [2011] 2 All ER 783, [2011] 1 FLR 2170, [2011] 1 FCR 221,
    [2011] HRLR 15, [2011] UKHRR 371, [2011] Imm AR 395, [2011]
    INLR 369, [2011] Fam Law 468, (2011) 108(7) LSG 17, (2011)
    155(5) SJLB 30, (2011) *Times*, 8 February 14.47
Ziderman v General Dental Council [1976] 1 WLR 330, [1976] 2 All ER
    334, (1975) 120 SJ 48, (1975) *Times*, 10 December 15.102
ZL and VL v SSHD [2003] 1 WLR 1230 .... 14.45
ZT (Kosovo) v SSHD [2011] EWCA Civ 193, [2011] 1 WLR 3200, [2011] 2
    All ER 772, (2011) 108(11) LSG 20, (2011) *Times*, 21 April 14.44
Zygmunt v General Medical Council [2008] EWHC 2643 (Admin), [2009]
    LS Law Medical 219 .... 15.153, 15.204

TABLE OF STATUTES

References are to paragraph numbers.

Academies Act 2010	11.03, 11.12
s 1A	11.13
s 1B	11.13
s 1C	11.13
s 9	11.14
s 10	11.14
Access to Justice Act 1999	
s 11	3.79
s 22	3.78
Acquisition of Land Act 1981	5.16, 5.39, 5.40, 5.41, 5.42
s 23	5.39, 5.40
s 23(4)	5.40
s 23(4)(b)	5.40
s 24	5.42
s 24(1)	5.41
s 24(2)	5.41
s 25	5.42
Administration of Justice Act 1960	
s 1	9.86, 9.88
s 2	9.87
Apprenticeships, Skills, Children and Learning Act 2009	11.03
Architects Act 1997	15.17
Asylum and Immigration (Treatment of Claimants etc) Act 2004	14.04, 14.55
Asylum and Immigration Appeals Act 1993	14.04
Audit Commission Act 1998	2.192
s 8	2.195
s 15(1)	2.200
s 17(1)	2.196
s 19A	2.198
Bail Act 1976	
s 4	9.73
s 4(2)	9.73
Betting, Gaming and Lotteries Act 1963	12.39
Bill of Rights 1689	2.69
Borders, Citizenship and Immigration Act 2009	14.04, 14.55
s 55	14.47
British Nationality Act 1981	4.20, 14.04
Broadcasting Act 1981	2.37
s 4(3)	2.37
Carers (Equal Opportunities) Act 2004	
s 1	6.102
Carers (Equal Opportunities) Act 2004—*continued*	
s 2	6.102
s 3	6.103
Carers (Recognition and Services) Act 1995	6.69, 6.95, 6.96, 6.97, 6.102
Carers and Disabled Children's Act 2000	6.98, 6.100, 6.101, 6.102
s 1	6.99
s 2	6.99, 6.100
Charities Act 1993	
s 2(c)	4.24
Child Support Act 1991	4.22
s 24	4.24
s 25	4.25
Child Trust Funds Act 2004	
s 21(10)	4.24
Childcare Act 2006	11.03
Children Act 1989	1.96, 1.98, 6.50, 6.60, 6.61, 6.62, 6.63, 6.65, 6.69, 6.70, 6.90, 6.130, 6.131, 8.77, 11.120
Pt III	6.48, 6.63
s 17	6.49, 6.52, 6.58, 6.63, 6.65, 6.69, 6.73, 6.107, 6.124
s 17–30	6.48
s 17(1)	6.49, 6.65
s 17(2)	6.52
s 17(6)	6.53
s 17(10)	6.50
s 17(11)	6.51
s 17A	6.64
s 20	6.54, 6.55, 6.57, 6.62, 6.131
s 20(1)	6.54, 6.56, 6.58, 6.60, 6.82
s 20(4)	6.56
s 21	6.64
s 22	6.64, 6.73
s 22(1)	6.82
s 23	6.64
s 23A	6.72
s 23B	6.72, 6.73, 6.74
s 23C	6.75, 6.90, 6.91, 6.124
s 23C(4)(a)	6.91
s 23C(4)(b)	6.91
s 23C(4)(c)	6.75, 6.91
s 23C(5)	6.75
s 23D	6.76
s 24	6.77, 6.79
s 24(2)	6.77
s 24A	6.78, 6.124
s 24B	6.73, 6.78, 6.79, 6.124

Children Act 1989—*continued*	
s 27	6.80
s 28A	6.48
s 193	6.57
Sch 2	6.48, 6.52, 6.65, 6.107
Sch 2, para 1	6.65
Sch 2, para 3	6.65
Children Act 2004	6.69, 10.13, 10.43, 11.03
Children (Leaving Care) Act 2000	6.70, 6.80
Children and Families Act 2014	11.03, 11.102
Children and Young Persons Act 1933	
s 39(1)	9.35
Children and Young Persons Act 2008	11.03
Children, Schools and Families Act 2010	11.03
Chiropractors Act 1994	15.17
s 29	15.73
Chronically Sick and Disabled Persons Act 1970	6.50, 6.63, 6.65, 6.121, 6.152
s 2	6.26, 6.33, 6.48, 6.63, 6.107
s 2(1)	6.09, 6.33
s 2(1)(e)	6.35
s 28A	6.63, 6.107
Community Care (Direct Payment) Act 1996	6.37
Compensation Act 2006	
s 13	4.24
Constitutional Reform Act 2005	2.60
Sch 2, Pt 1	4.19
Consumer Credit Act 1974	
s 41A	4.24
Contempt of Court Act 1981	
s 11	9.34
Courts-Martial (Appeals) Act 1968	
s 1	2.60
Crime (Sentences) Act 1997	10.54, 10.56, 10.73
s 30(2)	10.56
s 32	10.54
s 32A	10.73
s 254	10.54
s 254(2A)	10.54
Crime and Courts Act 2013	14.15
Crime and Disorder Act 1998	
s 51	9.34
Criminal Appeal Act 1968	9.28
Criminal Injuries Compensation Act 1995	4.16
Criminal Justice Act 1948	
s 37(1)(b)(ii)	9.64
s 37(1)(d)	9.64
Criminal Justice Act 1967	
s 22(1)	9.38
Criminal Justice Act 1987	9.32
Criminal Justice Act 1991	10.54, 10.56, 10.72
s 36	10.56
s 239(2)	10.56
Criminal Justice Act 2003	10.01, 10.51, 10.52, 10.54, 10.56, 10.65, 10.67, 10.69, 10.72
s 160	10.69
s 244	10.51
s 246	10.65
s 246(4)	10.65
s 248	10.56
s 250(4)	10.52
s 254	10.67
s 255	10.67, 10.68
Criminal Justice Act 2009	
s 5	10.125
s 7	10.125
Criminal Law Act 1967	10.107
s 3	10.107
Crown Proceedings Act 1947	2.08
Pt II	2.09
s 21(1)	2.78
s 38(2)	2.09, 2.78
Data Protection Act 1998	4.16, 15.120
s 28	4.25
s 49	4.24
Dentists Act 1984	15.17, 15.120
s 50C	15.73
Disability Discrimination Act 1995	6.25
s 49A	6.25, 6.42
s 49A(1)	6.36
Disability Discrimination Act 2005	6.25
Disabled Persons (Services, Consultation and Representation) Act 1986	
s 4	6.17, 6.33
s 8	6.33, 6.94
Education (Wales) Measure 2011	11.07
Education Act 1944	2.121, 11.03
Education Act 1981	2.85
Education Act 1996	11.02, 11.05, 11.09, 11.16, 11.110, 11.116, 11.158, 11.159
Pt IV	11.110
s 2(1)	11.09
s 4(1B)	11.13
s 4(1C)	11.13
s 5(2)	11.09
s 5(3)	11.09
s 6	11.09
s 7	11.04
s 9	11.53
s 19	11.55
s 328(2)	11.116
s 332B	11.105
s 463	11.16, 11.18
s 518	11.72
Education Act 2002	11.02, 11.06, 11.125
s 51A(3)	11.127
s 51A(4)	11.129
s 52(4)(b)	11.125
s 158	11.16
s 159	11.17
s 162A	11.16

Table of Statutes

Education Act 2002—*continued*	
s 163	11.16
Education Act 2005	11.03
Education Act 2011	11.03, 11.13, 15.17
Education (Wales) Act 2014	11.07
Education and Inspections Act 2006	11.03, 11.123
Pt 2	11.28, 11.30
Pt 7	11.123
s 15	11.28
s 15–17	11.28
s 15(4)	11.29
s 16	11.28, 11.29
s 17	11.29
s 52	11.132
s 60	11.27
s 89	11.123
s 92	11.124
s 93	11.124
s 94	11.124
Sch 2	11.28
Education and Skills Act 2008	11.03, 11.07
Education Reform Act 1988	11.03, 11.06
s 120(1)	11.23
s 235(2)(e)	11.23
Sch 6	11.23
Enduring Powers of Attorney Act 1985	8.73
Equality Act 2010	1.83, 1.201, 10.28
s 5	10.28
s 6	10.28
s 7	10.28
s 8	10.28
s 9	10.28
s 10	10.28
s 11	10.28
s 12	10.28
s 13	10.28
s 19	10.28
s 20	6.17, 10.28
s 85	11.74
s 149	1.83, 6.25, 6.147, 16.07
s 149(1)	6.42
s 149(3)	6.42
Estate Agents Act 1979	
s 7	4.24
European Communities Act 1972	1.202, 1.204, 5.44
s 2	1.204
Extradition Act 2003	1.89
Finance Act 2008	
s 124	1.81
Financial Services Act 2012	15.17
Financial Services and Markets Act 2000	
s 137	4.25
Freedom of Information Act 2000	2.200, 4.16
s 60	4.25
Further and Higher Education (Governance and Information) (Wales) Act 2014	11.07
Further and Higher Education Act 1992	11.19
Further Education and Training Act 2007	11.03, 11.20
Gambling Act 2005	12.59, 12.62, 12.67, 12.104
s 143	4.24
Government of Wales Act 1998	11.07
s 90	2.192
Health and Social Care Act 2001	1.143, 6.64
s 11	1.143
s 49(1)	6.113
s 49(2)	6.113
s 57	6.37
s 58	6.37
Health and Social Care Act 2008	
s 145	6.141
s 148	16.45
Health and Social Care Act 2012	16.55
Health Service Commissioners Act 1993	2.202
Sch 2, para 1A	2.153, 2.215
Health Services and Public Health Act 1968	
s 45	6.32
Higher Education Act 2004	11.03, 11.24
s 13	11.24
s 20	11.24
Highways Act 1980	5.39
Homelessness Act 2002	7.64, 7.75
s 11	7.44
Sch 1, para 17	7.41
Housing Act 1985	16.20
Pt 2	7.69
s 1	7.07
Housing Act 1988	16.20
Housing Act 1996	1.03, 2.25, 2.187, 2.203, 5.39, 6.59, 6.61, 7.10, 7.15, 7.18, 7.21, 7.23, 7.33, 7.36, 7.37, 7.38, 7.53, 7.66, 7.68, 7.73
Pt V	7.12, 7.80, 7.82
Pt VI	7.23, 7.31, 7.64, 7.65, 7.67, 7.69
Pt VII	1.117, 7.04, 7.11, 7.18, 7.34, 7.39, 7.43, 7.45, 7.49, 7.51, 7.55, 7.59, 7.63, 7.71, 7.78
s 1	7.07
s 2	7.07
s 8–10	7.23
s 125A	7.81
s 126	7.65
s 127(2)	7.83
s 128	7.82, 7.84
s 128(6)	7.84
s 129	7.12
s 129(4)(b)	7.84
s 129(5)	7.84
s 138(3)	7.85
s 159	7.65
s 159(7)	7.68
s 160A	7.66

Housing Act 1996—*continued*
  s 166(8) 7.68
  s 167 7.67, 7.74, 7.75, 7.76
  s 167(1A) 7.75
  s 167(2) 7.71, 7.72, 7.73, 7.75, 7.76
  s 167(2)(a)–(e) 7.76
  s 168 7.67
  s 170 7.23
  s 184 7.10, 7.34, 7.37, 7.38, 7.53
  s 184(2) 7.55
  s 188 7.45, 7.47
  s 188(1) 7.45
  s 188(3) 6.124, 7.45, 7.47
  s 189 6.57
  s 190–193 7.34
  s 190(2) 7.61, 7.71
  s 190(4) 7.61
  s 192(3) 7.71
  s 193 6.59, 7.51
  s 193(2) 7.71
  s 193(7) 7.34
  s 195(2) 7.71
  s 198 7.34
  s 199(1) 7.56
  s 200 7.34
  s 202 2.187, 7.33, 7.37, 7.41, 7.44, 7.47, 7.54, 7.61, 7.84
  s 202(1)(c) 7.57
  s 202(1)(d) 7.57
  s 202(1)(e) 7.57
  s 202(3) 7.54
  s 204 1.03, 7.39
  s 204(1) 7.33
  s 204(2) 7.41
  s 204(2A) 7.41
  s 204(3) 7.53
  s 204(4) 6.124
  s 204A 7.42, 7.44
Housing Act 2004 7.11
  Sch 1 7.11
  Sch 2 7.11
  Sch 5 7.11
  Sch 6 7.11
Housing and Regeneration Act 2008 7.03, 7.07, 7.08, 7.26
  Pt 2 7.26
  s 68 7.03
  s 69 7.03
  s 70 7.03
Human Rights Act 1998 1.07, 1.22, 1.34, 1.39, 1.40, 1.160, 1.161, 1.198, 1.200, 2.02, 2.81, 2.101, 2.104, 3.23, 3.24, 5.62, 6.10, 7.05, 7.19, 7.20, 8.35, 9.30, 10.01, 11.154, 13.15, 14.50, 15.19, 15.210
  s 2 1.163
  s 3 1.72, 1.163, 1.201, 1.205
  s 4 1.163, 2.02, 3.24, 13.15, 14.15
  s 6 1.160, 1.163, 1.199, 6.141, 6.142, 14.12, 15.41, 15.46
  s 6(3)(b) 1.163, 7.21
  s 6(5) 1.163, 7.21
  s 7 1.161, 1.163, 1.199, 6.142, 8.25, 8.32

Human Rights Act 1998—*continued*
  s 8 1.161, 1.163, 2.02, 2.99, 2.100
  s 8(3) 2.99
  s 8(4) 2.99
  s 9 3.24
  s 10 1.163
  s 12 1.191
  s 12(4) 1.191
  s 21(1) 13.15
  Sch 1 2.99

Immigration Act 1971 1.98
Immigration Act 2014 14.07, 14.12, 14.50
  s 19 14.07
Immigration and Asylum Act 1999 6.124, 14.04, 14.55
  s 4 6.90
  s 11 6.124
  s 94(1) 6.124
  s 94(3) 6.124
  s 95 6.124
  s 95(1)(a) 6.124
  s 98 6.124
  s 115 6.124
  Sch 3 6.90
Immigration and Nationality Act 2006 14.04, 14.55
Inquiries Act 2005 2.182

Jobseekers Act 1995 1.81
  s 17A 1.81
Justice and Security Act 2013
  s 15 1.03

Lands Tribunal Act 1949
  s 3(4) 4.25
Learning and Skills Act 2000 11.03, 11.19
Legal Aid, Sentencing and Punishment
  of Offenders Act 2012 10.72
  s 113 10.54
  s 119 10.73
Legal Services Act 2007 15.17
Licensing Act 1964 12.57, 12.98, 12.99
Licensing Act 2003 1.89, 12.01, 12.04, 12.18, 12.20, 12.24, 12.25, 12.40, 12.42, 12.59, 12.61, 12.62, 12.63, 12.64, 12.67, 12.68, 12.76, 12.80, 12.91, 12.95, 12.102, 12.104
  s 5 12.59
  s 13(3) 12.76
  s 35(2) 12.74
  s 182 12.62
Lloyd's Act 1982 15.17
Local Authorities (Goods and Services)
  Act 1970 6.105
  s 74(3) 6.105
Local Authority Social Services Act
  1970 6.34
  s 7 6.66
  s 7(1) 6.34

Local Democracy, Economic
    Development and Construction
    Act 2009
  s 34   13.73
  s 79(6)   5.84
Local Government Act 1933   13.42
Local Government Act 1972   1.85, 2.74,
              12.93, 13.46, 13.132, 13.135,
                                    13.138
  s 100A   12.93
  s 100E   12.93
  s 101   1.85, 12.18
  s 111   13.46, 13.48, 13.49, 13.50, 13.51,
                       13.68, 13.69, 13.71
  s 111(1)   13.47
  s 112   13.118
  s 135(1)   13.132
  s 135(2)   13.132
  s 135(3)   13.132
  s 135(4)   13.132
  s 137(2B)   13.69
  Sch 12, para 42   13.131
Local Government Act 1974   2.202
  s 29   2.153, 2.215
Local Government Act 1992   13.26, 13.31,
                               13.38, 13.39
Local Government Act 2000
  Pt I   13.53
  Pt III   13.109
  s 2   13.58, 13.68, 13.69, 13.70
  s 2(1)   13.56, 13.72
  s 3(2)   13.72
  s 78–79   4.24
  s 79(15)   13.113
  s 111   13.54
Local Government Act 2003   2.194
Local Government (Contracts) Act
    1997   13.132
Local Government (Miscellaneous
    Provisions) Act 1976   1.81, 12.21,
                              12.38, 12.104
  s 47   1.81
Local Government (Miscellaneous
    Provisions) Act 1982   12.16, 12.69,
                                12.70, 12.71
  Sch 3   12.19, 12.86
Local Government and Housing Act
    1989   13.69
  s 5   13.119
  s 20   13.131
  s 31   13.107
  s 33   13.69
Local Government and Public
    Involvement in Health Act
    2007   13.26, 13.31, 13.38
Local Government Finance Act 1988
  s 112–114   13.119
Localism Act 2011   5.91, 7.07, 7.64, 13.74,
                                    13.111
  s 1(4)   13.75
  s 2(1)   13.76
  s 2(3)   13.76
  s 3   13.76

Localism Act 2011—continued
  s 4   13.76
  s 5(1)   13.77
  s 5(2)   13.77
  s 5(3)   13.77
  s 25   5.116, 5.117, 5.118, 5.119
  s 25(2)   5.118

Medical Act 1983   15.17, 15.85
  s 22   15.83
  Sch 1
    para 16   15.26
  Sch 3A   15.73
    para 5   15.73
  Sch 3B   15.73
Mental Capacity Act 2005   8.02, 8.21, 8.47,
                   8.48, 8.72, 8.73, 8.74, 8.75, 8.76,
                                  8.78, 8.82, 16.32
  s 1(2)   8.72
  s 1(5)   8.72
  s 2(1)   8.72
  s 3   8.72
  s 4   8.72
  s 4A   8.47
  s 4B   8.47
  s 5   8.72
  s 6   8.72
  s 9–13   8.73
  s 16(2)(a)   8.47
  s 16A(2)   8.77
  s 19   8.73
  s 20   8.73
  s 21A   8.77
  s 24   8.73
  s 28   8.75
  s 45   8.73
  Sch A1   8.02, 8.44, 8.47, 8.77, 8.79
  Sch 1A   8.77, 8.79, 8.80
Mental Health (Care and Treatment)
    (Scotland) Act 2003   1.114
Mental Health Act 1983   1.166, 6.32, 6.115,
              8.01, 8.04, 8.07, 8.08, 8.09, 8.10,
              8.11, 8.15, 8.16, 8.17, 8.19, 8.20,
              8.24, 8.26, 8.27, 8.35, 8.36, 8.37,
              8.43, 8.45, 8.49, 8.59, 8.62, 8.66,
              8.74, 8.76, 8.77, 8.78, 8.79, 8.80,
                        8.82, 10.48, 10.49, 16.37
  Pt 1   8.09
  Pt 4   8.36, 8.75
  Pt 4A   8.46
  s 1(2)   8.09
  s 2   8.10, 8.11, 8.64, 8.80
  s 3   6.115, 6.118, 6.119, 8.10, 8.11, 8.12,
                 8.32, 8.33, 8.44, 8.64, 8.66, 8.67,
                        8.80, 16.40, 16.41, 16.42, 16.43
  s 6(3)   8.29, 8.30, 8.31, 8.33
  s 7   8.11, 8.43, 8.48
  s 8   8.48
  s 11   8.11, 8.44
  s 11(3)   8.12
  s 11(4)   8.12, 8.13, 8.31, 8.33
  s 12(2)   8.33
  s 13(3)   8.44
  s 15   8.28

Mental Health Act 1983—*continued*
s 17	8.43, 8.44, 8.45, 8.67
s 17(2A)	8.44
s 17(2B)	8.44
s 17A	8.43, 8.44, 8.45
s 17A(5)	8.44
s 17B	8.43, 8.44, 8.64
s 17B(2)	8.46
s 17B(2)(a)–(c)	8.64
s 17B(3)(a)	8.46
s 17B(3)(b)	8.46
s 17C	8.43, 8.44
s 17D	8.43, 8.44
s 17E	8.43, 8.44
s 17E(2)	8.45
s 17F	8.43, 8.44
s 17G	8.43, 8.44
s 20	8.35
s 20A	8.46
s 21	6.118
s 21A	8.80
s 23	8.21, 8.34
s 23(2)	8.35
s 23(2)(a)	8.12
s 23(4)	8.35
s 23(5)	8.35
s 25	8.35
s 25A	8.44
s 29	8.11
s 34	8.19
s 37	6.115, 8.10, 8.44, 8.53, 8.66, 8.71
s 38	8.53
s 39	8.53
s 40	8.53
s 41	8.53, 8.71
s 45A	6.115, 8.66
s 47	6.115, 8.44, 8.66, 10.48, 10.49
s 48	6.115, 8.44, 10.48, 10.49
s 57	8.38
s 58	8.38, 8.39
s 58(3)	8.38
s 58A	8.38, 8.39
s 62	8.38, 8.40
s 62(1)(a)–(d)	8.38
s 65(1)	8.49
s 65(1A)	8.49
s 66	8.49
s 66(1)	8.64
s 71	8.71
s 72	8.34
s 72(1)(c)	8.46, 8.47, 8.64
s 72(3A)	8.46, 8.64
s 78	8.59, 8.60
s 78(8)	8.49
s 117	6.09, 6.32, 6.115, 6.116, 6.117, 6.118, 8.45, 8.66, 8.67, 8.69, 8.70, 8.71, 16.38, 16.40, 16.41, 16.42, 16.43, 16.44, 16.45
s 117(2)	6.116, 16.44, 16.45
s 117(3)	6.119, 8.67, 16.39
s 118	8.60
s 139	8.24, 8.26, 8.30, 8.33
s 139(1)	8.33
s 139(2)	8.25, 8.31, 8.32

Mental Health Act 1983—*continued*
s 139(4)	8.25
s 145	8.17
s 145(1)	8.17
s 145(4)	8.17
Sch 2	8.59
Sch 2, para 1	8.59
Sch 2. para 1A	8.59
Mental Health Act 2007	8.02, 8.03, 8.43, 8.49, 8.76, 8.82

National Assistance Act 1948	6.114, 6.121, 6.128, 6.152, 16.45
Pt III	6.32, 6.33
s 21	6.09, 6.32, 6.33, 6.47, 6.119, 6.124, 6.125, 6.127, 6.128, 6.129, 6.152, 16.20, 16.21
s 21(1)	6.111, 6.114
s 21(1)(a)	6.125, 6.126, 6.152
s 21(1A)	6.124, 6.126
s 21(5)	6.109, 6.114
s 21(8)	6.111, 6.114, 16.17
s 22	6.33
s 24	6.119
s 26	6.33
s 29	6.09, 6.33, 6.47, 6.124
s 29(1)	6.112, 6.114
s 29(6)	6.112, 6.114
National Health Service Act 1977	7.30, 10.45
s 21	6.32
s 22	6.14
Sch 8	6.32
National Health Service Act 2006	6.105, 6.111, 6.112, 6.121, 16.10
Pt 3	6.105
s 1	16.16
s 1A	16.16
s 1B	16.16
s 1C	16.16
s 3	16.16
s 14Z2	16.05
s 65A	16.11
s 65B	16.11
s 65C	16.11
s 65D	16.11
s 65E	16.11
s 65F	16.11
s 65F(8)	16.13
s 65G	16.11
s 65H	16.11
s 65I	16.11
s 65J	16.11
s 65K	16.11
s 65L	16.11
s 65M	16.11
s 65N	16.11
s 65O	16.11
s 74	6.105
s 75	6.105
s 82	6.105
s 254	6.114
s 256	6.38
Sch 20	6.114

National Health Service and
  Community Care Act 1990   6.152,
                              8.48
  s 46   6.32, 6.105, 6.117, 8.70
  s 46(2)   6.105
  s 47   6.19, 6.20, 6.33, 6.47, 6.65, 6.117,
              6.118, 6.127, 6.152, 8.70
  s 47(1)   6.16, 6.152
  s 47(1)(b)   6.28, 8.70
  s 47(3)   6.17
  s 47(5)   6.16, 6.17
  s 47(6)   6.16
Nationality, Immigration and Asylum
    Act 2002   14.04, 14.55
  Pt 5   6.131
  s 55   3.35
  s 78   14.43
  s 82   14.09, 14.41
  s 83   6.132, 14.09, 14.41
  s 83(2)   14.09
  s 83A   14.09
  s 88   14.11
  s 89   14.11
  s 90   14.11
  s 91   14.11
  s 92   14.11, 14.12
  s 93   14.11
  s 94   14.11, 14.43
  s 94A   14.12
  s 94A(3)   14.12
  s 95   14.11
  s 96   14.11, 14.43
  s 97   14.10, 14.11
  s 98   14.11
  s 103   4.25
  s 103A   4.24
  s 117A   14.07
  s 117B   14.07, 14.50
  s 117C   14.07, 14.50
  s 117D   14.07
  Sch 3   6.136
  Sch 3, para 1(1)   6.124

Opticians Act 1989   15.17
  Sch 1A   15.73
Osteopaths Act 1993   15.17
  s 29   15.73

Parliamentary Commissioner Act 1967 2.202
  s 3   2.153, 2.215
Pensions Act 2004
  s 104   4.25
Pharmacy Act 1954
  s 3   15.79
Planning (Hazardous Substances) Act
    1990   5.20
  s 22   5.20
Planning (Listed Buildings and
    Conservation Areas) Act 1990
  s 62   5.20
  s 63   5.20
  s 64   5.20
  s 65   5.20

Planning (Listed Buildings and Conservation
    Areas) Act 1990—continued
  s 215   5.20
Planning and Compensation Act 1991 5.46
Planning and Compulsory Purchase
    Act 2004   5.17, 5.26, 5.86, 5.107
  s 38(6)   5.17, 5.86
  s 113   5.22, 5.23, 5.24, 5.107
  s 113(4)   5.13
  s 113(7)   5.24
Police Act 1996   15.17
Police and Criminal Evidence Act 1984 9.09
Police Reform and Social
    Responsibility Act 2011 1.56, 12.77,
                              12.104
Policing and Crime Act 2009 12.104
Prison Act 1952   10.03, 10.77, 10.142
  s 47   10.76, 10.77
Private Security Industry Act 2001 12.14
Prosecution of Offences Act 1985
  s 16(5)(a)   9.84
  s 16(5)(b)   9.84
  s 17   9.84
Protection of Children Act 1999
  s 9(6)   4.24
Public Audit (Wales) Act 2004 2.192
  s 22   2.195
  s 30(1)   2.200
  s 32   2.196
  s 33   2.198
Public Health Act 1936   12.38
Public Involvement in Health Act
    2007   13.111
Public Service Vehicles (Travel
    Concessions) Act 1955   13.90
Public Services Ombudsman (Wales)
    Act 2005   2.203

Race Relations Act 1976   11.75, 11.149
Road Traffic Regulation Act 1984 1.114

Safeguarding Vulnerable Groups Act
    2006
  s 4   4.17, 4.24, 4.25
School Inspections Act 1996 11.02
School Standard and Organisation
    (Wales) Act 2013   11.07
School Standards and Framework Act
    1998   11.02, 11.05, 11.10
  Pt III   11.34, 11.83
  s 1   11.58, 11.89
  s 20(1)   11.08
  s 21(1)   11.08
  s 25   11.42
  s 25(3)   11.28
  s 84   11.34
  s 85   11.34
  s 85A   11.39, 11.40
  s 86   11.34, 11.71, 11.76, 11.78
  s 86(1)   11.54
  s 86(2)   11.57
  s 86(3)(a)   11.58, 11.82

School Standards and Framework Act	
1998—*continued*	
s 86(8)	11.72
s 86A	11.40
s 87	11.34
s 87(4)(a)	11.61
s 87(4)(b)	11.61
s 87(4)(c)	11.61
s 88	11.34
s 88A	11.50
s 88D	11.69
s 88D(1)	11.67
s 88D(2)	11.67
s 89	11.34
s 89A(1)	11.67
s 89A(2)	11.67
s 90	11.34
s 91	11.34
s 92	11.34, 11.89
s 93	11.34
s 94	11.34, 11.54, 11.80, 11.151
s 95	11.34
s 95(1)	11.80
s 96	11.34
s 97	11.34
s 98	11.34, 11.35
s 98(4)	11.68
s 98(7)	11.61, 11.68
s 100	11.10, 11.60
s 101	11.60
s 102	11.11, 11.60
s 104	11.10, 11.60
s 151	11.43
School Standards and Organisation	
(Wales) Act 2013	11.31
Senior Courts Act 1981	2.64, 2.109
s 1	2.60
s 1(2)(c)	3.11
s 15(3)	14.55
s 18(1)	3.51
s 18(1)(a)	9.02
s 29	2.02
s 29(3)	9.25
s 30	2.64
s 30(1)(a)	2.62
s 30(1)(b)	2.62
s 30(2)	2.62
s 31	2.02, 3.01, 4.19
s 31(1)(b)	2.64, 7.92
s 31(1)(c)	2.63
s 31(2)	2.64, 2.70
s 31(2)(a)–(c)	2.64
s 31(3)	15.64
s 31(4)	2.24, 2.80, 2.81, 2.90, 2.98
s 31(4)(a)	2.80
s 31(4)(b)	2.80
s 31(5)	2.44, 2.52
s 31(5A)	2.44
s 31(5B)	2.44
s 31(6)	2.110, 3.15
s 31A	4.19
s 31A(1)	4.19
s 31A(2)	4.19
s 31A(3)	14.15

Senior Courts Act 1981—*continued*	
s 35A	2.105
s 37	2.02
s 43(1)	9.77, 9.78
s 51	3.74, 3.78
s 81(1)(e)	9.63
Social Security Act 1998	
s 14	4.24
s 15	4.25
Social Security Administration Act	
1992	1.89
s 116(2)(b)	1.89
Special Educational Needs and	
Disability Act 2001	11.03, 11.110
Special Immigration Appeals	
Commission Act 1997	14.04
Statutory Order (Special Procedure)	
Act 1945	5.40
Sunday Entertainments Act 1932	1.11
s 1	1.11
Sunday Observance Act 1780	2.61
Superannuation Act 1972	2.84
Supreme Court Act 1981	5.63, 5.64
s 31	5.64
s 31(3)	5.63
s 70(2)	5.70
Tax Credits Act 2002	
Sch 2, para 2(2)	4.24
Sch 2, para 4(1)	4.24
Taxes Management Act 1970	
s 33(2A)(a)	2.97
s 56	4.24
Teaching and Higher Education Act	
1998	11.03
Town and Country Planning Act 1990	5.08, 5.11, 5.16, 5.18, 5.39
s 77	5.18
s 78	5.18
s 97	5.18, 5.48, 5.50, 5.53
s 102	5.18
s 107	5.48, 5.54
s 198	5.18
s 221(5)	5.18
s 284	5.18
s 285	5.18
s 286	5.20
s 287	5.18, 5.29
s 287(4)	5.21
s 288	5.08, 5.11, 5.18, 5.19, 5.31, 5.32, 5.35, 5.108, 5.112, 5.118
s 288(3)	5.28
s 288(3A)	5.11
s 288(3B)	5.11
s 289	5.08, 5.18, 5.34, 5.35
s 289(1)	5.35
s 336	5.11
Sch 9	5.18
Town Police Clauses Act 1847	12.104
Transport Act 1985	
Sch 4, para 14	4.24, 4.25
Transport and Works Act 1992	5.05
Travel Concessions Act 1964	13.90

Tribunals and Inquiries Act 1992	
s 11	4.24
s 704	4.24
s 706	4.24
Tribunals, Courts and Enforcement Act 2007	4.01, 4.05, 4.06, 4.14, 8.03, 8.55, 8.60, 14.09, 14.14, 14.15
s 2(1)	4.06
s 2(3)	4.06
s 2(3)(c)	4.06
s 2(3)(d)	4.06
s 2(4)	4.07
s 3	8.55
s 3(5)	4.09, 4.22, 8.55
s 4	4.09
s 5	4.09
s 6	4.09
s 7	4.07
s 9	4.14, 4.16, 8.50, 8.63
s 9(1)	4.12
s 9(2)(a)	4.12
s 9(2)(b)	4.12
s 9(4)	4.15
s 9(5)(a)	4.15
s 9(5)(b)	4.15
s 10	4.14, 4.18, 8.50
s 11	4.16, 8.50, 8.63, 14.13
s 11(1)	4.16
s 11(2)	4.16
s 11(3)	4.16
s 11(4)(a)	4.16
s 11(4)(b)	4.16
s 11(5)	4.12, 4.16, 8.50
s 11(8)	4.16
s 12	4.17, 8.55
s 12(2)(a)	8.55
s 12(3)	4.17

Tribunals, Courts and Enforcement Act 2007—*continued*	
s 12(4)(a)	8.55
s 12(4)(b)	8.55
s 12(4)(b)(i)	8.55
s 12(4)(b)(ii)	8.55
s 13(1)	8.63
s 13(8)	4.25, 8.63
s 15	1.03, 4.19, 8.50
s 15(3)	8.56
s 15(4)	8.56
s 15(5)	8.56
s 16	8.56
s 18	4.19
s 18(3)	4.19
s 18(6)	4.19, 4.20
s 18(8)(a)	4.19
s 18(8)(b)	4.19
s 19	4.19
s 19(3)	4.20
s 31(1)	4.20
s 31(2)	4.09
s 31(4)	4.20
s 94	14.11
s 96	14.11
s 141	2.44
Sch 2	4.09
Sch 3	4.09
UK Borders Act 2007	14.04, 14.55
Veterinary Surgeons Act 1966	15.17
War Pensions Administrative Provisions Act 1919	
s 8(2)	4.24

TABLE OF STATUTORY INSTRUMENTS

References are to paragraph numbers.

Allocation of Housing and Homelessness (Eligibility) (England) Regulations 2006, SI 2006/1294	7.66	Civil Procedure Rules 1998, SI 1998/3132—*continued*	
		r 3.2(a)	3.13
		Pt 7	2.81, 3.64
		PD 7	
Allocation of Housing and Homelessness (Miscellaneous Provisions) (England) Regulations 2006, SI 2006/2527	7.66	para 13.2(2)	3.77
		Pt 8	3.01
		r 8.6	3.38
		r 8.6(1)	3.38
Allocation of Housing and Homelessness (Review Procedures) Regulations 1999, SI 1999/71		r 10.3(2)	3.29
		PD 16	
		para 13.1(2)	3.23
		para 15	3.22
reg 8	7.10	para 15.1(2)	3.24
Alternative Provision Academies and 16 to 19 Academies (Consequential Amendments to Subordinate Legislation) (England) Order 2012, SI 2012/979		para 15.1(2)(a)	3.24
		para 15.1(2)(d)	3.24
		para 15.1(2)(e)	3.24
		para 15.1(2)(f)	3.24
		Pt 25	2.02, 2.03
	11.13	r 25.1(1)	2.05
Alternative Provision Academies (Consequential Amendments to Act) (England) Order 2012, SI 2012/976		r 25.1(1)(a)	2.03
		r 25.1(1)(b)	2.03
		r 25.3	9.62
	11.13	r 25(2)(1)	2.04
Asylum and Immigration Tribunal (Procedure) Rules 2005, SI 2005/230		r 25(2)(2)	2.04
		Pt 31	3.10, 3.11
		r 40.12	15.223
	4.11	r 44.2	7.103
		r 44.2(2)	7.103
British Indian Ocean Territory (Constitution) Order 2004		r 44.3	3.74, 3.78
		r 44.3(4)	9.82
		r 45.43	3.82
s 9	13.14, 13.16	r 45.44	3.82
		Pt 52	5.36
Civil Legal Aid (Merits Criteria) Regulations 2013, SI 2013/104		r 52.2	3.67
		r 52.3	3.66
reg 39	10.141	r 52.3(3)	3.67
Civil Procedure (Amendment No 4) Rules 2013, SI 2013/1412	5.04	r 52.3(4)	3.70
		r 52.3(6)	3.66
		r 52.4	3.67
Civil Procedure (Modification of Supreme Court Act 1981) Order 2004, SI 2004/1033	2.90, 2.98	r 52.4(3)	3.67
		r 52.5(2)(b)	3.71
		r 52.11(1)	3.72
Civil Procedure Rules 1998, SI 1998/3132	2.02, 2.18, 2.34, 2.137, 2.138, 2.152, 3.64, 5.128, 5.133, 9.62	r 52.11(2)	3.72
		r 52.11(3)	3.72
		r 52.11(5)	3.72
r 1.1	7.101	r 52.15	3.52
Pt 3	3.11	r 52.15(2)	3.52
r 3.1(2)(a)	2.110, 3.16	r 52.15(3)	3.53
r 3.1(3)	3.16	r 52.15(4)	3.53

Civil Procedure Rules 1998,
SI 1998/3132—continued
PD 52
    para 5.6   3.68
    para 5.24   3.69
    para 6.2   3.70
    para 7.7   3.71
    para 7.7B   3.71
    para 19   3.69
    para 21   3.67
Pt 54   2.02, 2.81, 3.01, 3.05, 3.10, 3.75
r 54.1(1)(f)   15.233
r 54.1(2)(f)   3.28
r 54.2   3.05, 3.13
r 54.2(a)–(c)   3.05
r 54.2(d)   2.63, 3.05
r 54.3   2.64, 3.05, 7.92
r 54.3(2)   2.80, 3.05
r 54.4   3.21
r 54.5   1.163, 2.109, 3.13, 10.139, 14.21
r 54.5(1)   2.109
r 54.5(3)   3.13
r 54.5(5)   5.11, 5.68
r 54.6   2.04, 3.22
r 54.6(1)   3.23
r 54.6(1)(b)   3.23
r 54.6(1)(c)   3.23, 3.42
r 54.6(2)   3.27, 3.28
r 54.7   3.28
r 54.7(b)   3.29, 15.233
r 54.8   3.29
r 54.8(1)(a)(i)   3.30
r 54.8(1)(a)(ii)   3.30
r 54.8(2)(a)   3.29
r 54.8(2)(b)   3.29
r 54.8(3)   3.29
r 54.8(4)(b)   3.30
r 54.8(5)   3.29
r 54.9(1)(a)   3.29
r 54.9(1)(b)   3.29
r 54.9(2)   3.29
r 54.10   3.48, 3.55
r 54.10(1)   3.43, 3.48
r 54.10(2)   2.03, 2.19, 3.40, 3.43
r 54.11   3.43
r 54.12   3.46
r 54.12(1)   3.43
r 54.12(1)(b)(ii)   3.45
r 54.12(3)   3.43, 3.49
r 54.12(4)   3.43, 3.49
r 54.12(5)   3.50
r 54.13   3.55
r 54.14   3.30, 3.56, 5.08, 15.233
r 54.15   3.45
r 54.15(1)   3.60
r 54.15(2)   3.60
r 54.15(3)   3.60
r 54.16   3.38
r 54.16(1)   3.60
r 54.17   3.29, 3.57
r 54.18   3.58
r 54.19(2)   2.52
r 54.20   3.05, 3.64
r 54.21(2)   5.05

Civil Procedure Rules 1998,
SI 1998/3132—continued
PD 54   3.01, 3.10, 3.22
    para 2.1   3.21
    para 5.1   3.23
    para 5.4   3.25
    para 5.6   3.23, 3.27
    para 5.6(g)   3.23
    para 5.6(h)   3.23
    para 5.6(i)   3.23
    para 5.7   3.26, 3.27
    para 8.2   3.55
    para 8.4   3.43
    para 8.5   3.43, 3.75
    para 8.6   3.75
    para 10.1   3.56
    para 13.2   3.57
    para 17   3.65
PD 54A
    para 12.1   3.10
PD 54D
    para 5.2   3.21
PD 54E   5.06, 5.10
Sch 1   9.63, 9.66, 9.67, 9.70, 9.74
Community Care, Services for Carers and Children's Services (Direct Payments) (England) Regulations 2003, SI 2003/762   6.37
Criminal Justice Act 1991 (Notice of Transfer) Regulations 1992, SI 1992/1670   10.54, 10.56, 10.72
Criminal Procedure Rules 2013, SI 2013/1554   9.63
r 19.7   9.63
r 19.7(2)   9.63

Disability Discrimination (Public Authorities) (Statutory Duties) Regulations 2005, SI 2005/2966   6.25

Education (Admission Appeals Arrangements) (Wales) Regulations 2005, SI 2005/1398   11.80
reg 6(2)   11.89
reg 8   11.81
Sch 2, para 1(8)   11.94
Sch 2, para 2(10)   11.94
Education (Admission Forums) (England) Regulations 2002, SI 2002/2900   11.39
Education (Admission Forums) (Wales) Regulations 2003, SI 2003/2962   11.39
reg 3   11.40
reg 5   11.40
Education (Admission of Looked After Children) (Wales) Regulations 2009, SI 2009/821   11.79, 11.80

Education (Admissions Appeals Arrangements) Regulations 2002, SI 2002/2899	
reg 6(2)	11.89
reg 8	11.81
Sch 2, para 1(8)	11.94
Sch 2, para 2(10)	11.94
Education (Determination of Admission Arrangements) (Wales) Regulations 2006, SI 2006/174	11.42
Education (Objections to Admission Arrangements) Regulations 1999, SI 1999/125	11.47
Education (Pupil Exclusions and Appeals) (Maintained Schools) (Wales) Regulations 2003, SI 2003/3227	11.125
Education (Pupil Exclusions and Appeals) (Pupil Referral Units) (Wales) Regulations 2003, SI 2003/3246	11.125
Education (School Information) (Wales) Regulations 1999, SI 1999/1812	
Sch 1, para 10	11.143
Environmental Assessment of Plans and Programmes Regulations 2004, SI 2004/1656	
reg 12	5.107
General Medical Council (Fitness to Practise) Rules Order of Council 2004, SI 2004/2608	
r 4(5)	15.92
Health Professions Council (Screeners) Rules Order of Council 2003, SI 2003/1573	15.94
Homelessness (Priority Need for Accommodation) England Order 2002, SI 2002/2051	
Art 2	6.57
Art 3	6.57
Immigration (European Economic Area) Regulations 2006, SI 2006/1003	14.04, 14.06
Immigration Rules 1994	
r 353	6.132, 6.135
r 353A	6.132, 6.135
Licensing Act 2003 (Hearings) Regulations 2005, SI 2005/44	12.91
reg 14	12.95
Local Authorities (Standing Orders) (England) Regulations 2001, SI 2001/3384	13.131
Local Authorities (Standing Orders) Regulations 1993, SI 1993/202	13.131
Local Authorities (Standing Orders) (Wales) Regulations 2006, SI 2006/1275	13.131
Local Authority Partnership Arrangements Regulations 2000, SI 2000/617	6.105
Local Authority Social Services and National Health Service Complaints (England) Regulations 2009, SI 2009/309	2.187, 6.151
Local Authority Social Services Complaints (England) Regulations 2006, SI 2006/1681	
reg 7	6.20
reg 9	6.20
Local Government (Miscellaneous Provisions) (Northern Ireland) Order 1985, SI 1985/1208	12.16, 12.70, 12.71
art 10	12.70
National Health Service (Direct Payments) (Amendment) Regulations 2013, SI 2013/2354	16.24
National Health Service (Direct Payments) Regulations 2013, SI 2013/1617	16.23, 16.24, 16.27, 16.28
reg 5(5)	16.25
reg 6(2)	16.26
National Health Service (Performers Lists) Regulations 2004, SI 2004/585	15.13
Nursing and Midwifery Order (2001), SI 2002/253	
art 22(6)	15.91
Parole Board (Amendment) Rules 2009, SI 2009/408	10.57
Prison Rules 1999, SI 1999/728	10.142, 10.143
r 7	10.06
r 8	10.34
r 11	10.100
r 20	10.05, 10.46
r 23	10.05
r 24	10.05
r 29	10.05
r 30	10.05
r 34	10.42
r 34(1)	10.39
r 34(2)	10.39
r 35(1)	10.38
r 35(2)(a)	10.38
r 35(2)(b)	10.38
r 35(3)	10.38

Prison Rules 1999, SI 1999/728—continued		School Discipline (Pupil Exclusions and Reviews) (England) Regulations	
r 38(1)	10.40	2012, SI 2012/1033	11.125
r 39	10.40	reg 7	11.127
r 39(1)	10.40	reg 7(1)(b)	11.127
r 39(2)	10.40	reg 7(3)	11.127
r 39(3)	10.40	reg 25	11.127
r 39(4)	10.40	reg 25(1)(b)	11.127
r 43	10.30	reg 25(3)	11.127
r 45	10.17, 10.18, 10.32, 10.33	Sch 1, para 2(1)	11.127
r 47(1)	10.107	School Information (England) Regulations 2008,	
r 51	10.76	SI 2008/3093	11.62
r 53(1)	10.78	Sch 2, para 17	11.143
r 53(2)	10.78	Sch 3, para 4	11.143
r 53(3)	10.78	School Organisation (Establishment and Discontinuance of Schools) (England) Regulations 2007,	
r 53(4)	10.78		
r 53A	10.77		
r 54(1)	10.78	SI 2007/1288	11.28
r 55	10.33, 10.81	School Organisation (Foundation Special Schools) (Application of Provisions Relating to Foundations) (England) Regulations 2007,	
r 55A	10.85		
r 55B	10.87		
r 58	10.81		
r 61	10.82		
r 73	10.42	SI 2007/1329	11.08
		Special Educational Needs and Disability Tribunal (General Provisions and Disability Claims Procedure) Regulations 2002,	
Regulatory Reform (Collaboration etc between Ombudsmen) Order 2007, SI 2007/1889	2.153, 2.215		
Rules of the Supreme Court 1965, SI 1965/828		SI 2002/1985	11.111
		Special Educational Needs Tribunal for Wales Regulations 2012,	
Ord 53, r 10	2.33		
Ord 79, r 9(2)	9.66, 9.68	SI 2012/322	11.111
Ord 79, r 9(2)(a)	9.67	Supreme Court Rules 2009, SI 2009/1603	
Ord 79, r 9(2)(b)	9.74		
Ord 79, r 9(3)	9.68, 9.74	r 5(5)	9.87
Ord 79, r 9(11)	9.63		
Ord 79, r 9(12)	9.70	Town and Country Planning (Development Management Procedure) (England) Order	
School Admissions (Admission Arrangements and Co-ordination of Admission Arrangements) (England) Regulations 2012, SI 2012/8	11.41, 11.42, 11.47, 11.79	2010, SI 2010/2184	5.93
		Town and Country Planning (Environmental Impact Assessment) Regulations 1988,	
		SI 1988/1199	5.46
reg 22	11.45	Town and Country Planning (Environmental Impact Assessment) Regulations 1999,	
Sch 2	11.41		
School Admissions (Alteration and Variation of, and Objections to, Arrangements) (England) Regulations 2007, SI 2007/496	11.42	SI 1999/293	5.46, 5.104
		Town and Country Planning (Environmental Impact Assessment) Regulations 2011,	
reg 4	11.44	SI 2011/1824	5.46
School Admissions (Appeals Arrangements) (England) Regulations 2012, SI 2012/9	11.80	Town and Country Planning (General Development Procedure) Order	
		1995, SI 1995/419	5.93
reg 7(5)(b)	11.130	art 22	5.93
reg 25(5)(b)	11.130	Traffic Management Permit Scheme (England) Regulations 2007,	
Sch 1	11.128, 11.129		
School Admissions (Infant Class Sizes) (England) Regulations 2012, SI 2012/10	11.89	SI 2007/3372	1.89

Tribunal Procedure (First-tier Tribunal)
(General Regulatory Chamber)
Rules 2009, SI 2009/1976 ... 4.11
Tribunal Procedure (First-tier Tribunal)
(Health, Education and Social
Care Chamber) Rules 2008,
SI 2008/2699 ... 4.11, 4.12, 8.50, 8.60, 11.111
  r 6(5) ... 8.63
  r 14 ... 8.63
  r 14(2) ... 8.63
  r 44 ... 8.50
  r 45 ... 4.12
  r 45(2)(a)–(c) ... 8.50
  r 45(3) ... 4.13
  r 46 ... 4.13, 8.50
  r 47 ... 8.50
  r 47(1) ... 4.13
  r 48(2) ... 4.13
  r 49 ... 8.50
  r 49(1)(a) ... 4.13

Tribunal Procedure (First-tier Tribunal)
(Social Entitlement Chambers)
Rules 2009, SI 2009/2685 ... 4.11

Tribunal Procedure (First-tier Tribunal)
(Tax Chamber) Rules 2009,
SI 2009/273 ... 4.11

Tribunal Procedure (First-tier Tribunal)
(War Pensions and Armed
Forces Compensation Chamber)
Rules 2008, SI 2008/2686 ... 4.11

Tribunal Procedure (Upper Tribunal)
(Lands Chamber) Rules 2010,
SI 2010/2600 ... 4.11

Tribunal Procedure (Upper Tribunal)
Rules 2008, SI 2008/2698 ... 4.11, 4.17, 14.16, 14.34
  Pt 4 ... 4.21
  r 10(3)(a) ... 14.39
  r 21(3)(a) ... 4.17
  r 21(3)(b) ... 4.17
  r 21(4) ... 4.17
  r 21(5) ... 4.17
  r 21(6) ... 4.17
  r 21(7) ... 4.17
  r 21(7)(b) ... 4.17
  r 22(1) ... 4.18
  r 22(2) ... 4.18
  r 22(3) ... 4.18
  r 22(4) ... 4.18
  r 28 ... 14.21, 14.29
  r 28A ... 14.30
  r 29 ... 14.32
  r 32 ... 14.36
  r 34 ... 4.18
  rr 41–43 ... 4.18
  r 45 ... 4.18

Part 1
GENERAL PRINCIPLES

CHAPTER 1

GROUNDS OF JUDICIAL REVIEW

INTRODUCTION

1.01 The grounds on which a judicial review challenge may be brought are based on a small collection of overlapping principles. These include principles of lawfulness, reasonableness, and fairness. The values that underlie these principles are the requirements of the rule of law and the prohibition on abuses of power.[1] In this way, judicial review is a key constitutional safeguard that cannot be dispensed with.[2]

1.02 The principles of lawfulness, reasonableness, and fairness unpack into a variety of different grounds, and are highly context-dependent. This chapter explains the various grounds of judicial review; the chapters in Part 2 of this book explain the legal context of specific areas of public law, and how the grounds of judicial review can apply in those areas.

Classifying the principles of judicial review

1.03 The modern process of judicial review has developed out of the High Court's traditional constitutional role, which is to supervise the actions of the executive and lower courts. Until recently, the High Court had a unique power to exercise prerogative remedies that could be used to either quash decisions or would mandate or prohibit certain actions.[3] This power has since been distributed around the legal system in England and Wales.[4]

1.04 Judicial review has a long history that can be traced back to the 17th century.[5] However, it was only after the Second World War that judicial review began to develop quickly;[6] and a series of important cases greatly expanded the judicial review

---

[1] *Ahmed v HM Treasury* [2010] UKSC 2 at [45]; *A v Secretary of State for the Home Department* [2004] EWCA Civ 1123 (CA) at [248] and [251]; *R v Somerset County Council, ex parte Dixon* [1998] Env LR 111, 121.

[2] *R (Cart) v Upper Tribunal* [2009] EWHC 3052 (Admin) at [38]; *R (Jackson) v Attorney General* [2005] UKHL 56 at [102]; *AXA General Insurance Ltd v HM Advocate* [2011] UKSC 46 at [51].

[3] The old terminology for quashing orders was certiorari, mandamus and prohibition orders. The language was updated in 1977 and 1981. Remedies are dealt with in Chapter 2.

[4] Judicial review applications can now be made before the Upper Tribunal (s 15 of the Tribunals, Courts and Enforcement Act 2007) and the Special Immigration Appeals Commission (s 15 of the Justice and Security Act 2013). The County Court also exercises a jurisdiction akin to judicial review in relation to homelessness cases (s 204 of the Housing Act 1996).

[5] See, for instance, *Dr Bonham's Case*, 8 Co Rep 107a, 114a CP [1610], *Warner v Suckerman* (1615) 3 Bulst 119, and *James's Case* (1631) Hob 17. See further *R (Cart) v Upper Tribunal* [2009] EWHC 3052 (Admin); [2010] 2 WLR 1012 at [44]–[53].

[6] The pre-Second World War period has been described as the 'long sleep of judicial review' (Sir Stephen Sedley 'The Sound of Silence: Constitutional Law without a Constitution' [1994] LQR 110) exemplified in

jurisdiction.⁷ From the burgeoning case-law, the grounds of judicial review were neatly classified by Lord Diplock in 1984 in the following terms:

> 'Judicial review has I think developed to a stage today when...one can conveniently classify under three heads the grounds upon which administrative action is subject to control by judicial review. The first ground I would call "illegality," the second "irrationality" and the third "procedural impropriety".'⁸

1.05 This threefold classification provides a useful framework for considering the grounds of judicial review. It should be noted that these classifications are not watertight, and there is a degree of overlap in how they operate in practice.⁹

1.06 However, this division highlights an important distinction between the various grounds of judicial review, which is that they focus on either the *substance* of the decision (irrationality) or the *procedure* that was adopted in making the decision (illegality and procedural impropriety). This is subject to an overall principle of restraint, namely that the court will not substitute its own view of the decision it is reviewing.¹⁰ It is possible to map judicial review in the following way:

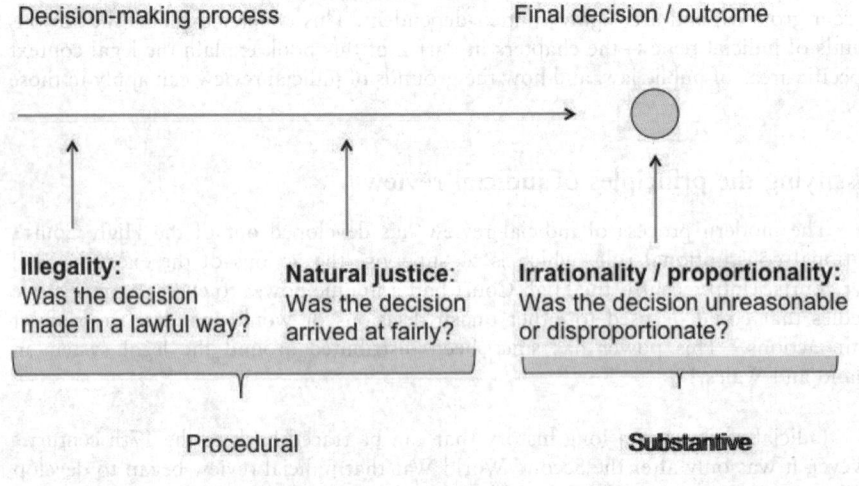

Local Government Board v Arlidge [1915] AC 120 where it was held that 'administrative bodies need follow only the procedural standards required by Parliament, not common-law standards of fair procedure as required in the courts'.

7   For instance, *Associated Provincial Picture Houses Ltd v Wednesbury Corporation* [1948] 1 KB 223 (on reasonableness), *Ridge v Baldwin* [1964] AC 40 (on natural justice), *Padfield v Minister of Agriculture, Fisheries and Food* [1968] AC 997 (on use of discretion and legislative purpose) and *Anisminic Ltd v Foreign Compensation Commission* [1969] 2 AC 147 (on jurisdictional error).

8   *Council of Civil Service Unions v Minister for the Civil Service* [1985] AC 374, 410 (often called 'the GCHQ case'). This case is considered to be seminal because it established that it was the nature of a power, not its source, which determined whether it could be subject to judicial review. Accordingly, a prerogative power could be subject to judicial review.

9   *Boddington v British Transport Police* [1998] 2 WLR 639, 644E.

10 It is 'forbidden' for a judicial review court to substitute its view for that of the primary decision maker. See: *R v Secretary of State for the Home Department, ex p Brind* [1991] 1 AC 696, 767G. In *Laker Airways Ltd v Department of Trade* [1977] QB 643, 724D–E, Lawton LJ said described his role as a referee: 'I can blow my judicial whistle when the ball goes out of play; but when the game restarts I must neither take part in it nor tell the players how to play.'.

Structure of this chapter

1.07 This chapter takes Lord Diplock's classification of the grounds of judicial review as its starting point. Within each category, various further grounds are identified. In addition to these categories, the chapter considers important further grounds arising from the Human Rights Act 1998 and European Union law.

1.08 In relation to each ground, a principle is stated and key cases are given. This is to assist the reader in identifying the relevant ground for their purposes. A commentary is then provided, which explains the extent and operation of the principle, and recent cases are also identified where relevant.

CATEGORY 1: IRRATIONALITY

1.09 Irrationality is a substantive category of judicial review because it focuses on whether a decision was unreasonable or unjustifiable. The focus of an irrationality challenge is not on the decision-making process, although to demonstrate that a public body has acted irrationally it may be necessary to explore how a decision was made. In this section, the following grounds are explored:

(1) *Unreasonableness*. The classic approach to irrationality is to show that a decision was so unreasonable that no reasonable decision-maker could have come to it. This is the *Wednesbury* formulation, which imports a high threshold that can be modified in certain circumstances.

(2) *Proportionality*. The principle of proportionality is developing in English law. It is dealt with under the category of irrationality because of the close relationship with *Wednesbury* unreasonableness. Proportionality is more structured and probing than *Wednesbury*, but it is still a flexible principle and only applies in a limited number of contexts.

(3) *Bad faith/improper motive*. An element of unreasonableness is that oppressive decisions can amount to abuses of power. The law prohibits decisions being taken in bad faith to prevent abuses of power, and this extends to a requirement that improper motives should not form the basis of decisions.

Unreasonableness

Principle

A public body cannot act unreasonably in the performance of its public functions. This is a high threshold, although the standard of review is context-dependent.

Key case

Associated Provincial Picture Houses Ltd v Wednesbury Corporation.[11]

Commentary

1.10 The principle that a public body cannot act unreasonably is a basic concept of public law in England and Wales. However, it is also a principle that is often

[11] [1948] 1 KB 223.

misunderstood. It is therefore valuable to consider the roots of the principle and to explore the approach of the courts over the years.

1.11 The starting point is *Associated Provincial Picture Houses Ltd v Wednesbury Corporation*. In that case, a cinema operator had been granted a licence to show films on Sundays by the local licensing authority. The licence included a condition that no child under 15 could be admitted, whether accompanied by an adult or not. This decision was taken having regard to the well-being and moral health of children likely to visit the cinema. The local licensing authority had a wide discretion in relation to licences and could impose 'such conditions as the authority thinks fit'.[12]

1.12 The legal issue in *Wednesbury* was, assuming that a public body has acted within the confines of its powers, are there circumstances when a court can still intervene to quash a decision? The Court of Appeal answered this question affirmatively. This confirmed that as well as scrutinising the *procedure* that was adopted in making a decision, a court can also scrutinise the *substance* of a decision. Lord Greene MR expressed this in the following terms:[13]

> 'The court is entitled to investigate the action of the local authority with a view to seeing whether they have taken into account matters which they ought not to take into account, or, conversely, have refused to take into account or neglected to take into account matters which they ought to take into account.

> Once that question is answered in favour of the local authority, it may still be possible to say that, although the local authority have kept within the four corners of the matters which they ought to consider, they have nevertheless come to *a conclusion so unreasonable that no reasonable authority could ever have come to it.*' (emphasis added)

1.13 This represented an important shift in the development of public law. Indeed, in subsequent cases judges were keen to explain away unreasonableness as simply a species of error of law. For instance, in *Edwards v Bairstow*,[14] Lord Radcliffe sought to describe an unreasonable decision on the basis 'that there has been some misconception of the law'.

1.14 However, Lord Diplock in the *GCHQ* case stated that unreasonableness was a ground of review in its own right and provided this further definition when explaining the term 'irrationality':[15]

> 'By "irrationality" I mean what can by now be succinctly referred to as "*Wednesbury* unreasonableness". It applies to a decision which is so outrageous in its defiance of logic or of accepted moral standards that no sensible person who had applied his mind to the question to be decided could have arrived at it.'

1.15 It is important to appreciate that *Wednesbury* establishes a layer of common law standards over and above ensuring compliance with the terms of a public body's statutory powers. Not only do decisions have to comply with the relevant statutory framework, decisions must also not be so unreasonable that no reasonable decision-maker could have come to it.

---

[12] Section 1 of the Sunday Entertainments Act 1932.
[13] *Associated Provincial Picture Houses Ltd v Wednesbury Corporation* [1948] 1 KB 223, 230.
[14] [1956] AC 14.
[15] *Council of Civil Service Unions v Minister for the Civil Service* [1985] AC 374, 410.

1.16 It is possible to criticise the Lord Greene's formulation of unreasonableness as tautological. However, the more immediate practical concern for public lawyers is that it sets a high threshold, although attempts to modify this have been made by adopting a 'sliding-scale' approach. These two matters are now considered.

1.17 *High threshold*: The *Wednesbury* formulation creates a high threshold for claimants seeking to establish that a decision is unreasonable. As a result, public bodies can be relatively well insulated from challenges on this ground alone. It is only in cases where a decision is manifestly unreasonable,[16] illogical[17] or oppressive[18] that a court will conclude that the decision was unlawful on this basis. Extreme delay or inaction by a public body has also been described as unreasonable.[19]

1.18 The reason for this high threshold is constitutional. The court's role in the context of a judicial review application is to supervise the decisions of the executive in order to maintain the rule of law. The court's role is not to substitute its view of the merits of a decision in place of the view of a decision-maker who has been authorised by Parliament to make that decision. This supervisory jurisdiction is distinct from an appellate jurisdiction where the test is whether a decision was 'wrong'.[20] This approach was emphasised by the House of Lords in *R v Secretary of State for the Home Department, ex p Brind*. In that case Lord Ackner stated that the 'standard of unreasonableness ... has to be expressed in terms that confine the jurisdiction exercised by the judiciary to a supervisory, as opposed to an appellate, jurisdiction'.[21]

1.19 An assessment of the reasonableness of a decision would cross this constitutional line if the threshold of unreasonableness was so low that the court was routinely quashing decisions it happened to disagree with. As was said in *Secretary of State for Education and Science v Tameside Metropolitan Borough Council*, it would be 'quite unacceptable ... to proceed from "wrong" to "unreasonable"'.[22]

1.20 The practical effect of the rule that forbids the court from substituting its view for the view of a decision-maker is that the threshold of unreasonableness is high and difficult to meet in many cases. The courts have used many terms to convey this high threshold, such as 'perversity',[23] 'taking leave of its senses',[24] 'devoid of plausible

---

[16] In addition to the *Wednesbury* and *GCHQ* formulations (above), see *HMB Holdings Ltd v Antigua and Barbuda* [2007] UKPC 37 at [31] and *Secretary of State for Education and Science v Tameside Metropolitan Borough Council* [1977] AC 1014 at 1064E–F.
[17] See for instance: *R v Parliamentary Commissioner for Administration, ex parte Balchin* [1998] 1 PLR 1, 13E–F (if a decision 'does not add up'); and *R (Interbrew SA) v Competition Commission* [2001] EWHC Admin 367 ('if the reasons make no sense').
[18] See *R (Khatun) v London Borough of Newham* [2004] EWCA Civ 55, [2005] QB 37 at [41] (oppressive decisions repugnant to public law standards).
[19] For instance see: *R (HA (Nigeria)) v Secretary of State for the Home Department* [2012] EWHC 979 (Admin) at [169] and [171]; *R (M) v Criminal Injuries Compensation Authority* [2002] EWHC 2646 (Admin) at [39].
[20] See *Re B (A Child)* [2013] UKSC 33.
[21] *R v Secretary of State for the Home Department, ex p Brind* [1991] 1 AC 696, 757F–G. See also *R (Khatun) v London Borough of Newham* [2004] EWCA Civ 55, [2005] QB 37 at [40]: 'the court has no role to impose what it perceives as ideal solutions under cover of the *Wednesbury* principle's application'.
[22] *Secretary of State for Education and Science v Tameside Metropolitan Borough Council* [1977] AC 1014 at 1074H–1075C.
[23] For example see: *Reid v Secretary of State for Scotland* [1999] 2 AC 512, 541G, 542C; *R v Hillingdon London Borough Council, ex parte Puhlhofer* [1986] AC 484, 518C.
[24] *R v Secretary of State for the Environment, ex parte Nottinghamshire County Council* [1986] AC 240, 247H and 248C–D.

justification',[25] 'verging on absurdity',[26] and 'a mountain to climb'.[27] It has been said that unreasonable decisions 'jump off the page at you'.[28]

1.21 *Sliding-scale*: Although the starting point is that unreasonableness is a high threshold, the concept contains an in-built latitude that can be applied flexibly depending on the context. This was described by Laws LJ in *R v Department of Education and Employment, ex p Begbie* as follows:[29]

> 'Fairness and reasonableness (and their contraries) are objective concepts: otherwise there would be no public law, or if there were it would be palm tree justice. But each is a spectrum, not a single point, and they shade into one another. It is now well established that the *Wednesbury* principle itself constitutes a sliding scale of review, more or less intrusive according to the nature and gravity of what is at stake.'

1.22 The clearest development of this sliding scale was in *R v Ministry of Defence, ex parte Smith*. This case concerned the policy that homosexuals could not serve in the armed forces. It is important to note that because this case was brought prior to the Human Rights Act 1998, the claimants could not directly rely on Article 8 ECHR before the domestic courts.

1.23 However, the Court of Appeal recognised that the case engaged human rights and so approached the case on a *Wednesbury* basis accepting the submission that 'the more substantial the interference with human rights, the more the court will require by way of justification before it is satisfied that the decision is reasonable'.[30]

1.24 What this required was an increased justification from the government for its decisions. This approach has since been termed 'anxious scrutiny'.[31] However, it is of note that even with this more intensive form of review, the court in *ex parte Smith* did not hold the policy to be unlawful.

1.25 Conversely, in cases where there are issues raised of a macro-economic nature or of national security the courts are likely to expect less in terms of justification of a decision or policy, and will adopt a lighter touch to review.

1.26 An example of this is *R v Secretary of State for the Environment, ex parte Nottinghamshire County Council*[32] where expenditure targets set for local authorities by central government were challenged as unreasonable. It was held that in the absence of some exceptional circumstance such as bad faith or improper motive on the part of the Secretary of State it was inappropriate for the courts to intervene on the ground of unreasonableness in a matter of public finances administration that had been one for the political judgment for the Secretary of State.

1.27 The position was summarised in *ex parte Smith* as follows:[33]

---

[25] *Bromley London Borough Council v Greater London Council* [1983] 1 AC 768, 821B.
[26] *R v Hillingdon London Borough Council, ex parte Puhlhofer* [1986] AC 484, 518C–D.
[27] *R v Lord Chancellor, ex parte Maxwell* [1997] 1 WLR 104, 109B.
[28] *R v Lord Chancellor, ex parte Maxwell* [1997] 1 WLR 104, 109E.
[29] *R v Department of Education and Employment, ex p Begbie* [2000] 1 WLR 1115, 1130.
[30] *R v Ministry of Defence, ex parte Smith* [1996] QB 517, 554.
[31] *R v Lord Saville of Newdigate, ex p A* [2000] 1 WLR 1855 at [37].
[32] [1986] AC 240.
[33] *R v Ministry of Defence, ex parte Smith* [1996] QB 517, 556.

'The greater the policy content of a decision, and the more remote the subject matter of a decision from ordinary judicial experience, the more hesitant the court must necessarily be in holding a decision to be irrational. That is good law and, like most good law, common sense. Where decisions of a policy-laden, esoteric or security-based nature are in issue even greater caution than normal must be shown in applying the test, but the test itself is sufficiently flexible to cover all situations.'

1.28 Accordingly, the contours of the unreasonableness principle are highly dependent on the context. Depending on the factors involved the court will either anxiously scrutinise the decision under challenge, or will adopt a light touch to review. However, a key indicator of unreasonableness will be those decisions that simply do not add up.

Recent examples

1.29 The foregoing commentary has highlighted that unreasonableness is a difficult threshold to meet. However, it does not mean that public bodies are immune from review on this ground. Indeed, there are several recent decisions where unreasonableness or irrationality has been a successful ground of review. These include:

(1) *R (May) v Birmingham City Council*.[34] This was a homelessness case where the local authority had rejected the claimant's further applications for housing on the basis that there had been no change in circumstances. It was held that this was irrational as there had been a change in circumstances, namely an unanticipated breakdown in the relationship between the claimant and her temporary accommodation provider.

(2) *R (V) v Secretary of State for the Home Department*.[35] In this case, it had been conceded that two previous refusals for indefinite leave to remain were unlawful. However, the defendant argued that any leave to remain should be taken to have begun at the date of the third decision. However, this simply repeated the errors of the second decision, and so it was irrational to rely on it.

(3) *R (Rhodes) v Police and Crime Commissioner for Lincolnshire*.[36] This case concerned the suspension of a temporary chief constable on the basis of an allegation that he had engaged in a dishonest enterprise. However, the claimant's character and standing or the likelihood of the allegations being proved had not been taken into account, and the claimant's version of events had not been sought. Accordingly, the decision to suspend was irrational and perverse.

(4) *R (Weddle) v Secretary of State for Justice*.[37] This claim concerned a life prisoner who sought to be re-categorised by showing that he was a reduced risk. In time, this could allow him to be released. However, there was a failure to provide the prison with the means to show that he was a reduced risk. It was irrational to have a policy of making release dependent on a prisoner undergoing rehabilitative courses without making reasonable provision for such courses.

---

[34] [2012] EWHC 1399 (Admin).
[35] [2013] EWHC 765 (Admin).
[36] [2013] EWHC 1009 (Admin).
[37] [2013] EWHC 2323 (Admin).

Proportionality

Principle

In some limited contexts, proportionality is the appropriate approach to review.

Key cases

De Freitas v Permanent Secretary of Ministry of Agriculture, Fisheries, Lands and Housing;[38] Huang v Secretary of State for the Home Department.[39]

Commentary

1.30 Whereas *Wednesbury* unreasonableness is a general public law standard, proportionality review is in its infancy as a separate ground of review and has a more fragmented application. The key difference between unreasonableness and proportionality is that proportionality provides a more structured and focused analysis of decisions, while maintaining an in-built flexibility in its application. In simple terms, proportionality review asks 'has a sledgehammer been used to crack a nut?'[40]

1.31 Proportionality has long been a principle of European law. The development of the principle of proportionality in the law of England and Wales was foreshadowed by Lord Diplock in the *GCHQ* case where, having described the various categories of review, he noted that further grounds may be added in the future:[41] 'I have in mind particularly the possible adoption in the future of the principle of "proportionality" which is recognised in the administrative law of several of our fellow members of the European Economic Community.'

1.32 *The development of proportionality*: Around the beginning of the 21st century, the limitations of *Wednesbury* unreasonableness were becoming increasingly apparent to the courts. In *Daly*, Lord Cooke noted:[42]

> '[Wednesbury was] an unfortunately retrogressive decision in English administrative law, in so far as it suggested that there are degrees of unreasonableness and that only a very extreme degree can bring an administrative decision within the scope of judicial invalidation.'

1.33 The intellectual difficulty of *Wednesbury* unreasonableness is that it was based on a tautology – an unreasonable decision is that which no reasonable decision-maker could make. However, the political difficulty of *Wednesbury* was clearest in cases where human rights were engaged. For instance, the claimants in the *Smith* case applied to the European Court of Human Rights and a violation of Article 8 was found. In its judgment, the court said the following:[43]

> '... the threshold at which the High Court and Court of Appeal could find the MOD's policy irrational was placed so high that it effectively excluded any consideration by the domestic courts of the question of whether the interference with the applicants' rights answered a pressing social need or was proportionate ...'

---

[38] [1999] 1 AC 69.
[39] [2007] UKHL 11.
[40] R v Secretary of State for the Home Department, ex p Brind [1991] 1 AC 696, 759D.
[41] Council of Civil Service Unions v Minister for the Civil Service [1985] AC 374, 410.
[42] R v Secretary of State for the Home Department, ex parte Daly [2001] UKHL 26 at [32].
[43] Smith v United Kingdom (2000) 29 EHRR 493 at [138].

1.34 As such, even in so-called sub-*Wednesbury* cases, where the more rigorous 'anxious scrutiny' approach was applied, there remained a risk that a claimant could apply to the ECtHR and a violation of human rights would be found. Enacting the Human Rights Act 1998 was intended to address this problem by 'bringing rights home' so that an individual did not have to go all the way to the ECtHR to have their human rights complaint properly addressed. The substantive difference was that where a person complained that a qualified right[44] had been violated the court's approach would be to assess the *proportionality* rather than the *rationality* of the decision.

1.35 Not all in the senior judiciary were happy about moves towards introducing proportionality review. In *Brind* an argument deployed by the claimants was that the proper standard of review was proportionality in relation to a challenge to restrictions on broadcasters airing the words of the IRA. However, Lord Ackner stated that proportionality would essentially shift the supervisory role of the judicial review court into an appellate court. He said that:[45]

> '... to stray into the realms of appellate jurisdiction involves the Courts in a wrongful usurpation of power. Yet in order to invest the proportionality test with a higher status than the *Wednesbury* test, an inquiry into and a decision upon the merits cannot be avoided.'

1.36 However, a creeping recognition of the role of proportionality was apparent from other decisions of the courts. A key decision in this process was the Privy Council case of *de Freitas v The Permanent Secretary of Ministry of Agriculture, Fisheries, Lands and Housing (Antigua and Barbuda)*.[46]

1.37 In that case, a civil servant had been dismissed for his campaigning activities against government corruption. A blanket restriction on political protest was held to be disproportionate and was thereby unconstitutional. Their Lordships were considering the phrase 'reasonably justifiable in a democratic society', which was part of a relevant provision in an Antiguan statute.

1.38 Having reviewed a number of authorities from countries such as Canada and South Africa, the following three-fold analysis was adopted and approved:[47]

> 'In determining whether a limitation is arbitrary or excessive he said that the Court would ask itself whether: (i) the legislative objective is sufficiently important to justify limiting a fundamental right; (ii) the measures designed to meet the legislative objective are rationally connected to it; and (iii) the means used to impair the right or freedom are no more than is necessary to accomplish the objective.'

1.39 This formulation has all the elements of a proportionality test. However, the *de Freitas* test was limited in its application. First, it was a Privy Council case deciding whether a measure was 'reasonably justifiable in a democratic society', which was a specific phrase from Antiguan law. The test was thereby limited on its facts. Secondly, the issue in *de Freitas* concerned fundamental rights – namely, freedom of expression. This is a context where the enactment of the Human Rights Act 1998 would catch up with this development. So while proportionality is the appropriate approach in rights

---

[44] See below for more on the distinction between absolute and qualified rights.
[45] *R v Secretary of State for the Home Department, ex parte Brind* [1991] 1 AC 696, 762.
[46] [1998] UKPC 30.
[47] *de Freitas v The Permanent Secretary of Ministry of Agriculture, Fisheries, Lands and Housing (Antigua and Barbuda)* [1998] UKPC 30, 80F–G.

cases, the principle does not extend significantly wider than that context (see below). This is consistent with the view expressed in *Brind* by Lord Ackner that:[48]

> 'Unless and until Parliament incorporates the European Convention on Human Rights into domestic law, a course which it is well-known has a strong body of support, there appears to me to be at present no basis upon which the proportionality doctrine applied by the European Court can be followed by the courts of this country.'

1.40 It was with the coming into force of the Human Rights Act 1998, on 22 October 2000, that proportionality review became the standard of review in domestic human rights claims. There was an expectation that, as a result of this change, *Wednesbury* would be cast aside as a standard of review. For instance, in *R (Alconbury Development Ltd) v Secretary of State for the Environment*, Lord Slynn said that:[49]

> 'I consider that even without reference to the HRA 1998 the time has come to recognise that the [proportionality] principle is part of English administrative law not only when judges are dealing with Community acts but also when they are dealing with acts subject to domestic law. Trying to keep the Wednesbury principle and proportionality in separate compartments seems to me to be unnecessary and confusing.'

1.41 The gauntlet was laid down by the appellants in the Court of Appeal case of *Association of British Civilian Internees v Secretary of State for Defence* where it was argued that proportionality had displaced *Wednesbury*. The court stated that:[50] '... we have difficulty in seeing what justification there now is for retaining the *Wednesbury* test ... [but] we consider that it is not for this court to perform its burial rites ...'

1.42 The Court of Appeal said that this was an issue best dealt with by the House of Lords (as it then was). The opportunity arose in *Somerville v Scottish Ministers* where it was argued that proportionality should be recognised as an independent ground of review. However, the House of Lords left the question undecided.[51]

1.43 Therefore, the current position is that proportionality review is not an independent ground of public law. The contexts in which proportionality is applied are described in detail below.

1.44 *Proportionality defined:* A proportionality analysis follows a defined template. This is derived from the *de Freitas* test cited above and the additional requirement to balance the interests of society with those of individuals and groups as identified by Lord Bingham in *Huang v Secretary of State for the Home Department*.[52]

1.45 These elements can be crystallised as follows:[53]

(1) The legitimate aim in question must be sufficiently important to justify the interference.

(2) The measures taken to achieve the legitimate aim must be rationally connected to it.

---

[48] *R v Secretary of State for the Home Department, ex parte Brind* [1991] 1 AC 696, 763.
[49] *R (Alconbury Development Ltd) v Secretary of State for the Environment* [2001] UKHL 23 at [51].
[50] *Association of British Civilian Internees v Secretary of State for Defence* [2003] EWCA Civ 473 at [34]–[35].
[51] *Somerville v Scottish Ministers* [2007] UKHL 44 at [56] and [147].
[52] *Huang v Secretary of State for the Home Department* [2007] UKHL 11 at [19]–[20].
[53] See *R (H) v Hull City Council* [2011] EWCA Civ 403 at [38].

(3) The means used to impair the right must be no more than is necessary to accomplish the objective.

(4) A fair balance must be struck between the rights of the individual and the interests of the community; this requires a careful assessment of the severity and consequences of the interference.

1.46 It can be seen that proportionality review is both more structured and more intrusive in its approach to the scrutiny of decisions. A comparison between proportionality and *Wednesbury* was given by Lord Steyn in the following terms:[54]

'Proportionality may require the reviewing court to assess the balance which decision-maker has struck; Proportionality may require attention to be directed to relative weight accorded to interests and considerations; even heightened scrutiny test developed in *Smith* is not necessarily appropriate to protection of human rights.'

1.47 *Sliding scale*: Like *Wednesbury* unreasonableness, proportionality review has its own sliding scale that provides latitude for certain kinds of decisions. This is derived from the EHtCR's concept of the 'margin of appreciation' that is afforded to decision-makers. In *Brown v Stott*,[55] Lord Bingham described this in the following terms:[56]

'Judicial recognition and assertion of the human rights defined in the Convention is not a substitute for the processes of democratic government but a complement to them. While a national court does not accord the margin of appreciation recognised by the European court as a supra-national court, it will give weight to the decisions of a representative legislature and a democratic government within the discretionary area of judgment accorded to those bodies.'

1.48 This idea of a discretionary area of judgment echoes the factors taken into account as part of *Wednesbury* review. Lord Hope made this clear in *R v DPP, ex p Kebilene* [2000] 2 AC 326:[57]

'It will be easier to recognise a discretionary area of judgment where the issues involve questions of social or economic policy, much less so where the rights are of high constitutional importance or are of a kind where the courts are especially well placed to assess the need for protection.'

1.49 During the early 21st century, the process of determining the correct approach to a discretionary area of judgment was often described in terms of the 'deference' that might be afforded to governmental decisions. However, the judiciary did not favour this term. Lord Hoffmann said in *R (ProLife Alliance) v BBC*:[58]

'The courts themselves often have to decide the limits of their own decision-making power ... This does not mean that their allocation of decision-making power to the other branches of government is a matter of "courtesy" or "deference". The principles upon which decision-making powers are allocated are principles of law...Independence makes the courts more suited to deciding some kinds of questions and being elected makes the legislature or executive more suited to deciding others ... the principle that majority approval is necessary

---

[54] *R (Daly) v Secretary of State for the Home Department* [2001] UKHL 26 at [27].
[55] [2003] 1 AC 681.
[56] *Brown v Stott* [2003] 1 AC 681, 703.
[57] *R v Director of Public Prosecutions, ex p Kebilene* [2000] 2 AC 326, 381.
[58] *R (ProLife Alliance) v BBC* [2003] UKHL 23 at [75]–[76].

for a proper decision on policy or allocation of resources is also a legal principle ... when a court decides that a decision is within proper competence of legislature or executive, it is not showing deference. It is deciding the law.'

1.50 Lord Bingham clarified this in the following terms:[59]

'... there has been a tendency, both in the arguments addressed to the courts and in the judgments of the courts, to complicate and mystify what is not, in principle, a hard task to define ...

The giving of weight to factors such as these is not, in our opinion, aptly described as "deference": it is performance of the ordinary judicial task of weighing up the competing considerations on each side and according appropriate weight to the judgment of a person with responsibility for a given subject matter and access to special sources of knowledge and advice. That is how any rational judicial decision-maker is likely to proceed.'

1.51 Whichever label is chosen to describe this process, the practical effect is that certain kinds of decisions will be less amenable to judicial intervention even when proportionality review is adopted. These kinds of decisions are typically decisions of high-policy and of resource allocation.

1.52 Exactly how this operates in practice can be difficult. A recent example is *R (Sinclair Collis Ltd) v Secretary of State for Health*. This case concerned a decision to ban the sale of tobacco from vending machines. On the issue of how intensely the decision should be reviewed in the context of proportionality, the Court of Appeal was split. Arden LJ said that 'the appropriate level of intensity ... is of a low level' due to the elements of high policy.[60] Lord Neuberger agreed, stating that the 'purpose of the ban was to improve public health, which is an area where a relatively broad margin of appreciation should be accorded to the Government'.[61]

1.53 However, Laws LJ held that because the Government had failed to consider less restrictive alternatives to the ban it followed that the ban had not been shown to be proportionate.[62] The approach of Laws LJ was that 'there can be no abrogation of the standards of proportionality however broad the margin of appreciation accorded to the decision-maker'. Although the court will leave a wider space for the decision-maker's own judgment, 'the questions the standards represent must still be asked and answered'. The point of Laws LJ's sharper approach is that it is not sufficient for a decision-maker to argue that a decision is proportionate simply on the basis that the court is probing areas that engage a wider discretionary area of judgment. If the decision is disproportionate, the court is under a duty to say so. This approach appears to be supported by the Supreme Court decision in *R (Quila) v Secretary of State for the Home Department*.[63]

1.54 *Sinclair Collis* is an example of the intensity of review depending on the circumstances, and that it is possible for there to be a difference in judicial opinion regarding where the line is drawn in specific cases. However, the overall model is akin to

---

[59] *Huang v Secretary of State of Home Department* [2007] UKHL 11 at [14]–[16].
[60] *R (Sinclair Collis Ltd) v Secretary of State for Health* [2011] EWCA Civ 437 at [173].
[61] *R (Sinclair Collis Ltd) v Secretary of State for Health* [2011] EWCA Civ 437 at [254].
[62] *R (Sinclair Collis Ltd) v Secretary of State for Health* [2011] EWCA Civ 437 at [80].
[63] See *R (Quila) v Secretary of State for the Home Department* [2011] UKSC 45 at [46] and [61].

the *Wednesbury* sliding scale: decisions of high policy and resource allocation will tend to engage a wider discretionary area of judgment, while cases of fundamental rights will narrow the discretionary area of judgment.

1.55 *Applications of proportionality*: As noted above, proportionality has a fragmented application in public law. The contexts in which proportionality applies are as follows:

(1) *Qualified ECHR rights*: The rights and freedoms protected by the ECHR fall into two main categories: absolute rights and qualified rights.[64] These rights are considered in more detail below. Where a decision interferes with a qualified right, this can be justified by reference to proportionality. The qualified rights are:
    (a) Article 8 (the right to respect for private and family life)
    (b) Article 9 (freedom of religion)
    (c) Article 10 (freedom of expression)
    (d) Article 11 (freedom of association)
    (e) Article 12 (freedom of marriage)
    (f) Article 1 of the First Protocol (protection of possessions).

(2) *EU law rights*: When rights protected by EU law are in issue, proportionality is the correct standard of review. A particular focus of proportionality in the EU context is the requirement that a decision-maker must choose the 'least restrictive alternative' for a decision to be proportionate.[65] As well as covering the fundamental rights and freedoms of the EU Treaty, this includes the rights protected by the EU Charter of Fundamental Rights. These are considered in more detail below.

(3) *Common law rights*: Where fundamental rights that are protected at common law are engaged, proportionality is the correct standard of review.[66] These rights are sometimes also described as constitutional rights. They include:
    (a) *Access to justice rights*. Within this category is included the right of access to the court[67] and the right of access to a lawyer.[68]

---

[64] There is a third category: absolute rights with exceptions, such as Article 5 ECHR (the right to liberty).
[65] See *Sinclair Collis Ltd v Secretary of State for Health* [2011] EWCA Civ 437.
[66] *R (Quila) v Secretary of State for the Home Department* [2010] EWCA Civ 1482 at [34].
[67] Access to court cases include: *R (Medical Justice) v Secretary of State for the Home Department* [2011] EWCA Civ 1710; *Ahmed v HM Treasury* [2010] UKSC 2; *R (Anufrijeva) v Secretary of State for the Home Department* [2003] UKHL 36; *R v Lord Chancellor, ex parte Witham* [1998] QB 575; *R v Secretary of State for the Home Department, ex parte Pierson* [1998] AC 539; *R v Secretary of State for the Home Department, ex parte Leech* [1994] QB 198.
[68] Access to a lawyer cases: *R (AM) v Director of Public Prosecutions* [2012] EWHC 470 (Admin); *R (T) v Secretary of State for the Home Department* [2010] EWHC 435 (Admin); *R v Secretary of State for the Home Department, ex parte Anderson* [1984] QB 778.

(b) *Due process rights.* This includes the principle of open justice,[69] the privilege against self-incrimination,[70] legal professional privilege[71] and trial by jury.[72] These rights are in addition to the overarching principles of natural justice that are considered below.

(c) *Human rights.* The common law recognises rights akin to those protected by the ECHR. Indeed, it has been held that the courts can develop such common law rights beyond those protected by the ECHR.[73] Accordingly, it may be possible to rely on the common law for the following absolute rights: right to life[74] and freedom from torture.[75] It is submitted that because of the absolute status of these rights, a proportionality test should not be applied, in line with the normal ECHR approach.

The following human rights are recognised at common law, and it is submitted that these would be treated as qualified and would attract a proportionality test: right of personal liberty (including habeas corpus),[76] right to privacy,[77] freedom of religion,[78] freedom of expression,[79] property rights,[80] citizenship rights,[81] the right to vote[82] and equality rights.[83]

(4) *Legitimate expectations*: When a court is considering whether a legitimate expectation has been breached, proportionality is applied. This was clearly set out in *R (Wood) v Secretary of State for Education*[84] where it was held that 'the

---

[69] *R (Guardian News and Media Ltd) v City of Westminster Magistrates' Court* [2012] EWCA Civ 420; *Al Rawi v Security Service* [2011] UKSC 34; *R (Mohamed) v Secretary of State for Foreign and Commonwealth Affairs (No 2)* [2011] QB 218; *R (Secretary of State for the Home Department) v Assistant Deputy Coroner for Inner West London* [2010] EWHC 3098 (Admin).
[70] *R v Rochford* [2010] EWCA Crim 1928 at [21] and *R v Director of the Serious Fraud Office, ex parte Smith* [1993] AC 1, 40D.
[71] *R (Morgan Grenfell & Co Ltd) v Inland Revenue Commissioners* [2002] UKHL 21 at [7] and [43]; *Quinn Direct Insurance Ltd v Law Society* [2010] EWCA Civ 805 at [23] and [29]; *R (Kelly) v Warley Magistrates' Court* [2007] EWHC 1836 (Admin).
[72] *R v Islington North Juvenile Court, ex parte Daley* [1983] 1 AC 347, 364B and *R (Misick) v Secretary of State for Foreign and Commonwealth Affairs* [2009] EWCA Civ 1549 at [20].
[73] *Rabone v Pennine Care NHS Trust* [2012] UKSC 2 at [113]; *R (Guardian News and Media Ltd) v City of Westminster Magistrates' Court* [2012] EWCA Civ 420 at [88].
[74] *R (Amin) v Secretary of State for the Home Department* [2003] UKHL 51 at [30].
[75] *A v Secretary of State for the Home Department* [2005] UKHL 71 at [11]–[12].
[76] *R (Lumba) v Secretary of State for the Home Department* [2011] UKSC 12; *A v Secretary of State for the Home Department* [2004] UKHL 56 at [36]; *B v Secretary of State for Justice* [2011] EWCA Civ 1608 at [53]; *R (Saadi) v Secretary of State for the Home Department* [2001] EWCA Civ 1512 at [69]; *R v Secretary of State for the Home Department, ex parte Khawaja* [1984] AC 74, 111F; and *Rahmatullah v Secretary of State for Foreign and Commonwealth Affairs* [2011] EWCA Civ 1540 at [43].
[77] *Douglas v Hello! Ltd (No 3)* [2005] EWCA Civ 595; *Wainwright v Home Office* [2003] UKHL 53 at [31].
[78] *McFarlane v Relate Avon Limited* [2010] EWCA Civ 880 at [22]; *R (Johns) v Derby City Council* [2011] EWHC 375 (Admin) at [37]–[45].
[79] *Rushbridger v HM Attorney General* [2003] UKHL 38 at [7]; *R v Shayler* [2002] UKHL 11 at [21]; *McCartan Turkington Breen v Times Newspapers Ltd* [2001] 2 AC 277 at 297F.
[80] *R (Eastenders Cash & Carry Plc) v Revenue & Customs Commissioners* [2012] EWCA Civ 15 at [88]; *R (Sainsbury's Supermarkets Ltd) v Wolverhampton City Council* [2010] UKSC 20 at [10]; *Attorney-General v Blake* [2001] 1 AC 268, 289G.
[81] *Pomiechowski v District Court of Legnica* [2012] UKSC 20 at [31]–[32]; *R (Bancoult) v Secretary of State for the Foreign and Commonwealth Office* [2001] QB 1067 at [39]; *R (Bancoult) v Secretary of State for Foreign & Commonwealth Affairs (No 2)* [2008] UKHL 61 at [89].
[82] *R (Preston) v Wandsworth London Borough Council* [2011] EWHC 3174 (Admin) at [40].
[83] *Percy v Board of National Mission of the Church of Scotland* [2005] UKHL 73, [2006] 2 AC 28 at [152]; *Association of British Civilian Internees & Far Eastern Region v Secretary of State for Defence* [2003] EWCA Civ 473, [2003] QB 1397; and *R (Rudi) v Secretary of State for the Home Department* [2007] EWCA Civ 132.
[84] [2011] EWHC 3256 (Admin).

standard of review which the court should adopt when the executive seeks to resile from its previous promise is that of proportionality'.[85]

(5) *Sanctions*: In relation to sanctions or penalties, proportionality has been the applicable standard of review even before the Human Rights Act 1998.[86] This applies in contexts such as disciplinary cases and cost awards.[87]

(6) *Duty to perform proportionality exercise*: In *RK v Chief Constable of South Yorkshire*[88] it was held that there had been no proper regard to the exercise of proportionality. In this case the police had failed to make an assessment of proportionality of disclosing information, and the decision was quashed on that basis.

Recent examples

1.56 Proportionality is routinely deployed in rights-based challenges. Recent examples include:

(a) *R (Lord Carlile of Berriew) v Secretary of State for the Home Department*.[89] A group of senior Parliamentarians challenged the decision to exclude a prominent Iranian politician, which had been made on the basis that to allow her to speak in Parliament would affect diplomatic relations. The court held that it could not gainsay this judgment and so the decision could not be found to be disproportionate.

(b) *R (Gallastegui) v Westminster City Council*.[90] The claimant was a protestor on Parliament Square who had been stopped from erecting a tent by powers under the Police Reform and Social Responsibility Act 2011. The court held that the measures were proportionate given the margin of appreciation that applied in cases where Parliament had itself considered the issue of proportionality.

(c) *Ogunnowo v Solicitors Regulation Authority*.[91] A solicitor challenged the conditions that had been imposed on his practice. The court held that these conditions were proportionate given the solicitor's lengthy disciplinary record.

(d) *R (Prothero) v Secretary of State for the Home Department*.[92] The requirement that sex offenders must provide bank account, debit and credit card details was held to be proportionate as a means of providing further protection to prevent other persons becoming victims.

(e) *R (R) v A Chief Constable*.[93] In this case a former prisoner challenged the practice of the police to collect DNA samples for a database on the basis that it was a disproportionate interference with Article 8 ECHR. The court held that the practice was proportionate given that the purpose was detecting serious crime.

---

[85] *R (Wood) v Secretary of State for Education* [2011] EWHC 3256 (Admin) at [41].
[86] *R (Electoral Commission) v City of Westminster Magistrates' Court* [2009] EWHC 78 (Admin) at [45].
[87] See respectively *Ghosh v General Medical Council* [2001] UKPC 29 at [34] and *R (Middleton) v Cambridge Magistrates' Court* [2012] EWHC 2122 (Admin).
[88] [2013] EWHC 1555 (Admin).
[89] [2013] EWCA Civ 199.
[90] [2013] EWCA Civ 28.
[91] [2013] EWHC 1882 (Admin).
[92] [2013] EWHC 2830 (Admin).
[93] [2013] EWHC 2864 (Admin).

Bad faith/improper motive

Principle

It is unlawful for a public authority to act in bad faith or with an improper motive.

Key case

Smith v East Ello Rural District Council;[94] *Board of Education v Rice*;[95] *Wheeler v Leicester City Council*.[96]

Explanation

1.57 The principle of unreasonableness prohibits oppressive decision-making. Two applications of this are the rules against bad faith or improper motive.

1.58 *Bad faith*: Public bodies cannot take decisions in bad faith. This means that it is unlawful to act dishonestly. This ground of judicial review can be seen as coming under the heading of unreasonableness as that concept includes decisions that are oppressive or arbitrary. Indeed, in *Holgate-Mohammed v Duke*[97] it was said that 'the first of the *Wednesbury* principles is that the discretion must be exercised in good faith'.[98] However, it has also been held that acting in bad faith would be a breach of natural justice.[99] It may also be said that the law's approach to bad faith is a result of judicial review being the process of controlling abuses of power.[100]

1.59 Whichever category bad faith comes within, it requires a claimant to specifically plead and prove by evidence that a decision-maker has acted improperly.[101] Bad faith is therefore a ground of judicial review that is likely to require the court to resolve a factual dispute.[102] Accordingly, such cases may require the court to order disclosure and cross-examination.[103]

1.60 *Improper motives*: An extension of the rule against bad faith includes taking into account improper motives. A striking illustration of this is *Wheeler v Leicester City Council*[104] where the local authority had sought to use its statutory powers in order to punish a rugby club for attempting to visit South Africa. This was in the context of widespread condemnation of South Africa's apartheid policy. The court held that the local authority's motives were improper and said that:[105]

---

[94] [1956] AC 736.
[95] [1911] AC 179.
[96] [1985] AC 1054.
[97] [1984] AC 437.
[98] *Holgate-Mohammed v Duke* [1984] AC 437, 443D.
[99] *Byrne v Kinematograph Renters Society Ltd* [1958] 1 WLR 762, 784.
[100] *R v Derbyshire County Council, ex parte Times Supplements Ltd* (1991) 3 Admin LR 241, 253A.
[101] *R (Birmingham and Solihull Taxi Association) v Birmingham International Airport* [2009] EWHC 1913 (Admin) at [36]; *R (Amraf Training Plc) v Secretary of State for Education and Employment* (2001) *The Times*, 28 June; *Cannock Chase District Council v Kelly* [1978] 1 WLR 1.
[102] See, for instance, *R v Derbyshire County Council, ex parte Times Supplements Ltd* (1991) 3 Admin LR 241, 247–248.
[103] See 3.7 for detail on disclosure and cross-examination in judicial review.
[104] [1985] AC 1054.
[105] *Wheeler v Leicester City Council* [1985] AC 1054.

'… this use by the council of its statutory powers was a misuse of power. The council could not properly seek to use its statutory powers of management or any other statutory powers for the purposes of punishing the club when the club had done no wrong.'

1.61 The principle that decision-makers should not pursue improper motives or purposes can be seen as complementing the positive duty on decision-makers to promote the purpose of a statute (the *'Padfield* principle'). This is discussed in more detail below. The doctrine of improper motives can also be seen as a species of the rule that legally irrelevant considerations should not be taken into account by decision-makers. This is also discussed below.

1.62 The *Wheeler* decision gives an indication of the paradigm case where improper motives are pursued, namely where a public body uses its powers for political gain. For instance, in *Magill v Porter*[106] a decision had been taken to designate some council houses for sale in order to gain electoral advantage. This was held to be unlawful because the decision was made to pursue political ends. There is a range of cases that supports the view that political motives are likely to be improper. However, in *R v Leeds City Council, ex parte Cobleigh*[107] it was noted that political considerations do not necessarily undermine a decision. It is submitted that even if political motives will not *necessarily* lead to a finding of unlawfulness, the overall effect of the authorities is that political motives will jeopardise the legality of a decision.[108]

1.63 Political motives are not the only improper motives. Other examples of where improper motives have been adopted include where planning powers have been used for purposes not provided by the relevant enabling statute, or where a court or tribunal has taken a decision on an improper whim such as its irritation with a party or a hurry to finish a case quickly. The unifying theme behind these cases is that the decision-maker has used its powers to take a decision that those powers were not designed for. It will be apparent that this principle is similar to the *Padfield* principle discussed below.

1.64 A practical issue in improper motive cases arises when a decision was made for mixed purposes. In such cases, the court will seek to identify what was the 'dominant purpose' behind a decision.[109] Determining exactly which purpose was true and dominant is a factual exercise and will require evidence from the public body to demonstrate the role of the various purposes involved. Where a public body is only able to show that a statutorily prescribed purpose was simply a collateral consequence of a decision, the decision may be found unlawful.[110] However, if a decision has an unlawful secondary purpose but a lawful primary purpose, the decision can still be lawful.[111]

Recent examples

1.65 The following cases are examples where bad faith or improper motive has been alleged. The cases illustrate that such claims need a strong factual basis.

---

[106] [2001] UKHL 67.
[107] [1997] COD 69.
[108] See further *Padfield v Minister of Agriculture, Fisheries & Food* [1968] AC 997, 1058F–G; *R v London Borough of Ealing, ex parte Times Newspapers* [1987] IRLR 129; *R v Secretary of State for Foreign and Commonwealth Affairs, ex parte World Development Movement Ltd* [1995] 1 WLR 386, 398C–D.
[109] *R v Crown Court at Southwark, ex parte Bowles* [1998] AC 641, 651; *R (Hicks) v Metropolitan Police Commissioner* [2012] EWHC 1947 (Admin) at [237].
[110] *R (Richards) v Pembrokeshire County Council* [2004] EWCA Civ 1000 at [44].
[111] *Porter v Magill* (1998) 96 LGR 157 (DC), 167.

(1) *R (Kelway) v Newcastle upon Tyne Combined Court*.[112] In this case, a litigant in person brought a wide-ranging challenge that included allegations that a district judge had tampered with a tape-recording of a hearing before Newcastle county court and related allegations of bad faith. The claim failed because of the lack of any prospects of success, and the claimant was made subject to a civil restraint order.

(2) *R (Bancoult) v Secretary of State for Foreign and Commonwealth Affairs*.[113] In this case, the decision to create a marine protected area around the Chagos Islands was challenged on the basis that there had been an improper motive. This was based on an article obtained from the WikiLeaks website that suggested that the purpose of the marine protected area was to prevent the Chagos Islanders returning to the islands. It was held that this document was inadmissible in light of the Vienna Convention on Diplomatic Relations 1961. Accordingly, the factual basis of the improper motive challenge was undermined.

(3) *R (Jackowski) v Poland*.[114] In this extradition case, a decision to extradite a Polish national was challenged on the basis that the Polish authorities should have dealt with all of the claimant's offending when he was previously extradited. It was argued that a further extradition order was made in bad faith. It was held that a strong case was required to amount to bad faith and that this case did not reach that threshold.

(4) *R (Hicks) v Commissioner of Police of the Metropolis*.[115] In this case, a group of protestors challenged the actions of the police in relation to the Royal Wedding. In particular, search warrants were challenged on the basis that there was an improper ulterior motive. However, it was held that the dominant purpose of the search warrants was the prevention of criminal damage and that this was lawful.

CATEGORY 2: ILLEGALITY

1.66 The category of illegality covers a wide range of grounds. It includes simple cases of illegality such as the *ultra vires* rule, as well as extended obligations that condition the lawful exercise of power. Grounds within this category are:

(1) *Ultra vires*. Public authorities must not make decisions beyond their powers. Arguments based on this principle require the relevant power to be located and construed, which will involve statutory interpretation. This principle includes the traditional but increasingly marginal issue of error of jurisdiction and the related ground of error of law.

(2) *Delegation of powers*. Where a public body has been given a power or a duty, it must not improperly delegate this function to a third party. Whether a delegation is proper will be determined by the context in which the power or duty was created, and how the delegation was made. This includes the related ground of acting under dictation, which prohibits decision-makers from mindlessly approving advice or recommendations from a third party.

---

[112] [2013] EWHC 2574 (Admin).
[113] [2013] EWHC 1502 (Admin).
[114] [2012] EWHC 3935 (Admin).
[115] [2012] EWHC 1947.

(3) *Fettering of discretion.* If a public body has been given a discretionary power it cannot tie its hands regarding how that power is exercised. This means that a decision-maker cannot apply a blanket policy, and must give each case individual consideration.

(4) *Mistake of fact.* Judicial review does not typically deal with disputes of fact. However, in limited circumstances, an error of fact can amount to an error of law. Similarly, there are narrowly defined situations where a precedent fact is disputed. Such facts unlock a public body's powers and obligations, and will be reviewed by the court.

(5) *Relevant/irrelevant considerations.* A public body must take into account all relevant consideration, and not take into account irrelevant considerations. The relevant legislative framework or what the public body chooses to take into account will identify such considerations. The court can also review whether unreasonable weight has been given to certain considerations.

(6) *Frustrating legislative purpose.* Statutory powers and duties reflect an underlying legislative purpose and public bodies must give effect to this purpose. Accordingly, using a power or duty to thwart the legislative purpose will be unlawful.

(7) *Sufficient inquiry.* When a public authority takes a decision it is under a duty to conduct reasonable inquiries to furnish itself with the information necessary to make an informed decision. Failure to do so, or a failure to consider the information properly, can render a decision unlawful.

(8) *Policy challenges.* Much of modern public law is concerned with the application of policy guidance. It is also possible to challenge such policy itself for instance where the policy would lead to unlawful decisions or if a policy creates a proven risk of injustice that inheres in the system itself.

Ultra vires

Principle

Public bodies cannot act beyond their legal powers.

Key cases

R (Bancoult) v Secretary of State for Foreign and Commonwealth Affairs;[116] Gibb v Maidstone & Tunbridge Wells NHS Trust.[117]

Explanation

1.67 All public authorities have limited powers. There can be no legal basis for acts or decisions taken beyond their powers. Such acts or decisions would be *ultra vires* and unlawful.[118] There is some debate about whether *ultra vires* is the unifying basis for judicial review as it is the principle that enables the courts to keep the executive acting within the confines of the law.[119] On this basis, whenever a decision is unlawful it is also *ultra vires*.[120]

---

[116] [2007] EWCA Civ 498.
[117] [2010] EWCA Civ 678.
[118] '*Ultra vires*' is Latin for 'beyond powers'. It is a concept borrowed by public law from company law in the 19th century. See *R (Bancoult) v Secretary of State for Foreign and Commonwealth Affairs* [2007] EWCA Civ 498 at [59] and *Gibb v Maidstone & Tunbridge Wells NHS Trust* [2010] EWCA Civ 678 at [50].
[119] See *R v Hull University Visitor, ex parte Page* [1993] AC 682, 701E and *Boddington v British Transport*

1.68 The classic format of *ultra vires* arguments is: first, determine the extent of a body's legal powers, which is often an issue of statutory interpretation; and, second, establish whether the body acted beyond those powers as construed.

1.69 *Step one: Locating and interpreting the vires.* There are three main sources of legal power – statutory powers, prerogatives powers and 'third source' powers. Statutory powers are derived from pieces of primary and secondary legislation[121] the application of which is often subject to policy or guidance;[122] prerogative powers are those powers that still reside with the monarch but are mainly exercised by the government;[123] and 'third source' powers, which include general administrative powers to carry on the ordinary business of government that are not exercises of the royal prerogative and do not require statutory authority.[124] Third source powers are controversial and their extent is unclear, although it has been said that they cannot be coercive, be inconsistent with statute or breach public law standards.[125]

1.70 Once the power has been located, there are two strands to the interpretative exercise. The first strand is to apply the one of the main techniques of statutory interpretation. The starting point is to identify the 'natural and ordinary meaning' of the words.[126] Some statutes have interpretation sections and are accompanied by explanatory notes that can assist with this, although it is often quite clear what words mean when read in the context of a particular piece of legislation.[127]

1.71 A further technique is to adopt a 'purposive approach' whereby the words are given a meaning that is consistent with the overall purpose of the Act and intention of Parliament. This approach can entail reference to parliamentary materials where the provision in question remains ambiguous or obscure.[128] This appeal to Parliament's intention may be more difficult with old statutes. However, it has been held that statutes

---

Police [1999] 2 AC 143, 164B; but compare with *R (Bancoult) v Secretary of State for Foreign & Commonwealth Affairs* [2007] EWCA Civ 498 at [59]–[61]; *Gibb v Maidstone & Tunbridge Wells NHS Trust* [2010] EWCA Civ 678 at [55]; *R v Department for Education and Employment, ex parte Begbie* [2000] 1 WLR 1115, 1129F–G; *R v Secretary of State for the Environment, ex parte Nottinghamshire County Council* [1986] AC 240, 249C–D; *R v Secretary of State for the Home Department, ex parte Brind* [1991] 1 AC 696, 751B.

[120] See *Anisminic Ltd v Foreign Compensation Commission* [1969] 2 AC 147, 195B–C; *R (Director of Public Prosecutions) v Birmingham City Justices* [2003] EWHC 2352 (Admin) at [37]. It is submitted that even if this is correct, this does not assist in categorising the grounds of judicial review.

[121] Such as statutory instruments, regulations, rules and orders. See Her Majesty's Stationary Office, *Statutory Instruments Practice* (4th edn, 2006) available at: www.opsi.gov.uk/si/si-practice.doc. This includes those powers that are implied or incidental to the statutory scheme.

[122] The meaning of policies is a matter for the court, while the application of policies is typically subject to a *Wednesbury* standard of review: *R (LE (Jamaica)) v Secretary of State for the Home Department* [2012] EWCA Civ 597 at [29]. Statutory guidance should be followed unless there is a good reason not to do so: *R (Munjaz) v Ashworth Hospital Authority* [2005] UKHL 58 at [46].

[123] Prerogative powers include powers relating to foreign affairs, the armed forces, the legislature, the judicial system, and certain emergency powers.

[124] *R (New London College Ltd) v Secretary of State for the Home Department* [2013] UKSC 51 at [28]. The exercise of such powers is reviewable in principle: *R (Abassi) v Secretary of State for Foreign and Commonwealth Affairs* [2002] EWCA Civ 1598 at [106].

[125] *R (New London College Ltd) v Secretary of State for the Home Department* [2013] UKSC 51 at [29]. This appears to be a development of the *Ram Doctrine* which provides that a minister of the Crown may exercise any powers that the Crown may exercise, except in so far as the minister is precluded from doing so, either expressly or by necessary implication (see HL *Hansard*, vol 643, col WA98).

[126] *McCormick v Horsepower Ltd* [1981] 1 WLR 993, 999; *Macarthys Ltd v Smith* [1979] 3 All ER 325, 332.

[127] This is sometimes called an 'informed interpretation'. See *Bennion on Statutory Interpretation* (5th edn, 2007), Code s 210.

[128] *Pepper v Hart* [1993] AC 593. See also *R (Spath Holme Ltd) v Secretary of State for the Environment, Transport and the Regions* [2001] 2 AC 349 and *Wilson v First County Trust Ltd (No 2)* [2003] UKHL 40.

are to be given an 'always-speaking construction' unless this is explicitly prohibited.[129] This means that legislation can be construed in light of present day circumstances rather than be reference to the original intent of Parliament. The purposive approach has been extended to the point where the court may apply a construction to legislation that rectifies errors in the drafting of a statute to reflect Parliament's true intention.[130]

1.72 The second strand of interpretation applies in cases where fundamental rights are engaged. In cases where a right protected by the ECHR is engaged, s 3 of the HRA requires courts to interpret legislation compatibly with the right so far as it is possible to do so. It is noted below that this is a strong obligation and can involve reading words into legislation.[131] There is a similar obligation in relation to EU law.[132] Where common law rights are engaged, the principle of legality entails that legislation should be read down in so far as it interferes with such rights.[133]

1.73 *Step two: Whether the actions were ultra vires:* Once the relevant power has been located and construed, the final issue is whether the action or decision was beyond the power as construed. This is essentially a question of fact that is to be answered in light of the evidence before the court.[134]

1.74 In addition to classic *ultra vires* arguments, there are two further concepts that come within the overall heading of whether a public authority has acted beyond its powers: first, the concept of acting beyond jurisdiction; and, second, errors of law.

1.75 *Acting beyond jurisdiction:* At one time, a principal issue in judicial review cases was whether a body had acted within or without its jurisdiction. In cases where a body had acted within its jurisdiction, a judicial review remedy would not be available even if the body had made an error of law or made the wrong decision.[135] This has been known as a 'narrow' or 'pre-*Anisminic*' approach to jurisdiction.[136] This position changed in light of the House of Lords decision in *Anisminic Ltd v Foreign Compensation Commission*[137] where it was held that *any* error of law took a tribunal outside its jurisdiction.[138]

1.76 As a result of *Anisminic*, most judicial review claims do not need to be concerned by the issue of whether an error of law was within or without the jurisdiction of a tribunal.[139] This does not mean that a body's jurisdiction is not a relevant starting point for considering the extent of its powers. Indeed, a decision taken without jurisdiction is simply a form of *ultra vires*. However, the complications of jurisdictional error no longer trouble modern public law in the way it used to.[140]

---

[129] *Re McFarland* [2004] UKHL 17 at [25].
[130] *Inco Europe Ltd v First Choice Distribution* [2000] 1 WLR 586, 592C–593A.
[131] *Ghaidan v Godin-Mendoza* [2004] UKHL 30.
[132] *Fleming v Revenue and Customs Commissioners* [2008] UKHL 2 at [25].
[133] *R v Secretary of State for the Home Department, ex parte Simms* [2000] 2 AC 115, 130C–G.
[134] *Moyna v Secretary of State for Work and Pensions* [2003] UKHL 44 at [24]–[26].
[135] *R v Northumberland Compensation Appeal Tribunal, ex parte Shaw* [1952] 1 KB 338, 346; *R v Governor of Brixton Prison, ex parte Armah* [1968] AC 192, 234.
[136] *R (Strickson) v Preston County Court* [2007] EWCA Civ 1132 at [26].
[137] [1969] 2 AC 147.
[138] *Anisminic Ltd v Foreign Compensation Commission* [1969] 2 AC 147, 174A–D.
[139] See *R (Cart) v Upper Tribunal* [2011] UKSC 28 at [18]; *O'Reilly v Mackman* [1983] 2 AC 237, 283E–F, *Re A Company* [1981] AC 374, 383C; *Palacegate Properties Ltd v Camden London Borough Council* [2000] 4 PLR 59, 78B.
[140] *R (Cart) v Upper Tribunal* [2011] UKSC 28 at [40]; [110]–[111].

1.77 Clear cases of jurisdictional error still arise in contexts where tribunals consider issues beyond their remit,[141] or where they refuse to consider issues within their remit.[142] Similarly, if a body is *functus officio*[143] or a condition precedent is not satisfied,[144] there will be a lack of jurisdiction.

1.78 *Errors of law:* The natural consequence of the *Anisminic* decision is that all errors of law are potential targets for judicial review challenges. The logic of this approach is that all errors of law are thereby *ultra vires*.[145] This can be readily shown in cases where public authorities have made an error of law by misconstruing their powers and acting beyond these powers.[146]

1.79 Courts will typically intervene to correct errors of law where the error relevant to the decision that is under challenge. Accordingly, the courts look for material misdirections in law.[147] For instance, if a body bases a decision on the legally flawed advice of an advisor a court is likely to find that the decision was based on a material error of law.[148]

1.80 It should be noted that there are residual categories of cases where it has been suggested that an approach to errors of law should remain on a narrow, pre-*Anisminic* basis. This includes judicial review challenges to decisions by visitors[149] and courts such as the county court.[150] It is submitted that this approach should be viewed on an alternative basis, namely that errors of law in these categories are reviewable in principle. However, such a challenge would only be entertained in limited circumstances, such as if the case raised an important issue of principle or practice, or there is some other compelling reason.[151] This was the approach adopted by the Supreme Court in relation to the Upper Tribunal in *Cart v Upper Tribunal*.[152] It is submitted that this

---

[141] *R (Bunce) v Pensions Appeal Tribunal* [2009] EWCA Civ 451 at [34]; *R (Srinivasans Solicitors) v Croydon County Court* [2011] All ER (D) 108 (Oct); *R (Secretary of State for Defence) v Pensions Appeal Tribunal* [2008] EWHC 3248 (Admin).

[142] *R (Parish) v Pensions Ombudsman* [2009] EWHC 969 (Admin); *R v Dorking Justices, ex parte Harrington* [1984] AC 743, 753B–754A.

[143] *Functus officio* means 'having discharged the duty' and applies where a body has exhausted its powers, and so cannot reopen or reconsider a matter. See *R v Parliamentary Commissioner for Administration, ex parte Dyer* [1994] 1 WLR 621, 629F; *R v Dorset Police Authority, ex parte Vaughan* [1995] COD 153; *Aparau v Iceland Frozen Foods Plc* [2000] 1 All ER 228, 235J–236A.

[144] A condition precedent refers to a condition that must be satisfied before a provision is engaged. For instance, the laying of an information triggers the jurisdiction of the Magistrates' Court – *R v Manchester Stipendiary Magistrate, ex parte Hill* [1983] 1 AC 328.

[145] *R v Hull University Visitor, ex parte Page* [1993] AC 682, 701F–G; *Boddington v British Transport Police* [1999] 2 AC 143, 154C.

[146] *R (Q) v Secretary of State for the Home Department* [2003] EWCA Civ 364 at [112]; *Council of Civil Service Unions v Minister for the Civil Service* [1985] AC 374, 410F.

[147] *R v Hull University Visitor, ex parte Page* [1993] AC 682, 702C–D; *R v Governor of Brixton Prison, ex parte Levin* [1997] AC 741, 749A; *Tesco Stores Ltd v Dundee City Council* [2012] UKSC 13 at [31].

[148] See *R (Lewis) v Redcar and Cleveland Borough Council (No 2)* [2010] UKSC 11 at [38]; *R (Patmore) v Brentwood Borough Council* [2012] EWHC 1244 (Admin) at [33]; *R (Cathco Property Holdings Ltd) v Cygnor Gwynedd Council* [2008] EWHC 1462 (Admin) at [77]. Compare with *R (Sullivan) v Warwick District Council* [2003] EWHC 606 (Admin).

[149] Visitors oversee certain institutions and can intervene in their affairs. See *R v Hull University Visitor, ex parte Page* [1993] AC 682, 704F; *R v Visitors to the Inns of Court, ex parte Calder & Persaud* [1994] QB 1; *R v Edmunsbury and Ipswich Diocese (Chancellor), ex parte White* [1948] 1 KB 195, 220–221; *R v Chief Rabbi, ex parte Wachmann* [1992] 1 WLR 1036, 1042H; *R v Charity Commissioners for England and Wales, ex parte Baldwin* (2001) 33 HLR 538.

[150] *R (Sivasubramaniam) v Wandsworth County Court* [2002] EWCA Civ 1738 at [42].

[151] *Cart v The Upper Tribunal (Rev 1)* [2011] UKSC 28.

[152] [2011] UKSC 28.

approach is consistent with cases that suggest that a pre-*Anisminic* approach to certain categories of cases should be abandoned.¹⁵³ However, this matter has yet to be authoritatively determined.

Recent examples

1.81 Some recent examples of *ultra vires* cases include:

(1) *R (Reilly) v Secretary of State for Work and Pensions*.¹⁵⁴ This case concerned whether certain regulations for jobseekers allowance were made within the powers of s 17A of the Jobseekers Act 1995. The regulations provided that if a person refused to participate in certain schemes, which involved working without pay, their jobseekers allowance would be removed. In this case, it was held that the regulations did not meet the requirements of the Act, and so were *ultra vires* and would be quashed.

(2) *R (Lewisham London Borough Council) v Secretary of State for Health*.¹⁵⁵ In this case, a decision by an NHS trust special administrator to reduce hospital services was challenged on the basis that the administrator was appointed in relation to a single trust and so could not make recommendations for other trusts. Accordingly, the decision to reduce services beyond the appointed trust was *ultra vires* the National Health Service Act 2006.

(3) *R (ToTel Ltd) v First-tier Tribunal (Tax Chamber)*.¹⁵⁶ An order purported to remove a right of appeal to the Upper Tribunal in VAT hardship cases. This was not permitted within the terms of s 124 of the Finance Act 2008, and so was *ultra vires*.

(4) *R (Shanks (t/a Blue Line Taxis)) v Northumberland County Council*.¹⁵⁷ A taxi operator challenged the power of a local authority to impose conditions on a licence where one was, or was associated with, a private hire operator. It was held that this was not beyond the power in s 47 of the Local Government (Miscellaneous Provisions) Act 1976, which provided that conditions could be imposed if 'reasonably necessary'. Accordingly, the conditions were not *ultra vires*.

Unlawful delegation of powers

Principle

A public body cannot improperly delegate its powers to another body.

Key case

Carltona Ltd v Works Commissioners.¹⁵⁸

---

¹⁵³ *O'Reilly v Mackman* [1983] 2 AC 237, 278D–F. See also *R (Woolas) v Parliamentary Election Court* [2010] EWHC 3169 (Admin); *R (Guardian News and Media Ltd) v City of Westminster Magistrates' Court* [2012] EWCA Civ 420.
¹⁵⁴ [2013] EWCA Civ 66.
¹⁵⁵ [2013] EWHC 2381 (Admin).
¹⁵⁶ [2012] EWCA Civ 1401.
¹⁵⁷ [2012] EWHC 1539 (Admin).
¹⁵⁸ [1943] 2 All ER 560.

Explanation

1.82 If Parliament gives statutory powers and duties to a body, that body cannot divest themselves of these powers and duties by delegating them to another body.[159] This principle is articulated through two rules: the rule against improper delegation and the rule against acting under dictation.

1.83 *Improper delegation*: The point at which delegation becomes 'improper' must be viewed in context. Four factors will often be relevant. First, the relevant statutory scheme, which may either permit or prohibit delegation of a decision to a third party. For example, the General Medical Council has a general statutory power to delegate its functions to a Registrar.[160] By contrast, the public sector equality duty in the Equality Act 2010 cannot be delegated.[161] Secondly, the law requires that delegation is made to an appropriate third party. For instance, the duty of the Crown Prosecution Service to assess each case could not be delegated to non-lawyers as they were not suitable for the task.[162]

1.84 Thirdly, the nature of the function being delegated is important. The courts are typically suspicious of the delegation of judicial decisions, as opposed to administrative decisions.[163] For instance, it was improper for school governors to delegate its disciplinary function to a staff committee.[164] However, the delegation of investigative functions has been held to be an administrative function and so readily delegable.[165] Fourthly, general public law principles are also relevant, such that a delegation may be unlawful if it is unreasonable.[166]

1.85 Delegation of certain decisions is necessary for the proper functioning of government, and this has long been recognised by the *Carltona* principle.[167] This provides the authority for a Secretary of State to have decisions taken in his or her name by civil servants of suitable seniority. Although the *Carltona* principle does not apply at the local government level, s 101 of the Local Government Act 1972 supplies a general power of delegation.

1.86 *Acting under dictation*: Linked to the rule against improper delegation is the rule that a public body must not act as a puppet to a third party.[168] This applies where a public body is required to make a judgment or exercise a discretion but unthinkingly

---

[159] *Birkdale District Electricity Supply Co Ltd v Southport Corporation* [1926] AC 355, 364.
[160] Paragraph 16 of Sch 1 to the Medical Act 1983.
[161] Section 149 of the Equality Act 2010. See *R (Brown) v Secretary of State for Work and Pensions* [2008] EWHC 3158 at [94]; and *R (Domb) v London Borough of Hammersmith & Fulham* [2009] EWCA Civ 941 at [52]. This is qualified in relation to central government where the *Carltona* principle allows this duty to be delegated – *R (Essex County Council) v Secretary of State for Education* [2012] EWHC 1460 (Admin) at [42].
[162] *R v Director of Public Prosecutions, ex parte Association of First Division Civil Servants* (1988) 138 NLJ Rep 158. See also *R (CC West Midlands) v Birmingham Justices* [2002] EWHC 1087 at [10].
[163] *R v Manchester Stipendiary Magistrate, ex parte Hill* [1983] 1 AC 328, 343D. See also *Barnard v National Dock Labour Board* [1953] 2 QB 18.
[164] *R v Secretary of State for Education, ex parte Prior* [1994] ELR 231.
[165] *R v Race Relations Board, ex p Selvarajan* [1975] 1 WLR 1686.
[166] *R v Institute of Chartered Accountants in England and Wales, ex parte Nawaz* [1997] CLY 1; *R v Secretary of State for the Home Department, ex parte Doody* [1994] 1 AC 531, 566F–G.
[167] *Carltona Ltd v Works Commissioners* [1943] 2 All ER 560; *R v Secretary of State for the Home Department, ex parte Oladehinde* [1991] 1 AC 254, 300A–B.
[168] See, for instance, *R v Teignmouth District Council, ex parte Teignmouth Quay Co Ltd* [1995] 2 PLR 1, 8C–D; *R v Secretary of State for Trade and Industry, ex parte Lonrho plc* [1989] 1 WLR 525, 538C.

acts on the advice of a third party.[169] An example would be magistrates who are advised on matters of law by a legal advisor – the magistrates must make their own decision and cannot simply abdicate the decision to the legal adviser.[170]

1.87 Similarly, if a public body has involved a third party in its decision-making process, it must not simply rubberstamp the views of the third party.[171] An example was where the granting of a film licence by a local authority was decided solely on whether British Board of Film Classification gave a certificate. This amounted to acting under dictation.[172] The underlying theme is that the public body must make its *own* decision even if a third party is involved in the process. Acting under dictation may be described as a species of improper delegation in the sense that both concepts challenge the making of evaluative or judicial decisions by third parties.

1.88 The rule against acting under dictation also extends to decisions that purport to rob a decision-maker of their discretion. For instance, guidance that cuts across statutory duties or that confines decision-making may be unlawful on the basis that it would force decisions to be made under dictation.[173]

Recent examples

1.89 Recent examples of the rule against delegation include:

(1) *Thames Water Utilities Ltd v Transport for London*.[174] The issue in this case was whether a statutory undertaker, who had been engaged in some emergency water works, could delegate the responsibility of obtaining a work permit to a third party. It was held that the Traffic Management Permit Scheme (England) Regulations 2007 did not permit such a delegation.

(2) *Mohammed v Department of Work and Pensions*.[175] Certificates made under s 116(2)(b) of the Social Security Administration Act 1992 and signed by officials in relation to the claimant's alleged benefit fraud were challenged as being a product of improper delegation. It was held that the delegation was proper, as the delegation was to lawyers acting in accordance with guidance and within the overall responsibility of the Secretary of State.

(3) *Edwards v United States*.[176] This was an extradition case where an official who was below the rank of a senior civil servant had signed a certificate. The court held that the *Carltona* principle enabled the official to sign the certificate on behalf of the Secretary of State and the principle had not been excluded by the terms of the Extradition Act 2003.

---

[169] See, for instance, *R v Chief Constable of the Thames Valley Police, ex parte Police Complaints Authority* [1996] COD 324; and *R v Parole Board, ex parte Watson* [1996] 1 WLR 906, 916F.
[170] See for instance, *R v Birmingham City Justice, ex parte Chris Foreign Foods (Wholesalers) Ltd* [1970] 1 WLR 1428.
[171] *R (L) v Secretary of State for the Home Department* [2003] EWCA Civ 25 at [67].
[172] *Ellis v Dubowski* [1921] 3KB 621. Compare this with *Mills v London City Council* [1925] 1 KB 213 where the council reserved the ultimate film licence decision to itself and there was no acting under dictation.
[173] *Laker Airways Ltd v Department of Trade* [1977] QB 632; *R v Worthing Borough Council, ex parte Burch* (1985) 50 P & R 53; *R v Secretary of State for the Environment, ex parte Lancashire County Council* [1994] 4 All ER 165.
[174] [2013] EWHC 187 (Admin).
[175] [2012] EWHC 4220 (Admin).
[176] [2012] EWHC 3771 (Admin).

(4) *R (Raphael) v Highbury Corner Magistrates' Court*.[177] A nightclub owner challenged a decision to place conditions on his nightclub licence. This was on the basis that the delegation by the licensing committee of nightclub licences to a sub-committee was unlawful. It was held that the delegation was proper within the terms of the Licensing Act 2003.

Fettering discretion

Principle

Where a public body has a discretion, it cannot tie its hands by reference to guidance or policy.

Key case

British Oxygen Company Ltd v Minister of Technology.[178]

Explanation

1.90 Alongside the rule against acting under dictation, the law requires that decision-makers do not fetter their discretion. The principle behind this rule is that each case must be considered in its own right.[179] Accordingly, a piece of guidance or policy that purports to decide all cases in a certain way without any flexibility will be unlawful.[180] For example, a blanket policy of detaining all foreign national prisoners was held to be unlawful on this basis.[181]

1.91 The key issue in cases of alleged fettering of discretion will be whether the policy or guidance allows for individual consideration of cases or whether it automatically determines the outcome.[182] This is a question of how the policy is applied in practice and evidence may show that an apparently flexible policy is being applied inflexibly.[183] A willingness by a public authority to allow an individual an opportunity to make representations may be evidence that there has not been fettering.[184] A public body will fetter its discretion if it treats guidance as binding even if it is not.[185] Furthermore, guidance must not be followed if it is inconsistent with the relevant statutory scheme.[186]

1.92 The rule against non-fettering requires consideration of the proper role of guidance and policy. On the one hand, the rule of law requires consistency in decision-making and relative certainty in the application of the law. On the other hand, flexible decision-making avoids harsh or oppressive decisions that take into account

---

[177] [2011] EWCA Civ 462.
[178] [1971] AC 610.
[179] *British Oxygen Company Ltd v Minister of Technology* [1971] AC 610, 625; *Re Findlay* [1985] AC 318, 338E–F.
[180] *R (S) v Secretary of State for the Home Department* [2007] EWCA Civ 546 at [50].
[181] *R (Lumba) v Secretary of State for the Home Department* [2011] UKSC 12 at [21] and [35].
[182] *R v Hampshire County Council, ex parte W* [1994] ELR 460, 476B.
[183] *R (MP) v Secretary of State for Justice* [2012] EWHC 214 (Admin) at [186]; *R v North West Lancashire Health Authority, ex parte A* [2000] 1 WLR 977, 993H; *R v Warwickshire County Council, ex parte Collymore* [1995] ELR 217, 223D–E.
[184] *R (H) v Ashworth Hospital Authority* [2001] EWHC Admin 872 at [136].
[185] *R v Police Complaints Board, ex parte Madden* [1983] 1 WLR 447.
[186] *R (Milner) v South Central Strategic Health Authority* [2011] EWHC 218 (Admin) at [45] and [57].

individual circumstances. This is a recognised tension in public law.[187] In addition to the rule against fettering discretion, it has been held that public bodies should normally follow their guidance, but should depart from guidance where there is a good reason to do so.[188]

Error of fact

Principle

Where a public body makes an error of fact, this can amount to an error of law.

Key cases

E v Secretary of State for the Home Department;[189] *R (A) v Croydon London Borough Council*.[190]

Explanation

1.93 Most judicial review claims concern errors of law. This is an important element of the Administrative Court's jurisdiction being supervisory rather appellate. Cases reiterate that judicial review applications are not appeals on the facts.[191] Accordingly, judicial review cases where a court interferes with findings of fact are limited in scope. There are two situations where errors of fact are elevated to errors of law: first, where there is a material error of fact; second, where there has been an error of precedent fact.

1.94 *Material error of fact*: The legal requirements to establish a material error of fact were summarised by the Court of Appeal in *E v Secretary of State for the Home Department*[192] as follows:[193]

(1) There must have been a mistake as to an existing fact, including a mistake as to the availability of evidence on a particular matter. This means that the particular fact in question must be have existed at the time of the error – it may be necessary to adduce fresh evidence to demonstrate this.[194]

(2) The fact or evidence must have been 'established', in the sense that it was uncontentious and objectively verifiable. This means that the decision-maker will

---

[187] *R (Alvi) v Secretary of State for the Home Department* [2012] UKSC 33 at [111]; *R v Ministry for Agriculture Fisheries & Food, ex parte Hamble Fisheries (Offshore) Ltd* [1995] 2 All ER 714, 722A–C.
[188] *R (Munjaz) v Ashworth Hospital Authority* [2005] UKHL 58 at [46].
[189] [2004] EWCA Civ 49; [2004] QB 1044.
[190] [2009] UKSC 8.
[191] *R (Malik) v Manchester Crown Court* [2008] EWHC 1362 (Admin) at [31]; *Kemper Reinsurance Company v Minister of Finance* [2000] 1 AC 1, 14H–15A; *R v Secretary of State for the Home Department, ex parte Launder* [1997] 1 WLR 839, 857C; *R v Secretary of State for Education and Science, ex parte Islam* (1993) 5 Admin LR 177, 179G–180A; *R v Northumberland Compensation Appeal Tribunal, ex parte Shaw* [1952] 1 KB 338, 357.
[192] [2004] EWCA Civ 49.
[193] *E v Secretary of State for the Home Department* [2004] EWCA Civ 49 at [66]. The Court of Appeal has described these categories as 'closely and carefully circumscribed': *Montes v Secretary of State for the Home Department* [2004] EWCA Civ 404 at [21]. However, the High Court has said that the categories are not 'strict preconditions' nor a 'precise code' for mistake of fact: *R (K & AC Jackson and Son) v Department for the Environment Food and Rural Affairs* [2011] EWHC 956 (Admin) at [60].
[194] *E v Secretary of State for the Home Department* [2004] EWCA Civ 49 at [68].

have overlooked a clear piece of evidence that cannot be disputed between the parties. An example is where a planning decision overlooked the relevant planning history of a site.[195]

(3) The claimant (or his advisers) must not been have been responsible for the mistake. This means that the claimant must not seek to rely on further evidence that he knew existed but was withheld from the decision-maker. This requirement goes to the issue of fairness, as a claimant cannot expect to show that a mistake of fact was unfair if he caused the mistake himself.

(4) The mistake must have played a material (not necessarily decisive) part in the tribunal's reasoning. This factor requires a claimant to show that the mistake caused or contributed towards an incorrect decision.[196] Many decisions are multi-faceted, and so an error of fact that was largely immaterial is unlikely to amount to an error of law.[197]

1.95 Material error of fact is a ground of review that does not fit neatly into a particular category of judicial review. It can be treated as a species of legal error, although the Court of Appeal in *E* approached the matter as an issue of fairness.[198] However, it is clear that factual errors can come to light where a body has come to an irrational conclusion on the facts.[199]

1.96 *Precedent fact*: A precedent fact is a fact that brings a case within a particular statutory scheme and triggers consideration under that scheme. For instance, for a local authority to have its duties engaged under the Children Act 1989, it must first be established whether they are dealing with 'a child'.[200] This is a precedent fact and the legal position is that a judicial review court can assess whether it is correct because it forms the legal basis of the exercise of the public body's statutory powers.[201] Furthermore, the court can decide the issue for itself.[202] This inevitably involves calling evidence in a manner that is unusual for judicial review cases.[203]

1.97 Identifying what amounts to a precedent fact typically involves consideration of three factors. First, whether the fact in question is 'objective' in the sense that the question whether the fact is correct has a right or wrong answer.[204] Second, whether the fact unlocks or triggers public law powers and duties.[205] Third, whether the matter was

---

[195] *R (Connolly) v Secretary of State for Communities and Local Government* [2009] EWCA Civ 1059 at [37]; compare with *Macarthur v Secretary of State for Communities and Local Government* [2013] EWHC 3 (Admin).
[196] *E v Secretary of State for the Home Department* [2004] EWCA Civ 49 at [63]. See, for instance, *R (Kensington & Chelsea Royal London Borough Council) v Secretary of State for Communities and Local Government* [2012] EWHC 1785 (Admin).
[197] *R v Independent Television Commission, ex parte Virgin Television Limited* [1996] EMLR 318.
[198] *E v Secretary of State for the Home Department* [2004] EWCA Civ 49 at [66].
[199] *Begum v Tower Hamlets London Borough Council* [2003] UKHL 5 at [99]; *R v Monopolies & Mergers Commission, ex parte South Yorkshire Transport Ltd* [1993] 1 WLR 23, 32H–33A; *Hemns v Wheeler* [1948] 2 KB 61, 66.
[200] *R (A) v Croydon London Borough Council* [2009] UKSC 8.
[201] *Eshugbayi Eleko v Government of Nigeria* [1931] AC 662, 669; *Liversidge v Anderson* [1942] AC 206, 273.
[202] *R (FZ) v Croydon London Borough Council* [2011] EWCA Civ 59 at [4].
[203] Indeed, following the Supreme Court decision in *R (A) v Croydon London Borough Council* [2009] UKSC 8 child age assessments have been transferred to the Upper Tribunal.
[204] *R (A) v Croydon London Borough Council* [2009] UKSC 8 at [14], [27]–[29]; *R (FZ) v Croydon London Borough Council* [2011] EWCA Civ 59 at [4].
[205] *R (FZ) v Croydon London Borough Council* [2011] EWCA Civ 59 at [4].

to be left to the judgment of the relevant public authority.[206] Whether these factors are satisfied in a particular case may be answered by reference to the relevant statutory scheme or Parliament's intention.[207]

1.98 Examples of precedent facts include 'child' under the Children Act 1989;[208] 'illegal entrant' under the Immigration Act 1971;[209] 'pending removal';[210] 'state aid';[211] and 'administrators of the pension scheme'.[212] By contrast, 'fresh claim',[213] 'refugee'[214] and 'offender'[215] have been held to not be precedent facts.

Recent examples

1.99 Some recent examples of mistake of fact include:

(1) *ML (Nigeria) v Secretary of State for the Home Department*.[216] This case concerned an asylum appeal where the decision of the first instance judge contained several errors, such as citing documents and evidence that did not exist. These were material errors of fact and these justified quashing the decision.

(2) *R (Ground Rents (Regisport) Ltd) v Upper Tribunal (Administrative Appeals Chamber)*.[217] In this case the claimant challenged the Upper Tribunal's refusal of permission to appeal on the basis that the tribunal had made a mistake regarding when one landlord had ceased to be the landlord and had transferred the freehold to a new landlord. The court held that there was plainly a mistake of fact, that the claimant was not responsible for the mistake, and that this had formed a decisive part of the Upper Tribunal's reasoning. The decision was quashed.

(3) *R (Pharmacy Care Plus Ltd) v Family Health Services Appeals Unit*.[218] In this case a pharmaceutical company sought to challenge a decision that was taken on the basis that two linked companies were in fact entirely separate. This error played a material role in the decision, and so the decision should be quashed.

(4) *Macarthur v Secretary of State for Communities and Local Government*.[219] This case concerned the grant of planning permission for a wind farm, partly on the basis that the planning inspector had made an error of fact in his conclusions about the limited impact of the visual amenity caused by the turbines. However, the claimant was unable to show that the supposed error of fact was based on a fact which was established, uncontentious and objectively verifiable.

---

[206] *R (A) v Croydon London Borough Council* [2009] UKSC 8 at [53].
[207] *R (A) v Croydon London Borough Council* [2009] UKSC 8 at [53].
[208] *R (A) v Croydon London Borough Council* [2009] UKSC 8.
[209] *R v Secretary of State for the Home Department, ex parte Khawaja* [1984] AC 74.
[210] *Tan Te Lam v Superintendant of Tai A Chau Detention Centre* [1997] AC 97, 112C–114E.
[211] *R v Commissioners of Customs and Excise, ex parte Lunn Poly Ltd* [1999] EuLR 653, 661A–662C.
[212] *R (Britannic Asset Management Ltd) v Pensions Ombudsman* [2002] EWHC 441 (Admin) at [10].
[213] *R (MN (Tanzania) v Secretary of State for the Home Department* [2011] EWCA Civ 193.
[214] *R v Secretary of State for the Home Department, ex parte Bugdaycay* [1987] AC 514, 522G–523B.
[215] *Barnard v Gorman* [1941] AC 378.
[216] [2013] EWCA Civ 844.
[217] [2013] EWHC 2638 (Admin).
[218] [2013] EWHC 824 (Admin).
[219] [2013] EWHC 3 (Admin).

Relevant/irrelevant considerations

Principle

A public body must only take into account legally relevant considerations.

Key case

R (Alconbury Developments) v Secretary of State for the Environment Transport and the Regions.[220]

Explanation

1.100 The law requires that when a public authority takes a decision only legally relevant considerations should be taken into account, and irrelevant considerations should be disregarded.[221]

1.101 Typically, there are two possible routes to challenge a decision on the basis of this principle. First, whether a particular factor was (or was not) taken into account, which involves identifying what are the legally relevant considerations in a particular case. Second, even if the relevant considerations have been identified, whether a particular factor has been given too much or too little weight.

1.102 *Route 1: Relevant considerations missed or irrelevant considerations considered.* There are two categories of relevant consideration.[222] The first category includes those considerations that have a mandatory relevance because either legislation or guidance requires the decision-maker to take them into account. In addition, legitimate expectations must also be taken into account,[223] and usually so must limited resources although this varies on the context.[224] Given that the decision-maker must take into account these factors, if there has been a failure to do so the decision will be unlawful.[225] Accordingly, the court applies a hard-edged test to this question and does not apply a *Wednesbury* test.

1.103 The second category includes those considerations that a decision-maker does not have to take into account but may take into account if it chooses to do so.[226] If a claimant seeks to challenge a failure to take into account a non-mandatory

---

[220] [2001] UKHL 23.
[221] R (Alconbury Developments) v Secretary of State for the Environment Transport and the Regions [2001] UKHL 23.
[222] See Creednz Inc v Governor General [1981] 1 NZLR 172, 183 approved in Re Findlay [1985] AC 318, 333H–334C. See also R (Hurst) v London Northern District Coroner [2007] UKHL 13 at [57]; R (Badger Trust) v Welsh Ministers [2010] EWCA Civ 807 at [50].
[223] R (Lumba) v Secretary of State for the Home Department [2011] UKSC 12 at [309]; Paponette v Attorney General of Trinidad and Tobago [2010] UKPC 32 at [46]; R (Bibi) v Newham London Borough Council [2001] EWCA Civ 607 at [49] and [51]; R (Patel) v Secretary of State for the Home Department [2012] EWHC 2100 (Admin) at [79]–[80].
[224] Health and Safety Executive v Wolverhampton City Council [2012] UKSC 34 at [25].
[225] Associated Provincial Picture Houses Ltd v Wednesbury Corporation [1948] 1 KB 223, 228; Secretary of State for Education and Science v Tameside Metropolitan Borough Council [1977] AC 1014, 1064H–1065B.
[226] R (Al Rawi) v Secretary of State for Foreign and Commonwealth Affairs [2006] EWCA Civ 1279 at [131]; R (Greenpeace Ltd) v Secretary of State for the Environment, Food and Rural Affairs [2005] EWCA Civ 1656 at [26].

consideration, it must be shown that the failure was *Wednesbury* unreasonable.[227] Examples of such failures include where the decision-maker has overlooked an obviously relevant document.[228]

1.104 *Route 2: Improper weight given to considerations.* Even if the decision-maker has identified all of the relevant considerations, it may be that the considerations were given an improper weight. While identifying relevant considerations is a matter for the court applying the standards of review noted above, the question of weight is a matter for the decision-maker.[229] This is subject to any statutory requirement to pay 'special' or 'particular' regard to a factor, which will require most weight to be given to that factor.[230]

1.105 The decision-maker's assessment of weight is subject to challenge only on *Wednesbury* grounds.[231] Accordingly, if a decision-maker has unreasonably given too little[232] or too much weight[233] to a particular factor, the decision will be unlawful. It is important to recall that the *Wednesbury* standard can be more intrusive where fundamental rights are engaged, and this applies in the context of relevant considerations.[234]

1.106 *Materiality.* In addition to the two routes described to challenge a decision-maker's approach to relevant or irrelevant considerations, it should be noted that the court will also assess whether the alleged factor was material to the eventual decision. In cases where a relevant consideration was overlooked, the court will ask whether the decision 'might' have been different if the factor was taken into account.[235] In cases where an irrelevant consideration was taken into account, the court will exceptionally not find the decision to be unlawful if it is clear that the decision-maker would have reached the same decision.[236]

Recent example

1.107 A recent case on relevant considerations is *R (UK Uncut Legal Action Ltd) v Revenue and Customs Commissioners*.[237] In this case, a campaign group challenged the decision by HMRC to settle a long-running dispute with two large corporate taxpayers. When the decision to settle was ratified one of the factors taken into account was the potential embarrassment to the Chancellor of the Exchequer that might arise if the matter was not settled. It was argued that this was an irrelevant consideration. HMRC

---

[227] *R (Khatun) v London Borough of Newham* [2004] EWCA Civ 55 at [35].
[228] *R (Coghlan) v Chief Constable of Greater Manchester* [2004] EWHC 2801 (Admin) at [48]; *R (Ireneschild) v Lambeth London Borough Council* [2007] EWCA Civ 234 at [41] and [77].
[229] *R (Sainsbury's Supermarket Ltd) v Wolverhampton City Council* [2010] UKSC 20 at [70].
[230] See, for instance, *R (Garner) v Elmbridge London Borough Council* [2011] EWCA Civ 891 at [4] and [8]; *R v City of Westminster Housing Benefit Review Board, ex parte Mehanne* [2001] UKHL 11 at [13]. Although compare with *R (Manchester City Council) v Secretary of State for Environment, Food & Rural Affairs* [2007] EWHC 3167 (Admin) at [31].
[231] *Tesco Stores Ltd v Secretary of State for the Environment* [1995] 1 WLR 759, 764G–H; *Secretary of State for the Home Department v AP (No 1)* [2010] UKSC 24 at [12].
[232] See, for instance, *R v Mid-Hertfordshire Justices, ex parte Cox* (1996) 8 Admin LR 409, 413H.
[233] See, for instance, *R (Gallagher) v Basildon District Council* [2010] EWHC 2824 (Admin) at [41].
[234] *R (Samaroo) v Secretary of State for the Home Department* [2001] EWCA Civ 1139 at [39].
[235] *R v Parliamentary Commissioner for Administration, ex parte Balchin* [1998] 1 PLR 1, 15C; *R v Royal Borough of Kensington and Chelsea, ex parte Kassam* (1994) 26 HLR 455, 465.
[236] *R (FDA) v Secretary of State for Work and Pensions* [2012] EWCA Civ 332 at [67]–[68] and [78]–[81].
[237] [2013] EWHC 1283 (Admin).

accepted that embarrassment was an irrelevant consideration, but it was argued that it had not tainted or affected the decision. This was accepted by the court, and so the decision was not unlawful on this basis.

Frustrating legislative purpose

Principle

A public body may not use a power in such a way that frustrates the legislative purpose.

Key case

Padfield v Minister of Agriculture, Fisheries & Food.[238]

Explanation

1.108 Decisions made by a public body within a particular statutory scheme must be consistent with the purpose of the legislation. The underlying assumption is that Parliament is presumed to grant discretionary powers to public authorities on the basis that such powers promote the policy and objects of the legislation.[239] Accordingly, using statutory powers to thwart the policy of the legislation will be unlawful. This principle was authoritatively defined by the House of Lords in *Padfield v Minister of Agriculture, Fisheries & Food* [1968] AC 997.[240] The principle applies to primary and secondary legislation[241] as well as the use of prerogative powers.[242]

1.109 In *Padfield* cases, typically there will be two main issues: first, identifying the purpose of the legislation or power; and second, establishing that a decision or action was contrary to that purpose.

1.110 *Identifying the purpose*: This is a question of statutory interpretation.[243] In some cases, identifying the purpose of the legislation or power will be straightforward as it will be specified in the text. For instance, the long title, preamble or explanatory notes to an Act may give an indication of the overall intention behind the legislation. Similarly, the section of the legislation that creates the relevant power may explicitly circumscribe the purposes for which it may be used.[244]

1.111 If it is not possible to determine the purpose of the legislation or power by reference to the text, it may be possible to refer to the parliamentary debates. This approach can entail reference to parliamentary materials where the provision in question remains ambiguous or obscure.[245]

---

[238] [1968] AC 997.
[239] *Padfield v Minister of Agriculture, Fisheries & Food* [1968] AC 997, 1030B–D.
[240] See also *R (Lumba) v Secretary of State for the Home Department* [2011] UKSC 2 at [199]; *R (Haworth) v Northumbria Police Authority* [2012] EWHC 1225 (Admin) at [4]; *R (VC) v Newcastle City Council* [2011] EWHC 2673 (Admin) at [25].
[241] See *R (Saadat) v Rent Service* [2001] EWCA Civ 1559 at [15].
[242] *R v Secretary of State for the Home Department, ex parte Fire Brigades Union* [1995] 2 AC 513, 552D.
[243] See paras **1.70** and **1.71** above for the general approach to statutory construction.
[244] See, for instance, *McEldowney v Forde* [1971] AC 632, 655C; and *R v Secretary of State for Foreign Affairs, ex parte World Development Movement Ltd* [1995] 1 WLR 386.
[245] *Pepper v Hart* [1993] AC 593. See also *R (Spath Holme Ltd) v Secretary of State for the Environment, Transport and the Regions* [2001] 2 AC 349 and *Wilson v First County Trust Ltd (No 2)* [2003] UKHL 40.

1.112 *Action contrary to the purpose*: Having identified the purpose of the power in question, the court must decide whether the exercise of that power fell outside the identified purpose. In most cases this will be a straightforward question of fact.[246]

1.113 In some cases there will be an issue where a decision was made for mixed purposes. As noted above, the court will seek to identify what was the 'dominant purpose' behind a decision.[247] This is a question of fact. Where a public body is only able to show that a statutorily prescribed purpose was simply a collateral consequence of a decision, the decision may be found unlawful.[248] However, if a decision has an unlawful secondary purpose but a lawful primary purpose, the decision can still be lawful.[249]

Recent examples

1.114 Two recent examples of the *Padfield* principle include:

(1) *R (Attfield) v Barnet London Borough Council*.[250] A public authority's use of the Road Traffic Regulation Act 1984 was challenged on the basis that charging for parking in order to raise a surplus for other transport purposes was contrary to the purpose of the Act. The court held that the Act was not a fiscal measure and so to raise a surplus by charging for parking was unlawful as it was contrary to the purpose of the Act.

(2) *M v Scottish Ministers*.[251] In this case, the failure of the Scottish Ministers to make necessary regulations to bring into effect some provisions of the Mental Health (Care and Treatment) (Scotland) Act 2003 were challenged. The failure to exercise the discretionary power to bring the Act into effect was contrary to the Scottish Parliament's intention and had thwarted the intention behind the Act. Accordingly, the failure was unlawful.

Sufficient inquiry

Principle

Public bodies are under a duty to ask themselves the right question and take reasonable steps to acquaint themselves with the relevant information.

Key case

Secretary of State for Education and Science v Tameside Metropolitan Borough Council.[252]

---

[246] See, for instance, *R (Haworth) v Northumbria Police Authority* [2012] EWHC 1225 (Admin) at [104]; *R (Manydown Ltd) v Basingstoke & Deane Borough Council* [2012] EWHC 977 (Admin) at [141]; *R (Cala Homes (South) Ltd) v Secretary of State for Communities & Local Government* [2010] EWHC 2866 (Admin) at [52].
[247] *R v Crown Court at Southwark, ex parte Bowles* [1998] AC 641, 651; *R (Hicks) v Metropolitan Police Commissioner* [2012] EWHC 1947 (Admin) at [237].
[248] *R (Richards) v Pembrokeshire County Council* [2004] EWCA Civ 1000 at [44].
[249] *Porter v Magill* (1998) 96 LGR 157 (DC), 167.
[250] [2013] EWHC 2089 (Admin).
[251] [2012] UKSC 58.
[252] [1977] AC 1014.

Explanation

1.115 Public bodies are under a duty to ask the right question and take reasonable steps to acquaint themselves with the relevant information to answer that question correctly.[253] This is often described as the *Tameside* duty as it derives from the House of Lords decision in *Secretary of State for Education and Science v Tameside Metropolitan Borough Council*.[254]

1.116 When a public authority is engaged in the decision-making process, the *Tameside* duty requires a public authority to make sufficient inquiries to find the relevant information, consider that information[255] and then come to decision consistent with that information.[256] It is a necessary condition for a decision to be lawful.[257] This is assessed against a rationality or *Wednesbury* standard.[258] In practice, this may involve the public body consulting outside bodies[259] or the person who may be affected by the decision.[260]

1.117 Like all judicial review grounds, the *Tameside* duty must be assessed in context. For instance, there will be situations where the statutory scheme points away from such a duty[261] or where an issue is not live and so it need not be investigated.[262] Similarly, there may be statutory duties that place an obligation equivalent to the *Tameside* duty on public authorities.[263]

1.118 The duty of sufficient inquiry requires that information is presented fairly to decision-makers, particularly where officials are responsible for collating information or providing reports.[264]

Policy challenges

Principle

It is possible to challenge a policy itself if a proven risk inherent in the system is created.

---

[253] *Secretary of State for Education and Science v Tameside Metropolitan Borough Council* [1977] AC 1014, 1065B. See also, *R (Law Society) v Legal Services Commission* [2010] EWHC 2550 (Admin) at [109].
[254] [1977] AC 1014.
[255] Failures to properly consider information include: *R (Mackenzie) v Secretary of State for Justice* [2009] EWCA Civ 669 at [34]; *R v Lambeth London Borough Council, ex parte K* (2000) 3 CCLR 141, 149H; *Dyason v Secretary of State for the Environment* [1998] 2 PLR 54; *O'Reilly v Coventry Coroner* [1996] COD 268.
[256] *R v Secretary of State for the Home Department, ex parte Iyadurai* [1998] Imm AR 470, 475. See also *R (Das) v Secretary of State for the Home Department* [2013] EWHC 682 (Admin) at [42]–[43].
[257] *R (RP) v Brent London Borough Council* [2011] EWHC 3251 (Admin) at [239].
[258] *R (Khatun) v London Borough of Newham* [2004] EWCA Civ 55 at [35]; *R (Kanssen) v Secretary of State for the Environment, Food and Rural Affairs* [2005] EWHC 1024 (Admin) at [35]; *R (Badger Trust) v Secretary of State for the Environment, Food and Rural Affairs* [2012] EWHC 1904 (Admin) at [62] and [67]. Compare with the authorities that apply a fairness test – *R (Q) v Secretary of State for the Home Department* [2003] EWCA Civ 364 at [90] and *Naraynsingh v Commissioner of Police* [2004] UKPC 20 at [23].
[259] *R v Secretary of State for Education, ex parte London Borough of Southwark* [1995] ELR 308, 323C.
[260] *R (Khatun) v London Borough of Newham* [2004] EWCA Civ 55 at [27].
[261] *R (Anglian Water Services Ltd) v Environment Agency* [2003] EWHC 1506 (Admin) at [36].
[262] *R v Sedgemoor District Council, ex parte McCarthy* (1996) 28 HLR 607.
[263] For example, in relation to homelessness under Part 7 of the Housing Act 1996. See *R v Barnet London Borough Council, ex parte Babalola* (1996) 28 HLR 196.
[264] *R (Hindawi) v Secretary of State for Justice* [2011] EWHC 830 (QB) at [73], [80] and [111]; *R (Georgiou) v London Borough of Enfield* [2004] EWHC 779 (Admin) at [85]; *R (Quark Fishing) v Secretary of State for Foreign and Commonwealth Affairs* [2002] EWCA Civ 1409.

Key case

R (Tabbakh) v The Staffordshire and West Midlands Probation Trust.[265]

Explanation

1.119 The role of policy or guidance in administrative law cannot be underestimated. Most decisions taken by public authorities are made within a framework of policy. This is partly to help guide decision-makers in the exercise of statutory discretions; it is partly because policy can be altered more easily than legislation.

1.120 The common law's approach to the application of policies has been noted above. The position is that policies must not be operated inflexibly so as to amount to a fetter on discretion.[266] However, policy must normally be followed to ensure consistency in decision-making. Accordingly, policy can be departed from where there is good reason to do so.[267] The meaning of policy is for the court to determine, although the application of policy is subject to a *Wednesbury* standard.[268] Policy should normally be published[269] and should be properly understood by the public authority that is applying it.[270]

1.121 However, the foregoing relates to challenges to individual decisions taken in light of policy guidance. It is also possible to challenge the guidance itself, and the common law has developed three principal routes of challenge.[271] These routes are in addition to other grounds such as whether the policy is *ultra vires* or violates an ECHR right.

(1) *Policy leading to unlawful decisions*. Policies that, if followed, would lead to unlawful acts or decisions, or which permit or encourage such acts, will be unlawful.[272] Where a non-statutory policy is interwoven with questions of social and ethical controversy this approach should be exercised with caution.[273]

(2) *Significant risk of treatment violating Article 3*. If a policy exposes a person to a significant risk of the treatment prohibited by Article 3 (torture or inhuman or degrading treatment or punishment), then the policy will be unlawful.[274] The policy must be viewed as a whole, although the extent to which the risk must be foreseeable by the public authority has been left open.[275]

(3) *Injustice inherent in the system itself*. Where there is potential unfairness in how a policy operates, the policy may be found unlawful 'to obviate in advance a proven risk of injustice which goes beyond aberrant interviews or decisions and inheres in the system itself'.[276] Cases suggest that this test has been slightly widened so as to

---

[265] [2013] EWHC 2492 (Admin).
[266] *R (MP) v Secretary of State for Justice* [2012] EWHC 214 (Admin) at [186]; *R v North West Lancashire Health Authority, ex parte A* [2000] 1 WLR 977, 993H; *R v Warwickshire County Council, ex parte Collymore* [1995] ELR 217, 223D–E.
[267] *R (Munjaz) v Ashworth Hospital Authority* [2005] UKHL 58 at [46]. See also *R (Lumba) v Secretary of State for the Home Department* [2011] UKSC 12 at [26] and [202].
[268] *R (LE (Jamaica)) v Secretary of State for the Home Department* [2012] EWCA Civ 597 at [29].
[269] *R (Lumba) v Secretary of State for the Home Department* [2011] UKSC 12 at [302]; *R (Refugee Legal Centre) v Secretary of State for the Home Department* [2004] EWCA Civ 1481 at [19].
[270] *R (LE (Jamaica)) v Secretary of State for the Home Department* [2012] EWCA Civ 597 at [29].
[271] See *R (Tabbakh) v The Staffordshire and West Midlands Probation Trust* [2013] EWHC 2492 (Admin) at [42]–[52].
[272] *Gillick v West Norfolk and Wisbech Area Health Authority* [1986] AC 112, 177E, 181F and 193G–194B.
[273] *Gillick v West Norfolk and Wisbech Area Health Authority* [1986] AC 112, 194B and 206F–G.
[274] *R (Munjaz) v Mersey Care NHS Trust* [2005] UKHL 58.
[275] *R (Munjaz) v Mersey Care NHS Trust* [2005] UKHL 58 at [29].
[276] *R (Refugee Legal Centre) v Secretary of State for the Home Department* [2004] EWCA Civ 1481 at [7].

allow a policy to be quashed if it created an 'unacceptable risk' or 'a serious possibility' of injustice.[277] However, it has been suggested[278] that this wider test should be avoided:

> 'Challenges on this third route need to prove a risk of injustice. Accordingly, detailed evidence is required to show how the policy is operating in practice. The impact of a policy can be difficult to gauge, and this evidential issue has been said to justify the high threshold required in these cases.'[279]

CATEGORY 3: PROCEDURAL IMPROPRIETY

1.122 The third main category of judicial review grounds is procedural impropriety, which embodies the underlying principle of natural justice.[280] This longstanding principle protects basic fairness in how public bodies make decisions.[281] The concept covers issues of fairness, both substantive and procedural. The grounds within the category include the following:

(1) *Procedural fairness*. The common law seeks to ensure that the standards of natural justice are met when public authorities take decisions. What this means depends on the context, but procedural fairness often entails a right to know the case one has to meet, a right to be heard and a duty to comply with stated procedural requirements.

(2) *Bias*. It is contrary to the principle of natural justice that a decision-maker is biased when it takes a decision. The common law has developed strict rules to prevent against bias, such that even if there is the appearance of bias a decision may be unlawful on that basis.

(3) *Legitimate expectations*. Public law has developed the private law concept of estoppel to ensure that public authorities honour their promises or practices. The doctrine of legitimate expectation has developed to the point where expectations can be both procedural and substantive, and the tests applied to whether frustrating those expectations is an abuse of power are the principles of fairness and proportionality.

(4) *Consultation*. Where a public authority conducts a consultation, the common law imposes certain requirements. These include requirements that the consultation must take place at a formative stage, that sufficient information must be given to understand the proposals, that there is adequate time to respond and that the responses are properly taken into account.

(5) *Reasons*. There is no general duty to provide reasons for decisions in all situations. However, the case-law suggests that adequate reasons are required in many situations so that it is clear why a decision was made and whether it can be challenged.

---

[277] *R (Medical Justice) v Secretary of State for the Home Department* [2010] EWHC 1925 (Admin) at [36]; *R (Suppiah) v Secretary of State for the Home Department* [2011] EWHC 2 at [137]; *MK v Secretary of State for the Home Department* [2012] EWHC 1896 (Admin) at [154]–[156].
[278] *R (Tabbakh) v The Staffordshire and West Midlands Probation Trust* [2013] EWHC 2492 (Admin) at [51].
[279] *R (Tabbakh) v The Staffordshire and West Midlands Probation Trust* [2013] EWHC 2492 (Admin) at [52].
[280] See *Council of Civil Service Unions v Minister for the Civil Service* [1985] AC 374, 410 where Lord Diplock describes this as the 'third head' of judicial review.
[281] See *R v University of Cambridge* (1723) 1 Stra 557, 567; *Cooper v Wandsworth Board of Works* (1863) 14 CB (NS) 180, 190; and *Board of Education v Rice* [1911] AC 179, 182.

Procedural fairness

Principle

A public body must make decisions using a fair procedure. The content of this duty depends on the circumstances.

Key case

Ridge v Baldwin;[282] R v Secretary of State for the Home Department, ex parte Doody.[283]

Explanation

1.123 The fundamental driver behind the duty to act fairly is the principle of natural justice. However, this is a flexible principle and what this amounts to in each case is more difficult to define precisely.[284] The concept of procedural fairness has developed several rules that can apply in each case. However, these rules are not exhaustive as the 'categories of unfairness are not closed, and precedent should act as a guide, not a cage'.[285] These are:

(1) *The right to know the case one has to meet*. It has been regularly said that a fundamental feature of due process is to know and be able to effectively challenge the opposing case.[286] This principle can only be departed from with statutory authority.[287] It is seen as a corollary of the right to be heard.[288] The right to be told means that there is an entitlement to see the relevant documents or information and make representations before the decision is made.[289] However, the requirement for finality means that once the parties have had their say the decision-maker is entitled to come to their own decision.[290]

The right to be told is typically breached in situations where claimants have been taken by surprise by a conclusion reached by a decision-maker, such as where

---

[282] [1964] AC 40.
[283] [1994] 1 AC 531.
[284] See for instance *R (Eisai Ltd) v National Institute for Health and Clinical Excellence* [2008] EWCA Civ 438 at [27]; *Bushell v Secretary of State for the Environment* [1981] AC 75, 95D; and *Ceylon University v Fernando* [1960] 1 WLR 223, 231.
[285] *R v Inland Revenue Commissioners, ex parte Unilever Plc* [1996] STC 681, 690F.
[286] *Al-Rawi v Security Service* [2011] UKSC 34 at [12]–[14]; *R (British Sky Broadcasting Ltd) v Central Criminal Court* [2011] EWHC 3451 (Admin) at [28].
[287] *Al-Rawi v Security Service* [2011] UKSC 34.
[288] *R (Ramda) v Secretary of State for the Home Department* [2002] EWHC 1278 (Admin) at [25]; *Malloch v Aberdeen Corporation* [1971] 1 WLR 1578, 1588F; *Kanda v Government of Malaya* [1962] AC 322, 337.
[289] *R (Roberts) v Parole Board* [2005] UKHL 45 at [43]; *R (Primary Health Investment Properties Ltd) v Secretary of State for Health* [2009] EWHC 519 (Admin) at [120]; *Crompton v General Medical Council* [1981] 1 WLR 1435, 1441E; *Kanda v Government of Malaya* [1962] AC 322, 336.
[290] *Hoffmann-La Roche (F) & Co AG v Secretary of State for Trade and Industry* [1975] AC 295, 369D-E; *R v Secretary of State for Education, ex parte S* [1995] ELR 71, 81G–H; *R (Ramda) v Secretary of State for the Home Department* [2002] EWHC 1278 (Admin) at [25].

a particular factor is going to tell against a claimant and there has been no opportunity to respond.[291] Such surprise has been described as 'the enemy of justice'.[292]

There has been an ongoing tension in cases where national security is concerned where a statute has authorised the use of 'closed material procedures' whereby the claimant is not permitted to see certain evidence and a 'special advocate' is instructed on the claimant's behalf.[293] The claimant is entitled to the 'gist' of the evidence against him in order to allow instructions to be given.[294] However, the right to such information is not absolute.[295]

(2) *The right to be heard.* As well as being told the case one has to meet, fairness requires that a person has an opportunity to have an input into decisions that may affect them.[296] In essence, this is about allowing a person to have 'a fair crack of the whip'.[297] This overall duty is a general principle of public law.[298] Applications of the principle include the immigration context,[299] in prisons,[300] decisions of central[301] and local government,[302] as well as tax.[303] It should be noted that this principle has been qualified where the affected person has another route of challenge such as an appeal.[304]

The content of the right to be heard will vary from case to case. However, key elements of the right have been held to include the right to an oral hearing,[305] a right to time to prepare,[306] a right to cross-examine[307] and a right to allow

---

[291] *Sayce v TNT (UK) Ltd* [2011] EWCA Civ 1583 at [15]; *R (Gates Hydraulics Ltd) v Secretary of State for Communities and Local Government* [2009] EWHC 2187 (Admin) at [30]; *Hadmor Productions Ltd v Hamilton* [1983] 1 AC 191, 233B–C; *R v Immigration Appeal Tribunal, ex parte Sui Rong Suen* [1997] Imm AR 355, 363.

[292] *R (Anufrijeva) v Secretary of State for the Home Department* [2003] UKHL 36 at [30]; *R v Chance, ex parte Coopers & Lybrand* (1995) 7 Admin LR 821, 835H.

[293] See for instance ss 6 to 16 of the Justice and Security Act 2013.

[294] *Secretary of State for the Home Department v AF* [2009] UKHL 28.

[295] *Tariq v Home Office* [2011] UKSC 35.

[296] *Kanda v Government of Malaya* [1962] AC 322, 337; *O'Reilly v Mackman* [198] 2 AC 237, 279F–G.

[297] *Fairmount Investments Ltd v Secretary of State for the Environment* [1976] 1 WLR 1255, 1265H–1266A. See also *E v Secretary of State for the Home Department* [2004] EWCA Civ 49 at [65]; *R (Gates Hydraulics Ltd) v Secretary of State for Communities and Local Government* [2009] EWHC 2187 (Admin) at [30].

[298] *Re Application for Judicial Review by JR17* [2010] UKSC 27 at [50]; *R (Shoesmith) v Ofsted* [2011] EWCA Civ 642 at [66]; *R v Secretary of State for the Home Department, ex parte Doody* [1994] 1 AC 531, 560D–G; *Re Hamilton* [1981] AC 1038, 1045B–D; *Hoffmann-La Roche (F) & Co AG v Secretary of State for Trade and Industry* [1975] AC 295, 368D–E.

[299] *R (London Reading College Ltd) v Secretary of State for the Home Department* [2010] EWHC 2561 (Admin) at [42]; *R (L) v Secretary of State for the Home Department* [2003] EWCA Civ 25 at [30].

[300] *R (Hirst) v Secretary of State for the Home Department* [2001] EWCA Civ 378 at [78]; *R (SP) v Secretary of State for the Home Department* [2004] EWCA Civ 1750.

[301] *Manning v Ramjohn* [2011] UKPC 20; *R (Shoesmith) v Ofsted* [2011] EWCA Civ 642.

[302] *R v Devon County Council, ex parte O (Adoption)* [1997] 2 FLR 388; *R v London Borough of Hackney, ex parte. Decordova* (1995) 27 HLR 108, 113.

[303] *R (Lunn) v Revenue & Customs Commissioners* [2011] EWHC 240 (Admin) at [36]; *R (Sporting Options Plc) v Horserace Betting Levy Board* [2003] EWHC 1943 (Admin) at [148].

[304] *R (Palmer) v Secretary of State for the Home Department* [2004] EWHC 1817 (Admin) at [28]; *Lawrence v Financial Services Commission* [2009] UKPC 49 at [34].

[305] *Osborn v The Parole Board* [2013] UKSC 61.

[306] *R (Medical Justice) v Secretary of State for the Home Department* [2011] EWCA Civ 1710 at [10]; *R (W) v Croydon London Borough Council* [2011] EWHC 696 (Admin) at [39]; *R (Agogo) v North Somerset Magistrates' Court* [2011] EWHC 518 (Admin).

[307] *R (Bonhoeffer) v General Medical Council* [2011] EWHC 1585 at [130]; *R (Evans) v Chief Constable of Sussex* [2011] EWHC 2329 (Admin); *R (S) v Knowsley NHS Primary Care Trust* [2006] EWHC 26 (Admin) at [91]; *Bushell v Secretary of State for the Environment* [1981] AC 75, 116D.

representation and assistance.³⁰⁸ It is important to emphasise that the availability of these different elements will depend on what is required to allow the decision-maker to come to a fair conclusion having regard to all the circumstances of the case. Accordingly, in some cases an oral hearing will not be required for example.³⁰⁹

Relevant factors in determining what fairness requires include: where facts are in dispute and credibility is an issue; where an assessment of the character of a person is required; where it is necessary to allow the opposing case to be put properly; where there is a significant potential impact as a result of the decision.³¹⁰ Of course, the ultimate requirement is that the procedure adopted is fair and this is often an intuitive judgment.³¹¹

(3) *Duty to comply with procedural requirements.* In many areas of administrative and judicial decision-making there will be rules or regulations that specify a procedure that has to be followed. Failure to follow these procedural rules will normally be described as acting *ultra vires* rather than a separate form of unfairness (although such a description would not be inappropriate).³¹²

However, it should be noted that the common law can add additional requirements to statutory schemes that do not meet the requirements of fairness. This has been described as the common law 'supplying the omission'.³¹³ Examples include importing a discretion to hear late objections,³¹⁴ implying a right to be heard,³¹⁵ and requiring advance disclosure of documents.³¹⁶ It should be noted that the fact that there is a statutory scheme may mean that a court is disinclined to add further requirements, such as extending duties to consult.³¹⁷ Furthermore, a statute can expressly exclude procedural rights if clear words are used to that effect.³¹⁸

(4) *Delay as unfairness.* In some circumstances, the sheer delay and inaction of a decision-maker can be described as unfair. Fairness requires a prompt investigation of the issues in a case and so gross or inordinate delay may be a ground of challenge in its own right.³¹⁹

---

308 *R (AS) v Great Yarmouth Youth Court* [2011] EWHC 2059 (Admin) at [8]–[9]; *R (Wagstaff) v Secretary of State for Health* [2001] 1 WLR 292, 322F; *R v Secretary of State for the Home Department, ex parte Tarrant* [1985] QB 251, 278B.
309 See *R (Downs) v Secretary of State for Justice* [2011] EWCA Civ 1422; *R (Shaffi) v Secretary of State for the Home Department* [2011] EWHC 3113 (Admin) at [75]; *R (Sandhar) v Office of the Independent Adjudicator for Higher Education* [2011] EWCA Civ 1614 at [45]. See also *Osborn v The Parole Board* [2013] UKSC 61.
310 *Osborn v The Parole Board* [2013] UKSC 61 at [2], [54]–[96].
311 *R v Secretary of State for the Home Department, ex parte Doody* [1994] 1 AC 531, 560D–G. See also *Wiseman v Borneman* [1971] AC 297, 308H–309C.
312 *Council of Civil Service Unions v Minister for the Civil Service* [1985] AC 374, 411A–B.
313 *Cooper v Wandsworth Board of Works* (1863) 14 CB (NS) 180, 194; *Wiseman v Borneman* [1971] AC 297, 317G. See also *R (Lumba) v Secretary of State for the Home Department* [2011] UKSC 12 at [201]; *R (Khatun) v London Borough of Newham* [2004] EWCA Civ 55 at [30]–[31]; *R (S) v London Borough of Brent* [2002] EWCA Civ at [14]; *R v Secretary of State for the Home Department, ex parte Pierson* [1998] AC 539, 588H.
314 *Belfast City Council v Miss Behavin' Ltd* [2007] UKHL 19 at [8].
315 *Malloch v Aberdeen Corporation* [1971] 1 WLR 1578, 1582G–H.
316 *R (Bentley) v HM Coroner District of Avon* [2001] EWHC Admin 170.
317 *R (Hillingdon London Borough Council) v Lord Chancellor* [2008] EWHC 2683 (Admin) at [42]; *R (Buckinghamshire County Council) v Kingston upon Thames London Borough Council* [2011] EWCA Civ 457.
318 *Wiseman v Borneman* [1971] AC 297, 318C.
319 See *Durity v Attorney General of Trinidad and Tobago* [2008] UKPC 59 at [29]; *R v Lambeth London Borough Council, ex parte Crookes* (1997) 29 HLR 29; and *Goose v Wilson Sandford and Co* (1998) The Times, 19 February.

1.124 There are three further factors that inform the application of the principles of fairness described. First, it is possible to waive natural justice rights. Where a claimant has consented to a modified procedure, this can act as a waiver of natural justice rights. This waiver prevents a breach of procedural fairness arising in the first place.[320] The consent must be voluntary, informed and unequivocal.[321]

1.125 Secondly, the issue of unfairness is a matter of law. The question of what fairness requires in any given case is a matter of law.[322] Therefore, the court is not considering whether the decision-maker had acted in a *Wednesbury* unreasonable sense when reviewing whether procedures were fair, but rather views the matter for itself.[323] This does not mean that weight will not be given to the decision-maker's view of what it considers to be fair.[324]

1.126 Thirdly, it is important to recognise the role of the 'no difference' principle. Where a decision-maker has acted in a procedurally unfair manner, the courts will usually look to whether the flaw made a difference to the outcome. The 'no difference' principle suggests that where the outcome would be no different the claim will be unsuccessful.[325] Defendants in judicial review claims often seek to rely on this principle.

1.127 However, it is important to position this principle properly in the way a judicial review claim operates. There is case-law that suggests that if a decision is made unfairly, then a finding of unlawfulness will follow.[326] Whether a remedy is provided to the claimant is a different matter. This is a matter for the court's discretion and is dealt with in more detail elsewhere in this book. It is likely that a technical breach of fairness that made no difference to the outcome will not attract a remedy such as a quashing order.[327] It should be noted however that courts need to be sure that the breach made no difference, and a risk that the breach did prejudice the claimant may prevent the 'no difference' principle from applying.[328] Accordingly, the 'no difference' principle is more accurately located as a defence to the remedy rather than the substance of a judicial review claim.

---

[320] *R (Hill) v Institute of Chartered Accountants in England and Wales* [2013] EWCA Civ 555.
[321] *R (Hill) v Institute of Chartered Accountants in England and Wales* [2013] EWCA Civ 555 at [23].
[322] *R (Shoesmith) v Ofsted* [2011] EWCA Civ 642 at [62]; *Gillies v Secretary of State for Work and Pensions* [2006] UKHL 2; *Osborn v The Parole Board* [2013] UKSC 61 at [65].
[323] *R (Mahfouz) v General Medical Council* [2004] EWCA Civ 233 at [19].
[324] *R v Panel on Take-overs and Mergers, ex parte Guinness Plc* [1990] 1 QB 146, 184C–E; *R v Lord Saville of Newdigate, ex parte A* [2000] 1 WLR 1855 at [41]; *R (A) v Lord Saville of Newdigate* [2001] EWCA Civ 2048 at [7]; *R (Brooks) v Parole Board* [2003] EWHC 1458 (Admin) at [34].
[325] *R v Chief Constable of the Thames Valley Police, ex parte Cotton* [1990] IRLR 344.
[326] *Boddington v British Transport Police* [1999] 2 AC 143, 174B–D; *General Medical Council v Spackman* [1943] AC 627, 644–645.
[327] Decisions to this effect include *R v East Dereham Justices, ex parte Clark* [1996] COD 196; *R v South Northamptonshire District Council, ex parte Crest Homes Plc* (1995) 93 LGR 205, 210; *R v Secretary of State for Foreign and Commonwealth Affairs, ex parte Everett* [1989] 1 QB 811, 819B; *R v Tanbridge District Council, ex parte Al Fayed* [2000] 1 PLR 58, 62C–D; *R (Varma) v Duke of Kent* [2004] EWHC 1705 (Admin); *R (Siborurema) v Office of the Independent Adjudicator* [2007] EWCA Civ 1365 at [66].
[328] *Kanda v Government of Malaya* [1962] AC 322, 337; *R v Leicester City Justices, ex parte Barrow* [1991] 2 QB 260, 290D–E; *R v Secretary of State for the Home Department, ex parte Georghiades* (1993) 5 Admin LR 457, 468H–469A; *R v Chelsea College of Art and Design, ex parte Nash* [2000] ELR 686 at [50]; *R (Clegg) v Secretary of State for Trade and Industry* [2002] EWCA Civ 519 at [30].

Bias

Principle

It is unlawful for a decision to be made by a person who is, or appears to be, biased.

Key cases

R v Gough;[329] Magill v Porter.[330]

Explanation

1.128 Decision-makers may be disqualified from taking certain decisions if they are, or appear to be, predisposed towards a particular position. The rule against bias typically applies in three situations: first, where there is actual bias; second, where there is the appearance of bias; and, third, where the circumstances are such that a person is automatically disqualified.

1.129 *Actual bias*: Cases of actual bias are relatively rare. The rule is straightforward – if actual bias is proved, the person must be disqualified.[331] In practice this will require proof that the person was either influenced by partiality or prejudice or was actually prejudiced when making the decision.[332] Such proof can be difficult establish.[333]

1.130 *Apparent bias*: The test for whether there is an appearance of bias is 'whether the fair minded observer, having considered the facts, would conclude that there was a real possibility that the tribunal was biased'.[334] This test is synonymous with the Article 6 ECHR requirement for an impartial tribunal.[335]

1.131 The hypothetical fair-minded observer is assumed to be informed and know the facts of the particular case and not just those facts that are in the public domain.[336] The observer is taken to be neither complacent not unduly suspicious.[337]

1.132 In principle, once a decision-maker has been found to be apparently biased the decision itself should be regarded as tainted and cannot be permitted to stand.[338] However, there are cases where the court has taken a more pragmatic view and asked

---

[329] [1993] AC 646.
[330] [2001] UKHL 67.
[331] R v Gough [1993] AC 646, 661G; Laker Airways Inc v FLS Aerospace Ltd [2000] 1 WLR 113, 117H.
[332] Re Medicaments and Related Classes of Goods (No 2) [2001] 1 WLR 700 at [38].
[333] Locabail (UK) Ltd v Bayfield Properties Ltd [2000] QB 451 at [3].
[334] Magill v Porter [2001] UKHL 67 at [103]. See also Helow v Secretary of State for the Home Department [2008] UKHL 62 at [39]; and Belize Bank Ltd v Attorney General of Belize [2011] UKPC 36 at [34].
[335] Magill v Porter [2001] UKHL 67 at [103]; R v Abdroikov [2007] UKHL 37 at [17]; Davidson v Scottish Ministers [2004] UKHL 34 at [47].
[336] Belize Bank Ltd v Attorney General of Belize [2011] UKPC 36 at [36]–[37]; Helow v Secretary of State for the Home Department [2008] UKHL 62; Virdi v Law Society [2010] EWCA Civ 100 at [37]–[44]; and Taylor v Lawrence [2002] EWCA Civ 90 at [61]–[63].
[337] Lawal v Northern Spirit Ltd [2003] UKHL 35 at [14].
[338] R (Al Hasan) v Secretary of State for the Home Department [2005] UKHL 13 at [43].

whether the apparent bias had any impact on the decision.[339] It is submitted that this creates a further layer in apparent bias cases, namely whether the bias infected the decision being made.[340]

1.133 *Automatic disqualification*: There are certain circumstances where a decision-maker will be disqualified even without showing that they are biased. Typically, this will involve situations where a person shares a direct interest to one of the parties (for instance, a financial interest) or to the issues involved.[341] Other situations include where a judge is also a member of the party involved in the litigation.[342] The approach to automatic disqualification cases is subject to a *de minimis* exception where the potential effect of an interest is so small that it could not possibly affect the decision-maker.[343] It has been suggested that this category of cases may not be distinct from apparent bias cases.[344]

Recent examples

1.134 Recent cases of bias include:

(1) *Mengiste v Endowment Fund*.[345] In this case, a judge had shown apparent bias against one party's solicitors. The judge had made findings about the solicitors without hearing evidence, without warning, and the repetition of the criticisms and their severity made them extreme and unbalanced.

(2) *O'Neill (Charles Bernard) v HM Advocate*.[346] A judge's sentencing remarks in a sexual offence case that the appellants were 'evil, determined, manipulative and predatory paedophiles of the worst sort' did not render him apparently biased when he presided over the appellants' subsequent murder trial. The fair-minded and informed observer would understand the context in which the remarks were made.

(3) *Ighalo v Solicitors Regulation Authority*.[347] In this case, a solicitor who had been struck off alleged that a member of the tribunal had been biased as he had previously acted for the Solicitors Regulation Authority as an adjudicator in an unrelated case. It was held that the mere fact of this previous role could not give rise to a finding of apparent bias.

(4) *R (Shaw) v HM Coroner for Leicester City and South Leicestershire*.[348] There was no apparent bias arising from the personal friendship between an assistant deputy coroner and the former chief executive of an NHS trust involved in an inquest where the deceased had died in one of its hospitals since the deceased had had no involvement the hospital's management team and the executive had left the post before the death.

---

[339] See *BAA Ltd v Competition Commission* [2010] EWCA Civ 1097; *ASM Shipping Ltd v Harris* [2007] EWHC 1513 (Comm).
[340] *R (Royal Brompton and Harefield NHS Foundation Trust) v Joint Committee of Primary Care Trusts* [2012] EWCA Civ 472.
[341] *R v Gough* [1993] AC 646, 661B–F; *Dimes v Proprietors of Grand Junction Canal* (1852) 3 HL Cas 759.
[342] *R v Bow Street Metropolitan Stipendiary Magistrate, ex parte Pinochet Ugarte (No 2)* [2000] 1 AC 119, 133B–G; *Meerabus v Attorney General of Belize* [2005] UKPC 12 at [24].
[343] *Locabail (UK) Ltd v Bayfield Properties Ltd* [2000] QB 451 at [10].
[344] *R (Kaur) v Institute of Legal Executives Appeal Tribunal* [2011] EWCA Civ 1168 at [44]–[46].
[345] [2013] EWCA Civ 1003.
[346] [2013] UKSC 36.
[347] [2013] EWHC 661 (Admin).
[348] [2013] EWHC 386 (Admin).

Legitimate expectations

Principle

It can be unlawful to frustrate a legitimate expectation.

Key cases

R v North and East Devon Health Authority, ex parte Coughlan;[349] *R (Nadarajah) v Secretary of State for the Home Department.*[350]

Explanation

1.135 Where a public authority promises to do a certain thing, or indeed has a longstanding practice of acting in a certain way, this may give rise to a legitimate expectation that a certain action or decision will occur.[351] Fairness can mean that it is unlawful to frustrate this legitimate expectation. This doctrine has two forms: procedural and substantive, both of which are measured against the standard of proportionality. The procedural form means that the public authority will act in a certain way or adopt a certain procedure, whilst the substantive form can entitle a person to a particular benefit or outcome.

1.136 Legitimate expectation arguments have two stages: First, establishing whether there is a legitimate expectation; second, whether it is lawful to frustrate that expectation.

1.137 *Stage one: identifying a legitimate expectation.* Whether there is a legitimate expectation is an issue of law for the court to decide for itself.[352] Typically, legitimate expectations arise where a public body has made a promise or representation to a person, or where a regular practice exists which the claimant can reasonably expect to continue.[353] To establish a substantive legitimate expectation, a rigorous standard is applied.[354] The clearer the promise or practice the more likely it will be held to be a legitimate expectation. This will be read in context and the court will look for whether there is a relevant qualification or ambiguity.[355] However, while there are many cases that emphasise the role of certain requirements, it has been suggested these are not separate conditions that must be satisfied in every case; the ultimate test is whether there has been an abuse of power.[356] It is submitted that even if this is correct, the court will normally expect a clear, unequivocal, and unqualified representation to be present.[357]

---

[349] [2001] QB 213.
[350] [2005] EWCA Civ 1363.
[351] *R (Nadarajah) v Secretary of State for the Home Department* [2005] EWCA Civ 1363 at [68]–[69]; *R (Bibi) v Newham London Borough Council* [2001] EWCA Civ 607 at [19].
[352] *R (Lichfield Securities Ltd) v Lichfield District Council* [2001] EWCA Civ 304 at [19].
[353] *Council of Civil Service Unions v Minister for the Civil Service* [1985] AC 374, 401B; *R (Bhatt Murphy) v Independent Assessor* [2008] EWCA Civ 755 at [29] and [33].
[354] *R (Godfrey) v Southwark London Borough Council* [2012] EWCA Civ 500 at [51].
[355] *R (HSMP Forum Ltd) v Secretary of State for the Home Department* [2008] EWHC 664 (Admin) at [52]–[53]; *Paponette v Attorney General of Trinidad and Tobago* [2010] UKPC 32 at [30].
[356] *R (Bibi) v Newham London Borough Council* [2001] EWCA Civ 607 at [27]; *Rowland v Environment Agency* [2003] EWCA Civ 1885 at [68(2)].
[357] See for instance *R (Davies) v Revenue and Customs Commissioners* [2011] UKSC 47 at [29]; *R (Bancoult) v Secretary of State for Foreign and Commonwealth Affairs (No 2)* [2008] UKHL 61 at [60]–[61]; *R (Royal Brompton and Harefield NHS Foundation Trust) v Joint Committee of Primary Care Trusts* [2012] EWCA Civ 472 at [104] and [107].

1.138 Other elements often required are that are requirements of knowledge[358] of the promise or practice and detrimental reliance.[359] However, it should be noted that there is case-law that suggests that both these requirements are not necessary. In terms of knowledge, the Court of Appeal has suggested that there are significant difficulties in this requirement because one of the underlying principles of legitimate expectations is ensuring good administration and that where a public authority has given a plain assurance, it should be held to it.[360] In terms of detrimental reliance, it has been said that this is not required but that it is highly relevant to the issue of whether it would be fair to frustrate the expectation.[361]

1.139 There are certain situations that are unlikely to give rise to legitimate expectations. These include where to comply with the expectation would require an action contrary to statute,[362] where the maker of a promise has no ostensible authority to do so,[363] or where there have been certain statements in Parliament.[364] However, this must be qualified by reference to the *Pepper v Hart* principle, whereby the court will expect that the Government's position as to the interpretation of a statute will be consistent with those statements made in Parliament during the passing of an Act.[365]

1.140 *Stage two: frustrating a legitimate expectation.* The standards that are applied to whether it is lawful to frustrate a legitimate expectation are typically fairness[366] and proportionality.[367] The court will normally seek to identify the public interest factors in each case and then see whether departing from the requirement of good administration and straight dealing with the public is justified.[368]

1.141 It is submitted that in cases where a person is seeking to rely on a substantive legitimate expectation this will be more difficult for the court to uphold given that it is binding the public authority to a particular outcome. However, the analysis in both procedural and substantive legitimate expectation cases is the same, with the court seeking to prevent abuses of power.

---

[358] *R (Weaver) v London & Quadrant Housing Trust* [2008] EWHC 1377 (Admin); *R v Secretary of State for the Home Department, ex parte Hindley* [2001] 1 AC 410, 419B-C; *R v Ministry of Defence, ex parte Walker* [2000] 1 WLR 806.
[359] *Gokool v Permanent Secretary for the Ministry of Health and Quality of Life* [2009] UKPC 54 at [21].
[360] *R (Bhatt Murphy) v Independent Assessor* [2008] EWCA Civ 755 at [30].
[361] *R (Bancoult) v Secretary of State for Foreign & Commonwealth Affairs (No 2)* [2008] UKHL 61 at [60]; *R v Department for Education and Employment, ex parte Begbie* [2000] 1 WLR 1115, 1124B–D; *R v Secretary of State for the Home Department, ex parte Popatia* [2000] INLR 587 at [82]; *R (Bibi) v Newham London Borough Council* [2001] EWCA Civ 607 at [31].
[362] *R (Albert Court Residents' Association) v Westminster City Council* [2011] EWCA Civ 430 at [34]; *R v Department for Education and Employment, ex parte Begbie* [2000] 1 WLR 1115, 1125D.
[363] *South Bucks District Council v Flanagan* [2002] EWCA Civ 690 at [18]; *Rowland v Environment Agency* [2002] EWHC 2785 (Ch) at [68].
[364] *R v Director of Public Prosecutions, ex parte Kebilene* [2000] 2 AC 326 (DC), 339F; *R (Wheeler) v Office of the Prime Minister* [2008] EWHC 1409 (Admin).
[365] *Pepper v Hart* [1993] AC 593, 616G; *R (Westminster City Council) v National Asylum Support Service* [2002] UKHL 38 at [6]; *Wilson v First County Trust Ltd* [2003] UKHL 40 at [113].
[366] *R v North and East Devon Health Authority, ex parte Coughlan* [2001] QB 213 at [57].
[367] *Nadarajah v Secretary of State for the Home Department* [2005] EWCA Civ 1363 at [68]; *R (Wood) v Secretary of State for Education* [2011] EWHC 3256 (Admin) at [41]; *R (B) v Nursing & Midwifery Council* [2012] EWHC 1264 (Admin) at [44].
[368] *R (HSMP Forum Ltd) v Secretary of State for the Home Department (No 2)* [2008] EWHC 711 (Admin) at [77]. See also *R v North and East Devon Health Authority, ex parte Coughlan* [2001] QB 213 at [57(c)]; *R (Capital Care Services (UK) Ltd v Secretary of State for the Home Department* [2012] EWCA Civ 1151; *R (Charlton) v Secretary of State for Education and Skills* [2005] EWHC 1378 (Admin) at [161]; *R (Wood) v Secretary of State for Education* [2011] EWHC 3256 (Admin) at [53] and [67].

Recent examples

1.142 Some recent cases where legitimate expectation arguments have been made include:

(1) *R (Che) v Secretary of State for the Home Department*.[369] In this case it was held that a letter sent to an asylum-seeker saying that his case was to be reviewed contained a promise that was clear, unambiguous and devoid of relevant qualification. However, this had to be viewed in light of the claimant's knowledge, which was that he made his outstanding submissions by the time the letter had been received. Accordingly, there was no legitimate expectation in this case.

(2) *United Kingdom Association of Fish Producer Organisations v Secretary of State for Environment, Food and Rural Affairs*.[370] This case sought to challenge a decision to reduce fishing quotas. In terms of the legitimate expectations argument, this failed at the first hurdle as there had been no clear, unambiguous and without qualification undertaking by the Secretary of State that the fixed quota allocation system would continue in its existing form.

(3) *R (Simpson) v Chief Constable of Greater Manchester*.[371] Police officers challenged promotion decisions on the basis that they expected that if they had passed promotion selection assessments they would be promoted when a position became available. It was held that the selection policy and past practice amounted to a clear, unambiguous and unqualified promise, and that officers had shown detrimental reliance. The chief constable was unable to justify not promoting the officers, and so their legitimate expectations had been breached.

(4) *R (Patel) v General Medical Council*.[372] An oversees trainee doctor sought reassurances from the GMC that they would recognise his qualifications before he undertook the relevant training courses. The GMC subsequently changed its recognition criteria. The court held that the doctor had a clear, unequivocal, and unqualified assurance from the GMC that if he completed the course in a reasonable time his qualification would be recognised. There was no public interest that outweighed the unfairness of refusing to honour the assurance given and to recognise the qualification. Accordingly, there had been a breach of the doctor's legitimate expectation.

Consultation

Principle

When a consultation is conducted it must comply with certain legal requirements.

Key cases

R v Brent London Borough Council, ex parte Gunning;[373] *R v North and East Devon Health Authority, ex parte Coughlan*.[374]

---

[369] [2013] EWHC 2220 (Admin).
[370] [2013] EWHC 1959 (Admin).
[371] [2013] EWHC 1858 (Admin).
[372] [2013] EWCA Civ 327.
[373] (1985) 84 LGR 168.
[374] [2001] QB 213.

Explanation

1.143 Where a public body undertakes a consultation exercise, it must be conducted properly. Often consultations are conducted because a statute requires it before a decision is made.[375] However, where this is not the case a duty to consult will arise where there is a 'pressing and focused' impact on a particular group[376] or if there is a legitimate expectation that a consultation would take place.[377] The overall test is whether the consultation process was so unfair as to be unlawful.[378]

1.144 The requirements of a lawful consultation were developed in *ex parte Gunning*, where the High Court adopted the principles argued for by Stephen Sedley QC.[379] These have become known as the 'Sedley requirements' and have been approved by the Court of Appeal.[380] The requirements are as follows:

(1) Consultation must take place when the proposal is still at a formative stage.

(2) Sufficient reasons must be put forward for the proposal to allow for intelligent consideration and response.

(3) Adequate time must be given for consideration and response.

(4) Consultation responses must be conscientiously taken into account.

1.145 *Consultation at a formative stage*: This requirement is straightforward as it would be pointless to conduct a consultation exercise if the outcome has been pre-determined. This does not mean that the public body cannot have narrowed the consultation options to few choices, including a preferred option.[381] The point is that the consultation occurs before the decision has been taken. If the decision-maker has formed a preliminary view about an issue, this should be made clear to consultees in order to allow responses to focus on this.[382] But this should stop short of making a decision 'in principle'.[383] Proving that a decision-maker has truly closed its mind to consultation responses is a matter for evidence and is unlikely to be proven easily.

1.146 *Sufficient reasons to allow for a response*: A proper response to a consultation cannot be given if the consultees do not know on what basis a proposal is being made. The reasons must not be misleading.[384] Accordingly, it is important that the criteria that will be applied in deciding which proposal to adopt are made clear.[385] If a particular proposal relies on complicated technical information, this should be presented in a way

---

[375] For example, s 11 of the Health and Social Care Act 2001.
[376] *R (Bhatt Murphy) v Independent Assessor* [2008] EWCA Civ 755 at [49]. See also *R (Luton Borough Council) v Secretary of State for Education* [2011] EWHC 217 (Admin).
[377] *R v Save Guana Cay Reef Association* [2009] UKPC 44 at [32].
[378] *Devon County Council v Secretary of State for Communities and Local Government* [2010] EWHC 1456 (Admin).
[379] *R v Brent London Borough Council, ex parte Gunning* (1985) 84 LGR 168 at 169.
[380] *R v North and East Devon Health Authority, ex parte Coughlan* [2001] QB 213 at [108].
[381] *Nichol v Gateshead Metropolitan Council* (1988) 87 LGR 435; *R (Bailey) v London Borough of Brent* [2011] EWHC 2572 (Admin) at [90].
[382] *R (Sardar) v Watford Borough Council* [2006] EWHC 1590 (Admin) at [29].
[383] *R (Sardar) v Watford Borough Council* [2006] EWHC 1590 (Admin).
[384] *R (Madden) v Bury Metropolitan Borough Council* [2002] EWHC 1882 (Admin).
[385] *R (Capenhurst) v Leicester City Council* [2004] EWHC 2124 (Admin) at [46]; *Robin Murray & Co v The Lord Chancellor* [2011] EWHC 1528 (Admin) at [37(4)].

that can be easily understood.[386] This does not mean that the public body has to publish advice it has received from its officials,[387] or all of the submissions made by other consultees.[388]

1.147 *Adequate time*: What is 'adequate' in terms of the length of the consultation can vary, subject to any statutory consultation requirements. This means that some opportunity is required, and so in a case where school building projects were cancelled with no notice, this requirement was breached.[389] It has been held that a consultation period which lasted from 15 December 2010 to 14 January 2011, and included the Christmas and New Year breaks was not too short.[390] However, four and five days have been held to be too short.[391]

1.148 *Responses taken into account*: The public body conducting the consultation exercise must read the responses and take them into account. For instance, if a key stakeholder makes a main point in its response, and the public authority does not refer this point, this will be evidence that the responses were not taken into account.[392] This does not mean that the public body has to make its decisions with the consensus of the consultation responses.[393]

1.149 Added to these requirements is a need to ensure that the public body is consulting with the right individuals, namely those who will be affected by the decision in question. However, this can be done by reference to interest groups such as trade unions.[394]

1.150 If the result of the consultation is that the public authority fundamentally changes its position, there can be a requirement to conduct a fresh consultation.[395] Such fundamental changes are those that it would be conspicuously unfair for the decision-maker to proceed with without seeking further representations.[396]

Recent examples

1.151 Some recent examples of cases where consultations were challenged include:

(1) *R (Save our Surgery Ltd) v Joint Committee of Primary Care Trusts*.[397] In this case, a consultation exercise that related to the possible closure of paediatric cardiac surgery services was challenged. Underlying the consultation were certain 'sub-scores' for each hospital that had not been disclosed. However, these were key to understanding the proposals. This failure meant that informed responses were not possible on this point and so the consultation was unlawful.

---

[386] *R (Breckland District Council) v The Boundary Committee* [2009] EWCA Civ 239.
[387] *R v North and East Devon Health Authority, ex parte Coughlan* [2001] QB 213 at [112].
[388] *R (Smith) v East Kent Hospital NHS Trust* [2002] EWHC 2640 (Admin) at [45].
[389] *R (Luton Borough Council) v Secretary of State for Education* [2011] EWHC 217 (Admin) at [83]–[97].
[390] *R (Green) v Gloucestershire County Council* [2011] EWHC 2687 (Admin) at [137].
[391] *R v Secretary of State for Education and Employment, ex parte National Union of Teachers*, unreported, 14 July 2000; *R v Devon County Council, ex parte Baker* [1995] 1 All ER 73.
[392] *R (Morris) v Newport City Council* [2009] EWHC 3051 (Admin) at [37]–[38].
[393] *R (Smith) v East Kent Hospital NHS Trust* [2002] EWHC 2640 (Admin) at [61].
[394] See *British Medical Association v Secretary of State for Health* [2008] EWHC 599 (Admin); *R (Staff Side of the Police Negotiating Board) v Secretary of State for Work and Pensions* [2011] EWHC 3175 (Admin).
[395] *R (Smith) v East Kent Hospital NHS Trust* [2002] EWHC 2640 (Admin) at [45].
[396] *R (Elphinstone) v Westminster City Council* [2008] EWHC 1287 (Admin) at [62]; *R (Devon County Council) v Secretary of State for Communities and Local Government* [2010] EWHC 1456 (Admin) at [81] and [98].
[397] [2013] EWHC 439 (Admin).

(2) *HS2 Action Alliance Ltd v Secretary of State for Transport*.[398] In this case, a number of claimants sought to challenge a decision regarding the route of a high-speed rail network. The claimants were successful on a single ground relating to consultation. It was held that insufficient information on blight and discretionary compensation had been provided to consultees, and that there had been a failure to conspicuously consider the response of a key stakeholder.[399]

(3) *R (Bancoult) v Secretary of State for Foreign and Commonwealth Affairs*.[400] The decision to create a marine protected area, which was taken after a four-month consultation, was not flawed on the basis of the consultation exercise. The information provided was sufficient for the exercise and the omission of any reference to traditional Mauritian fishing rights did not alter this.

(4) *R (T) v Sheffield City Council*.[401] A decision to stop paying subsidies to 20 nurseries in its area complied with the common law consultation requirements. The consultation was taken at a formative stage, the documentation showed that reasons were provided for the proposals and the local authority had taken the responses into account properly.

Reasons

Principle

In many situations, decision-makers must give adequate reasons for their decisions.

Key case

South Buckinghamshire District Council v Porter (No 2).[402]

Explanation

1.152 Where a public authority is required to give reasons for its decisions, these reasons should be adequate so that the parties know why the decision was taken and on what basis the decision may be challenged.[403] Additionally, the giving of reasons focuses the mind of the decision-maker.[404]

1.153 *Duty to give reasons:* There is no general duty on public authorities to give reasons for their decisions.[405] This is despite observations that there is a trend in this

---

[398] [2013] EWHC 481 (Admin).
[399] The appeal in this case did not alter this finding. See *HS2 Action Alliance Ltd v Secretary of State for Transport* [2013] EWCA Civ 920.
[400] [2013] EWHC 1502 (Admin).
[401] [2013] EWHC 2953 (QB).
[402] [2004] UKHL 33.
[403] *R v Westminster City Council, ex parte Ermakov* [1996] 2 All ER 302, 309f; *R v London Borough of Islington, ex parte Hinds* (1995) 27 HLR 65, 75; *R (Wye Valley Action Association Ltd) v Herefordshire Council* [2011] EWCA Civ 20 at [47]; and *R v University of Cambridge, ex parte Evans* [1998] ELR 515, 520H–521B.
[404] *R (Macrae) v Herefordshire District Council* [2012] EWCA Civ 457 at [41]; *R (Chisnell) v Richmond Upon Thames London Borough Council* [2005] EWHC 134 (Admin) at [42].
[405] *R (Lunn) v Revenue & Customs Commissioners* [2011] EWHC 240 (Admin) at [55]; *R (Birmingham City Council) v Birmingham Crown Court* [2009] EWHC 3329 (Admin) at [46]; *R (Hasan) v Secretary of State for Trade and Industry* [2008] EWCA Civ 1312 at [8]; *Stefan v General Medical Council* [1999] 1 WLR 1293, 1300G.

direction.[406] Accordingly, if a public authority is not under an explicit statutory duty to provide reasons, it will be have to be established whether the common law imports such a duty. Typically, this will occur when fairness requires it[407] or where a public authority is required to justify its reasoning.[408] This may occur when the authority is seeking to depart from its policy guidance[409] or if rejecting expert evidence.[410] Where Article 6 ECHR is engaged, this can give rise to a duty to provide reasons.[411] The same can also be said where common law rights are in play.[412]

1.154 There are certain contexts where a duty to provide reasons generally exists. This includes certain decisions in the following contexts: community care decision allocating a personal budget,[413] termination of an authorised tax agency,[414] certain prisons decisions,[415] coroners,[416] professional regulators,[417] use of forcible medication[418] and decisions by courts and judges.[419] By contrast, it has been held that in the following contexts reasons are not required: suitability of housing,[420] extending time for an ABSO,[421] findings of fact by disciplinary panels and in extradition cases[422] and the termination of a secondment.[423]

1.155 *Adequacy of reasons*: If it is possible to establish that there is a duty to give reasons, such reasons must be adequate. This will typically mean that the reasons do not

---

[406] *North Range Shipping Ltd v Seatrans Shipping Corp* [2002] EWCA Civ 405 at [15]; *Stefan v General Medical Council* [1999] 1 WLR 1293, 1301A–B; *R (Wooder) v Feggetter* [2002] EWCA Civ 554 at [39]–[41]; *R v Kensington and Chelsea Royal London Borough Council, ex parte Grillo* (1996) 28 HLR 94, 105; and *R v Higher Education Funding Council, ex parte Institute of Dental Surgery* [1994] 1 WLR 242, 259A–B.
[407] *R v Secretary of State for the Home Department, ex parte Duggan* [1994] 3 All ER 277; *R v Higher Education Funding Council, ex parte Institute of Dental Surgery* [1994] 1 WLR 242, 258D–E; *R (Wooder) v Feggetter* [2002] EWCA Civ 554 at [42]; *Gupta v General Medical Council* [2001] UKPC 61 at [14].
[408] *R (Birmingham City Council) v Birmingham Crown Court* [2009] EWHC 3329 (Admin) at [47]; *R v Higher Education Funding Council, ex parte Institute of Dental Surgery* [1994] 1 WLR 242, 258B–E.
[409] *Gransden v Secretary of State for the Environment* (1987) 54 P & CR 86; *R v Islington London Borough Council, ex parte Rixon* [1997] ELR 66.
[410] *R (Nottingham Healthcare NHS Trust) v Mental Health Review Tribunal* [2008] EWHC 2445 (Admin) at [17]; *R (I) v Secretary of State for the Home Department* [2005] EWHC 1025 at [54]; *R (C) v Merton London Borough Council* [2005] EWHC 1753 (Admin) at [31]; *R (Beeson) v Dorset County Council* [2001] EWHC Admin 986.
[411] *Anya v University of Oxford* [2001] EWCA Civ 405 at [12].
[412] See *R v Secretary of State for the Home Department, ex parte Doody* [1994] 1 AC 531; *R v Director of Public Prosecutions, ex parte Manning* [2001] QB 330 at [33]; *R (Wooder) v Feggetter* [2002] EWCA Civ 554 at [24] and [38]; *R (Faulkner) v Secretary of State for the Home Department* [2005] EWHC 2567 (Admin).
[413] *R (Savva) v Kensingston and Chelsea Royal London Borough Council* [2010] EWCA Civ at [20].
[414] *R (Lunn) v Revenue & Customs Commissioners* [2011] EWHC 240 (Admin) at [57].
[415] *R (Ali) v Director of High Security Prisons* [2009] EWHC 1732 (Admin) at [23] (classification decision); *R (Rowen) v Governor of Kirkham Prison* [2009] EWHC 3756 (Admin) (home detention curfew).
[416] *R (Cash) v Northamptonshire Coroner* [2007] EWHC 1354 at [45].
[417] *Stefan v General Medical Council* [1999] 1 WLR 1293 (GMC's health committee).
[418] *R (Wooder) v Feggetter* [2002] EWCA Civ 554.
[419] *Flannery v Halifax Estate Agencies Ltd* [2000] 1 WLR 377, 381B; *Eagil Trust Co Ltd v Pigott-Brown* [1985] 3 All ER 119, 122A; *English v Emery Reimbold and Strick Ltd* [2002] EWCA Civ 1138 at [17].
[420] *Akhtar v Birmingham City Council* [2011] EWCA Civ 383 at [46]; *R v Kensington and Chelsea Royal London Borough Council, ex parte Grillo* (1996) 28 HLR 94; *R (Giles) v Fareham Borough Council* [2002] EWHC 2951 (Admin) at [12].
[421] *R (Birmingham City Council) v Birmingham Crown Court* [2009] EWHC 3329 (Admin) at [50].
[422] *Gupta v General Medical Council* [2001] UKPC 61; *Rey v Government of Switzerland* [1999] 1 AC 54, 66F–67A.
[423] *R (Tucker) v Director General of the National Crime Squad* [2003] EWCA Civ 2.

show why the decision was reached.[424] This does not mean that reasons must address every issue raised or considered; only the reasons on the principal important controversial issues are required.[425] This is a matter of context and depends on the circumstances of the case.[426] For instance, the formulaic recitation of standard reasons may not be sufficient.[427] It has been held that even if the reasons given are inadequate, it is necessary to show that this has prejudiced the claimant.[428]

1.156 *Timing of reasons*: If requesting reasons from a public authority, this should be done in a timely manner prior to legal proceedings. Otherwise, it is likely that the court may hold that there could be no failure to provide reasons.[429] Where a public authority is requested or ordered to provide reasons, there can be issues regarding whether the explanation for a decision is tailored in light of legal proceedings.[430] Such *ex post facto* or retrospective reasons have to be treated with care.[431]

1.157 The court should be circumspect if material gaps are filled with later evidence, particularly in cases where there is statutory duty to give reasons.[432] This does not mean that witness statements cannot usefully explain the reasons for a decision.[433] Ultimately it is for the court to determine whether the reasons provided are consistent with the evidence of the decision-making process and previously stated reasons.[434]

---

[424] *R (C) v Financial Services Authority* [2012] EWHC 1417 (Admin) at [67]; *R v Brent London Borough Council, ex parte Baruwa* (1997) 29 HLR 915, 929; *South Bucks District Council v Porter (No 2)* [2004] UKHL 33 at [36].

[425] *South Bucks District Council v Porter (No 2)* [2004] UKHL 33 at [36]; *Bolton Metropolitan Borough Council v Secretary of State for the Environment* [1995] 3 PLR 37, 43C; *City of Edinburgh Council v Secretary of State for Scotland* [1997] 1 WLR 1447, 1465B–C; and *R (Ashworth Hospital Authority) v Mental Health Review Tribunal for the West Midland and North West Region* [2001] EWHC Admin 901 at [77].

[426] *R (Asha Foundation) v Millennium Commission* [2003] EWCA Civ 88 at [27].

[427] *R (Morris) v Newport City Council* [2009] EWHC 3051 (Admin) at [40]; *R (London Fire and Emergency Planning Authority) v Secretary of State for Communities and Local Government* [2007] EWHC 1176 (Admin) at [64]; *R (Reading Borough Council) v Admissions Appeal Panel for Reading Borough Council* [2005] EWHC 2378 (Admin) at [13]; and *R v Royal Borough of Kensington and Chelsea, ex parte Kassam* (1994) 26 HLR 455, 462.

[428] *R (C) v Financial Services Authority* [2012] EWHC 1417 (Admin) at [67]; *South Bucks District Council v Porter (No 2)* [2004] UKHL 33 at [36]. Compare with, *R (Adams) v Commissioner for Local Administration* [2011] EWHC 2971 (Admin) at [33] and *Brabazon-Drenning v United Kingdom Central Council for Nursing, Midwifery and Health Visiting* [2001] HRLR 91.

[429] *R (Savva) v Kensington and Chelsea Royal London Borough Council* [2010] EWCA Civ 1209 at [23]; *R v Crown Court of Southwark, ex parte Samuel* [1995] COD 249; *R v Crown Court at Stafford, ex parte Wil Gilbert (Staffs) Ltd* [1999] 2 All ER 955, 960A; *R v Lancashire County Council, ex parte M* [1995] ELR 136, 139H.

[430] *R (Nash) v Chelsea College of Art and Design* [2001] EWHC Admin 538 at [34]; *R (Young) v Oxford City Council* [2002] EWCA Civ 990 at [20]; *R (Leung) v Imperial College of Science, Technology and Medicine* [2002] EWHC 1358 (Admin) at [29]–[30]; and *R (B) v Merton London Borough Council* [2003] EWHC 1689 (Admin) at [42].

[431] *R (Macrae) v Herefordshire District Council* [2012] EWCA Civ 457 at [40]; *R (Mavalon Care Ltd) v Pembrokeshire County Council* [2011] EWHC 3371 at [54]; *R (M) v Haringey Independent Appeal Panel* [2010] EWCA Civ 1103 at [22]; *R (Hereford Waste Watchers Ltd) v Hereford Council* [2005] EWHC 191 (Admin) at [48]; *R (Richards) v Pembrokeshire County Council* [2004] EWCA Civ 1000 at [58]–[63].

[432] *R v Westminster City Council, ex parte Ermakov* [1996] 2 All ER 302, 312E; *R (Metropolitian Borough of Wirral) v Chief Schools Adjudicator* [2001] ELR 574 at [58]; *R v Doncaster Metropolitan Borough Council, ex parte Nortrop* (1996) 28 HLR 862, 874.

[433] *R (KM) v Cambridgeshire County Council* [2012] UKSC 23 at [38]; *Bank Mellat v HM Treasury (No 2)* [2011] EWCA Civ 1 at [46] and [82]; *R (Hewitson) v Guildford Borough Council* [2011] EWHC 3440 (Admin) at [27]; *R v Brent London Borough Council, ex parte Baruwa* (1997) 29 HLR 915, 929; *Office of Fair Trading v IBA Health Ltd* [2004] EWCA Civ 142 at [106].

[434] *R (Goldsmith) v London Borough of Wandsworth* [2004] EWCA Civ 1170 at [91]; *R (I) v Independent*

Recent examples

1.158 Recent examples of challenges to decisions on the basis of inadequate reasons include:

(1) *R (Wildie) v Wakefield Metropolitan District Council.*[435] A decision to grant planning permission for a caravan site in the green belt was challenged for failure to provide adequate reasons. The local authority had departed from the planning officer's advice, and proper reasons were required to ascertain whether the relevant policy had been interpreted and applied correctly. Such reasons were minimal and no special circumstances were identified, and so the decision was unlawful on this basis.

(2) *Ozyurekliler v Secretary of State for Communities and Local Government.*[436] A decision of a planning inspector to uphold an enforcement notice was challenged on the basis that the reasons given were inadequate. It was held that the decision letter had to be read as a whole and in a reasonably flexible manner and not as a contract or statute, and that the letter was addressed to a knowledgeable readership that was well aware of all the issues involved. The reasons stated were clear, intelligible and appropriate, and so the challenge was refused.

(3) *R (Jackson) v General Medical Council.*[437] A doctor sought to be erased from the register on a voluntary basis due to his health. However, the GMC panel refused this and sought to proceed with full fitness to practice proceedings that were estimated to last 45 days. The panel had not explained why it thought that the doctor was well enough to attend the hearing and so the decision was unlawful.

(4) *R (Mirza) v Secretary of State for the Home Department.*[438] In this case, an asylum-seeker challenged a decision to refuse him leave to remain on the basis of a failure to give reasons that there had been compliance with the relevant rules. It was held that the reasons were clear and concise, and that there was no need to explicitly check off each factor in the rules so long as it was clear that it was applied.

CATEGORY 4: RIGHTS AND FREEDOMS

1.159 In addition to the traditional grounds of judicial review, it is also unlawful for public bodies to act in breach of certain rights and freedoms protected by law. These rights are either protected by statute or common law.

1.160 Within this category, the following is dealt with:

(1) *ECHR rights.* These are the rights and freedoms protected by the European Convention on Human Rights that have been incorporated into domestic law by the Human Rights Act 1998.

Appeal Panel for G Technology College [2005] EWHC 558 (Admin) at [11]; *R (LE (Jamaica)) v Secretary of State for the Home Department* [2012] EWCA Civ 597 at [22].
[435] [2013] EWHC 2769 (Admin).
[436] [2013] EWHC 2648 (Admin).
[437] [2013] EWHC 2595 (Admin).
[438] [2013] EWHC 2207 (Admin).

(2) *Common law rights*. The common law protects rights and freedoms alongside the ECHR. These rights have been developed by the case-law arising from the Human Rights Act but they are freestanding rights that are ripe for further development.

(3) *EU law rights*. The UK's membership of the European Union brings with it certain rights and freedoms that can provide grounds for a judicial review. The EU Charter of Fundamental Rights has developed these rights, although this is a provision that is in its infancy in domestic law.

ECHR rights

Principle

A decision will be unlawful if it violates the rights protected by the European Convention of Human Rights.

Key provision

Section 6, Human Rights Act 1998.

Explanation

1.161 The Human Rights Act 1998 (the HRA) came into force in October 2000. The HRA incorporated most, although not all,[439] of the Articles of the ECHR and thereby gave effect to the rights and freedoms protected by the ECHR in domestic law. This has had a seismic impact on judicial review because a new set of tools was available to challenge the decisions of public authorities.[440] The HRA has been described as a constitutional statute and fulfilling the function of a Bill of Rights.[441]

1.162 It is important to distinguish between the provisions of the HRA that give effect to the Articles of the ECHR, and the Articles themselves. The mechanics of the HRA provide a complex and subtle framework within which the Articles are applied. In explaining how the HRA operates, the technical provisions will described followed by a brief overview of the relevant Articles of the ECHR.

1.163 *The mechanics of the HRA*: The technical provisions of the HRA provide a tight and elegant framework within which the Articles of the ECHR are applied.[442] The overall approach is that the ECHR rights should be rendered practical and effective.[443] The key provisions are as follows:

(1) Section 2 requires a court or tribunal determining a question under the HRA in connection with a Convention right to 'take account' of any jurisprudence or

---

[439] Unincorporated provisions of the ECHR include Article 1 (on territoriality), Article 13 (on just satisfaction), Protocol VI (abolition of death penalty) and Protocol VII (certain additional rights).

[440] It is important to note that the HRA is not simply a vehicle for judicial review claims. For instance, it is possible to bring a civil claim for damages under the HRA within one year of the act complained of (ss 7 and 8 HRA).

[441] See *McCartan Turkington Breen v Times Newspapers Ltd* [2001] 2 AC 277, 297G and *Thoburn v Sunderland City Council* [2002] EWHC 195 (Admin) at [62]–[64].

[442] See *Wilson v First County Trust Ltd* [2003] UKHL 40 at [179] where Lord Rodger described the structure of the HRA as 'tight and elegant'.

[443] *R v Shayler* [2002] UKHL 11 at [61]; *Jones v Ministry of Interior of Saudi Arabia* [2004] EWCA Civ 1394 at [87]; *Clue v Birmingham City Council* [2010] EWCA Civ 460 at [67].

decision of the Strasbourg institutions. The approach of the domestic courts has been to adopt a so-called 'mirror principle' as developed in *R (Ullah) v Special Adjudicator*.[444]

The approach is that domestic courts should normally keep pace with the ECtHR in its interpretation of the ECHR rights. This is because the object of the HRA was to enable claimants in the UK to obtain redress under the ECHR at the domestic level without having to apply to the ECtHR.[445]

The approach was summarised by Lord Neuberger in *Manchester City Council v Pinnock (No 1)*[446] at [48]:

> 'This court is not bound to follow every decision of the European court. Not only would it be impractical to do so: it would sometimes be inappropriate, as it would destroy the ability of the court to engage in the constructive dialogue with the European court which is of value to the development of Convention law ...Where, however, there is a clear and constant line of decisions whose effect is not inconsistent with some fundamental substantive or procedural aspect of our law, and whose reasoning does not appear to overlook or misunderstand some argument or point of principle ... it would be wrong for this court not to follow that line.'

(2) Section 3 sets out the interpretative obligation requiring the courts to read, and give effect to, legislation in a way which is compatible with those Convention rights, 'so far as it is possible to do so'. This obligation is a strong one and has a far-reaching character.

A key decision on the scope of s 3 is *Ghaidan v Godin-Mendoza*[447] where it was said that the interpretative obligation can require the court to 'depart from the unambiguous meaning the legislation would otherwise bear' and from 'the intention reasonably to be attributed to Parliament in using the language in question'. However, the interpretation given 'must be compatible with the underlying thrust of the legislation being construed'.[448] There are limits to the role of s 3, and so a court cannot rewrite provisions so as to create judge-made legislation.[449]

(3) Section 4 outlines the ability to seek and obtain a declaration of incompatibility if legislation cannot be interpreted compatibly with Convention as per s 3.[450] The case-law suggests that the focus of the court should be to seek a compatible interpretation and that a declaration of incompatibility should be a last resort.[451]

A declaration would only be appropriate in situations where the court is stretching to use s 3 to render a statute compatible in a context where Parliament has clearly expressed its views or an interpretation would render the provision

---

[444] [2004] UKHL 26. See also *R v Horncastle* [2009] UKSC 14 at [11] and *R (Chester) v Secretary of State for Justice* [2013] UKSC 63 at [25]–[35].
[445] *Re McCaughey* [2011] UKSC 20 at [59].
[446] [2010] UKSC 45.
[447] [2004] UKHL 30.
[448] *Ghaidan v Godin-Mendoza* [2004] UKHL 30 at [31]–[33]. See also *Principal Reporter v K* [2010] UKSC 56 at [60]–[61].
[449] For instance, in *Chester v Secretary of State for Justice* [2010] EWCA Civ 1439 the court was not prepared to use s 3 to recognise prisoners' right to vote.
[450] Three recent examples: *R (T) v Chief Constable of Greater Manchester* [2013] EWCA Civ 25 (blanket disclosure of criminal convictions incompatible with Article 8); *R (F (A Child) v Secretary of State for the Home Department* [2010] UKSC 17 (life-long notification requirements for sex offenders with no review incompatible with Article 8); and *R (Wright) v Secretary of State for Health* [2009] UKHL 3 (people listed as unsuitable to work with children with no right to make representations incompatible with Article 8).
[451] *R v A (No 2)* [2001] UKHL 25 at [44].

unworkable.[452] The effect of a declaration of incompatibility is to raise the issue with Parliament and triggers a fast-track procedure to remedy the defective legislation under s 10 HRA.

(4) Section 6 makes it unlawful for a 'public authority' to act in a way that is incompatible with a Convention right unless it could not have acted differently as a result of a statutory provision.

Section 6 is important for two reasons. First, it is the provision that explicitly states that acting contrary to the ECHR rights is unlawful. It thereby creates a standard of legality that cannot be breached. Accordingly, when a public authority breaches a Convention right, s 6 ensures that this is unlawful in public law terms.

Secondly, a public authority includes a court or tribunal, and any person certain of whose 'functions are functions of a public nature' (s 6(3)(b)). This means that organisations that are not traditionally considered to be public bodies can come within the terms of the HRA and be subject to a judicial review challenge. The court takes a factor-based approach to resolve whether a person is exercising 'functions of a public nature'.[453] Relevant factors include whether the body: receives public funding, provides a public service or acts in the public interest, has coercive or statutory powers, and is subject to government control. These factors are not exhaustive. It should be noted that s 6(5) provides that if a person is exercising functions of a public nature but the act complained of is 'a private act' then HRA will not apply.

(5) Sections 7 and 8 relate to procedural aspects of bringing a claim under HRA. Section 7 requires that only 'victims' can bring such claims – this is a narrower test than the convention standing test for judicial review, which only requires a 'sufficient interest' to be shown. Section 7 also makes reference to a one-year period for bringing proceedings (which can be extended if just and equitable).[454] This relates to specific HRA proceedings, and not to judicial review proceedings, which must still be brought promptly and in any event with three months (CPR, r 54.5).

(6) Section 8 empowers a court to make an order that it considers to be just and appropriate, and this includes making an award of damages. The approach to damages under s 8 is akin to the approach of the ECtHR in relation to the monetary remedy of 'just satisfaction'. In *Anufrijeva v London Borough of Southwark*[455] it was held that the level of damages should reflect the amount that would be awarded by the ECtHR, although ombudsmen compensation levels provided useful guidance. However, some cases have emphasised that the primary purpose of HRA proceedings is to bring the violation to an end, so damages may be unnecessary.[456]

1.164 *The ECHR rights*: The rights and fundamental freedoms that are protected by the ECHR and given effect to in domestic law fall into three categories:

---

[452] *R v Shayler* [2002] UKHL 11 at [52].
[453] See *Aston Cantlow and Wilmcote with Billesley Parochial Church Council v Wallbank* [2003] UKHL 37 at [7], [11]–[12]; *YL v Birmingham City Council* [2007] UKHL 27 and *R (Weaver) v London & Quadrant Housing Trust* [2009] EWCA Civ 587 at [35].
[454] See *Rabone v Pennine Care NHS Trust* [2012] UKSC 2 at [75] (on the relevant principles to the one-year time limit under s 7).
[455] [2003] EWCA Civ 1406.
[456] See *R (Greenfield) v Secretary of State for the Home Department* [2005] UKHL 14; *R (H) v Secretary of State for the Home Department* [2003] UKHL 59.

(1) The 'absolute rights'. Any interference with these rights is unlawful. The principal absolute right is Article 3, which prohibits torture and inhuman or degrading treatment. A key issue in Article 3 cases is determining whether treatment meets a minimum level of severity.

(2) The 'limited rights'. These rights can be described as absolute with exceptions. For instance, the right to liberty protected by Article 5 is absolute except when certain prescribed limitations apply (such as imprisonment following a criminal conviction). In addition to Article 5, the limited rights include Article 2 (the right to life) and Article 6 (right to a fair trial).

(3) The 'qualified rights'. These rights are structured in such a way so that the court can balance individual rights against the public interest. An interference with a qualified right will not be unlawful if it can be justified on the basis that it is in accordance with the law and is necessary in a democratic society. In assessing this latter requirement, the court applies the principle of proportionality (see above). The qualified rights include: Article 8 (right to respect for private and family life; Article 9 (freedom of thought, conscience and religion, Article 10 (freedom of expression), Article 11 (freedom of assembly and association) and Article 1 of the First Protocol (protection of property).

1.165 The application of the ECHR rights is highly context-specific. The specialist chapters in Part 2 describe how each of the relevant rights applies in those various contexts. In this chapter, the key features of the principal ECHR rights are considered to inform the correct overall approach to these rights. The important initial factors when considering whether an ECHR right will provide a ground for judicial review are whether the right has been interfered with and, if so, whether the interference can be justified.

1.166 *Article 2 (right to life).*[457] The protection given by Article 2 applies in situations where the state uses lethal force without justification or where the state has failed to protect an individual where the authorities knew or ought to have known of 'a real and immediate risk' to life.[458] It has been held that this duty extends to protect mentally ill patients where there was a real and immediate risk of suicide even if that person is not detained under the Mental Health Act 1983.[459]

1.167 Article 2 also imposes a procedural duty on states to investigate loss of life when an individual is in the care of the state. Where this duty is engaged a so-called 'Article 2 inquest' will be conducted, which is somewhat more far reaching than inquests that do not engage Article 2.[460]

1.168 *Article 3 (prohibition of torture or inhuman and degrading treatment).* Article 3 is intended to protect against acts of cruelty inflicted by the state. To violate Article 3, a minimum level of severity must be established. The more vulnerable the individual, the more likely it is that the threshold of minimum severity will be met.[461] The assessment of

---

[457] See *R (Middleton) v West Somerset Coroner* [2004] UKHL 10 at [2]–[3] for an overview of the principles.
[458] The full test is derived from *Osman v United Kingdom* (23452/94) [1999] 1 FLR 193, as described in *Van Colle v Chief Constable of Hertfordshire* [2008] UKHL 50.
[459] *Rabone v Pennine Care NHS Foundation Trust* [2012] UKSC 2.
[460] Article 2 inquests are also referred to as *Middleton* inquests because of *R (Middleton) v West Somerset Coroner* [2004] UKHL 10 which defined when such an inquest is necessary. See also *R (Smith) v Oxfordshire Assistant Deputy Coroner* [2010] UKSC 29.
[461] *Price v United Kingdom* [1988] 55 DR 224.

the minimum threshold is relative and depends on all the circumstances of the case including the duration of treatment, the physical or mental effects and the sex, age and state of health of the individual.[462]

1.169 To amount to 'torture' the treatment must be particularly severe. Article 1 of the United Nations Convention Against Torture defines torture in terms of severe pain and suffering with the purpose of extracting a confession or to intimidate a person. An example is 'Palestinian hanging' where a person's arms are tied behind the back and then the person is suspended by the arms.[463] Inhuman treatment is less severe than torture but still includes intense physical or mental suffering, while degrading treatment includes actions that create a feeling of fear, anguish and inferiority or humiliates and debases the victim.[464] It should be noted that there have been several recent findings of inhuman and degrading treatment where mentally ill people have been held in immigration detention.[465]

1.170 In addition to the absolute duty not to subject an individual to treatment that engages Article 3, there are also positive duties to safeguard against such treatment[466] and to investigate possible breaches of Article 3.[467] This positive aspect of Article 3 is commonly used in the immigration context where removal decisions are challenged on the basis that there is a real risk of inhuman and degrading treatment in the receiving country.[468]

1.171 *Article 5 (right to liberty and security).* Article 5 prohibits deprivations of liberty unless a relevant exception applies. These exceptions include detention following a criminal conviction; detention for persons of an unsound mind; and detention with a view to deportation or extradition.

1.172 A deprivation of liberty is distinguished from a restriction of liberty, which does not engage Article 5.[469] In assessing this the court will look at the concrete situation of the individual and account must be taken of a whole range of criteria such as the type, duration, effects and manner of implementation of the measure in question.[470]

1.173 Article 5 issues arise in a variety of situations, including: control orders imposed on suspected terrorists;[471] police stop-and-search powers;[472] police containment

---

[462] *Ireland v United Kingdom* [1978] 2 EHRR 25 at [162]; see also *Selmouni v France* [1988] EHRLR 510 at [160].
[463] *Aksoy v Turkey* (App 21987/93) (1997) 23 EHRR 553.
[464] *Pretty v United Kingdom* (2002) 35 EHRR 1 at [52]. See also *R (Limbuela) v Secretary of State for the Home Department* [2005] UKHL 66 at [7].
[465] *R (S) v Secretary of State for the Home Department* [2011] EWHC 2120; *R (BA) v Secretary of State for the Home Department* [2011] EWHC 2748; *R (D) v Secretary of State for the Home Department* [2012] EWHC 2501; *R (HA (Nigeria)) v Secretary of State for the Home Department* [2012] EWHC 979 (Admin).
[466] See for instance *Oneryildiz v Turkey* (48939/99) (No 2) (2005) 41 EHRR 20 and *Z v United Kingdom* (29392/95) [2001] 2 FL 612; *E v Chief Constable of the Royal Ulster Constabulary* [2008] UKHL 66.
[467] See for instance: *R (Mousa) v Secretary of State for Defence* [2011] EWCA Civ 1334.
[468] *R (Ullah) v Special Adjudicator* [2004] UKHL 26.
[469] *Guzzardi v Italy* (1981) 3 EHRR 333 at [92]; *Secretary of State for the Home Department v JJ* [2007] UKHL 45 at [12].
[470] *Guzzardi v Italy* (1981) 3 EHRR 333 at [92]; *Engel v The Netherlands* (1976) 1 EHRR 647 at [58]–[59].
[471] See *Secretary of State for the Home Department v JJ* [2007] UKHL 45; *Secretary of State for the Home Department v E* [2007] UKHL 46; *Secretary of State for the Home Department v MB* [2007] UKHL 47; *Secretary of State for the Home Department v AP* [2010] UKSC 24. Control orders are now called Terrorism Prevention and Investigation Measures ('TPIMs').
[472] *R (Gillan) v Commissioner of Police of the Metropolis* [2006] UKHL 12. Compare with *Gillan v United Kingdom* (4158/05) (2010) 50 EHRR 45.

techniques in public order situations;[473] cases before the Parole Board;[474] immigration detention;[475] extradition cases;[476] and detention of those with mental capacity issues.[477]

1.174 The case-law that has arisen from legal challenges in the above situations has struggled with the role of the *purpose* of restricting an individual's liberty. For instance, in *Austin* the House of Lords held that proportionality of a measure could be considered and as such the extended 'kettling' by police of individuals caught up in a protest did not violate Article 5 since it was for the purpose of maintaining public order.[478] However, in *Cheshire West* the Court of Appeal considered whether locking a child with severe learning difficulties in a bedroom for benevolent reasons could avoid a finding that there had been a deprivation of liberty. The conclusion was that 'purpose' in this context meant the objective aim and that benign reasons did not avoid a deprivation of liberty.[479]

1.175 An important part of Article 5 is a procedural obligation to ensure that the lawfulness of detention can be speedily reviewed by a court (Article 5(4)). Therefore, an unreasonable delay to allow a detention to come before a court can violate Article 5(4).[480]

1.176 *Article 6 (right to a fair trial)*: Article 6 has a two-tier structure that divides between standards that apply in criminal cases and civil cases. However, the overall requirement is that claimants are entitled to a fair hearing.

1.177 A key difference between the criminal and civil elements of Article 6 is that it is a requirement that legal aid is provided in criminal cases if a person is unable to pay for it (Article 6(3)(c)). In most cases it will be obvious whether a matter is civil or criminal. However, in contexts such as disciplinary procedures or certain aspects of the criminal trial process it can be unclear which category a case falls under.

1.178 For instance, the House of Lords held that a police disciplinary offence amounted to a criminal charge.[481] However, the procedure for dealing with whether a defendant is fit to stand trial was not criminal for the purposes of Article 6 as the outcome would not be a penal sanction.[482] It is submitted that the guiding principle for determining whether a case is 'civil' or 'criminal' is whether the potential outcome of the proceedings is penal.[483]

---

[473] *Austin v Commissioner of Police of the Metropolis* [2009] UKHL 5; *R (Moos) v Commissioner of Police of the Metropolis* [2012] EWCA Civ 12.
[474] *R (Black) v Secretary of State for Justice* [2009] UKHL 1; *R (Faulkner) v Secretary of State for Justice* [2010] EWCA Civ 1434 and *R (Sturnham) v Parole Board* [2013] UKSC 23.
[475] *R (Saadi) v Secretary of State for the Home Department* [2002] UKHL 41. Article 5 protection in the context of immigration detention is generally considered to be weaker than the common law protections: *R (Lumba) v Secretary of State for the Home Department* [2011] UKSC 12.
[476] *Sullivan v United States* [2012] EWHC 1680 (Admin) (a flagrant denial of Article 5 rights on return to US would render extradition unlawful).
[477] *Cheshire West and Chester Council v P* [2011] EWCA Civ 1257.
[478] *Austin v Commissioner of Police of the Metropolis* [2009] UKHL 5 at [34].
[479] *Cheshire West and Chester Council v P* [2011] EWCA Civ 1257 at [71] and [74]–[76]. See also *Surrey County Council v CA* [2011] EWCA Civ 190 at [50]–[52].
[480] *R (A) v Secretary of State for the Home Department* [2002] EWHC 1618 (Admin) (delay in case being heard by Mental Health Review Tribunal).
[481] *R (Greenfield) v Secretary of State for the Home Department* [2005] UKHL 14.
[482] *R v H* [2003] UKHL 1.
[483] *R v H* [2003] UKHL 1 at [19]; *Ali v Birmingham City Council* [2010] UKSC 8.

1.179 If a case does not fall within the criminal category, Article 6 will only be engaged in terms of the civil category if there has been a 'determination of civil rights and obligations'. The principles for determining whether there has been such a determination are:

(1) A 'dispute' over a 'right' or 'obligation'[484] that has a basis in domestic law.[485] This requirement requires the claimant to show that the legal dispute is arguably founded on domestic law[486] and procedural bars to claims are discounted.[487] The source of law or the body that decides the dispute is not significant.[488]

Examples include refusal of a licence to operate a gas-supply installation;[489] an out-of-time request for a lawyer's readmission to the Bar;[490] temporary suspension of medical practice rights;[491] a claim of a foreign-trained medic to become a registered doctor in another country;[492] a claim for compensation for allegedly unlawful detention;[493] proceedings concerning a change of name;[494] and the inability to contest rejection of a construction tender on national security grounds.[495]

(2) The right or obligation must be 'civil' in nature.[496] This has an autonomous meaning, which means that the domestic definition of a right or obligation does not determine whether it is 'civil' for the purposes of Article 6. What matters is the character of the right at issue, and whether the outcome of the proceedings will have a direct impact on private law rights and obligations.[497] An important factor is the economic nature of a right, although this is not decisive.[498]

The private law elements must be predominant over the public-law elements for an action to be qualified as civil.[499] This has meant that social welfare decisions typically fall outside Article 6.[500] For instance, a homelessness decision regarding the duty to secure accommodation is not a determination of civil rights.[501] Similarly, challenges to inclusion on a list of people suspected of a connection with terrorism and the resulting freezing of assets does not involve a determination of civil rights.[502]

1.180 The application of these principles has developed on a case-by-case basis.[503] Where Article 6 is engaged, its requirements are similar to the requirements of natural justice (see above). Hearings must be fair – this means knowing the case that has to be

---

[484] *Benthem v Netherlands* (8848/80) (1986) 8 EHRR 1 at [32]–[36].
[485] *Roche v United Kingdom* (32555/96) (2006) 42 EHRR 30 at [116]–[126].
[486] *Georgiadis v Greece* (21522/93) (1997) 24 EHRR 606 at [27]–[36].
[487] *Roche v United Kingdom* (32555/96) (2006) 42 EHRR 30 at [116]–[126]. This includes where there is an immunity from suit – *Osman v United Kingdom* (23452/94) (2000) 29 EHRR 245 at [136]–[140].
[488] *Ringeisen v Austria (No. 1)* (1979-80) 1 EHRR 455.
[489] *Benthem v Netherlands* (8848/80) (1986) 8 EHRR 1.
[490] *H v Belgium* (1986) 8 EHRR CD510.
[491] *Le Compte v Belgium* (1982) 4 EHRR 1.
[492] *Chevrol v France* (49636/99).
[493] *Georgiadis v Greece* (21522/93) (1997) 24 EHRR 606.
[494] *Mustafa v France* (63056/00).
[495] *Tinnelly v United Kingdom* (20390/92) (1999) 27 EHRR 249.
[496] *Ringeisen v Austria (No. 1)* (1979-80) 1 EHRR 455 at [94].
[497] *Baraona v Portugal* (1991) 13 EHRR 329 at [38]–[44].
[498] *Procola v Luxembourg* (1996) 22 EHRR 193 at [37]–[40].
[499] *Deumeland v Germany* (1986) 8 EHRR 448 at [59]–[74].
[500] *Savva v Royal London Borough of Kensington and Chelsea* [2010] EWHC 414 (Admin).
[501] *Ali v Birmingham City Council* [2010] UKSC 8.
[502] *R (Maftah) v Secretary of State for Foreign and Commonwealth Affairs* [2011] EWCA Civ 350.
[503] A useful summary of the case-law is available via the Council of Europe. See Vitkauskas and Dikov, *Protecting the right to a fair trial under the European Convention on Human Rights* (2012), pp 11–16.

met;[504] having an opportunity to make representations;[505] and being able to extend time to bring a case.[506] Hearings must be before an independent and impartial tribunal – a Secretary of State may not be independent and impartial, nor might a judge if he has expressed critical views in the past.[507] However, if there are such failings, the possibility of judicial review or an appeal can cure the breach by allowing an independent and impartial tribunal to reconsider the matter.[508]

1.181 It is important to bear in mind that Article 6 is based on 'benign and flexible' principles, rather than inflexible rules.[509] Accordingly, whether a fair hearing has been achieved will always depend on all the circumstances of the case.[510]

1.182 *Article 8 (the right to respect for private and family life, home and correspondence).* Article 8 has a broad application. Lord Bingham described Article 8 in the following terms:

> 'The content of this right has been described as "elusive" and does not lend itself to exhaustive definition ... But the purpose of the article is in my view clear. It is to protect the individual against intrusion by agents of the state, unless for good reason, into the private sphere within which individuals expect to be left alone to conduct their personal affairs and live their personal lives as they choose.'[511]

1.183 The content of Article 8 includes both positive and negative obligations. The positive obligations on a state to protect Article 8 rights are relatively limited – it has been held that the obligation can require measures to be taken to provide support, or an obligation to produce a scheme to protect private life.[512] This applies most clearly in the prison context.[513] Article 8 also gives rise to certain procedural obligations such as providing an opportunity to make representations before a decision is made that would affect a person's private and family life.[514]

1.184 However, Article 8 is a much more powerful tool to resist state interference with private and family life. For example Article 8 is engaged in a variety of situations such as: immigration decisions to remove an individual;[515] extradition decisions;[516] certain

---

[504] *Secretary of State for the Home Department v AF (No 3)* [2009] UKHL 28.
[505] *R (Wright) v Secretary of State for Health* [2009] UKHL 3 at [28].
[506] *Pomiechowski v District Court of Legnica* [2012] UKSC 20 at [37].
[507] *R (Anderson) v Secretary of State for the Home Department* [2002] UKHL 46; *Hoekstra v HM Advocate* [2000] UKHRR 578.
[508] *R (Alconbury Developments Ltd) v Secretary of State for the Environment, Transport and the Regions* [2001] UKHL 23; *R (Begum) v Tower Hamlets London Borough Council* [2003] UKHL 5.
[509] *R v Spear* [2001] QB 804, 819; *R (Husain) v Asylum Support Adjudicator* [2001] EWHC Admin 852 at [70].
[510] *R (Fleurose) v Securities and Futures Authority* [2001] EWCA Civ 2015 at [14].
[511] *R (Countryside Alliance) v Attorney General* [2007] UKHL 52 at [10].
[512] *R (McDonald) v Kensington and Chelsea Royal London Borough Council* [2011] UKSC 33 at [15]; *Anufrijeva v Southwark London Borough Council* [2003] EWCA Civ at [16].
[513] *R (Howard League for Penal Reform) v Secretary of State for the Home Department* [2002] EWHC 2497 (Admin) at [66]. Compare with *R (Children's Rights Alliance for England) v Secretary of State for Justice* [2012] EWHC 8 (Admin) at [198].
[514] *Principal Reporter v K* [2010] UKSC 6 at [41]; *R (DL) v Newham Borough Council* [2011] EWHC 1127 (Admin) at [140]; *R (CF) v Secretary of State for the Home Department* [2004] EWHC 111 (Fam) at [157].
[515] *R (Razgar) v Secretary of State for the Home Department* [2004] UKHL 27; *Beoku-Betts v Secretary of State for the Home Department* [2008] UKHL 39.
[516] *R (HH) v Westminster City Magistrates' Court* [2012] UKSC 25; *Norris v Government of the United States for America (No 2)* [2010] UKSC 9.

activities within prisons;[517] the retention of certain forms of data by police;[518] defending possession proceedings;[519] health and social care cases;[520] and child care proceedings.[521] In respect of the role of Article 8 in these subject areas, please see the specific area chapters in Part 2 of this book.

1.185 In cases where Article 8 is engaged, and the measure is both in accordance with law and following one of the broadly-worded legitimate aims given in Article 8(2), the courts will ask whether the interference is necessary in a democratic society. This assessment is conducted using a proportionality analysis (described above).

1.186 Most cases that rely on Article 8 turn on the court's balance between individual rights and the broader public interest. In some circumstances, the starting point automatically favours the public interest and so weighty factors will need to be demonstrated by the claimant to establish a breach of Article 8. This is particularly the case in extradition cases and where tenants seek to defend possession proceedings using Article 8.[522]

1.187 By contrast, the balance is tilted in child care proceedings where weighty reasons will be required by a public authority to remove a child from its parents.[523] The underlying principle is the discretionary area of judgment afforded to decision-makers depending on the legislative framework and the policy content of the decision (see above).

1.188 *Article 10 (freedom of expression)*: Article 10 protects free speech and rights to receive and impart information. Like Article 8, it is a qualified right and so where it is engaged, the court will conduct a balancing exercise to determine whether the interference is proportionate.

1.189 Article 10 is typically engaged in situations involving the media, for instance where broadcasters are ordered to produce documents,[524] or where there are restrictions on advertising and publicity[525] and limitations on journalists' activities.[526] Courts are often required to balance Article 8 and Article 10 rights where journalists seek to report

---

[517] *R (AB) v Secretary of State for Justice* [2009] EWHC 2220 (Admin); *R (Suzuluk) v Governor HM Prison Full Sutton* [2004] EWHC 514 (Admin); *R (D) v Secretary of State for the Home Department* [2003] EWHC 155 (Admin); *R v Secretary of State for the Home Department, ex parte Daly* [2001] UKHL 26.

[518] *R (GC) v Metropolitan Police Commissioner* [2011] UKSC 21; *R (F (A Child) v Secretary of State for the Home Department* [2010] UKSC 17; *R (L) v Commissioner of Police of the Metropolis* [2009] UKSC 9; *R (Wood) v Commissioner of Police of the Metropolis* [2009] EWCA Civ 414.

[519] *Manchester City Council v Pinnock (No 1)* [2010] UKSC 45; *Hounslow London Borough Council v Powell* [2011] UKSC 8; *Corby Borough Council v Scott* [2012] EWCA Civ 276; and *Thurrock Borough Council v West* [2012] EWCA Civ 1435.

[520] *R (McDonald) v Kensington and Chelsea Royal London Borough Council* [2011] UKSC 33; *R (Condliff) v North Staffordshire Primary Care Trust* [2011] EWCA Civ 910.

[521] *Re B (A Child)* [2013] UKSC 33; *Johansen v Norway* (1996) 23 EHRR 33, *K and T v Finland* (2001) 36 EHRR 18, *R and H v United Kingdom* (2012) 54 EHRR 2, [2011] 2 FLR 1236 and *YC v United Kingdom* (2012) 55 EHRR 33.

[522] See *R (HH) v Westminster City Magistrates' Court* [2012] UKSC 25 and *Corby Borough Council v Scott* [2012] EWCA Civ 276.

[523] *Re B (A Child)* [2013] UKSC 33.

[524] *R (BSB Ltd) v Chelmsford Crown Court* [2012] EWHC 1295 (Admin); *R (Malik) v Manchester Crown Court* [2008] EWHC 1362 (Admin).

[525] *R (Animal Defenders International) v Secretary of State for Culture, Media and Sport* [2008] UKHL 15; *R (Northern Cyprus Tourism Centre Ltd) v Transport for London* [2005] EWHC 1698 (Admin); *R (London Christian Radio Ltd) v Radio Advertising Clearance Centre* [2012] EWHC 1043 (Admin); *R (Core Issues Trust) v Transport for London* [2013] EWHC 651 (Admin).

on the private lives of individuals.[527] Other contexts can include political expression, such as a protestor resisting removal from a place;[528] and decisions to refuse entry to the UK to individuals wishing to express political views.[529]

1.190 When Article 10 rights are engaged, the nature of the justification required varies from case to case. For instance, the courts are typically reluctant to interfere with decisions where a public authority has made a judgment on whether a particular measure is necessary, such as banning an advert on the grounds of taste and decency.[530]

1.191 Section 12 of the HRA makes special provision for Article 10 in cases where the court is considering whether to grant a remedy that might affect the exercise of Article 10. This requires the court to have particular regard to the importance of Article 10 (s 12(4)) and provides some limitations on granting relief.

1.192 *Article 14 (prohibition of discrimination)*: The anti-discrimination provision by Article 14 is framed so that a person must be able to enjoy the protection of the ECHR rights without discrimination. Accordingly, any Article 14 claim requires a claimant to show that any alleged discrimination comes within the 'ambit' of another ECHR right.

1.193 It has been suggested that the correct analysis of an Article 14 claim should answer the five questions developed in *Michalak v London Borough of Wandsworth*[531] at [20]:

(1) Do the facts fall within the ambit of one or more of the Convention provisions? It has been held that this means where 'a personal interest close to the core of such a right is infringed'.[532]

(2) If so, was there different treatment as respects that right between the complainant on the one hand and other persons put forward for comparison ('the chosen comparators') on the other?

(3) Were the chosen comparators in an analogous situation to the complainant's situation?[533] The case-law indicates that comparators must be closely analogous.[534]

(4) If so, did the difference in treatment have an objective and reasonable justification: in other words, did it pursue a legitimate aim and did the differential treatment bear a reasonable relationship of proportionality to the aims sought to be achieved?[535]

(5) Is the basis for the different treatment of the complainant as against that of the chosen comparators based on any ground such as sex, race, colour, language or

---

[526] *R (BBC) v Secretary of State for Justice* [2012] EWHC 13 (Admin); *R (Hirst) v Secretary of State for the Home Department* [2002] EWHC 602 (Admin).
[527] See *Campbell v MGN Ltd* [2004] UKHL 22; *Douglas v Hello! Ltd (No 3)* [2005] EWCA Civ 595.
[528] *Hall v City of Westminster* [2010] EWCA Civ 817.
[529] *R (Lord Carlile) v Secretary of State for the Home Department* [2013] EWCA Civ 199; *R (Naik) v Secretary of State for the Home Department* [2011] EWCA Civ 1546; *R (Farrakhan) v Secretary of State for the Home Department* [2002] EWCA Civ 606.
[530] *R (Animal Defenders International) v Secretary of State for Culture, Media and Sport* [2008] UKHL 15.
[531] [2002] EWCA Civ 271.
[532] *R (Clift) v Secretary of State for the Home Department* [2006] UKHL 54 at [16].
[533] *AL (Serbia) v Secretary of State for the Home Department* [2008] UKHL 42 at [20]–[25].
[534] See *R (Waite) v Hammersmith and Fulham London Borough Council* [2002] EWCA Civ 482; *R (Purja) v Ministry of Defence* [2003] EWCA Civ 1345; *Malcolm v Benedict Mackenzie* [2004] EWHC 339 (Ch).
[535] See *Stec v United Kingdom* (65731/01) (2006) 43 EHRR 47; *Burnip v Birmingham City Council* [2012] EWCA Civ 629.

other status within the meaning of Article 14? There are several cases that have dealt with whether certain categories of people come within the term 'other status'. The overall focus is whether an individual has a 'personal characteristic'.[536] Such a characteristic need not be involuntary.[537]

1.194 It is submitted that the questions cited provide useful guidance on how to approach Article 14. However, it should be emphasised that a formulaic approach should be avoided and the House of Lords in *R (Carson) v Secretary of State for Work and Pensions* [2005] UKHL 37 specifically warned against going mechanically through a series of questions.

1.195 *Article 1 of the 1st Protocol (protection of property)*: This Article is often abbreviated to 'A1P1' and protects the peaceful enjoyment of possessions. The definition of 'possessions' is fairly broad and has been held to include non-contributory welfare benefits,[538] rights and expectations under a civil service pension scheme[539] and legitimate expectations.[540] However, a right to practise in the NHS due to inclusion on a list is not a possession as this is not transferable or marketable.[541]

1.196 A1P1 is a qualified right, and interference with property rights can be justified if in the public interest. Accordingly, a proportionality test is applied to assess whether a fair balance has been struck. In *Thomas v Bridgend County Borough Council*[542] a road-building scheme was held to interfere with A1P1 rights, and the relevant statutory compensation scheme provided for a disproportionate cap on awards. This was because the exclusion of claims within three years of the opening date of the scheme lead to bizarre results.[543] Similarly unfair or erroneous decisions that interfered with possessions have been held to violate A1P1.[544]

1.197 However, it should be noted that A1P1 rights are often engaged in contexts where public authorities or the legislature have taken high-level policy decisions. Accordingly, a wide discretionary area of judgment can apply, which means that inferences with A1P1 have been frequently justified on proportionality grounds.[545]

Common law rights

Principle

The common law protects many rights akin to ECHR rights.

---

[536] *Kjeldsen, Busk Madsen and Pedersen v Denmark* (1976) 1 EHRR 711 at [56]. Followed in *R (S) v Chief Constable of the South Yorkshire Police* [2004] UKHL 39.
[537] *R (RJM) v Secretary of State for Work and Pensions* [2007] EWCA Civ 614.
[538] *R (RJM) v Secretary of State for Work and Pensions* [2008] UKHL 63 at [34].
[539] *R (Public and Commercial Services Union) v Minister for the Civil Service (No 3)* [2011] EWHC 2041 (Admin) at [37].
[540] *Rowland v Environment Agency* [2003] EWCA Civ 1885.
[541] *R (Malik) v Waltham Forest NHS Primary Care Trust* [2007] 1 WLR 2092.
[542] [2011] EWCA Civ 862.
[543] *Thomas v Bridgend County Borough Council* [2011] EWCA Civ 862 at [56].
[544] *R (Infinis Plc) v Gas and Electricity Markets Authority* [2011] EWHC 1873 (Admin) at [103] and *R (London Reading College Ltd) v Secretary of State for the Home Department* [2010] EWHC 2561 (Admin) at [67].
[545] See for instance, *AXA General Insurance Ltd v HM Advocate* [2011] UKSC 46; *R (Huitson) v Revenue and Customs Commissioners* [2011] EWCA Civ 893; *Wilson v First County Trust Ltd* [2003] UKHL 40; *Marcic v Thames Water Utilities Ltd* [2003] UKHL 66.

Key cases

R v Secretary of State for the Home Department, ex parte Simms;[546] *R (Quila) v Secretary of State for the Home Department*.[547]

Explanation

1.198 Since the enactment of the Human Rights Act 1998, there has been a rapid development of the case-law on the ECHR rights. However, the Human Rights Act 1998 and its related jurisprudence is not the only source of human rights protection in domestic law. In particular, the common law recognises a number of rights that are similar to those contained within the ECHR. Some of these rights are not as developed as their ECHR counterparts. However, the seeds have long been sown and are ripe for future development. This section briefly outlines these common law rights.

1.199 There are two legal advantages to common law rights. First, to rely on a common law right a claim does not have to come within the procedural limitations of the Human Rights Act. These limitations include the narrower definition of a public body due to s 6 HRA, and the narrower standing test based on 'victim' status due to s 7 HRA. Secondly, the content and scope of common law rights are not limited by reference to the European Court of Human Rights.[548] This means that domestic courts are able to develop common law rights without needing to observe the 'mirror principle' and so such rights can be more closely tailored to domestic requirements.

1.200 In addition, it is important to note the political antipathy towards the HRA and the ECHR. A manifesto pledge of the Conservative Party is to repeal the HRA and leave the Council of Europe. This book makes no comment about this political position. However, it is submitted that even if the HRA was repealed, the common law would still supply a form of human rights protection at the domestic level.

1.201 *The common law rights*: Where common law rights are engaged, and such rights are not absolute in nature, the correct standard of review is proportionality (see above).[549] Additionally, where the court is faced with interpreting a statutory provision with ambiguous wording that interferes with common law rights this can be 'read down' due to the principle of legality.[550] This is similar to, although not as strong as, the interpretative obligation contained in s 3 HRA.[551] The principle of legality means that Parliament cannot override fundamental rights or the rule of law using general or ambiguous words.[552] The rights include:

(1) Respect for life.[553] In the context of a case concerning inquests, Lord Bingham said that 'a profound respect for the sanctity of human life underpins the common law'. He explained that this means that a state must take appropriate steps to protect

---

[546] [2000] 2 AC 115.
[547] [2010] EWCA Civ 1482.
[548] See *Rabone v Pennine Care NHS Trust* [2012] UKSC 2 at [113]; *R (Guardian News and Media Ltd) v City of Westminster Magistrates' Court* [2012] EWCA Civ 420 at [88]; *Osborn v The Parole Board* [2013] UKSC 61 at [57].
[549] *R (Quila) v Secretary of State for the Home Department* [2010] EWCA Civ 1482 at [34].
[550] *R v Secretary of State for the Home Department, ex parte Simms* [2000] 2 AC 115, 131E–G.
[551] *Ahmed v HM Treasury* [2010] UKSC 2 at [112] and [117].
[552] *AXA General Insurance Ltd v HM Advocate* [2011] UKSC 46 at [152].
[553] *R (Amin) v Secretary of State for the Home Department* [2003] UKHL 51 at [30].

life. The state owes a particular duty to those involuntarily in its custody. Reasonable care must be taken to safeguard their lives and persons against the risk of avoidable harm.

However, the common law goes further and recognises the overarching importance of the law of humanity.[554] This includes a freedom from destitution.[555]

(2) *Freedom from torture.*[556] In *A v Secretary of State for the Home Department*,[557] a case that concerned the use of evidence obtained by torture, Lord Nicholls said 'for centuries the common law has set its face against torture'.[558] The other Law Lords emphatically supported this view.[559] The place of the prohibition of torture in domestic law has also been discussed by the courts in relation to the international definition.[560] It is submitted that while the common law definition of torture will draw on concepts from international law, context is important. For instance, a wider definition of torture was found in a case concerning Home Office policy in relation to torture survivors.[561]

(3) *Right of personal liberty (including habeas corpus).*[562] The right of personal liberty is usually traced back to Magna Carta. It has been described as being of 'fundamental importance' and protects against arbitrary detention.[563] As such, any imprisonment is prima facie unlawful and must be justified by explicit statutory authority.[564] The right of personal liberty encompasses the concept of *habeas corpus*, which is an ancient remedy that requires a person under arrest to be brought before the court to examine the legality of a person's detention.[565] There is also a related freedom of unauthorised stop and search.[566]

(4) *Due process rights.* The common law has developed sophisticated and detailed rights based on the principle of natural justice. These are considered above. However, there are related rights that sit alongside the principle of natural justice. These include the constitutional principle of open justice, which requires that legal

---

[554] *R v Secretary of State for Social Security, ex parte Joint Council for the Welfare of Immigrants* [1997] 1 WLR 275, 292F–G; *R (Othman) v Secretary of State for Work and Pensions* [2001] EWHC Admin 1022 at [52] and [56].

[555] *Yildiz v Secretary of State for Social Security* [2001] EWCA Civ 309 at [18]; *R v Wandsworth London Borough Council, ex parte O* [2000] 1 WLR 2539; and *R (Limbuela) v Secretary of State for the Home Department* [2005] UKHL 66.

[556] *A v Secretary of State for the Home Department* [2005] UKHL 71 at [11]–[12].

[557] [2004] UKHL 56, [2005] 2 AC 68.

[558] *A v Secretary of State for the Home Department* [2005] UKHL 71 at [64].

[559] *A v Secretary of State for the Home Department* [2005] UKHL 71 at [83] (Lord Hoffmann); at [129] (Lord Rodger); and at [152] (Lord Carswell).

[560] See *Jones v Ministry of Interior of Saudi Arabia* [2006] UKHL 26; and *R (Mohamed) v Secretary of State for Foreign and Commonwealth Affairs (No 1)* [2008] EWHC 2048 (Admin).

[561] *R (EO & Ors) v Secretary of State for the Home Department* [2013] EWHC 1236 (Admin) at [75]–[82].

[562] *R (Lumba) v Secretary of State for the Home Department* [2011] UKSC 12; *A v Secretary of State for the Home Department* [2004] UKHL 56 at [36]; *B v Secretary of State for Justice* [2011] EWCA Civ 1608 at [53]; *R (Saadi) v Secretary of State for the Home Department* [2001] EWCA Civ 1512 at [69]; *R v Secretary of State for the Home Department, ex parte Khawaja* [1984] AC 74, 111F; and *Rahmatullah v Secretary of State for Foreign and Commonwealth Affairs* [2011] EWCA Civ 1540 at [43].

[563] See *A v Secretary of State for the Home Department* [2004] UKHL 56 at [36]; *R (Lumba) v Secretary of State for the Home Department* [2011] UKSC 12 at [341]; *B v Secretary of State for Justice* [2011] EWCA Civ 1608 at [53].

[564] *R (Abbasi) v Secretary of State for Foreign and Commonwealth Affairs* [2002] EWCA Civ 1598 at [60]; *Eshugbayi Elko v Government of Nigeria* [1931] AC 662, 670; *R v Secretary of State for the Home Department, ex parte Khawaja* [1984] AC 74, 111F.

[565] See *Rahmattullah v Secretary of State of Foreign and Commonwealth Affairs* [2011] EWCA Civ 1540 at [43]; *H v Lord Advocate* [2012] UKSC 24 at [32]; *R (Hilali) v Governor of Whitemoor Prison* [2008] UKHL 3.

[566] *Secretary of State for the Home Department v GG* [2009] EWCA Civ 786 at [12]; *R (W) v Metropolitan Police Commissioner* [2005] EWHC 1586 (Admin) at [21].

proceedings are conducted transparently and in public.[567] The common law also provides protection against self-incrimination, and thereby supports the right to silence,[568] as well as legal professional privilege.[569] Trial by jury in criminal cases is also a closely guarded principle.[570]

(5) *Access to justice.* In order to render any common law rights practical and effective, there must be access to justice. This has been recognised as a constitutional right and requires effective and unimpeded access to the court.[571] Closely related to this is the right of access to a lawyer.[572]

(6) *Right to privacy.*[573] A right to privacy is recognised at common law, having been developed through the tort of breach of confidence. Article 8 ECHR has played an important role in this developments but the right exists at common law as an underlying value in its own right.

(7) *Freedom of religion.*[574] The common law provides vigorous protection for the right of people to hold and express their religious beliefs. However, the common law does not protect the *content* of any religious belief.

(8) *Freedom of expression.*[575] The freedom to express views, whether political or otherwise, is a core value of the legal system in England and Wales. This means that the common law supports the activities of journalists and politicians, whether popular or unpopular, freely to express a variety of political opinions. This freedom includes the right to assemble and associate, such as in a trade union.[576]

(9) *Property rights.*[577] The common law is often associated with its strong protection for property rights. The courts will typically interpret legislation that limits private property rights narrowly, such as in the context of compulsory purchase law.[578] This has been described as a principle of high constitutional importance.[579]

---

[567] See *R (Guardian News and Media Ltd) v City of Westminster Magistrates' Court* [2012] EWCA Civ 420; *Al Rawi v Security Service* [2011] UKSC 34; *R (Mohamed) v Secretary of State for Foreign and Commonwealth Affairs (No 2)* [2011] QB 218; *R (Secretary of State for the Home Department) v Assistant Deputy Coroner for Inner West London* [2010] EWHC 3098 (Admin).
[568] See *R v Rochford* [2010] EWCA Crim 1928 at [21] and *R v Director of the Serious Fraud Office, ex parte Smith* [1993] AC 1, 40D.
[569] See *R (Morgan Grenfell & Co Ltd) v Inland Revenue Commissioners* [2002] UKHL 21 at [7] and [43]; *Quinn Direct Insurance Ltd v Law Society* [2010] EWCA Civ 805 at [23] and [29]; *R (Kelly) v Warley Magistrates' Court* [2007] EWHC 1836 (Admin).
[570] See *R v Islington North Juvenile Court, ex parte Daley* [1983] 1 AC 347, 364B and *R (Misick) v Secretary of State for Foreign and Commonwealth Affairs* [2009] EWCA Civ 1549 at [20].
[571] See *R (Medical Justice) v Secretary of State for the Home Department* [2011] EWCA Civ 1710; *Ahmed v HM Treasury* [2010] UKSC 2; *R (Anufrijeva) v Secretary of State for the Home Department* [2003] UKHL 36; *R v Lord Chancellor, ex parte Witham* [1998] QB 575; *R v Secretary of State for the Home Department, ex parte Pierson* [1998] AC 539; *R v Secretary of State for the Home Department, ex parte Leech* [1994] QB 198.
[572] See *R (AM) v Director of Public Prosecutions* [2012] EWHC 470 (Admin); *R (T) v Secretary of State for the Home Department* [2010] EWHC 435 (Admin); *R v Secretary of State for the Home Department, ex parte Anderson* [1984] QB 778.
[573] *Douglas v Hello! Ltd (No 3)* [2005] EWCA Civ 595; *Wainwright v Home Office* [2003] UKHL 53 at [31].
[574] *McFarlane v Relate Avon Limited* [2010] EWCA Civ 880 at [21]; *R (Johns) v Derby City Council* [2011] EWHC 375 (Admin) at [37]–[45].
[575] *Rushbridger v HM Attorney General* [2003] UKHL 38 at [7]; *R v Shayler* [2002] UKHL 11 at [21]; *McCartan Turkington Breen v Times Newspapers Ltd* [2001] 2 AC 277 at 297F.
[576] *McEldowney v Forde* [1971] AC 632, 657F.
[577] *R (Eastenders Cash & Carry Plc) v Revenue & Customs Commissioners* [2012] EWCA Civ 15 at [88].
[578] *R (Sainsbury's Supermarkets Ltd) v Wolverhampton City Council* [2010] UKSC 20 at [10].
[579] *Attorney General v Blake* [2001] 1 AC 268, 289G.

(10) *Citizenship rights*.[580] British citizens have a right to come and remain within the jurisdiction as he or she chooses.[581] Accordingly, a citizen cannot be exiled from the country.[582] Citizens are also entitled to vote, subject to the limits on the franchise.[583]

(11) *Equality rights*.[584] Whether there is a right to substantive equality at common law is debatable.[585] However, statutory equality duties as provided for in the Equality Act 2010 have arguably rendered the need for such a right unnecessary. The common law has a developed recognition of formal equality that targets unequal treatment.[586] This is sometimes described in terms of a duty to 'treat like cases alike' subject to the public interest.[587]

EU law rights

Principle

Rights protected by EU law can take priority over domestic law.

Key case

R v Secretary of State for Transport, ex parte Factortame Ltd (No 2).[588]

Explanation

1.202 The law of the European Union has supplemented the law of the UK since 1972. The European Communities Act 1972 (the 'ECA 1972') has been described as a constitutional statute given how it has modified the traditional understanding of sources of law.[589]

1.203 EU law is derived from the Treaty on European Union (TEU), the Treaty on the Functioning of the European Union (TFEU) and the Directives and Regulations passed by the European Parliament and Commission. The Court of Justice of the European Union (CJEU) deals with questions regarding the interpretation of EU law.[590]

1.204 *Basic principles of EU law*: There are several basic principles regarding EU law that must be noted at the outset. First, EU law has direct effect in domestic law,[591] and it

---

[580] *R (Bancoult) v Secretary of State for the Foreign and Commonwealth Office* [2001] QB 1067 at [39].
[581] *Pomiechowski v District Court of Legnica* [2012] UKSC 20 at [31]–[32].
[582] *R (Bancoult) v Secretary of State for Foreign & Commonwealth Affairs (No 2)* [2008] UKHL 61 at [89].
[583] *R (Preston) v Wandsworth London Borough Council* [2011] EWHC 3174 (Admin) at [40].
[584] *Percy v Board of National Mission of the Church of Scotland* [2005] UKHL 73, [2006] 2 AC 28 at [152].
[585] See *Matadeen v Pointu* [1999] 1 AC 98; *Association of British Civilian Internees & Far Eastern Region v Secretary of State for Defence* [2003] EWCA Civ 473, [2003] QB 1397; and *R (Rudi) v Secretary of State for the Home Department* [2007] EWCA Civ 132.
[586] *R (E) v Nottinghamshire Healthcare NHS Trust* [2009] EWCA Civ 795 at [90].
[587] *R (Zeqiri) v Secretary of State for the Home Department* [2002] UKHL 3 at [56].
[588] [1991] 1 AC 603.
[589] *Thoburn v Sunderland City Council* [2002] EWHC 195 (Admin) at [62]–[69].
[590] This is done by a reference to the CJEU. See Article 267 TFEU and Part 68 of the Civil Procedure Rules. On whether to make a reference see *R (ZO (Somalia)) v Secretary of State for the Home Department* [2010] UKSC 36 at [51]; *Bloomsbury International Ltd v Department for Environment, Food and Rural Affairs* [2011] UKSC 25 at [51]; and *R v International Stock Exchange, ex parte Else* [1993] QB 534, 545D–F.
[591] Section 2 of the European Communities Act 1972; *R v Secretary of State for Transport, ex parte Factortame Ltd* [1990] 2 AC 85, 151C.

prevails over any provision of domestic law that is inconsistent with it.[592] The principle of direct effect applied when the content of the provision is clear and precise,[593] the provision must be self-executing[594] and not contingent on some external event.[595] For instance, Directives can have direct effect if they have not been implemented properly into domestic law, while Regulations have immediate direct effect subject to the conditions stated.[596]

1.205 Second, EU law rights must be given effective protection at the domestic level. This means establishing a system of remedies and procedures that ensure respect for the relevant right.[597] Part of ensuring such protection is to require domestic legislation to be given an interpretation that conforms with EU law wherever possible.[598] This is akin to the interpretative obligation of s 3 HRA (above).[599]

1.206 Third, in addition to the principle of effective interpretation, other general principles have been recognised. These include proportionality,[600] legal certainty,[601] legitimate expectations,[602] equality and equal treatment,[603] and the provision of reasons.[604]

1.207 *EU law rights*: The EU Treaties provide for a series of fundamental freedoms that cannot be interfered with unless this can be justified by reference to the proportionality principle. These freedoms are principally directed towards enabling the internal market to operate effectively and they include:

- freedom of movement;[605]

---

[592] *A v Chief Constable of West Yorkshire* [2004] UKHL 21 at [9]; *Thoburn v Sunderland City Council* [2002] EWHC 195 (Admin) at [69]; *R v Secretary of State for Transport, ex parte Factortame Ltd (No 2)* [1991] 1 AC 603.
[593] *Van Gend en Loos* [1964] ECR 585.
[594] *Molkerei-Zentrale Westfalen v Hauptzollamt Paderborn* [1968] ECR 143.
[595] *Reyners v Belgium* [1974] ECR 631.
[596] See further Article 288 TFEU.
[597] *Tariq v Home Office* [2011] UKSC 35 at [15]; *FA (Iraq) v Secretary of State for the Home Department* [2011] UKSC 2 at [12].
[598] *Marleasing SA v La Comercial Internacionale de Alimentacion SA* [1990] ECRI–4135 at 4159; *Hashwani v Jivraj* [2011] UKSC 40 at [8]; *Russell v Transocean International Resources Ltd* [2011] UKSC 57 at [22]; *Vodafone 2 v Revenue and Customs Commissioners* [2009] EWCA Civ 446 at [37]–[38].
[599] *Ghaidan v Godin-Mendoza* [2004] UKHL 30 at [45] and [48]; *Alstom Transport v Eurostar International Ltd* [2012] EWHC 28 (Ch) at [37].
[600] *R v Ministry of Agriculture, Fisheries and Food, ex parte FEDESA* [1990] I-4023 at [13]; *R (Countryside Alliance) v Attorney General* [2007] UKHL 52 at [162]–[166]; *R (Sinclar Collis Ltd) v Secretary of State for Health* [2011] EWCA Civ 437 at [20], [115] and [210]; *Zalewska v Department of Social Security* [2008] UKHL 67 at [31]; *Centros Ltd v Erhvervs-og Selskabsstyrelsen* [2000] Ch 446 at [34]; and *R v Secretary of State for the Environment, ex parte Oldham Metropolitan Borough Council* [1998] ICR 367, 384H-385A.
[601] *Duff v Minister of Agriculture* [1996] ECR I-4559 at [24]; *Gondrand Freres* [1981] ECR 1931.
[602] *R v Ministry for Agriculture, Fisheries & Food, ex parte Hamble Fisheries (Offshore) Ltd* [1995] 2 All ER 714, 726A–B; *Milk Marketing Board of England and Wales v Tom Parker Farms Ltd* [1999] EuLR 154, 164F–G.
[603] *Klensch v Secretary of State* [1986] ECR 3477 at [8]–[11]; *Patmalniece v Secretary of State for Work and Pensions* [2011] UKSC 11; *R (Partridge Farms Ltd) v Secretary of State for Environment, Food & Rural Affairs* [2008] EWHC 1645 (Admin).
[604] *R v Secretary of State for the Home Department, ex parte Dannenberg* [1984] QB 766; *R v Secretary of State for Health, ex parte Pfizer Ltd* (1999) 2 CCLR 270, 2841.
[605] Articles 45–48 TFEU; *R (Preston) v Wandsworth London Borough Council* [2011] EWHC 3174; *B v Secretary of State for the Home Department* [2000] UKHRR 498; *R (Conde) v Lambeth London Borough Council* [2005] EWHC 62 (Admin); *R v Secretary of State for the Home Department, ex parte Adams* [1995] All ER (EC) 177.

- freedom of establishment;[606]
- freedom of services;[607]
- freedom of import and export;[608]
- freedom from discrimination.[609]

1.208 In addition to these rights, the EU Charter of Fundamental Rights establishes a framework of rights similar to, but more extensive than, the ECHR.[610] The Charter only applies in cases where EU law is being implemented.[611] The Charter is structured into seven chapters that have the following headings: Dignity, Freedoms, Equality, Solidarity, Citizens Rights, Justice and General Provisions. The rights contained in the Charter have analogues to ECHR rights. For instance:

- The right to life in Article 2 ECHR is reflected in Article 2 of the Charter.
- The prohibition against torture in Article 3 ECHR is reflected in Article 4 of the Charter.
- The right to liberty in Article 5 ECHR is reflected in Article 6 of the Charter.
- The right to respect for private and family life in Article 8 ECHR is reflected in Article 7 of the Charter.

1.209 Article 52(3) of the Charter provides that 'in so far as this Charter contains rights which correspond to rights guaranteed by the [ECHR], the meaning and scope of those rights shall be the same as those laid down by the [ECHR]'. Accordingly, this would appear to mean that the absolute rights in the ECHR would not be subject to a proportionality test, while the qualified rights would be.

1.210 There are several rights in the Charter that appear to go beyond the protections of the ECHR. For instance, there are rights of the elderly to lead a life of dignity,[612] to social and housing assistance to ensure a decent existence,[613] access to preventative health care,[614] and to good administration.[615] In short, the Charter provides for socio-economic rights in a way that is not provided for by the ECHR. However, Article 51 of the Charter suggests that these are not new obligations. Indeed, the preamble states that the Charter 'reaffirms' the rights. Accordingly, it may be that the

---

[606] Articles 49–55; *R v HM Treasury, ex parte Daily Mail & General Trust Plc* [1989] QB 446; *Centros Ltd v Erhvervs-og Selskabsstyrelsen* [2000] Ch 446.
[607] Articles 56–62 TFEU; *R (Low) v Secretary of State for the Home Department* [2010] EWCA Civ 4; *R (Theophilus) v London Borough of Lewisham* [2002] EWHC 1371 (Admin).
[608] Articles 28–29 TFEU; *R (Countryside Alliance) v Attorney General* [2007] UKHL 52; *R (Sinclar Collis) v Secretary of State Health* [2011] EWCA Civ 437; *R (International Transport Roth GmbH) v Secretary of State for the Home Department* [2002] EWCA Civ 158; *R v Ministry of Agriculture, Fisheries & Food, ex parte Hedley Lomas (Ireland) Ltd* [1997] QB 139; *R v Chief Constable of Sussex, ex parte International Trader's Ferry Ltd* [1999] 2 AC 418.
[609] Articles 18–19 TFEU; *R v Secretary of State for Employment, ex parte Equal Opportunities Commission* [1995] 1 AC 1; *R v Secretary of State for Employment, ex parte Seymour-Smith* [1999] 2 AC 554; *Harmon CFEM Facades (UK) Ltd v Corporate Officer of the House of Commons* (1999) 67 Con LR 1.
[610] Initially the UK maintained that it had opted out of the Charter. However, it was eventually conceded that the Charter could be relied upon in domestic law in *NS v Secretary of State for the Home Department* [2010] EWCA Civ 990 at [6]–[7]; *NS v Secretary of State for the Home Department* [2011] EUECJ C-493/10 and NS [2011] EUECJ C-411/10.
[611] Article 6(1), TEU; Article 51 of the Charter.
[612] Article 25 of the Charter.
[613] Article 34(3) of the Charter.
[614] Article 35 of the Charter.
[615] Article 41 of the Charter.

Charter is interpreted as simply bringing together those rights recognised elsewhere in EU law. It remains to be seen which interpretation is adopted.

1.211 There are limited examples of the Charter being applied in practice. In *R (H) v Deputy Prosecutor of the Italian Republic, Genoa*[616] the court recognised that Article 24(2) protects the best interests of the child. In *R (Medhanye) v Secretary of State for the Home Department*[617] it was held that to remove a person to Italy was compatible with the right to dignity under Article 1 of the Charter.

---

[616] [2012] UKSC 25.
[617] [2012] EWHC 1799 (Admin).

CHAPTER 2

REMEDIES

INTRODUCTION

2.01 This chapter considers public law remedies, both interim and final, that may be available on a claim for judicial review. The Administrative Court has a wide range of powers available which originate from statutory and common law sources. All remedies in judicial review are discretionary.[1]

2.02 In summary the remedies are:

- Interim orders, including injunctions, declarations and stays of proceedings: Senior Courts Act 1981, s 37 and the Civil Procedure Rules (CPR) Parts 25 and 54.
- The prerogative orders of quashing, prohibition, and mandatory, injunctions and declarations which may be granted in combination or together: Senior Courts Act 1981, ss 29 and 31 and CPR Part 54.
- Under common law there may be a right to restitution or damages if the claimant can show a recognised tort or breach of contract.
- Under the Human Rights Act 1998 declarations of incompatibility (s 4) and damages for an action breaching Convention Rights (s 8).
- Under EC Law there is full protection of Community Law rights, which may require additional and modified remedies to be available.

INTERIM RELIEF

2.03 At any time in judicial review proceedings the court may grant interim relief as provided for in CPR, Part 25. This includes interim injunctions,[2] interim declarations[3] and the jurisdiction to grant a stay.[4]

Procedure

2.04 Typically, interim remedies are sought when the claim is lodged. CPR, r 54.6 states that the claimant must specify any remedy (including interim) that is being claimed. Interim relief, however, may be sought at any stage of the proceedings.[5] It can also be granted before a claim has been made if the matter is urgent or it is necessary to

---

[1] *R (Hashemi) v The Upper Tribunal (Immigration and Asylum Chamber)* [2013] EWHC 2316 (Admin) at 81.
[2] CPR, r 25.1(1)(a) – including against the Crown: *Re M* [1994] 1 AC 377.
[3] CPR, r 25.1(1)(b).
[4] CPR, r 54.10(2).
[5] CPR, r 25.2(1).

do so in the interests of justice.⁶ A Practice Direction⁷ sets out the procedure to be followed. Although it only refers to interim injunctions the procedure which it sets out is appropriate for other forms of interim relief.

2.05 The most common form of interim relief is an interim injunction and stay of proceedings but the full orders listed in CPR, r 25.1(1) are available.

2.06 In cases of real urgency an application can be made to the out of hours judge. Where an interim application is refused on the papers it can be renewed at an oral hearing.

2.07 In practice it is not uncommon for the Administrative Court to deal with a claim for interim relief in an urgent case by ordering an expedited substantive hearing or a rolled up hearing. That enables it to be able to provide a remedy and to resolve the prospect of lengthy and contested satellite litigation.

Actions against the Crown

2.08 The interim power includes the ability on the part of the court to grant injunctions against ministers of the Crown on claims for judicial review. Initially it was thought that Part II of the Crown Proceedings Act 1947 restricted the court's powers. However, the House of Lords have held that the court has power to make coercive orders, prohibitory and mandatory, against ministers of the Crown: see *M v Home Office*.⁸ That includes the power to grant interim injunctions against ministers where it is necessary to protect rights under EC law. The only occasion now where such a power could not be used is where the power is entirely internal to the state. In those circumstances Community law has no application.⁹ Such occasions are likely to be increasingly few.

2.09 Further, in *M v Home Office*¹⁰ and *Davidson v Scottish Ministers*¹¹ the House of Lords has held that Part II of the 1947 Act applies only to 'civil proceedings' as defined in s 38(2) of the Act and which do not include claims for judicial review. Despite that, the most appropriate remedy against the Crown in both interim and final form is that of a declaration. Although the power to grant injunctions against the Crown exists in practice, it is used sparingly.

Principles on interim relief

2.10 The principles that a court will follow on interim remedies have been heavily influenced by private law.¹² In essence it is an approach of a modified 'balance of convenience'. It is modified to take into account the wider public interest that arises in public law cases. What is required is, firstly, an arguable case for the grant of judicial review and, secondly, the avoidance of the greater risk of injustice. The court will

---

6   CPR, r 25.2(2).
7   Practice Statement (Administrative Court: Listings and Urgent Cases) [2002] 1 WLR 810.
8   [1994] 1 AC 377.
9   *R v Ministry of Agriculture, Fisheries and Food, ex p First City Trading Ltd* [1997] 1 CMLR 250 where Community principles could not be used to review the UK's Beef Transfer Scheme which granted emergency aid to abattoirs after the BSE crisis.
10 [1994] 1 AC 377.
11 [2005] UKHL 74.
12 *American Cyanamid Co v Ethicon Ltd* [1975] AC 396 HL – a balance of convenience is the right approach.

consider the overall case, taking into account the strength of the claim, the importance of maintaining the status quo,[13] the wider public interest and, if relevant, which will be rare in public law cases, the prospect of any monetary order providing an adequate ultimate remedy. Where a public authority is involved 'the balance of convenience has to be looked at more widely and take into account the interests of the public in general to whom these duties are owed.'[14]

Cross undertaking in damages

2.11 The claimant's cross undertaking in damages is clearly more difficult in a public law case. In the case of *Huddleston v Durham County Council*[15] a cross undertaking was not required because of the wider public interest. 'The consequences of work starting without such an environmental assessment may, in my judgment, be such as to make irreversible any harm that might be caused. In those circumstances, it seems to me that there is probably a much wider issue than the narrow one between the applicant and the second respondent in relation to the immediate effect upon the applicant and his family. That wider issue is one that the court can properly have regard to and have regard to notwithstanding the fact that the applicant is not in a position to offer any undertaking as to any financial loss. It may well be, and in my judgment it is likely, that the second respondent could fairly readily satisfy the court that steps will be taken that will prevent any great harm of the kind that is spoken of by English Nature and by the Environment Agency.' Interim relief was granted. It has been said that the requirement for a cross undertaking is essentially a matter for the judge in the exercise of his discretion: *R v Inspectorate of Pollution, ex p Greenpeace*.[16] Consideration of the wider issues arising from the grant of an injunction has been held to be highly relevant in relation to the provision of cross-undertakings by public authorities as to the costs of third parties arising as a consequence of injunctions: *Financial Services Authority v Sinaloa Gold*.[17] In this case, the Supreme Court declined to require local authorities to make cross-undertakings as to third party costs, indicating that to do so might prevent public officials from acting out of a fear for endangering public funds.[18]

Injunctions

2.12 The leading authority on interim relief in public law cases remains *R v Transport Secretary, ex p Factortame (No 2)*.[19] The House of Lords adopted a two stage approach. First, there should be a consideration as to the adequacy of damages as a remedy. There, when the Crown was seeking to enforce the law it may not be appropriate to impose upon the Crown the usual undertaking in respect of damages. The same would apply to a local authority. Second, if there is doubt as to the adequacy of either or both of the respective remedies in damages, then the court proceeds to what is usually called the balance of convenience, and for that purpose will consider 'all the circumstances of the case'. 'In this context, particular stress should be placed upon the importance of upholding the law of the land, in the public interest, bearing in mind the need for stability in our society, and the duty placed upon certain authorities to enforce the law in

---

[13] *R (GSTS Pathology LLP) v Revenue & Customs* [2013] EWHC 1801 (Admin) at 115.
[14] *Smith v Inner London Education Authority* [1978] 1 All ER 411 – a dispute between parents and the LEA over whether to go to comprehensive schooling where the claimant parents had no real prospect of success at full trial.
[15] [1999] EWHC Admin 757.
[16] [1993] EWCA Civ 9.
[17] [2013] UKSC 11.
[18] *Financial Services Authority v Sinaloa Gold* [2013] UKSC 11 at 33–41.
[19] [1991] 1 AC 603.

the public interest. This is, of itself, an important factor to be weighed in the balance when assessing the balance of convenience. So, if a public authority seeks to enforce what is on its face the law of the land, and the person against whom such action is taken challenges the validity of that law, matters of considerable weight have to be put into the balance to outweigh the desirability of enforcing, in the public interest, what is on its face the law, and so to justify the refusal of an interim injunction in favour of the authority, or to render it just or convenient to restrain the authority for the time being from enforcing the law.'

2.13 In *R v Environment Agency, ex p Mayer Parry*[20] the court applied the principles set out in *R v Transport Secretary, ex p Factortame (No 2)* even when the issue was 'what is the law of the land?'[21] The court was asked to grant a mandatory injunction and other interim remedies by way of interim relief. Taking into account the interests of the public to whom a duty was owed the court refused an application for interim relief where the public interest in the receipt of revenue from Packaging Waste Recovery Notes (PRNs) enabling the Secretary of State to meet his obligations under the EC Directive was a forceful consideration and to allow the accreditation of PRNs was likely to lead to administrative difficulties. The court refused to declare or direct alternative payment prior to the substantive hearing and took the view that the public interest was in maintaining the status quo.

2.14 Inevitably, the courts will be more reluctant to grant an interim mandatory injunction compelling a public body to take specific action rather than grant an interim injunction that has the effect of preventing a public body from doing something. The court has said that a claimant seeking an interim mandatory injunction needs to establish a very strong case since an order of that kind is 'one stage removed' from the interim relief that is normally granted.[22] It has been done to keep a residential home open pending appeal.[23]

2.15 Examples of where interim injunctions have been granted are in immigration removal cases,[24] housing/welfare cases, restraining the designation of a protected site on the basis of a claim for incompatibility with primary legislation,[25] and to continue funding for a college placement in a special educational needs case.[26]

2.16 In *R v London Borough of Barnet, ex p Jewish Girls High Ltd*,[27] the court refused to continue an injunction that would have prevented the completion of a sale of land which it had found to be within the powers of the local authority. In making the decision, the court considered that there had been significant prejudice to the public interest in restraining the sale of the land.[28]

---

[20] [2000] EWHC Admin 388.
[21] The court had earlier referred to the ECJ questions on the meaning of recycling under EC Directives on waste and the packaging of waste.
[22] *R v Westminster City Council, ex p Augustin* [1993] 1 WLR 730.
[23] *R v Service Houses and Wandsworth London Borough Council, ex p Goldsmith* [2000] 3 CCLR 354 (granted by the Court of Appeal).
[24] *R (Pharis) v Secretary for State for the Home Department* [2004] EWCA Civ 654.
[25] *William Sinclair v English Nature* [2001] EWHC Admin 408.
[26] *R (S) v Norfolk County Council* [2004] EWHC Admin 404.
[27] [2013] EWHC Admin 523.
[28] *R (Jewish Girls High Ltd) v London Borough of Barnet* [2013] EWHC 523 (Admin) at 22–26.

The European dimension

2.17 There is a difference between the test for interim relief as a matter of European law and as a matter of domestic law. The differences were explored in *R v Secretary of State for Health, ex p Imperial Tobacco Ltd*.[29] Various tobacco companies applied to the court for interim relief pending a ruling from the European court on the validity of a directive. The Court of Appeal refused interim relief and held that the appropriate test was one of European law. The House of Lords held that had they been required to determine the matter they would have referred the issues raised to the European Court. As it was, the issue had been rendered redundant as a result of an opinion on the part of the Advocate General finding the directive invalid.

Interim declarations

2.18 This is a comparatively recent power since the introduction of the CPR. In *R v Environment Agency, ex p Mayer Parry Recycling Ltd*[30] an interim declaration was considered by reference to the balance of convenience. In *R (Ashworth Hospital Authority) v Mental Health Review Tribunal for West Midlands and the North West Region*[31] 'the court should not deprive a person of liberty by injunction or compel him to submit to treatment, except in the most exceptional cases' by way of interim relief.

Stays

2.19 CPR, r 54.10(2) makes it clear that where permission to proceed is given the court can also give directions, including ones that relate to a stay of proceedings to which the claim relates.

2.20 A wide interpretation is given by the courts to proceedings. Proceedings will include not only judicial proceedings, but administrative decisions and the process of arriving at such decisions.[32] 'The purpose of a stay in a judicial review is clear. It is to suspend the "proceedings" that are under challenge pending the determination of the challenge. It preserves the status quo. This will aid the judicial review process and make it more effective. It will ensure, so far as possible, that, if a party is ultimately successful in his challenge, he will not be denied the full benefit of his success', see *R (H) v Ashworth Hospital and others*.[33] The court made it clear that a stay would apply against all orders, even those which have been fully implemented due to the fact that a successful judicial review challenge does in some sense re-write history.

Bail

2.21 Both the High Court and the Court of Appeal have the power to grant bail in judicial review on the basis of the power 'to make ancillary orders temporarily releasing an applicant from detention and that on an appeal in those proceedings this court by

---

[29] [2002] QB 161.
[30] [2000] EWHC Admin 388.
[31] [2001] EWHC Admin 901.
[32] *R v Secretary of State for Education and Science, ex p Avon* [1991] 2 WLR 702 including a stay on the 'process by which the challenged decision has been reached, including the decision itself'. *Cala Homes (South) v Secretary of State for Communities and Local Government* [2010] EWHC 3278 for a recent example of where the balance of convenience favoured that an earlier stay be lifted as agreement on an early date, for an expedited 'rolled up' hearing had been reached and the Secretary of State had given appropriate undertakings.
[33] [2002] EWCA Civ 923.

virtue of s 15(3) of the 1981 Act can make the like order': *R v Secretary of State for the Home Department, ex p Sezek*.[34] By contrast, the Administrative Court has no jurisdiction to interfere with a Crown Court decision not to grant bail, the appropriate course of action to challenge such a decision being an appeal.[35]

THE PREROGATIVE REMEDIES: MANDATORY, PROHIBITING AND QUASHING ORDERS

Mandatory order

2.22 A mandatory order exists to compel the performance of a public duty. It will not be granted to enforce a private law duty, such as restitution of money owing.[36] A mandatory order issues from the High Court and is directed to any person, corporation or inferior tribunal requiring him, or it, to do something specified in the order which relates to an office and is in the nature of a public duty.[37]

2.23 The modern mandatory order is used to compel the performance of a public duty on the part of a public authority or decision-maker. It may compel a court or tribunal to exercise its jurisdiction to determine a case or, where a body has discretion, it may require the body to consider the exercise of the discretion when the occasion arises.[38] A public body may have declined to exercise a jurisdiction on a misconstruction of its statutory remit. In that event, the court will usually order the body to hear and determine the matter according to law.[39]

2.24 A mandatory order can require a public authority to perform a specific act if a statute imposes a clear and unqualified duty to carry it out. In practice such cases are rare. The courts have granted a mandatory order requiring a local authority to pay sums specified by a statutory instrument.[40] Where the statutory duty is on the face of it absolute, the court may read into it an implied exception on public policy grounds. The courts will not grant a mandatory order which will facilitate the commission of a criminal act[41] or allow a person to profit from a criminal act.[42]

2.25 In the case of housing provision a public law duty may give rise to a private law right. In such a case the House of Lords has considered whether the remedy should come through JR or an ordinary claim.[43] It found that no private law right arose as the

---

[34] [2001] EWCA Civ 795.
[35] *Uddin v General Medical Council* [2012] All ER (D) 23.
[36] *R v Barnet Magistrates' Court, ex p Cantor* [1998] 2 All ER 333. Here the court quashed a finding by the magistrates' court that the claimant, who was a beneficiary of a discretionary trust, should pay prosecution costs. The claimant's mother had paid the costs on the claimant's behalf and the court recognised that the claimant had a claim for the repayment of the costs. However, the court would not make a mandatory order and instead made a declaration that the money had been paid as a result of an unlawful order.
[37] *Padfield v Minister of Agriculture, Fisheries and Food* [1968] AC 997 per Lord Reid at 1034, HL.
[38] *R v Tower Hamlets LBC, ex p Chetnik Developments* [1988] AC 858.
[39] Eg *R v Nottingham County Court, ex p Byers* [1985] 1 WLR 403 at 407.
[40] *R v Liverpool City Council, ex p Coade* (1986) *The Times*, 10 October. The wages owed to the claimant by the education authority could be claimed in JR under SCA 1981, s 31(4).
[41] *R v Registrar-General, ex p Smith* [1990] 2 WLR 782. The court refused the claimant's application for JR of the Registrar's refusal to release the details of his biological mother where there was a risk the claimant might attack his mother when he tracked her down.
[42] *R v Chief National Insurance Cssr, ex p Connor* [1981] QB 758. A widow was not allowed to profit by a widow's benefit where she had murdered her husband.
[43] *O'Rourke v London Borough of Camden* [1998] AC 188.

Housing Act which enabled the power was a programme of social benefit of a public nature. Therefore, the court found that the appropriate path was to seek a remedy in Judicial Review. Lewis considers that the principle is likely to be applied generally.[44]

2.26 The court is more willing to grant a mandatory order to compel a public body to take an action of a procedural nature.[45] It will not order a public body to exercise a discretion, still less to exercise a discretion in a particular way.[46] In *Padfield v Minister of Agriculture, Fisheries and Food*[47] the court indicated that the minister should exercise his power to refer a complaint to a committee of investigation. Even in that case the mandatory order required the minister only to consider whether to make the reference. It did not order the minister to make it.

2.27 In *R v Secretary of State for Trade and Industry, ex p Lonrho*[48] the Divisional Court required the minister to make a reference to the Monopolies and Mergers Commission. The Divisional Court was reversed by the Court of Appeal whose decision was upheld by the House of Lords. The House of Lords found that the Divisional Court decision would have the effect of transforming a discretion into a duty.

2.28 In *R (Atamewan) v Secretary of State for the Home Department*,[49] the Administrative Court made a mandatory order that the Secretary of State use her best efforts to secure the return to the UK of a claimant who had been the victim of human trafficking and unlawfully removed to Nigeria.[50]

2.29 In the consideration of European Law the courts will be more willing to take positive action to protect enforceable rights of the individual in domestic courts. In such cases the courts may be required to determine what action must be taken to allow enjoyment of those rights.[51]

2.30 In cases where statutes impose an obligation on a public body to provide services the courts must be careful not to intrude upon the administrative role of a public body by determining the allocation of public funds and finite resources. The courts have refrained from making such orders and instead have construed such obligations: to include a discretion as to how to perform such a duty;[52] or to be a 'target duty';[53] or to be a duty to make reasonable effort or best endeavours;[54] or to be read with a gloss that a body which fails to act may have a just cause or excuse, so that the failure will not constitute a breach.[55]

---

[44] Clive Lewis, *Judicial Remedies in Public Law*, para 6-052 (4th edn, Sweet & Maxwell).
[45] *R (ES) v London Borough of Barking and Dagenham* [2013] EWHC 691 (Admin). The court remitted the case to a local authority in order to make a decision as to accommodation and support. An interim order for accommodation and support were made to stand until a new decision was made.
[46] *R (AS (Lebanon)) v Secretary of State for the Home Department* [2012] EWHC 1349 (Admin) at 37.
[47] [1968] AC 997.
[48] DC in *The Times*, 18 January 1989, CA in (1989) New LJ 150 and HL in [1989] 1 WLR 525.
[49] [2013] EWHC 2727 (Admin).
[50] *R (Atamewan) v Secretary of State for the Home Department* [2013] EWHC 2727 (Admin) at 103.
[51] *R v Secretary of State for Transport, ex p Factortame Ltd (No 2)* [1991] 1 AC 603 at 643–645, paras 18–19.
[52] *R v Lancashire CC, ex p Guyer* [1980] 1 WLR 1024 at 1033 per Stephenson LJ – a discretion found in how a local authority performed its duty to protect a right of way. Lancashire CC had only to act to protect a right of way where there was no serious dispute over the status of the highway.
[53] *R v Inner London Education Authority, ex p Ali* (1990) 2 Admin LR 822. Where an education authority fails to meet required education provision through no fault of its own no breach of duty occurs.
[54] *R v Bristol Corpn, ex p Hendy* [1974] 1 WLR 498 at 501 per Lord Denning MR. The local authority 'have only to do the best they can'.
[55] *R v Inner London Education Authority, ex p Ali* (1990) 2 Admin LR 822; *Meade v Haringey LBC* [1979]

2.31 The courts will often make a declaration rather than resort to a mandatory order on the basis that the public body may be relied on to comply with the duty set out in the declaration without the need for a coercive order.[56] Where a declaration is made the court may give the claimant liberty to apply for further relief if the respondent does not act upon it.[57]

2.32 As with all the JR remedies, the grant of a mandatory order is within the discretion of the court. It may be sought where there is an alternative remedy but the remedy is less beneficial and effective.[58] Disobedience of a mandatory order is a contempt of court and is punishable by fine or imprisonment.[59]

2.33 In the case of a corporate body the order should be addressed to each member of the body, and the individuals who have control of the body should be named in the writ of attachment.[60] Findings of contempt can be made against a government department or a minister acting in his official capacity.[61] In such cases the finding of contempt will not be enforced punitively against the minister. The finding of contempt is considered to be sufficient in itself to force the department or minister to act to obey the order. RSC Order 53, r 10 provided that no action or prosecution might be begun against any person in respect of actions taken to obey a mandatory order. It is thought that this principle still applies following the introduction of the CPR although there is no longer any express provision to that effect.

2.34 The CPR makes no provision for the awarding of an interim remedy where the claimant seeks a mandatory order; but a mandatory interim injunction can now be granted in a claim for JR.[62]

2.35 Mandatory orders will not lie to compel the performance of a moral duty[63] or order anything contrary to law. According to De Smith[64] the narrow technicalities that once applied to the grant of mandamus no longer restrict the remedy of a mandatory order.[65] It is desirable that the claimant should be able to show that he has demanded performance of a duty and that that duty has been refused by the authority obliged to

---

1 WLR 637 at 650 per Eveleigh LJ. Provided the Council (as education authority) have a 'just and reasonable excuse' for their action there would be no breach of duty.
56 Eg *R v Secretary of State for Home Dept, ex p Anderson* [1984] QB 778 at 795 per Robert Goff LJ; *R (van Hoogstraten) v Governor of Belmarsh Prison* [2003]1 WLR 263 at para 47. The prison authorities refused to let an individual (Di S) visit Mr van Hoogstraten in prison. Di S was an Italian advocate who Mr van Hoogstraten claimed had a right to visit him as a legal advisor. The court made a declaration that Mr van Hoogstraten's visitor should be allowed access to him but refused to make a mandatory order in case the prison found grounds to refuse Di S access on grounds of his character. *Sunderland City Council, R (on the application of) v South Tyneside Council* [2011] EWHC 2355 (Admin): The court made a declaration as to which was the responsible local authority for the care of a young man with special care needs.
57 *R v Liverpool City Corps, ex p Ferguson and Ferguson* [1985] IRLR 501. The court quashed a decision of the education authority not to pay teachers who could not work because schools were closed due to strike action by janitorial staff. The court set a date by which the authority should pay the arrears to the teachers and gave them liberty to apply for further relief.
58 *R v Thomas* [1892] 1 QB 426 at 431 per Wills J, DC, 'under which circumstances the remedy by appeal would not be as satisfactory and effectual as the remedy by mandamus'.
59 *R v Poplar MBC, ex p Metropolitan Asylums Board (No 2)* [1922] 1 KB 95 at 105 per Lord Sterndale MR, CA.
60 *R v Poplar MBC, ex p Metropolitan Asylums Board (No 2)* [1922] 1 KB 95 at 105–106 per Lord Sterndale MR, CA.
61 *M v Home Office* [1994] 1 AC 377 at 427 per Lord Woolf.
62 *R v Kensington and Chelsea Royal LBC, ex p Hammell* [1989] QB 518 at 529–531.
63 Eg to make good an officer's pay: *ex p Napier* (1852) 18 QB 692.
64 *De Smith's Judicial Review* (6th edn, Sweet & Maxwell).
65 Clive Lewis, *Judicial Remedies in Public Law*, para 6-066 (4th edn, Sweet & Maxwell).

discharge it. Before applying for JR the claimant should address a specific demand or request to the defendant that he perform the duty imputed to him.[66] The Pre-Action Protocol for Judicial Review obliges a claimant to take this step by writing a letter to the defendant before claim.

2.36 The court has declined to grant mandatory orders which would force a decision-maker to make a decision in a particular manner, instead leaving the decision-maker to reconsider the matter: *SM v Secretary of State for the Home Department*.[67] The court has also opted not to make mandatory orders where there is already a change in motion as to the challenged policy: *R (MA) v Secretary of State for Work and Pensions*.[68]

Prohibiting order

2.37 A prohibiting order is an order issuing from the High Court and directed to an inferior court, tribunal, public authority or other body whose decisions are justifiable which forbids that body to act in excess of its jurisdiction or contrary to law. Whereas quashing orders exist to quash a decision already made, prohibiting orders are used to prevent the respondent from acting or continuing to act in such a way as to exceed or abuse its jurisdiction.[69]

Examples of when a prohibiting order has been granted

2.38 These have included against magistrates to prevent them exceeding their jurisdiction;[70] a prison board of visitors seeking to hear a charge that they had no power to deal with;[71] a local authority to prohibit it acting on a licensing resolution regarding taxis;[72] a minister to prevent him making an invalid clearance order;[73] a rent tribunal seeking to proceed with a case outside its jurisdiction;[74] Electricity Commissioners seeking to hold an inquiry in order to bring into force an *ultra vires* scheme of supply;[75] and a chief medical officer likely to act with bias.[76]

---

[66] *R v Horsham DC, ex p Wenman* [1995] 1 WLR 680 at 709 per Brooke J: 'Lawyers acting for a party should not regard it as unnecessary to write a letter before action merely because they believe it to be inevitable that the response will deny their clients' claim.'.
[67] *SM v Secretary of State for the Home Department* [2013] EWHC 1144 (Admin) at 58–59.
[68] [2013] EWHC 2213 (QB) at 92.
[69] *R v Horseferry Road Justices, ex p Independent Broadcasting Authority* [1987] QB 54. The court quashed a summons by the magistrates' court where the court found no criminal offence was intended to be created by s 4(3) of the Broadcasting Act 1981. An informant (Norris McWhirter) alleged that ITV had committed an offence under the Act by inserting a single frame into an edition of Spitting Image, which showed a puppet of the informant in an unflattering light.
[70] *R v Horseferry Road Justices, ex p Independent Broadcasting Authority* [1987] QB 54.
[71] *R v Board of Visitors of Dartmoor Prison, ex p Smith* [1987] QB 106 at 127.
[72] *R v Liverpool Corps, ex p Liverpool Taxi Fleet Operators' Assoc* [1972] 2 QB 299 at 309 per Lord Denning MR.
[73] *R v Minister of Health, ex p Davis* [1929] 1 KB 619 at 628, CA.
[74] *R v Tottenham and District Rent Tribunal, ex p Northfield (Highgate) Ltd* [1957] 1 QB 103 at 107 per Lord Goddard CJ DC.
[75] *R v Electricity Cssrs, ex p London Electricity Joint Committee Co (1920) Ltd* [1924] 1 KB 171 at 197 per Bankes LJ, CA.
[76] *R v Kent Police Authority, ex p Godden* [1971] 2 QB 662 at 670, [1971] 3 All ER 20, CA: prohibition against a chief medical officer examining a police officer to determine whether the officer was to be compulsorily retired when the doctor was likely to be biased having recently examined the officer for another purpose.

Earliest time for application

2.39 An application for JR seeking a prohibiting order may be made as soon as the complete absence of jurisdiction is apparent on the record of the inferior court,[77] and without the question of jurisdiction having been raised in the inferior court.[78] The applicant will not have to raise an objection before the inferior court even when the defect is not clear upon the record in cases: (i) where the question is one of law not dependent on disputed facts;[79] or (ii) when he contends that the tribunal is so constituted such that there is a likelihood of bias.[80]

2.40 A prohibiting order must be invoked at an early stage when there remains something to be done that the court can prohibit. Similarly a quashing order will not lie unless a decision has been made that a court can quash.[81] However, sometimes both are pursued where a quashing order is required to quash an order made in excess of a tribunal or court's jurisdiction, and a prohibiting order is required to prevent the tribunal or court from continuing to exceed its jurisdiction.

Quashing orders

2.41 A quashing order is an order of the High Court by which it quashes a decision of an inferior court or tribunal, public authority or other body, which is susceptible to judicial review.

2.42 In order to found a claim for a quashing order a decision must exist to be quashed.[82] A quashing order is not available against a view expressed in correspondence or against a recommendation.[83] It can lie against a preliminary decision (*R v Postmaster General, ex p Carmichael*[84]). The form of the decision is immaterial. The decision can be in the form of a report or even of inactivity.[85] The decision must have had some legal effect and must affect identifiable 'subjects'.[86]

2.43 The primary role of the quashing order in modern public law is to quash an *ultra vires* decision. The order is technically an order bringing the decision of the decision-making body to the High Court so that the court may decide whether the decision is valid. Where the decision is found to be *ultra vires* a quashing order may be issued that will quash the decision. By quashing the decision the order confirms that the

---

[77] *London Corps v Cox* (1867) LR 2 HL 239: 'Where ... it is apparent on the record that the [court] never had jurisdiction ... the case is ripe for decision without waiting for any further pleading' per Lord Cranworth at 293.
[78] *London Corps v Cox* (1867) LR 2 HL 239 at 291 per Willes J.
[79] *R v Tottenham and District Rent Tribunal, ex p Northfield (Highgate) Ltd* [1957] 1 QB 103 at 108, [1956] 2 All ER 863, DC.
[80] *R v Kent Police Authority, ex p Godden* [1971] 2 QB 662 at 670, [1971] 3 All ER 20, CA. *R (Al-Hasan) v Secretary of State for the Home Department* [2005] UKHL 13 [2005] 1 WLR 688 where a deputy prison governor conducted a disciplinary hearing relating to disobeying an order given when he was present.
[81] *R (Siwak) v London Borough of Newham* [2012] EWHC 1520 (Admin) at 28–31 where consultation was still in progress, there had not yet been a decision that could be challenged.
[82] *R v St Lawrence's Hospital Statutory Visitors, ex p Pritchard* [1953] 1 WLR 1158 at 1166 per Parker J: 'this motion fails on the ground that there is no decision or determination to be quashed'.
[83] *R v Secretary of State for Employment, ex p Equal Opportunities Commission* [1995] 1 AC 1 at 25 per Lord Keith. In that case a declaration was appropriate remedy at 37 per Lord Browne-Wilkinson.
[84] [1928] 1 KB 291.
[85] *R v Hillingdon LBC, ex p Streeting* [1980] 1 WLR 1425 at 1432: The director of housing at the authority wrote to the claimant 'I do not propose to notify any other housing authority that your application for assistance in obtaining accommodation has been made'.
[86] *R v Criminal Injuries Compensation Board, ex p Lain* [1967] 2 QB 864 at 892 per Lord Parker CJ.

decision is a nullity to be deprived of legal effect. The House of Lords has said that a quashing order is the primary and most appropriate remedy for achieving the nullification of a public law decision.[87]

2.44 If, on an application for JR, the High Court quashes the decision to which the application relates, it may remit the matter to the court, tribunal or authority which made the decision with a direction to reconsider the matter and reach a decision in accordance with the findings of the High Court.[88] On some occasions the High Court may substitute its own decision for the decision challenged in the application. This course is open to the court only if: (i) the decision in question was made by a court or tribunal; (ii) the decision quashed was quashed on the ground of an error of law; and (iii) without the error of law there would have been only one decision that the original court or tribunal could have reached.[89] Unless the High Court otherwise directs, a decision substituted under s 31(5A) of the SCA 1981 has effect as if it were the decision of the original court[90] or tribunal.[91]

2.45 A quashing order lies to quash any decision of a public law body exercising public law powers. A quashing order can quash a licence,[92] directions to remove an immigrant,[93] the resolution of a local authority to adopt a particular policy,[94] a grant of planning permission[95] or a grant of a tenancy.[96]

2.46 A quashing order can be twinned with a declaration. This is useful where the precise consequences of quashing a decision need to be made clear. It may be paired with other JR remedies where appropriate. The judicial review jurisdiction and the prerogative remedies lay against any body exercising public law powers, whether derived from statute, the prerogative[97] or other non-statutory sources.[98]

---

[87] Cocks v Thanet DC [1981] UKHL 10, [1982] 3 All ER 1135, [1983] 2 AC 286 at 5.
[88] Senior Courts Act 1981 s 31(5) (s 31(5) subsequently substituted by s 31(5), (5A), (5B) of the Tribunals, Courts and Enforcement Act 2007, s 141).
[89] Senior Courts Act 1981, s 31(5A) as substituted.
[90] Senior Courts Act, s 31(5B) as substituted.
[91] CPR, r 54.19 (3) – the CPR enables the court not only to reverse the decision but also to require what is just to be done in a particular case, see *R v Northumberland Compensation Appeal Tribunal, ex p Shaw* [1952] 1 KB 338 at 347, [1952] 1 All ER 122 at 127–128, CA per Denning LJ. But where certain facts have been admitted by counsel during the JR proceedings the court will not make a direction based on such admissions: *R v Vaccine Damage Tribunal, ex p Loveday* (1985) The Times, 20 April, CA.
[92] *R v North Hertfordshire DC, ex p Cobbold* [1985] 3 All ER 486. A licence to hold an open-air concert was quashed as the condition requiring agreement on policing levels could not be met and could not be severed from the licence as a whole (Mann J).
[93] *R v Immigration Officer, ex p Shah* [1982] 1 WLR 544 at 550 per Woolf J.
[94] *R v Liverpool City Council, ex p Secretary of State for Employment* [1989] COD 404. The decision of the Council to withhold grants from an organisation wishing to join an Employment Training Scheme in order to put pressure on the organisation was unlawful.
[95] *R v Great Yarmouth BC, ex p Botton Bros Arcades Ltd* (1988) 56 P&CR 99. No duty existed to hear objectors but fairness required they be heard and so certiorari would issue to quash the decision (Otton J).
[96] *R v Port Talbot BC, ex p Jones* [1988] 2 All ER 207, (1987) 20 HLR 265 at 277 per Nolan J. A decision of the Council to allocate a council house to a member of the council outside the ordinary criteria for allocation was quashed. The applicant was the leader of the council, which made the wrongful allocation.
[97] *R v Secretary of State for Foreign and Commonwealth Affairs, ex p Everett* [1989] QB 811 at 817 per O'Connor LJ: whether an act under the prerogative was amenable to JR was a question of the nature of the act. The issuing of a passport was an administrative act affecting an individual's freedom to travel and was not likely to raise issues of foreign policy and thus was amenable to Judicial Review.
[98] *Reg v Criminal Injuries Compensation Board, ex p Lain* [1967] 2 QB 864; *R v Panel on Take-overs and Mergers, ex p Datafin plc* [1987] QB 815 at 835–836, 846–849. The panel considered itself to be a body deriving its authority entirely from the consent of parties but the court found that in fact it carried on public law duties with public law sanctions and was thus amenable to JR. *R v Norfolk CC, ex p M* [1989] QB 619 at 628 per Waite J: the register of sex offenders and suspected sex offenders operated by the Council was,

2.47 It was thought quashing orders could not lie against non-binding acts, such as advisory opinions and reports, of those exercising public law powers;[99] but it is now clear that a quashing order may be issued in appropriate circumstances to quash a recommendation.[100] The courts may grant a declaration that a non-binding advisory circular is *ultra vires*,[101] and that a report is void.[102] There does not appear to be any reason now why a quashing order would not be available in similar circumstances. A hypothetical order would confirm that an unlawful act had occurred and confirm that the circular or report should not be relied upon.

2.48 It is sometimes suggested that quashing orders serve no purpose in the case of nullities, since a nullity is without a legal effect for the order to quash. However, the quashing order serves a purpose in this respect, that it establishes the invalidity of the act and makes clear that it is a nullity without legal effect. The quashing order clarifies the position and allows parties to act, confident that the court recognises the lack of legal effect of the challenged decision.

2.49 The Divisional Court has held that a quashing order is available to quash a decision which is a nullity.[103] The court held that an unlawful acquittal was a nullity which did not allow the acquitted person to rely upon the concept of 'double jeopardy' or *autrefois acquit* to resist a fresh prosecution. The court found that the quashing order was a 'convenient way of preventing the continuance of an ostensible effect'.[104] However, the court indicated that the more suitable remedy to force the continuation of the trial by the Justices was for the DPP to seek a mandatory order compelling the trial to continue. Where the same result would otherwise have been reached, the Administrative Court has refused to grant a quashing order, finding that to do so would constitute an unmerited windfall for a claimant: *R (Ivlev) v Entry Clearance Officer, New York*.[105] Further, the Administrative Court has declined to grant a quashing order and remit a case where it would serve no useful purpose to do so.[106]

---

despite its administrative character, available to a significant enough part of the public to impose a duty upon the Council to act fairly in its operation. M (against whom two complaints had been made but no charges preferred) was added to the register without prior consultation or details of the reasons for the Council's decision to add him. The Council's decision to add him to the register was quashed.

[99] *R v Statutory Visitors to St Lawrance's Hospital Caterham, ex p Pritchard* [1953] 1 WLR 1158. The report of a board of visitors to a hospital was found not to be amenable to Judicial Review. This DC decision is now considered qualified.

[100] *R v Agricultural Dwelling-House Advisory Committee for Bedfordshire Cambridgeshire and Northamptonshire, ex p Brough* (1986) 19 HLR 367. The advisory report of a committee advising a local housing authority on an application for a dwelling by an agricultural worker was found to be amenable to JR and was quashed, as the opinion was likely to be followed by the housing authority. *R (London Borough of Lewisham) v Secretary of State for Health* [2013] EWHC 2329 (Admin) at 94: The recommendations made by a trustee as to the reconfiguration of NHS services were quashed due to the trustee exceeding his jurisdiction regarding which services were within his remit.

[101] *Gillick v West Norfolk and Wisbech Area Health Authority* [1986] AC 112 at 193–194 per Lord Bridge: 'But the occasions of a departmental non-statutory publication raising … a clearly defined issue of law, unclouded by political, social or moral overtones, will be rare. In cases where any proposition of law implicit in a departmental advisory document is interwoven with questions of social and ethical controversy, the court should, in my opinion, exercise its jurisdiction with the utmost restraint …'.

[102] *Grunwick Processing Laboratories v Advisory, Conciliation and Arbitration Service* [1978] AC 655 at 705 per Lord Keith. A recommendation by ACAS that a union should be recognised was based upon insufficient consultation of the relevant workforce (only one third were consulted) and thus was void.

[103] *R v Hendon Justices, ex p DPP* [1994] QB 167 at 178 per Mann LJ.

[104] *R v Hendon Justices, ex p DPP* [1994] QB 167 at 178 per Mann LJ: 'We recognise the defiance of logic in stating that the order can go, but in practice decisions which are nullities are quashed as a convenient way of preventing the continuance of any ostensible effect.'.

[105] [2013] EWHC 1162 (Admin) at 114.

[106] *R (Roberts) v The Welsh Ministers* [2011] EWHC 3416 (Admin) at 159.

2.50 The Court of Appeal held that judicial review was available to determine whether a draft order in council which was laid before Parliament for approval but was not yet submitted to Her Majesty in Council was within the powers conferred in the enabling Act.[107] The appropriate remedy was considered to be a declaration as a quashing order might be perceived as an attempt to restrain Parliament in its discussions.

2.51 A quashing order may be insufficient in cases where the claimant is challenging a decision to refuse to exercise a discretionary power. In such a case a quashing order would merely establish that the decision-maker has acted unlawfully, but would not of itself compel the public body to consider exercising the discretionary power. In such a case the quashing order may need to be coupled with a mandatory order compelling the authority to consider exercising its discretion or to hear the case according to law.[108]

2.52 The court may grant a quashing order with leave to apply for further relief in case the public authority does not act according to law.[109] The court has the power to quash the decision and remit the matter to the original decision-maker with a direction to decide the matter in accordance with the court's judgment.[110]

2.53 Where a public body is under a duty to act and has refused to act the court may, instead of making a mandatory order, make a quashing order and accompany it with a declaration setting out the extent of the public body's obligations. In a case where a local health authority refused to provide psychiatric care services, the court quashed the refusal, and made a declaration clarifying the extent of the health authority's duties and invited the health authority to reconsider the claimant's case in light of the judgment.[111]

2.54 Where a public authority misconstrues its jurisdiction and threatens to exceed it the appropriate remedy is a prohibiting order, or injunction, sometimes in conjunction with a quashing order to quash the decision to act beyond its powers.[112] In the case of *R (London Borough of Lewisham) v Secretary of State for Health*,[113] the court quashed a decision made in reliance upon recommendations by a trustee who had exceeded their powers. However, the court may simply issue a quashing order to quash the decision to act on the basis that the public authority is unlikely to continue to act unlawfully when the quashing order has established the illegality.[114]

Severance

2.55 Where only part of a decision is invalid, and that part can be separated from the valid part of the decision, the court may grant a quashing order to quash the invalid part whilst leaving the valid part untouched.[115]

---

[107] *R v HM Treasury, ex p Smedley* [1985] QB 657 at 666–667.
[108] *R v Tower Hamlets LBC, ex p Chetnik Developments Ltd* [1987] 1 WLR 593 at 605–606 (affirmed by the HoL [1988] AC 858 – a quashing order was granted to quash the Council's decision to refuse a discretionary refund and a mandatory order was made to make the Council hear and determine the matter according to law).
[109] *R v Police Complaints Board, ex p Madden* [1987] 1 WLR 447 at 472; *R v Hillingdon LBC, ex p Royco Homes Ltd* [1974] 2 QB 720 at 732.
[110] Senior Courts Act 1981, s 31(5); CPR, r 54.19(2).
[111] *R v Ealing Local Health Authority, ex p Fox* [1993] 1 WLR 373 at 387.
[112] *R v Horseferry Road Justices, ex p Independent Broadcasting Authority* [1986] 3 WLR 132, [1987] QB 54 at 73 per Lloyd LJ.
[113] [2013] EWHC 2329 (Admin).
[114] *R v Commission for Racial Equality, ex p Hillingdon BC* [1982] AC 779 at 793.
[115] The same principles apply as in declarations; *R v Secretary of State for Transport, ex p GLC* [1986] QB 556.

2.56 In *DPP v Hutchinson*[116] the House of Lords held that there were two aspects to the test of severance in public law: the ability to sever the act textually and in its substance. A legislative act was severable textually if the offending clause, phrase, sentence or word could be removed from the text without compromising the coherence or grammar of the provision. The act was severable in substance if what remained was unchanged in its legislative purpose, operation and effect. If both tests were satisfied, the act could be severed. In certain cases an act would not be textually severable but would be severable in substance. The court might in such cases still be able to sever the act and find it only partially invalid.

2.57 In *Hutchinson* the byelaw was not severable and was, therefore, found to be invalid in its entirety. *Hutchinson* related to delegated legislation but it is thought that it can be extended to other public law acts and decisions. In *R v IRC, ex p Woolwich Equitable Building Society*[117] a regulation imposing income tax liability could be altered by severing the paragraph that was *ultra vires*. However, the offending paragraph specified the rate of tax to be paid as being that in the 1985–86 tax year. The paragraph could not be severed in substance, since its removal would require the substitution of another tax rate from another year which would change the purpose and effect of the regulation. In *Woolwich* the entire regulation had to be quashed.

2.58 The test of severability has been used in determining whether conditions attached to licences or planning permissions can be severed leaving a functioning licence or permission intact without having to quash the whole decision. The courts have considered whether the condition can be removed without altering the character of the licence or permission. If the licence or provision would be fundamentally different, it has to be quashed.[118]

2.59 In *Hutchinson* Lord Bridge considered that severance might not be applicable to the resolution of a public authority to appropriate land where the power of the authority did not extend to all of the land.[119] In such cases Lord Bridge considered the language of severance to be inappropriate. Instead the resolution should be construed to determine which land was affected.

Restrictions on quashing orders

2.60 Some restrictions remain upon quashing orders. Quashing orders may not lie against superior courts.[120] Superior courts include the Supreme Court, the Court of Appeal, the High Court, Masters of the Supreme Court,[121] and the Courts-Martial Appeal Court.[122] The Supreme Court (as constituted prior to the Constitutional Reform Act 2005) was the Court of Appeal, the High Court of Justice and the Crown Court.[123]

---

[116] [1990] 2 AC 783 – byelaw imposed by the Secretary of State for Defence relating to the military base at Greenham Common took away the rights of commoners which rights he was not allowed to limit by the terms of the enabling Act.
[117] [1990] 1 WLR 1400.
[118] *R v North Hertfordshire DC, ex p Cobbold* [1985] 3 All ER 486; *Hall v Shoreham-by-Sea Urban DC* [1964] 1 WLR 240.
[119] *DPP v Hutchinson* [1990] 2 AC 783 at 810.
[120] *R v Oxenden* (1691) 89 ER 545; *Suratt and others v Att-Gen of Trinidad and Tobago* [2008] 2 WLR 262 at para 49.
[121] *Murrell v British Leyland Trustees* [1989] COD 389.
[122] Section 1 of the Courts-Martial (Appeals) Act 1968. Courts martial in times of martial law operate entirely outside the law and are not subject to JR: *Re Clifford and O'Sullivan* [1921] 2 AC 570.
[123] Section 1 of the Senior Courts Act 1981.

The courts have also refused to grant quashing orders where the effect of the illegality would be immaterial or inconsequential.[124]

Examples of where quashing orders have been granted

2.61 These have included orders against a department of state,[125] an individual minister's order,[126] a local authority's grant of planning permission[127] or a licence,[128] a valuation officer,[129] an immigration officer,[130] licensing justices,[131] the Gaming Board (as was, now the Gambling Commission),[132] the Police Complaints Board,[133] an election court,[134] rent tribunals,[135] a medical appeal tribunal,[136] a diary produce quotas tribunal,[137] the Health and Safety Commission,[138] a prison board of visitors,[139] a prison governor in respect of a disciplinary award,[140] the Commission for Racial Equality[141] (as was), and the mental health commissioners.[142]

---

[124] *R (Ivlev) v Entry Clearance Officer, New York* [2013] EWHC 1162 (Admin); *R (Adams) v The Commission for Local Administration in England* [2011] EWHC 2972 (Admin) at 33.

[125] *Board of Education v Rice* [1911] AC 179 at 182 per Lord Loreburn LC, HL.

[126] *R v Secretary of State for the Environment, ex p Brent LBC* [1982] QB 593 at 646–647 per Ackner LJ [1982] 2 WLR 693: the Secretary of State had fettered his discretion when making an order under the Local Govt, Planning and Land Act 1980; *R v Secretary of State for Home Dept, ex p Dannenberg* [1984] QB 766 at 777 per Dunn LJ [1984] 2 All ER 481, CA: the deportation order made by the Secretary of State failed to give reasons and was invalid on its face and had to be quashed; *R v Secretary of State for the Environment, ex p Binney* (1983) *The Times*, 8 October: Where there were two large groups of residents, one opposing and one supporting a road scheme, no reasonable minister could find an inquiry was unnecessary.

[127] *R v Hillingdon LBC, ex p Royco Homes Ltd* [1974] QB 720, [1974] 2 All ER 643 at 732 per Lord Widgery CJ, DC.

[128] *R v London CC, ex p Entertainments Protection Association* [1931] 2 KB 215 at 234 per Scrutton LJ, CA: a council granted a cinema licence beyond its jurisdiction contrary to the Sunday Observance Act 1780.

[129] *R v Paddington Valuation Officer, ex p Peachey Property Corps Ltd* [1966] 1 QB 380 at 400–401 per Lord Denning MR, [1965] 2 All ER 836, CA.

[130] *R v Chief Immigration Officer, Lympne Airport, ex p Amrik Singh* [1969] 1 QB 333 at 342 per Lord Parker CJ, [1968] 3 WLR 945, DC; *R v Chief Immigration Officer, Gatwick Airport, ex p Kharrazi* [1980] 1 WLR 1396 at 1404 per Lord Denning MR, CA.

[131] *R v Dudley Justices, ex p Curlett* [1974] 1 WLR 457 at 460 per Lord Widgery CJ, [1974] 1 WLR 457, DC: the granting of an alcohol license with a condition unknown to law, *R v Barnsley MBC, ex p Hook* [1976] 1 WLR 1052 at 1058 per Lord Denning MR, CA: the decision of the Council to revoke a street trader's license offended the principles of natural justice.

[132] *R v Gaming Board for Great Britain, ex p Benaim and Khaida* [1970] 2 QB 417 at 430–432 per Lord Denning MR, [1970] 2 WLR 1009, CA (relief refused on the facts).

[133] *R v Police Complaints Board, ex p Madden* [1983] 1 WLR 447 at 471 per McNeill J.

[134] *R v Cripps, ex p Muldoon* [1984] QB 68 at 89 per Robert Goff LJ, DC; affirmed [1984] QB 686, [1984] 2 All ER 705, CA.

[135] *R v Fulham, Hammersmith and Kensington Rent Tribunal, ex p Zerek* [1951] 2 KB 1 at 13 per Lord Goddard CJ, DC.

[136] *R v Medical Appeal Tribunal, ex p Gilmore* [1957] 1 QB 574 at 585 per Denning LJ, CA.

[137] *R v Dairy Produce Quotas Tribunal, ex p S Dimelow Farms* (1988) *The Times*, 7 November.

[138] *R v Health and Safety Commission, ex p Spelthorne BC* (1983) *The Times*, 18 July.

[139] *R v Blundeston Prison Board of Visitors, ex p Fox-Taylor* [1982] 1 All ER 646. Where the board of visitors were aware of evidence to aid a prisoner in his disciplinary hearing but did not inform the prisoner of the existence of the witness there was a breach of natural justice. The court quashed the finding of the board.

[140] *Leech v Deputy Governor of Parkhurst Prison* [1988] AC 533 at 568 per Lord Bridge, [1988] 1 All ER 485, HL, 'it can hardly be doubted that governors and deputy governors dealing with offences against discipline may occasionally fall short of the standards of fairness which are called for in the performance of any judicial function. Nothing, I believe, is so likely to generate unrest among ordinary prisoners as a sense that they have been treated unfairly and have no effective means of redress'.

[141] *R v Commission for Racial Equality, ex p Hillingdon LBC* [1982] QB 276 at 289 per Lord Denning MR, CA (affirmed [1982] AC 779, HL), 'the Commission for Racial Equality is a public body, its proceedings can be challenged by judicial review, no matter whether they are regarded as judicial or administrative. There is no need to go into the many cases on the subject. We have had them so often. The central principle is that a

Injunctions to restrain a person from acting in office

2.62 The High Court may grant an injunction to restrain a person from acting in certain public offices[143] in which he is not entitled to act[144] and, where necessary, declare the office vacant.[145]

2.63 The order must be sought by way of JR.[146] The conduct of the applicant may be considered before the awarding of an injunction.[147]

DECLARATIONS AND INJUNCTIONS

2.64 An application for a declaration or an injunction[148] may be made by way of an application for JR.[149] In such a case the court may grant the declaration or injunction if it considers that it would be just and convenient to grant it having regard to the factors in SCA 1981, s 31(2)(a)–(c).

2.65 The jurisdiction to grant declaratory or injunctive relief is concurrent with the jurisdiction to grant these remedies in private law claims.[150] However, a person seeking to establish that a public authority has by its decision infringed his rights that are protected under public law should pursue a remedy through JR and not by way of an ordinary claim.[151]

Injunction

2.66 An injunction is a discretionary, equitable remedy awarded by superior courts or, with some limitations, by a county court judge, to restrain an imminent threat or the commission or continuance of, an unlawful act or to compel the taking of steps to repair an unlawful omission or to restore the damage inflicted by an unlawful act. An injunction can therefore be prohibitory or mandatory.[152]

2.67 An injunction will not be issued to secure the provision of services which the court cannot effectively supervise,[153] or where damages are an adequate remedy.

---

public body must exercise its powers and carry out its duties in accordance with the intentions of Parliament, express or implied. It must not go beyond the bounds. If it does, its conduct is ultra vires and the courts can interfere to put it right'.

[142] *R v Mental Health Commission, ex p W* (1988) *The Times*, 27 May. The Commissioners had no power to refuse a course of treatment to a patient diagnosed with a sexual perversion.

[143] A substantive office of a public nature and permanent character which is held under the Crown or which has been created by a statutory provision or royal charter: Senior Courts Act 1981, s 30(2).

[144] Senior Courts Act 1981, s 30(1)(a).

[145] Senior Courts Act 1981, s 30(1)(b).

[146] Senior Courts Act 1981, s 31(1)(c), CPR, r 54.2(d).

[147] *Everett v Griffiths* [1924] 1 KB 941 at 958 per McCardie J.

[148] Not including an injunction under Senior Courts Act 1981, s 30 to restrain a person from acting in an office in which he is not entitled to act: CPR, r 54.2.

[149] Senior Courts Act 1981, s 31(1)(b) and s 31(2) and CPR, r 54.3.

[150] Eg *Gillick v West Norfolk and Wisbech Area Health Authority* [1986] AC 112, [1985] 3 All ER 402, HL.

[151] *O'Reilly v Mackman* [1983] 2 AC 237, [1982] 3 All ER 1124, HL.

[152] On mandatory injunctions see *Redland Bricks Ltd v Morris* [1970] AC 652, [1969] 2 All ER 576, HL.

[153] *Attorney-General v Colchester Corporation* [1955] 2 QB 207, [1955] 2 All ER 124 (no mandatory injunction to order continuance of a ferry service); *Dowty Boulton Paul Ltd v Wolverhampton Corps* [1971] 2 All ER 277, [1971] 1 WLR 204 (no injunction to order maintenance of an airfield); Cf. Unusual case in *Warwickshire CC v British Railways Board* [1969] 3 All ER 631, [1969] 1 WLR 1117, CA (prohibitory injunction to restrain invalid closure of a railway line).

2.68 Injunctions, both final and interim, may be granted against an officer of the Crown and he may be held in contempt if he breaches an injunction.[154] An injunction can be granted by a court even though compliance with the injunction may lead to practical difficulties.[155]

2.69 An injunction will not be granted to restrain proceedings in Parliament[156] but it seems that a body can be restrained from spending public money to introduce or oppose a private Bill in Parliament.[157] The courts may issue an injunction in relation to a statutory instrument even when that instrument has been laid before both Houses of Parliament.[158]

Declarations

2.70 The court may grant an injunction or make a declaration instead of, or in addition to, one of the prerogative orders if it is just to do so and considering: (i) the nature of the matter in which the prerogative remedies may be granted; (ii) the nature of the persons and/or bodies against whom relief may be granted by the prerogative orders; and (iii) all the circumstances of the case.[159]

2.71 An injunction or declaration can be sought as the sole remedy in a JR claim.[160] The court's jurisdiction to award such a remedy is no longer confined to cases where the prerogative orders would be available.[161]

2.72 A declaration can be granted by the court in the exercise of its discretion instead of one of the prerogative remedies where, for example, the applicant has delayed in applying for JR[162] or where the award of another remedy would be disruptive and lead to uncertainty and delay.[163] Declarations are often issued against Ministers instead of prerogative orders as they are expected to observe the decision of the court and comply with declaratory judgements.[164] Declarations have been used to resolve disputes between two public authorities;[165] to decide whether advice contained in departmental circulars

---

[154] *M v Home Office* [1994] 1 AC 377, [1993] 3 All ER 537, HL.
[155] *Bradbury v Enfield LBC* [1967] 3 All ER 434 at 441, [1969] 1 WLR 1311 at 1324, CA, per Lord Denning MR ('even if chaos should result, still the law must be obeyed').
[156] The Bill of Rights (1689) 'the freedom of speech and debates or proceedings in Parliament ought not to be impeached or questioned in any court or place out of Parliament'.
[157] *Attorney-General v London and Home Counties Joint Electricity Authority* [1929] 1 Ch 513; but see *Bilston Corporations v Wolverhampton Corps* [1942] Ch 391, [1942] 2 All ER 447.
[158] *Hoffman-La Roche & Co AG v Secretary of State for Trade and Industry* [1975] AC 295, [1974] 2 All ER 1128, HL.
[159] Section 31(2) of the Senior Courts Act 1981.
[160] *R v Secretary of State for Employment, ex p Equal Opportunities Commission* [1995] 1 AC 1, HL; *R v Bromley LBC, ex p Lambeth LBC* (1984) *The Times*, 16 June. Local authorities applied for, and received, a declaration that their contributions to Association of London Authorities were *intra vires*.
[161] *R v Bromley LBC, ex p Lambeth LBC* (1984) *The Times*, 16 June and the dicta of the Court of Appeal in *Law v National Greyhound Racing Club* [1983] 1 WLR 1302 at 1310.
[162] *R v Rochdale MBC, ex p Schemet* [1994] ELR 89, 91 LGR 425. The court found that the council's change of policy on school transport was unlawful but delay by the Schemet family meant certiorari would not be granted as the council had already budgeted in line with the new policy.
[163] *R v Secretary of State for Social Services, ex p Assoc. of Metropolitan Authorities* [1986] 1 All ER 164, [1986] 1 WLR 1. The Minister had failed to consult the Association as mandated before making regulations regarding public housing. The Association sought a quashing order in JR but were not granted one. A declaration was made.
[164] *M v Home Office* [1994] 1 AC 377 at 397, [1993] 3 All ER 537 at 543, HL, per Lord Woolf.
[165] Eg *R v London Transport Exec, ex p GLC* [1983] QB 484, [1983] 2 All ER 262. The GLC was granted

was correct in law;[166] and to direct a tribunal as to the decision it should reach.[167] In relation to decisions made by expert panels and tribunals, it should be noted that the courts are reluctant to interfere with decisions made by such panels, recognising that those panels are often best placed to determine those issues.[168]

2.73 A declaration cannot be merely academic. It must be effective at the time of the hearing or it must be certain to have effect in the future.[169] To ignore a declaratory judgement does not constitute a contempt of court but if a declaration is ignored the court may enforce it by way of injunction.

2.74 The cases, therefore, where a declaration or injunction is available in public law but the prerogative remedies of quashing, prohibiting or mandatory orders are not are narrow and limited. In *R v Bromley LBC, ex p Lambeth LBC*[170] the court considered that a prerogative order would not be available as the applicant was not affected by the decision of the respondent. Lambeth LBC simply wanted a declaration that payments to a particular organisation would be lawful under the Local Government Act 1972. JR was pursued against Bromley LBC because it had earlier brought JR proceedings against a different local authority to stop payment to the same organisation when it was operating under a different constitution.

2.75 Hodgson J held that the declaratory jurisdiction lay within the realm of public law, although prerogative remedies were unavailable, since it extended to the powers of statutory bodies. Woolf J (as he then was) also held that the court had a jurisdiction to grant declaratory relief on some public law point of general importance even if no decision yet existed against which a prerogative remedy could be sought.[171]

2.76 Quashing orders can lie against administrative acts[172] and in particular against delegated legislation.[173]

---

declarations confirming that instructions from the GLC to the London Transport Executive were lawful and could be lawfully implemented. Also, *R (Sunderland City Council) v South Tyneside Council* [2011] EWHC 2355 (Admin).

[166] *Royal College of Nursing of the United Kingdom v Dept of Health and Social Security* [1981] AC 800, [1981] 1 All ER 545, HL. The Royal College sought a declaration that DHSS guidance on a new method of abortion administered by nurses rather than doctors, as required in the Abortion Act 1967, was wrong in law. The DHSS sought a declaration to the contrary. Held: the DHSS's declaration was granted and the Royal College's refused; *Gillick v West Norfolk and Wisbech Area Health Authority* [1986] AC 112, [1985] 3 All ER 402, HL. Declarations were sought that a DHSS Memorandum of Guidance on contraceptive advice and treatment was unlawful. Declarations were refused.

[167] Eg *Barty-King v Ministry of Defence* [1979] 2 All ER 80.

[168] *Ansari v General Pharmaceutical Council* [2012] All ER (D) 126 (Apr). By contrast, the Court has granted orders where the expert panel has failed to provide reasons for their decision (*Duthie v The Nursing and Midwifery Council* [2012] EWHC 3021 (Admin)) or departed from established procedures (*R (B) v The Nursing and Midwifery Council* [2012] EWHC 1264 (Admin)).

[169] *Nottinghamshire CC v Secretary of State for the Environment* [1986] AC 240, [1986] 1 All ER 199, HL.

[170] *The Times*, 16 June 1984.

[171] *R v Secretary of State for the Environment, ex p Greater London Council* [1985] JPL 868. Appeal against a Queen's Bench Master's decision to strike out the GLC's application. Although the Master accepted that the GLC was not a 'person aggrieved' there were special circumstances that made it desirable that the approach of the planning inspector be tested by way of Judicial Review (Woolf J).

[172] Eg *R (Javed) v Secretary of State for the Home Dept* [2001] EWCA Civ 789, [2002] QB 129. The Asylum (Designated Countries etc) Order 1996 was reviewable in JR.

[173] *R v Secretary of State for Health, ex p United States Tobacco Intl Inc* [1991] 3 WLR 529. United States Tobacco had regulations banning oral snuff quashed on the basis of one of five grounds (unfairness).

2.77 The order might be used to quash normative acts and is not confined to decisions affecting only specified individuals.[174] Since the power to make delegated legislation is derived from statute, public law principles apply to the use of such powers. Lewis considers that the need for a separate public law procedure with shorter time limits in order to protect certainty relating to the decisions of public authorities, applies with 'especial force to legislative measures'.[175]

2.78 Another case where the declaratory remedy is available and a quashing order is not is in proceedings against the Crown. A quashing order lies against a Minster of the Crown and a minister exercising power derived from the prerogative[176] but not against the Crown itself. Section 21(1) of the Crown Proceedings Act 1947 provides that the courts have power to make certain orders, including declarations, against the Crown in civil proceedings; but, as set out earlier, JR is not included in the definition of civil proceedings in the Act.[177] Strictly, there is no power to make a declaration in JR against the Crown itself and the appropriate route to be followed to obtain one would be through an ordinary action. The occasions when a declaration would be needed against the Crown personally are likely to be very limited and concern the personal exercise by the Crown of prerogative powers. It is not a matter of great practical importance as statutory powers are usually vested in Ministers of the Crown and their exercise of those powers is challengeable through judicial review.

Orders against the Crown

2.79 No court can compel the Sovereign to perform any duty: so a mandatory order cannot lie against the Crown.[178] In *R (MM) v Secretary of State for the Home Department*, the court confirmed that it could not compel the Secretary of State to amend her decision, but only remit the matter for her consideration.[179] Where it is sought to establish a right against the Crown the appropriate procedure is that in accordance with the Crown Proceedings Act 1947. No order will lie against any person acting as an agent of the Crown and discharging duties on behalf of the Crown.[180] This exception is of limited practical importance[181] because a mandatory order can be made where the government official has a particular duty in relation to subjects.[182] If a statute requires 'the minister' to do something, a mandatory order can be made to force the minister to act.[183] This remedy is preserved in the Crown Proceedings Act 1947, s 40(5).[184]

---

[174] *Minister for Health v King (on the Prosecution of Yaffe)* [1931] AC 494.
[175] Clive Lewis, *Judicial Remedies in Public Law*, 4th edn 2-175.
[176] Lewis (supra) 6-015, *Council of Civil Service Unions v Minister of Civil Service* [1985] AC 374, *R v Secretary of State for Foreign and Commonwealth Affairs, ex p Everett* [1989] EHRR 52.
[177] Section 38(2) of the CPA 1947.
[178] *R v Powell* (1841) 1 QB 352 at 361 per Lord Denman CJ and *R v Treasury Lords Cssrs* (1872) LR 7 QB 387 at 394 per Cockburn CJ: 'Court cannot claim even in appearance to have any power to command the Crown; the thing is out of the question'.
[179] *R (MM) v The Secretary of State for the Home Department* [2013] EWHC 1900 (Admin) at 148.
[180] *R v Customs Cssrs* (1836) 5 Ad & El 380 at 383 per Littledale J; *R v Secretary of State for War* [1891] 2 QB 326, CA.
[181] *M v Home Office* [1994] 1 AC 377 at 417, [1993] 3 All ER 537 at 560, HL, per Lord Woolf.
[182] The distinction was drawn in *R v Secretary of State for War* [1891] 2 QB 326 at 334, CA, Charles J.
[183] *R v Customs and Excise Cssrs, ex p Cooke and Stevenson* [1970] 1 All ER 1068 at 1072–1073.
[184] The CPA does not limit the discretion of the court to grant relief by way of mandatory order in cases where the relief might have been granted before the commencement of the Act, notwithstanding that by reason of its provisions some other and further remedy is available.

DAMAGES AND RESTITUTION

Damages

2.80 A claim for damages may be attached to a claim for JR.[185] The court may award damages to the applicant if he has joined a claim for damages with his JR claim[186] and the court is satisfied that if the claim had been made in an action begun by the claimant at the time of his making the JR claim he would have been awarded damages.[187]

2.81 Section 31(4) of the SCA 1981 is not intended to create a new right but rather to remove the need for duplicate proceedings under Part 7 and Part 54. A claim under s 31(4) can be made only in conjunction with a claim for the prerogative remedies or for a declaration or injunction. It cannot be made in isolation. Damages can be awarded only if they would have been available in an ordinary claim where there was a right to damages in private law or under the HRA 1998. The change allows, for convenience, the rolling into a public law claim of a claim for damages under private law or the HRA 1998.

2.82 That an act of a public body is found to be *ultra vires* does not entitle an individual to damages for loss *per se*. The claimant must demonstrate that the unlawful act is identifiable as a recognised tort or as a breach of contract.[188] The general principles relating to tortious and contractual liability apply to public bodies exercising public law powers and powers derived from private law rights in contract and property.

2.83 When considering tortious acts committed by public bodies the courts will consider the special context of public administration.[189] The imposition of a duty of care is intended to lead to an improvement in the standard of care observed by a public authority in providing services.[190] The court will be mindful of cases where the imposition of a duty may make an authority unduly cautious in the exercise of its powers, or where a duty might lead to unproductive litigation which would distract the authority from its duty to provide the relevant service.[191]

2.84 In deciding whether to impose a duty upon a public authority the court will consider the availability of alternative remedies such as a statutory right of appeal.[192] In

---

[185] Senior Courts Act 1981, s 31(4); CPR, r 54.3(2).
[186] Senior Courts Act 1981, s 31(4)(a).
[187] Senior Courts Act 1981, s 31(4)(b).
[188] X v Bedfordshire County Council [1995] 2 AC 633 at 730 per Lord Browne-Wilkinson: 'the breach of a public law right by itself gives rise to no claim for damages. A claim for damages must be based on a private law cause of action'; R v Knowsley Metropolitan Borough Council, ex p Maguire (1992) 90 LGR 653: there is no general right to damages for maladministration. The claimant had no right to damages due to the authority's unlawful refusal to issue him with a taxi licence.
[189] X v Bedfordshire County Council [1995] 2 AC 633 per Lord Browne-Wilkinson at 739. The court will not hold a public authority vicariously liable for the actions of an employee where to do so would interfere with or 'discourage' the performance of the authority's duties. However occasions where vicarious liability will not be found will be rare: per Lord Slynn in *Phelps v Hillingdon LBC* [2001] 2 AC 619 at 653.
[190] *Phelps v Hillingdon LBC* [2001] 2 AC 619 at 672 per Lord Clyde the imposition of a duty 'may have the healthy effect of securing that high standards are sought and secured'; *Barrett v Enfield London Borough* [2001] 2 AC 550 at 568 per Lord Slynn approving Sir Thomas Bingham MR (as was).
[191] X v Bedfordshire County Council [1995] 2 AC 633. See also *Financial Services Authority v Sinaloa Gold* [2013] UKSC 11.
[192] *Rowley v Secretary of State for Work and Pensions* [2007] 1 WLR 2861 at para 73 per Dyson LJ: 'I accept, of course, that the mere fact that there is an alternative remedy is not necessarily a reason for denying the existence of a common law duty of care. It is important to see how comprehensive a remedy is provided and to consider it in the context of the statutory scheme as a whole. Ultimately, what has to be decided is

Jones v Department of Employment[193] the existence of a statutory right of appeal was a factor in the court's decision that an adjudication officer owed no duty of care to a claimant in processing a claim.

2.85 In *X v Bedfordshire County Council* the House of Lords found that a statutory complaints procedure and a reference to the local government ombudsman were more appropriate remedies than a negligence action in relation to maladministration in dealing with children at risk or with special educational needs.[194]

2.86 Article 6 of the European Convention on Human Rights guarantees the individual's access to the courts. The European Court has found that the failure of UK courts to find a duty of care in domestic law in a particular context does not infringe an individual's article 6 rights;[195] but, an individual may allege the infringement of other rights, such as the article 8 right to family and private life, which may go into the balance against policy considerations.[196]

2.87 In *Chief Constable of Hertfordshire Police v Van Colle, Smith v Chief Constable of Sussex*[197] the possibility of such a claim was not sufficient to set aside the rule that the police do not owe a common law duty in relation to their investigative functions.

2.88 In relation to statutory duties there is the problem that not all statutory duties give rise to a claim in damages. The issue becomes whether Parliament intended to confer a right to sue for damages where there has been a breach of a duty imposed by statute.[198] By a process of considering statutory construction the court will try to discern

---

whether, having regard to the purpose of the legislation, Parliament is to be taken as having intended that there should be a right to damages for negligence. The more comprehensive the remedy provided by Parliament, the less likely it is that Parliament is to be taken as having had that intention'. *Jain v Trent Strategic Health Authority* [2009] UKHL 4 per Lord Scott at para 28 'This line of authority demonstrates, in my opinion, that where action is taken by a State authority under statutory powers designed for the benefit or protection of a particular class of persons, a tortious duty of care will not be held to be owed by the State authority to others whose interests may be adversely affected by an exercise of the statutory power. The reason is that the imposition of such a duty would or might inhibit the exercise of the statutory powers and be potentially adverse to the interests of the class of persons the powers were designed to benefit or protect, thereby putting at risk the achievement of their statutory purpose'.

[193] [1989] QB 1 at 19 per Glidewell LJ Cf. *R v HM Treasury, ex p Petch* [1990] COD 19 where a duty in negligence could lie in parallel with a duty under the Superannuation Act 1972. Although Popplewell J held it was not negligence in its ordinary sense.

[194] *X v Bedfordshire County Council* [1995] 2 AC 633 at 751 and 762 per Lord Browne-Wilkinson: 'In my judgment ... the courts should hesitate long before imposing a common law duty of care ... The statute [Education Act 1981] provides its own detailed machinery for securing that the statutory purpose is performed. If, despite the complex machinery for consultation and appeals contained in the Act, the scheme fails to provide the benefit intended that is a matter more appropriately remedied by way of the Ombudsman looking into the administrative failure than by way of litigation. For these reasons I reach the conclusion that an education authority owes no common law duty of care in the exercise of the powers and discretions relating to children with special educational needs specifically conferred on them by the Act of 1981'.

[195] *TP and KM v United Kingdom* (2002) 34 EHRR 2 at paragraphs 92–103; *Z v United Kingdom* (2002) 34 EHRR 97 at 87–104.

[196] CA in *D v East Berkshire Community NHS Trust* [2004] QB 558 at paras 78–85.

[197] [2008] 3 WLR 593 at 136–139.

[198] *R v Deputy Governor of Parkhurst Prison, ex p Hague* [1992] 1 AC 58 at 159 per Lord Bridge: 'the fundamental question: "Did the legislature intend to confer on the plaintiff a cause of action for breach of statutory duty?"'; *X v Bedfordshire County Council* [1995] 2 AC 633 at 731 per Lord Browne-Wilkinson: 'The basic proposition is that in the ordinary case a breach of statutory duty does not, by itself, give rise to any private law cause of action. However, a private law cause of action will arise if it can be shown, as a matter of construction of the statute, that the statutory duty was imposed for the protection of a limited class of the public and that Parliament intended to confer on members of that class a private right of action for breach of the duty'; *Cullen v Chief Constable* [2003] 1 WLR 1763 at 41.

if an intention to create a private law remedy in damages can be found. As part of that process the relevant considerations include 'the object and scope of the provisions, the class (if any) intended to be protected by them, and the means of redress open to a member of such a class if the statutory duty is not performed'.[199] The difficulty in discerning an intention is such that the value of the exercise has been doubted. However, the intention of Parliament remains a cogent consideration in the courts' conclusions.

2.89 Public bodies are also liable for the tort of misfeasance in public office. The tort consists of a deliberate and dishonest abuse of power by a public officer or body.[200] It may be committed maliciously; or where it acted in the knowledge that the action was *ultra vires* and that where the public body acted the claimant or a class of persons[201] would probably suffer loss. To establish the tort the victim must show some special damage suffered. A prisoner whose correspondence was inspected in bad faith by prison officers was unable to demonstrate loss.[202] A prisoner moved from the open prison estate to the closed estate established such restraint of freedom caused him to sustain special damage.[203]

2.90 Claims for restitution, or the recovery of sums paid can also be attached to a claim for JR.[204]

Restitution

2.91 A restitutionary claim may be pursued by or against a public body where sums have been collected or paid out in pursuance of a power found to be *ultra vires*. Where a citizen pays monies to a public authority in the form of taxes or other dues, and the demand by the public authority is *ultra vires*, those sums are recoverable as of right.[205]

2.92 In *Woolwich v IRC No 2* the Inland Revenue repaid tax levied pursuant to regulations found to be *ultra vires* and paid interest on the taxes from the date of judgement; but refused to pay interest for the period from the date of payment to the date of judgment. The building society sought to show it was entitled to recover the money and so was entitled to the interest for the whole period. The majority of the House of Lords decided that the building society was entitled to recover money paid pursuant to a demand that was narrowly *ultra vires* in that there was no authority for the demand once the regulations were quashed. Two members of the majority in the House of Lords also expressed the view that the same principle applied where the tax was not due for some other reason such as misconstruction of the regulations or statute.[206]

---

[199] Per Bingham LCJ in *Olotu v Home Office* [1997] 1 WLR 328 at 336.
[200] See *Three Rivers DC v Governors of the Bank of England* [2003] 1 AC 1.
[201] The claimant or class of persons need not be identifiable. In *Akenzua v Secretary of State for the Home Department* [2003] 1 WLR 741 the fact that the murder victim of a released individual, or a group of potential victims, was unidentifiable was not a reason to strike out the claim.
[202] *Watkins v Home Office* [2006] 2 AC 395 at 23 per Lord Bingham.
[203] *Karagozlu v Commissioner of Police for the Metropolis* [2007] 1 WLR 1881 at 45 per Sir Anthony Clarke MR.
[204] Senior Courts Act 1981, s 31(4) as amended by the Civil Procedure (Modification of Supreme Court Act 1981) Order 2004 – as of 1 May 2004 a restitutionary claim can be included in a Judicial Review claim.
[205] *Woolwich Building Society v Inland Revenue Cssrs (No 2)* [1993] AC 70.
[206] *Woolwich Building Society v Inland Revenue Cssrs (No 2)* [1993] AC 70, per Lord Goff at 177 and per Lord Slynn at 205.

2.93 In cases where money was paid under an agreement that was later found to be *ultra vires* the law has been changed by House of Lords decisions. Previously the law was thought to be that money paid under a mistake of law was not recoverable.[207] In *Kleinwort Benson Ltd v Lincoln City Council*[208] the House of Lords overruled *Bilbie v Lumley*[209] and found that the previous rule was not part of English law.

2.94 A person who pays money under a mistake is *prima facie* entitled to recover it on the ground of unjust enrichment. Money is paid under a mistake of law even where the parties were unaware of the *ultra vires* status of the agreement or where the settled view of the law was that such agreements were lawful. There appears to be no limitation on claiming money paid under a settled understanding of the law when that understanding is later departed from by a decision of the court.[210] In *Sempra Metals Ltd (formerly Metallgesellschaft Ltd) v Inland Revenue Cssrs*[211] it was found that interest, including compound interest, may be awarded.

2.95 In *Hemming (t/a Simply Pleasure Ltd) v Westminster City Council*, the claimants were entitled to recover the difference between the amount paid to the council, and the amount that would have been paid had the council correctly calculated the appropriate licence fee.[212]

2.96 The courts have recognised some defences to a claim for recovery of money paid through a mistake of law. Where the recipient of the money has changed his position in reliance on the payment so that repayment would be inequitable, the court will not order restitution.[213] It is likely that where the money was paid under a compromise agreement or in settlement of a legal claim, there will be a defence.[214] It is not a defence that the defendant honestly believed that he was entitled to retain the money or that the money was paid under a fully performed void contract.[215]

2.97 In *Woolwich v IRC*[216] the court left open the possibility of a defence where the taxpaying company passed on the cost of an *ultra vires* tax demand to its customers.[217] In the case of *ultra vires* tax demands a public policy defence may develop,[218] since an error of law on the part of a public authority may result in it being liable to repay large sums of tax which may already have been spent. Such a situation could have a severe effect on a local authority's budget. Some statutory provisions deal with this problem by precluding repayment where the error was based on a general practice.[219]

2.98 A claim for restitution can be pursued through JR under SCA 1981, s 31 (4) where it is subordinate to a public law claim, which seeks to determine whether an

---

[207] See *Bilbie v Lumley* (1802) 2 East 469.
[208] [1999] 2 AC 349.
[209] Supra.
[210] *Kleinwort Benson Ltd v Lincoln City Council* [1999] 2 AC 349 (Lords Browne-Wilkinson and Lloyd dissenting on this point).
[211] [2008] 1 AC 561.
[212] [2012] EWHC 1260 (Admin).
[213] *Lipkin Gorman (a firm) v Karpnale Ltd* [1991] 2 AC 548.
[214] *Kleinwort Benson Ltd v Lincoln City Council* [1999] 2 AC 349 at 1112.
[215] *Kleinwort Benson Ltd v Lincoln City Council* [1999] 2 AC 349 at 1112.
[216] Supra.
[217] *Woolwich Building Society v Inland Revenue Cssrs (No 2)* [1993] AC 70.
[218] Lord Goff in *Kleinwort Benson Ltd v Lincoln City Council* [1999] 2 AC 349 at 1122 and Lord Goff again in *R v Tower Hamlets LBC, ex p Chetnik Developments Ltd* [1988] AC 858 at 882.
[219] Taxes Management Act 1970, s 33(2A)(a).

action was *ultra vires*.[220] Any claim for restitution remains subject to the procedural requirement of being brought within three months of the grounds arising.[221]

HRA damages

2.99 Damages are also available under s 8 of the Human Rights Act 1998 where they 'afford just satisfaction' to a claimant[222] who has suffered loss as a result of a public authority infringing his human rights under the European Convention on Human Rights adopted into UK law by the HRA 1998 Schedule 1.[223] The court must take account of any other remedy granted in respect of the infringement.[224] The court must also take into account the principles applied by the European Court of Human Rights in finding a right to damages and in quantifying such damages.[225]

2.100 In *A v Essex County Council UKSC*[226] a claim was made for damages under s 8 of the HRA as a result of a severely autistic claimant being asked to leave school in January 2002 but no replacement school placement was made available to him until July 2003. It was argued that that was a breach of the claimant's right to education under article 2 of Protocol 1 of ECHR. The court dismissed the claim on the factual basis that it stood no realistic prospect of success as there was no minimum right to education but there was no issue about the availability if damages had the claim been established.

2.101 In the giving of 'just satisfaction' damages will not always be necessary. Remedies in judicial review may be enough to give just satisfaction by guaranteeing an end to the violation.[227] In considering the right to damages in relation to the HRA 1998 the purpose of the Act should be considered. It is not a tort statute. It exists to protect Human Rights and not merely to provide compensation. The award of damages would not normally be necessary to secure a high degree of compliance with the statute by public bodies.

2.102 In considering quantum in HRA damages claims, the court should be guided by the approach of the European Court of Human Rights where damages awards are those considered equitable to the individual without precise calculation.[228] UK courts should follow ECtHR principles and should not draw parallels with damages awarded in comparable domestic torts.[229] In the case of *R (Bernard) v Enfield Borough Council*[230] the court took as its guide awards made by the Local Government Ombudsman.

---

[220] Senior Courts Act 1981, s 31(4) as amended by the Civil Procedure (Modification of Supreme Court Act 1981) Order 2004 – as of 1 May 2004 a restitutionary claim can be included in a Judicial Review claim.
[221] *Hemming (t/a Simply Pleasure Ltd) v Westminster City Council* [2012] EWHC 1260 (Admin) (16 May 2012) at 12.
[222] Human Rights Act 1998, s 8(3).
[223] Human Rights Act 1998, Sch 1 – The Articles.
[224] Section 8(3) of the Human Rights Act 1998 and see *Anufrijeva v Southwark LBC* [2004] 2 WLR 603 at para 55.
[225] Section 8(4) of the Human Rights Act 1998.
[226] [2010] UKSC 33.
[227] *Anufrijeva v Southwark LBC* [2004] 2 WLR 603 at para 53; *R (Bernard) v Enfield LBC* [2002] EWHC 2282 at para 39 (damages awarded where a family were forced to live in substandard conditions for a period of 20 months).
[228] *R (Faulkner) v Secretary of State for Justice* [2013] UKSC 23 at 29–39: where damages arose out of unlawful detention violating the claimant's human rights, reference should be had to the practice of the European Court of Human Rights.
[229] *R (Greenfield) v Secretary of State for the Home Department* [2005] 1 WLR 673 at paras 18–19.
[230] [2002] EWHC 2282.

2.103 In determining whether damages should be awarded the court may have regard to the gravity or severity of the violation, the manner in which the violation occurred and its impact on the individual.[231] Where anxiety and frustration are the harm suffered, it is unlikely that an award of damages will be justified.[232] Where a significant monetary loss has been suffered, for example where unlawful discrimination has caused the loss of employment, an award of damages is likely and the court will be able to assess such compensation.[233]

2.104 In a HRA JR and damages claim and in JR damages claims generally the court may deal with the substantive JR claim first and defer the consideration of damages to a separate occasion.[234]

2.105 Interest on damages is also recoverable.[235] Interest, whether from statute,[236] or in damages,[237] cannot be recovered on an application for judicial review where the unlawful decision successfully challenged had resulted in the late payment of a grant by the respondent authority.[238] The private law claim and its attendant damages are usually such that the practice is to deal with the public law claim first before dealing with the private law rights and the claim to damages.[239]

DISCRETION

2.106 Prerogative orders, declaratory orders and injunctions are discretionary remedies. The court has a wide discretion whether to grant relief at all and in what form to grant it.[240] The principles affecting the exercise of discretion are common to all the JR remedies. In deciding whether to exercise its discretion the court will take account of the conduct of the party applying for relief.

Conduct of the claimant

2.107 A taxpayer was refused relief amounting to quashing an authority's refusal to refund rates because of his previous unwarranted refusal to pay rates owed and because the authority was not being unjustly enriched.[241] In *Windsor and Maidenhead Royal Borough Council v Brandrose Investments Ltd*[242] the Council was refused relief where

---

[231] *Anufrijeva v Southwark LBC* [2004] 2 WLR 603 at paras 66–70.
[232] *Anufrijeva v Southwark LBC* [2004] 2 WLR 603 at paras 65 and 75.
[233] *Anufrijeva v Southwark LBC* [2004] 2 WLR 603 at 59; *R (Hooper) v Secretary of State for Work and Pensions* [2003] 1 WLR 2623 at para 147.
[234] *Anufrijeva v Southwark LBC* [2004] 2 WLR 603.
[235] *R v Liverpool City Council, ex p Coade*, The Times, October 10, 1986.
[236] Senior Courts Act 1981, s 35A (added).
[237] Unless there is an express or implied contractual provision to this effect which sounds in damages.
[238] *R v Secretary of State for Transport, ex p Sherriff & Sons* (1988) *Independent*, 12 January. The claimants had taken out a loan relying on the making of a grant by the minister to pay off the loan. The grant was delayed and interest accrued on the loan. The court found that the grant could not be construed as a debt.
[239] *R v Governor of Brockhill Prison, ex p Evans (No 2)* [1998] 4 All ER 993 (lawfulness of detention dealt with before claim for damages for false imprisonment); *R v Coventry CC, ex p Phoenix Aviation* [1995] 3 All ER 37 (court dealt with *ultra vires* claim before claim for breach of contract); *R v Chief Constable of Lancashire, ex p Parker* [1993] QB 577 (claim over validity of search warrant before claim for damages for trespass and aggravated damages).
[240] See *R (Edwards) v Environment Agency* [2008] UKHL 22 at para 63.
[241] *Dorot Properties Ltd v London Borough of Brent* [1990] COD 378.
[242] [1983] 1 WLR 509.

the litigation was found to be pointless. An authority was refused relief where it sought to challenge ministerial confirmation of its own policy based on the authority's own procedural error.[243]

2.108 The court will refuse to exercise its discretion in JR on the ground of the claimant's misconduct. Misconduct may consist in a failure to disclose material facts[244] and even in an inadvertent mis-statement of facts.[245]

Delay

2.109 Delay is a ground of refusal to exercise discretion in JR. Delay is governed by the Senior Courts Act 1981 and the CPR, r 54.5. A claim for JR must be commenced promptly, and in any event not later than three months after the grounds relied on arose.[246] The period runs from the time when the grounds first arose.[247] A finding at the permission stage that a claim was not made promptly is conclusive. It cannot be reopened at the full hearing.[248]

2.110 The court may allow a claim to proceed, even if was not made promptly, if the claimant can show a good reason.[249] However, by s 31(6) of the SCA 1981, if the court considers there has been 'undue delay' in the making of an application it may refuse to grant leave to make the application or refuse any relief if it considers that such relief would cause 'substantial hardship' or 'substantially prejudice' the rights of another or would be 'detrimental to good administration'.

2.111 In *R v Dairy Produce Quota Tribunal for England and Wales, ex p Caswell*[250] Lord Goff, giving the judgement of the House of Lords, held that 'detrimental to good administration' must be different from case to case as the need for finality would differ. Relevant factors in assessing detriment would be: the length of delay, the extent and effect of the decision under challenge, and the impact if the decision were to be reopened.

2.112 In *Caswell* the decision related to the fixing of the claimant's dairy quota. The reopening of the decision would lead to other challenges which, if successful, would require the reopening of quota allocation decisions for the previous four years as the quotas were derived from a national capped quota.

2.113 In *R (Nash) v Capita Plc*, a delay of two years resulted in the court refusing to grant the claimant permission for judicial review, and ruling that the claim was out of time on the basis that the challenge should have been brought to earlier distinct substantive decisions in 2010/2011 which enabled the procurement process to be initiated. Instead the challenge had been brought to particular decisions to award a contract to a particular contractor which were consequent upon the earlier substantive decision.[251] By contrast, in *R (Kilroy) v Parrs Wood High School*, the court held that

---

[243] *R v Secretary of State for Education and Science, ex p Birmingham City Council* (1984) 83 LGR 79.
[244] *R v Kensington Income Tax Cssrs, ex p Princess Edmond de Polignac* [1917] 1 KB 486.
[245] *R v North East Thames Regional Health Authority, ex p De Groot* [1988] COD 25.
[246] CPR, r 54.5(1).
[247] *R (Nash) v Capita Plc & Ors* [2013] EWHC 1067 (Admin) (29 April 2013) at 37.
[248] *R v Criminal Injuries Compensation Board, ex p A* [1999] 2 WLR 974.
[249] CPR, r 3.1(2)(a).
[250] [1990] AC 738.
[251] [2013] EWHC 1067 (Admin) (29 April 2013) at 37.

public interest demanded that a case brought only one day before the end of the three months since the cause of action accrued be allowed to proceed.[252]

2.114 In *R v Swale Borough Council, ex p RSPB*[253] the court refused to exercise its discretion on the basis of 'substantial prejudice to others' in the RSPB's challenge to the grant of planning permission to reclaim mudflats on the River Medway. The Society's challenge came out of time. The port authority had already entered into a dredging contract with another party. If relief were granted to the RSPB, the spoil already dredged would have to be dumped at sea or otherwise than upon the mudflats. There would be greater expense and the overall scheme would be delayed, with further losses.

2.115 In *R (Gavin) v London Borough of Haringey* the court refused to quash a planning permission when there was prolonged delay in bringing the claim as the developer had already made substantial financial commitments to get the development under way. The court refused to quash the planning permission but gave a declaratory judgement that there had been a failure to comply with the relevant procedural requirements.[254]

2.116 The court's discretion is so broad that the court may refuse to grant relief even where the claim is within time. In *R v Brent LBC, ex p O'Malley*[255] the claimant challenged the decision of a local authority to dispose of housing stock on the basis that it had failed to follow the appropriate consultation procedures. Despite the illegality of the decision the court would not grant relief as the third party interests of the majority of the tenants, who supported the disposal scheme, and good administration would be prejudiced if relief were to be granted.

In *Allman v Coroner for West Sussex* the court explained the refusal to grant relief even when the claim was brought in time as follows:

> 'The 3-month period is a long stop provision, a claimant must file the claim promptly and will be shut out if the claim is filed within the 3-month period but is not filed promptly.'[256]

---

[252] [2011] EWHC 3489 (Admin) at 30–32.
[253] (1991) 2 Admin L.Rep 790.
[254] *R (Gavin) v London Borough of Haringey* [2004] 2 P & CR 13.
[255] (1997) 10 Admin L.Rep 265.
[256] *Allman v Coroner for West Sussex* [2012] EWHC 534 (Admin) at 27.

2.117 Undue delay,[257] unreasonable[258] or unmeritorious[259] conduct, acquiescence in the irregularity complained of[260] or waiver of the right to object[261] may all result in the court's declining to grant relief.

2.118 The effect of granting relief is a further consideration.[262] The court would not grant relief the effect of which would be to facilitate unlawful activity.[263]

2.119 The court may refuse to exercise its discretion where the grant of the remedy is unnecessary,[264] futile,[265] where there is no injustice or where both the claimant and defendant have contributed to the unlawful situation.[266] Further, the court will not assess whether individual rights are breached when the legality of a policy is only considered in the abstract.[267] The court refused a declaration that the Inner London Education Authority was in breach of its statutory duty when the authority was to be abolished a few weeks after the date of the judgement.[268] However, the House of Lords has held that a quashing order should be granted to quash a deportation order on specified dates which were long past the date of judgement.[269]

2.120 Cases arise where prerogative relief will be of no use to the claimant but the court nevertheless issues a declaratory judgement to clarify the law for decision-makers in the

---

[257] *Hanson v Church Cssrs for England* [1978] QB 823 at 831, [1977] 3 All ER 404 at 408, CA, per Lord Denning MR; *R v Rochdale MBC, ex p Schemet* [1994] ELR 89, 91 LGR 425 – delay resulted in the court making a declaration rather than a quashing order.

[258] *R v Crown Court at Knightsbridge, ex p Marcrest Ltd* [1983] 1 All ER 1148, [1983] 1 WLR 300, CA; *Fullbrook v Berkshire Magistrates' Court Committee* (1970) 69 LGR 75; *ex p Fry* [1954] 2 All ER 118 at 120, [1954] 1 WLR 730 at 734, AC, per Hallett J.

[259] *R v Chief National Insurance Cssr, ex p Connor* [1981] QB 758, [1981] 1 All ER 769, DC. The denial of a widow's allowance where the individual had stabbed her husband to death; *Goordin v Secretary of State for the Home Dept* (1981) 125 Sol Jo 624, *The Times*, 11 August, CA. It is wrong to apply for a judicial remedy 'when political capital is sought to be made ... out of judicial review': *R v GLC, ex p Royal Borough of Kensington and Chelsea* (1982) *The Times*, 7 April (precept issued by the GLC).

[260] *R v Secretary of State for Education and Science, ex p Birmingham CC* (1984) 83 LGR 79 cf. *R v Port Talbot BC, ex p Jones* [1988] 2 All ER 207. A councillor who acquiesced in a decision was allowed to challenge it in JR as leader of the council acting on behalf of the wider community.

[261] *Whelan v R* [1921] 2 IR 310; *R v Williams, ex p Phillips* [1914] 1 KB 608; *R v Nailsworth Licensing Justices, ex p Bird* [1953] 1 WLR 1046.

[262] *R v Brent Health Authority, ex p Francis* [1985] QB 869, [1985] 1 All ER 74, DC; *R v Hillingdon Health Authority, ex p Goodwin* [1984] ICR 800.

[263] *R v Hereford and Worcester County Council, ex p Smith (Tommy)* [1994] COD 129, CA. A gypsy sought JR of an authority restricting access to lay bys. JR was refused on three grounds including that JR should not be granted to further the unlawful camping overnight on lay bys.

[264] *R v Boundary Commission for England, ex p Foot* [1983] QB 600, [1983] 1 All ER 1099, CA.

[265] *R v Commonwealth Public Services Commission, ex p Killeen* (1914) 18 CLR 586 (Aust); *Secretary of State for Social Services, ex p Assoc. Metropolitan Authorities* [1986] 1 All ER 164, [1986] 1 WLR 1 (certiorari refused but declaration given since challenged regulations had since been consolidated in regulations which were not challenged. *R v Ministry of Agric. Fisheries and Ford, ex p Live Sheep Traders Ltd* [1995] COD 297, DC (the court will not make declaration that repealed legislation is unlawful. Cf. *R v Northavon DC, ex p Palmer* (1993) 25 HLR 674 at 6 Admin LR 195, Sedley J granted permission to apply for JR even though the declaration sought was academic in order that the claimant might attach a claim for damages. 'Procedurally debatable' but not to grant permission would be 'a denial of justice' Sedley J at 679 and 200.

[266] *R (Hashemi) v The Upper Tribunal (Immigration and Asylum Chamber)* [2013] EWHC 2316 (Admin) at 81, see also *R (Stern) v Horsham District Council* [2013] EWHC 1460 (Admin) where both the claimant and defendant were concurrently in error.

[267] *R (MM) v Secretary of State for the Home Department* [2013] EWHC 1900 (Admin) at 151.

[268] *R v Inner London Education Authority, ex p Ali and Murshid* [1990] COD 317.

[269] *R v Secretary of State for the Home Dept, ex p Bugdaycay* [1987] AC 514.

future.[270] Such cases would mean that pursuit of judicial review would not be merely an academic exercise. The court may give guidance as to the state of the law without making a formal declaration.[271]

2.121 Other relevant considerations include whether practical problems,[272] including administrative confusion or inconvenience[273] to the public and the effects on third parties,[274] would result from the order or whether the form of the order would require the close supervision of the court or be practically incapable of performance.[275] The court may refuse to grant relief where the claimant has suffered no injustice or prejudice, for instance where a breach of natural justice had not prevented a claimant from receiving a fair hearing.[276] Similarly, where a technical breach of procedural requirements has occurred the court may refuse to exercise its discretion where the claimant has not suffered any prejudice.[277] The court will assess the degree of prejudice suffered by looking to the underlying purpose of the statutory requirements that have been breached.

2.122 The court may not quash a decision, despite an error of law[278] or failure to consider relevant, matters[279] where the decision-maker would have reached the same conclusion if he had been correctly informed of the law or had been fully aware of the relevant considerations.[280] Similarly a decision in breach of natural justice may not be quashed if the same decision would have been reached if natural justice had been

---

[270] See section on Declarations.
[271] *R v Bromley Licensing Justices, ex p Bromley Licensed Victuallers* [1984] 1 WLR 585; *R v Bromley Magistrates' Court, ex p Smith* [1995] 1 WLR 944; *R (Sacupima) v Newham LBC* [2001] 1 WLR 563 at 565G–H; *R (MA) v Secretary of State for Work and Pensions* [2013] EWHC 2213 (QB).
[272] *Chief Constable of North Wales Police v Evans* [1982] 3 All ER 141, [1982] 1 WLR 1155. The court had the power to order the CC to reinstate a probationary constable but Lord Brightman, at 156 and 1176, felt to do so would 'border on usurpation of the powers of the chief constable' and a declaration was made.
[273] *R v Paddington Valuation Officer, ex p Peachey Property Corps Ltd* [1964] 1 WLR 1186 at 1195, DC per Widgery J: 'administrative chaos and public inconvenience ... would follow the quashing of a valuation list' (later affirmed by the CA in [1966] 1 QB 380 at 418; *R v Rochdale MBC, ex p Schemet* (1992) 91 LGR 425, Roch J refused to quash an unlawful policy as it would affect two years of Rochdale's education budget and instead made a declaration to prevent the authority pursuing the unlawful policy into the future.
[274] *R v Panel on Take-overs and Mergers, ex p Datafin plc* [1987] QB 815 at 842 per Sir John Donaldson MR: 'I wish to make it clear beyond a peradventure that in the light of the special nature of the panel, its functions, the market in which it is operating, the time scales which are inherent in that market and the need to safeguard the position of third parties, who may be numbered in thousands, all of whom are entitled to continue to trade upon an assumption of the validity of the panel's rules and decisions, unless and until they are quashed by the court, I should expect the relationship between the panel and the court to be historic rather than contemporaneous'.
[275] *R v Peak Park Joint Planning Board* (1976) 74 LGR 376 at 380, DC, per Lord Widgery CJ 'the court does not allow mandamus to go if the form of the order may require day to day supervision and the detailed examination of circumstances'.
[276] *R v Monopolies and Mergers Commission, ex p Brown (Matthew)* [1987] 1 WLR 1235 at 1247; *R v Secretary of State for Foreign and Commonwealth Affairs, ex p Everett* [1989] QB 811 at 819.
[277] *R v Cornwall County Council, ex p Nicholls* [1989] COD 507. That the report before an education authority was not in the form specified in the Education Act 1944 did not prejudice its decision. *R (Shinwari) v Secretary of State for the Home Department* [2013] EWHC 2148 (Admin) at 20-21: where there is no unlawful decision, there is no basis for corrective justice.
[278] *R v Deputy Governor of Parkhurst Prison, ex p Hague* [1992] 1 AC 58 (the HoL reversed the CA decision on a separate issue; *R v Knightsbridge Crown Court, ex p Marcrest Properties* [1983] 1 WLR 300.
[279] *R v Mansfield Justices, ex p Sharkey* [1985] QB 613 at 630. The court refused to exercise its discretion, as the decision would remain unchanged in a case where the magistrates' court had not considered all the relevant factors in the case of bail conditions imposed upon miners involved in disorder during strikes.
[280] *R (Stern) v Horsham District Council* [2013] EWHC 1460 (Admin).

observed.[281] The obvious risk with this approach is that the court might assume that the decision-maker would see the same merits in the case as the court.

2.123 The courts will not refuse a remedy where there might be any doubt about whether the decision-maker would have come to the same decision if he had not been in error.[282] Also, there is a public interest in holding public bodies to account when they do not observe the appropriate public law principles in exercising their discretionary powers. Quashing orders in these cases emphasise to public authorities the need to take care to act lawfully.

2.124 Courts should refuse to grant relief only where the decision would undoubtedly have been the same without the error and the granting of relief would be contrary to the public interest.[283]

2.125 The court has complete discretion whether to take action on a decision and may decline to do so in the interest of the wider public even though it declares the decision to be unlawful.[284] In the *Argyll Group* decision the Master of the Rolls made clear the need to consider wider public policy implications over the interests of the claimant.

2.126 In balancing the various factors in determining whether to exercise its discretion to grant a remedy the court will base its decision upon the circumstances applying at the time of the hearing and not those operating at the time of the decision.[285] Discretion must be exercised consistently and on clear principles if JR discretion is not to become arbitrary and unpredictable.

THE ROLE OF MEDIATION AND OTHER ALTERNATIVE REMEDIES IN JUDICIAL REVIEW

2.127 The term ADR is a familiar one. However, this acronym is used for two related but different ideas.

2.128 The first, *alternative dispute resolution*, focuses on processes which are seen as alternatives to dispute resolution by the courts. The alternative is often seen as being

---

[281] Eg *Glynn v Keele University* [1971] 1 WLR 487 at 495–496. A student who stripped in the students union at Keele University was not given an opportunity to make a plea in mitigation to the Vice-Chancellor before being excluded from University residences but the facts were not disputed and even if the claimant had had an opportunity to mitigate the penalty would have been the same. In this case the Vice-Chancellor of the Chancery Division applied JR principles in the court of Chancery.

[282] *Berkeley v Secretary of State for the Environment* [2001] 2 AC 603 at 616 at para 8. Per Lord Hoffmann in a case where the decision-maker had failed to take account of an environmental impact assessment.

[283] *R v Bacon's School Governors, ex p Inner London Education Authority* [1990] COD 414, *The Independent*, 29 March 1990. A school board of governors voted to close the school, one of the governors had an indirect monetary interest in the decision. The decision was confirmed by a second vote excluding the disqualified governor. The second decision was allowed to stand as administratively necessary and it was unlikely the disqualified governor had any influence on the second vote.

[284] *R v Monopolies and Mergers Commission, ex p Argyll Group plc* [1986] 1 WLR 763 at 774–775 where Sir John Donaldson MR listed relevant factors in consideration of good public administration, CA; *R v Secretary of State for Social Services, ex p Assoc. of Metropolitan Authorities* (1992) 25 HLR 131 at 139–140 (Tucker J declined to quash regulations whose quashing would lead to uncertainty and delay; a declaration was made instead). *R v Restormel BC, ex p Corbett* [2001] EWCA Civ 330, [2001] 1 PLR 108 at 27 per Schiemann LJ (court declined to quash an unlawful grant of planning permission where to do so would unjustly deprive the landowner of compensation).

[285] *R v Secretary of State for Foreign and Commonwealth Affairs, ex p Everett* [1989] QB 811 at 818 per O'Connor LJ.

necessary because of the costs of litigation. In many areas governed by public law the particular matter in dispute may be of a relatively small financial amount, while nevertheless important for the claimant, and the costs involved in a full judicial review may be seen as disproportionate. Indeed, even for cases where the matter is of greater financial significance there is pressure to reduce costs, particularly to the public purse. For alternative dispute resolution, the primary aim is, therefore, to provide the equivalent of court justice, but delivered more cheaply and in an accessible manner. This, it is often argued will result in greater access to justice for the more disadvantaged and less articulate members of society.

2.129 The second, *appropriate dispute resolution*, focuses more on the nature of the process and the remedy which can be obtained. It is often argued that an adversarial process, where one side wins and the other loses as a result of the application of judicial principles, is less appropriate than a more flexible process which applies wider principles or standards designed to achieve a fair result in the particular circumstances of the case. It is also argued that a more comprehensible and accessible system is needed for claimants for whom the legal process and judicial review is not only impenetrable but also a positive deterrent to seeking a remedy.

2.130 Any particular system of dispute resolution outside of the courts can seek to further either or both of these ideas, and can have advantages and disadvantages accordingly. Both are part of what has been termed 'proportionate dispute resolution' which seeks to reduce the number of administrative errors and provide an appropriate range of mechanisms to resolve the different type of disputes effectively, fairly and efficiently.[286]

2.131 The remainder of this chapter provides a brief explanation of the more prominent alternatives to judicial review.

MEDIATION

Introduction

2.132 Mediation has now become a feature of the legal landscape in many areas of law. For example, it is a well-known and useful tool in family law areas and is often invoked in commercial disputes. However, it has been less well used in public law areas. This is, however, changing as pressure on the public purse increases and there are calls for disputes, such as appeals in relation to planning permissions, to be resolved more quickly.

2.133 Mediation is not adjudication or arbitration. Instead, it is a flexible process where the aim is to provide a solution acceptable to all parties. The mediator can facilitate this negotiated process by utilising various techniques, but control of the process remains with the parties and the mediator must remain neutral.

2.134 Certainly, the process may be cheaper by producing a quicker outcome, and with less formal processes and representation, than an action in the courts. However, if the parties are represented as they would be in court, which may well be necessary to redress a power imbalance, and the mediator must also be paid for, the cost advantage may be

---

[286] *Transforming Public Services: Complaints Redress and Tribunals*, Cm 6243, 2004.

less significant. Much will depend on the type of legal action involved. The main advantage is that the process provides a different solution or remedy acceptable to both or all sides.[287] While the solution may involve some compromise, it can also be a constructive process finding an alternative way of achieving the aims of the parties. As with cost, the possible advantage of a speedier outcome will depend on the type of public law action involved.

2.135 Previously mediation was not part of mainstream tools for public law. However, there has been increasing recognition of its value, not least from policy makers concerned with reducing costs and delay in public administration. However, it is still limited in its actual use, and the policy advice remains just that – largely advisory and the process is not yet compulsory. Indeed, despite formal schemes, for example in the Court of Appeal, and various trials having taken place and, as seen below, the threat of adverse costs implications, the evidence is that it is very rare for mediation to be suggested by judges in the Administrative Court.[288]

Support for mediation

2.136 Support for mediation processes can be drawn from the general literature on its use in relation to disputes and legal processes generally. It is not the intention to repeat this here. However, support for its use in public law processes can also be drawn from some more specific sources.

General

2.137 In *Cowl v Plymouth City Council*,[289] Woolf CJ stated that:

> '1. The importance of this appeal is that it illustrates that, even in disputes between public authorities and the members of the public for whom they are responsible, insufficient attention is paid to the paramount importance of avoiding litigation whenever this is possible. Particularly in the case of these disputes both sides must by now be acutely conscious of the contribution alternative dispute resolution can make to resolving disputes in a manner which both meets the needs of the parties and the public and saves time, expense and stress.
> 2. The appeal also demonstrates that courts should scrutinise extremely carefully applications for judicial review in the case of applications of the class with which this appeal is concerned. The courts should then make appropriate use of their ample powers under the CPR to ensure that the parties try to resolve the dispute with the minimum involvement of the courts. The legal aid authorities should co-operate in support of this approach.
> 3. To achieve this objective the court may have to hold, on its own initiative, an inter partes hearing at which the parties can explain what steps they have taken to resolve the dispute without the involvement of the courts. In particular the parties should be asked why a complaints procedure or some other form of ADR has not been used or adapted to resolve or reduce the issues which are in dispute. If litigation is necessary the courts should deter the parties from adopting an unnecessarily confrontational approach to the litigation. If this had happened in this case many thousands of pounds in costs could have been saved and considerable stress to the parties could have been avoided.'

---

[287] A conclusion supported by empirical study, see Bondy and Mulcahy, *Mediation and Judicial Review: An empirical research study*, The Public Law Project, 2009, p 86.
[288] Ibid, p 5.
[289] [2001] EWCA Civ 1935; [2002] 1 WLR 803.

2.138 The case arose out of a proposal to close a residential home. The Council had an internal complaints procedure which it had, in a letter to the court, indicated its willingness to use and it undertook not to move the claimants from the home for a period of six weeks. Nevertheless, the judicial review hearing was expedited because the claimants contended that they were in urgent need of protection. As the Court of Appeal noted,

> '14. It appears that one reason why the wheels of the litigation may have continued to roll is that both parties were under the impression that unless they agreed otherwise the complainants were entitled to proceed with their application for judicial review unless the complaints procedure on offer technically constituted an "alternative remedy" which would fulfil all the functions of judicial review. This is too narrow an approach to adopt when considering whether an application to judicial review should be stayed. The parties do not today, under the CPR, have a right to have a resolution of their respective contentions by judicial review in the absence of an alternative procedure which would cover exactly the same ground as judicial review. The courts should not permit, except for good reason, proceedings for judicial review to proceed if a significant part of the issues between the parties could be resolved outside the litigation process. The disadvantages of doing so are limited. If subsequently it becomes apparent that there is a legal issue to be resolved, that can thereafter be examined by the courts which may be considerably assisted by the findings made by the complaints panel.'

2.139 The issue of closure of residential homes is of course subject to established legal principles, and so was amenable to resolution by litigation. Nevertheless, the Court of Appeal rejected robustly the suggestion that an alternative resolution method was not appropriate.

> '15. ... the claimants prepared a supplemental skeleton argument which set out ten reasons why the complaint procedure is not a suitable alternative remedy to judicial review. We have examined each of those reasons carefully and in our judgment they establish no basis on which the claimants could reasonably object to the matters in issue being dealt with by the complaints procedure, as modified at the hearing before us. As an alternative, they certainly could have been the subject of mediation.'

2.140 This comment emphasises the utility of mediation even where the matter may be the subject of legal rights, contrary to the view held by traditionalists. Indeed, the Court of Appeal returned to this theme and emphasised further their stringent views.

> '25. We do not single out either side's lawyers for particular criticism. What followed was due to the unfortunate culture in litigation of this nature of over-judicialising the processes which are involved. It is indeed unfortunate that, that process having started, instead of the parties focussing on the future they insisted on arguing about what had occurred in the past. So far as the claimants were concerned, that was of no value since Plymouth were prepared, as they ultimately made clear was their position, to re-consider the whole issue. Without the need for the vast costs which must have been incurred in this case already being incurred, the parties should have been able to come to a sensible conclusion as to how to dispose the issues which divided them. If they could not do this without help, then an independent mediator should have been recruited to assist. That would have been a far cheaper course to adopt. Today sufficient should be known about ADR to make the failure to adopt it, in particular when public money is involved, indefensible.'

2.141 The court concluded with an exhortation to practitioners.

> '27. This case will have served some purpose if it makes it clear that the lawyers acting on both sides of a dispute of this sort are under a heavy obligation to resort to litigation only if it is really unavoidable. If they cannot resolve the whole of the dispute by the use of the complaints procedure they should resolve the dispute so far as is practicable without involving litigation. At least in this way some of the expense and delay will be avoided. We hope that the highly skilled and caring practitioners who practise in this area will learn from what we regard as the very unfortunate history of this case.'

2.142 Of course such exhortations, while they may be influential in supporting a culture change, are unlikely to be effective in the short term unless backed up by a sanction. The immediate sanction can bite at two stages.

2.143 First, at the permission stage. In *R (S) v Hampshire County Council*,[290] following a core assessment report the local authority refused to provide services for S, a child with behavioural difficulties. It was contended that the assessment had been unlawful, procedurally unfair and discriminatory. The local authority submitted that S should be refused permission to apply for judicial review because there was an adequate alternative remedy which had not been pursued, in that the covering letter accompanying the report had invited discussion if any concerns as to S's needs had been raised, but S's mother had not complained or taken issue with the contents of the assessment at all. The court held that the existence of an alternative remedy enabled the court to conclude that permission should be refused; that the complaints procedure for core assessment reports was there to provide a speedy, informal and cheap method of resolving disputes; and that was the appropriate route by which to notify the local authority of points of dispute and to seek to have them resolved. This approach was endorsed by the Court of Appeal in *R (C & ANR) v Nottingham City Council*,[291] where in refusing permission on appeal, Jackson LJ stated that:

> 'For my part, I would echo in this case all of the sentiments which Lord Woolf CJ expressed in *Cowl*. In this case also, the parties are under a heavy obligation to resort to litigation – and, I would add, to continue with litigation – only if that is really unavoidable. In the present case litigation is far from unavoidable.'

2.144 Secondly, in the award of costs. The effect of the *Cowl* case is that when dealing with costs the courts will take into account whether ADR was considered or used, so a litigant who refuses to engage in more appropriate procedures runs the risk of not recovering the costs even if successful in the litigation.

2.145 However, the costs sanction will only be successful where one party seeks to invoke the alternative process. If both simply proceed with litigation in the normal way then this principle is unlikely to be invoked. In addition, a failure to engage in the alternative process is not necessarily fatal to recovery of costs. In *Hurst v Leeming*,[292] the claimant submitted that no such order should be made because both before and after the commencement of these proceedings he invited the defendant to proceed to mediation but this was refused. In awarding the costs to the defendant, Lightman J held that:

---

[290] [2009] EWHC 2537 (Admin).
[291] [2010] EWCA Civ 790.
[292] [2002] EWHC 1051 (Ch).

(a) the fact that heavy costs had already been incurred was not a justification for refusing to mediate, but it was a factor to be taken into account in the mediation process;
(b) the fact that a party believed he had a watertight case was no justification for refusing mediation;
(c) the fact that a full and detailed refutation of the opposite party's case had already been supplied was also not a sufficient justification for refusing mediation;
(d) nevertheless, the defendant was justified, on the facts of this case, in taking the view that mediation was not appropriate because it had no realistic prospect of success, by reason of the character and attitude of the claimant.

It was stressed that a litigant would normally be taking a great risk by refusing mediation on this ground. However, this was an exceptional decision and reflected how seriously disturbed the claimant's judgment was in relation to his case.

The pre-action protocol for judicial review

2.146 As explained in Chapter 3, Practice and Procedure, when judicial review proceedings are instituted, it is necessary to indicate whether there has been compliance with the pre-action protocol. The aim of it is to allow both parties to understand the complaint and justification for the decision, and thereby allow the opportunity for settling the issue or narrowing down the areas of dispute.

2.147 Mediation can be seen as a logical extension of this process. Again, the sanction for failure to comply with the protocol applies at two stages.

2.148 First, at the permission stage. In *R (S) v Hampshire County Council*,[293] not only was the existence of an alternative remedy sufficient to enable the court to conclude that permission should be refused, but it was also held that the complete failure on S's part to comply with the pre-action protocol in relation to the assessment, meant there was no attempt whatsoever to seek to avoid litigation and so this also warranted refusal of permission. There was never any adequate opportunity for the local authority to consider and respond to points of dispute before the proceedings were launched, and *Cowl* was applied.

2.149 Secondly, a failure to comply may be taken into account in decisions on costs.

The view in The Judge Over Your Shoulder

2.150 This document was published by the Treasury Solicitor to warn government departments and advise how to avoid judicial challenge. It advises that ADR avoids confrontation, encourages reconciliation, and is usually cheaper and less public than judicial review, and that:

> 'Whether mediation or some other form of ADR is appropriate to the case will depend on the nature of the decision being challenged, whether there is any room for manoeuvre, what other parties are affected and so on. The point to remember, however, is that the pre-action

---

[293] [2009] EWHC 2537 (Admin).

protocol is intended to offer opportunities, including ADR, for settling disputes without recourse to litigation. It will be to your advantage as decision-maker to grasp those opportunities.'

2.151 That advantage also extends to those challenging the decision in most circumstances. It is perhaps understandable that those being challenged may, in the hope that it will simply 'go away', be tempted to forget about the dispute until it is listed for hearing, by which time it is too late to engage in effective mediation. It is less understandable for those challenging the decision to allow the opportunity for earlier resolution to pass. They should seek to encourage mediation, except of course where the aim of the challenge is to achieve delay, for example in regard to the implementation of a decision.

Suggestions that courts and ombudsman should have power to require mediation

2.152 As noted above, in considering whether to grant permission to seek judicial review, and in awarding costs, the courts can take into account whether or not alternative remedies were attempted. They do not at present have powers to require mediation or other alternative remedies to be attempted before litigation proceeds. Nevertheless, there are calls from some quarters that such a change should be made to the CPR to permit judges to direct such attempts before judicial review proceeds.

2.153 Equally, although the use of ombudsmen is, as explained below, seen as itself being an alternative to litigation, there are now powers for the Ombudsmen to appoint and pay a mediator or other appropriate person to assist in the conduct of an investigation.[294] Again, some consider that this should be extended to require such mediation.

Particular advantages in public law

2.154 There are a number of reasons why mediation could be particularly beneficial in public law matters:

(a) **Cost** – while this is normally split between the parties, there may be an advantage for the private sector/applicant to have a prompt decision by meeting the cost of the mediator, with the other costs borne by each side. Not only will this result in less delay for some matters, but it may result in a lower overall cost than if the matter proceeded to litigation. It is also more likely to encourage the public body to engage in mediation rather than incur further legal costs. Of course, much will depend on the particular matter. There may not be a saving for a short simple judicial review matter. In other matters it may appear to increase costs. For example, in planning disputes, it has been suggested that the additional cost of paying for a mediator when an Inspector is provided free of charge will act as a barrier to mediation. However, significant savings may well be made by the applicant in relation to the other costs of delay, attendance at the inquiry, etc.

(b) **Speed** – again much will depend on the particular matter at issue, but a binding decision may be achieved in advance of the time by which it would be reached by

---

[294] The Parliamentary Commissioner Act 1967, s 3; the Local Government Act 1974, s 29; and the Health Service Commissioners Act 1993, para 1A of Sch 2; as amended by the Regulatory Reform (Collaboration etc between Ombudsmen) Order 2007 (SI 2007/1889).

the litigation or appeal process. Even if the mediation is not completely successful, it may well narrow down the issues and thereby reduce the time taken in the litigation or appeal process.

(c) **Control** – an important aspect of the mediation process is that the parties keep control of the outcome. That may well be important in terms of the meaning and limits of policy for public authorities. For example, rather than risking an adverse decision from an Inspector as to the meaning or implementation of a policy, which will then be invoked in subsequent applications, a local planning authority may well prefer to accept a mediated outcome which, while not ideal, is nevertheless an acceptable application of the policy. Similarly, an applicant can use the process to obtain a permission which, while not identical to that applied for, is nevertheless acceptable.

(d) **Relationships** – avoiding confrontation is important in any continuing relationship and for the image created by public bodies, so the mediation process is perfectly suited to avoiding developing a confrontational relationship.

(e) **Creative solutions** – mediation has the clear advantage of permitting a fresh look at the aims of all parties and developing a more creative outcome, rather than simply having a yes/no decision. It also avoids the rigidity of legal principles and even the precedent value of ombudsmen's and Inspectors' decisions.

(f) **Confidentiality** – while much of the business of public authorities will be public in any event, there is nevertheless often a need for confidentiality, *eg* planning obligations which are dealt with very unsatisfactorily in the current inquiry process, and the mediation process is again particularly suited to maintaining confidentiality.

(g) **Discipline and focus** – in the financially overstretched public sector context, and with competing demands on the time and resources available, mediation provides a compact and focussed productive process.

(h) **Satisfaction and compliance** – the essence of successful mediation is that the outcome is acceptable to both/all sides.

(i) **Search for consensus in public sector** – in public administration at present the language and policy is one of seeking partnership, agreements, involving stakeholders etc. The mediation process is ideally placed to achieve that.

Objections to the use of mediation in public law

2.155 There are various objections to the use of mediation in any legal dispute. Again, this is not the place to engage in a long exposition of the general literature as to the objections to mediation processes in relation to disputes and legal processes generally. However, some more specific objections to its use in public law processes can be identified.

2.156 Indeed, the relative lack of use, despite the exhortations identified above, raises the issue of whether there is good reason for this. It has been argued that the use of mediation in the public law context is more problematic for various reasons and that public law is different.

It is wrong to consider public law as a single category

2.157 It is often said that public law is too wide a term, and that the substantive issues covered by public law differ widely. At one level, both assertions are correct. However, in so far as both seek to establish that public law is essentially different from private law and not amenable to mediation, the only valid justification is that we must be sensitive to whether the subject matter is amenable to mediation.

2.158 Of course a dispute over two rival interpretations of the meaning of a statutory provision, or a policy in national guidance or a development plan, ultimately requires a court or similar process to decide which is correct. But only a relatively few disputes in public law are actually about such interpretation or matters of enforcement of absolute rights. Most are concerned with particular decisions within a well understood, if flexible, legal and policy framework.

Duties and discretions

2.159 A related point which is often raised is that there is an important difference between statutory duties and discretion. For the former, it is said that only litigation is appropriate since this is a matter of legal right, not to be undermined by a settlement or negotiation, however consensual.

2.160 Of course mediation is easier to operate in regard to discretionary powers where there is a choice between a range of legitimate decisions. Clearly this category accounts for many decisions made by public authorities.

2.161 Nevertheless, mediation can still have a role to play in matters of statutory duty, in relation to resolution of disputes of fact; what constitutes satisfactory compliance with the duty in terms of good use of resources; and in clarifying areas of continuing dispute. It is also wrong to think that duties are always absolute – much depends on the context.

2.162 Equally, there will be matters where discretion is being exercised but mediation is not appropriate such as where there are simply two conflicting aims and no scope for either a third way or a compromise.

Not just two parties but the public as well

2.163 Equally, it is often argued that mediation is not appropriate because the dispute does not, as in most commercial disputes, concern simply two parties – the complainant and the public authority – but also involves the public. That is misconceived as a general objection because:

(a) a 'normal' mediation can be multi-party;

(b) while the public authority represents the 'public interest', it can nevertheless be recognised that there are separate third party interests to be taken into account;

(c) it may actually assist third parties to understand the issues or have their narrow/specific interest dealt with discretely;

(d) in relation to local government, if the mediation process can be in advance of the local planning authority decision on a controversial application, it may reduce the practice of elected members refusing planning applications in order to allow third parties to object at an appeal, and the strength and weakness of the third parties' position properly understood by all sides;

(e) it is the experience of some that the public inquiry, the main alternative to resolving disputes in planning matters, is all but incomprehensible to most of the lay public.

2.164 It can also be noted that in 1997 the Government stated in a consultation paper on planning that:

> 'Successful mediation would obviate the need for an appeal or inquiry, but openness and fairness, and the law, demand that a fresh application and decision should be made, in the normal way, in respect of any amended scheme emerging from mediation. Third parties would not normally be involved directly in mediation, but would have the opportunity to comment on the revised scheme. When mediation narrows, but does not dispose of, an appeal then third parties can still make representations to the Inspector.'

2.165 This of course represents a view where the mediation involves only the applicant and the local planning authority. However, it is certainly possible and indeed desirable in some circumstances, to involve clearly identified third party interests in the mediation process, since this can introduce more certainty and faster decision-making into the process.

2.166 In both circumstances, the normal rules as to what is a significant amendment requiring re-consultation apply.

Authority to settle

2.167 Most mediators consider it an essential part of the process that the participants have authority to settle the matter in the course of the mediation.

2.168 It is normally regarded as essential that those attending the mediation have the power to settle, so that it makes the process meaningful and minimises the chance of a party apparently reaching an agreement and then reneging on it or seeking further concessions.

2.169 It is often thought that this causes problems for the public authority. For example a leading textbook notes:[295]

> 'Complications may well arise with public bodies. Given the decision-making structures of national or local government, it is unlikely that any individuals will be able to attend a mediation with completely unfettered authority to settle. More likely, those who attend will be authorised to agree settlement terms subject to obtaining final approval from the appropriate committee .... Although not ideal ... mediation can and does still operate effectively in these circumstances. It may, however, be helpful to obtain a commitment in advance that the appropriate committee will meet within a specified and short period following the mediation so that the matter is not left unresolved for too long.'

2.170 While that shows that the issue is not insuperable, the difficulty may in any event be overstated. It is an objection which is thought to have greater force in regard to local government than for other public bodies. As far as local government is concerned, because:

---

[295] Mackie, Miles, Marsh and Allen, *The ADR Practice Guide*, pp 95–96.

(a) it is already the case that those officers involved in the proceedings are already delegated to take the relevant decision as to any settlement of modification of the authority's position, eg in relation to the conduct of legal proceedings or planning appeals;

(b) delegated authority is usually given in general terms;

(c) where it is not done, or the issue is recognised to be sensitive politically, then it is usually structured as an officer decision after consultation with the appropriate Chair or Cabinet member;

(d) the trend in local government law generally is to have executive decision-making so that not only the officer but also the relevant elected member with authority could attend the mediation, although this does not of course apply in the regulatory controls such as planning.

Other tailor-made processes/remedies

2.171 It may be thought that other tailor-made and designed alternatives to the courts would be more appropriate – such as public inquiries and/or ombudsmen. However, not only do they also have disadvantages, often in terms of control, costs, speed and effectiveness, but it is instructive that not only the ombudsmen, through 'informal settlements' and recent powers to finance mediation described above, but also the Planning Inspectorate are both actively encouraging mediation as a cost effective alternative to their own procedures.

Summary

2.172 Despite the strong exhortations from the courts and policymakers to use mediation, it is by no means the case that mediation is suitable for all public law issues.

2.173 Certainly, it is suitable for any functional area where discretion exists, or finding agreed facts is important. It has been widely used in relation to neighbour/tenancy issues, and could also be used in some social services issues as it is in matrimonial disputes.

2.174 In recent years there has been much encouragement in planning, environmental and compulsory purchase matters. This has included a pilot project and repeated exhortations in reports and adopted policy.[296] However, this has failed to deliver much activity, and Sir Henry Brooke has characterised the policy guidance as 'pious incantations' and the Government's response to the Barker Report's suggestion to promote mediation as 'a thoroughly flaccid response'.[297]

2.175 There are a number of possible reasons why it has not been utilised more. One clear barrier is what is perceived as an additional cost, since the cost of an appeal, as opposed to representation, is met by the public purse, but not the cost of mediation. However, it is capable of reducing overall costs, and the issue is on whom the costs should fall.

---

[296] For example, see consultation documents in 1997, 2001 and 2002; Major Infrastructure Inquiry Rules 2002; Planning and Access for Disabled Circulars 2002 and 2005; Compulsory Purchase Circular 02/2003; Crichel Down Rules Circular 06/2004; PPS 11 Regional Planning (2004); PPS 12 Development Plans (2004); Planning Obligations Circular 05/2005; Planning Policy Wales; the Barker Report (2006).

[297] Sir Henry Brooke, 'Mediation and Planning: The Role of Mediation in Planning and Environmental Disputes', [2008] JPEL 1390.

2.176 Another reason may be that it is seen purely as an alternative to a final dispute resolution and it is judged solely on that basis. However, it is a technique which can be used to produce useful results in a number of situations, and can be a success in relation to appeals even if it fails to resolve the matter conclusively and simply narrows down issues, in a more formal and rigorous way than, for example, the statement of common ground which it is necessary to provide in advance of a planning appeal.[298]

2.177 It is an issue which will not go away, and the relevance and utility of mediation is all the greater given the reality of resourcing of the public sector today. It is capable of reducing costs, while it has the similar advantage of allowing an independent expert to be involved but with control remaining with the parties.

OTHER ALTERNATIVE REMEDIES

2.178 Alternative remedies for disputes or complaints may be provided in different ways. In a work on judicial review it is not the place to provide a full account of the policy background and practice in relation to each of these. Instead, the main elements will be briefly explained and the relationship with judicial review outlined.

2.179 Three important themes throughout these alternatives are:

(a) the extent to which they deal with individual grievances or with more general systemic or administrative faults;
(b) the extent to which they concentrate on merits or simply the legality of decisions;
(c) the relationship of the principles applied to those applied by the courts.

Tribunals

2.180 Tribunals can now be viewed not so much as an alternative to the courts, which they were originally, but as specialised courts with their own procedures. They have developed from an ad hoc system of specialist supervisory and adjudicative bodies. Depending on the terms of reference of the particular tribunal, it reviews the legality and/or the merits of decisions. They concentrate on individual grievances. Tribunals are dealt with in detail in Chapter 4.

Inquiries

2.181 Inquiries take two forms. The first is the ad hoc inquiry into a single event or issue. The second is the mechanism by which appeals against adverse decision or proposals are made.

2.182 The first is usually a fact-finding exercise, although recommendations can be made to ministers or those establishing the inquiry.[299] These do not usually provide a specific remedy to an aggrieved individual, and are usually concerned with the merits of a particular decision or with more general issues. The inquiries, and the decisions, are themselves amenable to judicial review.

---

[298] Andy Grossman, 'Mediation in Planning – from talking the Talk to Walking the Walk', [2009] JPEL Occ Paper 24.
[299] Inquiries Act 2005.

2.183 The second is most often used in the areas of planning, highways, compulsory purchase, and other environmental matters. While originally these were also conceived as fact-finding exercises, and the Inspector reported to the minister who made the decision, now the vast majority of such appeals are determined by the Inspector.

2.184 Partly as a result of the search for speedier and cheaper determination of such appeals, the vast majority are determined without an actual formal inquiry, with cross-examination of the evidence. Most are dealt with by informal hearing or written representations.

2.185 These inquiries are therefore concerned with merits and not usually with more general policy issues. Again, these inquiries or determinations are subject to either statutory appeal to the court or judicial review.

2.186 As noted above, there are calls for mediation to be used in appropriate cases to deal with an appeal, instead of an inquiry or another mechanism, and successful pilot projects have been promoted by the Planning Inspectorate.

Internal complaints systems

2.187 Internal complaints systems were not previously regarded as effective mechanisms, largely because they were perceived to lack the necessary independence and impartiality. Nevertheless they have become an established part of the dispute landscape for four main reasons:

(1) First, from a more general management and audit perspective it is considered that organisations can learn from the mistakes highlighted by the complaints process, and so improve performance generally and minimise future errors.

(2) Secondly, external review by ombudsmen has resulted not only in exhortations from public bodies to have such internal systems to minimise external complaints, but has also increased the use of 'local settlements' by means of internal review when the external complaint is notified to the public body.

(3) Thirdly, clearly influenced by considerations of relative cost and speed, there has been strong policy support for such mechanisms, although of course a tension exists between these aims if the internal complaints system rejects the complaints and it nevertheless proceeds to external review.

(4) Fourthly, this policy has been given statutory force in some instances and the processes given formal recognition, such as for local authority standards committees, explained below, or for the National Health Service or under the Housing Act 1996.[300]

2.188 Such internal review is of course usually concerned with the merits of individual complaints but it may, if properly used, spill over into more general policy and administrative reviews. Other than in special cases such as local Standards Committees, such internal procedures are not usually concerned with enforcing legal principles, or have an independent element.

---

[300] Local Authority Social Services and National Health Service Complaints (England) Regulations 2009 (SI 2009/309); Housing Act 1996, s 202.

Standards

2.189 Within local government there is a further check on the legality of actions. Each authority is under a duty to appoint a monitoring officer whose roles include the duty, where it appears to him that any proposal, decision or omission by the authority or its employee has given rise to or is likely to or would give rise to a contravention of any enactment or rule of law to prepare a report to the authority with respect to that proposal, decision or omission. Approaching the monitoring officer can thus provide a means of raising the issue with the authority, and testing the willingness to change the course of action, without the expense of commencing proceedings. However, care must be taken to ensure that doing this does not result in unacceptable delay in commencing judicial proceedings promptly.

Audit

2.190 Audit is a term usually associated with financial reporting and management analysis. As with the private sector, this plays an important role across the whole public sector. Standard financial reporting has always been necessary to ensure probity, and more recent developments such as economy and impact studies, Best Value, performance indicators etc are intended not only to deliver value for money but also to ensure that the implementation of policy is delivered properly and effectively.

2.191 Such accountability is of course at a general level and may be valuable for those with a specific interest in a policy or issue being audited. However, in relation to local government there are also long established powers relating to the legality of decisions which are available to the auditor and which members of the public may request to be used. This has the following advantages for anyone thinking about instituting a judicial challenge: the reaction of the auditor may be a good guide to how successful an independent challenge would be; if the auditor accepts the complaint then the authority may reverse the decision to avoid an audit challenge or adverse report; and it would pass the costs of any eventual court action on to the auditor.

2.192 In England responsibility for audit arrangements is currently governed by the Audit Commission Act 1998 and is undertaken by the Audit Commission for Local Authorities and the National Health Service in England. In Wales, the Auditor General for Wales has responsibility under the Public Audit (Wales) Act 2004. Private sector firms may be appointed by the Commission or the Auditor General as auditors for any authority. In August 2010 the Government announced that in England the Audit Commission would be scrapped, and local authorities would be able to appoint their own external auditors. At the time of this work going to press, the Local Audit and Accountability Bill is before Parliament. The following is a description of the current position but the provisions of the Bill largely retain to detailed powers of the auditor.

2.193 The duties of the auditor, historically called the district auditor, in respect of the legality of decisions were described as follows:[301]

> 'The district auditor holds a position of much responsibility. In some respects he is like a company auditor, he is a watchdog to see that the accounts are properly kept and that no one is making off with the funds. ... In other respects, however, the duties of a district auditor go far beyond those of a company auditor. He must see whether, on the financial side, the councillors and their officers have discharged their duties according to law. He must listen to

---

[301] *Asher v Secretary of State for the Environment* [1974] Ch 208 at 219, Lord Denning MR.

any elector who makes objection to the accounts. He must make his own investigation also. If he finds that the councillors or the officers, or any of them, have expended money improperly, or unreasonably, or allowed it to be so expended, it is his duty to surcharge them ....'

2.194 The surcharge provisions, by which individual councillors could be forced to repay unlawful sums, were controversial and were eventually repealed by the Local Government Act 2003, but the rest of this description remains good.

2.195 The public can raise issues with the auditor who must consider whether in the public interest he should make a report on any matter in order that it may be considered by the body concerned or brought to the attention of the public.[302] He is also to consider whether the public interest requires an immediate report rather than a report at the conclusion of the audit. The authority is then under a duty to give consideration to it.

2.196 Where it appears to the auditor that an item of account is 'contrary to law' he may apply to the court for a declaration to that effect.[303] Essentially this means if the action represented by the item of account is unlawful and in principle includes a breach of the fiduciary duty a court can declare that is the position.[304]

2.197 The threat of such action on the part of the auditor is clearly very important, and where the auditor expresses a view in a report, as opposed to actually seeking a declaration, it is open to an authority to seek judicial review of that view and itself ask for a declaration.[305] While the court had reservations about using judicial review in this way, as opposed to waiting for an application for a declaration by the district auditor, the auditor acquiesced on the basis that the matter should be determined quickly so the court proceeded to hear the applications.

2.198 As a further power, the auditor may issue an advisory notice if he has reason to believe that the body or an officer of the body is about to make or has made a decision, or is about to take or has begun to take a course of action, which involves or would involve the body incurring expenditure which is unlawful.[306] Such a notice requires the authority to give the auditor not less than a maximum of 21 days' notice in writing before taking that decision or action.

2.199 The auditor is also a useful tool for obtaining information, since he has a right of access to all documents relating to an audited body which appear to him to be necessary for the purposes of his statutory functions.

2.200 In addition, all persons interested may inspect the accounts to be audited and all books, deeds, contracts, bills, vouchers and receipts relating thereto, and they may make copies of them.[307] Indeed, in *Veolia*,[308] an environmental activist claimed to be entitled to inspect and take copies of schedules to the waste management contract between the authority and the company. The company asked the local authority not to disclose the documents on the ground of commercial confidentiality and brought proceedings to

---

[302] Audit Commission Act 1998, s 8 and the Public Audit (Wales) Act 2004, s 22.
[303] Audit Commission Act 1998, s 17(1); Public Audit (Wales) Act 2004, s 32.
[304] For an explanation of the fiduciary duty, see para **13.104**.
[305] *R v District Auditor, ex p West Yorkshire Metropolitan CC* [1985] RVR 191; and *R v District Auditor, ex p Leicester City Council* [1985] RVR 191.
[306] Audit Commission Act 1998, s 19A; Public Audit (Wales) Act 2004, s 33.
[307] Audit Commission Act 1998, s 15(1); Public Audit (Wales) Act 2004, s 30(1).
[308] *Veolia ES Nottinghamshire Ltd v Nottinghamshire County Council* [2009] EWHC 2382 (Admin).

compel the authority to keep the documents confidential. The High Court held that the legislative materials supported a broad approach, and that Parliament's intention in using the words 'relating to' was simply that there should be an enquiry as to the factual connection between the limited category of documents mentioned on the one hand and the accounts to be audited on the other. The contract itself, and any invoice paid under it, related to the accounts. The court found that the concern about commercial confidentiality was understandable, but there was no duty to keep commercial confidentiality under the statutory provision. This permits wider access to information than would be possible under the Freedom of Information Act 2000.

Ombudsmen

2.201 While the auditor is primarily concerned with general issues of financial and management accountability, but have a more minor role for individual grievances, the ombudsmen are the opposite. Established primarily as an individual grievance remedying institution, they have developed a more general administrative audit role and promote good administrative practice. Nevertheless, they remain primarily concerned with providing a remedy where appropriate for an individual who has suffered injustice.

2.202 Since the Parliamentary Commissioner for Administration was created in 1967, there has been a proliferation of ombudsmen. This term 'ombudsman' does not appear in the formal statutory title of the three main Ombudsmen – the Parliamentary Commissioner,[309] the Health Services Commissioner,[310] and the Commission for Local Administration.[311] However, these are known generally as the Parliamentary Ombudsman, the Health Services Ombudsman and the Local Government Ombudsman.

2.203 The term 'ombudsman' is now becoming more widely understood and is given statutory recognition in some instances, such as the Public Services Ombudsman for Wales,[312] and the Housing Ombudsman.[313] Indeed the general concept has been widely accepted and, while these and various other bodies are statutory bodies with a formal remit to deal with public sector bodies, there are numerous other non-statutory ombudsmen dealing with the public and private sectors,[314] and statutory ombudsmen dealing with the private sectors.[315]

2.204 The detailed remit, and exclusions from jurisdiction, of each of these bodies is beyond the scope of this work. Indeed, each scheme has its own detailed rules relating to jurisdiction, exclusions, access, procedure, and remedies. However, the following comments can be made about the three main ombudsmen schemes.

2.205 Their remit is to investigate allegations of injustice through maladministration, although the Health Services Ombudsman has a wider jurisdiction to also include clinical judgement.

2.206 The term maladministration has never been defined by statute but has been left deliberately flexible. In the second reading debate on the Parliamentary Commissioner

---

[309] Parliamentary Commissioner Act 1967.
[310] Health Service Commissioners Act 1993.
[311] Local Government Act 1974.
[312] Public Services Ombudsman (Wales) Act 2005.
[313] Housing Act 1996.
[314] For example the Waterways Ombudsman.
[315] For example the Pensions Ombudsman.

Bill, the Minister stated that the characteristics of maladministration include 'bias, neglect, inattention, delay, incompetence, ineptitude, perversity, turpitude, arbitrariness and so on', and this has become known as the 'Crossman catalogue'.[316] It remains a flexible concept to deal with different and changing situations. It is thus wider than, but overlaps with, judicial principles and although it is largely about how decisions are reached it can involve the merits of 'bad rules'.

2.207 This overlap raises the issue of what the relationship between the courts and the ombudsmen should be, and the main issue is whether it should be cheaper, more accessible justice in accordance with legal principles, or a different concept. Clearly it is different in the sense that it is a wider concept, but where they do overlap the issue is whether authorities should be subjected to two regimes and the complainant should be allowed to choose between two different mechanisms with different remedies available.

2.208 This issue involves three issues – the statutory position; the judicial approach; and the respective remedies.

2.209 First, for all three of the main ombudsmen, there is a statutory exclusion to the effect that they should not investigate where the person aggrieved has or had a right of appeal or review to a tribunal, or where the person has or had a remedy in any court of law. However, this is subject to the qualification that an investigation may be undertaken if the ombudsman is satisfied that in the circumstances of the case it is not reasonable to expect the complainant to resort to that remedy. This has been interpreted liberally by the ombudsmen not only on the basis that the cost of challenges to the courts are a sufficient reason, but also on the basis that since 1967 the principles of judicial review have expanded and so the overlap is now much greater than it was thought to be.

2.210 Secondly, this approach to the wide discretion has been supported by the courts.[317] In addition, as with the approach to mediation described above, the courts have encouraged the use of this alternative to judicial review.[318] This approach raises two main issues.

(1) Given the respective time scales, where complaints to the ombudsmen can be made after the three months period for judicial review has expired, and any investigation is unlikely to be completed within that time scale in any event, such an approach relies either on the courts extending the three month period for bringing an action, which is risky, or proceedings must be commenced and then stayed, which undermines the cost advantages.

(2) The objection that this means that authorities which are acting in a manner which the courts define as lawful, may nevertheless be told they should not act in that way, is rejected not only on the basis that this must be is what Parliament intended by enacting this system, but also because the remedies provided by the two systems are different.

2.211 Thirdly, the remedies provided under the ombudsmen schemes appear less effective. The schemes rely on persuasion in that the ombudsmen have power only to

---

[316] HC Deb Vol 754, c 51 (1966).
[317] See eg *R v Local Commissioner for Local Government for North and North East England, ex p Liverpool City Council* [2001] 1 All ER 462.
[318] See *R v Lambeth London Borough Council, ex p Crookes* (1995) 29 HLR 28; R (*Scholarastica UMO v Commissioner for Local Administration* [2003] EWHC 3202 (Admin).

recommend particular redress. Again the substance of this is not defined and is left very flexible. It may range from recommending a formal apology to a substantial award of financial compensation. There is, however, no formal power to impose a particular remedy or to quash or overturn decisions which have been made.

2.212 In practice, the public bodies do comply in the vast majority of cases. Where there is non-compliance then additional powers are given to issue a special or further report. This will be raised in Parliament in the case of the Parliamentary Ombudsman, and in the case of the Local Ombudsman additional publicity for it and the response, at the expense of the authority, can be required by the ombudsman.

2.213 Over the years there have been calls for judicial enforcement of Ombudsmen's decisions, particularly in the case of the Local Government Ombudsmen, on the basis that any non-compliance, however infrequent, undermines the authority of the institution and deprives the complainant of what an independent body thinks appropriate. These calls, however, have been resisted largely on the basis that it would undermine the flexibility and informality of investigations.

2.214 The ombudsman, therefore, is both an alternative dispute resolution mechanism in that the principles applied overlap with those of the courts but a remedy can be provided more cheaply, and also an appropriate dispute resolution mechanism in that the more flexible investigatory procedure is more appropriate to the issues at stake and the principles of maladministration are not restricted to existing legal principles but can be tailored to the particular situation.

2.215 Nevertheless, while this is itself a valuable alternative to litigation, it is instructive to note that, in the search for speed, economy and more flexible dispute resolution, there are now powers for the ombudsmen to appoint and pay a mediator or other appropriate person to assist in the conduct of an investigation.[319]

2.216 This is a clear reminder that no one mechanism is appropriate for all public law disputes or grievances. Judicial review is certainly a valuable and important tool, but a range of alternatives exist which may provide cheaper and more appropriate solutions.

---

[319] Parliamentary Commissioner Act 1967, s 3; Local Government Act 1974, s 29; and the Health Service Commissioners Act 1993, para 1A of Sch 2; as amended by the Regulatory Reform (Collaboration etc between Ombudsmen) Order 2007 (SI 2007/1889).

CHAPTER 3

PRACTICE AND PROCEDURE

JUDICIAL REVIEW IN THE ADMINISTRATIVE COURT

3.01 The procedure for bringing a judicial review claim is governed by CPR Part 54 backed up with reference to PD 54. They need to be read with part 8 CPR and s 31 of the Senior Courts Act 1981 which tied an application to the High Court for prerogative relief as well as an application for a declaration and/or an injunction to an application for judicial review. Part 54 develops judicial review further in that it makes it clear that it does not depend only on the prerogative remedies but also on the nature and the functions of the body that is subject to challenge.

Pre-Action Protocol

3.02 Prior to bringing a claim for JR a claimant should first comply with the Pre-Action Protocol for Judicial Review.[1]

3.03 The Pre-Action Protocol requires a letter to be sent by the claimant to the defendant before making a claim for JR.[2] A standard form of the letter is to be found in Annex A to the Protocol and should be used in normal circumstances.[3] Relevant factors include:

- The letter should contain the date and details of the decision, act or omission being challenged, a summary of the facts and an outline of the alleged unlawfulness.[4]
- If the claimant seeks particular information, which he considers relevant to the claim, the details of the information sought should be contained in the letter.[5]
- A copy of the letter before claim should be sent to any interested parties.[6]
- A claim should not normally be made until after the proposed reply date given in the letter before claim unless the circumstances of the case require the claim be made sooner.[7]
- The letter of claim should set out the details of the actions which it is desired the defendant should take, ie what remedy is sought.[8]
- The letter before claim should specify a proposed reply date, usually 14 days.[9]

---

1   See http://www.justice.gov.uk/civil/procrules_fin/contents/protocols/prot_jev/htm.
2   Para 8 of Pre-Action Protocol.
3   Para 9 of Pre-Action Protocol.
4   Para 10 of Pre-Action Protocol.
5   Para 10 of Pre-Action Protocol.
6   Para 11 of Pre-Action Protocol.
7   Para 12 of Pre-Action Protocol.
8   See model letter at Annex A to Pre-Action Protocol.
9   Para 13 and model letter at Annex A of Pre-Action Protocol.

- The reply to the letter before claim should also be made in a standard form in most cases.[10] The reply should set out the public body's response to the claim and whether the claim will be resisted in whole or in part.[11]
- The protocol does not suspend the time limits for making a claim for JR. As such the Protocol is not appropriate where a claim would become out of time if the Protocol was followed. In such cases the claim should be filed and the claim form used to explain why the Pre-Action Protocol was not followed.
- Neither is the Protocol appropriate in 'urgent cases' where there is a need for an interim order to compel or prohibit a public body from acting. The Protocol gives examples of urgent cases such as an immigration claim where the claimant is due to be removed from the UK and a housing claim where a local authority has failed to secure interim accommodation for a homeless claimant.
- Failure to comply with the pre-action protocol may affect prospects of recovering costs.[12] In *R (Kemp) v Denbighshire Local Health Board*[13] the claimant had succeeded in obtaining funding relating to his nursing home costs but because he failed to comply with the pre-action protocol, no order for costs was made given that there was no evidence that the defendant would not have offered a review had a pre-action protocol letter been written. In addition, in *R (Ewing v Office of the Deputy Prime Minister)*,[14] Lord Justice Brooke stated at paragraph 54 that, 'Needless to say, if the claimant skips the pre-action protocol stage, he must expect to put his opponents to greater expense in preparing the summary of their grounds for contesting the claim, and this may be reflected in the greater order for costs that may be made against him if permission is refused ...'

3.04 Judicial review is a two-stage process. The claimant must first obtain permission to apply for judicial review. To obtain permission, an application must be made to the court outlining the grounds on which judicial review is sought.

PRE-ISSUE CONSIDERATIONS

3.05 Applications for Judicial Review fall within the jurisdiction of the Administrative Court.[15] The JR procedure under Part 54 must[16] be used in a claim for JR where the claimant is seeking one of the prerogative orders[17] or an injunction restraining a person from acting in any office in which he is not entitled to act.[18] The JR procedure may be used in a claim for JR where the claimant is seeking either an injunction or a declaration.[19] A claim for JR may include a claim for damages but may not seek damages alone.[20]

---

[10] See model letter at Annex B to Pre-Action Protocol.
[11] See model letter at Annex B to Pre-Action Protocol.
[12] *R (Bahta) v Secretary of State for the Home Department* [2011] EWCA Civ 895 at 59–71.
[13] [2006] EWHC 181 (Admin).
[14] [2006] 1 WLR 1260.
[15] *Practice Direction – Judicial Review* (2000) PD 54, para 2.1.
[16] CPR, r 54.2 is prescriptive and mandatory but CPR, r 3.10 gives the court general power to rectify procedural errors and the court will always seek to advance the overriding objective in preference to procedural formalism and technicalities.
[17] CPR, r 54.2(a)–(c).
[18] CPR, r 54.2(d).
[19] CPR, r 54 3.
[20] CPR, r 54.3(2), a claim seeking only damages will be transferred out of the Administrative Court under CPR, r 54.20.

Standing

3.06 Whether a claimant had sufficient standing to bring proceedings used to be a significant issue. Now the approach to standing is sufficiently generous that it is rarely an issue. Fundamentally, however, the court should not grant permission unless it considers that the claimant has sufficient interest (Senior Courts Act 1981, s 31(3)). The standing question at the permission stage is whether the claimant is a 'busybody' with 'no interest whatsoever', *R (Dixon) v Somerset CC*.[21] Recent examples of cases in which standing has been disputed concerned groups formed specifically for the purpose of pursuing judicial review. Permission has been granted to such bodies where they are found to have sufficient interest due to their representing affected individuals.[22] By contrast, in *R (Unison) v NHS Shared Business Services Ltd*, the trade union UNISON failed to show that it had been 'affected in some identifiable way' by the decision challenged, and as such was found not to have standing.[23] Short of an abuse of process, the court will not refuse permission for an otherwise arguable challenge but will take care to satisfy itself that the claim genuinely reveals an arguable point.[24] Auld LJ stated in *R (Noble) v Thanet DC*:[25]

> 'In [dismissing the appeal] I add a note of dissatisfaction at the way the availability of the remedy of judicial review can be exploited – some might say abused – as a commercial weapon by rival potential developers to frustrate and delay their competitors' approved developments, rather than for any demonstrated concern about potential environmental or other planning harm ... However seemingly complicated the issues are, or how sophisticated and technical the statement of facts and grounds supporting the initial claim for judicial review, they should be subject to rigorous examination by the single judge at the permission stage of a claim for judicial review.'

Duty of candour/disclosure

3.07 A claimant is under a duty to disclose all material facts in the claim form.[26] These include all facts known to the claimant at the time he applies for permission. The court may take account of those facts that he would have known had he made the proper and necessary inquiries before applying for permission.[27] The extent of inquiries the claimant should have made will depend on the circumstances of the case, including the nature of the case, the order for which the applicant is applying, the degree of legitimate urgency and the time available for making inquiries.[28] Non-disclosure is sufficient for the court to refuse the remedy sought,[29] to set aside permission[30] or refuse permission, and the claimant may be penalised in costs.

---

21 [1998] Env LR 111, 116–117, 330–331.
22 *R (Save Our Surgery Ltd) v Joint Committee of Primary Care Trusts* [2013] EWHC 439 (Admin): a shell company formed to represent affected individuals did have standing; cf *R (Broadway Care Centre Ltd) v Caerphilly County Borough Council* [2012] EWHC 37 (Admin): a care home did not have standing to represent its residents; *The Children's Rights Alliance for England v Secretary of State for Justice* [2012] EWHC 8 (Admin): a charity did not have standing where there was no victim.
23 *R (Unison) v NHS Shared Business Services Ltd* [2012] EWHC 624 (Admin) at 13.
24 *Bhatti, R (on the application of) v Bury MBC* [2013] EWHC 3093 (Admin) at 37–41.
25 [2005] EWCA Civ 782.
26 *R v Lloyds Corpn, ex p Briggs* [1993] 1 Lloyd's L Rep 176; *R v Jockey Club Licensing Committee, ex p Wright (Barrie John)* [1991] COD 306 and *R (Burkett) v Hammersmith and Fulham LBC* [2002] 1 WLR 1593 at para 50.
27 *R v Jockey Club Licensing Committee, ex p Wright (Barrie John)* [1991] COD 306.
28 *R v Jockey Club Licensing Committee, ex p Wright (Barrie John)* [1991] COD 306.
29 *R v Kensington General Cssrs, ex p Polignac (Princess)* [1917] 1 KB 486.
30 *R v SoS Home, ex p Sholola* [1992] Imm AR 135; *R v SoS Home, ex p Chinoy* (1991) 4 Admin LR 457, [1991] COD 381, DC; applications to set aside permission may now only be made rarely.

3.08 When setting out the facts and issues of law which demonstrate that the public body's action was unlawful the claimant should disclose any outstanding appeals against the decision,[31] or any rights of appeal that exist but have not been pursued and set out why judicial review is, in the circumstances, appropriate. The claim should identify any legislative provisions which purport to oust the court's jurisdiction and explain why the claimant contends the jurisdiction is not ousted.[32]

3.09 Equally, a defendant is required to satisfy the requirement of the duty of candour which applies from the outset and which applies to all information relevant to the issues of the case, not just documents. The point was explained by Lord Donaldson MR in *R v Lancashire County Council, ex p Huddleston* [1986] All ER 941 when he said this:

> 'This development [ie the remedy of judicial review and the evolution of a specialist administrative or public law court] has created a new relationship between the courts and those who derive their authority from public law, one of partnership based on a common aim, namely the maintenance of the highest standards of public administration ... The analogy is not exact, but just as the judges of the inferior courts when challenged on the exercise of their jurisdiction traditionally explain fully what they have done and why they have done it, but are not partisan in their own defence, so should be the public authorities. It is not discreditable to get it wrong. What is discreditable is a reluctance to explain fully what has occurred and why ... Certainly it is for the applicant to satisfy the court of his entitlement to judicial review and it is for the respondent to resist his application, if it considers it to be unjustified. But it is a process which falls to be conducted with all the cards face upwards on the table and the vast majority of the cards will start in the authority's hands.'

3.10 The Practice Direction to CPR Part 54 states (at para 12) that 'disclosure is not required unless the court orders otherwise'. What this means is that CPR Part 31 (which sets out the rules applicable on standard disclosure) will not ordinarily apply on an application for judicial review unless the court orders otherwise (CPR, PD 54A, para 12.1). One occasion when a court will order otherwise is when cross-examination is necessary to enable the court to establish the facts of a case for itself; *R (N) v M and others*,[33] *R (Wilkinson) v Broadmoor Special Hospital Authority*.[34] Disclosure is required to enable proper and effective cross-examination to take place.

3.11 In that exceptional category of judicial review involving inquiry into issues of fact, where disclosure has to be given, it is suggested that the best practice is to do so in accordance with the principles set out in CPR, r 31:

- the parties are required to help the court further the overriding objective which is to deal with cases justly. Dealing with a case justly includes dealing with the case in ways which are proportionate, CPR, r 3, s 1(2)(c);
- parties are required to disclose only the documents which:
    (i) they rely upon;
    (ii) adversely affect their own, or another party's, case;
    (iii) support another party's case;
- document means anything in which information of any description is recorded. It will include, for example, not only letters and emails, but drafts, calendars,

---

[31] *R v Humberside CC, ex p Bogdal* [1992] COD 467; *R v Mid-Worcestershire Justices, ex p Hart* [1989] COD 397.
[32] *R v Cornwall CC, ex p Huntingdon* [1992] 3 All ER 566 (substantive decision affirmed by CA at [1994] 1 All ER 694).
[33] [2003] 1 WLR 562.
[34] [2002] 1 WLR 419.

manuscript and post-it notes, voicemails, computer disks, documents stored on servers and back-up systems and documents that have been deleted and blogs;

- disclosure is required if a party has or at any time has had a document so that the existence of destroyed or lost documents or documents which have been passed on must be disclosed; and
- parties are required to undertake a reasonable search for disclosable documents.

3.12 In *R (Al Sweady) v Secretary of State for Defence*[35] the court emphasised that legal representatives have a duty to ensure that proper disclosure is given where there is to be cross-examination or in any case where the court makes findings of fact. The court made it plain that any infringements of the three basic human rights (Articles 2, 3 and 5) would be subject to intense scrutiny and that in such a case the duty of disclosure is 'even more acute'.

In *Durham County Council v D* the court emphasised that that non-disclosure and restrictions on disclosure are only permitted when strictly necessary. Further, the relevant rules to be relied upon in judicial review cases are the Civil Procedure Rules, not the Data Protection Act.[36]

Time limits for bringing a claim

3.13 The claim form must be filed promptly and in any event within three months of the date when the grounds for the claim arose.[37] The court has jurisdiction to grant an extension of time.[38] An extension cannot be agreed between the parties without the court's consent.[39] The time limits run from the date the grounds for JR arose,[40] not when the claimant became aware of the decision being challenged. That the claimant was delayed in becoming aware of the grounds for challenge is a factor which may be relevant to the question of whether there is good reason to extend the time limit.

3.14 Claims must be brought 'promptly' and the courts have emphasised that a claim will not necessarily be prompt merely because it has been made within the three-month period.[41] Promptness has not been tested as a test for delay with regard to European Convention or EU law but is likely to be compatible. The ECtHR rejected a challenge to the former provisions dealing with time-limits which are materially identical to the current provisions of the CPR as it considered the requirement was proportionate in pursuit of a legitimate end of ensuring claimants acted quickly to avoid prejudicing the rights of others.[42] The ECJ has held that it is compatible with EU law for domestic law to lay down reasonable time-limits[43] and has not challenged a similar rule to the JR time-limit.[44] However, cases brought challenging a European Directive are not required to be made promptly, only within the three-month period. *R (Buglife) v Medway Council* confirmed this by reference to the European Court of Justice's decision

---

[35] [2009] EWHC 2387 (Admin).
[36] *Durham County Council v D* [2012] EWCA Civ 1654 at 21–24.
[37] CPR, r 54.5.
[38] CPR, r 3.2(a). Where a shorter time-limit is provided by statute or subordinate legislation that shorter time-limit applies: CPR, r 54.5(3).
[39] CPR, r 54.2. That a defendant does not object to a claim being brought out of time may be relevant to the court exercising its discretion.
[40] *R (Nash) v Capita Plc* [2013] EWHC 1067 (Admin) (29 April 2013) at 37.
[41] Eg *R v Independent Television Cssrs, ex p TV NI Ltd* (1991) *The Times*, 20 December.
[42] Application no 4167/98 *Lam v UK*.
[43] Case C-33/76 *Rewe v Landwirtschaftskammer Saarland* [1976] ECR 1989 at para 5.
[44] Case C-208/90 *Emmot v Minister for Social Welfare and the Att-Gen* [1991] ECR I-4269.

in *Uniplex (UK) Ltd v NHS Business Services Authority* (C-406/09), which subjected a claimant to a three-month time limit unqualified by a promptness requirement.[45]

3.15 Where the court considers there has been undue delay it may refuse to grant permission or decide that it would be inappropriate to grant relief sought on the application[46] if it considers the granting of relief would cause substantial hardship, or prejudice the rights of any person or be detrimental to good administration.[47] A relevant factor in determining whether delay is determinative is the public interest in the case being heard.[48] The court may consider delay even when the defendant indicates that no point would be taken on delay.[49] In *R (Law Society) v LSC*[50] Moses LJ stated at paragraph 116 that:

> 'The need for promptness in judicial review is well-known. Good public administration requires finality. This is because public authorities need to have certainty as to the legal validity of their decisions and actions, and third parties need to be able to rely on those decisions and actions. Promptness has been recognised to be particularly important where the interest of other parties is concerned: see for example *R v Monopolies and Mergers Commission, ex parte Argyll Group plc* [1986] 1 WLR 763 at 782–783; *R v Independent Television Commission, ex parte TVNI Limited* [1996] JR 60; and the authorities cited in Fordham's Judicial Review Handbook, Fifth Edition, 26.2.2.'

3.16 The court may grant an extension of time for the bringing of a claim.[51] Any extension granted may be subject to any conditions which the court considers appropriate.[52] Undue delay should be determined once and for all and should not be an issue at both the permission stage and the substantive hearing.[53]

Alternative remedy[54]

3.17 It is worthy of note that a claim in judicial review should be a last resort, see *Cowl v Plymouth City Council*.[55] The courts cannot compel an Alternative Dispute Resolution ('ADR') but a failure to provide or pursue an alternative remedy may affect the grant of permission and/or the grant of relief to an otherwise successful claim and/or the award of costs. Differing methods of ADR include complaints procedures, mediation, complaint to a relevant ombudsman and round table meetings.[56] In *R (Bhatti) v Bury MBC*, the court refused to grant permission to amend the grounds under which judicial review was sought, indicating that a pertinent consideration was that an alternative remedy was available.[57]

---

[45] *R (Buglife) v Medway Council* [2011] EWHC 746 (Admin) at 63.
[46] *R v Swansea City Council, ex p Main* (1981), The Times, 23 December.
[47] SCA 1981, s 31(6).
[48] *R (Kilroy) v Parrs Wood High School* [2011] EWHC 3489 (Admin) at 30–32: the case was brought one day before the end of the three-month period.
[49] *R v Dairy Produce Quota Tribunal, ex p Wynn Jones* [1987] 2 EGLR 9.
[50] [2010] EWHC 2550 (Admin).
[51] CPR, r 3.1(2)(a).
[52] CPR, r 3.1(3).
[53] *R v CICB, ex p A* [1999] 2 AC 330 per Lord Slynn at 341, HL.
[54] Where an alternative remedy exists: *R v SoS for the Home Dept, ex p Swati* [1986] 1 WLR 477; or existed and should have been used: *R (Carnell) v Regents Park College and Conference of Colleges Appeal Tribunal* [2008] ELR 268 at paras 31–33.
[55] [2002] 1 WLR 803.
[56] See Chapter 2 from para 2.122.
[57] *R (Bhatti) v Bury MBC* [2013] EWHC 3093 (Admin) at 30–41.

3.18 The Court of Appeal has emphasised the importance of using alternative administrative means, such as an internal complaints procedure.[58] In its discretion the court may refuse to grant a remedy at the substantive hearing if an alternative remedy exists or existed and should have been used.[59] However, it has been indicated that to refuse a remedy after a full substantive hearing and costs would not be in line with the overriding objective.[60]

3.19 The claim form should state whether an alternative remedy exists and whether or not the claimant is pursuing it.[61] Reasons should be given as to why JR is the appropriate remedy instead of the alternative remedies.[62]

Academic challenges

3.20 It is well established that although the Administrative Court has a discretion to entertain claims that have become academic, such discretion should be exercised cautiously and only where there are good public interest reasons for doing so. Recently in *R (Raw) v London Borough of Lambeth*,[63] Stadlen J stated at paragraph 68 that:

> 'I have given anxious consideration to whether that is a course which I should follow in this case. I have come to the conclusion that it is not. My first concern is that as a matter of first principle given that part of the policy lying behind the general rule against entertaining academic claims is to discourage the proliferation of such claims, it seems to me that there is a risk of defeating that objective if, having declined to adjudicate upon a claim on the ground that it is academic the court proceeds to set out what its views would have been if it had adjudicated on it. Albeit such views would be of no binding effect, the fact that the court might be prepared to express them in the form of obiter dicta might nonetheless encourage future claims. Allied to this is the related consideration that on one view expressions of view by the court in the form of obiter dicta, after it has declined to entertain a hypothetical claim, are potentially even more unsatisfactory than obiter dicta in the form of views expressed as part of such an adjudication. Such obiter dicta may place the losing party in the invidious position of deciding whether to ignore the court's views on the ground that they are obiter dicta, to implement them even though they consider them to be wrong or to incur the expense of seeking permission to appeal against them even though the outcome of such an appeal, even if favourable to that party, would still take the form of further obiter dicta.'

In *Parsipoor v Secretary of State for the Home Department*,[64] the Court of Appeal contributed to the discussion as to academic claims, Lloyd LJ stating at 36 that:

> 'In general, cases which are or have become academic as between the parties should not be brought or continued, so as to take up the resources of the court or the parties or of those providing funding for the litigation.'

Lloyd LJ went on to acknowledge that this general rule is subject to exceptions, including where the issue might arise in other cases.

---

58   *R (Cowl) v Plymouth CC* [2002] 1 WLR 803.
59   *R v Brentford General Cssrs, ex p Chan* [1986] STC 46; *R v Birmingham CC, ex p Ferrero Ltd* [1993] 1 All ER 539.
60   *R v Chief Constable of Merseyside Police, ex p Bennion* [2001] ACD 114.
61   *R v Humberside CC, ex p Bogdal* [1992] COD 467.
62   *R v SoS for the Home Dept, ex p Swati* [1986] 1 WLR 477 at 483 per Sir John Donaldson MR (as was), CA.
63   [2010] EWHC 507 (Admin).
64   [2011] EWCA Civ 276.

THE CLAIM FORM AND SERVICE

3.21 The court's permission to proceed is required in a claim for JR.[65] The claimant must file a claim form in the Administrative Court Office.[66] Since the regionalisation of the Administrative Court in April 2009 a claim can be filed in London, Cardiff, Manchester, Birmingham or Leeds. Further, Form N464 allows an application to be made for transfer of the judicial review hearing to a more convenient local court centre if the requirements set out in PD 54D 5.2 are met. The requirements include the reason for the preference, the region in which both parties and their representatives are based, the ease and cost of travel, the speed within which the decision is sought, whether it is desirable to administer or determine the claim in another reason. Venue is also something that the judge determining the permission application needs to consider in appropriate cases. The claim is brought in the name of the Crown on the application of the claimant against the public body.[67]

Issuing the claim

3.22 A claim for JR is made using the JR claim form (N461) with the additional information prescribed in CPR, r 54.6, PD 16 para 15 and PD 54.

3.23 The claim must state:

(a) the claimant and claimant's solicitor;

(b) the decision, act or omission challenged;

(c) the name and address of any person the claimant considers an interested person. Where the JR relates to ongoing proceedings all other parties to the original proceedings must be named as interested persons (CPR, r 54.6(1) and PD 54, para 5.1);

(d) that the claimant is pursuing JR (CPR, r 54.6(1)(b);

(e) any remedy sought, (including any interim remedy) that is being claimed (CPR, r 54.6(1)(c)) and any relief sought under the HRA 1998 (PD 16, para 15.1(2));

(f) a detailed statement of grounds for seeking JR, which should be set out on the Claim Form or accompany it;[68]

(g) a statement of the facts relied upon;

(h) an application for extending the time to file the claim form if necessary;

(i) any directions sought; and

(j) a statement of truth.

R (Khan) v Secretary of State for The Home Department emphasised that permission applications must fulfil all of these requirements, must be made promptly and must only address relevant issues.[69]

---

[65] CPR, r 54.4.
[66] PD 54, para. 2.1.
[67] PD Administrative Court [2000] 1 WLR 1654.
[68] See PD 54, para 5.6 and also for (g), (h), and (i).
[69] *R (Khan) v Secretary of State for The Home Department* [2011] EWHC 2763 (Admin) at 2–8.

3.24 If the Human Rights Act 1998 is engaged further requirements arise:

(a) the form must state any relief sought under the HRA 1998 (PD 16, para 15.1(2));
(b) where the HRA is raised as an issue or a remedy under the HRA is sought precise details of the infringement alleged and the Convention right relied upon must be given (PD 16, 15.1(2)(a));
(c) where a declaration of incompatibility under s 4 of the HRA is sought, precise details of the legislative provisions and the alleged incompatibility (PD 16, 15.1(2)(d));
(d) where a HRA claim is founded on the finding of another court or tribunal, the details of that other court's finding (PD 16, 15.1(2)(e)); and
(e) where a HRA claim is founded on a judicial act which is alleged to have infringed a Convention right as provided by s 9 of the HRA, details of the judicial act and of the court in question (PD 16, 15.1(2)(f)).

3.25 Similarly if the claim raises a devolution issue, the claim form must specify that fact, and give a summary of the facts, circumstances and points of law on the basis of which it is alleged a devolution issue arises.[70]

3.26 PD 54, para 5.7 provides that the claim form must be accompanied by:

(a) any written evidence in support of the claim or any application to extend time;
(b) a copy of any order that the claimant seeks to have quashed;
(c) where the claim relates to the decision of a lower court or tribunal, an approved copy of the reasons for that decision;
(d) copies of any document relied upon by the claimant;
(e) copies of any relevant statutory material; and
(f) a list of the essential documents for advance reading by the court, with page references for the passages relied upon.

3.27 Two copies of a paginated and indexed bundle containing all the documents required under PD 54, paras 5.6 and 5.7 must be filed when the claim is issued (para 5.9 and CPR, r 54.6(2)).

Service

3.28 The claim form and the other documentation described above (see CPR, r 54.6(2)) must be served on the defendant and the other interested parties within seven days after the date of issue (CPR, r 54.7). Service must be by the parties and will not be completed by the court. An interested party is any person (other than the claimant and defendant) who is directly affected by the claim.[71] A person is directly affected if he would be affected by the grant of a remedy.[72] Any person may apply for permission to file evidence or make representations at the hearing of a Judicial Review.[73]

---

[70] PD 54, para 5.4.
[71] CPR, r 54.1(2)(f).
[72] *R v Rent Officer Service, ex p Muldoon* [1996] 3 All ER 498, [1996] 1 WLR 1103 at 1105, HL. *R v MMC, ex p Milk Marque Ltd and NFU* [2000] COD 329 at para 5 per Moses J – that a decision is of 'the utmost significance and importance' does not necessarily mean that the person is 'directly affected'.
[73] CPR, r 54.17.

Acknowledgement of service

3.29 The defendant (and anyone else served with a claim form) must file an acknowledgement of service.[74] The acknowledgement of service must be filed not more than 21 days after service of the claim form.[75] The acknowledgment must be served on the claimant and any other person named in the claim[76] as soon as practicable, and no later than seven days after it is filed.[77] These time limits cannot be extended by agreement between the parties.[78] A party who fails to file an acknowledgement may be precluded from taking part in any permission hearing.[79] That party will not be excluded from the substantive hearing as long as he complies with CPR, r 54.14 or any other directions made by the court.[80] Where a person takes part in the substantive JR the court may take his failure to file an acknowledgement of service into account when deciding what order to make as to costs.[81]

3.30 The acknowledgement of service must: (i) set out the summary grounds for contesting the claim (if contested); and (ii) the name and address of any person the filing party considers to be an interested party.[82] The acknowledgement may include an application for directions.[83] The Court of Appeal has given guidance as to what the summary grounds of defence should contain. In *Ewing v Office of the Deputy Prime Minister*[84] Carnwath LJ stated, at para 34:

> 'Neither the rules nor the practice direction expand on what is meant by "summary grounds". However, the "summary" required under this rule must be contrasted with the "detailed grounds for contesting the claim" and the supporting "written evidence", which are required following the grant of permission (CPR, r 54.14). In construing the rule, it is necessary also to have regard to its purpose, and place in the procedural scheme ... The purpose of the "summary of grounds" is not to provide the basis for full argument of the substantive merits, but rather ... to assist the judge in deciding whether to grant permission, and if so on what terms ... It should be possible to do what is required without incurring "substantial expense at this stage".'

3.31 Brooke LJ added, at paras 52–54:

> 'If they [the defendants] wish to incur greater expense in preparing a document that is more elaborate than the rules require at this stage, they should not expect to recover the extra expense from a claimant whose application is dismissed at the permission stage ... Needless to say, if the claimant skips the Pre-Action Protocol stage, he must expect to put his opponents to greater expense in preparing the summary of their grounds for contesting the claim, and this may be reflected in the greater order for costs that is made against him if permission is refused.'

---

[74] In accordance with CPR, r 54.8 – the correct form is N462 (as of April 2009). The acknowledgement should specifically deal with any argument to be advanced on grounds of delay since delay is an issue to be determined at the permission stage: *R v CICB, ex p A* [1999] 2 AC 330, [1999] 2 WLR 974, HL.
[75] CPR, r 54.8(2)(a).
[76] CPR, r 54.7(b).
[77] CPR, r 54.8(2)(b).
[78] CPR, r 54.8(3) and CPR, r 54.8(5) excludes CPR, r 10.3(2).
[79] CPR, r 54.9(1)(a).
[80] CPR, r 54.9(1)(b).
[81] CPR, r 54.9(2).
[82] CPR, r 54.8(4)(a)(i) and (ii) – there is no requirement for the defendant to file evidence but there is nothing to stop a defendant filing evidence in an appropriate case.
[83] CPR, r 54.8(4)(b).
[84] [2005] EWCA Civ 1583.

URGENT CASES

3.32 The Administrative Court has introduced a procedure for urgent cases.[85] Claimants should complete a form requesting their case be considered urgently. The form requires the claimant to state: (a) the need for urgency; (b) the timescale sought for the consideration off the permission application; and (c) the date by which the substantive hearing should take place.[86] Where an interim injunction is sought, a claimant must, in addition, provide: (a) a draft order; and (b) the grounds for the injunction.[87] The Administrative Court has emphasised that despite the urgent nature of the application being submitted, the claimant must ensure that the 'specific decision being challenged should appear clearly' in the application.[88]

3.33 The claimant must serve (by fax and post) the claim form and application for urgency on the defendant and interested parties, advising them of the application and that they may make representations. Those additional items are required where an interim injunction is sought which must be served by the claimant on the defendant in the same manner.[89]

3.34 The application for urgent consideration will be considered by a judge who, within the time requested, will make such orders as he considers appropriate.[90] Applications can be made and are dealt with out of hours in cases of real urgency.

3.35 In applications for interim relief where the claimant is about to be removed from the UK the Court of Appeal has given specific guidance.[91] Specific guidance has also been issued in relation to asylum seekers who have been refused support because they did not make their claims as soon as reasonably practicable (see s 55 of the Nationality, Immigration and Asylum Act 2002).[92]

3.36 In cases where the matter is so urgent that the JR would be moribund without an immediate hearing the judge may order what is known as a 'rolled up' hearing with the permission application to be heard orally with a substantive hearing immediately thereafter. Equally a rolled up hearing can be ordered if a speedy resolution to the dispute is needed. The judge will then set an accelerated timetable for the case to proceed including tight timetables for the production of evidence from the defendant and any interested parties and abridgement of time for the production of skeleton arguments. Cases in which urgent relief have been granted include cases in which local authorities have been compelled to provide accommodation and support to families in need.[93] The court has declined to hear urgent applications where removal directions were challenged, but were subsequently cancelled, thereby removing the element of urgency.[94]

---

[85] Practice Statement (Administrative Courts: Listing and Urgent Cases) [2002] 1 WLR 810.
[86] Ibid.
[87] Ibid.
[88] *Rrapaj v Director of Legal Aid Casework* [2013] EWHC 1837 (Admin) at 50.
[89] Ibid.
[90] Ibid.
[91] *R (Madan) v SoS Home* [2007] 1 WLR 2891.
[92] *R (Q, D, KH, OK, JK H, T and S) v SoS Home* [2003] EWHC 2507 (Admin) Maurice Kay J and Practice Statement (Judicial Review: Asylum Support) [2004] 1 WLR 644 Collins J.
[93] *R (ES) v London Borough of Barking and Dagenham* [2013] EWHC 691 (Admin). The court remitted the case to a local authority in order to make a decision as to accommodation and support. An interim order for accommodation and support was made to stand until a new decision was reached.
[94] *Rrapaj v Director of Legal Aid Casework* [2013] EWHC 1837 (Admin) at 51.

INTERIM ORDERS

Directions

3.37 In addition to the case management directions given at the permission stage there can be occasions when it is necessary to seek further directions from the court either before or after the permission stage. Directions may be required either due to some additional information becoming available or thought to be available but not being released by the other side, circumstances that make an expedited hearing need to be sought or a case where the nature of factual dispute is such as to require the cross examination of a witness. Although the latter is a rare occasion it can occur. The Administrative Court has the power to deal with all such applications where the interests of justice require it. In relation to the matter of preliminary issues, the court has made clear that it will only order the hearing of a preliminary issue where there is a single determinative issue that could be decided upon after a relatively short hearing.[95]

3.38 Until the substantive judicial review hearing interim orders should normally be able to be dealt with on the papers. All parties are under a duty to be candid. Under CPR, r 54.16 no written evidence may be relied upon unless it has been served in accordance with the rules or in accordance with the directions of the court or the court gives permission. Although Rule 8.6(1) which deals with written evidence is expressly disapplied under CPR, r 54.16 the other provisions of Rule 8.6 that deal with requiring or permitting a party to give oral evidence or to attend for cross examination are available. Although cross examination is rarely sought or permitted and should be treated as the exception in judicial review cases if the interests of justice in an individual case require it cross-examination can be ordered and does occur.[96] The same principles apply to disclosure.[97] It follows that neither disclosure nor cross examination is automatic.

3.39 Expedition may be ordered if the individual circumstances of the case require it. Most judicial review cases can be said to be urgent so the circumstances would have to take the case out of the ordinary queue. Examples of when expedition may be ordered include cases involving the liberty of an individual, the removal of an asylum seeker from the jurisdiction and cases where expedition is necessary in the interests of good public administration.

3.40 There is also the power to stay proceedings under CPR, r 54.10(2). If granted the stay would operate to restrain a public body from acting.[98] In effect it suspends the proceedings. It cannot be used to compel a public body to act.

---

[95] *Youssef v Secretary of State for Foreign and Commonwealth Affairs* [2011] EWHC 3014 (Admin) at 14–20.
[96] *R (the Friends of Basildon Golf Course) v Basildon District Council* [2009] EWHC 66 – overturned by the Court of Appeal but not on the judicial review procedure followed where a witness gave oral evidence and was cross examined about the processes that he had followed as part of an EIA screening opinion. See also earlier paras 3.10 to 3.12 inclusive.
[97] *R v Inland Revenue Commissioners, ex p National Federation of Self Employed and Small Businesses* [1982] AC 617 'Upon general principles, [disclosure] should not be ordered unless and until the court is satisfied that the evidence reveals grounds for believing that there has been a breach of public duty; and it should be strictly limited to documents relevant to the issue which emerges from the affidavits.' Lord Scarman at 654E–F.
[98] *R v Secretary of State for Education, ex p Avon CC* [1991] 1 QB 558.

Interim relief

3.41 Applications for interim relief will also be considered at the permission stage. Where there is an application for interim relief the judge may order a hearing for interim relief and permission. The court can grant interim relief pending the oral hearing or for a fixed period. The court can at the same time grant leave to the defendant to apply to discharge the interim injunction.[99] Interim relief can be granted before permission to proceed with the claim is given.[100]

3.42 Any applications for interim relief should be set out clearly in the claim form.[101] It does not automatically follow that if permission is granted that any interim relief sought will be forthcoming.[102] In most cases, if not all, interim relief will only be considered at a hearing where all the affected parties are present. The grant of interim relief in JR proceedings will normally follow the same principles as interim remedies in general proceedings.[103]

PERMISSION

3.43 The court will consider whether to grant permission without an oral hearing on the papers[104] when it will make an order either granting or refusing permission and giving any directions to the parties for the future course of the proceedings.[105] The judge's order and the reasons for his decision are then served upon the claimant, defendant and any other person who filed an acknowledgement of service.[106] Where the court refuses permission on the papers or gives permission to proceed subject to conditions or on certain grounds only,[107] the claimant may not appeal but may request the decision be reconsidered at an oral hearing.[108] The request for such a hearing must be filed within seven days of the service of the reason for the decision.[109] The claimant, defendant and any other person who filed an acknowledgement will be given at least two days' notice of the hearing date. No party other than the claimant need attend a permission hearing unless the court directs otherwise.[110] If other parties attend the court is unlikely to make a costs order against the claimant.[111]

3.44 Permission should be granted if, on material before the court, without inquiring in depth, there is an *arguable* case for granting the relief the claimant seeks.[112] This initial filter exists 'to prevent the time of the court being wasted by busybodies with misguided or trivial complaints of administrative error and to remove the uncertainty in

---

[99] *R (Lawer) v Restormel BC* [2007] EWHC 2299 (Admin), [2008] HLR 20.
[100] *M v Home Office* [1994] 1 AC 377 at 423.
[101] CPR, r 54.6(1)(c).
[102] *R v SoS Home Dept, ex p Doorga* [1990] COD 109, [1990] Imm AR 98, CA.
[103] CPR, r 25 and the principles in *American Cyanamid Co v Ethicon Ltd* [1975] AC 396, [1975] 1 All ER 504, HL.
[104] PD 54, para 8.4.
[105] CPR, r 54.10(1). The court may direct a stay of the originating proceedings CPR, r 54.10(2).
[106] CPR, r 54.11.
[107] CPR, r 54.12(1).
[108] CPR, r 54.12(3).
[109] CPR, r 54.12(4).
[110] PD 54, para 8.5.
[111] *R (Mount Cook Land Ltd et al v Westminster CC)* [2003] EWCA Civ 1346.
[112] *IRC v Nat Fed of Self-Employed and Small Businesses Ltd* [1982] AC 617 at 644, HL, per Lord Diplock; *R v SoS for the Home Dept, ex p Swati* [1986] 1 All ER 717, [1986] 1 WLR 477, CA.

which public authorities might be left ...'.[113] The granting of permission is within the court's discretion. The Supreme Court confirmed in *R (Cart) v Upper Tribunal; R (MR (Pakistan)) v Upper Tribunal (Immigration & Asylum Chamber)* that the rational approach to adopt when considering whether to grant permission to cases challenging Immigration Upper Tribunal decisions was to adopt the 'second appeals' criteria; namely identifying whether there was an important point of principle or some other compelling reason that permission should be granted.[114]

The Court of Appeal has indicated that permission should be granted where a point exists which merits investigation on a full hearing, with both parties represented and with all relevant evidence and arguments on the law.[115] Initially it was thought the permission procedure would be used to filter out only the weakest of cases and permission would be granted if from the papers there appeared to be a point which might turn out to be an arguable case.[116] In short, permission should only be granted where the court is satisfied that the papers actually disclose that there is an arguable point (not merely that an arguable point might emerge on further consideration of the papers). Though permission will not necessarily be determined on a brief review of the papers an in-depth examination is inappropriate.[117]

3.45 In granting permission for JR the court may limit the grounds which the claimant may argue. This was the position prior to the introduction of the CPR and remains the case after its introduction.[118] Even if a ground has been refused at the permission stage it is within the court's discretion to allow the issue to be argued at the substantive hearing if it is in the interests of justice and the overriding objective.[119]

3.46 It is within the court's discretion to direct that there be an oral hearing of the application for permission and a claimant can ask to have any refusal of permission reconsidered at an oral hearing.[120]

3.47 The court retains its inherent jurisdiction to set aside orders, including orders to grant permission to apply for JR.[121] The inherent jurisdiction of the court to set aside permission will be used sparingly, for instance where permission has been granted before the defendant has put in an acknowledgement of service.[122]

3.48 On granting permission for JR the court may give any appropriate directions for the future conduct of the claim.[123] The court can order a stay of the proceedings to

---

[113] Per Lord Diplock in *R v IRC, ex p National Federation of Self-Employed and Small Businesses Ltd* [1982] AC 617 at 643.
[114] [2011] UKSC 28 as per Lady Hale at 57.
[115] *R v SoS Home, ex p Begum* [1990] COD 107; [1990] Imm AR 1.
[116] Lord Diplock in *R v IRC, ex p Nat Fed of Self-Employed and Small Businesses Ltd* [1982] AC 617 at 644a.
[117] *R (Davey) v Aylesbury Vale DC* [2008] 1 WLR 878 at para 12 per Sedley LJ 'While there may be cases in which it is necessary or helpful to explore issues in depth at this stage, such cases must be quite exceptional. The proper place for a full exploration of evidence and argument is at the hearing of a claim which has been shown at the permission stage to be arguable.'
[118] *R v Staffordshire CC, ex p Ashworth* (1996) 4 Admin L Rep 373; *R v Advertising Standards Authority, ex p City Trading* [1997] COD 202 (Pre-CPR). CPR, r 54.12(1)(b)(ii).
[119] *R (Smith) v Parole Board* [2003] 1 WLR 2548 at para 12–16 and CPR, r 54.15.
[120] CPR, r 54.12.
[121] *R v SoS Home, ex p Chinoy* (1991) 4 Admin LR 457, [1991] COD 381, DC.
[122] *R (Webb) v Bristol CC* [2001] EWHC 696 (Admin).
[123] CPR, r 54.10.

which the JR claim relates.[124] Where permission is granted, directions will be given for an oral hearing, unless the parties consent otherwise.[125]

RENEWAL OF THE APPLICATION FOR PERMISSION

3.49 If permission is refused or the scope of the claim is limited to only certain of the grounds raised, a claimant is entitled to request an oral hearing by renewing his application (CPR, r 54.12(3)). The Notice of Renewal (form 86b) must be filed within seven days of the service of the decision (CPR, r 54.12(4)). The renewal form should set out grounds for renewal in light of the judge's reasons for refusing permission on the papers (*Practice Statement*[126]). Although not granted as of right, it is extremely rare for a request for an oral hearing to be refused.

The oral hearing

3.50 An oral hearing will be listed for a 30 minute hearing and all parties will be given at least two days' notice of the hearing date (CPR, r 54.12(5)). Where it is believed that 30 minutes will be insufficient for the permission hearing, a written estimate of the predicted time and a request for a special fixture should be made to the Listing Office.[127] Whilst generally neither the defendant nor any interested party is needed to attend – PD54, para 8.5 – the court may require them to do so if it considers it necessary, and in any event, they may often wish to do so. Oral permission hearings should be short and not a full-scale dress rehearsal of the substantive hearing, *R (Mount Cook) v Westminster CC*.[128]

Appeal on permission

3.51 The procedure for applying for permission is the same in the High Court in both civil and criminal matters. However, if permission is refused in the High Court the appeal process is different for criminal and civil matters. The refusal of permission to apply for JR in civil matters may be appealed to the Court of Appeal. The same right does not exist in criminal matters.[129] 'Criminal matters' are those that arise in the context of criminal proceedings where, if the proceedings were carried to their conclusion, they might result in the conviction of a person.[130] If the High Court considers that the claim raises an important point of law but that the claim would fail it may grant permission and then dismiss the substantive claim and certify that the claim raises a point of law of general public importance.[131] The claimant may then petition the Supreme Court for permission to appeal against the dismissal of the substantive claim where he could not petition against the refusal to grant permission for judicial review.

3.52 Where permission is refused in a civil matter, after an oral hearing, the claimant may apply to the Court of Appeal for permission to appeal against that refusal.[132] The

---

[124] CPR, r 54.10(1).
[125] *Parsipoor and another v Secretary of State for the Home Department* [2011] EWCA Civ 276 at 25–29.
[126] [2002] 1 All ER 633, 636d.
[127] See the ACO Notes for Guidance [2005] JR 5 at 10.4.
[128] [2003] EWCA Civ 1346, at [71] per Auld LJ.
[129] SCA 1981, s 18(1).
[130] *Amand v Home Secretary* [1943] AC 147.
[131] *R v DPP, ex p Camelot plc* (1998) 10 Admin L Rep 93.
[132] CPR, r 52.15.

claimant must make the application for permission to appeal within seven days of the decision of the High Court.[133] The claimant must lodge:

(a) an appellant's notice;
(b) an additional copy of the notice and additional copies to be sealed and returned for the defendant and any interested parties;
(c) the order of the High Court refusing permission;
(d) the claim form;
(e) a copy of the original decision being challenged;
(f) any written evidence in support of the applicant's application;
(g) a copy of the High Court bundle; and
(h) a transcript of the High Court judgment.

3.53 The Court of Appeal will usually grant permission for JR rather than granting permission to appeal.[134] The JR will then proceed in the High Court unless the Court of Appeal orders otherwise.[135] In exceptional circumstances the Court of Appeal may decide to hear the substantive JR itself rather than return it to the High Court. Unusually, the Court of Appeal has also reconstituted itself to become a criminal division of the court where the application had not been made to the correct division.[136]

3.54 Where the Court of Appeal refuses permission to appeal against the High Court's refusal to grant permission there is no further appeal.[137] When the Court of Appeal grants permission to appeal and then hears the appeal but refuses permission to apply for JR then the Supreme Court does have jurisdiction to entertain a petition for leave to appeal and if permission is granted the appeal itself.[138]

SUBSTANTIVE HEARING

3.55 Where permission is granted, the court will give case management directions (CPR, r 54.10). It can even transfer the case to another tribunal.[139] These directions may include provisions about serving the claim form and evidence on other persons. Where a claim is made under the HRA, a direction may be made for giving notice to the Crown or for joining the Crown as a party (see PD 54, para 8.2). Once permission has been granted, other parties cannot apply to have permission set aside (CPR, r 54.13) although the court can use its inherent jurisdiction to do so.[140]

3.56 If permission is granted, a defendant or any other person served with the claim form who wishes to contest the claim (or support it on additional grounds) must file and serve detailed grounds and any written evidence relied upon within 35 days after service of the order giving permission (CPR, r 54.14). A party relying upon any documents not already filed must file a paginated bundle of those additional documents with his

---

[133] CPR, r 52.15(2).
[134] CPR, r 52.15(3).
[135] CPR, r 52.15(4).
[136] *R (Hicks) v Court At Snaresbrook & Anor* [2012] EWCA Crim 2515 at 30–32.
[137] *R v SoS Trade and Industry, ex p Eastaway* [2000] 1 WLR 2222 at 2226 per Lord Bingham, see *R (Burkett) v Hammersmith and Fulham LBC* [2002] 1 WLR 1593 at para 12.
[138] *R (Burkett) v Hammersmith and Fulham LBC* [2002] 1 WLR 1593 at para 13.
[139] *R (MM) v Secretary of State for Work and Pensions* [2012] EWHC 2106 (Admin) at 59–61.
[140] *R v Commissioner for Local Administration, ex p Field* [2000] COD 58.

detailed grounds (PD 54, para 10.1). Claimants and their legal advisors are under an obligation to reconsider the merits of the claim in the light of written evidence served by other parties.

3.57 Any person may apply to file evidence or make representations at the hearing (CPR, r 54.17). Prior to the CPR a person was regarded as sufficiently affected to justify being joined only if they were affected without the intervention of an intermediate agency: *R v Liverpool CC, ex p Muldoon*.[141] If permission to be joined is granted to a third party, it may be given with conditions and the court may make directions (PD 54, para 13.2).

3.58 It is possible to determine the application for judicial review without a hearing where all parties agree (CPR, r 54.18).

Additional grounds

3.59 Where a claimant seeks to rely on additional grounds beyond those for which permission was given, notice must be given to the court and to the other persons who have been served with the claim form no later than seven clear days before the substantive hearing (or the warned date for the hearing) (PD 54, para 11.1). Permission must be sought for the additional grounds (CPR, r 54.15). The hearing on whether new grounds can be added will either be at the commencement of the substantive judicial review or by way of a further interim hearing. In considering whether to allow amendments to the grounds of JR the court will consider the general issues of whether any injustice will be caused to the defendant and whether the defendant can be compensated in costs. Generally new grounds are more likely to be allowed where issues of law are raised which do not require new evidence.

In *R (Bhatti) v Bury MBC*, the Administrative Court refused to grant permission to amend grounds where they bore no resemblance to the initially challenged decision, stating:

> 'It would be a wrong exercise of discretion to permit these proceedings to be used as a mechanism for a challenge to new decisions taken on a different basis following the commencement of these proceedings in circumstances where such a challenge does not involve even an incidental consideration of the decision originally challenged in these proceedings, and where there is no evidential basis for asserting that the withdrawal of the original decision was in any relevant sense "tactical".'[142]

If new grounds are allowed to be added but new evidence is required the court is likely to adjourn the hearing to allow the defendant to provide new evidence. In such circumstances the claimant is likely to be liable in costs for the additional work at the end of the substantive hearing whatever its outcome.

Skeleton arguments

3.60 The claimant must file and serve a skeleton argument not less than 21 working days before the hearing date (or warned date).[143] Other parties must file and serve their

---

[141] [1996] 1 WLR 1103, HL.
[142] *R (Bhatti) v Bury MBC* [2013] EWHC 3093 (Admin) at 41.2.
[143] PD 54, para 15.1.

skeleton arguments not less than 14 working days before the hearing or warned date.[144] The claimant's skeleton argument must be accompanied by a paginated and indexed bundle of all the relevant documentation.[145] Skeleton arguments must contain:

(a) a time estimate for the complete hearing, including delivery of the judgment;
(b) a list of issues;
(c) a list of legal points to be taken (together with relevant authorities and page references for passages relied upon);
(d) a chronology (with page references to the bundle of documents);
(e) a list of the essential documents for advance reading by the judge; and
(f) a list of persons referred to.[146]

The hearing

3.61 Hearings are conducted in public, subject to general principles justifying a hearing in private. The hearing is conducted on the basis of written material and legal submissions to the court. There are rare cases where the court will require witnesses to attend for cross-examination.[147] In addition to the materials before the decision-maker, it was held in *R v SoS for the Environment, ex p Powis*[148] that the court will consider the following categories of fresh evidence:

(a) evidence bearing on any question of fact as to whether the decision-maker had jurisdiction;
(b) evidence on whether any procedural requirements were observed; and
(c) evidence to prove misconduct – examples are bias on the part of the decision-maker, and fraud or perjury by a party.

3.62 The court considers whether the grounds for seeking JR are made out, and whether, in its discretion, it ought to grant relief.

3.63 The position where the decision-making authority has expressed more than one reason for a decision and the claimant successfully impugns/challenges one or some of them arose in *R v Broadcasting Complaints Commission, ex p Owen*.[149] May LJ said that where the reasons could be separated, and the court is satisfied that, despite one reason being bad in law, the same decision would have been reached for the valid reasons, then, within its discretion, the High Court would not intervene by way of JR.

CONVERSION TO A COMMON LAW CLAIM

3.64 The court has power under CPR, r 54.20 to order JR proceedings to continue as proceedings brought under CPR Part 7. This power may be exercised where the relief claimed is a declaration, an injunction, or damages, and the court considers that such relief should not be granted on an application for JR but might be granted in an

---

[144] PD 54, para 15.2.
[145] PD 54, para 16.1.
[146] PD 54, para 15.3.
[147] *R (Wilkinson) v Responsible Medical Officer Broadmoor Hospital* [2002] 1 WLR 419.
[148] [1981] 1 WLR 584 at 595 per Dunn LJ.
[149] [1985] QB 1153 at 1177.

ordinary claim. The purpose underlying the CPR, and this power of conversion, is to provide 'a framework which is sufficiently flexible to enable all issues between the parties to be determined'.[150]

CONSENT ORDERS

3.65 Where the parties come to an agreement to dispose of the application it is possible to obtain an order from the court to put that agreement into effect without needing to attend at court. The procedure is in PD 54, para 17. A document setting out the proposed order and containing a short statement of the matters relied on as justifying the making of the order, quoting the authorities and statutory provisions relied on, should be signed by all the parties. The original of this document, together with two copies, should be handed in to the appropriate Administrative Court Office, which will put it before the judge. If the judge is satisfied that an order can be made, the proceedings will be listed for a public hearing where the order will be pronounced without the parties needing to attend. If the judge is not satisfied that it would be proper to make the order, the proceedings will be listed in the usual way. Where a party succeeds, even by way of a consent order, they can be awarded costs, even if the consent order was agreed upon prior to the final hearing.[151] A consent order can be agreed upon after the final hearing has taken place and, if agreed to by the court, can limit the publication of the final judgment.[152]

APPEALS

3.66 Appeals against a decision of the court granting or refusing the JR claim may only be appealed to the Court of Appeal with permission.[153] Permission will only be given where there is a real prospect of success or there is some compelling reason why the appeal should be heard.[154] An issue of general public importance would be one such compelling reason.

3.67 Permission should be sought from the court of first instance (the High Court) initially.[155] If permission is refused by the court of first instance, an application for permission to appeal may be made to the Court of Appeal by filing an appellant's notice setting out the grounds for appeal and including the application for permission to appeal within 21 days of the decision of the lower court or within such time as directed by the lower court.[156] The applicant for permission must serve the appellant's notice on each respondent within seven days of filing the notice.[157] The respondent is not required to take any action until permission to appeal is granted unless directed to take some action by the court.[158]

---

[150] Per Lord Woolf in *R (Heather) v Leonard Cheshire* [2002] HRLR 30 at para 39.
[151] *R (Bahta) v Secretary of State for the Home Department* [2011] EWCA Civ 895 at 59–71.
[152] *R (S) v General Teaching Council for England* [2013] EWHC 2779 (Admin) at 31.
[153] CPR, r 52.3.
[154] CPR, r 52.3(6).
[155] CPR, r 52.2.
[156] CPR, r 52.3(3) and 52.4.
[157] CPR, r 52.4(3) and PD 52, para 21.
[158] PD 52, para 22.

3.68 The applicant must file in the Court of Appeal office:

(a) an appellant's notice with two additional copies for the court and one copy for each respondent;
(b) a skeleton argument;
(c) a sealed copy of the order being appealed;
(d) the order of the court below refusing permission to appeal and the reasons;
(e) any written evidence in support of the application to appeal; and
(f) those parts of the bundle in the JR below which are reasonably necessary to deal with the appeal (including the claim form, written evidence, any decision letter and the key documents).[159]

3.69 The documents required to be included in the appeal bundle are set out at PD 52, para 19. The appellant does not need to serve the appeal bundle on the respondents at this stage. He must serve the appellant's notice and his skeleton argument on the respondent unless the court directs otherwise.[160]

3.70 The application for permission to appeal is usually dealt with on the papers by a Lord Justice of Appeal, though the court may direct that an oral permission hearing be held with or without the respondent present. Where permission is refused, the applicant can, within seven days, apply for an oral hearing to reconsider the refusal.[161] If permission is granted the applicant must serve the appeal bundle (already filed with the Court of Appeal) on the respondents within seven days of the order giving permission to appeal.[162]

3.71 If permission to appeal was given in the lower court the appellant's notice and bundle should be filed within 14 days of the lower court's decision and should be served within seven days of filing. The respondent may file a notice asking the Court of Appeal to uphold the decision of the court below on different or additional grounds.[163] The respondent must file a skeleton argument in the Court of Appeal and serve it on the other parties.[164]

3.72 If permission is granted, the appeal is a review of the decision of the court below[165] and the appeal will be allowed only where the court below was wrong or the decision unjust because of some procedural irregularity.[166] No party may rely on any matter not contained within the appeal notice unless the court gives permission.[167] The Court of Appeal will not allow grounds to be argued that were not raised in the lower court.[168] Nor will fresh evidence usually be admitted.[169] The Court of Appeal retains the discretion to depart from these limitations where the justice of the case requires it.[170]

---

[159] PD 52, para 5.6.
[160] PD 52, para 5.24.
[161] CPR, r 52.3(4).
[162] PD 52, para 6.2.
[163] CPR, r 52.5(2)(b).
[164] PD 52, para 7.7 and 7.7B.
[165] CPR, r 52.11(1).
[166] CPR, r 52.11(3).
[167] CPR, r 52.11(5).
[168] *R (H) v SoS Home* [2002] 3 WLR 967 at para 47.
[169] CPR, r 52.11(2).
[170] *E v SoS Home* [2004] QB 1044 at paras 81–82.

3.73 There is a further appeal to the Supreme Court where permission is given either by the Court of Appeal or the Supreme Court.

COSTS

3.74 The most important provision in relation to costs is s 51 of the Senior Courts Act 1981, which provides the court with full discretion to determine the issue of costs, subject to enactments and rules of court. CPR, r 44.3 confirms that the court has discretion to order one party to pay the costs, the amount of those costs and when they are to be paid.

The permission stage

3.75 Paragraphs 8.5 and 8.6 of the Part 54 Practice Direction relate to the permission hearing and state that the defendant or other interested party need not attend a hearing on the question of permission unless the court directs otherwise. Additionally, where the defendant or any interested party does attend a permission hearing, the court will not make an order for costs against the claimant in cases where the defendant has attended and argued successfully that permission should not be granted save that: (1) the court will order that the claimant pays the costs of the preparation and filing of the acknowledgement of service, and (2) in exceptional circumstances: *Mount Cook Land and Another v Westminster City Council*[171] where Auld LJ sets out a non-exhaustive list of exceptions.[172] The rationale for ordering the claimant to pay the costs associated with the acknowledgement of service is because the defendant is obliged to file one.

3.76 Costs are usually not awarded to the claimant when the Administrative Court decides that permission should be granted. That applies both to a decision on the papers and after an oral hearing. This is because the costs issue can be dealt with at the substantive hearing, but more likely because the order is silent in relation to costs it is deemed to contain an order for costs in the case. Exceptionally, if the claimant has followed the pre-action protocol and receives no response from the defendant so that the claimant is obliged to issue proceedings and at that stage the defendant springs to life and files an acknowledgement of service that reveals the hopelessness of the claimant's case the defendant may not obtain any order for costs and the claimant may receive his even though he decided to discontinue after receipt of the acknowledgement of service from the defendant. Where permission is refused on consideration of the papers, if the defendant expressly asks for costs, the claimant will usually pay the costs of preparation and filing of the acknowledgement of service unless there are exceptional circumstances.[173]

Substantive hearing

3.77 The general rule in costs provides that the unsuccessful party will be ordered to pay the costs of the successful party. However, the court may decide to make a different order having regard to all the circumstances of the case, but, in particular, to the conduct of the parties and whether a party has succeeded in part of the claim. The conduct in this context means whether the parties have followed any relevant pre-action protocol to try

---

[171] [2003] EWCA Civ 1346.
[172] See para 76(5) and (6).
[173] *Mount Cook Land Limited v Westminster City Council* [2003] EWCA Civ 1346.

to settle the proceedings and the manner in which they have pursued or defended the case. For many judicial review hearings the court will want to conduct a summary assessment of costs 44 PD 7 (paragraph 13.2 (2)). The court will normally do so in any case lasting less than one day. A schedule of costs must be served not less than 24 hours before the hearing. The court will not make a summary assessment of the costs of a publicly funded litigant but so assess the costs payable by them. In all other cases the issue of costs is likely to go off for detailed consideration by the costs judge.

3.78 Other relevant considerations include:

- Discontinuance. This falls into two parts:
  (1) before permission is considered. In those cases the general rule is that no order for costs is made. The exception is where there is a plain and obvious case: *R v Royal Borough of Kensington and Chelsea, ex p Ghrebregiosis*[174] and see the example given in paragraph **3.76**, and
  (2) discontinuance after permission is granted but before a substantive hearing. In *R v Liverpool City Council, ex p Newman*[175] it was held that there was a general rule that the defendant would recover his costs where it could be shown that the discontinuance was as a result of the claimant's recognition of the likely failure of his challenge but the situation was different where some step had been taken by the defendant which rendered the claim unnecessary to be continued. In *R v Boxall v Mayor and Burgess of Waltham Forest London Borough Council*[176] the court said:

  > 'The overriding objective is to do justice between the parties without incurring unnecessary Court time and consequently additional costs. At each end of the spectrum there will be cases where it is obvious which side would have won had the substantive issues been fought to a conclusion. In between, the position will, in differing degrees, be less clear. How far the Court will be prepared to look into the previously unresolved substantive issues will depend on the circumstances of the particular case, not least the amount of costs at stake and the conduct of the parties. In the absence of a good reason to make any other order the fall-back is to make no order as to costs.'

  The court should take care to ensure that it does not discourage parties from settling judicial review proceedings, for example, by a local authority making a concession at an early stage.

- Partial success. In *PR (Bateman) v Legal Services Commission*[177] the claimants succeeded in quashing a decision of the Legal Services Commission but were deprived of 25% and 15% of their costs respectively of the issues on which they failed. CPR, r 44.3 can 'properly and where appropriate should be applied in such a way as positively to encourage litigants to be selective as to the points they take and positively to discourage litigants taking a multiplicity of bad points', see Munby J at para 18.

- Sanctions. The ordinary costs orders can be departed from because of a party's conduct. The conduct does not have to be causative of the loss (contrast wasted costs orders). In *Aegis Group PLC v Commissioners Inland Revenue*,[178] a late

---

[174] (1994) 27 HLR 602.
[175] (1993) 5 Admin LR 669.
[176] (2001) 4 CCLR 258.
[177] [2001] EWHC Admin 797.
[178] [2005] EWCH 1468 (Ch).

- response to a judicial review pre-action protocol letter with no adequate explanation for the delay resulted in the defendant recovering only 85% of his costs. Conduct can include refusing ADR. In practice this means mediation or failure to follow a complaints procedure, see *Halsey v Milton Keynes General NHS Trust*.[179]
- Indemnity. Costs can be awarded on an indemnity basis where there has been 'unreasonable behaviour of such a high degree that it can be characterised as exceptional', *Terry v LB Tower Hamlets*.[180] Examples include taking 'almost every possible point under the sun', see *R v Costwold DC, ex p Kissel*,[181] or failure to give proper disclosure – *R (Banks) v SSEFRA*.[182]
- Under s 51 of the Senior Courts Act 1981 the court has power to award costs against a non-party. This is an exceptional power but will ordinarily be exercised where the third party has controlled the proceedings or hopes to benefit from them so as to be the real party *Dymocks Franchise Systems (NSW) Pty Ltd v Todd*.[183]
- Legal Aid. The fact that a party is in receipt of public funding is not to be taken into account in deciding whether and what costs order to make, see s 22 of the Access to Justice Act 1999. Lord Justice Kay in a report of a working party entitled 'Litigating the Public Interest' stated at paragraphs 36–8 and 103 (http://www.liberty-human-rights.org.uk/publications/6-reports/litigating-the-public-interest.pdf):

    > 'The view was also expressed that many members of the judiciary are not sufficiently aware of the difference that not ordering costs *inter partes* makes both to lawyers doing legal aid work and to the CLS. For lawyers the rates of pay that their work will attract are considerably higher where the work is paid by their client's opponent. Just as the success fee in CFA cases is used to subsidise those CFA cases that the lawyer does not win, so cases paid at *inter partes* rates effectively subsidise cases paid at legal aid rates. For the CLS an *inter partes* costs order made on a legally-aided matter means that they are likely to have to pay out little themselves on the case and therefore have more funds available for other cases. An order that the lawyers in a legally-aided matter be paid by the CLS is a straight drain on the Commission's funds. Making an *inter partes* costs order against a public authority on a legally-aided matter is not a simple matter of robbing Peter to pay Paul.'

- In terms of assessment, the commonly used formula now is that there be 'detailed assessment of the claimant's [or other assisted party's] publicly funded costs'. The SCCO costs guide suggests 'there be detailed assessment of the costs of the claimant which are payable out of the Community Legal Service Fund' [annex to the SCCO Costs Guide 2006].[184]
- A successful defendant or interested party defending a claim against a publicly funded client may in certain situations apply to have their costs paid by the LSC where they will not recover them against the client. The requirements are that it must be 'just' and 'equitable' for the Order to be made. The application *must* be made within three months of the making of the relevant costs order.

---

[179] [2004] EWCA Civ 576, [2004] 1 WLR 3002, [2004] 4 All ER 920.
[180] Unreported, 15 December 2003 QBD.
[181] Unreported, 28 February 1997.
[182] [2004] EWHC 416 (Admin).
[183] [2004] UKPC 39, [2004] 1 WLR 2807.
[184] Appendix A6 to the Supreme Court Costs Office Guide 2006.

Protective costs order

3.79 Certain public law cases have issues of broader public interest which are unlikely to be resolved unless the claimant's exposure to liability to pay the defendant's costs is capped. An unsuccessful publicly funded litigant is entitled to a 'costs protection' on the basis that they can only be required to pay more than the amount 'which is a reasonable one' for them to pay having regard to their means and their conduct in relation to the dispute (Access to Justice Act 1999, s 11). This is known as a Protective Costs Order (PCO). There has been a growth of litigation concerning Protective Costs Orders. The principles were stated by Lord Phillips in *R (Corner House Research) v Secretary of State for Trade and Industry*.[185]

'We would therefore restate the governing principles in these terms:

1. A protective costs order may be made at any stage of the proceedings, on such conditions as the court thinks fit, provided that the court is satisfied that:
   i) the issues raised are of general public importance;
   ii) the public interest requires that those issues should be resolved;
   iii) the applicant has no private interest in the outcome of the case;
   iv) having regard to the financial resources of the applicant and the respondent(s) and to the amount of costs that are likely to be involved it is fair and just to make the order;
   v) if the order is not made the applicant will probably discontinue the proceedings and will be acting reasonably in so doing.
2. If those acting for the applicant are doing so pro bono this will be likely to enhance the merits of the application for a PCO.
3. It is for the court, in its discretion, to decide whether it is fair and just to make the order in the light of the considerations set out above.'

3.80 Certain of the principles have been controversial, in particular in environmental cases. In the case *of R (Buglife) v Thurrock Thames Gateway Development Corporation and others*[186] the Court of Appeal upheld an order capping the amount that the claimant charity would have to pay if it lost the case at £10,000. This was in a challenge to a planning permission granted for a distribution hub which was likely to destroy/affect nationally valuable invertebrates. The Master of the Rolls said that there was 'no difference in principle between the approach to PCOs in cases which raise environmental issues and the approach in cases which raise other serious issues and *vice versa*' (para 17).

3.81 However in *R (Garner) v Elmbridge BC, Gladedale Group and Network Rail Infrastructure*[187] the Court of Appeal considered an appeal by Mr Garner, an architect whose practice specialised in historic building conservation, who sought to challenge a grant of planning permission for the redevelopment of Hampton Court Station opposite to and in the setting of the grade 1 Hampton Court Palace. The Aarhus Convention and an EU Directive were directly engaged. Mr Garner sought a PCO. Sullivan LJ said:[188]

'Turning then to the two grounds on which Nicol J refused a PCO, I accept the appellant's submission that in an Article 10a[189] case there is no justification for the application of the issues of "general public importance/public interest requiring resolution of those issues" in

---

[185] [2005] 1 WLR 2600 at 74.
[186] [2008] EWCA Civ 1209.
[187] [2010] EWCA Civ 1006.
[188] Para 39.
[189] Directive 83/337/EEC which was directly applicable.

the *Corner House* conditions. Both Aarhus and the directive are based on the premise that it is in the public interest that there should be effective public participation in the decision-making process in significant environmental cases (those cases that are covered by the EIA and IPPC directives); and an important component of that public participation is that the public should be able to ensure, through an effective review procedure that is not prohibitively expensive, that such important environmental decisions are lawfully taken. In summary, under community law it is a matter of general public importance that those environmental decisions subject to the directive are taken in a lawful manner, and, if there is an issue as to that, the general public interest does require that that issue be resolved in an effective review process. The *Corner House* principles are judge-made law and in accordance with the *Marleasing* principle those judge-made rules for PCOs must be interpreted and applied in such a way as to secure conformity with the directive.'

On the second ground which was whether the costs of the proceedings were to be considered on subjective or objective bases Sullivan LJ continued:

'Even if it is either permissible or necessary to have some regard to the financial circumstances of the individual claimant, the underlying purpose of the directive to ensure that members of the public concerned having a sufficient interest should have access to a review procedure which is not prohibitively expensive would be frustrated if the court was entitled to consider the matter solely by reference to the means of the claimant who happened to come forward, without having to consider whether the potential costs would be prohibitively expensive for an ordinary member of "the public concerned"'.[190]

3.82 Since the first edition of this book the CPR has been amended to take into account Aarhus Convention claims. CPR, r 45.43 prescribes that subject to rule 45.44 a party to an Aarhus Convention claim may not be ordered to pay costs exceeding the amount prescribed in the Practice Direction. PD 45 limits the costs that a claimant is liable for to £5,000 if he is claiming as an individual and £10,000 if claiming as a non-governmental organisation or business. Where a defendant is ordered to pay costs the equivalent amount specified in the PD is £35,000.

---

[190] Para 46.

CHAPTER 4

THE TRIBUNAL SYSTEM

INTRODUCTION

4.01 The passing of the Tribunals, Courts and Enforcement Act 2007 has brought about a change in the framework of administrative law tribunals. The changes that it has brought about and is bringing about will alter the nature of the cases brought in the Administrative Court. In the circumstances it is appropriate to explain what is still a relatively new tribunal system first of all in this chapter.

THE ROLE OF THE TRIBUNAL SYSTEM

Background

4.02 In May 2000 the Government asked Sir Andrew Leggatt to investigate and report on the delivery of justice through the tribunals to ensure that tribunals were 'fair, timely proportionate and effective', that the 'administrative and practical arrangements for supporting those decision-making procedures' were human rights compliant by being fair and impartial, that there were 'adequate arrangements' for improving people's knowledge and understanding of those rights in relations to disputes, and that tribunals functioned in such a way that made those rights and responsibilities a reality.

4.03 Leggatt was also asked to ensure that the arrangements for the funding and management of the tribunals and other bodies by Government Departments 'are efficient, effective and economical' whilst paying 'due regard both to judicial independence, and to ministerial responsibility for the administration of public funds'. Finally, that 'performance standards for tribunals are coherent, consistent and public; and effective measures for monitoring and enforcing those standards are established' and that 'Tribunals overall constitute a coherent structure for the delivery of administrative justice'.[1] Leggatt's Report, Tribunals for Users: One System – One Service, made a large number of criticisms of the present system and a correspondingly large number of recommendations. The main focus of his criticisms of administrative tribunals was their lack of independence from the departments they were intended to review, and the lack of uniformity in their structure.

4.04 The Government's response to Leggatt was a White Paper in July 2004,[2] in which the Government spelled out its five-year strategy around the following principles:

---

[1] See Leggatt's final report: 'Tribunals for Users – One System, One Service'.
[2] 'Transforming Public Service: Complaints, Redress and Tribunals' (Cm 6243).

(a) developing **policies that help empower citizens** and communities to manage their own problems, protecting them from crime and anti-social behaviour, and narrowing the justice gap;

(b) moving out of courts and tribunals disputes that could be resolved elsewhere through better use of **education, information, advice** and **proportionate dispute resolution;**

(c) **changing radically the way we deliver services** so that the courts, tribunals, legal services and constitutional arrangements are fit for purpose and cost effective; and

(d) **re-shaping the Department of Constitutional Affairs' organisation and infrastructure** so that it is aligned structurally to meet the needs of the public and works well with the rest of government.[3]

4.05 The resulting legislation, the Tribunals, Courts and Enforcement Act 2007 (TCEA), has far-reaching implications for all those involved with the tribunals, whether as individual applicants or government departments or agencies, or those who sit on the various tribunals. The policy intent behind Part 1 (which deals with the new structure of tribunals) is to 'create a new, simplified statutory framework for tribunals, bringing existing tribunal jurisdictions together and providing a structure for new jurisdictions and new appeal rights'.[4]

LEGISLATION

4.06 The TCEA creates the new role of Senior President of Tribunals (SPT) (TCEA 2007, s 2(1)).[5] To reflect the history leading up to the creation of the new system the SPT must, in carrying out the functions of that office have regard to: (a) the need for the tribunals to be accessible, and (b) the need for proceedings before the tribunals to be fair as well as being handled quickly and efficiently (s 2(3)). The members of the tribunals must be 'experts in the subject matter of the law to be applied in which they decide matters' (s 2(3)(c)). Furthermore, the SPT must recognise 'the need to develop innovative methods of resolving disputes that are of a type that maybe brought before tribunals' (s 2(3)(d)).

4.07 The term 'tribunal' refers to the First-tier Tribunal (FTT), the Upper Tribunal (UT), the employment tribunal (ET), the Employment Appeals Tribunal (EAT) and the Asylum and Immigration Tribunal (AIT) (TCEA 2007, s 2(4)). The two new tribunals (FTT and UT) are to be divided into a number of chambers each containing a certain limited number of jurisdictions, to reflect the specialist expertise of those sitting (s 7). In November 2008 the first two chambers of the FTT came into existence.

4.08 At the time of writing the structure is as follows:[6]

First-tier Tribunal:

- Social Entitlement Chamber: Asylum Control, Social Security and Child Support, and Criminal Injuries Compensation.

---

[3] White Papers, p 5.
[4] Explanatory Notes, p 2.
[5] The first holder being Sir Robert Carnwath, a Court of Appeal Judge, the present incumbent being Sir Jeremy Sullivan.
[6] See First-tier and Upper Tribunal (Chambers) Order 2010, arts 2 and 9.

- Health, Education and Social Care: Care Standards, Mental Health, Special Educational Needs and Disability, Primary Care Lists.

- War Pensions and Armed Forces Compensation Chamber: War Pensions and Armed Forces Compensation.

- The General Regulatory Chamber: Charity, Claims Management Services, Consumer Credit, Environment, Environment, Estate Agents, Gambling Appeals, Immigration Services, Information Rights, Local Government Standards in England, and Transport.

- Immigration and Asylum Chamber: Immigration and Asylum

- Tax Chamber.

Upper Tribunal:

- Administrative Appeals

- Tax and Chancery

- Lands

- Immigration and Asylum.

4.09 The SPT presides over both the UT and the FTT. This means that an independent member of the judiciary heads the tribunals. Furthermore, the UT is a superior court of record (TCEA 2007, s 3(5)), which allows the expert tribunal to develop its own case-law where appropriate. The appointment of judges (the legal members) and members (experts, like medical practitioners and lay people) is subject to s 4 and Schedule 2 of the TCEA. Judges may be appointed if they satisfy the eligibility criteria (five years' legal experience or, if not, exceptionally, if the Lord Chancellor considers them to be suitable).[7] By s 31(2) certain judges are transferred-in – ie these are members of existing tribunals who automatically became FTT Judges when that tribunal's functions are assumed by the FTT. Similar provisions apply to the UT: s 5 and Schedule 3. Under s 6 certain judges automatically become judges of both FTT and UT: these include judges of the Appeal Courts in England and Wales, as well as Scotland and Northern Ireland, High Court Judges, Circuit Judges and District Judges.

4.10 Most of the present tribunals, some of them already part of the FTT, were appealed to the High Court whether by way of statutory appeal (for instance in the case of the Care Standards Tribunal) or judicial review (JR) (for instance, the Mental Health Review Tribunal).

4.11 Each Chamber has its own rules of procedure:

- Tribunal Procedure (First-tier Tribunal) (Social Entitlement Chambers) Rules 2009[8]

---

[7] The appointment is subject to a competition held by the Judicial Appointments Commission.
[8] SI 2008/2685.

- Tribunal Procedure (First-tier Tribunal) (Health, Education and Social Care Chamber) Rules 2008[9]
- Tribunal Procedure (First-tier Tribunal) (War Pensions and Armed Forces Compensation Chamber) Rules 2008[10]
- Tribunal Procedure (First-tier Tribunal) (General Regulatory Chamber) Rules 2009[11]
- Asylum and Immigration Tribunal (Procedure) Rules 2005[12]
- Tribunal Procedure (First-tier Tribunal) (Tax Chamber) Rules 2009.[13]

Apart from the Lands Chamber, which has its own sets or rules,[14] the other Upper Tribunal Chambers are governed by the Tribunal Procedure (Upper Tribunal) Rules 2008.[15]

Review of decisions

4.12 First, each FTT is empowered to review its own decision whether by its own initiative or on an application by a person with a right of appeal: TCEA 2007, s 9(1) and (2)(a) and (b). This is subject to the exception of 'excluded decisions', which cannot be reviewed.[16] This power has been incorporated into the Rules so far brought into force in the Social Entitlement Chamber (SEC) and Health Education and Social Care Chamber (HESC). By way of illustration, the HESC Rules[17] deal with the issue of reviews in Part 5. Under Rule 45, the tribunal 'may set-aside a decision which disposes of proceedings, or part of such a decision and re-make the decision or relevant part of it, if: (a) the tribunal considers it in the interests of justice to do so; and (b) one or more of the conditions in paragraph (2) are satisfied. These conditions are: (a) a document relating to the proceedings was not sent to, or was not received at an appropriate time by a party or a party's representative; (b) a document relating to the proceedings was not sent to the tribunal at an appropriate time; (c) a party or a party's representative, was not present at a hearing related to the proceedings; or (d) there has been some other procedural irregularity in the proceedings'.

4.13 A party wishing for a decision (or part of a decision) to be set aside must make a written application which must be received not later than 28 days 'after the date on which the tribunal sent notice of the decision to the party' (Rule 45(3)). An application for permission to appeal to the UT under Rule 46 of the HESC Rules gives the tribunal an opportunity under Rule 47(1) to consider whether the decision that is the subject of the proposed appeal should be reviewed. However, this power is subject to Rule 49(1)(a) which allows the tribunal to review a decision under Rule 47(1) if, and presumably, only if, 'it is satisfied that there was an error of law in the decision'. In special educational needs cases an application for a review of a decision may be made 'if circumstances relevant to the decision have changed since the decision was made' (Rule 48(2)).

---

[9] SI 2008/2699.
[10] SI 2008/2686.
[11] SI 2009/1976.
[12] SI 2005/230.
[13] SI 2009/273.
[14] Tribunal Procedure (Upper Tribunal) (Lands Chamber) Rules 2010, SI 2010/2600.
[15] SI 2008/2698.
[16] These 'excluded decisions' are listed at Tribunals, Courts and Enforcement Act (TCEA) 2007, s 11(5).
[17] The Tribunal Procedure (First-tier Tribunal) (Health, Education and Social Care Chamber) Rules 2008 (SI 2008/2699).

4.14 The net effect of the right to review has yet to be seen. However, those dealing with reviews are likely to be the more senior members of the FTT judiciary. Some decisions will be easy: for instance, in the mental health jurisdiction the failure to notify a nearest relative of a hearing will be reviewable since it will be both a failure to serve a document and a procedural irregularity. Equally, making an order that is plainly unlawful – for instance, adjourning a hearing to ensure that a non-statutory recommendation is complied with – will also be easily reviewable. However, more difficulty arises where there is a challenge to the adequacy of the reasons given by the tribunal, and/or where the coherence of the decision is challenged. If the reviewing judge considers the reasons given to be inadequate or incoherent he will be obliged to review the decision on the grounds that it is in the interests of justice to do so and the inadequacy of the reasons constitutes some other procedural irregularity. In reaching his decision the reviewing judge will have to consider whether the decision of the tribunal was obviously wrong in law or whether the decision made was unreasonable on *Wednesbury* principles. The Explanatory Notes to the TCEA, ss 9 and 10 state that the power to review is 'intended to capture decisions that are clearly wrong, so avoiding the need for an appeal. The power has been provided in the form of a discretionary power for the tribunal so that only appropriate decisions are reviewed. This contrasts with cases where an appeal on a point of law is made, because, for instance, it is important to have an authoritative ruling'.[18] This makes perfect sense in the context of the new tribunal system where there is a desire for the UT to create its own case-law. This point was emphasised the first time the UT was called upon to judicially review a case in which the FTT had reviewed itself. In *R (RB) v The First-tier Tribunal* [2010] UKUT 160 (ACC) in which the Senior President presided, the UT observed: 'The power to review decisions is an important and valuable one. It is common ground that the powers of review on a point of law are intended, among other things, to provide an alternative remedy to an appeal. In a case where the appeal would be bound to succeed, a review will enable appropriate corrective action to be taken without delay'.[19] It could not have been intended that the power of review should enable the FTT to usurp the UT's function of determining appeals on contentious points of law. Nor could it have been intended to enable a later FTT panel (or the same judge on a later occasion) to take a different view of the law from an earlier FTT decision where both views are tenable. '[I]f a power of review is to be exercised to set aside the original decision because of perceived error of law, this should only be done in clear cases'.[20] One critical observation the UT made concerned the length and detail of the FTT's review decision. The UT took the view that if an error is clear it should be possible to give reasons in a couple of paragraphs, drawing attention to an overlooked authority or statutory provision, or to agree with a ground of appeal.

4.15 Under the TCEA 2007, s 9(4), once the FTT has reviewed a decision, it may in the light of the review either: (a) correct accidental errors in the decision or in a record of the decision, (b) amend reasons given for the decision, or (c) set the decision aside. Where the decision is set-aside the FTT must either: (a) re-decide the matter concerned, or (b) refer the matter to the UT.[21] There is nothing in the Act that requires the renewed decision to be made by the individual judge reviewing the decision. The Act simply requires the FTT to re-decide or refer the matter. The reviewing judge may, for instance, quite properly set aside a plainly wrong decision, but consider it necessary for the new

---

[18] Taken from the Explanatory Notes to the Tribunals, Courts and Enforcement Act 2007.
[19] RB at para 22.
[20] RB at para 24.
[21] TCEA 2007, s 9(5)(a) and (b).

decision to be made by a full tribunal having heard evidence from witnesses. In those circumstances, the reviewing judge will remit the case.

Appeals to the Upper Tribunal

4.16 Under the TCEA 2007, s 11, any party to a case before the FTT has a right of appeal[22] to the UT 'on any point of law arising from a decision made by the First-tier Tribunal other than an excluded decision'.[23] That right may only be exercised with permission,[24] such permission may be given by either the FTT or the UT on an application by a party.[25] The excluded decisions are listed at s 11(5), and include: (a) an appeal against a FTT decision which itself was an appeal under the Criminal Injuries Compensation Act 1995, appeals against national security certificates under (b) the Data Protection Act 1998, and (c) the Freedom of Information Act 2000, and (f) 'any decision of the First-tier Tribunal that it is of a description specified in any order made by the Lord Chancellor'. Importantly, a decision made by the FTT under s 9 of the Act (ie to review or not to review, actions taken or not taken if a review is carried out, setting aside an earlier decision of the FTT or referring or not referring a matter to the UT) is excluded under (d) and (e).

4.17 If a case is brought before the UT the proceedings are governed by the Tribunals, Courts and Enforcement Act (TCEA) 2007, s 12 and the Rules.[26] Section 12 provides that if the UT, in deciding an appeal, finds that the making of the decision concerned involved the making of an error on a point of law, the UT may (but need not) set aside the decision of the FTT and, if it does it must either remit the case to the FTT with directions for its reconsideration or remake the decision. If the UT remits the decision it may direct that the members of the FTT who are chosen to reconsider the case are not to be the same as those who made the decision that has been set aside and can give procedural directions in connection with the reconsideration of the case by the FTT.[27] If the UT decides to re-make the decision, it may: (a) make any decision which the FTT could make if the FTT were remaking the decision, and (b) may make such findings of fact as it considers appropriate. The application for permission to appeal to the UT itself must be in writing and, generally, the application must be received by the UT no later than one month after the FTT that made the decision under challenge sent its notice of refusal of permission to appeal or refused to admit the application for permission to appeal.[28] In the case of an application under the Safeguarding Vulnerable Groups Act 2006, s 4 (ie from a decision of the Independent Barring Board) the period is three months from the date the decision challenged was sent to the appellant.[29] Rule 21(4) and (5) specify the formalities for the application. Rule 21(6) concerns the extension of time for making the application if it was made out of time (the applicant must give a reason). Rule 21(7) concerns the situation where the application was made too late to the tribunal below and it refused to admit the application; again the reason must be given and the UT '*must only admit the application*' if it is satisfied that it is in the interests of justice to do so.[30]

---

[22] TCEA 2007, s 11(2) subject to (8).
[23] TCEA 2007, s 11(1).
[24] TCEA 2007, s 11(3).
[25] TCEA 2007, s 11(4)(a) and (b).
[26] Tribunal Procedure (Upper Tribunal) Rules 2008 (SI 2008/2698).
[27] TCEA 2007, s 12(3).
[28] Rule 21(3)(b).
[29] Rule 21(3)(a). Until 3 November 2008 the appeal was to the Care Standards Tribunal.
[30] Rule 21(7)(b).

4.18 If the UT refuses permission to appeal it is obliged to send written notice of the refusal and written reasons for it.[31] These decisions will generally be made without a hearing (see Rule 34). However, where an application for appeal is refused or where permission is given, but only on limited grounds or subject to conditions,[32] without a hearing, and the case is a HESC mental health or special educational needs case or a safeguarding of vulnerable groups case, the appellant may apply for the decision to be reconsidered at a hearing.[33] Interestingly, as with the FTT, the UT has express powers to correct, set aside and review its own decisions.[34] Under Rule 45 the UT may review its decision when a party applies for permission to appeal. However, the UT may do so if, and only if: (a) when making the decision the UT has overlooked a legislative provision or binding authority which could have had a material effect on the decision; or (b) since the UT's decision a court has made a decision that is binding on the UT and which could have had a material effect on the UT's decision had it been made before that decision. The obvious purpose, once again, is to ensure that obvious mistakes at the UT can be rectified without the additional delay and expense of an appeal to the Court of Appeal.

Judicial Review in the UT[35]

4.19 Section 15 of the Tribunals, Courts and Enforcement Act 2007 grants the UT the powers to grant the following kinds of relief, ie: (a) a mandatory order, (b) a prohibiting order, (c) a quashing order, (d) a declaration, and (e) injunctions. There are two routes by which a judicial review case will come before the UT. An application may be made to the UT, which the UT can consider if, but only if, the conditions under s 18 of the Act are met or if the UT is authorised to proceed even though all the conditions have not been met. The restrictions on judicial review, under s 18, are four in number: (1) the UT can only be asked to grant a remedy it has the power to grant; (2) the application must not call into question anything done by the Crown Court; (3) the case falls within a class specified in a direction given in accordance with the Constitutional Reform Act 2005, Part 1 of Sch 2, ie the Lord Chief Justice (or someone to whom he delegates the power) may, with the agreement of the Lord Chancellor, specify a class of case which the UT may deal with, rather than the High Court;[36] (4) the Judge presiding at the hearing is required to be a High Court Judge in England and Wales, or a Judge of the Court of Appeal, or 'such other persons as may be agreed from time to time between the Lord Chief Justice and the SPT'.[37] If the UT does not have the function of deciding the application (ie any of conditions 1 to 4 are not met) then it must order the transfer of the application to the High Court.[38] The other route for a judicial review case to the UT is under the Tribunals, Courts and Enforcement Act 2007, s 19, which amends the Senior Courts Act 1981, s 31[39] to provide that where an application is made to the High

---

[31] Rule 22(1).
[32] Under Rule 22(1)(2).
[33] Rule 22(3) and (4).
[34] Section 10 of the TCEA 2007, and Rules 41 to 43 which are similar to those discussed above in relation to the FTT.
[35] For an in-depth analysis of judicial review (and other issues) in the Upper Tribunal see Coppel and Hanif, *Tribunal Practice* (Jordan Publishing, 2012) ch 14.
[36] This has been done for all cases the UT will hear, barring the excluded categories in the Lord Chief Justice's Practice Direction Classes of Cases Specified under the Tribunals, Courts and Enforcement Act 2007, s 18(6), 31 October 2008.
[37] TCEA 2007, s 18(8)(a) and (b). In Scotland the judge must be one of the Court of Session, and in Northern Ireland a High Court Judge or Appeal Court Judge. In those jurisdictions the agreement in (b) must be between the Lord President or the Lord Chief Justice of Northern Ireland and the SPT.
[38] TCEA 2007, s 18(3).
[39] Now the Senior Courts Act 1981, s 31A.

Court for judicial review or for permission to apply for judicial review and all four of the following conditions are met the High Court must transfer the application to the UT.[40]

4.20 The conditions are: (1) the application includes nothing other than relief or permission to apply for relief under the Tribunals, Courts and Enforcement Act 2007, s 31(1), an award under s 31(4), or interest or costs, (2) the application does not call into question anything done by the Crown Court, (3) the application must fall within the Tribunals, Courts and Enforcement Act 2007, s 18(6), ie within a case directed by the Lord Chief Justice and the Lord Chancellor, and (4) that the application does not call into question any decision made under the Immigration Acts, British Nationality Act 1981, or any instrument under those Acts, or any other nationality law provision. However, if conditions 1, 2 and 4 are met, but not 3, the High Court may order a transfer to the UT if it appears to it to be just and convenient to do so.[41]

4.21 The UT Rules now contain provisions concerning judicial review.[42] Since 1 November 2013 judicial reviews of immigration decisions that would previously have been to the High Court are now to be made to the Upper Tribunal.[43] In one of the first reported decisions of the UT one of the issues before the tribunal was whether it had jurisdiction to hear an appeal against the FTT's decision not to review an earlier decision on the disclosure of documents. The UT stated 'In the circumstances of this case, this issue could not entirely deprive us of jurisdiction in any event because, if there is no right of appeal, we could treat the appeal as an application for permission to apply for judicial review and waive the requirement to serve the First-tier Tribunal'.[44]

Judicial review of UT as a 'superior court of record'

4.22 Section 3(5) of the Tribunals, Courts and Enforcement Act 2007 declares that the UT is a superior court of record. Does this mean that it is not amenable to judicial review, and, if it is, to what extent and under what circumstances? This was the question that concerned the Divisional Court and the Court of Appeal in *R (Rex Cart) v The Upper Tribunal and others*.[45] The substantive issue in the case arose out of an application to revise a variation direction given by the Secretary of State under the Child Support Act 1991.[46] The UT refused to grant permission to the applicant to appeal on the grounds that the Secretary of State had failed to give written notice of variation. That was challenged by way of judicial review to the High Court. The Divisional Court held that the UT is amenable to judicial review but only on the pre-*Anisminic* grounds of jurisdictional error[47] or a denial of the right to a fair hearing. That decision was upheld on appeal by the Court of Appeal, albeit for different reasons.

---

[40] TCEA 2007, s 19 inserting s 31A(1) and (2).
[41] TCEA 2007, s 19(3).
[42] SI 2008/2698, Part 4.
[43] See Lord Chief Justice's Practice Directions, 21 August 2013.
[44] *Dorset Healthcare NHS Trust v MH* [2009] UKUT 4 (Administrative Appeals Chamber).
[45] In the Court of Appeal [2010] EWCA Civ 859. In the Queen's Bench Divisional Court at [2009] EWHC 3052 (Admin) and at [2010] 2 WLR 1012. This includes an excellent outline of the new tribunal system by Laws LJ.
[46] The facts of the case are summarised in the High Court decision at paras 26 and 27. The original decision is [2009] UKUT 62.
[47] *Anisminic Ltd v Foreign Compensation Commission* [1969] 2 AC 147.

THE TRIBUNAL SYSTEM: AN OVERVIEW OF APPEALS[48]

Onward Appeals – pre and post transfer

4.23 The following is a useful overview of the system of appeals reproduced from the Appendix to the judgments in *Cart*:

First-tier Tribunal

4.24

War Pensions and Armed Forces Compensation Chamber
(established November 2008)

Tribunal	Previous onward appeal	New onward appeal	Basis of appeal to UT
Pension Appeals Tribunal (England and Wales)	Pensions Appeal Tribunal (War Pensions Administrative Provisions Act 1919, s 8(2))	Administrative Appeals Chamber (UT)	Point of law (right of appeal to UT extended to include appeal against assessment of award. Previous appeal only against entitlement decision with JR against assessment)

Health, Education and Social Care Chamber
(established November 2008)

Tribunal	Previous onward appeal	New onward appeal	Basis of appeal to UT
Care Standards Tribunal (except appeals under the Safeguarding Vulnerable Groups Act 2006, s 4)	High Court (Protection of Children Act 1999, s 9(6))	Administrative Appeals Chambers (UT)	Point of law
Mental Health Review Tribunals for England	No right of appeal; case stated procedure or judicial review by High Court	Administrative Appeals Chambers (UT)	Point of law

---

[48] Table taken from *R (C) v The Upper Tribunal* [2010] EWCA Civ 859.

Tribunal	Previous onward appeal	New onward appeal	Basis of appeal to UT
Special Educational Needs and Disability Tribunal	High Court (Tribunals and Inquiries Act 1992, s 11)	Administrative Appeals Chamber (UT)	Point of law
Family Health Services Authority	High Court (Tribunals and Inquiries Act 1992, s 11)	Administrative Appeals Chambers (UT)	Point of law

General Regulatory Chamber
(established September 2009)

Tribunal	Previous onward appeal	New onward appeal	Basis of appeal to UT
Charity Tribunal	High Court (Charities Act 1993, s 2(c))	Tax and Chancery Chamber (UT)	Point of law
Consumer Credit Appeals Tribunal	Court of Appeal (Consumer Credit Act 1974, s 41A)	Administrative Appeals Chamber (UT)	Point of law
Estate Agents Appeals Panel	High Court (Estate Agents Act 1979, s 7)	Administrative Appeals Chamber (UT)	Point of law
Transport Tribunal (appeals against decisions of the Driving Standards Agency)	Court of Appeal (Transport Act 1985, para 14 of Sch 4)	Administrative Appeals Chambers (UT)	Point of law
Gambling Appeals Tribunal – transfer date January 2010	High Court (Gambling Act 2005, s 143)	Administrative Appeals Chamber (UT)	Point of law
Claims Management Services Tribunal – transfer date January 2010	Court of Appeal (Compensation Act 2006, s 13)	Administrative Appeals Chamber (UT)	Point of law

Tribunal	Previous onward appeal	New onward appeal	Basis of appeal to UT
Information Tribunal (except appeals against national security certificates) – transfer date January 2010	High Court (Data Protection Act 1998, s 49)	Administrative Appeals Chamber (UT)	Point of law
Immigration Services Tribunal – transfer date January 2010	No right of appeal: JR to High Court	Administrative Appeals Chamber (UT)	Point of law
Adjudication Panel for England – transfer date January 2010	High Court (Local Government Act 2000, ss 78–79)	Administrative Appeals Chambers (UT)	Point of law and wider appeal rights for a person penalised by a decision

Tax Chamber (established April 2009 at the same time as other changes to the tax appeals system by HMRC)

Tribunal	Previous onward appeal	New onward appeal	Basis of appeal to UT
General Commissioners of Income Tax	High Court (Taxes and Management Act 1970, s 56)	Tax and Chancery Chamber (UT)	Point of law, and wider appeal rights against amount of certain penalties
Special Commissioners of Income Tax	(Taxes and Management Act 1970, s 56)		
VAT and Duties Tribunals	(Tribunals and Inquiries Act 1992, s 11)		
Section 706 Tribunal Section 704 Tribunal	(Tribunals and Inquiries Act 1992, s 11)		

Social Entitlement Chamber
(established November 2008)

Tribunal	Previous onward appeal	New onward appeal	Basis of appeal to UT
Social Security and Child Support Appeal Tribunals	Social Security/Child Support Commissioners (Social Security Act 1998, s 14/Child Support Act 1991, s 24)	Administrative Appeals Chamber (UT)	Point of law under Tax Credit Act 2002, para 2(2) or 4(1) of Sch 2; Child Trust Funds Act 2004, s 21(10)
Criminal Injuries Compensation Panel	No right of appeal: JR by High Court	No right of appeal: JR by Administrative Appeals Chamber (UT)	Point of law
Asylum Support Tribunal	No right of appeal: JR by High Court	No right of appeal: JR by the High Court	

Immigration and Asylum Chamber
(established February 2010)

Tribunal	Previous onward appeal	New onward appeal	Basis of appeal to UT
Asylum and Immigration Tribunal	Reconsideration by AIT and review by High Court (Nationality Immigration and Asylum Act 2002, s 103A)	Immigration and Asylum Chamber (UT)[49]	Point of law

---

[49] See also Practice Direction of the Lord Chief Justice, 21 August 2013, transferring immigration judicial reviews to the Upper Tribunal from the High Court.

Upper Tribunal
4.25

Administrative Appeals Tribunal
(established November 2008)

Tribunal	Previous onward appeal	New onward appeal	Basis of onward appeal
Social security/Child Support Commissioners	Court of Appeal (Social Security Act 1998 s 15; Child Support Act 1991, s 25)	Court of Appeal	Point of law
Care Standards Tribunal (appeals under Safeguarding Vulnerable Groups Act 2006, s 4)	Court of Appeal (Safeguarding Vulnerable Groups Act 2006, s 4)	Court of Appeal	Point of law
Transport Tribunal (appeals against decisions of Traffic Commissioners)	Court of Appeal (Transport Act 1985, para 14 of Sch 4)	Court of Appeal	Law and fact
Information Tribunal: appeals against national security certificates under Data Protection Act 1998, s 28 and Freedom of Information Act 2000, s 60 – transfer date January 2010	No onward appeal	No onward appeal (excluded decision under TCEA 2007, s 13(8))	n/a

Tax and Chancery
(established April 2009)

Tribunal	Previous onward appeal	New onward appeal	Basis of onward appeal
Financial Services and Markets Tribunal	Court of Appeal (Financial Services and Markets Act 2000, s 137)	Court of Appeal	Point of law

Tribunal	Previous onward appeal	New onward appeal	Basis of onward appeal
Pensions Regulator Tribunal	Court of Appeal (Pensions Act 2004, s 104)	Court of Appeal	Point of law

Lands Chambers
(established April 2009)

Tribunal	Previous onward appeal	New onward appeal	Basis of onward appeal
Lands Tribunal	Court of Appeal (Lands Tribunal Act 1949, s 3(4))	Court of Appeal	Point of law

Immigration and Asylum Chambers
(established February 2010)

Tribunal	Previous onward appeal	New onward appeal	Basis of onward appeal
Asylum and Immigration Tribunal – reconsiderations	Court of Appeal (Nationality, Immigration and Asylum Act 2002, s 103)	Court of Appeal	Point of law

Part 2
SPECIFIC AREAS

CHAPTER 5

PLANNING AND ENVIRONMENT

INTRODUCTION

5.01 A decision on the part of a local planning authority is susceptible to challenge by judicial review.[1] Although that has been accepted for a long time there has been an increased use of judicial review to challenge planning decisions in recent years. The obvious reason is that, whereas applicants for planning permission have the right to appeal to the Secretary of State, third parties do not. The remedy of judicial review is thus the only remedy open to third parties.

5.02 As the planning system has become more front-loaded the absence of a right of appeal on the part of third parties can be seen as being increasingly anachronistic. That, coupled with enhanced environmental awareness, has meant that third parties have become more active in bringing challenges to a planning permission granted by a local planning authority and in relation to decisions made such as the decision to issue a general vesting declaration after a compulsory purchase order. Subject to obtaining favourable advice, such proceedings can be funded by the Legal Services Commission or conditional fee agreements may be entered into or a protective costs order obtained. There can be less cost to the third party in bringing judicial review proceedings than through appearing at a public inquiry and often, if successful, the result that they really want, namely the quashing of the planning permission.

5.03 The importance of the planning system as a vehicle for economic growth has been recognised by the government in the pressure that it has placed upon the courts to enhance the speed and efficiency with which planning cases are dealt with.

The Planning Court

5.04 In July 2013 the Coalition Government introduced reforms to the procedure for judicial review in planning cases.[2] Those have culminated in the establishment, as from 6 April 2014, of the Planning Court. That will function within the Queens Bench Division with a specialist list. It is an evolution of the Planning Fast Track which was introduced into the Administrative Court in July 2013. The aim is to ensure that important planning cases are brought on quickly before specialist judges.

5.05 CPR r 54.21(2) defines a 'Planning Court claim' as

'a judicial review or statutory challenge which –

---

[1] R v Sheffield City Council ex p Mansfield [1979] 37 P&CR 1.
[2] Civil Procedure (Amendment No 4) Rules 2013, SI 2013/1412.

(a) involves any of the following matters –
  (i) planning permission, other development consents, the enforcement of planning control and the enforcement of other statutory schemes;
  (ii) applications under the Transport and Works Act 1992;
  (iii) wayleaves;
  (iv) highways and other rights of way;
  (v) compulsory purchase orders;
  (vi) village greens;
  (vii) European Union environmental legislation and domestic transposition, including assessments for development consents, habitats, waste and pollution control;
  (viii) National, regional or other planning policy documents, statutory or otherwise; or
  (ix) Any other matter that the judge appointed under CPR r 54.22(2) determines; and

has been issued or transferred to the Planning Court.'

5.06 The Planning Liaison Judge will be able to categorise Planning Court cases as 'significant': PD 54E, para 3.1. That will include claims that:

'(a) relate to commercial, residential, or other development which have significant economic impact either at a local level or beyond their immediate locality;
(b) raise important points of law;
(c) generate significant public interest; or
(d) by virtue of the volume or nature of technical material, are best dealt with by judges with significant experience of handling such matters.'

5.07 Parties are able to make representations as to whether the matter should be classed as significant on issuing the claim or filing the acknowledgement of service. It is understood that a broad interpretation to the word will be taken.

5.08 Paragraph 3.4 of the Practice Direction sets target timescales for hearing significant cases. They are:

'(a) applications for permission to apply for judicial review are to be determined within 3 weeks of the expiry of the time for filing the acknowledgement of service;
(b) oral renewals of applications for permission to apply for judicial review are to be heard within one month of receipt of the request for renewal;
(c) applications for permission under s 289 of the Town and Country Planning Act 1990 are to be determined within one month of issue;
(d) substantive statutory applications, including applications under s 288 of the Town and Country Planning Act 1990, are to be heard within six months of issue; and
(e) judicial reviews are to be heard within ten weeks of the expiry of the period for the submission of detailed grounds by the defendant or any other party as provided in Rule 54.14.'

Practice Direction 54E para 3.6 provides that the Planning Liaison Judge will be able to direct expedition of any Planning Court claim if it is necessary to deal with the case justly.

5.09 Parties have to be prepared to meet the target timescales. In *London and Henley (Middle Brook Street) Ltd v Secretary of State for Communities and Local Government*[3] Lindblom J took

---

[3] [2013] EWHC 4207.

'this opportunity to remind parties in proceedings such as these of the new targets for planning cases in the Administrative Court which have been published on its website, and in particular the guidance on listing. The guidance makes it clear that parties will be consulted before substantive hearings are listed, but – and this is important for parties to note – listing will respect general timetable and targets. Dates may be imposed and counsel's availability will not be a reason for hearing a case significantly outside the target timetable.'[4]

5.10 The procedural rules for claims within the Planning Court are not changed from those in general Administrative Court cases. However, PD 54E para 3.5 provides that the Planning Court may make case management directions including a direction to any party intending to contest the claim to file and serve a summary of his grounds for doing so. That would be a significant change in that at present there is no obligation on a defendant in a statutory application or appeal to disclose their case until the filing of skeleton arguments. Summary grounds are, of course, necessary to determine whether permission to proceed with the claim should be granted. It may well be that active case management is used to deliver a consistent way of dealing with all cases but, in particular, the significant ones.

At the time of writing it is early in the history of the court but already there has been an improvement in the time within which cases are decided.

Other amendments

5.11 Amendments made to CPR r 54.5(5) provide:

'(5) Where the application for judicial review relates to a decision made by the Secretary of State or local planning authority under the planning acts, the claim form must be filed not later than six weeks after the grounds to make the claim first arose.'[5]

The logic for this reform has been to bring judicial review in line with the statutory provisions for challenging Secretary of State decisions under s 288 of the Town and Country Planning Act. However, the circumstances of a statutory challenge are not entirely analogous with judicial review. Under statutory provisions a party to a planning appeal has six weeks to challenge the Secretary of State's decision letter. In such cases the party litigating is fully informed of the circumstances of the case having just been through the planning appeal process and is challenging the terms of a single decision letter. The potential judicial review litigant will, by definition, not be a fully informed party (they are challenging someone else's planning application and permission) and will have to consider and review multiple documents perhaps having to instruct their own expert advisors. While 'unblocking' the judicial review system is undoubtedly a welcome goal it is uncertain what effect the revisions to the planning provisions will have. What is clear is that the alignment between the statutory route of challenge to a planning decision and judicial review has continued with amendments sought to be brought into effect under what is, at the time of writing, the Criminal Justice and Courts Bill 2014. That introduces a sift process into challenges under s 288 of the Town and Country Planning Act 1990, which is now amended to include sub-ss (3A) and (3B), which impose the requirement to obtain leave to proceed with a challenge and a time limit of six weeks respectively within which the challenge is to be brought. The Bill is now at the Report stage in the House of Lords and is likely to be enacted early in 2015.

---

[4] At [17].
[5] CPR r 54.5 (A1) states 'the planning acts' has the same meaning as in s 336 of the Town and Country Planning Act 1990.

5.12 Amendments to the Bill have been introduced at various stages. They include changes to provide greater consistency to statutory challenges under s 287 Town and Country Planning Act, s 63 of the Listed Buildings and Conservation Areas Act, s 113 of the Planning and Compulsory Purchase Act and the Planning Act 2008 so that all proceedings will require leave to proceed.

5.13 Other amendments have been made to allow for quashing part only of decisions, to enable the challenge to costs decisions to be brought within the main statutory challenge rather than having to be by way of separate judicial review and amendment to s 113(4) of the 2004 Act to permit the calculation of time within which a challenge should be brought as 'from' the relevant date.

5.14 There is currently provision in the Bill that provides that if the High Court or the Planning Court consider that the outcome for the claimant would not have been substantially different if the conduct complained of had not occurred it must refuse permission to apply for judicial review.

5.15 There is also a proposal to provide the ability to leapfrog appeals from the High Court to the Supreme Court if a point of law of general public importance is involved and that the proceedings relate to a matter of national importance or consideration of such a matter:

- the result of the proceedings is so significant (whether considered on its own or together with other proceedings or likely proceedings) that a hearing by the Supreme Court is justified;
- the judge is satisfied that the benefits of the earlier consideration by the Supreme Court outweigh the benefits of consideration by the Court of Appeal.

5.16 Before going on to look at the various areas of challenge an outline review of the statutory framework is necessary. Both the Town and Country Planning Act 1990 and the Acquisition of Land Act 1981 provide statutory grounds of challenge to decisions or orders. The availability of an alternative remedy would be a powerful reason for not allowing a challenge to the grant of planning permission to proceed. The same preclusive effect would apply to a challenge to a compulsory purchase order.

STATUTORY FRAMEWORK

Planning decisions

5.17 All planning applications are to be determined in accordance with the development plan unless material considerations indicate otherwise: s 38(6) of the Planning and Compulsory Purchase Act 2004. The consequence of that is that there is a plan-led, but not plan-determined, system to development control. The issue of material considerations is dealt with below.

5.18 Section 284 of the Town and Country Planning Act 1990 is a preclusive section. It precludes a challenge to the High Court on revocation or modification[6] of a planning permission, a discontinuance order, a tree preservation order,[7] an order made under

---

[6] Sections 97 and 102.
[7] Section 198.

s 221(5),[8] certain orders under Sch 9[9] and any decision by the Secretary of State on appeal under s 78 or under s 77 other than by s 287 and s 288 of the Act. Section 289 provides the right of statutory challenge to the High Court in respect of a decision on an enforcement notice appeal. Section 285 of the Act precludes an enforcement notice being challenged in any other way.

5.19 There are certain exceptions to the preclusive provisions. Where they apply the usual process of judicial review is applicable. The exceptions include the decision-making process of the local planning authority in determining a planning application when a third party wants to challenge that process or decision, an order confirmed by special parliamentary procedure, interim orders by the Secretary of State during the course of proceedings[10] and costs orders.[11]

5.20 There are other preclusive provisions that also prevent the challenge to the validity of planning permissions or decisions in certain circumstances,[12] decisions on the part of the Secretary of State under s 22 of the Planning (Hazardous Substances) Act 1990, and various orders in relation to the listed buildings and conservation areas under ss 62-65 of the Planning (Listed Buildings and Conservation Areas) Act 1990, and notices under s 215 requiring the proper maintenance of land. The time limits in the various ouster clauses are strictly enforced by the courts.[13]

5.21 An application has to be made within a six-week period under s 287(4). That is calculated from the day following publication of the order in question. That means that the proceedings have to be filed and served within the six-week period. The time period is absolute.

5.22 The Court of Appeal confirmed the principle that time to challenge under s 113 PCPA 2004 begins on the date of adoption of the development plan document.[14] A challenge under s 113 therefore has a 'day less' than under other statutory provisions.

5.23 In *R (Manydown Co Ltd) v Basingstoke and Deane Borough Council*[15] Lindblom J held that a decision not to promote land owned by a council in a plan-making process was beyond the ambit of s 113; however, such a decision was plainly susceptible to proceedings for judicial review. Accordingly as such a challenge would be outside the remit of s 113 the 'day less' time limit would not apply.

5.24 If a challenge under s 113 of the 2004 Act is upheld, sub-s (7) provides:

'(7) The High Court may –

---

[8] Advertisement regulation orders.
[9] Discontinuance of mineral workings under paras 1, 2, 5 or 6 of Sch 9.
[10] Such as a refusal to adjourn an inquiry.
[11] *Balogh v Secretary of State for the Environment* [1996] 1 PLR 32 where the court held that remained the case even where there was another appeal against the merits of the decision proceedings under s 288 although the two proceedings could be heard together.
[12] See s 286, which prohibits a challenge to the decision on the basis that it should have been made by some other local planning authority.
[13] *Khan v Newport Borough Council* [1991] COD 157 – CA refused permission on the basis of a six-week time period within which to challenge a TPO, *R v Dacorum District Council ex p Cannon* [1996] 2 PLR 45 – JR refused of listed building enforcement notices because of the availability of an appeal with full alternative remedy with time limit.
[14] *Barker v Hambleton DC* [2012] EWCA Civ 610 and *Hinde v Rugby BC and SSCLS* [2011] EWHC 3684.
[15] [2012] EWHC 977 (Admin).

(a) quash the relevant document;
(b) remit the relevant document to a person or body with a function relating to its preparation, publication, adoption or approval.'

The issue of whether the remedies of quashing and remittance were alternatives or available simultaneously was considered in *University of Bristol v North Somerset Council*.[16] It was held that the remedies were alternatives for if a policy in a DPD were quashed it could not therefore be remitted as it would simply not exist.[17]

5.25 Following the July 2013 reforms to the CPR the test of promptness would appear to have fallen away in planning judicial reviews.

5.26 To bring the challenge the right is exercisable by 'a person aggrieved'. As with the interest in respect of 'standing' to bring judicial review proceedings the approach of the courts has been increasingly liberal.[18]

5.27 The basis for challenge is set out in statute. That is that

- the document is not within the powers of the Act, or
- a procedural requirement has not been complied with.

5.28 Under s 288(3) there is the same six-week period within which to challenge a relevant order under that section. That is, in the case of a decision letter, from the date on which it is date-stamped by the Secretary of State and signed on his behalf. Again, the time limit is absolute.

5.29 The grounds of challenge are the same as those set out under s 287 above.

5.30 Even if the grounds are made out there remains a residual discretion in a case where the Secretary of State has failed to take into account a material consideration on the part of the court as to whether to quash the decision[19] or the judge concludes that there is a real possibility that the consideration is a matter that would have made a difference to the decision.

5.31 In *Arben Simoni v Secretary of State for Communities and Local Government*[20] there was a s 288 challenge to an inspector's decision to uphold a LPA's refusal of permission for the continued use of premises as a hand carwash. The court held that the inspector's decision was clear, cogent and sufficient. Conclusions about a canopy at the carwash were a classic area of planning judgment where the court should not interfere with an inspector's decision except in the most perverse of conclusions.

5.32 The case is useful for the succinct way in which Dobbs J summarised the principles which govern s 288 applications.

'20. The following principles apply to a s 288 claim:

---

[16] [2013] EWHC 231 (Admin).
[17] HHJ Robinson at para 7.
[18] It will include a subsequent purchaser of a property even though not the original applicant: *Times Investment Ltd v SOSE* [1991] 61 P&CR 98.
[19] *Bolton MBC v Secretary of State for the Environment* [1990] 61 P&CR 343 'if the matter was fundamental to the decision'.
[20] [2012] EWHC 323 (Admin).

(1) Questions of planning judgment and of weight are within the exclusive province of the decision maker and it is not for the court to substitute its own judgment: see *Tesco Stores v Secretary of State for the Environment* [1995] 1 WLR 759 at page 780;
(2) Where it is alleged that the decision maker failed to have regard to a material planning consideration, the omission of the consideration must materially affect the decision taken: see *Bolton MDC v Secretary of State for the Environment* [1990] 60 P&CR 343 at page 352.
(3) There is no obligation on the decision maker to refer to every material consideration but only the main issues in dispute: *Bolton MDC v Secretary of State for the Environment* [1995] 3 PLR 37 at page 43.
(4) An application under s 288 of the 1990 Act is not an opportunity for a review of the planning merits of an inspector's decision. Sullivan J (as he then was) stated in *R (Newsmith Stainless Ltd) v Secretary of State for the Environment, Transport and the Regions* [2001] EWHC Admin 74, paragraph 6 that, whilst an allegation that the inspector's conclusion is perverse is in principle within the scope of a challenge under s 288, the court must be astute to ensure that such challenges are not used as a cloak for what is, in truth, a re-run of the arguments of the planning merits.
(5) It is only necessary for the decision-maker to state his reasons in sufficient detail to enable the reader to know what conclusion he has reached on the principle important controversial version issues: see *South Buckinghamshire CC v Porter (No 2)* [2004] 1 WLR 1953. The decision letter has to be read as a whole in a reasonably flexible manner and not as a contract or as a statute.'

5.33 The discretion to quash is even narrower where there is a breach of European legislation as set out below.

5.34 Under s 289 there is the right to challenge an enforcement notice decision. That proceeds differently to challenges brought under the two previous sections.

5.35 First, the decision challenged is brought on a point of law only: s 289(1). The challenge has to be brought within a period of 28 days, although, unlike the position under s 288, there is power to extend time.[21]

5.36 Secondly, leave has to be sought from the court to bring the proceedings. There are procedural requirements to be followed as to which documents to file when seeking permission. They are the use of Form TCP(L) to make the initial application for permission accompanied by a draft appellant's notice and if permission is granted use of an appellant's notice which is form N161. The procedure is set out in CPR Part 52, PD para 22.6C. The test is whether there is an arguable case to proceed. The court may give directions when it grants leave and impose such terms as to costs as it thinks fit. The relevant appellant's notice must be served and filed within seven days of the grant of permission. There is no further right of appeal to the Court of Appeal.[22]

5.37 Once permission is granted the matter proceeds to a substantive hearing in a way similar to a substantive judicial review hearing. If successful, the matter is remitted to the Secretary of State for redetermination.

---

[21] *R v Wandsworth BC v Secretary of State for Transport, Local Government and the Regions* [2004] 1 P&CR 507 where time was extended by two weeks where the s 288 route rather than the s 289 had mistakenly been used in the first instance and there was no question of delay being used as an attempt to string proceedings out; CPR r 3.1(2).
[22] *Prashar v Secretary of Sate for Communities Transport and the Regions* [2001] 3 PLR 116, CPR Practice Direction relating to Part 52, para 4.8.

5.38 All of this is relevant as judicial review is a remedy of the last resort. If there is a suitable alternative remedy that can give appropriate relief that should be used before taking any judicial review proceedings. If the issue of alternative remedy is to be raised in judicial review proceedings by a defendant then it should be in the summary grounds of resistance so that it can be addressed at the permission stage.[23]

Compulsory purchase decisions

5.39 A compulsory purchase order can be made under a variety of authorising statutory provisions such as the Highways Act 1980, the Housing Act 1996 and the Town and Country Planning Act 1990 to name but a few. In terms of challenging a compulsory purchase order provision is made by the Acquisition of Land Act 1981, s 23 for 'any person aggrieved'[24] by a compulsory purchase order or a certificate under Part III or Sch 3 to make an application to the High Court on the basis that any relevant requirement has not been complied with.

5.40 An application to the High Court has to be made within six weeks from the date on which the order becomes operative.[25] The calculation of the period of time is carried out[26] as for proceedings to be brought under the TCPA. The time period is similarly absolute both in terms of its commencement[27] and end.

5.41 The court may grant an interim order suspending the CPO[28] or at the final hearing quash the compulsory purchase order or any provision within it or the certificate either generally or as it affects the property of the applicant.[29]

5.42 Apart from the statutory remedies under s 24, s 25 of the Acquisition of Land Act 1981 restricts the questioning of the compulsory purchase order in any legal proceedings whatsoever.

5.43 What the Acquisition of Land Act, however, does not do is to preclude judicial review proceedings being brought in relation to the issue of the general vesting

---

[23] *R v Falmouth and Truro Health Authority ex p South West Water Ltd* [2001] QB 445: 'the critical decision in an alternative remedy case certainly one that requires a stay, is the one taken at the grant of permission stage.'
[24] *Lomax and Others v Secretary of State for Transport, Local Government and the Regions and Rochdale Metropolitan Borough Council* [2002] 21 EG 143 where Richards J was satisfied that an objector who had withdrawn his objection to the CPO inquiry was still a person aggrieved and able to challenge confirmation of the decision under s 23.
[25] That is if the Statutory Order (Special Procedure) Act 1945 applies, or if it does not, six weeks from when the notice of confirmation of the order or making of the order is first published in accordance with the Acquisition of Land Act 1981, or if it is a certificate the date on which notice of the giving of the certificate is first published: see s 23(4).
[26] *Okolo v Secretary of State for the Environment* [1997] 4 All ER 242.
[27] *Enterprise Inns plc v Secretary of State for the Environment, Transport and the Regions and Liverpool CC* [2001] 81 P&CR 236: 'Parliament has deliberately prescribed a window rather than simply an end date in s 23 (4)(b) and in those circumstances it is not sufficient to show that the application was made before an end date. It must come within the window.'
[28] Section 24(1) ALA 1981.
[29] Section 24(2) ALA 1981.

declaration and, presumably, other subsequent steps to the confirmation of the compulsory purchase order which can then be challenged on conventional public law principles.[30]

JUDICIAL REVIEW PROCEEDINGS

The influence of EC law

5.44 Through the European Communities Act 1972 all the rights and obligations that EU law creates are incorporated into domestic law. Anything in domestic law inconsistent with EU rights or obligations is abrogated or must be modified to avoid inconsistency. Basic EU rights, obligations and principles including principles of direct effect, effective protection of rights and compatible interpretation are incorporated into domestic law and are capable of informing all grounds of judicial review.

5.45 Another strand that is important is the ability of the European Parliament to make regulations and issue directives, take decisions, make recommendations or deliver opinions.[31] Directives are binding on member states as to the result to be achieved and require national measures to be adopted to give effect to them. How the result is to be achieved through a choice of form and methods is left to the member state. All regulations are directly applicable so that they become part of the national law without any need for member states to transpose them into national law.

5.46 Decisions of the ECJ are thus binding on the High Court in the same way as decisions of the higher courts of the UK. The application of compatible interpretation was illustrated in *Wells v Secretary of State for Transport, Local Government and the Regions*,[32] where an old planning permission that was being reviewed under the Planning and Compensation Act 1991 was held to be subject to the requirements of environmental impact assessment as a result of art 4 of the Directive read in conjunction with Annexes I and II. That meant that all such projects must be made subject to an assessment with regard to their effects before (multi-stage) development consent is given. That decision was taken further in the case of *R (Barker) v Bromley London Borough Council*[33] when the House of Lords held that the Town and Country Planning (Environmental Impact Assessment) Regulations 1988 failed to adequately implement Directive 85/337/EEC. That was because the then Regulations made no provision for environmental assessment in accordance with a development consent when it was discovered as part of a multi-stage consent that environmental assessment was required as there were likely to be significant environmental effects there was no provision at any other than the outline planning permission stage to require one. As a result amendments to the Town and Country Planning (Environmental Impact Assessment) Regulations 1999 were introduced. In turn they have now been replaced by the Town and Country Planning (Environmental Impact Assessment) Regulations 2011. They apply the EU Directive 'on the assessment of the effects of certain public and private projects on the environment' to the planning system in England.

---

[30] *R (Iceland Foods Ltd) v Newport City Council* [2010] EWHC 2502 (Admin) where the High Court dismissed a claim for judicial review but held that a general vesting order when executed could be the subject of a challenge by way of judicial review.
[31] Article 249, EC.
[32] (Case C-201/02) [2004] ECR 1-273.
[33] [2006] UKHL 52.

5.47 If there has been a material misdirection as to EU Law then the decision will be quashed: *R v Secretary of State for the Environment ex p Royal Society for the Protection of Birds*[34] when it was held that the Secretary of State was not allowed to take into account economic considerations when classifying a special protection area or designating its boundaries applying Directive 79/409/EEC but economic considerations may constitute imperative reasons of overriding public interest of the kind referred to in art 6(4) of Directive 92/43/EEC.

5.48 However, economic considerations can be relevant in specific circumstances: *Health and Safety Executive v Wolverhampton City Council*.[35] Under s 97 TCPA 1990, in deciding whether it is expedient to revoke or modify planning permissions, the LPA must have regard to 'any other material considerations'. Does that include the threat of consequent compensation under s 107 TCPA?

5.49 Victoria Hall Ltd applied to the council to erect four blocks (blocks A–D) of student accommodation at a site in Wolverhampton – 95 metres away from a liquid petroleum gas storage facility. The HSE was consulted by the council, and advised refusal on health and safety grounds. Without going back to the HSE, or seeking its own advice on health and safety, the council granted permission without informing the HSE it had so done. By the time the HSE became aware of the development, work on three of the blocks – A, B and C – was well advanced. Work on block D, which was the closest block to the LPG facility, had not commenced.

5.50 The HSE complained that the council's procedural failures had deprived it of the opportunity to ask the Secretary of State to call in the application for planning permission. They asked the council to remedy this by making a revocation order under s 97, at least to prevent the construction of block D. The LPA was reluctant to make that order, inter alia, because of the likely compensation costs.

5.51 The Court of Appeal unanimously ordered the council to reconsider the question of revocation. However, the court was divided on whether compensation would be a material issue in that reconsideration. Pill LJ, dissenting, relied on Richards J in the *Alnwick District Council* case,[36] which decided that 'in so far as financial consequences do not relate to the use and development of land, they are not capable of amounting to material considerations'.

5.52 Lord Carnwath formulated what he called the 'simple' view:

> 'In simple terms, the question is whether a public authority, when deciding whether to exercise a discretionary power to achieve a public objective, is entitled to take into account the cost to the public of so doing. Posed in that way, the question answers itself. As custodian of public funds, the authority not only may, but generally must, have regard to the cost to the public of its actions, at least to the extent of considering in any case whether the cost is proportionate to the aim to be achieved, and taking account of any more economic ways of achieving the same objective. Of course, the weight attributable to cost considerations will vary with the context. Where, for example, the authority is faced with an imminent threat to public security within its sphere of responsibility, cost could rarely be a valid reason for doing nothing, but could well be relevant to the choice between effective alternatives. So much is not only sound administrative *practice, but common sense*.'

---

[34] [1997] QB 206.
[35] *Health and Safety Executive v Wolverhampton City Council* [2012] UKSC 34.
[36] 79 P&CR 130.

5.53 Section 97 did not require a different approach. Its mention of 'expediency' and other 'material considerations' is broad enough to encompass the cost consequences of revocation: 'The word "expedient" implies no more than that the action should be appropriate in all the circumstances. Where one of those circumstances is a potential liability for compensation, it is hard to see why it should be excluded.'[37]

5.54 This case clarifies the previously contradictory cases from lower courts on the question of whether compensation under s 107 is capable of being a material consideration.

5.55 Further, the need to interpret as far as possible national legislation in the light of the wording and purpose of directives has been a common theme. In *Marleasing SA v La Comercial Internacional de Alimentación SA*[38] the European Court of Justice defined this obligation as follows:

> 'It follows that, in applying national law, whether the provisions in questions were adopted before or after the directive, the national court called upon to interpret it is required to do so, as far as possible, in light of the wording and the purpose of the directive in order to achieve the result pursued by the latter and thereby comply with the third paragraph of Article 189 of the Treaty.'

5.56 Domestic legislation should be interpreted having regard to the wording and purpose of the Directive so as to achieve the result pursued by the Directive. As a result the *Marleasing* approach has been followed by the courts on many occasions.[39] The courts do recognise that the obligation to interpret legislation is not without boundaries. The case of *Commissioner for HM Revenue and Customs v IDT Card Services Ireland* made it clear that the obligation imposed by the ECJ is only to interpret national law in conformity with a Directive so far as possible. The phrase 'so far as possible' provides certain parameters and the court must 'go with the grain of the legislation'.[40]

5.57 The case of *R v Durham County Council ex p Huddleston*[41] illustrates a further example of where a direct effect solution was adopted as primary legislation was incompatible with EC Directive and convergent construction not possible.

5.58 If there is breach of European Law then the discretion on the part of the court to quash the decision was extremely limited. The case of *Berkeley v Secretary of State for the Environment*[42] made it clear that art 10 of the EC Treaty obliged the national court to ensure that Community rights are fully and effectively enforced. It was only if there was substantial compliance with the Directive and domestic regulations that the impugned decision could be saved. As there had not been substantial compliance in *Berkeley* the decision could not be saved. There has been an increasing shift from that position as evidenced below.

5.59 This case of *Walton v Scottish Ministers*[43] concerned a belated challenge to the Aberdeen bypass. The project had already been subject to EIA. The attempt to bring the

---

[37] *Health and Safety Executive v Wolverhampton City Council* [2012] UKSC 34, per Lord Carwath at para 26.
[38] (Case C-106/89) [1990] ECR I–4135, 1439.
[39] *Horner v Lancashire County Council* [2007] EWCA Civ 784.
[40] *Ghaidan v Godin-Mendoza* [2004] UKHL 30.
[41] [2000] 1 WLR 1484.
[42] [2000] UKHL 36.
[43] [2012] UKSC 44.

project within the SEA Directive on the basis that a decision to enlarge the project was a modification of the regional transport strategy was rejected. The court pointed out that the SEA and EIA Directives require environmental assessments in different but complementary circumstances. SEA is concerned with plans and programmes which set the framework for future development consent of projects whereas EIA is concerned with the environmental impact of specific projects.

5.60 Lord Carnwath addressed the issue of remedies and discretion. He sought to distinguish *Berkeley v Secretary of State for the Environment, Transport and the Regions*.[44] He said that the factual circumstances in *Walton* were dramatically different from those in *Berkeley*, the potential prejudice to public and private interests flowing from a quashing order would be very great and it would be extraordinary if the court were prevented from weighing that prejudice in the balance. He saw 'nothing in principle or authority to require the courts to adopt a different approach merely because the procedural requirement arises from a European rather than a domestic source.'

5.61 The decision in *Walton* reflects a more general reluctance on the courts' part to allow the EIA process to become 'an obstacle course'.[45]

5.62 In addition, the Human Rights Act 1998[46] enacted into domestic law protection for the European Convention of Human Rights (ECHR). Compulsory purchase cases subsequent to that enactment, in particular, show considerable reliance upon Convention Rights as part of any challenge to a decision.[47] Often the issue of proportionality is raised against a compulsory purchase order. The court's approach must go beyond that traditionally adopted to judicial review in a domestic setting. There is no shift to a merits review but the intensity of review is greater than was previously appropriate. The domestic court now has to make a value judgement: an evaluation by reference to the circumstances prevailing at the relevant time. Proportionality must be judged objectively by reference to those circumstances.[48]

Sufficient interest/person aggrieved

5.63 A claimant for judicial review must have a 'sufficient interest' in the subject matter to which the application relates.[49] The approach to standing has though become increasingly liberal over the years such that provided a genuine interest in the litigation can be shown the requirement is likely to be satisfied.

5.64 Under s 31 of the Supreme Court Act 1981 standing is seen as a precondition to the grant of permission: 'a discrete issue which could be decided irrespective of the merits of the claim.'[50] It has been used in the past as a threshold test to filter out

---

[44] [2001] 2 AC 603.
[45] *R (Jones) v Mansfield District Council* [2003] EWCA Civ 1408 at para 58; *Younger Homes (Northern) Ltd v FSS and Calderdale MBC* [2004] EWCA Civ 1060 at paras 46–47.
[46] The long title of which reads – An Act to give further effect to rights and freedoms guaranteed under the European Convention of Human Rights.
[47] *R (Pascoe) v First Secretary of State* [2006] EWHC 2356 – challenges brought under arts 1 and 8 – no requirement under CPO to use the least intrusive means: *Smith & others v SSTI and London Development Agency* [2007] EWHC 1013 Admin – a decision to conform a CPO may be proportionate even though not the lease intrusive interference with art 8 rights.
[48] *R (SD) v Governors of Denbigh High School* [2006] UKHL 15 at para 30.
[49] Section 31(3) of the Supreme Court Act 1981.
[50] *R (Edwards) v Environment Agency* [2004] EWHC 736 Admin.

busybodies so as to prevent abuse of the process,[51] but it may be affected by all of the circumstances in the claim so as to influence whether the claimant is entitled to the remedy claimed.[52]

5.65 In *R (Kides) v South Cambridgeshire DC*[53] the Court of Appeal could not see 'how it can be just to debar a litigant who has a real and genuine interest in obtaining the relief which he seeks' even if the claimant was put up[54] to front the claim to secure public funding.

5.66 While a financial or legal interest is not required[55] to establish standing commercial challenges in planning cases have often been the motivating force behind a challenge: *R v Canterbury City Council ex p Springimage Ltd*.[56] It is clear on the authorities that if the commercial interest of a person may realistically be affected by a decision in a way not common to the general run of the public, then that provides not only a particular interest on the part of the person concerned, but also a sufficient one for the purposes of judicial review'. The government reforms have as one of their objectives to reduce the challenges from a commercial competitor.

The need to be prompt and avoid undue delay

5.67 The issue of delay has a particular resonance in the planning context where the pressure is to complete the financing and delivery of the project in question. The approach of the courts has varied. While things seemed to be constant after *R (Burkett) v London Borough of Hammersmith and Fulham*[57] there were signs of the judicial pendulum swinging back towards a shorter time period than three months by emphasising the importance of promptness in challenging planning decisions before the government introduced changes in July 2013.

5.68 As set out the time limit for planning related judicial reviews is now set at six weeks.[58] This new time limit of six weeks does not include a requirement for promptness. It is, like the three-month time limit, an absolute deadline.

Grounds of review

5.69 The basic grounds of challenge for a judicial review are illegality (error of law), irrationality (unreasonableness) and procedural unfairness. There is often an overlap between the grounds which are not mutually exclusive.

5.70 As set out above the role of material considerations can be critical in taking a planning decision. What is or is not a material consideration is a matter of law and ultimately for the court.[59] There is no statutory definition of what a material consideration is. To be material the consideration has to relate to planning. Otherwise,

---

51   *R v Somerset County Council v Dixon* [1998] Env LR 111 – a busybody being someone with no legitimate concern at all per Sedley J.
52   *R v Somerset CC ex p Dixon* (supra).
53   [2002] EWCA Civ 1370, Parker LJ at para 133.
54   See para 21.
55   *R v Secretary of State for the Environment v Rose Theatre Trust Co* [1990] 1 QB 504 at 520D.
56   [1993] 3 PLR 58.
57   [2002] UKHL 23.
58   CPR r 54.5(5).
59   *Bolton MBC v Secretary of State for the Environment* [1991] JPL 241.

the parameters of materiality have been defined by the courts[60] and a broad approach has been approved.[61] Once it is established as a material consideration the weight to be attached to it is entirely a matter for the decision-maker. If the decision-maker takes into account something that is not a material consideration the decision-maker is vulnerable to having his decision quashed. Likewise, if the decision-maker fails to take into account a material consideration he is similarly vulnerable to a challenge to the decision. Such a stance on the part of a decision-maker would be both illegal and irrational thus illustrating the overlapping nature of the grounds of challenge.

5.71 In *R (Vieira and Saph) v London Borough of Camden & Bozi*[62] Messrs Vieira and Saph lived next to Ms Vanessa Boz on the Regent's Park Road in London. Ms Boz erected a conservatory and trellis screen, and put in an application for retrospective planning permission. Camden – the relevant LPA – consulted the claimants, who objected on the grounds of overlooking and loss of privacy. Following negotiation, Ms Boz amended the application and submitted revised drawings of the trellis. The claimants were not reconsulted on the new drawings. Planning permission was granted.

5.72 Camden's statement of community involvement provided that, inter alia, everyone who has commented on a planning application should be notified of 'any significant revisions made to the application'.

5.73 The claimants claimed that this provision had created a procedural legitimate expectation that they would be reconsulted on the new drawings, and that the expectation had not been met.

5.74 Lang J held that there had been a breach of a legitimate expectation on the basis that it was unfair to deny the claimant the opportunity to know the precise details of the application and to be able to comment upon it. It was prejudicial also to the claimant to be denied the potential benefit of participating in a reconsideration of how the application should be determined. The local authority sought to argue that no relief should be granted because it was inevitable that planning permission would be granted. The court rejected this argument, quashing the planning permission. The grant of permission was not inevitable because there remained a question of whether the amendments to the scheme made it acceptable.

5.75 In *R (Godfrey) v Southwark LBC*,[63] another case about legitimate expectations, the Court of Appeal considered an appeal against a decision of Lindblom J refusing permission to bring judicial review proceedings in relation to a community centre on a site known as Downtown on the Rotherhithe Peninsular in East London.

5.76 The site had been a district centre providing community facilities, including a freestanding community hall of around 400m². In 2002, the council prepared a planning brief relating to the site, which made it clear that any developer would be expected to improve the site's community facilities or create new infrastructure, which may include building a new community hall on the site. In 2007 the council adopted a development

---

[60] *Stringer v Minister of Housing and Local Government* [1971] 1 All ER 65, *Great Portland Estates plc v Westminster City Council* [1985] AC 661.
[61] *R (Rank) v East Cambridgeshire District Council* [2003] JPL 454 – a consideration is material for the purposes of s 70(2) if it was not irrelevant to the determination and if it might make a difference to the way in which the authority dealt with the application at para 15 of the judgment.
[62] [2012] EWHC 287.
[63] [2012] EWCA Civ 500.

plan which identified the uses for the site as a community centre and health centre. Planning permission was granted by the council in 2010 for redevelopment of the site, which included a community centre of around 124m² contained within the health centre.

5.77 Local residents challenged the grant of permission on a number of grounds. The Court of Appeal's judgment concentrates on the fourth ground, namely that there was a substantive legitimate expectation that better and larger facilities would be provided. The appellant argued that previous consultation between the council and local community, combined with the terms of the planning brief, had given rise to a substantive legitimate expectation that any grant of planning permission would include a freestanding community hall at least as large as the existing hall on site.

5.78 The Court of Appeal held that a rigorous standard is to be applied when a substantive legitimate expectation is claimed on the basis of a representation or promise by a public authority. The duty of public authorities to exercise powers in the public interest must be kept in mind. Only when the failure to give effect to the promise would be so unfair as to amount to an abuse of power, should it override other considerations. Further, an earlier approach of the local planning authority to an issue, even if amounting to a planning policy, cannot have primacy over the statutory duty of the council (eg under s 70(2) TCPA 1990 and s 38(6) PCPA 2004) to assess the current situation. The UDP policy did not require a particular size of provision for community facilities and the council was required to assess current needs against that policy.

5.79 The bar to acquiring a substantive legitimate expectation is very high, and the claimants were a long way from meeting it on these facts. The heart of their case was based on documents and informal representations made by the LPA from up to 10 years previous. Those were not material considerations for the LPA in conducting its *present* statutory task.

Ministerial statements and policy

5.80 The Cala Homes saga brought into stark relief the materiality of any 'government statement' in planning. There were two cases on the issue of the policy of the government to revoke regional spatial strategies ('RSS'). The first, *R (Cala Homes (South) Ltd) v Secretary of State for Communities and Local Government*[64] quashed the decision of the Secretary of State to 'revoke' the RSS; and the second, *R (Cala Homes (South) Ltd) v Secretary of State for Communities and Local Government*,[65] upheld the guidance of the Secretary of State that the proposed abolition of RSS through the then Localism Bill was a material consideration in planning decisions.

5.81 The issue of RSS revocation was first raised as the formal policy of the Conservative Party in August 2009. In early 2010, prior to the general election, the Conservatives published Open Source Planning, which indicated that Labour policy was anti-democratic and had not delivered. The Infrastructure Planning Commission was criticised for taking decisions about major infrastructure out of the hands of elected politicians. The document does not mention the word 'localism'. The aim of the Conservative's reforms was said to be:

---

[64] [2010] EWHC 2866 (Admin).
[65] [2011] EWCA Civ 639.

> 'The creation of an Open Source planning system means that local people in each neighbourhood ... will be able to specify what kind of development and use of land they want to see in their area. This will lead to a fundamental and long overdue rebalancing of power, away from the centre and back into the hands of local people. Whole layers of bureaucracy, delay and centralised micro-management will disappear as planning shifts away from being an issue principally for insiders' to one where communities take the lead in shaping their own surroundings.'

5.82 The Open Source Planning 'Green Paper' was endorsed in the Coalition's policy statement: 'Our Programme for Government'. Among the goals listed was the abolition of regional planning.

5.83 The Secretary of State issued a statement on 6 July 2010 that purported to exercise power to 'revoke' RSS having previously issued a statement on 27 May 2010, which said that the intention of Government to revoke RSS was to be treated as a material consideration in planning decisions. Presumably at the time there was thought in DCLG that a distinction could be drawn between a power to 'revoke' and actual 'abolition', because the July statement stated:

> 'The abolition of Regional Strategies will require legislation in the "Localism Bill" which we are introducing this session. However, given the clear coalition commitment, it is important to avoid a period of uncertainty over planning policy, until the legislation is enacted. So I am revoking Regional Strategies today in order to give clarity to builders, developers and planners.'

5.84 Sales J's judgment in the Administrative Court gives two reasons why he considered that the Secretary of State's decision to 'revoke RSS' was unlawful. The first reason of Sales J was that the power in the Local Democracy, Economic Development and Construction Act 2009, s 79(6) to amend RS 10 did not extend to withdrawing the entire RS in every region, when the Act itself stated expressly that there shall be an RS for each region. Such an approach would subvert the clear intention of Parliament, and was, therefore, beyond the more limited powers devolved to the Secretary of State.

5.85 The second reason was that if there was a requirement as a matter of European Law to produce a strategic environmental appraisal ('SEA') for the preparation of plans, including strategic plans, then it was illogical that there should not also be such an appraisal for the withdrawal of an entire tier of the development plan system.

5.86 The effect of the court's decision was that RSS was resurrected as part of the development plan. Or rather, because the original decision to revoke RSS was never lawful, then RSS never in fact ceased to be part of the development plan. As a matter of law[66] a decision had to have regard to the content of RSS in determining planning applications, so mindful no doubt of the clear statements of intention of Government, in response to the court's decision, on 10 November DCLG issued the following statement:

> 'Whilst respecting the court's decision this ruling changes very little. ... On 27 May 2010, the Government wrote to local planning authorities and to the Planning Inspectorate informing them of the Coalition Government's intention to rapidly abolish regional strategies and setting out its expectation that the letter should be taken into account as a material planning consideration in any decisions they were currently taking. That advice still stands.'

---

[66] Planning and Compulsory Purchase Act 2004, s 38(6).

5.87 A challenge was then launched against the issue of that letter as policy. The challenge was in effect based upon the contention that in issuing such policy the Executive was seeking to subvert the intention of Parliament, which had not yet been expressed on the proposed revocation of RSS, as well as to deliberately seek to 'go behind' the decision of Sales J in *Cala No 1*.

5.88 Proceedings in *Cala No 2* were issued in early December 2010 and an interim injunction sought and obtained preventing the reliance upon the November statement. The injunction was subsequently discharged on 16 December 2010.

5.89 In dismissing the application for judicial review shortly afterwards Lindblom J held on 7 February 2011 that the 10 November 2010 letter was not unlawful. He considered that it was axiomatic that a decision-maker could take account of Government policy, both in its final form as well as in draft, and that a direct analogy could be made between that approach and taking account of the draft legislative programme of Government. Indeed in many instances it might be entirely prudent to do so.

5.90 In the Court of Appeal Sullivan LJ, giving the lead judgment, endorsed the approach of Lindblom J that it was both lawful, and in some instances prudent, for a decision-maker to take account of the intention of Government in the Localism Bill. Much was made of the fact that the advice of Government was not that the intention to revoke had to be taken into account but rather that it 'may' be in circumstances to be decided by the decision-maker.

5.91 This decision in *Tewkesbury Borough Council v Secretary of State for Communities and Local Government*[67] rejects the misconception and even bolder belief that the Localism Act has brought about such a fundamental change in the planning system and that, the role of the Secretary of State has been eliminated in determining planning applications. The case concerned proposals for 1,000 dwellings at Bishops Cleeve. The Secretary of State had allowed two non-determination appeals upon the basis of an inadequate five-year housing land supply, and, that the potential harm to the landscape was capable of being outweighed by other material considerations. Males J pointed out that while the Act made provision for the abolition of regional strategies there was nothing in it to suggest that relevant national policies would no longer apply, or, that the Secretary of State would no longer perform his function in determining planning application appeals applying the same principles and policies as before. The National Planning Policy Framework (NPPF), expressly reaffirmed such policies as the five-year housing land supply. There was no question of empowering local authorities to develop plans without regard to those national policies. The Secretary of State had stated in the decision letter that although the Act had brought about changes that would give local communities more say over developments in their areas than was previously the case this greater say would depend on the expeditious preparation of local plans, which made provision, including, in particular, a five-year housing land supply, for the future needs of that area. Accordingly, he had acted in accordance with and not in contradiction to that approach. The judge pointed to the prematurity principle[68] as being available to regulate the position, which had been correctly taken into account by the inspector and the Secretary of State.

---

[67] [2013] EWHC 286 (Admin).
[68] See also recent applications in *Larkfleet Ltd v SSCLG & South Kesteven DC* [2012] EWHC 3592 (Admin), and *R (Save Our Parkland Appeal) v East Devon DC & Axminster Carpets* [2013] EWHC 22 (Admin) that prematurity argument is not applicable where plan is not yet formally submitted for examination.

Error of law

5.92 Given that most planning decisions involve matters of planning judgement that are exclusively for the decision-maker[69] errors of law might appear to be a less frequent ground of challenge. There have been three areas, in particular, however, where recent challenges have increased under this ground.

Duty to give reasons for the grant of planning permission

5.93 The Town and Country Planning (General Development Procedure) Order 1995 was repealed by the Town and Country Planning (Development Management Procedure) (England) Order 2010. Article 22 of the 1995 Order required local planning authorities to give a summary of their reasons and a summary of the relevant development policies in their decision notices where they have approved planning permission or reserved matters. The requirement to give reasons for the grant of planning permission has now been withdrawn. There remains a requirement to give reasons for the imposition of any condition on a grant of planning permission and a requirement to give full reasons for a refusal of planning permission.

5.94 The removal of the requirement to give reasons for the approval of planning permission means that a previously burgeoning area for legal challenge has fallen away.

The interpretation of planning policy

5.95 What a planning policy means is an old chestnut in challenges to planning decisions. In *R v Derbyshire County Council ex p Woods*[70] the Court of Appeal held that it was for the court to determine as a matter of law what the words are capable of meaning:

- if in all the circumstances the words are capable of bearing more than one meaning and the LPA adopts and applies a meaning that it is capable as a matter of law as bearing then they will not have gone wrong;
- if a decision-maker attaches a meaning to the words that they are not properly capable of meaning he will have made an error of law.

5.96 Such an approach was consistent with *Northavon District Council v Secretary of State for the Environment*[71] where it was observed that 'the words spoke for themselves and were not readily susceptible to precise legal definition. Whether a proposed development was within the description was in most cases likely to be a matter of fact and degree and planning judgment.' The same approach was also taken in *Virgin Cinema Properties Ltd v Secretary of State for the Environment*.[72]

5.97 Later cases had sought to provide limits to the approach. 'The courts must be wary of an approach whereby decision-makers can live in the planning world of Humpty Dumpty, making a particular planning policy mean whatever the

---

[69] *Tesco Stores Ltd v Secretary of State for the Environment* [1995] 1 WLR 759.
[70] 1997 JPL 958.
[71] 1993 JPL 761.
[72] 1998 2 PLR 24.

decision-maker decides that it should mean.'[73] Humpty Dumpty was invoked by Lord Reed in the Supreme Court in *Tesco Stores v Dundee City Council*.[74]

5.98 Tesco challenged the decision of the local planning authority to grant planning permission to a competitor for the development of an out-of-centre superstore which was only 800 metres from the local Tesco. Tesco argued that the grant of planning permission was based on a misunderstanding of one of the policies in the development plan.[75] The main issue in the case was whether it was up to the court to interpret the meaning of policies in the development plan or whether a local authority may adopt its own interpretation which will be immune from challenge except on *Wednesbury* principles.

5.99 The Supreme Court held that, in principle, policy statements should be interpreted objectively in accordance with the language used read in its proper context. The meaning of a policy is a matter for the court to interpret. The application of a particular policy to a particular set of facts falls within the judgment of the local planning authority and can only be challenged on the basis of irrationality. Such an error in interpretation would only be material if there was a real possibility that determination of the application might otherwise have been different.

5.100 Before this case, it was considered settled law that the interpretation of planning policy was primarily a matter for the decision-maker.[76] Following the *Tesco* case, there is now scope for challenges to planning decisions on the grounds that the decision-maker has erred by misinterpreting a relevant policy.[77]

5.101 Following the decision in the *Tesco* case challenges are being brought against the interpretation of local plan policies and national policy. In *Hunston Properties Ltd and another v St Albans City and District Council*[78] the Court of Appeal was required to determine the correct interpretation of para 47 of the NPPF. It is of note that upon granting permission to appeal against the High Court decision Sullivan LJ was not persuaded there was a real prospect of success but there was a compelling reason for the appeal to be heard so that there could be a 'definitive answer to the proper interpretation of paragraph 47'. This illustrates the change post-*Tesco* whereby the interpretation of national planning policy has changed from being a matter predominantly for decision-makers to becoming a matter worthy of consideration by the upper courts.

---

[73] *Cranage Parish Council v First Secretary of State* [2004] EWHC 2949 Admin at para 50.
[74] [2012] UKSC 13.
[75] The particular issue of interpretation before the court was: did 'suitable' mean 'suitable for the development proposed by the Applicant' (as the Council contended), or 'suitable for meeting identified deficiencies in retail provision in the area' (as Tesco contended)?
[76] See *R v Derbyshire DC ex parte Woods* [1997] JPL 958.
[77] For examples of cases where the courts have taken up the power to interpret see: *UK Coal Mining Ltd v Secretary of State for Communities and Local Government* [2013] EWHC 2142 (Admin); *R (Zurich Assurance Ltd t/a Threadneedle Property Investments) v North Lincolnshire Council* [2012] EWHC 3708 (Admin); *R (SAVE Britain's Heritage and the Victorian Society) v Sheffield City Council and the University of Sheffield* [2013] EWCA Civ 1108; *R (Cherkley Campaign Ltd) v Mole Valley District Council* [2013] EWHC 2582 (Admin) (under appeal); *Islington LBC v Secretary of State for Communities and Local Government* [2013] EWHC 2320 (Admin); *R (TW Logistics) v Tendring District Council and Anglia Maltings (Holdings) Ltd* [2013] EWCA Civ 9.
[78] [2013] EWCA Civ 1610.

EC-based challenges

5.102 These can be brought on a variety of grounds. The following provide a range of illustrations of the applicable principles.

5.103 *R (Alconbury Developments Ltd) v Secretary of State for the Environment, Transport and the Regions*[79] raised the fundamental issue about whether the decision-making processes on the part of the Secretary of State for the Environment, Transport and the Regions in a planning context, where the Secretary of State is the decision-maker, were compatible with art 6 of the ECHR. The basis was that the Secretary of State was not an independent and impartial tribunal as he would take account of his own policies that he had formulated. The Divisional Court held that the Secretary of State was not independent and impartial and granted declarations of incompatibility in relation to the call-in and appeal sections of the Town and Country Planning Act.[80] The House of Lords unanimously rejected that position and held that the part of the planning system under challenge was compatible.

5.104 In *R (Baker) v North East Somerset District Council*[81] a challenge was brought to planning permissions that had been granted for modifications/extensions to existing green waste composting facilities. No environmental impact assessment (EIA) was sought as the proposed modifications were under the threshold set out in the Town and Country Planning (Environmental Impact Assessment) Regulations 1999, which triggered the requirement for such a statement. A challenge was brought which considered whether Directive 85/337/EC (as amended) was properly transposed. Having regard to EC jurisprudence and the Directive the court found that it was wrong to have regard only to the modification itself. There should be regard to the cumulative effect on the whole development as a result of the modifications to it. A case-by-case appraisal of the modifications, which was provided for in the Regulations, was no answer as that excluded the public and part of the purpose of the Directive was to secure public involvement in EIA development. As a result the permissions were quashed.

5.105 Whilst not an EC-based challenge the decision in the case of *R (Mellor) v SSCLG*[82] provides that a competent authority does not have to make available to the public reasons for a negative screening opinion. However, if a member of the public asks for such a document the competent authority is under an obligation to supply it. The reasons stated can be short but one can see future litigation about the extent of the duty.[83] It is another illustration of the role of EC jurisprudence.

5.106 Allegations of unlawfulness through breach of an EC Directive were made as part of the case in *Ardagh Glass v Chester City Council*.[84] The latest hearing was another chapter in a long-running saga about Europe's largest glass-making factory built entirely without planning permission. Judicial review was sought of (1) the council's failure to take enforcement action within the four-year period after which the development would become immune from enforcement and the expiry of which was looming, and (2) that

---

[79] [2001] UKHL 23.
[80] Sections 77 and 78 together with various sections under the Transport and Works Act 1992.
[81] [2009] EWHC 595 Admin: the determination of the ECJ became academic due to supervening events. Costs proceeded to be determined by the CA in *R (Mellor) v SoS CLG* [2009] EWCA Civ 1201.
[82] C75-08.
[83] The decision of the ECJ was confirmed as stating the law by the Supreme Court in *R (Mellor) v Secretary of State for Communities & Local Government* [2009] EWCA Civ 1201.
[84] [2009] EWHC 745 Admin, High Court decision upheld by CA in *Ardagh Glass v Chester City Council* [2010] EWCA Civ 172.

the EIA Directive prohibited the grant of retrospective development consent. The court ordered service of enforcement notices and held that art 2(1) of Directive 85/337 did not appear to rule out the possibility of retrospective development consent provided that it was preceded by a full and proper EIA with a full and genuine opportunity for the public to understand the proposals, express their views and for those views to be taken into account. Such an approach complied with the objectives of the Directive.

5.107 Breaches of an EC Directive and Regulations were also used as a basis for a challenge under s 113 of the Planning and Compulsory Purchase Act 2004 in respect of planning policies contained in the East of England plan relating to housing development around certain towns in the London Arch.[85] It was held that contrary to Directive 2001/42 and the Environmental Assessment of Plans and Programmes Regulations 2004, no proper environmental assessments had been performed before the policies were adopted. Article 5 of the Directive and reg 12 required that reasonable alternatives to the proposals should be described and evaluated before a choice was made as to how a plan should be modified. The information that accompanied the policies meant that, in exceptional circumstances, such as sustainable development including housing, encroachment into the Green Belt would be probably necessary. Within Hatfield, Welwyn Garden City and Hemel Hempstead no reasonable alternatives that might affect development in the Green Belt had been identified and examined. Part of the South East England Plan was quashed.

Irrationality

5.108 Irrationality is a ground often relied upon but for reasons set out with great clarity in *R (Newsmith) v Secretary of State for the Environment, Transport and the Regions*[86] one that is difficult to succeed upon in planning challenges (where the claimant was described as facing a 'particularly daunting task'[87] given that the decision was one of planning judgement reached on the evidence and after a site inspection). Although the decision itself related to a challenge under s 288 the observations apply equally to a planning decision taken by a committee. The traditional test set out in *R v Monopolies and Mergers Commission ex p South Yorkshire Transport Ltd*[88] as to whether 'the decision is so aberrant that it cannot be classed as rational' still applies.[89]

5.109 The role of the court is supervisory only. It has repeatedly made it clear that it is no part of its role to substitute its own decision on the merits given that there will always be a broad range of planning judgements that the decision-maker could arrive at: *R v Leominster District Council ex p Pothecary*.[90]

5.110 Inconsistency in decision-making can be a basis for a challenge to a planning decision. Both the planning history of the site and a decision of a planning inspector on appeal on the same site can be material.[91] Where a planning authority departs from its previous decision on the same site it may need to be prepared to give an explanation for

---

[85] *Hertfordshire CC, City and District of St Albans v SSCLG* [2009] EWHC 1280 (Admin).
[86] [2001] EWHC 74.
[87] At para 8.
[88] [1993] 1 WLR 23.
[89] At 32H.
[90] [1998] P&CR 346.
[91] *North Wiltshire District Council v Secretary of State for the Environment* [1992] 3 PLR 113 at 112 F to H, *R (Chisnell) v Richmond on Thames LBC* [2005] EWHC 134.

that change of course.[92] But if the background is well known to members there is no duty on the part of the reporting officer to set out every fact to the members: *R v Mendip District Council ex p Fabre*.[93]

5.111 In *Fox Strategic Land and Property Ltd v Secretary of State for Communities and Local Government & Cheshire East Council*[94] the Secretary of State had refused an appeal against the refusal of planning permission on the basis that while the proposed housing development would contribute towards meeting a shortfall in housing land (and, therefore, was compliant with the RSS post-*Cala Homes*), that benefit was outweighed by the proposal's conflict with saved development plan policies in respect of settlement boundaries and restrictions on development in the countryside.

5.112 His decision was inconsistent with a previous decision he had made in respect of a similar development in the same town. In particular, the Secretary of State raised new points such as prematurity[95] and localism.[96] No explanation was given for the difference in approach. The Secretary of State did not address the apparent conflict between the two decisions and instead concluded that his earlier decision carried no weight. The High Court granted the claimant's challenge on a number of grounds. First, the Secretary of State had erred by failing to give weight to his previous decision. The two cases were concerned with very similar facts and the Secretary of State could not, without giving clear reasons, determine one appeal in a way that was contradictory to another. No reasons were given for the Secretary of State's conclusion in one case that the application conflicted with spatial policy objectives and in the other that a very similar application did not. Secondly, the Secretary of State had failed in his earlier decision to mention the 'prematurity' argument and the effect that granting permission would have on the local development framework process. Finally, the Secretary of State had failed to apply the correct test in Planning Policy Statement 7 ('PPS7' – loss of agricultural land). The judge commented that when the Secretary of State is faced with two appeals relating to similar proposals in the same town, he would significantly reduce the risk of inconsistent decisions if he heard the appeals together.

5.113 The Secretary of State appealed to the Court of Appeal. The Court of Appeal dismissed the appeal on similar grounds to the High Court. Again, the Court of Appeal stressed the need for consistency in the planning process and deciding like cases alike. A decision-maker is free to disagree with a previous decision but he must have regard to that decision and give reasons for departing from it. However, the Court of Appeal disagreed with the High Court that the Secretary of State had failed to apply the correct test in PPS7. On reading the decision letter as a whole it was clear that he had taken the correct approach to the policy and one instance of a hyperbolic expression was not a ground for quashing the decision. In any event, as the judge below had held that the

---

[92] *R v Aylesbury Vale District Council ex p Chaplin* [1997] 3 PLR 55.
[93] [2000] 80 P&CR 500.
[94] [2012] EWHC 444 and [2012] EWCA Civ 1198 (CA).
[95] Note that *Fox* and *Cala No 3* were s 288 challenges that arose at a time when 'prematurity' was being used as a consistent ground for rejection. In *Wainhomes (South West) Holdings Ltd v SSCLG* [2012] EWHC 914 (Admin) this conclusion was upheld by the High Court concerning a housing development (1,300 dwellings) at St Austell upon the basis that housing on such a scale being released for development would be premature in advance of Cornwall Council establishing the appropriate level of future housing.
[96] Localism – 'a principle which at this stage has nothing about it against which one can measure a proposal' (HH Judge Gilbart QC).

approach to PPS7 was not a sufficient reason to quash the decision, there was no reason to allow the appeal and restore the Secretary of State's decision.[97]

5.114 Legitimate expectations can be another facet of inconsistency. The role of the concept in planning is limited. Planning law provides a comprehensive code imposed in the public interest (see the House of Lords decision in *Pioneer Aggregates (UK) Ltd v SSE*[98]). As such, the concept of legitimate expectation in planning operates only in exceptional circumstances. This was made clear in the case of *Henry Boot v Bassetlaw*:[99]

> 'It is possible that circumstances might arise where it was clear that there was no third party or public interest in the matter and a court might take the view that a legitimate expectation could then arise from the local planning authority's conduct or representations. But, one suspects that such cases will be very rare ... Even more than many areas of public law which concern an individual and a public body, planning law is likely to have to reflect the fact that third parties and the public generally may have interests in any decision.'[100]

5.115 The public nature of and public involvement in the planning processes was emphasised in *R v East Sussex CC ex p Reprotech (Pebsham)*[101] 'a determination is not simply a matter between the applicant and the planning authority in which they are free to agree on whatever procedure they please. It is also a matter which concerns the general public interest and which requires other planning authorities, the Secretary of State on behalf of the national interest and the public itself to be able to participate.'[102] That was said as part of the rationale as to why the private law concept of estoppel had no role to play in planning law. The principle though applies to the concept of legitimate expectations equally as was recognised in the case of *R (Wandsworth BC) v SSTLGR*.[103]

Procedural unfairness

5.116 Most of the judicial review challenges which use this ground of challenge have been brought on the basis of bias or apparent bias and apparent pre-determination. The test applied has been that set out in *Porter v Magill*,[104] namely what a fair-minded and informed observer would have made of proceedings.[105] However, the basis on which challenges based on grounds of pre-determination have had to be reconsidered in light of s 25 of the Localism Act 2011:

> '25 Prior indications of view of a matter not to amount to predetermination etc
> (1) Subsection (2) applies if –
> (a) as a result of an allegation of bias or predetermination, or otherwise, there is an issue about the validity of a decision of a relevant authority, and

---

[97] By way of a postscript, the Secretary of State has now issued (February 2013) a 'minded to allow' decision upon the basis of a lack of an adequate five-year housing land supply.
[98] [1985] 1 AC 132.
[99] [2002] EWCA Civ 983.
[100] At para 56.
[101] [2002] UKHL 8.
[102] Lord Hoffmann at para 29.
[103] [2003] EWHC 622 Admin: 'the circumstances in which it will be appropriate to find a legitimate expectation in the planning field are limited, and the decision-taker is engaged in a task that is very different from an attempt to decide whether or not there is an estoppel in private law' at para 22.
[104] [2001] UKHL 67.
[105] *R v Secretary for State for the Environment & Anr, ex p Kirkstall Valley Campaign Ltd* [1996] 3 All ER 304, *Georgiou v Enfield London Borough Council* [2004] LGR, 779, *Condron v National, Assembly for Wales* [2006] EWCA Civ 1573, *R (on the Application of Island Farm Development Ltd & Anr) v Bridgend County Borough Council* [2006] EWHC Admin 2189.

(b) it is relevant to that issue whether the decision-maker, or any of the decision-makers, had or appeared to have had a closed mind (to any extent) when making the decision.

(2) A decision-maker is not to be taken to have had, or to have appeared to have had, a closed mind when making the decision just because –

(a) the decision-maker had previously done anything that directly or indirectly indicated what view the decision-maker took, or would or might take, in relation to a matter, and
(b) the matter was relevant to the decision.

(3) Subsection (2) applies in relation to a decision-maker only if that decision maker –

(a) is a member (whether elected or not) of the relevant authority, or
(b) is a co-opted member of that authority.'

5.117 There has been little judicial consideration as yet of s 25 so it remains to be seen precisely how it will impact on the determination of challenges based on pre-determination. It is likely, however, that s 25 will act to reaffirm the high evidential threshold that is required to establish that there has been bias or pre-determination by a decision-maker. The existing body of case-law illustrates that local councillors are allowed to express opinions on planning matters prior to a decision being reached: s 25 confirms this common law provision.

5.118 The impact of s 25 was considered briefly in *EU Plants Ltd v Wokingham Borough Council*.[106] That case concerned a s 288 challenge to a tree preservation order where one of the grounds of challenge was that the chairman of the planning committee who confirmed the TPO demonstrated bias or apparent bias. In the circumstances of the case Beatson J found he did not have to consider s 25; however he remarked that s 25(2) would not prevent courts from looking at the criticised conduct in the round.[107] The implication of this, it is suggested, is that s 25(2) is simply a starting point and if the conduct complained of when considered in light of all the relevant evidential circumstances in fact suggests bias then a challenge could be upheld on those grounds.

5.119 In light of the proceeding paragraphs the existing case-law on this issue is likely to remain valid. The same basic principles will continue to apply and the impact of s 25 will simply be one additional factor for the courts to consider.

5.120 The case of *Persimmon Homes Teesside Ltd v R (Lewis)*[108] reiterated the importance of understanding the local government context in which planning decisions are taken. 'Councillors are not in a judicial or quasi-judicial position but are elected to provide and pursue policies. Members of a Planning Committee would be entitled, and indeed expected, to have and to have expressed views on planning issues.'[109] The Court of Appeal upheld an appeal against a decision which had quashed a planning permission on the basis of apparent bias given that the decision to grant permission had been taken during a period leading up to a local election and various members of the Liberal Democratic party had expressed very positive and supportive views about the application which subsequently they had to determine. The court held that it was for the

---

[106] [2012] EWHC 3305 (Admin).
[107] At para 64.
[108] [2008] EWCA Civ 746.
[109] At para 69.

court to assess whether committee members made the decision with closed minds or that the circumstances gave rise to such a real risk of closed minds that the decision ought not in the public interest be upheld. The importance of appearances was more limited in the local government context than in a judicial context.

5.121 It was thought that that decision would slow the challenges by third parties on the basis of apparent predetermination. The case of *R (Gardner) v Harrogate BC (Mr and Mrs Atkinson)*[110] showed that not to be the case. The Local Government Ombudsman had reported that the grant of permission was procedurally flawed because there was apparent bias on the part of the chair of the council's area planning development control committee on whose casting vote the planning permission was granted. The court applied the fair-minded and informed observer test but again emphasised the surrounding context. In that case the context was that the applicant for planning permission was a fellow councillor who was regarded by the chair with 'liking, affection and loyalty'. The Ombudsman's report was one from which the court should be slow to depart and the fact that the council acknowledged that the grant of planning permission was improper and that other councillors expressed concerns were factors that did not give the court good reason to do so.

5.122 Most local planning authorities now have well-established procedures to be followed in making planning determinations so that those together with a full understanding of the local government context will make it difficult for the claimant to succeed under this head.[111]

5.123 Central government decision-making has not escaped challenge on the basis of procedural unfairness. In a climate of economic austerity the Planning Inspectorate's desire to limit the cost of hearings has generated a number of challenges where the procedure employed has been called into question.

5.124 In *Ashley v SSCLG & LB Greenwich & Taylor Wimpey (CA)*,[112] the claimant objected to a housing development on the grounds of noise and loss of amenity to the neighbouring houses. Planning permission was refused on the basis of the noise considerations and the matter proceeded to an appeal by way of written representations. The claimant was invited to provide written comments by a certain date after which point he was informed that no further representations could be made. On the last day before the deadline for representations, the appellant developer submitted detailed expert evidence on the noise issue. No copy was provided to the claimant and no prior notice of the report was given. The Inspector concluded that there was no objection to the expert evidence and that it adequately addressed the issue of noise and allowed the appeal.

5.125 The claimant challenged the decision on the basis of procedural unfairness. The developer resisted the challenge on the basis that all the claimant had to do was attend the council's offices the day after the deadline, see the report and then apply to make further representations.

5.126 At first instance, the challenge failed but the Court of Appeal allowed the appeal. The Court of Appeal found that there was no duty incumbent on the claimant to attend

---

[110] [2008] EWHC 2942 Admin.
[111] Apparent procedural irregularity has been accepted and overlooked, see *R (on the application of Hewitson) v Guildford BC* [2012] JPL 951; *R (Derwent Holdings Ltd) v Trafford BC* [2011] EWHC 491 (Admin).
[112] [2012] EWCA Civ 547.

the council's offices. He had not attended on the basis that the deadline had passed. Further, he was not aware that the expert evidence had been submitted. The claimant had not had a fair crack of the whip because he had been denied the opportunity to comment on the expert evidence. Pill LJ expressed the view that the Planning Inspectorate's guidance on written representations should be revised to prevent this sort of unfairness occurring in the future by an overly strict approach to deadlines.

5.127 The case of *R (on the application of Halite Energy Group Ltd) v Secretary of State for Climate Change and Energy*[113] looked at the issue of procedural fairness in a development consent order hearing. The examining authority had recommended approval of the project but their recommendation was rejected by the Secretary of State. The authority had not ensured that all material matters of concern had been raised with the parties in a fair and transparent way and had not provided an opportunity for them to comment upon a principal controversial issue before it reached its conclusion, which departed from what the main parties had agreed in the statement of common ground. The unfair approach on the part of the authority had infected the decision on the part of the Secretary of State who had taken no steps to correct the situation. That meant that the decision of the Secretary of State had to be quashed.

Protective costs orders

5.128 The Jackson Reforms were implemented on 1 April 2013. They considered how to deal with environmental cases. As a result amendments to the CPR dealt with in the Practice and Procedure chapter have been made which introduce a fixed recoverable costs regime for cases that engage the Aarhus Convention. That means that a claimant can have his/her costs capped at a fixed sum of £5,000 (if an individual) or £10,000 (if a NGO). The respondent has a reciprocal costs cap at £35,000.

5.129 The reforms are the Government's response to the problems caused by the Aarhus Convention otherwise known as the Convention on Access to Information, Public Participation in Decisions Making and Access to Justice to Environmental Matters. The preamble states:

> 'Recognising also that every person has the right to live in an environment adequate to his or her health and well being, and the duty, both individually and in association with others, to protect and improve the environment for the benefit of present and future generations, ...
>
> Considering that, to be able to assert this right and observe this duty, citizens must have access to information, be entitled to participate in decision making and have access to justice in environmental matters, and acknowledging in this regard that citizens may need assistance in order to exercise their rights.'

5.130 Article 9 of the Convention states:

> '2. Each Party shall, within the framework of its national legislation, ensure that members of the public concerned:
>
> (a) having a sufficient interest or, alternatively,
> (b) maintaining an impairment of a right ...

---

[113] [2014] EWHC 17.

Have access to a review procedure before a court of law and/or another independent and impartial body established by law to challenge the substantive and procedural legality of any decision, act or omission subject to the provisions of Article 6 ...

3. In addition, and without prejudice to the review procedures referred to ... Each party shall ensure that, where they meet the criteria, if any, laid down in its national law, members of the public have access to administrative or judicial procedures to challenge acts and omissions of private persons and public authorities which contravene provisions of its national law relating to the environment.

4. In addition and without prejudice to paragraph 1 above, the procedures referred to in paragraphs 1, 2, and 3 above shall provide adequate and effective remedies, including injunctive relief as appropriate, and be fair, equitable, timely and not prohibitively expensive.'

5.131 The difficulty for the domestic courts was how to interpret 'not prohibitively expensive'. As a result the Supreme Court made a reference to the European Court in the case of *R (on the application of Edwards) v Environment Agency*.[114] The court gave judgment on 11 April 2013. It said:

> 'judicial proceedings should not be prohibitively expensive means that persons covered by those provisions should not be prevented from seeking, or pursuing a claim for, a review by the courts that falls within the scope of those articles by reasons of the financial burden that might arise as a result. Where a national court is called upon to make an order for costs against a member of the public who is an unsuccessful claimant in an environmental dispute or, more generally, where it is required – as courts in the United Kingdom may be – to state its views, at an earlier stage in the proceedings, on a possible capping of the costs for which the unsuccessful party may be liable, it must satisfy itself that that requirement has been complied with, taking into account both the interest of the person wishing to defend his rights and the public interest in the protection of the environment.
>
> In the context of the assessment, the national court cannot act solely on the basis of that claimant's financial situation but must also carry out an objective analysis of the amount of costs. It may also take into account the situation of the parties concerned, whether the claimant has a reasonable prospect of success, the importance of what is at stake for the claimant and the protection of the environment, the complexity of the relevant law and procedure, the potentially frivolous nature of the claim at its various stages, and the existence of a national legal aid scheme or a costs protection regime.
>
> By contrast the fact that a claimant has not been deterred, in practice, from asserting his claim is not of itself sufficient to establish that the proceedings are not prohibitively expensive for him.
>
> Lastly, that assessment cannot be conducted according to different criteria depending on whether it is carried out at the conclusion of first instance proceedings, an appeal or a second appeal.'

5.132 In February 2014 the ECJ gave their judgment in *European Commission v United Kingdom of Great Britain and Northern Ireland*.[115] The Commission alleged that despite the criteria laid down by the judgment of the Court of Appeal in *R (Corner House Research) v Secretary of State for Trade & Industry*[116] the case-law in the UK on

---

[114] Case C-260/11, [2013] 1 WLR 2914.
[115] Case C-530/11.
[116] [2005] 1 WLR 2600.

'protective costs orders' remained contradictory and gave rise to legal uncertainty. In any event the courts only rarely granted such orders. The European Court upheld this complaint:

> 'Thus, the very conditions under which the national courts rule on applications for costs protection do not ensure that national law complies with the requirement laid down by Directive 2003/35 in several respects. First, the condition, laid down by the national case-law, that the issues to be resolved must be of public interest is not appropriate and, even should it be accepted, as the United Kingdom pleads, that condition was removed by the judgment of the Court of Appeal in *R (Garner) v Elmbridge Borough Council and Others*. That judgment, which was delivered after the period laid down in the reasoned opinion expired, could not be taken into account by the Court. Second, in any event, the courts do not appear to be obliged to grant protection where the cost of the proceedings is objectively unreasonable. Nor, finally, does protection appear to be granted where only the particular interest of the claimant is involved. These various factors lead to the conclusion that in practice the rules of case-law applied do not satisfy the requirement that proceedings not be prohibitively expensive within its meaning as defined in *Edwards and Pallikaropoulos*.
>
> It is apparent from the foregoing that that regime laid down by case-law does not ensure the claimant reasonable predictability as regards both whether the costs of the judicial proceedings in which he becomes involved are payable by him and their amount, although such predictability appears particularly necessary because, as the United Kingdom acknowledges, judicial proceedings in the United Kingdom entail high lawyers' fees.'

5.133 The action that was determined in Case C-530/11 was brought in 2010 and, therefore, pre-dated the Jackson Reforms and amendments to the CPR. Consequently, the issue of whether the amendment to the CPR has been sufficient to comply with the mixed subjective/objective test that the European Court is promulgating remains to be determined.

5.134 The Criminal Justice and Courts Bill also proposes changes to the PCO regime in that they will only be able to be made after permission has been granted unless the matter is an Aarhus claim. In that event PCOs will remain as now. In other cases, possibly not many but there will be some, the claimant, as currently proposed, will have to bear its own costs during the permission stage.

5.135 The role of judicial review in challenging planning decisions is likely to remain active. It will be interesting to see whether the reforms bring any change in the volume of planning work before the courts.

CHAPTER 6

COMMUNITY CARE

PREFACE

6.01 This area of the law does not benefit from a single source of legislation. It is founded upon various statutory provisions and guidance resulting in a complicated mirage of laws. This is despite the general importance of this area of law: it does not seek to govern or regulate particular forms of behaviour, rather it implements societal responsibilities for the benefit of those who are disabled or those who require assistance. This complexity has been caused by the implementation of various legislations that reflected (at the relevant time) the constantly evolving relationship between the state and the citizen. Lord Justice May expressed his consternation when considering community care law in *Crofton v NHS Litigation Authority*:[1]

> 'We cannot conclude this judgment without expressing our dismay at the complexity and labyrinthine nature of the relevant legislation and guidance, as well as (in some respects) its obscurity. Social security law should be clear and accessible. The tortuous analysis in the earlier part of this judgment shows that it is neither.'

6.02 Support for the review has been far reaching. McCombe J in *R v Wirral Borough Council, ex p F, J, S, R & Others*[2] stated that:

> 'The law in this field is exceptionally tortuous. It is encouraging to note, from the Law Commission's spring 2009 newsletter, that it is in the process of reviewing the law relating to the provision of adult social care in order to "modernise and consolidate this outdated area of the law". This would be very welcome.'

6.03 Whatever the outcome of the review, it is clear that the number of individuals seeking recourse to a wide ambit of community care services is increasing. The ageing population is the likely cause. As such, this area of law is likely to be at the forefront of judicial review litigation for some time.

6.04 In terms of the future, para 28 of the Coalition Agreement[3] contains the Government's commitment on social care and disability. It states that, 'The Government believes that people needing care deserve to be treated with dignity and respect. We understand the urgency of reforming the system of social care to provide much more control to individuals and their carers, and to ease the cost burden that they and their families face.'

---

[1] [2007] EWCA Civ 71 at para 111.
[2] [2009] EWHC 1626 (Admin).
[3] http://www.cabinetoffice.gov.uk/media/409088/pfg_coalition.pdf.

6.05 In respect of the present law, however, the Administrative Court has battled and succeeded in attempting to simplify this unduly complex area. As such, the court has played an important role in providing redress and holding public bodies to account in respect of community care provisions. This is despite the common perception that society has become far too litigious and overly preoccupied with asserting rights rather than accepting individual responsibilities.

6.06 Such an argument may have some merit in other areas of litigation, however, it is the author's view that community care law has been greatly assisted by the court's intervention. The recent paper prepared by Platt, Sunkin and Calvo, titled 'Judicial Review Litigation as a Incentive Change in Local Authority Public Services in England & Wales'[4] considered this very issue. The paper analysed the relationship between judicial review litigation and the quality of local authorities as indicated by the government's performance measures. In their conclusions the authors provided that:

> '... Far from being a negative irritant, our research indicated that judicial review may actually help authorities to improve. The findings also have important implications in relation to the funding of legal services. They highlight the extent to which judicial review is used to help meet the needs of the most vulnerable people who depend on having access to high quality and properly funded expert services. In short, they underscore the link, rather the tension, between access to justice and improvements in the quality of local government.'

6.07 The above findings are difficult to dispute.

INTRODUCTION

6.08 There is no definition of what is meant by 'community care law', however, it embraces the loose interpretations of social and health care. In a broad sense, community care services can include support at home, access to respite care and day care, family placements, the provision of sheltered housing and placement in residential or nursing homes. In most cases, the responsibility of such services fall to the local authority, but are increasingly provided by the NHS.

6.09 The most common community care services that local authorities provide, or arrange services for, are those provided under:

- The Mental Health Act 1983, s 117 ('MHA 1983');
- The National Assistance Act 1948, ss 21 and 29 ('NAA 1948'); and
- The Chronically Sick and Disabled Persons Act 1970, s 2(1) ('CSDPA 1970').

6.10 When a local authority carries out its obligations under one or various statutory regimes, it is prerequisite that it follows good and reasonable decision-making processes, thereby complying with public law principles. In order for any decision to be deemed lawful the decision-maker must observe the requirements of (see Chapter 1):

- rationality;
- legality;

---

[4] ESRC research paper February 2009, http://www.iser.essex.ac.uk/files/iser_working_papers/2009-05.pdf.

- procedural propriety (including compliance of policy, guidance and directions and proper consultation); and
- compatibility with rights under the European Convention of Humans Rights ('ECHR') as enshrined by the Human Rights Act 1998 ('HRA').

6.11 With the above in mind, this chapter will provide an overview of community care law, consider specific significant areas, and finally analyse relevant cases that seek to exemplify how community care decisions are challenged by way of judicial review.

6.12 Part 1 provides an overview of community care law with references to challenges by way of judicial review in the Administrative Court. Part 2 considers specific areas of community care law, and more importantly disputes, which seek resolution by the Administrative Court. Finally, Part 3 analyses how judicial review, as a remedy, has been utilised as a means of challenging decisions. In particular, Part 3 seeks to exemplify how *specific* grounds of judicial review are used to challenge community care decisions.

PART 1 – AN OVERVIEW OF COMMUNITY CARE LAW

The community care decision-making process

6.13 The process of decision-making relating to community care can be divided up into basic stages. The flowchart on the following page best illustrates the steps.

6.14 The important stages can be described as:

- **Community care assessment of needs** – the obligation is upon the local authority but often in practice cooperation between health and social services is required.

  A local authority is required to assess the community care needs of any person in respect of whom it has a power to provide community care services – *R v Berkshire CC, ex p P*.[5] By virtue of s 22 of the National Health Service Act 1977 ('NHSA 1977'), Primary Care Trusts ('PCT') and local authorities must cooperate in exercising their respective functions.
- A decision as to whether or not the individual's needs require provision of community care services (ie the **eligibility** stage).
- A **service provision decision**, ie a decision as to what services are going to be provided. Once a decision has been made it is necessary to provide services to meet the individual's needs. The local authority is then under an individual duty to make those arrangements as soon as is reasonably practicable – *R v Kirkham MBC, ex p Daykin and Daykin*.[6]
- The **care planning** stage. When care plan(s) are created for the implementation of a provision of services to meet the identified and eligible needs highlighted in the service provision decision.

---

[5] 1 CCLR 143.
[6] (1997–8) 1 CCLR 512, 527B.

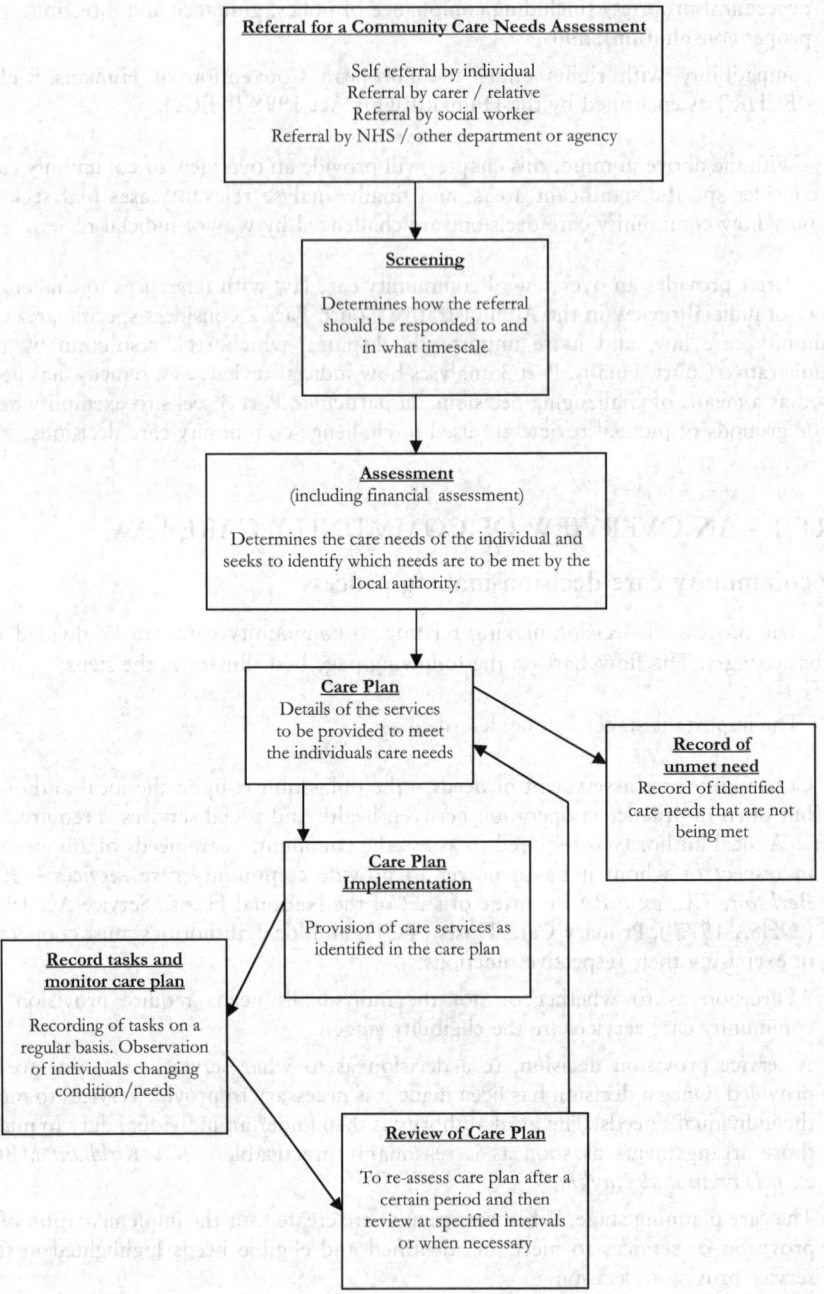

6.15 Professor Luke Clements and Pauline Thompson[7] have argued that there are five key 'underpinning principles' of community care law which ought to apply throughout the above process, ie the decision making process, namely non-discrimination, dignity, independent living, choice and cost effectiveness.

---

7   Community Care and the Law (4th edn), Legal Action Group, para 4.42.

The statutory framework

6.16 Section 47(1) of the National Health Service and Community Care Act 1990 ('NHSCCA 1990') provides:

> '(1) Subject to subsections (5) and (6) below, where it appears to a local authority that any person for whom they may provide or arrange for the provision of community care services may be in need of any such services, the authority –
> (a) shall carry out an assessment of his needs for those services; and
> (b) having regard to the results of that assessment, shall then decide whether his needs call for the provision by them of any such services.'

The assessment

6.17 The duty to assess a person's needs for community care services arises *where it appears* that the person *may be in need of such services*.[8] The elementary aspects of this duty are as follows:

(a) the identification of a need is matter of judgment for the social worker who carries out the assessment. In *R (B) v Cornwall CC & The Brandon Trust*[9] the court emphasised the importance that a local authority cannot avoid its obligation to assess needs by failing to make an appropriate assessment itself, for example by relying on a 'self assessment';

(b) it is trite that the duty to assess is *not* dependent on a request by any individual;

(c) the duty is activated upon the 'possibility of need'. In *R v Bristol CC, ex p Penfold*[10] the Court of Appeal reinforced the notion that the threshold for entitlement to an assessment was very low and that the duty to undertake an assessment is a strong obligation, rather than an absolute/mandatory duty;

(d) the duty is a social services function and cannot be delegated to another body, see *Daykin*;[11]

(e) the duty has been deemed to apply even when the disabled person is not ordinarily resident in a local authority's area, see *R v Berkshire County Council, ex p Parker*.[12] However, there is no obligation to undertake an assessment as to provision of accommodation and support services when the possibility of the claimant's release from prison was merely speculative: see *R (NM) v London Borough of Islington*;[13]

(f) if, during the assessment of needs, it seems that the person is disabled, there is a specific duty to ensure that a decision is made as to the services without the need for a request, s 4 of the Disabled Persons (Services, Consultation and Representation) Act 1986;

(g) there is a duty to inform a relevant PCT, health authority or local housing authority to invite them to assist in the assessment if there is need for services provided by those bodies, s 47(3) of the NHSCCA 1990;

(h) there is no prescribed timetable to complete an assessment. The Local Government Ombudsman ('LGO') considered that an adaptation assessment that took three

---

[8] See SAP (single assessment process) policy guidance, annex f.
[9] [2009] EWHC 491 (Admin).
[10] [1998] 1 CCLR 315.
[11] Formal partnership agreements are permitted with a NHS body.
[12] (1996) 95 LGR 449.
[13] [2012] EWHC 414 (Admin).

months was 'simply unacceptable'.[14] Policy guidance and Department of Health indicators do assist certain groups of individuals, namely: (i) disabled children whose initial assessment should be concluded within 7 working days and core assessment within 35 working days; and (ii) older people in relation to whom a single assessment process ('SAP') should commence within 48 hours of initial contact with conclusion within a month;

(i) if an individual's needs are considered to be urgent, a local authority may use its power under s 47(5) of the NHSCCA 1990[15] to provide services on a temporary basis until the completion of the assessment, see *R (AA) v Lambeth LBC*;[16]

(j) resources of a person in need of community care services are not relevant to their needs as such, save that if services and/or accommodation are actually being provided. Resources become relevant at the stage of charging for community care services;

(k) similarly, in *Penfold* at para 322G of the judgment, it was made clear that it is unlawful for a local authority to take resources into account when deciding whether or not to carry out a community care assessment. In *R v Birmingham CC, ex p Taj Mohammed*[17] it was explicitly held that resources could not be taken into account when deciding whether or not to approve a disabled facilities grant; and

(l) a local authority's resources are relevant to its thresholds for assessment of need and whether or not it is necessary to meet the need, i.e. when framing the eligibility criteria (*R v Gloucestershire CC, ex p Barry*[18]). Once, however, it has been determined that it is necessary to provide services to meet a need, a local authority cannot rely upon its own limited resources as a justification for failing to meet the need (see eg *Batantu v Islington Borough Council*[19]).

(m) a local authority must make reasonable adjustments when conducting the assessment by virtue of s 20 of Equality Act 2010, see *R (MM) v Secretary of State for Work and Pensions*.[20]

6.18 In respect of what an assessment should address, the Community Care Assessment Directions 2004 require a local authority to consult with the person being assessed; consider whether consultation with a carer is appropriate; take reasonable steps to reach agreement with the person (and carer) in terms of services to be provided to meet their needs; and to provide information about the amount of charge that the person may be required to make in respect of any services that may be provided.

6.19 Within the context of community care assessments, the case of *Lambeth LBC v Irenenschild* [2007] EWCA Civ 234 must be borne in mind. The Court of Appeal made

---

[14] Complaint number 05/c/07195 – Northumberland CC, 18 April 2006, paras 7, 29 and 30. See also complaint number 07A11108 – Surrey County Council, November 2008 where the Council agreed to pay the complainant £5,000 in respect of delays in assessment that would have allowed her to leave residential care and return to her family home. Finally, complaint number 06A08746 – LB of Ealing, May 2008, where the Council agreed to pay the complainant £16,700 which was the value of the direct payments she had missed during a period in which the Council had delayed in reassessing her needs. The LGO stated that the reassessment could have been achieved in six months.

[15] Section 47(5) provides, 'Nothing in this section shall prevent a local authority from temporarily providing or arranging for the provision of community care services for any person without carrying out a prior assessment of his needs in accordance with the preceding provisions of this section if, in the opinion of the authority, the condition of that person is such that he requires those services as a matter of urgency'.

[16] [2001] EWCA Admin 741.
[17] (1998) 1 CCLR 441.
[18] [1997] AC 584.
[19] LTL 9/11/2000.
[20] [2013] EWCA Civ 1565.

forceful comments regarding challenges to community care assessments under s 47 of the NHSCCA 1990. The judge at first instance had found that an assessment had been unlawful for a number of reasons, in particular because the assessor had failed to obtain, and to take into account, an Occupational Therapist ('OT') report and because she had failed to take into account the statutory Fair Access to Care Guidance 2002 ('FAC'). The Court of Appeal allowed the appeal, but the decision is important for the views expressed as to the circumstances under which such challenges should be brought. Lady Justice Hallett emphasised that assessments cannot be the subject of:

> '... over zealous textual analysis. Courts must be wary, in my view, of expecting so much of hard pressed social workers that we risk taking them, unnecessarily, from their front line duties ... a community care assessment ... is operational and inevitably judgmental. It must be carried out quickly. I accept the Appellants' argument that a social worker preparing such an assessment cannot be expected to engage in a detailed analysis of the material obtained (often from many sources), decide what particular points have and have not been specifically addressed by the "service user" thus far, and then take steps to ensure that any points which have been missed or not sufficiently addressed are drawn to the attention of the "service user" for his or her response.'[21]

6.20 More recently in *R v Wirral BC, ex p F & Others*,[22] McCombe J at paras 76 to 80 criticised further and said:

> 'While the Administrative Court is astute to correct any illegality of approach on a public authority's part, it is not the proper forum in which to probe into the adequacy of community care assessments in the manner which Mr Prescott belatedly sought to do in this case ... If any of these individual claimants truly have a grievance in respect of their community care provision it has not been identified here. None of them, for example, says, "I need help in

---

[21] Paras 57 and 71. See also *R (L) v Barking and Dagenham LBC* [2001] EWCA Civ 533 in which Schiemann LJ said at para 27 in these terms, 'It seems to us however that, leaving aside for the moment any undertakings to the court, the court is not the appropriate organ to be prescriptive as to the degree of detail which should go into a care plan or as to the amount of consultation to be carried out with Ms L's advisers. In practice these are matters for the Council, and if necessary its complaints procedure. If the Council has failed to follow the Secretary of State's guidance and is arguably in breach of its statutory duties in relation to the way it carries out its assessment and what it puts into its care plans then aggrieved persons should in appropriate cases turn first to the Secretary of State. Where there is room for differences of judgment the Secretary of State and his advisers may have a useful input. The court is here as a last resort where there is illegality. Here there is not ....'

[22] [2009] EWHC 1626. F & Others were adults who suffered from various disabilities. They lived in accommodation, within the local authority's area, let to them by a company (S). S considered that the local authority had improperly failed to meet its legal obligations to F in the social services field and as a result had deprived them of funds which would in turn reimburse S for the assistance provided by it to them. F, via S and their litigation friends, wrote to the local authority alleging that it was in breach of its duty under the National Health Service and Community Care Act 1990, s 47 in that it had failed to comply with its legal duty by carrying out an assessment of each of their needs. F asked that the matter be referred immediately to the second stage of the statutory complaints procedure, that of 'investigation', under the Local Authority Social Services Complaints (England) Regulations 2006, reg 9, and that within 14 days the local authority would carry out a multi-disciplinary assessment of each of them in accordance with its legal obligations under s 47. The local authority responded by stating that it was felt that the first stage of the complaints procedure, that of 'local resolution' under reg 7, was more appropriate and it proceeded to set out the current position in respect of each of F and others, indicating that, contrary to the allegation made in the complaint letters, in the cases of all but one of them (who was unknown to the local authority as a welfare claimant at all), assessments had been completed or reviewed or that current social work was being carried out. Two days later, without any further request for engagement of the complaints procedure, F sent judicial review pre-action protocol letters to the local authority alleging again that it had failed to carry out any assessment of F's needs under s 47 and making no reference to the local authority's letter stating that assessments had indeed been carried out, and F subsequently issued their judicial review claim. The local authority submitted that complaints as to the details of individual assessments or care plans or both were not appropriate for judicial review.

getting myself a hot meal" or "I cannot get out to do my shopping" and "the Council should be providing this". All has been fought out amongst the abstraction of form filling and the contents of official documents. The process was initiated by an entirely unjustified global complaint that no assessments had been carried out at all. If a claimant has a true claim that his or her eligible needs are not being met by the Council, there is a full and adequate complaints procedure in which that can be resolved ... Even in cases in which such a proper claim exists the courts have pointed out on many occasions that the remedy of judicial review will not be granted where there is an alternative remedy: see especially *Pulhofer v Hillingdon LBC*,[23] *R (L) v Barking & Dagenham LBC*[24] and *Lambeth LBC v Ireneschild*[25] ... If any of the assessments or care plans is truly inadequate in these cases and such inadequacy is giving rise to a true failure on the part of the Council to meet an eligible need, then the relevant claimant has a proper remedy through the statutory complaints procedure.'

6.21 This decision makes it extremely difficult to challenge community care assessments by way of judicial review without having recourse to the complaint procedure as the alternative remedy. It is questionable, however, whether the court would criticise the instigation of proceedings where a failure to meet eligible needs is placing the service user within the realms of real and tangible physical and/or mental harm.

Eligibility

6.22 The Department of Health has issued policy guidance with a view to standardising individual local authority eligibility criteria for community care services, namely FACS.

6.23 The eligibility framework is graded into four bands:[26]

(a) Critical – when
- life is, or will be, threatened; and/or
- significant health problems have developed or will develop; and/or
- there is, or will be, little or no choice and control over vital aspects of the immediate environment; and/or
- serious abuse or neglect has occurred or will occur; and/or
- there is, or will be, an inability to carry out vital personal care or domestic routines; and/or
- vital involvement in work, education or learning cannot or will not be sustained; and/or
- vital social support systems and relationships cannot or will not be sustained; and/or
- vital family and other social roles and responsibilities cannot or will not be undertaken.

(b) Substantial – when
- there is, or will be, only partial choice and control over the immediate environment; and/or
- abuse or neglect has occurred or will occur; and/or
- there is, or will be, an inability to carry out the majority of personal care or domestic routines; and/or

---

[23] [1996] AC 484.
[24] [2001] EWCA Civ 533.
[25] [2007] EWCA Civ 234.
[26] http://www.dh.gov.uk/en/Publicationsandstatistics/Publications/PublicationsPolicyAndGuidance/DH_4009653.

- involvement in many aspects of work, education or learning cannot or will not be sustained; and/or
- the majority of social support systems and relationships cannot or will not be sustained; and/or
- the majority of family and other social roles and responsibilities cannot or will not be undertaken.

(c) Moderate – when
- there is, or will be, an inability to carry out several personal care or domestic routines; and/or
- involvement in several aspects of work, education or learning cannot or will not be sustained; and/or
- several social support systems and relationships cannot or will not be sustained; and/or
- several family and other social roles and responsibilities cannot or will not be undertaken.

(d) Low – when
- there is, or will be, an inability to carry out one or two personal care or domestic routines; and/or
- involvement in one or two aspects of work, education or learning cannot or will not be sustained; and/or
- one or two social support systems and relationships cannot or will not be sustained; and/or
- one or two family and other social roles and responsibilities cannot or will not be undertaken.

6.24 In *Barry* the court concluded that the threshold of eligibility can lawfully differ between local authorities, and that resources can be a relevant factor in its determination. A variation of the threshold must be done at the social services committee level. For an example of this, see the case of *R v Wigan MBC, ex p Tammadge*.[27]

6.25 Based on the demand of services, it is becoming growing practice for local authorities to shift the threshold to 'critical needs' only. The case of *R v Harrow London Borough Council, ex p Chavad*,[28] however, deemed that the local authority's decision to *only* provide services for 'critical' needs was held to be unlawful as the decision-maker had failed to consider, with any particular weight, the duties under the Disability Discrimination Act 1995 ('DDA 1995').[29]

These duties have now been rearticulated in the Equality Act 2010, which at s 149 includes a public sector equality duty to have due regard to the need to eliminate discrimination, advance equality of opportunity and foster good relations. This duty has been used to successfully challenge budget-setting in the context of community care

---

[27] (1998) 1 CCLR 581.
[28] [2007] EWHC 3064.
[29] See also *R (W) v Birmingham City Council* [2011] EWHC 1147 (Admin). Section 49A of the DDA 1995 places a duty on all public bodies to have due regard to the need to promote equality of opportunity between disabled persons and other people. As a result, public bodies must acquire a Disability Equality Scheme pursuant to Regulation (Disability Discrimination (Public Authorities) (Statutory Duties) Regulations 2005 (SI 2005/2966), that promotes involvement in public life (see also the Social Care Sector and the Disability Equality Duty: A guide to the Disability Equality and Disability Discrimination Act 2005 for social care organisations). It also worth noting that Article 19 of the UN Convention on the Rights of Persons with Disabilities contains a declaration regarding the right of disabled individuals to live independently in the community. Article 14 of the ECHR can be deployed to build arguments.

services. For instance in *Hunt v North Somerset Council*[30] it was held that the local authority had not shown due regard to the objectives in s 149 when it sought to reduce its youth services budget. This was because the council members had not considered the relevant equality impact assessment.

6.26 The recent case of *R (JL a child, by his mother and litigation friend LL(1), LL(2)) v Islington LBC and Others*[31] ('JL') is of particular relevance as it considered the question of the lawfulness of the eligibility criteria for children services. JL was a 14-year-old autistic child who lived with his mother who also had health problems. The claimant challenged the eligibility criteria that reduced his number of hours from 1,248 to 624 hours per year. Mrs Justice Black held that the criteria was unlawful because: (i) the local authority was operating a banding system which (indirectly) imposed a maximum ceiling of 12 hours irrespective of need under s 2 of the CSDPA 1970; (ii) the decision to reduce the number of hours was made by an eligibility assessment tool rather than a core assessment; and (iii) the local authority used one criteria without distinguishing between the different services and their statutory source.

6.27 Note, however, that it has been deemed to be lawful to reduce and/or withdraw services following a reassessment of an individual's needs if the local authority's threshold of eligibility has changed, see *Barry*. This is to be balanced against the Department of Health's guidance[32] that refers to caution in withdrawing services to which service users have become dependent and would not be able to cope without its availability.

The decision and care planning

6.28 Once a local authority has made a decision under s 47(1)(b) of the NHSCCA 1990 that an individual's needs are such that community care services are required, then the local authority must make arrangements for those identified services to be provided. Those identified needs require also to be 'eligible needs', based on a local authority's individual eligibility criteria outlined above.

6.29 Once the needs have been assessed and deemed to be eligible, the local authority is under an *absolute/mandatory duty* to provide those services, see *Barry*. Failure to comply with this duty can be remedied by seeking an interim relief order in the form of a mandatory order, see case of *Tammadge*. There are, however, particular circumstances when an 'assessed need' will not require a local authority to provide services: when those needs do not achieve the threshold of eligibility as discussed above or, when those needs can be and are to be, provided by other statutory organisations, eg a housing authority/association or the NHS.

6.30 There is no formal statutory requirement to prepare a care plan. However, it has been considered to be at the very heart of the community care process. Bear in mind that the FACS guidance provides that:[33]

> '... If an individual is eligible for help then, together with the individual, councils should develop a care plan. The written record of the care plan should include as a minimum:

---

[30] [2013] EWCA Civ 1320.
[31] [2009] EWHC 458.
[32] LAC (2002) 13, paras 47 and 60.
[33] Paragraph 60 of the FACS policy guidance.

- A note of the eligible needs and associated risks.
- The preferred outcomes of service provision.
- Contingency plans to manage emergency changes.
- Details of services to be provided, and any charges the individual is assessed to pay, or if direct payments have been agreed.
- Contributions which carers and others are willing and able to make.
- A review date.

There should be an initial review within three months of help first being provided or major changes made to current services. Thereafter, reviews should be scheduled at least annually or more often if individuals' circumstances appear to warrant it. Reviews may be considered on request from services users, providers of services and other appropriate individuals or agencies.'

6.31 The practice guidance also illustrates the necessity of a written care plan:[34]

'Care plans should be set out in concise written form, linked with the assessment of need. The document should be accessible to the user, for example, in Braille translated into the user's own language. A copy should be given to the user but it should also, subject to constraints of confidentiality, be shared with other contributors to the plan ....'

Services

6.32 'Community care services' are defined in s 46 of the NHSCCA as services which the local authority may provide or arrange to be provided under:

(a) Part III of the National Assistance Act 1948 – accommodation and welfare services for persons in need of care and attention and/or who are 'aged eighteen or over who are blind, deaf or dumb or who suffer from mental disorder of any description, and other persons aged eighteen or over who are substantially and permanently handicapped by illness, injury, or congenital deformity or such other disabilities';

A local authority is empowered to provide 'normal' housing under s 21 of the NAA 1948 – see *Penfold* and *Tammadge* [1998];[35]

(b) Section 45 of the Health Services and Public Health Act 1968 – promotion of welfare of elderly people;

(c) Section 21 and Sch 8 to the National Health Service Act 1977 ('NHSA 1977') – services in relation to the care of expectant or nursing mothers, prevention, provision of centres for training and occupation of persons whose care is preventative, who are ill, or who have been ill, and home help and laundry facilities for those who are ill, or handicapped; and

(d) Section 117 of the MHA 1982 – after care services for those who have been discharged from compulsory detention under this Act.

6.33 Beyond the above, there are various services that can be provided. What is set out below seeks to summarise the extent of those services:

(a) As regards accommodation, s 21 of the NAA 1948, which falls within Part III of that Act, provides that 'local authorities may, with the approval of the Secretary of State, and to such extent as he directs must, make arrangements for providing

---

[34] Care Management & Assessment – A Practitioner's Guide, HMSO, 1991, para 4.37.
[35] See Chapter 26 for further details.

residential accommodation for persons aged 18 or over who by reason of age, illness, disability or any other circumstances are in need of care and attention which is not otherwise available to them'. By virtue of Appendix 1 to LAC (93) 10 the Secretary of State directs local authorities to make arrangements under s 21 in relation to persons ordinarily resident in their area. Under s 22 of the NAA 1948, the local authority can charge for such accommodation. Where accommodation is provided by virtue of s 21, the National Assistance Act 1948 (Choice of Accommodation) Directions 1992 creates an obligation to consult with the service user. An opportunity to challenge proposed accommodation should be given before a decision is made.[36]

Whether a potential service user is ordinarily resident in a particular local authority's catchments area is a recurring problem. *R (Greenwich LBC) v SS Health*[37] concerned an individual, D, who had lived in Bexley in a residential home as a self-funder. In 2006 due to problems at the home she had to move as a matter of urgency. The only suitable placement put forward by Bexley was a home in Greenwich, to which she moved. Four and a half weeks later she became entitled to funding under s 21 of the NAA 1948. The ordinary residence dispute was referred to the Secretary of State who accepted that D had not chosen the new home but nevertheless held that D had ceased to be ordinarily resident in Bexley. Her house had been sold and she was no longer living in the area, and therefore, her ties were severed. Greenwich challenged the decision on the basis that they were not responsible for monies in relation to the same. The court rejected Greenwich's challenge, holding that the question was *fact dependant* and since the Secretary of State had applied the correct criteria, and given adequate reasons, the decision could not be quashed.

More recently in *R (Buckinghamshire CC) v Kingston upon Thames Royal London Borough Council and SL & others*,[38] the claimant local authority sought to judicially review a decision of the defendant local authority to move the service user into its area. SL had been placed by Kingston in a school for children with learning difficulties, however, she was then placed in a National Society for Epilepsy Centre after which she moved into supported living in a privately rented bungalow in the Buckinghamshire area. Kingston initially funded the care, but sought that Buckinghamshire take over the funding, asserting that SL had become ordinarily resident in its area. Buckinghamshire refused, and sought a declaration that the decision to move SL was unlawful and that Kingston should indemnify it for any expense it had incurred or would incur in consequence of that decision.

The court held that Kingston did not owe any duties of fairness to Buckinghamshire to notify it of SL's proposed move, to consult with it, or give it an opportunity to participate in the decision. Kingston was under no duty to act fairly towards Buckinghamshire when carrying out the community care assessment or before making any decision consequent to it. Its duties towards other persons or bodies were limited to those stated expressly in s 47 of the 1990 Act, in the Community Care Assessment Directions 2004 and ss 21 and 26 of the 1948 Act. While the fact that a decision might impact adversely upon an individual or body was a factor in deciding whether there was a duty to act fairly towards that person, its significance depended on the factual circumstances. In the instant case, it was neither important nor determinative.

Note that commencing 19 April 2010, new statutory guidance came into place on the identification of the ordinary residence of people in need of community care

---

[36] See *R (W) v Croydon Borough Council* [2011] EWHC 696 (Admin).
[37] [2006] All ER (D) 178.
[38] [2010] EWHC 1703 (Admin).

services.[39] Other directions that also took effect on that date included: (1) Ordinary Residence Disputes (National Assistance Act 1948) Directions 2010; (2) Ordinary Residence Disputes (Community Care (Delayed Discharges etc) Act 2003) Directions 2010; and (3) Ordinary Residence Disputes (Mental Capacity Act 2005) Directions 2010.

The guidance can be summarised as providing some key principles when two or more local authorities fall into dispute over a person's ordinary residence, namely:
(1) the fundamental main concern of local authorities should be the well-being of the service user;
(2) the services (including accommodation) must not be delayed or adversely affected as a result of uncertainty over which local authority is responsible; and
(3) one local authority must accept responsibility for the provision of services while the dispute is being resolved in accordance with the directions issued by the Secretary of State.

The Ordinary Residence Disputes (National Assistance Act 1948) Directions 2010 is relevant insofar as it sets out which one of the local authorities is to provide services:
(a) if the person is already in receipt of services, the local authority providing them should continue to do so;
(b) if the person is not in receipt of services, the local authorities in dispute may agree which of them will provide services pending the resolution of the dispute;
(c) if the local authorities in dispute cannot agree, the local authority in which the person is living must provide the services; and
(d) if the person is not living anywhere, the local authority in whose area the person is physically present (the 'local authority of the moment') must do so.

(b) With respect to more general welfare services, s 29 of the NAA 1948, which falls within Part III of that Act, provides that 'local authorities may with the approval of the Secretary of State, and to such extent as he directs must, make arrangements for promoting the welfare of persons aged 18 or over who are blind, deaf, dumb, suffer from mental disorder or are substantially and permanently handicapped by illness, injury, or congenital deformity or such other disabilities as may be prescribed by the Minister'.

(c) Section 29 services include a range of services, and can include workshops, hostel accommodation, and recreational facilities. Similarly, by virtue of Appendix 2 to LAC (93) 10 the Secretary of State directs local authorities to make arrangements under s 29 in relation to persons ordinarily resident in their area for the purposes of providing facilities for occupational, social, cultural and recreational activities and facilities for social rehabilitation and adjustment to disability including assistance in overcoming limitations of mobility or communication.

(d) Section 2 of the Chronically Sick and Disabled Persons Act 1970 ('CSDPA') provides that:

> 'Where a local authority having functions under s 29 of the National Assistance Act 1948 are satisfied in the case of any person to whom that section applies who is ordinarily resident in their area that it is necessary in order to meet the needs of that person for that authority to make arrangements for all or any of the following matters, namely –

---

[39] http://www.dh.gov.uk/en/SocialCare/Deliveringadultsocialcare/Ordinaryresidence/index.

(a)	the provision of practical assistance for that person in his home;
(b)	the provision for that person of, or assistance to that person in obtaining, wireless, television, library or similar recreational activities;
(c)	the provision for that person of lectures, games, outings or other recreational facilities outside his home or assistance to that person in taking advantage of educational facilities available to him;
(d)	the provision for that person of facilities for, or assistance in, travelling to and from his home for the purpose of participating in any services provided under arrangements made by the local authority under ... s 29 or, with the approval of the local authority, in any services provided otherwise than as aforesaid which are similar to services which could be provided under such arrangements;
(e)	the provision of assistance for that person in arranging for the carrying out of any works of adaptation in his home or the provision of any additional facilities designed to secure his greater safety, comfort or convenience ... then ... It shall be the duty of that authority to make those arrangements in exercise of their functions under the said s 29'; and

(e) Section 4 of the Disabled Persons (Services, Consultation and Representation) Act 1986 provides that:

'When requested to do so by –

(a) a disabled person;
(b) his authorised representative; or
(c) any person who provides care for him in the circumstances mentioned in s 8, a local authority shall decide whether the needs of the disabled person call for the provision by the authority of any services in accordance with s 2(1) of the 1970 Act (provision of welfare services).'

6.34 In performing its functions under the above legislation, local authorities are required by virtue of s 7(1) of the Local Authorities Social Services Act 1970 ('LASSA') to act under the guidance of the Secretary of State. The Secretary of State has issued policy guidance pursuant to LASSA, which local authorities are effectively required to follow.[40] The Secretary of State has also issued other guidance (not pursuant to LASSA) to which local authorities must have regard and deviation from which, may be deemed to be unlawful: see *Rixon*.[41]

---

[40] As per Sedley J in *R v Islington LBC, ex p Rixon* [1998] 1 CCLR 119: 'Parliament by s 7(1) has required local authorities to follow the path chartered by the Secretary of State's guidance, with liberty to deviate from it where the local authority judges on admissible grounds that there is good reason to do so but without the freedom to take a substantially different course.'

[41] In the *Rixon* case Sedley J (as he then was) said, 'What is the meaning and effect of the obligation to "act under the general guidance of the Secretary of State"? clearly guidance is less than direction, and the word "general" emphasises the non-prescriptive nature of what is envisaged. Mr McCarthy, for the local authority, submits that such guidance is no more than one of the many factors to which the local authority is to have regard. Miss Richards submits that, in order to give effect the words "shall ... act", a local authority must follow such guidance unless it has and can articulate a good reason for departing from it. In my judgment Parliament in enacting s 7(1) did not intend local authorities to whom ministerial guidance was given to be free, having considered it, to take it or leave it. Such a construction would put this kind of statutory guidance on a par with the many forms of non-statutory guidance issued by departments of state. While guidance and direction are semantically and legally different things, and while "guidance does not compel any particular decision" (*Laker Airways v Department of Trade* [1977] QB 643, 714 per Roskill LJ), especially when prefaced by the word "general", in my view Parliament by s 7(1) has required local authorities to follow the path charted by the Secretary of State's guidance, with liberty to deviate from it where the local authority judges on admissible grounds that there is good reason to do so, but without freedom to take a substantially different course.'

6.35 As outlined above, s 2(1)(e) of CSDPA 1970 incorporates obligations pertaining to adaptations and additional facilities to a service user's property. The duty, however, is a specific one which arises when an assessment has deemed it necessary for this service to be provided.

6.36 Finally, it has been found to be lawful for a local authority to implement the cheapest option to meet an individual's need when there are two or more alternatives. In *R (McDonald) v Kensington & Chelsea LBC*,[42] the local authority had reduced a care package from £703 to £450 per week. The basis of the reduction was that during the night she required assistance to use a commode, as she needed to urinate frequently due to a bladder condition. It was argued that the needs of the service user could be met by the use of incontinence pads, which were cheaper. The service user argued a breach of her Art 8 right. The High Court held that the local authority was entitled to take the cheaper option so long as it met her needs and that there was no breach of Art 8. On appeal the Court of Appeal held that the authority was 'responsible also for acting on behalf of the interests of all clients whose welfare it supports with limited resources and that its decision to meet the claimant's reassessed need was a reasonable decision'. The claim under Art 8 was dismissed also. The Supreme Court affirmed this decision. A converse approach, however, was applied in the case of *R v Birmingham City Council & Birmingham University*[43] which also surrounded the issue of incontinence pads. In this matter the court held that the defendants had failed to have due regard to the duty under s 49A(1) of the DDA 1995.

Direct payments

6.37 The power under the Community Care (Direct Payment) Act 1996 has since been superseded by the provisions of s 57 and 58 of the Health and Social Care Act 2001. The Community Care, Services for Carers and Children's Services (Direct Payments) (England) Regulations 2003[44] essentially provides that direct payments can only be made to those service users who appear to be capable of managing the payments alone or with assistance. In addition, the local authority must be satisfied that the person's needs for the relevant service can be met by securing the provision of direct payments. Local authorities often determine the amount that a person receives as a direct payment by reference to a Resource Allocation Scheme (RAS). In *R (KM) v Cambridgeshire County Council*,[45] the Supreme Court stated that local authorities must consider what was the reasonable cost of securing provision of the services identified at the assessment stage and that the use of a RAS was lawful as long as the result was cross-checked.

6.38 The recent case of *R v Secretary of State for Health & Others, ex p Harrison* [2009] EWHC 574 confirmed that the NHS had no power to make direct payments under the statutory provisions that govern it. At the time of publication, a further application in this case has been sought to clarify whether the NHS can make indirect payments by transferring funds to social services pursuant to s 256 of the National Health Service Act 2006 ('NHSA 2006').

---

[42] [2011] UKSC 33.
[43] [2009] EWHC 688.
[44] SI 2003/762.
[45] [2012] UKSC 23.

Personalisation and independent living

6.39 The personalisation agenda is a radical re-engineering of the provision of care services. It signals a major change in the paradigm of the relationship between the citizen and the state. At the heart of the model are three concepts, namely: (i) control; (ii) choice of service; and (iii) flexibility of support.

6.40 The above terms have become a catchall phrase, which began its existence as a result of the Green Paper 'Independence, Well-Being and Choice' and the White Paper 'Our Health, Our Care, Our Say'. Further reports crystallised this school of thought in 'Putting People First: a shared commitment to the transformation of adult social care'[46] (2007) and the Local Government Circular (2008) 'Transforming Social Care'.[47] Paras 21 and 26 of the Circular provide:

> 'Reforming social care to achieve personalisation for all will require a huge cultural, transformational and transactional change in all parts of the system, not just in social care, but also for services across the whole of local government and the wider public sector. The scale and purpose of this ambition should not be underestimated. The experience with direct payments makes this clear. For the past ten years, direct payments have successfully given some people the ability to design the services they want but their impact has been very limited. The latest figures show that about 54,000 people out of a potential million recipients receive support through a direct payment. Evidence shows major variations in take up across the country, with success determined less by the characteristics of people who use services or the features of direct payments themselves, than by local leadership, professional culture and the availability of support ...
>
> The purpose of this reform is to ensure people have choice and control over the support they need to live the lives they want. It is necessary to tackle all four together to deliver the Government's aims of better health and better care for people who need treatment and support, as well as better value for taxpayers.'

6.41 The essential principles include:

(a) that service users should have choice and control over the support delivered in a manner that promotes independence, well-being and dignity;

(b) the emphasis of self assessment with social workers acting as 'brokers' and 'advocates' rather than 'gate keepers' of social services;

(c) to promote self-directed support to enable individual arrangements to be designed by the service user; and

(d) that the above transformations are to be implemented by the continuation of direct payments, individual budgets and personal budgets.

6.42 There are some fundamental foundations to the concept of 'personalisation' and 'independent living', namely:

---

[46] Produced by six government departments, namely the local government association, the association of adult social services, the NHS, the representatives of independent sector providers and the commission of social care inspections.
See http://www.dh.gov.uk/en/Publicationsandstatistics/Publications/PublicationsPolicyAndguidance/DH_081118.

[47] http://www.dh.gov.uk/en/publicationsandstatistics/lettersandcirculars/localauthoritycirculars/dh_081934.

(a) The UN Convention on the Rights of Persons with Disabilities,[48] in particular, see Art 19: Living independently and being included in the community which provides that:

> '(a) Persons with disabilities have the opportunity to choose their place of residence and where and with whom they live on an equal basis with others and are not obliged to live in a particular living arrangement;
> (b) Persons with disabilities have access to a range of in-home, residential and other community support services, including personal assistance necessary to support living and inclusion in the community, and to prevent isolation or segregation from the community;
> (c) Community services and facilities for the general population are available on an equal basis to persons with disabilities and are responsive to their needs.'

(b) Section 149(1) and (3) of the Equality Act 2010, which includes the following:

> '(1) A public authority must, in the exercise of its functions, have due regard to the need to—
>
> (a) eliminate discrimination, harassment, victimisation and any other conduct that is prohibited by or under this Act;
> (b) advance equality of opportunity between persons who share a relevant protected characteristic and persons who do not share it;
> (c) foster good relations between persons who share a relevant protected characteristic
>
> (3) Having due regard to the need to advance equality of opportunity between persons who share a relevant protected characteristic and persons who do not share it involves having due regard, in particular, to the need to –
>
> (a) remove or minimise disadvantages suffered by persons who share a relevant protected characteristic that are connected to that characteristic;
> (b) take steps to meet the needs of persons who share a relevant protected characteristic that are different from the needs of persons who do not share it;
> (c) encourage persons who share a relevant protected characteristic to participate in public life or in any other activity in which participation by such persons is disproportionately low.'

(c) Article 8 of the ECHR considerations, in particular the case of *R (A & B) v East Sussex County Council No 2*[49] in which Munby J reinforced the right of a disabled individual to participate in the life of the community and to have what he described as 'access to essential economic and social activities and to an appropriate range of recreational and cultural activities', thereby prevented isolation and being deprived of the possibility of developing a personality.

6.43 The parameters of the personalisation agenda are yet to be known. However, the Government has made it clear in 'A Vision for Adult Social Care' that it is one of seven principles on which its vision for a modern system of social care is based. The Law Commission has highlighted personalisation as being part of its reform agenda although it states that its approach is to create, as far as possible, a neutral legal framework that is not wedded to any particular policy and that is capable of accommodating different policies and practices in the future.

---

[48] See http://www.un.org/disabilities. Ratified by the UK in 2009.
[49] (2003) 6 CCLR 194.

6.44 In *R (S) v Royal Borough of Kensington & Chelsea*[50] the elderly claimant was in receipt of £170.45 per week for her care (assessed in July 2009). In November 2009 she was admitted to hospital and discharged which resulted in a further assessment in December 2009. Despite the assessment noting the claimant's decline in skills the local authority left the payment unchanged. The claimant challenged the methodology for calculating the payments using a formula called 'Resource Allocation System' and that the local authority had failed to give adequate reasons for its decision. The court concluded at para 48 that, '… without being able to properly understand the use made of the RAS, the service user and anyone acting on her behalf, is left totally in the dark as to whether the monetary value of £170.45 is adequate to meet the assessed need of a 28-point score. The process of conversion made by the Panel is not explained to the service user. It should have been underpinned by an evidential base, and it was not.'

6.45 Interestingly, the court rejected the argument that the system failed to discharge the local authority's statutory duty to meet assessed need because it imposed an unlawful cap on the budget. The court stated at para 51 that, 'Personal budgets are new and in many ways represent a fundamental shift in community care. It must be incumbent on those responsible for this provision, to be transparent, and to explain individual decisions in a precise and clear manner. I fail to see how such an obligation would be unduly burdensome.' That decision was upheld by the Court of Appeal in [2010] EWCA Civ 1209 which said that the figure generated by the RAS was a start rather than an end of the process and that 'when a local authority converts an established right – the provision of services to meet an assessed need – into a sum of money, the recipient is entitled to be told how the sum has been calculated.' It also worthy of note that the Audit Commission produced a report in October 2010 'Financial management of personal budgets: challenges and opportunities for councils'.[51] The report provides that personal budgets can promote health and well-being, user satisfaction and opportunities for costs saving (see page 3). The report also observes that only 6% of the social care budget (nationally) is currently being spent through personal budgets and recommends that details of the resource allocation scheme processes are published by local authorities and they should increase provision of information and support for those utilising the scheme.

It should be noted that the Government has sought to close the Independent Living Fund, which has assisted services users to access personalised services. This was successfully challenged in *Stuart Bracking v Secretary of State for Work and Pensions*[52] on the basis that insufficient evidence had been produced to show that had been due regard to the public sector equality duty.[53] At the time of writing, the Government is considering the position.

---

[50] [2010] EWHC 414 (Admin).
[51] See: www.aduit-commission.gov.uk/SiteCollectionDocuments/20101028financialimplicationsofpersonalbudgets.pdf.
[52] [2013] EWCA Civ 1345.
[53] Equality Act 2010, s 149.

PART 2 – SPECIFIC AND SIGNIFICANT AREAS OF COMMUNITY CARE LAW

6.46 Having considered the overview of the community care decision-making process, the following will set out specific areas, which require a detailed analysis in view of their prevalence in community care disputes.

Children

6.47 The community care structure regarding children, to some degree, is very separate from the adult community care system. This is best seen by reference to s 47 of the NHSCCA 1990[54] and ss 21 and 29 of the NAA 1948, both of which only apply to adults.

6.48 The main remit of services pertaining to disabled children is found within Part III of the Children Act 1989[55] ('CA 1989') and Schedule 2 of the CA 1989. Note, however, that in some instances there are community care provisions that apply both to children and adults.[56]

Statutory framework

Section 17 of the Children Act 1989

6.49 Section 17(1) of the CA 1989 imposes on a local authority a broad duty to safeguard and promote the welfare of children in need. It provides that:

> 'It shall be the general duty of every local authority (in addition to other duties imposed on them by this Part) –
>
> (a) to safeguard and promote the welfare of children within their area who are in need; and
> (b) so far as consistent with that duty, to promote the upbringing of such children by their families, by providing a range of level of services appropriate to those children's needs.'

6.50 Section 17(10) defines a child 'in need' in the following manner:[57]

> 'For the purposes of this Part a child shall be taken to be in need if –
>
> (a) he is unlikely to achieve or maintain, or to have the opportunity of achieving or maintaining, a reasonable standard of health or development without the provision for him of services by a local authority under this Part;
> (b) his health or development is likely to be significantly impaired, or further impaired, without the provision for him of such services; or
> (c) he is disabled.'

---

[54] With reference to the duty to assess.
[55] Sections 17–30.
[56] Section 2 of the CSPA 1970, read with s 28A, relates to the system of services to disabled children.
[57] See para 24.7, p 677 of Clements & Thompson, *Community Care & the Law* (LAG, 4th edn), for a detailed analysis of a child in need. They opine that children with Aspergers's Syndrome who have above average IQs could still be defined as disabled children for the purposes of CA 1989 and entitled to services under CSDPA 1970 if an assessment bears out an eligible need. As would children with Attention Deficit Hyperactivity Disorder (ADHD) and Attention Deficit Disorder (ADD).

6.51 Section 17(11) defines 'disabled child' as:

'... a child is disabled if he is blind, deaf or dumb or suffers from mental disorder of any kind or is substantially and permanently handicapped by illness, injury or congenital deformity or such other disability as may be prescribed; and in this Part –

"development" means physical, intellectual, emotional, social or behavioural development; and

"health" means physical or mental health.'

6.52 Section 17 was considered in detail by the House of Lords in *R (G) v Barnet LBC*[58] which confirmed that there is a general duty to provide an appropriate range and level of services.[59] As aptly stated by Mrs Justice Black in *JL* at para 58, the duty, '... does not itself impose a mandatory duty on a local authority to take specific steps to satisfy the assessed needs of a particular individual child in need, regardless of the local authority's resources. A child in need is eligible for the provision of services but has no absolute right to them'. The duty can be described as a 'target duty' rather than a specific law duty.[60] In *R (ES) v Barking & Dagenham LBC*[61] the court confirmed that the effect of the decision in *G* was that a local authority was a duty to take reasonable steps to assess the needs of children in appropriate cases, for instance where there had been a change in circumstances. In *MN v London Borough of Hackney*[62] the court confirmed that s 17 was not engaged until the local authority had determined that a child within its area was 'in need'.

6.53 Local authorities have a power to provide accommodation to children and their families pursuant to s 17(6) of the CA 1989.[63]

Section 20 of the Children Act 1989

6.54 Section 20 of the Children Act 1989 is entitled 'Provision of accommodation for children: general' and provides:

'(1) Every local authority shall provide accommodation for any child in need within their area who appears to them to require accommodation as a result of –[64]
    (a) there being no person who has parental responsibility for him;
    (b) his being lost or having been abandoned; or

---

[58] [2004] 2 AC 208.
[59] This was applied in *R (T, D and B) v Haringey LBC* [2005] EWHC 2235 (Admin) and *Blackburn-Smith v Lambeth LBC* [2007] EWHC 767 (Admin).
[60] However, s 17 (2) and Sch 2 set out specific duties and powers although these duties gave the local authorities a degree of discretion as to provision. See also on this Ouseley J in *R (T) v LB Haringey* [2005] EWHC 223 at para 73.
[61] [2013] EWHC 691 (Admin).
[62] [2013] EWHC 1205 (Admin).
[63] See also the Department of Health, 'The Children Act 1989, Guidance and Regulations, Volume 6, Children with Disabilities', HMSO, 1991, para 3.3.
[64] See *H and others v LB Wandsworth* [2007] EWHC 1082 (Admin) where the court observed that a factual spectrum exists which begins with the undoubted provision of accommodation and ends with matters which are not the provision of accommodation, such as the provision of practical assistance with accommodation. In *JL* the court considered that overnight stays does not fall within the remit of s 20(1). However Black J did say at para 97 that, 'I do not have to go so far as to say that short breaks can never come within that section. That issue would have to be determined if it arose in a particular case'.

(c) the person who has been caring for him being prevented (whether or not permanently, and for whatever reason) from providing him with suitable accommodation or care.[65]

(3) Every local authority shall provide accommodation for any child in need within their area who has reached the age of sixteen and whose welfare the authority consider is likely to be seriously prejudiced if they do not provide him with accommodation.

(4) A local authority may provide accommodation for any child within their area (even though a person who has parental responsibility for him is able to provide him with accommodation) if they consider that do so would safeguard or promote the child's welfare.

(6) Before providing accommodation under this section, a local authority shall, so far as is reasonably practicable and consistent with the child's welfare –
  (a) ascertain the child's wishes and feelings regarding the provision of accommodation; and
  (b) give due consideration (having regard to his age and understanding) to such wishes [and feelings] of the child as they have been able to ascertain.

(7) A local authority may not provide accommodation under this section for any child if any person who –
  (a) has parental responsibility for him; and
  (b) is willing and able to –
     (i) provide accommodation for him; or
     (ii) arrange for accommodation to be provided for him,
  objects ....'

6.55 In *R (FL) v Lambeth LBC*[66] the court helpfully summarised s 20 as follows:

'94. ... Ward LJ in *R(A) v Croydon London Borough Council* [2009] LGR 113 at para 75 set out a series of judgments that arise under s 20. These were adopted by Baroness Hale in *R(G) v Southwark LBC* [2009] 1 WLR 1299 at para 28. Those judgments are:

(i) Is the applicant a child? There is no dispute that she is in this case.
(ii) Is the applicant a child in need? Again no issue in this case, she is.
(iii) Is she within the local authority's area? Again no dispute in this case, she is.
(iv) Does she appear to the local authority to require accommodation? That is in issue.
(v) Is that need the result of: ... (c) the person caring for them being prevented from providing her with suitable accommodation or care? That is in issue.
(vi) What are the child's wishes and feelings regarding the provision of accommodation for her? There is little if any dispute the claimant wants to be accommodated independently from her mother in semi-independent accommodation or similar and does not want to be placed in foster care.
(vii) What consideration (having regard to her age and understanding) is duly to be given to those wishes? That is in issue.
(viii) Does any person with parental responsibility who is willing to provide accommodation for her object to the local authority intervention? Her mother does not object while being content to have her home.
(ix) If there is objection does the person in whose favour a residence order is in force agree to the child being looked after by the local authority? This is not applicable.'

---

[65] In *Barnet* Lord Nicholls said that 'prevented ... for whatever reason' is to be interpreted widely stating 'it includes a case where the person caring for the child is intentionally homeless. A child is not to be visited with the shortcomings of his parents'. In *R (L) v Nottinghamshire CC* [2007] EWHC 2364 Burton J made it clear that he would be inclined to the view that serious ill health on the part of the mother and her inability to control her child would also be sufficient to prevent the mother from providing accommodation. This view was adopted by Baroness Hale in *R (M) v Hammersmith & Fulham LBC* [2008] UKHL 14 when she took the view that the mother may not have been prevented from providing her daughter with any accommodation or care but she was from providing her daughter with 'any suitable' accommodation or care.
[66] [2010] EWHC 49 (Admin).

6.56 The distinct terminology between s 20(1) and 20(4) is clear. Section 20(1) provides that a local authority 'shall' provide for accommodation compared to 'may' under s 20(4). As such, the cases of *A v Croydon*[67] and *R (M) v Gateshead MBC*[68] have established that s 20(1) gives rise to an absolute duty which applies if a child is ordinarily resident in the area and requires accommodation for the reasons set out in the subsection. In *JL* the court concluded at para 71 that s 20(1) did impose an absolute duty on a local authority, and as such, an eligibility criterion could not be used to determine whether it had a duty to act under that section.

6.57 There are, however, a number of conditions that need to be fulfilled before the s 193 duty is triggered. One such provision is that the housing authority is satisfied that the applicant has a priority need, by virtue of Articles 2 and 3 of the Homelessness (Priority Need for Accommodation) England Order 2002 (made under s 189, HA 1996), a person to whom a local authority owes a duty to provide accommodation under s 20 CA 1989 is deemed not to have a priority need. In short, therefore, this means that where s 20 CA 1989 applies, the housing authority does not have a duty to secure accommodation for the child in question.

6.58 It is important to bear in mind the importance of the first two considerations under s 20(1), namely whether any of the three criteria are met under s 20(1) are met,[69] and whether the child 'appears to' the local authority 'to require accommodation' by reason of satisfying one of the three criteria. A local authority is able to conclude that a child does not require accommodation when he or she is sufficiently resourceful to be able to obtain accommodation via support under s 17 of the CA 1989 despite them having no accommodation.[70] It has been held that whilst it is not for the court to substitute its own decision for that of the local authority, the profound impact of a decision under s 20 requires an intense review (see *R (L) v Leeds City Council*[71] and *R (O) v London Borough of Hammersmith and Fulham*[72]).

6.59 Distinct to the above community care duties, a housing authority has obligations and power under the Housing Act 1996 ('HA 1996'). Under s 193 a housing authority has a duty to 'secure that accommodation is available for occupation' where it is 'satisfied that an applicant is homeless, eligible for assistance and has a priority need, and are not satisfied that he became homeless intentionally'. There can be considerable confusion when both a local authority and a housing association/authority provide concurrent services.

6.60 In *R (S) v LB Sutton* [2007] EWCA Civ 790 S lived in a hostel for homeless women and was re-housed (following eviction) by the local authority as a homeless person. It was not disputed that the local authority had failed to assess her needs under CA 1989 and as an alternative to have directed her to contact the housing authority. The local authority accepted that if it had carried out an assessment it would have placed S in the hostel for homeless women under CA 1989. In view of the same, the Court of

---

[67] [2008] EWCA Civ 1445.
[68] [2006] QB 650.
[69] If no criteria is met then there is no duty under s 20(1) as per *R (M) v LB Barnet* [2008] EWHC 2354 (Admin) where the court held that the criteria was not met as her parents were able and willing to provide her with suitable accommodation and care but M did not wish to live with them.
[70] See cases of *R (G) v Southwark LBC* [2008] EWCA Civ 877; *R (A) v Coventry CC* [2009] EWHC 34 (Admin); and [2009] 1 WLR 1299 (appeal of G).
[71] [2010] EWHC 3324 (Admin).
[72] [2011] EWHC 679 (Admin).

Appeal deemed that she had in fact been placed at the hostel, '... in fulfillment of the respondent's obligations under s 20(1)' CA 1989 and had been a 'looked after child'.

6.61 In *R (M) v Hammersmith and Fulham LBC*[73] Baroness Hale stated that the social services authorities owed CA 1989 duties, whilst HA 1996 duties were owed by a housing authority. Thereby, neither department had the power to carry out the other's function. The court equally stressed that the Homelessness Code of Guidance for Local Authorities provided that there was need for joint protocols between a housing authority and social services.

6.62 Finally in the recent decision in *R (MM) v LB Lewisham*,[74] the court considered the local authority's decision that MM did not meet the criteria in s 20 of the CA 1989 because she was housed at a woman's refuge. The refuge referred her to social services, describing her as vulnerable. Social services recommended that MM be referred to a support scheme, however no further action was taken. The court was critical of how social services had handled the referral. It provided that any reasonable local authority acting lawfully would have been bound to conclude that MM required accommodation under s 20 of the CA 1989, given her urgent need for accommodation, health and vulnerability. The court urged local authorities to ensure that '(a) Child in need assessments are not carried out in a summary manner as occurred in this case; (b) that its Housing Department do not simply fail to respond to applications in respect of children; (c) that steps are taken to ensure that the imminence of a child attaining 18 years is not taken as a basis for failing to take any action; and (d) that there is due and proper contact between its housing authority and its Social Services authority.'

Section 2 of the Chronically Sick and Disabled Persons Act 1970[75]

6.63 Section 2 of the CSDPA 1970 creates specific duties to provide certain services to persons who are 'ordinarily resident in the local authorities' area' in order to meet the needs of that person. Section 28A provides that the Act applies with respect to disabled children in relation to whom a local authority has functions under Part III of the CA 1989. As considered above it includes practical assistance in the home and provision of recreational and educational facilities. In *Bexley* the court held that if there was an option of providing services under the CSDPA 1970 or under s 17 of the CA 1989, then the duty under the 1970 Act goes beyond the duty in the 1989 Act because it is a specific duty rather than a target duty. As stated above, once it is deemed that it is necessary to provide services under the CSDPA 1970 the local authority is under an enforceable duty to provide those services.

6.64 Other relevant duties include those under:

(i) Section 23 of the Children Act 1989 (provision of accommodation and maintenance by local authorities for children whom they are looking after).

(ii) Section 22 of the Children Act 1989 (general duty to children looked after by the local authority).

(iii) Section 21 of the Children Act 1989 (provision of accommodation for children in police protection or detention or on remand).

---

[73] [2008] UKHL 14.
[74] [2009] EWHC 416 (Admin).
[75] See para 32(d) above for a general and detailed analysis.

(iv) Section 17A of the Children Act 1989 (as amended by the Health & Social Care Act 2001) (direct payments).

The assessment process

6.65 There is no specific or explicit duty on a local authority to assess under the CA 1989 equivalent to that found in s 47 of the NHSCCA 1990.[76] In *Barnet*, however, the House of Lords has made clear that there is a obligation to assess under the CA 1989, as per Lord Hope at para 77:[77]

> '... The duty of the local authority to take reasonable steps to identify the extent to which there are children in need in their area is to be found in para 1 of the Schedule. That will involve assessing the needs of each child who is found to be in need in their area as para 3 makes clear.'

6.66 The obligation is heavily supported by policy guidance under the 'Framework for the Assessment of Children in Need'[78] ('assessment guidance'). As discussed above, s 7 of the Local Authority Social Services Act 1970 requires local authorities in their social services functions to act under the general guidance of the Secretary of State. See the case of *Rixon* which reinforced that local authorities are bound to follow the guidance unless there is good reason not to.[79]

6.67 The assessment guidance is clearly an important document, of which the following are relevant parts, namely:

(a) social services departments have the lead responsibility for undertaking assessments of children in need [para 4.18];

(b) an 'initial assessment' should be undertaken within a maximum of seven working days of a child being referred to social services [para 3.9] and a 'core assessment' (if necessary after initial assessment) should be undertaken within a maximum of 35 working days [para 3.11];

(c) the direct involvement of the child is fundamental to the process [para 3.4]. It must include 'seeing, observing, talking, doing and engaging' [para 3.42]. 'As part of an initial assessment, the child should be seen. This includes observation and talking with the child in an age appropriate manner' [para 3.10];

(d) exclusive requirements for assessment of groups of vulnerable individuals, ie those who 'require particular care and attention during assessment' [paras 3.58–3.60];[80]

---

[76] See Sch 2 of the CA 1989, however, which does state that an assessment under s 17 may take place at the same time as an assessment under other legislation such as the CSDPA 1980.

[77] Lord Nicholls also stated at para 32 that, 'The first step towards safeguarding and promoting the welfare of a child in need by providing services for him and his family is to identify the child's need for those services. It is implicit in s 17(1) that a local authority will take reasonable steps to assess, for the purposes of the Act, the needs of any child in its area who appears to be in need. Failure to carry out this duty may attract a mandatory order in an appropriate case, as occurred in *R (AB and SB) v Nottinghamshire County Council* (2001) 4 CCLR 295. Richards J ordered a local authority to carry out a full assessment of a child's needs in accordance with the guidance given by the Secretary of State in Framework for the Assessment of Children in Need and their Families (March 2000).'

[78] Department of Health, Department for Education and Employment and Home Office, TSO, 2000.

[79] Para 123 J to K.

[80] They include children whose families 'have a long history of contact with social services'; children in transition; children 'about whom there are concerns that they are becoming or might become involved in prostitution'; and children who are drug users and whose level of use is unknown to family and teachers. Such groups of children require, 'a high degree of cooperation and coordination ... in planning and

(e) the conclusion of the assessment must result in [para 4.1]:
  (i) analysis of needs and parenting capacity to respond to those needs;
  (ii) identification of and whether intervention is required to secure well being of child; and
  (iii) a plan of action (outlining what services are to be provided) detailing who is responsible, a timetable and process of review; and
(f) continuing and review assessment are required under para 1.53, 'assessment should continue throughout a period of intervention'.

6.68 The weight of the guidance has been heavily emphasised by the court. In *R (AB and SB) v Nottingham City Council*[81] Richards J stated that:

> '... it is important, moreover, to be clear about the three-stage process: identification of needs, production of care plan, and provision of identified services. It seems to me that where an authority follows a path that does not involve the preparation of a core assessment as such, it must nevertheless adopt a similarly systematic approach with a view to achievement of the same objectives. Failures to do so without good cause will constitute an impermissible departure from the guidance ....'[82]

6.69 Similarly, in *R (J) v Newham LBC*[83] the court ordered a mandatory order for the local authority to undertake a s 17 assessment within 35 days. Also in *R (LH and MH) v Lambeth*[84] the court concluded that the completed care plan failed to accord with the relevant statutory obligations because it failed to specify adequate support to meet LH's identified needs. The Council's decision that the 'package of support' offered, much of which remains to be identified, was to be preferred to the residential placement was seriously flawed and irrational. Crane J granted a declaration that the defendant was in breach of the Children Act 1989 as supplemented by the Children Act 2004 and the Carers (Recognition of Services) Act 1995.

Leaving care

6.70 The relevant 'leaving care' provisions in the Children Act 1989 were incorporated by the Children (Leaving Care) Act 2000. The rationale behind the implementation derived from a consultation paper produced in 1999.[85] As succinctly put by Clements and Thompson, the main purpose of the Act:

> '... is to help young people who have been looked after by a local authority moved from care into living independently in as stable a fashion as possible. It seeks to promote this aim by amending key provisions of the CA 1989 to place specific duties on social services authorities in respect of "eligible" and "relevant" children.'[86]

---

preparing for assessments, in undertaking and completing them' and 'responsibility for action and providing services must be clearly identified and recorded, with specific timescales'.
[81] (2001) 4 CCLR 294.
[82] Para 306G–I.
[83] [2001] EWHC 992 (Admin).
[84] [2006] EWHC 1190 (Admin). The local authority produced a core assessment and carer's assessment. The social worker recommended that LH should attend a residential school but the placement was not arranged. LH's judicial review application was adjourned pending a further assessment. In the new assessment the social worker concluded that a residential placement was no longer appropriate. Instead, the social worker thought that a 'parenting skills programme' and an adjustment to the respite arrangements would suffice.
[85] 'Me, Survive, Out There? – New Arrangements for Young People Living in and Leaving Care'.
[86] Paragraph 24.23, page 683, *Community Care and the Law* (LAG, 4th edn).

6.71 Leaving care encompasses three differing circumstances, namely:

(i) the 'relevant child' – an individual who is aged 16 or 17 (a child), but who is no longer being looked after by the local authority;

(ii) the 'former relevant child' – an individual who has reached the age of 18 and who, before that date, was either a relevant child, or a 'looked after' child who was also an 'eligible child' immediately before ceasing to be 'looked after'; and

(iii) the 'qualifying child or young person over 16' – an individual who is under 21 and who, when aged 16 or 17, was, but is no longer, looked after, accommodated or fostered.

Eligible and relevant child

6.72 Section 23A of the CA 1989 stipulates that the responsible local authority shall have duties (set out in s 23B) in respect of a relevant child who is aged 16 or 17 and who would have been 'eligible'[87] before last ceasing to be looked after by a local authority.[88]

6.73 A relevant child is a 'looked after child' by virtue of s 22 if:

(a) the child is in the care of the relevant local authorities; or

(b) has been provided with accommodation by the relevant local authority in the exercise of any social service functions excluding those functions under ss 17, 23B and 24B.

6.74 The duties owed to a relevant child are as follows:

(i) Section 23B provides that an assessment of needs and pathway plan should be undertaken by a responsible local authority ('RLA') to safeguard and promote the child's welfare within three months of their 16th birthday. The local authority must support him or her by maintaining him, provide suitable accommodation or by other means unless is it satisfied that his welfare does not require it; and

(ii) Regulation 11 also provides that the RLA 'must provide' assistance to meet the relevant child's needs with regards to education, training or employment as outlined in the pathway plan.

Former relevant child

6.75 A 'former relevant child' is by virtue of s 23C a young person aged 18–21 who has been an eligible child and/or a relevant child. The same section of the Act outlines the duties which exist until the relevant child is 21:

(i) a RLA 'must take reasonable steps' to keep in touch and re-establish contact if it is lost, to continue the appointment of a personal adviser and to continue to keep the young person's pathway plan under regular review; and

---

[87] A is a child aged 16 or 17 who has been looked after by a local authority for a period or periods totalling at least 13 weeks beginning after the age of 14 and continuing after he reached the age of 16.

[88] A further class of relevant children includes those who do not fall within this definition but did not for the sole reason that, on their 16th birthday, they were in penal or hospital detention.

(ii) under s 23C(4)(c) to provide 'other assistance to the extent that his welfare requires it' which can be in kind or, in exceptional circumstances, in cash.[89]

6.76 Under s 23D all eligible, relevant and former relevant children must be provided with a personal advisor who will provide advice, information and support to young persons and keep them informed of their progress and well being. They must also be involved in the assessment of needs and the production of a pathway plan.

Young people over 16 and qualifying children

6.77 Under s 24, advice and assistance is to be provided by a RLA to those who are 'qualifying', namely those who include an individual aged 16 to 20, for whom a special guardianship order was in place or in force when he reached the age of 18 and was looked after until that order was made. Alternatively, it includes a person aged 16 to 20 and whilst aged 16 to 17 was looked after by accommodation[90] or fostering.[91]

6.78 The duties outlined below include a general obligation to keep in touch with care leavers to the extent that is appropriate for the discharge for their functions under ss 24A and 24B. In practice, this duty to 'keep in touch' can last for some time, if not extended over many years.

6.79 Section 24 provides duties of advice and assistance[92] to such individuals and those relating to employment, education and training as outlined above. Specifically, under s 24B there is a duty to contribute to the expenses incurred by him in living near a place of education, training or employment, or to make a grant to enable him to meet expenses connected with his education or training.[93]

Guidance

6.80 Guidance has been provided by the Department of Health[94] to which appropriate weight must be given. Paragraph 11 of Chapter 1 provides:[95]

'The culmination of young people's experience of being looked after by a local authority, private foster carers, a voluntary organisation or in a children's home is a successful return to

---

[89] Section 23C(5).
[90] Subsection 24(2) defines 'accommodated' as accommodated by a voluntary organisation or in a private children's home or, for at least three months, by any health authority or LEA or care home or similar.
[91] 'Fostered' means 'privately fostered'. Those who are fostered by the local authority meet the separate definition of being looked after.
[92] Note that under s 24B, a person who qualifies for advice and assistance also qualifies for help with accommodation during a vacation where he is in full-time further or higher education and his term-time accommodation is not available to him. That duty subsists until the person turns 24 years of age.
[93] Obviously only if his needs require it.
[94] Department of Education and Skills, *Children (Leaving Care) Act 2000 Regulations and Guidance*, 2001.
[95] See guidance for further details. There are also frequent reminders that although a social services department will take the lead, it will need to liaise with other agencies internally and externally: housing and education departments, health authorities, Connexions and the Careers service, Benefits Agency, the Employment Service, Job Centre Plus, Youth Offending Teams and the voluntary sector. Note s 27 of the Children Act 1989, which empowers a local authority to request help in its discharge of these functions from any other local authority and other agencies – such requests must be complied with if they are compatible with the other agency's own duties. There is considerable emphasis on the need for preparation for leaving care, starting well in advance. This is dealt with in Chapter 4 of the guidance. Preparation for leaving care should be incorporated in the care plan for young people as soon as they start to be looked after, accommodated or privately fostered.

their family or the establishment of a stable and positive relationship with another responsible person. Alternatively, where this is necessary, they should be enabled to become as self-supporting as possible.'

6.81 Important aspects of the guidance are as follows:

(i) that young people who qualify for leaving care provision should already have a care plan, which will have been reviewed regularly and updated as part of the process for children who are looked after [chapter 5, para 13];

(ii) the assessment of needs is subject to the detailed requirements of the Regulations;

(iii) regulation 5 provides that the authority is to prepare a written statement in which the needs of each eligible and relevant child will be assessed, including details of those involved, the timetable, how the outcome is to be recorded and the procedure if there is a disagreement;

(iv) regulation 6 states that the RLA is to seek and have regard to the views of the child or young person and to take all reasonable steps to enable him to attend and participate in any meetings;

(v) regulation 7 provides some timescales, namely eligible children must be assessed within three months of turning 16 or otherwise becoming eligible;

(vi) regulation 7 also prescribes a list of matters to be considered;[96]

(vii) that any multi-agency assessment will follow the spirit of the Framework for the Assessment of Children in Need and their Families; and

(viii) insofar as lack of engagement is concerned, the RLA should give clear and specific details of the steps, which it has taken to try to engage with the child and explain why it has not been reasonably practicable to do everything contemplated by the Regulations.

Leaving care decisions and judicial review

6.82 The starting point for any practitioner must be the case of *H v LB of Wandsworth and others*.[97] As fittingly stated by the court at paras 64 and 103:

> '... in certain circumstances, the local authority may consider that what the child requires is not "accommodation" (which would give rise to the duty under s 20(1)), but "help with accommodation", which would not. If they then provide no more than help (eg some limited funding) then neither a duty under s 20(1), nor the statutory consequence of the child becoming a looked after child under s 22(1) arise ... there is clearly a factual spectrum between undoubted provision of accommodation at one end, to mere or incidental help with accommodation at the other. At the first end of the spectrum, a social services department may actually house a person rent-free in accommodation which they actually own. At the other end of the spectrum, they may merely provide practical assistance by introducing a person to a private landlord and perhaps help with completing the necessary documents.'

6.83 The majority of reported cases converge on the actual assessment and pathway plan, and whether the necessary statutory and/or guidance requirements have been

---

[96] These include health and development; support available from family or other relationships; financial needs; practical and other skills; need for education, training or employment; and the needs for care and support and accommodation. Regulation 7 also provides that the RLA must seek and take into account the views of parents and those with PR and carers; school, college or LEA; any independent visitor; healthcare providers; personal adviser; and anyone else with relevant views.

[97] [2007] EWHC 1082 Admin.

satisfied. An example of such a case was *R (P) v Newham LBC* [2004] EWHC 2210 (Admin) where the court held that a RLA had acted unlawfully by failing to provide a personal pathway plan before the severely disabled person in care turned 19 years of age.

6.84 In *R (J) v Caerphilly County Borough Council*[98] a 17-year-old had been in care for four years. He was unwilling to engage with the RLA. His pathway plan ought to have been put into place by September 2003 but not produced until November 2004. The court reinforced the importance of involving the child in the assessment and planning process.[99] Munby J considered it 'wholly unsatisfactory' for the RLA to have produced the plan before discussing or engaging the child. He also found that the assessment and plans were inadequate.

6.85 At para 43 the court said:

> 'The deficiencies in this are all too apparent. Where are the details of the "nature and level of personal support" to be provided to J? Where is the "detailed plan" for J's education and training? Where are the details of the "programme to develop the practical and other skills necessary for [J] to live independently"? Where are the details of the "financial support" to be provided to him? How are his "mental health needs" to be met? Too often, as can be seen, the answer is that the plan is to arrange an appointment with someone else, or to "explore options", or to "develop" a programme. In no case is the "date by which" any of these actions will be carried out specified. Everything is either to be done "ASAP" or is "ongoing". There seems in some instances to be a lack of clarity in distinguishing between the plan and the contingency plan. What are identified in Parts 1, 3 and 5 as aspects of the contingency plan would seem more appropriately to be required as part of the main plan.'

6.86 The court also referred to the case of *R (AB and SB) v Nottingham CC*,[100] in which Richards J emphasised the rigour and detail required of a local authority embarking upon an assessment such as this. At the end of the process, what is needed is a document, as the court put it at paras 20 and 43:

> 'it should be possible to see what help and support the child and family need and which agencies might be best placed to give that help ... it was essentially a descriptive document rather than an assessment, and in any event sufficient detail was still lacking both as regards the assessment itself and as regards the care plan and service provision. There was no clear identification of needs, or what was to be done about them, by whom and by when.'

6.87 In concluding, the court outlined at para 45:

> 'To repeat, because the point is so important, and a clear statement of what is required may assist not merely this but other local authorities: *A pathway plan must clearly identify the child's needs, and what is to be done about them, by whom and by when*. Or, if another aphorism would help, *A pathway plan must spell out who does what, where and when*. As the *Children Leaving Care Act Guidance* makes clear in para 7.7: "The Pathway Plan should be explicit in setting out the objectives and actions needed to achieve these; this should include who is responsible for achieving each action and time-scale for achieving it." I draw attention to and wish to emphasise the word "explicit". At the risk of stating the obvious, the pathway plan here was very far indeed from being explicit.'

---

[98] [2005] EWHC 586 (Admin).
[99] See above stated guidance, particularly para 4 of Chapter 4.
[100] [2001] EWHC Admin 235.

6.88 In *R (C) v LB Lambeth*[101] the court was similarly asked to find that the RLA had failed to discharge their duties in respect of pathway plans. In particular, two criticisms were made without prejudice to the generality: namely (a) there was no timescale provided for addressing her needs and her training and educational needs; and (b) that there was a failure to connect the absence of educational progress with the housing difficulties; and that in itself reflected the associated difficulties, mental health, behavioural and otherwise that this young person had.

6.89 The court (allowing the declarations that the pathway plans failed to comply with the Regulations and mandatory orders requiring the local authority to produce a lawful assessment and pathway plan) concluded that the deficiencies in the process were obvious. In particular, the RLA had embarked on the process too late; the pathway plan should have been completed by September 2003; the steps taken to involve the child in the process were also inadequate; the pathway plans were hopelessly inadequate and contained little more than aspirations; and the RLA used standard pro forma pathway plans which failed to address financial support and would have been better advised to have used the Department of Health's pro forma prepared in 2002; a pathway plan had to clearly identify the child's needs, and what was to be done about them, by whom and by when.

6.90 Finally in *R (O) v Barking and Dagenham London Borough Council*[102] the court considered the question of whether the local authority or NASS was responsible for accommodating an adult who was a 'former relevant child' within the meaning of s 23C of the CA 1989. The claimant was a 19-year-old failed asylum seeker who had made fresh representations to the Secretary of State. No decision had been made in respect of this application, ie whether it amounted to a fresh claim. The local authority had accommodated and supported him as a child under the Children Act 1989 until he reached 18, after which his support was terminated. The local authority accepted that the claimant was a 'former relevant child' within the meaning of s 23C of the 1989 Act, however, the main issue of contention was whether the local authority or NASS was primarily or solely responsible for providing him with accommodation, either until he was removed from the country or until the Secretary of State had reached a conclusion. The local authority argued that: (i) it was prevented by Sch 3 of the Nationality Immigration and Asylum Act 2002 from providing the claimant with leaving care services under the 1989 Act; and (ii) as the claimant would be entitled to hard cases support from NASS under s 4 of the Immigration and Asylum Act 1999, he would not be destitute so as to require support to avoid a breach of his human rights.

6.91 The court held that s 23C(4)(c) of the CA 1989 was not concerned with the provision of accommodation, and a local authority could not use this section to provide accommodation to former relevant children. The only respect in which accommodation may be provided and paid for by a local authority under s 23C for former relevant children is in connection with work or educational needs under s 23C(4)(a) and (b). Accordingly, the claim failed, as the local authority had no duty to provide accommodation to the claimant.

6.92 The Court of Appeal completely disagreed,[103] and concluded that: (i) the judge had erred in holding that the above sub-section did not afford the local authority the power to provide accommodation to a former relevant child (see para 28 of

---

[101] [2008] EWHC 1230 (Admin).
[102] [2010] EWHC 634 (Admin).
[103] [2010] EWCA Civ 1101.

Tomlinson LJ's judgment); and (ii) the local authority is not entitled, when considering whether a formal relevant child's welfare requires that he be accommodated by it, to take into account the possibility of support from NASS.

6.93 This decision impacts on care leavers where young people, for example those seeking asylum or those coming out of custody, are unable to access suitable accommodation through the normal housing routes.

Carers

6.94 Section 8 of the Disabled Persons (Services, Consultation and Representation) Act 1986 provides that: 'Where (a) a disabled person is living at home and receiving a substantial amount of care on a regular basis from another person (who is not a person employed to provide such care by anybody in the exercise of its functions under any enactment), and (b) it falls to the local authority to decide whether the disabled person's needs call for the provision by them of any services for him under any welfare enactment, the local authority shall, in deciding that question, have regard to the ability of that person to continue to provide such care on a regular basis'.

6.95 The Carers (Recognition & Services) Act 1995 provides recognition for carers by requiring the social services authority (if so requested) to carry out a separate assessment of the carer at the same time as it assesses the person for whom the care is provided. The carer can be of any age. As aptly stated by relevant policy guidance:

> '... many young people carry out a level of caring responsibilities which prevents them from enjoying normal social opportunities and from achieving full school attendance. Many young carers with significant caring responsibilities should therefore be seen as children in need ....'[104]

6.96 In order to qualify for an assessment under the Act, a carer must satisfy the following criteria:

- a community care assessment (or reassessment) of the person for who he or she cares must be in the process of being carried out (ie a side by side assessment);
- the carer must be providing (or intending to provide) a substantial amount of care on a regular basis. People who provide care as a result of a contract of employment or as a volunteer placed by a voluntary organisation are excluded; and
- the carer must request a carer's assessment. The guidance, however, requires social workers to 'inform any carer who appears eligible under this Act of their right to request an assessment'.

6.97 The Act entitles qualifying carers to an assessment of their ability to provide and continue to provide care. If, as a result of such an assessment, it transpires that the carer is no longer able (or willing) to provide the same level of care, then the authority will have to decide whether to change the service user's care plan by increasing the level of services provided. Note that practice guidance accompanying the Act states that social workers should not 'assume a willingness by the carer to continue, or to continue to provide the same level of support'.

---

[104] Policy Guidance Letter CI (95), Annex X, para 1.1, adopted under Carers Act 1995.

6.98 Free standing carer's assessments are available under the Carers and Disabled Children's Act 2000, which enables carers of adults in need of community care services, and carers of disabled children (irrespective of whether community care assessment of person cared for is being carried out), to request a carer's assessment which must then be provided.

6.99 Section 1 provides for free standing carer's assessments; that is a carer can be assessed even if the person who s/he cares for refuses a community care assessment. The requirements are that the carer is over 15 years of age, is caring for someone aged 18 or over and the carer requests an assessment. The assessment enables the local authority to decide whether to provide services to the carer under s 2.

6.100 Section 2 enables the local authority to provide services to carers following a carer's assessment. Potentially there is little restriction upon the services that can be made available, provided the service helps 'the carer care for the person cared for'. The explanatory notes to the Act indicate that the services may take the form of physical help, for example assistance around the house, or other forms of support such as training or counselling for the carer.

6.101 Respite/short break care is not, however, a carer's service. This has been explained by the DOH in the following way, '... people who care may be assessed as needing a break from their caring role. This need will be clearly recorded on their own assessment documentation ... [and imperatively] ... *the additional service remains a community care service delivered to the cared for person, not the carer service under the [2000] Act ...*' [emphasis added].

6.102 Section 1 of the Carers (Equal Opportunities) Act 2004 places an obligation on social services authorities to inform carers of the rights to be assessed under the Carers (Recognition & Services) Act 1995 or the Carers & Disabled Children Act 2000. Section 2 requires that in any assessment under either of the above stated Acts that consideration be given as to whether the carer: (i) works or wishes to work; and (ii) is undertaking, or wishes to undertake, education, training or any leisure activity.

6.103 Section 3 aims to facilitate cooperation between local (social services) authorities and other bodies in connection with the authorities' provision of service for carers and the provision by those other bodies of services that may benefit carers. It provides:

- that a local authority may request another authority or health body (PCT etc) to assist it in planning the provision of services to carers and persons being cared for. These other bodies are required to give 'due consideration' to such a request; and
- that where a local authority forms the view that a carer's ability to provide care might be enhanced by the provision of services by another authority or health body it may request that the other body is to provide the service, to which request the other body must give due consideration.

The social care and healthcare overlap

Cooperation

6.104 Unfortunately, given the overlap of statutory provisions, there is an area of confusion that relates to the interplay of services provided by a local authority and the NHS.

6.105 Despite this, however, there are specific obligations upon both the NHS and local authorities to cooperate with each other. Some have already been considered above, others include:

(i) Section 46 of the NHSCCA 1990 which imposes a requirement on local authorities to prepare and keep under review a plan for the provision of community care services in their area. Section 46(2) states that in performing these duties, including the duty to review, the local authority must consult, inter alia, with any Health Authority and Local Health Board.

(ii) Part 3 of the NHSA 2006 combines a number of provisions governing the relationship between local authorities and the NHS. Section 82 states that NHS bodies and local authorities must cooperate with one another in order to secure and advance the health and welfare of the people of England and Wales.

(iii) Section 74 of the NHSA 2006 incorporates Health Authorities, Special Health Authorities and Primary Care Trusts under the Local Authorities (Goods and Services) Act 1970. Section 74(3) provides that each local authority must make services available to each NHS body acting in its area, so far as is reasonably necessary and practicable to enable the NHS body to discharge its functions under this Act.

(iv) Section 75 and the NHS Bodies and Local Authority Partnership Arrangements Regulations 2000 empowers NHS bodies and local authorities to engage in a partnership arrangements including pooled fund arrangements and the delegation of functions by local authorities to NHS bodies and vice versa.

Division between social care and medical care services

6.106 In *R v North and East Devon Health Authority, ex p Coughlan*,[105] the Court of Appcal acceded to the argument that there are circumstances in which a local authority may have the responsibility for providing nursing care for a chronically sick patient as part of its role as a social service provider. A local authority has no responsibility to provide medical care.

6.107 In *R (D and another) v Haringey London Borough Council* [2005] EWHC 2235 the court considered the scope of s 17 and Sch 2 of the Children Act 1989 and of ss 2 and 28A of the CSDPA 1970. The court accepted and highlighted the distinction between health and social care provisions and concluded that whilst s 2 of the CSDPA makes a provision for a local authority to provide 'practical assistance' in the home, it could not extend to the provision of day or night respite care provided by a nurse.

6.108 In establishing the same the court identified a number of relevant factors, namely:

(a) the question whether the care is incidental or ancillary to the provision of some other service which a social services authority is lawfully providing the scale and type of care;

(b) whether or not the service is of a nature which such authority can be expected to provide;

(c) the gravity of the consequences of a failure in care; the duration of the care need; whether the care is incidental to or arises out of other medical treatment; and

---

[105] [1999] All ER (D) 801.

(d) the nature of the training an individual needs to provide the care.

6.109 This approach may be contrasted, however, with the Court of Appeal's broader interpretation of s 21(5) of the NAA 1948 at para 27 of *Coughlan*.

Can a local authority provide healthcare provision?

6.110 There are some statutory bars to the provision of care services by local authorities.

6.111 Section 21(8) of the NAA 1948 applies to the provision of accommodation under s 21(1). Services in connection with accommodation can include nursing services, *Coughlan*.[106] A local authority cannot provide services, which are authorised or required to be provided under the NHS Act 2006.

6.112 Section 29(6) of the NAA 1948 applies to the making of arrangements under s 29(1) for promoting the welfare of adults who are blind, deaf, dumb, or suffer from mental disorder or are substantially and permanently handicapped by illness, injury or congenital deformity or other prescribed disabilities. Section 29(6) makes it unlawful for a local authority to provide accommodation or services pursuant to such arrangements where that accommodation or services is required to be provided under the NHS Act 2006 or to be provided by or under any other enactment; it is not sufficient that provision of the accommodation or services is merely authorised under the NHS Act 2006.

6.113 Finally, s 49(1) of the Health and Social Care Act 2001 makes it unlawful for a local authority to provide or arrange for any person to be provided with nursing care by a registered nurse in connection with the provision of community care services. Interestingly, s 49(2) defines nursing care by a registered nurse so as to exclude services which, although provided by a registered nurse, do not need to be provided by a registered nurse, having regard to their nature and the circumstances in which they are provided.

6.114 However, although these statutory bars are potentially far-reaching, it is important to recognise their limits. Thus, where s 21(8) of the NAA 1948 applies it only applies to bar a local authority from providing accommodation and services in connection with accommodation under s 21(1) and 21(5) of the NAA 1948. Likewise s 29(6) only bars a local authority from providing accommodation and services under s 29(1). These provisions do not prevent the local authority from providing other care to an individual under other community care powers such as s 254 and Sch 20 of the NHSA 2006; nor do they exclude the local authority's duties to do so. The fact that an individual is receiving some types of care from an NHS body does not mean that the local authority can assume that all types of care that are needed by that individual are being met or should be met by that NHS body.

Section 117 after care service

6.115 Duties under the MHA 1983 are a perfect example of the joint working cooperation between the NHS and a local authority. Section 117 of the Act places a duty jointly on Primary Care Trusts and social services authorities, in cooperation with

---

[106] Para 27(c).

relevant voluntary agencies, to provide after-care services for patients who have been detained in hospital for treatment under s 3, under a s 37 hospital order, under a s 45A hospital direction or after transfer from a prison under sections 47 or 48 of the MHA 1983.

6.116 The duty is triggered when the patient comes to an end of the detention and leaves hospital and continues until the health and local social services authorities are content that the patient is no longer in need of those services.[107] The House of Lords in the case of *R v Secretary of State for the Home Department, ex p H* [2003] UKHL 59 held that:

> 'The duty of the health authority, was not absolute, whether it arose under s 117 of the 1983 Act or in response to the tribunal's order. The authorities had to use their best endeavours to procure compliance with the conditions laid down by the tribunal.'

6.117 Section 117 after care services are community care services as outlined at s 46 of the NHSCCA 1990. The assessment obligations under s 47 apply, and the services can include home care, residential care, social work support in helping patients with employment, relationships, accommodation, provision of domiciliary services, use of day centres and residential facilities. With regards to which authorities are responsible, in *R v Mental Health Review Tribunal, ex p Hall* Scott Baker LJ held that:

> 'For the purposes of s 117 of the 1983 Act, the relevant health and social services authorities were those for this area where the patient was ordinarily resident at the time of his detention, unless he had no place of residence. In the latter case, the relevant authorities would be those of the area where the patient was sent on discharge, but the placing authority where the patient resided did not cease to be the appropriate local social services authority by virtue of the fact that he was sent to a different authority on discharge.'

6.118 In *R (MM) v Greenwich LBC & Bromley LBC* [2010] EWHC 1462 (Admin) the court clarified the extent of this duty in the following manner:

> '61. Section 117 requires the relevant authorities to provide a patient on discharge from s 3 with "after-care services". "After-care services" are not defined in the statute ....
>
> 63. In relation to the scope of s 117 services, the respected commentary on the 1983 Act by Richard Jones says (Mental Health Act Manual, 12th Edition, at para 1-1053):
>
>> "It is suggested that an after-care service is a service which is (1) provided in order to meet an assessed need that arises from a person's mental disorder; and (2) aimed at reducing that person's chance of being re-admitted to hospital for treatment for that disorder."
>
> 64. ... The duty derives from a provision in mental health legislation; and it is described as a duty to provide "after-care services". As Ms Richards submitted, s 117 is not concerned with the provision of support and accommodation at large, but rather with the provision, to the specified category of patients who have been detained on account of their mental disorder, of services tailored to meet needs arising from that disorder. An after-care service must, in my judgment, be a service that is necessary to meet a need arising from a person's mental disorder.

---

[107] Section 117(2) of the MHA 1983 provides that the relevant bodies will not be satisfied in the case of a community patient while he remains a patient.

...

66. That, it seems to me, is the principle. In practice, the assessment of needs that do arise from a mental disorder may of course give rise to difficult issues. It is for the relevant authorities – the local authority and the health authority – to reach their own view as to what need the person has, and, in making an assessment under s 47 of the 1990 Act, they enjoy a discretion as to what if any services are required to meet such needs. As Lord Phillips MR said in *R (K) v Camden and Islington Health Authority* [2001] EWCA Civ 240 at [29]:

> "The nature and extent of those [after-care] facilities must, to a degree, fall within the discretion of the [authorities] which must have regard to other demands in [their] budget."

The reference to "nature", as well as "extent", of the services in my view emphasises both the potential broad scope of s 117 and the wide discretion of the authorities within that scope. The recognition of this discretion, given to the authorities by Parliament, appears to me to be vital.

...

68. I consider that my construction of the s 117 – restricting its scope to services necessary to meet a need arising from a person's mental disorder – is generally supported by those authorities. In *Clunis v Camden and Islington Health Authority* [1998] 3 All ER 180, Beldam LJ, after noting that the term is not defined in the 1983 Act, said of "after-care services" (at page 191E–F):

> "They would normally include social work, support in helping the ex-patient with problems of employment, accommodation or family relationships, the provision of domiciliary services and the use of day centre and residential facilities. No doubt some assessment of the patient's needs would in the first instance be made by the hospital that discharged him."

69. In *Richmond Borough Council v Watson* [2000] EWCA Civ 239, Otton LJ (quoting Beldam LJ from that earlier case) said:

> "[T]he words 'after-care services' in [the 1983 Act] can include residential accommodation which is specifically designed to care for the needs of persons who have been detained under s 3 and who have left hospital."

...

70. When that case proceeded to the House of Lords (as *R (Stennett) v Manchester City Council* [2002] UKHL 34), Lord Steyn, again having quoted Beldam LJ in *Clunis*, commented that "caring residential accommodation ... (ensuring, for example, that prescribed medication is taken)" fell within the scope of after-care services, and indeed that appears to have been common ground by then (see [9] and [15]). He too referred to residential accommodation being available under s 21 (at [7]).

71. These authorities do not directly deal with bare accommodation – but they are at least consistent with the construction I consider correct. Indeed, although on their facts they all concern "accommodation plus", they appear particularly careful not to include mere accommodation in their comments; and there are several references to the residual power to accommodate in s 21.

...

75. In addition to authority, I consider that the construction of s 117 I favour is supported by the following.

76. First, relevant government guidance indicates that, in the view of the respective departments, services under s 117 are designed to meet needs that are related to the former patient's mental disorder. In relation to England, the Department of Health's guidance, The National Framework for NHS Continuing Healthcare and NHS-funded Nursing Care (July 2009) states, at para 116, that:

> "... [A] person in receipt of after-care services under s 117 may also have needs for continuing care that are not related to their mental disorder and that may, therefore, not fall within the scope of s 117."

So far as Wales is concerned, there is in substance the adoption of Mr Jones' suggested construction of s 117. The Welsh Assembly Government's Code of Practice for Wales, at para 3.12, provides:

> "After-care services are provided to meet an assessed need arising from the patient's mental disorder and are aimed at reducing the likelihood of the patient being readmitted to hospital for treatment for that disorder."

77. Second, local authorities cannot charge for services provided under s 117 (*Stennett*). That is a reflection of the nature of the services that are required to be provided under that provision, ie services provided to particularly vulnerable people particularly to cover the aspired transition from s 3 detention to living in the community by providing services to satisfy needs deriving from the mental disorder in respect of which they had been detained. Of course, in some cases, that might be a long-term requirement. However, it simply cannot have been the intention of Parliament to have required local authorities (let alone health authorities), free of charge, to provide a roof over the head of former s 3 patients so long as they simply required housing.

78. Third, as the legal authorities remark, even if mere housing is not available under s 117, there is provision for former patients to obtain ordinary housing, under s 21. Although a residual duty, s 21 seems to me a far more appropriate vehicle for requiring authorities to provide mere housing, than the provisions relating to mental health.

79. For all of those reasons, I consider that an authority's responsibility to provide services under s 117 is restricted to those services necessary to meet a need arising from a person's mental disorder.'

6.119 Note the recent case of *R (JM) v London Borough of Hammersmith & Fulham; and R (Hertfordshire CC) v London Borough of Hammersmith & Fulham*.[108] There the court considered the question of which local authority was responsible for meeting the accommodation costs of an individual detained under s 3 of the Mental Health Act 1983 who is then discharged back into the community. The issue focused on the apparent difference between the use of the word 'resident' in s 117(3) as compared to the words 'ordinarily resident' in ss 21 and 24 of the National Assistance 1948 Act. Mitting J concluded that there was no perceptible difference between the three phrases, 'resident', 'ordinarily resident' and 'normally resident'. All three connoted settled presence in a particular place other than under compulsion.

---

[108] [2010] EWHC 562 (Admin).

In *R (Sunderland City Council) v South Tyneside Council*[109] the Court of Appeal confirmed that determining where a person was resident for the purposes of s 117 was a question of determining the place where the person had in fact resided, as long as that place was voluntarily accepted by him. In the absence of voluntary acceptance, it may be that a person is found to be ordinarily resident in a place that they do not actually live in. For instance, in *R (Cornwall Council) v Wiltshire Council*[110] it was held that because an adult only had the capacity of small child it was location of his parents that was determinative of the question of ordinary residence, following *R v Waltham Forest LBC ex p Vale*.[111]

Analysis

6.120 This is a heavily commented area. Of particular interest, Clements and Bowen[112] have argued that where a person's needs as assessed by the social services authority are not being met fully by the NHS, either in terms of the nature or the quantity of the service provided, the social services authority may then be under a duty to address this deficit. They identify three situations in which this problem might arise: where an NHS body refuses to provide the relevant service because of a lack of financial resources; because of a lack of physical or human resources; or where the NHS body assesses the person's needs differently. The third possibility is when the local authority identified a need for more extensive respite care than the Primary Care Trust believed to be necessary or was willing to provide.

6.121 Commonly, however, it is believed that it is in the service user's best interest to be found eligible for NHS support provisions given that it is free at the point of source. Nevertheless, it is important to bear in mind that those found eligible for residential services under NAA 1948 or for residential home based care under CSDPA 1970 are entitled to enforce those duties in judicial review proceedings. This is significant when compared to the duty to provide NHS services under the NHSA 2006, which is a target duty which a Court will not enforce compared to the individually enforceable duties under the NAA or CSDPA.

Community care support for asylum seekers and migrants

6.122 Recently a number of reports have highlighted that certain improvements are required in the legislative framework relating to asylum seekers and their recourse to community care and housing services. The report entitled 'Deserving Dignity' prepared by the Independent Asylum Commission (2008) criticised the policy of destitution as a lever to encourage return and sought the end of detention of child and age-disputed young persons. 'Improving the care of unaccompanied asylum seeking children' (January 2008) investigated alternatives to the detention of children and presented a code of practice. In June 2008 the report prepared by the UK Commissioners to the UN Committee on the Rights of the Child (report on UK children's rights record) stressed the poor treatment of some of the UK's most vulnerable children, which it concluded was in clear breach of the UN Convention on the Rights of the Child.

---

[109] [2012] EWCA Civ 1232.
[110] [2012] EWHC 3739 (Admin).
[111] (1985) *The Times*, 25 February.
[112] *NHS continuing care and independent living: the law reviewed*, Legal Action, June 2007, pp 39–42.

6.123 It is quite understandable, therefore, that this specific area has been at the forefront of socio-political and legal debate.

Statutory framework

6.124 The basic provisions are as follows:

(i) to recap, under s 21 of the NAA 1948 a local authority is to make arrangements for providing residential accommodation for reasons of age, illness, disability or any other reason which makes them a person in need of care and attention. Subs 1A specifically provides that:

> '(1A) A person to whom s 115 of the Immigration and Asylum Act 1999 (exclusion from benefits) applies may not be provided with residential accommodation under subsection (1)(a) if his need for care and attention has arisen solely –
>
> (a) because he is destitute; or
> (b) because of the physical effects, or anticipated physical effects, of his being destitute.'

(ii) section 95 of the Immigration and Asylum Act 1999 ('IAA 1999') transfers responsibility for providing support to asylum seekers from local authorities to the Secretary of State for the Home Department ('SSHD'). By s 94(3), a claim for asylum shall be treated for the purposes of s 94(1) as having been determined at the end of such period as may be prescribed, beginning with the date on which the SSHD notifies the claimant of her decision on the claim, or, if the claimant appeals against the SSHD's decision, the date on which the appeal if disposed of. By s 95(1)(a), the SSHD may provide, or arrange for the provision of, support for asylum seekers who appear to the SSHD to be destitute. A person is 'destitute' for the purposes of s 95(1)(a) if he does not have, and cannot obtain, both adequate accommodation and food and other essential items. By s 98, the SSHD may provide or arrange for the provision of support for asylum seekers who it appears to the SSHD may be destitute. Support under this section may only be provided until the Secretary of State is able to determine whether support may be provided under s 95; and

(iii) schedule 3, para 1(1) of the Nationality, Immigration and Asylum Act 2002 ('NIAA 2002') states:

> 'The person to whom this paragraph applies shall not be eligible for support or assistance under ...
>
> (a) s 21 or 29 of the National Assistance Act 1948 ...,
> (g) s 17, 23C, 24A or 24B of the Children Act 1989 ...,
> (j) s 188(3) or 204(4) of the Housing Act 1996 ...,
> (k) s 2 of the Local Government Act 2000,
> (l) a provision of the Immigration and Asylum Act 1999.'

Paragraph 3 provides for an exception where support is necessary to prevent a breach of the individual's Convention rights. Paragraph 6 is headed 'Third class of ineligible person: failed asylum-seeker' and provides that a person is not eligible for support or assistance if: '(a) he was (but is no longer) an asylum seeker, and (b) he fails to cooperate with the removal directions issued in respect of him'. Para 7 is headed 'Fourth class of ineligible person: person unlawfully in UK' and provides that a person is within para 1 if: (a) he is in the UK in breach of the immigration laws within the meaning of s 11, and (b) he is not an asylum-seeker. By s 11 of the same Act a person is in the UK in breach of the immigration laws if (and only if) he: (a) is in the UK, and (b) does not have the right of abode, (c) nor have leave to enter or remain, nor benefit from any of the specific listed exemptions.

Section 21 support

6.125 The best starting point is the case of *R (M) v Slough BC*[113] which related to a Zimbabwean national who was HIV positive. He had overstayed on his visa and alleged that in view of his medical condition, and the lack of treatment in Zimbabwe, to return him would infringe his rights under Art 3 of the ECHR. He also sought accommodation from the local authority and argued that there was no immediate risk to him provided that he complied with his healthcare regime and that his accommodation needed refrigeration for his medication. The House of Lords held that his needs did not bring him within the scope of s 21(1)(a) 'as a person who is in need of care and attention not otherwise available to him'. In doing so, the court emphasised that a natural and ordinary meaning of 'care and attention' was required, which meant doing something which the person could not, or should not, be expected to do for himself. The need, therefore, for a refrigerator for the keeping of medication was not a need for 'care and attention' in that sense.

6.126 Baroness Hale stated[114] that:

> 'Although the respondent is HIV positive, his medical needs are being catered for by the National Health Service. So even if they did amount to a "need for care and attention" within the meaning of s 21(1)(a) he would not qualify. But for the reasons given above, I do not think that they do amount to such a need. There may of course come a time when they do, but people with the virus can now live normal lives for many years and we must hope that the respondent is able to do so. As he does not fall within s 21(1)(a) it is unnecessary to decide whether he would be excluded by s 21(1A). Unless and until one knows what care and attention a claimant needs, one cannot sensibly ask whether his need for it arises solely from destitution or its actual or anticipated effects.'

6.127 Post M, in *R (N) v Coventry City Council*[115] the court refused his application for judicial review and rejected the claimant's argument that the local authority should carry out an assessment under s 47 of the services which *would be* available in South Africa. The court clearly held that the authority was only required to assess what services it might provide,[116] as such, the local authority's assessments were deemed to be lawful in the light of the approach in *M*. At para 51 the court emphasised that even if the assessments had been wrong, in the light of the failure of the asylum claim, and the possibility of a return to South Africa, support would not have been necessary to avoid

---

[113] [2008] UKHL 52.
[114] Paragaph 36.
[115] [2008] EWHC 2786 (Admin). The claimant was a South African who was HIV positive and suffered from cognitive disturbance. He claimed asylum and while waiting for his claim to be decided, he applied to a local authority for support under s 21 assistance. His medical condition was stable and he had family help. The authority assessed his needs under s 47 of the NHSCA 1990, and decided that he was not in need of care and attention. His asylum claim was then refused. The authority then decided that, in accordance with para 3 of Sch 3 to the NIAA 2002 it was not necessary to provide him with assistance in order to avoid a breach of his Convention rights since he could return to South Africa.
[116] Paragraph 39 of the judgment.

a breach of Convention rights, in the light of the defendant's undertaking to assist him in obtaining a free flight there, and to accommodate him for 21 days while arrangements for his return were made.

6.128 *R v Lewisham LBC, ex p Pajaziti*[117] involved an asylum seeker who was in receipt of support from the National Asylum Support Service ('NASS') (on the condition of dispersal). He requested that he remain in London on health grounds. NASS declined to support him. He then sought NAA 1948, s 21 support from the local authority and relied upon medical evidence stating that both he and his wife suffered major depressive episodes and that the most powerful intervention would be to accommodate them in London. The Court of Appeal provided that the essential question was whether need for care and attention by the provision of residential accommodation was made more acute by virtue of the psychiatric disorder. As the claimants were ill, the crucial question was whether their need for that separate head of care and attention was made more acute by the depressive disorder and the fact that, absent any NAA 1948, s 21 assistance, they would have had to cope with that disorder on the streets. The authority had not answered that question, and it followed that its decision was materially flawed.

6.129 In *R v Leeds CC, ex p Gnezele; R (Dayina) v Leeds CC*[118] both individuals who were refused asylum were pregnant and nursing mothers. They sought NAA 1948, s 21 support. The court concluded that they were not entitled to such support and were only permitted to care and attention due to destitution, not due to being expectant or nursing mothers. Further guidance on the correct approach to NAA 1948, s 21 was provided by the Supreme Court in *SL v Westminster City Council*.[119] In that case it was held that a failed asylum seeker was not 'in need of care and attention' for the purposes of NAA 1948, s 21. In *SL* the court also commented on the guidance given in *M v Slough BC* and noted that it would be unwise to interpret the guidance in the *M* case as a compendious statement of all the elements of the 'care and attention' or 'looking after' concepts as those words were merely illustrative. What amounts to providing care and attention is informed by the duty to provide residential accommodation. It could not be confined to care and attention that could *only* be delivered in residential accommodation, but the fact that accommodation had to be provided for those who were deemed to need care and attention strongly indicated that something well beyond mere monitoring of an individual's condition was required.

Unaccompanied asylum-seeking children

6.130 Unaccompanied asylum seeking children ('UASCs') present a real and practical problem to local authorities. Of paramount obvious importance is the age of a person who claims to be a UASC. If under the age of 18, the local authority will potentially owe him or her a range of obligations under the CA 1989. Otherwise (if over the age of 18) the responsibility falls to the Home Office ('HO'). The United Kingdom Border Agency and the Association of Directors of Social Services have developed an 'Age Assessment Joint Protocol' in which it is explicit that local authorities (rather than the HO) will make age assessment decisions.

6.131 As one can imagine, age assessment decisions are extremely difficult. Relevant decisions include:

---

[117] [2007] EWCA Civ 1351.
[118] [2007] EWHC 3275 (Admin).
[119] [2013] UKSC 27.

(i) R (A) v Croydon London Borough Council.[120]

Claimants were young individuals who claimed to be children from abroad. The local authority rejected those claims. On an application for judicial review the court upheld the local authorities' decisions. The Court of Appeal also upheld the decision.

The Court of Appeal concluded that the age of a young person is a question for the local authority within the parameters of review on *Wednesbury* unreasonable grounds, it is not for the court to make a decision upon. The court held that it was necessary to read the following words (in italics) into s 20, namely that '*Every local authority shall provide accommodation for any person whom the local authority have reasonable grounds for believing to be a* child in need'.[121] It was for the local authority to make that decision as stated above. Finally, the court concluded that if s 20 of CA 1989 provided a right to accommodation, which was a civil right (for the purposes of Article 6 of the ECHR), supervision by the court on judicial review grounds complied with Article 6.

(ii) R (A (by his litigation friend Valbona Mejzninin)) v Croydon London Borough Council.[122]

This case related to a dispute relating to the significance of a report by an expert consultant pediatrician. The local authority rejected the report for reasons, which the court concluded, lacked cogency and were unsound. The local authority put forward the contention that such reports were not helpful as they *could only* indicate the general range of age. The court emphasised the fact that the defendant was required to individual consideration to the report and clearly explain (based on its contents) the reasons for the rejection.

(iii) R (Liverpool City Council) v Hillingdon London Borough Council.[123]

This case surrounded a dispute between two local authorities as to which authority was responsible for a failed asylum seeker who claimed to be a child. The claimant was assessed as being an adult, however, in the course of an asylum appeal the AIT assessed his age as 15 years. He moved between two detention centres. There was an agreement that there would be a re-assessment of the failed asylum seeker's age, pursuant to the Joint Protocol, however, neither could agree who ought to be responsible for carrying it out. The claimant applied for judicial review, and at first instance, the court held that the claimant was responsible for the individual. The claimant appealed. The court outlined a number of issues pertaining to the character of such an assessment to be carried out by a local authority under s 20. Lord Justice Dyson considered that in some situations (although not on this appeal) it is possible for two authorities to owe concurrent duties to a child.[124]

(iv) R(A) v Croydon LBC and R(WK) v SSHD & Kent CC.[125]

The conjoined applications sought to judicially review the decision of the local authority that they were over the age of 18. Both had been examined by medical experts who considered them to be under 18. Despite the same, the local authority did not change its initial decision. The key points in the judgment were:

---

[120] [2008] EWCA Civ 1445.
[121] Paragraph 30 of the judgment.
[122] [2008] EWHC 2921 (Admin).
[123] [2009] EWCA Civ 31.
[124] Paragraphs 44 and 45 of the judgment.
[125] [2009] EWHC 939 (Admin).

- the decision on age is one for the local authority's age assessors;[126]
- paediatric reports are not trump cards and that paediatricians are no better placed than social workers to assess age;[127]
- the decision of Stephen Morris QC to that effect in *R(A) v Croydon LBC*[128] last December was wrong;[129] and
- all other cases should now proceed. Collins J made an express order that all age dispute claims should progress on the law as it currently stands (ie applying his judgment and the Court of Appeal's judgment in *A v Croydon; M v Lambeth*[130]). The court also made an order that claimants in such cases should not be removed from the UK pending the outcome of the Supreme Court appeal in *A v Croydon; M v Lambeth* (considered below). He also observed that a similar order or undertaking should be made in relation to the age dispute cases which have been issued.

(v) *R (A) v Croydon LBC & one other action; R(M) v Lambeth LBC & one other action* [2009] UKSC 8.

As above, A and M were both unaccompanied asylum seeking children who disputed their respective local authorities' decision that they were 18 or over. The claimants were unsuccessful at the Administrative Court and the Court of Appeal.

The Supreme Court held unanimously that where there is a dispute about a young person's age between a local social services authority and a young person seeking assistance under the Children Act 1989 (as is common with unaccompanied young asylum seekers) the Administrative Court should decide the case on the balance of probabilities. This means the Administrative Court will no longer ask 'was the local authority's decision reasonable?' but 'was the local authority's decision correct?'

The court accepted the argument of M (in the case of *M v Lambeth*) that, as a matter of construction of s 20 of the Children Act 1989, whether a person is a child is a question which must be objectively decided. In addition, the court found it unnecessary to decide, A's contention (in *A v Croydon*), that traditional judicial review was inadequate for the purposes of Art 6 of the ECHR on the grounds that accommodation under s 20 was a civil right and social workers were not independent and impartial.

---

[126] See para 21, 'The evidence from Croydon and Kent and ... Cambridgeshire show that ... those responsible can be trusted to carry out their tasks properly so that the authorities and the Home Office can rely on their conclusions'.

[127] See para 47, 'No paediatrician other than the very few prepared to produce reports for claimants will agree to become involved and ... a medical view is not likely to be any more reliable or helpful than that formed by a properly trained and experienced social worker. Nor is it the case that opinions obtained from Drs Michie and Birch can be regarded as reliable'; paras 34 and 35, 'It is for them [LAs & SSHD] to decide how much weight to attach to such a report and it is in a given case open to the decision-maker to attach no weight. I would expect that only in rare cases would such a report persuade the decision-maker to reach a different view'; para 75, 'Thus Kent and so the Secretary of State are entitled to attach little if any weight to reports which make assessments based to a significant degree on a contradictory [to their own] findings'; and para 25, 'It is Dr Stern's view that a paediatrician is unlikely to be able to reach a conclusion which is superior to that reached by an experienced social worker, provided, of course, that the social worker is properly trained and experienced and conducted the necessary interview in an appropriate fashion'.

[128] [2008] EWHC 2921 (Admin).

[129] See para 47, 'I do not accept that the approach adopted by Mr Morris was correct (para 6). There is no obligation on the authority to obtain medical advice [in order to disagree with a medical report on age]'.

[130] [2008] EWCA Civ 1445.

In practice, the judgment means that age dispute cases will become trials of fact with witness examination. This is a distinct digression from the usual position that the Administrative Court is the not suitable arena to resolve factual disputes.[131] As stated by Lady Hale at para 33:

> 'The final arguments raised against such a conclusion are of a practical kind. The only remedy available is judicial review and this is not well suited to the determination of disputed questions of fact. This is true but it can be so adapted if the needs arises: see *R (Wilkinson) v Broadmoor Special Hospital Authority*.[132] That the remedy is judicial review does not dictate the issue for the court to decide or the way in which it should do so, as the cases on jurisdictional fact illustrate. Clearly, as those cases also illustrate, the public authority, whether the children's services authority or the UK Border Agency, has to make its own determination in the first instance and it is only if this remains disputed that the court may have to intervene. But the better the quality of the initial decision-making, the less likely it is that the court will come to any different decision upon the evidence.'

(vi) Post *Croydon*, in *R (PM) v Hertfordshire CC*,[133] the claimant who was an asylum seeker applied for judicial review of a decision of the defendant local authority to withdraw accommodation and support that it had provided under s 20 of the Children Act 1989. The claimant asserted that he was 14 years of age and the local authority had initially considered that it was more likely than not that PM was a child, and accordingly provided him with accommodation and support. The Secretary of State refused PM's asylum claim, finding that he had fabricated his age to strengthen his claim. PM appealed to the First-tier Tribunal Immigration and Asylum Chamber, which rejected his appeal, holding that he was over 18. The local authority considered that it had to respect the tribunal's decision and so withdrew its support for M on the basis that he was over 18.

Higginbottom J concluded that:

(1) The tribunal's conclusion that PM was an adult was not binding on all, and that under Part 5 of the Nationality, Immigration and Asylum Act 2002, the tribunal had no primary jurisdiction to determine age;

(2) The local authority could not simply adopt the tribunal's finding as to age. The 1989 Act places a burden upon local authorities to assess the age of young people who may be under 18 years old, and who may therefore be entitled to s 20 support. The local authority was not bound by the tribunal's finding. Before ceasing support under the 1989 Act, they were obliged to review their earlier age assessment, taking account of:
  (a) Any evidence as to age that may have been put before the tribunal that was not previously put before the local authority; and
  (b) The tribunal judge's reasoning and process by which he came to the conclusion that the claimant was an adult.

---

[131] This proposition has been made plain in case-law, namely in *R v Horsham DC, ex p Wenman* [1995] 1 WLR 680 at 709G, '... judicial review proceedings are wholly inappropriate as the forum for the resolution of issues of disputed facts ...' and *R v West Sussex County Council, ex p Wenman* (1993) 5 Admin LR 145 at 154BA–B, '... [judicial review] is not appropriate for he kind of fact finding exercise on disputed facts that a court at first instance, or a statutory body with statutory responsibilities to investigate facts, is equipped to perform ...' It is equally trite that the court has (on some occasions) acceded to resolve factual disputes when it inhibits a correct legal conclusion, *R (Corner House Research) v Director of Serious Fraud* [2008] EWHC 714 (Admin) at [8] or when the resolution is crucial to the case, *R v SOSDE, ex p LBI* [1997] JR 21 at 127.

[132] [2004] EWCA Civ 1545, [2002] 1 WLR 419.

[133] [2010] EWHC 2056 (Admin).

(3) Under the 1989 Act, the local authority had been bound substantively to review its earlier age assessment, taking account of the tribunal's determination in a limited manner, before ceasing support.

This case is interesting. Whilst the Secretary of State treated the claimant as an adult (and the tribunal agreed with that conclusion) and his rights of appeal were exhausted and his removal imminent, the local authority still had to conduct an age assessment to determine whether he was a child.

(vii) *FZ v London Borough of Croydon*[134] where Sir Anthony May, President of the Queen's Bench Division, said that at the permission stage in an age assessment the court should ask whether the material before the court raises a factual case which, taken at its highest, could not properly succeed in a contested factual hearing. If so, permission should be refused. The court stated if the decision-maker formed the provisional view that the applicant was lying as to his age, the applicant must be given the opportunity to address matters that led to that view. In the absence of formal central government guidance, the court should not be prescriptive of the way in which that might be done.

Further representations by failed asylum seekers

6.132 This situation arises when a failed asylum seeker submits further representations under Immigration Rule 353.[135] If the SSHD decides to treat those further representations as a fresh claim, the person becomes an asylum seeker (again) and, therefore, entitled to the provision of support and to a right of appeal against a refusal of the fresh claim for asylum. Naturally, if the SSHD refuses to accept the further representations as constituting a fresh claim, then no right of support or appeal arises.

6.133 In *R v Croydon, ex p AW*[136] a failed asylum seeker attempted to argue that it should not have been open to a local authority to decline to provide support on the basis of any inadequacy in a purported fresh claim. The local authority argued that they were entitled to consider the adequacy of the contents of the further submissions alleging that they amount to a fresh claim. In such circumstances, the local authority could legitimately withhold support if the representations were not adequate. The court agreed and reinforced this approach. Lloyd Jones J concluded at paras 73 and 74 that:

---

[134] [2011] EWCA Civ 59.
[135] See Chapter 14 Immigration for further details of this provision. In short, Immigration Rule 353 provides, 'When a human rights or asylum claim has been refused or withdrawn or treated as withdrawn under para 333C of these Rules and any appeal relating to that claim is no longer pending, the decision maker will consider any further submissions and, if rejected, will then determine whether they amount to a fresh claim. The submissions will amount to a fresh claim if they are significantly different from the material that has previously been considered. The submissions will only be significantly different if the content: (i) had not already been considered; and (ii) taken together with the previously considered material, creates a realistic prospect of success, notwithstanding its rejection. This paragraph does not apply to claims made overseas.' Rule 353A should be read alongside rule 353, 'Consideration of further submissions shall be subject to the procedures set out in these Rules. An applicant who has made further submissions shall not be removed before the Secretary of State has considered the submissions under para 353 or otherwise. This paragraph does not apply to submissions made overseas.' Further submissions by a person seeking asylum can be met by the Secretary of State in one of three ways: (i) they are accepted: the person is granted leave to enter or remain; (ii) they are rejected, but they are recognised as constituting a fresh claim for asylum. As a result the person has a right of appeal from the refusal under s 83 of the Nationality, Immigration and Asylum Act 2002 ('the 2002 Act') in the ordinary way; or (iii) they are rejected, and the SoS refuses to recognise them as a fresh claim. There is no appeal from the Secretary of State's decision that they do not amount to a fresh claim – but that decision is subject to judicial review in the Administrative Court.
[136] [2005] EWHC 2950 (Admin).

'... local authorities now are required to take decisions relating to the immigration status of individuals as a matter of course. ... in considering whether the provision of support to failed asylum-seekers is necessary in order to prevent a breach of Convention rights it will be necessary for the public body concerned to have regard to all relevant circumstances including, where appropriate, the matters which are alleged to constitute a fresh claim for asylum. In many cases – possibly the great majority – it may well be inappropriate for a public body to embark on any consideration of the purported fresh grounds. However, there may well be cases in which the purported fresh grounds are manifestly nothing of the sort and where it would be appropriate for the public body to take account of that fact in arriving at its decision in relation to asylum support ...'

6.134 Subsequent cases have largely followed this approach. In *R (B) v Southwark LBC*[137] the court reinforced *AW* and concluded that the issue for a local authority was whether the outstanding human rights application pending was 'manifestly unfounded', however, it was not to assess the general merits of the application, which was a matter for immigration authorities. In a similar vein, but in a more narrow approach, in *R (N) v Lambeth LBC*[138] the court reaffirmed *AW* and clarified that 'only in the clearest cases would it be appropriate for the public body concerned to refuse relief on the basis of the manifest inadequacy of the purported fresh grounds'.

6.135 An amendment to the Immigration Rule 353 now means that an individual who makes further submissions shall not be removed from the country. In *Gnezele*, Mitting J made the following obiter observations:[139]

'To the extent that that falls on local authorities it may be that the effect of r 353A will be to impose upon them the burden of providing accommodation to those who have made representations, until they have been determined by the Secretary of State, whether or not the representations are well founded or even abusive. Those are matters for another day. They do not arise for decision directly in this case in the light of my finding that it is upon the Secretary of State that the power and, in so far as it exists, the duty to provide accommodation for these claimants existed or continues to exist.'

6.136 Outside the ambit of 'further submissions' in *Birmingham CC v (1) Clue; (2) SSHD; & (3) Shelter*[140] the Jamaican national claimant entered the UK with her daughter with a visitor visa. The claimant applied for further leave (before the expiry the visitor visa) to remain as a student. This was dismissed, however, the claimant remained in the UK for some time and subsequently applied to remain on the basis that her eldest daughter had been in the UK for more than seven years pursuant to the Secretary of State's policy DP 5/06. She applied for assistance but was refused under Sch 3 of the 2002 Act, save to enable the family to return to Jamaica. The court granted the application on the basis that the local authority did not have regard to the underlying reasons of policy DP 5/96, namely that when applying Sch 3, the local authority should not consider the merits of an outstanding application for leave to remain. It is required to be satisfied that the application is not 'obviously hopeless or abusive'.

---

[137] [2006] EWHC 2254 (Admin).
[138] [2006] EWHC 3427 (Admin).
[139] Paragraph 31.
[140] [2010] EWCA Civ 460.

Private care homes

6.137 An area that is closely linked to community care law is the legal relationship between local authorities and private care home providers. Such providers are increasingly used to supply residential accommodation to the elderly, and there will usually be a complicated set of contractual obligations that, most importantly, set the rates at which the local authority will pay for residential places.

Scope of judicial review

6.138 Given that the relationship between the local authority and the care home provider is contractual, it might be assumed that a care home provider's remedy against a local authority only existed in private law. As was said in *YL v Birmingham County Council*:[141]

> 'If an outside private contractor is engaged on ordinary commercial terms to provide the cleaning services, or the catering and cooking services, or any other essential services at a local authority owned care home, it seems to me absurd to suggest that the private contractor, in earning its commercial fee for its business services, is publicly funded or is carrying on a function of a public nature. It is simply carrying on its private business with a customer who happens to be a public authority. The owner of a private care home taking local authority funded residents is in no different position. It is simply providing a service for which it charges a commercial fee.'

6.139 However, a number of decisions have established that it is only where the dispute is 'fundamentally contractual' that judicial review would be necessarily inappropriate. For instance, in *Davis v West Sussex County Council*[142] the dispute concerned the local authority's conduct during an investigation into alleged abuse at the care home. It was held that this investigation would have occurred whether or not there was a contract and the claimant would not have been able to seek quashing orders in private law proceedings.

6.140 In *R (Supportways Community Services Ltd) v Hampshire County Council*,[143] the Court of Appeal confirmed that where the claim is fundamentally contractual in nature and it involves no allegation of fraud or improper motive against a public body it would be right, as a matter of principle to limit a claimant to private law remedies.[144] Mummery LJ went on to say at [56]:

> '... in order to attract public law remedies, it would be necessary for the applicant for judicial review to establish, at the very least, a relevant and sufficient nexus between the aspect of the contractual situation of which complaint is made and an alleged unlawful exercise of relevant public law powers.'

6.141 It is important to clarify the role of the Human Rights Act 1998 in the context of private care homes. In *YL v Birmingham County Council*[145] the House of Lords held that a care home provider was not a public body for the purposes of s 6 of the HRA. However, the effect of this decision was reversed by s 145 of the Health and Social Care

---

[141] [2008] 1 AC 95 at [27].
[142] [2012] EWHC 2152.
[143] [2006] EWCA Civ 1035.
[144] *R (Supportways Community Services Ltd) v Hampshire County Council* [2006] EWCA Civ 1035 at [38].
[145] [2008] 1 AC 95.

Act 2008, which provides that where a person provides accommodation in a care home that person is taken 'to be exercising a function of a public nature in doing so'.

6.142 As a result of this position, it follows that a resident of a private care home would have a remedy under the HRA against the care home provider. For instance, in *R (Chatting) v Viridian Housing*[146] an elderly resident was able to challenge the transfer of responsibilities using art 8 ECHR. However, it does not follow that the care home provider can raise HRA grounds against local authorities. In *R (Broadway Care Centre Ltd) v Caerphilly County Borough Council*,[147] it was held that a decision to terminate a care home contract was not amenable to judicial review nor was the care home a 'victim' for the purposes of s 7 HRA.

Rates disputes

6.143 Perhaps the most important aspect of the relationship between local authorities and care home providers is the rate that the local authority will pay for the residential accommodation. The decision regarding the appropriate rate requires a complex analysis of the market rate, relevant policy guidance, changes in other relevant factors such as the capital cost of land and buildings. There have been a series of challenges to the way in which local authorities have decided the appropriate rates.

6.144 For instance, in *R (Mavalon Care Ltd) v Pembrokeshire County Council*[148] the court required a local authority to retake a decision because it had failed to have regard to relevant guidance and a previous decision on the same matter and had not justified its departure from its stated methodology. The previous decision in this case was *R (Forest Care Home Ltd) v Pembrokeshire County Council*[149] where the local authority had failed to take into account relevant factors, including the potential adverse consequences of the decision for providers and residents while the manner in which the local authority dealt with the issue of capital costs was methodologically wrong.

6.145 The court in *Forest Care* summarised the approach that should be adopted at [46], which requires that the local authority's discretion when choosing accommodation must be exercised with regard to the relevant policy guidance, as well as the impact of the decision on service-users. The court's approach to a challenge to a commissioning decision would be one of review rather than a reconsideration of the merits of the choice.

6.146 It is important for the local authorities to have regard to the actual costs of care. In *R (Care North East Newcastle) v Newcastle City Council*[150] the local authority had erred in law by failing to inform itself of the actual costs of providing services.[151] However, in *R (Care North East Northumberland) v Northumberland County Council*[152] the local authority had informed itself of the actual costs of providing care. In this case, the Court of Appeal endorsed the approach outlined in *R (South West Care*

---

[146] [2012] EWHC 3595 (Admin).
[147] [2012] EWHC 37 (Admin).
[148] [2011] EWHC 3371.
[149] [2010] EWHC 3514 (Admin).
[150] [2013] EWCA Civ 1740.
[151] See also *R (East Midlands Care Ltd) v Leicestershire County Council* [2011] EWHC 3096 (Admin), *R (Sefton Care Association) v Sefton Council* [2011] EWHC 2676 (Admin) and *R (Redcar and Cleveland Independent Providers Association and Others) v Redcar and Cleveland Borough Council* [2013] EWHC 4 (Admin).
[152] [2013] EWCA Civ 1740.

Homes Ltd) v Devon County Council[153] that as long as some inquiry was made into the actual costs, it was for the decision-maker to decide how much attention to pay to it.[154]

6.147 In a further challenge by South West Care Homes, the court emphasised that the public sector equality duty[155] was relevant to decisions regarding the cost of care. In that case, there had been a failure to have due regard to this duty and so the decision relating to fees was quashed.[156]

PART 3 – COMMON EXAMPLES OF JUDICIAL REVIEW CHALLENGES OF COMMUNITY CARE DECISIONS

6.148 Having undertaken a broad overview of community care law and considered some specific significant areas, it is now imperative to gauge how judicial review, as a remedy, has been utilised as a means of challenging decisions. The below, therefore, seeks to exemplify how community care decisions are challenged by specific grounds of judicial review.

6.149 A major percentage of community care decisions which are subject to judicial review proceedings have one common feature, namely that during the lifetime of judicial review proceedings, the care plan or pathway plan will be substantially modified and possibly improved. In some cases the improvements are insufficient to persuade the claimant to dispose of their legal challenge, and as such, the hearing proceeds as a challenge to the latest plan, and not to the plan which originally was the subject of judicial review proceedings.

6.150 In many cases, however, proceedings bring about a satisfactory level of improvement, which then leads to settlement, and in that way they can serve a useful purpose to both sides. This process of negotiation and evolution is a reminder of the very purpose of community care provisions, ie to assist and facilitate help to disabled individuals.

6.151 It is important to bear in mind that judicial review must be used as a remedy of last resort after local resolution procedures have been exhausted, or alternatively when a substitute remedy is not available. Common examples include the local authority complaints process and the LGO. Note the existence of the new Social Services and NHS Complaints Procedure Regulations 2009, which applies to complaints against either the NHS or local authority. The aim is to provide a simpler, quicker and more efficient complaint handling and resolution, with proper investigation and timely response and action. Consider the recent case of *R v Wirral BC, ex p F & Others*[157] stated above.

6.152 In usual circumstances, judicial review (within the context of social welfare law) ought to be confined to cases: (i) of genuine urgency, for example when interim relief is sought; (ii) involving human rights arguments; (iii) when alternative remedy is not

---

[153] [2012] EWHC 1867 (Admin).
[154] See also *Bevan & Clarke LLP & Ors v Neath Port Talbot County Borough Council* [2012] EWHC 236 (Admin).
[155] Equality Act 2010, s 149.
[156] See *R (South West Care Homes Limited) v Devon County Council*.
[157] [2009] EWHC 1626.

equally convenient, expeditious or effect, see *R v Devon County Council, ex p Baker*[158] and *R(JL)*;[159] and/or cases (iv) that require clarification of statutory instruments or provisions.

The following table summarises key cases involving community care.

Key Cases

Grounds of Judicial Review	Case Name	Details
Illegality Assessing need – general principles	*R v Berkshire CC, ex p P*[160]	The local authority ('LA') refused to undertake s 47 assessment because he was in a care home funded by the PCT. LA said that s 47(1) presupposed the physical availability of services to the applicant for the duty to assess to be invoked.
		Held, allowing the application and declaring that LA should make the appropriate assessment, that on a proper construction of s 47(1) of the 1990 Act there is no condition that the duty to assessment is dependent upon the physical availability of services. The duty to assess arises where the local authority has the legal power to make provision or provide community care to an individual.
	R v Islington LBC, ex p Rixon[161]	R contended that LA had failed to comply with guidance by DOH under CSDA 1970 and acted unlawfully by deviating.
		Held, allowing the application, that under the NHSCCA 1990, s 47 a local authority was subject to a duty to assess based on need. The LA was required to follow DOH guidance. If LA wishes to depart clear reasons must be given.
	R v Sefton MBC, ex p Help the Aged[162]	LA argued that entitled to have regard to its resources when assessing a person's need for accommodation under the NAA 1948.

---

[158] [1995] 1 All ER 73.
[159] [2009] EWHC 458 (Admin), [2009] 2 FLR 515.
[160] Laws J (1997–98) 1 CCL Rep 141.
[161] Sedley J (1997–98) 1 CCL Rep 119.
[162] Jowitt J (1997) 36 BMLR 110.

Grounds of Judicial Review	Case Name	Details
		Held, dismissing the applications, that S was entitled to have regard to its resources when deciding whether a person was in need under s 21(1)(a) following the House of Lords ruling in *R v Gloucestershire CC Ex p Barry*.[163] Any policy framework for prioritising need cannot fetter the discretion of the authority.
	R v North Yorkshire CC, ex p William Hargreaves[164]	H applied for judicial review of the decision to offer his sister a place for respite care, as part of the council's community care service, which was not the placement of her choice. Held: Application allowed. Provided that a care user was capable of making her preference known as regards respite care, a council was under an obligation to take account of that preference.
Procedural Impropriety	*R (Ireneschild) v Lambeth LBC*[165]	The LA appealed against the decision assessment of X was unlawful. X was severely disabled and required ground floor access. LA disagreed because this did not comply with the housing allocation policy. The court quashed the decision and ordered the LA to carry out the assessment again. The local authority submitted that the judge had erred on various findings. Appeal allowed as had not shown that there was a failure to take into account relevant consideration or guidance.
	R (Goldsmith) v Wandsworth LBC[166]	G was an elderly woman in residential care accommodation who the local authority decided should be moved to a nursing home. Decision made after a fall at the care home. Panel recommended move. An assessment was undertaken which conversely concluded that she was safe at home. LA instructed doctor who confirmed, without seeing her, that she needed nursing care. G contended that LA's decision-making process was defective and they had failed to apply their own policy.

---

[163] [1997] AC 584.
[164] Dyson J (1997–98) 1 CCL Rep 104.
[165] [2007] EWCA Civ 234.
[166] Brooke, Chadwick, Wall LLJ [2004] EWCA Civ 1170.

Grounds of Judicial Review	Case Name	Details
		Appealed allowed. LA was under a duty to take a rounded decision, which took into account all relevant factors, rather than treat a doctor's views on the resident's nursing needs as determinative. In the instant case, the local authority's decision-making process was sufficiently defective to vitiate its decision. It had based its decision that G should be put in a nursing home on the assessment of a panel to which it had referred the case and the apparent confirmation of that assessment by a doctor which it had later instructed. It made its decision without having before it the community care assessment, which was carried out afterwards and contradicted its view.
Irrationality	R v Staffordshire CC ex p Farley[167]	F, aged 86, applied for an interim injunction, pending the full hearing of her application for judicial review, to reinstate a community care package that had been provided by LA in accordance with its duties under the NHSCCA 1990 and the CSDPA 1970. She was assessed in S's original care plan as requiring a night sitter as she needed regular toileting throughout the night. In November 1996, however, that care plan was changed and the night sitting provision was withdrawn. Instead F was supplied with an attendant between 10pm and 10.30pm to help prepare for bed and ensure she was comfortable for the night. Held, granting the application, that it was appropriate in judicial review proceedings to grant an interim injunction. There was no evidence that F's circumstances or needs had changed and the decision to withdraw the night care services was *Wednesbury* unreasonable.

---

[167] 8 April 1997, Forbes J.

Grounds of Judicial Review	Case Name	Details
	R v Sutton LBC, ex p Tucker[168]	The care plan was held to be woefully inadequate. There was a failure to arrange supported accommodation to allow discharge from hospital to take place. There was no statement of the overall objectives in the care plan or the obligations of the service providers or carers and the lack of objectives meant there was a lack of criteria to assess if they objectives had been met. Key matters such as costing or possible alternative provision had not been recorded. The procuring of short term and interim outcomes instead of long-term objectives meant that there had been such a departure from the guidance of the Secretary of State that the actions of the authority had been *Wednesbury* unreasonable or irrational.
	R v Secretary of State for the Home Department, ex p Zakrocki[169]	H applied for judicial review of the Secretary of State's refusal to extend their leave to remain in the UK to enable them to care for an elderly relative, a British citizen, who was entitled to care under the care in the community policy and for whom social services could make no suitable alternative arrangements.
		Held, allowing the application, that the objective of the care in the community policy was to promote domiciliary care, and that in the absence of suitable alternative arrangements it was unreasonable, in the *Wednesbury* sense, for the Secretary of State to refuse Z leave to remain in the UK to care for their relative.

---

[168] (1998) 1 CCLR 251.
[169] Carnwath J (1997–98) 1 CCL Rep 374.

Grounds of Judicial Review	Case Name	Details
	R (Khana) v Southwark LBC[170]	J, a 91 year old Iraqi Kurd suffering from paranoid schizophrenia and severely impaired mobility, appealed against the refusal of her application for judicial review of LA's decision to make her an offer of full time residential care. J and her husband had been granted permission to enter the United Kingdom on condition that they did not have recourse to public funds; hence they were entitled to community care services pursuant to the NAA 1948 and the NHSCCA 1990. J, her husband and daughter lived in a one bedroom second floor flat. Following an assessment of J's needs, S offered a joint placement in a residential home for J and her husband, the primary carer. It was J's contention that her needs would be best met by the provision of a two bedroom ground floor flat so that her daughter could continue to live with them. First instance the application was refused. J appealed alleging that LA had acted in a way that no reasonable local authority could and had behaved unlawfully in failing to take her wishes into account. Held, dismissing the appeal, that whilst LA was under a duty to consider J's preferences and beliefs, the assessment of J's accommodation needs and how those needs were best met were ultimately matters for LA who had made an offer of accommodation of the only type which it considered would meet J's assessed needs. LA was required to take J's wishes into account but was under no obligation pursuant to s 21 of the 1948 Act to provide an alternative that would satisfy J's preference if that alternative would not meet all of the assessed needs, *R v Kensington and Chelsea RLBC ex p Kujtim*.[171]

---

[170] Henry LJ, Mance LJ, McKinnon J [2001] EWCA Civ 999.
[171] [1999] 4 All ER 161.

Grounds of Judicial Review	Case Name	Details
	R (Collins) v Lincolnshire HA[172]	H suffered from a severe learning disability caused by cerebral palsy. She sought judicial review of a decision of the health authority to cease providing long term care for her. The health authority planned to transfer H and other long term residents from NHS care into the community. H maintained that: (a) the health authority had misunderstood and misapplied government policy, and (b) by reneging on a promise that H's present home was for life the authority had abused its power and had breached C's human rights. Held, dismissing the application, that: (1) the general aim of government policy was to remove people with learning disabilities from long term institutional care in order to promote their independence. In applying this policy all cases had to be individually assessed. The authority's policy documents and reports demonstrated that it had not simply proposed that all persons with learning disabilities should be discharged into the community from NHS care but that such a move should be made where there were no individual health reasons for keeping a person in NHS care. In H's case there were no such reasons and it could not be said that the health authority had misunderstood and misapplied government policy, and (2) the authority was acting in what it regarded to be H's best interests and upon its belief that C would benefit substantially from the move rather than from any financial motive. Furthermore, the promise made to H in the present case was to a degree uncertain and lacking in clarity. Accordingly, there had been no abuse of the authority's power and no breach of H's human rights.
	R (Tucker) v Sutton LBC[173]	The Court granted JR where the defendant had unlawfully and/or irrationally failed: (i) to provide a care plan (contrary to statutory policy guidance issued by the Secretary of State, which was binding on it), and (ii) to make a service provision decision (pursuant to its statutory duty).

---

[172] Judge David Pannick QC [2001] EWHC Admin 685.
[173] Hidden J (1998) 1 CCLR 251.

CHAPTER 7

HOUSING

INTRODUCTION

7.01 This chapter focuses on the circumstances in which the Administrative Court is called upon to adjudicate on public law matters in this frequently changing area of law.

7.02 Preference will be given to practical and procedural questions rather than to a detailed exposition of the substantive legislative codes which underpin all aspects of the provision, management and condition of social housing.

7.03 This chapter adopts the meaning of 'social housing' provided by the Housing and Regeneration Act 2008, s 68: namely, low cost rental or low cost ownership accommodation. 'Low cost', for the purposes of the Housing and Regeneration Act 2008 means accommodation available at below market rates for those people whose needs are not met adequately by the commercial housing market.[1]

7.04 By concentrating on the work of the Administrative Court, it is not to be forgotten that a substantial body of public law has developed since the transfer to the County Court of the lion's share of homelessness cases as a consequence of the Housing Act 1996, Part VII. Indeed, by the mid-1990s one third of all judicial review applications to the High Court concerned homelessness decisions.[2] Whilst many of the seminal homelessness cases were decided before this transfer of jurisdiction took place, their full import is outside the terms of reference of this chapter.

7.05 Similarly, save to acknowledge its impact on the judicial review of social housing decisions, this chapter does not address in separate detail the Human Rights Act 1998.

THE ROLE OF PUBLIC LAW IN SOCIAL HOUSING

7.06 Public law is at the heart of and permeates nearly every aspect of the provision and management of social housing. Historically, social housing has been provided by local housing authorities, who are creatures of statute. However, the increasing decentralisation of the provision and management of social housing has led to a wider range of social housing providers exercising public functions and accordingly susceptible potentially to judicial review.

7.07 Historically, social landlords were registered with the Housing Corporation, the powers of which passed to the Tenant Services Authority (TSA) (England) and the Welsh Ministers (Wales), under the Housing and Regeneration Act 2008. On 1 April 2012,

---

[1] Housing and Regeneration Act 2008, ss 69 and 70.
[2] De Smith's *Judicial Review* (6th edn), 17-045.

the Localism Act 2011 brought to an end the TSA and transferred its functions to the Homes and Communalities Agency (HCA). In England, therefore, these bodies are now registered with the special committee of the HCA. In Wales, bodies providing social housing remain maintained by the Welsh ministers.

7.08 Landlords are rigorously regulated. Part 2 of the Housing and Regeneration Act 2008 and Pt 1 of the Housing Act 1996 govern the registration and regulation of social landlords in England and Wales respectively. In England, social landlords are registered with the special committee of the HCA and are known as private registered providers of social housing (PRPs). In Wales, bodies providing social housing are registered with the Welsh ministers and are known as registered social landlords (RSLs). This does not, however, mean that the HCA and the Welsh ministers are the only bodies involved in overseeing the actions and policies of social landlords: the courts have power to scrutinise the decisions and activities of social landlords.

7.09 Despite being underpinned by a legislative framework, the relationship between social housing providers and occupiers (both current and prospective) is underpinned by conventional public law principles. Although there are various ways of classifying the grounds on which administrative decisions can be challenged before the Administrative Court, it is convenient to adopt the 'triumvirate' set out by Lord Diplock in the *Council of Civil Service Unions v Minister for the Civil Service*:[3]

(1) illegality;
(2) irrationality;
(3) procedural impropriety.

7.10 Indeed, some of the statutory provisions represent an attempt to codify these principles. For example, the Allocation of Housing and Homelessness (Review Procedures) Regulations 1999, Reg 8[4] provides for a right to make oral or written representations where a reviewing officer considers that there is a deficiency or irregularity in the original decision,[5] but he is minded nonetheless to reach a decision contrary to the interests of the applicant. A small but important body of jurisprudence has built up around the proper ambit of this right to be heard,[6] with each case emphasising that procedural fairness lies at the heart of the 1999 Regulations.[7]

7.11 Various complex and evolving statutory codes regulate social housing, but whilst public law principles underpin the rights and duties of providers and users alike, the use of judicial review as a means of challenging decisions about social housing has become increasingly curtailed. The legislative tendency is now to draft self-contained statutory codes which have their own internal review and appeal mechanisms, the most obvious example of which is the transfer of the vast majority of homelessness cases from the Administrative Court to the County Court by virtue of Part VII of the Housing Act 1996. Similarly, the Housing Act 2004 was enacted in order to improve housing standards and to assist urban renewal. Whilst the powers and duties exercised by local

---

[3] [1985] AC 374, 410.
[4] SI 1999/71.
[5] Made under the Housing Act 1996, s 184.
[6] *Hall v Wandsworth LBC* [2004] EWCA Civ 1740; [2005] 2 All ER 192; *Lambeth LBC v Johnston* [2008] EWCA Civ 690; *Banks v Kingston-Upon-Thames RLBC* [2008] EWCA Civ 1443; *Makisi v Birmingham City Council* [2011] EWCA Civ 355, [2011] HLR 27, which established that a person requesting a review of a homelessness decision is entitled to demand an oral hearing.
[7] Eg *Banks v Kingston-Upon-Thames RLBC* [2008] EWCA Civ 1443 at [65].

authorities under the Housing Act 2004 involve issues of public law, there is a comprehensive statutory code that provides for the consideration of representations and the right of appeal to the Residential Property Tribunal.[8]

7.12 Similarly, the failure to request a review[9] of a decision to seek possession of premises held under an Introductory Tenancy[10] is likely to preclude a judicial review of the decision by the local housing authority to commence possession proceedings.[11]

7.13 In each of these circumstances, the Administrative Court is highly unlikely to entertain judicial review proceedings given the existence of an alternative remedy in the form of the schemes established by statute. Judicial review is, after all, the remedy of last resort.[12]

7.14 Nevertheless, judicial review continues to play an important role in the supervision of social housing providers and the enforcement of rights of both actual and prospective occupiers of social housing.

7.15 The specific areas most frequently encountered are homelessness, the allocation of social housing and challenges to decisions in relation to introductory tenancies under the Housing Act 1996. It is on these three substantive areas that this chapter focuses.

7.16 The judicial review of social housing decisions also raises its own peculiar procedural and costs issues, which will also be examined.

JURISDICTION

7.17 It is always necessary as a first step to determine whether the decision is one that is amenable to judicial review. It is not the status of the body in question, but the function being exercised which is crucial.

7.18 In the vast majority of housing cases, it should be apparent whether the decision-maker is a body who carries out public functions. For example, a local housing authority (for the purposes of the Housing Act 1996) which make decisions as to the allocation of social housing or the duties owed to persons claiming under the Housing Act 1996, Part VII (homelessness) are, quite obviously, susceptible to judicial review of acts or omissions taken within the context of that legislation.[13]

7.19 However, the advent of the Human Rights Act 1998 and the decentralisation of social housing provision (less than half of all social housing is now managed by local authorities) have led to some 'blurring at the edges'.

---

[8] See Schs 1, 2, 5 and 6 of the Housing Act 2004.
[9] Under the Housing Act 1996, s 129.
[10] A probationary tenancy governed by Chapter 1 of Part V of the Housing Act 1996.
[11] *R (Chelfat) v Tower Hamlets LBC* [2006] EWHC 313 (Admin); [2006] ACD 61.
[12] See for example *R v Hammersmith and Fulham LBC, ex p Burkett* [2002] UKHL 23; [2002] 1 WLR 1593.
[13] Although note the availability of alternative remedies.

7.20 Until *R (Weaver) v London and Quadrant Housing Trust*[14] there was a conflicting and confusing line of authority on the test of a public authority within the meaning of the Human Rights Act 1998, and also which bodies fall within the jurisdiction of the Administrative Court.

7.21 Mrs Weaver was an assured tenant of the Trust[15] and alleged that its decision to terminate her tenancy was amenable to judicial review and that it engaged her right to a home under Article 8 of the European Convention on Human Rights. The success of these arguments depended upon Mrs Weaver establishing that the Trust was a public body attracting the operation of public law principles and that it was a public authority for the purposes of the Human Rights Act 1998, s 6(3)(b). Equally importantly, the court had to determine whether the termination of the tenancy was a private act within the meaning of the Human Rights Act 1998, s 6(5), even if the Trust was a public authority.

7.22 The Court of Appeal considered that the starting point was to analyse the housing association's function of allocating and managing housing. Particular regard was to be had to the extent to which in carrying out the relevant function the body was publicly funded, or was exercising statutory powers, or was taking the place of central government or local authorities or was providing a public service.[16]

7.23 The court appeared to be particularly persuaded by the following factors:

(a) It was Government policy to provide affordable housing to those who cannot secure their housing needs in the market.

(b) Registered Social Landlords were subject to regulation by the Housing Corporation, an executive non-departmental public body responsible to the Secretary of State.[17]

(c) Housing management guidance was subject to consultation with and approval by the Secretary of State.

(d) There was statutory regulation of Registered Social Landlords, particularly as to the disposal of land or housing.[18]

(e) Registered Social Landlords received grants from the Housing Corporation, the source of which were public funds.

(f) There was a statutory obligation for Registered Social Landlords to cooperate with housing authorities. For example under the Housing Act 1996, s 170, a Registered Social Landlord is required to cooperate 'to such extent as is reasonable in the circumstances' with a local housing authority where the latter seeks to allocate housing under Part VI of that Act.

(g) Virtually all provision of new social housing is delivered by Registered Social Landlords, and increasingly they are becoming responsible for the management of former housing authority stock by voluntary transfer.

---

[14] [2010] 1 WLR 363, [2009] EWCA Civ 587, CA. Note that permission to appeal to the Supreme Court was refused. Whilst the Supreme Court considered that the point was appropriate for it to consider, it was not a 'suitable case on its facts'.
[15] Which was a Registered Social Landlord under the Housing Act 1996.
[16] *Aston Cantlow and Wilmcote with Billesley Parochial Church Council v Wallbank* [2003] UKHL 37, [2004] 1 AC 546.
[17] Although note that the mere fact of regulation tells us nothing about whether the body is a public one. *YL v Birmingham City Council* [2007] UKHL 27, [2008] 1 AC 95 per Lord Neuberger [135].
[18] See the Housing Act 1996, ss 8–10.

7.24 It was further concluded that:

(a) the provision of subsidised housing was a governmental function;
(b) the housing association was acting in the public interest; and
(c) it had charitable objectives which placed it outside the traditional area of private commercial activity.

7.25 Ultimately, it would appear that the question of reviewability of decision-making in the sphere of social housing depends upon an overall assessment of the functions of the body in question, and the legislative framework within which it operates.[19] Nevertheless, it is suggested that the factors which are set out in the preceding paragraphs provide a good general guide to follow in the event that there is any dispute as to whether the acts or omissions of social housing providers are amenable to judicial review.

7.26 The *Weaver* case was decided on a set of facts prior to the enactment of the Housing and Regeneration Act 2008. Since then, the question of whether social housing providers are amenable to judicial review should be easier to resolve. The 2008 Act created the TSA, which is took over the regulatory powers of the Housing Corporation and was responsible for the regulation of all affordable housing providers including local authorities and other social housing providers[20] until those functions were transferred to the HCA under the Localism Act 2011.

7.27 Given that all social housing providers are currently required to be registered with the HCA (or the Welsh ministers), and may be subject to enforcement action in the event that standards are not met, it is difficult to envisage circumstances in which social housing providers so registered with the HCA will not be amenable to judicial review.

7.28 It should be noted, however, that the immediate practical effect of *Weaver* is likely to be limited in scope. Whilst it establishes that the decisions of Registered Social Landlords to seek possession orders against assured tenants are likely to be amenable to judicial review, the number of people affected by this apparent broadening of the ambit of judicial review, is likely to be small. Indeed, even if a social housing provider is seen acting in a public law sphere, the Administrative Court will not ordinarily be the forum in which arguments about the legality of possession proceedings will be fought out; it will be the County Court.[21] Additionally, whilst a social housing provider may be susceptible to judicial review, relief may be refused if there is an alternative private law remedy available. In *R (McIntyre) v Gentoo Group Ltd*,[22] the requirement under an assured tenancy agreement that a registered social landlord could not unreasonably withhold its consent in deciding whether its tenants could exchange homes with each other involved a contractual relationship that possessed a public law dimension. As such, a decision to refuse such consent or impose conditions upon an exchange or

---

[19] Although note that in refusing permission to appeal the Supreme Court considered that the point of law was suitable for the Supreme Court, it was not suitable for determination on the facts of the case: [2009] 5 November, UKSC.
[20] See generally Part 2 of the Housing and Regeneration Act 2008.
[21] *Kay v Lambeth LBC* [2006] UKHL 10, [2006] 2 AC 465; and *Doherty v Birmingham City Council* [2008] UKHL 57, [2009] 1 AC 367. See also *R (McIntyre) v Gentoo Group Ltd* [2010] EWHC 5 (Admin), (2010) 154(2) SJLB 29, [2010] 2 P & CR DG6, a post-*Weaver* decision in which the claimant sought to challenge a RSL's decision to impose conditions on an exchange of tenancy. Whilst judicial review was not ruled out entirely as a means of challenging such a decision, it should normally be brought by private action.
[22] [2010] EWHC 5 (Admin).

transfer was capable of being challenged by judicial review. However, relief was refused because private law remedies were available and had not been used.[23]

JUDICIAL ATTITUDE

7.29 In order properly to set the context for the remainder of this chapter, it is worth considering whether there is a prevailing attitude amongst the judiciary towards cases which involve issues of social housing. In so far as it is possible to identify any general trend in relation to social housing, the courts have inclined towards an attitude of judicial deference to the decision-maker, recognising that Parliament has entrusted the distribution of limited social resources to local authorities and central government.[24]

7.30 Whilst the jurisprudence abounds with examples of judges expressing a desire not to interfere with the exercise of powers by local housing authorities to manage or allocate social housing save in the most obvious cases, this judicial deference is perhaps best illustrated by the oft-quoted speech of Lord Brightman in the homelessness case of *R v LB Hillingdon ex p Puhlhofer*:[25]

> 'My Lords, I am troubled at the prolific use of judicial review for the purpose of challenging the performance by local authorities of their functions under the Act of 1977. Parliament intended the local authority to be the judge of fact. The Act abounds with the formula when, or if the housing authority is satisfied as to this, or that, or has reason to believe this, or that. Although the action or inaction of a local authority is clearly susceptible to judicial review where they have misconstrued the Act, or abused their powers or otherwise acted perversely, I think that great restraint should be exercised in giving leave to proceed by judicial review. The plight of the homeless is a desperate one, and the plight of the applicants in the present case commands the deepest sympathy. But it is not, in my opinion, appropriate that the remedy of judicial review, which is a discretionary remedy, should be made use of to monitor the actions of local authorities under the Act save in the exceptional case.'

7.31 More recently, in *R (Ahmad) v Newham LBC*,[26] a case concerning the legality of an allocation scheme under the Housing Act 1996, Part VI, the House of Lords reinforced this mind-set through Lord Neuberger:

> 'However, it seems unlikely that the legislature can have intended that Judges should embark on the exercise of telling authorities how to decide on priorities as between applicants in need of rehousing, save in relatively rare and extreme circumstances. Housing allocation policy is a difficult exercise which requires not only social and political sensitivity and judgment, but also local expertise and knowledge.'

7.32 Judicial deference is not necessarily an entirely negative concept. It occurs when judges assign varying degrees of weight to the judgment of the elected branches of central and local government, out of respect for their superior expertise, competence or democratic legitimacy. Nevertheless, it is relevant for the practitioner to note that whilst

---

[23] Ibid at [115] and [116].
[24] Although note that the use of the expression 'judicial deference' has recently been deprecated by the House of Lords: *Huang v Secretary of State for the Home Department* [2007] UKHL 11, [2007] 2 AC 167, per Lord Bingham at [16].
[25] (1986) 1 AC 484 HL per Lord Brightman at p 518.
[26] [2009] UKHL 14.

the court will not hesitate to intervene in the appropriate case, it can often appear that the claimant has a particularly high hurdle to overcome before obtaining the relief he seeks.[27]

HOMELESSNESS

7.33 Following the enactment of the Housing Act 1996, homeless applicants were given a right of appeal on a point of law to the County Court where an applicant has requested a review under the Housing Act 1996, s 202, of a homelessness decision. This is an essential pre-requisite of an appeal to the County Court. The right to appeal arises in two circumstances: (i) where the applicant is dissatisfied with the decision on review; or (ii) where the review decision itself is not communicated to the applicant within any time prescribed by the Secretary of State.[28]

7.34 An applicant has the right to request a review of the following decisions:

(a) a decision by the local housing authority under the Housing Act 1996, s 184 following enquiries into whether the applicant is eligible for assistance under the Housing Act 1996, Part VII;

(b) any decision as to what duty (if any) is owed to the applicant under the Housing Act 1996, ss 190 to 193;

(c) any decision relating to or arising out of the referral of the application to another authority;[29]

(d) any decision as to the suitability of accommodation offered to the applicant in the discharge of its duties under any of the aforementioned provisions or under the Housing Act 1996, s 193(7).

7.35 The reason for setting out these classes of decision is as follows: for the applicant who is dissatisfied or who has not been notified of a relevant decision, the first – and usually the only – port of call will be the County Court.

7.36 Nevertheless, there are two circumstances in which the Administrative Court is likely to become involved in homelessness cases: (i) where exceptional circumstances pertain such that the court is prepared to exercise its residual discretion; and (ii) where the Housing Act 1996 does not provide a right of review and subsequent appeal to the County Court.

Exceptional circumstances

7.37 The exercise of the Administrative Court's jurisdiction to intervene in the context of homelessness decisions has not been taken away by the Housing Act 1996, but will

---

[27] For a more detailed examination of judicial attitudes, see Jeff A King *Institutional approaches to judicial restraint* (2009) Oxford Journal of Legal Studies, p 409. See also *R (Adow) v LB Newham* [2010] EWHC 951 (Admin): the court held that the practical difficulties of public authorities had to be recognised, particularly in the area of housing where, with limited resources and high demands, they had to make decisions quickly, humanely and in accordance with the law that was not always clear. However, where the law was clear and the authority realised that its procedures required amendment, the court was prepared to express its displeasure and would have been prepared to award costs on an indemnity basis.

[28] Housing Act 1996, s 204(1).

[29] See Housing Act 1996, ss 198 and 200.

only be exercised in exceptional circumstances.[30] For example: in *R (Lynch) v Lambeth LBC*,[31] Ms Lynch sought to challenge a decision under the Housing Act 1996, s 184 by the housing authority that she and her family were not homeless. Whilst she requested a review of the decision and sought to appeal to the County Court, she launched judicial review proceedings in the Administrative Court principally on the basis that the original decision was so defective (particularly in its lack of reasoning) that it was incapable of being reviewed.[32] The statutory review process, Ms Lynch reasoned, was therefore ineffective.

7.38 The court held that whilst the original decision under s 184 of the Housing Act 1996 was inadequate, that meant that it was defective rather than a nullity.[33] These defects were capable of being remedied by the statutory review procedure.[34] Importantly, the court confirmed the general proposition that whilst there is a residual remedy available in the Administrative Court in relation to Housing Act cases, it will only be exercised in exceptional circumstances.[35]

7.39 This approach is consistent not only with the practical considerations of avoiding the Administrative Court from being overburdened with cases which could otherwise have been dealt with by the County Court, but also with the principle that all alternative remedies should be exhausted before judicial review proceedings are commenced: it is the remedy of last resort.[36] It is also relevant to note that the prospects of persuading the Administrative Court to intervene are further reduced by virtue of the fact that appeals to the County Court under Part VII of the Housing Act 1996 are on a point of law,[37] with the grounds of appeal being essentially the same as judicial review.[38]

7.40 Despite the narrow construction of the residual jurisdiction of the Administrative Court, there may occasionally be circumstances in which a point of law is of such wider significance that the Administrative Court will permit a claim by way of judicial review rather than under the statutory scheme. In *R v Brent LBC, ex p Sadiq*,[39] the court granted relief on a judicial review claim notwithstanding the availability of an alternative remedy in the County Court. Moses J was particularly influenced by the fact that it was likely that the Court of Appeal would probably have considered the point raised by the challenge in any event.[40]

---

[30] *R (Lynch) v Lambeth LBC* [2006] EWHC 2737 (Admin), [2007] HLR 15. See also *Nipa Begum v Tower Hamlets LBC* [2000] 1 WLR 306; [2002] 32 HLR 445, CA; *R v Merton LBC ex p Sembi* [2000] 32 HLR 439, QBD; *R v Brent LBC ex p O'Connor* (1998) 31 HLR 923, QBD; *R v Brent LBC ex p Sadiq* [2001] 33 HLR 525, QBD; *R (Ahmed (Ashfaq)) v Waltham Forest LBC* [2001] EWHC Admin 540; and *R (Savage) v Hillingdon London Borough Council* [2010] EWHC 88 (Admin).
[31] [2006] EWHC 2737 (Admin); [2007] HLR 15.
[32] Although see *R v Camden LBC, ex p Mohammed* (1998) 30 HLR 315, QBD, at 323 in which it was held that judicial review might be available if the original decision was so defective that any internal review under the Housing Act 1996, s 202 would be unfair.
[33] [2006] EWHC 2737 (Admin), [2007] HLR 15 at [26].
[34] Ibid.
[35] Supra at [27].
[36] See in a different context *R v Hammersmith and Fulham LBC, ex p Burkett* [2002] UKHL 23, [2002] 1 WLR 1593. See also the homelessness case of *R v Brent LBC, ex p O'Connor* (1999) 31 HLR 923, QBD, at p 924 and *R (on the application of McIntyre) v Gentoo Group Ltd* [2010] EWHC 5 (Admin).
[37] See the Housing Act 1996, s 204.
[38] *Tower Hamlets LBC v Begum (Runa)* [2003] UKHL 5, [2003] 2 AC 430 at [17].
[39] (2001) 33 HLR 47, QBD.
[40] Ibid at [42].

7.41 A further example of the exceptional circumstances in which the Administrative Court will entertain a judicial review claim is provided by *R (Van der Stolk) v Camden LBC*,[41] the claimant was a single man with significant and worsening mental health problems. He approached the local authority for assistance, but was found to have made himself intentionally homeless from tied accommodation. The claimant sought a review under the Housing Act 1996, s 202 and did not appeal to the County Court within 21 days of being notified that the original decision had been upheld.[42] Whilst the court recognised that the statutory code provided for a right to appeal to the County Court, the severe and deteriorating nature of the claimant's mental health established that there were exceptional circumstances which permitted the Administrative Court to intervene.[43]

7.42 In *R (W) v Sheffield City Council*,[44] the claimant was the victim of a dispute between two housing authorities, neither of which would accept responsibility for housing him pending the resolution of the disagreement. He had sought a review and was prosecuting an appeal in the County Court against one of the local authorities, against which the claimant could have sought an interim injunction under the Housing Act 1996, s 204A. However, notwithstanding the existence of this alternative remedy, the court was prepared to entertain the judicial review claim, particularly in the light of unnecessary hurdles put in the way of the claimant and the failure of the competing housing authorities to accept responsibility for accommodating him.[45]

Decisions outside the statutory code

7.43 Apart from the extremely limited circumstances in which the Administrative Court will intervene by way of exercise of its residual jurisdiction, there are a number of discrete areas of homelessness law in which the court regularly does become involved. These decisions raise issues which lie – strictly speaking – outside the statutory code laid down by Part VII of the Housing Act 1996.

Interim accommodation

7.44 The most important use of judicial review in this arena is the challenge to decisions about the provision (or refusal) of temporary accommodation pending the making of a review decision under the Housing Act 1996, s 202.[46] Prior to 30 September 2002, when the jurisdiction to consider issues of temporary accommodation pending an appeal to the County Court was transferred to the County Court,[47] the Administrative Court would have been the jurisdiction of choice for all questions of interim accommodation.

7.45 Pending the outcome of enquiries as to whether an applicant is eligible for assistance under Part VII of the Housing Act 1996, a housing authority is under a duty

---

[41] [2002] EWHC 1261 (Admin).
[42] Housing Act 1996, s 204(2). Note that the County Court is now able to extend time for appealing where there is a good reason for doing so: s 204(2A), inserted by Sch 1, para 17 of the Homelessness Act 2002.
[43] Ibid at [46] and [47].
[44] [2005] EWHC 720 (Admin).
[45] Ibid at [34].
[46] M Sunkin et al, 'Mapping the Use of Judicial Review to Challenge Local Authorities in England and Wales' [2007] PL 545 at 555.
[47] See Housing Act 1996, s 204A, inserted by the Homelessness Act 2002, s 11.

to ensure that accommodation is available to the applicant.[48] This duty ceases on notification of the decision, even if the applicant requests a review, although the authority has discretion to continue to secure that accommodation remains available pending a decision on the review.[49] There is no right of review of the decision as to whether to continue to provide accommodation under the Housing Act 1996, s 188; any challenge must be made by way of judicial review.[50]

7.46 The housing authority is not obliged of its own motion to consider whether to accommodate pending a review, but may wait to see whether the applicant requests that it exercise the power.[51]

7.47 Given that there is an unfettered right to request a review under the Housing Act 1996, s 202, a council may decide to exercise its discretion to accommodate under s 188(3) only in exceptional circumstances.[52] However, in each case the authority must apply the following tests, as laid down in *R v Camden LBC ex p Mohammed* and must do so in a way that demonstrates that more than mere lip service has been paid to them:[53]

(a) the merits of the applicant's case (that the original decision was flawed)[54] and the extent to which it can be said that the decision was either contrary to the merits or one which involved a fine balance of judgment;

(b) whether consideration is required of new material or argument which alters the original decision; and

(c) the personal circumstances of the applicant.

7.48 The overarching test is to ensure that the right balance is struck between the rights of other homeless persons and a proper consideration of the possibility that the applicant's challenge to the original decision is well founded.

Challenge to policy

7.49 Given the wide variety of circumstances in which people present themselves as homeless to local housing authorities and the significant resource implications of processing such applications, it makes practical sense for authorities to adopt and apply policies in relation to homelessness. In most cases, a claim by way of judicial review rather than a statutory review and appeal under Part VII of the Housing Act 1996 will be the appropriate vehicle by which to challenge the legality of a policy.[55] However,

---

[48] Section 188(1) of the Housing Act 1996.
[49] Section 188(3) of the Housing Act 1996.
[50] *R v Camden LBC, ex p Mohammed* (1998) 30 HLR 315, QBD.
[51] *R (Ahmed) v Waltham Forest LBC* [2001] EWHC Admin 540, at [16].
[52] *R v Camden LBC, ex p Mohammed* (1998) 30 HLR 315, QBD; *R v Hammersmith & Fulham LBC, ex p Fleck* (1998) 30 HLR 679, QBD, at p 683; *R (Spencer) v Lambeth LBC* [2006] EWHC 3611 (Admin).
[53] *R (Paul-Coker) v Southwark LBC* [2006] EWHC 497; [2006] HLR 32, QBD, at [49]; and see *R (Kelly and Mehari) v Birmingham City Council* [2009] EWHC 3240 (Admin), in which there had been a systematic failure of the housing authority to mention, let alone apply, the statutory tests under the Housing Act 1996, s 188.
[54] The bracketed words were added in *R v Newham LBC, ex p Lumley* (2001) 33 HLR 11, QBD, at [54].
[55] See *Kensington and Chelsea RLBC, ex p Byfield* (1997) 31 HLR 913, QBD, at p 922.

practitioners should be wary of cloaking what is in essence a challenge to a particular homelessness decision in the guise of an attack on the underlying policy which informed it.[56]

7.50 In practice, the level of scrutiny applied to homelessness policies can appear to be slight. However, the courts are ever mindful of the observations of Lord Brightman in *R v Hillingdon LBC, ex p Puhlhofer*,[57] that, whilst recognising the plight of the homeless, the remedy of judicial review should only be available in exceptional circumstances.

7.51 Importantly, whilst the rights to request a review and to appeal under Part VII of the Housing Act 1996 are available only to the applicant himself, judicial review as a remedy is available to third parties, provided that they establish sufficient interest in the subject matter. In *R (Hammia) v Wandsworth LBC*,[58] the local authority had a policy of requiring homeless applicants to relinquish their tenancy before accepting the 'full' homeless duty under the Housing Act 1996, s 193. The claimant was the husband of a woman (with whom he held a joint tenancy) who applied as homeless following allegations of domestic violence. In line with the council's policy, the homeless applicant served a Notice to Quit on the claimant, against whom the local authority eventually brought possession proceedings. The possession proceedings were adjourned pending the outcome of judicial review proceedings, which challenged the legality of the authority's policy. The court held that the council's policy introduced an additional and unlawful pre-condition for accepting that a homeless applicant should be accommodated pursuant to the Housing Act 1996, s 193; in short, it placed an additional hurdle to an applicant which did not arise out of the statutory scheme.[59]

7.52 This decision is important not only as to the extent to which local housing authorities are entitled to give effect to the statutory homelessness code by the adoption of policies, but also as to the right of third parties to challenge such policies. Indeed, it is entirely possible that judicial review provides an avenue by which interest groups acting on behalf of homeless persons can take on policies which they consider to be unlawful.[60]

Statutory appeal ineffective

7.53 The County Court's powers under the Housing Act 1996, s 204(3) are limited to confirming, quashing or varying the housing authority's review decision or – if a review decision is not made – the original decision under the Housing Act 1996, s 184. The County Court has no inherent jurisdiction to order a local authority to carry out a statutory review. Consequently, where a housing authority has failed or refused to carry out any review, judicial review remains the appropriate method of securing a mandatory order that they do so.[61]

---

[56] See *Kensington and Chelsea RLBC, ex p Byfield* (1997) 31 HLR 913, QBD, at p 922.
[57] [1986] AC 484, HL at 518.
[58] [2005] EWHC 1127 (Admin); [2005] HLR 45. See also *Savage v Hillingdon LBC* [2010] EWHC 88 (Admin).
[59] Ibid at [24].
[60] Cf: *R v Secretary of State for the Environment, ex p Shelter and the Refugee Council* [1997] COD 49, a challenge to the lawfulness of the removal of rights of persons subject to immigration control under the homelessness legislation.
[61] *R (Aguiar) v Newham LBC* [2003] EWHC 1325 (Admin).

Refusal to extend time to review

7.54 A request for a review under the Housing Act 1996, s 202 must be made within 21 days of the date on which the applicant is notified of the authority's decision 'or such longer period as the authority may in writing allow'.[62] The discretion to extend time is wide and the authority may (but are not obliged to) balance the length of delay and reasons for it against the prospects of success. They are entitled to reach a decision without forming a provisional view of the underlying merits of the case if, in all the circumstances, they consider it reasonable not to do so.[63] The decision to refuse to extend time for requesting a review is only challengeable by way of judicial review.

Local connection

7.55 As part of their enquiries as to a person's eligibility for assistance under Part VII of the Housing Act 1996 and any duty owed to him, housing authorities may enquire whether the applicant has a local connection with another authority with a view to referring the person to that other local authority.[64]

7.56 A person has a local connection with an area if he has a connection:

(a) because he is, or in the past was, normally resident there, and that residence is or was of his own choice;

(b) because he is employed there;

(c) because of family associations; or

(d) because of special circumstances.[65]

7.57 If a housing authority decides that the applicant has a local connection and refers him to another authority, the applicant has a right of review of this decision.[66] However, there is no right of review where an authority refuses to make a local connection referral. Any such challenge should be made by way of judicial review.[67]

7.58 The referral of a homeless applicant to another authority can and does lead to disputes between housing authorities as to the basis on which the referral is made. Additionally, it is open to the referee authority to challenge the substantive decision of the referring authority as to whether any duty is owed to the homeless applicant. This can only be done by judicial review.[68]

Refusal to entertain a homelessness application

7.59 An application for assistance under Part VII of the Housing Act 1996 can be made in any number of ways and need not be in writing.[69] It does not need to be expressed as explicitly seeking assistance under Part VII. The application can be made on behalf of the applicant (ie a social services referral, a community group, friends or

---

[62] Section 202(3) of the Housing Act 1996.
[63] *R (C) v Lewisham LBC* [2003] EWCA Civ 927, [2004] HLR 4 at [49]; see also *R (Slaiman) v Richmond-Upon-Thames LBC* [2006] EWHC 329 (Admin); [2006] HLR 20 at [22] to [24].
[64] Section 184(2) of the Housing Act 1996.
[65] Section 199(1) of the Housing Act 1996.
[66] Section 202(1)(c), (d) and (e) of the Housing Act 1996.
[67] *Hackney London Borough Council v Sareen* [2003] EWCA Civ 351; [2003] HLR 54, CA at [36].
[68] Eg *R (Bantamagbari) v Westminster City Council* [2003] EWHC 1350 (Admin).
[69] *R v Chiltern DC ex p Roberts* (1991) 23 HLR 387.

family). A local housing authority is obliged to accept an application for homelessness assistance if there is reason to believe that the applicant may be homeless or threatened with homelessness.[70] If an authority fails to accept an application where the above test is met, then an applicant can challenge that failure in judicial review proceedings.

7.60 The circumstances in which a housing authority may reject an application as incompetent were considered in *Rikha Begum v London Borough of Tower Hamlets*:[71]

(a) it is for an applicant to identify, in the subsequent application, the facts which are said to render that application different from the earlier application;

(b) if no new facts are revealed in the application document, the authority may, indeed at least normally should, reject it as incompetent;

(c) if the subsequent application document purports to reveal new facts which are, to the authority's knowledge and without further investigation, not new, fanciful or trivial, the same conclusion applies;

(d) where the subsequent application document appears to reveal new facts which are, in light of the information then available to the authority, neither trivial or fanciful, the authority must treat the application as a valid application. In such a case the authority would not be entitled to investigate the accuracy of the alleged new facts before deciding whether to treat the application as valid, even where there may be reason to suspect the accuracy of the allegations.

Advice and assistance

7.61 *R (Savage) v Hillingdon LBC*[72] concerned a challenge to the purported exercise of a housing authority's duties under s 190(2) and (4) of the 1996 Act (duties to persons who are homeless, eligible for assistance and in priority need but are homeless intentionally). The court doubted that the manner in which an authority chose to discharge such duties could be dealt with by way of review under s 202 of the 1996 Act. Accordingly, such a challenge should be brought under judicial review proceedings.

Pre-emptive strikes

7.62 The question of intentional homelessness is a complex area of law and one which has given rise to a fairly substantial body of case-law. Consequently, for those persons who are at risk of losing their homes or who feel that they must soon leave accommodation, there is a temptation to obtain some assurance that if they apply to the local housing authority as homeless, they will not be found to be intentionally homeless.

7.63 The most obvious means of pre-empting a decision as to intentionality is to seek a declaration in judicial review proceedings that the prospective applicant will not be found intentionally homeless if he applies to the local authority. However, it is extremely unlikely that any such attempts to obtain a guarantee will be successful. To do so would be to take away from the housing authority the power entrusted to them by Parliament to make decisions as to whether a person is entitled to assistance under Part VII of the Housing Act 1996.[73]

---

[70] Housing Act 1996, s 183(1).
[71] [2005] 1 WLR 2103. See also *R (Gardiner) v Haringey LBC* [2009] EWHC 2699 (Admin); *R (May) v Birmingham City Council* [2012] EWHC 1399 (Admin).
[72] [2010] EWHC 88 (Admin).
[73] See *R v Hillingdon LBC, ex p Tinn* (1988) 20 HLR 305, QBD, at 312.

ALLOCATION

7.64 The allocation of social housing is governed principally by Part VI of the Housing Act 1996, as amended by the Homelessness Act 2002 and the Localism Act 2011. The amendments brought about by the Localism Act provide local housing authorities in England with increased powers in relation to the allocation of housing. The Act made two important changes to the law on allocations. Firstly, an authority's allocation scheme is not to apply to tenants, without a reasonable preference, who wish to transfer their accommodation with another tenant.[74] Secondly, authorities in England are given the power either to exclude specified classes of people from applying or to specify by class the only people entitled to an allocation of housing.[75] Despite these changes, the case-law, which has developed under Part VI of the 1996 Act, is likely to remain applicable.

7.65 A local authority allocates housing accommodation for the purposes of Part VI of the Housing Act 1996 if it:[76]

(a) selects a person to be a secure or introductory tenant[77] of accommodation held by them; or

(b) nominates a person to become a secure or introductory tenant (or licensee) of accommodation held by another person, such as a housing action trust; or

(c) nominates a person to be an assured tenant of accommodation held by a private registered provider of social housing or a registered social landlord.

7.66 The allocating authority must only allocate housing to eligible persons.[78]

7.67 The allocation of housing accommodation by local authorities must be carried out in accordance with the provisions of Part VI of the Housing Act 1996, particularly those sections relating to the establishment and operation of an allocation scheme.[79] An authority must have a scheme for determining priorities and procedures in the allocation of their housing.[80] It is in relation to the drafting and operation of allocation schemes that most jurisprudence has developed.

7.68 On the face of it, local housing authorities have a very broad discretion as to the allocation of social housing.[81] However, an allocation, which is made other than in accordance with the adopted allocation scheme, will be unlawful.[82] For example, in *Begum (Amirun) v Tower Hamlets LBC*,[83] the housing authority sought to earmark a property for a particular applicant before applying the provisions of the allocation scheme. The court held that a housing authority must apply its policy, and exercise any residual discretion, when it allocates the accommodation in question, not before.[84] Thus, the decision to allocate 'in advance' fell foul of the Housing Act 1996.

---

[74] Housing Act 1996, s 159(5).
[75] Housing Act 1996, s 160ZA.
[76] Section 159 of the Housing Act 1996.
[77] Tenancy includes licence: see the Housing Act 1996, s 126.
[78] In Wales, s 160A of the Housing Act 1996. In England, s 160ZA of the Housing Act 1996.
[79] Sections 166A (England), 167 (Wales) and 168 (England and Wales) of the Housing Act 1996.
[80] Sections 166A (England), 167 (Wales) of the Housing Act 1996.
[81] See s 159(7) of the Housing Act 1996.
[82] Section 166A(14) (England) and s 167(8)(Wales) of the Housing Act 1996.
[83] [2002] EWHC 633 (Admin), [2003] HLR 8.
[84] Ibid at [29].

7.69 However, one should compare the *Begum* decision with the more recent judgment in *Birmingham City Council v Qasim*[85] in which the Court of Appeal held that tenancies granted in breach of the housing authority's allocation scheme were not invalid. In *Qasim*, an officer of the council was granting secure tenancies to persons of his choosing, without authority and in contravention of the statutory allocation scheme. The Court of Appeal held that power to grant a tenancy was conferred by Part II of the Housing Act 1985 and was separate from the allocation of housing, which was governed by Part VI of the Housing Act 1996. Whilst the two activities would often be closely connected, and the distinction between allocation and disposal was rather technical, allocation was simply a preliminary step to disposal. It was possible to have a lawful allocation without a subsequent disposal if, for example, an applicant decided not to accept the property.

7.70 Similarly, if an authority makes a decision to refuse accommodation to an applicant, they must apply the allocation scheme. In *Sahardid v Camden LBC*,[86] the allocating authority's scheme provided that a homeless applicant with a child under five years old was only entitled to one-bedroom accommodation, whereas this entitlement was enlarged to a two-bedroom property when the child reached the age of five. The authority offered the appellant one-bedroom accommodation, but failed to consider the age of her son, who was five years and three days old when the offer was made. This failure was found to be a clear error of law in that the authority had not applied the terms of its own allocation scheme.[87]

7.71 The authority's allocation scheme must be framed so as to give reasonable preference to the following groups:[88]

(a) homeless persons (within the meaning of Part VII of the Housing Act 1996);

(b) people to whom a duty is owed under Part VII of the Housing Act 1996;[89]

(c) occupants of unsanitary or overcrowded or otherwise unsatisfactory housing;

(d) people who need to move on medical or welfare grounds (including grounds relating to a disability);

(e) people who need to move to a particular locality where, if that need were not met, they would suffer hardship.[90]

7.72 The question of reasonable preference was considered in *R (Mei Ling Lin) v Barnet LBC*.[91] The local housing authority had established a points-based allocation scheme which awarded applicants a certain number of points depending upon a number of criteria, based generally on the statutory preference categories under the Housing Act 1996, s 167(2). Applicants were requested to bid for accommodation as and when it became available, with the accommodation being allocated to the applicant with the highest number of points. Homeless families were housed under assured shorthold tenancies controlled by Registered Social Landlords and were given 10 'homeless family points' for as long as they occupied it, save where the RSL's lease expired, in which case

---

[85] [2010] HLR 19; [2009] EWCA Civ 1080, CA.
[86] [2005] HLR 11.
[87] Ibid at [29].
[88] Section 166A(3) (England) and 167(2) (Wales) of the Housing Act 1996.
[89] Sections 190(2), 193(2) or 195(2), together with people occupying accommodation provided under s 192(3) of the Housing Act 1996.
[90] Eg the need may arise from a requirement to give or receive care or to receive specialised medical treatment.
[91] [2007] EWCA Civ 132, [2007] HLR 30.

they were awarded 300 'lease end points' for a limited period of time. However, existing tenants who requested a transfer and who were not expressly included in any of the categories of statutory preference were able to accumulate up to 350 points (including 100 points for merely requesting the transfer), the effect of which was to defeat most homeless applicants. The claimant asserted that the scheme did not afford her 'reasonable preference'.

7.73 The case went up to the Court of Appeal. The salient points are as follows:

(a) the test is not whether the homeless are *excluded* from accommodation under Part VI of the Housing Act 1996, but whether they were given reasonable preference relative to people who did not fall within the s 167(2) categories;[92]

(b) 'reasonable preference' is not about prospects of success or outcomes but about giving the applicant a reasonable head start in his search for social housing;[93]

(c) whether a preference is 'reasonable' is a matter for the local housing authority;[94]

(d) having regard to the above, the award of 10 points to homeless families did constitute a reasonable preference because it placed such a person in a better position than somebody who did not qualify for these points.[95]

7.74 A scheme fails to comply with the requirements of the Housing Act 1996, s 166A (in England) or s 167 (in Wales) if it does not explain what criteria apply for awarding reasonable preference or indicate when they will be applied.[96]

7.75 Nevertheless, the scope for challenge has been curtailed considerably by the House of Lords (as it then was) in the recent case of *R (Ahmad) v Newham LBC*.[97] The London Borough of Newham operated a two-part allocation scheme which involved either Choice Based Lettings[98] or a direct offer. The House of Lords was required to determine the following issues:

(a) whether the Housing Act 1996, s 167[99] required a local housing authority to accord priority as between 'reasonable preference' applicants by reference to the relative gravity of their needs;

(b) whether Newham's scheme was unlawful because the Choice Based Lettings involved allocating a significant proportion of housing to a class of applicants who did not satisfy any of the requirements in paras (a) to (e) of the Housing Act 1996, s 167(2).

---

[92] Ibid at [25].
[93] Ibid at [25], [50]; see also *R v Wolverhampton MBC ex p Watters* (1997) 29 HLR 931 at 938.
[94] Ibid at [28], [50], [51].
[95] Ibid at [28]–[30].
[96] *R (Cali, Abdi and Hassan) v Waltham Forest LBC* [2006] EWHC 302 (Admin); [2007] HLR 1.
[97] [2009] UKHL 14.
[98] Introduced by the Homelessness Act 2002; see the Housing Act 1996, s 167(1A) in particular.
[99] Note that the *Ahmad* decision was made prior to the amendments introduced by the Localism Act 2011. Nevertheless, the principles will remain applicable.

7.76 Their Lordships answered the questions as follows:

(a) Section 167 of the Housing Act 1996 does not impose any requirement for an authority to rank reasonable preference applicants depending upon the weight of their need.[100]

(b) In the case of transfer applicants (who did not fall within the reasonable preference categories under s 167(2)(a)–(e)), it was entirely legitimate to operate an allocation scheme which, in some circumstances, meant that they were given preference over reasonable preference candidates. Section 167(2) of the Housing Act 1996 only required that those groups be given a 'reasonable preference'. It did not require that they should be given absolute priority over everyone else. Still less did it require that an individual household in one of those groups should be given absolute priority over an individual household which wished to transfer.[101]

7.77 The important point for judicial review practitioners to note is that the House of Lords made it very clear that matters of housing allocation require difficult judgments to be made, which depend upon juggling different social, political and economic priorities. It seemed very unlikely that Parliament would have intended that the courts should embark on an assessment of how priorities were to be accorded, save in the rarest and most exceptional circumstances.[102]

7.78 Thus, it would appear that the circumstances in which an allocation scheme (or a decision made under it) will be quashed or even scrutinised closely by the court will now be few and far between. It is only where a scheme is patently irrational that the courts are likely to intervene.[103] For example, in *R (Aweys) v Birmingham City Council*,[104] the House of Lords held that the authority's allocations policy was unlawful by reason of irrationality. Under the scheme, the authority would discharge its duty under Part VII of the Housing Act 1996 by leaving a family in their existing accommodation until suitable permanent accommodation could be found, even if that accommodation had been found to be unsuitable for their needs. A family in such a situation would be accorded a lower priority than a homeless family in temporary accommodation which had not been the subject of a finding that it was unsuitable. The authority had not justified the difference in treatment given that a family in unsuitable accommodation was in greater need than a family housed in suitable accommodation albeit temporarily.

7.79 However, practitioners should be aware that whatever the latitude enjoyed by allocating authorities, allocation decisions should still be made in accordance with the adopted scheme.

INTRODUCTORY TENANCIES

7.80 Introductory tenancies (introduced by Part V of the Housing Act 1996) provide a good example of the important, yet increasingly circumscribed role played by housing judicial review proceedings before the Administrative Court.

---

[100] Ibid at [39].
[101] Ibid at [18]–[20], per Baroness Hale.
[102] See generally the speech of Lord Neuberger, especially at [46] and [62].
[103] *R (Ariemuguvbe) v Islington LBC* [2009] EWCA Civ 1308, which re-iterated the broad discretion that is available to housing authorities in the allocation of housing.
[104] [2009] UKHL 36, [2009] 1 WLR 1506.

7.81 An introductory tenancy is, in essence, a probationary tenancy offered by a local housing authority or housing action trust in order that they can monitor the actions and behaviour of their tenants for a period of one year (although this may be extended by the landlord by a maximum of six months: Housing Act 1996, s 125A).

7.82 The landlord may bring the introductory tenancy to an end relatively efficiently and speedily by serving a notice seeking possession which complies with the requirements of the Housing Act 1996, s 128. The requirements of the Housing Act 1996, s 128 may be summarised as follows:

(a) that the notice states that an order for possession of the dwelling house will be sought;
(b) the reasons for the landlord's decision to apply for such an order;
(c) the notice shall specify a date after which possession proceedings may be commenced; this may not be earlier than the date on which the tenancy could, apart from Chapter I of Part V of the Housing Act 1996, have been brought to an end by the service of a notice to quit given by the landlord on the same date as the notice of proceedings;
(d) the notice must inform the tenant of the right to request a review of the decision to commence possession proceedings and that such a request must be made within 14 days of service of the notice seeking possession;
(e) the tenant must also be told that he can obtain legal assistance from a solicitor, the Citizens Advice Bureau or a housing aid or law centre.

7.83 Provided that these requirements have been met, and possession proceedings are commenced, the court must grant possession of the dwelling house (Housing Act 1996, s 127(2)).

7.84 It is the penultimate requirement of s 128 (s 128(6)) that is of most relevance because it refers expressly to the right of an introductory tenant to request a review of the decision to commence possession proceedings, in much the same way as the dissatisfied homeless applicant may do under s 202 of the same Act. Indeed, similar issues are likely to arise as to the lawfulness of the decision on review. In brief, the principal questions that are likely to surface are as follows:

(a) the adequacy of reasons (Housing Act 1996, s 129(5)): however, it should be noted that the reasons given for confirming the decision to commence proceedings need not be the same as those contained in the notice seeking possession, provided that the tenant is given the proper opportunity to respond to any new allegations upon which the landlord proposes to rely;[105]
(b) the procedural fairness of the review: the tenant has a right to make oral or written representations and to be legally represented throughout the review process (Housing Act 1996, s 129(4)(b));
(c) the rationality of the decision: in practice, it will be only in the most obvious and exceptional case that it will be established that no reasonable landlord would have upheld the decision to seek possession (eg in *R (Chowdhury) v Newham LBC*,[106] the tenant blamed his rent arrears on a failure of the housing authority to pay housing benefit. The court upheld the authority's view that the tenant had a

---

[105] *R (Laporte) v Newham LBC* [2004] EWHC 227.
[106] [2003] EWHC 2837 (Admin).

responsibility properly to inform himself as to the requirement of the housing benefit system and to ensure that any application was complete. Consequently, the landlord's decision that the tenant was unsuitable to remain in social housing was not irrational).

7.85 Questions arising out of possession proceedings for dwellings held under introductory tenancies can be dealt with either in the County Court or the Administrative Court. However, the clear legislative and jurisprudential steer is that challenges are principally to be considered in the County Court.[107] For example, the Housing Act 1996, s 138(3) provides that if a person takes proceedings in the High Court which he could have commenced in the county court, he is not entitled to any costs.

7.86 Similarly, it would appear that where a tenant fails to take issue with lawfulness of a decision to commence proceedings (either by failing to request a review or by failing to commence proceedings after an unsuccessful review) it will subsequently be too late to challenge the lawfulness of the review or the substantive decision to start possession proceedings (*R (Chelfat) v Tower Hamlets LBC*).[108]

7.87 A clear exception to this general proposition is the case where a tenant seeks to raise public law arguments as a defence to possession proceedings in the county court. Whilst as a general proposition it is open to a defendant to run a public law defence to possession proceedings (*Manchester City Council v Pinnock*).[109]

7.88 In practice, most deficiencies in an internal review can be rectified if the landlord carries out a second review.[110] In such circumstances, whilst the question of costs may still be 'live', any judicial review claim challenging the original decision is likely to be wholly academic.

PROCEDURE

7.89 The judicial review of housing decisions presents some particular procedural issues, if only by virtue of the urgency of many of the claims and the precarious position in which claimants sometimes find themselves.

7.90 The two main areas of procedural relevance are urgent applications and interim relief and costs.

Interim relief

7.91 Given that housing judicial review claims often (but not exclusively) concern issues as fundamental as the roof over a person's head, the question of interim relief is particularly relevant to a full understanding of this area of law. Practitioners will most regularly encounter the need to apply for or to resist an application for interim relief in the context of homelessness.

---

[107] *Manchester City Council v Pinnock* [2010] UKSC 45 at [88].
[108] [2006] EWHC 313.
[109] [2010] UKSC 45 and see *Wandsworth LBC v Winder* [1985] AC 461, 17 HLR 196, HL.
[110] *R (McDonagh) v Salisbury DC* [2001] EWHC Admin 567.

7.92 It is possible to combine a claim for judicial review with an application for interim injunctive relief.[111] In urgent cases, Form N463 (Request for Urgent Consideration) must be completed together with the draft claim form and a copy of a draft order. Justification for the urgency of the case must also be given and the applicant is required to give the date and time when it was first appreciated that an immediate application might be necessary, to provide reasons for any delay in making the application, and to state what efforts have been made to put the defendant and any interested party on notice of the application. These requirements will be strictly enforced.[112]

7.93 In practice, it is not at all unusual for such interim applications to be determinative of the claim. In many cases, the claimant will simply be seeking somewhere to stay for a limited period of time and by the time the substantive judicial review claim is to be heard, the issues between the parties may have been resolved or may no longer be relevant.[113]

7.94 In practice, it has appeared that the court is willing to grant interim relief fairly readily, especially in relation to claims by homeless persons. This willingness is likely to have been borne out of a desire to preserve the *status quo* pending the resolution of the substantive claim and the, perhaps understandable, wish to provide a claimant with somewhere to live so that he is better able to prosecute the claim.

7.95 Practitioners should nevertheless be wary of the temptation to commence proceedings, which have dubious merit in order simply (or primarily) to secure a short lived benefit for their clients. The court has deprecated such practices and in recent years has appeared more willing to investigate the substantive merits before granting interim relief. Alternatively, claimants who launch a poorly founded claim may ultimately be penalised in costs. The practice of applying for interim relief as a matter of course even where the substantive merits are weak has been subject to criticism. In *R (Lawer) v Restormel Borough Council*,[114] an interim injunction made without notice was set aside where there had been material non-disclosure by the claimant and where the substance of the claim was hopeless. In *R (Hamid) v Secretary of State for the Home Department*[115] (an immigration case), the Administrative Court issued a stern warning that it would not hesitate to refer lawyers to the Solicitors Regulation Authority if they failed to comply with the procedural requirements concerning urgent applications.

7.96 Occasionally, the responsibility for prolonging the *status quo* for perhaps too long may lie with the Administrative Court itself. For example, in *R (Casey) v Restormel Borough Council*,[116] Munby J (citing the Magna Carta) expressed concern at the length of time which the defendant local authority had to wait before its application to discharge the interim injunction was heard. The judge also referred to *R (Lawer) v Restormel Borough Council*[117] in which there was a similarly unacceptable delay.[118]

---

[111] Section 31(1)(b) of the Senior Courts Act 1981; CPR r 54.3.
[112] *R (Hamid) v Secretary of State for the Home Department* [2012] EWHC 3070 (Admin).
[113] M Sunkin et al, 'Mapping the Use of Judicial Review to Challenge Local Authorities in England and Wales' [2007] PL 545 at 556: housing and homelessness cases are much more likely to drop from the judicial review process than planning, childcare and education cases.
[114] [2007] EWHC 2299 (Admin) at [70]–[77].
[115] [2012] EWHC 3070 (Admin).
[116] [2007] EWHC Admin 2554 at [28].
[117] [2007] EWHC 2299 (Admin).
[118] *R (Casey) v Restormel Borough Council* [2007] EWHC Admin 2554 at [31].

7.97 It is to be hoped that the delays to which to the parties were subjected in the Casey and Lawer cases will be reduced, if not eliminated as a consequence of the regionalisation of the Administrative Court.

7.98 In an application for interim relief, the court will have regard to a number of principles, which can be extracted from the authorities:

(a) There must be a strong prima facie case demonstrating a breach of the authority's statutory obligations before the court will grant an injunction.[119] In *De Falco*, the court expressly disapproved of the application of the *American Cyanamid*[120] balance of convenience test in such cases on the basis that it was not appropriate to apply such private law concepts to the field of administrative law.[121]

(b) An injunction will usually follow if permission is granted to move for judicial review. See *R v Cardiff City Council, ex p Barry*.[122] Thus, if there is an arguable case at the permission stage of judicial review proceedings, there is a strong chance of obtaining interim relief pending the substantive hearing.

Costs

7.99 Public money is almost invariably in play in housing judicial review claims. Moreover, decisions are often (but by no means always) reviewed by the decision-maker as a consequence of changing circumstances or in the light of the strength of the claimant's challenge. Thus, proceedings do not always run their full course.

7.100 As we have already seen, in the field of housing judicial review claims, the granting of interim relief or permission to move to a substantive hearing will often be determinative of both the legal and practical issues between the parties. Consequently, a body of case-law has developed to deal with the situation in which costs are incurred but where the claim does not proceed to a full hearing.

7.101 One should be ever mindful of avoiding protracted satellite litigation when the substantive claim has been resolved. It is unlikely to promote the overriding objective of the Civil Procedure Rules[123] or be a proportionate course of action if the parties engage in what for all intents and purposes is a fully contested substantive hearing merely to seek a ruling as to who would have been successful when the only 'live' issue is one of costs.

7.102 In *M v Croydon LBC*,[124] the appellant (M) appealed against a decision making no order for costs where the respondent local authority conceded the relief sought. M had applied for asylum claiming to have been born in 1996 and aged 12. The local authority assessed him as 14. The matter was disputed between the parties culminating with the issue of proceedings by M. The local authority eventually conceded that M was born in 1996 but were not prepared to agree to pay his costs of the proceedings. The judge held that the just result was no order for costs as the outcome was not clear from the outset given the dynamic development of the law in that area while the claim was live.

---

[119] *De Falco v Crawley BC* [1980] QB 460 at 467.
[120] *American Cyanamid Co v Ethicon Ltd* [1975] AC 396 HL.
[121] Ibid.
[122] (1990) 22 HLR 261 at 263.
[123] CPR r 1.1.
[124] [2012] EWCA Civ 595, [2012] 1 WLR 2607, [2012] 3 All ER 1237.

7.103 The appeal was allowed and the Court of Appeal confirmed that:

(a) The position where cases settled in the Administrative Court should be no different from general civil litigation, where the general rule under the CPR r 44.2(2) applied.[125]

(b) Where a claimant obtained all the relief he sought, whether by consent or after a contested hearing, he was the successful party who was entitled to all his costs, unless there was a good reason to the contrary.[126]

(c) In a case where the claimant has only succeeded in part following a contested hearing, or pursuant to a settlement, the court will normally determine questions such as how reasonable the claimant was in pursuing the unsuccessful claim, how important it was compared with the successful claim, and how much the costs were increased as a result of the claimant pursuing the unsuccessful claim. However, where there has been a settlement, the court will normally be in a significantly worse position to make findings on such issues than where the case has been fought out. In many such cases the court will be able to form a view as to the appropriate costs order based on such issues; in other cases it will be much more difficult. Where the parties have settled the claimant's substantive claims on the basis that he succeeds in part, but only in part, there is often much to be said for concluding that there is no order for costs. However, where there is not a clear winner, much will depend on the particular facts. In some such cases it may help to consider who would have won if the matter had proceeded to trial as, if it is tolerably clear, it may for instance support or undermine the contention that one of the two claims was stronger than the other.[127]

(d) In a case where there has been some compromise which does not actually reflect the claimant's claims, the court is often unable to gauge whether there is a successful party in any respect and, if so, who it is. In such cases, therefore, there is an even more powerful argument that the default position should be no order for costs. However, in some such cases it may be sensible to look at the underlying claims and inquire whether it was tolerably clear who would have won if the matter had not settled. If it is, then that may well strongly support the contention that the party who would have won did better out of the settlement, and therefore did win.[128]

(e) The Court of Appeal stressed the importance of (i) early settlement; and (ii) agreeing the basis of any costs award. However, if the question of costs cannot be agreed, it is important that both the work and costs involved in preparing the parties' submissions on costs, and the material the judge is asked to consider, are proportionate to the amount at stake. No order for costs will be the default order when the judge cannot without disproportionate expenditure of judicial time, if at all, fairly and sensibly make an order in favour of either party.[129]

---

[125] This rule provides that: 'If the court decides to make an order about costs (a) the general rule is that the unsuccessful party will be ordered to pay the costs of the successful party; but (b) the court may make a different order.'
[126] [2012] EWCA Civ 595 at [49], [58] and [61].
[127] [2012] EWCA Civ 595 at [62].
[128] [2012] EWCA Civ 595 at [63].
[129] [2012] EWCA Civ 595 at [77].

7.104 The hard-pressed Administrative Court judge should make a reasonable and proportionate attempt to analyse the situation and not be overly tempted to adopt the fallback position of no order for costs.[130]

7.105 There is also an obligation in certain circumstances to put forward a more cost effective means of resolving the litigation prior to proceedings being commenced.[131] The defendant local authority was liable for the costs unnecessarily incurred, where they refused to consider an alternative resolution of the dispute. This requirement is likely to be given greater weight in the light of the duty to consider Alternative Dispute Resolution. However, the time for negotiating a mutually acceptable outcome without resorting to litigation is unlikely to be available where, for example, a prospective claimant is about to become street homeless.

---

[130] R (Scott) v London Borough of Hackney [2009] EWCA Civ 217, CA at [51].
[131] R (H) v Kingston-Upon-Thames RLBC [2002] EWHC 3158.

CHAPTER 8

MENTAL HEALTH

INTRODUCTION

8.01 Until relatively recently, judicial review or challenge by way of case stated was the only procedure by which there could be challenges to the Mental Health Review Tribunal, that being the only court or tribunal designed specifically for the purpose of deciding applications under the Mental Health Act (MHA). Cases concerning the other side of mental health law, involving those who lack the capacity to make certain decisions, if they reached a court at all, were decided under the inherent jurisdiction of the High Court; the Family Division in cases concerning treatment and welfare issues, and by the Chancery Division where the issues concerned property related matters, including wills.

8.02 However, with recent legislation the entire landscape of mental health law has changed. First, the Mental Capacity Act 2005 (MCA) has not only placed the common law relating to those lacking capacity on a statutory footing but has also created a new superior court of record, the Court of Protection, to deal with the interpretation of the new statutory code as well as resolving disputes that arise, and making declaratory decisions to enable those dealing with the mentally incapable to act on their behalf. The mental capacity landscape has been further clouded by the amendments made to the MCA by the Mental Health Act 2007 which introduced a new administrative procedure to enable those lacking capacity to be deprived of their liberty in a manner which is consistent with Art 5 of the European Convention of Human Rights (ECHR) the procedure under Sch A1 of the MCA, the Deprivation of Liberty Safeguards (universally referred to as DOLS), under which an appeal lies to the Court of Protection.

8.03 The Mental Health Act 2007 also brought about the end of the Mental Health Review Tribunal. Instead a virtually identical jurisdiction was passed onto the new tribunal system, which was created by the Tribunals, Courts and Enforcement Act 2007 (TCEA). The critical change is the two-tier system. At first instance the cases that were heard by the MHRT are now heard by a similarly constituted First-tier Tribunal (FTT), which is part of the Health, Education and Social Care Chamber (HESC). However, appeals from the FTT now lie to the Administrative Appeals Chamber of the Upper Tribunal (UT). This is a statutory appeal on a point of law. There is still the option of judicial review, which can be brought in the UT or, in appropriate cases, in the High Court. In addition, the new system enables each Tribunal to review its own decisions thereby creating a 'mezzanine level' between the FTT's first instance decision and an appeal to the UT.

8.04 As a result, the place of public law in the mental health sphere is somewhat more complicated than in many of the other areas of law dealt with in this book. Most of the bodies involved in cases under the MHA will be public bodies. So, too, will be many of those involved in MCA cases. Judicial review to the Administrative Court will only be appropriate in certain limited and selected instances. The aim of this chapter is to indicate to the puzzled practitioner which types of challenge arise in the mental health sphere and which judicial route needs to be taken to resolve them.

8.05 This chapter is not intended to explain in great detail the vast area of mental health and mental capacity law. What it is intended to do is to explain how the various judicial bodies discharge their functions within the area and where judicial review now stands.

8.06 As part of this introduction it is important to set out the most significant provision within the ECHR that concerns mental health law:

'Article 5 Right to Liberty and Security

(1) Everyone has the right to liberty and security of person. No one shall be deprived of his liberty save in the following cases and in accordance with a procedure prescribed by law ... (e) the lawful detention of ... persons of unsound mind ... (4) Everyone who is deprived of his liberty by arrest or detention shall be entitled to take proceedings by which the lawfulness of his detention shall be decided speedily by a court and his release ordered if the detention is not lawful.'

8.07 The term 'unsound mind' is nowhere defined in the Convention. It is, however, consistent with both 'mental disorder' and 'mental incapacity'.[1] In the case of mental disorder, the fact of a disorder itself does not justify deprivation of liberty. In *Winterwerp v The Netherlands*[2] the European Court of Human Rights (ECtHR) ruled that mental disorder from which the patient suffered had to be of a kind or degree which warranted detention. As we shall see that is reflected in the provisions of the MHA. There is some doubt as to whether *Winterwerp* applies to cases involving mental incapacity following the case of *G v E*, which is the subject of comment later in this chapter.

PUBLIC LAW AND THE MENTAL HEALTH ACT 1983

8.08 The purpose of the Mental Health Act is to create an essentially administrative procedure for the admission into detention and other forms of restriction of those who suffer from mental disorder, as well as having in place a proper procedure for regulating and regularising their treatment whilst in hospital or in the community. The Act ensures that there are safeguards to ensure that those detained or subject to orders have their detention reviewed and are discharged when the criteria for admission is no longer satisfied. The purpose of the Act, in other words, is to satisfy Article 5 of the ECHR. Indeed, in the landmark case of *HL v UK*[3] the ECtHR held up the MHA in order to criticise the pre-MCA regime for the treatment of the mentally incapacitated. At para [120], the court said:

'In particular, and most obviously, the Court notes the lack of any formalised admission procedures which indicate who can propose admission, for what reasons and on the basis of what kind of medical and other assessments and conclusions. There is [in HL's case] no requirement to fix the exact purpose of admission (for example for assessment or for

---

[1] This was confirmed by the Court of Appeal in *G v E* [2010] EWCA Civ 822.
[2] (1979) 2 EHRR 387.
[3] (2004) 40 EHRR 761.

treatment) and, consistently, no limits in terms of time, treatment or care attach to that admission. Nor is there any specific provision requiring a continuing clinical assessment of the persistence of the disorder warranting detention. The appointment of a representative of a patient who could make certain objections and applications on his or her behalf is a procedural protection to those committed involuntarily under the 1983 Act would be of equal importance for patients who are legally incapacitated and have, as in the present case, extremely limited communication abilities.'

8.09 In other words, the ECtHR was delivering a critique of the treatment of the 'Bournewood patient' by holding up the MHA as a paradigm against which Art 5 compliant procedures ought to be judged.[4] The MHA is divided into parts, each of which fulfills a particular role in ensuring that the orders made under the Act are lawful. So the first 'gateway' to an order for detention under the Act is 'mental disorder' which is expressly defined in Part I of the Act, which contains only one section. That definition (given in s 1(2)) is sufficiently wide to keep abreast with psychiatric diagnosis, but specific enough to satisfy the need for certainty and predictability under Art 5.

8.10 The second section of the Act fixes formalised admission procedures for compulsory admission to hospital and into guardianship. For instance, ss 2 and 3 of the Act are specifically designed to adhere to Art 5 as interpreted by the ECtHR in *Winterwerp v The Netherlands*,[5] by requiring that the mental disorder must be of a 'nature or degree' that would warrant or make it appropriate for the person to be detained in a hospital, and that it is necessary for him to be so detained for his own health and safety or for that of others. A legally sound reason for admission is thus created. Furthermore, the requirement of necessity means that the admission must be proportionate. Finally, there is a need for appropriate medical treatment to be available – therefore ensuring that the purpose for admission can be met. The sections each have time limits attached to them, ensuring their compliance with the Convention. Section 37 of the Act provides powers to the Crown Court or the magistrates court after conviction to order admission to and detention at hospital or to order guardianship in appropriate cases. The power is similar to s 3 but one imposed by the criminal courts.

8.11 What the Act also does is to ensure that there are functions to be discharged by certain actors within the statutory framework. In summary, the procedures for admission under ss 2, 3 and 7 of the MHA are governed by s 11. This places the obligation to carry out the procedure on the approved mental health professional (AMHP). The Act requires the AMHP to consult with another specific actor, the nearest relative (NR), who is intended to represent the patient's family or partner, with input into the decision-making process informed by the patient's social circumstances. The process may only proceed on the basis of the recommendations of two registered medical practitioners, thus ensuring that the procedure is based on a proper medical diagnosis or suspicion of a mental disorder (as the case may be). The NR can derail the admission process by their objection to it. If the objection is unreasonable, the AMHP may apply to displace the NR and replace them with another.[6] Once the application for admission is complete, and in the proper form, the documentation must be delivered to the hospital managers (HM). It is the HM 'who have the authority to detain patients under the Act'.[7] They have the primary duty to ensure that the provisions of the Act are

---

[4] So called because of the name of the NHS Trust in the HL case, and the domestic name of the case: *R v Bournewood Community and Mental Health NHS Trust, ex p L* [1999] 1 AC 458. The 'Bournewood patient' will be defined in the section of this chapter concerned with mental capacity.
[5] (1979–80) 2 EHRR 387.
[6] Under s 29 of the MHA.
[7] See Chapter 30 of the MHA Code of Practice for full details.

followed, that patients are detained only as the Act allows, and that they are treated only in accordance with the provisions of the Act.

8.12 What is clear from these procedures is that the legality of the admission is determined by whether the application procedure has been properly followed. At this stage in the proceedings procedural flaws may be challenged in the High Court.

Although the departure from proper practice may only be slight, it could still result in the detention that follows being unlawful. As the High Court put it in a case in 2012 in which an AMHP was held to have breached s 11(4) when admitting a patient under s 3 without having taken sufficient steps to consult with the patient's nearest relative:

> '[the section] provides constitutional protection for those that are faced with detention under the Mental Health Act. Compliance with the requirements of s 11(4) is therefore the price which is paid for the ability of those charged with the treatment of those with mental illnesses and disabilities to detain people without immediate recourse to a court and in a way which is compliant with Article 5 [of the ECHR]. Thus there is a heavy duty on those who carry out these tasks to ensure that those statutory provisions are complied with.'[8]

Some examples may assist in illustrating this point. Under s 11(3) of the MHA, the AMHP is obliged 'before or within a reasonable time after an application for admission of a patient for assessment is made ...' to 'take such steps as are practicable to inform the person (if any) appearing to be the nearest relative of the patient that the application is to be or has been made and of the power off the nearest relative under s 23(2)(a)'.[9] When the AMHP fails to do this in good faith the application is not invalidated, but if done in bad faith it may be.[10]

8.13 Another example concerns s 11(4) of the MHA where the AMHP may not make an application for admission for treatment or guardianship in either of the two following cases: first, where the NR has notified the AMHP (or the case of guardianship the Local Social Services Authority) that he objects to the admission; or, secondly, where the AMHP had not consulted a person (if any) appearing to be the NR (although the requirement does not apply if it appears to the AMHP that in the circumstances such a consultation would not have been reasonably practicable or would involve unnecessary delay). The courts have been willing to investigate factual issues that arise out of applications that may flout the requirements of these provisions. In one case the court made a decision as to how long a couple had lived together (thus determining status as NR).[11] In another, whether the consultation had been effective.[12]

8.14 Challenging the diagnostic requirements for admission through the High Court is problematic and is best left to an application to the managers or to the tribunal, where a full consideration of the medical opinion, with cross-examination and the use of an independent expert can take place.

---

[8] See *R (GP) v Derby City Council & Derbyshire Mental Health NHS Foundation Trust* [2012] EWHC 1451 (Admin) at para [36] (Judge Pelling, QC sitting as a High Court judge).
[9] The right of the NR to apply to the HM for discharge.
[10] See *R v Birmingham Mental Health Trust, ex p Phillips* (C/O/1501/95).
[11] *R v Hospital Managers of the Park Royal Hospital, ex p Robinson* (QBD Admin 26 November 2007).
[12] *BB v Cygnet Health Care & Lewisham LBC* [2008] EWHC 1259 (Admin) and *GD v Manager of the Dennis Scott Unit* (QBD Admin, 27 June 2008). I am grateful for the details of the unreported cases here, as well as the commentary from Laura Davidson's article 'Nearest Relative Consultation and the Avoidant AMHP' [2009] JMHL 70.

8.15 The medical evidence in support of admission will usually be a diagnosis of a recognised mental disorder and will be supported by a reference to one of the recognised diagnostic criteria.[13] The nature and degree of the disorder is disjunctive. Either may justify the order that follows, including detention.[14] There will often be a need for a high level of clinical judgment in determining nature and degree. The nature of the disorder is not simply which ICD-10 or DSM-IV category it falls into (if any). It is the history of the disorder over the patient's life, how chronic it has been, the patient's response to treatment, whether the patient's condition has deteriorated rapidly in the absence of treatment, the chronicity of the condition and possibly other factors that determine the nature of the disorder.[15] The degree of the disorder is the current manifestation of his disorder. Therefore, a patient with no history of a mental disorder may be detained under the MHA if he presently exhibits serious enough symptoms of such a disorder. Equally, and more controversially, a person who suffers from a disorder which is of a serious enough nature may be detained even if asymptomatic, in certain circumstances. For instance, a person who suffers from chronic and enduring paranoid schizophrenia and who is maintained in good health by medication, may be detained under the MHA if he were to discontinue his medication where a period of non-medication is likely to result in rapid deterioration into serious illness.[16]

8.16 Many of these decisions will be based almost entirely on the professional judgment of those deciding. Consequently, they are difficult in the extreme to challenge on the usual judicial review grounds. Only in extreme cases will the decision to detain a person with a mental disorder be *Wednesbury* unreasonable. However, challenges can be made by way of judicial review in the event of non-compliance with the rules laid down by the MHA, as we shall see below. Equally, the Code of Practice to the MHA must be adhered to unless there are very good reasons for not so doing. Although it falls short of having statutory effect, a breach of the code may assist in a challenge to the decision made in breach.[17]

8.17 Appropriate medical treatment must be available. Therefore, the availability of 'appropriate medical treatment' is another prerequisite for detention. The MHA does not define what 'appropriate' means in this context. The definition of medical treatment is given in the interpretation section, s 145. At s 145(1) medical treatment 'includes nursing, psychological intervention and specialist mental health habilitation, rehabilitation and care ...'. To this a caveat is added at s 145(4), namely: 'Any reference in this Act to medical treatment, in relation to mental disorder, shall be construed as a reference to medical treatment the purpose of which is to alleviate, or prevent the worsening of, the disorder or one or more of its symptoms or manifestations'. This definition is elaborated upon in the Code of Practice to the MHA at Chapter 6, which casts some additional light on the issue of appropriateness. At para 6.6 the Code states:

> 'Even if particular mental disorders are likely to persist or get worse despite treatment, there may well be a range of interventions which would represent appropriate medical treatment. It should never be assumed that any disorders, or any patients, are inherently or inevitably untreatable. Nor should it be assumed that likely difficulties in achieving long-term and

---

[13] More usual in the UK is reference to the ICD-10 Classification of Mental and Behavioural Disorders (WHO) or, sometimes, to the Diagnostic and Statistical manual of Mental Disorders (or DSM-IV), presently in its Fourth Edition.
[14] See *R v MHRT for South Thames Region, ex p Smith* [1998] EWHC 832 (Admin) Popplewell J.
[15] See *ex p Smith* (above) and *Smirek v Williams* [2000] EWCA Civ 3025.
[16] See *Smirek* (above) (per Hale LJ) and *R (H) v MHRT* [2001] EWCA Civ 415 (per Lord Phillips MR).
[17] *R (Munjaz) v Mersey Care NHS Trust* [2005] UKHL 58.

sustainable change in a person's underlying disorder make medical treatment to help manage their condition and the behaviours arising from it either inappropriate or unnecessary.'

8.18 This passage was concerned with the argument that those with treatment resistant conditions, including some personality disorders, could not be detained under hospital orders because no appropriate treatment could ever be available. However, it also illuminates another issue. The available treatment does not need to be the best treatment possible, or even, by the same measure, the best treatment available. At para 6.12 of the Code this is made clear, the medical treatment available at the time need only be 'an appropriate response to the patient's condition and situation'. Once again, the appropriateness test is dependent on the professional judgment of those supporting the order under the MHA. As the Code makes clear at para 6.14 what is appropriate '... will depend, in part, on what might reasonably be expected to be achieved given the nature and degree of the patient's disorder'. That treatment may not include any active therapeutic input in the form of medication or a psychological programme. It may consist 'only of nursing and specialist day-to-day care under the clinical supervision of an approved clinician, in a safe and secure therapeutic environment with a structured regime' (Code, para 6.16).

8.19 Consequently, detention in a hospital without active treatment may satisfy the appropriate treatment condition. Although (Code, para 6.17) 'simply detaining someone – even in a hospital – does not constitute medical treatment' para 6.16 does not require that treatment to be any more than nursing support in a safe environment. This is particularly important in the case of those with personality disorders[18] who may require 'relatively intense and long term, structured and coherent' treatment (Code, para 35.10). Any challenge by way of judicial review to an order made under the MHA on the basis of the 'availability of appropriate medical treatment', where the Responsible Clinician (RC)[19] is able to satisfy the tests outlined in the Code will be very difficult. The better mode of challenge is through the FTT, where the evidential basis and professional opinions of those supporting detention may be challenged in an adversarial way in front of an expert tribunal and with independent experts who contradict that view may be instructed.[20]

8.20 The appropriateness of medical treatment has also been considered in relation to whether a patient is eligible to be detained under the MCA/DOLS because he is detainable under the MHA. This issue will be revisited below in the MCA section of this chapter.[21] It is important, however, that the treatment must be for a mental disorder. This raises difficult questions as to the predominant purpose of the treatment proposed. Admission to hospital under the MHA can only be lawful if the core treatment proposed is for a mental disorder. This, however, can include the consequences of that disorder, such as the treatment of wounds inflicted by a mentally disordered person,[22] or the force-feeding of an anorexic patient.[23] However, it does not stretch to a case where a diabetic person, suffering from Korsakoff's syndrome and who is unable to manage his blood-sugar levels is detained in hospital so that that management can take place.[24]

---

[18] ICD-10, F-60. Also listed in DSM-IV in chapter on personality disorders.
[19] Defined in s 34.
[20] For a recent consideration of this issue as well as an example of how the matter may be challenged in the FTT, see *MD v Nottinghamshire Health Care NHS Trust* [2010] UKUT 59 (ACC) – Judge Jacobs sitting alone.
[21] *GJ v The Foundation Trust, A PCT and The Department of Health* [2009] EWHC 2972.
[22] See *B v Croydon HA* [1995] 2 WLR 294.
[23] *C (A Minor: Medical Treatment: Court's Jurisdiction)* [1997] 2 FLR 180.
[24] *GJ v The Foundation Trust, A PCT and the DOH* [2009] EWHC 2972 (Fam).

Whilst judicial review proceedings are not unknown to challenge the diagnostic element for detention under MHA, or the clinical decision as to what the primary purpose of the treatment is, in the absence of clear error the court will be slow to interfere with a competent professional's exercise of clinical judgment.

8.21 One of the RC's duties is to review the detention criteria (the *Winterwerp* conditions) on a continuous basis. Once he or she is of the view that those conditions are not met (for whatever reason) the RC has must discharge the patient from section.[25] A failure to do so will render the detention unlawful. The decision can be challenged by way of judicial review or by a writ of habeas corpus. The hospital managers can also discharge. If the matter comes before a Tribunal and the RC does not support further detention on the grounds that the criteria are not met, the tribunal should discharge, and a failure to do so ought to be challenged by appeal to the Upper Tribunal. The MCA now provides an alternative regime to the MHA for community placement and treatment. In the case of patients who lack capacity to make decisions as to residence and care the MCA provides a mechanism whereby the patient can be deprived of his liberty (or detained) in a community setting. Where that option is at least potentially available the 'decision-maker' must consider whether such an option is a less restrictive option than detention in a hospital under the MHA.[26] The importance of the AM case is that Charles J has expressly recognised that the concept of the 'primacy' of the Mental Health Act over the MCA, if it exists at all, relates only to the very narrow circumstances in *GJ*. Decision-makers at all levels, including the Court of Protection and the FTT, have a choice of regime and the ultimate decision as to which to use is likely to depend on the level of restrictions each involves – with the least restrictive being chosen where possible.

LEGAL REVIEW OF THE LAWFULNESS OF DETENTION

8.22 As we have seen, the admission of a person into detention is an administrative process governed by detailed rules, and conducted by actors with particular designated roles and duties. These include the hospital managers, who have a duty to ensure that admission is legally correct, and to review continued detention. These procedures are subject to the jurisdiction of the High Court by way of judicial review and habeas corpus.[27]

8.23 The writ of habeas corpus requires the detaining authority to show lawful justification for a person's detention, in default of which the person must be freed. As is well known, judicial review is a procedure that does not challenge the merits of a decision but rather its lawfulness. A decision can be challenged on the grounds that it is illegal (for instance there was an error of law), that there is procedural impropriety, that it is irrational (or *Wednesbury* unreasonable), that there has been an abuse of power, or that there has been a breach of the ECHR.

8.24 Section 139(1) of the MHA provides:

---

[25] *R v Drew* [2003] UKHL 25 and the Code of Practice (MHA) 29.16 and s 23 MHA.
[26] This would appear to be the corollary of *AM v South London & Maudsley NHS Foundation Trust & the Secretary of State for Health* [2013] UKUT 365 (AAC), Mr Justice Charles, CP. This decision should be read as part of the line of cases starting with *GJ*, and continuing with *DN v Northumberland, Tyne & Wear NHS Foundation Trust* [2011] UKUT 327 (AAC).
[27] See *R (GP) v Derby City Council & other* [2012] EWHC 1451 (Admin) and the very clear judgment of Judge Pelling QC.

'No person shall be liable, whether on the ground of want of jurisdiction or any other ground to any civil or criminal proceedings to which he would have been liable apart from this section in respect of any act purporting to be done in pursuance of this Act or any rules or regulations made under this Act unless the Act was done in bad faith or without reasonable care.'

8.25 Under s 139(2) no proceedings shall be brought against any person in any court in respect of such an act without the leave of the High Court (in civil proceedings) or the Director of Public Prosecutions (in criminal proceedings). That is, however, subject to s 139(4), namely that the section does not apply to the Secretary of State or NHS Trusts.[28] Whether an act (or omission) was done in bad faith or without reasonable care, does not preclude public law applications for judicial review or habeas corpus.[29] That being said, in *R (Wilkinson) v RMO Broadmoor Hospital*[30] the Court of Appeal suggested that a claim for damages under s 7 of the Human Rights Act 1998 would probably require leave. If leave is not obtained then no claim can proceed and any proceedings that have started without leave are a nullity.[31]

8.26 Section 139 does not breach Article 6(1) of the ECHR according to *Seal v Chief Constable of South Wales*[32] although the dissenting speech of Baroness Hale considered it to be a disproportionate interference with a right of access to the court in the absence of evidence that the person was vexatious.[33] It is probable that the limits imposed by s 139 are based on an outdated and discriminatory view of those who are subject to the MHA. It is likely that a challenge on those grounds in the ECtHR (or possibly domestically) may succeed.

The hospital managers and nearest relatives

8.27 The hospital managers have the central role in reviewing the admission and continued detention of a patient under the MHA and have the power to discharge a patient. The hospital managers exercise a public function and their decisions are amenable to judicial review.

8.28 The duties of the hospital managers in relation to the admission of patients under section are best outlined in the Code of Practice at Chapter 13.[34] The admission documents must be delivered to a person who is authorised by the hospital managers to receive them (13.4), those completing the documents (the AMHP) must take care to comply with the requirements of the Act and those acting on the authority of the documents (the hospital managers and those detaining the patient) should make sure they are in proper form. There is a distinction between receipt and scrutiny (13.6), the latter 'involves more detailed checking for omissions, errors and other defects and, where permitted, taking action to have the documents rectified after they have already been acted upon'.[35] There is an obligation on the person receiving the documents to go through the documents with the AMHP to check their accuracy (13.9). Also at 13.12 is a requirement that: 'Documents should be scrutinised for accuracy and completeness and to check whether they do not reveal any failure to comply with the procedural

---

[28] See the list in full at s 139(4).
[29] See *R(W) v Doncaster MBC* [2003] EWHC 192 (Admin) Stanley Burnton J.
[30] [2001] EWCA Civ 1545.
[31] See *Seal v Chief Constable of South Wales* [2007] UKHL 31.
[32] *Seal* at [20].
[33] See also *Salontaji-Drobnjak v Serbia* (ECtHR) 36500/05.
[34] Entitled 'Receipt and Scrutiny of Documents'.
[35] Section 15 of the MHA allows rectification in certain circumstances.

requirements of the Act in respect of applications for detention. Medical recommendations should also be scrutinised by someone with appropriate clinical expertise to check that the reasons given appear sufficient to support the conclusions stated in them.'

8.29 The managers are entitled to detain a patient once the admission documents appear to be in order or, to use the words of s 6(3) of the MHA the application 'appears to be duly made'. The MHT does not adjudicate on the validity of admission. The only way to challenge the validity of admission is by way of judicial review or by an application for habeas corpus. The status of a flawed admission under section from the date of admission until a court adjudicates that it was flawed is still uncertain. In *R v Managers of South Western Hospital, ex p M*[36] the court ruled that the admission was lawful unless and until overturned by the court.

8.30 The court reached the opposite conclusion in *Re S-C (Mental Patient: Habeas Corpus)*.[37] There the Court of Appeal made it clear that from the date of admission to the finding that the admission (and continued detention was unlawful) the detention was unlawful. What s 6(3) (particularly when read in conjunction with s 139) appears to do is provide a defence to those who detain a patient wrongly but in good faith.[38]

8.31 This issue has recently been considered by the High Court in *TTM v Hackney LBC*.[39] The AMHP who made the application for admission failed to notify the hospital managers that the patient's NR had objected to his admission. This was an innocent mistake. She honestly believed that the NR's objection had been lifted, but it had not. This rendered the admission unlawful under s 11(4) of the MHA. The brother applied for a writ of habeas corpus, which he obtained and the patient was released. The issue before Collins J[40] was whether TTM could pursue a claim for damages for breaches of his Art 5(5) and 8 rights? He also claimed that the court should declare s 139(2)[41] and s 6(3) incompatible with the ECHR. The claimant argued that the hospital managers had a duty to scrutinise the AMHP's application and they failed to do so. At the earlier hearing Burton J had concluded that the AMHP had made an 'honest mistake' and that the NR's objection had been withdrawn. Collins J went on:

> 'Lawfulness of detention, as it seems to me, does not depend on whether the AMHP reasonably believes that there is no objection but on whether in fact there was no objection. That is what has to be decided if there is an issue raised. Compensation should only follow (subject to the ECHR claim ...) if there is negligence or bad faith.'[42]

8.32 The judge concluded that on the findings made by Burton J, there was no evidence of negligence or bad faith. Since there was no reasonable prospect of success the judge declined to give leave for the claim, under s 139(2) (considered above). The judge then went on to consider whether there was a claim for damages for breach of Articles 5 and 8 of the ECHR?[43] The judge thought that the critical question was whether detention is regarded in domestic law as lawful until the decision granting habeas corpus is made and the patient is discharged from the s 3 order? This raises the

---

[36] [1993] QB 683.
[37] [1996] QB 599 (CA).
[38] See *Principles of Mental Health Law and Policy* – Gostin etc (Oxford 2010) at 12.136.
[39] [2010] EWHC 1349 (Admin) Andrew Collins J at first instance.
[40] The patient's release had been granted at an earlier hearing by Burton J.
[41] Considered above.
[42] TTM [37].
[43] A claim brought under s 7 of the Human Rights Act 1998.

issue whether an administrative decision which was found to have been unlawful is to be regarded as void ab initio or voidable so that it has effect until set aside? The judge rejected Lord Irvine's view[44] that when delegated legislation or administrative action is pronounced unlawful it must be recognised as never having had any effect at all. In *S-C* the Court of Appeal concluded that the detention was to be regarded as unlawful. However, Collins, J then considered what that finding actually meant. He relied on *R v Central London County Court, ex p London*,[45] a case about displacement of the nearest relative in which the Court of Appeal was concerned with whether unlawfulness of the administrative act should be regarded as prospective or retrospective. In *ex p London* the Court of Appeal concluded that detention was lawful (until found to be otherwise) but invalid. Collins J in TTM reached the same conclusion.

8.33 TTM has now been considered by the Court of Appeal. The court re-iterated that SC was authority for three propositions: (1) that the Hospital acted lawfully by reason of s 6(3) (because the application appeared to be properly made); (2) this, however, did not 'clothe the conduct of the AMHP in lawfulness'; and (3) the patient's detention was unlawful throughout.[46] Furthermore, the patient was deprived of his liberty as a direct consequence of AMHP's unlawful act in breach of s 11(4) of the MHA. Section 139(1) does not prevent the AMHP's conduct from being unlawful. What it does is to limit the civil liability of the AMHP (and the local authority) to cases where the act was done in bad faith or without reasonable care. The Court of Appeal read down s 139 to permit a claim for compensation in TTM. Although TTM was decided on the basis of a breach of s 11(4), the application went ahead where there was a known objection from the NR, the court also considered the provisions of s 12(2) of the MHA. The word 'practicable' should be construed with sufficient elasticity to account for situations where a s 3 application is made as a matter of urgency.[47] Furthermore, the court considered the two different types of breaches of procedural requirements in the case. First, there are breaches of procedural requirements which go to jurisdiction. In TTM the s 11(4) breach went to jurisdiction. The objection of the NR meant that the AMHP had no jurisdiction to make the application. Secondly, the breach of procedural requirements in the exercise of a jurisdiction. The breach of s 12(2) (if there was one) came under this category, because it went to the form of evidence needed to support an application.[48] Although the court did not wish to give a firm decision on the point (in the absence of detailed argument), it made it clear that a breach of the latter type of procedural requirement (for instance in exercising of a jurisdiction) would not make the outcome unlawful provided 'there was no breach of the underlying purpose behind' in this case s 12(2) of the MHA.

8.34 Since the legality of a patient's status under the MHA depends on his satisfying the criteria for admission, one of the RC's duties is to review that status on a continuous basis. Once he or she is of the view that those conditions are not met (for whatever reason) the RC has must discharge the patient from section: see *R v Drew*[49] and the Code of Practice[50] and s 23 of the MHA. If the RC reaches the conclusion that the patient no longer qualifies for detention (or guardianship or CTO) but does not discharge him, it is unlawful for that patient to remain under that status. If the RC offers

---

[44] *Boddington v British Transport Police* [1998] 2 All ER 203–2210G.
[45] [1999] QB 1260.
[46] *TTM v Hackney LBC, East London NHS Foundation Trust and Secretary of State for Health* [2011] EWCA Civ 4 at [56] per Toulson LJ.
[47] *TTM* at [81].
[48] [84] and [85].
[49] [2003] UKHL 25.
[50] Paragraph 29.16.

such an opinion to the FTT on review, it is submitted the FTT is obliged to ensure that the patient is discharged, either by informing the RC that continued detention is unlawful, or by ordering discharge under s 72. Any hospital policy that fetters the RC's ability to discharge a patient is also unlawful. These cases should be challenged by judicial review or habeas corpus.

8.35 A patient may apply to the hospital managers for discharge from detention or CTO (also under s 23(2) of the MHA). That power may be exercised by 'three or more members of that authority, trust, board or body authorised by them' or 'by three or more members of a committee or sub-committee which has been authorised by them' (section 23(4) and (5)). The managers' duties are listed in the Code of Practice at Chapter 30. The managers may review the detention of a detained patient at any time. They must review when the RC seeks to renew detention under s 20. They should review when a request is made by a patient or when the RC makes a report to them under s 25 barring discharge by the NR. The reviews must be conducted in a fair and reasonable manner. The Code requires them (at 31.23–31.32) to adopt a fair procedure, not make irrational decisions and to adhere to the MHA and Human Rights Act. The panel must have before it sufficient information to be able to make a decision including past history and future care plans. The patient must be provided with disclosure of evidence in advance, his NR informed, and to be legally represented. The managers are subject to judicial review where there is a breach of procedural or natural justice, or where there is a clear breach of the law.

TREATMENT AND THE CONTINUING DUTY TO REVIEW

8.36 The MHA also codifies compulsory treatment. Part 4 of the MHA and Chapters 23 and 24 of the Code of Practice are where that code is found. Compulsory treatment engages a number of Convention rights and the statutory code, notably Art 3 (the prohibition of torture and inhuman and degrading treatment) and Art 8 (privacy and family life). Article 8(2) prohibits public authorities interfering with family rights except in accordance with the law and where the interference is necessary in a democratic society, the protection of health or for the protection of the rights and freedom of others. In order to be in accordance with the law there must not only be a relevant domestic law but it must be accessible and its consequences and effects foreseeable (with legal advice if necessary). In order to fulfill that role the MHA specifies rules and procedures that must be followed. The limited scope of this chapter means that these rules shall not be gone through in detail here. However, if the rules are not followed then the treatment is likely to be unlawful and challengeable by way of judicial review and/or actions for damages.

8.37 It is important to remember that where detention is under the treatment sections of the MHA those detaining must provide a therapeutic environment. An anti-therapeutic environment may amount to arbitrary detention. In the Code of Practice at 3.130 this point is made: since detention is grounded in the patient's unsoundness of mind, its therapeutic purpose can only be achieved in 'a place equipped to provide minimally adequate care and treatment'. This must be born in mind by anyone whose role is to review detention – the RC, the hospital managers, the tribunal or the High Court.

8.38 The provision of 'urgent treatment' is the subject of s 62 of the MHA.[51] This provides that the patient's consent shall not be required for any treatment given to him for the mental disorder from which he is suffering if giving by or under the direction of the approved clinician in charge of his treatment unless ss 57, 58 or 58A apply. Sections 57 and 58 outline the second opinion procedure. The first category (s 57) concerns psychosurgery and the surgical implantation of hormones to reduce sex drive. In the case of any patient for whom this treatment is contemplated there must be valid consent (certified by a panel of three appointed by the Care Quality Commission) and it must be approved by a member of the second opinion panel (known as Second Opinion Appointed Doctor – or SOAD).[52] A decision not to authorise treatment is susceptible to judicial review.[53]

8.39 Sections 58 and 58A concern the administration of medicines for mental disorder and electro-convulsive therapy (ECT) respectively. Section 58 only applies to patients who are detained. It is only required once a period of three months has passed from the first day on which any form of medication for mental disorder has passed. Here treatment may be administered with the patient's consent, or without his consent, provided it is authorised by a Second Opinion Appointed Doctor (SOAD). A RC must always seek the patient's consent, however, even if he is entitled to treat the patient without consent with a SOAD's authorisation. Section 58A outlines the role of the SOAD, and there is no three month period during which the treatment can be administered without the use of s 58A.

8.40 To what extent can treatment plans for those detained under the MHA, including those certified by SOADs be challenged? A challenge to the treatment given under s 62 (or the other sections) may be challenged on the grounds that it was not for the patient's mental disorder – for instance the core purpose of the treatment is not concerned with the mental disorder.[54] Judicial review proceedings are not ideally suited to deal with cases in which there are genuine disputes over diagnosis and treatment and where oral evidence is required. However, following *R (Wilkinson) v Responsible Medical Officer for Broadmoor Hospital*,[55] it is recognised that the court on a judicial review may go beyond a *Wednesbury* exercise and decide the matter itself having heard all the evidence. However, the Court of Appeal has sounded a note of caution here, and many of the issues that will come before the High Court on treatment challenges can be considered without the need for live evidence,[56] and the High Court has gone further in suggesting that live evidence will only be required in a 'rare case'.[57] If one is seeking to challenge the decision to administer treatment without consent to a detained patient, those seeking to administer the treatment have to 'convincingly show' the court that the treatment is both medically necessary and in the patient's best interests.[58] With such a high standard it is submitted that it is usual for this to be satisfied (or not) on paper. The whole purpose of the SOAD procedure is to ensure that compulsory treatment is only administered if there is a convincing case of medical necessity, and that it is in the

---

[51] The definition of 'urgent' is encapsulated in s 62(1)(a)–(d).
[52] Section 58(3).
[53] *R v Mental Health Act Commission, ex p W* (1988) 9 BMLR 77.
[54] See *B v Croydon HA* [1995] 2 WLR 294, and *GJ v The Foundation Trust (etc)* [2009] EWHC 2972 (Fam) [2010] 3 WLR 840.
[55] [2001] EWCA Civ 1545.
[56] See *R (N) v M* [2002] EWCA Civ 1789.
[57] *R (Taylor) v Haydn-Smith etc* [2005] EWHC 1668 (Admin) Andrew Collins J. See also *M v South West Hospital & St Georges Mental Health Trust* [2008] EWCA Civ 1112.
[58] See *R (N) v M*, applying the ECtHR decision in *Herczegfalvy v Austria* (1992) 15 EHRR 437.

patient's best interests. The SOAD's decision, therefore can be reviewed, but the reviewing court's primary function is not to put itself in the shoes of the SOAD.

8.41 If the subject of the challenge is, in fact, the patient's detention in a hospital, rather than the proposed treatment regime then the Court of Appeal has stated that such a challenge is one that ought to be referred to the FTT in the first instance.[59]

8.42 In the case of patients subject to restrictions the Ministry of Justice has to consent to decisions that the RC would make in relation to patients not subject to such restrictions, such as leave and discharge. The Secretary of State's decisions in this area are susceptible to judicial review and challenge in the FTT.

TREATMENT IN THE COMMUNITY

8.43 When the MHA 1983 was amended by the MHA 2007 a new form of community treatment was introduced. Sections 17A–G now contain the regime for supervised community treatment (SCT) or (and more commonly known as) community treatment orders (CTO). These join the other two statutory provisions available for non-restricted mental health patients, namely guardianship (s 7) and leave of absence (s 17).

8.44 Prior to November 2008, it was common for RCs to allow detained patients ever increasing periods of s 17 leave.[60] The alternative under the old s 25A was discharge under supervision. The new provisions under ss 17A–17G create an alternative whereby the patient is discharged from liability to be detained, with conditions attached, and with the power of recall without the need to go through the admission process under s 11 first. In order for a patient to be subject to a CTO he must already be detained under either s 3 (including where he is on s 17 leave), s 37, s 47 or s 48. The RC has a discretion whether to grant s 17 leave or a CTO, provided the relevant criteria under s 17A(5) are met. If the RC considers it appropriate to grant ever increasing periods of leave he may do so. If he wishes to extend the period of leave beyond one week the only requirement that the Act imposes on the RC is to consider whether the patient should be dealt with by way of a CTO.[61] Provided he has considered the option, the granting of longer term leave is lawful. The advantage of extended s 17 leave over the CTO is that under the former the patient remains liable to be detained whereas he does not under a CTO. This means that where a RC wishes to test the patient in the community before discharging him onto a CTO, the patient on s 17 leave may still be deprived of his liberty (or held 'in custody' in the words of s 13(3) MHA). The RC may direct that the patient remain 'in custody' if it is necessary in the interests of his own health and safety or for the protection of others. Although the RC must consider whether instead of long-term s 17 leave a patient should be dealt with by CTO there is nothing in the MHA requiring him to do any more than that.[62] Where the patient lacks capacity and is in 'custody' in a hospital or care home, the managing authority of that institution should consider using Sch A1 of the MCA. If that patient is placed in a supported living arrangement, then those responsible ought to consider an application to the Court of Protection.

---

[59] *R (B) v Dr SS (RMO) SOAD & SSH* [2006] EWCA Civ 28.
[60] See *B v Barking, Havering and Brentwood Community Healthcare NHS Trust* [1999] 1 FLR 106, CA and *R (CS) v MHRT* [2004] EWHC 2958 (Pitchford J).
[61] Section 17(2A) and (2B).
[62] MHA s 17(2A).

8.45 The available statistics suggest that CTOs are more popular than was envisaged. The number of CTOs in the year 2009/10 was 4,107. In the 17 months from the date s 17A came into force (November 2008) there were 6,241 CTOs created, which is 367 per month.[63] The benefits of the CTO over leave are fairly clear. In order for the CTO to be granted there are rigorous criteria to be applied. The patient on a CTO is entitled to s 117 funding. He is no longer liable to be detained, which means that unlike the case of s 17 leave, the patient cannot be deprived of his liberty. Under s 17E(2) he may only be recalled if he breaches the mandatory conditions and requires medical treatment in hospital for his mental condition, failing which there would be a risk to his health or safety or another person. Such a recall must be based on objective medical evidence.

8.46 Challenges to a CTO may be made through the managers or the tribunal. The tribunal's powers are limited to discharging the CTO or making non-statutory recommendations to vary or add conditions.[64] Likewise the tribunal may not discharge a patient onto a CTO, but may make a recommendation for the RC to do so.[65] Legal challenge to conditions attached to a CTO where the existence of the CTO itself is not challenged, must be by way of judicial review. The two mandatory conditions are that the patient must make himself available for examination when it is time to renew the CTO (under s 20A), and when it is proposed that a certificate under Part 4A of the MHA is to be given (in respect of treatment – see below).[66] Those conditions cannot be challenged. Other conditions may be specified by the RC only with agreement from the AMHP and only then if those conditions are 'necessary or appropriate for one or more of the following purposes: (a) ensuring that the patient receives medical treatment; (b) preventing risk of harm to the patient's health or safety; (c) protecting other persons'.[67] Unless the conditions can be justified by the RC on those grounds, they can be challenged. Note, however, the threshold is low: the condition need only be necessary *or* appropriate.

8.47 One issue that has arisen at first instance in the FTT is where the actual working of the CTO involves a deprivation of the patient's liberty. The FTT has no jurisdiction to vary the conditions of the CTO, so it cannot remove the condition that amounts to a deprivation of liberty. It could discharge the CTO if it considers that s 72(1)(c) is not satisfied – because the power of recall is unnecessary (as the patient is already detained), but that may place the patient and the public at risk. It would seem appropriate in such circumstances for the RC and the responsible local authority to seek to formalise the deprivation of liberty through the Mental Capacity Act (assuming the patient lacks capacity) either by way of a welfare order of the Court of Protection or, if appropriate, using the DOLS. Other conditions the author has encountered have included 'not to drink excessive amounts of alcohol', which the FTT cannot strike down, but which was removed when its uncertainty was pointed out. Other conditions may be challenged on human rights grounds. For instance, a CTO that prevents a patient from entering certain geographical areas, or having contact with certain people may be challenged on ECHR grounds, notably Arts 8, 11, and generally 14.

More generally, once again is the impact the MCA has in this area. Those with capacity cannot be deprived of their liberty in the community by the use of CTO, guardianship or

---

[63] These figures as well as commentary on the operation of the MHA are printed in the Care Quality Commission's 'Monitoring the Use of the MHA in 2009/10' (2010).
[64] MHA, s 72(1)(c).
[65] MHA, s 72(3A).
[66] MHA, s 17B(3)(a) and (b).
[67] MHA, s 17B(2).

conditional discharge.[68] There is no Art 5 compliant method for doing so. However, in the case of those who lack capacity to make decisions as to their residence and care the MCA provides a mechanism.[69] This has led to patients who are subject to MHA orders also being made subject to MCA authorisation. This in turn has led to issues arising as to when the use of MHA powers is appropriate where there is a dispute between the patient as to the regime under which he should live. This prompted Peter Jackson J to comment:[70]

> '[I]t is not in my view appropriate for genuinely contested issues about the place of residence of a resisting incapacitated person to be determined either under the guardianship regime or by means of a standard authorisation under the DOLS regime. Substantial decisions of that kind ought properly to be made by the Court of Protection, using its power to make welfare decisions under s 16 [of the Mental Capacity Act].'

8.48 Guardianship under ss 7 and 8 of the MHA is another option for community care. There is no right to community care services under the National Health Service and Community Care Act 1990. The important issue concerning guardianship now is the extent to which it should be chosen instead of the orders that can be used under the Mental Capacity Act 2005 and the DOLS. Obviously, for a patient to be entered into guardianship he does not have to lack capacity, although many do. However, guardianship does not expressly authorise that a patient may be deprived of his liberty, whereas the MCA/DOLS can. This issue is considered in the section on the MCA.[71]

THE TRIBUNAL

8.49 Before the MHA 2007 amendments the Mental Health Review Tribunal (MHRT) dealt with applications and references by and in respect of patients under the provisions of the Act.[72] The MHRT could be challenged either by judicial review or by way of case stated under the old s 78(8).[73] Now the role of the MHRT falls within the new tribunal system. First instance applications[74] are now made to the FTT (Mental Health) which is part of the Health, Education and Social Care Chamber (HESC).

8.50 The FTT has almost entirely the same constitution and function as the old MHRT and there has been continuity of membership. The procedure in the FTT is governed by the Tribunal Procedure Rules.[75] Appeals are now made to the Upper Tribunal (Administrative Appeals Chamber) (UT) on a point of law other than in the

---

[68] See *Secretary of State for Health v RB* [2011] EWCA Civ 1608.
[69] See ss 4A and 4B MCA. Under s 4A deprivation of liberty is lawful if it is the result of a welfare order made by the Court of Protection under s 16(2)(a) of the MCA, or if it is in accordance with Sch A1 (the so-called DOLS). Section 4B is concerned with emergency life-saving or vital treatment where a person is deprived of his liberty pending an application for a standard authorisation under Sch A1.
[70] *C v Blackburn with Darwen BC, A Care Home & A Primary Care Trust* [2011] EWHC 3321 (COP) at para [37]. In this case C was subject to a guardianship order. His guardian could and did require him to live in a particular place – the care home. C did not want to live there and frequently left. He was made the subject of a standard authorisation under Sch A1 – making it lawful to deprive him of his liberty at the care home. The case came before Peter Jackson J under s 21A MCA (in effect an appeal against the DOL).
[71] See *C v Blackburn BC*, above.
[72] The old s 65(1) and (1A).
[73] Now repealed.
[74] Under s 66 MHA.
[75] Full title: Tribunal Procedure (First-tier Tribunal) (Health, Education and Social Care Chamber) 2008 (SI 2008/2699).

case of an 'excluded decision'.[76] The UT also has a statutory power to judicial review cases from the FTT.[77] The rules also provide for the FTT and UT to review their own decisions.[78] In the HESC Tribunal Rules the FTT has a number of powers which are designed to prevent unnecessary appeals. Clerical mistakes, accidental slips or omissions may at any time be corrected under rule 44. If it is in the interests of justice to do so and there have been the irregularities listed in rule 45(2)(a) to (c), the FTT may set aside a decision which disposes of the proceedings. When an application is made to appeal a decision of the FTT under rule 46, rule 47 provides that the FTT 'must first consider' whether 'taking into account the overriding objective ... whether to review the decision in accordance with rule 49'. Rule 49 provides that the Tribunal may only undertake a review of a decision in a mental health case if 'it is satisfied that there was an error of law in the decision'. Section 11(5) TCEA defines 'excluded decisions' that are relevant to the mental health jurisdiction as:

'(d) a decision of the First-tier Tribunal under section 9 – (i) to review or not to review, an earlier decision of the tribunal, (ii) to take no action, or not to take any particular action, in the light of a review of an earlier decision of the tribunal, (iii) to set aside an earlier decision of the tribunal or (iv) to refer, or not to refer, a matter to the Upper Tribunal.'

8.51 Since the UT cannot hear an appeal against an excluded decision, an application may be made to make an application for judicial review of such a decision to the UT (or the High Court[79]). In *R(RB) v The First-tier Tribunal*[80] the decision of the FTT (in the form of one of its senior judges) to set aside a decision of the FTT on review, and to remit it to a freshly constituted FTT, was an excluded decision. It was challenged by way of judicial review to the UT. The UT quashed the judge's decision on review, and set out some guidance as to how and when the power of review can properly be used. At para 31 the UT said:

'In the present case the question we ask ourselves is whether the reviewing judge properly directed himself as to the law governing the power of review. In particular, did he focus upon the need to make sure that the review did not usurp the Upper Tribunal's function in determining appeals on contentious points of law? This was a case where law had to be particularly clear if the review was to be justified.'

8.52 It is clear that in mental health cases where the liberty of the individual is at stake on the one hand, and there is a need to protect the individual and the wider public on the other, that to review a decision unless it is clearly wrong is a serious move. Furthermore, the FTT is an expert tribunal including not only a legally qualified judge, but also a Consultant Psychiatrist and a third member who will usually have expertise in the mental health field (often a nurse, a social worker/AMHP, or psychologist) to set aside any decision which turns on an assessment of facts, technical evidence or an evaluation of risk is likely to be justified only when clearly wrong.

---

[76] Section 11 of the Tribunals Courts and Enforcement Act 2007.
[77] Section 15 of the TCEA.
[78] Sections 9 and 10 of the TCEA respectively.
[79] This point has recently been emphasized once again in *Samuda v Secretary of State for Work & Pensions and Harris* [2014] EWCA Civ 1. This was a case where the Court of Appeal had to consider an appeal against the Upper Tribunal's decision not to grant permission to appeal to the Court of Appeal. That decision, the Court of Appeal concluded, was an 'excluded decision' and there was no right to appeal to the Court against that decision. The proper approach would be by way of judicial review: see Sir Stanley Burnton at para [12].
[80] [2010] UKUT 160 (AAC).

8.53 The *RB* case concerned a restricted patient detained under ss 37/41 in a secure psychiatric hospital. He suffered from 'a mental illness in the form of a persistent delusional disorder, which has caused him to be a life-long paedophile attracted to boys aged between approximately 9 and 13 years'. After 13 years of detention those treating him wanted him to be transferred to a care home with a restrictive regime so that he would only be able to leave if escorted. He could not be transferred because the care home was not a hospital in which patients under section could be placed. The MOJ declined to permit him to stay there on extended leave. The only option was a conditional discharge. The MOJ refused to consent to that option, so the matter came before the FTT. The issue the FTT had to decide was whether the restrictions placed upon RB would amount to him being detained/deprived of his liberty and, if so, whether such a 'discharge' was lawful. There were a number of authorities on or around the point which the FTT considered before granting a conditional discharge. The reviewing judge drafted a lengthy written decision in which he reviewed the authorities and found that: (a) the conditions imposed under the proposed conditional discharge would inevitably deprive the patient of his liberty, and the FTT had erred in finding otherwise, and (b) on the authorities his conditional discharge amounted to a transfer between one state of detention and another and was an order the tribunal could not make.[81]

8.54 Review, other than for obvious errors, is likely to prove difficult in mental health cases. The large majority of cases are essentially matters of fact or a judgment of risk. It is likely that reviews should be granted only where there has been a plain mistake as to the law – such as making an unlawful order, or applying the wrong legal test, or where the written reasons are plainly inadequate, that a review ought to be granted.

The Upper Tribunal

8.55 The Tribunals Courts and Enforcement Act 2007 (TCEA) establishes the new tribunal system (see Chapter 2, s 3), with the Upper Tribunal being 'a superior court of record' (s 3(5)). It has the powers to hear appeals from the FTT, and, in doing so, fulfils the function previously carried out by the High Court. Under s 12 of the TCEA if the UT finds that the making of the decision under appeal involved the making of an error on a point of law it 'may' set aside the FTT's decision, in which case it must then either remit the decision to the FTT with directions for its consideration (for instance whether there should be a newly constituted tribunal, or re-make the decision.[82] If it decides to re-make the decision then, under s 12(4)(a) and (b) the UT may make any decision the FTT could have made and 'make any such findings of fact as it considers appropriate'.

Where the UT is exercising a jurisdiction formerly exercised by the High Court, it need not regard itself as formally bound by decisions of the High Court. Subject to one qualification, the UT should approach decisions of the High Court as the High Court itself would approach them, for instance as a matter of 'judicial comity' that should follow the prior decisions unless convinced that the prior judgment is wrong.[83] The qualification relates to the specialist nature of the UT and the specialised issues arising

---

[81] The Upper Tribunal dismissed the Secretary of State for Justice's appeal against the FTT: see *Secretary of State for Justice v RB* [2010] UKUT 454 (AAC). However, the Court of Appeal subsequently overruled the Upper Tribunal: *Secretary of State for Justice v B* [2011] EWCA Civ 1608, [2012] 1 WLR 2043.
[82] Section 12(2)(a) and (b)(i) and (ii).
[83] The dicta of Lord Justice Carnwath, SPT in *Secretary of State for Justice v RB & Lancashire Care NHS Foundation Trust* [2010] UKUT 454 at para [40] – citing Lord Goddard CJ in *Huddersfield Police Authority v Watson* [1947] KB 842 at 848.

before it. As Baroness Hale of Richmond had emphasised in *AH v Sudan*[84] and *Cooke v Secretary of State for Social Security*[85] the higher courts need to respect the 'highly specialised character of some legislation before the tribunals'. 'Consistently with that approach, where such specialised issues arise before the Upper Tribunal, it may in a proper case feel less inhibited in revisiting issues decided even at High Court level, if there is good reason to do so.'[86]

Although the substantive decision in *RB* was reversed by the Court of Appeal the UT's approach to precedent was not challenged by the Secretary of State for Justice and remains good law.

8.56 As we have seen, the UT also has the power to judicially review decisions of the FTT. When doing so it acts, for all intents and purposes as the High Court, granting such relief as that court may grant, applying the same principles in both granting relief and permission for relief as the court would.[87]

8.57 The status of the UT was considered by the Court of Appeal in *R (Cart) v UT, SSJ and others*,[88] in particular, what was meant by the term 'superior court of record' and whether the UT was itself amenable to judicial review. What *Cart* has established is that the UT is part of 'a new tribunal structure' which (para [42]):

> 'while not an analogue of the High Court, is something greater than the sum of its parts. It represents a newly coherent and comprehensive edifice designed, among other things, to complete the long process of divorcing administrative justice from departmental policy, to ensure the application across the board of proper standards of adjudication, and to provide for the correction of legal error within rather than outside that system.'

8.58 The High Court retains its supervisory jurisdiction but the criteria that limits the exercise of that jurisdiction is the same as those limiting second appeals: ie there is an important point of principle or practice or there is some other compelling reason for judicial review.[89]

The First-tier Tribunal

8.59 Since November 2008 applications and references concerning patients subject to the provisions of the MHA have been heard by the FTT, which is part of the Health, Education and Social Care Chamber (HESC). Since the FTT is part of the tribunal system appeals against its decisions are made to the Upper Tribunal. The constitution of the membership of the FTT is specified in Sch 2 of the MHA. It is the same as with the old MHRT, namely a legal member (Tribunal Judge), a medically qualified member and another member (previously called a 'lay' member). All are appointed by the Lord Chancellor on the recommendation of the Judicial Appointments Commission.[90]

---

[84] [2007] UKHL 49 at para [30].
[85] [2001] EWCA Civ 734.
[86] *SSJ v RB* para [41].
[87] Section 15(3), (4) and (5) and s 16.
[88] [2010] EWCA Civ 859.
[89] *R (Cart) v Upper Tribunal* [2011] UKSC 28. Here, the Supreme Court harmonised what had appeared to be a different approach to the same legal provisions in Scotland: see *Eba v Advocate General for Scotland* [2011] UKSC 29.
[90] Schedule 2, para 1 and 1A.

Section 78 MHA enables the Lord Chancellor to make rules in relation to applications to the FTT, procedure within the FTT and to restrict membership of the FTT in certain cases to appropriately qualified.[91]

8.60 Section 78 must be read in conjunction with the relevant provisions of the TCEA, the Tribunal Rules,[92] and the Code of Practice.[93] The rules introduce into the FTT a more flexible procedure than under the previous MHRT Rules. As with the Civil Procedure Rules, the tribunal is required to ensure that it complies with the overriding objective,[94] as well as requiring parties to co-operate with the tribunal to achieve the same end.[95] To this end the FTT has significant case management powers under rule 4 designed to ensure the efficient running of cases, to minimise delays and to ensure that adjournments are made only where it is appropriate to do so. At the beginning of 2009, a number of full-time, salaried tribunal judges were appointed. Previously, the MHRT judiciary had been almost entirely made up of part-time legal members. The FTT judiciary is still predominantly part-time (or fee paid) deputy tribunal judges. The salaried (full-time) tribunal judges are now given a case management role and are usually called upon to make decisions over disclosure of documentation, vacating hearings, and convening hearings to determine pre-hearing issues. The tribunal judges also tend to consider whether FTT decisions should be reviewed and whether permission ought to be given for an appeal to the UT.

8.61 Since the FTT has been integrated into the Tribunal system, judicial review is no longer the automatic route to appeal. Of course, the mental health cases prior to 2008 all started as High Court challenges to MHRT decisions. In the future similar issues will be determined by the UT as appeals or, sometimes, under its judicial review jurisdiction. It is yet to be seen the extent to which the UT considers itself bound by pre-2008 High Court decisions. It is not within the subject matter of this work to outline the FTT procedures and case-law save where judicial review is relevant.

8.62 One of the Article 5 requirements that was made clear by litigation in the early 2000s was the need for timely hearings of applications under the MHA. In *R(C) v MHRT*[96] the MHRT's policy to list cases eight weeks from the date of the application was held to be a breach of Article 5(4). In *R (K) v MHRT*[97] a delay in the hearing of a patient's case was found to be the responsibility of the Government (due to the inadequate funding of staff) and damages were awarded. This delay has been held to include the appellate process.[98] Such delays would still come within the jurisdiction of the High Court and would be subject to judicial review in that Administrative Court. The same is true of issues concerning the effective right to have a case put before the tribunal.

8.63 The FTT decisions that are subject to judicial review are the 'excluded decisions'. These are defined above. The first case that came before the UT from the mental health jurisdiction considered whether the decision it was asked to consider was an excluded

---

[91] Most notably this applies to the consideration of restricted cases in which the tribunal judge is usually a serving or retired Circuit Judge or a Recorder with considerable criminal experience and usually a QC.
[92] The Tribunal Procedure (First-tier Tribunal) (Health, Education and Social Care Chamber) Rules 2008, SI 2008/2699.
[93] Published pursuant to s 118 MHA. The relevant chapter being 32.
[94] Outlined in detail in r 2.
[95] Rule 2(4).
[96] [2002] 1 WLR 176 (CA).
[97] [2002] EWHC 639 (Admin) Stanley Burnton J.
[98] See *Reid v UK* (2003) 37 EHRR 9.

decision, or not? The case, *Dorset Healthcare NHS Foundation Trust v MH*[99] concerned a common problem for tribunals, namely the disclosure of information to patients, and their representatives. The Trust agreed to disclose all the patient's records to the patient's solicitor save for a small number of documents which were withheld. The patient's solicitor made an application to the FTT for disclosure of all the material. The application was heard by a Deputy Regional Tribunal Judge (sitting on his own) and granted the patient access to her own records, including any third party material, subject to the Trust opposing disclosure on the grounds outlined in r 14 of the Tribunal Rules.[100] The decision was made without the DTJ seeking representations from the Trust. The Trust did not avail itself of the mechanism provided in the rules to challenge such a direction.[101] The Trust, instead, applied for a review under s 9 of the TCEA. The matter had already been set down before a fully constituted FTT for a hearing of the patient's application. The FTT considered reviewing the DTJ's decision but, instead, decided not to do so because '… the direction was made competently and by the tribunal at a level of authority equivalent to (or greater than) that which we enjoy today'.[102] The FTT decided that the matter ought to be referred to the UT for guidance on disclosure. The UT raised the issue as to whether it had jurisdiction (qua appeal court) to hear the case. The UT decided that s 11 of the TCEA is not to be construed as excluding an interlocutory decision to grant (or not grant) disclosure. In any event, the UT also stated that if a decision of the FTT is not within the scope of s 11, either because it is not a decision or it is an excluded decision, the UT is able to hear a challenge to that decision through its judicial review powers. This is what it did in *R (RB) v The First-tier Tribunal*[103] as discussed above. As outlined above, the decision to review a case and to set it aside is not appealable but can be challenged on public law grounds in the UT by way of judicial review. The question that then arises is what happens if the UT decides it will not grant permission for judicial review or, in the case of an appeal, it will not grant permission to appeal. These are both excluded decisions under s 13(1) and (8) of the TCEA. On the basis of the decision in *R (Cart)*[104] these can only be challenged in limited circumstances.

8.64 Judicial review is still relevant to the FTT process. Other issues arising out of the tribunal procedure are susceptible to judicial review. In *R (Modaresi) v Secretary of State for Health*[105] a number of these issues were considered. The case involved the submission of M's appeal against her s 2 detention by the Mental Health Act administrator of the hospital in which M was detained. The tribunal (wrongly, as it turned out) considered the application was made outside the 14-day period in which it should have been made, and declined to accept it because they said they had no jurisdiction to do so.[106] M's solicitor wrote to the Secretary of State for Health asking him to exercise his discretion to refer M's application to the tribunal (under s 67 MHA). However, by this time, M had been detained for a further period under s 3 MHA and she had another right to apply to the tribunal for discharge. On that basis the Secretary of State declined to refer her case on the grounds that her Art 5 rights were preserved

---

[99] [2009] UKUT 4 (AAC).
[100] Under r 14(2) the FTT may prohibit disclosure of documents or information to a person: (a) such disclosure is likely to cause that person or some other person serious harm, and (b) having regard to the interests of justice the FTT thinks it is proportionate to do so.
[101] Under r 6(5) the Trust may have challenged that decision before the hearing.
[102] This the UT described (rather charitably) as 'timid' see [19].
[103] [2010] UKUT 160 (AAC).
[104] [2010] EWCA Civ 859.
[105] [2013] UKSC 53.
[106] See s 66(1) MHA.

through her s 3 status. M challenged the jurisdiction issue concerning the time limits as well as the refusal of the Secretary of State to make a reference.

In the case of CTO, the FTT has no power to vary the conditions attached. Under s 17B of the MHA conditions may be attached by the RC (with the agreement of the AMHP) if he thinks them 'necessary *or* appropriate' (emphasis added) either to ensure that the patient receives treatment, to prevent the risk of harm to the patient's health or safety, or for the protection of other persons.[107] The FTT has the power to discharge a patient from a CTO under s 72(1)(c). Under s 72(3A) the FTT is not required to discharge a patient detained under an assessment or treatment order if it considers that the patient could or should be the subject to a CTO, but it may recommend that the RC consider making a CTO and can reconvene at a later date to consider the patient's case further if no CTO has been made. What the FTT cannot do is to make a CTO. It is also not able to vary conditions attached to a CTO, whether by revoking or adding conditions. Ultimately, a patient may challenge the conditions attached to his CTO by way of judicial review. It is submitted that it will be difficult to overcome the statutory language outlined above – 'necessary *or* appropriate' – unless the condition is plainly unnecessary and inappropriate. From the author's experience a condition 'not to drink excessive amounts of alcohol' appears impossible to uphold due to its uncertainty. However, faced with such a condition the FTT can do nothing other than discharge the patient (which is likely to be contrary to the patient's best interests) or include a strong comment in the written reasons as to why the condition should be removed or modified ('not to consume alcohol' would be certain, if difficult to police). It is also clear that a CTO does not provide lawful authority to deprive a patient of his liberty. It is submitted that conditions purporting to do so can be challenged by judicial review. In the case of a patient who lacks capacity issues concerning deprivation of liberty could be dealt with in conjunction with a CTO either in the Court of Protection by way of a welfare order, or, where the patient resides at a care home by way of the DOLS.[108]

8.65 The other area in which judicial review still plays an important part in mental health law, and, in particular, in relation to tribunal proceedings is in the area of aftercare. The subject of the provision of community care and services, as well as their funding, is dealt with elsewhere in this publication. The following is a summary of the relevance of that subject to mental health law. The Code of Practice[109] outlines the purpose of aftercare:

> '[27.5] After-care is a vital component in patients' overall treatment and care. As well as meeting their immediate needs for health and social care, after-care should aim to support them in regaining or enhancing their skills, or learning new skills in order to cope with life outside hospital.'

8.66 Section 117 of the MHA imposes a duty on certain bodies to provide after-care services free of charge to certain categories of mentally disordered persons who have been detained under the Act. Those bodies are the PCT or Local Health Board and LSSA in conjunction with any relevant voluntary agencies. The persons to whom the section applies are:

---

[107] Section 17B(2)(a)–(c).
[108] If the patient resides in a hospital he is likely not to be eligible for DOLS or the MCA: see *GJ (or J) v Foundation Trust*.
[109] Chapter 27.

'those who are detained under s 3 ... or admitted to hospital in pursuance of a hospital order made under s 37 ... or transferred to a hospital in pursuance of a hospital direction made under s 45A above or a transfer direction made under s 47 or 48 ... and then cease to be detained and (whether or not immediately after so ceasing) leave hospital.'

8.67 The duty falls upon the Local Social Services Authority (LSSA)/health body responsible for the area in which the person concerned is resident or to which he is sent on discharge by the hospital in which he is detained.[110] The duty only crystallises when the patient ceases to be detained. Consequently, a patient subject to s 3 is entitled to s 117 after-care if he is no longer actually detained but only liable to be detained. If the patient is granted extensive leave of absence under s 17, the duties to provide after-care services under s 117 arises. Long term leave is less likely now that the CTO regime is in force. Those subject to a CTO are entitled to s 117 after-care. Case-law has confirmed that although the NHS body has the power to take preparatory steps in anticipation of discharge from detention[111] there is no duty to do so.[112]

8.68 However, in *W v Doncaster MBC*[113] the Court of Appeal recognised that although the duty did not arise until discharge from detention in reality it was 'reasonable to suppose' that the relevant authorities had in place procedures to help cope with situations where they become responsible upon a patient's discharge. In *R v MHRT, ex p Hall*[114] the Court of Appeal considered the Code of Practice and stated that it suggested that 'at least in embryo, plans should be available before a tribunal takes place'.

8.69 In the present Code under the section After-care Planning (at 27.7) it states:

'When considering relevant patients' case, the tribunal and hospital managers will expect to be provided with information from the professionals concerned on what after-care arrangements might be made for them under s 117 if they were to be discharged. Some discussion of after-care needs, involving LSSAs and other relevant agencies, should take place in advance of the hearing.'

8.70 If, at the time of a tribunal hearing, there is insufficient information before it for the tribunal to consider the issue of aftercare, then the tribunal ought to adjourn and make directions for such information to be provided at the adjourned hearing.[115] This must not be done where the issue of after-care is academic – for instance where a discharge is unlikely whatever package maybe in place. A failure on the part of a health authority to use 'reasonable endeavours' to fulfill conditions imposed by the MHRT would probably be regarded as an unlawful use of its discretion; but a discretion it is nevertheless. The services provided under s 117 are community care services. If a person is in need of such services then an obligation falls on a LSSA to assess that person's needs.[116] Following the result of the assessments the LSSA must under s 47(1)(b) consider whether the person's needs call for the provision of community care services. It would seem that in the case of a patient discharged under s 117, and who has a right to be provided with services, the outcome of the s 47 assessment must always be that he needs to be provided with such services. However, the LSSA retains discretion to decide

---

[110] Section 117(3).
[111] *R(K) v Camden & Islington HA* [2001] EWCA Civ 240.
[112] *R(B) v Camden LBC* [2005] EWHC 1366 (Admin) Stanley Burnton J.
[113] [2004] EWCA Civ 378.
[114] (1999) 2 CCLR 383 and [1999] MHLR 63 (CA).
[115] *R (Ashworth Hospital) v MHRT and R(H) v Ashworth Hospital* [2002] EWCA Civ 923.
[116] This arises under ss 46 and 47 of the National Health Service and Community Care Act 1990.

the level of those services.[117] Consequently, although there is an absolute duty under s 117 to fund after-care there is no absolute duty to fund any and all conditions that the tribunal may impose.[118] Note also that patients discharged into after-care, including those subject to CTOs, will be subject to the Care Programme Approach.

8.71 There are practical problems for tribunals associated with a failure of those providing and/or funding aftercare services and which frustrate a patient's discharge. In *R(H) v Home Secretary*[119] an MHRT granted a conditional discharge to a patient detained under s 37, with restrictions under s 41, having concluded that he was no longer suffering from a mental illness. The hearing was adjourned so that the health authority could arrange services under s 117. This it was unable to do. When it reconvened, the tribunal made the same order but deferred the discharge until the package was in place. Much later the Home Secretary referred the patient (who was still detained) to the MHRT (under s 71). The MHRT found that the patient did suffer from a mental illness which required his detention. The patient brought judicial review proceedings. The House of Lords found that the lack of power of the MHRT to require a package to be put in place did not invalidate its coercive powers and was not a breach of Art 5(4). The proper approach where it decided to discharge if, and only if certain measures were in place, was to defer discharge and if, when it reconvened, those conditions had not been put in place, the MHRT should reconsider its decision and treat the original decision as provisional.

THE MENTAL CAPACITY ACT AND THE COURT OF PROTECTION

8.72 The Mental Capacity Act 2005 which came into force on 1 October 2007 was the culmination of a long period of discussion and debate about the reform of the law relating to those unable to make decisions. The detail of that discussion is beyond the scope of this work. The purpose of the Act is to empower people who lack mental capacity to 'make decisions for themselves wherever possible' and to protect them 'by providing a flexible framework that places individuals at the very heart of the decision-making process'. The intention is to 'ensure that they participate as much as possible in any decision made on their behalf, and that they are made in their best interests'. Also it 'allows people to plan ahead for a time in the future when they might lack the capacity' to make those decisions.[120] The main planks of the new code are: (1) a statutory presumption of capacity which must be rebutted on the balance of probabilities by those challenging capacity: s 1(2); (2) placing on a statutory footing the time and issue specific nature of capacity: s 2(1); (3) placing the functional test for capacity and the need to assist the person to make the decision so far as practicable before deciding that he lacks capacity (providing information, explaining, deferring the decision until the person is likely to be able to make the decision): s 3; (4) any decision made on behalf of a person lacking capacity must be in his best interests: s 1(5) and s 4; (5) providing a defence for those who act in connection with care or treatment and who otherwise would commit an assault or other tort on a person, if they have acted in accordance with the Act: ss 5 and 6.

---

[117] See the discussion on this subject in *Mental Health Act Manual*, Richard Jones (11th ed) at 1-1074.
[118] *R v Camden and Islington Health Authority, ex p K* [2001] EWCA Civ 240, per Lord Phillips MR.
[119] [2003] UKHL 59 and [2004] 2 AC 253.
[120] These quotations are taken from the Foreword to the Code of Practice to the Act, by Lord Falconer LC.

8.73 The Act also places the 'advance decision' (AD) on a statutory footing. Section 24 defines the AD as 'a decision made by a person, after he has reached 18 and when he has capacity to do so, that if: (a) at a later time and in such circumstances as he may specify, a specified treatment is proposed to be carried out or continued by a person providing health care for him, and (b) at that time he lacks capacity to consent to the carrying out or continuation of the treatment, the specified treatment is not to be carried out or continued'. New methods for delegated decision-making are also created by the Act. The lasting power of attorney (LPA) replaces the enduring power of attorney (EPA):[121] ss 9 to 13. LPAs have a greater scope than their predecessor, whereas the EPA was limited to property and affairs, the LPA also includes issues concerning welfare, care and treatment. The Act also creates the Court of Protection (s 45) which is a superior court of record, and which has the jurisdiction to determine issues that arise in respect of those mentally incapable (or reasonably suspected of being so until the issue is determined), as well as making declarations in relation to those issues. The court may make decisions on behalf of the person. Equally, the court may appoint deputies to make decisions on behalf of the person: see ss 19 and 20.

8.74 The Court of Protection deals with the overwhelming majority of cases that arise under the MCA. These are therefore not subject to judicial review and beyond the scope of this work.[122] Two issues that are relevant to this publication concern the interface between the Mental Health Act and the MCA, and the challenging of the decisions of public bodies when they conflict with best interest decisions under the MCA.

8.75 Section 28 of the MCA states:

'(1) Nothing in this Act authorises anyone –
   (a) to give a patient medical treatment for mental disorder, or
   (b) to consent to a patient's being given medical treatment for mental disorder if, at the time when it is proposed to treat the patient, his treatment is regulated by Part 4 of the Mental Health Act.'

8.76 In other words the MHA treatment 'code' discussed above has primacy over the MCA if a patient is a detained patient under MHA. However, this straightforward rule is complicated by the effects of amendment made to the MCA by the MHA 2007, when the deprivation of liberty safeguards (DOLS) were introduced.

8.77 The DOLS were intended to ensure that the criticisms made of the domestic law of England and Wales in the *Bournewood* case were answered. The *Bournewood* patient was a person deprived of his liberty in a hospital, incapable of consenting to being there, but not trying to leave so as to prompt detention under the MHA. Such persons were not protected by a regime that was compliant with Art 5(1) and (4) of the ECHR. The DOLS introduced a complicated administrative admissions regime, similar to the MHA, under Sch A1 of the MCA. In brief, these provisions enabled residents in hospitals and care homes to be deprived of their liberty provided standard authorisations were obtained by the managing authority of the hospital or care home from the supervisory authority (the PCT in the case of a hospital, local social services in the case of a care home). Urgent authorisations were also possible in emergency situations. The procedure requires a number of 'qualifying requirements' to be satisfied (under Part 3, Sch A1).

---

[121] A creation of the Enduring Powers of Attorney Act 1985.
[122] See Court of Protection Practice 2014 (Jordan Publishing, 2014) for the relevant primary and delegated legislation, COP Rules, and extremely valuable and authoritative commentary and case studies. The work is published on an annual basis.

The satisfaction of these requirements make a decision Art 5-compliant. The authorisations are for a limited time, and they must be reviewed. There is a right of challenge to the Court of Protection under s 21A. The court has the power to make orders depriving a person of his liberty under s 16A(2), but in doing so the court must also ensure that it considers the requirements necessary to make the order Art 5-compliant.[123]

8.78 With the MCA allowing persons to be deprived of their liberty the question arises as to when it is appropriate to exercise powers under the MCA and when to use the MHA? The MHA may only be used where the patient suffers from a mental disorder as defined by the Act. The MCA may only be used where the person lacks capacity to make decisions as to the relevant care or treatment. Not all those with mental disorder lack capacity. Not all those who lack capacity will suffer from a mental disorder, and even if they do, often the treatment they require will not be treatment for a mental disorder. The problem arises where these clear boundaries are blurred. This is particularly relevant when a decision has to be made whether a patient is to be subject to the MHA or the MCA/DOLS in hospital.

8.79 In *GJ v The Foundation Trust*,[124] the Court of Protection had to consider whether a patient subject to a standard authorisation in a psychiatric hospital was eligible to be detained under DOLS or whether, as his legal representatives argued, he ought to be under the MHA regime. Under paragraph 12 of Part 3 of Schedule A1 of the MCA the patient must satisfy the eligibility requirement in order to be deprived of his liberty under MCA. Whether a patient is eligible or not depends on Part 2 of Schedule 1A and, in case of *GJ* the issue was whether he came within Case E – namely that he was 'within the scope of the Mental Health Act but not subject to any mental health regime' and whether he objected to being a mental health patient. The MHA has primacy over the MCA when they overlap. However, in determining whether they overlap it is important to establish the core or primary purpose of the treatment that has led to the decision-maker requesting a DOLS authorisation (whether under the DOLS or through the Court of Protection).[125]

8.80 Then the court went on to consider what the expression 'within the scope of the Mental Health Act' meant. Schedule 1A, Part 2 paragraph 12 states that 'P is within the scope of the Mental Health Act if: (a) an application in respect of P could be made under s 2 or 3 of the Mental Health Act, and (b) P could be detained in a hospital in pursuance of such an application, were one made'. For the purposes of this provision it is to be assumed that the recommendations necessary to trigger the civil admission process under the MHA had been given. The court had to decide what 'could be detained' meant. The PCT and hospital (as supervisory body and managing authority respectively) argued that in order to overturn the authorisation the court had to find that no reasonable decision-maker could have concluded that GJ could not be detained under the MHA ('the high probability or effective certainty test'). GJ argued that the decision-maker

---

[123] It is submitted that the court ought to ensure that a welfare order that will deprive a person of his liberty is only made when the requirements in Part 3 of the DOLS are satisfied. The only authority on this issue from the higher courts so far is *G v E and others* [2010] EWCA Civ 822. The Court of Appeal rejected the submission that there was a threshold in DOL cases, such as in care proceedings under the Children Act 1989. Rather, the court must decide what was in the incapacitate person's best interests whilst ensuring that the decision was Art 5 compliant. It would seem that since the MCA itself has a test (ie Part 3 of Sch 1A) that is designed to ensure that a DOL decision is Art 5 compliant, the court ought to apply that test in the same way as a supervisory body must apply it.
[124] [2009] EWHC 2972, reported as *J v The Foundation Trust* at [2010] 3 WLR 840.
[125] *GJ* at [57].

ought to have asked himself whether it was possible that the patient could be detained under the MHA ('the possibility test'). Finally, the Secretary of State argued that the provision ought to be read as devolving the decision entirely to the decision-maker: that is to say, what does the decision-maker think? The court decided the 'what the decision-maker thinks test' was the correct one. This meant that the court had to decide and decided that GJ was rightly detained under the DOLS because the primary purpose of the detention was for the treatment of his diabetes.[126] The Upper Tribunal considered the issue of primacy in *DN v Northumberland, Tyne & Wear NHS Foundation Trust*,[127] and then, again, in *AM v South London & Maudsley NHS Foundation Trust, Secretary of State for Health*[128][129] In the latter case, Charles J, sitting as Chamber President in the Administrative Appeals Chamber added a 'postscript' in which he emphasised that the idea of 'primacy' of the Mental Health Act over the Mental Capacity Act was limited only to situations where they genuinely overlapped. There was no freestanding primacy as such whereby decision-makers were bound in general terms to choose one over the other, save that the least restriction principle should have great weight.

8.81 What if the Court of Protection makes a decision that a certain care plan is in the best interests of a person but the services necessary for that plan to be enacted are not made available by the public authorities that could provide them? It is possible for the public law issue arising out of the COP case to be decided simultaneously, and, if the case is heard by a High Court judge by the same judge sitting in the Family Division.

CONCLUSION

8.82 Something of a revolution took place in mental health law in 2008. The effects of the Mental Health Act 2007, which both amended the MHA 1983 and completed the MCA 2005 have brought into place two regimes which are intended to work in parallel but which perversely may overlap. These two regimes largely exclude the need judicial review. The MHA brings the tribunal within the new tribunal system, which is intended to create a new administrative justice system with its own statutory appeal court, the UT. This is intended to be the new face of public law. The MCA has its own court, the Court of Protection which determines the issues that arise under the MCA regime. The primacy of the MHA over the MCA is intended to solve problems that arise where there is an overlap. However, the two regimes necessarily involve public authorities and their decision-making processes may at some stage be amenable to public law challenge by way of judicial review. Those involved in litigation in this field, lawyers in particular, will be aware that when a case comes before a court or tribunal those proceedings will represent the tip of a large iceberg. An individual application to the Court of Protection concerning the placement of, for instance, a person suffering from autism may well be preceded by a long struggle between parents or carers to obtain services at home. The proceedings in the Court of Protection are likely to be tainted by the hostility those parents or carers will feel towards the local authority that has in the past frustrated their

---

[126] It is beyond the scope of this book to consider the ramifications of this decision. On the one hand, by devolving the decision to the clinician deciding whether the MCA or MHA should apply the court has given the clinician the right to exercise clinical judgment taking into account the circumstances of the case. However, another consequence is that the s 21A appeal means that the Court of Protection has to make a *de novo* decision, rather than reviewing the decision of the original decision-maker. This is more in keeping with the role of the tribunal in the MHA, and consequently it is probable that Mr Justice Charles' decision in *GJ* was in keeping with the intention behind the DOLS.
[127] [2011] UKUT 327 (AAC).
[128] [2013] UKUT 0365 (AAC).
[129] See para [76] onwards in *AM*.

access to suitable services, as they see it. That frustration will become anger when the same authority takes proceedings in the Court of Protection to move that person to a placement where the services can be provided. The use of judicial review at an earlier stage is likely to reduce the need for Court of Protection proceedings by bringing the issue concerning the provision of services to the surface before the care of the person breaks down to the point where the use of the MCA is needed. The role of the tribunals will also be interesting to watch in the years to come. The author's hunch is that the Upper Tribunal will wish to assert its status at the apex of a new administrative justice system by developing the law in a way that serves the purpose of the tribunals – by making it better suited to the needs of those who use the system. The tribunal should keep up with the trends in clinical practice – that is part of the expert function of a tribunal. In doing so the Upper Tribunal should shape the substantive law so that it has regard to the realities of those who use the tribunal, whether they be patients, clinicians, NHS Trusts, PCTS or the Ministry of Justice. The fact that so many people are now treated in the community through independent living means that many of the old precepts upon which mental health law has been based are outdated.

CHAPTER 9

CRIMINAL LAW

INTRODUCTION

9.01 Judicial reviews in a criminal context raise a number of issues that do not arise in other areas. The procedure can be different. There are specific statutory provisions that have an impact upon the jurisdiction of the court. This chapter seeks to identify the specific issues that arise in a criminal context.

WHETHER THE MATTER IS A CRIMINAL CAUSE OR MATTER

The importance of knowing whether a matter is a criminal cause or matter

9.02 The distinction between a criminal cause or matter and other cases is significant, as the procedure adopted when bringing proceedings in the Administrative Court depends on whether a matter is a criminal cause. In particular, there is no right of appeal to the Court of Appeal from any judgment of the Administrative Court in any criminal cause or matter, except in very limited circumstances.[1] In addition, although in principle it is possible for a single High Court judge to consider a criminal judicial review, the practice is that the Divisional Court will normally hear a judicial review relating to a criminal matter.[2]

9.03 The procedural distinctions that arise mean that practitioners will need to ensure that they know whether a case relates to a criminal cause or matter, so that they follow the correct procedure.

The decision that determines whether a matter is a criminal cause or matter

9.04 The court will not be concerned with the nature of the order made by the Administrative Court. Indeed, the orders that might be sought, when applying for a judicial review in a criminal cause or matter, are broadly the same as those that are sought in other matters. Instead, the court will consider whether the decision that was being challenged in the Administrative Court was a criminal cause or matter.[3]

---

[1] Senior Courts Act 1981, s 18(1)(a).
[2] In addition, matters relating to criminal justice that are not technically criminal will often be heard by a Divisional Court (eg *R (McFetrich) v Secretary of State for the Home Department* (2003) *The Times*, 28 July).
[3] *Carr v Atkins* [1987] QB 963 at 967B.

Determining whether a matter is a criminal cause or matter

9.05 The appeal courts have given a wide definition to the phrase 'criminal cause or matter'. For example, Lord Esher has held that the phrase:

> '[A]pplies to a decision by way of judicial determination of any question raised in or with regard to proceedings, the subject-matter of which is criminal, at whatever stage of the proceedings the question arises.'[4]

9.06 Similarly, Lord Wright held that:

> '[I]f the cause or matter is one which, if carried to its conclusion, might result in the conviction of the person charged and in a sentence of some punishment, such as imprisonment or fine, it is a "criminal cause or matter" ... Every order made in such a cause or matter by an English court, is an order in a criminal cause or matter, even though the order, taken by itself, is neutral in character and might equally have been made in a cause or matter which is not criminal. The order may not involve punishment by the law of this country, but if the effect of the order is to subject by means of the operation of English law the persons charged to the criminal jurisdiction of a foreign country, the order is, in the eyes of English law for the purposes being considered, an order in a criminal cause or matter.'[5]

There has, however, been some recent recognition that there is a degree of incoherence, and as such that a narrower approach may be appropriate.[6] In particular, there has been recognition that some matters are so collateral that they are not criminal (see below).

9.07 Although these judgments appear to suggest that the phrase 'criminal cause or matter' relates to a decision of a court, other authorities show that there is no need for the decision-maker to be a court. A decision to refer or to refuse to refer a matter to the criminal courts can be a criminal cause or matter. For example, under the legislative scheme that existed before the establishment of the Criminal Cases Review Commission, a refusal by the Secretary of State to refer a matter to the Court of Appeal was a criminal matter.[7] A decision of the Criminal Cases Review Commission is also a criminal matter.[8]

9.08 A decision to caution an offender is treated as a criminal cause or matter.[9] This conclusion was reached in the past because the Court of Appeal concluded that a caution was one manner of disposing of a criminal matter.[10]

9.09 The decision need not be a final decision of a criminal court for it to be a criminal cause or matter. For example, a decision relating to evidence that may be used in criminal proceedings is a criminal cause or matter even if the proceedings have not commenced. Thus, an order of a Crown Court judge in relation to the production of special procedure material under Sch 1 to the Police and Criminal Evidence Act 1984 is a criminal cause or matter, even if proceedings have not commenced.[11]

---

[4] Ex p Alice Woodhall (1888) 20 QBD 832 at 836.
[5] Amand v Home Secretary [1943] AC 147 at 162.
[6] R (Guardian News and Media Ltd) v City of Westminster Magistrates' Court [2011] 1 WLR 3253.
[7] R v Secretary of State, ex p Garner [1990] COD 457.
[8] R (Kevin Davis) v (1) Secretary of State for the Home Department and (2) Criminal Cases Review Commission [2011] EWHC 1509 (Admin).
[9] R (Aru) v Chief Constable of Merseyside [2004] 1 WLR 1697.
[10] Ibid at [10].
[11] Carr v Atkins [1987] QB 963.

9.10 At one stage it appears to have been thought that once the criminal courts have imposed a sentence, a decision about the effect of the penalty imposed by the criminal court should also be treated as a criminal cause or matter. Thus, a case considering the calculation of the number of days to be served as a result of the imposition of a sentence of imprisonment was treated as a criminal cause or matter.[12] More recent case-law suggests that this is wrong. For example, cases about the correct application of licence provisions have not been treated as criminal causes.[13] Similarly, a case about the compatibility of the sex offender registration scheme with the European Convention on Human Rights was not treated as a criminal cause.[14] As a consequence, current practice appears to be that decisions about the effect of a penalty are not treated as a criminal cause or matter.

9.11 It may be difficult to draw any firm conclusions from the case-law summarised in the paragraph above because it appears that there was little argument regarding the principles to be applied. However, the recent tendency to treat challenges to decisions regarding the effect of a sentence as not being criminal causes does better accord with the dicta of Lord Esher and Lord Wright set out above: that dicta suggests that decisions of the executive are not criminal causes. Clearly challenges to decisions such as the calculation of a prisoner's release date are essentially challenges to an executive decision as to the effect of a sentence. The judicial determination of the sentence is not in issue.

9.12 The practice of treating the effect of a sentence as not being a criminal cause is consistent with the case-law considering challenges to the exercise of a discretionary power regarding the effect of a sentence. A challenge to the exercise of such an executive discretion is not treated as a criminal cause or matter. Thus, a challenge to a deportation order made following a recommendation by a criminal court is not a criminal cause or matter, although the actual recommendation is a criminal cause or matter.[15] Similarly, a challenge to a decision to decline to release a prisoner who has been recommended for early release by the Parole Board is not a criminal cause or matter.[16]

9.13 Although the decision that is being challenged need not be a decision of a criminal court if the case is to be a criminal cause or matter, it must however relate in some way to a possible trial by a criminal court.[17] Thus, a general challenge to a police policy is clearly not a criminal cause or matter.[18] In addition, the proceedings must relate in some way to the 'enforcement and preservation of public law and order' rather than being merely domestic disciplinary proceedings.[19] Thus, as already noted, proceedings relating to an alleged breach of prison rules are not a criminal cause or matter.[20] Similarly, disciplinary proceedings against a solicitor are not a criminal cause or matter.[21]

9.14 Not every decision by a criminal court in relation to criminal proceedings is a criminal cause or matter: some decisions of the criminal courts are so collateral to the criminal proceedings that gave rise to the decision that the decision cannot be regarded

---

[12] *R v Secretary of State for the Home Department, ex p Francois* [1999] 1 AC 43.
[13] *R (Stellato) v Secretary of State for Justice* [2007] 2 AC 70.
[14] *R (F) v Secretary of State* [2011] 1 AC 331.
[15] *R v Secretary of State for the Home Department, ex p Dannenberg* [1984] QB 766.
[16] *R (Black) v Secretary of State for Justice* [2009] 1 AC 949.
[17] Per Lord Justice Shaw, *R v Board of Visitors of Hull Prison, ex p St Germain* [1979] QB 425 at 453C.
[18] Eg *R v Chief Constable of North Wales and Others, ex p Thorpe* [1999] QB 396.
[19] Per Lord Justice Shaw, *R v Board of Visitors of Hull Prison, ex p St Germain* [1979] QB 425 at 452B.
[20] *R v Board of Visitors of Hull Prison, ex p St Germain* [1979] QB 425.
[21] In *Re EF Hardwick* (1883) 12 QBD 148.

as a criminal cause or matter.[22] The Court of Appeal has held that a refusal of a district judge to allow a newspaper to have access to various documents was not a criminal cause or matter[23] and that the decision to enforce a recognizance is not a criminal cause or matter as '[a] recognizance is in the nature of a bond. The issue of a witness summons is, however, not so collateral that it is not a criminal cause or matter'.[24]

9.15 Challenges to the decisions of criminal courts may also not be a criminal cause or matter if the decision challenged relates to civil proceedings. For example, there are forms of civil proceedings that are brought in the magistrates' court. Thus, a decision to commit a person to jail for non-payment of non-domestic rates is not a criminal cause or matter.[25]

9.16 The definition of a criminal charge for the purposes of the European Convention on Human Rights is different to the domestic law definition. It would appear that a finding that proceedings are criminal for the purposes of art 6 makes no difference to the determination to whether a judicial review is a criminal cause or matter for procedural purposes.[26] That is perhaps not surprising as art 6 does not entitle a person to any particular form of appeal, which is essentially often the remit of judicial review in the criminal context.

DECISIONS THAT CANNOT BE CHALLENGED

Interim decisions

9.17 The High Court is very reluctant to allow judicial reviews of decisions of criminal courts where there has been no final decision in the proceedings. Judicial review is a discretionary remedy. That means that the High Court will not necessarily intervene to quash every decision where there are grounds for intervening. When deciding whether to quash a decision taken by a court during criminal proceedings, the High Court will take account of the stage that those proceedings have reached. Applicants for judicial review will normally be expected to wait for a final decision before bringing an application for judicial review. Indeed, Lord Justice May has held that because nothing will be lost if parties wait until the final determination of the matter, interim rulings should only be challenged before a final determination 'in a very special instance'.[27]

9.18 The authorities in this area were reviewed by the Divisional Court in *R (K) v Bow Street Magistrates' Court*[28] where the court was faced with an assertion that it had no jurisdiction to consider challenges to interim decisions.

9.19 It declined, however, to rule on these arguments. It concluded that the judicial review was premature because it was impossible to know how the legal issues raised would arise until the evidence was heard and findings of fact made. It does appear to be

---

[22] Per Sir John Donaldson MR, *Carr v Atkins* [1987] 1 QB 963 at 970F.
[23] *R (Guardian News and Media Ltd) v City of Westminster Magistrates' Court* [2011] 1 WLR 3253.
[24] *Day v Grant* [1987] QB 972.
[25] *R v Thanet Justices, ex p Dass* [1996] COD 77.
[26] *R (International Transport Roth Gmbh) v Secretary of State for the Home Department* [2003] QB 728 in which the Court of Appeal concluded that the decisions challenged were criminal for the purposes of article 6.
[27] *Streames v Copping* [1985] QB 920 at 929.
[28] (2005) *The Times*, 27 July.

difficult to see why there should not be jurisdiction given that, in general, there is jurisdiction to challenge decisions of magistrates.

9.20 Jurisdiction was accepted in *R (CPS) v Sedgmoor Magistrates' Court* [2007] EWHC Admin 1803 in which an interim decision to refuse to admit evidence was challenged. The Administrative Court held that judicial review proceedings should not have been brought and that the prosecution should have waited until proceedings were concluded before commencing an appeal by way of case stated. The court was, however, willing to consider the claim for judicial review because: (i) dismissing it would have resulted in further delay, (ii) there was no need for facts to be found by the magistrates to enable the judicial review to be determined, and (iii) the ruling challenged had the effect of determining the proceedings before the magistrates' court.

9.21 There are, however, some circumstances where it will be appropriate to challenge an interim decision. It would not be possible to identify all the circumstances; however, some principles can be seen in the decided cases. In particular the precedents set out in the paragraph below show that the High Court is likely to be concerned about the reason why the applicant cannot wait for a final determination of the criminal proceedings. It is less concerned about the type of decision being challenged. As a result, and as a matter of good practice, applicants for judicial review should always explain in their pleadings why they have not waited for a final decision of the court before bringing a judicial review application.

9.22 The High Court has held that a decision that has resulted in a person being detained may be challenged by judicial review even where there is no final conviction.[29] In addition, the High Court is more likely to exercise its discretion to quash an interim decision where quashing that decision is likely to result in the final determination of the matter.[30] This is particularly likely to be true in the context of proceedings against juveniles as the courts are keen to avoid putting juveniles through criminal trials if there is no need.[31] The same considerations may also apply in cases where there are juvenile witnesses where there will be a desire to avoid these witnesses giving evidence unnecessarily.

9.23 It does appear to be accepted that a challenge may be brought before a final conviction where a mode of trial has been determined wrongly. Thus a decision to decline jurisdiction where the matter could only be tried summarily could be challenged by judicial review before there had been a final conclusion of the matter.[32] Similarly an unreasonable decision to accept jurisdiction could be challenged by way of judicial

---

[29] Eg *R v Maidstone Crown Court, ex p Clark* [1995] 1 WLR 831.
[30] Eg *R v Horseferry Road Magistrates' Court, ex p Bennett* [1994] 1 AC 42 in which the House of Lords held that in certain circumstances judicial review proceedings should be brought in the High Court where it was said that a matter should be stayed as an abuse of process. See also *R v Horseferry Road Justices, ex p Independent Broadcasting Authority* [1987] QB 54 in which the High Court held that it should decide whether a criminal offence existed and *R (Latham) v Northampton Magistrates' Court* [2008] EWHC Admin 245 in which the issue of a summons was quashed as being unreasonable.
[31] *R v Chief Constable of Kent ex p L; R v DPP, ex p B* 93 CrAppR 416, DC. In this case the High Court considered an application for judicial review of a decision to prosecute juveniles. The court held that it would be more willing to quash a decision to prosecute in a case involving juveniles than it would be in a case involving adults. The same principles are likely to apply to judicial reviews of interim decisions taken during criminal proceedings.
[32] *R v Hatfield Justices, ex p Castle* [1981] 1 WLR 217.

review before there had been a final conviction on the basis that to do so would be a disproportionate use of the court's time and resources.[33]

9.24 If a claim for judicial review is brought to challenge an interim decision, it is important that both the prosecution and the defence seek to expedite the claim.[34] The normal timescales for judicial review are likely to result in excessive delay.

Decisions of the Crown Court

9.25 The jurisdiction of the Administrative Court to consider applications for judicial review from decisions of the Crown Court is governed by s 29(3) of the Senior Courts Act 1981. It provides that judicial review can be used to challenge all decisions of the Crown Court other than 'matters relating to trial on indictment'. The Administrative Court has rejected arguments that it has an inherent jurisdiction to consider judicial reviews of decisions of the Crown Court that would otherwise be excluded from the scope of judicial review by s 29(3) of the Senior Courts Act 1981.[35]

9.26 Clearly, there are some matters that do not relate to a trial on indictment, because no indictment is involved in the proceedings. For example, judicial review may be used to challenge the decisions of the Crown Court while exercising its jurisdiction to consider appeals from the magistrates' court.[36] Similarly, a decision to refuse legal aid in an application to remove a disqualification from driving is also subject to challenge in the Administrative Court.[37] There are also other matters that clearly cannot be challenged in the Administrative Court, such as conviction and sentence on a matter committed to the Crown Court for trial on indictment. In this context, the term 'trial' includes proceedings where a defendant pleads guilty to an indictment.[38] It also covers pre-trial hearings where no jury is sworn.[39]

9.27 When the Crown Court makes a decision that is ancillary to proceedings on indictment, it can be difficult to determine whether the Administrative Court has jurisdiction to consider the matter. For example, is it possible to challenge decisions made by the Crown Court that relate to legal aid in a case being tried on indictment?

9.28 The House of Lords has considered the scope of the Administrative Court's jurisdiction on at least four occasions.[40] Their Lordships have declined to define the statutory phrases used to limit the jurisdiction of the Administrative Court.[41] They have, however, stated that if the decision of the Crown Court was one affecting the conduct of a trial on indictment given in the course of the trial or by way of pre-trial directions, it cannot be challenged by judicial review.[42] If the decision was such a decision, an

---

[33] *R v Northampton Magistrates, ex p Commissioners for Customs and Excise* [1994] COD 382.
[34] *R (UK Real Estate Ltd) v London Borough of Camden* [2013] EWHC 3505 (Admin).
[35] *R v Chelmsford Crown Court, ex p Chief Constable of the Essex Police* [1994] 1 WLR 359 but cf *R v Maidstone Crown Court, ex p Harrow London Borough Council* [2000] QB 719 holding that there might be a judicial review challenging a lack of jurisdiction in circumstances where the challenge might be said to relate to trial on indictment.
[36] *R v Bournemouth Crown Court, ex p Weight* [1984] 1 WLR 980.
[37] *R v Recorder of Liverpool, ex p McCann* (1994) *The Times*, 4 May.
[38] *Re Smalley* [1985] AC 622.
[39] *R v Harrow Crown Court, ex p Perkins* (1998) *The Times*, 28 April.
[40] *Re Smalley* [1985] AC 622, *Re Sampson* [1987] 1 WLR 194, *R v Manchester Crown Court, ex p DPP* [1993] 1 WLR 1524, *Re Ashton* [1994] 1 AC 9.
[41] *Re Smalley* [1985] AC 622.
[42] Ibid.

aggrieved defendant normally has the opportunity to appeal to the Court of Appeal under the Criminal Appeal Act 1968. For example, a decision to refuse to grant legal aid has been held to be a matter that relates to a trial on indictment.[43] This is not surprising, because the Court of Appeal has held that it is entitled to quash a defendant's conviction where it is rendered unsafe by a trial judge's decision regarding legal aid.[44]

9.29 The absence of a right of appeal to the Court of Appeal does not necessarily mean that the Administrative Court will accept jurisdiction. For example, the court has no jurisdiction to consider a challenge to a decision to refuse to order costs after acquittal.[45] This is because the statutory limit on the jurisdiction of the court means that matters relating to a trial on indictment include orders made at the conclusion of a trial on indictment, if these orders are an integral part of the trial process.[46] Orders are an integral part of the trial process if they are based on what is learnt during the trial process.[47] Clearly costs orders are based on what is learnt during the trial process.

9.30 The absence of a right of appeal does not even necessarily result in the Administrative Court accepting jurisdiction if a person can claim to be a victim of a violation of the European Convention on Human Rights as a consequence of a Crown Court decision.[48] That is because there is no right under the rights incorporated into domestic law by the Human Rights Act 1998 to challenge the decision that is said to violate European Convention rights.[49]

9.31 If a claimant wrongly challenges a decision of the Crown Court by bringing judicial review proceedings when they are able to appeal, it is possible for the court to correct the problem by re-constituting itself as the Court of Appeal.[50]

9.32 Further assistance on the scope of the Administrative Court's jurisdiction is provided by Lord Browne-Wilkinson, who noted that decisions held to be open to challenge in the Administrative Court are those in which the order was made in a wholly different jurisdiction or where the order has been made against someone other than the accused.[51] The only possible exception to this is serious fraud cases, where the Administrative Court may be able to consider decisions to dismiss a case that has been transferred to the Crown Court under the special procedure provided by the Criminal Justice Act 1987.[52] Lord Browne-Wilkinson formulated the following guidance:

---

43 *R v Chichester Crown Court, ex p Abodunrin* (1984) 79 Cr App R 293.
44 *R v Kirk* (1983) 76 Cr App R 194.
45 *Re Meredith* (1973) 57 Cr App R 451, DC; *R v Harrow Crown Court, ex p Perkins* (1998) *The Times*, 28 April.
46 Per Lord Bridge in *Re Sampson* [1987] 1 WLR 194 at 198G.
47 Ibid at 197E.
48 *R (Regentford) Ltd v Canterbury Crown Court* [2001] HRLR 18.
49 *R (Shields) v Crown Court at Liverpool and the Lord Chancellor* [2001] UKHRR 610 at [58].
50 *R (Lichniak) v Secretary of State for the Home Department* [2002] QB 296.
51 *R v Manchester Crown Court, ex p DPP* [1993] 1 WLR 1524 at 1530C.
52 In *R v Manchester Crown Court, ex p DPP* [1993] 1 WLR 1524 at 1530G, Lord Browne-Wilkinson declined an opportunity to express a view on the correctness of *R v Central Criminal Court and Nadir, ex p Director of the Serious Fraud Office* [1993] 1 WLR 949. Although his Lordship noted that the decision in *ex p Director of the Serious Fraud Office* relied on cases that he held had been wrongly decided, he went on to say that the wording of the Criminal Justice Act 1987 might give rise to special considerations. Since the decision in *ex p DPP*, the Administrative Court has continued to consider judicial reviews of decisions to dismiss proceedings following a transfer under the provisions of the Criminal Justice Act 1987. See eg *R v Snaresbrook Crown Court, ex p Director of the Serious Fraud Office* (1998) *The Times*, 26 October.

'"Is the decision sought to be reviewed one arising in the issue between the Crown and the defendant formulated by the indictment (including the costs of such issue)?" If the answer is "Yes", then to permit the decision to be challenged by judicial review may lead to delay in the trial: the matter is therefore probably excluded from review by the section. If the answer is "No", the decision of the Crown Court is truly collateral to the indictment of the defendent and judicial review of that decision will not delay his trial: therefore it may well not be excluded by the section.'[53]

9.33 The decisions of the House of Lords have not prevented a degree of uncertainty about whether a matter is something that relates to a trial on indictment. Indeed, the lack of certainty has prompted Lord Justice Rose to call for legislation to clarify the scope of judicial review of Crown Court decisions.[54] There has been a consultation about such legislation. There are, however, a number of precedents that give examples of matters that have been held to relate to a trial on indictment or matters that do not relate to a trial on indictment. These precedents can, on a cursory reading, appear to be arbitrary. For example, although a decision to remit a legal aid contribution at the end of a trial is not subject to judicial review,[55] a decision to make a contribution order is subject to review.[56] These precedents, however, are a useful guide to whether the court will accept that it has jurisdiction to consider a challenge to a particular decision.

9.34 Matters held to be relating to a trial on indictment, and therefore excluded from judicial review and appeal by way of case stated, include the following:

(a) an order discharging a jury;[57]
(b) an order that an indictment lie on the file marked 'not to be proceeded with without leave of the court';[58]
(c) the decision of a judge to order a defence solicitor to pay the costs occasioned by the granting of a defence application for an adjournment;[59]
(d) a decision as to whether the trial of one indictment should proceed before the trial of another indictment faced by the same defendant;[60]
(e) a refusal to stay an indictment as an abuse of process;[61]
(f) an order quashing an indictment because the Crown Court lacks jurisdiction;[62]
(g) an order that matters should be stayed as an abuse of process;[63]
(h) an order regarding costs after the prosecution announce their intent to offer no evidence at a pre-trial hearing;[64]
(i) an order preventing the naming of a witness under s 11 of the Contempt of Court Act 1981;[65]

---

[53] *R v Manchester Crown Court, ex p DPP* [1993] 1 WLR 1524 at 1530F.
[54] *R v Manchester Crown Court, ex p H* [2000] 1 WLR 760.
[55] *R v Cardiff Crown Court, ex p Jones* [1974] QB 113.
[56] Per Lord Bridge, in *Re Sampson* [1987] 1 WLR 194 at 199F.
[57] *Ex p Marlowe* [1973] Crim LR 294.
[58] *R v Central Criminal Court, ex p Raymond* (1986) 83 Cr App R 94.
[59] *R v Smith (M)*, [1975] QB 531, but note doubts expressed by Lord Bridge in *Re Smalley* [1985] AC 622 at 644F.
[60] *R v Southwark Crown Court, ex p Ward* [1996] Crim LR 123.
[61] *R v Maidstone Crown Court, ex p Shanks & McEwan (Southern) Ltd* [1993] Env LR 340.
[62] *R v Manchester Crown Court, ex p DPP* [1993] 1 WLR 1524.
[63] *Re Ashton and Others; R v Manchester Crown Court, ex p DPP* [1994] 1 AC 9.
[64] *R v Harrow Crown Court, ex p Perkins* (1998) *The Times*, 28 April.
[65] *R v Central Criminal Court, ex p Crook* (1984) *The Times*, 8 November.

(j) a decision to refuse to dismiss a charge sent for trial under s 51 of the Crime and Disorder Act 1998;[66] and

(k) a decision to decline to make a compensation order.[67]

9.35 Matters that have been held to be matters that do not relate to a trial on indictment and therefore may be challenged by judicial review or appeal by way of case stated include the following:

(a) forfeiture orders made against a person who was not a defendant in the trial;[68]

(b) an order committing an acquitted defendant to prison unless he agrees to be bound over;[69]

(c) a decision to extend a custody time-limit;[70]

(d) an order enforcing the recognizance of a surety;[71] and

(e) an order lifting restrictions on the naming of juvenile defendants made under s 39(1) of the Children and Young Persons Act 1933.[72]

9.36 Ingenious arguments that seek to extend the Administrative Court's jurisdiction to consider decisions of the Crown Court have found little favour. For example, the Administrative Court has decided that it has no jurisdiction to consider a challenge to a warrant of committal to prison, if that challenge is in reality a challenge to sentence.[73]

9.37 One argument has succeeded, which is that the Administrative Court can exceptionally quash a decision that was made by the Crown Court in circumstances in which it lacked jurisdiction if no alternative remedy is available.[74] The Administrative Court has, however, sought to limit the scope of this jurisdiction. In particular, it is clear that an unlawful decision is not sufficient to enable the Administrative Court to intervene.[75] This is despite the fact that it might be thought that there is no jurisdiction to make an unlawful decision.

9.38 It was historically thought that one decision of the Crown Court that cannot be challenged by judicial review (though it might not relate to a trial on indictment) was a decision by a Crown Court judge in chambers to refuse bail.[76] This is because there was an alternative remedy as the High Court had jurisdiction to grant bail.[77] There is now a clear jurisdiction to consider judicial reviews of bail decisions because the High Court no longer has jurisdiction to grant bail.[78] This is true even when proceedings on indictment are pending.[79] That jurisdiction will, however, be exercised exceptionally.[80] In addition,

---

[66] *R (Snelgrove) v Woolwich Crown Court* [2005] 1 WLR 3223.
[67] *R (Faithfull) v Ipswich Crown Court* [2008] 1 WLR 1636.
[68] *R v Maidstone Crown Court, ex p Gill* (1987) 84 Cr App R 96.
[69] *R v Inner London Crown Court, ex p Benjamin* (1987) 85 Cr App R 267.
[70] *R v Norwich Crown Court, ex p Cox* (1993) 5 Admin LR 689.
[71] *Re Smalley* [1985] AC 622.
[72] *R v Manchester Crown Court, ex p H* [2000] 1 WLR 760.
[73] *R v Lewes Crown Court, ex p Sinclair* (1993) 5 Admin LR 1.
[74] *R v Maidstone Crown Court, ex p Harrow LBC* [2000] QB 719.
[75] *R (Faithfull) v Ipswich Crown Court* [2008] 1 WLR 1636.
[76] *Re Herbage* (1985) *The Times*, 25 October.
[77] Criminal Justice Act 1967, s 22(1).
[78] *R (M) v Isleworth Crown Court* [2005] EWHC Admin 363.
[79] *R (Mongan) v Isleworth Crown Court* [2007] EWHC Admin 1087.
[80] Ibid.

if the bail decision is a decision by a trial judge during the course of a trial to revoke bail that is a matter relating to trial on indictment and so judicial review is not available.[81]

GROUNDS FOR APPLYING FOR JUDICIAL REVIEW

9.39 The grounds for applying for judicial review are essentially the same as those that apply in other contexts. There are, however, some differences in the approach to those grounds when claims for judicial review are brought in a criminal context.

Decisions of prosecutors

9.40 Elsewhere in this book it will be noticed that the intensity of review when the Administrative Court considers a claim for judicial review depends upon the subject matter of the claim. This flexibility is perhaps clearest when the court considers challenges to decisions to bring a prosecution.

9.41 The decision of a public authority as to whether to prosecute a person is subject to judicial review.[82] Similarly it is possible to bring a judicial review of a decision to reinstate proceedings.[83] In practice, however, the High Court is unlikely to exercise its discretion to quash a decision to prosecute. For example, the High Court has held that it will only quash a decision to prosecute in the most extreme circumstances such as where the decision to prosecute was the result of fraud, corruption or mala fides.[84] The only exception to this general reluctance to quash decisions to prosecute may arise when the High Court considers prosecutions brought against juveniles. The High Court has held that it would be willing to quash a decision to prosecute a juvenile if that decision was clearly contrary to the policy of the prosecuting authority that was designed to protect the public interest.[85] More recently the Divisional Court has quashed a decision to prosecute brought by children who were not parties to the criminal proceedings in circumstances in which it was argued that the prosecution was contrary to the interests of those children.[86] The general reluctance to consider challenges to decisions to prosecute arises because it is in the public interest to discourage satellite litigation in a criminal context.

9.42 It is not only as a result of the High Court's reluctance to quash a decision to prosecute that a defendant is unlikely to seek a judicial review of a decision to prosecute. A defendant is also unlikely to seek judicial review as they will almost certainly be able to challenge the decision to prosecute during the criminal proceedings. Firstly, the defendant will be able to argue that the prosecution should be stayed as an abuse of process. Criminal proceedings that are 'oppressive and vexatious' should be stayed as an abuse of process.[87] As a result it is very difficult to conceive of circumstances where the High Court could quash a decision to prosecute during judicial review proceedings but

---

[81] *R (Uddin) v Crown Court at Isleworth* [2013] EWHC Admin 2752.
[82] Eg *R v Elmbridge Borough Council, ex p Activeoffice Ltd*, The Times, 29 December 1997 in which the applicant unsuccessfully tried to challenge a decision of a local authority to prosecute in a planning matter.
[83] Eg *R v DPP, ex p Burke* [1997] 2 CL 184 holding that there was no need for special circumstances before the CPS decided to reinstate proceedings. It was enough that the decision to discontinue was clearly wrong.
[84] Per Steyn LJ *R v Panel on Takeovers and Mergers, ex p Fayed*, The Times, 15 April 1992. See more recently *R (UK Real Estate Ltd) v London Borough of Camden* [2013] EWHC Admin 3505.
[85] *R v Chief Constable of Kent, ex p L* [1993] 1 All ER 756.
[86] *R (E) v DPP* [2011] EWHC 1465 (Admin).
[87] Per Lord Salmon *R v Humphries* [1977] AC 1 at 46D.

the criminal courts could not stay proceedings as an abuse of process.[88] If such circumstances did arise, it is now clear that criminal courts have jurisdiction to consider public law defences. In particular, it is able to consider arguments about 'the invalidity of subordinate legislation *or an administrative act under it*'[89] (emphasis added) unless the statute excludes this jurisdiction. The use of the phrase 'administrative act' clearly implies that a public law challenge to the decision to prosecute might be raised as a defence.

9.43 The availability of public law defences in the criminal courts is a matter that the High Court is likely to take account of when it considers whether to exercise its discretion to quash a decision to prosecute. As a result practitioners representing prosecuting authorities should normally raise the availability of an alternative remedy in opposition to a defendant's application for judicial review of a decision to prosecute.

9.44 Although the House of Lords has held that judicial reviews of decisions not to prosecute will only succeed in exceptional circumstances,[90] the High Court may be slightly more willing to entertain judicial review applications challenging a failure to prosecute.[91] As a result there have been a number of judicial reviews of decisions of the Crown Prosecution Service not to prosecute.[92] For example, the High Court quashed a decision not to prosecute where the Crown Prosecution Service had failed to take account of a reasoned judgment of a civil court that suggested that the evidence that would have been relied on during any criminal prosecution had merit.[93] The High Court quashed the decision not to prosecute because it was irrational in all the circumstances. In reaching its decision, the High Court took account of the Code for Crown Prosecutors. The High Court did, however, indicate that usually it would be reluctant to intervene to quash a decision not to prosecute. In part that is because there is a presumption that civil courts should not determine whether behaviour is criminal.[94] Recently, a decision not to prosecute was quashed where it was a breach of article 3 of the European Convention on Human Rights.[95]

9.45 When the High Court considers a judicial review of a decision to refuse to prosecute, it will take account of the availability of an alternative remedy when it decides whether to exercise its discretion to allow the judicial review. In particular, the possibility of a private prosecution will be considered in cases where it is as effective a remedy as judicial review. In determining the effectiveness the High Court will take account of the resources of the applicant.[96]

9.46 Historically it has been held that the High Court will not consider judicial reviews of decisions of the Attorney General regarding the entry of a *nolle prosequi*.[97] This is because the High Court has been reluctant to consider judicial reviews of the

---

[88] In *R v N* [2013] QB 379 the Court of Appeal accepted that in principle a decision to prosecute could be challenged in abuse proceedings.
[89] Per Lord Irvine *Boddington v British Transport Police* [1998] 2 WLR 639 at 651G.
[90] *R (Corner House Research) v DPP* [2008] 3 WLR 568.
[91] Eg *R v Commr of the Police for the Metropolis, ex p Blackburn* [1968] 2 QB 118 CA in which the applicant successfully challenged a police policy against prosecuting certain illegal gambling.
[92] Eg *R v CPS, ex p Waterworth* unreported, 1 December 1995, DC, *R v DPP, ex p Panayiotu* [1997] COD 83 and *R v DPP, ex p M and R v CPS, ex p Hitchins*, unreported, 13 June 1997, DC.
[93] *R v DPP, ex p Treadway*, (1997) The Times, 31 October .
[94] *R v DPP, ex p Camelot Croup plc* (1998) 10 Admin LR 93 at 104D.
[95] *R (B) v DPP* [2009] 1 WLR 2072.
[96] *R v DPP, ex p Camelot Croup plc* (1998) 10 Admin LR 93 at 105B.
[97] *R v Comptroller of Patents* [1899] 1 QB 909.

exercise of prerogative powers. There is, however, some indication that the High Court is showing a greater willingness to consider judicial reviews of the prerogative powers.

Legitimate expectation

9.47 It does appear easier to establish a legitimate expectation when challenging decisions of criminal courts regarding sentencing than it appears to be in some other contexts.

9.48 In *R v Nottingham Magistrates' Court, ex p Davidson*[98] Lord Bingham CJ held that:

> 'If a court at a preliminary stage of the sentencing process gives to a defendant any indication as to the sentence which will or will not be thereafter passed upon him, in terms sufficiently unqualified to found a legitimate expectation in the mind of the defendant that any court which later passes sentence upon him will act in accordance with the indication given, and if on a later occasion a court, without reasons which justify departure from the earlier indication, and whether or not it is aware of that indication, passes a sentence inconsistent with, and more severe than, the sentence indicated, the court will ordinarily feel obliged, however reluctantly, to adjust the sentence passed so as to bring it into line with that indicated.'[99]

9.49 The important point about the above is that it does not require reliance upon a statement for a legitimate expectation to arise. That contrasts with the approach to legitimate expectation in some other contexts.

9.50 The dicta does state that the court must give an indication as to the sentence that it will impose for a legitimate expectation to arise. However, the facts of *R v Feltham Justices, ex p Rees*[100] demonstrate that the indication need not be the sort of firm promise required in other areas. In that case the magistrates heard submissions about the adequacy of their powers. They then invited mitigation before stating that 'they' required more information. As a consequence, they adjourned stating that 'all options' were open. It might be thought that indicating 'all options' are open is sufficient to prevent a legitimate expectation arising. However, the court held that the approach of the magistrates' court implied that they would not commit the defendant to the Crown Court.

9.51 Another difference that arises when the courts consider claims relying on a legitimate expectation in a criminal context is that the conduct of one court can bind another court. As a consequence, a statement by a magistrates' court that a defendant will not be imprisoned can bind the Crown Court.[101] That contrasts with the normal reluctance to find that a promise by one public body binds another.

---

[98] [2000] 1 Cr App R (S) 167.
[99] Ibid at 169.
[100] [2001] 2 Cr App R (S) 1.
[101] *R v Isleworth Crown Court, ex p Irvin*, The Times, 5 December 1991.

ALTERNATIVE REMEDIES

Appeal to the Crown Court

9.52 A right to appeal to the Crown Court does not prevent an application for judicial review of a conviction in the magistrates' court.[102] Essentially it was held that the standards of procedural fairness are higher in criminal proceedings. Parliament has decided that a person is entitled to a fair trial in the magistrates' court and that will potentially be denied if a person cannot apply for a judicial review of a decision of a magistrates' court merely because they can appeal to the Crown Court.[103] An appeal to the Crown Court will only ensure one fair hearing.

9.53 The High Court must be informed of any appeal that is pending in the Crown Court.[104] As judicial review is a discretionary remedy, the possibility of an appeal to the Crown Court and the status of the appeal in the Crown Court is a matter that can be taken into account when the High Court considers whether it should intervene to quash a conviction. Thus a judicial review that was intended to procure delay of an appeal in the Crown Court in an attempt to secure the dropping of charges was rejected.[105] The High Court will also wish to ensure at the permission stage in an application for judicial review that there are good grounds for bringing an application for judicial review.[106]

Appeal by way of case stated

9.54 The courts have held that judicial review is only the appropriate method for applying to quash a conviction imposed by the Magistrates' Court or the Crown Court where an appeal by case stated was inapposite or inappropriate. For example, Mr Justice Brooke criticised claimants mounting a judicial review of a conviction in a magistrates' court:

> 'Our task in this case was made unnecessarily difficult because the applicants did not adopt the procedure prescribed by Parliament for referring a point of law which has arisen in the magistrates' court to the High Court for decision. If the justices had stated a case for our opinion, we would have known what their findings of fact had been and their reasons for the decisions they took and they would have identified the relevant points of law for our decision in the familiar way.'[107]

9.55 This approach has been endorsed in an application, which sought judicial review, of a conviction that was upheld by the Crown Court following an appeal.[108] The court did, however, go on to state that where a judicial review was brought, the court that had

---

[102] *R v Hereford Magistrates' Court, ex p Rowlands and Ingram; R v Harrow Youth Court, ex p Prussia* [1998] QB 110.
[103] Ibid.
[104] *R v Mid-Worcester JJJ, ex p Hart* [1989] COD 397, DC. In this case the High Court endorsed the comments of Alverstone LCJ in *R v Barnes* (1910) 102 LT 860 stating that the court considering a judicial review should be told of any pending appeal. The same comments suggested that in many cases the High Court will not wish to determine a judicial review until the appeal has been concluded.
[105] *R v Hereford Magistrates' Court, ex p Rowlands and Ingram; R v Harrow Youth Court, ex p Prussia* [1998] QB 110, DC considering and explaining *R v Peterborough Magistrates' Court, ex p Dowler* [1997] QB 911, DC.
[106] Per Lord Bingham CJ *R v Hereford Magistrates' Court, ex p Rowlands and Ingram; R v Harrow Youth Court, ex p Prussia* [1998] QB 110 at 866C.
[107] *R v Morpeth Ward JJ, ex p Ward* 95 CrAppR 215. It is significant to note, however, that despite these comments the High Court did consider the substantive merits of the judicial review application.
[108] *R v Gloucester Crown Court, ex p Chester*, The Independent, 6 July 1998, QBD.

made the original decision that was subject to challenge should at least write a letter stating whether they intended to resist the challenge.

9.56 As a result any challenge to a conviction should be by way of case stated where the High Court needs a full record of the findings of fact and law before the magistrates' court or the Crown Court. This means that it is normal to challenge a conviction based on a misconstruction of the statute that gives rise to the offence by an appeal by way of case stated.[109]

9.57 An appeal by way of case stated is also normally the correct procedure where a person seeks to challenge an acquittal.

9.58 In practice the availability of an appeal by way of case stated does not prevent a significant number of judicial reviews of convictions in the magistrates' courts or the Crown Court. This is because the High Court often does not need a record of the findings of fact and findings of law when it considers a challenge to the conviction. Instead it requires evidence about what happened during the trial of the matter and this evidence cannot normally be presented during an appeal by way of case stated. The procedure that the court adopts when considering applications for judicial review is usually the only appropriate way of presenting the High Court with the evidence that it needs in these circumstances.

9.59 For example, complaints about matters such as bias, a failure to adopt a procedure that satisfies the requirements of natural justice or a decision that is contrary to the applicant's legitimate expectation do not require a record of the court's findings of fact or law. Instead they require written evidence from persons present in court explaining the procedure adopted by the court. Judicial review is the procedure that allows a party to present this evidence.[110]

9.60 In addition to cases where the procedure in judicial review is preferable to that in appeal by way of case stated, there is one circumstance where a judicial review is the appropriate method of challenging a conviction. The justices or the Crown Court have discretion to refuse to state a case. In these circumstances it is possible to bring a judicial review of the failure to state a case. Where it is necessary to apply for a judicial review of the failure to state a case, the judicial review should also challenge the conviction. That enables the High Court to consider whether it is in a position to consider quashing the conviction on the basis of the information available to it.[111] The High Court will wish to avoid the unnecessary waste of time associated with ordering the justices or the Crown Court judge to state a case before being able to consider the merits of the conviction.

9.61 If a person wrongly applies for judicial review when they should have appealed by way of case stated or vice versa, the High Court can sometimes act in a way that avoids that person being prejudiced. For example, in one case where a party wrongly proceeded by way of judicial review, the High Court extended the time allowed for lodging an appeal by way of case stated. That then enabled the High Court to consider the case as if it was an appeal by case stated.[112]

---

[109] Eg *Vigon v DPP* [1998] Crim LR 289, DC.
[110] Although judicial review is normally the correct form of proceedings, it may be possible to bring an appeal by way of case stated if the justices were asked to rule on an issue such as bias. See *Johnson v Leicestershire Constabulary, The Times*, 7 October 1998.
[111] *R v Southwark Crown Court, ex p Brooke* [1997] COD 81.
[112] *R v Clerkenwell Stipendiary Magistrate, ex p DPP* [1984] QB 821 at 836D.

PROCEDURE

Bail as a form of interim relief

9.62 The first matter that needs to be considered when a claimant is detained is whether they wish to apply for bail. This may not be as straightforward an issue as it might appear to be. If a claimant is serving a criminal sentence applying for bail in the course of an unsuccessful judicial review claim may require them to return to prison without any reduction in the time that they serve.[113] They will be released from prison later than they would have been had bail not been granted. That may mean that in practice it is in the interest of the claimant to seek an expedited hearing of the claim for judicial review rather than bail.

9.63 When a person has sought permission to bring judicial review proceedings for a quashing order challenging proceedings in the Crown Court, that person is entitled to apply to the Crown Court for bail.[114] There is no equivalent power allowing the magistrates' court to grant bail.[115] The application to the Crown Court must be served at least two business days before the hearing.[116] The procedure for making an application is the same as when a defendant in proceedings in the magistrates' court seeks bail in the Crown Court.[117] If the Crown Court does grant bail, and an application of judicial review is determined or withdrawn, magistrates may issue a process enforcing the decision that is the subject of the judicial review.[118]

9.64 The power of an inferior court or tribunal to consider a bail application does not necessarily mean that the Administrative Court cannot also consider an application. Where a defendant applies for permission to seek an order quashing a conviction or sentence in the magistrates' court or challenging proceedings in the Crown Court, there is a statutory right to apply to the Administrative Court for bail.[119] The Administrative Court also has an inherent power to grant bail in the course of applications for judicial review.[120] It has become accepted that this is true whether the case is a criminal cause or matter or some other form of proceedings.[121]

9.65 There is some suggestion that a judicial review claimant should only apply for bail to the Administrative Court after they have tried to apply for bail by taking advantage of any alternative jurisdiction that permits an application for bail to an inferior court or tribunal.[122] In practice the Administrative Court is generally willing to hear bail applications despite the existence of an alternative right of application. That is perhaps not surprising as the Administrative Court will be best able to judge the merits of the judicial review, which is clearly a factor that will be relevant to the grant of bail.

---

[113] *R (Akhtar) v Governor of Newhall Prison* [2001] ACD 69.
[114] Senior Courts Act 1981, s 81(1)(e).
[115] *Ex p Blyth* [1944] 1 KB 532; holding that an express statutory provision is required if a person is to be bailed after conviction. This, however, contrasts with decisions of the High Court that it has an inherent power to grant bail during a judicial review.
[116] Criminal Procedure Rules (SI 2013/1554), Pt 19.7(2).
[117] Criminal Procedure Rules (SI 2013/1554), Pt 19.7.
[118] Civil Procedure Rules 1998 (SI 1998/3132) ('the CPR 1998'), Sch 1, RSC Ord 79, r 9(11).
[119] Criminal Justice Act 1948, s 37(1)(b)(ii) and (d).
[120] *R v Secretary of State for the Home Department, ex p Turkoglu* [1988] QB 398.
[121] See e g *Armand v Home Secretary* [1943] AC 147 for a case where in the context of a criminal habeas corpus application, it was assumed that there was an inherent power to grant bail. That inherent power may be limited following conviction: *ex p Blyth* [1944] 1 KB 532.
[122] *R v Secretary of State for the Home Department, ex p Kelso* [1998] INLR 603.

9.66 The procedure rules provide that bail applications should be made by claim form using Form 97.[123] However, in practice an application for bail is normally made by indicating that an application is being made for bail on the claim form, or alternatively filing an application notice seeking bail.

9.67 In a criminal case the bail application must be served on the prosecutor and on the Director of Public Prosecutions, if the prosecution continues.[124]

9.68 Service must take place at least 24 hours before the date set for the hearing.[125] The rules state that the application must be supported by a witness statement or affidavit.[126] In practice, this is usually unnecessary in the context of a claim for judicial review as the evidence in support of the judicial review claim can normally stand as the evidence in support of the bail application. Clearly, if this is to happen, the evidence in support of the judicial review claim must include matters relevant to the grant of bail.

9.69 In principle, there is no reason why bail should not be granted before permission to apply for judicial review has been ordered, as the inherent and statutory jurisdiction to grant bail extends to applications for permission.[127] In practice, however, the application for bail is normally considered at the same hearing as the application for permission, partly because a High Court judge is unlikely to be willing to grant bail unless they are satisfied that the application for judicial review is arguable.

9.70 In principle bail can be considered by the High Court judge who considers the paper application for permission. If bail and permission are refused it will be possible to make a renewed application for permission in the Administrative Court. It would appear, however, that in a criminal cause or matter bail cannot be sought from a High Court judge when an application for bail has previously been refused.[128] Practically, the judge should be asked not to determine bail when he considers a paper application, if he is minded to refuse permission.

9.71 Clearly, if a High Court judge refuses permission to apply for judicial review following an oral hearing, the Administrative Court is functus officio and so is unable to consider a bail application.

9.72 The fact that there is a need for bail is highly likely to justify a request for the judicial review claim to be given urgent consideration.

9.73 The right to bail under s 4 of the Bail Act 1976 does not apply to bail applications during judicial review proceedings in the Administrative Court.[129] That does not, however, mean that the Administrative Court will not grant bail. It simply means that there is no presumption that bail should be granted.

9.74 Prosecutors or others can make an application to the Administrative Court for an order varying the conditions imposed on bail by the High Court. At least 24 hours

---

[123] CPR 1998, Sch 1, RSC Ord 79, r 9 (2). Form 97 is not a standard court form which supports the practice of not submitting it.
[124] CPR 1998, Sch 1, RSC Ord 79, r 9 (2)(a).
[125] Ibid r 9(2).
[126] Ibid r 9(3).
[127] *R v Secretary of State for the Home Department, ex p Turkoglu* [1988] QB 398.
[128] CPR 1998, Sch 1, RSC Ord 79, r 9(12).
[129] Bail Act 1976, s 4(2).

notice of the application should be given to the person who has been granted bail.[130] An affidavit or witness statement should support this application.[131]

Role of the defendant

9.75 In judicial review proceedings, magistrates whose decision is challenged will often not be represented at any hearing. Indeed, it has been held that counsel should not represent justices unless there is some special factor such as an allegation of misconduct on the part of the justices.[132] However, the High Court will be very keen to have the views of the respondent when it determines the application.[133] As a result in most cases respondents should serve written evidence commenting on the application. In particular the written evidence should highlight any factual matters in the applicant's written evidence and grounds that are not agreed or any other matters that the court will find relevant.

9.76 The purpose of the written evidence described above should not be to advocate for any particular outcome. It is intended merely to assist the court. The effective defendant in any judicial review claim should be the opposing party in the magistrates' court. Hence, if a defendant to a criminal prosecution brings a judicial review claim, the effective defendant to a judicial review claim will be the prosecutor. They will have standing as an interested party.

Relief at the conclusion of proceedings

9.77 All of the normal remedies that are available in judicial review proceedings are also available in a criminal matter. However, in addition, s 43(1) of the Senior Courts Act 1981 provides the Administrative Court with a specific statutory power to vary a sentence imposed by a magistrates' court or the Crown Court following a committal for sentence or an appeal against a sentence if there has been a successful application for a quashing order. Before exercising the power, the Administrative Court must be satisfied that the sentence was one that the magistrates' court or Crown Court had no power to impose. When the Administrative Court exercises the power, it can impose any sentence that the court that passed sentence could have imposed.

9.78 Although s 43(1) requires the High Court to be satisfied that the sentence was not one that the magistrates' court or Crown Court had the power to impose, that does not mean that the power can only be exercised where the sentence imposed was in excess of the maximum prescribed by law. For example, a sentence imposed in breach of natural justice can be quashed and a fresh sentence imposed after the Administrative Court has heard the representations that magistrates would have heard had they not acted in breach of natural justice.[134]

---

[130] CPR 1998, Sch 1, RSC Ord 79, r 9(2)(b).
[131] Ibid, r 9(3).
[132] *R v Cambourne Justices, ex p Pearce* [1954] 2 All ER 850 at 856E. But note the remarks of Lord Justice Simon Brown asking Treasury Solicitors to instruct counsel to review the merits of a large number of judicial reviews of warrants of commitment in the light of his judgment in *R v Oldham Justices, ex p Cawley* [1996] 1 All ER 464 at 481G which suggests that the court increasingly finds that it is assisted by respondents being represented.
[133] For example in *R v Gloucester Crown Court, ex p Chester*, The Independent, 6 July 1998, QBD it was held that even where an applicant erred by bringing judicial review proceedings instead of an appeal by case stated the respondent should at least write a letter stating whether they opposed the application.
[134] *R v Pateley Bridge Justices, ex p Percy* [1994] COD 453.

COSTS AGAINST MAGISTRATES' COURTS

9.79 When magistrates are involved in proceedings in the High Court as the respondent or as the decision-maker in an appeal by way of case stated, the High Court will be reluctant to order costs against the magistrates.

9.80 Mr Justice Cazalet has stated that the principles that should be applied when determining whether costs should be awarded against magistrates are:

(i) that costs would only be awarded against justices in the rarest of circumstances when they have done something which calls for strong disapproval; and

(ii) that it was the practice not to grant costs against justices merely because they have made a mistake in law, but only if they have acted perversely or with some disregard for the elementary principles which every court ought to obey, and even then only if it was a particularly bad case.[135]

9.81 Thus, applying these principles, the High Court has awarded costs against magistrates in a case where they took a perverse decision in flagrant disregard of elementary principles.[136]

9.82 In general, magistrates should not be represented in cases where their decision is being challenged. If magistrates do attend at a hearing when they should not have attended the High Court will be required to take account of the reasonableness of their conduct before ordering costs.[137] In practice this means that the High Court will consider whether their decision to attend was a reasonable decision. This means that if the magistrates attend and are unsuccessful, they increase the risk that costs will be awarded against them. If they are successful, the High Court will be unwilling to order costs in their favour unless they can show that there were particularly good reasons why they should attend.

9.83 The High Court will be particularly reluctant to award costs against magistrates in cases when they have not appeared.[138] That does not mean, however, that there can never be a costs order against magistrates. For example, costs have been awarded in cases where the magistrates have caused an unnecessary substantive hearing by failing to sign a consent order[139] and where they failed to take a grant of permission sufficiently seriously in a case challenging a refusal to state a case.[140]

---

[135] *R v Bristol Magistrates' Court, ex p Hodge* [1997] QB 974 at 982C applying the test in *R v York City Justices, ex p Farmery* (1988) 153 JP 257.
[136] *R v Lincoln Justices, ex p Count* (1996) 8 Admin LR 233 in which magistrates refused to adjourn a case as there was no specific statutory power enabling them to adjourn.
[137] CPR r 44.4(3).
[138] *R v Newcastle under Lyme Justices, ex p Massey* [1994] 1 WLR 1684 at 1692A.
[139] *R v Newcastle under Lyme Justices, ex p Massey* [1994] 1 WLR 1684.
[140] *R v Huntingdon Magistrates' Court, ex p Percy* [1994] COD 323. See also *R v Metropolitan Stipendiary Magistrate, ex p Ali, The Independent,* 12 May 1997 where costs were awarded against a magistrate for continuing to refuse to state a case when the judge who had granted permission had said that it would be impossible to know if the magistrate had erred if they did not state a case.

Costs from central funds

9.84 The Divisional Court has the power to award costs to a defendant from central funds in any criminal cause or matter that it determines.[141] Similarly the House of Lords may make such an order in an appeal from the Divisional Court.[142] A similar power exists to award costs to a prosecutor who is not a public authority or a person acting on their behalf.[143]

9.85 The power to make an order for costs from central funds can be important in legally aided cases where the defendant is a magistrates' court. From a claimant's point of view a failure to obtain a costs order may result in their lawyers receiving a lower rate of remuneration. It may also result in less funds being available for other claims. These matters have persuaded courts to make orders for costs from central funds despite the fact that the claimant is in receipt of public funding.[144]

Appeal to the Supreme Court

9.86 A party to a judicial review in a criminal cause or matter can only appeal to the Supreme Court.[145] The Administrative Court can grant permission to appeal.[146] However, that is extremely unlikely. In practice it is likely to be necessary to obtain permission to appeal from the Supreme Court.[147] However, for reasons that are expanded upon below, the Supreme Court may lack jurisdiction to consider an application for permission to appeal.

9.87 An application for permission to appeal should be made to the Administrative Court within 28 days of the date that the court dismisses the claim for judicial review.[148] The Supreme Court should then be petitioned within 28 days of the decision of the Administrative Court refusing permission.[149] These time limits can only be extended where the party seeking permission to appeal was a defendant in the criminal proceedings.[150] Time can be extended when the delay is the result of delay in determining an application for public funding. Where the Registrar is informed that an application is being made for public funding, time is extended so that it runs until 28 days from the final decision on that application.[151]

9.88 Before the Supreme Court can be petitioned for permission to appeal the Administrative Court must issue a certificate that there is a point of law of general public importance.[152]

9.89 Technically it would appear that an application for a certificate of public importance is not subject to the same time limits as an application for permission to

---

[141] Prosecution of Offences Act 1985, s 16(5)(a); see para 9.5 onwards for a definition of the scope of a 'criminal cause or matter'.
[142] Prosecution of Offences Act 1985, s 16(5)(b).
[143] Prosecution of Offences Act 1985, s 17.
[144] Eg *R v Sheffield Magistrates' Court, ex p Ojo* (2000) 164 JP 659.
[145] Administration of Justice Act 1960, s 1.
[146] Ibid.
[147] Ibid.
[148] Administration of Justice Act 1960, s 2.
[149] Ibid.
[150] Ibid and *R v Weir* [2001] 1 WLR 421 holding that time could not be extended for a prosecutor to appeal.
[151] Supreme Court Rules 2009 (SI 2009/1603), r 5(5).
[152] Administration of Justice Act 1960, s 1.

appeal.[153] In practice, however, the application to the Administrative Court for it to certify a point of law of general public importance is made at the same time as the application for permission to appeal. That is primarily because the Administrative Court must certify a point of law of general public importance at the same time as they grant permission to appeal if they grant permission to appeal.

9.90 Great care must be taken to draft a question that both reflects the issues raised in the case and raises a point that is of significant general importance. The Administrative Court is unlikely to permit a prospective appellant to have more than one attempt to formulate a question and so it is important that the question is formulated the first time.

CONCLUDING REMARKS

9.91 Judicial review in criminal law is a specialist area governed by distinct rules. The decision of *R (Corner House Research) v DPP*[154] demonstrates the intention to avoid satellite litigation in this area. This may explain why the supervisory jurisdiction of the Administrative Court is used rarely in this area.

9.92 The apparent unwillingness of parties to criminal proceedings to bring proceedings in the Administrative Court suggests that a more accessible procedure for challenging errors of the inferior courts may be required.

---

[153] *Westley v Hertfordshire County Council*, unreported, 22 October 1998.
[154] [2008] 3 WLR 568.

CHAPTER 10

PRISON LAW

INTRODUCTION

10.01 Prison law has developed substantially as a discrete area of practice over the last 20 years, although its future is severely threatened by restrictions on the availability of legal aid funding to prisoners, which came into force on 2 December 2013. Prison law's earlier expansion can be attributed to a range of factors, including inception of the Human Rights Act 1998, and a vast increase in the prison population, including a large increase in the number of indeterminate sentence prisoners resulting from the Criminal Justice Act 2003 (CJA 2003).[1]

10.02 In theory, just about any decision taken by the prison authorities may be susceptible to judicial review. As a rule of thumb, the greater the effect of the decision on the prisoner, the more anxious the scrutiny that the court is likely to apply. However, this may not always be the case.[2]

10.03 A prisoner retains all of his rights except for those expressly removed from him or necessarily removed by his imprisonment.[3] The Prison Act 1952 (PA 1952) provides many of the powers exercised by the Secretary of State for Justice, but it is not prescriptive. Equally, while the Prison Rules 1999 are more specific as to what is required, they must generally be read subject to the Secretary of State's policies, which come in the form of Prison Service Orders (PSOs), or Prison Service Instructions (PSIs).[4] Failure to apply published policy may be unlawful and amenable to judicial review.[5] The Parole Board Rules 2004 are more prescriptive, but are also supplemented by policy statements and practice guidance issued by the Board.

10.04 What follows is not intended to be an exhaustive list of every decision that is amenable to judicial review within the context of prison law. However, we have

---

[1]   Chapter 5 CJA 2003 introduced the sentence of imprisonment for public protection (IPP), which enabled (and previously obliged) judges to pass indeterminate sentences much more easily, but with shorter tariffs than would attach to life sentences. The IPP sentence caused significant problems in terms of resourcing risk-reduction opportunities, and was abolished by the Legal Aid Sentencing and Punishment of Offenders Act 2012 (LASPOA 2012) (for background see *James v UK* (2013) 56 EHRR 12).
[2]   See, for example, *R (Jorgenson) v Secretary of State for Justice* [2011] EWHC 977 (Admin) in which it was accepted by Silber J at [44] that a decision to revoke an offender's licence and return him to prison should be subject to anxious scrutiny. Contrast *R (Carman) v Secretary of State for the Home Department* [2004] EWHC 2400 (Admin), a challenge to an offender's licence conditions, in which Moses J (as he then was) said at [33]: 'The licence conditions and assessment of risks to the public, on which they are based, are matters of fine judgment for those in the prison and the probation service experienced in such matters not for the courts. The courts must be steadfastly astute not to interfere save in the most exceptional case.'
[3]   *Raymond v Honey* [1981] 3 WLR 218.
[4]   PSOs are no longer issued, however many remain in force. PSIs include an expiry date, but in fact remain in force unless otherwise cancelled: see PSI 01/2011.
[5]   *Lumba (WL) (Congo) v SSHD* [2012] 1 AC 245 at [26], [202] and [313].

attempted to set out some of the more contentious areas that have resulted in judicial review claims in the past, those that may do so in the future, and to provide some context for prison law challenges.

REGIME

10.05 In general terms, the regime that a prisoner is able to access depends upon a system of entitlements, privileges and punishments. The Prison Rules 1999 create basic entitlements: for example to the same standard of medical care that would be available in the community,[6] access to food and clothing,[7] and exercise in the open air.[8] Additional privileges can be earned through the incentives and earned privileges (IEP) scheme, as set out below. Finally, aspects of the regime can be withdrawn as a punishment, as set out in the section of this chapter on discipline and prison adjudications.

Categorisation and recategorisation

10.06 Rule 7 of the Prison Rules 1999 empowers the Secretary of State to classify prisoners. He does so according to the risk that they present to the public, the risk of them absconding, and any control issues that they pose.[9] Prisoners are categorised A–D, with Category A being reserved for those who are so dangerous that for them escape must be made impossible, and Category D being for those who can be trusted in open prison conditions, where prisoners are able to work in the community and are trusted to return voluntarily.

10.07 The regime in Category A conditions is comparatively far more restrictive than elsewhere,[10] and decisions on suitability for Category A are taken by the Category A Team at the Ministry of Justice, which is headed by the Director of High Security Prisons. To be downgraded, a Category A prisoner must demonstrate evidence of a significant reduction in risk.[11] The recategorisation decision is of such consequence to a Category A prisoner that common law fairness may require there to be an oral hearing, and the circumstances in which this will occur have recently been extended by revisions to PSI 08/2013 to reflect the decision of the Supreme Court in *R (Osborn) v Parole Board*.[12] There have been a number of successful judicial review challenges arising from refusals by the Director of High Security to grant an oral hearing.[13] By contrast, in Category B–D cases there is no requirement to provide advance disclosure and an opportunity to make representations prior to the decision being made. However, prisoners are entitled to reasons for categorisation decisions and an opportunity to make representations through the complaints process (discussed later in this chapter).[14]

---

[6] Prison Rules 1999, r 20.
[7] Prison Rules 1999, rr 23 and 24.
[8] Prison Rules 1999, rr 29 and 30.
[9] PSI 40/2011, para 1.1.
[10] *R v Secretary of State for the Home Department, ex p Duggan* [1994] 3 All ER 277.
[11] PSI 08/2013, para 4.2.
[12] [2013] UKSC 61, [2013] 3 WLR 1020.
[13] See, for example, *R (Fox) v Secretary of State for Justice* [2012] EWHC 2411 (Admin).
[14] *R (Peries) v Secretary of State for the Home Department* [1997] EWHC 712 (Admin); *R (McLeod) v HM Prison Service* [2002] EWHC 390 (Admin); *R (Palmer) v Secretary of State for the Home Department* [2004] EWHC 1817 (Admin).

10.08 Categorisation decisions that do not involve Category A prisoners are generally taken by prison governors. The other exception is indeterminate sentence cases, where decisions on suitability for Category D (open conditions) are taken by the Public Protection Casework Section (PPCS) at the Ministry of Justice.[15] Recategorisation reviews generally take place annually, but will be conducted every six months during the last two years of the sentence.[16]

10.09 The courts accept that categorisation decisions involve questions of risk management that are for the Prison Service to regulate.[17] However, there are examples of claims having been allowed on a range of public law grounds, including illegality,[18] irrationality,[19] breach of legitimate expectation,[20] failure to provide reasons,[21] breach of procedural fairness (by failing to disclose sufficient information, including security intelligence relied on against the prisoner, to make meaningful representations),[22] and fettering of discretion.[23] In particular, there are a number of cases where the Prison Service has been found to have unlawfully operated a blanket policy or criterion.[24] The Secretary of State ordinarily guards against this by ensuring that policy instructions contain a direction to consider the individual case.

10.10 Note the new guidance PSO 37/2014, which applies to prisoners who are subject to immigration control and have a change in the deportation status. The rationale of the policy is that, '... the change in deportation status represents a *significant change* in circumstances and the prisoner must have their continued suitability for conditions as low security in open conditions reviewed ... the governor *must then assess whether the receipt of the notification will increase the prisoner's immediate risk of absconding...*' (paras 2.16–2.17).

Allocation

10.11 Allocation is concerned with where a prisoner will be held. As a general rule, prisoners will, wherever possible, be held closest to home, and where they are best able to access relevant risk-reduction work.[25] In exceptional circumstances Article 8 ECHR may be breached by an allocation decision.[26]

10.12 There are a number of special categories of offenders where other allocation options will come into play.

---

[15] Indeterminate sentence cases are referred to the Parole Board for advice on suitability for Category D, although the final decision rests with the Secretary of State. Following the decision in *R (Guittard) v Secretary of State for Justice* [2009] EWHC 2951 (Admin) the PPCS will now consider cases exceptionally outside of the parole process. The Secretary of State will accept the recommendations of the Parole Board, unless they are irrational: *R (Adetoro) v Secretary of State for Justice* [2012] EWHC 2576 (Admin).
[16] PSI 40/2011, para 5.5.
[17] See, for example, *R (Oge Dengbe) v Secretary of State for Justice* [2011] EWHC 266 (Admin) at [31].
[18] *R (Rowen) v Governor of HMP Kirkham* [2009] EWHC 3756 (Admin).
[19] *R (Manhire) v Secretary of State for Justice* [2009] EWHC 1788 (Admin).
[20] *R (Lowe) v Governor HMP Liverpool* [2008] EWHC 2167 (Admin).
[21] *R (Peries) v Secretary of State for the Home Department* [1997] EWHC 712 (Admin).
[22] In the Category A context, see *R (Lord) v Secretary of State for the Home Department* [2003] EWHC 2073 (Admin). In non-Category A cases, see the consideration of disclosure and 'gisting' in *R (McLeod) v HM Prison Service* [2002] EWHC 390 (Admin) at [45]–[52]; *R (Palmer) v Secretary of State for the Home Department* [2004] EWHC 1817 (Admin) at [24]–[26].
[23] *R (Oge Dengbe) v Secretary of State for Justice* [2011] EWHC 266 (Admin).
[24] See, for example, *R (Smith) v Governor HMP Lindholme* [2010] EWHC 1356 (Admin).
[25] PSI 36/2010, para 4.9.
[26] *McCotter v UK* (1993) 15 EHRR CD 98; *R (Shaheen) v Secretary of State for Justice* [2008] EWHC 1195 (Admin).

Mother and baby units

10.13 Mother and baby units (MBUs) are designated living accommodation that enable mothers to have their children with them while in prison. Currently there are seven units across the prison estate.[27] The government is required to make provision for MBUs, or some similar facility, pursuant to the Children Act 2004, Article 8(1) ECHR, and various international instruments.[28]

10.14 A decision on an offender's suitability for an MBU is determined by (1) whether it is in the best interests of the child, (2) the necessity to maintain good order and discipline, and (3) the health and safety of other babies and mothers on the unit.[29] Prison governors make these admission decisions with input from a range of stakeholders, including social services and the Probation Service.[30]

10.15 In *CF v Secretary of State for the Home Department*[31] a decision removing a child from her mother was quashed because the social worker had failed adequately to advance the child's interests. It was noted that 18 months was normally the ceiling for separation of mother and child, but not the norm. The court also noted that the prisoner's interests in remaining on the MBU (where conditions may be seen as preferable) might not coincide with the child's interests, which are the overriding consideration.

Vulnerable prisoner units and segregation

10.16 The majority of, if not all, prisons have vulnerable prisoner accommodation for the benefit of those who are at risk, or perceive that they are at risk, from the general prison population. This will most commonly, though not always, be associated with sex offenders. In some cases the accommodation takes the form of a separate unit within the prison, with its own regime and facilities.

10.17 Each prison also houses a segregation unit, also referred to as a care and separation unit. The authority to remove prisoners from association (ie to segregate them) derives from r 45 of the Prison Rules 1999, which provides that prisoners may be removed from association for the maintenance of good order and discipline, or in their own interests. There is further discussion on this subject under 'association' later in this chapter.

10.18 Decisions under r 45 are often secretive as the information relied upon by the prison may be sensitive. There is little opportunity for disclosure, although the independent monitoring board (IMB) provides some oversight over the decision. In *R (Bourgass) v Secretary of State for Justice*[32] it was held that the IMB's role provided a sufficient safeguard against the prejudice to the prisoner arising from non-disclosure. It may be possible to challenge the failure to provide reasons for the decision to segregate,[33] although prisoners are not entitled in all cases to such reasons.[34] The Court

---

[27] PSI 54/2011. At the time of writing the government has recently announced plans to close HMP Askham Grange, which houses a mother and baby unit.
[28] See, for example, the United Nations Convention on the Rights of the Child 1989.
[29] PSI 54/2011, para 1.4.
[30] PSI 54/2011, para 2.1.4.
[31] [2004] 2 FLR 517.
[32] [2011] EWHC 286 (Admin).
[33] *Hassan v Secretary of State for Justice* [2011] EWHC 1359 (Admin).
[34] *R (King) v Secretary of State for Justice* [2012] EWCA Civ 376 at [69]–[71].

of Appeal has suggested that segregation is highly unlikely to breach Article 3 ECHR and, while it will engage Article 8 ECHR, it may well be justified.[35]

Close supervision centres

10.19 Close supervision centres (CSCs) are specialist units for those who pose such a control problem that they cannot be held on normal location in the long term. Before admitting a prisoner to a CSC the governor must be satisfied that the prisoner poses a significant risk of serious harm.[36] The CSCs have operated for many years and remain controversial.[37] In *R (Bary) v Secretary of State for Justice*[38] a group of terrorism suspects unsuccessfully challenged their location on a 'detainee unit', which involved similar restrictions to a CSC. The court rejected, in particular, a claim that the conditions on the unit breached the claimants' Article 3 ECHR rights.

Sentence planning

Offending behaviour programmes

10.20 Offenders are required to have a sentence plan that is constructed to address their identified needs and risks.[39] One of the key aims is to reduce the risk of serious harm that the offender poses. This can be as important for the offender as it is for the public because the question of whether the offender has engaged with appropriate interventions in order to reduce risk is a key consideration for the Parole Board in determining whether or not to direct release.[40]

10.21 The principal method of an offender demonstrating a reduction in risk is through the completion of accredited[41] offending behaviour programmes, which are targeted at particular risk factors. These include the Thinking Skills Programme (TSP), the Controlling Anger and Learning to Manage It Programme (CALM), the Self-Change Programme (SCP),[42] and the Sex Offender Treatment Programme (SOTP). Although these programmes are neither a necessary nor sufficient condition for release,[43] in practice they may be the only realistic method of an offender satisfying the Parole Board that he or she is fit for release.[44]

10.22 The desirability of completing offending behaviour programmes has caused particular difficulties for offenders who maintain their innocence and whose release is dependent upon a direction by the Parole Board. That is because offence-focused programmes require the offender to discuss the motivations behind his/her offending, and so to accept his/her guilt. While the fact that a prisoner maintains innocence cannot

---

[35] *R (King) v Secretary of State for Justice* [2012] EWCA Civ 376.
[36] PSI 42/2012, para 1.2.
[37] A report on an unannounced inspection of HMP Wakefield by HM Chief Inspectorate of Prisons in May 2012 commented at [1.106] that: 'Environmental conditions in the unit remained inadequate ... The gated cage-like cells were small, cramped and without adequate natural light ... Cell toilets were not screened and were located directly in front of observation panels. Exercise yards consisted of grim cages without normalising features such as plants or other greenery.'
[38] [2010] EWHC 587 (Admin).
[39] PSI 41/2010, para 1.2.
[40] PSI 41/2012, para 2.1.
[41] Accredited by the Ministry of Justice as being effective in reducing risk.
[42] The SCP is targeted at offenders with a history of instrumental (rather than reactive) violence.
[43] *R (Gill) v Secretary of State for Justice* [2010] EWHC 364 (Admin) at [80].
[44] *R (Roberts) v Secretary of State for the Home Department* [2003] EWHC 3120 (Admin) at [40].

be held against him/her, and must not be used as a reason not to direct release, the fact that it will preclude access to offence-focused work may result in the same outcome.[45] The Administrative Court has held that there is nothing intrinsically unfair, unreasonable or irrational in requiring a prisoner to apply for and undertake a risk-reduction course even if this requires admission of guilt. However, there might be circumstances in which requiring a prisoner to apply for a course when it was known that the prisoner would never admit his/her guilt would be irrational or unreasonable,[46] but this would only arise in the most exceptional individual circumstances.[47]

10.23 In view of its importance to prisoners, and the competing consideration of finite resources, the provision of offending behaviour work has troubled the courts up to and including the ECtHR.[48] The courts have identified two overlapping public law duties with which the Secretary of State must comply.

10.24 First, the Secretary of State is under a public law duty to act rationally in the provision of courses or other means by which prisoners can demonstrate reduced risk so as to secure release.[49] Subject to resources, it is irrational to have a policy of making release dependent on a prisoner undergoing a rehabilitative course without making reasonable provision for such courses.[50] An individual prisoner is owed a duty in this regard and can bring proceedings in seeking to enforce that duty.

10.25 Second, the Secretary of State is under a public law duty to provide prisoners with reasonable access to courses to enable them to reduce their risk, and demonstrate that risk reduction to the Parole Board at or shortly after tariff expiry.[51] The Secretary of State was found to have breached that duty when introducing the IPP sentence, because insufficient resources were directed to meet the influx of prisoners requiring access to programmes.[52] In *James v UK*[53] the ECtHR considered that this also amounted to a breach of Article 5(1) ECHR, rendering ongoing detention arbitrary and unlawful, and requiring an individual remedy in damages. The Supreme Court in *R (Kaiyam) v Secretary of State for Justice*[54] declined to follow the ECtHR's conclusion that the failure to provide prisoners with reasonable access to courses amounted to a breach of Article 5(1). The Supreme Court instead held that it was implicit in the overall scheme of Article 5 that the state had a duty to provide a reasonable opportunity for a prisoner to rehabilitate himself and demonstrate that he no longer presented an unacceptable danger to the public. However, that duty was not owed under the express language of Article 5(1)(a) or Article 5(4). The duty should instead be implied as an ancillary duty under Article 5, thus not affecting the lawfulness of ongoing detention. A breach of this ancillary duty may occur where there is a failure to provide the appropriate systems and resources, resulting in lengthy delays accessing relevant courses. This ancillary duty under Article 5 is owed to individual prisoners whose individual rights under Article 5 have been breached. The duty confers a right in favour of each individual prisoner and

---

[45] *R (Roberts) v Secretary of State for the Home Department* [2003] EWHC 3120 (Admin).
[46] *Cannan v Governor of Sutton Prison* [2009] EWHC 1517 (Admin).
[47] *Hewlett v Secretary of State for Justice* [2009] EWHC 2979 (Admin) at [41].
[48] *James v UK* (2013) 56 EHRR 12.
[49] *R (Kaiyam) v Secretary of State for Justice* [2014] UKSC 66 at [41].
[50] *R (Cawser) v Secretary of State for the Home Department* [2003] EWCA Civ 1522; *R (Weddle) v Secretary of State for Justice* [2013] EWHC 2323 (Admin).
[51] *R (James) v Secretary of State for Justice* [2009] 2 WLR 1149; *R (Weddle) v Secretary of State for Justice* [2013] EWHC 2323 (Admin).
[52] *R (James) v Secretary of State for Justice* [2009] 2 WLR 1149.
[53] (2013) 56 EHRR 12.
[54] *R (Kaiyam) v Secretary of State for Justice* [2014] UKSC 66 at [36]–[42].

its satisfaction or otherwise depends upon the particular circumstances of the individual case. However, no system is likely to be able to avoid some periods of waiting and delay, and not all delay will breach the ancillary duty. It is not necessary to prove that there has been a systemic breach, or that the system of offending behaviour courses has wholly broken down in order to establish a breach of the ancillary duty. The appropriate remedy for a breach of this ancillary duty is not release, but an award of damages for legitimate frustration and anxiety.

10.26 A decision requiring a prisoner to complete an assessment for an offending behaviour programme and/or to complete the course itself is amenable to judicial review on the grounds of rationality. However, a prisoner will only succeed in such a challenge if the prisoner can demonstrate that there is no professional support for the decision-maker's view (1) that the assessment or course is in general terms useful, and (2) that, specifically in relation to that individual prisoner, it would be of advantage in terms of risk assessment if he/she was to undertake it.[55]

Dangerous and severe personality disorder units

10.27 Dangerous and severe personality disorder (DSPD)[56] units offer specialist treatment to high or very high-risk offenders who, by reason of severe disorders of the personality, are unable to benefit from 'traditional' offending behaviour programmes.[57] The assessment process includes a 'living phase' that lasts for up to 18 months. If found suitable for treatment, and the offender consents, the treatment phase lasts between three to five years. For that reason DPSD units are sometimes unpopular with prisoners, who may also be prevented from participating in alternative risk-reduction work while DSPD assessment is outstanding. In *R (Roose) v Parole Board*[58] the Divisional Court held that the Board was required to convene an oral hearing in view of a dispute as to the claimant's suitability for DSPD treatment.

Reasonable adjustments

10.28 The Prison Service must, pursuant to its duties under the Equality Act 2010 (EA 2010), ensure that prisoners are not discriminated against because of a protected characteristic.[59] It must make reasonable adjustments to avoid such disadvantage.[60] When determining whether an adjustment is reasonable the resources of the Prison Service as a whole should be considered, not merely the individual prison.[61] The protected characteristics are age, disability, gender reassignment, marriage and civil partnership, race, religion or belief, sex, and sexual orientation.[62]

10.29 The equalities legislation has a particular resonance in the sentence-planning context due to what may be at stake for the prisoner. It is estimated that between 7% and 14% of prisoners suffer with a learning disability as compared with 2% in the

---

[55] *R (Bealey) v Secretary of State for the Home Department* [2005] EWHC 1618 (Admin) at [22].
[56] Renamed Severe Personality Disorder (SPD) Units, but generally still known as DSPD Units.
[57] Probation Circular 21/2008.
[58] [2010] EWHC 1780 (Admin).
[59] Section 13 EA 2010 prohibits direct discrimination; s 19 EA 2010 prohibits direct discrimination. See also PSI 32/2011, which provides the Prison Service's policy on equalities.
[60] Section 20 EA 2010.
[61] PSI 32/2011, Annex G.4.
[62] Sections 5–12.

general population.⁶³ Prisons are required to ensure that the disability is 'fed in' to the sentence plan.⁶⁴ In *R (Gill) v Secretary of State for Justice*⁶⁵ the claimant (who had a learning disability) succeeded in establishing that the prison had discriminated against him in the sentence planning process by failing to ensure that he was provided with the same opportunities to demonstrate a reduction in his risk as were provided to non-disabled prisoners.

Living conditions

Property

10.30 Rule 43 of the Prison Rules 1999 provides that prisoners shall have their cash paid into an account controlled by the governor (but accessible to the prisoner). This applies to monies that an offender arrives with, but also to amounts paid in subsequently. Prisoner bank account statements will usually need to be supplied by those applying for legal aid to satisfy the means test.

10.31 PSI 12/2011 provides more specific guidance on the retention of prisoners' property. Prisoners may retain 'in possession' property appropriate to their IEP privilege level and subject to volumetric control. Governors have discretion to compile their own possessions lists for the regime at their prison.⁶⁶ Unconvicted prisoners will be allowed to convey and receive property during social visits;⁶⁷ however convicted prisoners will only be allowed to convey items.⁶⁸

Association

10.32 The Prison Rules 1999 do not make any provision for prisoners to associate. However, some degree of entitlement is implied, not least because r 45 makes provision for prisoners to be removed from association (ie segregated). In *R (King) v Secretary of State for Justice*⁶⁹ the Court of Appeal preferred to characterise association as a 'normal' privilege (ie not one that must be earned) rather than a right, because it is not provided for by the Prison Rules. In that case the Court of Appeal overturned a decision of the Administrative Court that association is a 'civil right' for the purposes of Article 6 ECHR.

10.33 As discussed earlier in this chapter, the removal of a prisoner from association can be directed under r 45 for the maintenance of good order and discipline, or for the prisoner's own protection. It can also be imposed as a punishment under r 55, which is discussed later in this chapter.

Incentives and earned privileges

10.34 Rule 8 of the Prison Rules 1999 provides that every prison shall establish a system of privileges, which includes arrangements under which money earned by

---

63 PSI 32/2011, Annex H.1.
64 PSI 32/2011, Annex H.14.
65 [2010] EWHC 364 (Admin).
66 PSI 12/2011, para 2.3.
67 PSI 12/2011, para 2.67.
68 PSI 12/2011, para 2.68.
69 [2012] 1 WLR 3602.

prisoners may be spent within the prison. It may also include arrangements under which prisoners are rewarded for their behaviour and their performance in work or other activities.

10.35 The current national IEP system is governed by PSI 30/2013, which came into force on 1 November 2013. The overriding purpose of the scheme is to encourage prisoners to work towards their rehabilitation, behave well, and help others.[70] There are four tiers of the scheme: enhanced, standard, entry, and basic. All newly sentenced prisoners will begin at entry level. To achieve enhanced level, prisoners must meet certain targets, including compliance with their sentence plan. To achieve standard level, prisoners must similarly meet certain standards of performance and behaviour. Basic level is for those who are not complying with the regime. This represents the minimum level of regime to which prisoners can lawfully be subject.[71]

10.36 One area of controversy in the administration of the IEP scheme has been the withholding of enhanced status from prisoners who maintain their innocence, and who consequently are deemed to be 'unready' for treatment. There have been a series of cases in which the courts have upheld the entitlement of the Prison Service to withhold enhanced status from such prisoners, because they are not complying with their sentence planning targets.[72]

10.37 However, in *R (Shutt) v Governor HMP Albany*[73] the Administrative Court held that a local IEP policy that amounted to a blanket ban on 'deniers' from achieving enhanced status was unlawful. The court drew a distinction between a policy that *permitted* the Prison Service to withhold enhanced status from such prisoners, and one that mandated it. The policy then in force[74] provided that unreadiness for treatment *could* result in the withholding of enhanced status, but did not require it. PSI 30/2013 purports to mandate the withholding of enhanced status from prisoners who are unready for treatment, and it remains to be seen whether this aspect of the policy is upheld as lawful.[75]

Correspondence and visits

10.38 Rule 35(1) of the Prison Rules 1999 provides that unconvicted prisoners can receive as many visits and letters as they wish, subject to any general limitations that may be imposed. Rule 35(2)(a) provides that convicted prisoners may send and receive letters weekly, while r 35(2)(b) provides that they shall be permitted to have visits fortnightly. Rule 35(3) provides that extra letters and visits shall be an earnable privilege under the IEP scheme.

---

[70] PSI 30/2013, para 1.6.
[71] Although, see the permission decision in *R (Nealon & Sims) v Governor HMP Wakefield*, unreported, 19 April 2010, in which it was held that the withdrawal of certain basic regime activities from those who refused to wear an identification card was permissible. Contrast *R v Governor HMP Frankland, ex p Russell & Wharrie*, unreported, 10 July 2000, in which it was held to be impermissible to provide fewer meals than ordinarily required to prisoners who refused to wear prison uniform.
[72] *R v Secretary of State for the Home Department, ex p Potter* [2001] EWHC 1041 (Admin); *R (Green) v Secretary of State for the Home Department* [2004] EWHC 596 (Admin); *R (Cannan) v Governor of HMP Full Sutton* [2009] EWHC 1517 (Admin); *R (Hewlett) v Secretary of State for Justice* [2009] EWHC 2979 (Admin).
[73] [2012] EWHC 851 (Admin).
[74] PSI 11/2011.
[75] PSI 30/2013, Annex D.

10.39 Rule 34(1) provides that the Secretary of State may impose restrictions upon the letters or other communications to be permitted between a prisoner and other persons. Rule 34(2) provides that visits may take place under closed conditions that restrict physical contact where appropriate.

10.40 To guarantee the common law and Article 6 ECHR right of access to the court,[76] r 38(1) provides that the legal adviser of a prisoner shall be afforded reasonable facilities for interviewing him, and may do so out of hearing but in the sight of an officer. To protect legal privilege, r 39(1) provides that a prisoner may correspond with his/her legal adviser and any court. Mail that is marked 'Rule 39' will not be opened unless the governor has reasonable cause to believe that it contains an illicit enclosure.[77] By Rule 39(3), correspondence may be opened, read and stopped if the governor has reasonable cause to believe that its contents endanger prison security or the safety of others, or are otherwise of a criminal nature. Rule 39(4) entitles a prisoner to be present when any correspondence is opened and shall be informed if it or any enclosure is to be read or stopped.

10.41 In *R (Daly) v Secretary of State for the Home Department*[78] the appellant challenged a policy whereby his legal correspondence was examined (but not read) during cell searches from which he was excluded. The Prison Service argued that this was justified by the needs of security. The appellant argued that mere knowledge that the prison was examining his mail might inhibit his willingness to communicate freely with his legal advisor. The House of Lords accepted that argument, and held that the policy in its blanket form infringed the appellant's common law right to maintain the confidentiality of his privileged correspondence.[79] Lord Bingham took the view that the same result was achieved whether reached by reliance upon the common law or upon Article 8(1) ECHR.

10.42 The right to enjoy visits is also guaranteed by Article 8(1) ECHR[80] and r 34 of the Prison Rules 1999 states that any restriction or condition imposed on a visit must be necessary and proportionate.[81] However, so far as individual visitors are concerned, r 73 provides that the Secretary of State may impose restrictions on visits for the purposes of security or good order. This has been lawfully deployed, for example, to restrict visits by the partner of an offender who was also his victim.[82]

10.43 Another controversial area in the context of prison visits is the entitlement of prisoners to have visits from their children. In *R (Westwater) v Secretary of State for Justice*[83] it was held that while a prisoner's contact with his children could be restricted by the Secretary of State, the guidance and procedures under the Children Act 2004 must be complied with in order to ensure that the parties' Article 8(1) ECHR rights are protected.

---

[76] *R (Thakrar) v Secretary of State for Justice* [2012] EWHC 3538 (Admin) at [11(2)], citing *Golder v UK* [1975] 1 EHRR 524.
[77] Prison Rules 1999, r 39(2).
[78] [2001] 2 AC 532.
[79] Per Lord Bingham of Cornhill at [19].
[80] *Klamecki v Poland* (2004) 39 EHRR 7.
[81] See *R (Wilkinson) v Home Office* [2002] EWHC 1212 (Admin) for an example of a visits ban that was ruled to be disproportionate.
[82] *R (S) v Secretary of State for Justice* [2013] EWHC 2889 (Admin).
[83] [2010] EWHC 2403 (Admin).

Reasonable adjustments

10.44 The duty to make reasonable adjustments imposed on the Prison Service requires the taking of reasonable steps to ensure non-discrimination in the way in which prisoners experience prison living conditions. This can include the provision of medical aids and private toilet facilities.[84]

Health and social care

Overview

10.45 Responsibility for prison healthcare transferred to the National Health Service (NHS) in April 2006.[85] It is the duty of the Secretary of State for Health to establish primary care trusts (PCTs), which are responsible for primary medical services. This includes access to general practitioners and pharmacy services. The PCT commissioners will procure secondary healthcare services, such as mental health services, from an appropriate provider.

10.46 That is not to say, however, that the Prison Service has ceased to have any duties in respect of prison healthcare. Rule 20 of the Prison Rules 1999 provides that the governor must work in partnership with local healthcare providers to secure the provision of the same quality and range of services as the general public receives from the NHS. This is likely to be viewed as a systemic duty rather than one owed in individual cases. Nevertheless it is a duty to ensure that proper care is available.[86] In certain limited circumstances, prisoners may be entitled to alternative care to that provided by the prison.[87]

10.47 Challenges alleging inadequate provision of healthcare on Article 3 ECHR and Article 8 ECHR grounds have met with little success.[88]

Mental health transfers

10.48 Section 47 of the Mental Health Act 1983 provides for the Secretary of State to make a transfer direction if there is medical opinion from at least two practitioners that the prisoner is suffering from a mental disorder that makes it appropriate for him or her to be detained in a hospital, and medical treatment is available. The transfer documents must address the relevant test.[89] The power to transfer is discretionary, and the Secretary of State must also be satisfied that it is in the public interest for him to make a transfer direction. Section 48 provides for transfer directions to be made in respect of remand prisoners and civil contemnors.

10.49 PSI 50/2007 introduced a revised Ministry of Justice and Department of Health procedure for the transfer of prisoners to and from hospital under ss 47 and 48. This *Good Practice Procedure Guide* was updated on 1 April 2011. Its executive summary

---

[84] *R (Hall) v University College London Hospitals NHS Foundation Trust, Secretary of State for Justice* [2013] EWHC 198 (Admin) at [36]–[37].
[85] National Health Service Act 1977.
[86] *R (Brooks) v Secretary of State for Justice, Isle of Wight Primary Care Trust* [2008] EWHC 3041 (Admin).
[87] *Steele v Home Office* [2010] EWCA Civ 724.
[88] See, for example, *R (Hall) v University College London Hospitals NHS Foundation Trust, Secretary of State for Justice* [2013] EWHC 198 (Admin) at [32]–[35].
[89] *R (DK) v Secretary of State for Justice* [2010] EWHC 82 (Admin).

recognises that a large proportion of prisoners will have suffered, or are suffering, from mental health problems, but assesses that the 'vast majority' can be treated within the prison. Only those who are 'acutely ill' and cannot be treated will be transferred.

10.50 The *Guide* contains a flowchart that sets out a model 14-day procedure for the processing of prisoners considered potentially suitable for a transfer direction, which begins with the first doctor's report, progresses through the commissioning stage, and concludes (in successful referrals) with a date for admission being fixed.

RELEASE AND RECALL

Licence and recall

10.51 The statutory provisions governing the release of prisoners are labyrinthine[90] and are beyond the scope of this chapter. However, nearly all offenders will, at some stage, be on licence. In the case of determinate sentence prisoners serving for offences committed after 4 April 2005, release will usually be at the halfway point of the sentence.[91] Indeterminate sentence prisoners will generally remain on licence for life.[92]

10.52 In the case of determinate sentence prisoners, those released on licence will be subject to the 'standard conditions' and may be subject to other conditions.[93] Detailed guidance on the implementation of licence conditions is contained within Probation Instruction (PI) 20/2012. The available conditions include relatively non-invasive conditions such as a requirement to live at a particular address, and extend to more onerous conditions such as a curfew, exclusion zones, and restrictions on contact with others. In recognition of the fact that licence conditions will frequently engage Article 8(1) ECHR, PI 20/2012 requires that they are necessary and proportionate.[94]

10.53 A number of challenges have been brought on Article 8 ECHR grounds against licence conditions.[95] However, the courts have indicated that it will only be in exceptional cases that they will interfere, as the management of risk is primarily the domain of expert probation officers making fine and difficult judgments, and exercising a classic form of administrative discretion.[96] Licence conditions should be treated as having been imposed by the Secretary of State even though a local Probation Service decides what conditions are necessary in a particular case.[97]

---

[90] See for example, *R (Noone) v Secretary of State for Justice* [2010] 1 WLR 1743 in which Lord Judge CJ said at [87]: 'It is outrageous that so much intellectual effort, as well as public time and resources, have had to be expended in order to discover a route through the legislative morass to what should be, both for the prisoner herself, and for those responsible for her custody, the prison authorities, the simplest and most certain of questions – the prisoner's release date.'
[91] Section 244 CJA 2003. This differs for those serving extended sentences, and for those serving for offences committed before 4 April 2005, eg historical sexual offences.
[92] However, in the case of IPP prisoners there is a power for the licence to be cancelled more than 10 years after release: Sch 18 CJA 2003.
[93] Section 250(4) CJA 2003.
[94] PI 20/2012, para 2.10.
[95] *R (Craven) v Secretary of State for the Home Department* [2001] EWHC Admin 850; *R (Davies) v Secretary of State for the Home Department* [2005] 1 Prison LR 228; *R (Mehmet) v London Probation Board* [2007] EWHC 2223 (Admin); *R (Gunn) v Secretary State for Justice and the Nottinghamshire Multi Agency Public Protection Arrangements Board* [2009] EWHC 1812 (Admin); *R (C) v Secretary of State for Justice* [2009] EWHC 2671 (Admin); *R (MA) v National Probation Service* [2011] EWHC 1332 (Admin).
[96] *R (MA) v National Probation Service* [2011] EWHC 1332 (Admin) at [37]; *R (Carman) v Secretary of State for the Home Department* [2004] EWHC 2400 (Admin) at [33], [52] and [120]–[121].
[97] *R (MA) v National Probation Service* [2011] EWHC 1332 (Admin) at [6].

10.54 By s 254 of the CJA 2003 and s 32 of the Crime (Sentences) Act 1997 (C(S)A 1997), offenders may have their licence revoked and thereby be recalled to prison. Reasons must be provided and there is a right to make representations. The test for revocation is a modest one: whether there is evidence upon which the Secretary of State reasonably believes that there has been a breach of licence.[98] Unproven allegations can result in recall, but the mere fact of a charge alone cannot. A distinction may be drawn between the mere fact of a charge, and the risk concerns that may arise from such a charge.[99] There is no independent mechanism for a review of licence revocation, although it will form part of the Parole Board's consideration if relevant to risk. The Parole Board is empowered to direct re-release when it comes to consider the case. The Secretary of State has the power to cancel the revocation if he is satisfied that the offender in fact complied with his licence conditions.[100] However this is unlikely to result in release.[101] Any benefit is likely to be limited to cases where the licence revocation otherwise extends the licence expiry date.[102]

The Parole Board

10.55 The Parole Board is an independent body whose primary function is to assess the risk that prisoners pose. The Board operates within the framework of the Parole Board Rules 2004, certain directions issued by the Secretary of State in relation to transfer to open conditions, and its own Practice Guidance in relation to decisions on release.

10.56 The Board's main functions are: (1) considering the early release of certain determinate prisoners,[103] (2) considering the release or transfer to open conditions of indeterminate sentence prisoners, and (3) considering re-release after recall for either type of prisoner. In the second and third of those functions the Board is acting as a 'court' for the purposes of Article 5(4) ECHR, and must therefore be independent of the executive and any parties to the case, provide a procedure appropriate to the deprivation of liberty at stake, and be empowered to direct release, not merely advise.[104] The Board also has a general power to advise on any matter referred to it by the Secretary of State to do with early release and recall,[105] including compassionate release.[106]

10.57 A controversial area to exercise the Board in recent years has been the requirement to provide an oral hearing. For many years it was the practice of the Parole Board to rarely grant an oral hearing in recall cases, but that changed after the decision of the House of Lords in *R (West) v Parole Board*.[107] Following the Parole Board Amendment Rules 2009, which removed the automatic entitlement of indeterminate sentence prisoners to an oral hearing, the Board developed Practice Guidance that an oral hearing would only be required where the application had sufficient prospects of success, or that the assessment of risk required there to be live evidence. That Guidance

---

[98] *R (Gulliver) v Parole Board* [2007] EWCA Civ 1386.
[99] *R (Oakes) v Secretary of State for Justice* [2009] EWHC 3470 (Admin); *R (Broadbent) v Parole Board* [2005] EWHC 1207 (Admin).
[100] Section 254(2A) CJA 2003 (as inserted by s 113 LASPOA 2012).
[101] *R (Gulliver) v Parole Board* [2007] EWCA Civ 1386.
[102] This applies to a number of offenders sentenced under the CJA 1991 for offences committed before 4 April 2005.
[103] This includes 'long-term' prisoners serving more than four years under the CJA 1991, and those serving extended sentences under the CJA 2003.
[104] *Weeks v UK* (1988) 10 EHRR 293 at [59] and [61].
[105] Section 239(2) CJA 2003.
[106] Section 36 CJA 1991; s 30(2) C(S)A 1997; s 248 CJA 2003.
[107] [2005] 1 WLR 350.

was strongly criticised by the Supreme Court in *R (Osborn) v Parole Board*,[108] in which it was held that oral hearings will be far more widely required than had previously been the case. Where a court is assessing whether the Parole Board has complied with the requirements of procedural fairness a primary merits review is conducted, not merely a *Wednesbury* assessment.[109]

10.58 A decision of the Board can be challenged on the grounds that it failed to consider and apply correctly the relevant legal test,[110] although some of the current case-law affords the Board a significant degree of latitude in how it applies the relevant tests and expresses that application.[111] Inadequate reasons may also result in an unlawful decision, although a nit-picking approach to decision letters of the Board has been disapproved.[112]

10.59 Decisions of the Board have also been overturned where: the Board failed to indicate that a significant matter in the prisoner's favour had been taken into account;[113] a decision was reached on factually inaccurate material in the dossier;[114] the Board failed to explore all release options of its own volition, rather than merely deciding on the release proposal put forward;[115] the Board allowed unfairly prejudicial material to remain in a parole dossier;[116] late disclosure of prejudicial material effectively prevented the prisoner from addressing the material;[117] the Board relied on material not disclosed to the prisoner.[118] Rule 8 of the Parole Board Rules 2004 does allow disclosure to be withheld. Consideration should be given to providing a 'gist' of the material or a redacted version.[119]

10.60 When assessing risk the Board is entitled to reject the unanimous recommendations of professional witnesses, but must accurately set out the evidence and give proper reasons for the rejection.[120] It may be unlawful for the Board to proceed on the basis that a particular version of the index offence had occurred where the outcome of a criminal trial and the sentencing remarks indicate otherwise.[121] However, the Board may rely on unproven allegations made against a prisoner to make factual findings adverse to the prisoner.[122]

10.61 The Board is not entitled to refuse a recommendation for open conditions or a release direction on the grounds that the offender maintains his/her innocence. However, the Administrative Court has stated that particularly in cases of serious persistent violent

---

[108] [2013] 3 WLR 1020.
[109] *R (Osborn) v Parole Board* [2013] UKSC 61; *Roose v Parole Board and Secretary of State for Justice* [2010] EWHC 1780 (Admin) at [19].
[110] *R (D'Cunha) v Parole Board* [2011] EWHC 128 (Admin) at [64]; *R (Hill) v Parole Board* [2012] EWHC 809 (Admin) at [15], [19]–[21] and [24].
[111] *R (Austin) v Parole Board* [2011] EWHC 2384 (Admin) at [56]–[57]; *R (Leach) v Parole Board* [2011] EWHC 2470 (Admin) at [41].
[112] *R (Gordon) v Parole Board* [2000] EWHC 414 (Admin); *R (Oyston) v Parole Board* [2000] EWCA Crim 3552.
[113] *R (Botmeh and Alami) v Parole Board* [2008] EWHC 1115 (Admin).
[114] *R v Parole Board, ex p Higgins* (1998), unreported.
[115] *R (Rawnsley) v Parole Board* [2010] EWHC 2689 (Admin).
[116] *R (McGetrick) v Parole Board, Secretary of State for Justice* [2013] EWCA Civ 182.
[117] *R (Weszka) v Parole Board* [2012] EWHC 827 (Admin).
[118] *R (AT) v Parole Board* [2004] EWHC 515; *R (Gregson) v Parole Board* [2009] EWHC 3639.
[119] *R (Rowe) v Parole Board* [2012] EWHC 1272.
[120] *R (O'Sullivan) v Parole Board* [2009] EWHC 2370 (Admin).
[121] *R (H) v Parole Board* [2011] EWHC 2081.
[122] *R (Allen) v Parole Board* [2009] EWHC 3492 (Admin) at [8].

or sexual crime, a continued denial of guilt will almost inevitably mean that the risk posed by the prisoner remains high or, at least, cannot be objectively assessed. In such cases the Board is entitled (perhaps obliged) to deny a recommendation.[123]

10.62 The Board is afforded a wide discretion by the courts as a specialist and uniquely qualified body tasked with assessing risk.[124] In normal circumstances, a court will ask itself only whether the decision falls within the range of decisions that a reasonable panel might make.[125]

10.63 On 1 April 2013, the Board published its current litigation strategy. This suggests that the Board, as a judicial body, intends to reduce the number of judicial review applications it will defend.[126]

10.64 Decisions by the Secretary of State on whether to accept the recommendations of the Board can be subject to judicial review.[127]

Home detention curfew

10.65 Section 246 of the CJA 2003 provides the Secretary of State with a power to release prisoners earlier than he is ordinarily required to. In practice this is given effect through the home detention curfew (HDC) scheme, which involves prisoners being released subject to an electronically monitored curfew. By s 246(4), certain offenders are excluded from consideration for early release on HDC. Others are 'presumed unsuitable' under the various policies governing the HDC scheme, but can make representations on why they should be eligible.

10.66 There are a large number of policies governing the HDC scheme but the most important are PSO 6700, PSI 31/2003 and PSI 31/2006. Those policies set out the process for risk assessment, and the considerations to which the governor must have regard when determining applications for early release on HDC. Where HDC is refused, the reasons for that decision must do more than merely repeating the criteria to be applied.[128]

10.67 A prisoner who is recalled for breaching the curfew under s 255 CJA 2003 will be re-released at his conditional release date. However, where there has also been a breach of licence the prisoner will be recalled under s 254, and so will be detained until his sentence expires, unless the Parole Board otherwise directs.

10.68 In *R (Whiston) v Secretary of State for Justice*,[129] which is under appeal, the Court of Appeal rejected an argument that the recall of a prisoner under s 255 engages Article 5(4) ECHR, reasoning that the highly restricted liberty inherent in the HDC

---

[123] *R v Secretary of State for the Home Department, ex p Hepworth* [1997] EWHC (Admin) 32; *R v Parole Board, ex p Oyston* [2000] Prison LR 45; *R (Bourke) v Secretary of State for Justice* [2012] EWHC 4041 (Admin).
[124] *R (Leach) v Parole Board* [2011] EWHC 2470 (Admin) at [18]; *R (D'Cunha) v Parole Board* [2011] EWHC 128 (Admin) at [18]; *R (O'Sullivan) v Parole Board* [2009] EWHC 2370 (Admin) at [18]; *R (Gordon) v Parole Board* [2000] EWHC 414 (Admin) at [31]; *R v Parole Board, ex p Hart*, unreported, 24 May 2000.
[125] *R (Gordon) v Parole Board* [2000] EWHC 414 (Admin) at [31].
[126] https://www.gov.uk/government/publications/parole-board-litigation-strategy-for-legal-practitioners.
[127] *R (Adetoro) v Secretary of State for Justice, Parole Board* [2012] EWHC 2576 (Admin); *R (Wilmot) v Secretary of State for Justice* [2012] EWHC 3139 (Admin).
[128] *R (Rowen) v Governor of Kirkham Prison* [2009] EWHC 3756 (Admin) at [6], [13], and [18].
[129] [2013] 2 WLR 1080.

scheme is too intimately connected with the original sentence to separately engage Article 5 ECHR. In *R (Foster) v Secretary of State for Justice*[130] the Divisional Court accepted that fairness could require an oral hearing to determine release and recall on HDC, but that any application would have to be very closely scrutinised.

Early removal scheme

10.69 Fixed-term foreign national prisoners (FNPs), who are confirmed to be liable to removal from the UK, can be removed from the UK up to 270 days (nine months) before the halfway point (for standard determinate sentence prisoners) or the two-thirds point (for extended determinate sentence prisoners) of their sentence.[131] Prisoners serving a term in default/civil term (including an outstanding confiscation order),[132] and young 'trainees' serving detention and training orders[133] are not eligible for removal under the early removal scheme (ERS). Prisoners must serve a minimum of a quarter of their sentence before they can be removed under the ERS, so the maximum 270 days can apply to sentences of three years or longer. For sentences of less than three years, the ERS period is proportionately shorter.[134]

10.70 The ERS is mandatory, meaning that all determinate sentenced FNPs who are liable to removal must be considered under the ERS,[135] and early removal should be confirmed unless there is a reason to refuse.[136] Early removal under the ERS should be refused where there are outstanding criminal charges against a prisoner,[137] and may be refused where compelling reasons of public safety (eg plans for further crime, evidence of repeated violence in prison, conviction for terrorism offences)[138] or public confidence in the ERS favours refusal.[139]

10.71 Prison governors are responsible for authorising early removal once confirmation has been given of the intention to remove the prisoner from the UK.[140] Where authorisation for removal is not authorised, there is no formal right of appeal by a prisoner, but he/she may complain using the internal complaints system (see below), and should be given written reasons for the refusal of early release.[141]

10.72 Prisoners serving long-term sentences under the CJA 1991, extended sentences under the CJA 2003, or extended determinate sentences under the LASPOA 2012, can be removed under the ERS at the authorisation of the governor. There is no requirement for the Parole Board to direct release for removal to take place.[142] The parole process must continue, however, to ensure that if removal is not carried out the prisoner is considered for parole in the normal way.[143]

---

[130] [2013] EWHC 1951 (Admin).
[131] Section 160 CJA 2003; PSI 04/2013, paras 1.1 and 2.2.
[132] PSI 04/2011, para 2.5.
[133] PSI 04/2011, para 2.19.
[134] PSI 04/2011, para 1.4.
[135] PSI 04/2012, paras 1.2, 1.5 and 2.1.
[136] PSI 04/2011, para 2.9.
[137] PSI 04/2011, para 2.8.
[138] PSI 04/2011, para 2.9.
[139] PSI 04/2011, paras 2.15–2.16.
[140] PSI 04/2012, paras 1.8 and 2.26.
[141] PSI 04/2012, para 4.22.
[142] PSI 04/2012, paras 1.9–1.10, 2.3 and 5.3.
[143] PSI 04/2012, paras 1.10 and 5.7.

Tariff expired removal scheme

10.73 The tariff expired removal scheme (TERS) allows indeterminate sentence FNPs, who are confirmed to be liable to removal from the UK, to be removed on or any date after the expiry of their tariff without reference to the Parole Board.[144] The TERS is mandatory, so all indeterminate FNPs must be considered for removal under the scheme by the PPCS at the Ministry of Justice.[145]

10.74 All indeterminate FNPs will be presumed suitable for removal under the scheme unless they meet the criteria for refusal.[146] A FNP may be considered unsuitable for removal for the same reasons as apply under the ERS, including the existence of outstanding criminal charges, and compelling reasons of public safety or public confidence which favour refusal.[147] Where authorisation for removal is not authorised, there is no formal right of appeal by a prisoner, but he/she may complain using the internal complaints system (see below), and should be given written reasons for the refusal of release under the TERS.[148]

10.75 The parole process must continue for indeterminate FNPs despite the possibility of removal under the TERS.[149]

PRISON DISCIPLINE

The prison disciplinary system

10.76 Section 47 of the PA 1952 empowers the Secretary of State to make rules for the discipline of prisoners. Prisoners can be charged with a wide variety of offences against prison discipline, including assault and possession of an unauthorised article.[150] Parallel systems running outside the formal disciplinary procedures, which allow the imposition of *de facto* punishments, have been declared unlawful.[151]

10.77 Adjudications can be heard either by prison governors, or by the independent adjudicator (IA), depending on whether the severity of the charge means that additional days should be added to the prisoner's sentence as punishment if the charge is proven.[152] There is discretion to refer cases to the IA even where additional days cannot be imposed.[153] Section 47 of the PA 1952 requires that the Prison Rules must ensure that a person who is charged with an offence is given a proper opportunity of presenting his/her case.

10.78 Rule 53(1) of the Prison Rules 1999 provides that where a prisoner is to be charged with an offence against discipline, the charge must be laid within 48 hours of

---

[144] Section 32A C(S)A 1997, as amended by s 119 LASPOA 2012. See also PSI 18/2012, paras 1.1 and 4.2.
[145] PSI 18/2012, paras 1.2 and 2.1.
[146] PSI 18/2012, para 2.1.
[147] PSI 18/2012, para 2.3.
[148] PSI 18/2012, para 3.12.
[149] PSI 18/2012, paras 1.10 and 4.4.
[150] Rule 51 of the Prison Rules 1999. The elements of the available offences are set out in detail in PSI 47/2011.
[151] *R (KB) v Secretary of State for Justice* [2010] EWHC 15 (Admin).
[152] Prison Rules 1999, r 53A. See PSI 47/2011, para 2.23 for guidance on cases that may be sufficiently serious to be referred to the IA.
[153] Prison Rules 1999, r 53A, following *R (Smith) v Governor of Belmarsh Prison* [2009] EWHC 109 (Admin).

the discovery of the offence. Failure to do so may result in a charge being dismissed.[154] Under r 53(2) and (3) the governor must inquire into a charge and this inquiry should commence no later than the next day after the charge is laid. The prisoner must be informed of the charge before the governor's inquiry begins.[155] The charge sheet provided to the prisoner should include sufficient detail that the substance of the charge is clear,[156] and will form the basis of the case considered by the adjudicator.[157] Once a charge has been laid it cannot be amended and if the incorrect charge is brought, a fresh charge can only be laid if it remains within the 48-hour window.[158] A prisoner who is to be charged with an offence against discipline may be kept apart from other prisoners pending the governor's first inquiry.[159]

10.79 PSI 47/2011 sets out the steps that should be taken by adjudicators, including: providing the prisoner and his/her legal representatives with copies of the adjudication papers;[160] asking the prisoner at the adjudication hearing whether he/she wishes to obtain legal advice;[161] adjourning to allow legal advice to be obtained (where appropriate);[162] taking a complete record of the hearing, including the reasons for the decision;[163] and allowing the prisoner to call defence witnesses (subject to relevance).[164] Prisoners are entitled to question witnesses,[165] provided such questioning is relevant to the charge.[166] Charges must be proved beyond reasonable doubt.[167]

Governor adjudications

10.80 In the vast majority of governor adjudications the charged prisoner is not legally represented. However, governors are required to consider the *Tarrant*[168] criteria when determining whether legal representation should be granted to a prisoner.[169] These criteria include the seriousness of the charge and the potential penalty, whether any points of law are likely to arise, the capacity of the prisoner to present his/her own case, procedural difficulties, including the need to question witnesses, the need for reasonable speed in the adjudication process, and the need for fairness in the adjudication process.[170] Successful applications for legal representation under the *Tarrant* criteria are rare.

10.81 Governors can impose a range of punishments where a prisoner is found guilty, including a caution, forfeiture of privileges, exclusion from work, and cellular

---

[154] PSI 47/2011, para 2.40; *R (Garland) v Secretary of State for Justice* [2011] EWCA Civ 1335. See also *R v Board of Visitors of Dartmoor Prison, ex p Smith* [1986] 3 WLR 61.
[155] Prison Rules 1999, r 54(1).
[156] PSI 47/2011, paras 1.16–1.97.
[157] *R (Shreeve) v Secretary of State for Justice* [2007] EWHC 2431 (Admin).
[158] PSI 47/2011, para 2.40.
[159] Prison Rules 1999, r 53(4).
[160] PSI 47/2011, para 2.9. See *R (MA) v Independent Adjudicator* [2013] EWHC 438 (Admin) at [78].
[161] PSI 47/2011, para 2.8.
[162] PSI 47/2011, para 2.8. Repeated and lengthy adjournments may compromise the fairness of the proceedings: PSI 47/2011, paras 2.16 and 2.40.
[163] PSI 47/2011, para 2.6.
[164] PSI 47/2011, para 2.37.
[165] PSI 47/2011, para 2.30.
[166] PSI 47/2011, para 2.33.
[167] PSI 47/2011, para 2.39.
[168] *R v Secretary of State for the Home Department, ex p Tarrant* [1984] 1 All ER 799.
[169] PSI 47/2011, para 2.17.
[170] See summary of the *Tarrant* criteria at PSI 47/2011, para 2.10.

confinement.[171] A medical practitioner must be consulted before cellular confinement is imposed.[172] Governors cannot impose additional days to be added to the prisoner's sentence.

10.82 The Secretary of State is empowered to quash a governor's finding of guilt, or remit or mitigate a governor's punishment.[173] The Deputy Director of Custody or the Director of High Security makes such decisions.[174]

10.83 Governors' findings of guilt can be quashed on grounds of apparent bias where the governor is required, in hearing the charge, to rule on the lawfulness of an order that he/she gave.[175] It may also be unlawful for a governor to hear a charge where he/she has heard prejudicial information at the preliminary stage.

Independent adjudications

10.84 Once a charge has been referred to the IA, the first hearing before the IA must take place within 28 days, unless there are exceptional circumstances.[176]

10.85 An IA can impose the full range of sanctions available to a governor, but may also impose up to 42 additional days.[177]

10.86 Article 6(3) ECHR is engaged by adjudications where additional days may be imposed on a prisoner as a punishment for the charge(s), as such charges amount to 'criminal charges' within the meaning of Article 6 ECHR.[178] These adjudications are referred to the IA (a district judge) for determination, and not to a prison governor.[179] The protections of Article 6(3) ECHR require that the prisoner be afforded legal representation at the adjudication hearing.

10.87 A prisoner can challenge the penalty imposed by the IA following a finding of guilt, but not the finding of guilt itself.[180] Both the Secretary of State and the Prison and Probation Ombudsman (see below) are unable to overturn an IA's finding of guilt. Judicial review is the prisoner's only recourse.

Challenging findings of guilt

10.88 Findings of guilt may be quashed on grounds of procedural fairness where errors in the adjudication process result in material unfairness to the prisoner, for example where the IA speaks to relevant witnesses outside the hearing, or where relevant evidence is not permitted to be called.[181] A failure by an IA to call independent CCTV evidence, instead relying on the disputed evidence of the reporting prison officer, proved fatal to a

---

[171] Prison Rules 1999, r 55.
[172] Prison Rules 1999, r 58.
[173] Prison Rules 1999, r 61.
[174] PSI 47/2011, para 3.5.
[175] *R (Carroll and Al-Hasan) v Secretary of State for the Home Department* [2005] 1 WLR 688.
[176] PSI 47/2011, paras 2.26 and 2.40.
[177] Prison Rules 1999, r 55A.
[178] *Ezeh and Connors v UK* [2004] 39 EHRR 3, confirmed by *Black v UK* (App No 60682/00), *Young v UK* (App No 56745/00) and *Whitfield v UK* (App Nos 46387/99, 48906/99, 57410/00 and 57419/00).
[179] PSI 47/2011, para 2.20.
[180] Prison Rules 1999, r 55B; PSI 47/2011, para 3.11.
[181] *R (Low) v Independent Adjudicator* [2009] EWHC 2253 (Admin).

finding of guilt.[182] A finding was quashed where a governor refused to allow a prisoner to ask questions of a witness that went to the elements of the charge.[183] A failure to provide adequate reasons may result in an unlawful finding of guilt.[184] Findings of guilt have also been quashed because the adjudicator refused to adjourn a hearing where the existence of previously unidentified and relevant witnesses only became apparent at the hearing, and where the prison had failed to inform the prisoner of witnesses to the incident of whom he was unaware.[185] However, adjudicators are not required to suggest to a legally represented prisoner that the prisoner's interests would be better served by seeking to call oral evidence where the prisoner does not propose to do so.[186]

10.89 Prison staff are under a duty to disclose all relevant information, including the identity of witnesses, prior to an adjudication hearing, and not to withhold information from the prisoner that could advantage his/her case. Where this is not done, the adjudication may be quashed.[187]

10.90 A finding of guilt may be quashed on the basis that the reasons provided were inadequate.[188] Such reasons must be intelligible, accurate, and must enable the reader to understand why the matter was decided as it was, and what the conclusions were on the issues that were raised.[189]

10.91 In IA adjudications, frustrating access to a prisoner's chosen lawyer may amount to a violation of Article 6 ECHR,[190] as may failing to provide relevant adjudication paperwork to a prisoner's legal representative in advance of the hearing.[191] Where there has been a violation of a prisoner's Article 6 ECHR rights in finding against him/her at adjudication, that does not automatically entitle the prisoner to have the finding of guilt quashed.[192]

10.92 Where a finding of guilt is quashed, if it remains possible to remit the case for a rehearing before a different adjudicator, this can be done.[193]

10.93 The courts will be slow to interfere with an adjudication finding, and the findings of fact involved in reaching that finding, where there was material upon which it was open to the adjudicator to conclude as he/she did.[194]

---

[182] *R (Cox) v Independent Adjudicator* [2013] EWHC 2753 (Admin).
[183] *R (Russell) v Secretary of State for the Home Department* [2000] Prison LR 145.
[184] *R (Anderson) v Independent Adjudicator* [2010] EWHC 2260 (Admin).
[185] *R (Smith) v Independent Adjudicator* [2011] EWHC 3981 (Admin).
[186] *R (Bates) v Independent Adjudicator, Secretary of State for Justice* [2011] EWHC 3236 (Admin) at [30].
[187] *R v Blundeston Board of Visitors, ex p Fox-Taylor* [1982] 1 All ER 646. See also Annex D of PSI 47/2011 where this case is summarised.
[188] *R (Smith) v Independent Adjudicator* [2011] EWHC 3981 (Admin).
[189] *R (Shepherd) v Governor of HMP Whatton* [2010] EWHC 2474 (Admin) at [19].
[190] *R (Van Hoogstraten) v Governor of HMP Belmarsh* [2002] EWHC 1965 Admin.
[191] *R (MA) v Independent Adjudicator* [2013] EWHC 438 (Admin) at [80].
[192] *R (Smith) v Governor of HMP Belmarsh and Secretary of State for the Home Department* [2009] EWHC 109 (Admin).
[193] *R (Beever) v Independent Adjudicator of HMP Frankland* [2010] EWHC 1559.
[194] *R (Bates) v Independent Adjudicator, Secretary of State for Justice* [2011] EWHC 3236 (Admin) at [43]; *R (Maloney) v Governor of HMP Rochester* [2000] Prison LR 23 at [44].

COMPLAINTS PROCESSES

The internal complaints system

10.94 The stated aim of the internal complaints system is to ensure that prisoners' needs and welfare are being looked after, thereby reducing tension and promoting better relations.[195] Prison Service policy seeks to resolve issues at the lowest level in the most expeditious manner, including by informal resolution, where possible.[196]

10.95 Prisons are required to make it simple and easy to submit a complaint, and prisoners must be informed of how to do so during the early days in custody.[197] Complaints should normally be submitted within three months of the incident or circumstances giving rise to the complaint, or the date on which they became known to the prisoner. However, there is discretion to consider complaints submitted after this time limit in exceptional circumstances where there are good reasons for the delay, or where the issues raised are so serious as to override the time factor.[198]

10.96 There is no fixed target for replies to complaints. Replies should be based on the urgency of the individual case.[199] However, prisoners must receive a response within a maximum of five working days. An interim reply can be regarded as meeting this target, although interim replies should be used sparingly, and a full reply must be given in the shortest period possible. Prisoners must be kept updated as to the progress of their complaints.[200]

10.97 Responses to complaints must address the issues raised, and must be answered by someone capable of providing an adequate and meaningful reply.[201] If the complaint is upheld, the problem must be put right and where necessary consideration must be given as to whether an apology is appropriate.[202] Where the complaint is not upheld, the prisoner must be given an explanation of the reason for not upholding it.[203]

10.98 Prisoners may appeal against the response to a complaint. An appeal should normally be made within seven days of the prisoner having received the initial response, unless there are exceptional reasons why this is difficult or impossible. Prisoners must receive a response to their appeal within five working days of the appeal being logged. Someone at a higher level in the management structure than the person who provided the initial response must answer appeals, and the appeal response should decide whether the original decision was fair and reasonable and whether the explanation given to the prisoner was satisfactory.[204] An appeal response must add to the explanation of why the original decision was made. Where an appeal is upheld, the response must explain why the original response is being overturned.[205]

---

[195] PSI 02/2012, para 1.3.
[196] PSI 02/2012, para 1.4.
[197] PSI 02/2012, paras 2.1.1–2.1.2.
[198] PSI 02/2012, para 2.1.4.
[199] PSI 02/2012, para 2.3.1.
[200] PSI 02/2012, para 2.3.2–2.3.5.
[201] PSI 02/2012, para 2.2.1.
[202] PSI 02/2012, para 2.2.2.
[203] PSI 02/2012, para 2.2.3.
[204] PSI 02/2012, para 2.7.
[205] PSI 02/2012, para 2.9.1.

10.99 Prisoners who are deemed to have abused the complaints process can be subject to a process to restrict such abuse, but the right to complain cannot be removed altogether.[206]

10.100 Rule 11 of the Prison Rules 1999 also entitles prisoners to make a confidential complaint to the governor or IMB relating to their imprisonment. This procedure may be used for particularly serious matters where a prisoner is concerned about complaining through the administrative or wing staff, but it cannot be used to bypass the normal complaints process.[207]

The Prison and Probation Ombudsman

10.101 The Prison and Probation Ombudsman (PPO) is independent of the National Offender Management Service (NOMS) and the Ministry of Justice. The PPO is sponsored by the Ministry of Justice and reports to the Secretary of State.[208]

10.102 The PPO receives and investigates complaints from prisoners who have failed to obtain satisfaction from the prison complaints system.[209] The PPO can consider complaints regarding decisions and actions (including failures or refusals to act) relating to the management, supervision, care, and treatment of prisoners in custody, by prison staff and people acting as agents or contractors of NOMS.[210] The PPO may choose not to accept a complaint, or not to continue an investigation, where the PPO considers that no worthwhile outcome can be achieved or the complaint raises no substantial issue.[211] If the PPO decides that a complaint is ineligible, written reasons will be provided.[212]

10.103 Prisoners must exhaust the internal prison complaints system before making a complaint to the PPO.[213] A complaint to the PPO must be made within three months of exhausting the internal prison complaints system.[214] The PPO will not normally accept complaints where there has been a delay of more than 12 months between the complainant becoming aware of the relevant facts and submitting their case.[215] The PPO retains a discretion to investigate outside the normal time limits where there is good reason for the delay, or where the issues raised are so serious as to override the time factor.[216]

10.104 Where the PPO accepts a complaint he can consider both the merits of prisoners' complaints, as well as the procedures involved.[217] The PPO will gather evidence where necessary, and is entitled to unfettered access to relevant documentation, and is also able to access relevant premises and conduct interviews.[218] The PPO will reach a determination on whether the complaint should be upheld. If so, written findings

---

[206] PSI 02/2012, para 2.1.11.
[207] PSI 02/2012, para 2.5.
[208] PPO Terms of Reference (September 2013), paras 1-3: http://www.ppo.gov.uk/docs/Terms_of_Reference_September_2013_(updated_to_inc._STC_comps).pdf.
[209] PPO Terms of Reference, para 10.
[210] PPO Terms of Reference, para 12(i).
[211] PPO Terms of Reference, para 15.
[212] PPO Terms of Reference, para 19.
[213] PPO Terms of Reference, para 17.
[214] PPO Terms of Reference, para 21.
[215] PPO Terms of Reference, para 22.
[216] PPO Terms of Reference, para 23.
[217] PPO Terms of Reference, para 13.
[218] PPO Terms of Reference, paras 8-9.

and conclusions will be provided. If not, written reasons will be given. The PPO may choose to write a full report on the complaint.[219] The PPO is entitled to resolve the complaint as he sees fit, including by mediation,[220] and local resolution.[221] The PPO may make recommendations but they are not binding on the Prison Service.[222]

10.105 Prison governors are required to make information about the PPO (including the deadline for submitting complaints) available to all prisoners and staff,[223] and must allow prisoners wishing to make a complaint to do so.[224] Correspondence to and from the PPO must be treated as confidential.[225]

10.106 Prison staff must comply with the PPO's requests for information and assistance when conducting investigations or enquiries.[226] An agreement is in place between NOMS and the PPO to provide only relevant information, including from security information reports, to the PPO in the course of his investigations.[227] A procedure is in place for determining requests by the PPO to see the full details of security information.[228]

INVESTIGATIONS/FAILURES TO INVESTIGATE

Use of force

10.107 The authority entitling prison staff to use force against prisoners derives from s 3 of the Criminal Law Act 1967 (which permits reasonable force to be used in preventing crime or affecting an arrest), the common law power to use reasonable force in self-defence, and r 47(1) of the Prison Rules 1999.

10.108 PSO 1600 sets out the Prison Services' policy on the use of force by prison staff against prisoners. The policy governs the use of control and restraint (C&R) techniques, de-escalation skills, personal safety techniques and the use of batons.

10.109 Staff are encouraged to avoid danger and to defuse potentially violent situations through the use of de-escalation skills. The use of force is therefore a last resort that should be used where it has not been possible to avoid its use by deploying other techniques.[229] Defensive strikes and the use of batons should be considered exceptional measures.[230]

10.110 Where staff resort to the use of force, PSO 1600 states that the use of force will be unlawful unless it is justified.[231] Force will be justified where:

---

[219] http://www.ppo.gov.uk/what-to-expect-when-you-make-a-complaint.html.
[220] PPO Terms of Reference, para 24.
[221] PSI 58/2010, s 6.
[222] PPO Terms of Reference, para 25.
[223] PSI 58/2010, s 3.
[224] PSI 58/2010, s 4.
[225] PPO Terms of Reference, para 18; PSI 58/2010, paras 4.8–4.9.
[226] PSI 58/2010, s 5.
[227] PSI 58/2010, para 1.9.
[228] PSI 58/2010, para 1.10.
[229] PSO 1600, paras 2.13–2.18, 4.2–4.3 and 4.24.
[230] PSO 1600, paras 4.6 and 4.12.
[231] PSO 1600, para 2.1.

- it is reasonable in the circumstances. Reasonableness is a matter of fact, and relevant factors to be taken into account include the size, age and sex of both the prisoner and the member of staff concerned in the use of force, and whether any weapons are present.[232]
- it is necessary. Force will not be necessary merely because a prisoner refuses to obey a lawful order. Whether force is necessary depends on the risk of harm involved, eg force is more likely to be necessary where there is a risk to life than where there is a risk to the good order of the establishment or to property.[233]
- no more force than is necessary is used. This means that the use of excessive force, where only some force is required, will be unlawful.[234] The purpose of using force is to get away from the violent situation as quickly as possible.[235] Where more force is used than is required to achieve that aim, the force will be unlawful.[236]
- the force used is proportionate to the seriousness of the circumstances. Action taken is unlikely to be regarded as proportionate where less injurious, but equally effective alternatives exist.[237]

10.111 Where the use of force is justified, staff should only use approved C&R techniques, unless this is impractical.[238] Where staff use non-approved force techniques, the lawfulness of that use of force will depend on whether the use of force was reasonable.[239] The use of an improvised and unauthorised technique may render the use of force unlawful.[240]

10.112 When applying C&R techniques or using force, staff must pay particular attention to the signs and symptoms that may indicate that a prisoner is in medical distress.[241] Conditions such as positional asphyxia can result in rapid death from the application of C&R.[242] Where staff identify signs of medical distress, an incident will need to be treated as a medical emergency rather than a C&R incident.[243] C&R can be used on pregnant prisoners, but specific planning and techniques must be employed.[244] Healthcare staff must attend planned C&R interventions, and should attend unplanned C&R incidents where possible.[245] Following the use of restraint against a prisoner he/she must be seen by a qualified healthcare professional as soon as possible, and no later than 24 hours after the incident.[246]

---

[232] PSO 1600, paras 2.2–2.3.
[233] PSO 1600, paras 2.2 and 2.4–2.7.
[234] PSO 1600, paras 2.2 and 2.8.
[235] PSO 1600, para 4.5.
[236] PSO 1600, para 4.8.
[237] PSO 1600, paras 2.2 and 2.9.
[238] PSO 1600, para 2.10.
[239] PSO 1600, para 2.11.
[240] *Glowacki v Long and Chief Constable of Lancashire* [1998] EWCA Civ 1034.
[241] PSO 1600, para 3.1.
[242] PSO 1600, paras 3.2–3.3 and Annex D.
[243] PSO 1600, para 3.1.
[244] PSO 1600, paras 4.36–4.37.
[245] PSO 1600, paras 3.4–3.6, 4.28–4.29 and 6.1–6.8.
[246] PSO 1600, para 6.9.

10.113 PSO 1600 provides guidance on the use of a range of force techniques, including batons,[247] C&R,[248] ratchet handcuffs,[249] and advanced C&R for incidents of serious and concerted indiscipline.[250]

10.114 Where force has been employed the individual concerned must be able to account for their own decisions and actions.[251] A report justifying the use of any type of force must be completed in all cases.[252] This must explain why force was required and why the level of force was required.[253] All staff involved in using force must complete a form and PSO 1600 envisages detailed contents being provided.[254] Use of force forms must be monitored,[255] and the supervising officer must also conduct a debrief with a member of staff who has used force, and must follow up any concerns over the use of force.[256] A debrief with the prisoner should also take place.[257]

Assaults

10.115 According to PSI 64/2011, there are approximately 15,000 violent incidents in prisons each year.[258] Assaults against prisoners can be investigated in a number of different ways depending largely on their severity and complexity.

10.116 Where an incident or alleged misconduct takes place, an appropriate manager, having assessed the circumstances, will determine whether to investigate, and, if so, how.[259] This is based on a judgment of the nature and seriousness of the incident or allegation, and how much is known about its circumstances.[260] Managers may decide not to investigate at all, for example because the incident is minor and can be dealt with without an investigation, or because even in a serious case the facts are clear and unambiguous.[261] PSO 1300 does, however, indicate that in most cases there will be lessons to be learned from incidents and an investigation would prove useful.[262] The purpose of any prison investigation must be to inquire into what has taken place, to establish the facts, to learn from them and to establish any accountability.[263]

10.117 Where a decision is made to investigate, there are two broad types of investigation available: simple and formal.[264] Simple investigations are for where there is no need for a formal process or the need is uncertain.[265] A formal investigation will be necessary if the incident has major consequences such as disorder, damage and injury, serious harm was caused to any person, or the investigation has some specialist element,

---

[247] PSO 1600, paras 4.10–4.21.
[248] PSO 1600, paras 4.22–4.33.
[249] PSO 1600, paras 4.38–4.46.
[250] PSO 1600, paras 4.54–4.59.
[251] PSO 1600, para 2.11.
[252] PSO 1600, paras 2.12 and 8.1–8.2.
[253] PSO 1600, paras 4.9 and 8.1.
[254] PSO 1600, para 8.9.
[255] PSO 1600, paras 8.12–8.16 and Annex G.
[256] PSO 1600, para 8.18.
[257] PSO 1600, paras 8.19–8.20.
[258] PSI 64/2011, chapter 7.
[259] PSO 1300, para 1.1.1.
[260] PSO 1300, para 1.3.1.
[261] PSO 1300, para 1.3.2.
[262] PSO 1300, para 1.3.2.
[263] PSO 1300, para 1.2.
[264] PSO 1300, para 1.5.
[265] PSO 1300, para 1.5.1.

such as sexual or racial harassment or discrimination.[266] PSO 1300 requires that all simple and formal investigations must be conducted according to the principles of natural justice and procedural fairness.[267] Detailed guidance on conducting simple and formal investigations is provided in PSO 1300.

10.118 Investigations can also be conducted on an informal basis outside PSO 1300, or under the Prison Service's violence reduction policy.[268] Violence reduction investigations may be necessary in order to learn lessons, prevent future occurrences and improve local delivery of safer custody.[269]

10.119 Judicial review can be sought of the decision on what type of investigation to conduct. The court will apply a rationality standard of review.[270]

10.120 Article 3 ECHR imposes a duty on the state to conduct an effective official investigation where credible evidence suggests that one or more individuals have been subjected by or with the connivance of the state to treatment falling within Article 3 ECHR. An effective investigation must comply with certain minimum requirements; it must be capable of leading to the identification and punishment of those responsible, be independent and thorough, the state must take all reasonable steps to secure the evidence concerning the incident, and the investigation must permit effective access for the complainant to the investigatory procedure.[271] Article 3 ECHR may also require that an investigation is capable of learning lessons for the future.[272] A prison may be required to conduct an Article 3 ECHR-complaint investigation into a prison assault. However, the case-law suggests that good reason must be shown, the obligation is resource-sensitive, alternative investigations may well suffice to meet Article 3 ECHR, it will be relevant whether all or most of the facts are already known, and the situations in which an Article 3 ECHR investigation is required will be relatively unusual.[273]

Deaths

10.121 A death in prison may be the result of a wide range of circumstances, including self-harm/suicide, violence inflicted by third parties, and natural causes.

10.122 The procedures immediately following a death in custody are set out in detail in PSI 64/2011, including contacting the deceased's next of kin, reporting the incident to appropriate stakeholders, reviewing the cell-sharing risk of the deceased's cellmate

---

[266] PSO 1300, para 1.6.1. See also PSI 64/2011, chapter 14, which states that: 'There are a range of options available to investigate serious incidents of harm to self or others. Consideration must be given to the circumstances in which the harm occurred, the lessons that can be learned from the incident and its management, and the need to support those harmed and sanction perpetrators of harm.'
[267] PSO 1300, para 1.1.4.
[268] PSI 64/2011, chapter 7. See *R (NM) v Secretary of State for Justice* [2012] EWCA Civ 1182.
[269] PSI 64/2011, chapter 7.
[270] *R (NM) v Secretary of State for Justice* [2012] EWCA Civ 1182.
[271] *R (AM) v Secretary of State for the Home Department* [2009] EWCA Civ 219; *R (MM) v Secretary of State for the Home Department* [2012] EWCA Civ 668. See also the recent case-law of the ECtHR on the Article 3 ECHR investigative obligation: *El-Masri v Macedonia* (App No 39630/09).
[272] Contrast *R (AM) v Secretary of State for the Home Department* [2009] EWCA Civ 219 with the more recent decision in *R (MM) v Secretary of State for the Home Department* [2012] EWCA Civ 668.
[273] *R (P) v Secretary of State for Justice* [2010] QB 317; *R (NM)v Secretary of State for Justice* [2012] EWCA Civ 1182; *R (MM) v Secretary of State for the Home Department* [2012] EWCA Civ 668; *R (Mousa) v Secretary of State for Defence* [2010] EWHC 3304 (Admin).

(where applicable), securing all relevant documentation on the deceased, and providing the necessary support to both staff and prisoners in the aftermath of the death.[274]

10.123 Article 2 ECHR enshrines the right to life. It requires that an investigation is conducted into any death in prison where it appears that agents of the state are, or may be, in some way implicated,[275] including all self-inflicted deaths.[276] The obligation to investigate is heightened and must involve increased thoroughness where a death occurs in state custody.[277] Where Article 2 ECHR imposes the obligation to investigate, the investigation must be: independent; effective; reasonably prompt; initiated of the state's own motion; it must involve a sufficient element of public scrutiny to secure accountability, maintain public confidence in the authorities' adherence to the rule of law, and prevent any appearance of collusion in or tolerance of unlawful acts; and the deceased's next of kin must be involved to the extent necessary to safeguard their legitimate interests.[278]

10.124 To be effective the investigation must ensure as far as possible that the full facts are brought to light, that culpable and discreditable conduct is exposed and brought to public notice, that those at fault are made accountable, that suspicion of deliberate wrongdoing (if unjustified) is allayed, that dangerous practices and procedures are rectified, and that lessons are learned and mistakes corrected so as to save the lives of others.[279] Reasonable steps must be taken to secure all relevant evidence concerning the death and its circumstances,[280] and sufficient expert evidence must be called, where required.[281]

10.125 In normal circumstances, an inquest is the means by which the state meets its obligation under Article 2 ECHR to conduct an effective investigation into a death in prison.[282] Where a person dies in prison custody there must be an inquest[283] held with a jury (provided that the coroner has reason to suspect that the death was a violent or unnatural one, or the cause of death is unknown).[284] The inquest will consider by what means and in what circumstances the deceased came by his/her death.[285] The jury's verdict must include a determination of the central issues in the case.[286]

---

[274] PSI 64/2011, chapter 12.
[275] R (Middleton) v West Somerset Coroner [2004] 2 AC 182 at [3] and [19].
[276] R (Middleton) v West Somerset Coroner [2004] 2 AC 182 at [5]; R (JL) v Secretary of State for the Home Department [2009] 1 AC 588 at [9], [32], [38], [59], [101] and [113].
[277] R (Amin) v Secretary of State for the Home Department [2004] 1 AC 653 at [31]; R (Sacker) v West Yorkshire Coroner [2004] 1 WLR 796 at [11]; R (Middleton) v West Somerset Coroner [2004] 2 AC 182 at [5].
[278] Jordan v UK [2001] 37 EHRR 52 at [105]–[109] and [133]; R (Amin) v Secretary of State for the Home Department [2004] 1 AC 653 at [25] and [32].
[279] R (Amin) v Secretary of State for the Home Department [2004] 1 AC 653 at [31]; R (Sacker) v West Yorkshire Coroner [2004] 1 WLR 796 at [11].
[280] Edwards v UK (2002) 35 EHRR 19 at [71]; Kakoulli v Turkey (2007) 45 EHRR 12 at [123].
[281] R (Stanley) v HM Coroner for Inner North London [2003] EWHC 1180 (Admin) at [45]–[48]; R (Warren) v HM Assistant Coroner for Northamptonshire [2008] EWHC 966 (Admin) at [42]–[43].
[282] R (Middleton) v West Somerset Coroner [2004] 2 AC 182 at [20] and [47].
[283] Sections 1 and 6 of the Coroners and Justice Act 2009 (CJA 2009).
[284] Section 7 CJA 2009.
[285] R (Middleton) v West Somerset Coroner [2004] 2 AC 182 at [35]; s 5 CJA 2009.
[286] R (Middleton) v West Somerset Coroner [2004] 2 AC 182 at [20]; R (Hurst) v London Northern District Coroner [2007] 2 AC 189 at [34]; R (Lepage) v HM Assistant Deputy Coroner for Inner South London [2012] EWHC 1485 (Admin) at [52].

10.126 Following a death in prison custody the police will investigate, and their investigation will take primacy over other investigations. The police will also investigate for the coroner, and will provide the coroner with a report on the death.

10.127 All deaths in prison are also investigated by the PPO, who will conduct a fatal incident investigation (FII).[287] The PPO will decide on the extent of the investigation, depending on the circumstances of the death, and the PPO's remit will include all relevant matters for which NOMS is responsible, or would be responsible if not contracted elsewhere,[288] as well as the clinical care received by the deceased.[289] The purposes of an FII are to: establish the circumstances and events surrounding the death; examine whether any change in operational methods, policy, practice or management arrangements would help prevent a recurrence; examine relevant health issues and assess clinical care; provide explanations and insight for the bereaved relatives; assist the coroner's inquest to fulfil the investigative obligation arising under Article 2 ECHR by ensuring as far as possible that the full facts are brought to light and any relevant failing is exposed, any commendable action or practice is identified, and any lessons from the death are learned.[290] PSI 58/2010 provides guidance on prisons' disclosure of documents to the PPO following a death in custody,[291] as well as the PPO's disclosure policy for FIIs.[292]

10.128 On conclusion of an FII, the PPO produces a report, a copy of which is passed to the coroner and the family for consideration prior to the inquest taking place, and which is also sent to the prison and the relevant health body. The report may make recommendations.[293]

10.129 Where a young person dies in prison custody the establishment must have procedures in place for informing the local safeguarding children board, who will undertake a serious case review.[294]

10.130 Prison staff must co-operate fully with investigations by the police, the PPO, the Health and Safety Executive (where applicable), and the coroner, including in relation to the disclosure of documents.[295]

10.131 Prisons must analyse the evidence generated by the investigations into all deaths in order to learn lessons aimed at reducing future deaths.[296]

Near deaths

10.132 Near-fatal and life-threatening injuries in custody can arise in a range of circumstances, including self-harm/suicide and violence inflicted by third parties.

---

[287] PPO Terms of Reference, para 29(i).
[288] PPO Terms of Reference, para 30.
[289] PPO Terms of Reference, para 33.
[290] PPO Terms of Reference, para 31.
[291] PSI 58/2010, para 1.10, ss 8 and 9, and Annex B.
[292] PSI 58/2010, Annex B. See also: http://www.ppo.gov.uk/disclosure-policy.html.
[293] PPO Terms of Reference, para 36.
[294] See PSI 08/2012 for detailed guidance.
[295] PSI 64/2011, chapters 2 and 12.
[296] PSI 64/2011, chapter 14.

10.133 Where a prisoner sustains near-fatal injuries in prison, for example as a result of an attempted suicide, Article 2 ECHR (see above for details) may in certain circumstances require an Article 2-compliant investigation into the incident, which meets the criteria identified above in relation to Article 2 investigations into deaths.[297] Such an investigation into a near death has become known as a 'D-type inquiry', following the case of R (D) v Secretary of State for the Home Department in which the attempted suicide by a prisoner, resulting in permanent brain damage, was held to require a far-reaching semi-public investigation.[298]

10.134 A D-type investigation involves a number of minimum requirements:[299]

- Written evidence must be published, oral evidence taken and submissions heard in public.[300] The investigative obligation will not be met merely by the publication of a report that has been investigated in private,[301] even where the injured person and his/her representatives are provided with the evidence and afforded opportunities to suggest questions and lines of enquiry, and comment on the draft report.[302]
- The injured person and his/her representatives must be given reasonable access to all relevant evidence in advance of the inquiry.[303]
- There is no requirement that the injured person and his/her representatives must be allowed to cross-examine witnesses,[304] although there should be a mechanism by which they can put questions, eg through counsel to the inquiry or the inquiry's chairperson.[305] They should also be permitted to make oral submissions on lines of enquiry and the questions to be asked.[306]
- The injured person and his/her representatives must be entitled to be present during oral evidence.[307]
- The inquiry must have the power to compel witness attendance.[308]
- The injured person must receive adequate funding for legal representation to allow him/her to be involved in the investigative procedure to the extent necessary to satisfy his/her legitimate interests.[309]

10.135 Whether a D-type inquiry will be required to discharge the investigative duty under Article 2 ECHR will be a fact-sensitive question.[310] Case-law subsequent to R (D) v Secretary of State for the Home Department makes clear that while the near suicide of a prisoner that results in the possibility of serious long-term injury automatically triggers

---

[297] R (D) v Secretary of State for the Home Department [2006] EWCA Civ 143 at [11]; R (Amin) v Secretary of State for the Home Department [2004] 1 AC 653 at [31].
[298] [2006] EWCA Civ 143. The D inquiry, including terms of reference, evidence and final report, is available on the PPO's website: http://www.ppo.gov.uk/disclosure-policy.html.
[299] R (D) v Secretary of State for the Home Department [2006] EWCA Civ 143 at [9].
[300] R (D) v Secretary of State for the Home Department [2006] EWCA Civ 143 at [24] and [35].
[301] R (D) v Secretary of State for the Home Department [2006] EWCA Civ 143 at [21] and [35]; R (Sacker) v HM Coroner for West Yorkshire [2004] 1 WLR 796 at [20]; Edwards v UK (2002) 35 EHRR 487 at [82]–[83] and [87].
[302] R (D) v Secretary of State for the Home Department [2006] EWCA Civ 143 at [21], [42] and [46].
[303] R (D) v Secretary of State for the Home Department [2006] EWCA Civ 143 at [46].
[304] R (D) v Secretary of State for the Home Department [2006] EWCA Civ 143 at [42].
[305] R (D) v Secretary of State for the Home Department [2006] EWCA Civ 143 at [41].
[306] R (D) v Secretary of State for the Home Department [2006] EWCA Civ 143 at [42].
[307] R (D) v Secretary of State for the Home Department [2006] EWCA Civ 143 at [42].
[308] R (D) v Secretary of State for the Home Department [2006] EWCA Civ 143 at [43]–[45].
[309] R (D) v Secretary of State for the Home Department [2006] EWCA Civ 143 at [47].
[310] R (D) v Secretary of State for the Home Department [2006] EWCA Civ 143 at [34].

the investigative obligation under Article 2 ECHR,[311] this obligation may, but does not necessarily, require a *D*-type inquiry.[312] The investigative obligation cannot be met by an internal Prison Service investigation of the facts.[313] Minimum requirements must be met by the overall investigation process – including independence, involvement of the injured prisoner and his/her family, initiation of the investigation must by the state, reasonable promptness, and a sufficient element of public scrutiny – but how they are met involves a degree of flexibility depending on the particular facts.[314] A *D*-type investigation may be required where the public interest and public exposure requires it, where it is necessary to have the full powers of a *D*-type inquiry to ensure that the investigation is efficacious, or where the initial investigation discloses serious conflicts of evidence.[315] It has been stated that the necessity for a *D*-type inquiry will be comparatively rare,[316] or exceptional,[317] and generally speaking there is no need for inquiries into near-suicides to take place in public.[318]

10.136 A *D*-type inquiry is not required where there is no real and immediate risk to a prisoner's life, for example where a prisoner is known to be a regular self-harmer. Such a case does not fall within the ambit of a near-death case,[319] although an Article 3 ECHR-compliant investigation may be required (see above).

10.137 To determine whether a *D*-type investigation is required, consideration should be given to the facts of *R (D) v Secretary of State for the Home Department* (and the facts of the cases cited by the Court of Appeal) and the facts of *R (JL) v Secretary of State for the Home Department*. In both cases *D*-type inquiries were held, with the Court of Appeal in *R (D) v Secretary of State for the Home Department* directing such an inquiry, and the House of Lords indicating in *R (JL) v Secretary of State for the Home Department* that the Secretary of State was right to hold such an inquiry on the facts of that case.[320]

10.138 PSI 64/2011 recognises that there are a range of options available to investigate serious incidents of harm to self or others.[321] A formal investigation under PSO 1300 could be used to consider the circumstances resulting in a near death, depending on whether the facts of the case required a more rigorous *D*-type investigation.

LITIGATION PRACTICALITIES

Exhausting alternative remedies

10.139 The internal prison complaints process should be utilised for any decision where a complaint could result in the decision in question being overturned. Given the

---

[311] *R (JL) v Secretary of State for the Home Department* [2009] 1 AC 588 at [15], [37(i)], [38]–[41], [66] and [113].
[312] *R (JL) v Secretary of State for the Home Department* [2009] 1 AC 588 at [37(iii)], [43]–[45], [77], [96], [104] and [113].
[313] *R (JL) v Secretary of State for the Home Department* [2009] 1 AC 588 at [37(ii)] and [42].
[314] *R (JL) v Secretary of State for the Home Department* [2009] 1 AC 588 at [43], [74]–[76], [78]–[82] and [107].
[315] *R (JL) v Secretary of State for the Home Department* [2009] 1 AC 588 at [45].
[316] *R (JL) v Secretary of State for the Home Department* [2009] 1 AC 588 at [95]–[96] and [108].
[317] *R (JL) v Secretary of State for the Home Department* [2009] 1 AC 588 at [104].
[318] *R (JL) v Secretary of State for the Home Department* [2009] 1 AC 588 at [95]–[108].
[319] *R (P) v Secretary of State for Justice* [2010] 2 WLR 967 at [35]–[41].
[320] *R (JL) v Secretary of State for the Home Department* [2009] 1 AC 588 at [50] and [73].
[321] PSI 64/2011, chapter 14.

time involved in resolving a complaint, which can include an appeal, careful attention needs to be paid to ensure that the three-month time limit under CPR r 54.5 is met. The same reasoning applies to a review application to the Secretary of State against a governor's adjudication finding. It may be possible to argue that a letter before claim will act as a prisoner's complaint where an official complaint form has not been submitted.

10.140 There may be circumstances in which a complaint to the PPO would be beneficial, although the benefits of such a complaint must be carefully weighed against the risks involved. The Administrative Court may conceivably criticise a prisoner for failing to pursue a complaint to the PPO. In the adjudication context the Court has indicated that where the complaint concerns the merits or procedure, the PPO process should be followed. However where the challenge is properly concerned with matters of policy, a claim for judicial review will be the appropriate course.[322] A complaint to the PPO is likely to take the case outside the three-month time limit for judicial review, although were this the case, the Administrative Court might be persuadable to extend time beyond three months. It should be borne in mind that a negative response from the PPO may be harmful to an intended application for judicial review.

10.141 Public funding for judicial review may be refused where alternative remedies have not been pursued. This includes exhaustion of ombudsman schemes and other forms of alternative dispute resolution.[323] It remains to be seen whether funding will be successfully withheld for failure to make a complaint to the PPO.

Identifying the correct defendant

10.142 Close attention should be paid to the source of the decision or omission being challenged, including by reference to the powers conferred on the Secretary of State and prison governors by the PA 1952 and the Prison Rules 1999.

10.143 Many decisions are made by officials, for example within the Prison Service and NOMS, who have received delegated authority from, and therefore make decisions on behalf of, the Secretary of State. A challenge to a national policy, even where it is administered by a local official, should be directed at the Secretary of State, as well as the local decision-maker. By contrast, a challenge to the fact-specific application of a policy should be directed at the local official, eg a prison governor. Similarly, where a decision has been conferred directly on a prison governor by the Prison Rules 1999, or has been devolved to a governor by the Secretary of State, the correct defendant will be the governor. For example, challenges to non-Category A categorisation decisions, or governor adjudications, should both be brought against the relevant governor.

10.144 Relevant defendants in prison law judicial reviews are likely to include the Secretary of State, prison governors, the independent adjudicator, the Parole Board, and the Probation Service or relevant probation trust.

Public funding

10.145 Historically, prison law work has been funded as part of the Criminal Defence Service. Solicitors' firms with contracts to undertake public law work, those pursuing

---

[322] *R (Gifford) v Governor HMP Bure & Secretary of State for Justice* [2014] EWHC 911 (Admin).
[323] Civil Legal Aid (Merits Criteria) Regulations 2013, reg 39.

prison law work under the general criminal contract, and those pursuing prison law work under a 'stand-alone' prison law contact, could apply for public funding certificates to pursue prison law judicial review applications. Judicial review work relating to prison law matters could be carried out as 'associated CLS work' under the general criminal contract. Public funding was assessed and, where appropriate (subject to means and merits assessment), granted by the Legal Services Commission (latterly the Legal Aid Agency).

10.146 For firms conducting prison law work under the general criminal contract or under a stand-alone contract, a great deal of prison law work was completed under the advice and assistance scheme, which allowed public funding to be granted to a prisoner who required advice and assistance regarding his/her 'treatment or discipline in prison'. Grant of funding was subject to the sufficient benefit test, as well as a means assessment. Having worked on a prison law matter under advice and assistance funding, if judicial review became necessary a Legal Help file could be opened or an application could be made for a public funding certificate.

10.147 Changes to public funding for prison law, brought into effect by secondary legislation on 2 December 2013, significantly reduces the ability of prisoners to pursue proceedings in the Administrative Court. Advice and assistance funding will no longer be available for a wide range of treatment and release matters, including categorisation (including for those held in Category A), allocation (eg to a CSC, MBU or DPSD Unit), segregation, searching, visits, reasonable adjustments for disabled prisoners, Parole Board hearings where the Board has no power to direct release (eg pre-tariff consideration of open conditions), resettlement, and licence conditions.[324] The effect is to remove advice and assistance funding for whole swathes of prison law work.

---

[324] For details of the matters being taken out of scope, see the government's paper 'Transforming Legal Aid: Next Steps'.

CHAPTER 11

EDUCATION

INTRODUCTION

11.01 In family life and for society, relatively few issues attract greater importance than the provision of education. The law of education is highly complex and closely entwined with political policy. Where competing public, private and commercial interests converge and conflict, judicial review has become a prevalent means of challenge. In this chapter, we start by providing a brief overview of the education system, followed by a more detailed consideration of the areas in which public law challenges are common, including relevant practice issues, before concluding with a brief examination of the impact of human rights law in this area.[1]

OVERVIEW

The legislative framework

11.02 In England and Wales, the main principles and framework of the schools system are set out in the Education Act 1996 (EA 1996), the School Inspections Act 1996 (SIA), the School Standards and Framework Act 1998 (SSFA) and the Education Act 2002 (EA 2002).

11.03 These Acts consolidated the principles of the Education Act 1944 (EA 1944) and successive statutes such as the Education Reform Act 1988 (ERA). Since 1996, several major pieces of education legislation have been introduced, including the following:

- Teaching and Higher Education Act 1998
- Learning and Skills Act 2000
- Special Educational Needs and Disability Act 2001
- Higher Education Act 2004
- Children Act 2004
- Education Act 2005
- Education and Inspections Act 2006
- Childcare Act 2006
- Further Education and Training Act 2007
- Education and Skills Act 2008

---

[1] For more detailed consideration of the law of education see *Education and the Courts* (3rd edn: Jordan Publishing 2012), *Education Law and Practice* (3rd edn: Jordan Publishing 2010), *The Law of Education* (2nd edn: Jordan Publishing 2004) and *The Law of Education* (LexisNexis: looseleaf).

- Children and Young Persons Act 2008
- Apprenticeships, Skills, Children and Learning Act 2009
- Children, Schools and Families Act 2010
- Academies Act 2010
- Education Act 2011
- Children and Families Act 2014.

11.04 Section 7 of the EA 1996 confirms the principles of education as being those of providing free, efficient full-time education, suitable to the age, ability and aptitude, and any special educational needs that the child may have, for all children during defined, compulsory stages of education.

11.05 The EA 1996 continues to provide the basis for the management of schools in England and Wales, whilst the SSFA introduced a new framework for the legal status of schools.

11.06 The EA 2002 restated the division of compulsory education into four key stages,[2] whilst at the same time creating a legislative distinction between key stages 1 to 3 and key stage 4 of compulsory education (5–7, 7–11, 11–14 and 14–16 years respectively). The EA 2002 also consolidated earlier legislation, altered the basis on which teachers and support staff could be employed and introduced changes regarding admissions to and exclusions from maintained schools.

11.07 The Government of Wales Act 1998 began a series of radical changes to education law in Wales, with transfer of functions from Westminster to Cardiff on an ongoing basis. The National Assembly for Wales (and now the Welsh Assembly Government) can make its own Measures, Orders and Regulations, many of which operate in parallel to statutory provisions in England. The Education and Skills Act 2008 (ESA) further enhanced Welsh independence from Westminster on matters of education. Since education became a devolved function, a significant body of Welsh legislation has already been passed, notably the Education (Wales) Measure 2011, the School Standard and Organisation (Wales) Act 2013, the Further and Higher Education (Governance and Information) (Wales) Act 2014 and the Education (Wales) Act 2014. Where appropriate, the applicable legislation or guidance for Wales is noted below.

Categorisation of schools and colleges

State schools

11.08 State schools in England and Wales are categorised by ownership, funding, pupil age and intake. Section 20(1) of the SSFA provides that schools maintained by local authorities (LAs) shall be divided into the following categories:

(a)   community schools;[3]

---

[2] Key stages were first introduced by the Education Reform Act 1988 upon the introduction of the National Curriculum and the delegation of budgets to schools. The ERA also made important reforms to higher education, taking polytechnics and higher education colleges out of local authority control.

[3] A 'community school' is a mainstream (as opposed to special) school belonging to the LA, including those formerly described as 'county schools'.

(b) foundation schools;[4]
(c) voluntary schools,[5] comprising:
   (i) voluntary aided schools;[6] and
   (ii) voluntary controlled schools;[7]
(d) community special schools;[8] and
(e) foundation special schools.[9]

11.09 Within the above categories, schools are also defined by their pupils' age range namely as either:

(a) a nursery school;[10]
(b) a primary school;[11]
(c) a middle school;[12]
(d) a secondary school (or high school);[13]
(e) a sixth-form.[14]

11.10 Schools defined by their selective pupil intake fall into two main groups; grammar schools and those which otherwise select on the basis of aptitude. Grammar schools select pupils of high ability by examination, usually at 11+, and are designated as such by the SSFA.[15] Some maintained schools select pupils for admission on the basis of aptitude. This is permitted where, at the beginning of the 1997–1998 school year, the school made provision for selection of its pupils by ability or aptitude (the so called 'pre-existing arrangements' exemption). These arrangements must have operated continuously and without significant change to the basis of selection.[16]

11.11 Specialist schools are funded, both by the DfE and sponsorship, with a view to developing talent within PE, sport, performing arts, visual arts, modern foreign

---

[4] A 'foundation school' is a category of maintained school, as defined by the SSFA, s 21(1), and is owned by a trust, foundation body or statutory corporation.
[5] A 'voluntary school' was historically one provided by a church or philanthropist.
[6] A 'voluntary aided school' is a maintained school owned and run by a voluntary organisation.
[7] A 'voluntary controlled school' is a maintained school, the original buildings of which are owned by a voluntary organisation.
[8] A 'special school' is one specifically organised to make educational provision for pupils with special educational needs. LA provision for special educational needs is made either through a community special school or a foundation special school.
[9] See note 8 above, SFFA, s 21(1), and the School Organisation (Foundation Special Schools) (Application of Provisions Relating to Foundations) (England) Regulations 2007 (SI 2007/1329).
[10] A 'nursery school' is a school used wholly or mainly for providing education for children who have attained the age of two, but are under compulsory school age, as provided by the EA 1996, s 6.
[11] A 'primary school' is a school providing primary education; ie education suitable to the requirements of children between two and compulsory school age, children above compulsory school age who are under ten and a half years and older children whom it is expedient to educate with the latter group, as provided by the EA 1996, s 2(1).
[12] A 'middle school' teaches children from about age 8–9 to age 12–13 and is likely to straddle one or more Key Stage boundaries. See EA 1996, s 5(3).
[13] A 'secondary school' is a school providing secondary education; ie education suitable to the requirements of children above compulsory school age who are over ten and a half years and older or whom it is expedient to educate with children over that age, as provided by EA 1996, s 5(2).
[14] A 'sixth-form' denotes education of those over compulsory school age. A 'sixth form' may be part of a secondary school or a separate 'sixth-form college', the latter representing a further education establishment, as opposed to a school.
[15] Section 104, SSFA.
[16] SSFA as amended, s 100.

languages, design technology, engineering or information technology. A specialist school may select up to 10% of its intake by means of carefully-set aptitude tests in one or more specialism.[17]

Academies and free schools

11.12 Following the introduction of the Academies Act 2010 (AA 2010), an ever-increasing number of state schools are funded directly by central government, as opposed to being maintained by LAs. Most of the secondary schools in England are now academies, which are state schools funded by the DfE (the Welsh Assembly is yet to permit academies to be created in Wales), of which there are an increasing number of different types of 'academy', described as 'academy schools', 'free schools, 'alternative provision academies', university technical colleges or 'studio schools'.

11.13 Every new 'academy' is either an 'academy school'[18] or a '16–19 academy'[19] or an 'alternative provision academy'.[20] Some of the older types of 'academy' have retained their original label (such as 'city technology college'), but most of the older institutions' have updated their classification or branding to match the scheme set out in the AA 2010, as amended by the Education Act 2011. Academy schools are, legally, 'independent schools', save that '16–19 academies' and 'alternative provision academies' are not, or not always, called 'independent schools'.[21]

11.14 Free schools are a category of 'academy', which were created in 2010, not by specific legislation but uniquely promoted through guidance and policy documentation. The governing legal framework derives from ss 9–10 of the AA 2010, which provides for the establishment of 'new schools'. Free schools are independent of LAs, but – as with other academies – highly dependent upon funding from the DfE and each will enter into a funding agreement with the Secretary of State before opening. Legally, free schools are the same as academies founded or operated under the AA 2010. The main practical difference between a free school and a normal academy is that a new free school is usually an addition to the local stock of educational establishments, whereas a new academy school often replaces one or more existing schools.

11.15 Decision-making by the Secretary of State in this context, whether or not to enter into academy arrangements or to make an academy order, is amenable to challenge by judicial review on conventional grounds. While academies are independent schools, the nature of their establishment, public funding and the statutory framework under which they operate all point to them being public bodies, some decisions of which are amenable to judicial review.[22]

---

17 SSFA as amended, s 102.
18 AA 2012 as amended, s1A.
19 AA 2012 as amended, s1B.
20 AA 2012 as amended, s1C.
21 Alternative Provision Academies (Consequential Amendments to Act) (England) Order 2012, SI 2012/976 and Alternative Provision Academies and 16 to 19 Academies (Consequential Amendments to Subordinate Legislation) (England) Order 2012, SI 2012/979; EA 1996, s 4(1B) confirms that a '16 to 19 academy' is not a school; nor is it, technically, 'an institution within the further education sector' under the Education Acts. EA 1996, s 4(1C) provides that an 'alternative provision academy' is a school. An 'alternative provision academy' may provide education full-time or part-time and will therefore not always meet the definition of an 'independent school'.
22 Although not authoritatively settled as yet, the issue is likely to be determined consistently with *R v Governors of Haberdashers Aske's Hatcham College Trust Ex p T* [1995] ELR 350. Here Dyson J held that city technology colleges (CTCs) were different from private schools, in that the Secretary of State for

Independent schools

11.16 Independent schools, as defined,[23] are typically financed by means of fees payable by parents and, in some cases, donations and grants from benefactors. The EA 2002 requires providers to register with the DfE and the Welsh Assembly Government respectively.[24] Schools must meet standards covering the quality of education; spiritual, moral, social and cultural development of pupils; welfare, health and safety of pupils; suitability of the people running the school; standards of premises; provision of information and handling of complaints. The authorities are empowered to require an independent school to be inspected by Ofsted in England or Estyn in Wales.[25]

11.17 The curriculum and governance of an independent school is the responsibility of the proprietor and typically administered under the auspices of a board of governors. The curriculum is one of the major aspects considered in a school inspection and both the range and the depth of the curriculum offered must be appropriate for the age, aptitude, ability and any special educational needs of the pupils in the school. A school which fails to meet the required standards may be deleted from the register.[26]

11.18 The relationship between the parent of a pupil registered at an independent school and the body responsible for administering the school is usually contractual. On this basis, independent schools are not generally amenable to judicial review by parents, although it is an implied term that decisions, where appropriate, will be reached in accordance with the principles of natural justice.[27]

Further education

11.19 Under the Further and Higher Education Act 1992 ('FHEA'), most 'further education' institutions became independent of home LAs as 'further education corporations' and 'designated institutions'. These institutions included FE colleges (both general and specialist) and sixth-form colleges. Under the Learning and Skills Act 2000 (LSA), former voluntary aided schools which had joined the further education sector in 1992 as 'designated institutions' also became incorporated. As public corporations, FE institutions are subject to company law and are typically administered under the direction of a governing body (with a role similar to the board of directors of a company). The governing body will be responsible, within the limits imposed by its statutory obligations, for all decisions affecting the institution.

11.20 Under the FHEA, adult education centres which provided largely part-time further education courses for adults continued to be maintained by home LAs. Under the

---

Education was able to exercise a certain amount of control over the running of the schools, decisions made by a CTC on pupil admissions were susceptible to judicial review. The position may, however, be less clear cut in the case of some free schools.

[23] EA 1996, s 463.
[24] Section 158, EA 2002.
[25] For England, see EA 2002, s 162A (details at www.ofsted.gov.uk). For Wales, see EA 2002, s 163 (details at www.estyn.gov.uk).
[26] It is an offence to conduct an independent school which is not registered: EA 2002, s 159.
[27] See *R(B) v Fernhill Manor School* [1994] ELR 67; *R(T) v Governors of Haberdashers' Aske's Hatcham College Trust* [1995] ELR 350 (city technology college amenable to review); *R(S) v Cobham Hall School* [1998] ELR 389 (decision to withdraw an assisted place amenable to review); *R(R) v Muntham House School* [2000] ELR 287 (non-maintainable fee-paying school not amenable to review, although it fell outside the definition of an 'independent school' under EA 1996, s 463).

LSA, any provision made by an LA is now funded by the Learning and Skills Council (LSC) in England, and the Department for Children, Education, Lifelong Learning and Skills (DCELLS) in Wales.[28]

11.21 Legal challenges by way of judicial review against FE institutions are unlikely to prove common. Whilst being statutory bodies and amenable to public law challenge in principle, FE institutions are likely to employ appropriate multi-layered appeal and complaints procedures, which need to be exhausted.[29] In *R (Griffiths) v Lewisham College*,[30] Collins J allowed an application for judicial review where the defendant college had failed to adhere to its own disciplinary procedures in connection with a permanent exclusion. The claimant had not, amongst other matters, been given the stipulated notice period, a clear, advance statement of the nature of the conduct complained of or a proper opportunity to dispute the facts relied upon. A subsequent appeal hearing did not cure these defects, as its scope of review was unduly limited.

Higher education

11.22 Higher education in England and Wales is provided by a single, unified sector of institutions which are independent, self-governing bodies constituted by Royal Charter or by statute to develop their own programmes of study and award individual degrees.

11.23 A programme of 'higher education' is defined as any course fulfilling one of the following descriptions:[31]

(a) a course for the further training of teachers or youth and community workers;
(b) a post-graduate course (including a higher degree course);
(c) a first degree course;
(d) a course for the Diploma of Higher Education;
(e) a course for the Higher National Diploma or Higher National Certificate of the Business & Technician Education Council, or the Diploma in Management Studies;
(f) a course for the Certificate in Education;
(g) a course in preparation for a professional examination at higher level;
(h) a course providing education at a higher level (whether or not in preparation for an examination).

11.24 The governance of a HE establishment is amenable to judicial review, subject to an aggrieved party exhausting alternative means of redress.[32] In particular, universities and other HE institutions must participate in the scheme for dealing with student

---

[28] For further information visit http://www.dcsf.gov.uk/furthereducation. For Wales, visit http://new.wales.gov.uk/topics/educationandskills/.
[29] For example, see *R (Carnell) v Regent's Park College and other* [2008] ELR 268 (permission refused in claim against Higher Education body, where claimant had failed to exhaust alternate remedies).
[30] [2007] EWHC 809 (Admin).
[31] Sections 120(1), 235(2)(e) and Sch 6 of the ERA 1988.
[32] *R (Shi) v King's College London* [2008] ELR 414; *R (Carnell) v Regent's Park College and other* [2008] ELR 268; *R (Clarke) v Cardiff University* [2009] NPC 105 (successful challenge against BVC provider upon grounds of substantive unfairness); *K (Martin) v University College London* [2012] ELR 487 (unsuccessful challenge to establishment's acceptance of withdrawal, following change of mind by student).

complaints set up under Part 2 of the Higher Education Act 2004 (HEA).[33] The operator of the student complaints scheme under s 13 of the HEA is the 'Office of the Independent Adjudicator for Higher Education' (OIA).

11.25 Anyone who was or is registered as a student at a participating HE institution can complain to the OIA about the following matters; a programme of study or research for which he or she is or was registered; a service provided to him or her by a HE institution; a final decision by a HE institution's disciplinary or appeal body. There is, however, no general obligation on the OIA to express an opinion on the strength of a particular allegation, for example a complaint of disability discrimination, although it is possible for it to do so in the exercise of its discretion.[34]

11.26 An aggrieved student must exhaust any internal complaints procedure before approaching the OIA. The OIA will not investigate a complaint if it relates to a matter of academic judgment[35] or if the matter is or has been the subject of court proceedings. A claim for judicial review, in the event of dissatisfaction, will lie against the HE institution and/or OIA on conventional public law grounds.[36]

SUBSTANTIVE AREAS OF CHALLENGE

School organisation

11.27 Detailed consideration of the law relating to school organisation, including establishment of new or alteration of existing state schools, is beyond the scope of this work.[37] For the most part, the threatened closure of a school is the most likely subject matter of a public law challenge in this context.[38]

---

[33] The traditional role of the 'Visitor', who used to investigate student and staff complaints, was abolished in the HEA, s 20.
[34] *R (Maxwell) v Office of the Independent Adjudicator & University of Salford* [2010] ELR 637 (upheld on appeal [2012] ELR 538).
[35] It is extremely difficult, in any event, to challenge an exercise of academic judgement: see *R (Vijayatunga) v Her Majesty the Queen in Council* [1989] 3 WLR 13; *R (Bashir) v Cranfield University* [1999] ELR 317; *R (Persaud) v Cambridge University* [2001] ELR 480; *R (Echendu) v University of Leeds* [2012] ELR 449; *R (Kwao) v University of Keele* [2013] ELR 266.
[36] *R (Siborurema) v Office of the Independent Adjudicator* [2008] ELR 209 (unsuccessful procedural challenge, establishing amenability of adjudicator to review); *R (Arratoon) v Office of the Independent Adjudicator* [2009] ELR 186 (unsuccessful complaint against relief: adjudicator could not be criticised for failing to make a recommendation which had not been sought by the complainant); *R (Budd) v Office of the Independent Adjudicator* [2010] ELR 579 (unsuccessful challenge on procedural grounds); *R (Sandhar) v Office of the Independent Adjudicator* [2012] ELR 160 (apparent bias: unsuccessful challenge to independence of adjudicator owing to collective funding of position by higher education institutions); *R (Cardao-Pito) v Office of the Independent Adjudicator* [2012] ELR 231 (successful procedural challenge based on inadequacy of reasoning regarding compensation recommendations); *R (Mustafa) v Office of the Independent Adjudicator* [2013] ELR 446 (unsuccessful challenge to adjudicator's rejection of a compliant on the grounds that the subject matter – the existence and extent of plagiarism – was a matter of academic judgement); *R (Burger) v Office of the Independent Adjudicator* [2013] EWCA Civ 1803 (affirming [2013] ELR 331) (errors on the part of the deputy adjudicator were not material as the ultimate decision would have been the same in any event); *R (Wilson) v Office of the Independent Adjudicator* [2014] ELR 273 (unsuccessful challenge to partial rejection of complaints and of measure of compensation recommended).
[37] See the *Law of Education* (Butterworths: looseleaf), Division A, Chapter 3 for further detail.
[38] Although the establishment of institutions can also form the subject matter of challenge: *R (Chandler) v Camden LBC and others* [2009] BLGR 4127, approved [2010] ELR 192 (failed challenge to the proposed establishment of a city academy); *R (Moyse) v Secretary of State for Education* [2012] ELR 551 (academies: Secretary of State not bound to accept majority parental view against conversion); *R (British Humanist Association & Others) v Richmond upon Thames LBC & Others* [2013] ELR 79 (unsuccessful challenge to LA approval of plans to establish voluntary-aided Catholic primary and secondary schools); *R (Governing*

11.28 Parents reasonably expect schools to remain open and, accordingly, Part 2, ss 15–17 of the Education and Inspection Act 2006 (EIA) requires LAs and governors to publicise proposed closures (or discontinuances as they are described within the EIA). Detailed requirements for the publishing of proposals are provided at Sch 2 and in the regulations made under s 15 of the EIA.[39] Every closure proposal must begin with consultation under s 16 of the EIA. Schedule 2 of the EIA provides for the detailed consideration of such proposals by the home LA and the procedure for independent review by the adjudicator.[40]

11.29 Rural primary schools and special schools have added protection from closure,[41] although the latter are subject to a fast-track closure scheme where the pupils are thought by the Secretary of State to be at risk to their health, safety or welfare.[42]

11.30 It remains to be seen whether, as intended, improved consultation and closer independent scrutiny, as provided under Part 2 of the EIA, bolsters public assurance and reduces the number of judicial review applications in this context.[43]

11.31 The opening, altering and closing of state schools in Wales is principally governed by Part 3 of the School Standards and Organisation (Wales) Act 2013, supplemented by comprehensive statutory guidance in a code of practice published by the Welsh Government in July 2013; the 'School Organisation Code'.

Body of Warren Comprehensive School) v Secretary of State for Education [2014] EWHC 338 (Admin) (academies: Secretary of State's decision to impose an academy order was premature on the basis of failure to adequately consider alternate federation agreement). Likewise, cessation of projects – *R (Luton Borough Council & Ors) v Secretary of State for Education* [2011] ELR 222 (successful challenge of decision to stop certain school building projects on the basis of inadequate consultation and failure to have regard to equality legislation) – and LA interventions regarding governance – *R (Governing Body of Uplands Junior School) v Leicester City Council* [2014] ELR 143 (unsuccessful challenge to LA's decision to intervene in the governance of school following non-compliance with a warning notice issued under the Education and Inspections Act 2006, s 60).

[39] School Organisation (Establishment and Discontinuance of Schools) (England) Regulations 2007 (SI 2007/1288).
[40] Appointed under SSFA 1998, s 25(3).
[41] EIA, ss 15(4) and 16.
[42] EIA, s 17.
[43] Examples of cases decided before and following the above legislative changes include: *R (N) v Leeds CC* [1999] ELR 324 (claim dismissed where consultation effective); *R (T) v Secretary of State for Education* [2000] Ed CR 652 (use of wrong language in decision letter implied application of wrong test by minister upon approval of reorganisation plan); *R (Beaumont) v Kirklees MBC* [2001] ELR 204 (council resolution to close school quashed owing to substantial risk of bias); *R (B and C) v Lambeth LBC* [2001] HWHC 515 (Admin) (unsuccessful claim based upon alleged failure to have appropriate regard to SEN requirements of pupils); *R (WB) v School Organisation Committee for Leeds* [2003] ELR 67 (unsuccessful challenge based upon inadequate notice of consultation meeting); *R (Louden) v School Organisation Committee for Bury* [2002] EWHC 2749 (Admin) (claim on various grounds dismissed on merits and by reference to delay); *R (P) v Schools Adjudicator* [2007] BLGR 346 (unsuccessful challenge of decision to approve the discontinuance of a maintained primary school); *R (Elphinstone) v Westminster CC and others* [2009] ELR 24 (unsuccessful challenge based upon allegedly defective consultation); *R (Parr) v Hertfordshire CC* [2008] EWHC 3379 (Admin) (successful challenge to primary school closure decision where proposal failed to adequately address SEN provision); *R (McDougal) v Liverpool CC* [2009] ELR 510 (unsuccessful challenge to comprehensive school closure).

School admissions

Introduction

11.32 School admission arrangements remain one of the most contentious and extensively litigated areas within the education sphere. For many parents, especially in rural areas, there is only one school that is both suitable for their child's education and within an appropriate travelling distance. For others, particularly those living in urban areas, there are often several suitable, accessible schools and a real element of choice exists. The school admissions process attempts to resolve the inherent conflicts within an administrative system based on parental preference, but where places at preferred establishments are limited and often oversubscribed.

11.33 Judicial review has played a significant role in shaping the law and practice relating to school admissions and continues to offer an appropriate means of challenge in some cases. This section provides an overview of the legal framework and its guiding principles, highlighting reported cases of continuing relevance.

The legal framework

11.34 The principle legislation is Part III of the SSFA, ss 84–98 as amended, which is supplemented by comprehensive statutory guidance, namely the School Admissions Code and the School Admission Appeals Code.[44]

11.35 The school admissions system in England[45] applies to community, foundation and voluntary schools and to academies, whilst nursery school admissions are handled separately.[46] The application of the system to academies derives contractually from the institution's public funding agreement, whilst other 'state' schools are included in the system by statute.

Co-ordination of school admissions

11.36 Each school is served by an 'admission authority' which has initial responsibility for allocating places. The admission authority must know how many children it can and will admit in each relevant year and, in the event of oversubscription, it must have a transparent policy by which it will accord precedence to applications. To enable multiple and/or out-of-area applications, each admission authority must also co-ordinate its annual admissions process with those of its neighbouring admission authorities.

11.37 The admission authority for each of the five main school categories is summarised below:

School	Admission authority
Academies	Academy Trust

---

[44] The 2012 School Admissions Appeals Code applies to school admission appeals lodged on or after 1 February 2012, while the 2012 School Admissions Code applies to school admissions from the school year 2013–2014 onwards. Save where indicated, such Codes apply with immediate effect; *R (Buckinghamshire CC) v School Admissions IAP for Buckinghamshire* [2010] ELR 172.
[45] In Wales, see the School Admissions Code and the School Admission Appeals Code for Wales (July 2009).
[46] See SSFA as amended, s 98.

School	Admission authority
Community schools	Local authority
Foundation schools	Governing body
Voluntary-aided schools	Governing body
Voluntary-controlled schools	Local authority

11.38 Academies and free schools all comply with the School Admissions Code and the School Admissions Appeals Code, as if they were maintained schools, as a stipulation of their funding agreements. The admission of pupils can be controversial at a free school if, for example, the proposers wish to give priority to their children or those of teaching and/or non-teaching staff. Any such adjustments to the usual criteria are a matter for individual negotiation on proposal of the institution. Where an academy or free school replaces an existing school, the pupils from the existing school will, in practice, be enrolled automatically. Every academy or free school will have or use an independent appeal panel for the hearing of appeals by parents (and by prospective sixth-form pupils) against refusal of admission.

11.39 In recognition of the need among parents for certainty and clarity, admission authorities are required to work closely together. School admissions forums are no longer required in England,[47] but co-ordination of annual admission rounds will continue.[48]

11.40 In Wales, as before, LAs are obliged to establish an admission forum to advise it on the exercise of its admission functions and the admission authorities for maintained schools in its area.[49] The role of an admissions forum is set out in reg 3 of the Education Admissions (Admission Forums) (Wales) Regulations 2003, while the formalities regarding membership are set out in reg 5. The LA and admission authorities must have regard to the advice of the admissions forum in carrying out their respective functions.[50]

11.41 In England, each LA must organise a 'qualifying scheme' to co-ordinate arrangements for pupil admissions to primary and secondary schools in its area.[51] The process, as summarised in the School Admissions Code, is as follows:[52]

- All schools must have admission arrangements that clearly set out how children will be admitted, including the criteria that will be applied if there are more applications than places at the school. Admission arrangements are determined by admission authorities.

- Admission authorities must set ('determine') admission arrangements annually. Where changes are proposed to admission arrangements, the admission authority

---

[47] Education Act 2011, s 34 repealing (not in Wales) some of SSFA 1998, s 85A.
[48] School Admissions (Admission Arrangements and Co-ordination of Admission Arrangements) (England) Regulations 2012, SI 2012/8.
[49] SSFA 1998, s 86A.
[50] SSFA 1998, s 85A.
[51] SSFA 1998, s 88M and s 88N and, now, the School Admissions (Admission Arrangements and Co-ordination of Admission Arrangements) (England) Regulations 2012, SI 2012/8 (especially Sch 2), which apply to the co-ordination of school admissions from the school year 2014–2015 onwards.
[52] For Wales, see the corresponding summary in Chapter 2 of the School Admissions Code 2009.

must first publicly consult on those arrangements.[53] If no changes are made to admission arrangements, they must be consulted on at least every seven years. Consultation must be for a minimum of eight weeks and must take place between 1 November and 1 March of the year before those arrangements are to apply. This consultation period allows parents, other schools, religious authorities and the local community to raise any concerns about proposed admission arrangements.

- Once all arrangements have been determined, arrangements can be objected to and referred to the schools adjudicator by 30 June. Any decision of the adjudicator must be acted on by the admission authority and admission arrangements amended accordingly. The LA will collate and publish all the admission arrangements in the area in a single composite prospectus.

- In the normal admissions round parents apply to the local authority in which they live for places at their preferred schools. Parents are able to express a preference for at least three schools. The application can include schools outside the local authority where the child lives: a parent can apply for a place for their child at any state-funded school in any area. If a school is undersubscribed, any parent that applies must be offered a place. When oversubscribed, a school's admission authority must rank applications in order against its published oversubscription criteria and send that list back to the local authority. Published admission arrangements must make clear to parents that a separate application must be made for any transfer from nursery to primary school, and from infant to junior school.

- All preferences are collated and parents then receive an offer from the local authority at the highest preference school at which a place is available. For secondary schools, the offer is made on or about 1 March (known as national offer day) in the year in which the child will be admitted. For primary schools, the offer is made on or about 16 April, in the year in which the child will be admitted.

- Parents, and in some circumstances children, have the right to appeal against an admission authority's decision to refuse admission. The admission authority must set out the reasons for the decision, that there is a right of appeal and the process for hearing such appeals. The admission authority must establish an independent appeals panel to hear the appeal. The panel will decide whether to uphold or dismiss the appeal. Where a panel upholds the appeal the school is required to admit the child.

The schools adjudicator

11.42 The schools adjudicator[54] has a key role in ensuring a fair admissions system by enforcing statutory requirements and the mandatory provisions of the School Admissions Code. An objection to an admission arrangement may be referred to the adjudicator, as prescribed.[55]

11.43 Section 151 of the ESA places a new duty on the adjudicator to consider the legality of admission arrangements referred to him via the LA report or the Secretary of

---

[53] Except where the change is an increase to a school's published admission number or is made to comply with any mandatory requirements of the Code or the School Admissions (Admission Arrangements and Co-ordination of Admission Arrangements) (England) Regulations 2012.
[54] The Adjudicator is appointed under SSFA, s 25. In Wales, the role of the Adjudicator is undertaken by the National Assembly.
[55] School Admissions (Admission Arrangements and Co-ordination of Admission Arrangements) (England) Regulations 2012, Chapter 6. For Wales, see Education (Determination of Admission Arrangements) (Wales) Regulations 2006 (SI 2006/174).

State. The adjudicator may also consider any admission arrangements that come to his attention by other means, if he considers they may not be compliant.

11.44 For obvious reasons, it is desirable that admission arrangements are consistent from one year to the next and the circumstances in which these can be altered or varied are closely circumscribed.[56] An admission authority must implement any direct decision and may revise its admission arrangements in light of a decision by the adjudicator upholding, or partially upholding, an objection to the admission arrangements of another school.

11.45 A decision by the adjudicator must be upheld in the admission arrangements for two subsequent school years, promoting continuity and preventing a school from being required to meet the same objection in successive years.[57]

11.46 In *R (Governing Body of London Oratory School) v Schools Adjudicator*,[58] the claimant challenged the decision of the adjudicator that he had jurisdiction to determine an objection, concerning interview arrangements, from the governors of a local primary school. The adjudicator had upheld a similar objection made in the previous year. On judicial review, the court had quashed this decision on a number of grounds, but declined substantive relief on the basis that it was too late for the claimant to be reasonably required to change its admission process by omitting interviews. In the circumstances, the court had not remitted the matter back to the adjudicator as there was only one decision that the adjudicator could lawfully take at that point, irrespective of the merits, namely to dismiss the primary school's objection for reasons of practicability.

11.47 Dismissing the claimant's application for judicial review, Crane J held that there had been no earlier decision by the adjudicator for the purposes of regulations,[59] the original adjudication having been quashed. The underlying purpose of the statutory framework was to ensure that parties, if practicable, were able to obtain an adjudicator's decision on the merits of their objections and the adjudicator has not, in these circumstances, erred in accepting jurisdiction to consider the matter afresh.

11.48 If the adjudicator receives an objection, he may consider admission arrangements for the school as a whole, not simply the specific complaint raised, and also their effect upon other admission arrangements in the relevant area. The adjudicator may also consider admission arrangements that he considers to be complex, including those using convoluted points systems, and amend or replace the same.

11.49 However, the latitude afforded to the adjudicator is not boundless. In *R (Wandsworth LBC) v Schools Adjudicator*,[60] the claimant acted as admission authority for a college (EBC) that operated a selective admissions policy under which it could choose up to 33% of its pupils on the basis of aptitude. Objections were made to the

---

[56] See School Admissions (Admission Arrangements and Co-ordination of Admission Arrangements) (England) Regulations 2012, regs 19–20.
[57] See School Admissions (Admission Arrangements and Co-ordination of Admission Arrangements) (England) Regulations 2012, reg 22.
[58] [2005] ELR 484.
[59] In this case, the Education (Objections to Admission Arrangements) Regulations 1999, for which now see the School Admissions (Admission Arrangements and Co-ordination of Admission Arrangements) (England) Regulations 2012, Chapter 6.
[60] [2004] ELR 274.

adjudicator on the basis that the policy resulted in an unequal spread of ability across the area and, in particular, produced a damaging effect upon a local secondary school. The claimant demonstrated by intake analysis that the policy caused no distorting effect on local admissions and that the respective intakes of the two establishments were broadly comparable. Notwithstanding, the adjudicator decided to require EBC to reduce its proportion of selective places to 30% in light of the objections. Allowing the claimant's application for judicial review, Goldring J held that the adjudicator had acted unlawfully:[61]

> 'Once the defendant decided that the objectors were wrong in their fundamental complaint regarding an imbalance in intake, it seems to me it made it difficult rationally to justify any interference with it ... The objective of creating a more balanced intake by reference to the intake into other schools in Wandsworth became by definition impossible to achieve as far as EBC was concerned for it was balanced already ....'

11.50 Other challenges have succeeded on conventional public law grounds. In *R (Watford GS for Girls & another) v Schools Adjudicator*,[62] the adjudicator had reduced the permitted percentage of pupils that could be selected on the basis of aptitude by the claimant school from 35% to 25% following objections by some local schools. Allowing the claimant's application, Collins J held that the adjudicator had failed to take into account all relevant considerations. Following earlier parental objection, the school had been forced to reduce its selection on the basis of aptitude from 50% to 35%. No further objections had been received by parents and, otherwise, the aim of having more pupils accepted on the basis of proximity to the school might be achieved in other ways. Accordingly, the adjudicator's decision was quashed.

11.51 In *R (Governing Body of Drayton Manor High School) v Schools Adjudicator*,[63] the claimant school applied for judicial review of the adjudicator's decision to change one of the criteria it applied in the event of oversubscription. Whilst the adjudicator had been entitled on the evidence to find that the criterion indirectly discriminated against poorer families, it was unable to ascertain whether he had addressed the school's counter submission that the substituted criterion would disadvantage other groups. Accordingly, the decision was quashed on the basis that the adjudicator had failed to provide adequate reasons and/or take account of a fundamental part of the school's case. It was not possible to demonstrate on the evidence that its scheme was inequitable and thus in need of rectification.

Parental preference, admission numbers and oversubscription

11.52 At the heart of the admissions system are three key considerations: parental preference, admission numbers and oversubscription. In terms of individual participation, the admissions system must provide parents with an opportunity to make informed decisions about school places and to fully communicate their preferences. In terms of administration, the number of available school places must be ascertained and a fair and transparent allocation method adopted where the number of places exceeds demand.

---

[61] [2004] ELR 274 at [72].
[62] [2004] ELR 40. See also *R (Governing Body of London Oratory School) v Schools Adjudicator* [2005] ELR 162 (a case concerning selection by a faith school on the basis of interview; a practice now outlawed under SSFA, s 88A).
[63] [2009] ELR 127.

Parental preference

11.53 The underlying aim of legislative developments in this area, in particular since the 1980s, has been to actively promote choice and involvement by parents in the education of their children within the state sector. Due regard to parental wishes is an overriding obligation in public education provision, as provided by s 9 of the EA 1996:[64]

> 'In exercising or performing all their respective powers and duties under the Education Acts, the Secretary of State and local education authorities shall have regard to the general principle that pupils are to be educated in accordance with the wishes of their parents, so far as that is compatible with the provision of efficient instruction and training and the avoidance of unreasonable public expenditure.'

11.54 In the context of school admissions, this guiding principle of 'parental preference' is enshrined in s 86(1) of the SSFA which provides that every LA must enable the parent of a child in its area to 'express a preference as to the school at which he wishes education to be provided for his child ... and to give reasons for his preference'. The right to express a 'preference' in respect of nursery, primary and secondary school provision is vested in the parent, not the child.[65]

11.55 However, a LA is not under an absolute obligation to educate a pupil in accordance with parental preference. A LA must do no more than have regard to this guiding principle, weighing parental preference in the balance together with and against other relevant considerations. The obligation is no more than a 'target' duty, as confirmed in the case of *R (Watt) v Kesteven CC*.[66]

11.56 A Roman Catholic parent sought a declaration that the defendant LA was liable to pay school fees in respect of Catholic boarding school places for his sons, having declined to send his children to a local independent secondary school on religious grounds. The LA was in fact willing to fully fund the places at an independent school, with which arrangements had been agreed, or otherwise to make a contribution to the

---

[64] EA 1996, s 9 is to be construed widely, so as to include any expenditure incurred by a public body; '*public expenditure*' is not limited to the costs of the LA or to the costs arising under its education budget: *Haining v Warrington Borough Council* [2014] ELR 212.
[65] See SSFA, s 94.2A (the wider implications of which are considered at **11.151** below).
[66] [1955] 1 QB 408. See also *R (W) v Gwynedd CC* (1993) *The Times*, June 25, 1993 (failed challenge against school's refusal to confirm to a parent that his daughter would not be placed against her will into classes that were taught in Welsh); *R (Ali) v Inner London Education Authority* [1990] 2 Admin LR 822 (an alleged failure to provide sufficient places for primary school children in the Tower Hamlets area was not amenable to review because, in the circumstances, there was no prospect of the court exercising its discretion to grant relief); *R (O) v Hackney LBC* [2007] ELR 405 (LA had not acted unlawfully in rejecting a parent's wishes, having provided a place at a suitable school which it was reasonably practicable for the pupil to attend). For examples of challenges in the context of the 'suitability' of education provided see: *R (G) v Westminster City Council* [2004] ELR 135 (whether the duty arising under s 19 of the EA 1996 to make arrangements for the provision of suitable education had been triggered); *R (Southern) v Oxfordshire CC* [2004] ELR 489 (unsuccessful challenge of LA refusal to make a discretionary grant to assist a child of exceptional intelligence); *R (Jones and others) v Ceredigion CC* [2004] ELR 506 (successful challenge to transport funding refusal where no suitable arrangements existed for pupils to be registered locally); *R (R and other) v Leeds CC* [2006] ELR 25 (conversely, LA entitled to withdraw free school transport for out-of-area school where suitable local provision existed); *R (C) v Brent LBC* [2006] ELR 435 (unsuccessful challenge to LA decision as to suitability of pupil referral unit placement); *R (R) v Kent CC* [2007] ELR 648 (unsuccessful challenge to the suitability of provision for a pupil who had been subject to bullying at the school named by the defendant LA).

fees payable at the boarding school, as there was no grammar school provision within the area in which the family resided. Dismissing the parent's appeal, Lord Denning MR stated:[67]

> '[The section] does not say that pupils must in all cases be educated in accordance with the wishes of their parents. It only lays down a general principle to which the county council must have regard. This leaves it open to the county council to have regard to other things as well, and also to make exceptions to the general principle if it thinks fit to do so. It cannot, therefore, be said that a county council is at fault simply because it does not see fit to comply with the parent's wishes ....'

11.57 Once ascertained, the LA and the governing body of a maintained school are obliged to comply with the expressed preference of a parent regarding school admission, unless a lawful exception applies.[68] The circumstances under which parental preference can be overridden are limited as follows:

- if compliance with the preference would prejudice the provision of efficient education or the efficient use of resources;
- the school is a grammar school or otherwise selects some pupils on ability or aptitude as permitted; or
- the child has within the previous two years been excluded from two or more schools.

Prejudice to the provision of efficient education or the efficient use of resources

11.58 Under s 86(3)(a) of the SSFA the duty to make educational provision in accordance with parental preference will not apply 'if compliance with the preference would prejudice the provision of efficient education of the efficient use of resources'. For the most part, this qualification on parental choice is only a relevant issue where an application is made in respect of a school that is oversubscribed, as considered below. In the context of infant school admissions, specific regard must be had to the statutory restriction of class sizes.[69]

11.59 Such prejudice may, however, arise in other more specific circumstances. In *R (N and E) v Governors of the Hasmonean High School*,[70] the Court of Appeal considered the position of two prospective pupils whose admission had been refused by the defendant's appeal committee taking into account their respective special educational needs and the existing demands on the school's resources. The parents alleged that allocation on this basis amounted to selection by ability and was thus unlawful. The defendant considered that the prejudicial effect likely upon admission of either pupil outweighed parental preference. Dismissing the parents' application for judicial review, the Court of Appeal held that whilst academic ability was clearly a factor in the decision not to admit, there was compelling evidence that the difficulty in providing a suitable, appropriately supported education for each pupil had been a significant factor. The admission of either pupil to the school, which was already oversubscribed, was also likely to be detrimental to the education of the other children and the appeal committee had not erred in these circumstances.

---

[67] [1955] 1 QB 408 at p 424.
[68] See SSFA, s 86(2).
[69] See SSFA, s 1.
[70] [1994] ELR 343.

Selection

11.60 Parental choice is qualified where compliance with any preference would be incompatible with permissible selective admission arrangements. Save as provided below, any admissions policy based on selection is prohibited:

- grammar school arrangements;[71]
- any arrangements for selection based upon aptitude which were in place for the school year 1997–98 and which have not changed;[72]
- where the arrangements are designed to secure that in any year the pupils admitted to the school in any relevant age group are representative of all levels of ability among applicants for admission and no level of ability is substantially over or under represented (so called 'banding' arrangements);[73] or
- where the school has one or more specialism (music, sport, art etc) and selective admissions by ability or aptitude do not exceed 10% in any relevant age group.[74]

Exclusion

11.61 Where a child has been permanently excluded from two or more schools, a parent can still express a preference regarding admission, but the requirement to comply with that preference is removed for a period of two years from the date on which the latest exclusion took place. This exception does not apply to the following:

- children with statements of special educational needs;[75]
- children who were below compulsory school age when excluded;[76]
- children who were reinstated following a permanent exclusion;[77] or
- children who would have been reinstated if it had been practicable to do so.[78]

Informing and ascertaining parental preference

11.62 To properly give effect to parental preference, parents must be placed in a position to make informed decisions when applying for places. LAs must publish online – with hard copies available for those who do not have access to the internet – a composite prospectus for parents by 12 September in the offer year,[79] which contains the admissions arrangements and any supplementary information forms for each of the state-funded schools in the local authority area to which parents can apply (for instance all schools, including academies).

11.63 As part of the co-ordination role described above, each LA will ascertain parental preference by sending out a form which allows parents to rank choices of schools. LAs must provide a common application form that enables parents to express their preference for a place at any state-funded school, with a minimum of three preferences

---

[71] See SSFA, s 104.
[72] See SSFA, s 100.
[73] See SSFA, s 101.
[74] See SSFA, s 102.
[75] See SSFA, s 98(7).
[76] See SSFA, s 87(4)(c).
[77] See SSFA, s 87(4)(a).
[78] See SSFA, s 87(4)(b).
[79] See regs 5, 6 and Sch 2 of the School Information (England) Regulations 2008.

in rank order, allowing them to give reasons for their preferences. Forms must afford parents the opportunity to positively express reasons for their preference, without making assumptions.

11.64 In *R (Clark & others) v Rotherham BC*,[80] the Court of Appeal upheld a public law challenge to the defendant's allocation of secondary school places. The LA provisionally allocated places to children by home catchment area. Parents were advised that if they were happy with allocation on this basis, no further action was required. If a different school was preferred, parents were advised to complete and return a specified form. A number of parents, whose expressed preferences had been declined, claimed that the authority's policy and the individual decisions refusing to admit the children to their preferred school were unlawful on the ground that the statutory requirements had not been met. Upholding the parents' objection, Lord Bingham LCJ rejected the legality of a system based upon inference or acquiescence:[81]

> 'Because parents who were happy with the provisionally-allocated school (in whose catchment area they lived) were not invited to express a preference, it followed that they were not invited to give reasons. On no reasonable reading of the language used could it be said that the authority made arrangements which enabled parents happy to accept their provisional allocation to give reasons. The system which the authority established was not in any meaningful sense such as to give them that opportunity. That was, in truth, because they were not invited to express a preference either.'

11.65 Similarly, in *R (K) v Newham LBC*,[82] a devout Muslim, whose daughter was about to commence her secondary school education, successfully applied for judicial review of the authority's decision not to allocate a place at a single sex school in accordance with his religious beliefs. Whilst the authority had issued a leaflet to parents outlining its school selection policy and confirming that preference for same sex education was one of its criteria for selection, the authority had simply inferred such a preference where parents indicated a same sex school as their first choice. Moreover, there had been no indication whether the claimant's religious beliefs had been considered in reaching the decision. Collins J held that there ought to be a means of separately identifying religious preference and that attention ought to be drawn to that in guidance literature provided by the authority. Furthermore, where applications were made to a single sex school, there ought to be some means of ensuring that the authority knew who deliberately made the choice to apply for single sex education. It was clear that neither the authority nor the appeal panel appreciated the importance of the claimant's religious convictions and the decision was remitted.

11.66 Accordingly, there is a need for a positive expression of parental preference where stipulated; arrangements based upon silence or acquiescence will not suffice.

Admission numbers

11.67 If a school has an available place for a prospective pupil, expressed parental preference must be given effect to. Accordingly, the starting point for each admissions authority is to determine the number of pupils in each relevant age group that it proposes to admit to the school in that academic year (its 'published admission number' or 'PAN').[83] The authority must also establish the number of boarding school and day

---

[80] [1998] ELR 152.
[81] [1998] ELR 152 at 183.
[82] [2002] ELR 390.
[83] See SSFA, s 88D(1). For Wales, see SSFA, s 89A(1).

places as appropriate.[84] The admission number does not include pupils already of compulsory school age and already within the school, for example those simply moving up a year within the same establishment.

11.68 Some exceptions apply. Admission arrangements for nursery places are dealt with separately.[85] A child with a statement of special educational needs will be allocated a school place in accordance with his or her assessment.[86]

Oversubscription

11.69 Many challenges have arisen out of the selection criteria applied by admission authorities in the event of oversubscription. Necessarily, when a school has more applications than the number of places that have been determined in accordance s 88D of the SSFA, some scheme or policy must be applied to determine which applications should be successful.[87]

11.70 In *Choudhury v Governors of Bishop Challoner RC Comprehensive School*, the House of Lords recognised the inevitability of making choices that were popular with some parents, but not with others:[88]

> '... when a school is over-subscribed ... [and] ... "compliance with the preference" of all applicants would prejudice proper education at the school through overcrowding ... it is absolutely necessary that the school should have an admissions policy of some kind in order to select from all those who have expressed such preference which of them are to be accepted and which rejected. Since whatever admissions criteria are adopted the selection of some only of the applicants will necessarily result in defeating the parental preference of those who are rejected, what reason is there for Parliament to object to any given set of criteria being adopted? ... if the school is over-subscribed, the parental wishes of some parents must be defeated whatever criteria are adopted ....'

11.71 Provided that the various statutory requirements and mandatory aspects of the School Admissions Code are observed, admissions authorities retain considerable latitude when determining admission criteria, as confirmed by Lloyd LJ in *R (Governors of John Ball Primary School) v Greenwich LBC*:[89]

> '... I do not regard efficient education or the efficient use of resources as being the sole source of lawful policy. Local education authorities were always entitled to have an admission policy ... see *Cumings v Birkenhead Corporation* [1972] 1 Ch 12, per Lord Denning at p 37C. In my judgment a local education authority can have any reasonable policy they think fit, provided it does not conflict with their duties under [s 86 of the SSFA], or any other enactment ....'

11.72 *R (Governors of John Ball Primary School) v Greenwich LBC* concerned the prohibition on discrimination against pupils from other LAs, so-called 'out-of-area' applications, as provided by s 86(8) of the SSFA. Discrimination may be alleged to arise

---

[84] See SSFA, s 88D(2). For Wales, see SSFA, s 89A(2).
[85] See SSFA, s 98(4).
[86] See SSFA, s 98(7).
[87] Extensive guidance on the setting of fair oversubscription is contained in the respective Schools Admissions Codes for England & Wales.
[88] [1992] 2 AC 182 per Lord Browne-Wilkinson at 193D–G.
[89] (1990) 88 LGR 589 at 599.

directly, as in the case of John Ball Primary School, or indirectly, for example, where a geographical restriction is placed on the grant of scholarships or other awards provided under s 518 of the EA 1996.[90]

11.73 The prohibition on out-of-area discrimination is strict and cannot be justified with reference to any other educational duty.[91] Whilst catchment areas may lawfully follow part of a LA boundary,[92] those which do so closely may be susceptible to challenge.[93]

11.74 It is unlawful for a school to discriminate against a child on the grounds of his or her religion or belief.[94] However, in the event of oversubscription, faith schools are permitted to use faith-based oversubscription criteria in order to give a higher priority to children who are members of, or who practise, their faith or denomination.[95] Such criteria must be framed so as not to conflict with other legislation, such as equality and race relations legislation, and the mandatory provisions of the School Admissions Code. Such criteria are liable to be strictly construed.[96]

11.75 Admissions may be determined by faith, but not by ethnicity. In *R (E) v Governing Body of JFS and others*,[97] a child whose father was Jewish by birth, but whose mother was Jewish by conversion, applied for a place at a publicly maintained Jewish school. The school was oversubscribed and its policy was to give priority to children who were recognised as Jewish by the Office of the Chief Rabbi. The Office of the Chief Rabbi did not recognise the validity of the mother's conversion to Judaism because it had not been conducted by an Orthodox synagogue. It only regarded a child as Jewish if his or her mother was Jewish and the child was thus refused admission to the school. On appeal, the Court of Appeal held that requirement imposed by the school was a test of ethnicity which contravened the Race Relations Act 1976. The matter ultimately concluded on further appeal to the Supreme Court.[98] By a majority, the court rejected the school's argument that the matrilineal test derived from religious law, and what had motivated the school was compliance with that law. The court confirmed that the motive of a discriminator for applying the discriminatory criteria was irrelevant. A person, who discriminated on the ground of race, as defined by the Act, could not rely on the fact that the ground of discrimination was one mandated by religion. The court also concluded that, had the school's policy not amounted to directed discrimination, it would otherwise have amounted to unlawful indirect discrimination, as it could not be regarded as a proportionate means of achieving a legitimate aim.

11.76 Typically, in the context of prejudice for the purposes of s 86 of the SSFA and faith school admissions, the authority's focus will be on the likely effect upon an

---

[90] See *R (G) v Lambeth LBC* [1994] ELR 207.
[91] See *R (C and others) v Bromley LBC* [1992] 1 FLR 174 and *R (Kingwell) v Royal Borough of Kingston-upon-Thames* [1992] 1 FLR 182. (In each case, reliance was unsuccessfully placed on target duties to make sufficient educational provision within the LA area.)
[92] See *R (Razazan) v Wiltshire CC* [1997] ELR 370 and *R (LT) v Rotherham MBC* [2000] LGR 338.
[93] See *R (LT) v Rotherham MBC* [2000] LGR 338 per Lord Justice Stuart-Smith at 344–345.
[94] See Equality Act 2010, s 85.
[95] See *Choudhury v Governors of Bishop Challoner RC Comprehensive School* [1992] 2 AC 182 and the Schools Admission Code at paras [1-36]–[1-38]. For Wales, see Schools Admissions Code, paras [2.42]–[2.44].
[96] *R (T) v Governors of La Sainte Union Convent School* [1996] ELR 98 per Sedley J at 101D.
[97] [2009] 4 All ER 375.
[98] [2010] 2 WLR 153.

oversubscribed establishment. The 'efficient use of resources' within an admission area may, however, entail consideration of problems at other schools, eg where numbers would be short or distorted.[99]

11.77 For example, in *R (F) Lancashire CC*,[100] the parents of a Roman Catholic child had expressed a preference for their son to attend a non-denominational secondary school. Almost a quarter of the schools in the LA area were Roman Catholic voluntary aided schools, a particularly high percentage. Faced with the prospect of a shortage of places for non-Roman Catholic children, the LA introduced an admissions policy giving priority to non-Roman Catholic children over Roman Catholic children for places at non-denominational secondary schools in the event of oversubscription. The school was oversubscribed and the parents challenged the arrangement by judicial review. The court upheld the authority's policy on the grounds that unless such an arrangement existed, it would not be possible to offer places to a number of children in the area in which they lived.

11.78 If a maintained faith-school is undersubscribed, the school must admit a child of another faith or of no faith by virtue of s 86 of the SSFA unless to do so would otherwise prejudice the provision of efficient education or the efficient use of resources.[101]

11.79 Children in care are recognised to be among the most vulnerable in society and all admission authorities must give highest priority within their oversubscription criteria to such pupils.[102] This obligation also applies, with certain modifications, to faith schools and those operating selective admission arrangements.

School admission appeals

11.80 Under s 94 of the SSFA an appeal lies to an Independent Appeal Panel (IAP) for parents aggrieved by a refusal to comply with an expressed preference.[103] The appeal must be organised by the admission authority and constituted and conducted in accordance with the School Admissions (Appeals Arrangements) (England) Regulations 2012.[104] As indicated above, the legislative framework is supplemented by a detailed Admission Appeals Code.

11.81 The decision of an IAP is susceptible to judicial review and the admission authority must provide an indemnity to the members in respect of any legal costs.[105]

11.82 The overwhelming majority of all school admission appeals are in practice about s 86(3)(a) of the SSFA, for instance the competing contentions of admission authorities, schools and parents regarding the pervasive issue of 'prejudice'. An IAP must adopt a

---

[99] For example, the provisional view of Kay J in *R (Taylor) v Blackpool BC* [1999] ELR 237 (application was dismissed with reference to delay).
[100] [1995] ELR 33.
[101] As in the case of *R (N and E) v Governors of the Hasmonean High School* [1994] ELR 343 above.
[102] In England, see School Admissions (Admission Arrangements and Co-ordination of Admission Arrangements) (England) Regulations 2012 and the Schools Admission Code at para [1.7]. For Wales, see the Education (Admission of Looked After Children) (Wales) Regulations 2009 (SI 2009/821) and the Schools Admissions Code, paras [3.22]–[3.42].
[103] Save in respect of a 'twice-excluded child' – SSFA, s 95(1).
[104] (SI 2012/9). For Wales, see the Education (Admission Appeals Arrangements) (Wales) Regulations 2005 (SI 2005/1398), as amended.
[105] School Admissions Appeal Code, para [1.13]. For Wales, see the Education (Admission Appeals Arrangements) (Wales) Regulations 2005, reg 8.

two-stage process in respect of appeals,[106] save in respect of decisions based upon infant class size prejudice and multiple appeals, as considered below.

11.83 The first stage involves establishment of the relevant facts, namely:

- whether the school's admission arrangements comply with the Part III of the SSFA and the mandatory aspects of the School Admissions Code;
- whether the admission arrangements were correctly applied in the individual's case; and
- whether 'prejudice' would arise were the child to be admitted.

11.84 Relevant considerations include any preferences expressed by the parent, the published admission arrangements and the reasons expressed in favour or against admission.

11.85 The IAP is entitled, in its consideration of all relevant circumstances, to consider the lawfulness of the published admissions arrangements,[107] though it will rarely be necessary for these to be subject to public law scrutiny:[108]

> '... Appeal panels are obliged to take appropriate account of procedural or substantive errors, if they are relevant to the question they have to determine. This may readily apply to relevant errors which are established or self-evident. By contrast, although general admission arrangements are not, as I have said, immune from examination, it will scarcely ever be necessary to go further than to consider whether their application to the particular child was perverse ....'

11.86 Examples of an incorrect application of individual criteria include *R (S) v Governors of Dame Alice Owens School*.[109] The relevant admission policy provided for specified numbers of pupils to be admitted from three alternate categories; those who passed an entrance exam, those who demonstrated specified connections with the school and those who demonstrated aptitude for either music or sport. Whilst fulfilling the third criteria, the pupil was refused a place when the school chose to admit more pupils from the second category. McCullough J held, allowing the application for judicial review, that the merits of applications satisfying the third criteria fell to be considered before any unfulfilled places might be offered to applicants from other groups in accordance with the published policy.

11.87 Whilst it will primarily be for the admission authority to address the issue of prejudice by way of evidence, there is no strict onus or burden of proof in this

---

[106] See *R (Croydon LBC) v Commissioner for Local Administration* [1989] 1 All ER 1033 (as approved in *R (W (A Minor)) v Education Appeal Committee of Lancashire CC* [1994] ELR 530); see also *R (M) v IAP of Haringey* [2010] ELR 823.
[107] See *R (Hounslow LBC) v Schools Admissions Panel for Hounslow* [2002] 1 WLR 3147 per May LJ at [22] where the Court of Appeal considered its earlier decision in *R (H) v Sheffield CC* [1999] ELR 511.
[108] Per May LJ at [61].
[109] [1998] Ed CR 101; [1998] COD 108; for an example of a failed challenge on the basis of the application of individual criteria see *R (S) v IAP of St Thomas Catholic Primary School* [2010] EWHC 3785 (Admin); see too *R (Lambeth LBC) v IAP for Lambeth* [2013] ELR 145 (an inadequately reasoned decision was set aside when, on proper application of the admission criteria, the appeal should have been dismissed).

context.[110] The IAP must consider all of the material placed before it and unless it is satisfied that giving effect to the expressed preference would result in prejudice, it must uphold the appeal.[111]

11.88 If prejudice has been established, the IAP must move on to the second stage of balancing the arguments. This represents an independent, discretionary exercise, weighing the degree of prejudice to the school against the appellant's case for the child being admitted to the preferred school before arriving at a reasoned decision based upon all relevant factors.[112]

Infant admissions

11.89 The size of an infant class is limited to 30 with a single schoolteacher by virtue of regulations made under s 1 of the SSFA.[113] An IAP can only uphold an appeal where the admission decision was made on the ground of prejudice in this context if either of the following requirements can be established by the parent:[114]

(a) it finds that the admission of additional children would not breach the infant class size limit; or

(b) it finds that the admission arrangements did not comply with admissions law or were not correctly and impartially applied and the child would have been offered a place if the arrangements had complied or had been correctly and impartially applied; or

(c) it decides that the decision to refuse admission was not one which a reasonable admission authority would have made in the circumstances of the case.

11.90 In multiple appeals where a number of children would have been offered a place on one or more of the above grounds, and to admit that number would seriously prejudice the provision of efficient education or efficient use of resources, the IAP must proceed to a second stage, comparing each appellant's case for their child to be admitted and decide which of them, if any, to uphold. Where the school could admit a certain number of children without breaching the infant class size limit (or without needing to take measures to avoid breaching it that would prejudice the provision of efficient education or efficient use of resources) the IAP must uphold the appeals of at least that number of children.

11.91 In *R (LBC) v Schools Admissions Panel for Hounslow*, May LJ described the appropriate process for such appeals as follows:[115]

---

[110] See *R (Croydon LBC) v Commissioner for Local Administration* [1989] 1 All ER 1033 per Woolf LJ at 1041a–c and *R (G and B) v Brighouse School Appeal Committee* [1997] ELR 39 per Sedley J at 44f–h.
[111] See the Admission Appeals Code at paras [3.2]–[3.5]. For Wales, Admission Appeals Code at para [5.15].
[112] See the Admission Appeal Code at paras [3.8]–[43.9]. For Wales, see Admission Appeals Code at para [5.15] For example, see *R (Jacobs) v Essex CC* [1997] ELR 190 (successful challenge of decision failing to have regard to separate living arrangements of estranged parents with reference to catchment criteria); *R (H) v A* [2013] EWHC 2506 (Admin) (complaint of failure to make reasonable adjustments during entrance examination; unsuccessful on facts, as same outcome inevitable). Relevant factors may include legitimate expectation: *R (K) v Beatrix Potter School* [1997] ELR 468 (dismissal of challenge to IAP decision following the making of an offer to pupil in error, which was promptly withdrawn).
[113] School Admissions (Infant Class Sizes) (England) Regulations 2012, SI 2012/10.
[114] See Admission Appeal Code at paras [4.4]–[4.8]. For Wales, see the Education (Admission Appeals Arrangements) (Wales) Regulations 2005 (SI 2005/1398), Reg 6(2) and the Admission Appeals Code at Annex C.
[115] [2002] 1 WLR 3147 at [63]. See also *R (Hampshire CC) v IAP for Hampshire* [2007] ELR 266 (successful challenge by LA of IAP decision on the grounds of failure to have regard to its primary contentions and in

'... parents need to make a particular case which is so compelling that the decision not to admit the child is shown to be perverse. A local education authority opposing an appeal will need to explain their admission arrangements, explain their particular problems in relation to the school in question, and show that, unfortunate though it may be, it was objectively fair not to admit the child in question. They may wish to show that they had to refuse admission to several children with good cases, but that admitting one or more of those children would have entailed refusing one or more of those who were admitted because of the class size limit. As to the Panel, their task is not simply to rubber stamp the local education authority's decision, but they can only uphold the appeal if they conclude that it was perverse in the light of the admission arrangements to refuse to admit the particular child. Their task is not to take again the original decision ....'

11.92 When considering ground (c), the IAP can properly have regard to additional evidence in certain circumstances, including but not limited to information that the admissions authority ought reasonably to have been aware of, but it cannot conduct a rehearing.[116] By contrast, grounds (a) and (b) are in effect 'slip clauses' which empower the IAP to put right any error made by the admissions authority on the information that had been available to it.[117]

Multiple appeals

11.93 The Admissions Code provides comprehensive guidance regarding the conduct of multiple appeals, for instance where there are two or more appeals by children against admission decisions in respect of the same school.[118] In *R (Tarmohamed) v Education Committee of Leicester CC*,[119] the court recognised that if more than one parent's preference outweighed the relevant prejudice, but the cumulative admission of all such children could not be coped with by the school, there was no alternative but to rank the children in order of priority. That entailed a third stage at which the individual applicants were compared. The decision ensures that multiple appeals are conducted simultaneously, consistently and in accordance with the principles of natural justice.

Reasons

11.94 The IAP must communicate its decision, including the grounds upon which it was made, in writing to the appellant and the admission authority ('the decision letter').[120] The decision letter must be expressed clearly and enable parties to see what matters were taken into consideration, to understand what view the IAP took on questions of fact or law which it had to resolve and to understand, in broad terms, the basis on which the IAP reached its decision.[121]

11.95 The decision letter must reflect the type of appeal that was being considered, for instance it should be appropriately tailored in the case of infant admissions and/or

---

taking into account irrelevant considerations); cf *R (DD) v IAP for Islington LBC* [2013] ELR 483 (panel correct, on facts, to consider infant class-size limit, not just with reference to admission year, but also with reference to the subsequent two academic years).

[116] *R (JC) v Richmond LBC* [2001] ELR 21 per Kennedy LJ at [50]–[53].
[117] *R (JC) v Richmond LBC* [2001] ELR 21 per Kennedy LJ at [41].
[118] See paras [2.18]–[2.20]. For Wales, see Admission Appeals Code at paras [5.18]–[5.22].
[119] [1997] ELR 48 per Sedley J at 59b–e.
[120] See Admission Appeals Code paras [2.24]–[2.25]. For Wales, see Admission Appeals Code at paras [6.1]–[6.6].
[121] *R (T) v Hackney LBC* [1991] COD 454; *R (M) v Lancashire CC* [1995] ELR 136 ('broad grounds must be set out rather than what may be termed detailed reasons'); *R (B) v Birmingham CC Education Appeals Committee* [1999] ELR 305 (standard letter an appropriate staring point, to be modified as required); *R (L) v IAP of St Edward's College* [2001] ELR 542.

multiple appeals, and make reference to the two-stage process as appropriate. It must contain a summary of the relevant factors raised and considered by the IAP,[122] details of how these were resolved[123] and a summary of any legal advice received.[124] The level of detail required will depend on the nature of the issues that have been raised.[125]

11.96 If the letter does not explain the decision or otherwise satisfy the court that the IAP conducted the appeal in a procedurally and substantively lawful manner, the decision is liable to be quashed. In some cases, however, the court may decline relief where the complaint is one of form rather than substance.[126]

Special educational needs and learning disability

Introduction

11.97 The role of judicial review in the context of special educational needs and learning disability has been significantly curtailed over recent years.[127]

11.98 In 1993, the Special Educational Needs Tribunal (SENT) was introduced. In the first instance, appeals were heard by an Appeal Committee of the relevant Local Authority (LA) or by the Secretary of State. In September 2002, SENT became the Special Educational Needs and Disability Tribunal (SENDIST) and latterly SENDIST became part of the First-tier Tribunal (Special Educational Needs and Disability Discrimination) on 3 November 2008 ('the Tribunal').

11.99 In common with other public law areas, the existence of the Tribunal, which offers a specialist appeals process, precludes many prospective applications for judicial review particularly those cases involving the assessment, provision, review or maintenance of statements identifying special educational needs provision.

11.100 However, the overwhelming majority of children with special educational needs do not have a statement based upon the degree of their learning difficulties. In January 2013, some 229,390 (or 2.8% of) pupils across all schools in England had statements, whilst there were 1,316,220 pupils (16% of pupils across all schools in England) with special educational needs in respect of which a statement had not been made.[128]

11.101 In this section, consideration is given to the jurisdiction of the Tribunal in the context of special educational needs and learning disability and to those areas in which judicial review still has a residual role to play.

---

[122] R (K and S) v Admissions Appeal Panel of Cardiff CC and other [2003] EWHC 436 (Admin).
[123] R (L) v IAP of St Edward's College [2001] ELR 542; R(C) v Admission Panel of Nottinghamshire CC and Other [2004] EWHC 2988 (Admin).
[124] R (I) v IAP for G Technology College [2005] EWHC 558 (Admin).
[125] R (C) v South Gloucestershire Appeals Committee [2000] ELR 220. See also R (E) v Education Appeal Committee of Lancashire CC [1994] ELR 530; R (Taylor) v Education Committee of Blackpool BC [1999] ELR 237; R (M) v Lancashire CC [1994] ELR 478; R (D) v Northamptonshire CC [1998] ELR 291; R (C) v Admission Panel of Nottinghamshire CC and another [2005] ELR 182; R (T) v IAP for Devon CC and Governing Body of X College [2007] ELR 499; R (Reading BC) v IAP for Reading BC and others [2006] ELR 186; R (S and B) v IAP of Birmingham CC [2007] ELR 57.
[126] R (L) v IAP of St Edward's College [2001] ELR 542; R (L) v Governors of the Buss Foundation Camden School for Girls [1991] COD 98.
[127] For more detailed consideration of law relating to special educational needs and its development, please see Special Educational Needs and the Law (2nd edn: Jordan Publishing 2007).
[128] SFR30/2013, updated 1 May 2014 (DfE).

11.102 It should be noted, however, that on 1 September 2014 the Children and Families Act 2014 came into force in England. Part 3 of that Act made significant changes to the system for children and young people with special educational needs, including those who are disabled, so that services consistently support the best outcomes for them. The Act extends the SEN system from birth to 25, giving children, young people and their parents greater control and choice in decisions and ensuring needs are properly met and will involve, among other matters, replacing old statements with a new birth-to-25 education, health and care plan.

11.103 At the time of writing no case-law had been decided under the new statutory provisions, so the analysis below reflects the regime before 1 September 2014. Transitional provisions apply which mean that the pre-1 September 2014 regime could be effective for some until 2018. It is anticipated that disputes will continue, for the most part, to be adjudicated upon within the Tribunal system, although the Act extends a statutory right to mediation, among other measures aimed at promoting alternate dispute resolution. It is likely (as intended) that such measures will further curtail the role of judicial review in this context.

The Tribunal

11.104 Forming part of the Health, Education and Social Care Chamber (HESC), the Tribunal is wholly independent. The Government cannot influence the Tribunal's decision and the panel will have no connection with any LA.

11.105 The Tribunal considers parental appeals against a decision by a LA about a child's special educational needs or learning disability provision where agreement cannot be reached.[129]

11.106 Individual appeals are heard by a panel of three appointed people. The panel is chaired by a tribunal judge (who is a lawyer), and the other two members are non-legal (specialist) members who have knowledge and experience of special educational needs and disability.

11.107 The Tribunal also considers some claims regarding alleged disability discrimination in schools, nursery schools and nursery classes in schools, as well as some functions of the LA in providing education for children. In the case of admissions and permanent exclusions from LA maintained schools, appeals are instead dealt with by independent appeal panels. Accordingly, a second appeal route is available (to the Upper Tribunal) in respect of some school admission and permanent exclusion decisions, whereas judicial review may be appropriate in other cases.

11.108 The position at first instance is summarised below:

	Independent (private) and non maintained schools	Maintained (LA) schools including voluntary schools
Admissions	Tribunal	LA admissions appeal panel
Permanent exclusions	Tribunal	LA exclusions appeal panel

---

[129] Each LA must make arrangements for avoiding or resolving disagreements between parents and schools about special educational needs provision: EA 1996, s 332B. These arrangements apply to all schools, including an independent school named in the statement of child maintained by the LA.

	Independent (private) and non maintained schools	Maintained (LA) schools including voluntary schools
Fixed-term exclusions	Tribunal	Tribunal
Education and associated services	Tribunal	Tribunal

11.109 Academies make individual arrangements for admission appeals and appeals against permanent exclusions and these must be investigated locally by parents or advisers on a case-by-case basis.

11.110 The primary legislative sources are Part IV of the EA 1996 and the Special Educational Needs and Disability Act 2001 (the latter making important changes to the EA 1996).

11.111 Practice and procedure in the Tribunal is governed by the Special Educational Needs and Disability Tribunal (General Provisions and Disability Claims Procedure) Regulations 2002 (as preserved) and by the Tribunal Procedure (First–tier Tribunal) (Health, Education and Social Care Chambers) Rules 2008.[130]

11.112 At first instance, a parent (but not a child)[131] is able to appeal about the following decisions made by the LA concerning special educational needs provision:

- Failure or refusal by a LA to carry out a statutory assessment of child's SEN following a parental and/or school request.
- Refusal by a LA to make a statement of SEN after a statutory assessment.
- Failure or refusal by a LA to reassess a child's SEN after a period of six or more months following a parental and/or school request.
- A LA decision not to maintain (to cancel) a statement of SEN.
- A LA decision not to change a statement of SEN following reassessment.
- Refusal by a LA to change the school named in a child's statement of SEN (if the statement is one year or more old).

11.113 If the LA has made a statement, or has changed a previous statement, a right of appeal also lies against any or all of the following:

- The description of the child's SEN (part 2).
- The detail of special educational provision (help) necessary to meet the child's SEN (part 3).
- The school or type of school named in part 4 of the statement.
- The LA not naming a school in part 4.

11.114 The following matters do not fall within the jurisdiction of the Tribunal:

- The way the LA carried out the assessment or the length of time that it took.
- How the LA or the school arranges to provide the help set out in the child's statement.

---

[130] For Wales, see the Special Educational Needs Tribunal for Wales Regulations 2012, SI 2012/322.
[131] (R) S v SENT & City of Westminster [1996] ELR 102.

- The way the school is meeting the child's needs at School Action or School Action Plus (SEN provision in 'early years' schooling).
- The description in parts 5 and 6 of the statement of a child's non-educational needs or how the LA plans to meet those needs.
- The LA refusal to amend the statement following an annual review.
- The LA refusal to name an independent school, a non-maintained school or a different type of school (where the LA has been asked to make a change to part 4 and the statement is at least one year old).

11.115 In relation to the last two complaints, the Tribunal offers the following advice to parents: '… you would need to ask your LA to reassess your child and appeal to us if they refused that reassessment or if you remained dissatisfied at some later point in the process of amending your child's statement ….'[132]

11.116 The force of this guidance is illustrated by *R (W) v Kent County Council*.[133] The parents of a child with special educational needs challenged the refusal of the LA to amend their son's statement to name the residential school at which he had been enrolled or, alternatively, to meet the fees payable. The school named as being suitable within part 4 of the child's statement attracted substantially higher fees, but the LA considered (as observed by an earlier SENDIST panel) that the preferred option of the parents did not offer an environment apposite for the child's assessed needs. Rejecting the application on this and other grounds, Silber J observed as follows:

> '… The Council contend that the claimant's parents had an alternative remedy as they could have sought a statutory assessment pursuant to the 1996 Act. So it would have been open to the claimant's parents to obtain redress by requesting reassessment in accordance with the statutory procedure set out in s 328(2) of the 1996 Act, which enables a parent to request the local education authority to make a re-assessment of the SSEN.
>
> Further, any parent dissatisfied with any such re-assessment decision could appeal to what is now the First-Tier Tribunal (Health, Education and Social Care Chamber) and what was previously SENDIST. On such an appeal, the Tribunal would be obliged to carry out a merits review which, of course, is of much wider scope than that which is permitted on the present application or on any judicial review application. In addition, there is a right of appeal to SENDIST against a refusal of re-assessment. These statutory remedies constitute suitable alternative remedies especially as they permit a merits review followed by an opportunity to appeal any subsequent decision of this tribunal …
>
> … I came across the apposite comment that "where Parliament has introduced a new procedure to deal with a particular problem which it perceives to exist, the court should hesitate long before considering that procedure to be less satisfactory" (per Collins J in *R (G) v Immigration Appeal Tribunal* [2004] 3 All ER 286 [11]). The alternative procedure falls exactly into that category and that fortifies my conclusion that as there was an appropriate alternative remedy for the claimant, I must reject the claim ….'

11.117 The right of appeal to Upper Tribunal will generally preclude the judicial review of a first instance decision within the HESC, as with the statutory appeal route from a

---

[132] How to Appeal a SEN decision: A Guide for Parents (SENDIST 2008) at p 4.
[133] [2009] ELR 536.

SENDIST decision that was available before reform of the Tribunals Service,[134] particularly as the power to grant interim relief in such cases exists, where exceptional circumstances can be demonstrated.[135]

11.118 It remains the position that careful consideration will need to be given to the very small number of cases in which, by reason of the need for interim relief, judicial review may remain appropriate.[136]

11.119 For example, in *R (G) v Barnet LBC*[137] the Administrative Court was concerned with an application for permission for judicial review in respect of the LA's handling of the renewal of a child's statement. Ouseley J addressed the question of whether judicial review was appropriate in a case where a statutory appeal to the SENDIST was available. Whilst having regard to earlier authorities, he found that the particular case was 'exceptional' as the LA proposed significant changes, on short notice, in respect of the provision for a child with severe physical and mental disabilities:

> '... The substantive remedy before SENDIST does not mean that there are no circumstances, however exceptional, in which this court on the grant of permission to apply for judicial review should not require that some of interim relief be provided.
>
> ... I regard this as one such exceptional case. I bear in mind that the availability of the substantive remedy means that the power is to be exercised sparingly, and the fact that there is no statutory provision for a stay by SENDIST means that it should be exercised even more sparingly. However that may be, this is an exceptional and unusual special educational needs case, where the educational needs are provided for 52 weeks of the year exclusively at a residential school. The care is not provided at the child's family home in the evenings, or at weekends or during any school holidays. The severity of the child's needs mean that it would be very difficult for any provision to be made at home, and although [counsel for the respondent] dangles the prospect of social services' assistance as a means of making good some of the problems, I consider that that does not by itself assuage the severity and urgency of the situation which the parents face here. The position, so far as they are concerned, is that in a very short space of time, by the end of July, this severely disabled child whose most recent statement of education needs required 52 weeks a year of residential care, would be at home with them where they could not cope ....'

Residual jurisdiction of the High Court

11.120 In cases concerning special educational needs and learning disability that fall outside of the jurisdiction of the Tribunal, individual consideration will need to be given as to both the appropriateness and merits of pursuing judicial review on a conventional basis. Reported examples include:

- Failure by the LA to appropriately consider and consult upon a revised funding allocation for a grant-maintained school, which left the school unable to provide for the identified needs of pupils with statements.[138]

---

[134] *R (South Glamorgan CC) v SENT* [1996] ELR 326.
[135] *R (JW) v The Learning Trust* [2010] ELR 115.
[136] In contrast to the powers of the Upper Tribunal, the First-tier Tribunal has no power to grant interim relief pending a final determination: see *MH v Nottinghamshire CC* [2009] UKUT 178 (ACC) (following *R (White) v Ealing LBC* [1998] ELR 203 per Dyson J at 220 E–F).
[137] [2006] ELR 4; see also *R (HR) v Medway Council* [2010] ELR 513 (unsuccessful attempt to obtain interim relief in connection with naming of a school within a SEN Statement).
[138] *R (Governing Body of Queensmead School) v Hillingdon LBC* [1997] ELR 331.

- Failure by the Secretary of State to consult effectively over the withdrawal of a school's approved status, so as to preclude its continued acceptance of pupils with statements.[139]
- Failure to fund out-of-area transport costs having named the school to which the child travelled within his statement.[140]
- Failure to have proper regard to the individual needs of a child with SEN when refusing to provide free transport to a preferred further education placement.[141]
- Declaration granted as to which LA had responsibility for maintaining a child's SEN statement following an out-of-area residential placement.[142]
- Failure to appropriately implement statement of SEN.[143]
- Failure to conclude an assessment and report to the Learning and Skills Council to enable consideration of educational funding support.[144]
- Failure, when making a report to the Learning and Skills Council, to recommend placement with a particular provider of education or otherwise suggest which providers could reasonably meet a child's needs.[145]
- Declaration as to whether a local authority had been correct to end a child's status as being 'looked after' under the Children Act 1989 when placing him in a full-time residential school in accordance with his SEN Statement.[146]
- Refusal of respite care provision pending decision on funding for residential placement for 20-year-old man with severe autism.[147]
- Failure to admit pupil in accordance with statement of SEN.[148]

11.121 Consideration will need to be given, as usual, to the exhaustion of LA complaints and procedures and, thereafter, a request for intervention by the Secretary of State as appropriate. A careful balancing exercise needs to be conducted with reference to the issues of delay and whether other routes provide appropriate and sufficiently timely redress. Where an extension of time is required, due weight is likely to be given to time spent exploring alternative resolution and generic difficulties such as obtaining public funding.[149]

Pupil discipline and exclusion

Introduction

11.122 Pupil discipline and, in particular, exclusion decisions are amongst the most important yet highly contentious matters in education. Historically, the latter sanction has proved a particularly prevalent source of public law challenges, as considered below.

---

[139] *R (McCarthy) v SoS for Education and Employment* [1996] *The Times*, July 24.
[140] *R (H) v Brent LBC* [2002] ELR 509.
[141] *R (A) v North Somerset Council* [2010] ELR 139.
[142] *R (L) v Waltham Forest LBC* [2008] LGR 495; followed in *R (JK) v Haringey LBC* [2009] ELR 421 (permission to appeal declined [2010] EWCA Civ 495).
[143] *R (N) v North Tyneside BC* [2010] ELR 312 (allowing the claimant's appeal against [2010] ELR 130).
[144] *R (A) v Bromley LBC* [2008] EWHC 2449 (Admin).
[145] *R (P) v Windsor & Maidenhead RBC and the Learning & Skills Council* [2010] EWHC 1408 (Admin).
[146] *R (O) v East Riding of Yorkshire CC* [2010] ELR 318 (proceeding by way of appeal).
[147] *R (RC) v Manchester City Council* (unreported, 21 June 2014) Judge Goss QC.
[148] *R (N) v Governing Body of A School* [2014] EWHC 1238 (Admin).
[149] *R (H) v Brent LBC* [2002] ELR 509 above, per Michael Supperstone QC at [15].

11.123 In such a highly legislated area, it is perhaps surprising that this aspect of school governance remains rooted in the common law, as clarified and supplemented in Part VII of the EIA. The EIA replicates the common law position that teachers (and duly authorised staff) exercise parental responsibility and may discipline their pupils in any reasonable way.[150] Maintained schools, but not academies, must set out their 'behaviour and discipline policy' and periodically review the same.[151]

11.124 There are a number of ways in which schools seek to maintain discipline and safety. The common methods include confiscation of personal property,[152] detention[153] and, in appropriate cases, physical restraint.[154] Those which most commonly come to the attention of the administrative court are exclusion decisions, including those associated with school uniform policy.

Exclusion

11.125 Pupil exclusions are a serious matter and, hence, the relevant decision-making and appeal processes are closely regulated by statute. Exclusion of pupils for a fixed period or permanently is permitted under s 52 of the EA 2002. Under s 52, a number of regulations have been issued.[155] These must be observed by head teachers, governing bodies, LAs and Review Panels (RPs) as appropriate. These parties must also have regard to government guidance issued under s 52.[156]

Challenging RP decisions

11.126 Since the statutory appeal route must generally be exhausted before judicial review proceedings can be contemplated,[157] it is appropriate to consider the RP process in a little detail.

11.127 In the case of a permanent exclusion, a 'relevant person' may seek a review of the governors' or proprietor's decision not to reinstate.[158] In England, this replaces and effectively mirrors the previous independent appeal panel (IAP) regime, but it is now described as a 'review'. Any such application must be made within 15 school days after requisite notice is given of the decision.[159] The review must be organised and funded by

---

[150] For example, see *Fitzgerald v Northcote* (1865) 4 F&F 856 and *Gateshead Union Guardians v Durham CC* [1918] 1 Ch 146.
[151] See EIA, s 89.
[152] See EIA, s 94.
[153] See EIA, s 92.
[154] See EIA, s 93.
[155] The current provisions are, in England, the School Discipline (Pupil Exclusions and Reviews) (England) Regulations 2012, SI 2012/1033 ('the 2012 Regulations') and, in Wales, the Education (Pupil Exclusions and Appeals) (Maintained Schools) (Wales) Regulations 2003 and the Education (Pupil Exclusions and Appeals) (Pupil Referral Units)) (Wales) Regulations 2003, as amended.
[156] See EA 2002, s 52(4)(b). The relevant guidance in England is the DfE publication 'Exclusion from maintained schools, academies and pupil referral units in England' ('the DfE Guidance'). The DfE Guidance is revised and updated regularly, most recently in 2012. For Wales, see 'Exclusion from schools and pupil referral units', updated in September 2012 ('the NAFW Guidance').
[157] See *R (DR) v Head Teacher of St George's Catholic School*; *R (AM) v Governing Body of Kingsmead School* [2003] LGR 371 and *R (A) v Fernhill Manor School* [1994] ELR 67 (a fair hearing before an IAP may be sufficient to cure irregularities below). In exceptional cases, recourse might properly be had to judicial review without exhausting the IAP process: see *R (M) v Governors of St Gregory's RC Aided High School* [1995] ELR 290 (appeal before Governors not properly constituted), *R (K) v Governors of the W School and West Sussex CC* [2001] ELR 311 (family health considerations were relevant).
[158] Under the Education Act 2002, s 51A(3) and the 2012 Regulations, reg 7 or 25.
[159] 2012 Regulations, Sch 1, para 2(1).

the local authority[160] (or, in the case of an academy, by the academy proprietor[161]). The 'relevant person' has the right to require an SEN expert to be called in to advise the review panel.[162]

11.128 The constitution and procedures of a RP are set out in Sch 1 to the 2012 Regulations. There may be a clerk to advise the panel, as prescribed.[163] If so, the clerk must be trained. If there is no clerk, the local authority must organise the hearing and write the minutes.

11.129 After the hearing, the RP must notify the parties of their decision and of the reasons for that decision without delay.[164] The decision may be:

- to uphold the responsible body's decision not to reinstate the pupil;
- to recommend the responsible body to reconsider its decision not to reinstate the pupil; or
- to quash the responsible body's decision not to reinstate the pupil and direct the responsible body to reconsider (if its considers the decision was flawed when considered in light of the principles applicable to judicial review[165]).

11.130 The RP may also, where they find that the responsible body's decision must be quashed (in the case of a maintained school), order a downward adjustment of £4,000 in that school's budget share[166] or (in the case of an academy) order the proprietor to pay £4,000 to the local authority.[167] This 'fine' applies (in either case) only if the school's responsible body does not then reinstate the pupil.

11.131 Decisions under the old IAP regime remain relevant and are considered below, save as regards 'reinstatement' (which the RP no longer has power to direct).

Procedural fairness

11.132 Hearings are subject to and must be conducted in accordance with the principles of natural justice and this is where most public law challenges will lie. In *R (S) v Brent LBC*,[168] the Court of Appeal considered three consolidated judicial review appeals arising from exclusion decisions. Although the appeals principally related to the lawfulness of the prevailing government guidance issued under the precursor to s 52 of the EIA, the court proceeded to make a number of useful statements regarding the appropriate conduct of IAP hearings:

- the LA must maintain an objective stance; it is not part of its function to press for a particular finding or outcome in respect of a pupil;[169]

---

[160] 2012 Regulations, reg 7.
[161] 2012 Regulations, reg 25.
[162] 2012 Regulations, reg 7(1)(b) and (3) (or, at academies, reg 25(1)(b) and (3)).
[163] 2012 Regulations, Sch 1, para 4.
[164] 2012 Regulations, Sch 1, para 19.
[165] As expressly provided by the Education Act 2002, s 51A(4).
[166] 2012 Regulations, reg 7(5)(b).
[167] 2012 Regulations, reg 25(5)(b).
[168] [2002] ELR 556.
[169] [2002] ELR 556 at [22]–[24].

- the IAP must avoid permitting the LA or any other party to unduly influence or monopolise the hearing through its representations;[170]
- the IAP must entertain any credible material, written or oral, which is reasonably and fairly capable of affecting what it has to decide;[171]
- if there is a material conflict of evidence involving an adult witness, there is no reason why the witness cannot be invited to attend and be questioned. If a witness declines to come for no reason, or for an unacceptable one, the IAP will be entitled to draw whatever inferences seem appropriate in the circumstances;[172]
- the IAP is entitled to restrict confrontational cross-examination of witnesses and to require questions to be put through or by the chair;[173]
- whilst there may be good reasons for seeking to preserve the anonymity of witnesses, for example in the context of bullying allegations, use by the IAP of anonymised statements has the potential to cause injustice. Use of such statements may be unfair; in particular, if they are damaging to the pupil in ways that he or she cannot be expected to address without knowing the maker.[174]

11.133 In *R (B) v Head Teacher of Dunraven School*,[175] the Court of Appeal had earlier given guidance on disclosure in the context of IAP hearings:

- if there are discrepancies within the material relied upon in support of the allegations made against the pupil, fairness will ordinarily dictate making sufficient disclosure to reveal such inconsistency;[176]
- it is unfair for the IAP to have access to damaging material to which the pupil has no access;[177]
- disclosure of such material is not dependent upon a request by the pupil; the duty to ensure fairness is not conditional upon applications or demands more appropriate to adversarial litigation.[178]

11.134 Far and above the most contentious issues before the courts have been the degree to which the matters complained of should be investigated and the proper application of the burden of proof to those facts ascertained. It has been held that an

---

[170] [2002] ELR 556 at [25] approving the observations of Newman J in *R (T) v Head Teacher of Wembley High School and Others* [2001] ELR 359. See also *R (W) v Governors of Bacon's City Technology College* [1998] ELR 488 (failure of the chair to indicate the panel's need to hear from a pupil directly, as opposed to his loquacious representative, gave rise to unfairness).
[171] [2002] ELR 556 at [27]. See also *R (W) v Governors of Bacon's City Technology College* [1998] ELR 488 (allowing a limited period of time for appeals was a dangerous policy as it would serve to unduly restrict the scope of inquiry and representations in some cases).
[172] [2002] ELR 556 at [28].
[173] [2002] ELR 556 at [28]. See also *R (W) v IAP for Bexley* [2008] ELR 301 per Burton J at [20]–[29] (it is for the IAP to hear all the evidence and consider any challenge to its reliability and weight).
[174] [2002] ELR 556 at [27]. See also *R (B) v Head Teacher of Dunraven School* [2000] ELR 156 (a governing body may, in some cases, be forced to elect to proceed in the absence of a statement or otherwise reinstate a pupil); *R (K) v Governors of the W School and West Sussex CC* [2001] ELR 311 (failure to provide witness evidence on which the decision was based to the applicant handicapped his defence) and *R (T) v Head Teacher of Elliott School* [2002] ELR 556 (decisions on admission are fact sensitive and the IAP, in each case, must be conscious of any possible unfairness).
[175] [2000] ELR 156.
[176] [2000] ELR 156 per Sedley LJ at [190]. Similarly, a head teacher with reason to doubt the reliability or impartially of a statement must draw such concerns to the attention of the IAP: *R (T) v Head Teacher of Elliott School* [2002] ELR 556 per Schiemann LJ at [37].
[177] [2000] ELR 156 per Sedley LJ at 190.
[178] [2000] ELR 156 per Sedley LJ at 193.

IAP is not determining a pupil's civil rights and obligations so as to engage art 6 of the ECHR and it is not determining a criminal charge so as to import the criminal burden of proof, even where the conduct giving rise to the exclusion is of a criminal character.[179]

11.135 The Regulations expressly provide that all factual determinations are to be made on the 'balance of probability', but the more serious the nature of the allegation and thus the possible sanction, the more compelling the evidence necessary to support it is likely to need to be.[180]

11.136 The nature and extent of the investigation required will depend on the facts of the case. In *R (S) v Roman Catholic Schools*, Moses J accepted the following principles as being of general application (whilst cautioning specifically about the evaluation of identification evidence):[181]

- the overriding principle is that a pupil must have a fair opportunity to exculpate him or herself;
- whether such an opportunity has been afforded will depend upon the issues raised in the inquiry;
- those conducting an inquiry must decide what critical issues of fact they should resolve and what inquiries could reasonably be made to resolve those issues;
- they must give careful and even-handed consideration to all the available evidence in relation to those issues; and
- those conducting an inquiry do not need, on every occasion, to carry out searching inquiries involving the calling of bodies of oral evidence.

11.137 The statutory constitution of appeals panels is in conformity with the impartial tribunal provisions of art 6(1) of the ECHR.[182] Whilst no mention was made of a clerk to the IAP in the former legislation, it is a long-established and lawful practice for panel to have a clerk.[183] There is no real danger of bias where, as is ordinarily the case, the clerk is employed by the LA.[184] A clerk may advise the IAP during its deliberations, but if this is done in private, the clerk should repeat the advice in open session thereby affording the interested parties with an opportunity to make representations.[185]

---

[179] *R v (LG) v IAP Tom Hood School* [2010] ELR 291 (affirming [2009] ELR 248). Specific guidance is now given in the context of parallel criminal investigation in both the English and Welsh guidance (within Chapter 12 and Chapter 5 respectively).

[180] See *R (S) v Governing Body of YP School* [2004] ELR 37; *R (H) v IAP for Y College* [2005] ELR 25; *R (Culkin) v Wirral IAP* [2009] ELR 287 (investigation sufficient to identify serious and persistent conduct); *R (A) v IAP for Sutton LBC* [2009] ELR 321 (error in not making finding as to the true nature of the conduct complained of rendering assessment of proportionality of sanction impossible); *R (G) v IAP of Bexley LBC* [2009] ELR 100 (IAP had made sufficient findings of fact to justify exclusion for one-off serious act of violence against a member of staff).

[181] [1998] ELR 304. See also *R (C) v IAP of Sefton MBC and Governors of Hillside High School* [2001] ELR 393 (unnecessary to carry out searching inquiries where assault substantially admitted) and *R (A) v Head Teacher of North Westminster Community School and others* [2003] ELR 378 (clear opportunity afforded by IAP, but no issues raised by pupil or representative at hearing).

[182] *R (B) v Head Teacher of Alperton Community School* [2001] ELR 359, affirmed in *R (S, T and P) v Brent LBC, Oxfordshire CC, Head Teacher of Elliott School and the Secretary of State for Education and Skills* [2002] ELR 556.

[183] The position having now been formalised in the 2012 Regulations, Sch 1, para 4.

[184] *R (S) v Head Teacher of C High School* [2002] ELR 73.

[185] See *R (I) v IAP for G* [2005] ELR 490.

11.138 Concerns regarding impartiality may arise from an IAP member having worked closely with the head teacher or governing body of the excluding school, or from being a teacher or governor of a school (or PRU), to which the pupil might be admitted if the exclusion is confirmed. Familiarity or past teaching involvement is liable to give concern.[186] The test to be applied is that set out by Lord Phillips MR in *Re Medicaments and Related Classes of Goods (No 2)*:[187]

> '... When the Strasbourg jurisprudence is taken into account, we believe that a modest adjustment of the test in *R v Gough* is called for, which makes it plain that it is, in effect, no different from the test applied in most of the Commonwealth and in Scotland. The court must first ascertain all the circumstances which have a bearing on the suggestion that the judge was biased. It must then ask whether those circumstances would lead a fair-minded and informed observer to conclude that there was a real possibility, or a real danger, the two being the same, that the tribunal was biased ... The material circumstances will include any explanation given by the judge under review as to his knowledge or appreciation of those circumstances. Where that explanation is accepted by the applicant for review it can be treated as accurate. Where it is not accepted, it becomes one further matter to be considered from the viewpoint of the fair-minded observer. The court does not have to rule whether the explanation should be accepted or rejected. Rather it has to decide whether or not the fair-minded observer would consider that there was a real danger of bias notwithstanding the explanation advanced. Thus in *R v Gough*, had the truth of the juror's explanation not been accepted by the defendant, the Court of Appeal would correctly have approached the question of bias on the premise that the fair-minded onlooker would not necessarily find the juror's explanation credible ....'

Reasons

11.139 Decision letters have proved a contentious area, as poorly drafted documents cause confusion and undermine the perceived reliability of the IAP process. Whilst a decision letter must give the panel's reasons for its decision in as much detail as possible,[188] including clear information about the offences or behaviour for which the pupil has been excluded, the courts have shown considerable reluctance to accept challenges on this basis alone. For example, it has been held unnecessary for the IAP to set out each and every option short of exclusion and give reasons for its rejection of the same.[189] The key consideration is whether the parties can understand why the decision has been made.[190]

11.140 If an internal exclusion policy was at variance with the statutory guidance, and the IAP considers it appropriate to give the local policy additional weight, it must explain why this is so in the decision letter.[191]

---

[186] See *R (M) v Board of Governors of Stoke Newington School* [1994] ELR 131 (decision of IAP quashed where panel included a teacher-governor who had been the head of year for the pupil in the academic year which formed a relevant part of the pupil's record) and *R (T) v Head Teacher of Elliott School* [2002] ELR 556 per Sedley LJ at [46].

[187] [2001] 1 WLR 700 at [85]–[86] applied in *R (Culkin) v Wirral IAP* [2009] ELR 287 per Nicol J at [40]–[43].

[188] See DfE Guidance [170]. Contrast the position in Wales, where the guidance simply states that 'The decision letter should give the panel's reasons for its decision in sufficient detail for the parties to understand why the decision was made'. NAFW Guidance, Part 4 [12.2].

[189] *R (H) v Camden LBC and the Governors of Hampstead School* [1996] ELR 360 and *R (W) v Solihull BC* [1997] ELR 489.

[190] *R (W) v Northamptonshire CC* [1998] ELR 291.

[191] *R (S and B) v IAP of Birmingham CC* [2007] ELR 57; *R (Culkin) v Wirral IAP* [2009] ELR 287 (absence of evidence as to existence or consideration of school behavioural policy was not a fatal flaw).

11.141 Where the adequacy of the reasons given by an IAP is challenged within judicial review proceedings, the court may exceptionally receive further evidence giving a fuller explanation of the decision. Even where the court is satisfied, as it must be, that such evidence represents the actual reasons operative in the minds of IAP members at the relevant time, it will not automatically receive such material, but rather it will always be a matter of discretion.[192]

11.142 The degree of scrutiny and caution to be applied by the court when considering additional material depends on the subject matter of the administrative decision in question. Where important human rights are concerned anxious scrutiny is required. Where the subject matter is less important, the court may be less demanding and readier to accept subsequent reasons.[193] The court must, however, bear in mind the qualifications and experience of the persons involved:[194]

> 'It is one thing to require comprehensiveness and clarity from lawyers and those who regularly sit on administrative tribunals; it is another to require those qualities of occasional non-lawyer tribunal chairmen and members.'

School uniform

11.143 The adoption of uniforms by schools is normal, lawful and, indeed, positively endorsed within official guidance. As stated within the School Admissions Code for England,[195] 'School uniform plays a valuable role in contributing to the ethos and setting the tone of a school, and the Government strongly encourages schools to consider the introduction of uniforms where they do not already have them'. It is a mandatory requirement that admission authorities include information regarding school uniform policies within composite prospectuses, including information about schemes to defray the costs of purchase for eligible families.

11.144 Conflict may arise where it is alleged that a uniform policy conflicts with anti-discrimination legislation and disciplinary sanctions, including exclusion, are imposed. Save where discrimination is established, it is permissible to exclude a pupil for infringements of uniform policy 'where these are persistent and in open defiance of such rules'.[196] This will always be a course of last resort.

11.145 The leading case is *R (Begum) v Headteacher and Governors of Denbigh High School*,[197] in which the House of Lords considered whether, in refusing to allow a Muslim girl to wear the jilbab instead of the permitted shalwar kameeze, the school and its governors had, among other matters interfered with the claimant's right to manifest

---

[192] *R (W) v Northamptonshire CC* [1998] ELR 291; *R (AF) v Brent and Vassie LBC* [2000] ELR 550 (admission of fuller and more accurate statement of reasons which IAP considered); *R (H) v IAP for Y College* [2005] ELR 25 (clerk's notes providing a permission degree of clarification, thus negating the need for supplementary witness evidence); *R (T) v IAP for Devon CC and Governing Body of X College* [2007] ELR 499 (inappropriate to admit evidence where there was a substantial risk that the additional material did not represent the actual reasons of the decision-maker); *R (Culkin) v Wirral IAP* [2009] ELR 287 (clerk's notes and decision letter collectively explaining the sanction of exclusion); *R (W) v IAP of Bexley LBC* [2008] ELR 301 (clerk's notes simply a clarification or supplementation of the decision letter on the facts).
[193] *R (Nash) v Chelsea College of Art and Design* [2001] EWHC 538 (Admin) per Stanley Burnton J at [35]; extracted in the asylum case, *R (B) v Merton LBC* [2003] 4 All ER 280.
[194] *R (Nash) v Chelsea College of Art and Design* [2001] EWHC 538 (Admin) per Stanley Burnton J at [36].
[195] (2008) at [1.90]–[1.91]. For Wales, Schools Admissions Code (Wales) at [3.71]–[3.72].
[196] DfE Guidance on Uniform (September 2013). For Wales, see NAFW Guidance [1.4] and Guidance for Governing Bodies on School Uniform and Appearance Policies (revised July 2011).
[197] [2007] 1 AC 100. See also *R (X) v Y School* [2007] ELR 278.

her religion under article 9 of the ECHR and whether the interference, if any, was justified. The claimant, an existing pupil of the school, had adhered to its uniform code for two years. She later came to believe that the shalwar kameeze was not an appropriate form of dress for herself as a Muslim girl upon reaching puberty. She, therefore, attended the school dressed in a jilbab, a form of dress which concealed the shape of her arms and legs. She refused to attend school unless permitted to wear a jilbab, whilst the school refused to allow her to attend unless she complied with the uniform code.

11.146 The claimant contended that the defendant had unjustifiably limited her right under art 9 to manifest her religion or beliefs and violated her right not to be denied education under art 2 of Protocol 1 of the ECHR. The claim was dismissed by Bennett J at first instance, accepted by the Court of Appeal, before being ultimately rejected by the House of Lords.

11.147 By a majority, the House of Lords held that the claimant's art 9 rights had not been infringed, whilst they were unanimous in stating that any interference was justified. The court confirmed that art 9 did not entail freedom to manifest one's religion at any time and place of one's own choosing. The right to manifest one's belief was qualified and what constituted interference would depend on all the circumstances of the case, including the extent to which an individual could reasonably expect to be at liberty to manifest her beliefs in practice. The court placed particular reliance on the fact that the claimant's family had chosen the school for her with knowledge of its uniform requirements and that she could have sought the help of the school and the LA in solving the problem, if necessary, by changing schools.

11.148 In *R (Playfoot) v Governing Body of Millais School*,[198] the High Court considered whether wearing a 'purity' ring at school was a manifestation of the claimant's belief in pre-marriage celibacy, whether the school's refusal to permit the wearing of the ring constituted interference with her right to manifest her belief, and if so, whether it was justified. Whilst extending time to pursue the challenge, the court rejected the claim relying, among other considerations, on findings that the wearing of a ring was not 'intimately linked' to the belief in chastity before marriage. There were also other means open to her to practise her belief, such as attaching the ring to a chain or to a bag, as the school had suggested. Otherwise, the school's policy was plainly prescribed by law, the rules were made for the legitimate purpose of protecting the rights and freedoms of others and this had been clearly communicated to the claimant. In the particular circumstances, the school was fully justified in acting as it did.

11.149 In *R (Watkins-Singh) v Governing Body of Aberdare Girls' High School*,[199] the High Court considered whether the exclusion of a Sikh pupil from school for wearing a religious bangle (a Kara) was unlawful. The pupil believed that, as supported by objective evidence, the wearing of the Kara bangle was of exceptional importance as an expression of her race and culture. The court held that the defendant had clearly failed to comply with its obligations under 71 of the Race Relations Act 1976 and that race equality played no part, as it should have done, in its decision-making process. As wearing the Kara was unobtrusive and was unlikely to make inroads into the school uniform policy, the discriminatory effect far outweighed any justification for the school's treatment of the claimant.

---

[198] [2007] ELR 484.
[199] [2008] ELR 561. See also *R (G) v St Gregory's Catholic Science College* [2011] ELR 446 (successful claim based on indirect discrimination; refusal to allow pupil to wear hair in cornrows).

11.150 Uniform cases are, as they have been expressly described by the courts, likely to be fact-sensitive. Schools have considerable freedom in determining their ethos and character. If the relevant issues have been identified and considered by policy makers, the courts are highly unlikely to interfere.

PARTICULAR CONSIDERATIONS

Standing and funding

11.151 In judicial review proceedings arising from educational provision, the appropriate claimant will invariably be the parent, save where a pupil is provided a direct right of appeal.[200] If a pupil is named with the intention of manipulating public funding, where otherwise this would be restricted on the grounds of financial eligibility, parties and their advisers can expect robust censure.[201]

Delay

11.152 It is well established that delay in the context of applications for judicial review of an education decision is highly unlikely to be excused. In most, if not each case there is liable to be an effect on other pupils or otherwise prejudice to efficient administration of relevant establishment. Undue delay has precluded the grant of permission or relief across the education spectrum, for example:

- School reorganisation and closure.[202]
- Higher education determinations.[203]
- Admission arrangements.[204]
- Registration issues.[205]
- Exclusion appeals.[206]

11.153 If funding difficulties are experienced, these must be evidenced.[207] Failure to do so is likely to result in refusal of an extension.[208]

---

[200] For example, the co-extensive right of appeal to a child who expresses a preference for a sixth-form school place, as created by recent amendment to SSFA, s 94.
[201] *R (B) v Head Teacher of Alperton Community School* [2001] ELR 359 (exclusion); *R (T) Hackney LBC* [1991] COD 454 (admissions); *R (JC) Richmond LBC* [2001] ELR 21 (admissions); *R (Bandtock) v Secretary of State for Education* [2001] ELR 333 (school closure); *R (S) v SENT & City of Westminster* [1996] ELR 102 (special educational needs).
[202] *R (N) v Leeds CC* [1999] ELR 324; *R (Melton and others) v Oxford CC* [2001] EWHC Admin 245.
[203] *R (Lakareber) v University of Portsmouth* [1999] ELR 135; *R (K) v University of Nottingham* [1998] ELR 184.
[204] *R (Ali) v Bradford MBC* [1994] ELR 299; *R (B) v Rochdale MBC* [2000] Ed. CR 117; *R (Taylor) v Blackpool BC* [1999] ELR 237.
[205] *R (X) v Governing Body of Gateway Primary School* [2001] ELR 321; *R (M) v Barking and Dagenham LBC* [2003] ELR 144.
[206] *R (M) v Secretary of State for Home Department* [1999] Ed. CR 656.
[207] *R (T) v Governors of La Sainte Union Convent School* [1996] ELR 98.
[208] *R (Lakareber) v University of Portsmouth* [1999] ELR 135 (distinguishing *R (Jackson) v Stratford-on-Avon DC and others* [1985] 3 All ER 769 on the basis of failure to provide information regarding funding enquiries).

HUMAN RIGHTS

11.154 Human rights jurisprudence has, to date, had a muted influence on education law. The ECHR which guarantees basic rights and freedoms is given effect in the United Kingdom by the Human Rights Act 1998 (HRA). Article 2 of First Protocol to the ECHR provides that:

> 'No person shall be denied the right to education. In the exercise of any functions which it assumes in relation to education and to teaching, the State shall respect the right of parents to ensure such education and teaching in conformity with their own religious and philosophical convictions.'

11.155 The principle, as stated by the European Court of Human Rights in the Belgian Linguistic Case (No 2),[209] is that art 2 of the First Protocol does not confer a right to an education which the domestic system does not provide:

> 'all member States of the Council of Europe possessed, at the time of the opening of the Protocol to their signature, and still do possess, a general and official educational system. There neither was, nor is now, therefore, any question of requiring each State to establish such a system, but merely of guaranteeing to persons subject to the jurisdiction of the Contracting Parties the right, in principle, to avail themselves of the means of instruction existing at a given time.'

11.156 It was authoritatively stated in *R (Begum) v Headmaster and Governors of Denbigh High School*,[210] that regard should be had, in the first instance, to domestic provision:

> 'The Strasbourg jurisprudence ... makes clear how art 2 should be interpreted. The underlying premise of the article was that all existing member states of the Council of Europe had, and all future member states would have, an established system of state education. It was intended to guarantee fair and non-discriminatory access to that system by those within the jurisdiction of the respective states. The fundamental importance of education in a modern democratic state was recognised to require no less. But the guarantee is, in comparison with most other convention guarantees, a weak one, and deliberately so. There is no right to education of a particular kind or quality, other than that prevailing in the state. There is no convention guarantee of compliance with domestic law. There is no convention guarantee of education at or by a particular institution. There is no convention objection to the expulsion of a pupil from an educational institution on disciplinary grounds, unless (in the ordinary way) there is no alternative source of state education open to the pupil (as in *Eren v Turkey* [2006] ECHR 60856/00). The test, as always under the convention, is a highly pragmatic one, to be applied to the specific facts of the case: have the authorities of the state acted so as to deny to a pupil effective access to such educational facilities as the state provides for such pupils?'

11.157 Similarly, in *A v Essex County Council*,[211] the Supreme Court considered the position of a severely disabled child with SEN who was left without schooling for an 18-month period while the LA secured a place at one of the few specialist schools which could cope with his behaviour. A complicated assessment of A's medical and psychiatric problems was necessary before any long-term plans could be made for his continuing

---

[209] (1968) 1 EHRR 252 at 281.
[210] [2006] 2 AC 363 per Lord Bingham of Cornhill at [24].
[211] [2010] 3 WLR 509.

education. This took eight months to undertake and it was a further ten months before A could be placed in a special residential school where he was able to receive the 24-hour supervision that he needed.

11.158 Dismissing A's appeal against the striking-out of his claim at first instance, the court held (by a majority) that whilst, during the 18-month period, there had been a failure to comply with the requirements of the EA 1996 and a failure to provide any significant education to A, that did not mean that there had been an infringement of his rights under art 2 of the First Protocol.

11.159 In such a case, it was hardly surprising that a LA might be unable, through lack of resources, to immediately satisfy the obligations imposed by the EA 1996. In so far as a state's system of education made provision for children with SEN, art 2 guaranteed fair and non-discriminatory access for those children to the special facilities that were available. But if the facilities were limited, so that immediate access could not be provided, regard must be had to that limitation.

11.160 Accordingly, whilst it is accepted that everyone is entitled to be educated to a minimum standard,[212] the right under art 2 extends no further.

CONCLUSIONS

11.161 In the exercise of any functions which it assumes in relation to education and to teaching, the state must respect the right of parents to ensure that such education and teaching conforms to their religious and philosophical convictions.[213] A conviction is only liable to be respected in so far as it is compatible with the provision of efficient instruction and training and the avoidance of unreasonable expenditure. It would appear that Convention rights are unlikely to be a more effective basis of challenge, procedurally or substantively, in the context admission or with regard to exclusion appeals.[214]

---

[212] *R (Holub) v Secretary of State for the Home Dept* [2001] ELR 401.
[213] *R (Watkins-Singh) v Governing Body of Aberdare Girls' High School* [2008] ELR 561 (failure to respect religious conviction); *R (K) v Newham LBC* [2002] ELR 390 (failure to ascertain parental conviction); *R (Begbie) v Secretary of State for Education and Employment* [2000] ELR 445 (right to education did not guarantee the right to an assisted place at an independent school); *L (Hughes) v Hereford and Worcester CC* [2000] ELR 375 (no requirement to provide special facilities to accommodate a particular conviction).
[214] *R (JC) v Richmond LBC* [2001] ELR 21 (admissions); *R (B) v Head Teacher of Alperton Community School* [2001] ELR 359 (exclusions).

CHAPTER 12

LICENSING

INTRODUCTION
Local decision-making

12.01 Many functions under the various licensing regimes are carried out by local authorities. These licensing functions range from hackney carriages, street traders to sex establishments. The scope of the licensing responsibilities vested in local authorities has also increased significantly following the implementation of the Licensing Act 2003. This places the responsibility for the licensing of alcohol sales, regulated entertainment and the provision of late night refreshment in the hands of local councils. Local councils discharge their licensing responsibilities through committees and sub committees comprising councillors and/or through council officials who have delegated powers. The statutory schemes usually involve rights of appeal from the decisions of councils to the magistrates' court (and in some instances the Crown Court). All these bodies are public bodies carrying out public functions and as such their actions may, in appropriate cases, be susceptible to challenges by way of applications for judicial review.

Specialist tribunals

12.02 Some of the other licensing functions are carried out by specialist tribunals. Examples of these include the Gambling Commission (who deal with certain licences in respect of gambling) and the Office of the Traffic Commissioner (who deal with, for example, the licensing of the road haulage industry). The applicability of judicial review claims to such bodies is not as prevalent as it is in respect of the licensing functions carried out by local councils. These bodies operate within specific tribunal systems which involve statutory rights of appeal to specialist tribunals.

Chapter outline

12.03 This chapter will consider, in the context of judicial review and Administrative Court proceedings, the status of a licence, those responsible for regulating them and some of the key areas that inform the decision-making process within the licensing sphere.

STATUS OF A LICENCE
Permission/authorisation

12.04 A licence is a permission or authorisation allowing the licence holder to carry on a particular activity. In effect, it sets out the scope of that which has been authorised by the regulator. Depending on the circumstances, a person seeking to carry on an activity may need multiple authorisations, for instance permissions under different regulatory regimes if the activity crosses different regulatory contexts.[1] Sometimes the scope of an activity is restricted by reference to conditions, which are imposed on the licence. Breach of an authorisation often engages significant criminal sanctions under the respective statutory codes. In the light of that, both domestic and European jurisprudence require that the licence must be sufficiently certain.[2] In the latter case Mitting J referred to the observations of Scott Baker LJ in *Crawley Borough Council v Attenborough*.[3] In *Attenborough*, the Administrative Court was considering the clarity of conditions which had been attached to a premises licence under the Licensing Act 2003. Scott Baker LJ explained that it must be apparent from reading the licence what the licence and its conditions mean. The licence and the conditions must be clear, not just to those having specialist knowledge of licensing but to those who have no knowledge of licensing at all. Indeed, breach of a condition carries criminal sanction and a vague and unclear licence could render the terms of it unenforceable.

Possession or property?

12.05 As explained, a licence is an authorisation or permission. In other words, it is a regulatory approval. Ordinarily understood, therefore, a licence in itself would not appear to be the 'possession' or 'property' of a licence holder. Notwithstanding this, the issue has generated not insubstantial litigation before the Administrative Court and higher appellate jurisdiction.

12.06 A question that often arises is whether a licence is the possession or property of the licence holder and whether, therefore, it engages the protection afforded by Article 1 of the First Protocol of the European Convention of Human Rights. Article 1 of the First Protocol provides:

> 'Every natural or legal person is entitled to the peaceful enjoyment of his possessions. No one shall be deprived of his possessions except in the public interest and subject to the conditions provided for by law and by the general principles of international law.
>
> The preceding provisions shall not, however, in any way impair the right of a State to enforce such laws as it deems necessary to control the use of property in accordance with the general interest or to secure the payment of taxes or other contributions or penalties.'

12.07 It was explained by the European Court of Human Rights in *Sporrong v Sweden*[4] that the Article comprises three rules.[5] Those three rules are as follows: the first rule is the principle of peaceful enjoyment of property. The second rule deals with deprivation of possessions. The third rule recognises that Member States are entitled to control the use of property in accordance with the general interest by enforcing such law as they deem necessary for that purpose. It should be recognised that merely because the Article is engaged this does not necessarily mean that there has been a violation of the right. The importance of the Article becoming engaged is that the burden thereafter shifts to the

---

[1] See, for example, *R (Kelly) v Liverpool City Council* before the Administrative Court on 5 September 2008 (unreported) per HHJ Langan QC and the Court of Appeal (permission hearing) at [2009] EWCA Civ 191 per Dyson LJ.
[2] See, for example, *R (the Mayor and Citizens of Westminster City Council) v Metropolitan Stipendary Magistrate* [2008] EWHC 1202 (Admin).
[3] [2006] EWHC 1278 (Admin).
[4] [1982] 5 EHRR 35.
[5] See also *Fredin v Sweden* [1991] ECHR 12033/86 in this regard.

public authority as the State to justify any interference in accordance with the Convention so as to show there has been no violation of the Article.

12.08 The issue was considered by the Administrative Court in *R (Royden) v Wirral Metropolitan Borough Council*.[6] This case concerned the decision of a council to remove the limit on the number of vehicles licensed as hackney carriage vehicles within its area. The claimant was a proprietor of a hackney carriage vehicle licensed by the council and he argued, amongst other things, that a hackney carriage vehicle licence was a 'possession' and that the council's decision constituted an interference with the peaceful enjoyment of that possession. The case was argued specifically on the basis that the result of the council's decision would be to eliminate the value of the claimant's licence. Christopher Bellamy QC (sitting as a Deputy High Court Judge) reviewed a number of decisions of the European Court of Human Rights and the European Commission. It was explained that he had 'some difficulty accepting that an authorisation granted by the State under public law to carry out a particular activity' could itself be property or a possession under the Convention.

12.09 The Deputy Judge adopted the reasoning from the European Court of Human Rights decision in *Tre Trakoter Aktiebolag v Sweden*.[7] In this case, a company (TTA) had a licence to sell alcoholic beverages at a restaurant, Le Cardinal. The licence was withdrawn by the relevant authorities in Sweden. The European Court found that Article 1 of the First Protocol was engaged. This was not because the licence itself constituted a 'possession' or 'property' but rather because the economic interests connected to the running of the restaurant were 'possessions' for the purpose of the Article. It was decided that:

> 'the Court takes the view that the economic interests connected with the running of Le Cardinal were "possessions" for the purposes of Article 1 of the Protocol. Indeed, the Court has already found that maintenance of the applicant company's business and that its withdrawal had adverse effects on the goodwill and value of the restaurants. Such withdrawal thus constitutes, in the circumstances of this case, an interference with TTA's right to the "peaceful enjoyment of [its] possessions".'

12.10 The interference in this case, however, was held to be justified in accordance with the Convention. It was held to be in compliance with Swedish law and proportionately undertaken in the pursuit of the general interest, namely the control of the sale of alcoholic beverages.

12.11 It therefore appears that a licence in itself does not constitute a possession or property for the purposes of the Convention. However, as in the *Tre Trakoter* case, economic interests connected to the running of a business or the underlying assets may well do so.

12.12 There is, however, domestic authority from the Court of Appeal which approached the issue on the basis that a licence did constitute a 'possession' or 'property' for the purposes of Article 1 of the First Protocol (see *Crompton v Department of Transport*,[8] a case concerning the revocation of a road haulage operators' licence). It is right to recognise that the issue of whether the licence was a 'possession' was not actually argued in *Crompton*. The Court of Appeal proceeded on the agreed basis that

---

[6] [2002] EWHC 2484 Admin.
[7] [1991] EHRR 309.
[8] [2003] EWCA Civ 64.

the licence did constitute a possession for the purposes of Article 1 of the First Protocol. Indeed, the approach by the Court of Appeal in *Crompton* is difficult to reconcile with the European jurisprudence (see, for example, the reasoning in *Tre Trakoter*) and the approach taken in the other domestic authorities. The erroneous approach in *Crompton*, namely, that a licence was a possession for the purposes of Article 1 of the First Protocol, has now been recognised by the Court of Appeal in *Waltham Forest NHS Primary Care Trust & Others v Malik*[9] (however, on its facts, the decision in *Crompton* was justified since the underlying economic interests were affected).

12.13 *Malik* was a case which considered whether the inclusion of a doctor on a NHS Primary Care Trust's approved list of medical practitioners was a possessory right for the purpose of Article 1 of the First Protocol. The Court of Appeal in *Malik* held that it was not a 'possession' for the purposes of Article 1. The court rejected the argument that a licence to practise a profession could be a 'possession' and also rejected the argument that future loss of income was a loss of a 'possession'. *Malik* has also been considered in different licensing contexts (see, for example, *Security Industry Authority v Stewart & Others*).[10]

12.14 In *Stewart & Others* the Administrative Court considered whether people who had licences to work as door supervisors under the regime in place before the Private Security Industry Act 2001, but who were disqualified under the 2001 Act by reason of the statutory criteria in that Act, were thereby unlawfully deprived of their 'possessions' for the purposes of Article 1 of the First Protocol. The court said that in the light of *Malik* the contention that earlier permissions were 'possessions' for the purposes of the Convention involved '*mountainous*' difficulties.

12.15 *Stewart & Others* illustrates a departure from the previous authority on the point, *Nicholds & Others v Security Industry Authority*,[11] a case which considered the same issue and legislation as in *Stewart & Others*. In *Nicholds & Others*, Kenneth Parker QC sitting as a Deputy High Court Judge held that, despite his reservations, he had to proceed on the basis that the permissions previously enjoyed by the claimants did constitute 'possessions'. This was in the light of decisions such as *Crompton* and *Malik* at first instance but it was, however, recognised in *Nicholds & Others* that an expectation of future income is not a 'possession' and would not engage the protection afforded by Article 1 of the First Protocol.

12.16 The issues have so far been considered from the perspective of a licence being withdrawn. However, a decision to refuse to grant a licence may also engage Article 1 of the First Protocol. This occurred in the *Miss Behavin'* litigation.[12] In this case, it was argued that a decision of Belfast City Council to refuse to grant a licence for a sex establishment under the Local Government (Miscellaneous Provisions) (Northern Ireland) Order 1985 (the equivalent to the 1982 Act in England and Wales) engaged Article 1 of the First Protocol. Lord Kerr CJ in the Northern Irish Court of Appeal held that the refusal of the council to allow the appellant to use its premises in a way that would permit their commercial exploitation engaged Article 1 of the First Protocol. In the House of Lords it was acknowledged that the Article may have been engaged.

---

[9] [2007] EWCA Civ 265.
[10] [2007] EWHC 2338 (Admin).
[11] [2006] EWHC 1792 (Admin).
[12] See Northern Irish Court of Appeal [2006] NI 181 and House of Lords [2007] UKHL 19.

However, given the circumstances being considered in that case (namely, the right to sell pornography), the House Lords considered the argument that there was a violation of the Article to be weak.

Summary of the principles

12.17 The following points summarise the above review of authorities:

(1) a licence is a regulatory approval. The scope of the authorisation must be sufficiently certain and clear from the licence;

(2) a licence is not a 'possession' or 'property' for the purposes of Article 1 of the First Protocol;

(3) however, connected economic interests may well be (see for example, *Tre Traktoer* where goodwill and the value of the restaurant were said to be such); but

(4) the economic interest must be existing or vested. By way of example, a mere right or expectation to future income will not engage Article 1 of the First Protocol.

ROLE OF LOCAL LICENSING BODIES

12.18 As explained earlier, a number of the licensing regimes specify that the functions are carried out by local councils. The responsibilities are often carried out through committees, sub committees or officers of the council. To lawfully carry out the licensing functions, the responsibilities must be properly delegated (note s 101 of the Local Government Act 1972 allows a council to delegate its responsibilities to committees, sub committees and individual officers of the council). The identity of the body within the council responsible for the function will depend on how matters have been delegated within the particular council. However, some statutes, see for example the Licensing Act 2003, also include specific provisions relating to the delegation of licensing responsibilities and who may carry out the particular functions.

Quasi-judicial function?

12.19 The local council committees comprise democratically elected local councillors. It has been generally accepted that proceedings before such committees are by their nature quasi-judicial. A clear statement of this proposition is found in *R v London Borough of Wandsworth, ex p Darker Enterprises Limited*,[13] a case which concerned an application for the renewal of a sex establishment licence under the Local Government (Miscellaneous Provisions) Act 1982, Sch 3. Turner J recognised that it is generally accepted that proceedings before such a sub-committee are quasi-judicial in their nature.

12.20 Similar observations were made by the Court of Appeal in *R v Preston Borough Council, ex p Quietlynn Ltd*,[14] a case concerning the licensing of sex establishments. In that case Simon Brown LJ explained that a local council was exercising an administrative function involving an element of judicial process when it considered applications for licences. However, more recently, the Court of Appeal in *R (Hope & Glory Public House Ltd) v Westminster Magistrates' Court & Others*[15] has explained

---

[13] (Unreported) 15 January 1999.
[14] (1984) 83 LGR 308.
[15] [2011] EWCA Civ 31.

that whilst a local council has a duty to carry out its decision-making process fairly under the Licensing Act 2003, the decision itself is not a judicial or quasi-judicial act. Rather, it is an administrative function and 'the exercise of a power delegated by the people as a whole to decide what the public interest requires'. This was endorsed by Hickinbottom J in the case of *Matthew Taylor v Manchester City Council & TCG Bars Limited*[16] where it was stated:

> 'Given the administrative nature of the authority's function, it is perfectly appropriate for the authority thus to liaise with the applicant licensee and the responsible authorities/interested parties to see whether a compromise can be reached ... relevant representations trigger an administrative investigation by the licensing authority into the effect the proposed changes will make to the promotion of the licensing objectives: that decision making process having been triggered, it is then for the authority to weigh the various strands of public interest and determine whether the promotion of those objectives requires the rejection of any part of the application or modification of the licence conditions.'

Local decision-making

12.21 One of the objects of the licensing regimes is to promote local decision-making by local people based on local knowledge. This is why Parliament vests the responsibilities for such issues in the hands of local councils. As such, the fact that a local council in a different part of the country has granted a similar, perhaps even identical, application would not generally oblige a local council in an another part of the country to do the same. By way of example, this has been specifically recognised in respect of the licensing of private hire vehicles: see *Chauffeur Bikes Limited v Leeds City Council*.[17] In this case, Poole J explained that the legislation, namely, the Local Government (Miscellaneous Provisions) Act 1976, permitted local councils to individually consider the issues. Poole J illustrated this point by explaining that the fact that a local council in Kent may have come to one conclusion on whether a particular vehicle should be licensed did not oblige one in Yorkshire to do the same. That said, depending on the context, it may be that the experience and practice of other local authorities cannot properly be ignored and would be a relevant consideration.[18]

12.22 It should always be borne in mind that licensing decisions are being taken by democratically elected councillors and not lawyers. In *R v Reading Borough Council, ex parte Johnson*[19] Goldring J considered the decision of a licensing committee to issue further hackney carriage licences in its district. It was explained that:

> 'Real deference should be paid to the decision of decision-takers who are democratically elected and who take their decision following at least adequate consultation (as in my view this undoubtedly was) with interested parties. That decision should not be judged in an over refined and over legalistic way.'

Local knowledge

12.23 Local knowledge plays a key part in the decision-making processes undertaken by local councils. In *ex p Johnson* the Administrative Court explained that local councillors

---

[16] [2012] EWHC 3467 (Admin).
[17] [2005] EWHC 2369 (Admin).
[18] See *R (Lunt) v Liverpool City Council* [2009] EWHC 2356 (Admin) per Blake J.
[19] [2004] EWHC 765 (Admin).

would be failing in their duty as councillors if they ignored their local knowledge when making licensing decisions. Goldring J explained that:

> 'I see nothing objectionable in local councillors, plainly familiar with [the area], using their local knowledge of how the taxi system operates in practice. Indeed, they would be failing in their duty as councillors if they ignored their local knowledge.'

12.24 The Administrative Court is often more reluctant to interfere with decisions that are highly dependent on local knowledge. In *R (4 Wins Leisure Limited) v Blackpool Licensing Committee & Others*,[20] proceedings in respect of the Licensing Act 2003, the issue was whether a trade competitor was a person with a business within the vicinity of the applicant's premises and whether, therefore, it was entitled to make representations in respect of the application for a licence. Sullivan J decided that:

> 'Whether or not premises can sensibly be said to be in the vicinity of another must be very much a question of fact and degree. Moreover, it is a question that is highly dependent upon local knowledge. That, no doubt, is why the question was left for local licensing committees to determine. It would only be in very unusual circumstances that this court, never having seen the site and being wholly unfamiliar with the area in question, would be able to say that such a judgmental conclusion of a local committee was unlawful on the ground of being irrational.'

12.25 However, a decision-maker must measure their own local knowledge and views against the evidence presented to them. In *R (Daniel Thwaites PLC) v Wirral Magistrates' Court & Others*[21] the decision of a Magistrates' Court hearing an appeal under the Licensing Act 2003 to refuse to grant extended hours of operation to a licensed premises was judicially reviewed. In that case, importantly, the police had no objection to the application. Black J explained that:

> 'It is clear from the Guidance that drawing on local knowledge, at least the local knowledge of local licensing authorities, is an important feature of the Act's approach. There can be little doubt that local Magistrates are also entitled to take into account their own knowledge but, in my judgment, they must measure their own views against the evidence presented to them. In some cases, the evidence presented will require them to adjust their own impression. This is particularly likely to be so where it is given by a responsible authority such as the Police.'

12.26 Indeed, the limits of acting on local knowledge should be appreciated. Local knowledge should not be equated with expertise in a specialist area of assessment (*R (Lunt & Others) v Liverpool City Council*).[22]

ROLE OF LOCAL COUNCILLORS

Strong and robust opinions

12.27 Local councillors are also politicians. In their roles as local politicians, councillors are likely to have views (perhaps strong views) about issues of local public interest and to have expressed them publicly. In general, such should not disqualify them from hearing and determining licensing matters.

---

[20] [2007] EWHC 2213 (Admin).
[21] [2008] EWHC 838 (Admin).
[22] [2009] EWHC 2356 (Admin) per Blake J.

12.28 This is supported by a number of decisions concerning the licensing of sex establishments. In *R v Reading Borough Council, ex p Quietlynn*,[23] the case concerned an application for a sex establishment licence. Members of a sub-committee who determined the application had previously decided it was opposed to sex establishments and some opposition had been expressed publicly. The issue in the case was whether the decision to refuse the licence was objectionable on the grounds of bias. Kennedy J explained that a councillor's role was to formulate and express views on subjects of local interest (such as the licensing of sex establishments) and that they should not be disqualified from deciding something, which Parliament has expressly decided to vest in local councillors, by merely carrying out this role. See also the approach in *R v Chesterfield Borough Council, ex p Darker Enterprises Ltd*.[24] The key point is that the councillors should be prepared to fairly consider the issues.

12.29 Notwithstanding the above as a matter of law, the court did explain in *ex p Quietlynn* that as a matter of practice it would be better if councillors who have been particularly vocal in respect of the relevant issues are not appointed to the committees deciding the applications. It is also important to recognise that the outcome of complaints of bias or predetermination largely depend on the facts of the individual case. This is an area of law that is highly fact sensitive.

A closed mind approach?

12.30 The authorities referred to earlier pre-date what is presently the leading case on issues of bias, namely, the House of Lords decision in *Porter v Magill*.[25] In this case, the House of Lords set out the general test to be applied when considering complaints of apparent bias; namely, whether the circumstances were such that it would lead a fair minded and informed observer to conclude that there was a real possibility that the decision-maker was biased.

12.31 The *Porter v Magill* test was applied by Richards J in *Georgiou v Enfield Borough Council & Others*[26] to the decisions of local councillors comprising planning committees; namely, whether the circumstances would lead a fair minded and informed observer to conclude that the members of the planning committee were biased in the sense of approaching the decision with a closed mind and without impartial consideration of the planning issues.

12.32 This approach was applied in the licensing context in *R (Aujla & Others) v Slough Borough Council*.[27] These proceedings were concerned with a decision of the council to de-limit the number of hackney carriage vehicle licences issued in its district. It was unsuccessfully alleged that this decision was tainted by bias since two of the councillors had a past and present connection with the private hire trade.

12.33 In *Aujla & others* the court considered whether the council had approached the matter with a closed mind, or predetermined it. It concluded that the ground had not been made out. Whilst not relevant to the issues in that case, Goldring J observed *obiter* that 'councillors are entitled to have robust views without the decision in which they participate being defective'. This observation provides some support post decisions such

---

[23] [1986] 85 LGR 387.
[24] [1992] COD 466.
[25] [2001] UKHL 67.
[26] [2004] EWHC 799 (Admin).
[27] [2005] EWHC 1866 (Admin) per Goldring J.

as *Porter* and *Georgiou* for the approach that was taken in the *Quietlynn Ltd* and *Darker Enterprises Ltd* line of authorities. Notwithstanding the high threshold for challenges on the ground of bias, it is important that any such issues are raised contemporaneously for a failure to raise the issue at first instance is likely, in itself, to be fatal.[28]

A less strict approach?

12.34 The decision of Collins J in *R (Island Farm Development) v Bridgend County Borough Council* appeared to signal a departure from the stricter application of the *Porter* test as modified in *Georgiou*. Collins J acknowledged that councillors would have views on issues of public interest and are likely to have expressed them publicly. This has also been recognised more recently, again in the planning field, by the Court of Appeal in *R (Lewis) v Persimmon Homes Teesside Ltd*.[29] It was held that there was an important difference between predisposition (which was legitimate) and predetermination (which was illegitimate). In considering complaints that a decision-maker had predetermined the outcome or approached the matter with a closed mind the court explained that the context of the case, in particular the role of elected councillors, should always be borne in mind. This means acknowledging, and bearing in mind, that local councillors do, and are entitled to, express their views publicly on issues of public interest.

Summary of the general principles

12.35 The key point appears to be that councillors should act fairly when considering matters and be willing to listen. The present position of the authorities might be summarised as follows:

(1) Local councillors are of course also politicians. In this role, they are likely to have views (perhaps strong views) about issues of local public interest and to have expressed them publicly. In general, the expression of strong views should not, without more, disqualify them from carrying out licensing functions in which the issues they have previously spoken about are relevant (see, for example, *R v Amber Valley District Council, ex p Jackson*;[30] *R v Reading Borough Council, ex p Quietlynn*;[31] *R (Aujla) v Slough Borough Council*[32] and *R (Island Farm Development) v Bridgend County Borough Council*).[33] It is important to recognise however that this is an area of the law which is highly fact sensitive and therefore each case will be largely dependant on its specific facts.

(2) In considering a complaint that the decision-maker had a closed mind then the role and responsibilities of local councillors and the context of the case are important and have to be borne in mind (see, for example, *R (Lewis) v Redcar & Cleveland Borough Council & Others*).[34]

(3) The responsibility of local councillors when acting as decision-makers is to approach the issues fairly and on their merits, even though they may approach those issues with a predisposition to an outcome. They are obliged to fairly consider the issues and to be prepared to change their views if so persuaded (see,

---

[28] See the case of *R (Alistair Lockwood Thompson) v Oxford City Council* [2013] EWHC 1819 (Admin).
[29] [2008] EWCA Civ 746.
[30] [1985] 1 WLR 298 per Woolf J.
[31] [1986] 85 LGR 387 per Kennedy J.
[32] [2005] EWHC 1866 (Admin) per Goldring J.
[33] [2006] EWHC 2189 (Admin) per Collins J.
[34] [2008] EWCA Civ 746 per Pill, Rix and Longmore LLJ.

for example, *R v Amber Valley District Council, ex p Jackson*;[35] *R (Island Farm Development) v Bridgend County Borough Council*[36] and *R (Lewis) v Redcar & Cleveland Borough Council & Others*).[37]

(4) There is an important distinction between predisposition to an outcome (which is legitimate) and predetermination of an outcome (which is illegitimate). The latter test of predetermination is a difficult test to satisfy (see, for example, *R (Lewis) v Redcar & Cleveland Borough Council & Others*[38] and see also *R (Chandler) v London Borough of Camden & Others*).[39]

12.36 The more recent authorities have considered the role of local councillors in the planning context and have approached the issues in the context that planning committees do not sit in a judicial or quasi-judicial capacity. It has been said that licensing committees do sit in a quasi-judicial capacity. There may, therefore, be some argument as to the differing status between a planning committee and a licensing committee and thus the context within which a complaint has to be considered and whether a licensing committee could seek support from the more recent legal decisions concerning planning authorities. However, the point remains that councillors exercise a constitutional role and are likely to be vocal in their area on issues of public interest. This context is important when considering arguments relating to predetermination.

ROLE OF THE APPEAL COURTS

12.37 It should be recognised that claims for judicial review are not appeals. A judicial review is a supervisory review of the decision-making process. Some of the licensing regimes do, however, provide for statutory rights of appeal to the magistrates' court and the Crown Court. The legislation itself usually provides for how and when an appeal should be made. The particular legislation should be carefully considered to ascertain whether it provides for such a right of appeal.

Time periods for appealing

12.38 The statutes often set out a fixed time period within which an appeal must be brought. It is usual for such provisions not to include a power to extend that time period. If that is so, then such a power cannot usually be implied into the legislation. Moreover, the court does not possess any inherent jurisdiction or discretion to extend time. As such, a court would not have jurisdiction to hear an appeal brought out of time. This was the situation in *Stockton on Tees Borough Council v Latif*[40] where an appeal was brought in respect of a hackney carriage and private hire licensing matter under the Local Government (Miscellaneous Provisions) Act 1976 which incorporated the Public Health Act 1936. A fixed period of 21 days was provided in which an appeal could be brought to the magistrates' court from the decision of a local council. The Administrative Court held that there was no power to extend the time limit. Christopher

---

[35] [1985] 1 WLR 298 per Woolf J.
[36] [2006] EWHC 2189 (Admin) per Collins J.
[37] [2008] EWCA Civ 746 per Pill, Rix and Longmore LLJ.
[38] [2008] EWCA Civ 746 per Longmore LJ at para 109.
[39] [2009] EWHC 219 (Admin) per Forbes J.
[40] [2009] EWHC 228 (Admin).

Symons QC (sitting as a Deputy High Court Judge) explained that Parliament had not provided for an extension of time and could have done so if that had been the intention.[41]

The nature of the appeal

12.39 Statutory appeals are unrestricted. Permission, therefore, is not usually required. The appeal involves a rehearing of the applications on its merits. In effect, the appeal court when hearing such an appeal stands in the shoes of the licensing committee or sub-committee who determined the matter. This is a well-established practice and has been explained in many cases. The leading case is *Sagnata Investments Ltd v Norwich Corporation*.[42] This case concerned an application for a permit to provide amusements with prizes under the now repealed Betting, Gaming & Lotteries Act 1963. The principle is, however, applicable to all forms of licensing which involve unrestricted statutory appeals from the decision of councils.

12.40 It has been applied in a variety of other licensing contexts. Other examples include *Darlington Borough Council v Paul Wakefield*[43] (a case involving the licensing of hackney carriage drivers) and *R (Blackwood) v Birmingham Magistrates' Court & Others*[44] (a case concerning an application for a premises licence under the Licensing Act 2003). In *Rushmoor Borough Council v Richards*[45] (a case involving an appeal against the decision of a council to vary an entertainment licence) Tuckey J confirmed that the appeal was a rehearing. The reasoning in this case is instructive as to the general approach to be taken to cases involving similar statutory appeals. Tuckey J explained that there was nothing in the particular legislation itself to suggest that the procedure was to be any different to the procedure that would usually be found in other situations where this type of process is in place; that is, a rehearing of the case on the appeal.

12.41 The rehearing, however, should be confined to the issues raised in the notice of appeal and effective case management by the appeal courts should identify the live issues in any event.[46]

Admissibility of fresh evidence

12.42 Since the appeal is by way of re-hearing then fresh evidence is admissible. In *Rushmoor Borough Council v Richards*[47] Tuckey J explained that the appeal court is not restricted to hearing evidence about events before the council's decision. It must consider all the relevant evidence, whether it relates to events before or after that decision. In *Noor Mohammed Khan v Coventry Magistrates' Court and Coventry City Council* the Court of Appeal made it clear that fresh evidence includes evidence pertaining to grounds not raised in pursuit of a revocation before the licensing committee. The magistrates' court's function was to consider the application by reference to the statutory licensing objectives untrammelled by any of the regulations that governed the procedure for a review under the Licensing Act 2003.

---

41   See also the approach in *R v Pembrokeshire Justices, ex p Bennell* [1968] 2 WLR 858.
42   [1971] 2 QB 614.
43   [1989] 153 JP 481.
44   [2006] EWHC 1800 (Admin).
45   (1996) *The Times*, 5 February.
46   See the Northern Irish case of *Re Sainsbury's Supermarket Ltd sub nom Sainsbury's Supermarket Ltd v Winemark the Wine Merchants Ltd* [2012] NIQB 45.
47   (1996) *The Times*, 5 February.

The appeal – a true rehearing?

12.43 An issue often arises in practice as to the extent to which the appeal court should have regard to the decision of the local council. This approach stems from the reasoning in *Stepney Borough Council v Joffe*[48] (a case involving the revocation by a local council of a street traders licence) in which Lord Goddard CJ held that:

> 'if there is an unrestricted right of appeal, it is for the court of appeal, in this case the metropolitan magistrate, to substitute its opinion for the opinion of the borough council. That does not mean to say that the court of appeal ought not to pay great attention to the fact that the duly constituted and elected local authority have come to an opinion on the matter and ought not lightly to reverse their opinion.'

12.44 The above observation was expressly endorsed by the Court of Appeal in the leading case of *Sagnata* as being the correct approach to the hearing of such appeals. Furthermore, in *R v Essex Quarter Sessions, ex p Thomas*[49] (a case which involved an appeal from a betting licensing committee to the quarter sessions), Lord Parker CJ stated that:

> 'Speaking for myself, I would hesitate, and I would expect any chairman of quarter sessions to hesitate, long before he differed from the local justices who had dealt with the matter in their locality with the greatest care.'

12.45 The appeal court will need to be aware of the decision and the reasons which have led it to hear the case in the first place. It is often said, however, that the above observations are difficult to reconcile with the practice that such appeals are by way of a rehearing in which the appeal court should substitute its own opinion on the merits for that of the council.

12.46 In *R v Preston Crown Court, ex p Chief Constable of Lancashire & Others*[50] the Administrative Court touched on a similar issue. This case was concerned with the composition of a Crown Court when hearing appeals from licensing justices. It principally held that the Crown Court should not comprise magistrates from the same area as those comprising the bench whose decision was under challenge. However, when considering the nature of the hearing before the Crown Court, Laws LJ also observed that:

> 'An appeal against a decision of licensing justices to the Crown Court is, as I have indicated, by way of rehearing. There is some contest on the skeleton arguments as to the extent to which, in reality, a rehearing is conducted. A dictum of Lord Parker advanced by Mr Saunders displays, or did in its time display, a certain reluctance on the part of the Crown Court (or Quarter Sessions) to part company from decisions reached by licensing justices. It seems to me plainly right, however, to proceed on the basis that the Crown Court conducts a rehearing in the full and proper sense ....'

12.47 This tension as to the correct approach has been considered in a number of recent decisions. A direct challenge to the *Stepney/Sagnata* approach was mounted in *R (Hope and Glory Public House Limited) v City of Westminster Magistrates' Court & Others*.[51] In this case, Burton J refused permission to bring a claim for judicial review after hearing

---

[48] [1949] 1 KB 599.
[49] [1966] 1 All ER 353.
[50] [2001] EWHC Admin 928.
[51] [2009] EWHC 1996 (Admin).

detailed argument on the point. In his judgment Burton J confirmed that the correct approach to such appeals was set out in *Sagnata* and *Stepney*. It was explained that the appeal is by way of a re-hearing – a fresh appeal with fresh evidence – but after hearing all the evidence the appellate decision-maker will have to be satisfied that the decision below was 'wrong'. The decision of Burton J was upheld by the Court of Appeal (*R (Hope and Glory Pubic House Limited) v City of Westminster Magistrates' Court & Others*).[52] The Court of Appeal explained that: 'in all cases, magistrates should pay careful attention to the reasons given by the licensing authority for arriving at the decision under appeal, bearing in mind that Parliament has chosen to place responsibility for making such decisions on local authorities. The weight which the magistrates should ultimately attach to those reasons must be a matter for their judgment in all the circumstances, taking into account the fullness and clarity of the reasons, the nature of the issues and the evidence given on appeal'. There is no requirement on the magistrates to state what weight they have given to the decision below.[53]

12.48 In *R (Townlink Ltd) v Thames Magistrates' Court*,[54] the Administrative Court was invited to interpret *Hope and Glory* in the context of judicial review. Lindblom J stated that the Appeal Court is required to consider 'the rightness of the decision itself' and relying on Lord Goddard's words in *Joffe*, he stated that the Appeal Court had nonetheless 'to come to [its] own conclusion on the merits of the appeal', and accordingly, 'to consider on the merits whether the decision of the licensing sub-committee ought to be upheld'. In *R (Developing Retail Ltd) v East Hampshire Magistrates' Court*,[55] while approving *Hope and Glory*, the court adopted a similar approach to *Townlink* in stating that the Appeal Court must 'consider whether, having taken the decision of the licensing authority into account, it is "wrong on the basis of the evidence put before [it]"'. There is no requirement for *Wednesbury* unreasonableness as the appeal is an evidential rehearing rather than a review of the licensing authority's decision. 'The magistrates therefore have power to review the decision on the grounds of error of law and also on its merits.' Thus there are three ways in which the decision of the licensing committee may be successfully challenged on appeal, namely; that they got the decision wrong in law; they got it wrong on the merits, or that the decision was not wrong at the time it was made, but having regard to the case on appeal to the magistrates, it was wrong.

12.49 The importance of considering matters afresh on appeal was emphasised in *Canterbury City Council v Ali*, where it was held that the magistrates had erred in law when allowing an appeal by a licensed taxi driver against the revocation of his licence by the local authority, since they had focused on finding flaws in the local authority's decision-making process rather than coming to their own conclusion on the issue of revocation. Carr J stated that the correct approach of the magistrates was to come to a fresh conclusion of their own and not to conduct an adverse review of the local authority's decision-making.

12.50 If the local council has a policy then the Appeal Court must apply that policy when arriving at its decision on appeal. In *R (Westminster City Council) v Middlesex Crown Court & Chorion PLC & Fred Proud*[56] Scott Baker J explained:

---

[52] [2011] EWCA Civ 31.
[53] See the case of *Little France Ltd v Ealing London Borough Council* [2013] EWHC 2144 (Admin).
[54] [2011] EWHC 898 (Admin).
[55] [2011] EWHC 618 (Admin).
[56] [2002] EWHC 1104.

'How should a Crown Court (or a Magistrates' Court) approach an appeal where the council has a policy? In my judgment it must accept the policy and apply it as if it was standing in the shoes of the council considering the application. Neither the Magistrates' Court nor the Crown Court is the right place to challenge the policy.'

The appeal – an alternative remedy

12.51 It should be borne in mind that the availability of an unrestricted right of appeal to the magistrates' court and the Crown Court is not available in respect of all decisions of local councils. Such rights of appeal must be expressly provided for in the relevant legislation. The availability of a statutory appeal process impacts on the appropriateness of judicial review.

12.52 As a general principle, judicial review is considered an option of last resort (see comments of Baroness Hale in *R (Cart) v Upper Tribunal*[57]) and one that should not be embarked upon unless all alternative remedies have been exhausted. Such alternative remedies include appeals to the magistrates' court and the Crown Court.

12.53 The availability of an alternative remedy is likely to lead the Administrative Court to refuse permission to proceed with a claim for judicial review or to refuse the relief sought. The issue of alternative remedies in the licensing context has been considered in a number of cases. As these cases illustrate the main consideration is the appropriateness of the alternative remedy:

(1) In *R v Huntingdon District Council, ex p Cowan*[58] (a case involving the licensing of sex establishments) Glidewell J explained that 'the court should always ask itself whether the remedy that is sought in the court, or the alternative remedy which is available to the applicant by way of appeal, is the most effective and convenient, in other words, which of them will prove to be the most effective and convenient in all the circumstances, not merely for the applicant, but in the public interest. In exercising discretion whether or not to grant relief, that is a major factor ...'.

(2) In *R v Nottingham City Council, ex p Howitt*[59] (a case concerning taxi licences) Dyson J held that the court must ask itself what is the real issue to be determined and whether the statutory appeal is suitable to determine that issue.

(3) In *R v Leeds City Council, ex p Hendry*[60] (a case concerning the licensing of the private hire industry) Latham J decided that the question to be asked in cases where there is an alternative statutory procedure is whether the real issues can sensibly be determined by the statutory procedure.

12.54 These authorities, and others, were reviewed by Beatson J in *R (JD Wetherspoon plc) v Guildford Borough Council*.[61] This case concerned a challenge to the council's decision to refuse to grant Wetherspoons' application to extend its permitted hours. On the particular circumstances of the case, the issue raised was one on which, in the court's judgment, there was a need for uniformity in the understanding of licensing authorities as to the scope of their policies in the light of guidance published by the Secretary of State. Therefore it was appropriate to proceed by way of judicial review.

---

[57] [2011] UKSC 28; [2012] 1 AC 663 at [19].
[58] [1984] 1 ALL ER 58.
[59] [1999] COD 530.
[60] (1994) *The Times*, 20 January.
[61] [2006] EWHC 815 (Admin).

12.55 In the recent case of *R (Great Yarmouth Port Co Ltd) v Marine Management Organisation*,[62] permission to proceed with a claim for judicial review against the decision to vary a construction licence was refused. Hickinbottom J made it clear that where a statutory right of appeal was available, then permission would only be granted in exceptional circumstances such as to make the alternative remedy clearly unsatisfactory. Such circumstances, he added, would be rare.

Case stated or judicial review?

12.56 The magistrates' court and Crown Court are carrying out public functions, and similarly to local councils, are susceptible in appropriate cases to challenges by way of judicial review. It should be borne in mind, however, that the decisions of the magistrates' court and the Crown Court may also be appealed to the Administrative Court by way of the case stated procedure.

12.57 In any case, a decision will need to be made as to which route is the most appropriate. This will depend upon the circumstances of the particular case. An often overlooked fact is that an appeal by way of case stated on a non-criminal matter (such as a licensing case) is final. In other words, there is no further right of appeal to the Court of Appeal or Supreme Court (see *Westminster City Council v O'Reilly*,[63] a case concerning special hours certificates issued under the previous liquor regime, the Licensing Act 1964).

POLICIES AND GUIDANCE

Licensing policies – an overview

12.58 The starting point is that a licensing authority is entitled to have a policy in respect of its licensing functions. Policies have become a key part of many licensing regimes. They inform those who may be affected by how the authority will exercise its powers and the policies also act as a guide to inform the decision-makers making the decisions. Such policies, therefore, promote consistency. Indeed, an absence of a published policy may leave an authority more open to criticism or challenge on the grounds of inconsistency or a lack of transparency.

12.59 In practice, policies range from the licensing of entertainment venues, sex establishments, the sale of alcohol through to the hackney carriage and private hire industry. The more recent licensing regimes under the Licensing Act 2003 and the Gambling Act 2005 now place a statutory obligation on licensing authorities to formulate and implement polices setting out how they will approach their licensing functions (see, for example, s 5 of the Licensing Act 2003).

12.60 Policies are not exclusive to the field of licensing law. They play an integral part in other areas of public administration and decision-making and decisions in those areas may be equally applicable to licensing cases. If an authority has a policy then it should be made public. It is contrary to good public administration for an authority to have a policy but not make it public.

---

[62] [2013] EWHC 3052 (Admin).
[63] [2003] EWCA Civ 1007 per Auld LJ.

Policies – summary of general principles

12.61 A summary of the fundamental principles relating to licensing policies is set out below:

(1) The starting point is that a licensing policy must have reasonable objectives and not run counter to the policy of the respective legislation. This is the well-known *Padfield* principle deriving from the House of Lords in *Padfield v Minister of Agriculture, Fisheries and Food*.[64] This principle was applied in the licensing context by Richards J in *British Beer & Pub Association & Others v Canterbury County Council*.[65] In this case the council's policy under the Licensing Act 2003 was over prescriptive and ran counter to the objectives of the 2003 Act.

(2) Licensing policies must be properly formulated after adequate consultation. Some statutes, such as the Licensing Act 2003, set out a statutory code of consultation which must be undertaken before a licensing policy is published including who must be consulted. In general terms, the key principles to consultation are set out in *R v North and East Devon Health Authority, ex p Coughlan*.[66] Those principles are: (1) consultation must be undertaken at a time when proposals are still at a formative stage, (2) it must include sufficient reasons for particular proposals to allow those consulted to give intelligent consideration and an intelligent response, (3) adequate time must be given for this purpose, and (4) the product of consultation must be conscientiously taken into account when the ultimate decision is taken.

Those principles have been applied to licensing functions. See for example, *Sardar & Others v Watford Borough Council*[67] and *Royden*.[68] These were cases which involved decisions of local councils as to limitations on the number of hackney carriage licenses issued in its district. In *Royden*, Christopher Bellamy QC (sitting as a Deputy High Court Judge) explained the importance of considering the *Coughlan* principles in the context of the particular case and circumstances under challenge. Adequacy depends very much on its context.

(3) A challenge to a licensing policy on the basis that it has been unlawfully established is a matter for the Administrative Court to resolve by way of judicial review proceedings. This was made clear in *R (Westminster City Council) v Middlesex Crown Court & Chorion plc & Fred Proud*[69] where Scott Baker J stated that 'neither the magistrates' court nor the Crown Court is the right place to challenge the policy. The remedy, if it is alleged that a policy has been unlawfully established, is an application to the Administrative Court for judicial review'.

(4) A review of the principles relating to policies is set out in the judgments of Richards J in *R (British Beer & Pub Association & Others v Canterbury City Council*[70] and Beatson J in *R (JD Wetherspoon) v Guildford Borough Council*.[71] These refer to the following general principles which govern the interpretation of policies. A legalistic approach to the interpretation of licensing policies is to be avoided. Such policies should not be treated as if they were statutes. A policy

---

[64] [1968] AC 997.
[65] [2005] EWHC 1318 (Admin). See also *R (Gordon-Jones) v The Secretary of State for Justice* [2014] EWHC 3997 (Admin).
[66] [2001] QB 213.
[67] [2006] EWHC 1590 (Admin).
[68] [2002] EWHC 2484 (Admin).
[69] [2002] EWHC 1104.
[70] [2005] EWHC 1318 (Admin).
[71] [2006] EWHC 815 (Admin).

should be considered mindful of its underlying purpose and the statutory framework to which it relates. Specific passages within policies should be read in the light of the policy as a whole and not merely considered in isolation. It should be recognised, however, that people reading such policies are going to vary in sophistication and there are limitations as to how far they can be expected to read in qualifications expressed elsewhere in a policy document or to be derived from an understanding of the statutory scheme. The meaning of passages must be judged in a common sense way. A policy must be applied in accordance with its meaning. It cannot fulfill its purpose of providing guidance if its intended meaning is different from the actual meaning of the words used.

(5) It is also a general rule that a licensing policy should not be applied inflexibly or rigidly. There needs to be a willingness on the part of the decision-maker to consider individual applications on their merits. In general, a decision-maker should always be willing to listen to see if the circumstances justify a departure from the policy. The classic statement is set out by Lord Reid in *British Oxygen Ltd v Minister of Technology*:[72]

> 'the general rule is that anyone who has to exercise a statutory discretion must not "shut his ears to the application" ... I do not think there is any great difference between a policy and a rule. There may be cases where an officer or authority ought to listen to a substantial argument reasonably presented urging a change of policy. What the authority must not do is to refuse to listen at all. But a Ministry or large authority may have had to deal already with a multitude of similar applications and then they will almost certainly have evolved a policy so precise that it could be called a rule. There can be no objection to that, provided the authority is always willing to listen to anyone with something new to say.'

However, this approach has been said to represent the general position and much will depend on the statutory context under scrutiny. In *Nicholds & Others v Security Industry Authority*,[73] Kenneth Parker QC explained that:

> 'In most instances where a discretionary power is conferred it would be wrong for the decision-maker to frame a rule in absolute terms because to do so would defeat the statutory purpose. However, it seems to me that there are certain exceptional statutory contexts where a policy may lawfully exclude exceptions to the rule because to allow exceptions would substantially undermine an important legislative aim which underpins the grant of the discretionary power to the authority. There is, for example, a well known line of cases concerning "taxi" licensing where licensing rules, which admitted of no exception for any "special" circumstances, were held lawful: see for example, *R v Manchester City Justices, ex p McHugh* [1989] RTR 285; 88 LGR 180; *R v Wirral MBC, ex p The Wirral Licensed Taxi Owners Association* [1983] 3 CMLR 150.'

In the recent case of *R (Singh) v Cardiff City Council*,[74] the court allowed a claim for judicial review of a penalty points system adopted by the local authority for misconduct by taxi drivers. Singh J accepted that there was nothing wrong in principle with such a system; however, the present policy was unlawful for it left no room for judgment or discretion and it did not allow for the alternative sanction of suspension. Singh J stated that:

---

[72] [1971] AC 610.
[73] [2006] EWHC 1792 (Admin).
[74] [2012] EWHC 1852 (Admin).

'One of the reasons why public law recognises and indeed encourages the adoption of policies to govern the exercise of discretionary powers is not only that they assist decision makers within the relevant authority. As importantly, if not more importantly, policies signal to members of the public how discretionary powers will be exercised. In that respect they form an important function in maintaining the rule of law, because they assist individuals to be able to regulate their conduct to predict with some reasonable certainty how they will be treated by a public authority, depending on what they do.'

(6) However, an inflexibly worded policy does not necessarily lead to the conclusion that the policy is unlawful as long as it is applied flexibly in practice and a licensing authority is prepared to listen to each case on its own particular merits. Similarly, a flexibly worded policy which is applied inflexibly in practice may lead to a successful challenge in judicial review proceedings (see, for example, the approaches in *R v Nottingham City Council, ex p Howitt*[75] and *R v City & County of Swansea, ex p Julie Amanda Jones*.[76] See also the cases of *R v Chester Crown Court, ex p Pascoe & Jones*[77] and *R v Licensing Justices at North Tyneside*[78] in which the reasons of the decision-maker did not show that they had considered an application on its merits).

(7) The burden rests on the person seeking a departure from a policy to persuade the decision-maker that the circumstance of the individual case justifies such a departure from the policy.[79]

Statutory guidance – an overview

12.62 Statutory guidance has also become an integral part of decision-making under the more modern licensing regimes such as the Licensing Act 2003 and the Gambling Act 2005. The 2003 Act requires the Secretary of State to issue guidance to licensing authorities on the discharge of their licensing functions. This guidance may not be issued unless a draft of it has been laid before, and approved by, each House of Parliament. Once issued, licensing authorities must have regard to it when carrying out its licensing functions under the 2003 Act (see s 182 of the Licensing Act 2003). The 2005 Act requires the Gambling Commission to issue guidance to local councils (who have responsibility for the licensing of premises under the 2005 Act). This may only be issued following consultation with specified bodies including the Secretary of State.

Guidance – summary of general principles

12.63 Such guidance is not novel. It plays a key part in other areas of public law. There is an overlap with many of the principles relating to policies particularly in respect of interpretation. Set out below are some of the fundamental principles which relate to statutory guidance:

(1) The key point is that statutory guidance cannot usurp or replace the statute. The focus should always be on the wording and purpose of the respective legislation. A number of recent cases illustrate this point. In *R (4 Wins Leisure Limited) v*

---

[75] [1999] COD 530, QBD.
[76] (1996) CO1996/3187/95 unreported.
[77] (1987) 151 JP 752.
[78] (1988) 153 JP 100.
[79] See a review of the authorities on this issue in the *Chorion* decision, supra.

Blackpool Licensing Committee & Others[80] Sullivan J explained that: 'it is important to remember that, whilst regard must be had to the guidance, it should not be allowed to usurp the clear language in the statute.'

Similar approaches have been taken in a number of other (licensing) judicial review proceedings. See, for example, Dobbs J in *R (South Northamptonshire Council) v Towcester Magistrates' Court*;[81] Andrew Nicol QC (sitting as a Deputy High Court Judge in *R (Betting Shop Services Ltd) v Southend on Sea Borough Council*[82] and Black J in *Daniel Thwaites PLC v Wirral Magistrates' Court & Others*[83] who stated that: 'there is no doubt that regard must be had to the guidance by the magistrates but that its force is less than that of a statute'. See the recent case of *Nuran Aksu & Murat Yazgan v London Borough of Enfield*[84] in which Edwards-Stuart J considered that a certain part of the Guidance was in fact incorrect for it could not be reconciled with the wording of the Licensing Act 2003.

(2) Whilst the statutory guidance cannot replace the statutory words it may, however, assist with interpreting the legislation. In *R (Blackpool Council) v Howitt and the Secretary of State for Culture Media and Sport*,[85] HHJ Denyer QC sitting as a Judge of the High Court used the statutory guidance issued under the Licensing Act 2003 to interpret the meaning of the phrase 'crime and disorder' as it related to the 2003 Act. Whilst, statutory guidance may assist with interpretation, interpretation always remains a matter for the court.

(3) The regard that is given to the guidance is a matter for the decision-maker. If, however, it departs from the guidance it should give proper reasons for doing so. In the *Daniel Thwaites plc* case, Black J held that: 'any individual licensing decision may give rise to a need to balance conflicting factors which are included in the Guidance and that in resolving this conflict, a licensing authority or magistrates' court may justifiably give less weight to some parts of the Guidance and more to others ... it may also depart from the Guidance if particular features of the individual case require that. What a licensing authority or magistrates' court is not entitled to do is simply to ignore the Guidance or fail to give it any weight, whether because it does not agree with the Government's policy or its methods of regulating licensable activities or for any other reason. Furthermore, when a magistrates' court is entitled to depart from the Guidance and justifiably does so, it must, in my view, give proper reason.'

(4) Similarly in *R (Bassetlaw District Council) v Worksop Magistrates' Court*[86] Slade J held that a district judge had erred in failing to give reasons for departing from the statutory guidance when determining an appeal under the Licensing Act 2003. The decision of the district judge was also overturned because passages in the guidance had been misconstrued and incorrectly applied.

12.64 Furthermore, many of the principles relating to the interpretation of policies (discussed earlier in this chapter) may also equally apply to statutory guidance. In particular, such guidance should not be read with the fine analysis with which one would read a statute and a legalistic approach to the guidance is to be avoided. A review of the

---

[80] [2007] EWHC 2213 (Admin).
[81] [2008] EWHC 381 (Admin).
[82] [2007] EWHC 105 (Admin).
[83] [2008] EWHC 838 (Admin).
[84] [2013] EWHC 249 (Admin).
[85] [2008] EWHC 3300 (Admin).
[86] [2008] EWHC 3530 (Admin).

principles may be found in the judgment of Beatson J in *R (JD Wetherspoon) v Guildford Borough Council*[87] which considered the guidance issued under the 2003 Act.

OBJECTORS AND REPRESENTORS

Objections and representations – an overview

12.65 Licensing decisions may affect not just the applicant for the licence (or an existing licence holder) but other interested parties as well (for instance, those who will also be affected by the activities authorised by the licence; examples include the police and local residents). Representations or objections may, therefore, be submitted by these people and bodies.

12.66 The admissibility of such objections and whether they should be properly taken into account by decision-makers is often a live and contentious consideration at any licensing hearing.

12.67 Some licensing regimes set out a statutory procedure that must be followed in terms of notifying people and bodies of licence applications. The purpose underpinning this is to ensure that the application is brought to the attention of those who may be affected by the application. Under the Licensing Act 2003 and the Gambling Act 2005 the respective statutes require applicants to advertise and provide notice of their applications. In effect, Parliament has legislated specific schemes of consultation under the Acts. The provisions also identify who may make representations in respect of the application and the time limits for such representations.

12.68 In the case of *Corporation of the Hall of Arts and Sciences v Albert Court Residents' Association*[88] the Court of Appeal, in quashing the decision of McCombe J, has made it clear that there is no power to consider late objections pursuant to the Licensing Act 2003 given the permissive nature of the statutory language. In this case, there was an application to vary a licence to include boxing and wrestling. The local authority ran a scheme whereby local residents would be notified of applications through a computerised system that served to identify premises near to the applicant. Despite their close proximity, the residents of Albert Court were not identified by the computer and the only representation received was by Environmental Health who later withdrew their representations having reached an agreement. The application was therefore granted by way of delegated authority, no hearing being required. Residents of Albert Court made representations after the deadline had past and insisted that a hearing was held. The local authority disagreed and declined to consider those representations or act upon them in any way. The residents sought a judicial review of that decision and were initially successful on the ground that the grant offended their legitimate expectation that they would be notified of the application. The Court of Appeal overturned that decision and Stanley Burnton LJ expressed real doubt that such a legitimate expectation existed at all. In any event, a legitimate expectation could not require a Local Authority to act contrary to statute, thus it could not override the statutory duty to grant, nor deprive the Albert Hall of its entitlement to a grant.

12.69 This decision is in contrast to other licensing regimes where no such statutory provisions exist. For example, there is no such consultation or codified representation

---

[87] [2006] EWHC 815 (Admin).
[88] [2011] EWCA Civ 430.

procedure in respect of applications for street trading licences pursuant to the Local Government (Miscellaneous Provisions) Act 1982.

The *Miss Behavin'* litigation

12.70 A challenge to the entitlement of the decision-maker to take particular objections or representations into account when arriving at its decisions arose in the Northern Irish *Miss Behavin'* litigation. These proceedings concerned an application for a sex establishment licence under the Local Government (Miscellaneous Provisions) (Northern Ireland) Order 1985, the equivalent provisions of the 1982 Act. Article 10 of this legislation specified that representations in respect of an application should be made within 28 days of the date of the application and that the council when considering that application should have regard to the representations which have been made within that time. A number of objections in the case were late and made outside the 28 day time period. The issue arose as to whether a council could take those objections, which were made out of time, into account when arriving at its decision in respect of the application. The matter proceeded by way of a claim for judicial review and ultimately came before the House of the Lords. It was held that the council was not precluded from taking into account objections which were late.

12.71 The following principal points emerge from the decision of the House of Lords and, in particular, the opinions of Lord Hoffman and Lord Neuberger of Abbottsbury:

(1) The relevant statutory provisions under the 1985 Order (and therefore the equivalent 1982 Act) are concerned only with the position of the objector. In other words, if an objector did not comply with the 28-day statutory deadline then they would not be entitled to complain if the council did not take their objection into account.

(2) The proper effect of the provisions is that late objections could, but need not, be taken into account. A local council has discretion whether or not to have regard to information which comes from outside the scope of a statutory objection. Much depends on the circumstances of the particular case. In exercising this discretion the council may have regard to all relevant matters including whether the objection was late for lack of good faith, any prejudice caused to the applicant or other relevant parties and/or disruption to council business. It may well be correct to disregard a late objection if it was intentionally last minute, or if it was received so late that taking it into account would lead to unfairness to the applicant (because he would not have had the chance to consider it) or to unacceptable disruption to the council's business.

(3) A local council should not be prohibited from taking all relevant matters into account, whether those matters have been communicated by an objector or others, whether it was communicated early or late, or in any other way. It would be a strange approach if such a provision, designed to allow the council to carry on its business in an orderly and expeditious manner, had the effect of requiring the council to shut its eyes to facts which would be considered relevant to the council's decision-making process.

(4) It would be unrealistic and unjust if a council was absolutely precluded from taking into account such objections. If an objection, which revealed to a council for the first time certain highly relevant information, was received one day late, it would be a little short of absurd if it could not be taken into account. It would be contrary to the purpose of the 1985 Order, and to the public interest generally, if

the council was obliged to ignore relevant information. Moreover, it would be the duty of council officers to open and read any letter of objection or representation received by the council. Such an officer would then be placed in an impossible situation if he or she had read a late letter of objection, with new and important information, but was effectively precluded from communicating this information to the committee.

(5) The issue of late objections is governed by general administrative law principles: it is a matter for the council whether to take it into account, and the court will not interfere with its decision in that regard, save on administrative law principles, for instance unless the decision took into account irrelevant factors or failed to take into account relevant factors or was a decision which no reasonable council could have made in the case.

(6) There could be circumstances in which a failure on the part of the council to take relevant information into account could itself be judicially reviewable. It would take clear statutory terms to oblige a council to ignore relevant information and material.

12.72 This decision was in line with the decision of Webster J in *Quietlyn Ltd v Plymouth City Council*[89] which approved the dictum of Woolf J in the earlier case of *R v Chester City Council, ex p Quietlynn*.[90] In the latter case it was held that:

> 'in coming to a determination, the authority must be entitled to take account of information which comes into its possession and which is relevant even though it is not from a statutory objector. It may, for example, be necessary for inquiries to be made of the fire authorities and if an oral objection was made by the fire authorities out of time it could not properly be ignored in reaching a decision. It will be necessary, however, in respect of such non-statutory information to act fairly and, if necessary, give the applicant notice of the material upon which it is proposed to rely.'

12.73 These authorities appear to promote the undesirability of subjecting a statutory scheme to a literal analysis and proceeding on the basis that Parliament has laid down a fixed and rigid procedure.

12.74 The issue, therefore, of whether, and in what circumstances, a licensing authority is entitled to take into account information which comes from outside a statutory scheme is dependent upon the wording of the relevant statutory scheme. In the context of street trading, the relevant scheme did not include mandatory wording as to the grant of a licence as in s 35(2) of the Licensing Act 2003. In the absence of such wording, the ability on the part of the licensing authority to take into account extraneous information is governed by the classic administrative law principles.

Importance of the statutory context

12.75 The information provided by the residents in the Albert Court case may well have been relevant and may well have assisted the decision-making process, yet the statutory scheme required that the application be granted. This illustrates the importance of statutory context to a particular case.

---

[89] [1988] QB 114.
[90] (1983) *The Times*, 19 October.

12.76 This is further illustrated by the decision in *R (4 Wins Leisure Limited) v Blackpool Borough Council*.[91] In that case the Administrative Court considered whether a council's refusal to allow a nightclub operator in Blackpool to make representations in respect of a trade competitors' application for a premises licence under the Licensing Act 2003 was lawful. Sullivan J explained:

> 'On behalf of the claimants, Mr Walsh submitted that such a "narrow" geographical approach to the meaning of "in the vicinity" would drive a coach and horses through the Act because it would mean that representations from businesses which might have a very real contribution in terms of assisting the licensing authority to see whether or not the licensing objectives would or would not be promoted by the application would not be treated as interested parties. I can well see that there may well be very good arguments for submitting that those who could make a useful contribution to that question should be allowed to be heard by the licensing authority. The difficulty is that it treats an interested party as though that term were not constrained by the further definition in s 13(3) ... one may have a business which has business interests that might indeed be affected, but if that business is not "in the vicinity" then, regardless of the impact on those business interests, it is not an interested party. Mr Walsh submits that that is an absurd position. He may well be right, but that is the effect of Parliament's definition.'

12.77 The requirement that a person must be an interested party living or working in the vicinity of the licensed premises was repealed by the Police Reform and Social Responsibility Act 2011 such that applications are now objectionable to persons who are not responsible authorities and whose representations are not frivolous or vexatious according to the licensing authority.

The strength of opposition

12.78 The mere fact that a large number of objections have been made in respect of an application should not on its own be a sufficient basis for refusing or determining an application. This is illustrated in the Scottish cases of *The Noble Organisation Limited v City of Glasgow District Council (No 3)*[92] and *The Noble Organisation Limited v Kilmarnock and Loudoun District Council*.[93] Both these cases involved applications for public entertainment licences to operate amusement centres. The applications were rejected essentially on the basis of the strength of local opposition to the amusement centres. In the latter case of *Kilmarnock*, Lord Hope approved the reasoning in the *Glasgow* case and explained that: 'the mere number of objections irrespective of their content can never be a good reason for refusing an application. What matters are the grounds on which the objection is based.' It was further explained that 'the licensing authority is not permitted to attach weight to the objection because of the number of persons associated with it regardless of its content.'

12.79 This Scottish approach was considered in *R v Liverpool City Council, ex p Luxury Leisure Limited*.[94] In that case the Court of Appeal rejected the argument that the decision-maker, in that case the Crown Court, had merely relied on the weight of local opposition. The decision does recognise, however, that the reasoning underlying the opposition is important. As Simon Brown LJ explained that: 'if of course the objections of the public are founded on a demonstrable misunderstanding of the true factual position, or otherwise indicate no more than an uninformed gut reaction to a

---

[91] [2007] EWHC 2213 (Admin) per Sullivan J.
[92] [1991] SCLR 380.
[93] [1992] SCLR 1006.
[94] [1999] LGR 345.

proposal, then I would accept that they can carry no weight whatever and must be ignored'. Aldous LJ observed that: 'opposition which is misinformed is of no weight, and remains of no weight even if held by many people.'

12.80 In general, objections and representations should only be taken into account if the basis of them relates to the statutory objects underpinning the particular scheme and would, therefore, assist the decision-maker in arriving at an informed decision based on statutory grounds. Indeed, the more recent licensing regimes, see for example the Licensing Act 2003, only allow representations to be admitted if they concern the licensing objectives under that Act.

12.81 In the *Glasgow* case, the Scottish courts left undecided the issue of whether the number of objections could ever be a relevant consideration. Much will depend on the circumstances. In appropriate cases it may well be right that the number of objections is a relevant factor. For instance, it could be relevant to the credibility of, or the weight to be given to, the objections which have been received. By way of example, it could be relevant if a number of similar objections all about similar issues and experiences have been raised by the objectors.

Fair notice of objection or representation

12.82 Procedural fairness requires the applicant to be given notice of any objections to, or representations in respect of, the application. This was explained by Lord Hoffman in the *Miss Behavin'* litigation: 'fairness obviously requires that the terms of any representations which the council proposes to consider should be communicated to the applicant so that he may have an opportunity to comment.' There is no proper distinction between an objection and a representation in this regard. Fairness requires proper notice irrespective of the technical classification (see *R v Inner Crown Court, ex p Provis*).[95]

12.83 What is proper notice will depend upon the circumstances of any one case. This has been explained in a number of cases (see, for example, *Quietlyn Ltd v Plymouth City Council*;[96] *R v Huntingdon District Council, ex p Cowan and another*[97] and *R v Inner Crown Court, ex p Provis*).[98] In the *Miss Behavin'* litigation Lord Neuberger of Abbottsbury explained that if: 'a late objection is to be taken into account by the council, then the applicant must be informed as to its contents in good time so as to be able to consider it and deal with it appropriately.'

12.84 These authorities consider the position of the applicant. There is additionally the position of an objector who could be, or is, affected by the activities carried on under the licence and is entitled to make representations and be heard in respect of the issues before the decision-maker. Whilst much will depend on the statutory scheme and the circumstances of any one case, in general, it would appear that fairness requires these people to be aware of the applicant's position on issues. By way of example, there may be licensing proceedings in which the applicant seeks to rely on expert evidence in support of its application. A fair process may require other objectors to be given the opportunity to consider this evidence in advance.

---

[95] (2000) *The Times*, 11 July.
[96] [1988] QB 114 per Webster J.
[97] [1984] 1 ALL ER 58 per Glidewell J.
[98] (2000) *The Times*, 11 July per Gibbs J.

HEARINGS AND EVIDENCE

12.85 The key point is that the decision-maker when determining licensing matters should act in accordance with the relevant statutory scheme and in doing so should adopt and follow a procedure which is fair. What is fair will depend on the circumstances of the particular case.

Being properly heard by the decision-maker

12.86 It is important that the decision-maker is aware of the issues to be determined and the representations which are advanced in respect of it. As such the decision-maker will be able to make a proper and informed decision. It is therefore important that the issues and the representations are accurately reported to the decision-making committee. In *R v Chester City Council, ex p Quietlynn Ltd*[99] Woolf J considered the provisions in respect of the licensing of sex establishments under Schedule 3 of the Local Government (Miscellaneous Provisions) Act 1982. Those provisions afforded an applicant a statutory right to be heard before the decision. Woolf J explained that when an authority is performing the type of function involved in considering whether to grant a licence, such applications must be considered fairly and in many cases it will be necessary for the decision-making body to have at least a summary of the applicant's representations whether they were made in writing or orally at a hearing before a different committee or sub-committee. In the Court of Appeal (see *R v Preston Borough Council, ex p Quietlynn Ltd*[100]), Simon Brown LJ explained that it was a requisite of the statutory provisions that the applicant's representations should be considered by the committee making the decision. In this case, they were not. No report of any kind was put before the decision-making committee. As such, Simon Brown LJ held that there was a breach of the procedural rules which vitiated the decision of the committee. Furthermore, it was said that this procedural irregularity could not be cured by the fact that members of the committee could probably be expected to have been familiar with the locality and could have asked, if they wished, for details of the applicant's representations from those members of the committee who had actually heard the applicant's representations.

12.87 See also the planning decision of *R v Liverpool City Council, ex p Ramm*[101] in which the decision of Simon Brown LJ in *Quietlynn* was cited to Moses J. It was held that no-one could 'seriously dispute' the accuracy of the proposition that it was essential for the decision-making body to apply its mind to material considerations and that if the decision-making body did not consider directly the source material and the representations then it must at least put its mind to a report as to what the source material and representations concern.

12.88 The contents of a report to the decision-making committee could also be the subject of challenge. The widely accepted approach has been set out by Judge LJ in a planning case (*Oxton Farm & Others v Selby District Council*).[102] Whilst that was a planning case, the principles are equally applicable to licensing proceedings before the council. Judge LJ explained that:

---

[99] (1983) *The Times*, 19 October.
[100] (1984) 83 LGR 308.
[101] (unreported) 28 January 1998.
[102] [1997] EGCS 60.

'there will no doubt be cases where judicial review is granted on the basis of what is or is not contained in the planning officer's report. This reflects no more than the court's conclusion in the particular circumstances of the case before it. In my judgment an application for judicial review based on criticisms on the planning officer's report will not normally begin to merit consideration unless the overall effect of the report significantly misleads the committee about material matters which thereafter are left uncorrected at the meeting of the planning committee before the relevant decision.'

12.89 That said, it is important to recognise that the duty of an officer reporting to a committee is broader than merely a duty not to mislead. It includes a positive duty to provide sufficient information and guidance to enable the decision-maker to reach a decision applying the relevant statutory criteria: see *R (Lowther) v Durham County Council & Others*[103] and a review of the relevant authorities by Hickinbottom J in *R (Miller) v North Yorkshire County Council & Others*.[104] Indeed, there is an obligation on those who assist the decision-makers such as licensing officers to explore relevant issues properly and fairly and to equip the decision-maker with relevant material so as to enable them to arrive at an informed decision.

12.90 It may be that a right to be heard by the decision-maker does not always necessarily have to include a right to be heard orally. However, this will depend on a number of factors not least the statutory scheme and the particular matters and circumstances in issue. In any event, the modern practice is for councils to hold committee meetings or hearings so that the applicant and any other relevant person or body can make their representations directly to the decision-maker. This is a sensible approach given the quasi-judicial nature of the licensing process.

The procedure at the meeting or hearing

12.91 The procedure to be followed at committee or sub committee meetings or hearings is usually a matter for each council. Some Acts, such as the Licensing Act 2003, enable regulations to be made which set out a core procedure that should be followed at a committee hearing. These regulations however still allow the licensing committees to regulate their own procedure.[105] Other statutes may be silent altogether as to the procedure that should be followed at hearings or meetings.

12.92 The modern practice of many local councils is for hearings or meetings to take place before the particular decision-making committee or sub-committee and for those affected by the proceedings to be afforded the opportunity of being heard by the decision-making body.

Matters are generally heard in public

12.93 The meetings of committees or sub-committees are generally held in public. Indeed, this is a requirement under ss 100A and 100E of the Local Government Act 1972 (subject to specified exceptions). However, these requirements do not necessarily extend to the committee's or sub-committee's deliberations when considering its decision. This was explained by Turner J in *R v London Borough of Wandsworth, ex p Darker Enterprises Ltd*[106] who explained that it accorded neither with the court's:

---

[103] [2001] EWCA Civ 781 per Pill LJ.
[104] [2009] EWHC 2172 (Admin).
[105] See, for example, the Licensing Act 2003 (Hearing) Regulations 2005, SI 2005/44.
[106] (Unreported) 15 January 1999.

'experience nor expectation that deliberations by such a body which take place before a decision is reached would take place, or could reasonably take place, in public. Moreover, it is hard to see how sub-committees could effectively conduct their discussions, in relation to decisions whether to grant or renew licences, if they were required to do so in public. I hold that the applicants have failed to establish that the respondents acted in breach of any relevant requirement of the Act of 1972. Even had I been satisfied that there was a breach, the applicants are unable to point to any particular mischief which they have suffered as the result. Reasons for the decision were given as the Act of 1982 required. They could have asked for no more.'

12.94 Indeed, as long as reasons are provided it difficult to see what prejudice or unfairness an applicant or other relevant party would suffer from the deliberations taking place in private.

12.95 Some of the modern licensing regimes such as the Licensing Act 2003 explain that hearings should take place in public. This is subject to the proviso that a licensing authority may exclude the public from all or part of the hearing where it considers that the public interest in so doing outweighs the public interest in the hearing, or that part of the hearing taking place in public.[107]

The approach of the decision-maker

12.96 The responsibility of decision-makers in these types of licensing proceedings is to apply the statutory test and considerations and to form a responsible judgment based on the relevant information. This has been explained in two cases by Lord Bingham of Cornhill CJ both of which involved 'fit and proper' tests (see *R v Warrington Crown Court, ex p RBNB (a company)*[108] and *McCool v Rushcliffe Borough Council*[109]). The latter was a case which concerned the licensing of a private hire driver. It was explained that:

'the borough council and the justices were entitled to rely on any evidential material which might reasonably and properly influence the making of a responsible judgment in good faith on the question in issue. Some evidence such as gossip, speculation and unsubstantiated innuendo would be rightly disregarded. Other evidence, even if hearsay, might by its source, nature and inherent probability carry a greater degree of credibility. All would depend on the particular facts and circumstances.'

12.97 The decision in *McCool* also confirms the widely understood principle that the strict rules of evidence as usually found in the criminal and civil jurisdictions do not apply to licensing proceedings. Licensing proceedings involve the exercise of an administrative function. The leading case on this is the Court of Appeal decision in *Kavanagh v Chief Constable of Devon*.[110] This was a case which concerned the licensing of firearms and, in particular, the principles on which a Crown Court should act when determining an appeal against the decision of the Chief Constable. Lord Denning MR explained as follows:

'It seems to me that the Crown Court is in the same position as the court of quarter sessions. The Crown Court is to try cases according to the same rules as the court of quarter sessions used to do. The court of quarter sessions, when trying criminal cases, applied the rules of

---

[107] See in this regard, Licensing Act 2003 (Hearings) Regulations 2005, SI 2005/44, reg 14 (as amended).
[108] [2002] UKHL 24.
[109] [1998] 3 ALL ER 889.
[110] [1974] QB 624.

evidence applicable to criminal cases. But from time immemorial the court of quarter sessions exercised administrative jurisdiction. When so doing, the justices never held themselves bound by the strict rules of evidence. They acted on any material that appeared to be useful in coming to a decision, including their own knowledge. No doubt they admitted hearsay, though there is nothing to be found in the books about it. To bring the procedure up to modern requirements, I think they should act on the same lines as any administrative body which is charged with an enquiry. They may receive any material which is logically probative even though it is not evidence in a court of law. Hearsay can be permitted where it can fairly be regarded as reliable.'

12.98 In *R v Licensing Justices of East Gwent, ex p Chief Constable of Gwent*[111] (a case which concerned the previous alcohol licensing regime in the Licensing Act 1964) the Administrative Court applied the *Kavanagh* approach and explained that it equally applied to other forms of licensing functions. In his judgment, Dyson J referring to *Kavanagh* also stated that the weight to be given to the evidence is a matter for the decision-maker (specifically, in this case, the weight which was to be given to the statements of people who had not attended to give oral evidence and as such had not had their evidence tested under questioning).

Judgment and the decision-maker's discretion

12.99 Challenges to the judgmental conclusions of licensing bodies involve a high threshold. This is well illustrated by a case under the previous liquor licensing regime set out in the Licensing Act 1964. In *R v Doncaster Justices, ex p Langfield*[112] an application was made for special orders of exemption (extensions to the permitted hours) to cover half time and immediate post-match periods in respect of matches at Doncaster Rovers Football Club. The police had not objected and had in fact given evidence which positively supported the application. In particular, the police stated that there had been no serious public order problem at the Club in the previous two seasons and that there was no evidence to show that the availability of alcohol at the ground had contributed to any unruly behaviour in the past. Despite that, the justices refused to grant the application. The justices' reasoning was founded principally on their own knowledge and experience as magistrates on the Doncaster bench that offences of a public disorder nature were committed during and after Doncaster Rovers football matches. They further took notice of their own experience that those who are arrested and subsequently appeared before the court would invariably plead as mitigation some intake of alcohol. The decision was subject to an application for judicial review which was dismissed. Nolan J recognised that the application before the justices was a strong one. Nonetheless, he held that the justices had not exceeded their jurisdiction or improperly exercised their discretion.

12.100 More recently in *Mark Carter-Pascoe v Birmingham Magistrates' Court & Others*[113] Lightman J held, on similar relevant facts to those in *Langfield*, that:

'In my view the Justices are perfectly entitled to form their own view on whether there was a significant risk of a public order problem. They are not bound by any view taken either way by the Police, though they must plainly take that view into account and give it proper weight. But, if they were minded to disagree with the view of the Police, they were bound to intimate

---

[111] (2000) 164 JP 339.
[112] (1984) 149 JP 26.
[113] [2002] EWHC 1202 (Admin).

to the Appellant that they were considering acting in this way and put the Appellant on notice that this was a possible outcome of the proceedings in order to obviate the risk that he might be taken by surprise.'

12.101 These authorities appear to reveal that a challenge to the judgmental conclusion of a licensing authority involves a 'high hurdle'. This is also identified in the approach of Sullivan J in the *4 Wins* litigation. In this case, the Administrative Court set out the *Wednesbury*/irrationality test as it related to the decisions of local licensing bodies. In that case it was said that a claimant had to persuade the Administrative Court that no reasonable licensing panel with the local knowledge that the licensing panel had could have come to the conclusion that it did.

12.102 These decisions (particularly those under the previous liquor licensing regime) should however be contrasted with the approach of the Administrative Court in *Daniel Thwaites PLC v Wirral Magistrates' Court & Others*[114] when considering the Licensing Act 2003. This case involved a judicial review claim in relation to an application under the 2003 Act to extend the licensable hours. The application was initially granted by the licensing authority but this was later overturned by the magistrates' court following an appeal by a local group of residents. Central to the decision of the magistrates' court was their concern that customers would migrate to the premises from other premises. In this case, the police had withdrawn its concerns and had therefore not opposed the application. The applicant brought judicial review proceedings to challenge the decision of the magistrates' court. In a detailed judgment which considered the policy behind the Licensing Act 2003 and the legal framework within which such licensing decisions should be made, Black J explained that:

> 'The fact that the police did not oppose the hours sought on this basis should have weighed very heavily with them whereas, in fact, they appear to have dismissed the police view because it did not agree with their own ... They proceeded without proper evidence and gave their own views excessive weight and their resulting decision limited the hours of operation of the premises without it having been established that it was necessary to do so to promote the licensing objectives.'

12.103 As explained earlier, Black J was of the view that whilst such a decision-maker may take account of its own local knowledge, it must be measured against the evidence presented to it. The decision in *Thwaites* also reinforces the proposition that the decision-maker must direct itself, and act, in accordance with the respective legal framework and the policy behind it. Moreover, it was explained in *R (Lunt & Others) v Liverpool City Council*[115] that the margin of discretion afforded to decision-makers under the *Wednesbury* test only applies to those decision-makers who have acted fairly and directed themselves properly as to the relevant considerations to be weighed in making the judgment.

THE FUTURE

12.104 What does the future hold for licensing law? In brief, the answer appears to be that there is potential for much litigation before the Administrative Court. Indeed, over recent years there has been an increase in licensing legislation which has completely changed and consolidated the way in which specific sectors are regulated and licensed.

---

[114] [2008] EWHC 838 (Admin).
[115] [2009] EWHC 2356 (Admin).

Both the Licensing Act 2003 and the Gambling Act 2005 have been notable entrants to the statute books. Both these Acts are far reaching and have overhauled the way in which alcohol, entertainment and gambling is regulated. A number of cases appear to be consistently making their way through the Administrative Court, notably in the context of the appeal court's approach to appeals and the familiar theme of costs. With the recent introduction of the Police Reform and Social Responsibility Act 2012 and the availability of late night levy's and early morning restriction orders, it is anticipated that there will be further case-law development. In contrast to the legal developments in terms of the licensing of alcohol, entertainment and gambling – other regulated sectors have been left untouched for many years. Indeed, the starting point for the licensing of the hackney carriage industry remains an Act of Parliament from 1847 (Town Police Clauses Act 1847). This has been supplemented by a statute from 1976 (Local Government (Miscellaneous Provisions) Act 1976). Many believe that the regulation of the hackney carriage and private hire industry requires modernising and bringing into line with the current commercial times. It remains to be seen, however, whether this area of the law will be developed by reference to modern legislation.

CHAPTER 13

LOCAL/CENTRAL GOVERNMENT

INTRODUCTION

13.01 Like central government, local government is a public body amenable to judicial review, and the principles explained in the general chapters of this book apply to them both. Indeed, many of the cases and issues dealt with elsewhere in this book relate to actions taken by or against local authorities. Nevertheless, central and local government differ in two important respects from other bodies.

13.02 First, unlike many bodies delivering public services or regulating activity, a local authority is a multifunctional, not a single issue, body. The functions exercised by an authority are diverse, although the precise functions allocated differ between unitary and two-tier authorities. While some of these specific functions are considered in other chapters of this book, this multifunctional nature raises issues relating to the appropriate relationship between the various powers conferred on local authorities and the factors which can be taken into account in exercising them.

13.03 Clearly, this characteristic is also shared by central government, but there is a difference between the legal bases of the two levels of government, affecting the extent of their powers and the ability to deal with 'cross-cutting' issues. This difference, and the nature of the powers of central and local government, is examined in this chapter.

13.04 Secondly, unlike most other public bodies, local government is an elected body and this democratic accountability raises issues relating to the extent to which the democratic imperative should be respected by the court, and the extent to which constraints should be placed on political action. While central government is not directly elected, it possesses the democratic legitimacy conferred by Parliament and similar issues arise, albeit that the response of the courts is not identical to the two levels of government.

THE LEGAL BASIS OF CENTRAL AND LOCAL GOVERNMENT

Residual and prerogative powers for central government

13.05 As explained in previous chapters, central government possesses not only the statutory powers conferred on it by Parliament but also many of the prerogative powers of the Crown, and other non-statutory non-prerogative powers, and the principles of judicial review have continued to develop in relation to these.[1]

---

[1] See eg *R (Bancoult) v Secretary of State for Foreign and Commonwealth Affairs (No 2)* [2008] UKHL 61. The residual power of central government has been confirmed recently in relation to the reorganisation of

13.06 The prerogative used to be reviewable only to the extent that it was open to the court to determine whether or not the prerogative existed, and not in regard to its exercise. This left wide discretion in respect to the exercise of these powers.

13.07 It is often said that the prerogative cannot be enlarged.[2] However, permitting it to be adapted to meet new situations allows the courts to come close to recognising new prerogatives.[3]

13.08 On the other hand, the courts have applied fairly rigorously the principle that the prerogative is displaced by statute legislating in regard to the same subject matter, thus respecting the right of Parliament to regulate areas previously subject to prerogative powers.[4]

13.09 However, given that the aim of judicial review is to ensure governmental power is exercised lawfully and properly, whilst the previous position could be understood historically a different judicial review regime for statutory and prerogative powers appeared anomalous in the modern democratic age. Pressure for change culminated in *Council of Civil Service Unions v Minister for the Civil Service*,[5] where Lord Scarman stated:

> 'the law relating to judicial review has now reached the stage where it can be said with confidence that, if the subject matter in respect of which prerogative power is exercised is justiciable, that is to say if it is a matter on which the court can adjudicate, the exercise of the power is subject to review in accordance with the principles developed in respect of the review of the exercise of statutory power.'

13.10 Indeed, in *M v Home Office*,[6] Lord Woolf stated, albeit *obiter*:

> 'As a result of even more recent developments, illustrated by the decision in [GCHQ], a distinction probably no longer has to be drawn between duties which have a statutory and those which have a prerogative source.'

13.11 That is not to say that all prerogative powers will be subject to the same degree of scrutiny. As Lord Scarman indicated, not all prerogatives are considered to be justiciable. Lord Roskill clarified this in the *Council of Civil Service Unions* case, albeit *obiter*:

> 'Prerogative powers such as those relating to the making of treaties, the defence of the realm, the prerogative of mercy, the grant of honours, the dissolution of Parliament and the appointment of ministers as well as others are not, I think, susceptible to judicial review because their nature and subject matter are such as not to be amenable to the judicial process. The courts are not the place wherein to determine whether a treaty should be concluded or the armed forces disposed in a particular manner or Parliament dissolved on one date rather than another.'

---

local government in *R (Shrewsbury and Atcham BC) v Secretary of State for Communities and Local Government* [2008] EWCA Civ 148; [2008] 3 All ER 548.

[2] *BBC v Johns* [1965] Ch 32 where Diplock LJ said: 'It is 350 years and a civil war too late for the Queen's courts to broaden the prerogative.'

[3] *R v Secretary of State for the Home Department, ex p Northumbria Police Authority* [1987] 2 All ER 282; [1988] 1 All ER 556. See also *Re Michelle Williamson's Application for Judicial Review* (NI Unreported Judgments, Court of Appeal, 16 March 2010); *R (New London College Ltd) v Secretary of State for the Home Department* [2013] UKSC 31.

[4] *R v Secretary of State for the Home Department, ex p Fire Brigades Union* [1995] 1 All ER 888.

[5] [1985] AC 374.

[6] [1993] 3 All ER 537.

13.12 Lord Diplock confirmed the justiciability point by noting that while judicial review was possible, many decisions would involve the application of government policy, and that such questions were not ones to which 'the judicial process is adapted to provide the right answer'. He therefore considered that such matters should be considered on a case-by-case basis.

13.13 As the law has developed since then, it has become clear that no areas remain immune from review in principle.[7] Indeed, the House of Lords has given very clear guidance on the point in *R (Bancoult) v Secretary of Stare for Foreign and Commonwealth Affairs (No 2).*[8]

13.14 The case concerned the validity of s 9 of the British Indian Ocean Territory (Constitution) Order 2004, made by prerogative Order in Council. One issue was whether this was amenable to review at all. The Government claimed that the courts had no power to review the validity of an Order in Council legislating for a colony, one strand of this reasoning being that it was primary legislation having unquestionable validity comparable with that of an Act of Parliament.

13.15 On this point Lord Hoffmann stated:[9]

> 'It is true that a prerogative Order in Council is primary legislation in the sense that the legislative power of the Crown is original and not subordinate. It is classified as primary legislation for the purposes of the Human Rights Act 1998: see paragraph (f)(i) of the definition in s 21(1). That means that it cannot be overridden by Convention rights. The court can only make a declaration of incompatibility under s 4. But the fact that such Orders in Council in certain important respects resemble Acts of Parliament does not mean that they share all their characteristics. The principle of the sovereignty of Parliament, as it has been developed by the courts over the past 350 years, is founded upon the unique authority Parliament derives from its representative character. An exercise of the prerogative lacks this quality; although it may be legislative in character, it is still an exercise of power by the executive alone. Until the decision of this House in *Council of Civil Service Unions v Minister for the Civil Service* [1985] AC 374, it may have been assumed that the exercise of prerogative powers was, as such, immune from judicial review. That objection being removed, I see no reason why prerogative legislation should not be subject to review on ordinary principles of legality, rationality and procedural impropriety in the same way as any other executive action. Mr Crow rightly pointed out that the *Council of Civil Service Unions* case was not concerned with the validity of a prerogative order but with an executive decision made pursuant to powers conferred by such an order. That is a ground upon which, if your Lordships were inclined to distinguish the case, it would be open to you to do so. But I see no reason for making such a distinction. On 21 February 2008 the Foreign Secretary told the House of Commons that, contrary to previous assurances, Diego Garcia had been used as a base for two extraordinary rendition flights in 2002 (Hansard (HC Debates), cols 547–548). There are allegations, which the US authorities have denied, that Diego Garcia or a ship in the waters around it have been used as a prison in which suspects have been tortured. The idea that such conduct on British territory, touching the honour of the United Kingdom, could be legitimated by executive fiat, is not something which I would find acceptable.'

13.16 Lord Bingham found that there was in fact 'no royal prerogative power to make an order in council containing s 9', but he also concluded that 'if (contrary to that

---

[7] For example, on the prerogative of mercy see *R v Secretary State for the Home Department, ex p Bentley* [1993] 4 All ER 442.
[8] [2008] UKHL 61.
[9] Paragraphs [34] and [35].

conclusion) there was power to make it, I agree with my noble and learned friends that the section is susceptible in principle to review by the courts'.[10] He found that it was unlawful on two grounds, namely irrationality and contradicting a clear representation of the Secretary of State in 2000.

13.17 For Lord Rodger, reliance on the historical approach to the prerogative was no longer acceptable and:[11]

> 'Nowadays, a broader form of review of other prerogative acts is established: *Council of Civil Service Unions v Minister for the Civil Service* [1985] AC 374. Therefore, like Lord Hoffmann, I see no reason in principle why, today, prerogative legislation, too, should not be subject to judicial review on ordinary principles of legality, rationality and procedural impropriety. Any challenge of that kind must, of course, be based on a ground that is justiciable.'

13.18 The concept of justiciability for Lord Rodger has moved from the nature of the power to the grounds raised in any challenge. Indeed, any reticence on the part of the courts to interfere with these powers has shifted from a focus on the power itself to recognising simply that due deference must be shown to the democratic role of the decision-maker. This was seen clearly in the view expressed by Lord Mance:[12]

> '... the prerogative power of the Crown to legislate by order in council on the advice of Her Majesty's ministers in relation to a territory such as BIOT is subject to judicial review. ... I see no good reason why they should not be reviewable in the same way as other steps, administrative or legislative, by the executive, and every reason why they should be, on the familiar grounds of legality, rationality and procedural propriety, due weight being of course given to the executive's effective role as primary decision-maker. A recognition that a legislative order in council is invalid by a judgment given in proceedings such as the present directed against the Minister responsible for the making of the order no more involves the making of an impermissible order against the Sovereign than a successful challenge to any other prerogative act undertaken in Her name.'

13.19 Thus, it can now be said that the basis of governmental power no longer provides the key to the extent to which it is susceptible to judicial review.

13.20 At the same time as the courts have been expanding the ability to review the exercise of the prerogative, there has been increasing recognition that central government can exercise other non-statutory powers.

13.21 To some extent this may be a matter of terminology. While some include in the term 'prerogative powers' only those powers which were historically unique to the Crown, others include all residual non-statutory powers. However, beyond both of these are powers for which there are various descriptions. Whether called 'third source', 'de facto', 'common law', or 'residual' powers, or even 'new prerogatives',[13] they all refer to powers which may be thought to operate under a wide approach to incidental powers, or what is termed the 'Ram doctrine', namely that a Minister can do anything a natural person can do provided it is not prohibited.[14] Authority for this is also said to stem from

---

[10] Paragraph [71].
[11] Paragraph [105].
[12] Paragraph [141].
[13] In contradiction to the established approach to prerogative powers where the categories are closed.
[14] The 'Ram doctrine' is named after the First Parliamentary Counsel who articulated the doctrine in 1945.

the common law powers which derive from the Crown's status as a corporation.[15] One example of such a wide power was given judicial recognition in *Malone v Metropolitan Police Commissioner*,[16] where telephone tapping was permitted on the basis that the Government could do anything 'except what is expressly forbidden'.[17]

13.22 However, the tension inherent in recognising wide powers lies in the fact that the Government is not simply another natural person, and some consider that the exercise of such power should be scrutinised by the courts carefully, to ensure there is no abuse of such powers and that they are exercised in the public as opposed to Government's interest.

13.23 This tension can be seen in the recent case of *R (Shrewsbury and Atcham BC) v Secretary of State for Communities and Local Government*,[18] which not only clarifies the approach to 'third source' powers but also illustrates the two approaches to how they should be treated by the courts.

13.24 In that case, the council applied for judicial review of the process adopted by the Secretary of State for considering proposals to abolish it by replacing the existing two-tier local government in the area with unitary authorities.

13.25 Following the publication of a White Paper in which it was stated that such reform was desirable, local authorities were invited by the Government to make proposals for future unitary structures. The council strongly opposed unitary structures advanced by other local authorities in the area. The Government stated that proposals which the Government considered met the relevant criteria would continue to a second stage where there would be wide consultation in the areas affected and, following that consultation, it would re-assess proposals to take account of the outcome of consultation and implement any proposals that succeeded.

13.26 It was acknowledged in the White Paper that the proposals could not be implemented unless and until new legislation was passed, since a policy decision had been made not to use the existing legislative machinery under the Local Government Act 1992. However, the exercise was undertaken prior to the enactment of the Local Government and Public Involvement in Health Act 2007. The challenge was made on the basis that the Secretary of State had no power to undertake the exercise.

13.27 The Court of Appeal considered itself obliged to follow a previous decision of the House of Lords which held that the powers of the Secretary of State were not confined to those conferred by statute or prerogative. As Carnwath LJ stated:[19]

> 'the answer seems to me to be dictated by the decision in [*R v Secretary of State for Health, ex p C* [2000] 1 FCR 471] in the judgment of Hale LJ ... . That decision, which is binding also on us, confirms that the powers of the Secretary of State are not confined to those

---

15 Written Reply in 2003 by Baroness Scotland, House of Lords, *Hansard*, Vol 645, col WA12, cited in De Smiths *Judicial Review*, 6th edn, para 5-023. She also stated that this flexibility was necessary because otherwise it would 'impose upon Parliament an impossible burden or produce legislation in terms that simply reproduced the common law'.
16 [1979] Ch 344.
17 This was subsequently held to violate Art 8 of the ECHR.
18 [2008] EWCA Civ 148; [2008] 3 All ER 548. For a discussion of third source powers see *R (New London College Ltd) v Secretary of State for the Home Department* [2013] UKSC 51.
19 Paragraph [44]. See also *R (Hillingdon LBC) v Secretary of State for Transport and Transport for London* [2010] EWHC 626 (Admin).

conferred by statute or prerogative, but extend, subject to any relevant statutory or public law constraints, and to the competing rights of other parties, to anything which could be done by a natural person.'

13.28 This confirms in principle the 'third source' approach. However, the court took the matter further and outlined the principles applicable to such power.

13.29 The majority warned that this residual category of ministerial power was exceptional, and should be strictly confined. As Carnwath LJ stated:[20]

> 'Unlike a local authority, the Crown is not a creature of statute. As a matter of capacity, no doubt, it has power to do whatever a private person can do. But as an organ of government, it can only exercise those powers for the public benefit, and for identifiably "governmental" purposes within limits set by the law.'

13.30 Nevertheless, on the facts of the case, Carnwath LJ also held that local government re-organisation as such did not fall within any residual non-statutory government power and so legislation was needed to give effect to the proposals. However, the Secretary of State's actions which fell short of the actual re-organisation were 'governmental' and undertaken for what she perceived to be the public benefit. The court therefore held that the Secretary of State could promote new legislation and lawfully take some preparatory steps in advance of doing so. That extended to the preparation and publication of the White Paper. He concluded:[21]

> 'I do not see that it is necessary to invoke a "third source" category for that purpose. I see it as simply a necessary and incidental part of the ordinary business of central government, part of which is the promotion of new policies through legislation. The issue is how far such preparatory steps can properly go before crossing into territory reserved to statute. That issue can only sensibly be considered in the context of the present statutory scheme. It therefore overlaps with the second ground of appeal, to which I now turn.'

13.31 That second ground of appeal was whether the actions of the Secretary of State were inconsistent with the existing statutory regime under the Local Government Act 1992 and how far preparatory steps could properly go before crossing into territory reserved to statute. Carnwath LJ held that while the inconsistency principle was well developed,[22] how 'far in any case it is necessary or appropriate to review the procedural steps will depend on the facts and circumstances, including the nature of the illegality and the substantive relief sought in respect of it'. On the facts of that case, he concluded that it would not be appropriate to grant relief because the actions had in effect been ratified by Parliament through the enactment of the Local Government and Public Involvement in Health Act 2007.

13.32 Nevertheless, although not upholding the challenge of the council, Carnwath LJ expressed his concern about the use of such powers:[23]

> 'As I have made clear, I have more concerns ... about the extent to which a wholly non-statutory procedure has been used to prepare the way for decisions, in an area which is accepted as the province of the legislature. I have also pointed out the potential risks of such

---

[20] Paragraph [48].
[21] Paragraph [49].
[22] *R v Secretary of State for the Home Department, ex p Northumbria Police Authority* [1989] QB 26; *De Keyser's Royal Hotel Ltd* (1920) AC 508; and *Laker Airways Ltd v Department of Trade* [1977] QB 643.
[23] Paragraph [70].

a course. I understand that one purpose was to limit the period of uncertainty accompanying structural change. But it seems to me a constitutional principle of some importance that local authorities should be able to rely on the safeguards of a statutory framework for the processes leading to decisions of this importance. However, in the end, I find it impossible to avoid the conclusion that Parliament has (if only retrospectively) given its stamp of approval to the procedure in this case, and there is no evidence that the authorities have been prejudiced in presenting their opposition.'

13.33 Although agreeing with Carnwath LJ as to the outcome of the case and much of the reasoning, Richards LJ disagreed on two points.

13.34 First, in relation to the extent of the common law powers, he stated:[24]

'As the first instance judge whose decision was upheld by the Court of Appeal in *R v Secretary of State for Health, ex p C* [2000] 1 FLR 627 I took a broad view of those powers, and nothing in the materials deployed before us in the present case has caused me to change my mind. The Court of Appeal's judgment in that case is not only determinative of the issue at this level (see paras 44 and 49 of Carnwath LJ's judgment) but was in my view correct.

The complex process of government includes a vast amount of work in relation to the formulation of policy, drafting new legislation and preparing for its implementation. Carnwath LJ states that it is not necessary to invoke a "third source" of power for such work, which is simply "a necessary and incidental part of the ordinary business of government" (para 49). To my mind, however, it is still necessary to explain the basis on which that ordinary business of government is conducted, and the simple and satisfactory explanation is that it depends heavily on the "third source" of powers, ie powers that have not been conferred by statute and are not prerogative powers in the narrow sense but are the normal powers (or capacities and freedoms) of a corporation with legal personality. The context is a special one, but the powers are the same.

I accept, of course, that such powers cannot override the rights of others and, when exercised by government, are subject to judicial review on ordinary public law grounds. But I think it unnecessary and unwise to introduce qualifications along the lines of those suggested by Carnwath LJ at para 48, to the effect that they can only be exercised "for the public benefit" or for "identifiably 'governmental' purposes". It seems to me that any limiting principle would have to be so wide as to be of no practical utility or would risk imposing an artificial and inappropriate restriction upon the work of government.'

13.35 The third judge, Waller LJ, noted the disagreement between the two and his own contribution was tentatively on the side of Carnwath LJ:[25]

'I doubt whether anything that I can say will influence any future debate, and since *ex p C* is binding, it is not appropriate to say very much. But it seems to me that once one accepts capacity, the limit so far as any challenge before the courts is concerned cannot be other than by reference to "the limits set by the law". The question is thus whether there should be an ability to challenge as unlawful an action taken "not for the public benefit" or which has not been taken for "identifiably governmental purposes".

I instinctively favour some constraint on the powers by reference to the duty to act only for the public benefit but until one has actual facts by reference to which the matter can be fully tested, it is unwise to say more.'

---

[24] Paragraphs [72] to [74].
[25] Paragraphs [80] and [81].

13.36 These different views were also seen in the more recent case of *R (New London College Ltd) v Secretary of State for the Home Department*. On the one hand Lord Sumption considered that:

> 'It has long been recognised that the Crown possesses some general administrative powers to carry on the ordinary business of government which are not exercises of the royal prerogative and do not require statutory authority: see BV Harris, "The 'Third Source' of Authority for Government Action Revisited" (2007) 123 LQR 225. The extent of these powers and their exact juridical basis are controversial. In *R v Secretary of State for Health ex parte C* [2000] 1 FLR 627 and *Shrewsbury and Atcham Borough Council v Secretary of State for Communities and Local Government* [2008] EWCA Civ 148, [2008] 3 All ER 548, the Court of Appeal held that the basis of the power was the Crown's status as a common law corporation sole, with all the capacities and powers of a natural person subject only to such particular limitations as were imposed by law. Although in *R (Hooper) v Secretary of State for Work and Pensions* [2005] UKHL 29, [2006] 1 All ER 487, [2005] 1 WLR 1681, para 47 Lord Hoffmann thought that there was "a good deal of force" in this analysis, it is open to question whether the analogy with a natural person is really apt in the case of public or governmental action, as opposed to purely managerial acts of a kind that any natural person could do, such as making contracts, acquiring or disposing of property, hiring and firing staff and the like.'

Although he accepted that the question did need to be resolved in that case 'because the statutory power of the Secretary of State to administer the system of immigration control must necessarily extend to a range of ancillary and incidental administrative powers not expressly spelt out in the Act', Lord Carnwath nevertheless felt it necessary to again record his view that:

> 'I cannot accept ... that there is some alternative, unidentified source of such powers, derived neither from the prerogative nor from any specific provision in the Act, but from the general responsibilities of the Secretary of State in this field. No authority was cited for that proposition and to my knowledge none exists. Mr Swift did not seek to rely on a possible "third source" of powers, by reference to the "controversial" line of authority mentioned by Lord Sumption (para 28). In my view he was wise not to do so (for the reasons given in my judgment for the majority in the *Shrewsbury* case [2008] EWCA Civ 148). (This sensitive issue has also been the subject of recent consideration by the House of Lords Select Committee on the Constitution: The pre-emption of Parliament HL Paper 165 – 1 May 2013).
>
> [35] Lord Sumption relies instead on a broader application of the incidental powers approach, which appears to be a variant of Mr Swift's main submission. The Secretary of State's power to administer the system of immigration control must, it is said, extend to "a range of ancillary and incidental powers", including administrative measures for identifying suitable sponsors, "even if these measures do not themselves fall within s 3(2) of the Act". This formulation, as I understand it, treats the licensing process as linked not to the specific provisions for regulating entry under s 1(4), but to the general system of immigration control under the Act. It thus takes it outside the scope of the s 3(2) procedure altogether.
>
> [36] I find this more difficult to accept. In *Hazell v Hammersmith LBC* [1992] 2 AC 1, considering the analogous principle in s 111 of the Local Government Act 1972, Lord Templeman extracted from the authorities, starting with *Attorney-General v Great Eastern Railway Co* (1880) 5 App Cas 473," ... the general proposition that when a power is claimed to be incidental, the provisions of the statute which confer and limit functions must be considered and construed." (p 31D). In that case the alleged power to enter into swap transactions had to be considered in the context of the specific provisions governing local authority borrowing. Similarly, in *Barry* the scheme for vetting door-staff was incidental, not to the council's regulatory powers in general, but to the particular power for

licensing places for public entertainment. In each case the source of the incidental power was found in a specific provision conferring specific functions.

[37] So in the present context, in my view the sponsorship licensing scheme is an adjunct, not of the immigration control system in general, but of the specific function of providing for entry for study under s 1(4). That is its only purpose within the statutory scheme. Section 1(4) states that such provision is to be "in such cases and subject to such restrictions as may be provided by the rules". On its face that leads back to s 3(2) which prescribes the procedure for making the rules.'

13.37 Thus, given the lack of unanimity and that strictly the views expressed are *obiter* albeit fully reasoned and deliberate, it will be for a future ruling to decide between the two approaches, and determine the flexibility which the courts will grant to central government outside of its statutory and prerogative powers. Whether a future court will embrace the 'third source', or adopt a more restrictive approach based on incidental or implied powers remains to be seen.

13.38 The second point on which Richards LJ disagreed in the *Shrewsbury and Atcham* case was in relation to whether the actions of the Secretary of State were inconsistent with the 1992 Act. As Richards LJ explained his position:[26]

'I do not read the 1992 Act as preventing the taking of action by Ministers by way of preparation for the introduction of a different statutory regime. Moreover the work done did not pre-empt Parliament's decision in relation to the proposed new legislation but prepared for it on a contingent basis. The process engaged in was not intended to produce, and was not capable of producing, a result with legal effects unless and until the proposed legislation was enacted and relevant measures were taken under it. It is true that the existing machinery of the 1992 Act was not used and, so far as one can see, was not intended to be used even as a fall-back in the event that Parliament did not enact the proposed legislation. But nothing done was, in my judgment, inconsistent with the 1992 Act. However improbable it was in practice, it would still have been possible in principle to fall back on the machinery of that Act if the new legislation had not been forthcoming and the Secretary of State had wished to pursue the matter.

On these issues, therefore, I would endorse the conclusion reached by Underhill J, even before the 2007 Act was enacted, that the Secretary of State acted lawfully. The Secretary of State's actions did not depend for their lawfulness on the retrospective effect of the Act. But if there were any doubt about that, then I agree with Carnwath LJ that the position was resolved against the Boroughs by the Act and the measures adopted under it.'

13.39 In relation to this point Waller LJ was less equivocal, agreeing firmly with Carnwath LJ:[27]

'One reason I have for supporting his view is that it seems to me that the action being taken was in an area which the 1992 Act was designed to cover. The action was not simply preliminary to bringing in an Act to change the 1992 Act with the intention thereafter of acting under a new statutory scheme. The action being taken was to treat the 1992 scheme as having already been repealed.'

13.40 This approach continues the trend seen in relation to the prerogative whereby the courts seek to respect the authority of Parliament when it legislates in the same sphere.

---

[26] Paragraphs [75] and [76].
[27] Paragraph [82].

Residual prerogative powers for local government?

13.41 For local government, it is clear that there is no longer any such residual prerogative power, and certainly no judicial recognition of non-statutory powers. Previously, some local authorities were established by Royal Charter, and as such were deemed to have inherited the relevant powers of the Crown.[28] However during the 19th century the influence of centralism was seen, and many local authorities were the creation of statute. Thus in *Att-Gen v Manchester Corporation*,[29] it was held that the prerogative power was in practice suspended.

13.42 The role of the public sector in the depression was subject to much debate and there was a rise of 'municipal socialism'. In *Att-Gen v Leicester Corporation*,[30] following the enactment of the Local Government Act 1933, the local prerogative was reasserted. Nevertheless, this does not accord with current judicial approaches to the prerogative and in *Hazell v Hammersmith and Fulham LBC*,[31] the 'loan swaps' case, the House of Lords held that the council was the creature of statute and possessed only those powers granted by statute.

13.43 Nevertheless, just as there are sound arguments why flexibility and discretion beyond specific statutory powers is necessary for central government, in the form of prerogative or other non-statutory powers, so there are sound reasons why local government also needs appropriate flexibility and discretion.

General power of competence

13.44 This is reflected in a debate in relation to local authority powers as to whether the narrow *ultra vires* doctrine, requiring express or implied/incidental statutory authority is unduly constraining on innovative local government activity.

13.45 Under the common law, the courts held that a corporation may do not only those things for which there is express or implied authority, but also whatever is reasonably incidental to the doing of those things.[32]

13.46 For local government this common law principle was incorporated into statute by s 111 of the Local Government Act 1972. It provides that:

> '(1) Without prejudice to any powers exercisable apart from this section but subject to the provisions of this Act and any other enactment passed before or after this Act, a local authority shall have power to do anything (whether or not involving the expenditure, borrowing or lending of money or the acquisition or disposal of any property or rights) which is calculated to facilitate, or is conducive or incidental to, the discharge of any of their functions.'

13.47 However, there has been confusion so as to be unclear whether the 'functions' referred to in s 111(1) must be expressly conferred by statute or can be impliedly conferred.

---

[28] *Case of Sutton's Hospital* (1612) 10 Co Rep 1; *Riche v Ashbury Railway Carriage and Iron Co* (1874) LR 9 Exch 224.
[29] [1906] 1 Ch 643.
[30] [1943] 1 Ch 86.
[31] [1992] 2 AC 1.
[32] *Att-Gen v Great Eastern Railway* (1880) 5 App Cas 473.

13.48 The broader view, that s 111 can apply not only to express powers but also implied powers, is not only in accord with the trend in most of the 20th century before s 111 was enacted, but accords with there being no indication that the enactment of s 111 was intended to reduce the width of the common law power. This wider view of s 111 is also reflected in a number of cases, as articulated by Woolf LJ in the Court of Appeal in *Hazell v Hammersmith and Fulham LBC*,[33] where he considered that 'functions' meant the 'specific statutory activities the council is expressly or impliedly under a duty to perform', and by the Divisional Court in *Allsop v North Tyneside Metropolitan Borough Council*.[34]

13.49 On the other hand more restrictive interpretations seemed to be adopted in some cases in the 1990s. In *R v Richmond Upon Thames London Borough Council, ex p McCarthy & Stone (Developments) Ltd*,[35] the House of Lords appeared to take a narrow approach and held that the giving of pre-planning application advice was not itself a 'function' of the council and so charging for it could not be justified by reference to s 111 as that would be 'incidental to the incidental'. However, no consideration was given to the possibility that the giving of pre-application advice was an 'implied function' of the local authority.[36] This debate can be seen as similar to that in relation to the width of interpretation of statutory powers of central government as a 'third source' or ancillary powers referred to above.

13.50 Another principle restricting the scope of s 111 is that of the 'comprehensive code'. Where the court considers that Parliament has made sufficiently detailed provision as to a statutory regime, it is considered that it is not possible to justify additional powers by reference to s 111.[37]

13.51 Whatever the position as a matter of strict interpretation of the cases, by the mid-1990s it was perceived that by restrictive judicial interpretation there had been a narrowing of the width of incidental powers under s 111.

13.52 At the same time there was a resurgence of the debate over the desirability of granting local government a power of general competence, as is done in many continental systems. A modification of the narrow doctrine of *ultra vires*, and consideration of a power of general competence had been recommended in a number of official reports.[38] While a power of general competence reverses the presumption in favour of an authority having the power to do something, rather than having to find positive statutory authority, its exercise would remain subject to the other wider principles of judicial review and it does not 'allow a council to do anything' as many of its critics suggest.

13.53 However, a power of general competence expressed as such remained politically unacceptable and, instead, the Government introduced the well-being powers under

---

[33] [1990] 2 QB 697.
[34] (1992) 90 LGR 462.
[35] [1992] 2 AC 48.
[36] The *Encyclopedia of Local Government Law* submits that the broad approach is to be preferred, and correctly suggests that *McCarthy & Stone* can be justified by reference to the principle that a power for a public authority to charge for its services must be conferred expressly or by necessary implication, see *Att-Gen v Wilts United Dairies Ltd* (1922) 38 TLR 781.
[37] *Hazell v Hammersmith & Fulham LBC* [1992] 2 AC 1; *Credit Suisse v Allerdale BC* (1996) 94 LGR 628; *R v Liverpool City Council, ex p Baby Products Association* [2000] LGR 171.
[38] See eg the Royal Commission on Local Government in England 1966–69, Cmnd 4039 & 4040 (Redcliffe-Maud).

Part 1 of the Local Government Act 2000, intending to reduce and contain the uncertainty arising from the narrow principle of *ultra vires*.

13.54 The underlying aims of these powers were to meet the concerns of local government by:

- reassurance that existing activities were legally possible and not constrained by the recent restrictive interpretations of s 111;
- allowing new ways of undertaking existing activity; and
- allowing new activities.

13.55 The general approach to the legislation was to provide a wide power which could be a 'power of first resort' and thus one which was overlapping with, but wider than, the existing statutory powers under the wide variety of Acts. The idea was that it would not be necessary to use the existing statutory powers and reliance would simply be placed on the new power. However, the enactment of such a power clearly had implications for existing statutory restrictions, and it was not intended that these would be swept away by the new power.

13.56 This general approach resulted in a wide power under s 2(1) of the 2000 Act to promote economic, social or environmental well-being:

> '(1) Every local authority are to have power to do anything which they consider is likely to achieve any one or more of the following objects –
>
> (a) the promotion or improvement of the economic well-being of their area;
> (b) the promotion or improvement of the social well-being of their area; and
> (c) the promotion or improvement of the environmental well-being of their area.'

13.57 The three objectives are separate but could be related, and were intended to be all-embracing, eg including cultural or health issues.

13.58 Until the Court of Appeal's decision in *Risk Management Partners Ltd v Brent LBC and London Authorities Mutual Ltd*,[39] the approach to the issues in relation to the well-being power was relatively uniform and could be summarised as follows:

- The general trend in interpreting the power had been to rely on underlying purpose, as seen from the Explanatory Notes and the Guidance, rather than its precise wording.
- The case-law supported the wide approach and the use of the power as one of 'first resort'.
- The case-law supported the view that normally a limitation would almost always be found in an express legislative provision.
- Nevertheless, it was important to note the, albeit rare, possibility that a limitation might arise by necessary implication, thus leaving some uncertainty.
- An express limitation or restriction in another enactment may not apply to s 2, depending on whether it is considered to be fundamental to the other scheme, thus again leaving scope for further litigation.

---

[39] [2009] EWCA Civ 490.

- While the power may, in principle, be invoked for making payments to individuals, and it is, of course, a matter for the council, the starting point of the courts is that it would be a relatively exceptional case where the power would be exercised purely for the benefit of an individual. It follows that there is not a duty enforceable by an individual in the sense of being able to force the authority to make any such payment.

- A local authority is not a 'person' for the purposes of promoting or improving its well-being under s 2, and the financial well-being of a local authority is not the same as the economic, social or environmental well-being of its area.

13.59 However, uncertainty and confusion has resulted from the Court of Appeal's decision in the *LAML* case.[40]

13.60 In relation to the role of the guidance and the explanatory notes, the court attributed less importance to these than in previous cases. Reiterating the formal position that such guidance 'cannot relieve the court of its duty itself to construe legislation',[41] it was concluded not only that they are not a proper aid to interpretation but also that they did not shed any real light on the question now before the court, containing 'nothing either way which touches on the question of whether embarking on a course of action which is expected to reduce the authority's costs can of itself and, for that reason alone, be regarded as doing something that will promote or improve the well-being of its area'.[42] Indeed, Pill LJ considered that:[43]

> 'Had it been intended to apply to an arrangement such as the disputed arrangement, I would have expected the power now claimed to have been conferred either specifically or by the use of an expression other than and more directed to the subject matter than the expression "promote the well-being".'

13.61 Thus, the Court of Appeal was not willing to take a purposive approach to either the power, or the guidance, preferring a narrower and more literal approach. The court moved from supporting a wide purposive approach which regards the power as one of first resort, and sought to define the term 'well-being', albeit largely negatively.

13.62 On the positive side, for Moore-Bick LJ the power:[44]

> 'gives a local authority power to take steps that have as their object, direct or indirect, some reasonably well defined outcome which it considers will promote or improve the well-being of its area. In other words, it gives authorities the power to do things themselves, or to procure or enable others to do things, that directly affect the well-being of their areas.'

13.63 Equally, Pill LJ found that the expression is a general one and that:[45]

> 'I accept that the words have, and were intended to have, a broad meaning and were intended to prevent an over-technical approach to the definition of powers. The Government's purpose was stated in the guidance (paragraphs 5 and 6) to be to reverse the "traditionally cautious approach" to "innovation and joint action".'

---

[40] *Risk Management Partners Ltd v Brent London Borough Council* [2009] EWCA Civ 490.
[41] Ibid per Hughes LJ at para 256.
[42] Ibid per Moore-Bick LJ at para 181.
[43] Ibid, para 116. This approach was followed in *R (Barnsley MBC) v Secretary of State for Communities and Local Government* [2012] EWHC 1366 (Admin).
[44] Ibid, para 180.
[45] Ibid, para 114.

13.64 Nevertheless, for Pill LJ:[46]

> 'Promotion of well-being is not an expression one would normally associate with a somewhat complex arrangement to save money, such as the LAML arrangement, rather than with action directly to promote or improve a healthy or prosperous condition. The documents specifically contemplate positive action in a variety of areas: community strategies to promote the well-being of the local community (explanatory note paragraph 13), a wide range of activities for the benefit of the local area (explanatory note paragraph 15), promotion of sustainable development by delivering the actions and improvements identified in the community strategy and action, for example, to combat climate change and to contribute to health improvement programmes (paragraph 6 of guidance).'

13.65 Similarly, for Moore-Bick LJ:

> 'In my view action to reduce the costs of goods or services purchased by the authority which does not have as its object the use of the money saved for an identified purpose which the authority considers would promote or improve well-being does not, on a natural reading of the words, fall within the section.'

13.66 Thus, at its narrowest, the case decided that, without express justification in the section or perhaps in the guidance, schemes for cost reduction and savings will not be acceptable without a specific and identified end use which itself meets the well-being criteria. As Moore-Bick LJ put it:[47]

> 'there must obviously be some degree of connection between the authority's actions and the promotion or improvement of the area's well-being to enable the authority to conclude that the action it proposes to take is likely to have that effect.'

13.67 Both judges gave some further justification for their conclusions and it is those justifications which caused the greatest uncertainty over the future use of the power.

13.68 For Pill LJ, the section did not represent a move away from the technicality in previous decisions in relation to s 111 of the 1972 Act, but was simply an alternative to it. As he stated:[48]

> 'Clearly, s 2 of the 2000 Act was intended to create a general power and thus, in appropriate circumstances, to limit the need to rely on s 111 of the 1972 Act and the somewhat technical arguments which have arisen on that section. However in analysing the breadth of the power conferred the approach adopted to the construction of statutory powers in such cases as *Hazell* and *Waltham Forest* retains in my view a relevance.'

13.69 This lead him to a view on guarantees when he stated that powers 'which have been held not to be incidental to functions of the authority, such as giving guarantees to companies, do not readily obtain sanction by the use of a general expression, the wording of which does not easily bear upon such activities.'[49] This completely ignores the fact that s 2 replaced the previous powers for economic development, and, in particular, s 33 of the Local Government and Housing Act 1989 which expressly authorised the giving of guarantees, and before that the same was done by s 137(2B) of

---

[46] Ibid, para 115.
[47] Ibid, para 178.
[48] Ibid, para 117.
[49] Ibid, para 117.

the 1972 Act. The intention behind s 2 was that it would replace these powers. It also ignores the fact that it was by no means clear that there was a prohibition on the giving of guarantees under s 111.[50]

13.70 In the judgment there was some confusion over whether Pill LJ was really making a finding on narrow *vires* or one of abuse of discretion akin to the fiduciary duty. While he stated that:[51]

> 'The guarantees and degree of speculation involved, in my view take the activity proposed beyond what Parliament intended by the well-being clause. It did not require a specific exclusion to place beyond the s 2 power the enterprise proposed.'

He also emphasised the degree of speculation suggesting that it was a matter of degree rather than of kind:[52]

> 'Of course, the risks involved may be lessened by the employment of professional agents and the reinsurance they may suggest but the substantial speculative element cannot be ignored. Any enterprise by a local authority involves risks but the local authority becoming insurer for itself and other authorities over a wide area of activity is of a different order.'

13.71 Equally, it is unclear whether the objection was the degree of speculation or whether he was finding that the mechanism was simply not insurance at all and so not implementing the power under s 111:[53]

> 'The present venture is not, however, merely a different way of obtaining insurance; it is a venture to set up an insurance company of which the local authority is a member and by which insurance is obtained not only for itself but for other local authorities.'

13.72 Moore-Bick LJ was influenced by s 3(2):[54]

> 'The fact that a local authority cannot use its powers under s 2(1) to raise money suggests two things: first, that any action taken under s 2(1) must be financed out of authority's existing resources; second, that taking steps to improve the authority's general financial position is not to be treated as something that will of itself promote or improve the well-being of its area.'

13.73 That the interpretation by the court was out of step with the political consensus is seen from the fact that the substantive issue was resolved by s 34 of the Local Democracy, Economic Development and Construction Act 2009 which authorises mutual insurance schemes and so solved the immediate practical problem.

13.74 The wider problem of providing an adequate general power remained, and the Coalition Government introduced a new power, called the general power of competence, by Part 1 of the Localism Act 2011.

---

[50] See discussion at Ch 9 of *Law relating to Local Government* by Crawford, Sauvain, Coulson and Clarke, DETR 2000.
[51] *Risk Management Partners Ltd v Brent London Borough Council* [2009] EWCA Civ 490, para 119.
[52] Ibid, para 120.
[53] Ibid, para 121.
[54] Ibid, para 179.

13.75 Described by the Secretary of State as 'probably the single most important item in the Bill', the general power of competence in s 1 of the Act provides that a 'local authority has power to do anything that individuals generally may do'. By s 1(4), the power may be exercised in

> 'any way whatever, including –
>
> (a) power to do it anywhere in the United Kingdom or elsewhere,
> (b) power to do it for a commercial purpose or otherwise for a charge, or without charge, and
> (c) power to do it for, or otherwise than for, the benefit of the authority, its area or persons resident or present in its area.'

13.76 As with the well-being power, the wide power comes with limitations. Since it was impossible within the timescale to enact comprehensive tailor-made restrictions, it is provided by s 2(1) that if exercise of an existing power of a local authority is subject to restrictions, those restrictions apply also to exercise of the general power so far as it is overlapped by the pre-commencement power. By s 2(3), the general power does not enable a local authority to do anything which the authority is unable to do by virtue of an existing limitation expressly imposed by a statutory provision, or anything that the authority is unable to do by virtue of an express limitation in a subsequent statutory provision that is expressed to apply to the general power or various powers including the general power. In addition, s 3 and s 4 apply the existing law on charging and limitations on trading to the new power.

13.77 Again similar to the well-being powers, in order to mitigate these limitations, s 5(1) provides power for the Secretary of State, if he thinks that a statutory provision (whenever passed or made) prevents or restricts local authorities from exercising the general power, to amend, repeal, revoke or disapply that provision by order. Equally, by s 5(2) if the Secretary of State thinks that the general power is overlapped (to any extent) by another power then, for the purpose of removing or reducing that overlap, he may by order amend, repeal, revoke or disapply any statutory provision (whenever passed or made). On the other side, by s 5(3) power is also given to the Secretary of State to make provision by order preventing local authorities from doing, in exercise of the general power, anything that is specified in the order. Detailed provision is made for the procedure of such orders.

13.78 There are various potential problems with this new power but the main issue must be whether it will alter judicial attitudes to a wide discretionary power, or whether the courts will, as in the *LAML* case, simply treat this power as yet another specific provision rather than one intended to introduce genuine general competence and wide legislative power.

Multifunctional government and judicial review

13.79 As noted above, unlike many bodies delivering public services or regulating activity, local and central government are multifunctional, and not single issue, bodies. It has been a common criticism of local government, and to a lesser extent central government, that it is seen, and has acted, as a series of separate functions or 'silos', rather than taking a coordinated approach to problems and issues, such as in the area of health where medical, social, educational, environmental, financial and other issues impinge.

13.80 Although much of this criticism can be attributed to the culture in public administration and financial structures, the legal framework has sometimes been seen as a problem in local government. While it allowed for consultation and coordination, each action had to be justified in terms of the purposes of, and considerations relevant to, the particular statutory power being exercised. This, it was said, resulted in a situation where a great amount of time and effort went into trying to finding a range of powers to use to achieve policies which were otherwise sensible and worthwhile. At worst this could result in an inability to undertake the activity, or it would deter more cautious authorities, and even for the more confident authorities it was at the very least considered to be waste of resources. This legal framework was seen as reinforcing the 'silo mentality' and inhibiting proper community leadership and the most effective use of resources.

13.81 This lack of integration and coordination of powers in local government was intended to be addressed by the well-being power, and is now provided for by the general power of competence. Given that the purposes for which this power can be used are so broad, and that a diverse range of considerations may be taken into account, depending on the particular purpose for which it being exercised, much of the perceived legal barrier to effective community leadership has been removed. While this is a step in the right direction, as shown above the power is not without its uncertainties. In addition, it is subject to the wider principles of judicial review.

13.82 In that respect, comparison can be drawn with the prerogative and other non-statutory powers exercised by central government. While these are not, and never were intended to be wide powers akin to general competence, they are wide discretionary powers which operate where there are no specific statutory powers, and give necessary flexibility to government and administration. As seen from *R (Bancoult) v Secretary of Stare for Foreign and Commonwealth Affairs (No 2)*,[55] these are reviewable in the same way as other administrative actions by the executive, on the grounds of legality, rationality and procedural propriety. However, while the courts have made clear that due weight will be given to the Government's role as primary decision-maker, it remains to be seen the extent to which the courts will respect local government's role as community leader.

DEMOCRATIC ISSUES

Political considerations

13.83 The issue of political considerations in decision-making as a general principle has been dealt with elsewhere in this work.[56] The remainder of this section deals with other aspects of the relevant legal principles which impinge on the making of political decisions.

Fiduciary duty

13.84 There are of course a number of principles which the courts apply to the exercise of discretion by public bodies. However, there is one controversial principle which the courts have applied to local authorities, namely the fiduciary duty.

---

[55] [2008] UKHL 61.
[56] See paras **1.128–1.134** and **5.120** and *Persimmon Homes (Teesside) Ltd v R (Lewis)* 2008 EWCA Civ 746 – for a specific example of the role of political considerations in the planning context.

13.85 A 'fiduciary duty' applies to any person acting as trustee for the benefit of another person. However, it is less clear that an analogous principle should be applied to a body which is elected, in order to give priority to the interests of taxpayers over those of electors. Indeed, critics of the principle point to the fact that it has not been applied to central government where the courts pay more respect to the democratic nature of the institution. It is also pointed out that most of local government funding comes from central taxation and non-domestic rates over which local government has no control.

13.86 Nevertheless, it is clear that the courts do invoke this concept and local authorities are under a special duty to consider the interests of local taxpayers. However the stringency with which the principle is applied remains a matter of debate for two reasons.

13.87 First, the cases in which it has been invoked can be seen as politically controversial. Thus, in *Roberts v Hopwood*,[57] the House of Lords reversed the Court of Appeal, which had deferred to the views of elected representatives, and found unlawful the council's decision, under its power to pay such wages as it 'may think fit', to pay a minimum wage of £4 per week to all employees, both men and women, when this was above market rates for male labourers. The case is often remembered for comments such as those of Lord Atkinson who found that:

> 'The council would, in my view, fail in their duty if, in administering funds which did not belong to their members alone, they put aside all these aids to the ascertainment of what was just and reasonable remuneration to give for the services rendered to them, and allowed themselves to be guided in preference by some eccentric principles of socialistic philanthropy, or by a feminist ambition to secure the equality of the sexes in the matter of wages in the world of labour.'

13.88 Many commentators took the view not only that this case was out of step with legitimate political thinking, but that it also exceeded the proper limits of judicial review.[58] Following the *Wednesbury* case in 1948,[59] many considered that *Roberts v Hopwood* and the fiduciary duty was to be considered an aberration.

13.89 Nevertheless, the duty formed the basis of the decision in *Prescott v Birmingham Corporation*.[60] There, the council had exercised its power to charge 'such fares as they may think fit' to introduce a scheme for free travel for old people on its public transport. Invoking *Roberts v Hopwood*, the Court of Appeal quashed the decision, Jenkins LJ stating:

> 'Local authorities are not, of course, trustees for their ratepayers, but they do, we think, owe an analogous fiduciary duty to their ratepayers in relation to the application of funds contributed by the latter. Thus local authorities running an omnibus undertaking at the risk of their ratepayers, in the sense that any deficiencies must be met by an addition to the rates, are not, in our view, entitled, merely on the strength of a general power, to charge different fares to different passengers or classes of passengers, to make a gift to a particular class of persons of rights of free travel on their vehicles simply because the local authority concerned are of opinion that the favoured class of persons ought, on benevolent or philanthropic grounds, to be accorded that benefit.'

---

[57] [1925] AC 578.
[58] See SA de Smith, *Judicial Review of Administrative Action*, 3rd edn, 1973 p 309.
[59] *Associated Provincial Picture Houses v Wednesbury Corporation* [1948] 1 KB 223.
[60] [1955] 1 Ch 210.

13.90 However, it may be thought that this was again out of touch with legitimate political thinking, evidenced by the fact that Parliament validated existing concessions by means of a 1955 Act and finally gave general powers to make such concessions in 1964.[61]

13.91 However, that the adoption of the principle was again not a mere aberration is seen from another political controversial case, *Bromley LBC v Greater London Council*.[62] The case concerned a challenge to supplementary rates levied by the GLC to finance its 'Fares Fair' policy whereby there would be a 25% cut in bus and underground fares in order to reverse the decline in use of public transport and reduce the volume of car traffic. The speeches of the House of Lords adopted such different reasoning that it is impossible to discern a *ratio*, but the majority invoked both the *Roberts v Hopwood* and *Prescott* cases, and the fiduciary duty.

13.92 Again, this decision, while very controversial when it was made and alleged to be out of touch with legitimate political thinking in transport policy, did not ultimately result in frustrating that policy with subsequent cases accepting that fares could be subsidised from the rates.[63]

13.93 The three main cases cited as authority for the doctrine are not only concerned with very controversial subject matter, but the application of the principle by the courts can be seen to be too close a judgment on the merits to be acceptable. That in itself indicates that while the fiduciary principle remains relevant, it is likely to be invoked only exceptionally.

13.94 The second reason for doubting the stringency with which the principle will be applied lies in the fact that, from a strict legal perspective, the cases in which it has been invoked can also be classified as the application of other principles. As noted above, in the *Bromley* case various lines of reasoning were put forward in the five speeches, so that it is possible to conclude that the case turned on the interpretation of the precise statutory power, or that it related to the process of decision-making and slavish adherence to a manifesto commitment. That it was not based on absolute inability to lower the fares and subsidise the operation from general taxation is seen from the subsequent case of *R v London Transport Executive, ex p Greater London Council*.[64]

13.95 Similarly, *Roberts v Hopwood* can be interpreted as narrow illegality or a purposes case in that the payments were not wages but included a 'gift' element, and the purpose was not one of proper remuneration for the task undertaken. Indeed, this view was adopted by Forbes J in *Pickwell v Camden London Borough Council*,[65] where he stated that:

> 'The case seems to me to decide no more than this, that where the inevitable inference which must be drawn is that an obviously excessive wage payment was agreed to be paid without any regard to any commercial consideration and solely on some extraneous principle, as, for instance, philanthropy, such a payment can only be regarded as a gift and is not covered by a statutory power to pay reasonable wages. Looking back as we do, over sixty years of

---

[61] Public Service Vehicles (Travel Concessions) Act 1955; Travel Concessions Act 1964.
[62] [1982] 1 AC 768.
[63] *R v Merseyside County Council, ex p Great Universal Stores* (1982) 80 LGR 639; *R v London Transport Executive, ex p Greater London Council* [1983] QB 484.
[64] [1983] QB 484.
[65] [1983] QB 962.

progress in the field of social reform and industrial relations some of their Lordships' observations may, with the benefit of this hindsight, appear unsympathetic. But what has changed over those years is our attitudes to what should be regarded as pure philanthropy; the basic legal principle, that a payment is illegal which cannot be justified by reference to the objects for which a statutory power is granted, still remains.'

13.96 Equally, *Prescott* can be interpreted as the making of an unauthorised gift to a specified class of persons.

13.97 On this basis, the fiduciary principle can be interpreted as an aid to construction of any particular power and its particular application to a given situation, rather than as a freestanding principle to allow the courts to quash decisions. This approach was adopted in *Pickwell* where Ormrod LJ stated that the *Bromley* case affirmed that the fiduciary duty was a relevant factor to be taken into account in determining the scope and use of the statutory powers:

> 'However, it would not be right to regard this case as authority for the general proposition that this fiduciary duty opens up a route by which the courts can investigate, and if thought appropriate, interfere with any exercise of their discretionary powers by local authorities. This would completely undermine the principle of the *Wednesbury* case ....'

13.98 Nevertheless it is clear from the cases that, as was stated in *Taylor v Munrow* by Lord Parker CJ:[66]

> 'the council must preserve a balance between the duty owed to that general body of ratepayers and the duty owed to [others].'

13.99 At the very least it must show that this balancing exercise has been carried out when considering the financial implications of any decision. It is also clear that a proper audit trail, showing the balancing exercise, must be provided. In *R v Hackney LBC, ex p Structadene Ltd*,[67] in quashing a decision to dispose of land, Elias J noted:

> 'As I have already indicated, the council has not provided any proper explanation why it took the decision which it did. Prima facie I consider that the applicant has made out its claim that the council acted in breach of its fiduciary duty and there is no evidence which effectively counters that allegation. I accept that in an appropriate case it is possible for a council successfully to contend that there are social or other benefits to the local community which outweigh the loss resulting from the failure to obtain the best price. The interests of the local taxpayers are not decisive but must be taken into account; see *Bromley London Borough Council v Greater London Council*. However, in the absence of any indication of what these advantages were perceived to be, I cannot speculate whether they existed or not. In general, however, in the absence of some such benefit, it will be a breach of the fiduciary duty if the council fails to obtain the best price for the local taxpayers: see the *Bromley* case per Lord Diplock, at p 829H. I therefore hold that the council is in breach of that duty.
>
> For essentially the same reason I am compelled to find that it acted *Wednesbury* unreasonably. A rational council would not have rejected an offer which was £100,000 more favourable than the offer which it in fact accepted, in the absence at least of cogent countervailing considerations. The evidence does not enable me to say what the relevant factors are which could render the decision a rational one.'

---

[66] [1960] 1 WLR 151.
[67] [2001] LGR 204.

13.100 Although couched in terms of the fiduciary duty, the underlying reasoning in that case equates a breach of it with irrationality. Nevertheless, it is not yet the case that the courts fully accept that the principle does not permit a substitution of its view as to the weight to be attached to the financial interests of taxpayers. In *R (Molinaro) v Kensington and Chelsea Royal London Borough Council*,[68] Elias J suggested that this was indeed possible:

> '39. There is no doubt that the council does have a fiduciary duty to its ratepayers. There are numerous authorities to that effect, many of which were considered in the case of *Bromley London Borough Council v Greater London Council*.
>
> 40. The imposition of the fiduciary duty does not, however, mean that financial considerations must outweigh all others. It is a matter of balancing competing interests. But the doctrine of fiduciary duties can sometimes be used to enable the court to consider the weight afforded to the relevant factors, and to ensure that the fiduciary obligation is given proper significance.'

13.101 However, the implication of the last sentence is qualified. He went on to state that:

> '43. Where the effect is as limited, as in the decision under consideration, then in my view the doctrine is not in truth engaged in any significant way. Of course, the council must still have regard to the financial consequences of its actions and it must weigh them in the balance with other relevant considerations, but the effect on local taxpayers of this decision, viewed against the council's finances as a whole, is very minimal.'

13.102 Indeed it may be that the *obiter* sentence will be ignored in the future. In that case Elias J also stated that:

> 'I accept Mr Birks' submission that in a case of this kind the fiduciary duty does not really add anything to the doctrine of irrationality. Of course, if there are no counterveiling benefits to offset the loss of rent, then it can be said that the decision was a breach of fiduciary duty but, equally, it will be irrational. That will be, however, an exceptional case (see, for an example, *R (Structadene Ltd) v Hackney London Borough Council*). But once it is shown that the financial consequences were drawn directly to the attention of the members, as well as other countervailing considerations, the court can only interfere with the decision if it was one which no reasonable council could make.'

13.103 That approach has been followed in *Charles Terence Estates v Cornwall County Council*,[69] where the Court of Appeal reversed a finding by the High Court of a breach of the duty. The court found that, when comparing the facts with the leading authorities in which the breach of fiduciary duty approach had been propounded and in which it had succeeded, the case, taken at its highest, established significantly less culpability. In the absence of expert evidence, there had been no basis for having concluded that the rents were not a reasonable price.

13.104 In short, the fiduciary principle remains an important symbol in the law relating to local government, and also an active part of the language in which challenges can be framed. Local authorities must ensure that due consideration is given to this factor. Nevertheless, in terms of strict legal analysis it is not a factor which should be given

---

[68] [2002] LGR 336.
[69] [2012] EWCA Civ 1439, [2013] 1 WLR 466.

priority over other relevant considerations and it is for the local authority to determine where the balance lies between these considerations, subject to a residual test of rationality.

Interests and probity

13.105 The principles of natural justice are considered elsewhere in this book,[70] and the issues of bias, predetermination and predilection are clearly relevant to the operation of democracy.

13.106 This section does not seek to repeat that material but simply highlights, within local government, that these issues are not only dealt with by the courts but also by the enforcement of a statutory code of conduct. This has proved to be a very controversial area of law, and for England was the subject of substantial amendment in the Localism Act 2011. The remainder of this section explains the development of the law.

13.107 Every councillor must agree to abide by the Code upon taking office. There have been other Codes of Conduct. Conduct generally including non-pecuniary interests, was dealt with under the National Code of Local Government Conduct, first issued on a non-statutory basis following a recommendation of the Redcliffe-Maud Royal Commission.[71] The Widdicombe Committee's recommendation that the Code should be given statutory status,[72] and that new councillors in their declaration of acceptance of office should undertake to be guided by it in the performance of their functions, was implemented by s 31 of the Local Government and Housing Act 1989. Enforcement at that stage was by the Local Government Ombudsman.

13.108 The existing arrangements were strongly criticised by the Nolan Committee on Standards in Public Life,[73] which concluded that a radical change in the ethical framework was needed. It proposed a code of conduct for councillors developed by each individual council within a general framework approved by Parliament; the establishment by each council of a Standards Committee with powers to recommend the discipline of errant members; the creation of new Local Government Tribunals to act as independent arbiters on matters relating to codes of conduct and to hear appeals; and the involvement of the courts in imposing penalties for misconduct to replace surcharge.

13.109 The general principle of reform identified by Nolan was accepted, but the resulting statutory scheme under Part III of the Local Government Act 2000 was more centralised with a prescriptive and detailed code, all elements of which were mandatory for each local authority to adopt. Every authority had also to establish a standards committee to promote and maintain high standards of conduct within the authority and to monitor the operation of the code, but alleged breaches of codes of conduct by members were to be investigated by a newly created Standards Board for England (then Standards for England) or the Commissioner for Local Administration in Wales. Provision was made for appeals to a new body, the Adjudication Panel.

13.110 Members of the Adjudication Panel for Wales are appointed by the National Assembly. In England, from January 2010 the Adjudication Panel for England became

---

[70] See Chapter 1, paras 1.48–1.51.
[71] Cmnd 5636, 1974.
[72] Committee on the Conduct of Local Authority Business, Cmnd 9797, 1986.
[73] Third Report on Standards of Conduct in Local Government in England, Scotland and Wales, Cm 2702–I, 1997.

the First-tier Tribunal (Local Government Standards in England) as part of the General Regulatory Chamber. A person who is brought before a case tribunal may be represented by counsel, a solicitor, or any other person they would like to represent them.

13.111 While this basic structure remains, there has been a move towards the original intention of Nolan. By the Local Government and Public Involvement in Health Act 2007, provision was made for more local determination of complaints. Then the Localism Act 2011 abolished the Standards Board regime for England removing Standards for England, standards committees of local authorities, the jurisdiction of the First-tier Tribunal in relation to local government standards in England, and model codes of conduct for councillors. Nevertheless, authorities in England are required to adopt a code of conduct for their members. The system in Wales remains.

13.112 This system raises two main issues for judicial review. First, whether and to what extent the decisions taken under the codes are amenable to judicial review. Secondly, what relationship the principles in them have to those applied by the courts.

13.113 While it is beyond the scope of this work to analyse the judicial interpretations of the codes and the proper approach to the sanctions which can be imposed, it is clear not only that the court will interfere where appropriate,[74] but also that a different approach is taken depending on whether the challenge is by means of judicial review or on appeal from a case tribunal under s 79(15) of the 2000 Act.[75]

13.114 The relationship of the principles under the codes with those applied by the courts was a matter which concerned the Nolan Committee. The Committee recommended that the test which should apply in the codes should be that of the common law.[76] However, in *R v Local Commissioner for Administration for North and North-East England, ex p Liverpool City Council*,[77] the Court of Appeal took the view that under the old Code the Ombudsman had been perfectly entitled to apply the test laid down in the Code rather than the test laid down in the common law. More recently in *Scrivens v Ethical Standards Officer*,[78] in rejecting one possible interpretation of the Code, Stanley Burnton J noted that it would provide an inconsistency with the law on bias and 'that is a consequence to be avoided'.

Relationship with officers

13.115 Much of public administration is carried on by professional administrators. Policy may of course be set by politicians, whether by Parliament, ministers or councillors, but the detailed administration is left to unelected officials in public bodies of various types. However, central and local government differs in that politicians often take administrative decisions themselves or together with officials.

13.116 The relationship between the elected and non-elected decision-maker raises two particular issues.

---

[74] *Livingstone v Adjudication Panel for England* [2006] EWHC 2533 Admin; *Sanders v Kingston* [2005] EWHC 1145 (Admin).
[75] *R (Mullaney) v Adjudication Panel for England* [2009] EWHC 72 (Admin), at 72 and 73.
[76] Third Report on Standards of Conduct in Local Government in England, Scotland and Wales, Cm 2702–I, 1997, para 111.
[77] [2001] 1 All ER 462.
[78] [2005] EWHC 124 (Admin).

13.117 First, the extent to which officers should be perceived as or should operate as a check on elected politicians.

13.118 In local government, while local authority is given power to appoint 'such officers as they think necessary for the proper discharge by the authority of such of their or another authority's functions as fall to be discharged by them',[79] various restrictions and checks are placed on the council and the ability to appoint political or politicised officers. Together with particular rules relating to the appointment and dismissal of chief officers, and limiting political activity by senior officers, the requirement to appoint specified officers seeks to ensure that the administration of local authority functions achieves a balance of political and professional expertise.

13.119 One aspect of this is that certain officers are charged with a duty to raise issues which could form the basis of a challenge by judicial review or other court action. For example, every local authority must appoint a monitoring officer who must, if it at any time appears to him that any proposal, decision or omission by the authority has given rise to or is likely to or would give rise to a contravention of any enactment or rule of law, prepare a report to the authority with respect to that proposal, decision or omission.[80] The authority is under a duty to provide that officer with such staff, accommodation and other resources as are, in his opinion, sufficient to allow those duties to be performed. Similarly, an authority must appoint a chief finance officer who shall make a report if it appears to him that the authority has made or is about to make a decision which involves or would involve the authority incurring expenditure which is unlawful; has taken or is about to take a course of action which, if pursued to its conclusion, would be unlawful and likely to cause a loss or deficiency on the part of the authority; or is about to enter an item of account the entry of which is unlawful.[81]

13.120 The second main issue about the relationship between the elected and non-elected decision-makers, concerns the extent to which it is legitimate for ministers or elected decision-makers in whom powers are formally vested to allow others to take decisions in their name.

13.121 The starting point is the principle that the exercise of discretion cannot be fettered by unauthorised delegation.[82] However, in practice powers are often conferred on ministers or other named office holders and the realities of administration mean that decisions are taken by officers within those departments or organisations, and the basic principle must accommodate that reality while seeking to uphold the underlying principle of ensuring that discretionary power is exercised properly.

13.122 In relation to central government, where powers are vested in a minister it is often suggested that exercise by an official is as an alter ego of the department and power is devolved rather than delegated.[83] As Lord Greene MR pointed out in *Carltona Ltd v Commissioner of Works*:[84]

> 'In the administration of government in this country the functions which are given to ministers ... are functions so multifarious that no minister could ever attend to them. To take

---

[79] Local Government Act 1972, s 112.
[80] Local Government and Housing Act 1989, s 5.
[81] Local Government Finance Act 1988, ss 112–114.
[82] See Chapter 1, para 1.82.
[83] *R v Secretary of State, ex p Oladehinde* [1991] 1 AC 254.
[84] [1943] 2 All ER 560.

the example of the present case no doubt there have been thousands of requisitions in this country by individual ministries. It cannot be supposed that this regulation meant that, in each case, the minister in person should direct his mind to the matter. The duties imposed on ministers and the powers given to ministers are normally exercised under the authority of the ministers by responsible officials of the department. Public business could not be carried on if that were not the case. Constitutionally, a decision of such an official is, of course, the decision of the minister. The minister is responsible. It is he who must answer before Parliament for anything that his officials have done under his authority, and, if for an important matter he selected an official of such junior standing that he could not be expected competently to perform the work, the minister would have to answer to Parliament.'

13.123 Although that approach stressed the role of Parliament in scrutiny of the appropriateness of the official chosen to decide, it is now clear that courts will examine the suitability of the official on the basis of *Wednesbury* unreasonableness.[85]

13.124 It has been less clear that the *Carltona* principle applies to local government or other public bodies.

13.125 In *Nelms v Roe*, the extension of the *Carltona* principle to other bodies appeared to be rejected by Lord Parker CJ:[86]

'I feel grave difficulties in extending that well-known principle to a case such as this, to the Commissioner of the Metropolitan Police. It is not, I think sufficient to say that it is a principle which it applicable whenever it is difficult or impractical for a person to act for himself, in other words whenever he has to act through others the principle applies. I see grave difficulties in going that far, and, as it seems to me, superintendent Williams was, by reason of his position, not the alter ego of the Commissioner but merely had implied delegated authority, by reason of his position, from the Commissioner.'

13.126 However, clarity has been given by Sedley LJ in *R (Chief Constable of the West Midlands) v Birmingham Justices*,[87] who considered that:

'9. Although the *Carltona* case is frequently cited as a source of the "alter ego" doctrine, it can be seen that Lord Greene's reasoning is not predicated on this. It is predicated on the proposition that the departmental head is responsible for things done under his authority. The relevance of the alter ego doctrine is that Crown servants were at that time taken in law to hold their positions by grace and not by contract, so that the minister was first among equals, not an employer with servants or a principal with agents. His implied power to delegate functions depended, therefore, on two things: the conferment of a power in terms which implicitly permitted their delegation and the existence of persons to whom he could delegate them without parting with ultimate responsibility.'

13.127 He also considered the reasoning in *Nelms v Roe* and concluded:

'12. With all possible respect, I do not consider that we are required to adopt this reasoning. As has been seen, the *Carltona* principle, which binds this court, does not depend upon the peculiar status of civil servants as the alter ego of their minister. It is sufficiently ample to allow a Chief Constable to discharge functions of the kind we are concerned with through an officer for whom he or she is answerable. To fall back instead on implied delegation and sub-delegation is capable of appearing to be a ratification by the court of an accomplished fact and to beg the question of power to delegate.'

---

[85] *R (Chief Constable of the West Midlands) v Birmingham Justices* [2002] EWHC 1087.
[86] [1970] 1 WLR 4.
[87] [2002] EWHC 1087.

13.128 However, to meet the criticism that this opened the principle too widely, Sedley LJ pointed out that there are other functions imposed upon individuals by virtue of their office which may not be delegable at all, for example the function of a health and safety inspector and he concluded:

> '14. For my part I can see good reason to differentiate, where Parliament has conferred powers on the holder of a named office, between those offices which are the apex of an organisation itself composed of office-holders or otherwise hierarchically structured, and those offices designated by Parliament because of the personal qualifications of the individual holder. Thus, … one can readily infer that when Parliament confers functions on a chief officer of police, all but the most important are likely to be delegable; whereas the likelihood is that powers conferred on a medical officer of health or on a statutory inspector, each professionally qualified as an individual, are to be exercised by the office-holder alone. This, with respect, seems to me a better legal test than overriding administrative convenience, although it may produce similar outcomes.'

13.129 Thus, provided the power does not require the exercise of a particular professional expertise, it can be delegated, subject to the residual test that the person chosen is not an irrational choice.

Role of standing orders

13.130 As explained previously,[88] all public authorities are required to comply not only with statutory procedural requirements but also with the procedural principles laid down by the common law. As also explained, while a breach of a procedural requirement may make the decision of no legal consequence, it does not always result in the decision being invalid. Much will depend on the importance of the requirement and the context of the breach.

13.131 These principles will apply to any decision-making process. For local authorities, however, there are also rules contained in the standing orders adopted by the authority, now usually contained with the authority's constitution. Not only does the local authority have power to make, vary and revoke standing orders to regulate its proceedings and business,[89] but power is given to the Secretary of State to require standing orders to contain particular provisions.[90] While a standing order is subordinate to any statutory requirement, the common law rules will apply only where there is no statutory or standing order requirement in relation to the issue.

13.132 A breach of a standing order is generally treated in the same way as any other procedural requirement and it may result in the decision having no legal effect. One exception to this is in relation to contracts. Authorities are required to make standing orders in respect of contractual matters.[91] However, protection is given to those contracting with the authority since breach of the orders does not invalidate any

---

[88] See para **1.122**.
[89] Local Government Act 1972, Sch 12, para 42.
[90] Local Government and Housing Act 1989, s 20, and see Local Authorities (Standing Orders) Regulations 1993, SI 1993/202; Local Authorities (Standing Orders) (England) Regulations 2001, SI 2001/3384; Local Authorities (Standing Orders) (Wales) Regulations 2006, SI 2006/1275 (W 121).
[91] Local Government Act 1972, s 135(1)–(3).

contract, and they are not bound to inquire whether the standing orders have been complied with.[92] However, this provision does not apply to contracts which are otherwise *ultra vires*.[93]

13.133 Since standing orders are not themselves statutory but are made under statutory powers, they can in turn be subject to judicial review and can be quashed by a court. In *R v Flintshire CC, ex p Armstrong-Braun*,[94] a standing order preventing a councillor from placing a matter on the agenda, unless seconded by another council member, was quashed by the Court of Appeal.

13.134 As Schiemann LJ put it, the court was concerned with:[95]

> 'the legal validity of a Standing Order made by the Flintshire County Council which prevents any councillor from putting a matter on the agenda for discussion unless he has the support of at least one other councillor. There is thus demonstrated in this case a tension between two desirable and understandable aims. It is desirable that a councillor should be able to raise matters of concern to him or his electors, and that he should be able to do so in a public forum which the public can attend, and of whose deliberations there is a public record. On the other hand it is desirable that a council, which has a vast amount of business to transact, should be able to get through its business with reasonable dispatch, otherwise the quality of persons who are prepared to give their time will, quite possibly decline because too much time will in their estimation, be spent on matters of no intrinsic interest.'

13.135 The court's approach was that this standing order fell within the meaning of regulating the proceedings or business of the council, within the meaning of the Local Government Act 1972, but that it could be quashed if it fell outside the policy and objects of the act or was otherwise legally objectionable. In that regard, it had been argued that the loss to democracy caused by such a Standing Order was inevitably great and disproportionate to any gain in administrative efficiency. For the council, it was pointed out that there was no right conferred on councillors by statute to have any matter considered. Schiemann LJ refused to conclude that the standing order was or was not contrary to the policy and objects of the 1972 Act construed as a whole. He identified arguments both ways and indicated that had he been required to do so he may have decided it in the claimant's favour. However, he concluded that it was unnecessary to decide whether or not such a standing order can ever be lawfully adopted because the 'same reasons as make it arguable that the adoption of such a Standing Order is, in principle, unlawful, indicate that before adopting such a Standing Order the matter should be given most anxious consideration'.[96] The council quite simply had not considered where the correct balance lay. The procedure for making the change to the standing order was a procedure which was so imperfect that it ought to be quashed, without prejudice to it being introduced in an identical form in the future.

13.136 For Sedley LJ, the issue that he 'found by far the hardest' was whether the new standing order fell outside what council can lawfully do to regulate its proceedings and business.[97] He noted that Schiemann LJ set out a powerful case for concluding that it does and that the council had not sufficiently addressed the question of whether this

---

[92] Local Government Act 1972, s 135(4).
[93] *North West Leicestershire DC v East Midlands Housing Association* [1981] 1 WLR 1396, but see also the Local Government Contracts Act 1997.
[94] [2001] EWCA Civ 345; [2001] LGR 344.
[95] Ibid, para 4.
[96] Ibid, para 37.
[97] Ibid, para 55.

hurdle should be placed in the path of a councilor. He noted the series of good reasons why it may unjustifiably silence an elected member. He also noted that 'the lone voice, though necessarily a nuisance to the majority, plays an important part in a democracy'.[98]

13.137 However, 'and not without hesitation', he accepted the council's submission that there may be grounds on which a rule such as the standing order can be adopted without violating these broader principles. Nevertheless he found that whether reasons are sufficient to justify a change of that kind in the standing order is a question for the members of the council, voting after careful consideration of the full range of relevant issues and of those alone. He concluded:[99]

> 'What seems to me clear beyond a peradventure is that in this case nobody, neither the members nor the officers, even appreciated the potential damage to local democracy, much less weighed it against the reasons, such as they were, for introducing the new Standing Order. ... His own submissions have demonstrated the exact contrary: a failure on the part of his client authority to perceive, much less to evaluate, the democratic damage capable of being done by the rule-change. As the history set out by Schiemann LJ demonstrates, the exercise was apparently treated simply as one administrative tidying up and went through on the nod. The queries about whether it was ultra vires were more or less brushed aside. The answer, had it been seriously looked into, might not have been that the new Standing Order 8 was in itself ultra vires – though as Schiemann LJ's judgment has demonstrated that is an entirely tenable view – but it would certainly have been that there was far more than administrative convenience at issue.'

13.138 In relation to whether it would be possible to come to the same conclusion after proper consideration he stated:[100]

> 'For my part, I would hold that if any proposal to resurrect Standing Order 8 either in its present form or in some related form is placed before the council or its Policy Committee, it cannot lawfully be entertained, much less be adopted, without consideration by members of objective advice on, as a minimum, the following. First, the legal and constitutional purposes of the Local Government Act 1972 and the related legislation. In the light of what has happened so far, there is no reason, in my judgment, to assume that such advice is unnecessary. Second, the difference in substantive effect between the model Standing Orders (or the existing ones) and the proposed Standing Order 8. It is now clear that this cannot possibly be dismissed either as insignificant or as too obvious to require examination. Third, the obligation of members collectively to regulate the proceedings and business of the council without regard to party or other advantage and in the sole interests of an efficient representative local democracy.'

and he added:[101]

> 'Although it does not arise at the moment for decision, it may well be that this needs to be regarded in law as a question of proportionality: is the proposed measure, having regard to its restrictive effect on the functioning of individual elected representatives, one which is necessary, in a democratic society to achieve the efficient functioning of the county council? In answering such a question, it will be appropriate, among many other things, to consider what net gain in council efficiency is likely to be achieved if the Standing Order is changed in this or some similar way. If the answer is little if any, that should be an end of it. If some appreciable administrative or procedural gain is perceived, it must be set with great care against the contra-indicators touched on in the judgments in this court.'

---

[98] Ibid, para 57.
[99] Ibid, para 58.
[100] Ibid, para 59.
[101] Ibid, para 60.

13.139 A clear warning has, therefore, been given to local authorities that standing orders must pay proper regard to the furthering of democracy and not err on the side of administrative efficiency.

CONCLUDING REMARKS

13.140 While the principles of judicial review apply to both central and local government, it is clear that local government raises specific issues. Not least among these is the extent to which the courts should accord local government a status as a multi-purpose body with democratic legitimacy, as opposed to simply an administrative body exercising a number of specific statutory powers.

13.141 While the courts have tended to adopt the latter approach, and are often criticised for this as being out of step with political thought, it is not surprising given the lack of clear constitutional position for local government within a system dominated by central government under the doctrine of parliamentary sovereignty.

13.142 While there have been various attempts to change this, for example by political concordats, becoming a signatory to the European Charter of Local Self-Government, or enacting the well-being powers, these have not succeeded. In response to this problem there is an increasing recognition that an instrument is necessary that will clearly state the purpose, mandate and role of local government. This is reflected in the current attempt by the Select Committee on Political and Constitutional Reform to achieve this aim, which has remained elusive in the British context.[102] Whether it will succeed remains to be seen.

---

[102] Political and Constitutional Reform Committee, Prospects for Codifying the Relationship between Central and Local Government, 3rd Report Session 2012–13, HC 656, and for a largely negative response see Government Response to the House of Commons Political and Constitutional Reform Committee Report, Cm 8623, May 2013.

CHAPTER 14

IMMIGRATION LAW

INTRODUCTION

14.01 For many years immigration and asylum claims have made up a significant proportion of the total number of claims lodged before the Administrative Court. There are a number of reasons for this including extensive delay in executive decision-making, regular changes in policy, rules, instructions and law rendering applications and decisions more prone to error, a lack of substantive statutory appeal rights and unmeritorious claims being brought.

14.02 This chapter provides an overview of the broader immigration legal framework, considers the new forum for immigration judicial reviews in the Upper Tribunal (Immigration and Asylum Chamber) ('UT'), reviews the specific procedural concerns in the context of immigration law before turning to the key principles affecting some frequently occurring substantive issues.

OVERVIEW OF THE IMMIGRATION, ASYLUM AND NATIONALITY LAW FRAMEWORK

14.03 Immigration law moves swiftly and is to be found in a complex array of interlinking sources: statutes, rules, published and unpublished policy, case authority (domestic, Strasbourg, Luxemburg and international), and the increasingly important European dimension. Those dealing with asylum also need to be familiar with a wide range of source material relating to country conditions including country of origin information reports and UT country guidance decisions.

14.04 The bedrock of UK immigration law is the Immigration Act 1971 and the Immigration Rules made under it. The 1971 Act has been significantly amended and added to by a number of statutes, the most important of which are: the British Nationality Act 1981, the Asylum and Immigration Appeals Act 1993, the Special Immigration Appeals Commission Act 1997, the Immigration and Asylum Act 1999, the Nationality, Immigration and Asylum Act 2002, the Asylum and Immigration (Treatment of Claimants etc) Act 2004, the Immigration and Nationality Act 2006, the UK Borders Act 2007, the Borders, Citizenship and Immigration Act 2009 and the Immigration Act 2014. These domestic legislative developments run in parallel to the integration of British immigration law with European law. The free movement provisions are contained in the Immigration (European Economic Area) Regulations 2006 (as amended). A number of Directives and Regulations impose common minimum standards and criteria in asylum claims and reception conditions. The relevant framework would be incomplete without reference to the Citizens' and Qualification Directives, and more recently the Charter of Fundamental Rights of the European Union.

14.05 The pace of legislative changes shows no sign of slowing down. The Immigration Act 2014 ('the 2014 Act') includes wholesale changes to the appeal structure by replacing a wide array of immigration decisions that attract a statutory right of appeal with more limited rights of appeal where there has been a refusal of a protection or human rights claim. The commencement arrangements for the 2014 Act ensure that these changes are implemented on a phased basis. The intention seems to be to limit statutory appeal rights, which may result in a significant increase in judicial review applications.

14.06 The Immigration Rules are 'detailed statements by a minister of the Crown as to how the Crown proposes to exercise its executive power to control Immigration'.[1] They have been amended substantially in recent years and continue to be amended regularly and in important respects. They should be checked carefully. The current version can be found on the new Home Office website.[2] There have been three particularly important developments in recent years as far as the rules are concerned. First, a points-based scheme ('PBS') was introduced in 2008 and has been substantially and regularly added to since that time. The aim was to introduce an Australian-style points system to manage migration in a simple and objective manner. The PBS has proven to be difficult for decision-makers to apply coherently and consistently because of the constant stream of changes to the requirements for each category and the inflexibility built into the Rules. Second, the Secretary of State for the Home Department ('SSHD') regularly amends and adds to the Immigration Rules. This has gained pace following the Supreme Court's decision in *Alvi v SSHD*,[3] which decided that anything akin to a rule must take the form of a formal amendment laid before Parliament.

14.07 Third, new immigration rules (HC 194) introduced on 9 July 2012 made sweeping changes to family migration. There have been numerous challenges to these Rules and the attempt by the Secretary of State to seek to include her view of the relevant balancing exercise under Art 8 of the ECHR within the Rules. For example, in *R (MM (Lebanon)) v SSHD*[4] the Court of Appeal overturned the conclusion in the court below that the measures severely restricting the ability of sponsors on low incomes to bring their spouses to the United Kingdom were disproportionate. Since the introduction of the 2012 changes there has been considerable uncertainty over the correct approach to Art 8 where the new rules are not met but see below at **14.50**. The relevant 2012 rules did not last long before they were themselves modified when the 2014 Act was passed. Section 19 of the 2014 Act introduced into the 2002 Act a new Part 5A containing new ss 117A–117D. These set out statutory guidelines that must be applied when a court or tribunal has to decide whether an immigration decision to remove someone from the UK would be in breach of his Art 8 rights.

14.08 The executive makes decisions relevant to immigration control either 'in-country' or 'out of country'. The Home Office is responsible for nationality, passports and immigration control. The SSHD is the minister in charge, and it is in her name that many officials make in-country decisions. Visas are required for citizens of many

---

[1] *Odeola v SSHD* [2009] UKHL 25, [2009] 1 WLR 1230, para 6.
[2] www.gov.uk/government/organisations/uk-visas-and-immigration.
[3] [2012] UKSC 33, [2012] 1 WLR 2208.
[4] [2013] EWHC 1900 (Admin), [2013] WLR(D) 280.

countries to visit the UK and visas are required for anyone who seeks entry for more than six months for whatever purpose. The decision-making process relevant to the granting of entry clearance or visas takes place in overseas posts run by the Foreign Office. Such decisions are taken by entry clearance officers.

APPELLATE STRUCTURE

14.09 The Tribunals, Courts and Enforcement Act 2007 ('the TCEA') reshaped the entire tribunal appeal structure. An appeal against an immigration decision lies to the First-tier Tribunal (Immigration and Asylum Chamber) ('FTT'). Prior to the 2014 Act in order for any decision of the executive to give rise to a statutory right of appeal there must generally be an 'immigration decision' as defined by s 82 of the Nationality, Immigration and Asylum Act 2002 ('the NIAA'). It was always important to check with precision the nature of the decision made and whether it constitutes an 'immigration decision' or another form of decision giving rise to a right of appeal.[5] Section 82 has now been substituted so as to restrict appeal rights to decisions to refuse a protection or human rights claim or to revoke protection status. Section 82 however continues to be in force at the time of writing in relation to decisions other than those made by the Secretary of State in relation to Tier 4 or deportation. Two systems are therefore in operation in parallel and practitioners need to carefully check the relevant transitional orders.

14.10 A small number of decisions are excluded from the normal system of appeals on national security grounds and the appeal must be made to the Special Immigration Appeal Commission ('SIAC').[6]

14.11 The right of appeal is excluded for an exhaustive list of reasons.[7] Some of the most common reasons are where there has been an earlier right of appeal or the Secretary of State has issued a certificate under ss 94 and 96 of the TCEA (see below).

14.12 A person may not appeal against an immigration decision from within the UK unless his appeal is one to which s 92 of the NIAA (as amended by the 2014 Act) applies. It used to be the case that once an appeal to the Tribunal in an 'in country' appeal is pending, then the appellant cannot be removed from or required to leave the UK. However the 2014 Act inserts a new s 94A whereby the Secretary of State may certify a human rights claim made by a person liable to deportation if she considers that despite the appeals process not having been begun or not having been exhausted, removal would not be unlawful under s 6 of the Human Rights Act 1998. Section 94A(3) provides that grounds upon which the Secretary of State may certify a claim where the person is liable to deportation include that the person would not face a real risk of serious irreversible harm if removed.

14.13 Appeals from decisions of the FTT, save 'excluded decisions', are to the UT on a point of law.[8] Excluded decisions in respect of which no appeal lies to the UT are as follows: (1) FTT decisions in the exercise of its power to review decisions; (2) decisions of the FTT set aside on review; (3) where the decision carried another right of appeal to

---

[5] Such as a refusal of asylum (s 83(2) of the NIAA), or refusal to extend leave or curtail leave as a refugee (s 83A of the NIAA).
[6] Section 97 of the NIAA.
[7] Sections 88–98 of the NIAA.
[8] Section 11 of the Tribunals, Courts and Enforcement Act 2007.

a court or tribunal; (4) bail decisions, procedural, ancillary or preliminary decisions on appeals. Any challenge to these decisions would have to be brought by way of judicial review.

JUDICIAL REVIEW JURISDICTION OF THE UT

14.14 The TCEA provides for a judicial review jurisdiction across the chambers of the Upper Tribunal. Initially, there was no enabling direction in order for that function to be in force in respect of decisions made under the Immigration Acts. In accordance with a direction from the Lord Chief Justice the UT has been able to consider judicial review applications arising from certain challenges not to treat submissions as a fresh human rights or asylum claim under para 353 of the Immigration Rules since 17 October 2011. The UT was also given jurisdiction to deal with judicial reviews that were transferred by the High Court, where the challenge is to the assessment of the age of a person who claims to be a minor from outside the United Kingdom.

14.15 Significantly, following the introduction of the Crime and Courts Act 2013 on 1 November 2013, the UT assumed jurisdiction in respect of a much wider range of applications for judicial review of immigration and related decisions taken (for the most part) by the SSHD. Pursuant to the TCEA and various enactments and instruments made under it, the UT has 'original' judicial review jurisdiction in those classes of case falling within the direction made by the Lord Chief Justice on 21 August 2013. This includes any application that calls into question: (1) a decision made under the Immigration Acts or any instrument having effect under an enactment within the Immigration Acts, or otherwise relating to leave to enter or remain in the UK outside the immigration rules, or (2) a decision of the FTT, from which no appeal lies to the UT. The Lord Chief Justice's direction specifically excludes challenges to the following: (1) secondary legislation or the immigration rules; (2) detention; (3) decisions concerning inclusion on the register of licensed sponsors; (4) citizenship; (5) UT decisions; (6) asylum support decisions; (7) SIAC decisions; (8) an application for a declaration of incompatibility under s 4 of the Human Rights Act 1998. Any application which comprises or includes a challenge to any of these must continue to be brought in the Administrative Court. A judge considering an application for permission made to the UT must transfer the application to the Administrative Court if the application is not within the Lord Chief Justice's direction. In such a case, the High Court may, nevertheless decide that the application should be transferred to the UT on a discretionary basis in accordance with s 31A(3) of the Senior Courts Act 1981.[9]

14.16 Part 4 of the Tribunal Procedure (Upper Tribunal) Rules 2008 as amended ('the 2008 Rules')[10] concerns judicial review in the UT. The Practice Directions, Immigration Judicial Review in the Immigration and Asylum Chamber of the Upper Tribunal ('the Practice Directions') as amended on 1 November 2013, were made by the Senior President in the exercise of powers conferred by the TCEA. Part 5 concerns applications which challenge removal and is to be read together with Part 4, which relates to urgent applications. The Practice Directions are supplemented by a Practice Statement, dated 1 November 2013, also made by the Senior President. Paragraph 2.1 records that an application for permission to bring proceedings may be made direct to the Upper Tribunal where the application is designated as an immigration matter in the Lord Chief

---

[9] See the Senior President's Practice Statement on Immigration Judicial Reviews in the Immigration and Asylum Chamber of the Upper Tribunal on or after 1 November 2013 at 2.5.
[10] SI 2008/2698 (as amended).

Justice's Direction. Where an application is made to the High Court, on a matter that falls within the Lord Chief Justice's Direction, it will be transferred to the UT. Practitioners should make themselves familiar with the 2008 Rules together with the practice directions and practice statement governing judicial review applications within the UT. These are all easily available on the UT website.

14.17 An underlying purpose of the changes is to reduce pressure on the Administrative Court so that it can properly consider the most serious cases, and to ensure that the more routine immigration cases, including challenges to removal directions, are determined by the specialist judges in the UT. In *Ashraf v* SSHD[11] Cranston J warned against any attempt to lodge applications in the Administrative Court by including an unmeritorious claim that detention is unlawful, when the real challenge was to removal. This may constitute an abuse of process, which could be addressed by costs and other professional penalties.

14.18 The UT is based at Field House, London. The UT also sits outside London at regional hearing centres of the Immigration and Asylum Chamber (Newport, Birmingham, Nottingham, Stoke, Manchester, Bradford, North Shields) and in the Administrative Court sitting outside London (Cardiff, Birmingham, Manchester, Leeds). Hearings listed to be heard at Field House can take place by way of video-link or an application can be made to apply for a transfer of venue from London. There is a Presidential Guidance Note on this.[12] Although this does not relate specifically to judicial review applications, there seems to be no reason why judicial review applications to be heard by video link or in regional centres should not be considered in light of the Guidance Note. The Practice Statement also anticipates the use of video link hearings for legal representatives based outside London.[13]

PRE-ACTION MATTERS TO CONSIDER

Pre-action protocol letters

14.19 In normal circumstances the pre-action protocol procedure ('PAP') must be followed. Exceptional cases should involve extreme urgency, although it is important and good practice to try to alert the SSHD to proposals to issue judicial review or seek injunctive relief with a timescale proportionate to the timing of the removal directions.

14.20 A structured, detailed letter drafted in accordance with the PAP has a number of advantages. First, it is more likely to give rise to a considered and sometimes favourable response from the SSHD. Second, it will be considered as a relevant matter when determining the issue of costs. For this reason it should be drafted with care, and in the knowledge that a judge will be considering how clearly it gives notice of the subject of the complaint. Third, the SSHD has a policy[14] to issue a removal decision and therefore a right of appeal to certain classes of applicants whose application was refused but not accompanied by a removal decision. By way of example, the policy states that a removal decision can be made where the application for leave to remain included a dependent child under 18 resident in the UK for three years or more or a British citizen. Fourth, it may be helpful to request information from the SSHD to assist in determining the merits

---

[11] [2013] EWHC 4028 (Admin).
[12] Guidance Note 2013 No 2: Video link hearings.
[13] See 2.12 of the Senior President's Practice Statement.
[14] Requests for removal decisions, valid from 23 August 2013.

of the claim. The public authority's 'duty of candour' has a particular importance in the context of immigration. Early application for a 'subject access request' under the Data Protection Act 1998 can be very helpful in obtaining relevant information that is either unknown to or not retained by the applicant. It is however important to be vigilant about time running out.

Time limits

14.21 Rule 28(3) of the 2008 Rules replicates CPR 54.5. An application must therefore be made promptly and must be sent or delivered to the UT so that it is received no later than three months after the date of the decision to which the application relates. It is wrong to presume that an application issued at the outer edge of the time limit will not be penalised for delay. Practitioners should always aim to bring proceedings at the earliest point and be in a position to account for actions or lack of action in the intervening period. Where there is an ongoing unlawful act or failure to act (for example delay in reaching a decision or issuing status documents) then time does not run.

14.22 An application for an extension of time can be made but satisfactory written reasons must be given why the application was not made promptly and in any event within three months of the decision under challenge. In addition any factual assertion made in the explanation must be supported by evidence or an explanation of why such evidence has not been lodged.[15] It is noteworthy that the Practice Statement states that in deciding what is prompt regard may be had to any relevant time limits in statutory appeals.

Alternative remedies

14.23 Where there is an out-of-country appeal it is well-established that judicial review is inappropriate because there is an adequate alternative remedy, unless the case is exceptional or cannot provide the appellant with 'fair, adequate or proportionate protection': see the Court of Appeal's judgment in *SSHD v Lim*.[16]

PROCEDURE IN THE UT

Urgent applications and interim relief

14.24 Where it is intended to request the UT to deal urgently with the application or where an interim injunction is sought, the applicant must serve with the application a written 'request for urgent consideration', in Form T483 (which is displayed on the UT's website). Guidance on urgent applications is contained within Part 4 of the Practice Directions. This provides that the application must state (1) the need for urgency; (2) the timescale sought for the consideration of the application (for example within 72 hours or sooner if necessary); and (3) the date by which the substantive hearing should take place. In *Hamid v SSHD*[17] the then President of the Queens Bench Division, Sir John Thomas, highlighted the pivotal importance of completing all the relevant information when requesting urgent consideration. Practitioners were also warned of the serious professional consequences that would follow where this is not complied with. Similar

---

[15] The Practice Statement states that an application for an extension of time *will* be refused unless satisfactory written reasons are given and this is supported by evidence (2.4).
[16] [2007] EWCA Civ 733.
[17] [2012] EWHC 3070 (Admin).

warnings emphasising compliance with professional obligations and the need for appropriate scrutiny by qualified lawyers, particularly in relation to applications on an ex parte basis have been given in subsequent cases.[18] These warnings should be heeded in relation to all judicial reviews lodged not just in the Administrative Court but in the UT as well. In *R (Okondu and Abdussalam) v SSHD*[19] the UT drew representatives' attention to *Hamid* and underscored its importance. This decision reminds representatives that their overriding duty is to the court or tribunal. It is therefore improper for any practitioner to advance arguments that they know to be false or which they know, or should know, are inconsistent with their own evidence.

14.25 Where an interim injunction is sought, the applicant must, in addition, provide: (1) the draft order; and (2) the grounds for the injunction. The draft order should specify what urgent action the court is asked to take and should suggest practical timescales proportionate to the urgency. The applicant must serve (by fax and post) the application form, the request for urgent consideration and the draft order and any grounds for an injunction on the SSHD and interested parties, advising them of the application and that they may make representations.

14.26 It is good practice to alert the UT that an urgent application is to be made. Once the UT specifies that a hearing shall take place within a specified time, the representatives of the parties must liaise with the UT and each other to fix a hearing of the application within that time. It is important to remember that an applicant's duty of full and frank disclosure requires that adverse factors of which the representatives are aware (such as country guidance decisions and a proper chronology of previous applications) are brought to the attention of the UT. In the immigration context this means a 'warts and all' disclosure to the judge of all relevant adverse matters.

Lodging the application

14.27 An application to the UT for judicial review is made on form T480 and must be accompanied by the relevant fee.[20] Guidance notes on completing the form are contained in T481. These forms can be downloaded from the UT's website. The application can either be lodged at Field House or one of the regional centres of the Tribunal.[21] These are located at the Administrative Court offices in Birmingham, Cardiff, Leeds and Manchester.

14.28 The application must include a number of matters but these are set out clearly within form T480. It has become established practice to attach a separate comprehensive document that sets out the outcome that the applicant is seeking and the facts and grounds relied on.

14.29 The Practice Direction sets out the additional materials to be filed with the application at Part 3. The application must be accompanied by: (1) any written evidence on which it is intended to rely (but the applicant may only rely on the matters set out in the application as evidence under this Practice Direction if the application is verified by a statement of truth); (2) copies of any relevant statutory material; and (3) a list of

---

[18] See *Awuku v SSHD* [2012] EWHC 3690 Admin; *B & J v SSHD* [2012] EWHC 3770 (Admin); *R (Butt and others) v SSHD* [2014] EWHC 264 (Admin).
[19] IJR [2014] UKUT 00377 (IAC).
[20] Currently £60 for permission to apply for judicial review and £215 on a request to reconsider at a hearing a decision on permission.
[21] See 2.1 of the Practice Statement for applications on or after 1 November 2013.

essential documents for advance reading by the Tribunal (with page references to the passages relied on). The applicant must file two copies of a paginated and indexed bundle containing all the documents required by r 28 of the 2008 Rules and the Practice Direction. Careful consideration should be given to the preparation of the bundle. Only those documents that are directly relevant to the application should be included although practitioners should be vigilant to comply with the duty of full and frank disclosure.

Removal directions

14.30 The Practice Direction makes it clear (15.1) that any application challenging removal must (a) indicate on its face that Part 5 of the Practice Direction applies; and (b) be accompanied by (i) a copy of the removal directions and the decisions to which the application relates; and (ii) any document served with the removal directions including any document which contains UKBA's factual summary of the case; and (c) contain or be accompanied by the detailed statement of the applicant's grounds for making the application. If the applicant is unable to comply with para 15.1(b) or (c) the application must contain or be accompanied by a statement of the reasons why. Where the applicant has not complied with Practice Direction 15.1(b) or (c) and has provided reasons for not complying, and the Tribunal has issued the application form, the Practice Direction requires the Tribunal's staff to (a) refer the matter to a judge for consideration as soon as practicable; and (b) notify the parties that they have done so. The Practice Direction also requires the applicant, notwithstanding r 28A of the 2008 Rules, immediately upon issue of the application, to send copies of the issued application form and accompanying documents to the address specified by the United Kingdom Border Agency.

14.31 Detailed instructions to caseworkers at chapter 60 of the 'Enforcement Instructions and Guidance' set out the notification periods that must be provided for a variety of cases: normal enforcement, family, third country/non-suspensive appeal and charter flights. Failures to provide an adequate opportunity for those served with removal directions to take legal advice have been strongly condemned by the Administrative Court. Where a claim for judicial review has been properly lodged in compliance with the relevant Rules, Practice Directions and Practice Statements then removal will normally be deferred.[22]

Responding to the application – the acknowledgment of service ('AoS')

14.32 Rule 29 of the 2008 Rules provides that a person who is sent an application for permission to bring judicial review proceedings and wishes to take part in the proceedings must send or deliver to the UT an AoS so that it is received no later than 21 days after the date on which the UT sent a copy of the application to that person.

14.33 In *R (Kumar) v SSHD*[23] the UT noted the continuing systemic inability of the SSHD to file AoS in immigration judicial review proceedings within the time limit contained in the 2008 Rules and set out a number of general temporary arrangements to be kept under review. In summary, the UT will not consider the application before the end of six weeks of service of the claim on the SSHD save where the UT considers it appropriate to do so, in response to an application for urgent consideration filed by the

---

[22] This is set out in detailed instructions to caseworkers at chapter 60 of the 'Enforcement Instructions and Guidance'.
[23] (Acknowledgment of Service; Tribunal Arrangements) IJR [2014] UKUT 00104 (IAC).

applicant (on Form T483); or a notice in writing from the applicant, copied to the SSHD, which states the need for urgency and the proposed timescale for considering the application; and in response to a request by the SSHD for expedition, pursuant to an arrangement between her and the Chamber President. Specific guidance is also given on costs where an AoS is not served.

Permission

14.34 Where the UT is entitled to grant the relief sought, the Practice Statement gives extensive guidance on how the UT will deal with the application at the permission stage. The UT judge may, on considering the permission application: (1) grant the application; (2) grant the application on some grounds and refuse it on others; (3) adjourn the application for permission to an oral hearing; (4) refuse the application. Where the application is refused the judge may also make any order for costs of the AoS, curtail the period for renewal of the application from the nine days permitted under the 2008 Rules, record that the application is considered to be totally without merit; and, if so, that any renewal of the application shall not operate as a bar on removal. The judge must give brief written reasons for refusing the application or any part of it and may give reasons for the other decisions made if considered appropriate to identify the issues or otherwise assist the preparation for the next hearing.

14.35 Where a judge refuses the application on some or all grounds without a hearing, the applicant may apply by notice in writing for that decision to be reconsidered at a hearing. However, where the application has been refused and the decision records that the application is considered to be totally without merit, the applicant may not request the decision to be reconsidered at a hearing. If permission is refused at a hearing at the conclusion of that hearing the judge will deliver a judgment giving the decision and explaining in summary terms why the application or any part of it has been refused and consider any application made at that hearing for permission to appeal to the Court of Appeal.

Substantive hearing

14.36 Where an applicant who has been given permission to bring judicial review proceedings intends to apply under r 32 of the 2008 Rules to rely on additional grounds at the substantive hearing, the applicant must give written notice to the UT and to any other person served with the application, not later than seven working days before that hearing. The applicant must serve a skeleton argument, together with an agreed bundle (containing all relevant evidence from the applicant and the respondent) on the UT not later than 21 days before the substantive hearing and the respondent and any other party wishing to make representations at the hearing must serve a skeleton argument on the UT and on the applicant, not later than 14 days before the hearing.

Consent orders

14.37 The majority of judicial review applications arising from well-prepared grounds settle once permission has been granted. It is not unusual for the Treasury Solicitor to propose a draft consent order inviting the applicant to withdraw his application upon a further decision being made within an appropriate time frame or upon leave being granted. Draft consent orders should be carefully scrutinised to ensure that all the relevant issues have been addressed including costs.

14.38 If the parties agree about the final order to be made, the applicant must file at the UT a document (with two copies) signed by all the parties setting out the terms of the proposed agreed order, together with a short statement of the matters relied on as justifying the proposed agreed order and copies of any authorities or statutory provisions relied on. The UT will consider the documents referred to and will make the order if satisfied that the order should be made. If the UT is not satisfied that the order should be made, a hearing date will be set. In *R (Muwonge) v SSHD (Consent Orders: Costs: Guidance)*[24] the UT has recently provided guidance on the appropriate practice and procedure to be followed where an AoS contains a concession. This makes it clear that where a draft consent order is tabled both parties should proactively take all necessary and appropriate steps to achieve consensual resolution within a period of at most three weeks. Where a consensual resolution is not achieved the UT sets out what is expected of the parties within a set timetable.

Costs

14.39 The Practice Statement gives guidance where the UT makes an order that the applicant is to pay a sum to the respondent in respect of the AoS or the costs of resisting an urgent application pursuant to r 10(3)(a) of the 2008 Rules and there has been no prior opportunity on the paying party to make representations or to have an inquiry into that party's means (4.1). In these circumstances, the order takes effect as a provisional order subject to representations to be made in writing within 10 working days of the order. Where no representations have been received within the time specified in the order, the order for costs becomes absolute (4.2).

14.40 In other cases where there is a dispute as to costs, the Practice Statement states (4.2) that the parties' representations shall be referred promptly to the judge making the order or such other judge as is available for determination. In *Muwonge* (above) the UT has indicated that where the Secretary of State's AoS includes a concession, a justifiable claim for costs is likely to be rare. Where it is claimed, the AoS should state briefly the justification for such a claim.

COMMON JUDICIAL REVIEW APPLICATIONS BEFORE THE UT

Fresh claims

14.41 In order to prevent repeat claims and appeals para 353 of the Immigration Rules sets out the circumstances where fresh claims will be accepted as constituting a fresh claim for asylum or human rights protection. This requires submissions to be 'significantly different' from the material that has previously been considered. The submissions will only be considered to be significantly different if the content: (1) had not already been considered; and (2) taken together with the previously considered material, created a realistic prospect of success, notwithstanding its rejection. If the para 353 test is satisfied, it is SSHD policy to make a fresh immigration decision. The immigration decision will trigger a right of appeal to the FTT in accordance with s 82 and s 83 of the Nationality, Immigration and Asylum Act 2002. If the test is not satisfied and the SSHD decides that the submissions do not constitute a fresh claim then the only available remedy is judicial review. In *WM (DRC) v SSHD*[25] the Court of Appeal described the test under para 353 as undemanding and 'somewhat modest'. If the

---

[24] IJR [2014] UKUT 00514 (IAC).
[25] [2006] EWCA Civ 1495.

objective analysis of the materials leads to the conclusion that the outcome might well be different from the first determination then it would not be open to the Secretary of State to conclude otherwise. Buxton LJ observed that the Secretary of State must ask herself the right question and said:[26]

> 'The question is not whether the Secretary of State himself thinks that the new claim is a good one or should succeed, but whether there is a realistic prospect of an adjudicator, applying the rule of anxious scrutiny, thinking that the applicant will be exposed to a real risk of persecution on return: see §7 above. The Secretary of State of course can, and no doubt logically should, treat his own view of the merits as a starting-point for that enquiry; but it is only a starting-point in the consideration of a question that is distinctly different from the exercise of the Secretary of State making up his own mind. Second, in addressing that question, both in respect of the evaluation of the facts and in respect of the legal conclusions to be drawn from those facts, has the Secretary of State satisfied the requirement of anxious scrutiny? If the court cannot be satisfied that the answer to both of those questions is in the affirmative it will have to grant an application for review of the Secretary of State's decision.'

14.42 The correct test on a judicial review application of a refusal to treat submissions as a fresh claim is to ask whether or not it was *Wednesbury* unreasonable for the SSHD to conclude that the further submissions, taken together with the previously considered material, did not create a realistic prospect of the claimant succeeding before a FTT judge, bearing in mind the need for anxious scrutiny.

Certification

14.43 Certification is the statutory means by which the SSHD can prevent an applicant from appealing from within the United Kingdom against a refusal that would ordinarily attract a right of appeal. The SSHD can invoke s 94 or 96 of the Nationality, Immigration and Asylum Act 2002 in order to certify a claim as 'clearly unfounded'. In such circumstances the applicant would have to leave the United Kingdom before such appeal could be exercised thereby depriving him/her of the suspensory protection of s 78 of the NIAA 2002.

14.44 A claim should only be certified if the SSHD, after reviewing the available material, is 'reasonably and conscientiously satisfied that the allegation must clearly fail'.[27] On judicial review the judge must consider for himself whether a claim is 'clearly unfounded' but only on the material available to the SSHD at the time she made her decision.[28] This point is not entirely free from doubt. It is sufficiently clear at least that where there is no dispute as to primary fact the judge should ask himself the relevant question.[29]

14.45 The position is more difficult where there is dispute as to primary fact including the credibility of the applicant. Some courts have held that it is only where the SSHD could be satisfied that nobody would find the applicant credible that she should certify a claim as clearly unfounded and if there was any reasonable doubt, the claim could not

---

[26] Ibid at para 11.
[27] Per Lord Bingham of Cornhill in *R (Yogathas) v SSHD* [2003] 1 AC 920.
[28] See *YH (Iraq) v SSHD* [2010] 4 All ER 448 at [19]–[21].
[29] See *ZT (Kosovo) v SSHD* [2011] 1 WLR 3200 per Lord Phillips §23, and also Lord Brown §76 and Lord Neuberger §83 (cf Lord Hope at §§54, 55 citing *Razgar* and Lord Carswell §65); as considered by Elias LJ in *R (MD (Gambia)) v SSHD* [2011] EWCA Civ 121 §52.

be described as clearly unfounded.[30] In *EM and others v SSHD* Lord Kerr observed that when determining whether an asylum claim is capable of succeeding, it is customary to take the facts at their highest in the claimant's favour and he adopted this approach in the consideration of the cases before the Supreme Court. Where, therefore, it is stated that a particular event took place or that a certain factual proposition is established, this is for the purposes of considering the applicant's case at the certification stage but does not betoken any final finding or conclusion.

14.46 There has been considerable judicial attention to the correct approach to certification, in contrast to fresh claims. It seems to be relatively settled following *MN (Tanzania) v SSHD*[31] that the two tests are different. The scope for review of fresh claims is the *Wednesbury* test subject to anxious scrutiny whereas the judge can decide for himself whether the claim is clearly unfounded.

Delay

14.47 The SSHD's failure to make timely decisions on applications that have been outstanding for years continues notwithstanding the attempt to resolve this through the Legacy programme. Delay in reaching an immigration decision may have serious adverse effects on children, whose best interests must be a specific and primary consideration in the exercise of the SSHD's discretion[32] and those effects may constitute a breach of Art 8 of the ECHR.[33] In addition the EU Charter of Fundamental Rights and the Common European Asylum System importantly provides for a right to good administration at Article 41. That includes the right for every person to have his or her affairs handled within reasonable time by the institutions and bodies of the Union. This only applies when Member States are implementing European Union law but has the potential to have far reaching effects when there is unreasonable delay in this context.

14.48 The SSHD operates a policy of prioritising certain cases. That policy lists the circumstances where it may be appropriate to prioritise. These include seriously mishandled cases. Challenges to the failure to properly apply this policy where there are exceptional features such as medical evidence supporting the adverse impact of continued uncertainty on an applicant's mental health have met with mixed success.[34] Where practitioners are considering challenging unreasonable delay in decision-making it is generally necessary to conduct a careful assessment of the specific adverse impact of delay on the individual concerned and any third parties including children, and the evidence available to support this.

14.49 There has been a spate of judicial review applications challenging the SSHD's application of policies relevant to the Legacy programme and its aftermath. The lead case is *R (Geraldo) v SSHD*[35] in which the court followed the Court of Appeal in *R (S, H & Q) v SSHD*[36] to the effect that mere administrative delay, uncoupled from any promise or commitment to deal with a case by a certain date, does not readily give rise

---

[30] See Lord Phillips in *ZL and VL v SSHD* [2003] 1 WLR 1230 at §58–60 and more recently *R (MN (Tanzania)) v SSHD* [2011] EWCA Civ 193.
[31] 'Case Resolution Directorate – Priorities and Exceptional Circumstances.'
[32] See s 55 of the Borders, Citizenship and Immigration Act 2009, the relevant statutory guidance and *ZH (Tanzania) v SSHD* [2011] UKSC 4; [2011] 2 AC 166.
[33] See for example *Mendizabel v France* (2010) 50 EHRR 50.
[34] See for example *R (FH) v SSHD* [2007] EWHC 1571 (Admin) in which Collins J regarded a particular case as exceptional and justifying immediate consideration.
[35] [2013] EWHC 2763 (Admin).
[36] [2009] EWCA Civ 142.

to an illegality relevant to a subsequent decision properly based on current policy calling for 'corrective' intervention by the court, and arguments of 'unfairness' based on administrative delay simpliciter do not give rise to any jurisdiction in the court to intervene. In *SH (Iran) v SSHD*, the Court of Appeal sought to lay to rest cases of this kind.[37]

Article 8 ECHR/refusal to issue an appealable decision

14.50 There continue to be numerous challenges to decisions unaccompanied by an 'immigration decision' (and therefore without a right of appeal to the FTT) addressing outstanding submissions based on Art 8 of the ECHR. As set out above the law on the proper approach to Art 8 following the implementation of the new Immigration Rules on family migration has been uncertain.[38] Although the Court of Appeal appeared to indicate in *MF (Nigeria) v SSHD*[39] that even where a decision to refuse an Art 8 claim under the new rules is found to be correct, judges must still consider whether the decision is in compliance with the Human Rights Act 1998, in *Shahzad*[40] the UT approved of the approach in the Administrative Court decision of *Nagre v SSHD*[41] as adopted in *Gulshan*.[42] This was to the effect that after applying the requirements of the rules, only if there may be arguably good grounds for granting leave to remain outside them is it necessary for Art 8 purposes to go on to consider whether there are compelling circumstances not sufficiently recognised under them. In *MM Lebanon (supra)* the Court of Appeal indicated that where the relevant rules provide a complete code for dealing with Convention rights such as deportation then the balancing exercise and the way the various factors are to be taken into account must be done in accordance with that code. The court however indicated that where the immigration rules are not a complete code 'then the proportionality test will be more at large'. This has been interpreted to mean by many that in non-deportation cases the relevant balancing exercise under Art 8 should still be carried out. In any event as indicated above the 2002 Act (as amended by the 2014 Act) requires a court or tribunal, when considering the public interest question pursuant to Art 8, to consider all relevant considerations in s 117B in all cases and s 117C in cases involving foreign criminals. The best interests of the child remain an integral part of the proportionality assessment, albeit it is incumbent on the applicant to rely on concrete evidence regarding any adverse impact on the child. A summary of the relevant principles governing the proper approach to the best interests of the child are set out in *Zoumbas v SSHD*.[43]

14.51 Where an applicant has already made a clear decision not to voluntarily return to his country of origin and the SSHD's policy on issuing removal decisions applies,[44] careful consideration should be given to inviting the SSHD to make a removal decision thereby triggering a right of appeal to the FTT.

---

[37] [2014] EWCA Civ 1469.
[38] See **14.25** above.
[39] [2013] EWCA Civ 1192, [2013] WLR(D) 380.
[40] (Art 8: legitimate aim) [2014] UKUT 00085 (IAC).
[41] [2013] EWHC 720 (Admin).
[42] (Article 8 – new Rules – correct approach) [2013] UKUT 640 (IAC).
[43] [2013] UKSC 74 at [10], which of course relies upon the seminal decision of *ZH (Tanzania) v SSHD* [2011] 2 AC 166.
[44] See **14.48** above.

OTHER CHALLENGES
Detention

14.52 It is important to distinguish between whether there is a power in law to detain and whether the discretion to detain under such power has been exercised reasonably, fairly and lawfully. The first category includes cases where the detainee is not liable to detention at all, for example because he is exempted from deportation by reason of being a British citizen. Judicial review is not appropriate for this first category as the application should be brought by way of habeas corpus. There are clear procedural advantages to the habeas route. The court prioritises such applications as very urgent and will normally list them within days. The writ of habeas corpus issues by right whereas judicial review remedies are discretionary.

14.53 The second category includes those cases in which the discretionary decision to detain has become unlawful in accordance with the *Hardial Singh* principles.[45] In *R (Lumba) v SSHD*[46] Lord Dyson JSC affirmed the *Hardial Singh* principles and encapsulated them thus: (1) the SSHD can only use the power to detain for the purpose of deporting the detainee; (2) the period of detention must be no longer than that which is reasonable in the circumstances; (3) if before the end of that period it becomes apparent that it will not be possible to effect deportation within it the power should not be exercised; and (4) the SSHD should act with reasonable diligence and expedition to effect removal. In *Lumba's* case Lord Dyson stated[47] that the *Hardial Singh* principles reflect the basic public law duties to act consistently with the statutory purpose and reasonably. But he also stated[48] that they are not exhaustive, and do not therefore preclude the operation of the public law duty of adherence to published policy. Failure by the SSHD to have regard to a material policy concerning detention would, it was held, render the detention unlawful and a false imprisonment, even where it is certain or inevitable that the person detained could and would have been detained had the power been exercised lawfully. But, if detention was certain or inevitable, while the SSHD will have committed the tort of false imprisonment, the person detained will only be entitled to nominal damages.

14.54 It is clear from the decisions on the *Hardial Singh* principles that the state of a person's mental health will affect the determination of what is a reasonable period for which to detain that person: see Baroness Hale in *Lumba's* case[49] and the SSHD's own policy documents on mental health and detention. Absent exceptional circumstances victims of torture should not be detained.[50]

14.55 Where there is a power to detain under the Immigration Acts there is a power to release. Although an application for bail is normally made to the FTT, where there is an application pending before the Administrative Court challenging the legality of the detention, the court may grant bail under its inherent jurisdiction.[51] An application for bail under the court's inherent jurisdiction is not a *Wednesbury* review of the decision

---

[45] *R v Governor of Durham Prison, ex p Hardial Singh* [1984] 1 WLR 704.
[46] [2011] UKSC 12, [2012] 1 AC 245, at [22].
[47] Ibid at para [22].
[48] Ibid at para [30].
[49] Ibid at para [218].
[50] *R (D & K) v SSHD* [2006] EWHC 980 (Admin). See also *R (EO and ors) v SSHD* [2013] EWHC 1236 (Admin).
[51] Senior Courts Act 1981 s 15(3), *R (Sezuk) v SSHD* [2001] INLR 675.

but an application on its merits. A grant of bail may provide the claimant some of the relief he is seeking but the court may still need to consider past detention and damages.

Secondary legislation or the immigration rules

14.56 A classic and successful recent challenge to the Immigration Rules themselves was recently taken in *MM v SSHD*.[52] This decision helpfully reviews a number of decisions challenging provisions of the Immigration Rules, including human rights challenges to the rules at [65]–[85].

Decisions of the UT

14.57 The majority of these challenges are to the refusal of the UT to grant permission to appeal from the FTT. Such challenges can of course only be made on second-tier appeal grounds, ie on the basis that the challenge not only discloses an error of law on the part of the relevant decision-maker but raises an important point of principle or practice, or there is some other compelling legal reason to allow the challenge to proceed: see *R (Cart) v Upper Tribunal*.[53] It has been clarified that the court should decide whether the second-tier appeals criteria is satisfied at the permission stage and not whether it is arguable that it will be satisfied at the substantive hearing.[54]

National security/SIAC

14.58 Cases in which the SSHD relies upon closed evidence in order to refuse naturalisation or deprive a person of their citizenship have been on the increase. In *R (AHK) v SSHD* the Court of Appeal found that those wishing to challenge a refusal of naturalisation had to opt whether to do so by way of judicial review or by proceedings before SIAC and a 'wait and see' approach should not be adopted. Where SIAC proceedings had already been commenced the SIAC appeal was a suitable alternative remedy that should be pursued expeditiously.

---

[52] See above at **14.7**.
[53] [2011] UKSC 28 as applied in *PR (Sri Lanka) v SSHD* [2012] 1 WLR 73.
[54] *R (HS) v Upper Tribunal* [2012] EWHC 3126 (Admin).

CHAPTER 15

PROFESSIONAL REGULATION

INTRODUCTION

15.01 This chapter concerns the role of judicial review in the context of professional regulation. An outline of the structure of regulatory law is provided following which the chapter identifies where judicial review is often deployed to challenge the decisions of the professional regulators.

15.02 Professional regulation is a wide area that includes the regulation of healthcare professionals, lawyers, accountants, surveyors and police officers, as well as other more niche professions. These professions are regulated by separate legislative structures and this impacts on how the regulators perform their functions. However, there are many common elements in how the principles of judicial review apply to the regulators. This chapter identifies those elements.

15.03 This chapter is structured in two parts. The first explains the nature of regulation and outlines the three primary roles of the regulators. The second explains how judicial review operates in relation to these roles and the limits of judicial review in relation to the regulators.

REGULATION AND THE REGULATORS

What is regulation?

Self regulation v statutory regulation

15.04 Professional regulation typically has two forms. The first is 'self-regulation'; the second is 'statutory regulation'. The best example of self-regulation is the old model of the General Medical Council, which was established in 1858. Self-regulation is where an organised group comes together to regulate the behaviour of its members without interference from the state.[1]

15.05 Self-regulation often emerges in order to maintain and promote a high level of professional competence as well as to enhance the status of professionals. This is because membership of the profession is normally linked to those who have certain specialist qualifications. As a consequence, the profession is likely to develop a positive reputation that the profession is keen to protect. As the Court of Appeal noted in *Bolton v Law Society*, 'a profession's most valuable asset is its collective reputation and the confidence which that inspires'.[2]

---

[1] N Gunningham and P Grabosky, *Smart Regulation: Designing Environmental Policy* (1998) pp 50–51.
[2] *Bolton v The Law Society* [1993] EWCA Civ 32 at [15].

15.06 Self-regulatory systems were permitted to exist by government on the basis that potential benefits included the development of professional standards, which were policed effectively because standard setting and enforcement was the responsibility of the relevant practitioners. Furthermore, peer pressure was seen to have created an environment of high standards of behaviour, which was more effective and responsive than traditional legal methods of regulation.[3]

15.07 There has also been an historical assumption that professional expertise was beyond the ability of unqualified people to understand or evaluate.[4] Furthermore, there is an underlying sense that self-regulation allows a profession to maintain its independence from government.[5]

15.08 However, this model of informal and non-statutory self-regulation is of largely historical interest for most professions. This is because the state has increasingly legislated to create models of statutory regulation. There are several reasons for this.

15.09 First, the self-regulators typically also performed a representative function on behalf of the profession. This was seen as a potential conflict to the role of setting and enforcing standards. Accordingly, many professions now have a representative body and a regulatory body. For solicitors this is the Law Society and the Solicitors Regulation Authority; for barristers, this is the Bar Council and the Bar Standards Board.

15.10 Secondly, the climate towards professionals is no longer as deferential. Recent times have witnessed shifting social and political attitudes that have reflected a decline in trust in experts and governing elites to safeguard public interests. A 'more demanding, less deferential, more vociferous' public who are more willing to challenge professional judgments is challenging traditional social deference.[6] Accordingly, professionals have had to become more focused on the public they serve, rather than simply maintaining their professional status. Moreover, professional control of information has been challenged by the development of the internet and greater access to information. UK policy-makers have encouraged people to take more responsibility. In the healthcare context this is known as 'responsibilisation' and can be seen, for example, in the proliferation of statistics and league tables related to public service performance.[7]

15.11 Thirdly, in many professions there have been a series of regulatory failures. In medicine, the Shipman Inquiry represented a most high-profile failure.[8] This arose following the conviction of Dr Harold Shipman, a general practitioner, for the murder of 15 of his middle-aged and older female patients by lethal injections of diamorphine. Subsequent revelations showed that he had in fact killed 215 of his patients. This report

---

[3] N Gunningham and P Grabosky, *Smart Regulation: Designing Environmental Policy* (1998) p 52.
[4] See, for example, J Warring and others, 'Modernising Medical Regulation: Where Are We Now?' (2010) 24 Journal of Health Organisation and Management 6, 540.
[5] See, for example, The Rt Hon Lord Justice Leveson, *An Inquiry into the Culture, Practices and Ethics of the Press: Report* (November 2012) pp 235 and 1735–9.
[6] C Ham and K Alberti, *The Medical Profession, the Public and* Government (2002) British Medical Journal 324, 838.
[7] M Dent, 'Patient Choice and Medicine in Health Care: Responsibilisation, Governance and Proto-professionalism' (2006) 8 Public Management Review 3, 449 and S Harrison, 'New Labour, Modernisation and the Medical Labour Process' (2002) 31 Journal of Social Policy 3, 465.
[8] *The Shipman Inquiry Fifth Report: Safeguarding Patients, Lessons from the Past – Proposals for the Future* (2004) Cm 6394. Previous inquiries highlighting regulatory failures included the Bristol Royal Infirmary Inquiry (2001) on the cardiac treatment of children; the Alder Hey Inquiry (2003) on the removal of organs from dead children without parental consent and the reports into Rodney Ledward, Clifford Ayling, Richard Neale, William Kerr and Michael Haslam.

criticised self-regulation as self-serving and lacking transparency and accountability, and cast serious doubts on the capacity of the profession to regulate itself satisfactorily.

15.12 In the context of press regulation, the Leveson Inquiry investigated allegations of poor standards in journalism and public life, including the hacking of individuals' voicemail inboxes, illegitimate payments to police officers for stories and inappropriately close relationships between politicians and newspaper editors.[9] The final report noted the weaknesses in the regulatory system, including the Press Complaints Commission.

15.13 Both these failures provided the opportunity for the state to undertake a more prominent regulatory role. In medicine, various reforms have taken place, and the regulatory landscape has become increasingly complex. There are at least three additional layers: first, internal NHS regulation, whereby Performers Lists are maintained;[10] second, systems regulation, whereby the Care Quality Commission regulates premises and organisations; and thirdly 'meta-regulation' whereby all of the healthcare professional regulators are themselves regulated by the Professional Standards Authority for Health and Social Care.[11] Further bodies can be added to this list, such as Monitor (the sector regulator for the NHS), the Health and Safety Executive, the Health Protection Agency, and the National Patient Safety Agency.

15.14 These layers of regulation do not guarantee good outcomes. The inquiry into Mid-Staffordshire NHS Trust showed that the quantity and complexity of regulation can stifle the basic essentials of good professional conduct, namely the provision of high-quality services in a safe and effective manner.[12]

15.15 However, the overall trend in the modern professional regulatory landscape is the move away from self-regulation towards forms of statutory regulation. Regulation is no longer about enhancing professional status; instead, it is about managing risk and promoting best practice where the public interest is paramount.[13]

Who are the regulators?

15.16 There are many professional regulators. Each regulator is concerned with the regulation of a particular set of professionals, and protects certain professional titles. For instance, it is an offence to hold oneself out as a general practitioner if one is not

---

[9] The Rt Hon Lord Justice Leveson, *An Inquiry into the Culture, Practices and Ethics of the Press: Report* (November 2012).
[10] National Health Service (Performers Lists) Regulations 2004.
[11] The Professional Standards Authority has the power to refer cases to the High Court where a sanction was 'unduly lenient'. See *Council for the Regulation of Health Care Professionals v Ruscillo* [2004] EWCA Civ 1356; [2005] 1 WLR 717 at [68] to [69].
[12] Robert Francis QC, *Report of the Mid Staffordshire NHS Foundation Trust Public Inquiry* (February 2013) (HC 898–1).
[13] This is different to providing an avenue of redress to complainants, which is not normally the focus of the regulators: *R (Zia) v General Medical Council* [2011] EWCA Civ 743 at [35].

registered with the General Medical Council.[14] In addition, some regulators also protect certain functions.[15] For instance, only a registered midwife may attend to a woman in childbirth.[16]

15.17 The table below lists some of the main regulators, and the primary legislation that governs their particular regulatory framework. It is important to note that each regulator has its own rules and regulations for disciplinary proceedings.

Regulator	Legislation	Regulations
Architects Registration Board	Architects Act 1997	Investigations Rules and Professional Conduct Committee Rules 2013
Bar Standards Board	Legal Services Act 2007	Disciplinary Tribunals Regulations 2009
Financial Conduct Authority	Financial Services Act 2012	Tribunal Procedure (Upper Tribunal) Rules 2008
General Chiropractic Council	Chiropractors Act 1994	General Chiropractic Council (Professional Conduct Committee) Rules Order of Council 2000
General Dental Council	Dentists Act 1984	General Dental Council (Fitness to Practise) Rules Order of Council 2006
General Medical Council	Medical Act 1983	General Medical Council (Fitness to Practise) Rules Order of Council 2004
General Optical Council	Opticians Act 1989	General Optical Council (Fitness to Practise) Rules 2005

---

[14] For a full list of protected titles in the healthcare context see App D of Law Commission, *Regulation of healthcare professionals and Regulation social care professionals in England* (Consultation Paper) (March 2012).

[15] For instance in *General Dental Council v Jamous* [2013] EWHC 1428 it was held that tooth-whitening comes within the practice of dentistry and so registration with the General Dental Council is required to perform this function.

[16] For a full list of protected titles in the healthcare context see, App E of Law Commission, *Regulation of healthcare professionals and Regulation social care professionals in England* (Consultation Paper) (March 2012).

Regulator	Legislation	Regulations
General Osteopathic Council	Osteopaths Act 1993	General Osteopathic Council (Professional Conduct Committee) Rules 2000
General Pharmaceutical Council	Pharmacy Order 2010	General Pharmaceutical Council (Fitness to Practise and Disqualification Rules) Order of Council 2010
Health and Social Care Professions Council	Health and Social Work Professions Order 2001	Health and Care Professions Council (Practice Committees) Rules 2009
Institute for Chartered Accountants in England and Wales	Royal Charter of the 11th May 1880 and Supplemental Charter of the 21st December 1948	Disciplinary Bye-Laws
Nursing and Midwifery Council	Nursing and Midwifery Order 2001	Nursing & Midwifery Council (Fitness to Practise) Rules 2004
Police Disciplinary Tribunal	Police Act 1996	Police (Conduct) Regulations 2012
Royal College of Veterinary Surgeons	Veterinary Surgeons Act 1966	The Veterinary Surgeons and Veterinary Practitioners (Disciplinary Committee) (Procedure and Evidence) Rules 2004
Secretary of State for Education	Education Act 2011	Teachers' Disciplinary (England) Regulations 2012
Society of Lloyd's	Lloyd's Act 1982	Enforcement Byelaw (No 6 of 2005)
Solicitors Regulation Authority	Legal Services Act 2007	Solicitors (Disciplinary Proceedings) Rules 2007

15.18 It should be noted that in addition to these regulators, there are numerous private organisations that perform regulatory functions such as requiring compliance with a code of conduct. These are most prevalent in relation to sport and include the following:

- the Football Association

- the Jockey Club
- the National Greyhound Racing Club
- the British Amateur Weightlifters Association
- the British Athletic Federation Limited
- the England and Wales Cricket Board
- the Federation Internationale de l'Automobile

15.19 The relationship between these organisations and their members is contractual. Accordingly, the obligations in terms of conduct and performance are a matter of private law and the actions of the organisation are unlikely to be amenable to judicial review.[17] Furthermore, the requirements of the Human Rights Act 1998 do not apply.[18] This does not mean that disciplinary proceedings before such organisations should not comply with the standards of natural justice and there is often an implied obligation of fairness in these contexts.[19] Indeed, it has been suggested that the court's supervisory jurisdiction can be deployed in these contexts.[20] However, this is achieved through a claim in private law.[21]

Key regulatory functions

15.20 There are certain functions that are common to all regulators. These fall into three categories:

- *Entry onto the register*. This requires the regulator to establish a register of professionals and routes for placing professionals on the register. This will require the regulator to decide what criteria must be satisfied before a professional will become registered. This will typically include specifying educational standards that must be attained, as well as additional requirements such as a certain amount of practical experience. Issues can arise when professionals from outside the United Kingdom seek to be registered and their qualifications do not match the equivalent domestic qualifications.

- *Maintaining the register*. The regulator will need to take steps to ensure that those professionals who have been entered on to the register maintain their standards of practice. This is typically done by requiring a certain amount of continuing professional development to be undertaken, as well as monitoring compliance with the relevant code of practice.

- *Removal from the register*. Each regulator will have a system for removing professionals from the register if that professional has fallen below the standards required, such as by breaching a standard in the code of practice. This is the main disciplinary role of the regulator, and there will be systems for the investigation and adjudication of allegations of poor professional conduct. Typical outcomes include being removed or suspended from the register, having conditions placed on the professional's practice or a fine or reprimand. There will usually be a route of appeal.

---

[17] See, for instance, *R v Disciplinary Committee of the Jockey Club, ex p Aga Khan* [1993] 1 WLR 909.
[18] *R (Mullins) v The Jockey Club* [2005] EWHC 2197 (Admin).
[19] See, for instance, *McInnes v Onslow Fane* [1978] 1 WLR 1520, 1535 F–H; *Modahl v British Athletic Federation* [2001] EWCA Civ 1447; *Flaherty v National Greyhound Racing Club Ltd* [2005] EWCA Civ 1117.
[20] *Bradley v Jockey Club* [2005] EWCA Civ 1056 at [17]–[18]; *McKeown v British Horseracing Authority* [2010] EWHC 508 (QB).
[21] See, for example, *Law v National Greyhound Racing Club Ltd* [1983] 1 WLR 1302.

15.21 Most regulators will have further powers in relation to their governance and other issues such as interfaces with other systems of regulation. However, the functions described above are the three key regulatory functions performed by the regulators. From the perspective of the professional the concerns are: getting on the register, staying on the register and avoiding removal from the register.

JUDICIAL REVIEW AND THE REGULATORS

15.22 Having set out the general contours of professional regulation in the first part, this part deals with two areas of practical concern in relation to judicial review. The first area addresses the various factors that can limit the role of judicial review in this context. These are important preliminary matters as many prospective judicial review claims may be limited due to the nature and timing of the decision under challenge, whether the regulator is amenable to judicial review, the availability of alternative remedies, as well as issues of restraint and standing.

15.23 The second area concerns how the grounds of judicial review relate to the key functions of the regulators. This identifies how the authorities have addressed issues through the three stages of entry onto the register, the maintenance of the register and removal from the register (see above). It should be emphasised that the general grounds of judicial review described in detail in Chapter 1 of this book apply to the decisions of the regulators. To adapt a well-known public law adage, the cases cited below should act as a guide, not a cage.[22]

The limits of judicial review

Targets

15.24 Any judicial review claim against a professional regulator must be clear about the nature of the decision that is under challenge. Within each regulator there will be an *administrative* branch that will deal with applications for registration and investigating disciplinary complaints, and an *adjudicative* branch that deals with the adjudication of disciplinary cases, ie a tribunal, panel or committee.

15.25 This distinction is important, as the administrative branch of the regulator should not be making findings of a judicial nature as this role is for the adjudicative branch. This would make a difference in a case where unlawful delegation was alleged, as administrative functions are more readily delegable than judicial functions.[23] It is important to recall that the legal framework for each regulator will often provide powers to delegate certain functions within a regulator.

15.26 For example, the General Medical Council has a general statutory power to delegate its functions to a registrar.[24] In *R v Institute of Chartered Accountants of England and Wales, ex p Taher Nawaz*, the Court of Appeal heard a challenge to a decision of an investigation committee to reprimand an accountant for failure to provide documents as part of a disciplinary investigation. It was argued that the delegation of functions to the Committee was improper. It was held that the relevant bye-law, which

---

[22] See *R v Inland Revenue Commissioners, ex p Unilever Plc* [1996] STC 681, per Sir Thomas Bingham MR.
[23] *R v Race Relations Board, ex p Selvarajan* [1975] 1 WLR 1686.
[24] Paragraph 16 of Sch 1 to the Medical Act 1983.

empowered delegation by the Committee of 'any or its powers :.. to such other person ... as it thinks fit' was constrained by a duty to act reasonably, and that the purported power to delegate was not excessive.²⁵

15.27 However, it is important that the internal decision-makers within each regulator keep within their remit. For instance, in *R v General Medical Council, ex p Richards* Sullivan J allowed a claim for judicial review on the basis that the screeners who initially consider allegations or complaints had attempted to resolve a conflict of evidence.²⁶ In doing so, the screeners had usurped the role of the substantive decision-making committee.

15.28 The role of screeners was given consideration in *Law Society of Scotland v The Scottish Legal Complaints Commission*. In that case, Lord Kingarth noted that their role is typically to sift out wholly unmeritorious claims and there is an obvious advantage if regulators are not put to the time and expense of investigating unmeritorious claims.²⁷ This role is typically limited to determine whether there is at least the basic information as to the basis of the complaint. Lord Kingarth indicated that there might be some flexibility in this role, but that ultimately screeners must limit their role to sifting.

15.29 These cases highlight the importance of establishing which decision-maker within a regulator should be challenged, and the possible consequences in terms of the grounds it is possible to argue. The legislative context for each regulator will be an important consideration.

15.30 The practical importance of identifying the correct target is whether a route of appeal is available. Typically, there will not be an appeal route for administrative decisions and so challenges must be brought by judicial review. This was the position in *ex p Richards* (above). In *Marcus v Nursing and Midwifery Council* the High Court made it clear that a statutory appeal does not normally extend to decisions of investigating committees.²⁸

15.31 A final issue must be mentioned in relation to the issue of identifying the correct target. As noted, there is a distinction between the investigation and adjudication of disciplinary matters. However, the institutional separation of these functions is not clear. This has raised concerns about whether this structure is compatible with Art 6 of the ECHR because the prosecutor and adjudicator are of the same body.

15.32 This issue was considered in *Tehrani v United Kingdom Central Council for Nursing Midwifery and Health Visiting* where it was held that the Professional Conduct Committee would probably not be sufficiently independent and impartial given the overlap in its prosecutorial and adjudicative functions and personnel. However, the availability of an appeal meant that an Art 6 violation was avoided.²⁹ Concerns about whether members of a panel are impartial have to be raised on a case-by-case basis, relying on the grounds of bias or disqualification.

---

²⁵ *R v Institute of Chartered Accountants of England and Wales, ex p Taher Nawaz*, unreported, 25 April 1997, CA.
²⁶ *R v General Medical Council, ex p Richards* (2001) The Times, 24 January; [2001] Lloyd's Rep Med 47.
²⁷ *Law Society of Scotland v The Scottish Legal Complaints Commission* [2010] ScotCS CSIH 79.
²⁸ *Marcus v Nursing and Midwifery Council* [2011] All ER (D) 104 (Nov).
²⁹ *Tehrani v United Kingdom Central Council for Nursing Midwifery and Health Visiting* 2001 SC 581, [2001] IRLR 208 at [85].

15.33 As a result of the structural concerns raised by *Tehrani*, most regulators now select members of their investigation committee and their disciplinary committees separately. The General Medical Council has gone one step further by establishing a Medical Practitioners Tribunal Service that is said to be operationally independent of the regulator. Indeed, the disciplinary cases brought by the Financial Conduct Authority are heard by the Upper Tribunal, which removes any concerns of structural overlaps.

Timing

15.34 The nature of the decision under challenge may also affect when it is appropriate to bring judicial review proceedings. There is normally reluctance by the courts to deal with challenges to interim or procedural decisions before a matter has run its course.[30] This will apply with particular force when a disciplinary hearing is underway and procedural decisions have been taken, for instance decisions relating to adjournments.

15.35 However, this overall approach is nuanced because there are exceptional occasions where an unlawful interim decision may interfere with the overall fairness of proceedings and the requirement that judicial review claims are brought promptly may require a challenge to be brought before a final decision has been made.[31]

15.36 In *R (Mahfouz) v General Medical Council*, a disciplinary panel had refused to adjourn a hearing to raise an issue of apparent bias before the High Court. In quashing the decision, the Court of Appeal said that while there is a general need to decide issues quickly, this need is relative. Furthermore, the issue was recognised as important and requiring detailed legal argument. It was held that the 'justice and the appearance of justice' required an opportunity to bring judicial review proceedings.[32]

15.37 This approach is consistent with authorities that suggest that issues of principle should be considered at the earliest available opportunity.[33] For instance, in *R v Chief Constable of Ministry of Defence Police, ex p Sweeney* the Court of Appeal said that judicial review should have been brought sooner in order to secure a stay of the disciplinary hearing.[34] Similarly, time limits are normally strictly enforced by the High Court. For instance, in *R v The Institute of Chartered Accountants in England and Wales, ex p Andreou* the Court of Appeal stated that public law litigation could not be undertaken at the slow pace adopted too often in private law disputes.[35]

15.38 Furthermore, a failure to raise an issue in a timely manner can be considered a factor in determining the fairness of any subsequent decisions.[36] For instance, in *R (Kashyap) v General Medical Council*, the claimant sought to challenge by way of

---

[30] *R v Chance, ex p Coopers & Lybrand* (1995) 7 Admin LR 821, 837C–E; *R (Mahfouz) v General Medical Council* [2003] EWCA Civ 233 at [44]; *R (Singh) v Stratford Magistrates' Court* [2007] EWHC 1582 (Admin) at [7]; *R (Commissioner of Police of the Metropolis) v Police Appeals Tribunal and Peart* [2011] EWHC 3421 (Admin).
[31] *R (Royal Brompton and Harefield NHS Foundation Trust) v Joint Committee of Primary Care Trusts* [2012] EWCA Civ 472 at [89].
[32] *R (Mahfouz) v General Medical Council* [2003] EWCA Civ 233 at [45].
[33] *R (Associated Newspapers Ltd) v Lord Justice Leveson* [2012] EWHC 57 (Admin) at [39]–[40]; *R v Lord Saville of Newdigate, ex p A* [2000] 1 WLR 1855 at [43].
[34] *R v Chief Constable of Ministry of Defence Police, ex p Sweeney* [1999] COD 122 CA.
[35] *R v The Institute of Chartered Accountants in England and Wales, ex p Andreou* (1996) 8 Admin. L.R. 557. This was an interim judgment prior to the judgment in *Andreou v Institute of Chartered Accountants in England and Wales* [1998] 1 All ER 14.
[36] *R (Hoffmann) v Commissioner of Inquiry* [2012] UKPC 17 at [66]; *R (Thompson) v Law Society* [2004] EWCA Civ 167 at [47].

judicial review a decision to refer his case-by-case examiners to a disciplinary panel. The challenge was brought almost a year and a half after the referral and after a 28-day hearing where it was found that his fitness to practise was impaired. The court held that the doctor had a choice after the referral was made – to either apply for judicial review or contest the allegations. He had chosen to contest the allegations and it was now too late to bring a judicial review challenge against the referral.[37]

15.39 Accordingly, the timing of certain challenges to regulators' decisions may require careful consideration. This is particularly the case when disciplinary proceedings are underway. It is submitted that issues should be raised early to ensure that a challenge is brought promptly. However, claimants should be aware that the court may be reluctant to intervene if the matter is a minor one and is unlikely to make a difference to the final outcome of the proceedings.

Amenability

15.40 Only bodies that are exercising public functions will be amenable to judicial review challenges. Whether a particular decision is a product of a public function is fact-sensitive, and it has been held that there is 'no simple litmus test'.[38] Furthermore, simply because a body is amenable to judicial review does not mean that all of its functions are reviewable.[39]

15.41 A key decision on the issue of amenability was *R v Panel on Take-overs and Mergers, ex p Datafin plc*. In this case, the Court of Appeal emphasised the necessity of some 'public element'.[40] Some statutory underpinning to a body will indicate this public element,[41] as will whether the function is governmental in nature[42] and whether but for the body's activities the government would intervene.[43] It should be noted that similar factors are taken into account in assessing whether a body comes within s 6 of the Human Rights Act 1998.[44]

15.42 On this basis, statutory regulators will be amenable to judicial review. This includes the healthcare regulators listed in the table above, as well as the Bar Standards Board, Solicitors Regulation Authority and the Financial Conduct Authority.

15.43 It is submitted that the Institute of Chartered Accountants of England and Wales is also generally subject to judicial review proceedings. In *Andreou v Institute of Chartered Accountants in England and Wales*, the Institute argued that a challenge to a

---

[37] *R (Kashyap) v General Medical Council* [2009] EWHC 2873 (Admin) at [11].
[38] *R (Beer) v Hampshire Farmers Market Ltd* [2003] EWCA Civ 1056 at [12].
[39] *R v Jockey Club, ex p RAM Racecourse Ltd* [1993] 2 All ER 225, 246J.
[40] *R v Panel on Take-overs and Mergers, ex p Datafin Plc* [1987] QB 815, 838E–F, applied in *R v Disciplinary Committee of the Jockey Club, ex p Massingberd-Mundy* [1993] 2 All ER 207.
[41] *R v Panel on Take-overs and Mergers, ex p Datafin Plc* [1987] QB 815, 847A–B; *R (A) v Partnerships in Care Ltd* [2002] EWHC 529 (Admin); *Mohit v Director of Public Prosecutions of Mauritius* [2006] UKPC 20 at [20].
[42] *R v Panel on Take-overs and Mergers, ex p Datafin Plc* [1987] QB 815, 835F; *R v Disciplinary Committee of the Jockey Club, ex p Aga Khan* [1993] 1 WLR 909, 932H.
[43] *R v Chief Rabbi, ex p Wachmann* [1992] 1 WLR 1036, 1041F–1042A; *R v Panel on Take-overs and Mergers, ex p Datafin Plc* [1987] QB 815; *R v Football Association Ltd, ex p Football League Ltd* [1993] 2 All ER 833, 848J; and *R v Disciplinary Committee of the Jockey Club, ex p Aga Khan* [1993] 1 WLR 909, 932B.
[44] See *Aston Cantlow and Wilmcote with Billesley Parochial Church Council v Wallbank* [2003] UKHL 37 at [7], [11]–[12]; *YL v Birmingham City Council* [2007] UKHL 27 and *R (Weaver) v London & Quadrant Housing Trust* [2009] EWCA Civ 587 at [35].

procedural decision taken as part of disciplinary proceedings should be brought by judicial review, rather than by a private law action. Although the case was allowed to proceed as a private law claim, the court noted that judicial review ought to be used to challenge the public law decisions of the Institute.[45] There are numerous cases involving the Institute that illustrate that the Institute is amenable to judicial review challenges.[46]

15.44 Regulators that are not typically amenable to judicial review include the private organisations listed at **15.18** above. There have been several cases on whether the Jockey Club and Lloyd's of London are amenable to judicial review.

15.45 In terms of the Jockey Club, in *R v Disciplinary Committee of the Jockey Club, ex p Aga Khan* it was held that decisions of its disciplinary committee were not amenable to judicial review.[47] In *R (Mullins) v Jockey Club Appeal Board* it was held that this also applies to the appeals from the disciplinary committee.[48]

15.46 In terms of Lloyd's of London, its statutory underpinning might suggest that it is prima facie amenable to judicial review. However, the authorities indicate otherwise. The latest decision from the Court of Appeal is *R (West) v Lloyd's of London* where a decision to approve syndicate membership buy-outs was challenged. It was held that regulating Lloyd's members was a private contractual matter and so not amenable to judicial review.[49] This confirms the general position held in *R v Lloyd's of London, ex p Briggs* and *R v Council of Lloyd's, ex p Johnson*.[50] Furthermore, it has been held that Lloyd's is not a public authority for the purposes of s 6 of the Human Rights Act 1998.[51]

15.47 However, in the earlier decision of *R v Committee of Lloyd's, ex p Moran*, it appears to have been assumed that Lloyd's was amenable to judicial review.[52] Similarly, in *R v Committee of Lloyd's, ex p Postgate* the underwriter challenged Posgate letters from the Committee of Lloyd's to the employers of an underwriter requiring his suspension. In this case, the application was successful as it was held that there was no power to write the letters.[53]

15.48 It is submitted that the more recent authorities should be preferred. In *ex p Moran* and *ex p Posgate* it is unclear whether the question of amenability was

---

[45] *Andreou v Institute of Chartered Accountants in England and Wales* [1998] 1 All ER 14; cited in *R (Coke-Wallis) v Institute of Chartered Accountants in England and Wales* [2011] UKSC 1 at [28].
[46] See for instance, *R v Institute of Chartered Accountants in England and Wales, ex p Brindle* [1994] BCC 297 (challenge to decision to proceed with disciplinary case despite extant and pending litigation); *R v Institute of Chartered Accountants of England and Wales, ex p Taher Nawaz*, unreported, 25 April 1997, CA (challenge to decision (challenge based on improper delegation and privilege against self-incrimination); *R v Institute of Chartered Accountants in England and Wales, ex p Friend & Co* (30 June 2000) (challenge to decision to reopen investigation in breach of legitimate expectation); *R (Gorlov) v Institute of Chartered Accountants of England and Wales* [2001] EWHC Admin 220 (challenge to failure to make costs award); *R (Hill) v Institute of Chartered Accountants in England and Wales* [2012] EWHC 1731 (QB) (challenge to decision to proceed without panel member).
[47] *R v Disciplinary Committee of the Jockey Club, ex p Aga Khan* [1993] 1 WLR 909. See also *R v Disciplinary Committee of the Jockey Club, ex p Massingberd-Mundy* [1993] 2 All ER 207 and *R v Jockey Club, ex p RAM Racecourses Ltd* [1993] 2 All ER 225.
[48] *R (Mullins) v Jockey Club Appeal Board* [2005] EWHC 2197 (Admin).
[49] *R (West) v Lloyd's of London* [2004] EWCA Civ 506.
[50] *R v Lloyd's of London, ex p Briggs* (1993) 5 Admin LR 698 DC and *R v Council of Lloyd's, ex p Johnson*, unreported, 16 August 1996, Brooke LJ.
[51] *Doll-Steinberg v Society of Lloyd's* [2002] EWHC 419 (Admin).
[52] *R v Committee of Lloyd's, ex p Moran* (1983) *The Times*, 24 June, Mustill J.
[53] *R v Committee of Lloyd's, ex p Posgate* (1983) *The Times*, 12 January, DC.

argued and these decisions were before *ex p Datafin*, which clarified the position on questions of amenability. Accordingly, it is unlikely that Lloyd's will be held to be amenable to judicial review.

15.49 Three bodies that perform disciplinary functions and have been specifically held not to be amenable to judicial review include the National Greyhound Racing Club (*Law v National Greyhound Racing Club Ltd*);[54] the Association of British Travel Agents (*R (Sunspell Ltd (t/a Superlative Travel)) v Association of British Travel Agents*)[55] and the Chief Rabbi (*R v Chief Rabbi of the United Hebrew Congregation of Great Britain and the Commonwealth, ex p Wachmann*).[56]

15.50 It should be noted that even if a body is held to be amenable to judicial review, the basis on which the review is conducted might be limited. This is a result of the decision in *R v Hull University Visitor, ex p Page* that held that a decision of a visitor was only open to review if he had acted outside his jurisdiction, abused his powers or acted in breach of the rules of natural justice.[57] This principle has been held to apply to the Visitors to the Inns of Court, which is the appellate body from the Bar Standards Board.[58] In *R v Visitors to the Inns of Court, ex p Calder & Persaud*, the Court of Appeal held that although the Visitors were not acting as High Court judges and were therefore reviewable this would only be on limited '*Page* grounds'. However, it should be noted that investigatory decisions of the Bar Standards Board would appear to be reviewable on normal grounds.[59]

15.51 Similarly, it has been held by the Court of Appeal in *R (Davies) v Financial Services Authority* that decisions of the Financial Services Authority (the precursor to the Financial Conduct Authority) would only be amenable to judicial review in exceptional cases. This is because the point could be raised before the Upper Tribunal.[60] This is another way of articulating the rule that judicial review is not available if there are alternative remedies available, but it highlights that the Financial Conduct Authority is unlikely to be amenable to judicial review except in exceptional circumstances.

Alternative remedies

15.52 Judicial review is often described as an avenue of last resort.[61] Accordingly, the supervisory jurisdiction of the High Court will not normally be deployed where a satisfactory alternative has been provided.[62] This is a matter for the court's discretion and an alternative remedy does not oust the judicial review jurisdiction.[63]

---

[54] *Law v National Greyhound Racing Club Ltd* [1983] 1 WLR 1302.
[55] *R (Sunspell Ltd (t/a Superlative Travel)) v Association of British Travel Agents* [2001] ACD 16.
[56] *R v Chief Rabbi of the United Hebrew Congregation of Great Britain and the Commonwealth, ex p Wachmann* [1992] 1 WLR 1036.
[57] *R v Hull University Visitor, ex p Page* [1993] AC 682, 704F.
[58] *R v Visitors to the Inns of Court, ex p Calder & Persaud* [1994] QB 1, CA.
[59] *R (Davies) v General Council of the Bar, ex p Percival* [1991] 1 QB 212.
[60] *R (Davies) v Financial Services Authority* [2004] 1 WLR 185; applied in *R (Griggs) v Financial Services Authority* [2008] EWHC 2587 (Admin) and *R (C) v Financial Services Authority* [2013] EWCA Civ 677.
[61] See *R (Cart) v Upper Tribunal* [2012] UKSC 28 at [19]; *R (G) v Immigration Appeal Tribunal* [2004] EWCA Civ 1731 at [27]; *R v Hammersmith and Fulham London Borough Council, ex p Burkett* [2002] UKHL 23 at [42].
[62] See *R (Cart) v Upper Tribunal* [2012] UKSC 28 at [71].
[63] *Leech v Deputy Governor of Parkhurst Prison* [1988] AC 533, 580C–D; *R (Cheltenham Builders Ltd) v South Gloucestershire District Council* [2003] EWHC 2803 (Admin) at [53].

15.53 In assessing the available alternative remedies, the court will typically consider whether the other means of redress are convenient and effective.[64] This will often be a question of how the alternative procedure operates[65] and what remedies are available.[66] However, convenience and effectiveness may not be enough to circumvent specified statutory procedures to challenge or review decisions.[67]

15.54 A classic example of where an alternative remedy will exist is where the decisions can be appealed. As Lord Scarman said in *Re Preston*:[68] 'it will only be very rarely that the courts will allow the collateral process of judicial review to be used to attack an appealable decision.'

15.55 In the context of professional regulation, some decisions are open to appeal. The most obvious example is decisions on sanction made by a disciplinary panel or tribunal. For instance, the legislation of the healthcare regulators provides for a statutory appeal, which takes the form of a rehearing and seeks to indentify any error of law or fact made by the panel or tribunal.[69]

15.56 The question of alternative remedy has been considered several times in the disciplinary context. For instance, in *R v Chief Constable of Ministry of Defence Police, ex p Sweeney*, a challenge was brought to a decision to commence disciplinary proceedings. Although the decision had been arguably wrong, judicial review was refused as there was an alternative remedy, namely an appeal by way of a complete rehearing.[70] Similarly, in *R v Law Society, ex p Bratsky Lesopromyshlenny Complex*, a decision to grant permission to bring judicial review was set aside because there was alternative remedy that had not been brought to the attention of the first judge.[71] In *R v Law Society, ex p Kingsley*, permission was set aside on a similar basis to the *ex p Bratsky* and it was noted that this was not an exceptional case that would warrant the court allowing the judicial review to continue.[72]

15.57 The approach that requires some exceptional circumstances to be show before a judicial review application will be allowed where there is an appeal available is apparent in the line of cases regarding challenges to the Financial Services Authority (now Financial Conduct Authority). The approach outlined by the Court of Appeal in *R (Davies) v Financial Services Authority* and then *R (C) v Financial Services Authority* was that where a specific appellate procedure had been provided even considerations of convenience and effectiveness may not be sufficient reason not to use the procedure provided by Parliament.[73]

---

64 *Kay v Lambeth Borough Council* [2006] UKHL 10 at [30] but compare with *R (C) v Financial Services Authority* [2013] EWCA Civ 677 at [20]–[36].
65 See, for example, *Primecrown Ltd v Medicines Control Agency* [1997] EuLR 657, 659F.
66 *R v Inland Revenue Commissioners, ex p Mead* [1993] 1 All ER 772, 783A–B; *R (Shoesmith) v OFSTED* [2011] EWCA Civ 642 at [97]–[98].
67 *R v Falmouth and Truro Port Health Authority ex p South West Water* [2001] QB 445, 477C–F.
68 *Re Preston* [1985] AC 835, 852.
69 See *Gupta v General Medical Council* [2001] UKPC 61; *Ghosh v General Medical Council* [2001] 1 WLR 1915 and *Threlfall v General Optical Council* [2004] EWHC 2683 (Admin) at [21].
70 *R v Chief Constable of Ministry of Defence Police, ex p Sweeney* [1999] COD 122, CA.
71 *R v Law Society, ex p Bratsky Lesopromyshlenny Complex* [1995] COD 216.
72 *R v Law Society, ex p Kingsley* [1996] COD 59.
73 *R (Davies) v Financial Services Authority* [2004] 1 WLR 185; and *R (C) v Financial Services Authority* [2013] EWCA Civ 677. See also *R (Griggs) v Financial Services Authority* [2008] EWHC 2587 (Admin).

15.58 An example where an alternative remedy was not appropriate is provided by *R v Ministry of Defence Police, ex p Byrne* where a finding that an officer had been drunk on duty was quashed as the officer had been denied access to documents relevant to the case. It was noted that although there was an alternative remedy, in the form of an internal appeals procedure, this was inappropriate because the head of the police force made the decision under appeal.[74]

15.59 Additionally, in *R (Aga) v General Medical Council* there was no alternative remedy open to the claimant, as the disciplinary panel had not imposed a sanction.[75] In this case, the panel found that the doctor's failure to recognise a condition in a patient should be characterised as misconduct. However, it was decided that his fitness to practise was not impaired and no sanction was imposed. Accordingly, the statutory appeal route was not open to the claimant and the only alternative was to bring judicial review proceedings.

15.60 The alternative remedy limitation will not apply in cases where complainants are seeking to challenge decisions by regulators not to refer their complaints to a disciplinary committee. There are several examples of such challenges and these are explored in more detail below.

Restraint

15.61 The doctrine of restraint applies with particular force to the decisions made by professional regulators, and in particular their adjudicative branch. This is because the regulators are best placed to make decisions about professional misconduct. Accordingly, in *Bolton v Law Society* it was said that:[76] 'In cases of professional misconduct ... it would require a very strong case to interfere with a sentence ... because the disciplinary committee are the best possible people for weighing the seriousness of the professional misconduct.'

15.62 This restraint applies to the findings of fact made by the regulator, and to the sanction given, as these are questions of judgment. This extends to specialist decisions, such medical judgments, which the panel may be best placed to assess the evidence.[77] However, it should be noted that this approach to restraint does not apply when the regulator decides questions of law because this is a matter for the court exercising its supervisory jurisdiction.[78] Accordingly it has been said that:[79]

> 'A tribunal either misdirects itself in law or not according to whether it has got the law right or wrong, and that depends on what the law is and not on what a lay tribunal might reasonably think it was. In this field there are no marks for trying hard but getting the answer wrong.'

---

[74] *R v Ministry of Defence Police, ex p Byrne* [1994] COD 429, DC.
[75] *R (Aga) v General Medical Council* [2012] EWHC 782 (Admin) at [1].
[76] *Bolton v Law Society* [1994] 1 WLR 512, 516H.
[77] *R v Milling (Medical Referee), ex p West Yorkshire Police Authority* [1997] 8 Med LR 392.
[78] See *R v Elmbridge Borough Council, ex p Health Care Corporation* [1991] 3 PLR 63, 68G ('the court itself has to come to the conclusion as to what the law is').
[79] *R v Central Arbitration Committee, ex p BTP Tioxide Ltd* [1981] ICR 843, 856B–D.

15.63 When seeking to challenge a decision made by a regulator, it is important to bear in mind that a judicial review court will typically exercise restraint on questions of judgment and discretion. This is particularly important if a challenge seeks to attack the factual basis of a decision.

Standing

15.64 A potential judicial review claimant needs to demonstrate that he or she has a 'sufficient interest' in the decision under challenge in order to bring proceedings.[80] This is not normally an issue in judicial reviews brought against regulators as professionals who have been subject to an adverse decision normally bring such challenges. However, where this has not been the case, standing has still been found.

15.65 For instance, in *R v General Council of the Bar, ex p Percival*, a head of chambers sought to challenge a decision by the Bar Council to pursue a lesser charge against a barrister. It was held that the head of chambers had standing to bring the challenge.[81] A similar case was *R v General Medical Council, ex p Richards* where a complainant successfully challenged the decision of the regulator not to proceed with her complaint.[82]

The grounds of judicial review

15.66 In this section, key functions of the regulators are described in relation to the grounds of judicial review that commonly arise in practice. It is important to bear in mind the limitations of judicial review, as described above. Perhaps the most important limitation is the availability of an alternative remedy, namely appeals from certain decisions affecting a professional's registration.

15.67 Another preliminary point is that many of the cases in professional regulation are first instance appeals to the High Court. The High Court has observed that it is important not to rely on these cases uncritically. In *Shah v General Pharmaceutical Council*, the appellant sought to show that there was 'a consistent body of jurisprudence' in relation to imposing reprimands on pharmacists. This was done by citing numerous previous first instance decisions, but as the judge noted:[83]

> 'There is no suggestion in any of the cases, for example, that later cases rely upon the earlier ones; there is no suggestion in the reports that the sanction of reprimand was imposed because that was some kind of norm in the circumstances revealed in the cases in question.'

15.68 A similar approach was taken in *EY v General Medical Council* where the appellant sought to rely on several first instance decisions in relation to how the Interim Orders Panel arrived at its conclusion. The judge noted that:[84]

> 'It can be dangerous to argue from case specific conclusions to general principle ... there seemed to the court to be some considerable danger that some central principles of public law about reasoning would be overlooked.'

---

[80] Section 31(3) of the Senior Courts Act 1981.
[81] *R v General Council of the Bar, ex p Percival* [1991] 1 QB 212.
[82] *R v General Medical Council, ex p Richards* (2001) *The Times*, 24 January; [2001] Lloyd's Rep Med 47.
[83] *Shah v General Pharmaceutical Council* [2011] EWHC 73 (Admin) at [24].
[84] *EY v General Medical Council* [2013] EWHC 860 (Admin) at [21], [34] and [38].

None of those first instance authorities on the nature of the reasoning to be adopted should be seen as more than illustrations of how the fundamentals of decision making and reasoning have been applied in individual cases, and they should not be seen as identifying any new or different approach.'

15.69 The lesson from these two cases is that while first instance decisions may provide useful examples of how judges have decided similar issues, they should not be overly cited in a manner that may obscure the applicable public law principles.

Entry onto the register

15.70 As noted above, each regulator has to determine the criteria for entry onto the professional register or to be recognised as a professional. There are three areas of relevance in this context: first, general issues regarding registration; second, challenges to exams; and third, the recognition of certain qualifications.

Issues regarding registration

15.71 Registration is an essential step for a professional to be recognised as such. The precise mechanics for registration will differ according to the legislation for each regulator. However, there are some important common themes between the regulators.

15.72 The most important theme for the purposes of judicial review applications is that there is normally an appeal available against registration decisions. Accordingly, an alternative remedy is provided that makes judicial review inapt in most cases.

15.73 At some of the healthcare regulators, this right of appeal is to a specific panel or committee set up for this purpose.[85] At the General Chiropractic Council and the General Osteopathic Council, the right of appeal is to the General Council.[86] A further appeal is then provided to the county court.[87] Registration appeals against the Solicitors Regulation Authority are made to the High Court.[88] Registration appeals against the Bar Standards Board go to the Visitors to the Inns of Court.[89]

15.74 Typically, a prospective registrant will need to satisfy requirements that include having the relevant qualifications, being in good health and being of good character. The burden is on the applicant to show that they meet the requirements.[90] In terms of the educational requirements, there will typically be a discretion for the regulator to accept different qualifications.[91]

15.75 Applicants are expected to be full and frank with their disclosures regarding any previous criminal convictions.[92] A failure to do so may amount to dishonesty.[93] It is only

---

[85] Dentists Act 1984, s 50C; Medical Act 1983 Schs 3A and 3B; and Opticians Act 1989 Sch 1A.
[86] Chiropractors Act 1994, s 29 and Osteopaths Act 1993 s 29.
[87] For example, see para 5 of Sch 3A to the Medical Act 1983.
[88] Regulation 3 of the Solicitors Admission Regulations 2011.
[89] Annex M to the Code of Conduct of the Bar of England and Wales.
[90] See *Jones v Commission for Social Care Inspection* [2005] 1 WLR 2461; *Butt v Solicitors Regulation Authority* [2010] EWHC 1381 (Admin).
[91] See *Islam v Bar Standards Board* [2012] All ER (D) 05 (Aug).
[92] See, for instance, *Re A Solicitor No 4 of 2009, Afsar* [2009] EWCA Civ 842; *Venton v Solicitors Regulation Authority* [2010] EWHC 1377 (Admin).
[93] See, for instance, in *Re A Solicitor Nos 21 and 22 of 2007, Ali and Naeem* [2008] EWCA Civ 769; *Chaudery v Solicitors Regulation Authority* [2012] EWHC 372 (Admin).

in rare cases that a person would be registered where there had been non-disclosure.[94] On an appeal, the amount of insight shown by an applicant is a relevant factor.[95] An important factor is also whether a person is fit to be registered, as it would be illogical to allow a person to be registered if their behaviour would lead to them to be struck off the register.[96]

15.76 These factors apply to registration appeals and it is important to emphasise the limited role of judicial review is this context. Judicial review claims are best deployed if it appears that the regulator has acted beyond its powers or unreasonably, and there is no available appeal. For instance, in *R (Law Society) v Master of the Rolls* the issue was whether the Law Society had the power to impose conditions on a solicitor's registration. It was held that the power only extended to the initial making of an entry on the register, and there was no general power to impose conditions.[97]

Exams

15.77 Challenges to examinations overseen by the professional regulators are not common, but can only be brought by judicial review where there is no appeal available. An example of a claimant not appreciating this is *R v Council of Legal Education Board of Examiners, ex p Joseph*. In this case, the claimant sought to challenge a decision of the Board of Examiners of the Council of Legal Education refusing to certify him as having satisfactorily completed his Bar exams. It was held that such a decision was not amenable to judicial review and it fell within the exclusive jurisdiction of the Visitors to the Inns of Court.[98]

15.78 Similarly, a challenge can be rendered academic if a fresh decision is taken. That is what occurred in *R v Institute of Chartered Accountants, ex p Bruce*. In this case, the claimant sought to challenge a decision to decline him an extension of time to sit an exam. In the end the Institute did give a limited extension of time and the claim was struck out as the original decision had been overtaken.[99]

15.79 An example of a fully argued challenge to an examination regime was in *R v Royal Pharmaceutical Society of Great Britain, ex p Mahmood*. In this case, the claimant sought to challenge a bye-law of the Royal Pharmaceutical Society that prevented him from sitting an examination for a fourth time. It was argued that the bye-law was *ultra vires* s 3 of the Pharmacy Act 1954, was irrational and was discriminatory. The challenge failed on all grounds, as the Society had such a power, and its exercise was neither irrational nor discriminatory.[100]

---

[94] Two examples where registration appeals were allowed despite non-disclosure of convictions are: *Mulla v Solicitors Regulation Authority* [2010] EWHC 3077 (Admin); *Davies v Solicitors Regulation Authority* [2010] EWHC 3645 (Admin).
[95] *Khan v Solicitors Regulation Authority* [2010] EWHC 1555 (Admin).
[96] *Jideofo v Law Society* [2007] WL 511 6865 and *Council for the Regulation of Healthcare Professionals v General Dental Council and Fleischmann* [2005] EWHC 87 (Admin) at [55].
[97] *R (Law Society) v Master of the Rolls* [2005] 1 WLR 2033.
[98] *R v Council of Legal Education Board of Examiners, ex p Joseph* [1994] COD 318.
[99] *R v Institute of Chartered Accountants, ex p Bruce*, unreported, 22 October 1986, CA.
[100] *R v Royal Pharmaceutical Society of Great Britain, ex p Mahmood* [2001] EWCA Civ 1245.

Recognition of certain qualifications

15.80 Issues can arise for regulators when they are asked to recognise qualifications by foreign professionals. This broadly falls into two categories of professional: first, professionals coming from *within* the European Economic Area (EEA); and, secondly, professionals coming from *beyond* the EEA.

15.81 In the case of certain professionals within the EEA, their registration will be determined by Directive 2005/36/EC (referred to as the 'Qualifications Directive'). This applies to nurses, dentists, vets, midwives, architects, pharmacists, doctors and lawyers. The intention behind the Directive is to promote freedom of movement and it allows for the 'automatic' recognition of qualifications after the relevant documents have been submitted. This is immediate where a professional will only be working temporarily in another country. The level of detail required is more onerous if the person intends to relocate permanently. A refusal to register under the Directive by a regulator will typically be a decision that can be appealed, and so the role of judicial review is limited in this regard.

15.82 When professionals seek to be registered from beyond the EEA, the processes are typically less detailed and the regulators usually have their own requirements that include proof of experience and an exam or assessment. Judicial review has been used in this context to challenge changes to the registration requirements to overseas applicants.

15.83 For instance, in *R v General Medical Council, ex p St Georges University* an overseas university sought to challenge the decision to withdraw its recognition of the university's degree in medicine as an 'acceptable overseas qualification' (s 22 of the Medical Act 1983). It was held that this decision was an exercise of academic and professional judgment and so reasons were not required, following *R v Higher Education Funding Council, ex p Institute of Dental Surgery*.[101] In any event, the reasons were adequate and it was held that there was no unfairness or breach of legitimate expectation in the manner in which the GMC had informed the university of its concerns.[102]

15.84 A similar issue arose in *R (Patel) v General Medical Council*.[103] In this case, a doctor had decided to study medicine at a Caribbean university. He had specifically asked the GMC whether this would be an acceptable overseas qualification, and he was told that it would be. He undertook the course, and then gained the necessary practical experience in the United Kingdom. When he came to register with the GMC, his application was refused as the registration criteria had changed without any transitional provisions.

15.85 Applying for judicial review of the decision, the claimant successfully argued that his legitimate expectation had been frustrated by the decision. The Court of Appeal held that he had been given a clear, unequivocal and unqualified assurance that his qualification would be recognised. The Medical Act 1983 did not exclude the principle of legitimate expectation and the statutory duty had to be exercised in accordance with established principles of substantive fairness. It had not been open to the GMC to change its policy without adopting some transitional provision for someone in the claimant's position. Furthermore, there was no public interest that outweighed the

---

[101] *R v Higher Education Funding Council, ex p Institute of Dental Surgery* [1994] 1 WLR 242.
[102] *R v General Medical Council, ex p St Georges University*, unreported, 30 November 1994, DC.
[103] *R (Patel) v General Medical Council* [2013] EWCA Civ 327, [2013] 1 WLR 2801.

unfairness of refusing to honour the assurance given and to recognise the claimant's qualification. The court emphasised that the relief granted was specific to the claimant and ordered the GMC to recognise his qualifications.[104]

Maintaining the register

15.86 Maintaining the register of professionals is largely achieved by establishing systems of continuing professional development (CPD) and any other systems to ensure that the requirements of registration are being maintained. This can include the payment of an annual fee, and ensuring that the required level of indemnity insurance is in place. For instance, in *Taylor v General Chiropractic Council*[105] a chiropractor was refused registration on the basis that he had not paid his fees. Accordingly, he was removed from the register. On appeal it was held that there was no discretion in this regard, nor was the level of the fee discriminatory.

15.87 Failure to comply with the ongoing requirements for registration can lead to disciplinary action. An example is *Rahman v Bar Standards Board* where a barrister had failed to comply with CPD requirements. On appeal an 18-month suspension was reduced to a three-month suspension.[106]

15.88 Judicial review challenges in this context are rare. For instance, applications to be restored to the register after some failure to comply with the registration requirements usually have a right of appeal, rendering judicial review inapt. Where such appeals are undertaken, the court is typically wary to disagree with the decision of a specialist tribunal unless there is an error of law.[107]

15.89 In *Raji v General Medical Council* such an error of law was identified, namely that it had been unfair to require a doctor to make dual submissions at the same hearing as to both restoration to the register and also suspension of future applications for restoration. The Privy Council held that the public law principle of fairness required that the issue of suspension should have been considered separately after the decision on restoration and the reasons for it had been announced.[108]

15.90 However, all of the cases cited in this section were appeals from the relevant regulator. This is indicative that there is normally an alternative to judicial review and accordingly judicial review is limited in this context.

Removal from the register

Allegations

15.91 The first stage of disciplinary proceedings to remove a professional from the register is the receipt of an allegation. This initial process requires the regulator to receive the relevant information and, having been satisfied that the complaint meets its referral criteria, the allegation will be referred to an investigatory committee or panel to

---

[104] *R (Patel) v General Medical Council* [2013] EWCA Civ 327 at [83]–[86].
[105] *Taylor v General Chiropractic Council* [2009] EWHC 301 (Admin).
[106] *Rahman v Bar Standards Board* [2013] EWHC 4202 (QB).
[107] *Thobani v Solicitors Regulation Authority* [2011] All ER (D) 12 (Dec).
[108] *Raji v General Medical Council* [2003] UKPC 24.

gather evidence and make the necessary enquiries. Some of the regulators are also able to treat information that comes to their attention as an allegation.[109]

15.92 The legal framework for each regulator varies and so the manner in which allegations are dealt with will vary. Some regulators have a time limit for allegations. For instance, at the General Medical Council an allegation will not normally be considered if the events giving rise to the allegation are more than five years old. This is subject to a public interest exception.[110] In *R (D) v General Medical Council* a claimant doctor sought judicial review of a decision to refer a case for initial consideration where the allegations were of sexual misconduct from over 20 years ago. The GMC said it was in the public interest to bring proceedings against the doctor, even though the police had concluded their investigation after they were satisfied that the complaint was malicious. The GMC said that the police had closed their investigation due to a lack of evidence.

15.93 The judge held that the GMC's position was fundamentally flawed, as the police had not concluded the allegation due to a lack of evidence but because the complaint was malicious. The GMC had not taken into account that the health authority had not thought it necessary to make any investigations at the time. In the circumstances, the decision would be quashed.[111]

15.94 Many regulators use systems of 'screeners' to determine whether a case should be referred for full investigation.[112] Even if the regulator does not have a formal system of screeners it will typically have some method of determining whether the information provided amounts to a valid allegation.

15.95 The proper role of screeners is relatively limited, although the information they can take into account when considering an allegation is very wide. There is not normally an appeal against decisions made at the initial consideration stage, and so judicial review is usually the only way to challenge such decisions.

15.96 In terms of the role of screeners, it has been noted that their task is to determine 'whether the allegation is capable of producing a finding of misconduct'.[113] The same test applies in deficient performance cases.[114]

15.97 However, the role of the screener does not extend to trying to resolve conflicts of evidence, as this is a matter for investigation or adjudication.[115] These limits were spelt out in *R v General Medical Council, ex p Toth* where a complainant sought judicial review of a decision by a screener not to refer his complaint against a doctor. In that case it was held that while a screener might conclude that a case should not proceed further because it did not amount to an allegation in law, it was not the function of the screener to look at the substantive issues of the complaint, such as the prospects of the complaint succeeding, or to investigate the fairness of a complaint being allowed to continue. The role of the screener was limited to acting as preliminary filter. Furthermore, any doubts

---

[109] See, for instance, art 22(6) of the Nursing and Midwifery Order 2001.
[110] See r 4(5) of the General Medical Council (Fitness to Practice) Rules Order of Council 2004.
[111] *R (D) v General Medical Council* [2013] EWHC 2839 (Admin). See also *R (Peacock) v General Medical Council* [2007] EWHC 585 (Admin) and *R (Gwynn) v General Medical Council* [2007] EWHC 3145 (Admin).
[112] See, for instance, the Health Professions Council (Screeners) Rules Order of Council 2003.
[113] *R (Pal) v General Medical Council* [2009] EWHC 1061 (Admin) at [33].
[114] *R (Remedy UK Ltd) v General Medical Council* [2010] EWHC 1245 (Admin) at [20].
[115] *R v General Medical Council, ex p Richards* (2001) *The Times*, 24 January, Sullivan J.

should be resolved in favour of allowing the complaint to proceed, particularly where the practitioner concerned continued to practise.[116] Similarly, decisions by screeners were quashed in *R (Holmes) v General Medical Council* and *R (Woods) v General Medical Council* when the screeners had applied the wrong test, such as making value judgments about the merits of the complaints.[117]

15.98 The initial consideration function at the Scottish Legal Complaints Commission was explained in *Law Society of Scotland v The Scottish Legal Complaints Commission* as an important duty to sift wholly unmeritorious claims that focuses on obtaining the basic information about a complaint.[118]

15.99 The matters that can be taken into account as part of an allegation are typically wide. For instance, allegations can relate to conduct that occurred out of the jurisdiction or before registration. In *R (L) v Prosthetists and Orthotists Board* a doctor sought judicial review of a decision to bring disciplinary proceedings relating to allegations of rape prior to his registration. The Court of Appeal held that past conduct can clearly impact upon the continuance of future registration and so dismissed the challenge.[119]

15.100 It is also possible that allegations that are referred can include conduct after the allegations were made. In *R (Bramall) v Law Society* it was held that even after the complaint was made to the Law Society, further conduct could be taken into account as part of the disciplinary process.[120]

15.101 The fact that a professional has been acquitted in criminal proceedings does not mean that the same conduct will not give rise to disciplinary proceedings. This was explained in *Sinha v General Medical Council*:[121]

> '... the mere fact of an acquittal in criminal proceedings cannot be the be all and end all of the matter for other purposes. Supposing, for example, that a professional man is acquitted of murder or grievous bodily harm by a jury on the direction of the judge on a purely technical and unmeritorious point. He is not guilty in the eyes of the criminal law. But that would not stop – nor should it stop – his professional body re-investigating the matter and deciding both that he had been guilty of serious professional misconduct, and that he should be disciplined according to the rule of the profession concerned. A professional body is, after all, charged with the duty to protect the public from members of the profession who fall below its standards.'

15.102 Accordingly, it is not abusive for disciplinary proceedings to revisit matters that have been dealt with in a criminal trial.[122] To the extent that this may interfere with the rule against double jeopardy, it has been held that this rule does not apply to tribunal proceedings as the rule only applies to other courts of competent jurisdiction.[123] In any event, an interference with the double jeopardy rule can be justified because of the

---

[116] *R v General Medical Council, ex p Toth* [2000] 1 WLR 2209.
[117] *R (Holmes) v General Medical Council* [2001] EWHC Admin 321; *R (Woods) v General Medical Council* [2002] EWHC 1484 (Admin).
[118] *Council of the Law Society of Scotland v Scottish Legal Complaints Commission* [2010] CSIH 79 at [34]–[35].
[119] *R (L) v Prosthetists and Orthotists Board* [2001] EWCA Civ 837.
[120] *R (Bramall) v Law Society* [2005] EWHC 1570 (Admin) at [52].
[121] *Sinha v General Medical Council* [2009] EWCA Civ 80 at [8].
[122] *Bhatt v General Medical Council* [2011] EWHC 783 (Admin).
[123] *R (Redgrave) v Commissioner of Police for the Metropolis* [2003] EWCA Civ 4. See also *Ziderman v General Dental Council* [1976] 1 WLR 330 and *R v Statutory Committee of the Pharmaceutical Society of Great Britain, ex p Pharmaceutical Society of Great Britain* [1981] 1 WLR 886.

importance of protecting the public.¹²⁴ By contrast, it has been held that the principle of *res judicata* prevents a professional from being brought before a disciplinary panel twice for the same breach of standards.¹²⁵

15.103 An example of the limits of what can be taken into account is where the conduct does not relate to the practice of a professional. In *R (Remedy UK Ltd) v General Medical Council* there was a challenge to a decision not to refer complaints against the Chief Medical Officer for England and a professor for their part in a flawed recruitment process. It was held that while the concept of fitness to practise may extend beyond clinical practice, the allegations related to administrative conduct that was not sufficiently close to the practise of medicine. Accordingly, it was right for the allegations not to be referred, as the GMC's disciplinary processes could not deal with them.¹²⁶

Investigations

15.104 After an allegation has been given initial consideration, it may be referred to an investigator or investigating committee. At the investigation stage, further enquiries will be made, such as gathering evidence regarding the allegations. This may include requiring the professional to undertake assessments or to provide the regulator with further information.

15.105 In this section the following issues will be considered: the role of judicial review at the investigation stage (including challenges to referrals); data issues; the question of delay and reopening cases. It should be noted that this section does not deal with interim orders, which in practice are an important factor for many professionals. Interim orders can be used to suspend or impose conditions on a professional pending a disciplinary hearing. However, there is typically an appeal route and so judicial review is inapt in relation to such decisions.¹²⁷

15.106 The purpose of the investigatory hearing is to establish whether the matter should be referred for adjudication by a disciplinary panel. In this way, the investigatory stage has similarities to the initial consideration stage in that both are essentially filters to ensure that only cases where there is a reasonable prospect of imposing a sanction will come before the disciplinary tribunal.

15.107 In *Henshall v General Medical Council*, the Court of Appeal noted that the filtering at the investigation stage takes a more rigorous form than that conducted by the screener, although not so rigorous as the determinative and forensic role of the adjudication stage. It is not the job of investigators to conduct an enquiry in an evidential sense, but rather to consider whether the evidence ought to be put before the disciplinary panel. Accordingly, disputes of fact should not be resolved at the investigatory stage.¹²⁸

15.108 The scope of any investigation should be linked to the allegations that have been made. For instance, in *R (McNicholas) v Nursing and Midwifery Council* it was noted that the power to conduct further investigations was not an 'at-large power' to

---

[124] *Council for the Regulation of Health Care Professionals v Ruscillo* [2004] EWCA Civ 1356 at [41] to [42].
[125] *R (Coke-Wallis) v Institute of Chartered Accountants in England and Wales* [2011] UKSC 1.
[126] *R (Remedy UK Ltd) v General Medical Council* [2010] EWHC 1245 (Admin).
[127] See *R (Madan) v General Medical Council (No 1)* [2001] EWHC Admin 322 at [6].
[128] *Henshall v General Medical Council* [2005] EWCA Civ 1520.

conduct investigations for their own sake. Such a power only arises in the context of the existing allegations against the professional.[129]

The role of judicial review at the investigation stage

15.109 Judicial review is typically the only route to challenge decisions taken at the investigation stage. This is because appeal routes do not usually exist at this stage. Indeed, in *Marcus v Nursing and Midwifery Council* the court noted that on appeal there is no power to address decisions made during an investigation.[130]

15.110 A good example of judicial review at the investigation stage is challenges to referral decisions. Both professionals and complainants commonly challenge such decisions, and the examples below tend to indicate that the court is more willing to order the regulators to refer cases rather than to prevent referrals.

15.111 For instance, in *R (David) v General Medical Council* a doctor challenged the referral of her case to the disciplinary panel on the basis that there was no sufficient evidence to establish misconduct. The court disagreed and held that there was a real prospect of finding misconduct. Furthermore the conflicts of evidence should be resolved at the adjudicative stage.[131] Similarly, in *R (Rycroft) v Royal Pharmaceutical Society of Great Britain* although a referral had taken an inordinate and unjustified amount of time, it would not be quashed unless the claimant pharmacist could show that such prejudice had been caused that no fair disciplinary process was possible.[132]

15.112 In *R (Holmes) v General Medical Council* the parents of a deceased patient challenged a decision not to refer an allegation to the disciplinary panel. The court held that the allegations should be investigated, and it was noted by the Court of Appeal that there should be caution exercised in not referring cases onwards.[133] Similarly in *R (Richards) v General Medical Council*, a complainant challenged a decision not to refer her complaint. The court quashed the decision as it was clear how the investigation panel could have come to the view that there were no questions raised about possible serious professional misconduct.[134]

15.113 Further examples of complainants successfully challenging referral decisions include *R v General Medical Council, ex p Toth*, *Woods v General Medical Council* and *Henshall v General Medical Council*.[135]

15.114 It has been suggested that challenges to referrals must meet a high threshold. For instance, in *R (Aurangzeh) v Law Society of England and Wales*, the court discussed the proper approach to challenges by professionals of decisions to refer cases to the disciplinary tribunal. It was said that:[136]

---

[129] *R (McNicholas) v Nursing and Midwifery Council* [2009] EWHC 627 (Admin).
[130] *Marcus v Nursing and Midwifery Council* [2011] All ER (D) 104 (Nov).
[131] *R (David) v General Medical Council* [2004] EWHC 2977.
[132] *R (Rycroft) v Royal Pharmaceutical Society of Great Britain* [2010] EWHC 2832 (Admin).
[133] *R (Holmes) v General Medical Council* [2002] EWCA Civ 1838.
[134] *R (Richards) v General Medical Council* [2001] Lloyd's Rep Med 47.
[135] *R v General Medical Council, ex p Toth* [2000] 1 WLR 2209, *R (Woods) v General Medical Council* [2002] EWHC 1484 (Admin) and *Henshall v General Medical Council* [2005] EWCA Civ 1520.
[136] *R (Aurangzeh) v Law Society of England and Wales* [2003] EWHC 1286 (Admin) at [4]–[8].

"In my view the question is whether as a matter of principle, it is right for the court to intervene by way of judicial review when the ambit and reach of the decision under challenge goes no further than to place the allegations in question before a disciplinary tribunal ... I have no doubt that the court must, in accordance with basic elementary principles have considerable reservations about the desirability of intervening in the manner suggested, save in circumstances where the facts call out for that intervention, for example where irreparable harm or unfairness is likely to occur or justice could only be met by intervention.

In my judgment, it is important to establish, as a matter of general principle, that, save in exceptional circumstances, which may be in the general category of those I have attempted to define, where what has occurred is that there has been a procedural failure and the matter is before the Tribunal, the proper conclusion is that the Tribunal will have ample opportunity to cure any of the failures which to that date it is said have occurred. There will be an occasion for justice then to be done. The decision of the Tribunal will be subject to review.'

15.115 A similar view was taken in *R (David) v General Medical Council* where it was said that caution should be taken to challenges to refer cases to disciplinary tribunals. However, this caution will be less if the challenge is to the interpretation or application of the relevant rules.[137] It is submitted that this is consistent with the general public law principle: that matters of law are for the court alone.[138]

15.116 There is a potential timing issue of challenges at the investigation stage. For instance, as the court in *Aurangzeh* made clear 'the whole process will be at risk of being bogged down and the disciplinary process will be at risk of being undermined by repeated applications for judicial review'.[139] A similar concern was raised in *Heath v Home Office Policy and Advisory Board for Forensic Pathology* where a challenge to a referral was unsuccessful. The court said that its role was not to monitor the procedural process and that any prejudice from delay could be prevented by hearing the matter promptly.[140]

15.117 As noted above at **15.34**, where there is likely to be an obvious miscarriage of justice judicial review proceedings should be brought promptly. However, it is important to be aware that the court will scrutinise whether the challenge is in reality a delaying tactic, as was the court's view in *Heath*.

Data issues

15.118 Having conducted its investigation the regulator will normally want to pass on the evidence generated to the disciplinary panel. This can create an issue regarding the use of personal or confidential data, and a regulator would be amenable to challenge for disclosing such information if it had done so unlawfully.

15.119 The correct approach to this issue was considered in *General Dental Council v Savery*.[141] The question in *Savery* was whether the GDC was required to apply for an order each time it sought transfer information within the organisation. The question was analysed in terms of common law obligations of confidentiality and Art 8 of the ECHR.

---

[137] *R (David) v General Medical Council* [2004] EWHC 2977 at [32]–[35].
[138] See, for example, *R v Elmbridge Borough Council, ex p Health Care Corporation* [1991] 3 PLR 63.
[139] *R (Aurangzeh) v Law Society of England and Wales* [2003] EWHC 1286 (Admin) at [7].
[140] *Heath v Home Office Policy and Advisory Board for Forensic Pathology* [2005] EWHC 1793 (Admin) at [42]–[43].
[141] *General Dental Council v Savery* [2011] EWHC 3011 (Admin), [2012] Med LR 204.

15.120 In terms of the common law aspect, it was held that this was no barrier to the regulator passing information to the disciplinary committee. Indeed, in this case, the Dentists Act 1984 provided specific authority for such disclosure. This was consistent with the public interest of the investigation of disciplinary issues. To the extent that any issue arose under the Data Protection Act 1998, this sanctioned disclosure for the exercise of any functions conferred on any person by or under any enactment. Accordingly, this did not provide a barrier either.

15.121 In terms of the Art 8 aspect, it was held that disclosure pursed a legitimate aim and was in accordance with the law. The real issue was whether disclosure was necessary in a democratic society and proportionate. It was held that there was a strong public interest in the proper administration of disciplinary proceedings, which would invariably outweigh patient confidentiality save in exceptional cases.

15.122 The court also said in an *obiter* statement that if a person's confidential information was to be disclosed that person should normally be notified. Only reasonable steps would be required in this regard.

15.123 The effect of *Savery* is that data issues should not normally arise as part of the investigatory process. However, there will be exceptional cases where such disclosure would be disproportionate and therefore violate Art 8. It is suggested that an example would be where medical records are disclosed that contain highly sensitive material that is irrelevant to the underlying allegations. A challenge in that context would need to be raised by way of judicial review by the person concerned.

Delay

15.124 An unfortunate recurring theme in disciplinary cases is delay on behalf the regulators. This delay typically occurs at the investigatory stage where the regulator has not proactively progressed the case. A number of decisions have challenged decisions to proceed with cases after a lengthy delay.

15.125 The overall position is that a judicial review claim brought on the basis of delay alone will need to demonstrate some prejudice arising from the delay. For instance, in *Johnson v Nursing and Midwifery Council* the investigation took two years and the eventual disciplinary hearing took place over another two years. The delayed proceedings were challenged by way of judicial review as an unlawful interference with the right to a hearing within a reasonable time protected by Art 6 of the ECHR. The court agreed and noted that 'the length of time which these disciplinary proceedings took remains disgraceful'.[142]

15.126 A delay of four and a half years occurred in *Okeke v Nursing and Midwifery Council* during which time the nurse was suspended from practice. The court identified the relevant factors for considering the reasonableness of delay were the importance of the matter to the claimant, the complexity of the case, and the conduct of the parties.[143] It was held that the delay was unreasonable and a violation of Art 6 of the ECHR.[144]

---

[142] *Johnson v Nursing and Midwifery Council* [2013] EWHC 2140 (Admin).
[143] *Dyer v Watson* [2002] UKPC D1, [2004] 1 AC 379.
[144] *Okeke v Nursing and Midwifery Council* [2013] EWHC 714 (Admin).

15.127 The role of prejudice was emphasised in *R (Rycroft) v Royal Pharmaceutical Society of Great Britain* where it took about two years and eight months for an initial complaint to be referred to an investigating committee.[145] Although the court recognised that the delay was inordinate and unjustified, the claimant could not establish that he had been so prejudiced by the delay that a fair process was impossible. It should be noted that in *R v Chief Constable of the Merseyside Police, ex p Merrill* it was held that prima facie delay caused prejudice and the greater the delay, the greater the prejudice.[146]

15.128 It has been held that unlawful delay can provide an exception to the alternative remedy rule. In *R v Chief Constable of the Merseyside Police, ex p Calveley* there was a two-year delay in arranging a disciplinary hearing. The Court of Appeal held that this was a rare case where despite the alternative remedy of an appeal, because of such a serious and abusive departure from police disciplinary procedure the judicial review challenge would be allowed.[147]

15.129 The question of delay does not arise if the claimant has been the cause of the delay. For instance, in *R (Calland) v Financial Ombudsman Service Ltd* it took over six and a half years to come to a final decision and the claimant was ordered to pay compensation to a third party. The claimant argued that the delay was unreasonable and breached his rights under Art 6 of the ECHR. However, this was a result of the claimant's continued objections to the investigation and refusal to cooperate. Accordingly, the delay was not unlawful.[148]

Reopening cases

15.130 Having investigated an allegation, if a regulator decides to take no action against a professional there may be occasions where the regulator attempts to reopen a case. Such decisions must be scrutinised carefully as they may be vulnerable to challenge.

15.131 In *R (B) v Nursing and Midwifery Council* a nurse had been subject to an investigation regarding failures at the care home where she worked. However, the NMC took the view that there was not enough information to suggest that the claimant was responsible for the inadequate care and informed the nurse that no further action would be taken.[149] However, the NMC purported to set aside that decision relying on a supposed 'slip rule' supposedly identified in *R (Jenkinson) v Nursing and Midwifery Council*.[150]

15.132 The court held that such slips were accidental errors that did not substantially affect the rights of the parties or the decision arrived at.[151] Furthermore, the decision also unlawfully frustrated the claimant's legitimate expectation as the NMC had departed from its published procedures.[152]

---

[145] *R (Rycroft) v Royal Pharmaceutical Society of Great Britain* [2010] EWHC 2832 (Admin), [2011] Med LR 23.
[146] *R v Chief Constable of the Merseyside Police, ex p Merrill* [1989] 1 WLR 1077, 1085.
[147] *R v Chief Constable of the Merseyside Police, ex p Calveley* [1986] 2 WLR 144.
[148] *R (Calland) v Financial Ombudsman Service Ltd* [2013] EWHC 1327 (Admin).
[149] *R (B) v Nursing and Midwifery Council* [2012] EWHC 1264 (Admin).
[150] *R (Jenkinson) v Nursing and Midwifery Council* [2009] EWHC 1111 (Admin).
[151] *Akewushola v Secretary of State for the Home Department* [2000] 1 WLR 2295.
[152] Compare with *R (Wood) v Secretary of State for Education* [2011] EWHC 3256 (Admin) where a teacher had been told that no further action would be taken against him. However, in the event a further decision was made to bar the teacher from working with children. This was held to be proportionate interference with his substantive legitimate expectations.

15.133 Similarly, in *R (Gwynn) v General Medical Council* a complaint against a surgeon had been closed at the investigation stage. However, four and a half years later the GMC purported to reopen the case and instituted disciplinary proceedings. The surgeon challenged this by way of judicial review and the court quashed the decision. The court held that the only possible way such a case could be reopened was if the complainant reverted back to the GMC. In this case, this did not happen and there was no other power to reopen the case. Even if there was such as power, it had not been exercised fairly or reasonably in this case.[153]

15.134 A slightly different case was *R (Independent Police Complaints Commission) v Commissioner of Police of the Metropolis* where the IPCC informed police officers that they were minded to close a disciplinary case against them. However, the case was never formally closed although the police officers thought it had been. Sometime later the IPCC sought further information from the officers in order to determine whether to bring disciplinary proceedings. The police officers declined on the understanding that the matter had been closed.

15.135 The court accepted that the case had not been closed by the IPCC and that an abuse of process argument could not be raised at the point of simply seeking further information. However, the requests were not sensible or practical given that the incident was six years old and the delay had been largely down to the IPCC. The officers' belief that the case was closed was not unreasonable and an order requiring further information would be oppressive.[154]

15.136 This case demonstrates that even if a case has not been formally closed, it can still be unreasonable to seek to revive an investigation after substantial delay.

Adjudication

15.137 Once a case has been referred from the investigating committee, the disciplinary case moves into the adjudicative stage. The disciplinary panel's role is the preservation and maintenance of public confidence in the profession rather than the administration of retributive justice.[155] This is consistent with the general purpose that the disciplinary function is about securing the public interest rather than providing redress to complainants.[156]

15.138 There are many legal issues at this stage and the full range of public law principles can be used to challenge the decisions of disciplinary panels. However, it is important to recognise that virtually all challenges will be by way of appeal rather than judicial review. The correct way to challenge most decisions by disciplinary panels is on appeal and so the alternative remedy limitation on judicial review will apply.

15.139 In this part of the chapter, the various steps of the adjudicative stage are described with a view to identifying the limited circumstances when judicial review might be deployed as well as frequently occurring public law issues that frequently arise.

---

[153] *R (Gwynn) v General Medical Council* [2007] EWHC 3145 (Admin) at [21]–[27].
[154] *R (Independent Police Complaints Commission) v Commissioner of Police of the Metropolis* [2009] EWHC 1566.
[155] *Raschid v General Medical Council* [2007] EWCA Civ 46 at [16]–[19].
[156] *R (Zia) v General Medical Council* [2011] EWCA Civ 743 at [35].

Preliminary issues

15.140 It can be appropriate to use judicial review to challenge the preliminary procedural decisions taken by the disciplinary panel. This is subject to the approach that courts will often prefer the proceedings to run their course and then raise matters on appeal (see above). The two most important preliminary issues are whether an adjournment should be made and whether the charge has been properly drafted.

Adjournments

15.141 It can be unfair to proceed to hear a disciplinary case if the professional is either not present or if not all of the evidence is ready. In these circumstances, an adjournment can be vital to ensure that the proceedings are conducted fairly. Since the power to adjourn is a discretionary matter, it has been held challenges to refusals to adjourn must show that the decision was outside the proper exercise of the discretion, that there was an error in principle, the decision was based on irrelevant considerations or it ignored relevant ones, or it was thoroughly unreasonable or unfair.[157]

15.142 A failure to adjourn where the professional has not attended may be unlawful depending on the reason for the non-attendance. A point of principle is where the professional has a medical condition that prevented attendance. In such cases, the normal approach is to adjourn, unless strong facts pointed to the contrary.[158] It can be a violation of Art 6 of the ECHR to proceed without the professional where there is unchallenged medical evidence that the professional is too ill to put his or her own case.[159]

15.143 In *Janik v Standards Board for England* exceptional circumstances existed which included that there was little objective evidence as to the medical condition and the case turned on documentary evidence and so oral evidence was unlikely to be necessary. Accordingly, the appeal was dismissed. However, in *Mahmood v General Medical Council* the doctor did not attend because he was in hospital suffering from chest pains at the time. It was unfair to continue in his absence and it could not be said that he was using his admission to hospital as a ploy to avoid the proceedings.[160]

15.144 By contrast, where a professional is found fit to attend but did not do so it is unlikely that it will be an abuse of process to proceed without the professional. In *Varma v General Medical Council* the medical evidence showed that the doctor could understand the nature of the proceedings and instruct lawyers. Accordingly, continuing with the case was not unlawful.[161] *Tinsa v General Medical Council* is a further example of where a failure to substantiate a mental illness meant that proceeding with the case was not unlawful.[162]

15.145 It is important that a professional is allowed to put before the disciplinary panel the evidence on which he seeks to rely and is given a proper opportunity to respond to

---

[157] *Khan v General Teaching Council for England* [2010] EWHC 3404 (Admin).
[158] *Janik v Standards Board for England* [2007] EWHC 835 (Admin).
[159] *Brabazon-Drenning v United Kingdom Central Council for Nursing, Midwifery and Health Visiting* [2001] HRLR 6.
[160] *Mahmood v General Medical Council* [2007] EWHC 474 (Admin).
[161] *Varma v General Medical Council* [2008] EWHC 753 (Admin). It should be noted that in this case a total of 21 adjournments had been granted to allow the appellant to prepare and present his case properly.
[162] *Tinsa v General Medical Council* [2008] EWHC 1284 (Admin).

allegations. In *R (Thompson) v General Chiropractic Council* the panel had listed a disciplinary hearing on a date when it was known that the claimant's expert could not attend. It was held that this was unfair and that the hearing should be relisted.[163] It should be noted that this was a successful judicial review application, rather than being an appeal.

15.146 In *Thacker v Solicitors Regulation Authority* the SRA presented to the tribunal a wide range of evidence that went far beyond the allegations against the solicitor. This was not a case that the solicitor had expected to meet and there should have been an adjournment to allow an opportunity to respond to these wider allegations.[164]

Charges

15.147 When a case is referred to a disciplinary tribunal, the initial allegations will be formulated into a series of distinct charges. Such charges should be specific and specify what professional standard has been breached. In *R (Wheeler) v Assistant Commissioner House of the Metropolitan Police* it was noted that:[165]

> '... the danger with a vague charge is that the parties, and in particular the respondent ... do not know with some precision what is alleged against them and therefore are not fully able to address those matters in the course of the hearing.'

15.148 Accordingly, charges should not generally be drafted as a long series of 'and/or' allegations that contains numerous alternatives.[166] Similarly, charges should reflect the factual basis upon which the proceedings have been brought. In *R (Council for the Regulation of Health Care Professionals) v Nursing & Midwifery Council*, it was alleged that a nurse had forged a document and the nurse admitted this allegation. However, misconduct was not found as dishonesty had not formed part of the charges against the nurse. The High Court held that this was a serious procedural error because if dishonesty had been on the charge sheet, the finding that there was no misconduct would have been unduly lenient.[167] This decision is consistent with the authorities that have held that a failure to particularise or formulate allegations of dishonesty amounts to a procedural flaw.[168]

15.149 The disciplinary panel can encounter problems if the charges are different to the allegations that have been previously investigated. However, it may be that whilst the wording of the charges may be different to the allegations in substance they are the same. This occurred in *R (Gorlov) v Institute of Chartered Accountants in England and Wales* where the claimant argued that the charges were materially different to the allegations that had been investigated. The court disagreed, and held that the allegations were substantively the same.[169]

---

[163] *R (Thompson) v General Chiropractic Council* [2008] EWHC 2499 (Admin).
[164] *Thaker v Solicitors Regulation Authority* [2011] EWHC 660 (Admin).
[165] *R (Wheeler) v Assistant Commissioner House of the Metropolitan Police* [2008] EWHC 439 (Admin) at [1.6].
[166] *Connolly v Law Society* [2007] EWHC 1175 at [104].
[167] *R (Council for the Regulation of Health Care Professionals) v Nursing & Midwifery Council* [2007] EWHC 1806 (Admin).
[168] *Singleton v Law Society* [2005] EWHC 2915; *Salha v General Medical Council* [2003] UKPC 80.
[169] *R (Gorlov) v Institute of Chartered Accountants in England and Wales* [2002] EWHC 2202 (Admin).

15.150 It is submitted that good practice would also require charges to specify which part of the relevant code of conduct has breached.[170] The wording of the grounds on which charges may be brought varies between the regulators. However, the substance of such charges covers some broad themes including whether a professional has been guilty of misconduct, whether their professional performance has been deficient or whether a professional has been convicted of a relevant offence. At the healthcare regulators, a further question is asked, namely whether the fitness to practise of the professional is impaired.

15.151 In terms of misconduct, this typically means sufficiently serious misconduct in the exercise of professional practice or conduct of a morally culpable kind that prejudices the reputation of the profession.[171] A single act may or may not cross the threshold of misconduct depending on the gravity of the action.[172] Misconduct will include allegations of dishonesty. As noted above, such allegations need to be specifically formulated and the correct test is derived from *Twinsectra Ltd v Yardley*.[173] This requires a subjective element to be present, namely whether the professional had a dishonest state of mind.[174]

15.152 In terms of deficient professional performance, this is a separate concept to negligence.[175] So, while poor judgment could not of itself constitute gross negligence it may in an appropriate case, and particularly if exercised over a period of time, constitute seriously deficient performance.[176] The standard to be expected is that applicable to the post to which the professional has been appointed and the work that is being carried out.[177] There may be an overlap between what amounts to misconduct or deficient professional performance, and so acts or omissions could be pursued under either head.[178]

15.153 The further question of impairment, which is relevant at the healthcare regulators, has been described in the case of *Yeong v General Medical Council*.[179] It was noted that the purpose of the impairment test was to ensure that the regulators make an assessment of whether the professional's fitness to practise is impaired at the time when the disciplinary findings are made. This means that the disciplinary panel must look forward and not back (although previous behaviour may well be relevant).[180] The role of professional insight will be important and any remedial steps that have been taken.[181]

---

[170] *R (Derbyshire Constabulary) v The Police Appeals Tribunal* [2012] EWHC 2280 (Admin).
[171] *R (Remedy UK Ltd) v General Medical Council* [2010] EWHC 1245 (Admin) at [37].
[172] *Calhaem v General Medical Council* [2007] EWHC 2606 (Admin) at [39].
[173] *Twinsectra Ltd v Yardley and Others* [2002] UKHL 12.
[174] For applications of the *Twinsectra* test see *Bultitude v Law Society* [2004] EWCA Civ 1853; *Bryant v Law Society* [2007] EWHC 3043 (Admin); and *Donkin v Law Society* [2007] EWHC 414 (Admin).
[175] *Calhaem v General Medical Council* [2007] EWHC 2606 (Admin) at [39].
[176] *R (Remedy UK Ltd) v General Medical Council* [2010] EWHC 1245 (Admin) at [37].
[177] *Holton v General Medical Council* [2006] EWHC 2960 (Admin) at [70]–[71].
[178] *Vranicki v Architects Registration Board* [2007] EWHC 506 (Admin) at [8].
[179] *Yeong v General Medical Council* [2009] EWHC 1923 (Admin).
[180] See *General Medical Council v Meadow* [2006] EWCA Civ 1390 at [28]–[32]; *Zygmunt v General Medical Council* [2008] EWHC 2643 (Admin) at [31]; *Cohen v General Medical Council* [2008] EWHC 581 (Admin) at [63]–[64].
[181] *Cohen v General Medical Council* [2008] EWHC 581 (Admin), at [69]–[71]; *Azzam v General Medical Council* [2008] EWHC 2711 (Admin) at [44].

The substantive hearing

15.154 Once a substantive hearing is underway, the disciplinary procedure must comply with public law standards. In practice, the most important source of standards is the principle of natural justice. This is considered alongside the other grounds of judicial review, as well as the applicability of Art 6 of the ECHR. Two initial matters are dealt with, which are the standard of proof and the role of legal assessors.

Standard of proof

15.155 The standard of proof in disciplinary proceedings is usually the civil standard. As such, findings of fact need to be proven on the balance of probabilities.[182] It is important to note that this is not a 'sliding scale' that depends on the seriousness of the allegations. However, the concept of a balance of probabilities ought to take into account the inherent likelihood of something happening.[183] It is submitted that authorities that suggest that a sliding scale or a criminal standard can be adopted in certain circumstances must be treated with caution.[184]

15.156 For instance, in *R (Independent Police Complaints Commission) v Assistant Commissioner Hayman* the assistant commissioner determined that, having regard to the seriousness of the allegations and sanction, it was appropriate for him to consider whether the allegations had been proved beyond a reasonable doubt. As a result, the facts were not proved. On an application for judicial review, it was held that this applied the incorrect standard and so the decision would need to be remitted and taken afresh.[185]

Legal assessors

15.157 A feature of many disciplinary panels or tribunals is the legal assessor. In *Libman v General Medical Council*, Lord Hailsham described the legal assessor's role in the following terms:[186]

> 'The legal assessor who assists the committee at its hearing is not a judge, and his advice to the committee is not a summing up, and no analogy with a criminal appeal against conviction before a judge and jury can properly be drawn. The legal assessor simply advises the committee ... on points of law ... Where a criticism is made of the legal adviser's ... advice the question is whether it can fairly be thought to have been of sufficient significance to the result to invalidate the decision ....'

15.158 Not only must the legal adviser give advice to the Panel on any question of law referred to them, but they must also intervene to advise the Panel in cases where procedural or legal problems may be arising.[187] The legal adviser's role includes a duty

---

[182] *Hutchinson v General Dental Council* [2008] EWHC 2896 (Admin).
[183] *Re B* [2008] UKHL 35 at [13]–[16] and [69]–[73]; and *Re Doherty* [2008] UKHL 33 at [27]–[29] and [44]–[52].
[184] See *Muscat v Health Professions Council* [2008] EWHC 2798 (QB) where a sliding scale was adopted; and *R (Doshi) v Southend on Sea Primary Care Trust* [2007] EWHC 1361 (Admin) where a criminal standard was applied.
[185] *R (Independent Police Complaints Commission) v Assistant Commissioner Hayman* [2008] EWHC 2191 (Admin).
[186] *Libman v GMC* [1972] AC 217, 221. Affirmed in *R (Campbell) v General Medical Council* [2005] EWCA Civ 250 [23]–[24]. See also *Gopakumar v General Medical Council* [2008] EWCA Civ 309.
[187] *R (Sinha) v General Medical Council* [2008] EWHC 1732 (Admin).

to identify points that might assist the absent practitioner.[188] There is also an implied power to allow an adviser to assist with the drafting of written findings.[189]

15.159 The courts have confirmed that in some cases the advice of the legal adviser must be disclosed and the defendant should be given an opportunity to comment on such advice in order to afford the equality of arms required by Art 6 of the European Convention on Human Rights.[190]

Natural justice

15.160 The category of natural justice has been considered in Chapter 1 of this book. In this section, examples of how the principle of natural justice has been applied in the context of professional discipline are given. It is worth noting that the seminal case of *Ridge v Baldwin* was a police discipline case where it was held that natural justice applies not only to judicial decisions but also to administrative decision-making.[191]

Right to be heard

15.161 The right to be heard is an important element of natural justice. In *Kanda v Government of Malaya*, a police officer had been disciplined for misconduct without a reasonable opportunity of being heard because the adjudicating officer had considered a damning report without disclosing the contents to the police officer. The Privy Council held that this was a breach of natural justice.[192] In *Crompton v General Medical Council* there was a similar breach of natural justice as the doctor was not allowed to see or make representations in relation to psychiatrists' reports.[193]

15.162 *Kanda* and *Crompton* are examples of where professionals had been denied access to documents. This is an essential part of the basis of the right to be heard, namely that an accused needs to see the evidence that is used against him. Accordingly, in *R v Ministry of Defence Police, ex p Byrne* it was held to be a breach of natural justice where materially relevant documents had been withheld from the police officer.[194] This point was also made in *McCarthy v Visitors to the Inns of Court* where it was held that it was beyond question that statements that were capable of being used to discredit a witness should be disclosed. The failure to do so in this case was unfair.[195] However, it should be noted that in *McCarthy* the decision was not quashed, as it would have made no difference to the outcome.

15.163 It is important to have an opportunity to refute allegations or findings In *General Medical Council v Spackman* where a doctor was struck off for having an adulterous affair with one of his patients but the GMC did not give him an opportunity to refute the findings of the divorce court.[196] Similarly, in *R v Chief Constable of the West Midlands Police, ex p Carroll*, a police officer was forced to resign over alleged misconduct. However, the finding of misconduct was not the result of any disciplinary

---

[188] *Compton v General Medical Council* [2008] EWHC 2868 (Admin).
[189] *Virdi v Law Society* [2010] EWCA Civ 100 at [33]–[34].
[190] *Nwabueze v General Medical Council* [2000] 1 WLR 1760.
[191] *Ridge v Baldwin* [1964] AC 40.
[192] *Kanda v Government of Malaya* [1962] AC 322.
[193] *Crompton v General Medical Council* [1981] 1 WLR 1435.
[194] *R v Ministry of Defence Police, ex p Byrne* [1994] COD 429.
[195] *McCarthy v Visitors to the Inns of Court* [2013] EWHC 3253 (Admin).
[196] *General Medical Council v Spackman* [1943] AC 627.

proceedings and so there had never been an opportunity to disprove the allegations. The Court of Appeal held that this was unfair and unlawful.[197]

Rights to be represented, to cross-examine, and to a public hearing

15.164 The content of the natural justice principle is typically to provide concrete practical procedural rights. However, these rights are often qualified. For instance, the right to be represented by a lawyer will often assist a professional in the presentation of their case. But in some contexts, this right can be excluded provided that fairness can be achieved without representation. For instance, in *Maynard v Osmond* a police constable challenged the non-availability of legal representation in police disciplinary hearings but it was held that this did not lead to any unfairness.[198] This approach has been held to be compatible with Art 6 of the ECHR.[199]

15.165 It should be noted that if a professional is represented, but the lawyer's conduct causes an adverse outcome for the professional, the outcome can be challenged. For instance, in *Dennis v United Kingdom Central Council for Nursing Midwifery & Health Visiting* a representative did not realise that 'misconduct' had a wider meaning than simply conduct as a nurse. It was held that the panel should have informed the representative of this obvious error and the failure to do so was a procedural error.[200]

15.166 Even if a professional is not represented, there should normally be an opportunity to test the evidence through cross-examination. In *R (Bonhoeffer) v General Medical Council* it was held that it was unfair to allow untested evidence to be used where a doctor faced serious charges amounting to criminal offences. There would have to be compelling reasons to deny the right to cross-examine in such circumstances.[201] There is a limited duty on a disciplinary panel to cross-examine witnesses if it is proceeding without the professional. In *McDaid v Nursing and Midwifery Council* it was held that the panel should try to expose weaknesses in the regulator's case, although this did not require full cross-examination akin to how the professional's representative would have conducted the questioning.[202]

15.167 Hearings should be in public unless there is some countervailing public interest to hear a case in private. Many regulators sit in private when considering a professional's health due to the sensitive nature of the topic. However, a panel cannot simply sit in private as a method of ensuring that a witness will give evidence. In *Miller v General Medical Council* a witness refused to give evidence unless the hearing was in private. Without considering any alternatives, such as screens, the panel decided to sit in private. This decision was successfully challenged as the panel had not probed the reasons for the witness's reluctance to give evidence in public, and had not followed the principles in *R v Legal Aid Board, ex p Kaim Todner*[203] regarding the importance of hearing cases in public.[204]

---

[197] *R v Chief Constable of the West Midlands Police, ex p Carroll* (1995) 7 Admin LR 45.
[198] *Maynard v Osmond* [1977] QB 240.
[199] *Pine v Law Society* [2001] EWCA Civ 1574; *R (Melia) v Merseyside Police* [2003] EWHC 1121 (Admin).
[200] *Dennis v United Kingdom Central Council for Nursing Midwifery & Health Visiting* [1993] 4 Med LR 252.
[201] *R (Bonhoeffer) v General Medical Council* [2011] EWHC 1585 (Admin).
[202] *McDaid v Nursing and Midwifery Council* [2013] EWHC 586 (Admin).
[203] *R v Legal Aid Board, ex p Kaim Todner* [1999] QB 966.
[204] *Miller v General Medical Council* [2013] EWHC 1934 (Admin).

The right to reasons

15.168 A much-contested area of judicial review is when there is a right to receive reasons for a decision. As explained in Chapter 1 there is no general right to reasons. Accordingly, the right has had to be defined in a context-specific manner. Accordingly, in *Gupta v General Medical Council* it was held that there is a duty on a disciplinary panel to give reasons for why a particular sanction was imposed, but not for findings of fact.[205] However, in *Stefan v General Medical Council* it was held that a health committee is obliged to give reasons for its decisions.[206] *Stefan* was relied upon in *Threlfall v General Optical Council* for the proposition that it is important for the parties and the appeal court to be able to understand why the disciplinary panel reached its decision.[207] Furthermore, in *Cheatle v General Medical Council* it was held that because there was contradictory evidence reasons should have been given for findings of fact.[208] It is submitted that *Threlfall* and *Cheatle* represent inroads into the exception provided for in *Gupta*. Where there is particular complexity in a case or if the panel is departing from the views of a specialist adviser, reasons will normally be required.[209]

15.169 If there is a duty to give reasons, the reasons must be adequate. This does not require the disciplinary panel to provide lengthy reasons. The reasons must generally inform the parties why they won or lost.[210] Inadequate reasons were found in *R (Scholten) v General Medical Council* cases where a particularly onerous interim suspension order was imposed without explaining whether the public interest and the professional's interests were balanced.[211] Similarly, failing to address with a professional's case properly in its reasons can be unlawful.[212]

Rule against bias

15.170 The rule against apparent bias was authoritatively defined in *Porter v Magill* in terms of 'whether the fair-minded observer, having considered the facts, would conclude that there was a real possibility that the tribunal was biased'.[213] The fair-minded observer is taken to be a person who will reserve judgment until the information has been fairly considered.[214] This is a test of general application and has been considered several times in the disciplinary context. Typically, a claimant will argue that there is real possibility that a panel member was biased.

15.171 For instance, in *Ighalo v Solicitors Regulation Authority* it was argued that because a panel member has previously been an adjudicator for the SRA, this created a real possibility of bias. However, the High Court held that since the panel member was

---

[205] *Gupta v General Medical Council* [2001] UKPC 61.
[206] *Stefan v General Medical Council* [1999] 1 WLR 1293.
[207] *Threlfall v General Optical Council* [2004] EWHC 2683 (Admin).
[208] *Cheatle v General Medical Council* [2009] EWHC 645 (Admin).
[209] See *Southall v General Medical Council* [2010] EWCA Civ 40 (reasons in complex cases); *Yanah v General Medical Council* [2006] EWHC 3843 (Admin) and *Cullen v General Medical Council* [2005] EWHC 353 (Admin) (reasons when departing from experts' view).
[210] *Southall v General Medical Council* [2010] EWCA Civ 40 and *Phipps v General Medical Council (Application for Permission to Appeal)* [2006] EWCA Civ 397.
[211] *R (Scholten) v General Medical Council* [2013] EWHC 173 (Admin). See also *Council for the Regulation of Healthcare Professionals v General Dental Council* [2006] EWHC 1870 (Admin).
[212] See *R (Wheeler) v Assistant Commissioner of the Metropolitan Police* [2008] EWHC 439 (Admin); *Ogango v Nursing and Midwifery Council* [2008] EWHC 3115 (Admin); and *D'Souza v Law Society* [2006] EWHC 987 (Admin).
[213] *Porter v Magill* [2001] UKHL 67.
[214] *Virdi v Law Society* [2010] EWCA Civ 100 to [42]–[44], citing *Helow v Secretary of State for the Home Department* [2008] UKHL 62 at [1]–[3].

no longer an adjudicator and had never been involved in the investigation of this case, there was no apparent bias.[215] Similarly, the payment of fees and expenses by the prosecuting authority is unlikely to give rise to apparent bias.[216] By contrast, where members of the regulatory body sit on the disciplinary panel this can give rise to apparent bias.[217]

15.172 Similarly, the conduct of panellists during hearings can lead to allegations of apparent bias. In *Muscat v Health Professions Council* it was argued that a panellist's questioning of the professional amounted to a real possibility of bias. This was because the panellist had shaken her finger at the professional and been strident in her questioning. However, the High Court found that these questions had been fair and unobjectionable, and so there was no apparent bias.[218] When assessing whether the behaviour of a panellist amounts to bias, it is important to look at any such behaviour in context.[219]

Waiver

15.173 An important qualification to the natural justice principle is where due process rights have been waived. In *R (Hill) v Institute of Chartered Accountants* a panellist was temporarily absent during a disciplinary hearing. The advocates for each party agreed to this. However, having been struck off, the accountant sought to challenge the panellist's absence on natural justice grounds. The Court of Appeal held that there was no breach of natural justice as the professional's waiver prevented such a breach from occurring in the first place.[220]

Article 6 of the European Convention on Human Rights

Does Article 6 apply?

15.174 There has been difficulty in establishing exactly when the protections of Art 6 apply in the disciplinary context. The first issue is whether the professional regulator is engaging in functions of a public nature so that s 6 of the Human Rights Act 1998 is satisfied. In the healthcare context, this was answered affirmatively in the case of *Tehrani v United Kingdom Central Council for Nursing Midwifery and Health Visiting*.[221] However, in the non-healthcare context it is possible that issues regarding whether a regulator is a public authority may arise.

---

[215] *Ighalo v Solicitors Regulation Authority* [2013] EWHC 661 (Admin).
[216] *Leathley v Bar Standards Board* [2012] All ER (D) 110 (Jan).
[217] See *R (Kaur) v Institute of Legal Executives Appeal Tribunal* [2011] EWCA Civ 1168 and *P (A Barrister) v General Council of the Bar* [2005] 1 WLR 3019. Compare these cases with *Holmes v Royal College of Veterinary Surgeons* [2011] UKPC 48 and *Colman v General Medical Council* [2010] EWHC 1608 (QB) where there was no bias despite an arguably prima facie overlap in personnel. In *Holmes*, there was in fact separation between the prosecuting and adjudicating bodies. In *Colman*, a deputy registrar was not a prosecutor and there was no apparent bias in the registrar assisting the panel with the drafting of its determination.
[218] *Muscat v Health Professions Council* [2008] EWHC 2798 (QB). See also *Roylance v General Medical Council (No 2)* [2000] 1 AC 311.
[219] See, for instance, *R (Ashby) v Royal Pharmaceutical Society of Great Britain* [2008] EWHC 1739 (Admin) at [39]–[40].
[220] *R (Hill) v Institute of Chartered Accountants* [2013] EWCA Civ 555.
[221] *Tehrani v United Kingdom Central Council for Nursing Midwifery and Health Visiting* 2001 SC 581. It should be noted that it was agreed between the parties that the regulator was a public authority (see [31]). In the healthcare context, this proposition has not been disputed in any reported case since.

15.175 To determine this issue, the court takes a factor-based approach to resolve whether a person is exercising 'functions of a public nature'.[222] Relevant factors include whether the body: receives public funding, provides a public service or acts in the public interest, has coercive or statutory powers, and is subject to government control. These factors are not exhaustive. It should be noted that s 6(5) provides that if a person is exercising functions of a public nature but the act complained of is 'a private act' then HRA will not apply. It is submitted that it is relevant whether the body is considered to be amenable to judicial review generally.[223]

15.176 The second issue, assuming that the HRA 1998 applies to the professional regulator, is whether the protections of Art 6 apply. Case-law indicates that the key consideration is whether the outcome of the proceedings is capable of affecting a practitioner's ability to continue working in their chosen profession.[224] This is because such an outcome amounts to a determination of civil rights.[225]

15.177 Accordingly, it would seem to follow that Art 6 applies in substantive hearings before disciplinary panels but not before interim orders panels or during the investigatory stage.[226] However, it has been held that interim suspension orders made by the General Medical Council do engage Art 6 as such orders deny a professional the right to work, albeit not permanently.[227] An explanation for this difference is that internal disciplinary proceedings do not necessarily deny a professional from working in the chosen industry completely, while regulatory proceedings can entail such a denial.[228]

15.178 The outcome-based approach has been strongly criticised. In *Threlfall v General Optical Council* it was said that it was:

> '... obvious that the applicability of Article 6 must be determined on the basis of the jurisdiction and powers of the tribunal rather than its ultimate decision. The adjectival law applicable to its proceedings must be determined before the proceedings begin rather than after they have been completed. Thus the question whether a person subject to disciplinary proceedings is entitled to a "fair and public hearing ... by an independent and impartial tribunal" must be determined before the hearing and *before* its result is known.'[229]

15.179 The resolution of this tension appears to be that if the jurisdiction that is being exercised 'could' result in the professional being unable to practise Art 6 is engaged. This is supported by the decision in *Tehrani* and confirmed by the Court of Appeal in *R (Thompson) v The Law Society*.[230]

---

[222] See *Aston Cantlow and Wilmcote with Billesley Parochial Church Council v Wallbank* [2003] UKHL 37 at [7], [11]–[12]; *YL v Birmingham City Council* [2007] UKHL 27 and *R (Weaver) v London & Quadrant Housing Trust* [2009] EWCA Civ 587 at [35].
[223] *R (McIntyre) v Gentoo Group Ltd* [2010] EWHC 5 (Admin) at [21].
[224] *Konig v Germany* (1979-80) 2 EHRR 170 at [86]–[97]; *Albert and Le Compte v Belgium* (1983) 5 EHRR 533 at [28]; *R (Wright) v Secretary of State for Health* [2009] UKHL 3, [2009] 1 AC 739. For a summary of recent authorities see *Re B* [2011] EWHC 2362 (Admin) at [38]–[99].
[225] *Albert and le Compte v Belgium* (1983) 5 EHRR 533.
[226] See *R (Malik) v Waltham Forest NHS* [2007] EWCA Civ 265 (interim suspension did not engage Art 6).
[227] *Madan v General Medical Council* [2001] EWHC Admin 577 at [50].
[228] See *Mattu v The University Hospitals of Coventry and Warwickshire NHS Trust* [2012] EWCA Civ 641 but compare with *Kulkarni v Milton Keynes Hospital NHS Trust* [2009] EWCA Civ 789 (recently distinguished in *R (Puri) v Bradford Teaching Hospitals NHS Foundation Trust* [2011] EWHC 970 (Admin). See also *R (G) v The Governors of X School* [2011] UKSC 30 where the overlap of such proceedings in considered and the 'substantial influence' test was endorsed.
[229] *Threlfall v General Optical Council* [2004] EWHC 2683 (Admin) at [33].
[230] *Tehrani v United Kingdom Central Council for Nursing Midwifery and Health Visiting* 2001 SC 581 at [44] and *R (Thompson) v The Law Society* [2004] EWCA Civ 167 at [83].

15.180 Accordingly, the applicability of Art 6 throughout the different stages of the fitness to practise process is as follows:

Stage in process	Decision	Does Article 6 apply?	Reason
Information received by regulator	Decision to consider information to be an allegation	No	Decision does not determine registrant's ability to practice.
Screening process	Decision to refer to Investigation Committee	No	Decision does not determine registrant's ability to practice.
Investigatory process	Decision to refer to Fitness to Practice Panel	No[231]	Decision does not determine registrant's ability to practice.
Fitness to Practice hearings (mainstream / health)	Decision to impose sanction	Yes	Decision determines registrant's ability to practice.
Resumed hearings	Decision to continue to impose suspension / conditions	Yes	Decision determines registrant's ability to practice.
Interim Order hearings	Decision to impose suspension / conditions	Yes[232]	Decision determines registrant's ability to practice.
Restoration hearings	Decision to restore a person to the Register	Yes	Decision determines registrant's ability to practice.
Fraudulent register entry hearings	Decision to remove registrant	Yes	Decision determines registrant's ability to practice.

15.181 It should be noted that there is an issue in cases of parallel proceedings. For instance, a professional may be subject to an internal disciplinary procedure as well as regulatory proceedings by the professional regulator. The question regarding Art 6 is whether the relevant procedural protections should apply in a situation where Art 6 would not normally apply. The Supreme Court confirmed that the correct approach is

---

[231] *David v General Medical Council* [2004] EWHC 2977 at [35].
[232] *Madan (No 2) v General Medical Council* [2001] Lloyd's Rep Med 539 at [50] and [80].

whether one set of proceedings (where Art 6 does apply) will have a substantial influence over proceedings where Art 6 would not normally apply.[233]

If Article 6 applies, what is the content?

15.182 Assuming that it is established that Art 6 applies, there is a further issue regarding the content of the protections that are provided. This issue arises because Art 6 is split into two-tiers – criminal and civil protections. In the criminal context, Art 6 entitles a person to representation and specific procedural rights, such as a right to cross-examine. In the civil context, the principal right is 'to a fair and public hearing within a reasonable time by an independent and impartial tribunal established by law'.

15.183 Given these two limbs of Art 6, the courts have not been content to classify regulatory proceedings as purely civil proceedings given that the nature of some allegations could clearly amount to criminal conduct. Accordingly, the criminal limb of Art 6 can be relevant in regulatory proceedings.[234] Indeed in *Albert and Le Compte v Belgium*, the ECtHR said that:

> 'For its part, the Court does not believe that the two aspects, civil and criminal, of Article 6(1) are necessarily mutually exclusive ... Dr Albert relied in addition on paragraph 2 and on sub-paragraphs (a), (b) and (d) of paragraph 3 [the criminal limb], but, in the opinion of the Court, the principles enshrined therein are, for the present purposes, already contained in the notion of a fair trial as embodied in paragraph 1 [the civil limb]; the Court will therefore take these principles into account in the context of paragraph 1.'[235]

15.184 The court went on to say:

> 'In the opinion of the Court, the principles set out in paragraph 2 and in the provisions of paragraph 3 invoked by Dr Albert (that is to say only sub-paragraphs (a), (b) and (d)) are applicable, *mutatis mutandis*, to disciplinary proceedings subject to paragraph 1 in the same way as in the case of a person charged with a criminal offence.'

15.185 Taking the relevant aspects of Art 6 together, the following rights appear to be applicable in the disciplinary context. First, in terms of the civil limb: the right to a fair hearing; the right to a public hearing;[236] the right to a hearing within a reasonable time;[237] the right to an independent and impartial tribunal established by law;[238] the right to have judgment pronounced publicly.[239] These requirements are similar to the

---

[233] *R (G) v The Governors of X School* [2011] UKSC 30 at [64]–[69].
[234] *R (Fleurose) v Securities and Futures Authority Ltd* [2001] EWCA Civ 2015; [2002] IRLR 297 at [9] and [14].
[235] *Albert and le Compte v Belgium* (1983) 5 EHRR 533 at [30].
[236] *Gautrin and others v France* (1999) 28 EHRR 196.
[237] *Johnson v Nursing and Midwifery Council* [2013] EWHC 2140 (Admin).
[238] See *Sadler v General Medical Council* [2003] UKPC 59 [2003] 1 WLR 2259 PC where it was held that GMC's Committee on Professional Performance was an independent and impartial tribunal satisfying Art 6. Compare with *R (Kaur) v Institute of Legal Executives Appeal Tribunal* [2011] EWCA Civ 1168. For what constitutes 'independence' see *Bryan v United Kingdom* (1995) 21 EHRR 342 at [37], *Zand v Austria* [1981] ECC 50 at [78]–[80]; and *Starrs v Ruxtion* 2000 JC 208. For what constitutes 'impartiality' see *Piersack v Belgium* (1983) 5 EHRR 169 at [30]; *Gautrin and others v France* (1999) 28 EHRR 196 at [58].
[239] *Gautrin and others v France* (1999) 28 EHRR 196 at [42]. This right can be waived (*Le Compte, Van Leuwen and de Meyere v Belgium* (1982) 4 EHRR 1 at [59]) but not if this runs counter to an important public interest (*Schuler-Zgraggen v Switzerland* (1993) 16 EHRR 405 at [58]). Any exceptions to this right must be interpreted narrowly: *Diennet v France* (1996) 21 EHRR 554 at [34].

common law concept of natural justice and include knowing the case that has to be met;[240] having an opportunity to make representations;[241] and being able to extend time to bring a case.[242]

15.186 Second, in terms of the relevant parts of the criminal limb (as identified in *Albert and Le Compte*): the right to a presumption of innocence;[243] the right to be informed promptly of the nature and cause of the accusation;[244] the right to have enough time to prepare a defence; the right to examine witnesses;[245] and the right to legal representation.[246]

15.187 The court has also developed a doctrine known as 'equality of arms', which allows all parties to proceedings to have a reasonable opportunity of presenting their case under conditions that 'do not place him at a substantial disadvantage vis-à-vis his opponent'.[247]

15.188 Overall, Art 6 is based on 'benign and flexible' principles, rather than inflexible rules.[248] Accordingly, whether a fair hearing has been achieved will always depend on all the circumstances of the case.[249]

15.189 However, if there are such failings, the possibility of judicial review or an appeal can cure the breach by allowing an independent and impartial tribunal to reconsider the matter.[250] It has been held that to cure any Art 6 defects, an onward appeal must be unrestricted and amount to an opportunity to rehear the case.[251] Therefore, an appeal on a point of law or judicial review may not be sufficient where matters of fact are in issue.[252]

Unreasonableness

15.190 It is elementary that a decision of a disciplinary panel can be challenged where a discretion has been exercised unreasonably, applying the principles derived from *Associated Provincial Picture Houses Ltd v Wednesbury Corporation*.[253] This is discussed in more detail in Chapter 1 of this book. The *Wednesbury* standard is variable

---

[240] *Secretary of State for the Home Department v AF (No 3)* [2009] UKHL 28.
[241] *R (Wright) v Secretary of State for Health* [2009] UKHL 3 at [28].
[242] *Pomiechowski v District Court of Legnica* [2012] UKSC 20 at [37].
[243] *Albert and Le Compte v Belgium* (1983) 5 EHRR 533; *Official Reciever v Stern* [2000] 1 WLR 2230 at [30].
[244] *Brozicek v Italy* (1989) 112 EHRR 371.
[245] *R (Bonhoeffer) v General Medical Council* [2011] EWHC 1585 (Admin) at [108].
[246] *R (G) v The Governors of X School* [2011] UKSC 30.
[247] See *Neumeister v Austria* (1968) 1 EHRR 81; *Dombo Beheer BV v The Netherlands* (1994) 18 EHRR 213; *Niderost-Huber v Switzerland* [1997] ECHR 18990/91 at [23]; and *SH v Finland* [2008] 28301/03.
[248] *R v Spear* [2001] QB 804, 819; *R (Husain) v Asylum Support Adjudicator* [2001] EWHC Admin 852 at [70].
[249] *R (Fleurose) v Securities and Futures Authority* [2001] EWCA Civ 2015 at [14].
[250] *R (Alconbury Developments Ltd) v Secretary of State for the Environment, Transport and the Regions* [2001] UKHL 23; *R (Begum) v Tower Hamlets London Borough Council* [2003] UKHL 5; *Tehrani v United Kingdom Central Council for Nursing, Midwifery and Health Visiting* [2001] ScotCS 19 at [55].
[251] See *Ghosh v General Medical Council* [2001] 1 WLR 1915; *Preiss v General Dental Council* [2001] 1 WLR 1926 and *Gupta v General Medical Council* [2002] 1 WLR 1691.
[252] See *Kingsley v United Kingdom* [2001] ECHR 526 and *Bryan v United Kingdom* (1995) 21 EHRR 342.
[253] *Associated Provincial Picture Houses Ltd v Wednesbury Corporation* [1948] 1 KB 223.

depending on the circumstances. In the context of disciplinary proceedings, a wide margin in afforded to such specialist tribunals.[254] The threshold has been described as one of perversity.[255]

15.191 An example is *R (Al-Zayyat) v General Medical Council* where the disciplinary panel held that a doctor was deliberately and voluntarily absent from the hearing. This was challenged by way of judicial review and the court held that there was psychiatric evidence that she could not participate in the hearing. As there was no sufficient evidential basis for the panel's decision, it was legally perverse.[256]

15.192 Similarly, in *R (Li) v General Medical Council* a doctor sought voluntary erasure from the register and a stay of proceedings. These were both refused and the disciplinary panel continued with a hearing despite medical evidence that the doctor could not participate. The decisions were held to be irrational as the refusal of voluntary erasure had taken into account irrelevant considerations and the medical evidence was unchallenged.[257]

15.193 A further example is *R (Chong) v Law Society* where an adjudicator's decision was described as perverse for failing to grapple with the gravamen of the complaint. This was in relation to an alleged deception regarding referral fees.[258]

Illegality

15.194 Illegality is a broad category of judicial review. The various grounds of judicial review within this category are described in Chapter 1 of this book. The most important principle in this context is the *ultra vires* principle, which precludes the regulators from acting beyond their powers.

15.195 The powers and duties of the regulators will be defined by their statutory scheme. In addition, the disciplinary panel or tribunal will operate in accordance with published procedural rules. Such rules must be followed and cannot be set aside if a professional argues that they are contrary to natural justice.[259] It has been held that a panel or tribunal can have implied powers incidental to its jurisdiction such as a power to regulate its procedure and a power to make such administrative arrangements as are appropriate for it to discharge its functions.[260] Therefore, it was not *ultra vires* for the Solicitors Disciplinary Tribunal to instruct or invite its clerk to assist it when it retired or drafted its findings and decisions.[261] Although the issue of *ultra vires* actions can be raised on a judicial review application[262] this can equally be raised on appeal. As noted elsewhere, the appropriate procedure will always depend on whether there is an alternative method of challenging the decision.

15.196 An important element of the illegality principle is clarifying the source of law in question. The legal status of rules that have been issued by the regulators but have not

---

[254] *Walker v General Medical Council* [2010] EWHC 3849 (Admin) at [10].
[255] *Loutfi v General Medical Council* [2010] EWHC 1762 (Admin) at [27].
[256] *R (Al-Zayyat) v General Medical Council* [2010] EWHC 3213 (Admin).
[257] *R (Li) v General Medical Council* [2013] EWHC 522 (Admin).
[258] *R (Chong) v Law Society* [2007] EWHC 641 (Admin) at [24]. The claim was dismissed on other grounds.
[259] See *R v Honourable Society of the Middle Temple, ex p Bullock* [1996] ELR 349.
[260] *Virdi v Law Society of England and Wales* [2010] EWCA Civ 100 at [30]–[31].
[261] *Virdi v Law Society of England and Wales* [2010] EWCA Civ 100.
[262] *R (Rutter) v The General Teaching Council for England* [2008] EWHC 133 (Admin) at [25].

been approved by Parliament is that they have the full force of law if authorised by statute. This applies irrespective of whether or not the relevant rules have been laid in Parliament or the person entrusted with issuing the rules is not an emanation of the state.[263]

15.197 It should be noted that the Visitors to the Inns of Court exercise a special jurisdiction derived from the Crown and exercisable by judges to regulate lawyers.[264] It has been held that the appointment of a member could be valid under the doctrine of *de facto* authority.[265] This is the doctrine that legally valid decisions can be taken even where there was no authority to do so, although the extent of this doctrine is unclear.[266]

15.198 In addition to the procedural rules that govern how the disciplinary panels conduct hearings, there is often further guidance or policy issued by the regulators to assist the panels with certain decisions. The most common example is indicative sanctions guidance, which is considered in more detail below. When guidance is referred to by panels, it is important that it is not treated as binding as this will amount to an unlawful fetter of their discretion.

15.199 For instance, in *Perry v Nursing and Midwifery Council* it was held that guidance directed at interim orders panels operated as an unlawful fetter as it required panels to prefer interim suspension orders rather than an interim conditions of practice order.[267] Similarly, in *R v Chief Constable of the Thames Valley Police, ex p Police Complaints Authority* it was held that a disciplinary board had unlawfully fettered its discretion by not continuing with proceedings because the Director of Public Prosecutions had decided not to prosecute the officers. By treating the Director's decision as binding the board had failed to make its own decision.[268]

15.200 Guidance is open to challenge in its own right. Two examples of where guidance was challenged are *R (Burke) v General Medical Council* and *R v General Medical Council, ex p Colman*. In *Burke* guidance relating to the withholding and withdrawal of life-prolonging treatments was challenged. At first instance, the aspects of the guidance were declared to be unlawful as it was among other things contrary to Art 8 of the ECHR.[269] The Court of Appeal reversed this decision and held that while a decision contrary to the wishes of a patient might violate Arts 2, 3 and 8 of the ECHR, the guidance itself was lawful.

15.201 In *ex p Colman*, a would-be holistic practitioner sought to challenge the GMC's guidance that banned advertising in the press. It was argued that this guidance was irrational on the basis that it was a restraint of trade – the Court of Appeal disagreed and held that it would be unconstitutional to review actions that were reasonable and *intra vires*.[270]

---

[263] *Swain v Law Society* [1983] 1 AC 598 and *Mohamed v Alaga* [1998] 2 All ER 720.
[264] *R v General Council of the Bar, ex p Percival* [1991] 1 QB 212, at 227.
[265] *Russell v Bar Standards Board* [2012] All ER (D) 122.
[266] See *Fawdry v Murfitt* [2003] QB 104.
[267] *Perry v Nursing and Midwifery Council* [2012] EWHC 2275 (Admin) at [46].
[268] *R v Chief Constable of the Thames Valley Police, ex p Police Complaints Authority* [1996] COD 324.
[269] *R (Burke) v General Medical Council* [2004] EWHC 1879 (Admin).
[270] *R v General Medical Council, ex p Colman* [1990] 1 All ER 489.

15.202 While these cases were not successful attacks on regulatory guidance, it is important to note that such challenges are possible. Further detail on such challenges is provided in Chapter 1.

Sanctions

15.203 A sanction may be imposed if a disciplinary panel makes findings of fact that leads to the conclusion that the professional is guilty of misconduct, poor performance or any other disciplinary ground. The availability of sanctions differs between the regulators. Most regulators can strike off (erase), suspend or impose conditions on a professional.[271] However, some regulators can also reprimand or fine a registrant.[272]

15.204 Choosing the appropriate sanction is a question of judgment for the disciplinary panel, and it is assessed at the time of the hearing.[273] Most regulators adopt a 'ladder approach' to sanctions. This involves considering lesser sanctions before greater sanctions.[274] It is submitted this is right in principle as it enables sanctions to be proportionate to the public safety risk a professional represented. Such an approach helps the tribunal to avoid excessive sanctions.[275] This is consistent with the principle that disciplinary sanctions are not to be applied for primarily punitive purposes.[276]

15.205 Many regulators make use of indicative sanctions guidance. Such guidance is meant to assist the disciplinary tribunal to choose the appropriate sanction, and provides a useful starting point in most cases[277] and it aids transparency.[278] Regard should normally be had to such guidance where it exists.[279] Although it is important that the tribunal does not treat guidance as binding and makes its own assessment in each case. To do otherwise may amount to an unlawful fetter on the tribunal's discretion.[280]

15.206 During a disciplinary hearing there is sometimes discussion that may include an indication about the sanction that will be sought in relation to a professional. In *Finegan v General Medical Council* it was held that a disciplinary panel is not obliged to provide such an indication.[281]

---

[271] Where conditions are imposed they must be precisely worded and workable (*Daraghmeh v General Medical Council* [2011] EWHC 2080 (Admin)) and must not be incompatible with registration (*Udom v General Medical Council* [2010] Med LR 37).
[272] For instance, the General Optical Council can impose fines while the General Dental Council can impose fines on companies.
[273] *Zygmunt v General Medical Council* [2008] EWHC 2643 (Admin).
[274] See, for instance, *MacLeod v Royal College of Veterinary Surgeons* [2006] UKPC 39 at [25]; *Luthra v General Medical Council* [2013] EWHC 240 (Admin) at [27].
[275] An excessive sanction can be a ground of appeal. See, for instance, *Dad v General Dental Council* [2000] 1 WLR 1538 and *Preiss v General Dental Council* [2001] 1 WLR 1926 where the sanctions imposed were excessive.
[276] *Raschid v General Medical Council* [2007] 1 WLR 1460 at [18] and *Meadow v General Medical Council* [2006] EWCA Civ 1390, [2007] 1 QB 462 at [32]; *Brennan v Health Professions Council* [2011] EWHC 41 (Admin).
[277] *Sanders v Ethical Standards Officer* [2005] EWHC 2132 (Admin) at [27].
[278] *Hazelhurst v Solicitors Regulation Authority* [2011] EWHC 462 (Admin) at [38].
[279] See *R (Coghlan) v Chief Constable of Greater Manchester Police* [2004] EWHC 2801 (Admin) where there had been a failure to take into account sanctions guidance.
[280] See *R v Police Complaints Board, ex p Madden* [1983] 1 WLR 447 where the guidance was treated as binding.
[281] *Finegan v General Medical Council* [1987] 1 WLR 121. This was confirmed in *R (Russell) v General Medical Council* [2008] EWHC 2546 (Admin).

15.207 An issue can arise when a professional has been made subject to a sanction by a foreign regulator. It has been held that if the domestic regulator imposes a different sanction, there is no duty to provide reasons for the departure. In *R (Alhy) v General Medical Council* a doctor had been suspended by his regulator in France in relation to offences concerning the deaths of two of his patients. He failed to inform the GMC about this, and the GMC's disciplinary panel decided to strike him off the register having taken into account the convictions and the failure to report. It was held that the panel's task is simply to assess the matters in accordance with the GMC legislation and its code of conduct.[282]

Appeals

15.208 Appeals against sanctions are the most common way to challenge decisions by disciplinary panels. Due to the alternative remedy principle, an appeal is usually more advisable than a challenge by way of judicial review. Furthermore, in contrast to judicial review, such appeals do not normally require permission. Of course, appeals are only available to the professional who has been made subject to sanction. A complainant or member of the public would need to use judicial review to challenge the findings of a disciplinary panel.

15.209 The approach to appeals is informed by the judgment of Sir Thomas Bingham MR in *Bolton v Law Society* which indicated that there is a high threshold to be met to challenge sanction decisions. This is because the disciplinary committee is in the best place to weigh the seriousness of any professional misconduct.[283]

15.210 The *Bolton* approach has been slightly qualified since the enactment of the Human Rights Act 1998. Accordingly, the correct analysis is that the disciplinary panel comprises an expert and informed tribunal, and so it is well placed to assess what measures are required to protect the public interest. Absent any error of law, the High Court must pay considerable respect to the sentencing decisions of the tribunal. Nevertheless if the High Court, despite paying such respect, is satisfied that the sentencing decision was clearly inappropriate, then the court will interfere.[284]

15.211 It should be noted that while appeals from the Solicitors Regulation Authority are done by way of 'review' and appeals from the healthcare regulators are appeals by way of a rehearing, in practice the approach is similar. This is because although the appeal by way of a rehearing is the appeal it is in reality a review of the evidence and material before the Panel.[285] The parameters for such appeals were set down in *Ghosh v General Medical Council* and *Gupta v General Medical Council*.

15.212 In *Ghosh* it was emphasised that the jurisdiction is truly appellate rather than supervisory, and so on appeal the court may substitute its view in place of the disciplinary tribunal's decision.[286] However, in *Gupta* it was held that appeals would normally be on the basis of the transcript of the hearing, and witnesses would only be

---

[282] *R (Alhy) v General Medical Council* [2011] EWHC 2277 (Admin).
[283] *Bolton v Law Society* [1994] 1 WLR 512, 516.
[284] *Law Society v Salsbury* [2008] EWCA Civ 1285 at [30]. See also *Harris v Solicitors Regulation Authority* [2011] EWHC 2173 (Admin) at [13].
[285] *Chyc v General Medical Council* [2008] EWHC 1025 (Admin) at [4]; and *Nagiub v General Medical Council* [2011] EWHC 366 (Admin) at [6]; *Sheill v General Medical Council* [2008] EWHC 2967 (Admin) at [12]–[15].
[286] *Ghosh v General Medical Council* [2001] UKPC 29.

called in exceptional circumstances. It was inevitable that preference would be given to the tribunal's findings on evidential issues.[287]

15.213 This has given rise to a delicate position whereby the appeal court has the power to come to its own judgment, but this judgment will be 'distinctly and firmly a secondary judgment'.[288] The reason for this was fully explained in *Threlfall v General Optical Council* where it was said that:[289]

> '... the Disciplinary Committee was in a far better position to assess the reliability of the evidence of live witnesses where it was in issue ... The Disciplinary Committee possesses professional expertise that a High Court judge lacks ... such a Disciplinary Committee is better qualified to assess evidence relating to professional practise, and the gravity of any shortcomings, and it therefore accords the decision of the Committee an appropriate measure of respect, but no more ... an Appellant must establish an error, of law or fact or of judgment, on the part of the tribunal.'

15.214 Importantly, this approach precludes the appellate court from applying the *Wednesbury* standard of reasonableness.[290]

15.215 All appeals must be brought within a certain time limit that will have been specified in the regulators' governing legislation. There is authority that where time limits are inflexible, Art 6 of the ECHR can be used to create discretion to extend time in exceptional circumstances. In *Adesina v Nursing and Midwifery Council*, the Court of Appeal held that this discretion would only be used where the appellant had personally done all he could to bring the appeal timeously.[291] In *Adegbulugbe v Nursing and Midwifery Council*, the appellant was unable to provide a sufficient explanation for the delay and so the late appeal was not entertained.[292]

Costs

15.216 Not all of the regulators have a costs jurisdiction. Those that do include the General Dental Council, the General Pharmaceutical Council, the Institute of Chartered Accountants in England and Wales and the Solicitors Regulation Authority. A power to award costs will not normally be found unless the relevant rules or regulations specifically provide for such a power.[293]

15.217 Costs do not normally follow the event because it is recognised that the regulator is performing a public protection role.[294] Accordingly, all the facts of the case should be taken into account before a costs award is made against a professional.[295]

---

[287] *Gupta v General Medical Council* [2001] UKPC 61.
[288] *Raschid v General Medical Council* [2007] EWCA Civ 46 at [20].
[289] *Threlfall v General Optical Council* [2004] EWHC 2683 (Admin) at [21]. See also *Gupta v General Medical Council* [2001] UKPC 61 at [10].
[290] *R (Chief Constable of Avon and Somerset Police) v Police Appeals Tribunal* [2004] EWHC 220 (Admin).
[291] *Adesina v Nursing and Midwifery Council* [2013] EWCA Civ 818, applying *Pomiechowski v Poland* [2012] UKSC 20.
[292] *Adegbulugbe v Nursing and Midwifery Council* [2013] EWHC 3301 (Admin). This case is also a chastening reminder that legal representatives must keep up to date with case-law and must prepare appeals properly. In this matter, Andrews J noted at [26]: 'The appeal has been shoddily prepared and its presentation falls well below the professional standards that are to be expected in any court.'
[293] See *R v South Yorkshire Police Authority, ex p Booth* [2000] Po LR 335.
[294] *Baxendale-Walker v Law Society* [2007] EWCA Civ 233.
[295] See, for instance, *Beresford v Solicitors Regulation Authority* [2009] EWHC 3155 (Admin).

15.218 Costs decisions can be challenged by way of judicial review. For instance in *R (Gorlov) v Institute of Chartered Accountants in England and Wales*, an accountant was successful in challenging a decision to not award costs to him after it was held that the disciplinary proceedings that had been brought against him were a nullity. Accordingly, it was irrational not to award costs.[296]

Postscript: Judicial review of the regulators by the regulators

15.219 The final issue to be discussed in this chapter concerns how and when regulators might judicially review themselves. A decision of a disciplinary panel may be riddled with legal errors but also favour the professional, and so is unlikely to be appealed. Some regulators rightly feel aggrieved about this, but do not have the benefit of a statutory right of appeal. The only remaining option appears to be judicial review.

15.220 When a decision-maker has discharged its legal functions, it is described as being *functus officio*. Whether a decision-maker is *functus* is usually an issue that arises when considering whether it has power to reconsider a decision. Unless there is specific provision stating otherwise, the regulator will not be able to set aside the decision. The result is that to overturn a decision, it would be necessary to seek a quashing order by way of judicial review.

15.221 The *functus* principle is engaged when a disciplinary tribunal has come to a final decision on culpability and sanction. In particular, this means when the tribunal has made its order, even if reasons are to follow, as happened in *Baxendale-Walker v Law Society*. The court said that 'by reference to the statutory jurisdiction of the tribunal and, as a matter of principle' the SDT had discharged its functions and so could not reconsider its decision.[297]

15.222 'Slip rules' cannot be used to avoid the *functus* principle. This was considered in *R (B) v Nursing and Midwifery Council* (as noted above) where the Investigating Committee of the NMC sought to set aside one of its decisions. Although not expressed in terms of the *functus* principle, it is clear from the judgment that the investigating committee had discharged its functions and that without statutory authority it could not set aside its decision.[298]

15.223 This basis of the decision in *B* was the Court of Appeal's judgment in *Akewushola v Secretary of State for the Home Department*. This provided that tribunals only have a limited power 'to correct accidental errors which do not substantially affect the rights of the parties or the decision arrived at', which is akin to CPR r 40.12.[299] Importantly, both *Akewushola* and the *B* case highlight that it is not possible to manoeuvre around the *functus* principle by relying on supposed 'slips' or 'accidental errors'.

15.224 Accordingly, it is clear that once the tribunal has made a decision it has discharged its functions and the *functus officio* principle bites. As a statutory appeal is not available to the regulatory body, the only option is to pursue judicial review.

---

[296] *R (Gorlov) v Institute of Chartered Accountants in England and Wales* [2001] EWHC Admin 220.
[297] *Baxendale-Walker v Law Society* [2006] EWHC 643 (Admin) at [23].
[298] *R (B) v Nursing and Midwifery Council* [2012] EWHC 1264 (Admin).
[299] *Akewushola v Secretary of State for the Home Department* [2000] 1 WLR 2295.

15.225 However, such a judicial review can create practical problems. The best example of a professional regulator judicially reviewing itself is *R v Statutory Committee of the Pharmaceutical Society of Great Britain, ex p Pharmaceutical Society of Great Britain*. In this case, the regulator was granted quashing and mandatory orders against its disciplinary committee.

15.226 Given that judicial review was the only available route to the regulator, it is understandable that no issue was taken in the PSGB case on whether the regulator could judicially review its disciplinary committee. There is unlikely to be a principled objection to a regulator taking a similar course. What follows are four suggestions for how such cases may be conducted.

15.227 First, the normal practice in judicial review cases is to engage with the pre-action protocol by sending a letter before claim. One of the purposes of the protocol is to encourage settlement and to narrow the issues – however, in cases where the *functus officio* principle bites settlement is not possible. The best that can be hoped for is a consent order approved by the court.

15.228 Accordingly, it may be sensible for the regulator to send a letter before action that is aimed both at the defendant and registrant (as an interested party). This may help narrow the issues and begin communication about whether a consent order is possible. This is the policy of the Treasury Solicitor in *functus* cases and there is evidence that it is a useful process.[300] It also provides extra cover if the court asks whether there should be any cost consequences for failing to engage with the protocol.[301]

15.229 Secondly, the regulator will need to decide about the details of the defendant. Referring to the '*Fitness to Practice Panel of the General XYZ Council*' is likely to be sufficient. However, there is a deeper problem here: to handle the case properly, the individuals who receive the judicial review ought to be sufficiently independent of the regulator.

15.230 This will not be an issue for some regulators where efforts have been made to separate the disciplinary functions from the other regulatory functions. For instance, the General Medical Council would be able to serve its judicial review on the Medical Practitioners Tribunal Service (MPTS), and the MPTS should be able to engage and fund legal advice independently of the GMC.

15.231 However, this architecture is not available to many smaller regulators. A decision would therefore need to be taken about how to achieve this on an ad hoc basis. It submitted that the following four steps could be taken: first, ensuring Chinese walls are in place to protect the privilege of any legal advice; secondly, ensuring that sufficient funds are available to fund the litigation properly; and, thirdly, drafting a witness statement by the disciplinary committee that reassures the court of these arrangements. It may be that the disciplinary committee takes the decision to adopt a neutral position in the litigation. However, it is important that such a decision is arrived at the basis of proper legal advice and not due to an organisational link to the regulator.

15.232 This set up may seem convoluted, but it is an essential part of demonstrating the independence of the regulator's disciplinary system. It is submitted that the court will

---

[300] See Bondy and Sunkin, *The Dynamics of Judicial Review Litigation* (2009) p 29.
[301] See *R (Bahta) v Secretary of State for the Home Department* [2011] EWCA Civ 895.

be unimpressed if it appears that the parties are not independent, and failure to do so will only increase the perception by some registrants that the disciplinary process is not truly independent.

15.233 Thirdly, it is important to list the registrant concerned as an interested party on the N461 form. He or she will obviously be directly affected by the claim and so will need to be listed (see CPR r 54.1(1)(f)). This will mean that registrant is also served with the claim (CPR r 54.7(b)) and will be informed of the requirements to serve a response if they wish to participate (CPR r 54.14).

15.234 Fourthly, the final practical matter to consider is costs. In the *Pharmaceutical Society* case, although the regulator was successful there was no order as to costs. This was a sensible result in that case, as the costs of both parties would have been paid from the same overall pot. Depending on the conduct of the parties, no order as to costs is likely to be a pragmatic starting point. However, it should be noted that if the registrant interested party attempts to derail the litigation through excessive evidence and hopeless arguments, there would be an obvious case to move away from this position.

15.235 The *functus officio* principle means that regulators are likely to confront the issue of how to judicially review their own disciplinary panels. However, the mechanics of doing so requires consideration. The most problematic matter for some regulators will be ensuring that their disciplinary panels have the appropriate separation and resources to defend a judicial review challenge. Other matters simply require an appropriate modification of elements such as the pre-action protocol. By moving through the steps described, the regulator will have brought together the most important elements to begin this unconventional form of judicial review.

CHAPTER 16

HEALTHCARE

INTRODUCTION

16.01 Over recent years there have been significant changes to the way in which healthcare services are provided in the United Kingdom. Most, but by no means all, healthcare services are provided by or on behalf of the National Health Service. These services were previously commissioned by primary care trusts and some other specialised commissioning groups. The vast majority of NHS commissioning is now managed by approximately 200 local clinical commissioning groups (CCGs) under the supervision of the NHS Commissioning Board (NHS CB).

16.02 NHS England itself commissions certain specialised services, primary care, offender healthcare (see below) and some services for the armed forces in four regions via 27 area teams. The CCGs and NHS England are supported in their commissioning roles by commissioning support units (CSUs). The overarching aim of NHS England is to ensure that the NHS delivers continuous improvements in outcomes for patients within the resources available. Such outcomes are defined by the NHS Outcomes Framework as guaranteed by the NHS Constitution, which are both important in identifying responsibilities, entitlements and general information about the way in which the NHS operates.

16.03 The delivery and quality of healthcare services have always been (and are likely to remain) issues of wide public and political concern – even more so following recent events such as those at mid-Staffordshire Hospital and Winterbourne View care home. The challenge of ensuring that the quality of healthcare services is as high as possible is immense. That challenge is likely to be heightened by an ageing population, finite resources, ongoing restructuring of the NHS and continued political intervention.

16.04 The focus of this chapter is not on the quality of day-to-day healthcare provision, which should, as a general rule, be dealt with under the NHS complaints procedure. Rather, this chapter seeks to identify some of the main issues that have become the subject of challenges by way of judicial review in recent years, and some more recent developments that are still in the process of implementation. They are illustrative only, but serve to demonstrate the complexities of this area of the law and why there is likely to be an increase in such challenges before the courts.

NHS RECONFIGURATION AND CONSULTATION

16.05 As a general rule, any significant changes to the way in which existing services are being provided or may be provided must not be made without consultation. There is an express statutory duty to consult when changes to the way services are commissioned are proposed. NHSA 2006, s 14Z2 provides as follows:

> **'Public involvement and consultation by clinical commissioning groups**
>
> *(1) This section applies in relation to any health services which are, or are to be, provided pursuant to arrangements made by a clinical commissioning group in the exercise of its functions ("commissioning arrangements").*
>
> *(2) The clinical commissioning group must make arrangements to secure that individuals to whom the services are being or may be provided are involved (whether by being consulted or provided with information or in other ways) –*
>
> (a) *in the planning of the commissioning arrangements by the group,*
> (b) *in the development and consideration of proposals by the group for changes in the commissioning arrangements where the implementation of the proposals would have an impact on the manner in which the services are delivered to the individuals or the range of health services available to them, and*
> (c) *in decisions of the group affecting the operation of the commissioning arrangements where the implementation of the decisions would (if made) have such an impact.*
>
> *(3) The clinical commissioning group must include in its constitution –*
>
> (a) *a description of the arrangements made by it under subsection (2), and*
> (b) *a statement of the principles which it will follow in implementing those arrangements.*
>
> *(4) The Board may publish guidance for clinical commissioning groups on the discharge of their functions under this section.*
>
> *(5) A clinical commissioning group must have regard to any guidance published by the Board under subsection (4).*
>
> *(6) The reference in subsection (2)(b) to the delivery of services is a reference to their delivery at the point when they are received by users.'*

16.06 The statutory duty is complemented by guidance,[1] which contains the following in its executive summary:

> 'NHS England will ensure that public, patient and carer voices are at the centre of our healthcare services, from planning to delivery. Every level of our commissioning system will be informed by insightful methods of listening to those who use and care about our services.
>
> …
>
> NHS commissioners should:
>
> …
>
> Engage with patients, carers and the public when redesigning or reconfiguring healthcare services, demonstrating how this has informed decisions.'

---

[1] *Transforming Participation in Health and Care* (September, 2013) NHS England.

16.07 Particular attention should also be given to the public sector equality duty[2] and whether the same should be addressed through a bespoke equality impact assessment (EIA).

16.08 A useful touchstone in any consultation process is the need to satisfy or establish the following:

- support from GP commissioners;
- strengthened public and patient engagement (including with local authorities);
- clarity on the clinical evidence underpinning the proposals;
- consistency with current and prospective patient choice.

16.09 Of course not all changes require consultation and not all consultation requires a formal 12-week period. Changes that are not significant and/or are temporary may not require any consultation at all.

16.10 In *R (Lewisham LBC) v Secretary of State for Health*[3] the court had cause to consider reconfiguration. The importance of consultation when any significant changes are proposed was made clear. The case was actually concerned with a challenge to a recommendation by a trust special administrator (TSA) to reduce services at a local hospital and of the subsequent decision of the Secretary of State to accept those recommendations. The central issue before the court was whether the TSA and the Secretary of State had acted *ultra vires* of the powers under NHSA 2006 where the hospital recommended for disclosure fell within the control of another NHS Trust.

16.11 Under NHSA 2006, ch 5A, a TSA may be appointed by the Secretary of State over an NHS trust to take over and make recommendations in relation to and in response to the failure to deliver services to the appropriate standard. It should be noted that the hospital in question was not actually a 'failing' entity. The court held that the powers of the TSA were confined to that particular trust and that any recommendations made in respect of services outside the trust were *ultra vires*.

16.12 This decision was upheld on appeal.[4] However, this is unlikely to be the end of this particular issue. Following the outcome of the original decision a new clause (cl 119) was inserted into the Care Bill that will give a TSA/Secretary of State powers to make decisions about hospitals and others services forming part of other trusts.

16.13 In its present form cl 119 adds a new sub-s (8) to s 65F of NHSA 2006 as follows:

> '*Where the administrator recommends taking action in relation to another NHS foundation trust or an NHS trust, the references in subsection (5) to a commissioner also include a reference to a person to which the other NHS foundation trust or the NHS trust provides services under this Act that would be affected by the action.*'

16.14 Theoretically, this could lead to the closure of local hospitals that are not failing should that be deemed necessary in order to address wider concerns arising in relation to

---

[2] Equality Act 2010, s 149.
[3] [2013] EWHC 2381.
[4] [2013] EWCA Civ 1409.

the original trust over which the TSA was appointed. Indeed it would appear to allow for far-ranging changes to healthcare service provision across a whole region.

NHS CONTINUING HEALTHCARE FUNDING

16.15 Primary care trust responsibility in relation to NHS continuing healthcare ceased with effect from 31 March 2013. From 1 April 2013 these responsibilities have been taken over by CCGs (except in the case of serving members of the armed forces and their families who are the responsibility of NHS CB).

16.16 NHS continuing healthcare is defined as a package of ongoing care that is arranged and funded solely by the NHS where the individual has been assessed as having a primary health need. The underpinning statutory duty is NHSA 2006, ss 1, 1A–1C and 3.

16.17 The availability of such services is important because a local authority will not be able to provide such services if they are otherwise available, pursuant to National Assistance Act 1948 s 21(8). It is also important for those that are found to be eligible because they must be provided free of charge. This is so even where a patient has the means to fund services by reason of damages received following a road traffic accident.[5]

16.18 The Secretary of State has issued guidance in relation to continuing healthcare entitled *National Framework for NHS Continuing Healthcare and NHS-funded Nursing Care* (Framework guidance). The Framework guidance defines a 'primary health' need as follows:

> '34. ... taken as a whole, the nursing or other health services required by the individual:
>
> a) are no more than incidental or ancillary to the provision of accommodation which LA social services are, or would be but for a person's means, under a duty to provide; and
> b) are not of a nature beyond which an LA whose primary responsibility it is to provide social services could be expected to provide.'

16.19 Where a person is assessed as being eligible for continuing healthcare funding, the CCG must commission all relevant services. In general, local authorities have a tendency to remove themselves from on-going decision-making save for when specific issues arise, such as safeguarding concerns.

16.20 One issue that has arisen is the question of whether a CCG is responsible for commissioning or providing accommodation for a person who is eligible for continuing healthcare funding. There is little, if any, useful guidance from the courts on this issue. As a matter of general approach the duties on the provision of social housing fall upon local authorities under the Housing Acts or s 21 of the National Assistance Act 1948.

16.21 However, the Framework guidance states as follows:

> '33. To assist in deciding which treatment and other health services it is appropriate for the NHS to provide under the 2006 Act, and to distinguish between those and the services that LAs may provide under s 21 of the National Assistance Act 1948, the Secretary of State has

---

[5] *R (Booker) v NHS Oldham & ors* [2010] EWHC 2593.

developed the concept of a "primary health need". Where a person has been assessed to have a "primary health need", they are eligible for NHS continuing healthcare. Deciding whether this is the case involves looking at the totality of the relevant needs. Where an individual has a primary health need and is therefore eligible for NHS continuing healthcare, the NHS is responsible for providing all of that individual's assessed health and social care needs – including accommodation, if that is part of the overall need.' *(Emphasis added)*

16.22 This would appear to give rise to a potential argument that, subject to an individual being assessed as eligible for continuing healthcare and requiring accommodation as part of their 'overall need', the CCG would be responsible for commissioning or otherwise providing what may be termed 'ordinary' accommodation.

16.23 Another issue that has yet to be the subject of any consideration by the courts is the power to provide direct payments as part of a personal health budget (PB). Such direct payments have been possible from the 1 April 2014. In theory these regulations would allow individuals to receive direct payments allowing them to buy their own healthcare services in the same way that already happens in the context of social care services.

16.24 The National Health Service (Direct Payments) Regulations 2013 (as amended) set out how the scheme should work. Directs payments can only be made to a person who is aged 16 or over and is not excluded. Key issues for consideration include whether directs payments would be appropriate for a person with his/her condition; the impact of that condition on that person's life; and whether a direct payment represents value for money.

16.25 Direct payments may be made in respect of a person who lacks capacity to consent if that person may or must be provided with a service by a health body, is not excluded and has a representative who consents to the same. In considering whether to make direct payments the same primary issues must be considered by the health authority (see **11.19** above). In addition reg 5(5) provides that the representative must:

'(a) agree to act on the patient's behalf in relation to the direct payment;
(b) act in the best interests of the patient when securing the provision of services in respect of which the direct payment is made;
(c) be responsible as a principal for all contractual arrangements entered into for the benefit of the patient and secured by means of the direct payment;
(d) use the direct payment in accordance with the care plan; and
(e) comply with the relevant provisions of these Regulations.'

16.26 A representative may nominate another person to receive a direct payment on a patient's behalf. In such circumstances, reg 6(2) provides that a nominee must:

'(a) be responsible as a principal for all contractual arrangements entered into for the benefit of the patient and secured by means of the direct payment;
(b) use the direct payment in accordance with the care plan; and
(c) comply with the relevant provisions of these Regulations.'

16.27 The health body must agree to making such payments and must, in relation to all direct payments, monitor and review the same by reference to the overarching principles as to their appropriateness for the patient, their impact on the patient's condition and whether they continue to represent value for money.

16.28 Whilst the principle of increasing choice and control is clearly laudable it is equally clear that decisions concerning direct payments to purchase healthcare services are bound to be contentious in many cases. Decision-makers within CCGs will have to be careful to manage the expectations of patients and family members through full and effective communication and clear polices and procedures in order to try and avoid a significant increase in complaints and judicial review claims.

MEDICAL TREATMENT POLICIES

16.29 A health body's policy concerning medical treatment is amenable to challenge by way of judicial review in the same way that any policy by a public authority is amenable. One of the most contentious is that which concerns the circumstances in which life-sustaining treatment ought to be provided.

16.30 A recent example of a challenge by way of judicial review is *R (Tracey) v Cambridge University Hospital NHS Foundation Trust*.[6] Mr Tracey challenged the decision to place a 'do not attempt cardio-pulmonary resuscitation' (DNACPR) notice on the file of his wife and the lawfulness of the trust's non-resuscitation policy. Mrs Tracey was admitted to hospital following a road traffic accident but two weeks earlier had been diagnosed with terminal lung cancer. As a consequence of her deterioration following admission a DNACPR notice was added to her file. The case concerned a challenge not to allow the matter to proceed to a substantive hearing but it is important because the Court of Appeal held that the following points were significant and therefore arguable:

(1) the alleged failure to communicate the policy to the family so as to enable them to effectively challenge it;

(2) the policy was not clear as to whether the final decision lay with the patient or, if she lacked capacity, the family; and

(3) the failure to consult with Mr Tracey before the first notice was signed off was a possible breach of his rights under Art 8.

16.31 This decision would suggest that it is prudent, to say the least, to proceed on the basis that Art 8 might be engaged by placing a DNACPR notice even in circumstances where it must also be acknowledged that a patient cannot demand a treatment that the relevant doctor thought was not clinically indicated. Whatever the legal obligations are (and a final determination of this issue is still awaited) it is clearly good practice to consult with the patient before the DNACPR notice is placed on the file. This is so even where the family had agreed to such a notice as happened in this particular case (albeit the family asserted that such agreement had been granted reluctantly).

16.32 Where the patient lacks capacity the decision-making process must comply with the framework contained in the Mental Capacity Act 2005 when considering whether it is in his best interests for him to be given, or not to be given, treatments necessary to sustain life. The Supreme Court in *Aintree University NHS Foundation Trust v James*[7] reiterated that the starting point was the strong presumption that it is in a person's best interests to stay alive. Decision-makers must look at welfare in the widest sense, including medical, social and psychological factors, trying to put themselves in the place

---

[6] [2014] EWCA Civ 33.
[7] [2013] UKSC 67.

of the individual patient to ask what his attitude is or would likely be. Full and effective consultation was seen as critical within the decision-making process. On the issue of futility it was held that a treatment may bring some benefit even if it has not effect on the underlying disease and was not futile if it enabled a patient to resume a quality of life that the patient would regard as worthwhile.[8] This decision must inform all policies and decisions made in relation to the withdrawal or withholding, or the giving, of life-sustaining treatment.

Recent illustrative cases include *County Durham & Darlington NHS Foundation Trust v PP & Others*[9] and an *NHS Foundation Trust v (1) M (2) K*.[10]

INDIVIDUAL FUNDING REQUESTS

16.33 Clinicians, on behalf of their patients, are entitled to make an individual funding request (IFR) to NHS CB for treatment that is not normally commissioned by the NHS CB under defined circumstances. The processes for consideration of IFRs are outlined in the standard operating procedures[11] and are subject to a policy, presently described as interim, entitled *NHS Commissioning Board – Interim Commissioning Policy: Individual funding requests* (2013). It applies to England only and is currently subject to review.

16.34 The 'defined conditions' are as follows:

'• The request does not constitute a request for a service development; and
- The patient is suffering from a medical condition for which the NHS CB has commissioning responsibility and a commissioning position and the patient's particular clinical circumstances falls outside the criteria set out in an existing commissioning policy for funding the requested treatment; or
- The patient is suitable to enter a clinical trial which requires individual explicit funding by the NHS CB as opposed to being part of a group of such trial patients; or
- The patient has a rare clinical circumstance, thus rendering it impossible to carry out clinical trials, and for whom the clinician wishes to use an existing treatment on an experimental basis.'

16.35 Such requests will be screened by reference to a number of factors (too many to outline for the purposes of this chapter) and, if successful, forwarded to the IFR Panel unless it is considered that there is no reasonable prospect of approval by the panel.

16.36 It will be seen that this very brief overview gives rise to potential challenges by way of judicial review although there are a number of significant difficulties with the same. An example of an unsuccessful challenge is *R (Condliff) v North Staffordshire Primary Care Trust*[12] in which a morbidly obese patient who did not qualify for gastric by-pass surgery made an IFR on the grounds of exceptionality. His claim for judicial review was focused on an argument that the trust's policy, which included reference to non-clinical, social considerations, breached Art 8. The Court of Appeal held Art 8 could not be relied on as giving rise to a positive duty to take into account welfare considerations wider than the comparative medical conditions and medical needs of

---

8 Ibid paras 39–44.
9 [2014] EXCOP 9.
10 [2013] EWHC 2402 (COP).
11 NHSCB/SOP/02.
12 [2011] EWCA Civ 910.

different patients. The trust was entitled to set an IFR policy that reflected what it reasonably considered to be the fairest way of treating patients. Nothing in the authorities led to the conclusion that the trust's policy was to be regarded as showing a lack of respect for C's private and family life so as to bring Art 8 into play.

AFTER-CARE SERVICES

16.37 The circumstances in which after-care services must be provided to those that were formerly detained under certain provisions of the Mental Health Act 1983 continue to form part of claims for judicial review before the courts. Issues surrounding which health body is responsible and the scope of after-care services have been the subject of a number of judicial review claims. Such disputes are likely to increase in number in these financially straightened times.

16.38 Mental Health Act 1983 s 117 provides as follows:

> '*After-care.*
>
> *(1) This section applies to persons who are detained under s 3 above, or admitted to a hospital in pursuance of a hospital order made under s 37 above, or transferred to a hospital in pursuance of a hospital direction made under s 45A above or a transfer direction made under s 47 or 48 above, and then cease to be detained and (whether or not immediately after so ceasing) leave hospital.*
>
> *(2) It shall be the duty of the Primary Care Trust or Local Health Board and of the local social services authority to provide, in co-operation with relevant voluntary agencies, after-care services for any person to whom this section applies until such time as the Primary Care Trust or Local Health Board and the local social services authority are satisfied that the person concerned is no longer in need of such services; but they shall not be so satisfied in the case of a community patient while he remains such a patient.*
>
> ...
>
> *(2B) Section 32 above shall apply for the purposes of this section as it applies for the purposes of Part II of this Act.*
>
> *(3) In this section "the Primary Care Trust or Local Health Board" means the Primary Care Trust or Local Health Board, and "the local social services authority" means the local social services authority, for the area in which the person concerned is resident or to which he is sent on discharge by the hospital in which he was detained.*'

16.39 The issue of where a person is resident for the purposes of s 117(3) was comprehensively considered in *R (Sunderland City Council) v South Tyneside Council*.[13] In that case Langstaff J held that there can be only one place of residence and that the word 'resident' should be given its ordinary meaning, subject to the statutory context. The approach was to apply to those facts the distillation of the authorities set out in *R v Barnet London Borough Council ex p Shah*[14] that ordinary residence referred to a man's abode in a particular place or country, which he had adopted voluntarily and for settled purposes as part of the regular order of his life for the time being, whether of short or long duration. In determining what formed part of the regular order of the person's life,

---

[13] [2011] EWHC 2355.
[14] [1983] 2 AC 309.

regard should be had to the purpose and other circumstances of a person's presence or absence from the address. A period of time in hospital, for example where a person had suffered an accident, did not make one cease to be resident where one had been resident before. It was not simply a question of duration, but was to be defined by qualitative considerations including the purpose of the stay and the extent to which it disturbed the normal pattern and order of life.[15]

16.40 The nature and scope of after-care services has also been a contentious issue. In *R (Mwanza) v (1) Greenwich LBC (2) Bromley LBC*[16] M argued that after being discharged from detention under s 3 the local authority owed him a duty to provide after-care services and that duty included an obligation to accommodate him. He submitted that the authority was bound to provide any service that prevented possible deterioration in his mental condition that would also reduce the chance of relapse and readmission. Hickinbottom J said[17] as follows:

> 'I do not accept Mr Armstrong's submission that s 117 requires the relevant authorities to provide a former s 3 patient with any and all services simply because those services do or may prevent deterioration or relapse of a mental condition, or require readmission, for the following reasons.'

16.41 He went on to set out the reasons as follows:[18]

> '... The duty derives from a provision in mental health legislation; and it is described as a duty to provide 'after-care services'. As Ms. Richards submitted, s 117 is not concerned with the provision of support and accommodation at large, but rather with the provision, to the specified category of patients who have been detained on account of their mental disorder, of services tailored to meet needs arising from that disorder. An after-care service must, in my judgment, be a service that is necessary to meet a need arising from a person's mental disorder.'

16.42 Of critical importance is the next part of his reasoning[19] as follows:

> 'It may be that, if a former patient were unemployed or homeless, that would increase the chance of deterioration in his mental condition – but, in my judgment, that would not require an authority under s 117 to provide employment or housing, as Mr Armstrong's submission suggested. The need for work or the need for a roof over one's head *simpliciter* are common needs, and do not arise from mental disorder. Section 117 does not impose a general responsibility on the relevant authorities to house or provide an income to a former patient. Of course, a patient's mental disorder may make it more difficult for him to look for housing or employment on discharge from s 3 – and it may therefore give rise to a need for assistance in doing so. But that is a different need and a different issue.'

16.43 It would now appear to be settled law that as a matter of principle s 117 does not give rise to a duty to provide or fund accommodation for someone following discharge from detention under s 3 in the absence of any evidence that the same is necessary to meet a need arising from a person's mental disorder. Becoming homeless may increase the chance of deterioration in a person's mental condition but that is not sufficient to give rise to a duty to accommodate under s 117. In reaching that decision, Hickinbottom

---

[15] See para 23.
[16] [2010] EWHC 1462 (Admin).
[17] Ibid at [62].
[18] Ibid at para [64].
[19] Ibid at para [65].

J relied on the decision of Lord Phillips MR in *R (K) v Camden and Islington Health Authority*.[20] He also questioned the decision of HHJ Gilbart QC (as he then was) in *R (B) v LB of Lambeth*,[21] which suggested otherwise and pointed out that that case proceed on the concession that such a duty arose where argument on the issue was not heard.

16.44 The decision in *Mwanza* must also be read in light of the more recent decision of Mostyn J in *R (Afework) v LB of Camden*.[22] The same issue arose – was the authority under a duty to provide accommodation (free of charge) under s 117. Mostyn J answered that question in the negative. In relation to the statutory language he said as follows:[23]

> '... The section applies to people who have been compulsorily detained under the Act but who have then ceased to be detained and who have left hospital. It even applies to people who may have been detained in hospital only for a very short period of time. Those people are owed a duty by the state – either the NHS body or the local authority. That duty is to provide them with "after-care services". This is a single compound noun with two components viz "after-care" and "services". The hyphenated linking of the word "after" with "care" within the first component shows that the services in question must be consequential to the detention in hospital. The services must relate to the reason, and only to the reason, for the detention in hospital. In my opinion that is the only possible logical interpretation that can be given to the qualification of the component "services" by the hyphenated component "after-care". If Parliament had intended that the services to be supplied to such persons should be of a more general nature, not specifically related to the reason for detention, then it would not have qualified the word "services" at all, or it would have used a qualifying component such as "caring".'

He concluded[24] as follows:

> 'Thus far I would not have concluded, having regard both to the literal meaning of the actual words used in s 117(2) and to the identified policy objective enacted in 1948, that s 117(2) could embrace a duty to provide any kind of accommodation whether basic or enhanced, unless the enhanced accommodation was a substitute for, or an extension of, the hospital environment in effect imposed on the patient.'

16.45 The judge went on to consider the amendments to the National Assistance Act 1948 brought about by s 148 of the Health and Social Care Act 2008 and concluded that Parliament in 2008 envisaged that some accommodation could be provided under s 117. However, he went on to find that he could not think of any circumstances where the duty would arise because 'basic or pure accommodation does not come within the concept of after-care services'.[25] He held as follows:[26]

> 'I therefore hold that as a matter of law s 117(2) is only engaged vis-à-vis accommodation if:
>
> i)   The need for accommodation is a direct result of the reason that the ex-patient was detained in the first place ("the original condition");

---

[20] [2001] EWCA Civ 240 at [29].
[21] [2006] EWHC 262.
[22] [2013] EWHC 1637.
[23] Ibid at para [8].
[24] Ibid at para [9].
[25] Ibid at para [16].
[26] Ibid at para [19].

ii) The requirement is for enhanced specialised accommodation to meet needs directly arising from the original condition; and
iii) The ex-patient is being placed in the accommodation on an involuntary (in the sense of being incapacitated) basis arising as a result of the original condition.'

16.46 In cases such as these it appears necessary for claimants in prospective judicial review claims to establish that the person's need for accommodation arises as a result of the reason they were detained in the first place – for example, due to a deterioration in his mental health caused by schizophrenia for which they were originally detained. Absent such a causal link a claim for judicial review based on a decision not to provide accommodation is unlikely to be successful.

IMMIGRATION AND HEALTHCARE

16.47 Asylum-seekers and others arriving in the United Kingdom without leave to remain represent some of the most vulnerable people in society. Many require healthcare services. As a general rule anyone with an outstanding application for asylum in the United Kingdom is entitled to use NHS services without charge. Significant numbers of people are classed as failed asylum-seekers or do not otherwise have leave to remain. As a general rule those who are not ordinarily resident in the United Kingdom must be charged for NHS services and if a person does not have leave to remain they cannot be ordinarily resident. However, health bodies continue to have a discretion to provide treatment to those who are not ordinarily resident or otherwise not entitled to it even where there is no prospect of them paying for the same.

16.48 There is a significant number of persons who are detained due to their immigration status in short-term holding facilities (both residential and non-residential), immigration removal centres and pre-departure accommodation. While the Home Office has a duty to enforce immigration policy, including, in certain circumstances, the detention of people without leave to remain, NHS England has acknowledged that healthcare services will continue to be made available.

16.49 Primary healthcare facilities and services are provided at most of these facilities and all detainees should be seen for a healthcare screening by a nurse within two hours of arrival. In some, but not all, detainees may be entitled to an appointment with a GP within 24 hours, giving them access to healthcare facilities on demand subject to the normal triage service found in GP surgeries in the community. NHS England is responsible for funding healthcare services, escort and bed-watches, consumables and non-fixed minor capital equipment.

16.50 The challenges of ensuring good quality healthcare services are provided to this section of the population are obvious. Such people may have only recently arrived in the country or may be moving around on a regular basis. They may have little if any healthcare documentation and may have difficulty communicating. It is therefore vital that there is effective communication between the Home Office and NHS England in relation to such people. Each organisation should have specific procedures to encourage information sharing, which also takes account of the confidentiality of that information and how it affects the patient and the safety of the public.[27]

---

27 See further: *Immigration Enforcement and NHS England Framework* (December 2013).

16.51 Many of the judicial review claims that have been brought concern alleged failures to meet needs arising from mental disorders. A good example is *R (S (by his litigation friend the Official Solicitor)) v Secretary of State for the Home Department*[28] in which the detention pending the removal of an overstayer who suffered from a serious mental disorder was found to be unlawful and in breach of both Art 3 and Art 8 of the European Convention on Human Rights.

16.52 S was detained in various removal centres but the place of detention is not particularly determinative. In addition to failing to observe her own policies concerning the detention of those suffering from mental disorders the court emphasised that everyone has an unqualified right not to be subjected to inhuman or degrading treatment whilst in detention. Where a mental disorder was exacerbated by the conditions of detention, including the failure to provide adequate healthcare, the detention itself may breach Art 3. Further, as a person's mental health was a crucial part of private life associated with moral integrity such circumstances may also give rise to a breach of Art 8.

16.53 It is therefore crucial that all reasonable steps are taken to assess and afford access to healthcare services as far as possible with the aim of replicating the provision afforded in the community. Failure to do so will give rise to claims based on breaches of fundamental rights for which substantial damages may be awarded.

PRISONERS AND HEALTHCARE

16.54 There are currently approximately 120 prisons and young offender institutions in England. Offenders in secure settings typically have poorer health and health outcomes than the average population. Issues causing concern have typically arisen over assessments, joint working arrangements between the prison and health authority, prisoner access to health services, quality of services offered and clinical governance issues. The incidence of poor mental health is particularly high. There are a number of other issues that are important to highlight about the provision of non-mental health related services and healthcare provision generally for prisoners.

16.55 In the past there has been some confusion as to who is responsible for healthcare in prisons particularly prisons owned and managed by private companies. From April 2013 NHS CB must be satisfied that it is meeting its duty under the Health and Social Care Act 2012 to arrange medical services for prisoners irrespective of custodial providers. In short, prisoners are entitled to the same level of quality and consistency in all prisons as is available in the community. NHS CB is responsible for planning, securing and monitoring services for prisons and other secure accommodation centres.

CONCLUSION

16.56 These are a just some of the issues that may be amenable to claims for judicial review. It has only been possible to provide an outline analysis of the same for the purposes of this chapter but it is clear that healthcare delivery, quality and funding are likely to continue to give rise to increasing legal challenges going forward.

---

[28] [2014] EWHC 50.

Part 3
APPENDICES

APPENDIX 1

PROCEDURAL GUIDE

CLAIMS FOR JUDICIAL REVIEW[1]

Legal background

Claims for judicial review are governed by CPR Pt 54.

A claim for judicial review is a means of vindicating rights in public law. It is defined in the CPR as 'a claim to review the lawfulness of (i) an enactment; or (ii) a decision, action or failure to act in relation to the exercise of a public function'. It is sometimes difficult to tell whether a particular complaint involves a matter of public law or of private law. Frequently, the complaint involves elements of both; where it does, the courts are allowing claimants greater flexibility in choosing their forum. But the distinction between public and private law remains important for a number of purposes.

There are a number of respects in which claims for judicial review differ from private law claims –

- There are short time-limits.
- The claimant requires the permission of the court to bring the proceedings.
- The proceedings are generally conducted without oral evidence.
- There is rarely disclosure of documents.
- Relief is discretionary.

A Practice Direction on Judicial Review accompanies Pt 54. In addition, there is available from the Administrative Court Office a helpful booklet entitled *Notes for Guidance on Applying for Judicial Review*.

Procedure

Availability	Where the substance of the claim is a matter of public law and the remedy sought is as stated above. Proceedings for judicial review are generally not appropriate where an alternative remedy is available, such as a statutory appeal	Judicial Review Protocol, paras 2–4; SCA, ss 29–31; Rules 54.2, 54.3
	Judicial review is available in criminal proceedings save in matters relating to trial on indictment	SCA 1981, s 29(3)

---

[1] Taken from *Civil Court Service 2014* (Reissue) (Jordan Publishing, 2014).

Letters before action	The prospective claimant should write a detailed letter before action, allowing 14 days for the prospective defendant to respond, save where the nature of the claim precludes this. The prospective defendant should write a similarly detailed response. The letters should be copied to any interested parties	Judicial Review Protocol, paras 8–17, Annexes A and B
Venue	Proceedings must be issued in the High Court. Judicial review remedies cannot be made by the County Court, although claims started in the High Court that should have been started in the County Court can be transferred.	CLSA 1990, s 1(10); CCA 1984, s 38(3) and s 40
	Proceedings should be issued in the Administrative Court Office in the Royal Courts of Justice, London or in the Administrative Court Office at Birmingham, Cardiff, Leeds or Manchester High Courts	PD54D
	The claimant or defendant can make an application to transfer the claim to a more convenient venue if the criteria set out in the Practice Direction 54D are met. Similarly the court can transfer a case to a different court centre of its own volition if it appears that the case is more conveniently heard at a different court centre	
Permission	A claimant needs the permission of the court to bring a claim for judicial review	SCA 1981, s 31(3); Rule 54.4
	The application for permission is generally made on the papers in the first instance	PD54A, para 8.4
	If permission is refused, or is granted subject to conditions or on certain grounds only, the application may be renewed to a judge orally but only if the initial refusal was on the papers	Rule 54.12

	Where a person served with the claim form has not filed an acknowledgment of service in accordance with the rules (see below), he will not be permitted to take part in the renewed permission hearing unless the court allows him to do so, but the defendant may take part in the substantive hearing, providing that he complies with any directions about filing his grounds and evidence	Rule 54.9
	If permission is refused at the oral hearing, the claimant may apply for permission to appeal to the Court of Appeal. Such application must be filed within 7 days of the decision of the High Court. If the Court of Appeal grants permission to apply for judicial review, the case will proceed in the High Court unless the Court of Appeal orders otherwise	Rule 52.15
	If the Court of Appeal refuses permission to appeal, no further appeal lies to the Supreme Court	AJA 1999, s 54
	Where permission is given, the court may give directions. The court will serve the order giving permission, and any directions, on the claimant, the defendant and on any interested party who has acknowledged service	Rule 54.10 Rule 54.11
	Neither the defendant nor any other party served with the claim form may apply to set aside the grant of permission to apply for judicial review	Rule 54.13
Time-limits	In most cases proceedings must be brought promptly and in any event within 3 months from the date when the grounds for the application first arose. However, in planning and procurement cases the time limit is six weeks, whilst judicial review claims against the Upper Tribunal must be brought within 16 days.	Rule 54.5 and 54.7A
	Where the claimant seeks the quashing of a judgment, order or conviction, time begins to run from the date of that judgment, order or conviction	PD54A, para 4.1
	If there is undue delay by the claimant, the court may refuse to grant permission or any relief	SCA, s 31(6)

	The claimant must serve the claim form on the defendant and on any interested party within 7 days after the date of issue	Rule 54.7
	An interested party is any other person who is directly affected by the claim	Rule 54.1(2)(f)
	The defendant and any interested party served with the claim form who wishes to take part in the judicial review must file an acknowledgment of service not more than 21 days after the claim form is served on him; and must serve his acknowledgment on the other parties within 7 days after it is filed. It is not served by the court	Rule 54.8
	If the application for permission is refused, or is granted subject to conditions or on certain grounds only, the application to renew the request for permission at an oral hearing must be made within 7 days after the court serves on the claimant its reasons for not (simply) granting permission	Rule 54.12(4)
	An application for permission to appeal to the Court of Appeal against the refusal of permission must be made within 7 days of the decision of the High Court	Rule 52.15
Contents of claim form	The claim form must specify the relief claimed and must include –	Rule 54.6
	the name and address of any interested party;	
	a detailed statement of the claimant's grounds for bringing the claim for judicial review;	
	a statement of the facts relied on;	
	any application to extend the time-limit for filing the claim form;	
	any application for directions; and	PD54A, para 5.6
	It should be accompanied by –	
	any written evidence relied on;	
	a copy of any order that the claimant seeks to have quashed;	
	where the claim relates to a decision of a court or tribunal, an approved copy of the reasons for reaching that decision;	

	copies of any documents on which the claimant proposes to rely;	
	copies of any relevant statutory material;	
	a list of essential documents for advance reading by the court (with page references to the passages relied on); and,	
	insofar as any of the above are not available, reasons why they are unavailable	PD54A, paras 5.7, 5.8
	The claim form should also give details of the claimant's solicitors	
	Where the claimant seeks to raise any issue under HRA 1998, the claim form must give the particulars required by PD16, para 16.1	PD54A, para 5.3
	Where the claimant seeks to raise a devolution issue, the claim form must say so and must specify the relevant statutory provision and the relevant facts	PD54A, para 5.4
Acknowledgment of service	The acknowledgment of service should state whether the defendant contests the claim and, if so, summarise his grounds for doing so	Rule 54.8(4)
Opposing the claim	The defendant, and any interested party who wishes to oppose or be heard on the claim, must serve detailed grounds and any evidence within 35 days after service of the order giving permission	Rule 54.14(1)
	The claimant must serve any reply within 14 days of service of the defendant's or interested party's evidence	Rule 54.14(2)
	No other evidence is admissible without the court's permission	Rule 54.16
Preparation for hearing	The claimant requires the court's permission to rely on any grounds other than those for which he has been given permission	Rule 54.15
	The claimant must give the other parties 7 clear days' notice of an application to rely on additional grounds	PD54A, para 11.1

	Any person wishing to apply to the court for permission to file evidence or to make representations at the hearing of the claim for judicial review should do so promptly	Rule 54.17
	The court may allow such an intervention and may do so subject to conditions	PD54A, paras 13.1, 13.2
	Disclosure is not required unless the court orders otherwise	PD54A, para 12.1
	The court may order cross-examination but this is rare	
	The claimant must file two copies of a paginated and indexed bundle	PD54A, paras 5.9, 5.10
	The bundle, and the claimant's skeleton argument, must be filed 21 working days before the hearing	PD54A, para 15.1
	The defendant and any interested party wishing to make representations must file skeleton arguments 14 working days before the hearing date	PD54A, para 15.2
	Skeleton arguments must contain –	
	a time estimate for the complete hearing, including judgment;	
	a list of issues;	
	a list of the legal points to be taken (together with any relevant authorities with page references to the passages relied on);	
	a chronology of events (with page references to the bundle of documents);	
	a list of essential documents for the advance reading of the court (with page references to the passages relied on) (if different from that filed with the claim form);	
	a time estimate for that reading; and	
	a list of persons referred to	PD54A, para 15.3
Transfer	Proceedings which commenced as a claim for judicial review may be ordered to continue as if they had not been commenced under Pt 54	Rule 54.20
	Proceedings which were commenced other than under Pt 54 may be transferred to the Administrative Court	PD54A, paras 14.1, 14.2; Rule 30.5

Agreed final orders	Where the parties agree about the final order to be made in a claim for judicial review, the claimant should file a document (with two copies) signed by all the parties setting out the terms of the proposed order, together with a short statement of the matters relied on as justifying the proposed order and copies of any authorities and provisions relied on	PD54A, para 17.1
	If the court is satisfied that the proposed order should be made, it may make it without a hearing	Rule 54.18
	If the court is not so satisfied, a hearing date will be set	PD54A, para 17.3
Forms	Claim Form N461	
	Application for urgent consideration N463	
	Acknowledgment of service N462	
	Form N464 Application for directions as to venue for administration and determination	
	Form N465 Response to application for directions as to venue for administration and determination	
	Application for permission to appeal a refusal of permission to bring claim for judicial review N161	

APPENDIX 2

STATUTORY MATERIALS

Statutes

Senior Courts Act, s 31	537
Tribunal Courts and Enforcement Act 2007, ss 15–18	539

Statutory Instruments

First-tier Tribunal and Upper Tribunal (Chambers) (Amendment No 2) Order 2013, SI 2013/2068	542
Upper Tribunal (Immigration and Asylum Chamber) (Judicial Review) (England and Wales) Fees (Amendment) Order 2013, SI 2013/2069	543

SENIOR COURTS ACT 1981, S 31

****

31 Application for judicial review

(1) An application to the High Court for one or more of the following forms of relief, namely –

 (a) a mandatory, prohibiting or quashing order;
 (b) a declaration or injunction under subsection (2); or
 (c) an injunction under section 30 restraining a person not entitled to do so from acting in an office to which that section applies,

shall be made in accordance with rules of court by a procedure to be known as an application for judicial review.

(2) A declaration may be made or an injunction granted under this subsection in any case where an application for judicial review, seeking that relief, has been made and the High Court considers that, having regard to –

 (a) the nature of the matters in respect of which relief may be granted by mandatory, prohibiting or quashing orders;
 (b) the nature of the persons and bodies against whom relief may be granted by such orders; and
 (c) all the circumstances of the case,

it would be just and convenient for the declaration to be made or for the injunction to be granted, as the case may be.

(3) No application for judicial review shall be made unless the leave of the High Court has been obtained in accordance with rules of court; and the court shall not grant leave to make such an application unless it considers that the applicant has a sufficient interest in the matter to which the application relates.

(4) On an application for judicial review the High Court may award to the applicant damages, restitution or the recovery of a sum due if –

- (a) the application includes a claim for such an award arising from any matter to which the application relates; and
- (b) the court is satisfied that such an award would have been made if the claim had been made in an action begun by the applicant at the time of making the application.

(5) If, on an application for judicial review, the High Court quashes the decision to which the application relates, it may in addition –

- (a) remit the matter to the court, tribunal or authority which made the decision, with a direction to reconsider the matter and reach a decision in accordance with the findings of the High Court; or
- (b) substitute its own decision for the decision in question.

(5A) But the power conferred by subsection (5)(b) is exercisable only if –

- (a) the decision in question was made by a court or tribunal;
- (b) the decision is quashed on the ground that there has been an error of law; and
- (c) without the error, there would have been only one decision which the court or tribunal could have reached.

(5B) Unless the High Court otherwise directs, a decision substituted by it under subsection (5)(b) has effect as if it were a decision of the relevant court or tribunal.

(6) Where the High Court considers that there has been undue delay in making an application for judicial review, the court may refuse to grant –

- (a) leave for the making of the application; or
- (b) any relief sought on the application,

if it considers that the granting of the relief sought would be likely to cause substantial hardship to, or substantially prejudice the rights of, any person or would be detrimental to good administration.

(7) Subsection (6) is without prejudice to any enactment or rule of court which has the effect of limiting the time within which an application for judicial review may be made.

****

TRIBUNAL COURTS AND ENFORCEMENT ACT 2007, SS 15–18

PART 1
TRIBUNALS AND INQUIRIES

"Judicial review"

15 Upper Tribunal's "judicial review" jurisdiction

(1) The Upper Tribunal has power, in cases arising under the law of England and Wales or under the law of Northern Ireland, to grant the following kinds of relief –

- (a) a mandatory order;
- (b) a prohibiting order;
- (c) a quashing order;
- (d) a declaration;
- (e) an injunction.

(2) The power under subsection (1) may be exercised by the Upper Tribunal if –

- (a) certain conditions are met (see section 18), or
- (b) the tribunal is authorised to proceed even though not all of those conditions are met (see section 19(3) and (4)).

(3) Relief under subsection (1) granted by the Upper Tribunal –

- (a) has the same effect as the corresponding relief granted by the High Court on an application for judicial review, and
- (b) is enforceable as if it were relief granted by the High Court on an application for judicial review.

(4) In deciding whether to grant relief under subsection (1)(a), (b) or (c), the Upper Tribunal must apply the principles that the High Court would apply in deciding whether to grant that relief on an application for judicial review.

(5) In deciding whether to grant relief under subsection (1)(d) or (e), the Upper Tribunal must–

- (a) in cases arising under the law of England and Wales apply the principles that the High Court would apply in deciding whether to grant that relief under section 31(2) of the Senior Courts Act 1981 (c 54) on an application for judicial review, and
- (b) in cases arising under the law of Northern Ireland apply the principles that the High Court would apply in deciding whether to grant that relief on an application for judicial review.

(6) For the purposes of the application of subsection (3)(a) in relation to cases arising under the law of Northern Ireland –

- (a) a mandatory order under subsection (1)(a) shall be taken to correspond to an order of mandamus,
- (b) a prohibiting order under subsection (1)(b) shall be taken to correspond to an order of prohibition, and

(c) a quashing order under subsection (1)(c) shall be taken to correspond to an order of certiorari.

16 Application for relief under section 15(1)

(1) This section applies in relation to an application to the Upper Tribunal for relief under section 15(1).

(2) The application may be made only if permission (or, in a case arising under the law of Northern Ireland, leave) to make it has been obtained from the tribunal.

(3) The tribunal may not grant permission (or leave) to make the application unless it considers that the applicant has a sufficient interest in the matter to which the application relates.

(4) Subsection (5) applies where the tribunal considers –

    (a) that there has been undue delay in making the application, and
    (b) that granting the relief sought on the application would be likely to cause substantial hardship to, or substantially prejudice the rights of, any person or would be detrimental to good administration.

(5) The tribunal may –

    (a) refuse to grant permission (or leave) for the making of the application;
    (b) refuse to grant any relief sought on the application.

(6) The tribunal may award to the applicant damages, restitution or the recovery of a sum due if –

    (a) the application includes a claim for such an award arising from any matter to which the application relates, and
    (b) the tribunal is satisfied that such an award would have been made by the High Court if the claim had been made in an action begun in the High Court by the applicant at the time of making the application.

(7) An award under subsection (6) may be enforced as if it were an award of the High Court.

(8) Where –

    (a) the tribunal refuses to grant permission (or leave) to apply for relief under section 15(1),
    (b) the applicant appeals against that refusal, and
    (c) the Court of Appeal grants the permission (or leave),

the Court of Appeal may go on to decide the application for relief under section 15(1).

(9) Subsections (4) and (5) do not prevent Tribunal Procedure Rules from limiting the time within which applications may be made.

17 Quashing orders under section 15(1): supplementary provision

(1) If the Upper Tribunal makes a quashing order under section 15(1)(c) in respect of a decision, it may in addition –

    (a) remit the matter concerned to the court, tribunal or authority that made the decision, with a direction to reconsider the matter and reach a decision in accordance with the findings of the Upper Tribunal, or
    (b) substitute its own decision for the decision in question.

(2) The power conferred by subsection (1)(b) is exercisable only if –

(a) the decision in question was made by a court or tribunal,
(b) the decision is quashed on the ground that there has been an error of law, and
(c) without the error, there would have been only one decision that the court or tribunal could have reached.

(3) Unless the Upper Tribunal otherwise directs, a decision substituted by it under subsection (1)(b) has effect as if it were a decision of the relevant court or tribunal.

18 Limits of jurisdiction under section 15(1)

(1) This section applies where an application made to the Upper Tribunal seeks (whether or not alone) –

(a) relief under section 15(1), or
(b) permission (or, in a case arising under the law of Northern Ireland, leave) to apply for relief under section 15(1).

(2) If Conditions 1 to 4 are met, the tribunal has the function of deciding the application.

(3) If the tribunal does not have the function of deciding the application, it must by order transfer the application to the High Court.

(4) Condition 1 is that the application does not seek anything other than –

(a) relief under section 15(1);
(b) permission (or, in a case arising under the law of Northern Ireland, leave) to apply for relief under section 15(1);
(c) an award under section 16(6);
(d) interest;
(e) costs.

(5) Condition 2 is that the application does not call into question anything done by the Crown Court.

(6) Condition 3 is that the application falls within a class specified for the purposes of this subsection in a direction given in accordance with Part 1 of Schedule 2 to the Constitutional Reform Act 2005 (c 4).

(7) The power to give directions under subsection (6) includes –

(a) power to vary or revoke directions made in exercise of the power, and
(b) power to make different provision for different purposes.

(8) Condition 4 is that the judge presiding at the hearing of the application is either –

(a) a judge of the High Court or the Court of Appeal in England and Wales or Northern Ireland, or a judge of the Court of Session, or
(b) such other persons as may be agreed from time to time between the Lord Chief Justice, the Lord President, or the Lord Chief Justice of Northern Ireland, as the case may be, and the Senior President of Tribunals.

(9) Where the application is transferred to the High Court under subsection (3) –

(a) the application is to be treated for all purposes as if it –
   (i) had been made to the High Court, and
   (ii) sought things corresponding to those sought from the tribunal, and

(b) any steps taken, permission (or leave) given or orders made by the tribunal in relation to the application are to be treated as taken, given or made by the High Court.

(10) Rules of court may make provision for the purpose of supplementing subsection (9).

(11) The provision that may be made by Tribunal Procedure Rules about amendment of an application for relief under section 15(1) includes, in particular, provision about amendments that would cause the application to become transferrable under subsection (3).

(12) For the purposes of subsection (9)(a)(ii), in relation to an application transferred to the High Court in Northern Ireland –

- (a) an order of mandamus shall be taken to correspond to a mandatory order under section 15(1)(a),
- (b) an order of prohibition shall be taken to correspond to a prohibiting order under section 15(1)(b), and
- (c) an order of certiorari shall be taken to correspond to a quashing order under section 15(1)(c).

FIRST-TIER TRIBUNAL AND UPPER TRIBUNAL (CHAMBERS) (AMENDMENT NO 2) ORDER 2013

SI 2013/2068

Made 20 August 2013

Laid before Parliament 29 August 2013

Coming into force 1 November 2013

1 Citation and commencement

This Order may be cited as the First-tier Tribunal and Upper Tribunal (Chambers) (Amendment No 2) Order 2013 and comes into force on 1st November 2013.

2 Amendments to the First-tier Tribunal and Upper Tribunal (Chambers) Order 2010

The First-tier Tribunal and Upper Tribunal (Chambers) Order 2010 is amended as follows.

3

In article 10 (functions of the Administrative Appeals Chamber), in paragraph (b), for 'or (d)', substitute ', (d) or (e)'.

4

In article 11 (functions of the Immigration and Asylum Chamber of the Upper Tribunal), for paragraphs (c) and (d), substitute –

'(c) an application for the Upper Tribunal to grant relief mentioned in section 15(1) of the Tribunals, Courts and Enforcement Act 2007 (Upper Tribunal's "judicial review" jurisdiction), or to exercise the power of review under section 21(2) of that Act (Upper Tribunal's "judicial review" jurisdiction: Scotland), which is made by a person who claims to be a minor from outside the United Kingdom challenging a defendant's assessment of that person's age;

(d) an application for the Upper Tribunal to exercise the powers of review under section 21(2) of the Tribunals, Court and Enforcement Act (Upper Tribunal's "judicial review" jurisdiction: Scotland), which relates to a decision of the First-tier Tribunal mentioned in paragraph (a);

(e) an application for the Upper Tribunal to grant relief mentioned in section 15(1) of the Tribunals, Courts and Enforcement Act 2007 (Upper Tribunal's "judicial review" jurisdiction), which is designated as an immigration matter –

(i) in a direction made in accordance with Part 1 of Schedule 2 to the Constitutional Reform Act 2005 specifying a class of case for the purposes of section 18(6) of the Tribunals, Courts and Enforcement Act 2007; or

(ii) in an order of the High Court in England and Wales made under section 31A(3) of the Senior Courts Act 1981, transferring to the Upper Tribunal an application of a kind described in section 31A(1) of that Act.'

UPPER TRIBUNAL (IMMIGRATION AND ASYLUM CHAMBER) (JUDICIAL REVIEW) (ENGLAND AND WALES) FEES (AMENDMENT) ORDER 2013

SI 2013/2069

Made 20 August 2013

Laid before Parliament 29 August 2013

Coming into force 1 November 2013

1 Citation, commencement and extent

This Order may be cited as the Upper Tribunal (Immigration and Asylum Chamber) (Judicial Review) (England and Wales) Fees (Amendment) Order 2013 and comes into force on 1st November 2013.

2

This Order extends to England and Wales only.

3 Amendments to the Upper Tribunal (Immigration and Asylum Chamber) (Judicial Review) (England and Wales) Fees Order 2011

The Upper Tribunal (Immigration and Asylum Chamber) (Judicial Review) (England and Wales) Fees Order 2011 is amended as follows.

4

In article 1 (citation, commencement, interpretation and extent), in paragraph (2) –

(a) omit the definition of 'fresh claim proceedings';

(b) before the definition of 'LSC' insert –

'"immigration judicial review proceedings" means judicial review proceedings (within the meaning of the Tribunal Procedure (Upper Tribunal) Rules 2008), which are designated as an immigration matter–

(a) in a direction made in accordance with Part 1 of Schedule 2 to the Constitutional Reform Act 2005 specifying a class of case for the purposes of section 18(6) of the Tribunals, Courts and Enforcement Act 2007; or

(b) in an order of the High Court in England and Wales made under section 31A(3) of the Senior Courts Act 1981, transferring to the Upper Tribunal an application of a kind described in section 31A(1) of that Act;'.

5

In article 2 (fees payable), for 'fresh claim' substitute 'immigration judicial review'.

6

In Schedule 1 (fees to be taken in fresh claim proceedings), in the heading of that Schedule and in paragraph 3.1, for 'fresh claim' substitute 'immigration judicial review'.

APPENDIX 3

CIVIL PROCEDURE RULES

Contents

Civil Procedure Rules, Part 54	545
Practice Direction 54A	553
Practice Direction 54B	558
Practice Direction 54C	558
Practice Direction 54D	558
Practice Direction 54E	561
Pre Action Protocol for Judicial Review	562

PART 54
JUDICIAL REVIEW AND STATUTORY REVIEW[1]

Section 1 – Judicial Review

54.1 Scope and interpretation

(1) This Section of this Part contains rules about judicial review.

(2) In this Section –

    (a) a 'claim for judicial review' means a claim to review the lawfulness of –
        (i) an enactment; or
        (ii) a decision, action or failure to act in relation to the exercise of a public function.
    (b)–(d)...
    (e) 'the judicial review procedure' means the Part 8 procedure as modified by this Section;
    (f) 'interested party' means any person (other than the claimant and defendant) who is directly affected by the claim; and
    (g) 'court' means the High Court, unless otherwise stated.

    (Rule 8.1(6)(b) provides that a rule or practice direction may, in relation to a specified type of proceedings, disapply or modify any of these rules set out in Part 8 as they apply to those proceedings)

54.1A Who may exercise the powers of the High Court

(1) A court officer assigned to the Administrative Court office who is –

    (a) a barrister; or

---

[1] As at 75th Update to the CPR.

(b) a solicitor, may exercise the jurisdiction of the High Court with regard to the matters set out in paragraph (2) with the consent of the President of the Queen's Bench Division.

(2) The matters referred to in paragraph (1) are –

(a) any matter incidental to any proceedings in the High Court;
(b) any other matter where there is no substantial dispute between the parties; and
(c) the dismissal of an appeal or application where a party has failed to comply with any order, rule or practice direction.

(3) A court officer may not decide an application for –

(a) permission to bring judicial review proceedings;
(b) an injunction;
(c) a stay of any proceedings, other than a temporary stay of any order or decision of the lower court over a period when the High Court is not sitting or cannot conveniently be convened, unless the parties seek a stay by consent.

(4) Decisions of a court officer may be made without a hearing.

(5) A party may request any decision of a court officer to be reviewed by a judge of the High Court.

(6) At the request of a party, a hearing will be held to reconsider a decision of a court officer, made without a hearing.

(7) A request under paragraph (5) or (6) must be filed within 7 days after the party is served with notice of the decision.

54.2 When this Section must be used

The judicial review procedure must be used in a claim for judicial review where the claimant is seeking –

(a) a mandatory order;
(b) a prohibiting order;
(c) a quashing order; or
(d) an injunction under section 30 of the Senior Courts Act 1981 (restraining a person from acting in any office in which he is not entitled to act).

54.3 When this Section may be used

(1) The judicial review procedure may be used in a claim for judicial review where the claimant is seeking –

(a) a declaration; or
(b) an injunction.

(Section 31(2) of the Senior Courts Act 1981 sets out the circumstances in which the court may grant a declaration or injunction in a claim for judicial review)

(Where the claimant is seeking a declaration or injunction in addition to one of the remedies listed in rule 54.2, the judicial review procedure must be used)

(2) A claim for judicial review may include a claim for damages, restitution or the recovery of a sum due but may not seek such a remedy alone.

(Section 31(4) of the Senior Courts Act 1981 sets out the circumstances in which the court may award damages, restitution or the recovery of a sum due on a claim for judicial review)

54.4 Permission required

The court's permission to proceed is required in a claim for judicial review whether started under this Section or transferred to the Administrative Court.

54.5 Time limit for filing claim form

(A1) In this rule –

"the planning acts" has the same meaning as in section 336 of the Town and Country Planning Act 1990;
"decision governed by the Public Contracts Regulations 2006" means any decision the legality of which is or may be affected by a duty owed to an economic operator by virtue of regulation 47A of those Regulations (and for this purpose it does not matter that the claimant is not an economic operator); and
"economic operator" has the same meaning as in regulation 4 of the Public Contracts Regulations 2006.

(1) The claim form must be filed –

(a) promptly; and
(b) in any event not later than 3 months after the grounds to make the claim first arose.

(2) The time limits in this rule may not be extended by agreement between the parties.

(3) This rule does not apply when any other enactment specifies a shorter time limit for making the claim for judicial review.

(4) Paragraph (1) does not apply in the cases specified in paragraphs (5) and (6).

(5) Where the application for judicial review relates to a decision made by the Secretary of State or local planning authority under the planning acts, the claim form must be filed not later than six weeks after the grounds to make the claim first arose.

(6) Where the application for judicial review relates to a decision governed by the Public Contracts Regulations 2006, the claim form must be filed within the time within which an economic operator would have been required by regulation 47D(2) of those Regulations (and disregarding the rest of that regulation) to start any proceedings under those Regulations in respect of that decision.

54.6 Claim form

(1) In addition to the matters set out in rule 8.2 (contents of the claim form) the claimant must also state –

(a) the name and address of any person he considers to be an interested party;
(b) that he is requesting permission to proceed with a claim for judicial review;
(c) any remedy (including any interim remedy) he is claiming; and
(d) where appropriate, the grounds on which it is contended that the claim is an Aarhus Convention claim.

(Rules 45.41 and 45.44 make provision about costs in Aarhus Convention claims)

(Part 25 sets out how to apply for an interim remedy)

(2) The claim form must be accompanied by the documents required by Practice Direction 54A.

54.7 Service of claim form

The claim form must be served on –

- (a) the defendant; and
- (b) unless the court otherwise directs, any person the claimant considers to be an interested party, within 7 days after the date of issue.

54.7A Judicial review of decisions of the Upper Tribunal

(1) This rule applies where an application is made, following refusal by the Upper Tribunal of permission to appeal against a decision of the First Tier Tribunal, for judicial review –

- (a) of the decision of the Upper Tribunal refusing permission to appeal; or
- (b) which relates to the decision of the First Tier Tribunal which was the subject of the application for permission to appeal.

(2) Where this rule applies –

- (a) the application may not include any other claim, whether against the Upper Tribunal or not; and
- (b) any such other claim must be the subject of a separate application.

(3) The claim form and the supporting documents required by paragraph (4) must be filed no later than 16 days after the date on which notice of the Upper Tribunal's decision was sent to the applicant.

(4) The supporting documents are –

- (a) the decision of the Upper Tribunal to which the application relates, and any document giving reasons for the decision;
- (b) the grounds of appeal to the Upper Tribunal and any documents which were sent with them;
- (c) the decision of the First Tier Tribunal, the application to that Tribunal for permission to appeal and its reasons for refusing permission; and
- (d) any other documents essential to the claim.

(5) The claim form and supporting documents must be served on the Upper Tribunal and any other interested party no later than 7 days after the date of issue.

(6) The Upper Tribunal and any person served with the claim form who wishes to take part in the proceedings for judicial review must, no later than 21 days after service of the claim form, file and serve on the applicant and any other party an acknowledgment of service in the relevant practice form.

(7) The court will give permission to proceed only if it considers –

- (a) that there is an arguable case, which has a reasonable prospect of success, that both the decision of the Upper Tribunal refusing permission to appeal and the decision of the First Tier Tribunal against which permission to appeal was sought are wrong in law; and
- (b) that either –
    - (i) the claim raises an important point of principle or practice; or
    - (ii) there is some other compelling reason to hear it.

(8) If the application for permission is refused on paper without an oral hearing, rule 54.12(3) (request for reconsideration at a hearing) does not apply.

(9) If permission to apply for judicial review is granted –

(a) if the Upper Tribunal or any interested party wishes there to be a hearing of the substantive application, it must make its request for such a hearing no later than 14 days after service of the order granting permission; and
(b) if no request for a hearing is made within that period, the court will make a final order quashing the refusal of permission without a further hearing.

(10) The power to make a final order under paragraph (9)(b) may be exercised by the Master of the Crown Office or a Master of the Administrative Court.

54.8 Acknowledgment of service

(1) Any person served with the claim form who wishes to take part in the judicial review must file an acknowledgment of service in the relevant practice form in accordance with the following provisions of this rule.

(2) Any acknowledgment of service must be –

(a) filed not more than 21 days after service of the claim form; and
(b) served on –
   (i) the claimant; and
   (ii) subject to any direction under rule 54.7(b), any other person named in the claim form, as soon as practicable and, in any event, not later than 7 days after it is filed.

(3) The time limits under this rule may not be extended by agreement between the parties.

(4) The acknowledgment of service –

(a) must –
   (i) where the person filing it intends to contest the claim, set out a summary of his grounds for doing so; and
   (ii) state the name and address of any person the person filing it considers to be an interested party; and
(b) may include or be accompanied by an application for directions.

(5) Rule 10.3(2) does not apply.

54.9 Failure to file acknowledgment of service

(1) Where a person served with the claim form has failed to file an acknowledgment of service in accordance with rule 54.8, he –

(a) may not take part in a hearing to decide whether permission should be given unless the court allows him to do so; but
(b) provided he complies with rule 54.14 or any other direction of the court regarding the filing and service of –
   (i) detailed grounds for contesting the claim or supporting it on additional grounds; and
   (ii) any written evidence,
   may take part in the hearing of the judicial review.

(2) Where that person takes part in the hearing of the judicial review, the court may take his failure to file an acknowledgment of service into account when deciding what order to make about costs.

(3) Rule 8.4 does not apply.

54.10 Permission given

(1) Where permission to proceed is given the court may also give directions.

(2) Directions under paragraph (1) may include –

(a) a stay of proceedings to which the claim relates;
(b) directions requiring the proceedings to be heard by a Divisional Court.

(Rule 3.7 provides a sanction for the non-payment of the fee payable when permission to proceed has been given)

54.11 Service of order giving or refusing permission

The court will serve –

(a) the order giving or refusing permission; and
(b) any directions,

on –

(i) the claimant;
(ii) the defendant; and
(iii) any other person who filed an acknowledgment of service.

54.12 Permission decision without a hearing

(1) This rule applies where the court, without a hearing –

(a) refuses permission to proceed; or
(b) gives permission to proceed –
   (i) subject to conditions; or
   (ii) on certain grounds only.

(2) The court will serve its reasons for making the decision when it serves the order giving or refusing permission in accordance with rule 54.11.

(3) Subject to paragraph (7), the claimant may not appeal but may request the decision to be reconsidered at a hearing.

(4) A request under paragraph (3) must be filed within 7 days after service of the reasons under paragraph (2).

(5) The claimant, defendant and any other person who has filed an acknowledgment of service will be given at least 2 days' notice of the hearing date.

(6) The court may give directions requiring the proceedings to be heard by a Divisional Court.

(7) Where the court refuses permission to proceed and records the fact that the application is totally without merit in accordance with rule 23.12, the claimant may not request that decision to be reconsidered at a hearing.

54.13 Defendant etc may not apply to set aside

Neither the defendant nor any other person served with the claim form may apply to set aside an order giving permission to proceed.

54.14 Response

(1) A defendant and any other person saved with the claim form who wishes to contest the claim or support it on additional grounds must file and serve –

(a) detailed grounds for contesting the claim or supporting it on additional grounds; and
(b) any written evidence,

within 35 days after service of the order giving permission.

(2) The following rules do not apply –

(a) rule 8.5(3) and 8.5(4) (defendant to file and serve written evidence at the same time as acknowledgment of service); and
(b) rule 8.5(5) and 8.5(6) (claimant to file and serve reply within 14 days).

54.15 Where claimant seeks to rely on additional grounds

The court's permission is required if a claimant seeks to rely on grounds other than those for which he has been given permission to proceed.

54.16 Evidence

(1) Rule 8.6(1) does not apply.

(2) No written evidence may be relied on unless –

(a) it has been served in accordance with any –
   (i) rule under this Section; or
   (ii) direction of the court; or
(b) the court gives permission.

54.17 Court's powers to hear any person

(1) Any person may apply for permission –

(a) to file evidence; or
(b) make representations at the hearing of the judicial review.

(2) An application under paragraph (1) should be made promptly.

54.18 Judicial review may be decided without a hearing

The court may decide the claim for judicial review without a hearing where all the parties agree.

54.19 Court's powers in respect of quashing orders

(1) This rule applies where the court makes a quashing order in respect of the decision to which the claim relates.

(2) The court may –

(a) (i) remit the matter to the decision-maker; and
    (ii) direct it to reconsider the matter and reach a decision in accordance with the judgment of the court; or
(b) in so far as any enactment permits, substitute its own decision for the decision to which the claim relates.

(Section 31 of the Senior Courts Act 1981 enables the High Court, subject to certain conditions, to substitute its own decision for the decision in question)

...

54.20 Transfer

The court may –

(a) order a claim to continue as if it had not been started under this Section; and
(b) where it does so, give directions about the future management of the claim.

(Part 30 (transfer) applies to transfers to and from the Administrative Court)

Section II – Planning Court

54.21 General

(1) This Section applies to Planning Court claims.

(2) In this Section, "Planning Court claim" means a judicial review or statutory challenge

which –

(a) involves any of the following matters –
  (i) planning permission, other development consents, the enforcement of planning control and the enforcement of other statutory schemes;
  (ii) applications under the Transport and Works Act 1992;
  (iii) wayleaves;
  (iv) highways and other rights of way;
  (v) compulsory purchase orders;
  (vi) village greens;
  (vii) European Union environmental legislation and domestic transpositions, including assessments for development consents, habitats, waste and pollution control;
  (viii) national, regional or other planning policy documents, statutory or otherwise;
  or
  (ix) any other matter the judge appointed under rule 54.22(2) considers appropriate; and
(b) has been issued or transferred to the Planning Court.

(Part 30 (Transfer) applies to transfers to and from the Planning Court)

54.22 Specialist list

(1) The Planning Court claims form a specialist list.

(2) A judge nominated by the President of the Queen's Bench Division will be in charge of the Planning Court specialist list and will be known as the Planning Liaison Judge.

(3) The President of the Queen's Bench Division will be responsible for the nomination of specialist planning judges to deal with Planning Court claims which are significant within the meaning of Practice Direction 54E, and of other judges to deal with other Planning Court claims.

54.23 Application of the Civil Procedure Rules

These Rules and their practice directions will apply to Planning Court claims unless this section or a practice direction provides otherwise.

54.24 Further provision about Planning Court claims

Practice Direction 54E makes further provision about Planning Court claims, in particular about the timescales for determining such claims.

54.25–54.27 (*revoked*)

...

PRACTICE DIRECTIONS
PRACTICE DIRECTION 54A – JUDICIAL REVIEW

This Practice Direction supplements CPR Part 54 (PD54A)

Judicial Review

1.1 In addition to Part 54 and this practice direction attention is drawn to –

- section 31 of the Senior Courts Act 1981; and
- the Human Rights Act 1998.

The Court

2.1 Part 54 claims for judicial review are dealt with in the Administrative Court.

(Practice Direction 54D ... contains provisions about where a claim for judicial review may be started, administered and heard)

...

Rule 54.5 – Time Limit for Filing Claim Form

4.1 Where the claim is for a quashing order in respect of a judgment, order or conviction, the date when the grounds to make the claim first arose, for the purposes of rule 54.5(1)(b), is the date of that judgment, order or conviction.

Rule 54.6 – Claim Form

Interested parties

5.1 Where the claim for judicial review relates to proceedings in a court or tribunal, any other parties to those proceedings must be named in the claim form as interested parties under rule 54.6(1)(a) (and therefore served with the claim form under rule 54.7(b)).

5.2 For example, in a claim by a defendant in a criminal case in the Magistrates' or Crown Court for judicial review of a decision in that case, the prosecution must always be named as an interested party.

Human rights

5.3 Where the claimant is seeking to raise any issue under the Human Rights Act 1998, or seeks a remedy available under that Act, the claim form must include the information required by paragraph 15 of Practice Direction 16.

Devolution issues

5.4 Where the claimant intends to raise a devolution issue, the claim form must –

(1) specify that the applicant wishes to raise a devolution issue and identify the relevant provisions of the Government of Wales Act 2006, the Northern Ireland Act 1998 or the Scotland Act 1998; and

(2) contain a summary of the facts, circumstances and points of law on the basis of which it is alleged that a devolution issue arises.

5.5 In this practice direction 'devolution issue' has the same meaning as in paragraph 1, Schedule 9 to the Government of Wales Act 2006, paragraph 1, Schedule 10 to the Northern Ireland Act 1998; and paragraph 1, Schedule 6 to the Scotland Act 1998.

Claim form

5.6 The claim form must include or be accompanied by –

(1) a detailed statement of the claimant's grounds for bringing the claim for judicial review;
(2) a statement of the facts relied on;
(3) any application to extend the time limit for filing the claim form;
(4) any application for directions ...
...

5.7 In addition, the claim form must be accompanied by –

(1) any written evidence in support of the claim or application to extend time;
(2) a copy of any order that the claimant seeks to have quashed;
(3) where the claim for judicial review relates to a decision of a court or tribunal, an approved copy of the reasons for reaching that decision;
(4) copies of any documents on which the claimant proposes to rely;
(5) copies of any relevant statutory material;
(6) a list of essential documents for advance reading by the court (with page references to the passages relied on).

5.8 Where it is not possible to file all the above documents, the claimant must indicate which documents have not been filed and the reasons why they are not currently available.

Bundle of documents

5.9 The claimant must file two copies of a paginated and indexed bundle containing all the documents referred to in paragraphs 5.6 and 5.7.

5.10 Attention is drawn to rules 8.5(1) and 8.5(7).

Rule 54.7 – Service of Claim Form

6.1 Except as required by rules 54.11 or 54.12(2), the Administrative Court will not serve documents and service must be effected by the parties.

6.2 Where the defendant or interested party to the claim for judicial review is –

(a) the Immigration and Asylum Chamber of the First-tier Tribunal, the address for service of the claim form is Official Correspondence Unit, PO Box 6987, Leicester, LE1 6ZX or fax number 0116 249 4240;

(b) the Crown, service of the claim form must be effected on the solicitor acting for the relevant government department as if the proceedings were civil proceedings as defined in the Crown Proceedings Act 1947.

(Practice Direction 66 gives the list published under section 17 of the Crown Proceedings Act 1947 of the solicitors acting in civil proceedings (as defined in that Act) for the different government departments on whom service is to be effected, and of their addresses)

(Part 6 contains provisions about the service of claim forms)

Rule 54.8 – Acknowledgment of Service

7.1 Attention is drawn to rule 8.3(2) and the relevant practice direction and to rule 10.5.

Rule 54.10 – Permission Given

Directions

8.1 Case management directions under rule 54.10(1) may include directions about serving the claim form and any evidence on other persons.

8.2 Where a claim is made under the Human Rights Act 1998, a direction may be made for giving notice to the Crown or joining the Crown as a party. Attention is drawn to rule 19.4A and paragraph 6 of Practice Direction 19A.

...

Permission without a hearing

8.4 The court will generally, in the first instance, consider the question of permission without a hearing.

Permission hearing

8.5 Neither the defendant nor any other interested party need attend a hearing on the question of permission unless the court directs otherwise.

8.6 Where the defendant or any party does attend a hearing, the court will not generally make an order for costs against the claimant.

Rule 54.11 – Service of Order Giving or Refusing Permission

9.1 An order refusing permission or giving it subject to conditions or on certain grounds only must set out or be accompanied by the court's reasons for coming to that decision.

Rule 54.14 – Response

10.1 Where the party filing the detailed grounds intends to rely on documents not already filed, he must file a paginated bundle of those documents when he files the detailed grounds.

Rule 54.15 – Where Claimant Seeks to Rely on Additional Grounds

11.1 Where the claimant intends to apply to rely on additional grounds at the hearing of the claim for judicial review, he must give notice to the court and to any other person served with the claim form no later than 7 clear days before the hearing (or the warned date where appropriate).

Rule 54.16 – Evidence

12.1 Disclosure is not required unless the court orders otherwise.

Rule 54.17 – Court's Powers to Hear any Person

13.1 Where all the parties consent, the court may deal with an application under rule 54.17 without a hearing.

13.2 Where the court gives permission for a person to file evidence or make representations at the hearing of the claim for judicial review, it may do so on conditions and may give case management directions.

13.3 An application for permission should be made by letter to the Administrative Court office, identifying the claim, explaining who the applicant is and indicating why and in what form the applicant wants to participate in the hearing.

13.4 If the applicant is seeking a prospective order as to costs, the letter should say what kind of order and on what grounds.

13.5 Applications to intervene must be made at the earliest reasonable opportunity, since it will usually be essential not to delay the hearing.

Rule 54.20 – Transfer

14.1 Attention is drawn to rule 30.5.

14.2 In deciding whether a claim is suitable for transfer to the Administrative Court, the court will consider whether it raises issues of public law to which Part 54 should apply.

Skeleton arguments

15.1 The claimant must file and serve a skeleton argument not less than 21 working days before the date of the hearing of the judicial review (or the warned date).

15.2 The defendant and any other party wishing to make representations at the hearing of the judicial review must file and serve a skeleton argument not less than 14 working days before the date of the hearing of the judicial review (or the warned date).

15.3 Skeleton arguments must contain –

(1) a time estimate for the complete hearing, including delivery of judgment;
(2) a list of issues;
(3) a list of the legal points to be taken (together with any relevant authorities with page references to the passages relied on);
(4) a chronology of events (with page references to the bundle of documents (see paragraph 16.1);
(5) a list of essential documents for the advance reading of the court (with page references to the passages relied on) (if different from that filed with the claim form) and a time estimate for that reading; and
(6) a list of persons referred to.

Bundle of documents to be filed

16.1 The claimant must file a paginated and indexed bundle of all relevant documents required for the hearing of the judicial review when he files his skeleton argument.

16.2 The bundle must also include those documents required by the defendant and any other party who is to make representations at the hearing.

Agreed final order

17.1 If the parties agree about the final order to be made in a claim for judicial review, the claimant must file at the court a document (with 2 copies) signed by all the parties setting out the terms of the proposed agreed order together with a short statement of the matters relied on as justifying the proposed agreed order and copies of any authorities or statutory provisions relied on.

17.2 The court will consider the documents referred to in paragraph 17.1 and will make the order if satisfied that the order should be made.

17.3 If the court is not satisfied that the order should be made, a hearing date will be set.

17.4 Where the agreement relates to an order for costs only, the parties need only file a document signed by all the parties setting out the terms of the proposed order.

Section II – Applications for Permission to Apply for Judicial Review in Immigration and Asylum Cases – Challenging Removal

18.1 (1) This Section applies where –

(a) a person has been served with a copy of directions for his removal from the United Kingdom by the UK Border Agency of the Home Office and notified that this Section applies; and

(b) that person makes an application for permission to apply for judicial review before his removal takes effect.

(2) This Section does not prevent a person from applying for judicial review after he has been removed.

(3) The requirements contained in this Section of this Practice Direction are additional to those contained elsewhere in the Practice Direction.

18.2 (1) A person who makes an application for permission to apply for judicial review must file a claim form and a copy at court, and the claim form must –

(a) indicate on its face that this Section of the Practice Direction applies; and
(b) be accompanied by –
 (i) a copy of the removal directions and the decision to which the application relates; and
 (ii) any document served with the removal directions including any document which contains the UK Border Agency's factual summary of the case; and
(c) contain or be accompanied by the detailed statement of the claimant's grounds for bringing the claim for judicial review; or
(d) if the claimant is unable to comply with paragraph (b) or (c), contain or be accompanied by a statement of the reasons why.

(2) The claimant must, immediately upon issue of the claim, send copies of the issued claim form and accompanying documents to the address specified by the UK Border Agency.

> (Rule 54.7 also requires the defendant to be served with the claim form within 7 days of the date of issue. Rule 6.10 provides that service on a Government Department must be effected on the solicitor acting for that Department, which in the case of the UK Border Agency is the Treasury Solicitor. The address for the Treasury Solicitor may be found in the Annex to Part 66 of these Rules)

18.3 Where the claimant has not complied with paragraph 18.2(1)(b) or (c) and has provided reasons why he is unable to comply, and the court has issued the claim form, the Administrative Court –

(a) will refer the matter to a Judge for consideration as soon as practicable; and
(b) will notify the parties that it has done so.

18.4 If, upon a refusal to grant permission to apply for judicial review, the Court indicates that the application is clearly without merit, that indication will be included in the order refusing permission.

PRACTICE DIRECTION 54B – APPLICATIONS FOR STATUTORY REVIEW UNDER SECTION 103A OF THE NATIONALITY, IMMIGRATION AND ASYLUM ACT 2002

Applications for Statutory Review under section 103A of the Nationality, Immigration and Asylum Act 2002

****

PRACTICE DIRECTION 54C – REFERENCES BY THE LEGAL SERVICES COMMISSION

This Practice Direction supplements CPR Part 54 (PD54C)

References by the Legal Services Commission

1.1 This Practice Direction applies where the Legal Services Commission ('the Commission') refers to the High Court a question that arises on a review of a decision about an individual's financial eligibility for a representation order in criminal proceedings under the Criminal Defence Service (Financial Eligibility) Regulations 2006.

1.2 A reference of a question by the Legal Services Commission must be made to the Administrative Court.

1.3 Part 52 does not apply to a review under this paragraph.

1.4 The Commission must –

(a) file at the court –
 (i) the individual's applications for a representation order and for a review, and any supporting documents;
 (ii) a copy of the question on which the court's decision is sought; and
 (iii) a statement of the Commission's observations on the question; and
(b) serve a copy of the question and the statement on the individual.

1.5 The individual may file representations on the question at the court within 7 days after service on him of the copy of the question and the statement.

1.6 The question will be decided without a hearing unless the court directs otherwise.

PRACTICE DIRECTION 54D – ADMINISTRATIVE COURT (VENUE)

This Practice Direction supplements CPR Part 54 (PD54D)

Administrative Court (Venue)

Scope and purpose

1.1 This Practice Direction concerns the place in which a claim before the Administrative Court should be started and administered and the venue at which it will be determined.

1.2 This Practice Direction is intended to facilitate access to justice by enabling cases to be administered and determined in the most appropriate location. To achieve this purpose it provides flexibility in relation to where claims are to be administered and enables claims to be transferred to different venues.

Venue – general provisions

2.1 The claim form in proceedings in the Administrative Court may be issued at the Administrative Court Office of the High Court at –

(1) the Royal Courts of Justice in London; or
(2) at the District Registry of the High Court at Birmingham, Cardiff, Leeds, or Manchester unless the claim is one of the excepted classes of claim set out in paragraph 3 of this Practice Direction which may only be started and determined at the Royal Courts of Justice in London.

2.2 Any claim started in Birmingham will normally be determined at a court in the Midland region (geographically covering the area of the Midland Circuit); in Cardiff in Wales; in Leeds in the North-Eastern Region (geographically covering the area of the North Eastern Circuit); in London at the Royal Courts of Justice; and in Manchester, in the North-Western Region (geographically covering the Northern Circuit).

Excepted classes of claim

3.1 The excepted classes of claim referred to in paragraph 2.1(2) are –

(1) proceedings to which Part 76 or Part 79 applies, and for the avoidance of doubt –
    (a) proceedings relating to control orders (within the meaning of Part 76);
    (b) financial restrictions proceedings (within the meaning of Part 79);
    (c) proceedings relating to terrorism or alleged terrorists (where that is a relevant feature of the claim); and
    (d) proceedings in which a special advocate is or is to be instructed;
(2) proceedings to which RSC Order 115 applies;
(3) proceedings under the Proceeds of Crime Act 2002;
(4) appeals to the Administrative Court under the Extradition Act 2003;
(5) proceedings which must be heard by a Divisional Court; and
(6) proceedings relating to the discipline of solicitors.

3.2 If a claim form is issued at an Administrative Court office other than in London and includes one of the excepted classes of claim, the proceedings will be transferred to London.

Urgent applications

4.1 During the hours when the court is open, where an urgent application needs to be made to the Administrative Court outside London, the application must be made to the judge designated to deal with such applications in the relevant District Registry.

4.2 Any urgent application to the Administrative Court during the hours when the court is closed, must be made to the duty out of hours High Court judge by telephoning 020 7947 6000.

Assignment to another venue

5.1 The proceedings may be transferred from the office at which the claim form was issued to another office. Such transfer is a judicial act.

5.2 The general expectation is that proceedings will be administered and determined in the region with which the claimant has the closest connection, subject to the following considerations as applicable –

(1) any reason expressed by any party for preferring a particular venue;
(2) the region in which the defendant, or any relevant office or department of the defendant, is based;
(3) the region in which the claimant's legal representatives are based;
(4) the ease and cost of travel to a hearing;
(5) the availability and suitability of alternative means of attending a hearing (for example, by videolink);
(6) the extent and nature of media interest in the proceedings in any particular locality;
(7) the time within which it is appropriate for the proceedings to be determined;
(8) whether it is desirable to administer or determine the claim in another region in the light of the volume of claims issued at, and the capacity, resources and workload of, the court at which it is issued;
(9) whether the claim raises issues sufficiently similar to those in another outstanding claim to make it desirable that it should be determined together with, or immediately following, that other claim; and
(10) whether the claim raises devolution issues and for that reason whether it should more appropriately be determined in London or Cardiff.

5.3

(1) When an urgent application is made under paragraph 4.1 or 4.2, this will not by itself decide the venue for the further administration or determination of the claim.
(2) The court dealing with the urgent application may direct that the case be assigned to a particular venue.
(3) When an urgent application is made under paragraph 4.2, and the court does not make a direction under sub-paragraph (2), the claim will be assigned in the first place to London but may be reassigned to another venue at a later date.

5.4 The court may on an application by a party or of its own initiative direct that the claim be determined in a region other than that of the venue in which the claim is currently assigned. The considerations in paragraph 5.2 apply.

5.5 Once assigned to a venue, the proceedings will be both administered from that venue and determined by a judge of the Administrative Court at a suitable court within that region, or, if the venue is in London, at the Royal Courts of Justice. The choice of which court (of those within the region which are identified by the Presiding Judge of the circuit suitable for such hearing) will be decided, subject to availability, by the considerations in paragraph 5.2.

5.6 When giving directions under rule 54.10, the court may direct that proceedings be reassigned to another region for hearing (applying the considerations in paragraph 5.2).

If no such direction is given, the claim will be heard in the same region as that in which the permission application was determined (whether on paper or at a hearing).

PRACTICE DIRECTION 54E – PLANNING COURT CLAIMS

This Practice Direction supplements CPR Part 54 (PD54E)

Planning court claims

General

1.1 This Practice Direction applies to Planning Court claims.

How to start a Planning Court claim

2.1 Planning Court claims must be issued or lodged in the Administrative Court Office of the High Court in accordance with Practice Direction 54D.

2.2 The form must be marked the "Planning Court".

Categorisation of Planning Court claims

3.1 Planning Court claims may be categorised as "significant" by the Planning Liaison Judge.

3.2 Significant Planning Court claims include claims which –

a) relate to commercial, residential, or other developments which have significant economic impact either at a local level or beyond their immediate locality;
b) raise important points of law;
c) generate significant public interest; or
d) by virtue of the volume or nature of technical material, are best dealt with by judges with significant experience of handling such matters.

3.3 A party wishing to make representations in respect of the categorisation of a Planning Court claim must do so in writing, on issuing the claim or lodging an acknowledgment of service as appropriate.

3.4 The target timescales for the hearing of significant (as defined by paragraph 3.2) Planning Court claims, which the parties should prepare to meet, are as follows, subject to the overriding objective of the interests of justice –

a) applications for permission to apply for judicial review are to be determined within three weeks of the expiry of the time limit for filing of the acknowledgment of service;
b) oral renewals of applications for permission to apply for judicial review are to be heard within one month of receipt of request for renewal;
c) applications for permission under section 289 of the Town and Country Planning Act 1990 are to be determined within one month of issue;
d) substantive statutory applications, including applications under section 288 of the Town and Country Planning Act 1990, are to be heard within six months of issue; and
e) judicial reviews are to be heard within ten weeks of the expiry of the period for the submission of detailed grounds by the defendant or any other party as provided in Rule 54.14.

3.5 The Planning Court may make case management directions, including a direction to any party intending to contest the claim to file and serve a summary of his grounds for doing so.

3.6 Notwithstanding the categorisation under paragraph 3.1 of a Planning Court claim as significant or otherwise, the Planning Liaison Judge may direct the expedition of any Planning Court claim if he considers it to necessary to deal with the case justly.

PRE ACTION PROTOCOL FOR JUDICIAL REVIEW

Introduction

This protocol applies to proceedings within England and Wales only. It does not affect the time limit specified by Rule 54.5(1) of the Civil Procedure Rules which requires that any claim form in an application for judicial review must be filed promptly and in any event not later than 3 months after the grounds to make the claim first arose or the shorter time limits specified by Rules 54.5(5) and (6) which set out that a claim form for certain planning judicial reviews must be filed within 6 weeks and the claim form for certain procurement judicial reviews must be filed within 30 days.[2][1]

1

Judicial review allows people with a sufficient interest in a decision or action by a public body to ask a judge to review the lawfulness of:

- an enactment; or
- a decision, action or failure to act in relation to the exercise of a public function.[3][2]

2

Judicial review may be used where there is no right of appeal or where all avenues of appeal have been exhausted.

Alternative Dispute Resolution

3.1

The parties should consider whether some form of alternative dispute resolution procedure would be more suitable than litigation, and if so, endeavour to agree which form to adopt. Both the Claimant and Defendant may be required by the Court to provide evidence that alternative means of resolving their dispute were considered. The Courts take the view that litigation should be a last resort, and that claims should not be issued prematurely when a settlement is still actively being explored. Parties are warned that if the protocol is not followed (including this paragraph) then the Court must have regard to such conduct when determining costs. However, parties should also note that a claim for judicial review 'must be filed promptly and in any event not later than 3 months after the grounds to make the claim first arose'.

---

[2] While the court does have the discretion under Rule 3.1(2)(a) of the Civil Procedure Rules to allow a late claim, this is only used in exceptional circumstances. **Compliance with the protocol alone is unlikely to be sufficient to persuade the court to allow a late claim.**

[3] Civil Procedure Rule 54.1(2).

3.2

It is not practicable in this protocol to address in detail how the parties might decide which method to adopt to resolve their particular dispute. However, summarised below are some of the options for resolving disputes without litigation:

- Discussion and negotiation.
- Ombudsmen – the Parliamentary and Health Service and the Local Government Ombudsmen have discretion to deal with complaints relating to maladministration. The British and Irish Ombudsman Association provide information about Ombudsman schemes and other complaint handling bodies and this is available from their website at www.bioa.org.uk. Parties may wish to note that the Ombudsmen are not able to look into a complaint once court action has been commenced.
- Early neutral evaluation by an independent third party (for example, a lawyer experienced in the field of administrative law or an individual experienced in the subject matter of the claim).
- Mediation – a form of facilitated negotiation assisted by an independent neutral party.

3.3

The Legal Services Commission has published a booklet on 'Alternatives to Court', CLS Direct Information Leaflet 23 (www.clsdirect.org.uk), which lists a number of organisations that provide alternative dispute resolution services.

3.4

It is expressly recognised that no party can or should be forced to mediate or enter into any form of ADR.

4

Judicial review may not be appropriate in every instance.

Claimants are strongly advised to seek appropriate legal advice when considering such proceedings and, in particular, before adopting this protocol or making a claim. Although the Legal Services Commission will not normally grant full representation before a letter before claim has been sent and the proposed defendant given a reasonable time to respond, initial funding may be available, for eligible claimants, to cover the work necessary to write this. (See Annex C for more information.)

5

This protocol sets out a code of good practice and contains the steps which parties should generally follow before making a claim for judicial review.

6

This protocol does not impose a greater obligation on a public body to disclose documents or give reasons for its decision than that already provided for in statute or common law. However, where the court considers that a public body should have provided relevant documents and/or information, particularly where this failure is a breach of a statutory or common law requirement, it may impose sanctions.

This protocol will not be appropriate where the defendant does not have the legal power to change the decision being challenged, for example decisions issued by tribunals such as the Asylum and Immigration Tribunal.

This protocol will not be appropriate in urgent cases, for example, when directions have been set, or are in force, for the claimant's removal from the UK, or where there is an urgent need for an interim order to compel a public body to act where it has unlawfully refused to do so (for example, the failure of a local housing authority to secure interim accommodation for a homeless claimant) a claim should be made immediately. A letter before claim will not stop the implementation of a disputed decision in all instances.

This protocol may not be appropriate in cases where one of the shorter time limits in Rules 54.5(5) or (6) applies. In those cases, the parties should still attempt to comply with this protocol but the court will not apply normal cost sanctions where the court is satisfied that it has not been possible to comply because of the shorter time limits.

7

All claimants will need to satisfy themselves whether they should follow the protocol, depending upon the circumstances of his or her case. Where the use of the protocol is appropriate, the court will normally expect all parties to have complied with it and will take into account compliance or non-compliance when giving directions for case management of proceedings or when making orders for costs.[43] However, even in emergency cases, it is good practice to fax to the defendant the draft Claim Form which the claimant intends to issue. A claimant is also normally required to notify a defendant when an interim mandatory order is being sought.

The letter before claim

8

Before making a claim, the claimant should send a letter to the defendant. The purpose of this letter is to identify the issues in dispute and establish whether litigation can be avoided.

9

Claimants should normally use the suggested **standard format** for the letter outlined at Annex A.

10

The letter should contain the date and details of the decision, act or omission being challenged and a clear summary of the facts on which the claim is based. It should also contain the details of any relevant information that the claimant is seeking and an explanation of why this is considered relevant. If the claim is considered to be an Aarhus Convention claim, the letter should state this clearly and explain the reasons, since specific rules as to costs apply to such claims.

---

[4] Civil Procedure Rules Costs Practice Direction.

11

The letter should normally contain the **details of any interested parties**[5] known to the claimant. They should be sent a copy of the letter before claim for information. Claimants are **strongly advised to seek appropriate legal advice when considering such proceedings and, in particular, before sending the letter before claim to other interested parties or making a claim.**

12

A claim should not normally be made until the proposed reply date given in the letter before claim has passed, unless the circumstances of the case require more immediate action to be taken.

The letter of response

13

Defendants should normally respond within 14 days using the **standard format** at Annex B. Failure to do so will be taken into account by the court and sanctions may be imposed unless there are good reasons.[6]

14

Where it is not possible to reply within the proposed time limit the defendant should send an interim reply and propose a reasonable extension. Where an extension is sought, reasons should be given and, where required, additional information requested. This will not affect the time limit for making a claim for judicial review[7] nor will it bind the claimant where he or she considers this to be unreasonable. However, where the court considers that a subsequent claim is made prematurely it may impose sanctions.

15

If the **claim is being conceded in full,** the reply should say so in clear and unambiguous terms.

16

If the **claim is being conceded in part or not being conceded at all,** the reply should say so in clear and unambiguous terms, and:

(a) where appropriate, contain a new decision, clearly identifying what aspects of the claim are being conceded and what are not, or, give a clear timescale within which the new decision will be issued;
(b) provide a fuller explanation for the decision, if considered appropriate to do so;
(c) address any points of dispute, or explain why they cannot be addressed;
(d) enclose any relevant documentation requested by the claimant, or explain why the documents are not being enclosed; and
(e) where appropriate, confirm whether or not they will oppose any application for an interim remedy.

---

5   See Civil Procedure Rule 54.1(2)(f).
6   See Civil Procedure Rules Pre-action Protocol Practice Direction paragraphs 2–3.
7   See Civil Procedure Rule 54.5(1).

If the letter before claim has stated that the claim is an Aarhus Convention claim but the defendant does not accept this, the reply should state this clearly and explain the reasons.

17

The response should be sent to **all interested parties**[8] identified by the claimant and contain details of any other parties who the defendant considers also have an interest.

A letter before claim

Section 1. Information required in a letter before claim

Proposed claim for judicial review

1

To

(Insert the name and address of the proposed defendant – see details in section 2)

2

The claimant

(Insert the title, first and last name and the address of the claimant)

3

Reference details

(When dealing with large organisations it is important to understand that the information relating to any particular individual's previous dealings with it may not be immediately available, therefore it is important to set out the relevant reference numbers for the matter in dispute and/or the identity of those within the public body who have been handling the particular matter in dispute – see details in section 3)

4

The details of the matter being challenged

(Set out clearly the matter being challenged, particularly if there has been more than one decision)

5

The issue

(Set out the date and details of the decision, or act or omission being challenged, a brief summary of the facts and why it is contented to be wrong)

6

The details of the action that the defendant is expected to take

(Set out the details of the remedy sought, including whether a review or any interim remedy are being requested)

---

[8] See Civil Procedure Rule 54.1(2)(f).

7

The details of the legal advisers, if any, dealing with this claim

(Set out the name, address and reference details of any legal advisers dealing with the claim)

8

The details of any interested parties

(Set out the details of any interested parties and confirm that they have been sent a copy of this letter)

9

The details of any information sought

(Set out the details of any information that is sought. This may include a request for a fuller explanation of the reasons for the decision that is being challenged)

10

The details of any documents that are considered relevant and necessary

(Set out the details of any documentation or policy in respect of which the disclosure is sought and explain why these are relevant. If you rely on a statutory duty to disclose, this should be specified)

11

The address for reply and service of court documents

(Insert the address for the reply)

12

Proposed reply date

(The precise time will depend upon the circumstances of the individual case. However, although a shorter or longer time may be appropriate in a particular case, 14 days is a reasonable time to allow in most circumstances)

Section 2. Address for sending the letter before claim

Public bodies have requested that, for certain types of cases, in order to ensure a prompt response, letters before claim should be sent to specific addresses.

> Where the claim concerns a decision in an Immigration, Asylum or Nationality case:
> – The claim may be sent electronically to the following email address UKVIPAP@homeoffice.gsi.gov.uk
> – Alternatively the claim may be sent by post to the following UK Border Agency postal address:
> > Judicial Review Unit
> > UK Border Agency
> > Lunar House
> > 40 Wellesley Rd
> > Croydon CR9 2BY

Where the claim concerns a decision by the Legal Services Commission:

- The address on the decision letter/notification;
  Legal Director
  Corporate Legal Team
  Legal Services Commission
  102 Petty France
  London SW1H 9AJ

Where the claim concerns a decision by a local authority:

- The address on the decision letter/notification; and
- Their legal department[9]

Where the claim concerns a decision by a department or body for whom Treasury Solicitor acts and Treasury Solicitor has already been involved in the case a copy should also be sent, quoting the Treasury Solicitor's reference, to:

The Treasury Solicitor,
One Kemble Street,
London WC2B 4TS

In all other circumstances, the letter should be sent to the address on the letter notifying the decision.

Section 3. Specific reference details required

Public bodies have requested that the following information should be provided in order to ensure prompt response.

Where the claim concerns an Immigration, Asylum or Nationality case, dependent upon the nature of the case:

- The Home Office reference number
- The Port reference number
- The Asylum and Immigration Tribunal reference number
- The National Asylum Support Service reference number

Or, if these are unavailable:

- The full name, nationality and date of birth of the claimant.

Where the claim concerns a decision by the Legal Services Commission:

- The certificate reference number.

B Response to a letter before claim

Information required in a response to a letter before claim

Proposed claim for judicial review

1

The claimant

(Insert the title, first and last names and the address to which any reply should be sent)

---

[9] The relevant address should be available from a range of sources such as the Phone Book; Business and Services Directory, Thomson's Local Directory, CAB, etc.

2

From

(Insert the name and address of the defendant)

3

Reference details

(Set out the relevant reference numbers for the matter in dispute and the identity of those within the public body who have been handling the issue)

4

The details of the matter being challenged

(Set out details of the matter being challenged, providing a fuller explanation of the decision, where this is considered appropriate)

5

Response to the proposed claim

(Set out whether the issue in question is conceded in part, or in full, or will be contested. Where it is not proposed to disclose any information that has been requested, explain the reason for this. Where an interim reply is being sent and there is a realistic prospect of settlement, details should be included)

6

Details of any other interested parties

(Identify any other parties who you consider have an interest who have not already been sent a letter by the claimant)

7

Address for further correspondence and service of court documents

(Set out the address for any future correspondence on this matter)

C Notes on public funding for legal costs in judicial review

Public funding for legal costs in judicial review is available from legal professionals and advice agencies which have contracts with the Legal Services Commission as part of the Community Legal Service. Funding may be provided for:

> Legal Help to provide initial advice and assistance with any legal problem; or
> Legal Representation to allow you to be represented in court if you are taking or defending court proceedings. This is available in two forms:
> – Investigative Help is limited to funding to investigate the strength of the proposed claim. It includes the issue and conduct of proceedings only so far as is necessary to obtain disclosure of relevant information or to protect the client's position in relation to any urgent hearing or time limit for the issue of proceedings. This includes the work necessary to write a **letter before claim** to

the body potentially under challenge, setting out the grounds of challenge, and giving that body a reasonable opportunity, typically 14 days, in which to respond.

– Full Representation is provided to represent you in legal proceedings and includes litigation services, advocacy services, and all such help as is usually given by a person providing representation in proceedings, including steps preliminary or incidental to proceedings, and/or arriving at or giving effect to a compromise to avoid or bring to an end any proceedings. Except in emergency cases, a proper **letter before claim** must be sent and the other side must be given an opportunity to respond before Full Representation is granted.

Further information on the type(s) of help available and the criteria for receiving that help may be found in the Legal Service Manual Volume 3: "The Funding Code". This may be found on the Legal Services Commission website at:

www.legalservices.gov.uk

A list of contracted firms and Advice Agencies may be found on the Community Legal Services website at:

www.justask.org.uk

APPENDIX 4

ADMINISTRATIVE COURT GUIDANCE

Contents

Notes for guidance on applying for judicial review	571
Administrative Court – guidance as to how the court will approach applications for costs following settlement of claims for judicial review	589
R (on the application of Hamid) v Secretary of State for the Home Department [2012] EWHC 3070R (on the application of Hamid) v Secretary of State for the Home Department [2012] EWHC 3070	591
R (Butt and Others) v SSHD [2014] EWHC 264 (Admin)	594

NOTES FOR GUIDANCE ON APPLYING FOR JUDICIAL REVIEW

1 Introduction
2 What is Judicial Review?
3 What is the Pre-action protocol?
4 Where should I commence proceedings?
5 When should I lodge my application for permission to apply for judicial review?
6 Is there a fee to pay and, if so, when do I pay it?
7 How do I apply for Judicial Review?
8 What do I do if my application is urgent?
9 What is an Acknowledgement of Service?
10 What happens after the defendant and/or the interested party has lodged an acknowledgement of service or the time for filing such has expired?
11 What happens if my application for permission is refused or if permission is granted subject to conditions or in part only?
12 What happens if my application for permission is granted?
13 What happens when my case is ready for hearing?
14 What if I need to make an application for further orders after the grant of permission?
15 Can my application be determined without the need for a hearing?
16 What if the proceedings settle by consent prior to the substantive hearing of my application?
17 What if I want to discontinue the proceedings at any stage?
18 Will I be responsible for costs of the defendant and/or the interested parties if my application is unsuccessful?

19   What can I do if I am unhappy with the Judge's decision?
20   Where can I get advice about procedural matters?

Section 1

General introduction

1.1 These notes are not intended to be exhaustive but are designed to offer an outline of the procedure to be followed when seeking to make an application for judicial review in the Administrative Court. For further details of the procedure to be followed you and your representatives/legal advisers should consult Part 54 of the Civil Procedure Rules (CPR) and the Practice Directions accompanying Part 54. For further details of the procedure to be followed for judicial review applications to the Planning Court you should consult rule 54.20 of the CPR and the Practice Direction 54E on Planning Court Claims.

Immigration and Asylum Judicial Reviews

1.2 Since 1 November 2013 Immigration Judicial Reviews (IJRs) that were previously dealt with in the Administrative Court have been dealt with by the Upper Tribunal Immigration and Asylum Chamber (UTIAC).

This is by virtue of the Lord Chief Justice's Direction of 21 August 2013 (which can be viewed at www.judiciary.gov.uk/publications-and-reports/practicedirections/tribunals/tribunals-pd) which provides full details of the categories of IJRs that are transferred. Please consult the UTIAC website at http://www.justice.gov.uk/tribunals/immigration-asylum-upper for details and guidance on applying for a Judicial Review by the UTIAC.

Should you require an urgent consideration of an Immigration matter outside of the UTIACs office hours this will be considered by the Administrative Court. Please consult 'Out of Hours applications in the Royal Courts of Justice' at our web page http://www.justice.gov.uk/courts/rcj-rolls-building/administrative-court

Section 2

What is judicial review?

2.1 Judicial review is the procedure by which you can seek to challenge the decision, action or failure to act of a public body such as a government department or a local authority or other body exercising a public law function. If you are challenging the decision of a court, the jurisdiction of judicial review extends only to decisions of inferior courts. It does not extend to decisions of the High Court or Court of Appeal. Judicial review must be used where you are seeking:

- a mandatory order (i.e. an order requiring the public body to do something and formerly known as an order of mandamus);
- a prohibiting order (i.e. an order preventing the public body from doing something and formerly known as an order of prohibition); or

- a quashing order (i.e. an order quashing the public body's decision and formerly known as an order of certiorari);
- a declaration;
- HRA Damages.

2.2 Claims can either be heard by a single Judge or a Divisional Court (a court of two judges). The Administrative Court sits at the following locations, although in appropriate cases arrangements may be made for sittings at alternative locations:

- The Royal Courts of Justice in London – (address for correspondence: Room C315, Royal Courts of Justice, Strand, London, WC2A 2LL);
- Birmingham Civil Justice Centre – (address for correspondence: Priory Courts, 33 Bull Street, Birmingham, B4 6DS);
- Cardiff Civil Justice Centre – (address for correspondence:2 Park Street, Cardiff, CF10 1ET);
- Leeds Combined Court Centre – (address for correspondence:1 Oxford Row, Leeds, LS1 3BG);
- Manchester Civil Justice Centre – (address for correspondence:1 Bridge Street West, Manchester, M3 3FX).

Section 3

What is the pre-action protocol?

3.1 The protocol sets out a code of good practice and contains the steps which parties should generally follow before making a claim for judicial review. The objective of the pre-action protocol is to avoid unnecessary litigation.

3.2 Before making your claim for judicial review, you should send a letter to the defendant. The purpose of this letter is to identify the issues in dispute and establish whether litigation can be avoided. The letter should contain the date and details of the decision, act or omission being challenged and a clear summary of the facts on which the claim is based. It should also contain the details of any relevant information that the claimant is seeking and an explanation of why this is considered relevant. A claim should not normally be made until the proposed reply date given in the letter before claim has passed, unless the circumstances of the case require more immediate action to be taken.

3.3 Defendants should normally respond to that letter within 14 days and sanctions may be imposed unless there are good reasons for not responding within that period.

NB – The protocol does not affect the time limit for permission to apply for judicial review – see Section 5 for details of time limits.

NB – You should seek advice as to whether the protocol is appropriate in the circumstances of your case. Use of the protocol will not be appropriate where the defendant does not have the legal power to change the decision being challenged. It also may not be appropriate in circumstances where the application is urgent.

NB – A letter before claim will not automatically stop the implementation of a disputed decision

NB – Even in emergency cases, it is good practice to fax the draft claim form that you are intending to issue to the defendant. You will also normally be required to notify a defendant when you are seeking an interim order; ie, an order giving some form of relief pending the final determination of the claim.

3.4 Any claim for judicial review must indicate whether or not the protocol has been complied with. If the protocol has not been complied with, the reasons for failing to do so should be set out in the claim form.

Section 4

Where should I commence proceedings?

4.1 Claims for judicial review under CPR Part 54 are dealt with in the Administrative Court.

4.2 Claims may be issued at the District Registry of the High Court at Birmingham, Cardiff, Leeds or Manchester as well as at the Royal Courts of Justice in London. Cases started in Birmingham will normally be determined at a court in the Midland region; in Cardiff in Wales; in Leeds in the North-Eastern Region; in London at the Royal Courts of Justice and in Manchester, in the North-Western Region.

4.3 The general expectation is that proceedings will be administered and determined in the region with which the claimant has the closest connection, subject to the following considerations as applicable –

(1) any reason expressed by any party for preferring a particular venue;
(2) the region in which the defendant, or any relevant office or department of the defendant, is based;
(3) the region in which the claimant's legal representatives are based;
(4) the ease and cost of travel to a hearing;
(5) the availability and suitability of alternative means of attending a hearing (for example, by videolink);
(6) the extent and nature of media interest in the proceedings in any particular locality;
(7) the time within which it is appropriate for the proceedings to be determined;
(8) whether it is desirable to administer or determine the claim in another region in the light of the volume of claims issued at, and the capacity, resources and workload of, the court at which it is issued;
(9) whether the claim raises issues sufficiently similar to those in another outstanding claim to make it desirable that it should be determined together with, or immediately following, that other claim; and
(10) whether the claim raises devolution issues and for that reason whether it should more appropriately be determined in London or Cardiff.

Can I get Legal Services Commission funding (Legal Aid) for my application?

4.4 Neither the Court nor the Administrative Court Offices have power to grant funding (previously legal aid). The responsibility for the provision of public funding is held by the Legal Services Commission.

4.5 Further information on the type(s) of help available and the criteria for receiving that help may be found on the Legal Services Commission website at http://www.legalservices.gov.uk/.

4.6 A list of contracted firms and Advice Agencies may be found on the Community Legal Services website at http://www.communitylegaladvice.org.uk/. Community Legal Advice can also provide you with a list of solicitors in your area if you telephone them on 0845 345 4 345.

Section 5

When should I lodge my application for permission to apply for judicial review?

5.1 Generally, unless Section 18 Practice Direction 54 applies in relation to the deferral of removal, the claim must be filed promptly and (subject to paragraphs 5.2–5.4), in any event **no later than three months** after the grounds to make the claim first arose. However, the time limit for lodging a Planning Court Judicial review is **six weeks** from the date the grounds arise; this is in line with other applications to the Planning Court.

5.2 Challenges to decisions under the Town and Country Planning Act 1990, The Planning (Listed Buildings & Conservation Areas) Act 1990, The Planning (Hazardous Substances) Act 1990 and The Planning (Consequential Provisions) Act 1990 must be filed not later than six weeks after the grounds to make the claim first arose (CPR 54.5(A1)(5)).

5.3 Where the application for judicial review relates to a decision governed by the Public Contracts Regulations 2006, the claim form must be filed within 30 days beginning with the date when the claimant first knew or ought to have known that grounds for starting the proceedings had arisen (CPR 54.5(A1)(6)).

5.4 Where the challenge is to a decision under the Inquiries Act 2005, the claim form must be filed within 14 days after the day on which the applicant becomes aware of the decision, unless that time limit is extended by the court(s.36 Inquiries Act 2005) (CPR 54.5(A1)(6)).

5.5 Where the applicant is challenging the decision of the Upper Tribunal, the claim form and supporting documents must be filed within 16 days from the date of the decision made by the Upper Tribunal (CPR 54.7A)

5.6 The court has the power to extend the period for the lodging of an application for permission to apply for judicial review but will only do so where it is satisfied there are very good reasons for doing so.

NB – The time for the lodging of the application may not be extended by agreement between the parties.

NB – If you are seeking an extension of time for the lodging of your application, you must make the application in the claim form, setting out the grounds in support of that application to extend time (CPR Part 54.5).

Section 6

Is there a fee to pay and if so, when should I pay it?

6.1 A fee of £140.00 is payable when you lodge your application for permission to apply for Judicial Review. A further £700.00[1] is payable if you wish to pursue the claim if permission is granted Civil Proceedings Fees (Amendment) Order 2014).

6.2 For judicial where the court refuses permission to proceed, the claimant may not appeal but may request the decision to be reconsidered at a hearing. If such a request is made, the claimant must pay an additional fee of £350.

NB – If you are in receipt of certain types of benefits you may be entitled to remission of any fee due as part of judicial review proceedings. If you believe you may be entitled to fee remission you should apply to the relevant Administrative Court Office using Form EX160 (Application for a Fee Remission) and lodge the application with your claim form.

NB – Cheques should be made payable to HMCTS. If you lodge your claim form at the court office in person, personal cheques must be supported by a cheque guarantee card presented at the time the claim form is lodged. Cheques and postal orders will be accepted via post at each of the Administrative Court's offices.

Fees may be paid by credit/debit card, cheque or cash in London when presented in person to the Royal Courts of Justice Fees Office. The Administrative Court Office in Cardiff will accept payment by cheque, cash or debit card only when presented in person at their office, and the Birmingham, Manchester and Leeds offices accept payment by cheque and credit/debit cards at their counters and over the telephone.

Section 7

How do I apply for judicial review?

7.1 An application for permission to apply for judicial review to the Planning Court must be made on claim form N461PC; any other application for permission to apply for judicial review must be made by claim form N461.

7.2 The claim form must include or be accompanied by –

---

[1] If the fee has been paid for a request to reconsider at a hearing a decision on permission to bring a judicial review and permission is subsequently granted at a hearing, only half of the judicial review fee is then payable.

- a detailed statement of the claimant's grounds for bringing the claim for judicial review;
- a statement of the facts relied on;
- any application to extend the time limit for filing the claim form; and
- any application for directions.

7.3 Where you are seeking to raise any issue under the Human Rights Act 1998, or a remedy available under that Act, the claim form must include the information required by paragraph 16 of the Practice Direction supplementing Part 16 of the Civil Procedure Rules.

7.4 Where you intend to raise a devolution issue, the claim form must specify that you (a) wish to raise a devolution issue (b) identify the relevant provisions of the Government of Wales Act 1998, and (c) contain a summary of the facts, circumstances and points of law on the basis of which it is alleged that a devolution issue arises. Cases involving Welsh devolution issues are expected to be lodged at the Administrative Court Office in Wales.

7.5 The claim form must also be accompanied by –

- any written evidence in support of the claim or application to extend time;
- a copy of any order that you are seeking to have quashed;
- where the claim for judicial review relates to a decision of a court or tribunal, an approved copy of the reasons for reaching that decision;
- copies of any documents upon which you propose to rely;
- copies of any relevant statutory material;
- a list of essential documents for advance reading by the court (with page references to the passages relied upon). Where only part of a page needs to be read, that part should be indicated, by side-lining or in some other way, but not by highlighting.

NB – Where it is not possible for you to file all the above documents, you must indicate which documents have not been filed and the reasons why they are not currently available. The defendant and/or the interested party may seek an extension of time for the lodging of its acknowledgement of service pending receipt of the missing documents.

What documents do I need to lodge?

7.6 You must file the original claim form and witness statement, together with a set of paginated and indexed copy documents for the courts use containing the documents referred to in paragraph 7.5 above (CPR Part 54.6 and Practice Direction 54). You should also file a complete set of copy documents (including a copy claim form and witness statement) in a paginated and indexed set for the courts use. Please ensure you paginate in consecutive page number order throughout your bundle. Also ensure that each page has a page number on it and provide an index, which lists the description of documents contained in your bundle together with their page reference numbers.

7.7 Please note that if your case is of a criminal nature then the Court will require you to lodge two paginated and indexed bundles of copy documents.

7.8 You must also lodge sufficient additional copies of the claim form for the court to seal them (i.e. stamp them with the court seal) so that you can serve them on the defendant and any interested parties. The sealed copies will be returned to you so that you can serve them on the defendant and any interested parties.

7.9 If you are represented by solicitors they must also provide a paginated, indexed bundle of the relevant legislative provisions and statutory instruments required for the proper consideration of the application. If you are acting in person you should comply with this requirement if possible.

NB – Applications that do not comply with the requirements of CPR Part 54 and Practice Direction 54 will not be accepted, save in exceptional circumstances. In this context a matter will be regarded as exceptional where a decision is sought from the Court within 14 days of the lodging of the application. In such circumstances an undertaking will be required to provide compliance with the requirements of the CPR within a specified period.

NB – If the only reason given in support of urgency is the imminent expiry of the three month time limit for lodging an application, the papers will nonetheless be returned for compliance with Part 54 and Practice Direction 54. In those circumstances you must seek an extension of time and provide reasons for the delay in lodging the papers in proper form.

Whom should I serve my application on?

7.10 The sealed copy claim form (and accompanying documents) must be served on the defendant and any person that you consider to be an interested party (unless the court directs otherwise) within 7 days of the date of issue (i.e. the date shown on the court seal). The Administrative Court Office will not serve your claim on the defendant or any interested party.

NB – An interested party is a person who is likely to be directly affected by your judicial review application.

NB – Please note that under the provisions of the Crown Proceedings Act 1947 service must be upon the Department responsible for the Defendant.

NB – Where the claim for judicial review relates to proceedings in a court or tribunal, any other parties to those proceedings must be named in the claim form as interested parties and served with the claim form (CPR 54 PD.5). For example, in a claim by a defendant in a criminal case in the Magistrates' or Crown Court for judicial review of a decision in that case, the prosecution must always be named as an interested party.

7.11 You should lodge a Certificate of Service in Form N215 in the relevant Administrative Court Office within 7 days of serving the defendant and other interested parties.

7.12 The date of deemed service is calculated in accordance with CPR Part 6.14 (see methods of service below).

7.12 The date of deemed service is calculated in accordance with CPR Part 6.14 (see methods of service below).

Method – First class post, Document Exchange (DX) or other service which provides for delivery on the next business day.	Deemed date of service – The second business day after it was posted, left with, delivered to or collected by the relevant service provider provided that day is a business day; or if not, the next business day after that: | Posted	Deemed served
Monday	Wednesday
Tuesday	Thursday
Wednesday	Friday
Thursday	Monday
Friday	Monday | **Please note:** If the service date falls on a Public Holiday the deemed service date is the first working day following the Public Holiday.
Method – Delivering the document to or leaving it at the relevant place.	Deemed date of service – Where it is delivered to or left at the relevant place before 12.00 midnight, on the second business day after that day.
Method – Fax	Deemed date of service – The second business day after the transmission of the fax (e.g. if the fax is sent at 10.30pm on Monday, it will be deemed served on Wednesday.
Method – Other electronic method e.g. email	Deemed date of service – The second business day after sending the email or other electronic transmission.
Method – Personal Service	Deemed date of service – The second business day after completing the relevant step required by CPR 6.5(3).

NB – The time for a Defendant and any Interested Party to lodge an acknowledgement of service (21 days) commences from the date that the claim is deemed served upon them.

Section 8

What do I do if my application is urgent?

8.1 If you want to make an application for your application for permission to be heard / considered by a Judge as a matter of urgency and/or to seek an interim injunction, you must complete a Request for Urgent Consideration, Form N463, which can be obtained from the HMCTS website or the relevant Administrative Court Office. The form sets out the reasons for urgency and the timescale sought for the consideration of the permission application, e.g. within 72 hours or sooner if necessary, and the date by which the substantive hearing should take place.

8.2 Where you are seeking an interim injunction, you must, in addition, provide a draft order; and the grounds for the injunction. You must serve the claim form, the draft order and the application for urgency on the defendant and interested parties (by FAX and by post), advising them of the application and informing them that they may make representations directly to the Court in respect of your application.

8.3 A judge will consider the application within the time requested and may make such order as he/she considers appropriate.

NB – The judge may refuse your application for permission at this stage if he/she considers it appropriate, in the circumstances, to do so.

8.4 If the Judge directs that an oral hearing must take place within a specified time the Administrative Court Office will liaise with you and the representatives of the other parties to fix a permission hearing within the time period directed.

8.5 Where a manifestly inappropriate urgency application is made, consideration may, in appropriate cases, be given to making a wasted costs order.

Section 9

What is an acknowledgement of service?

9.1 Any person who has been served with the claim form and who wishes to take part in the judicial review should file an acknowledgment of service (Form N462) in the Administrative Court Office, within 21 days of the proceedings being served upon them.

NB – Whilst there is no requirement upon you to serve the defendant and any interested party with a Form N462 for completion by them, it is good practice to do so.

9.2 The acknowledgement of service must set out the summary of grounds for contesting the claim and the name and address of any person considered to be an interested party (who has not previously been identified and served as an interested party).

9.3 The acknowledgement of service must be served upon you and the interested parties no later than 7 days after it is filed with the court.

NB – Failure to file an acknowledgement of service renders it necessary for the party concerned to obtain the permission of the court to take part in any oral hearing of the application for permission.

Section 10

What happens after the defendant and/or the interested party has lodged an acknowledgement of service, or the time for lodging such has expired?

10.1 Applications for permission to proceed with the claim for judicial review are considered by a single judge on the papers. The purpose of this procedure is to ensure that applications are dealt with speedily and without unnecessary expense.

10.2 The papers will be forwarded to the judge by the Administrative Court Office upon receipt of the Acknowledgement of Service or at the expiry of the time limit for lodging such acknowledgement – whichever is earlier.

10.3 The judge's decision and the reasons for it (Form JRJ) will be served upon you, the defendant and any other person served with the claim form.

10.4 If the judge grants permission and you wish to pursue the claim, you must lodge a further fee of £700.00 (or a further Application for Remission of Fee (Form EX160) with the relevant Administrative Court Office within 7 days of service of the judge's decision upon you.

NB – If you do not lodge the additional fee, your file will be closed.

Section 11

What happens if my application for permission is refused, or if permission is granted subject to conditions or in part only?

11.1 If permission is refused, or is granted subject to conditions or on certain grounds only, you may request a reconsideration of that decision at an oral hearing. In cases lodged after 1 July 2013, there is no right to renew if permission is refused and the case was deemed as totally without merit (CPR 54.12 (7)). The claimant must pay a fee of £350 when requesting a renewal hearing.

11.2 Request for an oral hearing must be made on the Notice of Renewal, Form 86b, (a copy of which will be sent to you at the same time as the judge's decision if you are eligible to renew) and must be filed within 7 days after service of the notification of the judge's decision upon you (CPR Part 54.11 & 54.12).

11.3 Where the judge directs an oral hearing or you renew your application after refusal following consideration on paper, you may appear in person or be represented by an advocate (if you are legally represented). If you are not legally represented you may seek the court's permission to have someone speak on your behalf at the hearing.

NB – Any application for permission to have someone speak on your behalf should be made to the judge hearing the application who will make such decision as he considers appropriate in all of the circumstances.

11.4 Notice of the hearing is given to you, the defendant and any interested party by the Administrative Court List Office. An oral hearing is allocated a total of 30 minutes of court time. If it is considered that 30 minutes of court time is insufficient, you may provide a written estimate of the time required for the hearing and request a special fixture.

11.5 Neither the defendant nor any other interested party need attend a hearing on the question of permission unless the court directs otherwise.

Section 12

What happens if my application for permission is granted?

12.1 On granting permission the court may make case management directions under CPR 54.10(1) for the progression of the case. Case management directions may include directions as to venue, as to the service of the claim form and any evidence on other persons and as to expedition.

12.2 Where a claim is made under the Human Rights Act 1998, a direction may be made for the giving of notice to the Crown or joining the Crown as a party. In that regard you attention is drawn to the requirements of Civil Procedure rule 19.4A and paragraph 6 of the Practice Direction supplementing Section I of Part 19.

When should the defendant/interested party lodge its evidence following the grant of permission?

12.3 A party upon whom a claim form has been served and who wishes to contest the claim (or support it on additional grounds) must, within 35 days of service of the order granting permission, file and serve on the Court and all of the other parties –

- Detailed grounds for contesting the claim or supporting it on additional grounds; and
- Any written evidence relied upon.

12.4 Any party who has done so may be represented at the hearing.

12.5 Where the party filing the detailed grounds intends to rely on documents not already filed, a paginated bundle of those documents must be filed at the Court when the detailed grounds are filed.

12.6 The Court has power to extend or abridge the time for lodging evidence.

Section 13

What happens when my case is ready for hearing?

13.1 When the time for lodging of evidence by the parties has expired, the case enters a warned list and all parties are informed of this by letter.

13.2 Where a direction has been given for expedition, the case will take priority over other cases waiting to be fixed and enters an expedited warned list.

What is the procedure for the listing of a case for hearing?

NB – The procedure is the same whether you act in person or are legally represented.

13.3 Where advocate's details have been placed on the court record, the parties will be contacted by the relevant Administrative Court List Office in order to seek to agree a date for the hearing. You and advocate's clerks will be offered a range of dates and will have 48 hours to take up one of the dates offered. If the parties fail to contact the List Office within 48 hours, the List Office will fix the hearing on one of the dates offered without further notice and the parties will be notified of that fixture by letter. Where a hearing is listed in this way the hearing will only be vacated by the Administrative Court Office if both parties consent and good reason is provided for the need to vacate the fixture, using the adjournment form available from Administrative Court Listing Offices.

13.4 There may be circumstances where you are unable to attend at court on the date fixed to hear your application, i.e. as a result of illness or accident. If you are unlikely to be able to attend court on the hearing date you must notify the relevant List Office immediately. You should contact the other parties to seek their consent to the adjournment using the adjournment form. If illness is the cause of your inability to attend, a medical certificate should also be provided. Your application for an adjournment will be considered by the Appropriate Officer of the relevant Administrative Court Office.

Please note there is a fee payable for any application to adjourn **unless** the application is made with the consent of all parties and lodged with the court no later than 14 days before the date of the hearing. If you are entitled to fee remission, you must lodge an Application for a Fee Remission (Form Ex160) with your adjournment form.

13.5 Where agreement to an adjournment cannot be reached, a formal application for adjournment must be made to the Court (on notice to all parties) using Form PF244 – Administrative Court Office or PC PF244 if your application relates to a Planning Court matter. Please note that there is a fee payable (£155.00) for any application to adjourn made without the consent of all parties, notwithstanding when it is lodged, unless you are entitled to fee remission, in which case you must lodge an Application for a Fee Remission (Form Ex160) with your application. Where all parties consent to an adjournment within 14 days of the date of the hearing, a fee of £50.00 is payable.

13.6 There are occasions when circumstances, outside the control of the List Office, may necessitate them having to vacate a hearing at very short notice. Sometimes this can be as late as 4.30pm the day before the case is listed. This could be as a result of a case unexpectedly overrunning, a judge becoming unavailable, or other reasons. The List Office will endeavour to re-fix the case on the next available date convenient to the parties.

What is the short warned list?

13.7 Whilst the Administrative Court usually gives fixed dates for hearings, there is also a need to short warn a number of cases to cover the large number of settlements that occur in the list. Parties in cases that are selected to be short warned will be notified that their case is likely to be listed from a specified date, and that they may be called into the list at less than a day's notice from that date. If the case does not get on during that period, a date as soon as possible after that period will be fixed in consultation with the parties.

What is a Skeleton Argument and do I need to lodge one?

13.8 A skeleton argument is a document lodged with the court by a party prior to the substantive hearing of any application for judicial review.

13.9 Whilst there is no requirement for a litigant in person to lodge a skeleton argument there is nothing to prevent you from doing so if you wish and if you consider that it would assist the Court.

13.10 If you wish to lodge a skeleton argument you must file it with the Court and serve it on the other parties not less than 21 working days before the date of the hearing of the judicial review or the short warned date, where a case has been "short warned".

13.11 The defendant and any other party wishing to make representations at the hearing of the judicial review must file and serve a skeleton argument not less than 14 working days before the date of the hearing of the judicial review (or the short warned date).

13.12 The skeleton argument must contain:

- A time estimate for the complete hearing, including delivery of judgment;
- A list of issues;
- A list of the legal points to be taken (together with any relevant authorities with page references to the passages relied on);
- A chronology of events (with page references to the bundle of documents);
- A list of essential documents for the advance reading of the court (with page references to the passages relied on) (if different from that filed with the claim form) and a time estimate for that reading; and
- A list of persons referred to.

What is a trial bundle and when should I lodge it?

13. You must file a paginated and indexed bundle of all relevant documents required for the hearing of the judicial review whether or not you file a skeleton argument. The bundle must be filed with the court and served on the other parties not less than 21 working days before the hearing.

NB – Two copies of the bundle are required by the Court when the application is to be heard by a Divisional Court.

NB – The bundle must also include those documents required by the defendant and any other party who is to make representations at the hearing.

Section 14

What if I need to make an application to the court for further orders/directions after the grant of permission?

14.1 Where case management decisions or directions are sought after permission has been granted, application should be made by way of an application under CPR Part 23, using Form PF244 – Administrative Court Office or PC PF244 if your application relates to a Planning Court matter. You will be required to pay a fee for such application (currently £155.00, or £50.00 if all parties provide their written consent to the order being made), unless you are entitled to fee remission (in which case you should complete and submit a form EX160 with you application).

Section 15

Can my substantive application be determined without the need for a hearing?

15.1 The court may decide a claim for judicial review without a hearing where all parties agree (CPR Part 54.18).

Section 16

What do I need to do if the proceedings settle by consent prior to the substantive hearing of the application?

16.1 If you reach agreement with the other parties as to the terms of the final order to be made in your claim, you must file at the court a document (with 2 copies) signed by all the parties setting out the terms of the proposed agreed order.

NB – There is a fee of £50.00 payable on lodging the consent order, unless you are entitled to fee remission, in which case you must complete and submit a Form EX 160 (Application for a Fee Remission) with your application.

NB – If you agree with the other parties that a mandatory order etc. is required, the draft order should be accompanied by a statement of reasons (i.e. a short statement of the matters relied on as justifying the proposed agreed order) and copies of any authorities or statutory provisions relied on. If settlement is reached before permission is considered, the draft consent order must include provision for permission to be granted.

NB – Such a statement is not required where the agreement as to disposal (usually by way of withdrawal of the application) requires an order for costs or a detailed assessment of the Claimant's Legal Services Commission costs – in those circumstances the parties should file a draft consent order setting out the terms of settlement signed by all parties.

16.2 The court will consider the documents submitted and will make the order if it is satisfied that the order should be made. If the court is not satisfied that the order should be made, the court will give directions and may direct that a hearing date be set for the matter to be considered further.

Section 17

What if I want to discontinue the proceedings at any stage?

Before service of the claim form etc. on the other parties,

17.1 If you have not yet served any of the parties with the sealed claim form and accompanying documents you may discontinue the proceedings by notifying the Court in writing of your intention to do so. The Court will accept a letter of withdrawal provided that you confirm in writing that you have not effected service on the parties.

After service of the claim form etc. on the other parties,

17.2 Discontinuance of a claim is governed by CPR Part 38. Discontinuance renders you liable for the costs incurred by the other parties until the date of discontinuance.

17.3 There is a right to discontinue a claim at any time, except where:

- An interim injunction has been granted or an undertaking has been given – in those circumstances the permission of the court is required to discontinue the proceedings (an example of this would be where bail had been granted pending determination of the application for judicial review).
- Interim payment has been made by defendant – in those circumstances the consent of the defendant or the permission of the court is required to discontinue the proceedings.
- There is more than one claimant – in those circumstances the consent of every other claimant or the permission of the court is required to discontinue the proceedings.

17.4 If you wish to discontinue the proceedings at any stage after the service of those proceedings upon the other parties you must file a Notice of Discontinuance in the requisite form (N279) at the relevant Administrative Court Office and serve a copy on every other party.

17.5 A defendant may apply to set aside the Notice of Discontinuance, within 28 days of being served with it (CPR Part 38.4).

NB – If the parties require any order for costs, then a draft order setting out the terms of the order sought is required. A Notice of Discontinuance would not be appropriate in those circumstances.

Section 18

Will I be responsible for the costs of the defendant and/or the interested parties if my application is unsuccessful?

18.1 The general rule is that the party losing a substantive claim for judicial review will be ordered to pay the costs of the other parties. However, the Judge considering the matter has discretion to deal with the issue of costs as he/she considers appropriate in all of the circumstances.

NB – Costs may be awarded in respect of an unsuccessful paper application. Any application by the defendant/interested party for costs will normally be made in the Acknowledgment of Service.

Section 19

What can I do if I am unhappy with the Judge's decision?

Civil matters

Appeal after refusal of permission

19.1 If you are unhappy with the Court's decision in a civil matter you can appeal to the Court of Appeal Civil Division (with permission of the Court of Appeal (CPR Part 52.15)). Application to the Court of Appeal for permission to Appeal must be made within 7 days of the refusal by the Administrative Court of permission to apply for judicial review.

Appeal after substantive hearing

19.2 In substantive applications, permission to appeal may be sought from the Administrative Court when it determines the claim for judicial review. If an application for permission to appeal is not made at the conclusion of the case, the application for permission to appeal must be made to the Court of Appeal Civil Division within 21 days (CPR Part 52.3 & 52.4).

19.3 Guidance as to procedure should be sought from the Civil Appeals Office, Royal Courts of Justice, Strand, London, WC2A 2LL.

Criminal matters

Appeal after refusal of permission

19.4 There is no further remedy in the domestic courts after a refusal of permission by the Administrative Court.

Appeal after substantive hearing

19.5 If you are unhappy with the Court's decision in a substantive claim for judicial review in a criminal matter, you can appeal to the Supreme Court but only with the leave of the Administrative Court or the Supreme Court and such leave may only be granted if:

(a) The Administrative Court certifies that a point of law of general public importance is involved in its decision; and

(b) It appears to the Administrative Court or the Supreme Court that the point is one which ought to be considered by the Supreme Court. (see The Administration of Justice Act 1960 s.1).

Section 20

Where can I get advice about procedural matters?

20.1 If in doubt about any procedural matter you can contact the relevant Administrative Court Office, telephone numbers below. Court staff cannot give legal advice as to the merits of a case.

- Birmingham Civil Justice Centre – 0121 250 6319;
- Cardiff Civil Justice Centre – 029 2037 6460;
- Leeds Combined Court Centre – 0113 306 2578;
- Manchester Civil Justice Centre – 0161 240 5313;
- The Royal Courts of Justice in London – 020 7947 6655.

20.2 The forms referred to in this guidance can be downloaded from the Justice website (www.justice.gov.uk)

ADMINISTRATIVE COURT – GUIDANCE AS TO HOW THE COURT WILL APPROACH APPLICATIONS FOR COSTS FOLLOWING SETTLEMENT OF CLAIMS FOR JUDICIAL REVIEW

JANUARY 2014

Guidance as to how the parties should assist the Court when applications for costs are made following settlement of claims for judicial review – December 2013

When this guidance applies

1. This guidance is applicable where the parties to judicial review have agreed to settle the claim but are unable to agree liability for costs and have submitted that issue for determination by the Court.
2. It applies to all consent orders submitted for approval by the court after 13 January 2014, and will guide the terms of other costs orders.
3. The previous guidance is withdrawn.

The problem

4. The Court faces a significant number of cases, poorly considered and prepared by the parties, which can consume judicial time far beyond what is proportionate to deciding a costs issue after the parties have settled the case. The judicial and other Court resources applied to these cases must be proportionate to what is at stake. That requires efficiency and co-operation from the parties. At the same time, parties want to have the costs orders resolved fairly and quickly.

How the parties should assist the court before sending in submissions on costs

5. The onus lies on the parties to reach agreement on costs wherever possible, and in advance of asking the Court to resolve the issues, in order to support the overriding objective and ensure that efficient use is made of judicial time. See *M v Croydon* [2012] EWCA Civ 595, paragraphs 75-77.
6. The parties should not make submissions to the Court on costs following a compromise of the proceedings without seeking to agree the allocation of costs through reasoned negotiation, applying those principles, mindful of the overriding objective in the CPR and the amount of costs actually at stake. This should give them a clear understanding of the basis upon which they have failed to reach agreement, so as to focus their submissions to the court on the points in dispute.
7. Liability for costs between the parties will depend on the specific facts in each case but the principles are set out in *M v Croydon*, paragraphs 59–63. These are annexed at the end of this guidance.

The terms of consent orders

8. The terms of consent orders require the approval of the court. Unless there are specific contrary reasons given with the draft consent order, the court is very unlikely to approve the order without varying its terms so as to incorporate the following provisions.

Timetable

9. Any party wishing to claim costs must file and serve submissions on costs within 14 days of the approval by the Court of the consent order settling the claim.
10. Any party wishing to resist a claim for costs must file and serve submissions in reply within 14 days of service of the submissions seeking costs.
11. Submissions, if any, in response to matters raised in those replies must be filed and served within 7 days of the service of the reply.

Content of submissions

12. Submissions should –
- confirm that the parties have used reasonable endeavours to negotiate a costs settlement;
- identify what issues or reasons prevented the parties agreeing costs liability;
- state the approximate amount of costs likely to be involved in the case;
- clearly identify the extent to which the parties complied with the pre-action protocol;
- state the relief the claimant (i) sought in the claim form and (ii) obtained;
- address specifically how the claim and the basis of its settlement fit the principles in *M v Croydon,* including the significance and effect of any action or offer by the defendant in relation to the claim.

Documents

13. Submissions should be of a normal print size and should not normally exceed two A4 pages in length unless there is good reason to exceed this, which is properly explained in the submissions.
14. They should be accompanied by the pre-action protocol correspondence (where this has not previously been included as part of the documents supporting the claim), the correspondence in which the costs claim is made and defended, along with any other correspondence necessary to demonstrate why the claim was brought in the light of the pre-action protocol correspondence or why the step which led to settlement was not taken until after the claim was issued.
15. Unless advised otherwise, the parties should assume that the Court has the claim form and grounds, the acknowledgment of service and evidence lodged by the parties. Further copies of these should not be provided unless requested by the Court.

R (ON THE APPLICATION OF HAMID) V SECRETARY OF STATE FOR THE HOME DEPARTMENT [2012] EWHC 3070

QBD, Divisional Court

Sir John Thomas P, Cranston J

30 October 2012

Sir John Thomas (P):

[1] This is the judgment of the court. On 13 January 2011, the Claimant entered the United Kingdom from Bangladesh as a student with clearance until 30 April 2014. On 30 March 2012, the leave was curtailed to expire on 29 May 2012. The Claimant was found to be working in a restaurant in Bournemouth. On Saturday 20 October 2012, he was notified that he was an overstayer and held in detention. The following day he was served with removal directions for a flight on Thursday 25 October 2012 at 9.15am. He then consulted immigration advisors and representations were made to the Secretary of State. Those representations were rejected and the removal affirmed. On Wednesday 24 October 2012, further representations were made by a firm of solicitors. They were considered on behalf of the Secretary of State and rejected. At 4.00pm that afternoon an application was made by the solicitors to the Administrative Court claiming that the court should defer the removal.

[2] This court, because of a very substantial number of such claims, has now revised its form N463. First the form requires in s 1 that the reasons for urgency be stated. Secondly, it requires in s 2 the Appellant to state the timetable in which the matter should be heard. Third, it requires the justification for immediate consideration to be given. In particular it requires the date and time when it was first appreciated that an immediate application might be necessary and, if there have been any delays, the reasons are to be stated. Also the form requires any efforts that have been made to put the Defendant and any interested party on notice to be set out.

[3] The form was revised because the Administrative Court faces an ever increasing large volume of applications in respect of pending removals said to require immediate consideration. Many are filed towards the end of the working day, often on the day of the flight or the evening before a morning flight. In many of these applications the person concerned has known for some time, at least a matter of days, of his removal. Many of these cases are totally without merit. The court infers that in many cases applications are left to the last moment in the hope that it will result in a deferral of the removal.

[4] The Court of Appeal in *R (Madan) v Secretary of State for the Home Department* [2007] EWCA Civ 770, [2008] 1 All ER 973, [2007] 1 WLR 2891 set out in the judgment given by Buxton LJ a number of principles that must be taken into account by legal advisers on attempts to obtain judicial review of removal decisions: see para 17 and in particular the following sub-paragraphs:

> 'i) CPR PD 54.18 makes provision for the hearing of judicial review applications in the Administrative Court against removal from the jurisdiction. Such applications must be made promptly on the intimation of a deportation decision, and not await the actual fixing of removal arrangements.

ii) The detailed statement required by PD 18.2(c) must include a statement of all previous applications made in respect of the Applicant's immigration status, and indicate how the present state of the case differs from previous applications.

iii) Counsel or solicitors attending ex parte before the judge in the Administrative Court are under professional obligations (a) to draw the judge's attention to any matter adverse to their clients' case, including in particular any previous adverse decisions; and (b) to take a full note of the judge's judgment or reasons, which should then be submitted to the judge for approval.

...

viii) Counsel will remember that where the application is made ex parte there is a particular obligation to draw the court's attention to relevant authority, including in particular Country Guidance cases.'

As Buxton LJ pointed out at para 8, there are circumstances in which professional misconduct can arise if an application is made with the view to postponing the implementation of a previous decision where there are no proper grounds for so doing.

[5] In this particular case (where we do not name the solicitor), no reasons for urgency were given, no information was given of the time at which it was appreciated the matter required immediate consideration and nothing was set out as to whether the Defendant had been notified. The judge who considered this application refused it as totally without merit.

[6] The court has required the attendance of the solicitor today. It has received an apology on his behalf. Neither he nor the caseworker appreciated that this information is now required. It is for that reason that on this occasion we do not name either the employee or the firm.

[7] However, we will for the future do the following. If any firm fails to provide the information required on the form and in particular explain the reasons for urgency, the time at which the need for immediate consideration was first appreciated and the efforts made to notify the Defendant, the court will require the attendance in open court of the solicitor from the firm who was responsible, together with his senior partner. It will list not only the name of the case but the firm concerned. Non-compliance cannot be allowed to continue.

[8] That will not be the only consequence of failing to complete the requirements set out in this form. First, one consequence may be that, if the form is not completed, the judge may simply refuse to consider the application. Second, if reasons are not properly set out or do not explain why there has been delay or the reasons are otherwise inadequate, the court may simply refuse to consider the application for that reason and that reason alone.

[9] These remarks apply equally to the form soon to be introduced for out of hours applications and the form for renewals when an application has been refused on the papers.

[10] These late, meritless applications by people who face removal or deportation are an intolerable waste of public money, a great strain on the resources of this court and an abuse of a service this court offers. The court therefore intends to take the most vigorous action against any legal representatives who fail to comply with its rules. If people

persist in failing to follow the procedural requirements, they must realise that this court will not hesitate to refer those concerned to the Solicitors Regulation Authority.

[11] That is a warning for the future. We hope it will be unnecessary to have to have any further hearings of this kind or to refer anyone to the Solicitors Regulation Authority, but we will not hesitate to do so where there is a failure to comply with the court's requirements.

Judgment accordingly.

R (BUTT AND OTHERS) V SSHD [2014] EWHC 264 (ADMIN)

In the High Court of Justice Queen's Bench Division Divisional Court

Tuesday, 28 January 2014

The President of the Queen's Bench Division
(Sir Brian Leveson)
Mr Justice Cranston

Between:

The Queen on the Application of Butt	Claimant
v	
Secretary of State for the Home Department	Defendant
The Queen on the Application of Kiran	Claimant
v	
Secretary of State for the Home Department	Defendant
The Queen on the Application of Siddique	Claimant
v	
Secretary of State for the Home Department	Defendant
The Queen on the Application of Patel	Claimant
v	
Secretary of State for the Home Department	Defendant

Mr Andreas Pretzell (instructed by M&K Solicitors) appeared on behalf of the First Claimant

Mr Zeeshan Mian (Solicitor Advocate) (instructed by Denning Solicitors) appeared on behalf of the Second Claimant

Miss Samantha Broadfoot (instructed by Eden Solicitors) appeared on behalf of the Third Claimant

Mr Andreas Pretzell (instructed by Malik & Malik Solicitors) appeared on behalf of the Fourth Claimant

Sir Brian Leveson:

1. THE PRESIDENT OF THE QUEEN'S BENCH DIVISION: In *R ex parte Hamid v Secretary of State for the Home Department* [2012] EWHC 3070 (Admin), the then President of the Queen's Bench Division Sir John Thomas, now Lord Chief Justice, delivered a judgment of the court in which he made the point at paragraph 10 that meritless applications by people who face removal or deportation are an intolerable

waste of public money, a great strain on the resources of this court and an abuse of a service this court offers. He went on to observe that:

> 'The court therefore intends to take the most vigorous action against any legal representatives who fail to comply with its rules. If people persist in failing to follow the procedural requirements, they must realise that this court will not hesitate to refer those concerned to the Solicitors Regulation Authority.'

2. In subsequent decisions *Awuku (No 2) v Secretary of State for the Home Department* [2012] EWHC 3690 (Admin) and *B & J v Secretary of State for the Home Department* [2012] EWHC 3770 (Admin), Sir John identified the importance of compliance with professional obligations and the need for appropriate scrutiny by qualified lawyers, particularly in relation to applications on an ex parte basis.

3. It should not be thought that the approach which the then President initiated has in any sense fallen into desuetude following his appointment as Chief Justice. In my judgment, it remains equally critical that solicitors who work in this field make applications only when based upon a proper consideration of the evidence, having assembled appropriate proof and taken care to ensure that the time of the court is not being wasted. If a firm is called to show cause in the future, the first occasion may very well be met with an opportunity to address failings. That opportunity will have to be seized and is likely to consist of a requirement for training and a report back to the Administrative Court of steps taken in that regard. Normally a second, and even more so a third, reference to this court is likely to lead to the papers being dispatched to the Solicitors Regulation Authority.

4. In these days of austerity, the court simply cannot afford to spend unnecessary time on processing abusive applications; still less is it a proper use of the time of out-of-hours and overnight judges, hard pressed at the very best of times, to deal with such applications. All those who practise in this field ought to be warned, because the most serious failings will not necessarily lead to this stepped approach but may lead directly to reference to the Solicitors Regulation Authority.

5. With those words, I deal shortly with the applications before the court today. The first, *R (Butt) v Secretary of State for the Home Department*, concerns M & K Solicitors, who had not previously come to the attention of this court but whose application was considered to be totally without merit and an abuse of process because the relevant decision was taken as long ago as 2010, with the pre-action protocol letter being dated 15 November 2012 and the claim issued 10 May 2013. Dealing with the application for permission, Cranston J said:

> 'All this simply beggars belief and to suggest that this was an ongoing refusal of the Secretary of State which somehow justifies coming to the court almost three years after the decisions being challenged demonstrates a level of incompetence which the senior partner of the firm can explain to the Divisional Court.'

6. It is commonplace that applications for judicial review must be made as soon as possible and no later than three months after the relevant decision. Of course there is liberty in certain circumstances to extend time, but to believe that such an extension could be granted after three years is utterly to fail to recognise the importance of speed and expedition in this court. It has not been suggested that the application was not an abuse of process.

7. In addition, reliance was placed upon an extremely scruffy handwritten letter from a bank. The circumstances do not matter, but it is not surprising either that the Secretary of State or that the court should have been extremely concerned as to the origins of this letter. To say that to produce such a document necessarily reverses the burden of proof equally misunderstands the approach which has to be adopted in this court.

8. The firm has given an undertaking as to its future conduct and as to appropriate steps which it will take to ensure that all those working within it are suitably aware of the importance to which the court attaches to timeous applications properly made and properly evidenced. They, along with other firms dealt with today, must write to the Administrative Court within six weeks explaining the steps they have taken to put that into effect.

9. The second case with which the court has had to deal, *R (Kiran) v Secretary of State for the Home Department*, is even less explicable than the last. This application initially was for urgent consideration and was sent to the immediates judge with the claimant seeking urgent interim relief. Turner J dealing with it said this:

> 'This application betrays a complete lack of understanding of the nature of an application for urgent consideration. There is no justifiable basis whatsoever for the request that the court should consider this application within 48 hours. An out of date form N463 has been filled in as a result of which no explanation is proffered as to why such urgency applies to applications relating to a decision reached more than two months ago.'

10. Quite apart from the use of the wrong form, the more serious failing in this application was identified when the matter came for consideration on the documents. The judge observed:

> 'This is not an appealable immigration decision. It informs the individual that they are an illegal entrant and they are liable to detention and removal. It also allows the imposition of reporting restrictions. It is when an immigration decision is made that there will be a right of appeal under Section 82(2)(g) of the Nationality, Immigration and Asylum Act 2002. At that point the claimant will be able to advance her explanation, including that what she said at the screening interview was inaccurately recorded. Thus the challenge to IS 151A is incompetent.'

11. Mr Zeeshan Mian, a solicitor advocate and senior partner in the firm, has offered an undertaking to ensure that the firm does not get into a similar unwanted situation in future by providing in-house training to all qualified fee earners, by personally scrutinising the merits of a claim before it is filed and to take these steps additionally to those which have already been taken, such as the appointment of a Head of Immigration Department to review all applications and claims and appointing a part-time in-house counsel.

12. It is sad to see a firm which has not previously come to adverse attention of the court appearing before us in these circumstances. We accept the undertaking that Mr Mian has made. We require him to write to the Administrative Court in six weeks to identify how all these various measures have been put into effect and the impact of the changes that have been made.

13. The third case which we have considered is *R (Siddique) v Secretary of State for the Home Department*. This case is more serious because the firm, Eden Solicitors, has previously appeared before a *Hamid* court. Indeed, on 25 November the firm wrote to

the Administrative Court enclosing certified copies of training certificates to demonstrate its compliance with its undertaking. Nevertheless, this application for judicial review was received by the Administrative Court on 12 December. In refusing permission, the reasons given were:

> 'The grounds are essentially of what were advanced before the FTT. Judge Borsada dismissed the case on the grounds that the claimant lacked credibility. This is a case to which CPR 54.7A applies. The Court will give permission to proceed only if it considers that there is an arguable case which has a reasonable prospect of success because both the decisions of the Upper Tribunal and the First-tier Tribunal are wrong in law *and* that either (i) the claim raises an important point of principle or practice; or (ii) there is some other compelling reason to hear it. No attempt is made to address CPR 54.7. The claim is an abuse of process and should never have been filed.'

Counsel instructed on behalf of the solicitors has been the first to recognise the validity of those observations.

14. We have anxiously considered whether the time has now come for that firm to be referred to the Solicitors Regulation Authority. On their behalf, Miss Broadfoot of counsel has offered that the firm will not merely follow up on the training for judicial review generally but will arrange for specific training in immigration law. They are also intending to review the internal checklist and flow chart and ensure that no application is made without having been checked by a senior partner. The particular application was made by a foreign-registered lawyer who is not authorised to commence judicial review proceedings. That itself is a failure which needs to be addressed.

15. For the final time, but specifically for the final time, we will accept this undertaking and require the firm again within six weeks to write to the Administrative Court Office identifying precisely what steps it has taken to ensure that these failings do not recur.

16. The final case before the court is slightly different. In one sense in *R (Patel) v Secretary of State for the Home Department*, the solicitors, Messrs Malik & Malik, present a particularly serious problem given that they have twice before appeared in *Hamid* courts. However, the explanation for what is conceded to have been an abusive application in this case is based upon the dishonesty of an employee who felt pressured to make the application and to deceive the senior partner into signing the appropriate cheque to pay the court fee.

17. It is not necessary to enter into the merits of the particular case. The relevant employee has undergone disciplinary proceedings and been dismissed. He himself has signed a statement for the court apologising fully and unreservedly and with the highest degree of shame and embarrassment, not blaming anyone but himself for his actions. The senior partner of the firm of solicitors also expressed his mortification in having to appear before the court in these circumstances. We recognise that the unauthorised actions of a trusted individual are difficult to stop. The firm will have to reflect upon what the senior partner needs to see before signing cheques on the firm's behalf, and will doubtless have learnt a salutary lesson in relation to this particular problem.

18. In the circumstances, although reading the papers before seeing this explanation we were minded to refer this firm to the Solicitors Regulation Authority, we have decided not to take that step but to accept the apology. Again, the firm will write to the Administrative Court Office identifying what steps it has taken to improve its

procedures to ensure that this will not happen again. It is almost inconceivable that Malik & Malik will survive a further referral to a *Hamid* court.

19. We add only this: these courts are not assembled because of our wish to embarrass or otherwise impugn solicitors whose work is conscientious, thorough and in accordance with the highest keepings of the profession. We are, however, determined to ensure that the overly frequent abusive applications in this field of law cease and we will take whatever steps are necessary to do so. This judgment will be circulated to all judges and deputy judges sitting on these applications in the Administrative Court.

20. Finally, for my part I regret that many of these applications have only received responses either yesterday or today. In future, we expect that any response to an application to appear before a *Hamid* court, should there be another one, is filed with the court at least seven days before the hearing.

21. MR JUSTICE CRANSTON: I agree.

APPENDIX 5

FORMS

Forms

N461 – Judicial Review Claim Form	600
N462 – Judicial Review Acknowledgment of Service	606
N463 – Judicial Review Application for Urgent Consideration	610
T480 – Judicial Review Claim Form in the Upper Tribunal Immigration and Asylum Chamber	612
T481 – Accompanying Notes to T480	618
T482 – Acknowledgment of Service in the Upper Tribunal Immigration and Asylum Service	622
T483 – Judicial Review Application for Urgent Consideration in the Upper Tribunal Immigration and Asylum Chamber	625

N461 – JUDICIAL REVIEW CLAIM FORM

Judicial Review Claim Form

In the High Court of Justice
Administrative Court

Notes for guidance are available which explain how to complete the judicial review claim form. Please read them carefully before you complete the form.

For Court use only	
Administrative Court Reference No.	
Date filed	

Seal

SECTION 1 Details of the claimant(s) and defendant(s)

Claimant(s) name and address(es)
- name
- address
- Telephone no.
- Fax no.
- E-mail address

Claimant's or claimant's solicitors' address to which documents should be sent.
- name
- address
- Telephone no.
- Fax no.
- E-mail address

Claimant's Counsel's details
- name
- address
- Telephone no.
- Fax no.
- E-mail address

1st Defendant
- name

Defendant's or (where known) Defendant's solicitors' address to which documents should be sent.
- name
- address
- Telephone no.
- Fax no.
- E-mail address

2nd Defendant
- name

Defendant's or (where known) Defendant's solicitors' address to which documents should be sent.
- name
- address
- Telephone no.
- Fax no.
- E-mail address

SECTION 2 Details of other interested parties

Include name and address and, if appropriate, details of DX, telephone or fax numbers and e-mail

name	name
address	address
Telephone no. / Fax no.	Telephone no. / Fax no.
E-mail address	E-mail address

SECTION 3 Details of the decision to be judicially reviewed

Decision:

Date of decision:

Name and address of the court, tribunal, person or body who made the decision to be reviewed.

name	address

SECTION 4 Permission to proceed with a claim for judicial review

I am seeking permission to proceed with my claim for Judicial Review.

Is this application being made under the terms of Section 18 Practice Direction 54 (Challenging removal)?	☐ Yes	☐ No
Are you making any other applications? If Yes, complete Section 8.	☐ Yes	☐ No
Is the claimant in receipt of a Community Legal Service Fund (CLSF) certificate?	☐ Yes	☐ No
Are you claiming exceptional urgency, or do you need this application determined within a certain time scale? If Yes, complete Form N463 and file this with your application.	☐ Yes	☐ No
Have you complied with the pre-action protocol? If No, give reasons for non-compliance in the box below.	☐ Yes	☐ No

Have you issued this claim in the region with which you have the closest connection? (Give any additional reasons for wanting it to be dealt with in this region in the box below). If No, give reasons in the box below.	☐ Yes	☐ No

Does the claim include any issues arising from the Human Rights Act 1998?
If Yes, state the articles which you contend have been breached in the box below. ☐ Yes ☐ No

SECTION 5 Detailed statement of grounds

☐ set out below   ☐ attached

SECTION 6 Aarhus Convention claim

I contend that this claim is an Aarhus Convention claim ☐ Yes ☐ No

If Yes, indicate in the following box if you do not wish the costs limits under CPR 45.43 to apply.

If you have indicated that the claim is an Aarhus claim set out the grounds below

SECTION 7 Details of remedy (including any interim remedy) being sought

SECTION 8 Other applications

I wish to make an application for:-

SECTION 9 Statement of facts relied on

Statement of Truth

I believe (The claimant believes) that the facts stated in this claim form are true.

Full name _____

Name of claimant's solicitor's firm _____

Signed _____ Position or office held _____
    Claimant ('s solicitor)   (if signing on behalf of firm or company)

SECTION 10 Supporting documents

If you do not have a document that you intend to use to support your claim, identify it, give the date when you expect it to be available and give reasons why it is not currently available in the box below.

Please tick the papers you are filing with this claim form and any you will be filing later.

☐ Statement of grounds	☐ included	☐ attached
☐ Statement of the facts relied on	☐ included	☐ attached
☐ Application to extend the time limit for filing the claim form	☐ included	☐ attached
☐ Application for directions	☐ included	☐ attached

☐ Any written evidence in support of the claim or application to extend time

☐ Where the claim for judicial review relates to a decision of a court or tribunal, an approved copy of the reasons for reaching that decision

☐ Copies of any documents on which the claimant proposes to rely

☐ A copy of the legal aid or CSLF certificate *(if legally represented)*

☐ Copies of any relevant statutory material

☐ A list of essential documents for advance reading by the court *(with page references to the passages relied upon)*

If Section 18 Practice Direction 54 applies, please tick the relevant box(es) below to indicate which papers you are filing with this claim form:

☐ a copy of the removal directions and the decision to which the application relates	☐ included	☐ attached
☐ a copy of the documents served with the removal directions including any documents which contains the Immigration and Nationality Directorate's factual summary of the case	☐ included	☐ attached
☐ a detailed statement of the grounds	☐ included	☐ attached

Reasons why you have not supplied a document and date when you expect it to be available:-

Signed _____ Claimant ('s Solicitor)_____

Click here to print form

N462 – JUDICIAL REVIEW ACKNOWLEDGMENT OF SERVICE

	Click here to reset form	Click here to print form

Judicial Review
Acknowledgment of Service

In the High Court of Justice
Administrative Court

Name and address of person to be served

name

address

Claim No.	
Claimant(s) (including ref.)	
Defendant(s)	
Interested Parties	

SECTION A
Tick the appropriate box

1. I intend to contest all of the claim ☐ ⎫
2. I intend to contest part of the claim ☐ ⎬ complete sections B, C, D and F
3. I do not intend to contest the claim ☐ complete section F
4. The defendant (interested party) is a court or tribunal and **intends** to make a submission. ☐ complete sections B, C and F
5. The defendant (interested party) is a court or tribunal and **does not intend** to make a submission. ☐ complete sections B and F
6. The applicant has indicated that this is a claim to which the Aarhus Convention applies. ☐ complete sections E and F

Note: If the application seeks to judicially review the decision of a court or tribunal, the court or tribunal need only provide the Administrative Court with as much evidence as it can about the decision to help the Administrative Court perform its judicial function.

SECTION B
Insert the name and address of any person you consider should be added as an interested party.

name

address

Telephone no.   Fax no.
E-mail address

name

address

Telephone no.   Fax no.
E-mail address

SECTION C
Summary of grounds for contesting the claim. If you are contesting only part of the claim, set out which part before you give your grounds for contesting it. If you are a court or tribunal filing a submission, please indicate that this is the case.

SECTION D
Give details of any directions you will be asking the court to make, or tick the box to indicate that a separate application notice is attached.

If you are seeking a direction that this matter be heard at an Administrative Court venue other than that at which this claim was issued, you should complete, lodge and serve on all other parties Form N464 with this acknowledgment of service.

SECTION E
Response to the claimant's contention that the claim is an Aarhus claim

Do you deny that the claim is an Aarhus Convention claim?   ☐ Yes   ☐ No

If Yes, please set out your grounds for denial in the box below.

SECTION F

*delete as appropriate

*(I believe)(The defendant believes) that the facts stated in this form are true.
*I am duly authorised by the defendant to sign this statement.

(if signing on behalf of firm or company, court or tribunal)

Position or office held

(To be signed by you or by your solicitor or litigation friend)

Signed

Date

Give an address to which notices about this case can be sent to you

name
address
Telephone no.
Fax no.
E-mail address

If you have instructed counsel, please give their name address and contact details below.

name
address
Telephone no.
Fax no.
E-mail address

Completed forms, together with a copy, should be lodged with the Administrative Court Office (court address, over the page), at which this claim was issued within 21 days of service of the claim upon you, and further copies should be served on the Claimant(s), any other Defendant(s) and any interested parties within 7 days of lodgement with the Court.

[Click here to print form]

Administrative Court addresses

- Administrative Court in **London**

    Administrative Court Office, Room C315, Royal Courts of Justice, Strand, London, WC2A 2LL.

- Administrative Court in **Birmingham**

    Administrative Court Office, Birmingham Civil Justice Centre, Priory Courts, 33 Bull Street, Birmingham B4 6DS.

- Administrative Court in **Wales**

    Administrative Court Office, Cardiff Civil Justice Centre, 2 Park Street, Cardiff, CF10 1ET.

- Administrative Court in **Leeds**

    Administrative Court Office, Leeds Combined Court Centre, 1 Oxford Row, Leeds, LS1 3BG.

- Administrative Court in **Manchester**

    Administrative Court Office, Manchester Civil Justice Centre, 1 Bridge Street West, Manchester, M3 3FX.

N463 – JUDICIAL REVIEW APPLICATION FOR URGENT CONSIDERATION

Judicial Review
Application for urgent consideration

This form must be completed by the Claimant or the Claimant's advocate if exceptional urgency is being claimed and the application needs to be determined within a certain time scale.

The claimant, or the claimant's solicitors must serve this form on the defendant(s) and any interested parties with the N461 Judicial review claim form.

To the Defendant(s) and Interested Party(ies)
Representations as to the urgency of the claim may be made by defendants or interested parties to the relevant Administrative Court Office by fax or email:-

For cases proceeding in

In the High Court of Justice Administrative Court	
Claim No.	
Claimant(s) *(including ref.)*	
Defendant(s)	
Interested Party(ies)	

London
Fax: 020 7947 6802   email: administrativecourtoffice.generaloffice@hmcts.x.gsi.gov.uk

Birmingham
Fax: 0121 250 6730   email: administrativecourtoffice.birmingham@hmcts.x.gsi.gov.uk

Cardiff
Fax: 02920 376461   email: administrativecourtoffice.cardiff@hmcts.x.gsi.gov.uk

Leeds
Fax: 0113 306 2581   email: administrativecourtoffice.leeds@hmcts.x.gsi.gov.uk

Manchester
Fax: 0161 240 5315   email: administrativecourtoffice.manchester@hmcts.x.gsi.gov.uk

SECTION 1 Reasons for urgency

SECTION 2 Proposed timetable *(tick the boxes and complete the following statements that apply)*

☐ a) The N461 application for permission should be considered within _____ hours/days

If consideration is sought within 48 hours, you must complete Section 3 below

☐ b) Abridgement of time is sought for the lodging of acknowledgments of service

☐ c) If permission for judicial review is granted, a substantive hearing is sought by _____ (date)

SECTION 3 Justification for request for immediate consideration

If it is decided that your application will be dealt with as an immediate application, we will notify you of the outcome by email as soon as the judge has reached a determination. You will subsequently be sent a hard copy of the judges order in the post. Please provide an email address to which you would like notification sent.

Email address:

Please note: if you do not provide a valid email address, you will only be notified of the outcome by post, which will take at least 2 – 3 days to be processed and delivered.

Date and time when it was first appreciated that an immediate application might be necessary.

Date   Time

Please provide reasons for any delay in making the application.

What efforts have been made to put the defendant and any interested party on notice of the application?

SECTION 4 Interim relief *(state what interim relief is sought and why in the box below)*

A draft order must be attached.

SECTION 5 Service

A copy of this form of application was served on the defendant(s) and interested parties as follows:

Defendant	Interested party
☐ by fax machine to time sent Fax no. time	☐ by fax machine to time sent Fax no. time
☐ by handing it to or leaving it with name	☐ by handing it to or leaving it with name
☐ by e-mail to e-mail address	☐ by e-mail to e-mail address
Date served Date	Date served Date

I confirm that all relevant facts have been disclosed in this application

Name of claimant's advocate   Claimant (claimant's advocate)

name   Signed

T480 – JUDICIAL REVIEW CLAIM FORM IN THE UPPER TRIBUNAL IMMIGRATION AND ASYLUM CHAMBER

Judicial Review
Claim Form

In the Upper Tribunal
Immigration and Asylum Chamber

Notes for guidance are available which explain how to complete the judicial review claim form. Please read them carefully before you complete the form.

For Upper Tribunal use only	
Upper Tribunal Reference No.	
Date filed	

Seal

SECTION 1 Details of the applicant(s) and respondent(s)

Applicant(s) name and address(es)
- name
- address
- Telephone no.
- Fax no.
- E-mail address

Applicant's or Applicant's solicitors' address to which documents should be sent.
- name
- address
- Telephone no.
- Fax no.
- E-mail address

Applicant's Counsel's details
- name
- address
- Telephone no.
- Fax no.
- E-mail address

1st Respondent
- name

Respondent's or (where known) Respondent's solicitors' address to which documents should be sent.
- name
- address
- Telephone no.
- Fax no.
- E-mail address

2nd Respondent
- name

Respondent's or (where known) Respondent's solicitors' address to which documents should be sent.
- name
- address
- Telephone no.
- Fax no.
- E-mail address

SECTION 2 Details of other interested parties

Include name and address and, if appropriate, details of DX, telephone or fax numbers and e-mail

name

address

Telephone no.

Fax no.

E-mail address

name

address

Telephone no.

Fax no.

E-mail address

SECTION 3 Details of the decision to be judicially reviewed

Decision:

Date of decision:

Name and address of the person or body who made the decision to be reviewed.

name

address

SECTION 4 Permission to bring Judicial Review proceedings

I am seeking permission to bring Judicial Review proceedings.

Is this application being made under the terms of Part 5 of the Senior President of Tribunals' Practice Directions entitled 'Immigration Judicial Review in the Immigration and Asylum Chamber of the Upper Tribunal'? ☐ Yes ☐ No

Are you making any other applications? If Yes, complete Section 7. ☐ Yes ☐ No

Is the applicant in receipt of a Civil Legal Aid certificate? ☐ Yes ☐ No

Are you claiming exceptional urgency, or do you need this application determined within a certain time scale? If Yes, complete form T483 and file this with your application. ☐ Yes ☐ No

Have you complied with the pre-action protocol? If No, give reasons for non-compliance in the box below. ☐ Yes ☐ No

Does the claim include any issues arising from the Human Rights Act 1998?
If Yes, state the articles which you contend have been breached in the box below. ☐ Yes ☐ No

SECTION 5 Detailed statement of grounds

☐ set out below   ☐ attached

SECTION 6 Details of remedy (including any interim remedy) being sought

SECTION 7 Other applications

I wish to make an application for:-

SECTION 8 Statement of facts relied on

Statement of Truth

I believe (The applicant believes) that the facts stated in this claim form are true.

Full name _____

Name of applicant's solicitor's firm _____

Signed _____ Position or office held _____
    Applicant ('s solicitor)   (if signing on behalf of firm or company)

SECTION 9 Supporting documents

If you do not have a document that you intend to use to support your claim, identify it, give the date when you expect it to be available and give reasons why it is not currently available in the box below.

Please tick the papers you are filing with this claim form and any you will be filing later.

☐ Statement of grounds ☐ included ☐ attached

☐ Statement of the facts relied on ☐ included ☐ attached

☐ Application to extend the time limit for filing the claim form ☐ included ☐ attached

☐ Application for directions ☐ included ☐ attached

☐ Any written evidence in support of the claim or application to extend time

☐ Copies of any documents on which the claimant proposes to rely

☐ A copy of the Civil Legal Aid certificate *(if legally represented)*

☐ Copies of any relevant statutory material

☐ A list of essential documents for advance reading by the court *(with page references to the passages relied upon)*

If Part 5 of the Senior President of Tribunals' Practice Directions entitled 'Immigration Judicial Review in the Immigration and Asylum Chamber of the Upper Tribunal' applies, please tick the relevant box(es) below to indicate which papers you are filing with this claim form:

☐ a copy of the removal directions and the decision to which the application relates ☐ included ☐ attached

☐ a copy of the documents served with the removal directions including any documents which contains the UK Border Agency factual summary of the case ☐ included ☐ attached

☐ a detailed statement of the grounds ☐ included ☐ attached

Reasons why you have not supplied a document and date when you expect it to be available:-

Signed _____ Applicant('s Solicitor) _____

Completed forms and accompanying documents, together with a copy should be lodged with the Upper Tribunal, Immigration and Asylum Chamber, Field House, 15-25 Breams Building, London EC4A 1DZ.
For information regarding filing with Welsh and regional offices of the Tribunal,
see www.justice.gov.uk/tribunals/immigration-asylum-upper

T481 – ACCOMPANYING NOTES TO T480

Upper Tribunal – Immigration and Asylum Chamber
Guidance notes on completing the Judicial Review claim form

This form should be used where your application is:

A class of case specified in paragraph 1 of the Lord Chief Justice's direction of 21 August 2013 (a copy of which is attached to these guidance notes).

This form should not be used where your claim comprises or includes a challenge of a kind described in paragraph 3 of the direction, or where your claim relates to a challenge to some other decision not within paragraph 1 of the direction. In either case, your claim should be filed on an Administrative Court claim form (N461) and sent to:

Administrative Court Office
Room C315
Royal Courts of Justice
Strand
London
WC2A 2LL

Birmingham Civil Justice Centre
Priory Courts
5th Floor
33 Bull Street
Birmingham
B4 6DS

Cardiff Civil Justice Centre
2 Park Street
Cardiff
CF10 1ET

Leeds Combined Court
1 Oxford Row
Leeds
West Yorkshire
LS1 3BG

Manchester Civil Justice Centre
1 Bridge Street West
Manchester
M60 9DJ

For more information regarding filing with Welsh and regional offices of the Administrative Court, see www.justice.gov.uk/courts/rcj-rolls-building/administrative-court

Set out below are notes to help you complete the form. You should read the notes to each section carefully before you begin to complete that particular section.

Use a separate sheet if you need more space for your answers, marking clearly which section the information refers to.

If you do not have all the documents or information you need for your claim, you must not allow this to delay sending or taking the form to the Upper Tribunal Immigration and Asylum Chamber, Field House, 15-25 Breams Building, London EC4A 1DZ within the correct time. Complete the form as fully as possible and provide what documents you have. The notes to Section 9 will explain more about what you have to do in these circumstances. For information regarding filing with Welsh and regional offices of the Tribunal, see www.justice.gov.uk/tribunals/immigration-asylum-upper

Time limit for filing a claim

- Unless Part 5 of the Senior President of Tribunals' Practice Directions entitled 'Immigration Judicial Review in the Immigration and Asylum Chamber of the Upper Tribunal' applies in relation to the deferral of removal, the claim must be filed **promptly and in any event no later than three months** after the date of the decision, action, or omission to which the application relates.

If the application challenges a decision at the First-tier Tribunal, it may be made later than the time required above, if it is made **within one month** after the date on which the Tribunal sent written reasons for its decision or notification than an 'in-time' application for the decision to be set aside had been unsuccessful.

Note: Part 5 of the Senior President of Tribunals' Practice Directions entitled 'Immigration Judicial Review in the Immigration and Asylum Chamber of the Upper Tribunal' are set out on the website (www.justice.gov.uk/about/hmcts/index.htm). Should you need a hard copies of these Practice Directions, please contact the Administrative Court office or your local Citizen's Advice Bureau.

If you need help to complete the form you should consult a solicitor or your local Citizen's Advice Bureau.

Section 1
Details of the applicants and respondent
Give the full name(s) and address(es) to which all documents relating to the judicial review are to be sent. Include contact information e.g. telephone numbers and any other reference numbers.

Please note that if the respondent is the Secretary of State for the Home Department (Home Office), the relevant name and address for service is The Treasury Solicitor, One Kemble Street, London WC2B 4TS.

Section 2
Details of other interested parties
Full details of interested parties must be included in the claim form; namely you should give details of any persons directly affected by the decision you wish to challenge.

Section 3
Details of the decision to be judicially reviewed
Give details of the decision you seek to have judicially reviewed. Give the name of the person or body whose decision you are seeking to Judicially Review, and the date on which the decision was made.

Section 4
Permission to bring Judicial Review proceedings
This section must be completed. You must answer all the questions and give further details where required.

Section 5
Detailed statement of grounds
Set out, in detail, the grounds on which you contend the decision should be set aside or varied.

Section 6
Details of remedy
Complete this section stating what remedy you are seeking:
  (a) a mandatory order;
  (b) a prohibiting order;
  (c) a quashing order; or
  (d) an injunction restraining a person from acting in any office in which he is not entitled to act.

A claim for damages may be included but only if you are seeking one of the orders set out above.

Section 7
Other applications
You may wish to make additional applications to the Upper Tribunal in connection with your claim for Judicial Review. Any other applications may be made either in the claim form or in a separate application (form T484). This form can be obtained from the Upper Tribunal or from the justice website website at www.justice.gov.uk
But see above, as to the effect of challenging decisions that are not within paragraph 1 of the Lord Chief Justice's direction.

Section 8
Statement of facts relied on
The facts on which you are basing your claim should be set out in this section of the form, or in a separate document attached to the form. It should contain a numbered list of the points that you intend to rely on at the hearing. Refer at each point to any documents you are filing in support of your claim.

Section 9
Supporting documents
Do not delay filing your claim for Judicial Review.
If you have not been able to obtain any of the documents listed in this section within the time limits referred to on the previous page, complete the notice as best you can and ensure the claim is filed on time. Set out the reasons why you have not been able to obtain any of the information or documents and give the date when you expect them to be available.

Direction given in accordance with Part 1 of Schedule 2 to the Constitutional Reform Act 2005 and section 18 of the Tribunals, Courts and Enforcement Act 2007

Jurisdiction of the Upper Tribunal under s. 18 of the Tribunals, Courts and Enforcement Act 2007 and Mandatory Transfer of Judicial Review applications to the Upper Tribunal under s. 31A(2) of the Senior Courts Act 1981

1. Subject to paragraphs 2 and 3 below, the Lord Chief Justice hereby specifies the following classes of case for the purposes of section 18(6) of the Tribunals, Courts and Enforcement Act 2007:

    any application for permission to apply for judicial review and any application for judicial review (including any application for ancillary relief and costs in such applications) that calls into question:

    i. a decision made under the Immigration Acts (as defined in Schedule 1 to the Interpretation Act 1978) or any instrument having effect (whether wholly or partly) under an enactment within the Immigration Acts, or otherwise relating to leave to enter or remain in the United Kingdom outside the immigration rules; or

    ii. a decision of the Immigration and Asylum Chamber of the First-tier Tribunal, from which no appeal lies to the Upper Tribunal.

2. Paragraph 1 above applies, with effect from 1 November 2013, in relation to:

    i. any case in which an application for permission to apply for judicial review was issued in the Administrative Court on or after 9 September 2013;

    ii. any case in which there has been a request, which has yet to be determined, for reconsideration at a hearing under CPR 54.12 of an application for permission that was refused without a hearing on or after 9 September 2013; and

    iii. any application issued in the Upper Tribunal on or after 1 November 2013.

3. Paragraph 1 above does not apply to any application which comprises or includes:

    i. a challenge to the validity of primary or subordinate legislation (or of immigration rules);

    ii. a challenge to the lawfulness of detention (but an application does not do so by reason only of the fact that it challenges a decision in relation to bail);

    iii. a challenge to a decision concerning inclusion on the register of licensed Sponsors maintained by the United Kingdom Border Agency, or any authorisation of such Sponsors;

    iv. a challenge to a decision as to citizenship under the British Nationality Act 1981 or any other provision of the law for the time being in force which determines British citizenship, the status of a British national (Overseas), British Overseas citizenship or the status of a British subject;

    v. a challenge to a decision made under or by virtue of section 4 (accommodation centres) or Part VI (support for asylum seekers) of the Immigration and Asylum Act 1999;

    vi. a challenge to a decision made under or by virtue of Part II (accommodation centres) or Part III (other support and assistance) of the Nationality, Immigration and Asylum Act 2002;

    vii. a challenge to a decision of the Upper Tribunal;

    viii. a challenge to a decision of the Special Immigration Appeals Commission; or

    ix. an application for a declaration of incompatibility under section 4 of the Human Rights Act 1998.

4. In paragraphs 1 and 3 above, references to a decision include references to any omission or failure to make a decision.

5. Any application to which paragraph 1 above applies, and any proceedings relating thereto, are hereby designated as an immigration matter.

6. (1) The direction of 17 October 2011 is hereby revoked.

   (2) The direction of 29 October 2008 is amended as follows.

   (3) In paragraph 2b, after "First-tier Tribunal" insert "(other than its Immigration and Asylum Chamber)".

   (4) This paragraph takes effect on 1 November 2013.

7. This direction is made by the Lord Chief Justice with the agreement of the Lord Chancellor. It is made in the exercise of powers conferred by section 18(6) and (7) of the Tribunals, Courts and Enforcement Act 2007 and in accordance with Part 1 of Schedule 2 to the Constitutional Reform Act 2005.

The Right Honourable Lord Judge
Lord Chief Justice of England and Wales
21 August 2013

T482 – ACKNOWLEDGMENT OF SERVICE IN THE UPPER TRIBUNAL IMMIGRATION AND ASYLUM SERVICE

Judicial Review
Acknowledgment of Service

Name and address of person to be served
- name
- address

In the	Upper Tribunal Immigration and Asylum Chamber
Upper Tribunal Ref. No.	
Applicant(s) *(including ref.)*	
Respondent(s)	
Interested Parties	

SECTION A
Tick the appropriate box

1. I intend to contest all of the claim ☐ ⎫
2. I intend to contest part of the claim ☐ ⎬ complete sections B, C, D and E
3. I do not intend to contest the claim ☐   complete section E

SECTION B
Insert the name and address of any person you consider should be added as an interested party.

- name
- address
- Telephone no.
- Fax no.
- E-mail address

- name
- address
- Telephone no.
- Fax no.
- E-mail address

SECTION C
Summary of grounds for contesting the claim. If you are contesting only part of the claim, set out which part before you give your grounds for contesting it.

SECTION D
Give details of any directions you will be asking the Upper Tribunal to make, or tick the box to indicate that a separate application notice is attached.

SECTION E

delete as appropriate

*(I believe)(The respondent believes) that the facts stated in this form are true.
*I am duly authorised by the respondent to sign this statement.

(if signing on behalf of firm or company)

Position or office held

(To be signed by you or by your solicitor or litigation friend)

Signed

Date

Give an address to which notices about this case can be sent to you

name

address

Telephone no.

Fax no.

E-mail address

If you have instructed counsel, please give their name address and contact details below.

name

address

Telephone no.

Fax no.

E-mail address

Completed forms, together with a copy, should be lodged with the Upper Tribunal Immigration and Asylum Chamber, Field House, 15-25 Breams Building, London EC4A 1DZ within 21 days of you being provided with a copy of the claim form and accompanying documents by the Appliant and further copies should be provided to the Applicant(s), any other Respondent(s) and any interested parties at the same time. (For information regarding filing with Welsh and regional offices of the Tribunal, see www.justice.gov.uk/tribunals/immigration-asylum-upper)

T483 – JUDICIAL REVIEW APPLICATION FOR URGENT CONSIDERATION IN THE UPPER TRIBUNAL IMMIGRATION AND ASYLUM CHAMBER

Judicial Review
Application for urgent consideration

This form must be completed by the Applicant or the Applicant's advocate if exceptional urgency is being claimed and the application needs to be determined within a certain time scale.

The applicant, or the applicant's solicitors must serve this form on the respondent(s) and any interested parties with the form T480 Judicial Review claim form.

To the Respondent(s) and Interested Party(ies)

Representations as to the urgency of the claim may be made by respondents or interested parties to the Upper Tribunal Immigration and Asylum Chamber by fax to 0870 324 0185. For fax numbers of Welsh and regional offices, see www.justice.gov.uk/tribunals/immigration-asylum-upper

In the	Upper Tribunal Immigration and Asylum Chamber
Claim No.	
Applicant(s) *(including ref.)*	
Respondent(s)	
Interested Parties	

SECTION 1 Reasons for urgency

SECTION 2 Proposed timetable *(tick the boxes and complete the following statements that apply)*

☐ a) The application for interim relief should be considered within _____ hours/days

☐ b) The form T480 application for permission should be considered within _____ hours/days

☐ c) Abridgement of time is sought for the lodging of acknowledgments of service

☐ d) If permission for judicial review is granted, a substantive hearing is sought by _____ (date)

SECTION 3 Justification for request for immediate consideration

Date and time when it was first appreciated that an immediate application might be necessary.

| Date | Time |

Please provide reasons for any delay in making the application.

What efforts have been made to put the respondent and any interested party on notice of the application?

SECTION 4 Interim relief *(state what interim relief is sought and why in the box below)*

A draft order must be attached.

SECTION 5 Service

A copy of this form of application was served on the respondent(s) and interested parties as follows:

Respondent

☐ by fax machine to
Fax no. _____   time sent
                        time _____

☐ by handing it to or leaving it with
name _____

☐ by e-mail to
e-mail address _____

Date served
Date _____

Name of applicant's advocate
name _____

Interested party

☐ by fax machine to
Fax no. _____   time sent
                        time _____

☐ by handing it to or leaving it with
name _____

☐ by e-mail to
e-mail address _____

Date served
Date _____

Applicant (applicant's advocate)
Signed _____

INDEX

References are to paragraph numbers.

Academic challenges	3.20
Academies	11.12, 11.13, 11.14, 11.15
Acknowledgement of service	3.29, 3.30, 3.31
Additional grounds	3.59
Alternative dispute resolution *see also*	
Mediation	2.127, 2.128, 2.131
advantages	2.150, 2.151
Alternative remedies	2.178, 2.179, 3.17, 3.18, 3.19
Appeals	3.66
case stated, by way of	9.54, 9.55, 9.56, 9.57, 9.58, 9.59, 9.60, 9.61
Crown Court, to	9.52, 9.53
documents to be filled	3.68, 3.69
licensing, and	12.37
permission for	3.67, 3.70, 3.71
permission, on	3.51, 3.52, 3.53, 3.54
review of decision	3.72
Supreme Court, to	9.86, 9.87, 9.88, 9.89, 9.90
tribunal system	4.23
Upper Tribunal, to	4.16, 4.17, 4.18
Appropriate dispute resolution	2.129, 2.130
Asylum seekers	
community care	6.122
Audit	2.190
accountability	2.191
advisory notice, issue of	2.198, 2.199
duties of auditor	2.193, 2.194
inspection of accounts	2.200
public interest, and	2.195
responsibility for arrangements	2.192
role of	2.190
threat of action	2.196, 2.197
Bad faith/improper motive	1.57, 1.58, 1.59, 1.60, 1.61, 1.63
mixed purposes	1.64
political gain	1.62
recent examples	1.65
Bail	2.21, 9.62, 9.63, 9.64, 9.65
application procedure	9.66, 9.67, 9.68, 9.69, 9.70, 9.71, 9.72, 9.73, 9.74
interim relief, as	9.62, 9.63, 9.64, 9.65
Bias	1.128
actual	1.129
apparent	1.130, 1.131, 1.132
automatic disqualification	1.133
recent examples	1.134
Candour/disclosure, duty of	3.07, 3.08
all information	3.09
court order	3.10
CPR 31	3.11, 3.12
Carers	6.94
assessment	6.96, 6.97, 6.98, 6.99
co-operation between bodies	6.103
recognition for	6.95
rights to be assessed	6.102
services	6.100
Case stated	
appeal by way of	9.54, 9.55, 9.56, 9.57, 9.58, 9.59, 9.60, 9.61
licensing, and	12.56, 12.57
Central government	
extent of common law powers	13.34, 13.35, 13.36, 13.37, 13.38
prerogative powers	13.05, 13.06, 13.07, 13.08, 13.09, 13.10, 13.19, 13.20
justiciable	13.11, 13.12, 13.13
meaning	13.21
Order in Council	13.14, 13.15, 13.16, 13.17, 13.18
statutory regime, and	13.31, 13.32, 13.33, 13.38, 13.39, 13.40
'third source'	13.23, 13.24, 13.25, 13.26, 13.27, 13.28, 13.29, 13.30
residual powers	13.05, 13.06, 13.07, 13.08, 13.09, 13.10
wide powers, recognising	13.22
Children	
community care	6.47
Claim form	3.21
documents to accompany	3.26
Classifying principles of judicial review	1.03, 1.04, 1.05, 1.06, 1.07, 1.08
Common law claim	
conversion to	3.64
Common law rights	1.198, 1.200
legal advantages	1.199
principle of legality	1.201
Community care	6.01
Administrative Court, and	6.05, 6.06
assessment	6.17
challenges to	6.19, 6.20, 6.21
matters to be addressed	6.18
assessment of needs	6.14

Community care—*continued*
  asylum seekers   6.122
    failed, further representations
        by   6.132, 6.133, 6.134, 6.135, 6.136
    s 21 support   6.125, 6.126, 6.127, 6.128, 6.129
    statutory framework   6.124
    unaccompanied children   6.130, 6.131
  care planning   6.14, 6.28
    duty to provide services   6.29
    FACs guidance   6.30, 6.31
  carers   6.94
  children   6.47
    assessment guidance   6.67, 6.68, 6.69
    assessment process   6.65, 6.66
    Children Act 1989, s 17   6.49, 6.51, 6.52, 6.53
    Children Act 1989, s 20   6.54, 6.55, 6.57, 6.58
    disabled   6.63, 6.64
    eligible and relevant child   6.72, 6.73, 6.74
    former relevant child   6.75, 6.76
    guidance   6.80, 6.81
    housing authority, and   6.59, 6.60, 6.61, 6.62
    leaving   6.70, 6.71
    leaving care decisions   6.82, 6.83, 6.84, 6.85, 6.86, 6.87, 6.88, 6.89, 6.90, 6.91, 6.92, 6.93, 6.101
    qualifying   6.77, 6.78, 6.79
    statutory framework   6.49, 6.51, 6.52, 6.53
    terminology   6.56
    young people over 16   6.77, 6.78, 6.79
  common services   6.09
  decision making process   6.13
  decisions   6.10, 6.28
  direct payments   6.37, 6.38
  eligibility   6.14, 6.22, 6.23
    children services   6.26
    critical needs   6.25
    reassessment of needs   6.27
    threshold   6.24
  examples of judicial review
    challenges of decisions   6.148, 6.149, 6.150, 6.151, 6.152
  future developments   6.04
  independent living   6.39
    fundamental foundations   6.42
  legislation   6.01
  meaning   6.08
  migrants   6.122
    s 21 support   6.125, 6.126, 6.127, 6.128, 6.129
    statutory framework   6.124
  overview of law   6.11, 6.12, 6.13
  personalisation   6.39, 6.40
    budgets   6.44, 6.45
    essential principles   6.41
    fundamental foundations   6.42
    parameters   6.43
  present law   6.05

Community care—*continued*
  review   6.02, 6.03
  service provision decision   6.14
  services   6.32
    cheapest option   6.36
    extent   6.33
    guidance of Secretary of State   6.34
  specific and significant areas   6.46
  statutory framework   6.16
  underpinning principles   6.15
Compulsory purchase decisions   5.39, 5.40, 5.41, 5.42, 5.43
Consent orders   3.65
Consultation   1.143, 1.144
  adequate time   1.147
  formative stage   1.145
  recent examples   1.151
  responses taken into account   1.148, 1.149, 1.150
  sufficient reasons to allow for
    response   1.146
Costs   3.74
  central funds, from   9.84, 9.85
  housing cases   7.99, 7.100
  magistrates' courts, against   9.79, 9.80, 9.81, 9.82, 9.83
  permission stage   3.75, 3.76
  protective order   3.79
  substantive hearing   3.77, 3.78
Court of Protection *see also* **Mental health**   8.74, 8.75, 8.76
Criminal cause or matter   9.03
  civil proceedings, and   9.15
  collateral decisions   9.14
  conviction   9.06
  Crown Court decisions   9.25
  decision determining   9.04
  decision of court   9.07, 9.08, 9.09
  decisions that cannot be challenged   9.17
  determining   9.05
  European Convention on Human Rights   9.16
  interim decisions   9.17, 9.18, 9.19, 9.20, 9.21, 9.22, 9.23, 9.24
  sentence   9.10, 9.11, 9.12
  trial by criminal court   9.13
Criminal law   9.01, 9.91, 9.92
  alternative remedies   9.52
  appeal to Supreme Court   9.86, 9.87, 9.88, 9.89, 9.90
  bail as form of interim relief   9.62, 9.63, 9.64, 9.65
  case stated, appeal by   9.54, 9.55, 9.56, 9.57, 9.58, 9.59, 9.60, 9.61
  costs from central funds   9.84, 9.85
  Crown Court, appeal to   9.52, 9.53
  decisions of prosecutors   9.40, 9.41, 9.43
    challenge during proceedings   9.42
    failure to prosecute   9.44, 9.45
    nolle prosequi   9.46
  defendant, role of   9.75, 9.76
  legitimate expectation   9.47, 9.48, 9.49, 9.50, 9.51
  procedure   9.62, 9.63, 9.64, 9.65

Index

Criminal law—*continued*
  relief at conclusion of proceedings   9.77, 9.78
Cross undertaking in damages   2.11
Crown Court decisions   9.25
  ancillary decisions   9.27, 9.28
  appeal to   9.52, 9.53
  appeal, right of   9.29, 9.30, 9.31
  grounds for applying for judicial review   9.39
  lack of jurisdiction   9.37
  refusal to grant bail   9.38
  scope of jurisdiction of Administrative Court   9.32
  trial on Indictment   9.25, 9.26, 9.33, 9.34, 9.35
  trial process   9.29
Crown, actions against   2.78, 2.79
  interim relief   2.08, 2.09

Damages *see also* **Remedies**   2.80, 2.81
  Article 6 rights, and   2.86, 2.87
  Article 8 rights, and   2.86, 2.87
  cross undertaking in   2.11
  Human Rights Act, under   2.99
  European Court of Human Rights approach   2.102
  gravity of violation   2.103, 2.104
  interest   2.105
  just satisfaction   2.99, 2.100, 2.101
  misfeasance in public office, and   2.89, 2.90
  statutory duties, and   2.88
  tortious acts of public bodies   2.83, 2.84, 2.85
  ultra vires, and   2.82
Declarations *see also* **Remedies**   2.70
  academic   2.73, 2.74
  Crown, proceedings against   2.78, 2.79
  discretion, and   2.72
  injunction, and   2.64, 2.65
  mandatory order, and   2.31
  public law jurisdiction   2.75
  quashing order, and   2.46
  sole remedy, as   2.71
Directions   3.37, 3.38, 3.39, 3.40

ECHR rights   1.161, 1.162
  categories   1.164
  context-specific application   1.165
  fair trial, right to   1.176, 1.177, 1.178, 1.179, 1.180, 1.181
  freedom of expression   1.188, 1.189, 1.190, 1.191
  liberty and security   1.171, 1.172, 1.173, 1.174, 1.175
  mechanics of HRA   1.163
  prohibition of discrimination   1.192, 1.193, 1.194, 1.196, 1.197
  prohibition of torture or inhuman and degrading treatment   1.168, 1.169, 1.170
  protection of property   1.195

ECHR rights—*continued*
  respect for private and family life, home and correspondence   1.182, 1.183, 1.184, 1.185, 1.186, 1.187
  right to life   1.166, 1.167
Education   11.01, 11.161
  admission criteria   11.71
  categories of schools and colleges   11.08
  delay in application   11.152, 11.153
  discrimination   11.72, 11.73, 11.74, 11.75
  exclusion   11.122, 11.123, 11.124, 11.125
    challenging IAP decisions   11.126, 11.127, 11.128, 11.129, 11.130, 11.131
    procedural fairness   11.132, 11.133, 11.134, 11.135
    processes   11.116
    reasons   11.139, 11.140, 11.141, 11.142
  funding   11.151
  further education   11.19, 11.20, 11.21
  higher education   11.22, 11.23, 11.24, 11.25, 11.26
  human rights   11.154
    Article 2, First Protocol ECHR   11.154, 11.155, 11.156, 11.157, 11.158, 11.159, 11.160
    IAP hearings   11.132, 11.133, 11.134, 11.135
    impartiality   11.138
    investigations   11.136
  independent schools   11.16, 11.17, 11.18
  learning disability   11.97, 11.99, 11.100, 11.101, 11.102, 11.103
    residual jurisdiction of High Court   11.120, 11.121
    Tribunal   11.104, 11.105
  legislative framework   11.02, 11.03, 11.04, 11.05, 11.06, 11.07
  parental preference   11.52, 11.53
    admission numbers, and   11.67, 11.68
    appeals   11.80, 11.81, 11.82, 11.83, 11.84, 11.85, 11.86, 11.87, 11.88
    ascertaining   11.62, 11.63, 11.64, 11.66
    exclusion   11.61
    guiding principle   11.54, 11.55, 11.56
    infant admissions   11.89, 11.90, 11.91, 11.92
    informing   11.62, 11.63, 11.64, 11.66
    lawful exception   11.57
    multiple appeals   11.93
    oversubscription   11.69, 11.70, 11.76, 11.77, 11.78, 11.79
    prejudice to efficiency   11.58, 11.59
    reasons   11.94, 11.95, 11.96
    selection   11.60
    single sex school   11.65
  pupil discipline   11.122, 11.123, 11.124
  school admissions   11.32, 11.33
    admission authority   11.36, 11.37
    admission forum   11.38, 11.39, 11.40
    admission numbers   11.52

Education—continued
  school admissions—continued
    consistency   11.44, 11.45
    co-ordination   11.36, 11.37
    legal framework   11.34, 11.35
    objections   11.46, 11.47, 11.48, 11.49,
                                11.50, 11.51
    oversubscription   11.52
    parental preference   11.52
    qualifying schemes   11.41
  school organisation   11.27, 11.28, 11.29,
                        11.30, 11.31, 11.143
  schools adjudicator   11.42, 11.43
  special educational needs   11.97, 11.99,
                11.100, 11.101, 11.102, 11.103
    residual jurisdiction of High
      Court   11.120, 11.121
    Tribunal   11.104, 11.105
  standing   11.151
  state schools   11.08, 11.09, 11.10, 11.11
  substantive areas of challenge   11.27,
                  11.28, 11.29, 11.30, 11.31
Errors of fact   1.93
  material   1.94, 1.95
  precedent   1.96, 1.97, 1.98
  recent examples   1.99
Errors of law
  ultra vires   1.78, 1.79, 1.80
EU Charter of Fundamental Rights   1.208,
                        1.209, 1.210, 1.211
EU law rights   1.202, 1.203
  basic principles of EU law   1.204
  effective protection at domestic
    level   1.205
  fundamental freedoms   1.207
  general principles   1.206

Fair trial, right to   1.176, 1.177, 1.178,
                        1.179, 1.180, 1.181
Fettering discretion   1.90
  policy, and   1.91, 1.92
First-tier Tribunals (Special Educational
    Needs and Disability
    Discrimination) see also
    Education; Tribunal system   11.98,
                          11.104, 11.105
  guidance to parents   11.115, 11.116
  judicial review, and   11.117, 11.118,
                                  11.119
  jurisdiction   11.107, 11.108, 11.109,
              11.110, 11.111, 11.112, 11.113,
                                  11.114
  panel   11.106
  practice and procedure   11.111
  rights of appeal   11.112, 11.113
Free schools   11.12, 11.13, 11.14, 11.15
Freedom of expression   1.188, 1.189, 1.190,
                                  1.191
Frustrating legislative purpose   1.108, 1.109
  action contrary to purpose   1.112
  identifying purpose   1.110, 1.111
  mixed purposes   1.113
  recent examples   1.114

Grounds of judicial review   1.01, 1.02
Habeas Corpus
  mental health, and   8.22, 8.23
Healthcare   16.01, 16.02, 16.03, 16.04,
                                  16.56
  after-care services   16.37, 16.38, 16.39,
              16.40, 16.41, 16.42, 16.43, 16.44,
                                  16.45, 16.46
  immigration, and   16.47, 16.48, 16.49,
                    16.50, 16.51, 16.52, 16.53
  individual funding requests 16.33, 16.36
    defined conditions   16.34, 16.35
  prisoners, and   16.54, 16.55
Home detention curfew   10.65, 10.66, 10.67,
                                  10.68
Homelessness   7.33
  advice and assistance   7.61
  challenge to policy   7.49, 7.50, 7.51, 7.52
  competing housing authorities 7.42
  decisions outside statutory code 7.43
  exceptional circumstances   7.37
  interim accommodation   7.44, 7.45, 7.46,
                                  7.47, 7.48
  local connection   7.55, 7.56, 7.57, 7.58
  mental health, and   7.41
  point of law   7.40
  pre-emptive strikes   7.62, 7.63
  refusal to entertain application 7.59, 7.60
  refusal to extend time to review   7.54
  review of decisions   7.34, 7.35, 7.36
  statutory appeal ineffective   7.53
  statutory review process   7.37, 7.38, 7.39
Housing   7.01, 7.02
  costs   7.99, 7.100
    alternative dispute resolution   7.105
    principles   7.102, 7.103, 7.104
    satellite litigation   7.101
  interim relief 7.91, 7.92, 7.93, 7.94, 7.95,
                                  7.96, 7.97
    principles   7.98
  procedure   7.89, 7.90
  public law   7.04, 7.05
Human rights
  damages under   2.99
  education, and   11.154
  licensing, and 12.06, 12.07, 12.08, 12.09,
              12.10, 12.11, 12.12, 12.13, 12.14,
                    12.15, 12.16, 12.17

Illegality   1.66
  range of grounds   1.66
Immigration
  healthcare, and   16.47, 16.48, 16.49,
                    16.50, 16.51, 16.52, 16.53
Immigration law   14.01, 14.02
  appellate structure   14.09, 14.10, 14.11,
                                  14.12, 14.13
  Article 8 ECHR   14.50, 14.51
  certification   14.43, 14.44, 14.45, 14.46
  delay   14.47, 14.48, 14.49
  detention   14.52, 14.53, 14.54, 14.55
  executive decisions   14.08

Immigration law—*continued*
  fresh claims 14.41, 14.42
  judicial review jurisdiction of UT 14.14,
       14.15, 14.16, 14.17, 14.18
    alternative remedies 14.23
    time limits 14.21, 14.22
  national security/SIAC 14.58
  overview 14.03
  pre-action matters to consider 14.19,
     14.20
  procedure in UT
    acknowledgment of service 14.32,
     14.33
    consent orders 14.37
    costs 14.39, 14.40
    lodging application 14.27, 14.28,
     14.29
    permission 14.34, 14.35, 14.38
    removal directions 14.30, 14.31
    substantive hearing 14.36
    urgent applications and interim
     relief 14.24, 14.25, 14.26
  statutes 14.04, 14.05
Immigration Rules 14.06, 14.07
  challenges 14.56
  decisions of UT 14.57
Injunctions 2.12, 2.13, 2.14, 2.15, 2.16,
    2.66, 2.67, 2.68
  balance of convenience 2.12, 2.13, 2.14,
    2.15, 2.16
  declarations, and 2.64, 2.65
  Parliament, and 2.69
  restraining person from acting in
    office 2.62, 2.63
Inquiries 2.181
  ad hoc 2.182
  appeals, and 2.183, 2.184, 2.185, 2.186
Interim orders 3.37
  directions 3.37, 3.38, 3.39, 3.40
Interim relief 2.03, 3.41, 3.42
  bail as 2.21, 9.62, 9.63, 9.64, 9.65
  cross undertaking in damages 2.11
  Crown, actions against 2.08, 2.09
  declarations 2.18
  European dimension 2.17
  injunctions 2.12, 2.13, 2.14, 2.15, 2.16
  principles 2.10
  procedure 2.04, 2.05, 2.06, 2.07
  stays 2.19, 2.20
Internal complaints system 2.187, 2.188
Introductory tenancies 7.80
  internal review 7.87, 7.88
  nature of 7.81
  possession notice 7.82, 7.83, 7.84, 7.85,
    7.86
Irrationality 1.09, 5.108, 5.109, 5.110,
    5.111, 5.112, 5.113, 5.114, 5.115
Issuing claim 3.22
  contents of claim 3.23
  devolution issue, and 3.25
  Human Rights Act 1998, and 3.24

Legitimate expectations 1.135, 1.136
  frustrating 1.140, 1.141

Legitimate expectations—*continued*
  identifying 1.137, 1.138, 1.139
  recent cases 1.142
Liberty and security 1.171, 1.172, 1.173,
    1.174, 1.175
Licensing 12.01
  appeal courts 12.37
  appeal
    alternative remedy 12.51, 12.52,
     12.53, 12.54, 12.55
    true rehearing, whether 12.43,
     12.44, 12.45, 12.46, 12.47, 12.48,
     12.49, 12.50
    fresh evidence 12.42
    nature of appeal 12.39, 12.40, 12.41
    time periods of appealing 12.38
  appealcourts
    appeal-alternativeremedy 12.52
  approach of decision-maker 12.96, 12.97,
    12.98
  authorisation 12.04
  case stated or judicial review 12.56
  discretion of decision-maker 12.99,
    12.100, 12.101, 12.102, 12.103
  evidence 12.85
  future developments 12.104
  hearings 12.85
    procedure 12.91, 12.92
    public 12.93, 12.94, 12.95
  human rights 12.06, 12.07, 12.08, 12.09,
    12.10, 12.11, 12.12, 12.13, 12.14,
    12.15, 12.16, 12.17
  judgment 12.99, 12.100, 12.101, 12.102,
    12.103
  local councillors 12.27
    closed mind approach, whether 12.30,
     12.31, 12.32, 12.33
    general principles 12.35, 12.36
    less strict approach 12.34
    strong and robust opinions 12.27,
     12.28, 12.29
  local decision-making 12.01, 12.21,
    12.22
  local knowledge 12.23, 12.24, 12.25,
    12.26
  objections 12.65, 12.66, 12.67, 12.68,
    12.69
    fair notice 12.82, 12.83, 12.84
    Miss Behavin' 12.70, 12.71, 12.72,
     12.73, 12.74
    statutory context 12.75, 12.76, 12.77
    strength of opposition 12.78, 12.79,
     12.80, 12.81
  permission 12.04
  policies 12.58, 12.59, 12.60
    general principles 12.61
  possession 12.05
  proper hearing by decisions-maker 12.86,
    12.87, 12.88, 12.89, 12.90
  property 12.05
  representations 12.65, 12.66, 12.67,
    12.68, 12.69
    fair notice 12.82, 12.83, 12.84

Licensing—*continued*
  representations—*continued*
    Miss Behavin'   12.70, 12.71, 12.72,
        12.73, 12.74
    statutory context   12.75, 12.76, 12.77
    strength of opposition   12.78, 12.79,
        12.80, 12.81
  role of local bodies   12.18
    quasi-judicial function   12.19, 12.20
  specialist tribunals   12.02
  status of licence   12.04
  statutory guidance   12.62
    general principles   12.63, 12.64

Local government
  comprehensive code, and   13.50
  general competence, power of   13.52,
    13.53, 13.54, 13.55, 13.56
  general power of competence   13.74,
    13.75, 13.76, 13.77, 13.78
  power to promote economic, social
    or environmental well-being   13.56,
    13.57
    approach to issues   13.58, 13.59
    guarantees   13.69, 13.70, 13.71,
    13.72, 13.73
    Guidance   13.60, 13.61, 13.62, 13.63,
    13.64, 13.65, 13.66, 13.67, 13.68
  residual prerogative powers   13.41, 13.42,
    13.43
  ultra vires   13.44, 13.45, 13.46, 13.47,
    13.48, 13.49, 13.51, 13.52

Local/central government   13.01, 13.02,
  13.03, 13.04, 13.140, 13.141,
  13.142
  Adjudication Panel   13.109, 13.110
  Codes of Conduct   13.107, 13.112,
    13.113, 13.114
  democratic issues   13.83
  fiduciary duty   13.84
    aid to construction, as   13.97, 13.98,
    13.99, 13.100, 13.101, 13.102,
    13.103, 13.104
    gift, and   13.95, 13.96
    meaning   13.85, 13.86
    political controversy, and   13.87,
    13.88, 13.89, 13.90, 13.91, 13.92,
    13.93, 13.94
  interests and probity   13.105, 13.106
  legal basis   13.05, 13.06, 13.07, 13.08,
    13.09, 13.10
  Nolan Committee   13.108, 13.109
    intention   13.111
  political considerations   13.83
  relationship with officers   13.115, 13.116,
    13.117, 13.118
    Carltona Principle   13.122, 13.123,
    13.124, 13.125, 13.126, 13.127,
    13.128, 13.129
    devolution of powers   13.122
    duties of officers   13.119, 13.120
    unauthorised delegation   13.121
  standing orders   13.130, 13.131, 13.133
    breach   13.132

Local/central government—*continued*
  standing orders—*continued*
    validity   13.134, 13.135, 13.136,
    13.137, 13.138, 13.139

Magistrates' court
  costs against   9.79, 9.80, 9.81, 9.82, 9.83
Mandatory interim injunction   2.34
Mandatory order   2.22
  action of procedural nature   2.26
  administrative role of public body   2.30
  corporate body, and   2.33
  declaration, and   2.31
  discretion and duty, and   2.26, 2.27, 2.28,
    2.29
  discretion of court   2.32
  housing provision   2.25
  nature of   2.22
  scope   2.24, 2.35, 2.36
  use of   2.23
Mediation   2.132
  authority to settle   2.167, 2.168, 2.169,
    2.170
  closure of residential homes   2.139
  compliance   2.154
  confidentiality   2.154
  costs, and   2.134, 2.144, 2.145, 2.154
  creative solutions   2.154
  discipline   2.154
  discretion, and   2.159, 2.160
  exhortations   2.140, 2.141, 2.142
  focus   2.154
  nature of   2.133
  not appropriate, when   2.162
  number of parties, and   2.163, 2.164,
    2.165, 2.166
  objections to use of   2.155
  other remedies   2.171
  permission stage, at   2.143, 2.148
  pre-action protocol, and   2.146, 2.147
  public law, and   2.157, 2.158
  reasons for   2.154
  relationships   2.154
  relative lack of use   2.156
  resolution of disputes of fact   2.161
  satisfaction   2.154
  search for consensus in public
    sector   2.154
  speed   2.154
  suggestion of power to require   2.152,
    2.153
  suitability   2.172, 2.173, 2.174, 2.175
  support   2.136, 2.137, 2.138
  use of   2.135
Medical treatment policies   16.29, 16.30,
  16.31, 16.32
Mental Capacity Act 2005   8.72, 8.73
  application   8.78, 8.79, 8.80, 8.81
  nearest relatives   8.27
  professional judgment   8.16
  public law and Mental Health Act   8.08
  recent legislation   8.02
  section 17 leave   8.44

Mental Capacity Act 2005—*continued*
   section 139 Mental Health Act   8.24,
                                        8.25, 8.26
   therapeutic environment   8.37
   treatment   8.36
   treatment in community   8.43
   treatment plans   8.40, 8.41, 8.42
   Upper Tribunal   8.55
      High Court jurisdiction   8.58
      powers   8.55, 8.56
      status   8.57
   urgent treatment   8.38
Mental health   8.01, 8.04, 8.05, 8.82
   admission procedures   8.10, 8.11, 8.12,
                                    8.13, 8.14, 8.15
   appropriate medical treatment   8.17, 8.18,
                                    8.19, 8.20, 8.21
   Article 5, ECHR   8.06
   'Bournewood patient'   8.09
   community treatment orders   8.43, 8.44,
                            8.45, 8.46, 8.47, 8.48
   continuing duty to review   8.36
   Court of Protection   8.73, 8.74, 8.75,
                                              8.76
   definitions   8.07
   DOLS   8.77
   First-tier Tribunal   8.49, 8.59
      aftercare   8.65, 8.66, 8.67, 8.68, 8.69,
                                            8.70, 8.71
      Article 5 requirements   8.62
      constitution   8.50
      excluded decisions   8.50, 8.51, 8.52,
                                    8.53, 8.54, 8.63
      procedure   8.60, 8.61
      relevance of judicial review   8.64
   habeas corpus   8.22, 8.23
   hospital managers   8.27
      duties   8.28, 8.29, 8.30, 8.31, 8.32,
                                    8.33, 8.34, 8.35
   lawfulness of detention   8.22
   treatment   8.39
   Tribunal   8.02, 8.03
Migrants
   community care   6.122
Multifunctional government   13.79
   legal framework   13.80, 13.81, 13.82

NHS continuing healthcare funding   16.15,
             16.16, 16.17, 16.18, 16.19, 16.20
   Framework guidance   16.21, 16.22
   personal health budget   16.23, 16.24,
            16.25, 16.26, 16.27, 16.28
NHS reconfiguration   16.05, 16.06, 16.10,
                  16.11, 16.12, 16.13, 16.14
   consultation process   16.08, 16.09
   public sector equality duty   16.07

Ombudsmen   2.201
   courts, relation with   2.207, 2.208, 2.209,
                2.210, 2.211, 2.212, 2.213
   jurisdiction   2.204, 2.205
   maladministration   2.206
   powers   2.215, 2.216

Ombudsmen—*continued*
   proliferation   2.202
   statutory recognition   2.203

Parole Board   10.55, 10.56, 10.57, 10.58,
          10.59, 10.60, 10.61, 10.62, 10.63,
                                          10.64
Permission to apply   3.04, 3.43
   appeal on   3.51, 3.52, 3.53, 3.54
   arguable case, where   3.44
   costs   3.75, 3.76
   directions, and   3.48
   inherent jurisdiction to set aside   3.47
   limited grounds of argument   3.45
   oral hearing   3.46, 3.50
   renewal of application for   3.49
Planning and environment   5.01, 5.02, 5.03,
          5.17, 5.18, 5.19, 5.20, 5.21, 5.22,
          5.23, 5.24, 5.25, 5.26, 5.27, 5.28,
          5.29, 5.30, 5.31, 5.32, 5.33, 5.34,
                        5.35, 5.36, 5.37, 5.38
   amendments   5.11, 5.12, 5.13, 5.14
   delay   5.67, 5.68
   duty to give reason for grant of
      planning permission   5.93, 5.94
   EC-based challenges   5.102, 5.103, 5.104,
                        5.105, 5.106, 5.107
   error of law   5.92
   grounds of review   5.69, 5.70, 5.71, 5.72,
          5.73, 5.74, 5.75, 5.76, 5.77, 5.78,
                                          5.79
   influence of EC law   5.44, 5.45, 5.46,
                                            5.47
      economic considerations   5.48, 5.49,
            5.50, 5.51, 5.52, 5.53, 5.54
      interpretation of national
          legislation   5.55, 5.56, 5.57,
                        5.58, 5.59, 5.60, 5.61
      proportionality   5.62
   interpretation of planning policy   5.95,
          5.96, 5.97, 5.98, 5.99, 5.100,
                                          5.101
   irrationality   5.108, 5.109, 5.110, 5.111,
            5.112, 5.113, 5.114, 5.115
   leapfrog appeals   5.15
   ministerial statements and policy   5.80,
          5.81, 5.82, 5.83, 5.84, 5.85, 5.86,
              5.87, 5.88, 5.89, 5.90, 5.91
   procedural unfairness   5.116, 5.117,
          5.118, 5.119, 5.120, 5.121, 5.122,
          5.123, 5.124, 5.125, 5.126, 5.127
   protective costs orders   5.128, 5.129,
          5.130, 5.131, 5.132, 5.133, 5.134,
                                          5.135
   statutory framework   5.16
   sufficient interest/person aggrieved   5.63,
                                    5.64, 5.65, 5.66
Planning Court   5.04
   claim   5.05
   procedural rules   5.10
   significant cases   5.06, 5.07, 5.08
   target *Times*cales   5.09

Planning decisions 5.17, 5.18, 5.19, 5.20,
    5.21, 5.22, 5.23, 5.24, 5.25, 5.26
  basis for challenge 5.27, 5.28, 5.29, 5.30,
    5.31, 5.32, 5.33, 5.34, 5.35, 5.36,
    5.37, 5.38
Planning permission
  duty to give reason for grant 5.93, 5.94
Planning policy
  interpretation 5.95, 5.96, 5.97, 5.98,
    5.99, 5.100, 5.101
Policy challenges 1.119, 1.120
  routes 1.121
Political gain 1.62
Practice and procedure 3.01
Pre-Action Protocol 3.02
  letter before claim 3.03
Pre-issue considerations 3.05
Prerogative remedies 2.22
Prison and Probation Ombudsman 10.101,
    10.102, 10.103, 10.104, 10.105,
    10.106
Prison discipline 10.76, 10.77, 10.78, 10.79
  challenging findings of guilt 10.88, 10.89,
    10.90, 10.91, 10.92, 10.93
  governor adjudications 10.80, 10.81,
    10.82, 10.83
  independent adjudications 10.84, 10.85,
    10.86, 10.87
Prison law 10.01, 10.02, 10.03, 10.04
  allocation 10.11
    close supervision centres 10.19
    mother and baby units 10.13, 10.14,
      10.15
    vulnerable persons units 10.16, 10.17,
      10.18
  assaults 10.115, 10.116, 10.117, 10.118,
    10.119, 10.120
  association 10.32, 10.33
  categorisation 10.06, 10.07, 10.08,
    10.09, 10.10, 10.12
  close supervision centres 10.19
  complaints processes 10.94, 10.95, 10.96,
    10.97, 10.98, 10.99, 10.100
  correspondence 10.38, 10.39, 10.40,
    10.41, 10.42, 10.43
  dangerous and severe personality
    disorder units 10.27
  deaths 10.121, 10.122, 10.123, 10.124,
    10.125, 10.126, 10.127, 10.128,
    10.129, 10.130, 10.131
  early removal scheme 10.69, 10.70,
    10.71, 10.72
  earned privileges 10.34, 10.35, 10.36,
    10.37
  health and social care 10.45, 10.46,
    10.47
  mental health transfers 10.48, 10.49,
    10.50
  home detention curfew 10.65, 10.66,
    10.67, 10.68
  incentives 10.34, 10.35, 10.36, 10.37
  licence and recall 10.51, 10.52, 10.53,
    10.54

Prison law—*continued*
  litigation practicalities
    exhausting alternative
      remedies 10.139, 10.140,
        10.141
    identifying correct defendant 10.142,
      10.143, 10.144
    public funding 10.145, 10.146,
      10.147
  living conditions 10.30, 10.31
    association 10.32, 10.33
    correspondence 10.38, 10.39, 10.40,
      10.41, 10.42, 10.43
    earned privileges 10.34, 10.35, 10.36,
      10.37
    incentives 10.34, 10.35, 10.36, 10.37
    property 10.30, 10.31
    reasonable adjustments 10.44
    visits 10.38, 10.39, 10.40, 10.41,
      10.42, 10.43
  mental health transfers 10.48, 10.49,
    10.50
  mother and baby units 10.13, 10.14,
    10.15
  near deaths 10.132, 10.133, 10.134,
    10.135, 10.136, 10.137, 10.138
  offending behaviour programmes 10.20,
    10.21, 10.22, 10.23, 10.24, 10.25,
    10.26
  property 10.30, 10.31
  reasonable adjustments 10.28, 10.29,
    10.44
  recategorisation 10.06, 10.07, 10.08,
    10.09, 10.10
  regime 10.05
  release and recall
    early removal scheme 10.69, 10.70,
      10.71, 10.72
    home detention curfew 10.65, 10.66,
      10.67, 10.68
    licence and recall 10.51, 10.52, 10.53,
      10.54
    Parole Board 10.55, 10.56, 10.57,
      10.58, 10.59, 10.60, 10.61, 10.62,
      10.63, 10.64
    tariff expired removal scheme 10.73,
      10.74, 10.75
  segregation 10.16, 10.17, 10.18
  sentence planning 10.20, 10.21, 10.22,
    10.23, 10.24, 10.25, 10.26
    dangerous and severe
      personality disorder
      units 10.27, 10.28, 10.29
    offending behaviour
      programmes 10.20, 10.21,
      10.22, 10.23, 10.24, 10.25, 10.26
  tariff expired removal scheme 10.73,
    10.74, 10.75
  use of force 10.107, 10.108, 10.109,
    10.110, 10.111, 10.112, 10.113,
    10.114
  visits 10.38, 10.39, 10.40, 10.41, 10.42,
    10.43

Index

Prison law—*continued*
    vulnerable prisoner units   10.16, 10.17, 10.18

Prisoners
    healthcare, and   16.54, 16.55

Private care homes   6.137
    scope of judicial review   6.138, 6.139, 6.140, 6.141, 6.142
        rates disputes   6.143, 6.144, 6.145, 6.146, 6.147

Procedural fairness   1.123, 1.124
    law, matter of   1.125
    no difference principle   1.126, 1.127

Procedural impropriety   1.122

Professional regulation   15.01, 15.02, 15.03
    disciplinary proceedings
        appeals   15.208, 15.209, 15.210, 15.211, 15.212, 15.213, 15.214, 15.215
        Article 6 ECHR
            application   15.174, 15.175, 15.176, 15.177, 15.178, 15.179, 15.180
            content   15.182, 15.183, 15.184, 15.185, 15.186, 15.187, 15.188, 15.189
        bias   15.170, 15.171, 15.172
        charges   15.147, 15.148, 15.149, 15.150, 15.151, 15.152, 15.153
        costs   15.216, 15.217, 15.218
        illegality   15.194, 15.195, 15.196, 15.197, 15.198, 15.199, 15.200, 15.201, 15.202
        natural justice   15.160
            cross-examination   15.164, 15.165, 15.166, 15.167
            public hearing   15.164, 15.165, 15.166, 15.167
            representation   15.164, 15.165, 15.166, 15.167
            right to be heard   15.161, 15.162, 15.163
            waiver   15.173
        preliminary issues   15.140
            adjournments   15.141, 15.142, 15.143, 15.144, 15.145, 15.146
        right to reasons   15.168, 15.169
        sanctions   15.203, 15.204, 15.205, 15.206, 15.207
        substantive hearing   15.154
            legal assessors   15.157, 15.158, 15.159
            standard of proof   15.155, 15.156
        unreasonableness   15.190, 15.191, 15.192, 15.193
    entry onto register   15.70
    exams   15.77, 15.78, 15.79
    issues regarding registration   15.71, 15.72, 15.73, 15.74, 15.75, 15.76
    judicial review   15.22, 15.23
        alternative remedies   15.52, 15.53, 15.54, 15.55, 15.56, 15.57, 15.58, 15.59, 15.60
        grounds   15.66, 15.67, 15.68, 15.69

Professional regulation—*continued*
    judicial review—*continued*
        judicial review of regulators by regulators   15.219, 15.225, 15.226, 15.227, 15.228, 15.229, 15.230, 15.231, 15.232, 15.233, 15.235
        costs   15.234
        functus officio   15.220, 15.221, 15.224
        slip rules   15.222, 15.223
    limits
        amenability   15.40, 15.41, 15.42, 15.43, 15.44, 15.45, 15.46, 15.47, 15.48, 15.49, 15.50, 15.51
        targets   15.24, 15.25, 15.26, 15.27, 15.28, 15.29, 15.30, 15.31, 15.32, 15.33
        timing   15.34, 15.35, 15.36, 15.37, 15.38, 15.39
        standing   15.64, 15.65
    key regulatory functions   15.20, 15.21
    maintaining register   15.86, 15.87, 15.88, 15.89, 15.90
    recognition of qualifications   15.80, 15.81, 15.82, 15.83, 15.84, 15.85
    regulators   15.16, 15.17, 15.18, 15.19
    removal from register
        allegations   15.91, 15.92, 15.93, 15.94, 15.95, 15.96, 15.97, 15.98, 15.99, 15.100, 15.101, 15.102, 15.103
        adjudication   15.137, 15.138, 15.139
        investigations   15.104, 15.105, 15.106, 15.107, 15.108
        data issues   15.118, 15.119, 15.120, 15.121, 15.122, 15.123
        delay   15.124, 15.125, 15.126, 15.127, 15.128, 15.129
        reopening cases   15.130, 15.131, 15.132, 15.133, 15.134, 15.135, 15.136
        role of judicial review   15.109, 15.110, 15.111, 15.112, 15.113, 15.114, 15.115, 15.116, 15.117
    restraint   15.61, 15.62, 15.63
    self regulation
    statutory regulation   15.04, 15.05, 15.06, 15.07, 15.08, 15.09, 15.10, 15.11, 15.12, 15.13, 15.14, 15.15

Prohibiting order *see also* Remedies   2.37
    earliest time for application   2.39, 2.40
    examples   2.38

Prohibition of discrimination   1.192, 1.193, 1.194, 1.196, 1.197

Prohibition of torture or inhuman and degrading treatment   1.168, 1.169, 1.170

Proportionality   1.30, 1.31
    applications   1.55
    deference, and   1.49, 1.50

Proportionality—*continued*
   development   1.32, 1.33, 1.34, 1.35, 1.36,
      1.37, 1.38, 1.40, 1.41, 1.42, 1.43
     de Freitas test   1.39
     elements   1.45
     policy, and   1.51, 1.52, 1.53, 1.54
     recent examples   1.56
     Wednesbury compared   1.46, 1.47, 1.48
Protection of property   1.195
Protective costs order   3.79
   environmental cases   3.80, 3.81, 3.82
   planning and environment   5.128, 5.129,
     5.130, 5.131, 5.132, 5.133, 5.134,
     5.135
   principles   3.79

Quashing order   2.41
   administrative acts, against   2.76
   decision in existence   2.42
   declaration, and   2.46
   discretionary power, and   2.51
   draft order in council   2.50
   examples   2.61
   leave to apply for further relief   2.52
   nature of   2.41
   non-binding acts   2.47
   normative acts   2.77
   nullities, and   2.48, 2.49
   public law body   2.45, 2.53, 2.54
   remitting matter   2.44
   restriction on   2.60
   ultra vires decision, and   2.43
Quashing orders *see also* Remedies

Reasons   1.152
   adequacy   1.155
   duty to give   1.153, 1.154
   recent examples   1.158
   timing   1.156, 1.157
Relevant/irrelevant considerations   1.100, 1.101
   categories   1.102, 1.103
   improper weight   1.104, 1.105
   materiality   1.106
   recent example   1.107
Remedies   2.01, 2.02
   damages and restitution   2.80, 2.81
   declarations and injunctions   2.64
   delay, and   2.109
     detriment   2.111, 2.112, 2.113, 2.114, 2.115
     discretion, breadth of   2.116
     effect of relief, and   2.118
     good reason   2.110
     grant of remedy unnecessary or futile   2.119, 2.120
     relevant considerations   2.121
     undue   2.117
   discretion   2.106
     balancing of factors   2.126
     conduct of claimant   2.107, 2.108
     delay   2.109

Remedies—*continued*
   discretion—*continued*
     natural justice, and   2.122, 2.123, 2.124, 2.125
     relevant consideration   2.121
   interim relief   2.03
   mandatory order   2.22
   prohibiting order   2.37
   quashing order   2.41
Respect for private and family life, home and correspondence   1.182, 1.183, 1.184, 1.185, 1.186, 1.187
Restitution   2.91
   Inland Revenue, and   2.92
   mistake, and   2.94, 2.95, 2.96, 2.97, 2.98
   ultra vires payments, and   2.93, 2.96, 2.97, 2.98
Right to life   1.166, 1.167
Rights and freedoms   1.159, 1.160

School uniform   11.143
   conflict   11.144
   jilbab   11.145, 11.146, 11.147
   Kara   11.149
   purity ring   11.148
Service   3.21, 3.28
Severance   2.55
   byelaw   2.57
   conditions attached to licenses or planning permissions   2.58
   test of   2.56
Skeleton arguments   3.60
Social care and healthcare overlap   6.104
   analysis   6.120, 6.121
   cooperation   6.104, 6.105
   division between social care and medical care services   6.106, 6.107, 6.108, 6.109
   local authority providing healthcare provision   6.110, 6.111, 6.112, 6.113, 6.114
   s 117 after care service   6.115, 6.116, 6.117, 6.118, 6.119
Social housing
   allocation   7.64, 7.65, 7.66
   discretion   7.68, 7.69, 7.70
   Part VI Housing Act 1996   7.67
   preferences   7.71
   reasonable preference   7.72, 7.73, 7.74, 7.75, 7.76, 7.77, 7.78, 7.79
   decision maker   7.18
   importance of judicial review   7.14, 7.15, 7.16
   judicial attitude   7.29, 7.30, 7.31, 7.32
   jurisdiction   7.17, 7.19
   meaning   7.03
   occupiers, and   7.09
   possession proceedings   7.12, 7.13
   public authority   7.20, 7.21, 7.22, 7.23, 7.24, 7.25, 7.26, 7.27, 7.28
   role of public law in   7.06, 7.07, 7.08
   statutory codes   7.11
   statutory provisions   7.10

Standards	
Local Government Act 2000	2.189
Standing	3.06
Stays	2.19, 2.20
Substantive hearing	3.55, 3.56, 3.57, 3.58, 3.62, 3.63
costs	3.77, 3.78
public	3.61
Sufficient inquiry	1.115, 1.116, 1.117, 1.118
Supreme Court	
appeal to	9.86, 9.87, 9.88, 9.89, 9.90
Time limits for bringing claim	3.13, 3.14, 3.15, 3.16
Tribunal system	2.180, 4.01, 4.05
appeals, overview of	4.23
background	4.02
Leggatt review	4.02, 4.03, 4.04
legislation	4.06
onward appeals	4.23
first-tier tribunal	4.24
Upper Tribunal	4.25
review of decisions	4.12, 4.13, 4.14, 4.15
effect	4.14
written application	4.13
role	4.02
rules of procedure	4.11
Senior President of Tribunals	4.06
structure	4.08, 4.09, 4.10
tribunal, meaning	4.07
Upper Tribunal	
appeals to	4.16, 4.17, 4.18
judicial review in	4.19, 4.20, 4.21

Tribunal system—*continued*	
Upper Tribunal—*continued*	
superior court of record, as	4.22
Ultra vires	1.67, 1.68, 1.73, 1.74
acting beyond jurisdiction	1.75, 1.76, 1.77
errors of law	1.78, 1.79, 1.80
fundamental rights, and	1.72
locating and interpreting vires	1.69, 1.70
purposive approach	1.71
recent examples	1.81
Unlawful delegation of powers	1.82, 1.83, 1.84, 1.85
acting under dictation	1.86, 1.87, 1.88
recent examples	1.89
Unreasonableness	1.09, 1.10, 1.11, 1.12, 1.13, 1.14, 1.15, 1.16, 1.17, 1.18, 1.19, 1.20, 1.21, 1.22, 1.23, 1.24, 1.25, 1.26, 1.27, 1.28
recent examples	1.29
Urgent cases	3.32, 3.33, 3.34, 3.35, 3.36
Wednesbury	1.11
human rights, and	1.40, 1.41
legal issue	1.12, 1.13, 1.14, 1.15, 1.16, 1.29
high threshold	1.17, 1.18, 1.19, 1.20
sliding scale	1.21, 1.22, 1.23, 1.24, 1.25, 1.26, 1.27, 1.28
limitations	1.32, 1.33, 1.34, 1.35
proportionality compared	1.46, 1.47, 1.48